토익 기본서

20일 만에 끝내는 기적의 토익 LC

목차

DAY	PAGE	PART 1 사진 묘사	PART 2 질의 응답
DAY 01	10	1인 사진/2인 사진	When 의문문/Where 의문문
DAY 02	28	다인 사진/사물·풍경 사진	What 의문문/Who 의문문
DAY 03	46	실내 사진 (1)	How 의문문 (1)
DAY 04	64	실내 사진 (2)	How 의문문 (2) / Why 의문문
DAY 05	82	야외 사진	일반 의문문 – 긍정
DAY 06	100		일반 의문문 – 부정
DAY 07	120		부가 의문문
DAY 08	138		간접 의문문/선택 의문문
DAY 09	158		청유문
DAY 10	178		평서문
DAY 11	196		우회적 응답 모음
DAY 12	214		
DAY 13	232		
DAY 14	250		
DAY 15	268		
DAY 16	286		
DAY 17	304		
DAY 18	322		
DAY 19	340		
DAY 20	358		

PART 3 짧은 대화	PART 4 담화
주제·목적 문제/장소·직업 문제/세부 사항 문제	
제안·요청 문제/다음 할 일 문제/의도 파악 문제	
시각 자료 연계 문제/3인 대화 문제	
	주제·목적 문제/장소·직업 문제/세부 사항 문제
	제안·요청 문제/다음 할 일 문제/의도 파악 문제
	시각 자료 연계 문제
회사 – 업무 요청/규정 관련	전화 메시지 – 주문·구매/배송·문의
회사 – 입사·채용/전근·퇴임	녹음 메시지/설명
회사 – 사내 교육/비품·장비	회의 발췌록 – 업무 지시/규정 변경
회사 – 출장·행사/상점 – 상품 구매·서비스	담화 – 제품 시연/발표
상점 – 멤버십·고객 의견/할인	안내 – 교통편 관련/콘퍼런스
상점 – 환불·고객 불만/병원·약국	광고 – 제품 광고/서비스 광고
호텔/식당 – 예약/요청 사항	관광 정보/소개
공항/역 – 체크인/변경 요청	라디오 방송 – 지역 행사 안내/기업 소개 관련
박물관·공연장/교통수단	뉴스 보도 – 업계 소식/연구 결과
	[해설집] 정답·스크립트·해석·해설

토익 LC, 이제 〈기적의 토익 LC〉로 학습하세요.

포인트 1

PART 1, 2, 3, 4를
골고루 학습하는 구성

책 앞 부분에 있는 PART 1, 2만 학습하다 그만두는 LC 공부는 이제 그만! 20일 동안 매일 두 PART씩(PART 1과 2, PART 2와 3, PART 2와 4, PART 3와 4) 골고루 학습할 수 있게 구성하여 학습 성취도를 높일 수 있도록 하였습니다.

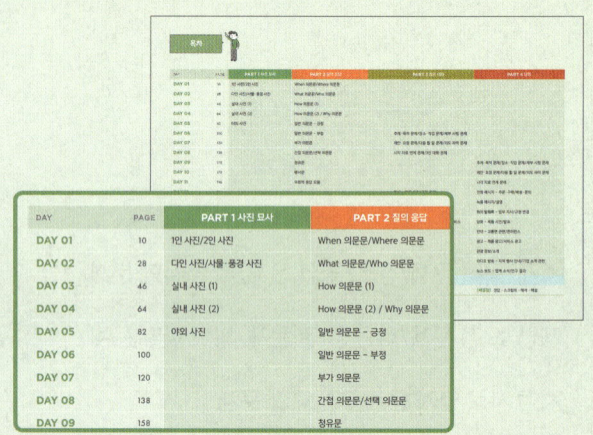

포인트 2

하루의 학습 포인트
미리 보기

하루에 학습할 주요 내용을 미리 보며 큰 그림을 그릴 수 있도록 보기 쉽게 정리하였습니다. 토익 시험 직전에는 이 부분만 훑어보며 마무리 학습용으로도 활용할 수 있습니다.

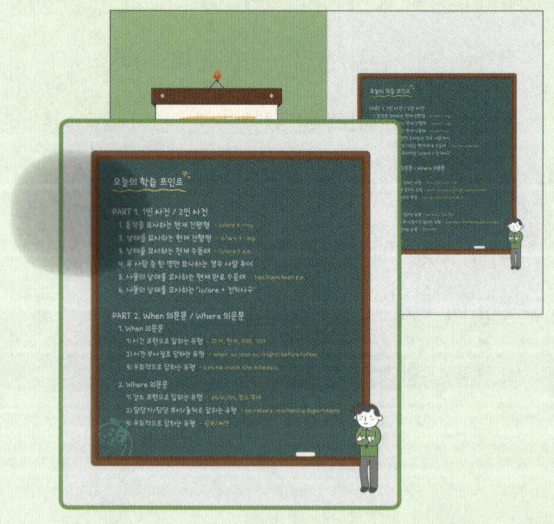

포인트 3

800+, 900+를 위한
고득점 포인트

목표 점수대에 따라 학습해야 할 출제 유형 및 개념을 구분하여, 800~900점 이상의 고득점을 위해 정복해야 하는 개념에는 '800+', '900+'를 표시하였습니다. 목표 점수에 따라 필요한 내용들만 우선 학습하여 좀 더 빠르게 효과적으로 학습할 수 있습니다.

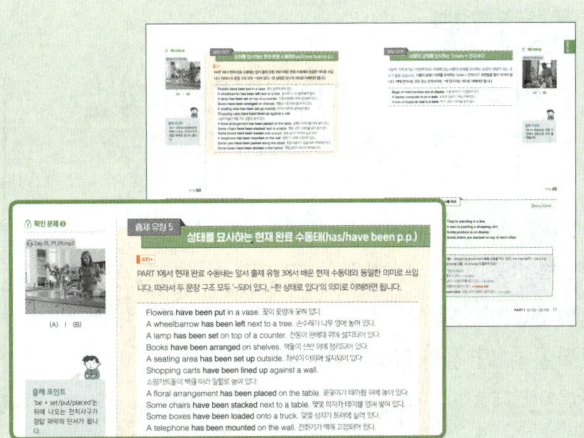

포인트 4

꼭 나오는 출제 유형만,
알찬 보조 학습 코너까지!

토익을 위해 필요한 출제 유형만 선별하여 수록하였습니다. 또한 보조 학습 코너의 <확인 문제>를 풀어 보며 학습한 내용을 바로바로 점검해 볼 수 있고, 토익 출제 경향을 알려주는 <출제 포인트>, 실수할 수 있는 부분을 짚어주는 <주의> 코너를 통해 더욱 알차게 학습할 수 있습니다.

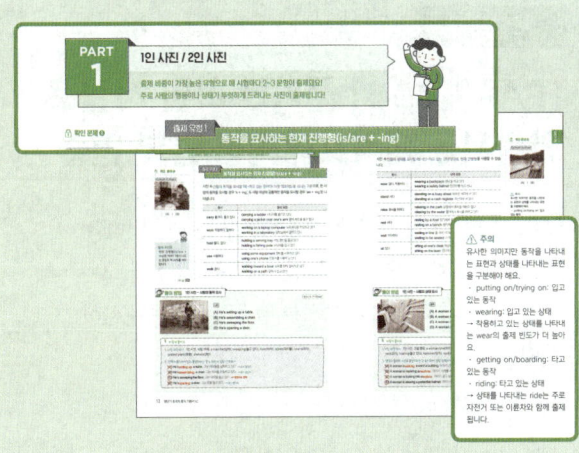

토익 LC, 이제 〈기적의 토익 LC〉로 학습하세요.

포인트 5

[PART 3&4] 대화/담화 유형별 빈출 어휘 수록

PART 3는 대화 상황별 빈출 어휘를, PART 4는 담화 유형별 빈출 어휘를 수록하였습니다. 대화 상황/담화 유형별 빈출 어휘를 우선 정복하고 PART 3, 4의 대화 및 담화를 들으면 훨씬 쉽게 이해할 수 있습니다. 빈출 어휘를 마스터하여 PART 3, 4를 정복하세요!

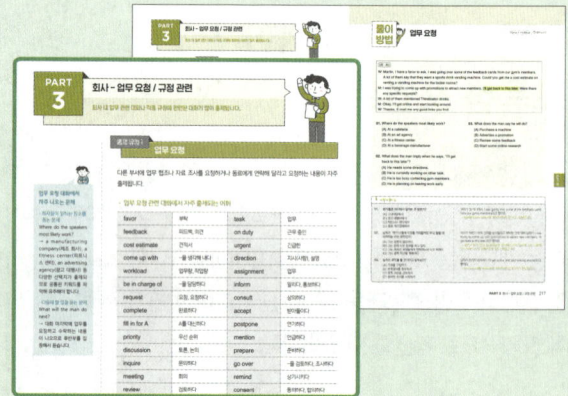

포인트 6

[PART 3&4] 풀기만 하면 저절로 외워지는 패러프레이징 반복 연습

PART 3, 4는 패러프레이징만 잘하면 반은 성공입니다! PART 3, 4에서 꼭 연습해야 하는 패러프레이징을 모든 연습 문제에서 학습할 수 있도록 별도의 코너로 구성하였습니다.

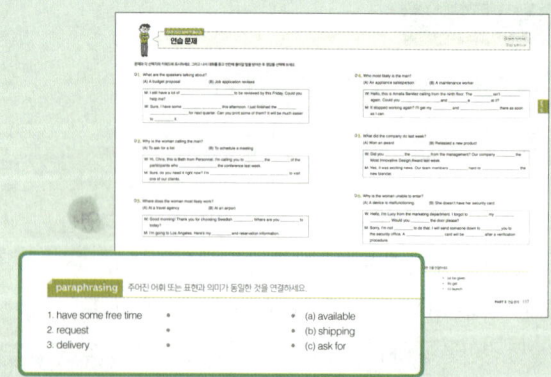

포인트 7
내 옆의 선생님 같은
친절한 풀이 방법

앞에서 학습한 출제 유형이 실제 토익 시험에서는 어떻게 문제로 출제되는지 알 수 있어요. '이렇게 풀어요'에 제시된 풀이 방법을 따라 하다 보면 쉽게 문제를 푸는 경험을 할 수 있습니다!

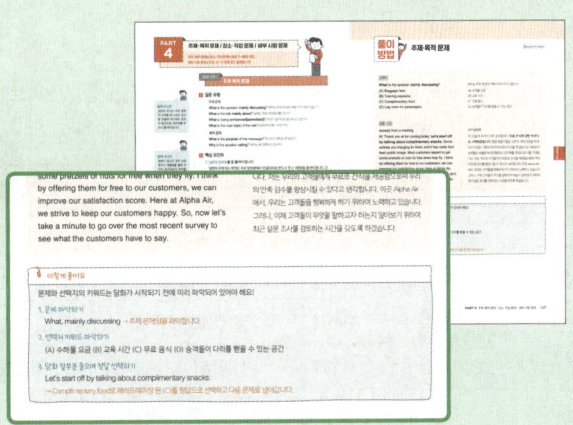

포인트 8
학습 시너지 효과를 높이는
적용 기술

개념이 실제로 적용되는 기술을 참고할 수 있도록 <영단기 700+ 기적의 필기노트>의 관련 페이지와 기술 넘버를 표시했습니다. <영단기 700+ 기적의 필기노트>와 함께 공부하면 학습 시너지 효과를 높일 수 있습니다.

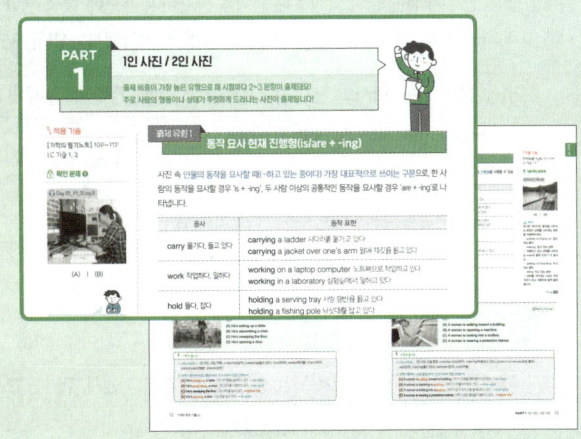

토익 시험의 모든 것

토익 시험 개요

TOEIC 시험이란?
TEST OF ENGLISH FOR INTERNATIONAL COMMUNICATION의 약자로, 모국어가 영어가 아닌 사람이 일상적인 생활 또는 업무에서 의사소통이 가능한지를 평가하는 시험입니다.

시험 구성
듣기(LC) 4개 파트 100문제와 읽기(RC) 3개 파트 100문제로 총 7개 파트에 걸쳐 200문제가 출제됩니다. 200문제 모두 선택지 중에서 정답을 찾는 객관식 문제로 출제됩니다.

구성	PART 구성	출제 내용	문항수	시간	점수
LC (Listening Comprehension)	PART 1	사진 묘사 (사진 보고 문제 풀기)	6	45분 내외	495점
	PART 2	질문-대답 (질문 듣고 답변 고르기)	25		
	PART 3	짧은 대화 (두세 사람의 대화를 듣고 질문에 답하기)	39		
	PART 4	설명문 (한 사람이 말하는 것을 듣고 질문에 답하기)	30		
RC (Reading Comprehension)	PART 5	문장 빈칸 채우기 (하나의 문장 안에 있는 빈칸에 알맞은 말(문법 & 어휘) 고르기)	30	75분	495점
	PART 6	지문 빈칸 채우기 (짧은 지문 안에 있는 빈칸에 알맞은 말(문법&어휘&문장) 고르기)	16		
	PART 7	싱글 지문 (1개의 지문을 읽고 질문에 답하기)	29		
		더블 지문 (2개의 지문을 읽고 질문에 답하기)	10		
		트리플 지문 (3개의 지문을 읽고 질문에 답하기)	15		
총계			200	약 120분	990점

출제 범위 및 주제
일상생활 및 업무에 대한 영어 의사소통 능력을 평가하기 때문에 특정 분야의 전문 지식 또는 이와 관련된 어휘는 출제하지 않습니다. 국제 업무 환경에 맞게 다양한 국가의 지명과 성명이 등장하며, 듣기 평가에서는 미국, 영국, 호주 발음이 고르게 섞여 출제됩니다. 다음의 주제를 참고해 봅시다.

기업 일반	이사회, 편지, 공지, 전화, 팩스, 이메일, 사무실 장비 및 가구, 규정, 계약, 협상, 합병 및 인수, 판매, 보증, 사업 계획, 회의
공식 연회	식사 및 연회, 장소 예약
엔터테인먼트	영화, 공연, 전시
재무	은행 업무, 투자, 세금, 회계, 청구
의료	건강 보험, 병원 방문 및 예약
부동산	건설 및 보수 내역, 부동산 구매 및 임대, 기타 설비
제조	제품 조립, 공장 경영, 품질 관리
인사	모집, 고용, 퇴임, 승진, 급여, 일자리 지원서, 구인 광고, 연금, 시상
구매	쇼핑, 주문, 배송, 송장
기술	전자 장비, 기술 지원, 컴퓨터, 연구실과 관련 장비
여행	여행 일정, 교통 관련 각종 공지, 렌터카, 호텔 예약, 연착 및 취소

시험 접수부터 성적 확인까지! 토익 가이드

1 토익 접수 방법
- 토익 시험의 인터넷 접수 기간을 한국 TOEIC 위원회 사이트(www.toeic.co.kr)에서 확인합니다.
- 사이트에서 인터넷 접수를 선택하고 시험일, 고사장, 수험 정보 등의 정보를 입력합니다.
- 시험 접수 시 최근 6개월 이내 사진(JPG 형식)이 필요하오니 미리 준비합니다.

TIP 시험 D-30부터는 특별 추가 접수에 해당하여 약 5천원 정도의 추가 비용이 발생합니다. 미리 시험을 접수하는 것이 좋습니다.

2 시험 당일 꼭! 챙겨야 할 준비물
- **규정 신분증**
  성인의 경우, 주민등록증, 운전면허증, 기간 만료 전 여권, 공무원증 등이 인정됩니다. 중고등학생에 한하여 학생증(국내 학생증만 허용)도 신분증으로 인정됩니다.
- **연필 (볼펜, 사인펜은 No!)**
  연필 끝을 뭉뚝하게 만들어 준비하면 답안 마킹을 더 쉽게 할 수 있습니다.
- **지우개**
- **아날로그 손목시계 (전자식 시계는 No!)**

3 입실 전 유의사항
- 시험 시간이 오전일 경우, 오전 9:20까지, 시험 시간이 오후일 경우 오후 2:20까지 입실합니다.

TIP 오전 시험은 오전 9:50 이후, 오후 시험은 오후 2:50 이후로는 절대 입실할 수 없으니 꼭 시간을 지켜 미리 입실합니다.
TIP 시험 시간 직전에는 독해 문제를 풀기보다는 듣기 연습을 충분히 하여 귀를 훈련시키는 게 더 효과적입니다.

4 시험 진행 안내

오전 시험	오후 시험	시험 진행
9:30~9:45 (15분)	2:30~2:45 (15분)	답안지 작성 오리엔테이션
9:45~9:50 (5분)	2:45~2:50 (5분)	쉬는 시간
9:50~10:05 (15분)	2:50~3:05 (15분)	신분증 확인
10:05~10:10 (5분)	3:05~3:10 (5분)	문제지 배부, 파본 확인
10:10~10:55 (45분)	3:10~3:55 (45분)	듣기 평가 (LC)
10:55~12:10 (75분)	3:55~5:10 (75분)	독해 평가 (RC)

5 성적 확인 및 성적표 발급 방법 알아보기
- 시험일로부터 10일 후 낮 12시에 한국 TOEIC 위원회 사이트(www.toeic.co.kr)에서 성적 확인이 가능합니다.
  (토요일 시행 시험 등 일부 회차 시험은 11일 후에 발표될 수 있습니다.)
- 성적 수령은 온라인 출력이나 우편 수령을 택할 수 있습니다.
- 온라인 출력 시, 성적 유효 기간 내 홈페이지를 통해 출력 가능합니다.
- 우편 수령 시, 성적 발표 후 접수 시 기입한 주소로 성적표가 우편 발송됩니다. (약 7~10일 소요)
- 온라인 출력과 우편 수령은 1회 발급만 무료이며, 이후에는 유료로 발급됩니다.

'멋진 당신, 오늘도 화이팅'

DAY 01

오늘의 학습 포인트

PART 1. 1인 사진 / 2인 사진
1. 동작을 묘사하는 현재 진행형 - is/are + -ing
2. 상태를 묘사하는 현재 진행형 - is/are + -ing
3. 상태를 묘사하는 현재 수동태 - is/are + p.p.
4. 두 사람 중 한 명만 묘사하는 경우 사람 주어
5. 사물의 상태를 묘사하는 현재 완료 수동태 - has/have been p.p.
6. 사물의 상태를 묘사하는 'is/are + 전치사구'

PART 2. When 의문문 / Where 의문문
1. When 의문문
    1) 시간 표현으로 답하는 유형 - 과거, 현재, 미래, 기타
    2) 시간 부사절로 답하는 유형 - when, as soon as, (right) before/after
    3) 우회적으로 답하는 유형 - Let me check the schedule.

2. Where 의문문
    1) 장소 표현으로 답하는 유형 - at/in/on, 장소 부사
    2) 담당자/담당 부서/출처로 답하는 유형 - secretary, marketing department
    3) 우회적으로 답하는 유형 - 권유/제안

PART 1 · 1인 사진 / 2인 사진

출제 비중이 가장 높은 유형으로 매 시험마다 2~3 문항이 출제돼요!
주로 사람의 행동이나 상태가 뚜렷하게 드러나는 사진이 출제됩니다!

적용 기술
[기적의 필기노트] 10P~11P
LC 기술 1, 2

확인 문제 ❶
Day 01_P1_01.mp3

(A) | (B)

출제 포인트
현재 진행형(is/are + -ing)은 PART 1에서 나오는 문장의 약 66%를 차지합니다.

출제 유형 1 — 동작 묘사 현재 진행형(is/are + -ing)

사진 속 인물의 동작을 묘사할 때(~하고 있는 중이다) 가장 대표적으로 쓰이는 구문으로, 한 사람의 동작을 묘사할 경우 'is + -ing', 두 사람 이상의 공통적인 동작을 묘사할 경우 'are + -ing'로 나타냅니다.

동사	동작 표현
carry 옮기다, 들고 있다	**carrying** a ladder 사다리를 옮기고 있다 **carrying** a jacket over one's arm 팔에 재킷을 들고 있다
work 작업하다, 일하다	**working** on a laptop computer 노트북으로 작업하고 있다 **working** in a laboratory 실험실에서 일하고 있다
hold 들다, 잡다	**holding** a serving tray 서빙 쟁반을 들고 있다 **holding** a fishing pole 낚싯대를 잡고 있다
use 사용하다	**using** some equipment 장비를 사용하고 있다 **using** one's phone 전화기를 사용하고 있다
walk 걷다	**walking** toward a boat 보트를 향해 걸어가고 있다 **walking** on a path 길에서 걷고 있다

풀이 방법 — 1인 사진 – 사람의 동작 묘사

Day 01_P1_02.mp3

US
(A) He's setting up a table.
(B) He's assembling a chair.
(C) He's sweeping the floor.
(D) He's opening a door.

이렇게 풀어요

1. **사진 파악하기** 1인 사진, 식당/카페, a man/he(남자), sweeping(쓸고 있다), floor(바닥), tables(테이블), chairs(의자), potted plant(화분), shelves(선반)

2. **선택지 들으며 사진과 불일치하는 것 소거하여 정답 선택하기**
   (A̶) He's setting up a table. 그는 테이블을 설치하고 있다. → 동사 불일치
   (B̶) He's assembling a chair. 그는 의자를 조립하고 있다. → 동사 불일치
   (C) He's sweeping the floor. 그는 바닥을 쓸고 있다. → 정답으로 선택
   (D̶) He's opening a door. 그는 문을 열고 있다. → 동사 불일치

출제 유형 2   상태 묘사 현재 진행형(is/are + -ing)

사진 속 인물의 상태를 묘사할 때(~인/~하고 있는 상태이다)도 현재 진행형을 사용할 수 있습니다.

동사	상태 표현
wear 입다, 착용하다	wearing a backpack 배낭을 메고 있다 wearing a safety helmet 안전모를 쓰고 있다
stand 서다	standing on a busy street 분주한 거리에 서 있다 standing at a cash register 계산대에 서 있다
relax 휴식을 취하다	relaxing in the park 공원에서 휴식을 취하고 있다 relaxing by the water 물가에서 휴식을 취하고 있다
rest 쉬다	resting by a river 강가에서 쉬고 있다 resting on a bench 벤치에서 쉬고 있다
wait 기다리다	waiting in line 줄 서서 기다리고 있다 waiting to be seated (자리에) 앉으려고 기다리고 있다
sit 앉다	sitting at one's desk 책상에 앉아 있다 sitting on the lawn 잔디에 앉아 있다

적용 기술
[기적의 필기노트] 10P~11P
LC 기술 1, 2

🔒 확인 문제 ❷

🎧 Day 01_ P1_03.mp3

(A) | (B)

⚠️ 주의
유사한 의미지만 동작을 나타내는 표현과 상태를 나타내는 표현을 구분해야 해요.
· putting on/trying on: 입고 있는 동작
· wearing: 입고 있는 상태
→ 착용하고 있는 상태를 나타내는 wear의 출제 빈도가 더 높아요.
· getting on/boarding: 타고 있는 동작
· riding: 타고 있는 상태
→ 상태를 나타내는 ride는 주로 자전거 또는 이륜차와 함께 출제됩니다.

(A) ❷ 정답

풀이 방법   1인 사진 – 사람의 상태 묘사

🎧 Day 01_ P1_04.mp3

[BR]

(A) A woman is walking toward a building.
(B) A woman is repairing a machine.
(C) A woman is looking into a toolbox.
(D) A woman is wearing a protective helmet.

이렇게 풀어요

1. **사진 파악하기**   1인 사진, 건설 현장, a woman/she(여자), wearing(착용하고 있다), protective helmet(보호 헬멧), vest(조끼), holding(들고 있다), hammer(망치), roof(지붕)

2. **선택지 들으며 사진과 불일치하는 것 소거하여 정답 선택하기**
   (A̶) A woman is walking toward a building. 여자가 건물을 향해 걸어가고 있다. → 동사 불일치
   (B̶) A woman is repairing a machine. 여자가 기계를 수리하고 있다. → 목적어 불일치
   (C̶) A woman is looking into a toolbox. 여자가 공구 상자 안을 들여다보고 있다. → 목적어 불일치
   (D) A woman is wearing a protective helmet. 여자가 보호 헬멧을 착용하고 있다. → 정답으로 선택

🔒 **확인 문제 ❸**

🎧 Day 01_ P1_05.mp3

(A) | (B)

출제 포인트

2인 사진에서 자주 출제되는 표현이 있습니다.
They are shaking hands. 그들은 악수하고 있다.
They are facing each other. 그들은 마주 보고 있다.

(A) ❸ 정답

출제 유형 3 상태 묘사 현재 수동태(is/are + p.p.)

800+

사람의 상태를 'is/are + p.p.(동사의 과거 분사형)'로 표현하는 문장은 출제 비중이 높지는 않지만, 이 형태로 자주 출제되는 동사들이 있습니다.

동사	상태 표현
seat 앉다, 앉히다	**seated** in a dining area 식당에 앉아 있다 **seated** next to each other 나란히 앉아 있다
stop 멈추다	**stopped** to watch a performance 공연을 보기 위해 멈춰 서 있다 **stopped** in front of a shop 가게 앞에 서 있다
gather 모이다, 모으다	**gathered** in a waiting area 대기실에 모여 있다 **gathered** around an entrance 입구 주위에 모여 있다
line up 줄을 서다	**lined up** outside 밖에 줄 서 있다 **lined up** to board a bus 버스를 타기 위해 줄 서 있다

 풀이 방법 2인 사진 - 두 사람의 공통점 묘사

🎧 Day 01_ P1_06.mp3

[BR]
(A) They are listening to a presentation.
(B) They are standing beside a window.
(C) They are entering a meeting room.
(D) They are seated at a table.

이렇게 풀어요

1. **사진 파악하기** 2인 사진, 실내 공간, they(그들), sitting(앉아 있다), looking at(보고 있다), document(서류), laptop computer(노트북 컴퓨터), ceiling(천장), potted plant(화분)

2. **선택지 들으며 사진과 불일치하는 것 소거하여 정답 선택하기**
   (A̶) They are listening to a presentation. 그들은 발표를 듣고 있다. → 동사 불일치
   (B̶) They are standing beside a window. 그들은 창문 옆에 서 있다. → 동사 불일치
   (C̶) They are entering a meeting room. 그들은 회의실에 들어가고 있다. → 동사 불일치
   (D) They are seated at a table. 그들은 탁자에 앉아 있다. → 정답으로 선택

출제 유형 4 — 두 사람 중 한 명만 묘사하는 경우 사람 주어

적용 기술
[기적의 필기노트] 12P
LC 기술 3

2인 사진에서는 **두 사람 중 한 명만 묘사하는 문장이 정답이 되는 경우가 종종 있으므로** 개개인의 동작이나 상태도 파악해야 합니다. 둘 중 한 명만 묘사하는 경우 보기에 나올 수 있는 사람 주어는 다음과 같습니다.

확인 문제 ❹

- 남자-남자 또는 여자-여자의 동성 사진일 경우

One of the men 남자들 중 한 명 One of the people 사람들 중 한 명 A man 한 남자	One of the women 여자들 중 한 명 One of the people 사람들 중 한 명 A woman 한 여자

- 남자-여자의 혼성 사진일 경우

A man / The man / He 남자	A woman / The woman / She 여자

출제 포인트
사진을 있는 그대로 가장 객관적으로 표현한 보기를 선택해야 합니다. 컴퓨터 모니터를 끄는지 켜는지와 같은 행동은 사진만으로는 파악할 수 없으므로 답이 될 수 없습니다.

정답 (B)

 **풀이 방법** 2인 사진 - 두 사람 중 한 명만 묘사

 Day 01_P1_08.mp3

AU

(A) One of the men is having a snack.
(B) One of the men is turning off a computer monitor.
(C) One of the men is opening a file cabinet.
(D) One of the men is distributing some documents.

이렇게 풀어요

1. **사진 파악하기** 2인 사진, 실내 공간, 왼쪽 남자 – having food(음식을 먹고 있다), holding a pencil(연필을 쥐고 있다), wearing glasses(안경을 끼고 있다), 오른쪽 남자 – working on a laptop(노트북으로 일하고 있다)

2. **선택지 들으며 사진과 불일치하는 것 소거하여 정답 선택하기**
   (A) One of the men is having a snack. 남자들 중 한 명이 간단한 식사를 하고 있다. → 정답으로 선택
   (B) One of the men is turning off a computer monitor. 남자들 중 한 명이 컴퓨터 모니터를 끄고 있다. → 동사 불일치 – 사진으로 알 수 없음
   (C) One of the men is opening a file cabinet. 남자들 중 한 명이 파일 보관함을 열고 있다. → 동사 불일치
   (D) One of the men is distributing some documents. 남자들 중 한 명이 서류를 나누어주고 있다. → 동사 불일치

확인 문제 ❺

Day 01_P1_09.mp3

(A) | (B)

출제 포인트

'be + set/put/placed'는 뒤에 나오는 전치사구가 정답 파악의 단서가 됩니다.

출제 유형 5
상태를 묘사하는 현재 완료 수동태(has/have been p.p.)

800+

PART 1에서 현재 완료 수동태는 앞서 출제 유형 3에서 배운 현재 수동태와 동일한 의미로 쓰입니다. 따라서 두 문장 구조 모두 '~되어 있다, ~한 상태로 있다'의 의미로 이해하면 됩니다.

Flowers **have been put** in a vase. 꽃이 꽃병에 꽂혀 있다.
A wheelbarrow **has been left** next to a tree. 손수레가 나무 옆에 놓여 있다.
A lamp **has been set** on top of a counter. 전등이 판매대 위에 설치되어 있다.
Books **have been arranged** on shelves. 책들이 선반 위에 정리되어 있다.
A seating area **has been set up** outside. 좌석이 야외에 설치되어 있다.
Shopping carts **have been lined up** against a wall.
쇼핑카트들이 벽을 따라 일렬로 놓여 있다.
A floral arrangement **has been placed** on the table. 꽃꽂이가 테이블 위에 놓여 있다.
Some chairs **have been stacked** next to a table. 몇몇 의자가 테이블 옆에 쌓여 있다.
Some boxes **have been loaded** onto a truck. 몇몇 상자가 트럭에 실려 있다.
A telephone **has been mounted** on the wall. 전화기가 벽에 고정되어 있다.
Some cars **have been parked** along the street. 몇몇 자동차가 길을 따라 주차되어 있다.
Some boats **have been docked** in the harbor. 몇몇 보트가 항구에 정박해 있다.

정답 ❺ (A)

 풀이 방법 1인 사진 - 사람 주어 + 사물 주어

Day 01_P1_10.mp3

US

(A) A man is riding a bicycle in the park.
(B) Some bicycles have been parked outdoors.
(C) Some trees have been lined along both sides of the road.
(D) A man is pouring water into a bottle.

이렇게 풀어요

1. **사진 파악하기** 1인 사진, 야외, a man(남자) - sitting on a bench(벤치에 앉아 있다), 배경 - water(물가), trees(나무), bicycles(자전거), parked(세워진)

2. **선택지 들으며 사진과 불일치하는 것 소거하여 정답 선택하기**
   (A) A man is **riding** a bicycle in the park. 남자가 공원에서 자전거를 타고 있다. → 동사 불일치
   (B) Some bicycles have been parked outdoors. 자전거 몇 대가 야외에 세워져 있다. → 정답으로 선택
   (C) Some trees have been lined along **both sides of the road**. 나무 몇 그루가 도로 양쪽을 따라 늘어서 있다. → 위치 불일치
   (D) A man is **pouring** water into a bottle. 남자가 병에 물을 따르고 있다. → 동사 불일치

16 기적의 토익 LC

출제 유형 6 · 사물의 상태를 묘사하는 'is/are + 전치사구'

사람이 크게 보이는 사진이더라도 주위에 있는 사물의 상태를 묘사하는 문장이 정답이 되는 경우가 종종 있습니다. 사물의 상태나 위치를 묘사하는 'is/are + 전치사구' 표현들을 알아 두어야 합니다. 이때 전치사는 모두 장소 전치사이며, '~에 있다'라는 의미로 이해하면 됩니다.

Bags of merchandise **are on display**. 상품 꾸러미가 진열되어 있다.
A laptop computer **is on a desk**. 노트북 컴퓨터가 책상 위에 있다.
A box of books **is next to a table**. 책 한 상자가 테이블 옆에 있다.

🔒 확인 문제 ❻

(A) | (B)

출제 포인트
be on display는 상점 사진에서 정답으로 자주 출제됩니다.

정답 ❻ (A)

👋 풀이 방법   2인 사진 – 사람 주어 + 사물 주어

[BR]
(A) They're standing in a line.
(B) A man is pushing a shopping cart.
(C) Some produce is on display.
(D) Some chairs are stacked on top of each other.

✓ 이렇게 풀어요

1. **사진 파악하기**   2인 사진, 슈퍼마켓, they(그들) – shopping groceries(식료품 쇼핑을 하고 있다), the man(남자) – carrying a basket(바구니를 들고 있다), 배경 – produce(농산물), on display(진열되어 있는)

2. **선택지 들으며 사진과 불일치하는 것 소거하여 정답 선택하기**
   (A) They're standing **in a line**. 그들은 한 줄로 서 있다. → 위치 불일치
   (B) A man is **pushing** a shopping cart. 남자가 쇼핑카트를 밀고 있다. → 동사 불일치
   (C) **Some produce is on display.** 몇몇 농산물이 진열되어 있다. → 정답으로 선택
   (D) **Some chairs** are stacked on top of each other. 몇몇 의자가 층층이 쌓여 있다. → 주어 불일치

PART 1 1인 사진 / 2인 사진

따라 하면 문제가 풀리는 연습 문제

Day 01_P1_13.mp3
정답 및 해석 p.2

01.

(1) 음원을 들으며 사진과 관련된 단어이면 O, 아니면 X에 표시하세요.

　(A) O | X　　(B) O | X　　(C) O | X

(2) 음원을 들으며 빈칸을 채우고 정답에는 O, 오답에는 X 표시하세요.

　(A) He is _____ a wheelbarrow.　　[　]
　(B) He is _____ a potted plant.　　[　]

02.

(1) 음원을 들으며 사진과 관련된 단어이면 O, 아니면 X에 표시하세요.

　(A) O | X　　(B) O | X　　(C) O | X

(2) 음원을 들으며 빈칸을 채우고 정답에는 O, 오답에는 X 표시하세요.

　(A) They're _____ along the river.　　[　]
　(B) A bicycle is _____ against a fence.　　[　]

03.

(1) 음원을 들으며 사진과 관련된 단어이면 O, 아니면 X에 표시하세요.

　(A) O | X　　(B) O | X　　(C) O | X

(2) 음원을 들으며 빈칸을 채우고 정답에는 O, 오답에는 X 표시하세요.

　(A) They are pulling _____.　　[　]
　(B) They are _____ a train.　　[　]

04.

(1) 음원을 들으며 사진과 관련된 단어이면 O, 아니면 X에 표시하세요.

　(A) O | X　　(B) O | X　　(C) O | X

(2) 음원을 들으며 빈칸을 채우고 정답에는 O, 오답에는 X 표시하세요.

　(A) A man is _____ coffee into a mug.　　[　]
　(B) A woman is washing dishes in a _____.　　[　]

토익에 나올 실전 문제

Day 01_ P1_14.mp3
정답 및 해설 p.2

01.

(A)　(B)　(C)　(D)

02.
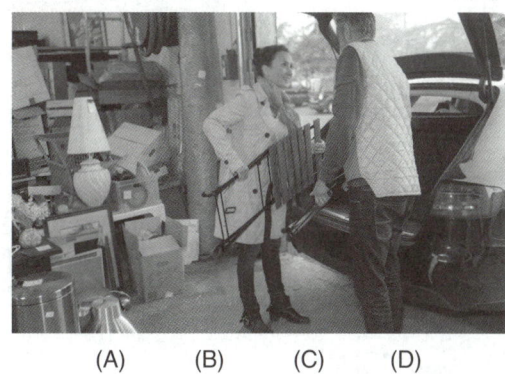
(A)　(B)　(C)　(D)

03.
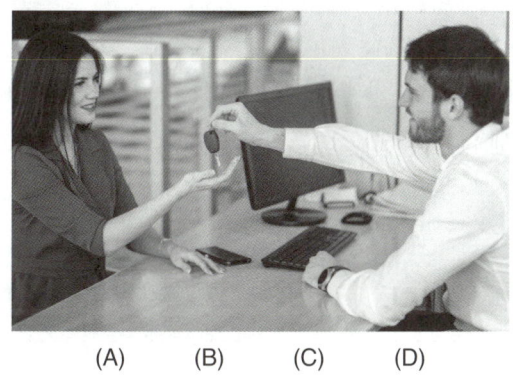
(A)　(B)　(C)　(D)

04.

(A)　(B)　(C)　(D)

05.
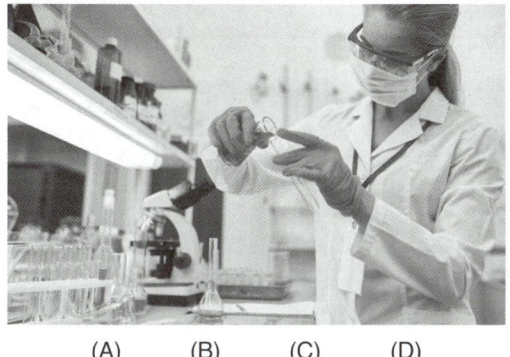
(A)　(B)　(C)　(D)

06.
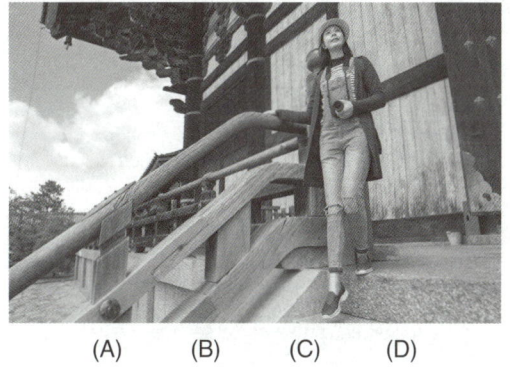
(A)　(B)　(C)　(D)

PART 2 | When 의문문 / Where 의문문

시간/시점을 묻는 When 의문문과 위치/장소/출처에 대해 묻는 Where 의문문은 매회 2문제 정도씩 출제돼요!

적용 기술

[기적의 필기노트] 25P
LC 기술 15

🎧 Day 01_P2_01.mp3

🔒 확인 문제 ❶

Mark your answer.

(A) (B)

⚠️ 주의

When 의문문에 two hours, three days 등 기간으로 답변하면 오답입니다.

출제 유형 1 — When 의문문

1 시간 표현으로 답하는 유형

시간 표현을 사용해 특정 시점으로 응답하는 것은 When 의문문에 대한 가장 대표적인 답변 방식입니다.

Q. **When** did you join the company? 언제 회사에 입사하셨나요?
A. **Last year**. 작년에요.

과거	last month/quarter 지난달/지난 분기 yesterday 어제 this morning 오늘 아침 a month ago 한 달 전 already 이미 a couple of days ago 며칠 전에
현재	right now 지금 당장 for now 지금은
미래	next month/quarter 다음 달/다음 분기 tomorrow 내일 in about 30 minutes 30분쯤 후에 soon 곧
기타	[in + 연도/월] in 2019 2019년에 in July 7월에 [on + 일/요일] on May 2 5월 2일에 on Monday 월요일에 [at/by/until + 시점] at three o'clock 3시에 by noon 정오까지 until this Friday 이번 주 금요일까지

(B) ❶ 정답

🧑 풀이 방법 — When 의문문 – 시간 표현으로 답하는 유형

🎧 Day 01_P2_02.mp3

[US - US]

When is the office rent due?
(A) For the newly hired accountants.
(B) Tomorrow, I think.
(C) Ski equipment rental service.

사무실 임대료를 언제까지 지불해야 하나요?
(A) 새로 채용된 회계사들을 위한 거예요.
(B) 내일일 거예요.
(C) 스키 장비 대여 서비스요.

┌─ 이렇게 풀어요 ─────────────────────────────
│ 1. 질문 내용 파악하기 **When** is the office **rent due**?
│   언제인지   임대료 지불 기한이
│ 2. 선택지 들으며 오답 소거하여 정답 선택하기
│   (A̶) For the newly hired **accountants**. → 연상 어휘 오답(office-accountants)
│   (B) **Tomorrow, I think.** → 정답으로 선택
│   (C̶) Ski equipment **rental** service. → 유사 발음 오답(rent-rental)
└──

2 시간 부사절로 답하는 유형

시간 표현을 나타내는 접속사를 사용하여 응답하는 경우입니다. 접속사의 의미를 잘 파악하여 시제가 일치하는 답변인지 확인해야 합니다.

Q. **When** are we opening the branch in Madrid? 우리가 언제 마드리드에 지점을 개점하나요?
A. **After** we hire the staff. 우리가 직원을 고용한 후예요.

when ~할 때	**When** the prices go down. 가격이 내려갈 때요.
as soon as ~하자마자	**As soon as** he gets back. 그가 돌아오자마자요.
(right) before ~하기 (바로) 전에	**Before** the meeting starts. 회의가 시작하기 전에요.
(right) after ~한 (직)후에	**Right after** I finish the project. 제가 프로젝트를 끝낸 직후에요.

800+

| not until ~할 때까지는 아닌 | **Not until** the manager is here.
매니저가 여기 올 때까지는 아니에요. |

🎧 Day 01_P2_03.mp3

🔒 **확인 문제 ②**

Mark your answer.

(A)　　　(B)

정답 ② (A)

풀이 방법　When 의문문 – 시간 부사절로 답하는 유형

🎧 Day 01_P2_04.mp3

BR - AU

When will Steve send the invitation cards?
(A) Right after the manager approves.
(B) We accept credit cards.
(C) To anyone on the list.

Steve가 언제 초대장을 보낼 건가요?
(A) 부장님이 승인하자마자요.
(B) 저희는 신용카드를 받습니다.
(C) 목록에 있는 모든 사람들에게요.

이렇게 풀어요

1. 질문 내용 파악하기　**When** will Steve **send** the invitation cards?
　　　　　　　　　　　　언제　　　　　　보낼 것인지

2. 선택지 들으며 오답 소거하여 정답 선택하기
　(A) Right after the manager approves. → 정답으로 선택
　(B) We accept credit cards. → 동일 단어 반복 오답 (cards-cards)
　(C) To anyone on the list. → 다른 의문사 답변 오답 (who)

🎧 Day 01_P2_05.mp3

🔒 **확인 문제 ❸**

Mark your answer.

(A)　　(B)

⚠️ **주의**

When 의문문에서는 질문의 시제와 정답 답변의 시제가 일치하지 않는 경우가 출제되기도 합니다. '언제 할 것인지' 묻는 미래 시제 질문에 '이미 했다'와 같이 과거 시제로 답하는 경우가 대표적인 예입니다.

800+

3 우회적으로 답하는 유형

특정 시점이나 시간 표현이 아닌, '이미 했다', '할 것이다', '모른다'고 하거나 모호한 시점으로 응답하는 경우도 출제됩니다. 또한, 상대방에게 되묻는 응답도 최근 자주 출제되므로 아래와 같이 다양한 예시를 알아 두세요.

> The sooner, the better. 빠르면 빠를수록 더 좋습니다.
> Let me check the schedule. 제가 일정을 확인해 보겠습니다.
> It depends on my schedule. 제 일정에 따라 다릅니다.
> How about tomorrow afternoon? 내일 오후 어때요?
> Check with Peter. Peter에게 확인해 보세요.

(B) 정답

👦 **풀이 방법**　When 의문문 – 우회적으로 답하는 유형

🎧 Day 01_P2_06.mp3

[BR - US]

When is Mr. Bacon's flight going to depart?
(A) He is from Vancouver.
(B) I will check the Web site now.
(C) An aisle seat, please.

Bacon 씨의 비행기가 언제 떠나나요?
(A) 그는 밴쿠버에서 왔어요.
(B) 제가 지금 웹사이트를 확인해 볼게요.
(C) 복도 좌석으로 주세요.

> ✏️ **이렇게 풀어요**
>
> 1. 질문 내용 파악하기　When is Mr. Bacon's flight going to depart?
>   　　　　　　　　　　　언제　　　　　비행기가 떠날 건인지
>
> 2. 선택지 들으며 오답 소거하여 정답 선택하기
>   (A̶) He is from Vancouver. → 다른 의문사 답변 오답(where)
>   (B) I will check the Web site now. → 정답으로 선택
>   (C̶) An aisle seat, please. → 연상 어휘 오답(flight-aisle seat)

22　기적의 토익 LC

DAY 01

출제 유형 2 · **Where 의문문**

1 장소 표현으로 답하는 유형

Where 의문문은 기본적으로 장소나 위치를 나타내는 전치사나 부사를 사용해 답변할 수 있습니다.

Q. **Where** will they be opening the new store? 그들은 어디에 새 매장을 열 건가요?
A. Probably **in Berlin**. 아마도 베를린에요.

at / in / on	at the station 역에서　at the customer service center 고객 서비스 센터에서 in the drawer 서랍에　in the yard 뜰에서　in Italy 이탈리아에서 on the third floor 3층에　on the board 게시판에
기타 전치사	next to the photocopier 복사기 옆에　opposite the hotel 호텔 건너편에 around the corner 모퉁이를 돈 곳에　in front of the post office 우체국 앞에 near the subway station 지하철역 근처에
장소 부사	indoors 실내에　outdoors 실외에　(right) here (바로) 여기 over there 저쪽에　upstairs 위층에　downstairs 아래층에

적용 기술

[기적의 필기노트] 26P
LC 기술 16

🎧 Day 01_P2_07.mp3

🔒 **확인 문제 ❹**

Mark your answer.

(A)　　(B)

⚠️ **주의**

When vs. Where
영국식 발음이나 호주식 발음의 경우, 모음 뒤의 r을 약하게 발음하므로 when[웬]과 where[웨-]의 구별이 어려운 경우가 있습니다. 이를 이용하여 오답을 유도하므로 주의해야 합니다.

정답 ❹ (A)

풀이 방법　Where 의문문 - 장소 표현으로 답하는 유형

🎧 Day 01_P2_08.mp3

[BR - US]

Where is the vending machine on this floor?
(A) At the end of this hallway.
(B) $2 each.
(C) No, it's not.

이 층에 자판기가 어디에 있나요?
(A) 이 복도 끝에 있어요.
(B) 한 개에 2달러입니다.
(C) 아뇨, 아니에요.

이렇게 풀어요

1. 질문 내용 파악하기　<u>Where</u> is the <u>vending machine</u> on this floor?
   　　　　　　　　　어디에　　　　　자판기가

2. 선택지 들으며 오답 소거하여 정답 선택하기
   (A) At the end of this hallway. → 정답으로 선택
   (B) $2 each. → 다른 의문사 답변 오답 (How much?)
   (C) No, it's not. → 의문사 의문문에 Yes/No로 답한 오답

PART 2　When 의문문 / Where 의문문　23

Day 01_P2_09.mp3

🔒 확인 문제 ❺

Mark your answer.

(A)   (B)

출제 포인트

Web site, online, Internet 등도 출처를 묻는 Where 의문문의 정답으로 출제될 수 있습니다.

800+

2 담당자/담당 부서/출처로 답하는 유형

'어디에 제출해야 하는지' 또는 '어디로 가야 하는지' 묻는 질문에 해당 업무를 담당하는 부서나 담당자 이름으로 답변할 수 있습니다.

Q. **Where** did you get the ticket? 그 표 어디서 사셨어요?
A. Actually, **a friend of mine** gave me. 사실은, 제 친구가 주었어요.

담당자	My **supervisor** told me. 제 상사가 제게 말해주었어요. I'll ask my **secretary**. 제 비서에게 물어볼게요. It's up to the **vice president**. 그건 부사장님이 결정할 거예요. The **manager** should have it. 매니저님이 가지고 있을 거예요.
담당 부서	The **marketing department** will handle it. 마케팅 부서에서 그 일을 처리할 거예요. Someone from the **personnel** will do it. 인사부의 누군가가 할 거예요.
출처	Actually, it was a **gift**. 사실은, 선물이었어요. My sister **gave** it to me yesterday. 제 여동생이 어제 제게 주었습니다.

(B)

풀이 방법   Where 의문문 – 담당자/담당 부서/출처로 답하는 유형

🎧 Day 01_P2_10.mp3

[AU - BR]

Where can I report this malfunctioning thermostat in my apartment?
(A) Ms. Malcom will handle it.
(B) It would be more energy-efficient.
(C) Maybe next Friday.

제 아파트의 오작동하는 이 온도 조절 장치를 어디에 말하면 되나요?
(A) Malcom 씨가 처리할 거예요.
(B) 그게 더 에너지 효율적일 거예요.
(C) 아마 다음 주 금요일이요.

✔ **이렇게 풀어요**

1. 질문 내용 파악하기 **Where** can I **report** this malfunctioning thermostat in my apartment?
   어디에   말할지

2. 선택지 들으며 오답 소거하여 정답 선택하기
   (A) Ms. Malcom will handle it. → 정답으로 선택
   (B) It would be more energy-efficient. → 연상 어휘 오답 (thermostat-energy-efficient)
   (C) Maybe next Friday. → 다른 의문사 답변 오답 (when)

3 우회적으로 답하는 유형

장소나 담당자로 답변하지 않고 아래와 같이 우회적으로 답변하는 경우도 있습니다.

Q. **Where** can I check this week's work schedule?
이번 주 근무 일정을 어디에서 확인할 수 있나요?

A. **It hasn't been confirmed yet.** 아직 확정되지 않았어요.

권유/제안	Stand in line over there. 저쪽에서 줄을 서 주세요. Leave them on the desk. 책상 위에 두세요. Ask the manager. 매니저에게 물어보세요.
기타	Everyone has been talking about it. 모든 사람들이 그 얘기를 합니다. It hasn't been decided yet. 아직 결정되지 않았어요. It depends on the situation. 상황에 따라 다릅니다.

🎧 Day 01_P2_11.mp3

🔒 **확인 문제 ❻**

Mark your answer.

(A)   (B)

출제 포인트
장소를 묻는 질문에 구체적인 장소로 답변하지 않고, 그 장소를 알 수 있는 지도(map)나 건물 안내도(building directory) 등을 제시하는 답변이 출제됩니다.
Q. **Where** is the Accounting Department located? 경리부가 어디 있나요?
A. Here's **the building directory.** 여기 건물 안내도가 있어요.

정답 ❻ (A)

풀이 방법   Where 의문문 – 우회적으로 답하는 유형

🎧 Day 01_P2_12.mp3

US - AU

Where did the delivery man leave the contract from Johnson Cosmetics?
(A) He will take a two-day leave.
(B) Check your mail box.
(C) The next-day delivery option.

배달원이 Johnson Cosmetics에서 온 계약서를 어디에 두었나요?
(A) 그는 이틀간 휴가를 가질 거예요.
(B) 당신의 우편함을 확인해 보세요.
(C) 익일 배송 옵션이요.

이렇게 풀어요

1. 질문 내용 파악하기   **Where** did the delivery man **leave the contract** from Johnson Cosmetics?
   어디에   계약서를 두었는지

2. 선택지 들으며 오답 소거하여 정답 선택하기
   (A̶) He will take a two-day **leave**. → 동일 단어 반복 오답 (leave-leave)
   (B) **Check your mail box.** → 정답으로 선택
   (C̶) The next-day **delivery** option. → 동일 단어 반복 오답 (delivery-delivery)

따라 하면 문제가 풀리는
연습 문제

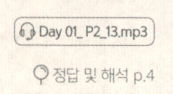

각 질문과 보기를 들으며 빈칸을 채운 뒤 정답에는 O, 오답에는 X 표시하세요.

01. _____ can I find Ms. Timber in the accounting department?
　(A) _____ is a senior _____. [　]
　(B) _____ through the _____ door on the right. [　]

02. _____ can I submit my job application?
　(A) _____ it _____. [　]
　(B) Probably _____ 4 P.M. [　]

03. _____ is Bernard going to meet with the new clients?
　(A) _____ met with them _____. [　]
　(B) They are open _____ _____. [　]

04. _____ are we announcing the company merger?
　(A) _____ _____ _____ the president _____ from the seminar. [　]
　(B) It will be _____ in the _____. [　]

05. _____ can I get this document photocopied?
　(A) There's a _____ on the _____ _____. [　]
　(B) Two _____ per _____ should be sufficient. [　]

06. _____ are you taking a coffee break?
　(A) Not for _____ _____. [　]
　(B) I want to _____ a _____. [　]

07. _____ can I find the notice about the personnel?
　(A) Yes, _____ _____ and turn left. [　]
　(B) It will be _____ on our Web site. [　]

08. _____ can I come in for my regular check-up?
　(A) Sorry, that book has already been _____ _____. [　]
　(B) Can you spare some time around three _____ _____? [　]

토익에 나올 실전 문제

🎧 Day 01_ P2_14.mp3
정답 및 해설 p.5

01. Mark your answer on your answer sheet.
(A) (B) (C)

02. Mark your answer on your answer sheet.
(A) (B) (C)

03. Mark your answer on your answer sheet.
(A) (B) (C)

04. Mark your answer on your answer sheet.
(A) (B) (C)

05. Mark your answer on your answer sheet.
(A) (B) (C)

06. Mark your answer on your answer sheet.
(A) (B) (C)

07. Mark your answer on your answer sheet.
(A) (B) (C)

08. Mark your answer on your answer sheet.
(A) (B) (C)

09. Mark your answer on your answer sheet.
(A) (B) (C)

10. Mark your answer on your answer sheet.
(A) (B) (C)

11. Mark your answer on your answer sheet.
(A) (B) (C)

12. Mark your answer on your answer sheet.
(A) (B) (C)

13. Mark your answer on your answer sheet.
(A) (B) (C)

14. Mark your answer on your answer sheet.
(A) (B) (C)

15. Mark your answer on your answer sheet.
(A) (B) (C)

16. Mark your answer on your answer sheet.
(A) (B) (C)

'멋진 당신, 오늘도 화이팅'

DAY 02

오늘의 학습 포인트

PART 1. 다인 사진 / 사물·풍경 사진
1. 사람이나 사물의 상태를 묘사하는 현재 완료 - has/have + p.p.
2. 여러 사람 중 일부만 묘사
3. 진행 중인 동작을 묘사하는 현재 진행 수동태 - is/are being p.p.
4. 상태나 위치를 묘사하는 'There is/are + 명사 + 전치사구/분사구'
5. 사물의 상태를 묘사하는 'be + p.p. + 전치사구'
6. 사물의 상태를 묘사하는 '주어 + 일반 동사 + 목적어/전치사구'

PART 2. What 의문문 / Who 의문문
1. What 의문문
    1) What + 명사 - What time, What day, What type
    2) What + 동사
    3) What 관용 표현 - What about ~?, What do you think of ~?
2. Who 의문문
    1) 사람 이름/직위/부서명으로 답하는 유형 - manager, accounting
    2) 부정 대명사와 인칭 대명사로 답하는 유형 - someone, no one, everyone, one of
    3) 우회적으로 답하는 유형 - It hasn't been decided yet.

PART 1 다인 사진 / 사물·풍경 사진

다인 사진은 공통점 혹은 일부를 묘사하는 표현이 정답으로 출제됩니다.
사물·풍경 사진은 매회 1문제씩 꾸준히 출제돼요!

확인 문제 ❶

🎧 Day 02_ P1_01.mp3

(A) | (B)

출제 유형 1 — 상태를 묘사하는 현재 완료 (has/have + p.p.)

900+

다인 사진에서 인물들의 공통적인 상태나 동작을 묘사할 때 주어는 주로 they, people 등으로 출제됩니다. 아래 풀이 방법의 정답 문장처럼 상태를 나타낼 때 사용되는 구조 중 하나가 'has/have + p.p.'인데 '~했다, ~한 상태이다'의 의미로 파악하면 됩니다.

> A bus **has stopped** on the street. 버스가 거리에 정차했다.
> Some people **have left** their bags on the grass.
> 몇몇 사람들이 그들의 가방을 잔디에 놓아두었다.
> Some people **have lined up** in front of a building. 몇몇 사람들이 건물 앞에 줄 서 있다.
> A man **has opened** a door. 한 남자가 문을 열어 놓은 상태다.

(B) ❶ 정답

풀이 방법 — 다인 사진 – 공통점 묘사

🎧 Day 02_ P1_02.mp3

[BR]
(A) The men are working at a building site.
(B) They have gathered near a building.
(C) They are looking into a computer monitor.
(D) They are resting on a bench.

이렇게 풀어요

1. **사진 파악하기** 다인 사진, 건물 밖, men/they(남자들/그들) – standing(서 있다), gathered(모여 있다), holding a cup(컵을 들고 있다), 배경 – buildings(건물들)

2. **선택지 들으며 사진과 불일치하는 것 소거하여 정답 선택하기**

   (A̶) The men are working **at a building site**. 남자들이 건설 현장에서 일하고 있다. → 위치 불일치
   (B) They have gathered near a building. 그들은 건물 근처에 모여 있다. → 정답으로 선택
   (C̶) They are **looking into** a computer monitor. 그들은 컴퓨터 화면을 들여다보고 있다. → 동사 불일치
   (D̶) They are **resting** on a bench. 그들은 벤치에서 쉬고 있다. → 동사 불일치

출제 유형 2 · 여러 사람 중 일부만 묘사

다인 사진은 최소 3명, 많을 경우 5~6명이 사진에 등장합니다. 이때 모든 사람들의 **공통적인 동작**이 아니라 **일부 몇몇 사람들의 동작이나 상태가 답이 되는 경우가 많습니다.** 일부를 나타낼 때 사용하는 주어 표현을 알아 두어야 합니다.

• 일부를 나타낼 때 사용하는 주어 표현

Some people 몇몇 사람들 Some men 몇몇 남자들 Some women 몇몇 여자들	A group of people 한 무리의 사람들 One of the people 사람들 중 한 명

Some people are listening to a presentation. 몇몇 사람들이 발표를 듣고 있다.
Some customers are paying for their meal. 몇몇 고객들이 식사비를 지불하고 있다.
A group of people are seated on the floor. 한 무리의 사람들이 바닥에 앉아 있다.

🔒 확인 문제 ❷

(A) | (B)

출제 포인트
모여 있는 사람을 나타내는 표현으로 **a crowd of people**이 자주 출제됩니다.

정답 ❷ (A)

풀이 방법   다인 사진 – 일부만 묘사

[US]

(A) One of the women is pushing a shopping cart.
(B) One of the women is putting an item in a bag.
(C) Some people are waiting in line.
(D) Some people are gathered at an entrance.

✔ 이렇게 풀어요

1. **사진 파악하기** 다인 사진, 도서관, a man(남자) – sitting(앉아 있다), some people(몇몇 사람들) – in line(줄 서 있는), 배경 – bookshelves(책장)

2. **선택지 들으며 사진과 불일치하는 것 소거하여 정답 선택하기**
   - (A) One of the women is **pushing** a shopping cart. 여자들 중 한 명이 쇼핑 카트를 밀고 있다. → 동사 불일치
   - (B) One of the women is putting an item **in a bag**. 여자들 중 한 명이 제품들을 가방에 넣고 있다. → 위치 불일치
   - (C) Some people are waiting in line. 몇몇 사람들이 줄을 서서 기다리고 있다. → 정답으로 선택
   - (D) Some people are gathered **at an entrance**. 몇몇 사람들이 입구에 모여 있다. → 위치 불일치

적용 기술

[기적의 필기노트] 17P
LC 기술 7

🔒 확인 문제 ❸

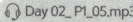
Day 02_ P1_05.mp3

(A) | (B)

⚠️ 주의

현재 진행 수동태는 사람이 없으면 대부분 오답이 되지만 사람 유무에 관계 없이 정답이 되는 경우도 있습니다.

· 전시된 상태나 배경을 나타낼 때 (display, decorate, exhibit, cast, occupy 등의 동사)
- Some merchandise **is being displayed** for sale. 몇몇 상품이 판매용으로 전시되고 있다.
· 기계에 의한 동작을 나타낼 때
- Luggage **is being moved** on the conveyer belt. 수하물이 컨베이어 벨트 위에서 옮겨지고 있다.

(B) ❸ 정답

출제 유형 3 : 진행 중인 동작을 묘사하는 현재 진행 수동태 (is/are being p.p.)

900+

사람의 동작을 묘사할 때 사물 주어를 이용하여 표현하는 보기가 정답으로 출제됩니다. 이 경우에 현재 진행 수동태(is/are being p.p.)를 사용합니다. 따라서 현재 진행 수동태가 정답이 되려면 반드시 사람이 사진에 있어야 합니다. 사람이 없는 사진에서 출제되는 현재 진행 수동태 문장은 오답입니다.

> A floor **is being swept**. 바닥이 쓸리고 있다. (사람이 바닥을 쓸고 있다.)
> Some doors **are being painted**. 문이 칠해지고 있다. (사람이 문을 칠하고 있다.)
> A bookshelf **is being assembled**. 책장이 조립되고 있다. (사람이 책장을 조립하고 있다.)
> Some fruits **are being weighed** on a scale.
> 과일이 저울에서 무게가 재어지고 있다. (사람이 과일을 저울에 놓고 무게를 재고 있다.)
> A set of musical instruments **is being set up** on a stage.
> 한 세트의 악기가 무대에 설치되고 있다. (사람이 악기를 무대에 설치하고 있다.)

👨 풀이 방법   다인 사진 - 사람 주어 + 사물 주어

Day 02_ P1_06.mp3

[BR]

(A) A dining table is being set up outside.
(B) Dishes are being served on a table.
(C) A server is pouring water into a cup.
(D) A woman is reading a menu.

✓ 이렇게 풀어요

1. **사진 파악하기** 다인 사진, 식당, customers(손님들) - sitting(앉아 있다), a man(남자)/a server(종업원) - serving(서빙하고 있다), 배경 - dishes(음식), table(테이블)

2. **선택지 들으며 사진과 불일치하는 것 소거하여 정답 선택하기**
   (A̶) A dining table is being set up outside. 식탁이 야외에 설치되고 있다. → 동사 불일치
   (B) Dishes are being served on a table. 음식들이 테이블에 제공되고 있다. → 정답으로 선택
   (C̶) A server is pouring water into a cup. 종업원이 컵에 물을 따르고 있다. → 동사 불일치
   (D̶) A woman is reading a menu. 여자가 메뉴를 읽고 있다. → 동사 불일치

출제 유형 4   상태나 위치를 묘사하는 'There is/are + 명사 + 전치사구/분사구'

- 'There is/are ~' 구문은 사물이나 사람의 상태나 위치를 묘사할 때 사용됩니다. 진주어인 명사가 'is/are' 뒤에 제시되므로 주의해야 합니다. 명사 뒤에는 장소 전치사구가 따라 나와 주어인 명사의 위치를 묘사합니다. 따라서 명사와 장소 전치사구 표현이 사진과 일치하는지 확인하는 것이 중요합니다.
- 장소 전치사구 대신에 현재 분사구(-ing) 또는 과거 분사구(p.p.)가 따라 나오는 보기는 출제 비중은 낮지만 난이도가 높은 문제입니다. 명사와 분사 사이에 'is/are'를 넣고 의미를 파악하면 해결하기 쉽습니다.

There is a water dispenser beside a door. 문 옆에 정수기가 있다.
There are dishes on the table. 테이블 위에 접시들이 있다.
There are trees along a roadway. 길을 따라 나무들이 있다.
There are lampposts along a walkway. 인도를 따라 가로등이 있다.

800+
There are umbrellas blocking a road. 길을 막고 있는 파라솔들이 있다.
There are clothes hanging from racks. 선반에 걸려 있는 옷들이 있다.
There are boxes stacked on the shelves. 선반에 쌓여 있는 상자들이 있다.

🔒 확인 문제 ❹

🎧 Day 02_P1_07.mp3

(A) | (B)

⚠️ **주의**
'There is/are + 명사 + 전치사구/분사구' 형태의 보기는 뒤의 명사와 전치사구까지 잘 들어야 합니다.

정답 (A)

👨‍🏫 풀이 방법   사물·풍경 사진 – 실내

🎧 Day 02_P1_08.mp3

[BR]
(A) All chairs are occupied.
(B) Curtains have been left open.
(C) There are laptop computers on a desk.
(D) Some file folders are scattered on the floor.

✅ **이렇게 풀어요**

1. **사진 파악하기** 사물·풍경 사진, 사무실, chairs(의자), desk(책상), laptop computers(노트북 컴퓨터), windows(창문)
2. **선택지 들으며 사진과 불일치하는 것 소거하여 정답 선택하기**
   - (A̶) All chairs are occupied. 모든 의자에 사람들이 앉아 있다. → 동사 불일치
   - (B̶) Curtains have been left open. 커튼이 열려 있다. → 주어 불일치
   - (C) There are laptop computers on a desk. 책상에 노트북 컴퓨터들이 있다. → 정답으로 선택
   - (D̶) Some file folders are scattered on the floor. 몇몇 파일 폴더들이 바닥에 흩어져 있다. → 위치 불일치

확인 문제 ❺

🎧 Day 02_P1_09.mp3

(A) | (B)

출제 유형 5
사물의 상태를 묘사하는 'be + p.p. + 전치사구'

`800+`

수동태 'be + p.p.' 뒤에 전치사구가 붙어서 사물의 상태 또는 위치를 묘사할 수 있습니다. 이때 전치사구가 사진과 일치하지 않아 오답이 되는 경우가 있으므로 반드시 문장을 끝까지 들어야 합니다.

Some vehicles **are parked on a street**. 몇몇 차량이 거리에 주차되어 있다.
Decorations **are arranged on a sofa**. 장식품이 소파 위에 놓여 있다.
Some photographs **are arranged on a windowsill**. 사진들이 창틀에 놓여 있다.
Boxes **are stacked in the room**. 상자들이 방 안에 쌓여 있다.
A train **is stopped at a platform**. 기차가 승강장에 멈춰 있다.
Some tall buildings **are located behind an outdoor market**.
몇몇 높은 건물들이 야외 시장 뒤에 있다.

(B) ❺ 정답

풀이 방법   사물·풍경 사진 – 야외

🎧 Day 02_P1_10.mp3

US
(A) A car has been parked in a garage.
(B) Chairs are set up in front of a building.
(C) Some potted plants are arranged on the balcony.
(D) Centerpieces are placed on tables.

✔ 이렇게 풀어요

1. **사진 파악하기** 사물·풍경 사진, 골목길, chairs and tables in front of a building(건물 앞에 의자와 테이블), a car(자동차), parked(주차된), buildings(건물), plants(식물)

2. **선택지 들으며 사진과 불일치하는 것 소거하여 정답 선택하기**
   (A̶) A car has been parked in a garage. 차가 차고에 주차되어 있다. → 위치 불일치
   (B) Chairs are set up in front of a building. 의자들이 건물 앞에 배치되어 있다. → 정답으로 선택
   (C̶) Some potted plants are arranged on the balcony. 화분 몇 개가 발코니에 배열되어 있다. → 위치 불일치
   (D̶) Centerpieces are placed on tables. 중앙부 장식품이 테이블 위에 놓여 있다. → 주어 불일치

출제 유형 6 | 사물의 상태를 묘사하는 '주어 + 일반 동사 + 목적어/전치사구'

900+

앞서 배웠던 문장 구조는 모두 be동사가 사용되지만, 현재 시제의 일반 동사를 사용해서 사진 속 사물의 상태를 나타내는 경우도 있습니다. 출제 빈도는 높지 않지만, surround(둘러싸다), line(줄지어 있다), cross(가로지르다), lead(~로 이어져 있다)와 같이 종종 출제되는 동사들은 알아 두어야 합니다.

> Mountains **surround** a town. 산이 마을을 둘러싸고 있다.
> A bridge **crosses** over a river. 다리가 강을 가로지르고 있다.
> Some stairs **lead to** a swimming pool. 몇몇 계단이 수영장으로 이어져 있다.
> The trail **leads up to** the hill. 오솔길이 언덕으로 이어져 있다.

확인 문제 ❻

Day 02_ P1_11.mp3

(A) | (B)

정답 ❻ (A)

풀이 방법 | 사물·풍경 사진

Day 02_ P1_12.mp3

US
(A) A roof is being repaired.
(B) A flag is being raised on a pole.
(C) Some benches are lined up.
(D) A fence surrounds a statue.

✓ 이렇게 풀어요

1. **사진 파악하기** 사물/풍경 사진, statue(조각상), fence(울타리), in front of(~ 앞에), building(건물)

2. **선택지 들으며 사진과 불일치하는 것 소거하여 정답 선택하기**
   - (A) A roof is being repaired. 지붕이 수리되고 있다. → 동사 불일치
   - (B) A flag is being raised on a pole. 깃발이 막대기에 게양되고 있다. → 주어 불일치
   - (C) Some benches are lined up. 벤치들이 줄지어 늘어서 있다. → 주어 불일치
   - (D) A fence surrounds a statue. 울타리가 조각상을 둘러싸고 있다. → 정답으로 선택

PART 1 다인 사진 / 사물·풍경 사진

연습 문제

01.

(1) 음원을 들으며 사진과 관련된 단어이면 O, 아니면 X에 표시하세요.

(A) O I X (B) O I X (C) O I X

(2) 음원을 들으며 빈칸을 채우고 정답에는 O, 오답에는 X 표시하세요.

(A) Some people are _____ at a _____ site. [   ]
(B) Some people are standing on the _____. [   ]

02.

(1) 음원을 들으며 사진과 관련된 단어이면 O, 아니면 X에 표시하세요.

(A) O I X (B) O I X (C) O I X

(2) 음원을 들으며 빈칸을 채우고 정답에는 O, 오답에는 X 표시하세요.

(A) They're _____ on a riverbank. [   ]
(B) A tent _____ _____ _____ _____ on the grass. [   ]

03.

(1) 음원을 들으며 사진과 관련된 단어이면 O, 아니면 X에 표시하세요.

(A) O I X (B) O I X (C) O I X

(2) 음원을 들으며 빈칸을 채우고 정답에는 O, 오답에는 X 표시하세요.

(A) There are _____ on a bed. [   ]
(B) Some curtains are pulled _____. [   ]

04.

(1) 음원을 들으며 사진과 관련된 단어이면 O, 아니면 X에 표시하세요.

(A) O I X (B) O I X (C) O I X

(2) 음원을 들으며 빈칸을 채우고 정답에는 O, 오답에는 X 표시하세요.

(A) A _____ is driving on a _____. [   ]
(B) Some _____ are _____ on a river. [   ]

토익에 나올 실전 문제

01.

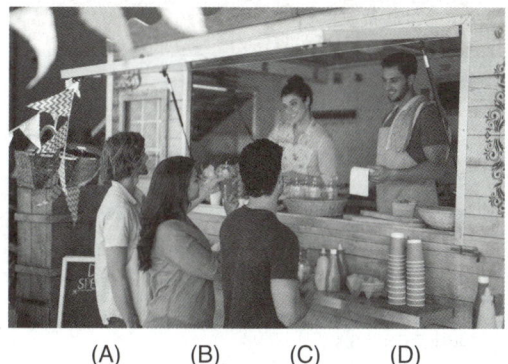

(A) (B) (C) (D)

02.

(A) (B) (C) (D)

03.

(A) (B) (C) (D)

04.

(A) (B) (C) (D)

05.

(A) (B) (C) (D)

06.

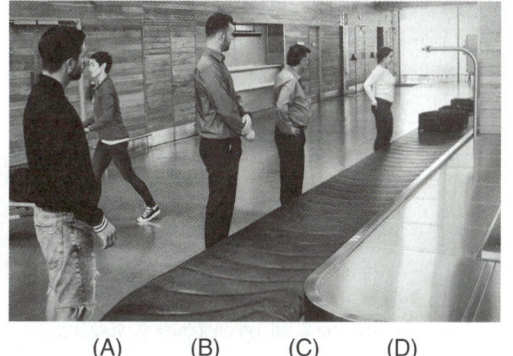

(A) (B) (C) (D)

PART 2 — What 의문문 / Who 의문문

What 의문문은 매회 1문제 정도 출제됩니다!
Who 의문문은 담당자를 묻는 문제가 자주 나오며 매회 2문제 정도 출제돼요!

적용 기술

[기적의 필기노트] 28P
LC 기술 17

🎧 Day 02_P2_01.mp3

🔒 확인 문제 ❶

Mark your answer.
(A)　　(B)

출제 유형 1 — What 의문문

1 What + 명사

What 다음에 나오는 명사에 따라 시간, 장소, 비용, 종류 등 다양한 내용을 물을 수 있습니다. 따라서 What 뒤의 명사를 반드시 들어야 해요.

What + time = When 시간을 묻는 표현	Q. **What's** the local **time** now in London? 런던의 지금 현지 시간은 몇 시인가요? A. A quarter past six. 6시 15분이요.
What date/day = When 날짜를 묻는 표현	Q. **What date** is the rent due? 며칠에 임대료를 내야 하죠? A. On the last day of every month. 매달 말일입니다.
What type/kind = Which 종류를 묻는 표현	Q. **What type** of phone do you want? 어떤 종류의 전화기를 원하세요? A. Something easy to use. 사용하기 편한 것이요.
What place/location = Where 장소를 묻는 표현	Q. **What place** do you recommend visiting? 어떤 장소를 방문하는 것을 추천하시나요? A. You should go to Time Square. 타임스퀘어에 가 보세요.
What + cost/estimate/ fee/price = How much 비용을 묻는 표현	Q. **What's** the **cost** to send this package? 이 소포를 보내는 데 비용이 얼마인가요? A. It's 50 dollars. 50달러입니다.

풀이 방법 — What 의문문 - What + 명사

🎧 Day 02_P2_02.mp3

[US - BR]

What plans do you have during your trip to Chicago?
(A) I really enjoyed it.
(B) It would be triple.
(C) I'm going to attend my cousin's wedding.

시카고를 여행하는 동안 무슨 계획이 있나요?
(A) 정말 즐거웠어요.
(B) 세 배일 거예요.
(C) 사촌의 결혼식에 참석할 거예요.

이렇게 풀어요

1. 질문 내용 파악하기 **What plan** do you have during your trip to Chicago?
　　　　　　　　　　　　　무슨　계획

2. 선택지 들으며 오답 소거하여 정답 선택하기
　(A) I really enjoyed it. → 시제가 맞지 않는 오답(미래-과거)
　(B) It would be triple. → 유사 발음 오답(trip-triple)
　(C) I'm going to attend my cousin's wedding. → 정답으로 선택

2 What + 동사

- What 뒤에 명사가 나오지 않는 경우에는 동사를 잘 들어야 합니다. 'What + 주어 + 동사'에서 동사가 정답을 결정하기 때문입니다.

    Q. **What** did the vice president **ask for**? 부사장님이 무엇을 요청했나요?
    A. Updated contact information of all employees. 전 직원의 최신 연락처요.

- What 다음에 나오는 동사의 시제도 유의해서 들어야 합니다.

    Q. **What** are you **planning to do** tomorrow? 내일 무엇을 할 계획인가요? [미래 시제]
    A. **I'll go** grocery shopping. (O) 식료품을 사러 갈 거예요.
    A. I already **bought** some. (X) 저는 이미 좀 샀어요.

🎧 Day 02_P2_03.mp3

🔒 확인 문제 ❷

Mark your answer.

(A)　　(B)

정답 ❷ (B)

풀이 방법　What 의문문 - What + 동사

🎧 Day 02_P2_04.mp3

US - BR

What did you discuss in the weekly meeting?
(A) In meeting room B on the second floor.
(B) Every other week, I think.
(C) It was mainly about the upcoming inspection.

주간 회의에서 무엇을 논의했나요?
(A) 2층의 회의실 B에서요.
(B) 제 생각엔 격주마다요.
(C) 주로 곧 있을 감사에 관한 것이었어요.

✓ 이렇게 풀어요

1. 질문 내용 파악하기　 in the weekly meeting?
   　　　　　　　　　　무엇을　　논의했나요

2. 선택지 들으며 오답 소거하여 정답 선택하기
   (A̶) In meeting room B on the second floor. → 동일 단어 반복 오답(meeting)
   (B̶) Every other week, I think. → 다른 의문사 답변 오답(how often)
   (C) It was mainly about the upcoming inspection. → 정답으로 선택

PART 2　What 의문문 / Who 의문문　39

🎧 Day 02_P2_05.mp3

🔒 **확인 문제 ❸**

Mark your answer.

(A)　　　(B)

800+

3 What 관용 표현

What 의문문에는 숙어처럼 관용 표현으로 굳어진 질문 형태가 있습니다. 듣는 즉시 이해할 수 있도록 표현과 의미를 통째로 암기해야 합니다.

Q. **What would you like to** drink? 무엇을 마시겠습니까?
A. I'll have coffee, thank you. 저는 커피를 마시겠습니다. 감사합니다.

이유/원인	What made you ~? 왜 ~?
권유	What about ~? ~하는 게 어때요? What do you say to ~? ~하는 게 어때요?
의견	What do you think of ~? ~에 대해서 어떻게 생각하세요?
외모	What does ~ look like? ~는 어떻게 생겼나요?
성격/상태	What is ~ like? ~는 어떤 사람인가요?
선택	What would you like to ~? 무엇을 ~하시겠어요?

(B)

풀이 방법   What 의문문 – What 관용 표현

🎧 Day 02_P2_06.mp3

BR - US

What do you think of the TV commercial for the new shoes line?
(A) It's very creative and attractive.
(B) Yeah, I live close to the commercial area.
(C) A little bit small and tight for me.

새 신발 라인에 대한 TV 광고를 어떻게 생각하나요?
(A) 아주 창의적이고 매력적이에요.
(B) 네, 저는 상업 지구 가까이에 살아요.
(C) 저한테 좀 작고 꽉 끼어요.

✓ **이렇게 풀어요**

1. 질문 내용 파악하기　**What do you think** of the **TV commercial** for the new shoes line?
　　　　　　　　　　　 어떻게 생각하나요　　　　　 TV 광고를

2. 선택지 들으며 오답 소거하여 정답 선택하기
　(A) It's very creative and attractive.　→ 정답으로 선택
　(B) Yeah, I live close to the commercial area.　→ 의문사 의문문에 Yes/No로 답한 오답
　(C) A little bit small and tight for me.　→ 연상 어휘 오답 (shoes-small and tight)

출제 유형 2 — Who 의문문

1. 사람 이름/직위/부서명으로 답하는 유형

Who 의문문에 대한 대표적인 답변은 사람 이름, 직위 등 사람을 지칭하는 명사로 답하는 것입니다. 자주 출제되는 직위나 부서명은 알아 두어야 합니다.

Q. **Who**'s going to pick up the vice president at the airport?
누가 부사장님을 공항에서 모셔올 건가요?

A. **My assistant** will. 제 비서가 할 거예요.

지위/직업	manager 매니저, 부장 branch manager 지점장 vice president 부사장 supervisor 상사, 관리자 assistant 비서, 부하 직원 sales representative 영업 사원 secretary 비서 technician 기술자 clerk 점원 accountant 회계사 inspector 검사관 architect 건축가 board of directors 이사진 real estate agent 부동산 중개인
부서	accounting 회계부 personnel/human resources 인사부 maintenance 시설 관리부 sales 영업부 payroll 급여 관리부 security office 보안 관리부
지인/가족	associate 동료 colleague 동료 client 고객 cousin 사촌 aunt 이모, 고모

적용 기술
[기적의 필기노트] 24P
LC 기술 14

🎧 Day 02_ P2_07.mp3

🔒 확인 문제 ④
Mark your answer.
(A)   (B)

출제 포인트
단체나 회사 전체를 나타내는 어휘도 정답이 될 수 있습니다.
Q. Who's in charge of the job fair? 누가 직업 박람회를 담당하고 있나요?
A. Several agencies have been assigned to it. 몇 개의 대행사들이 그 일에 배정되었어요.

정답 🔊 (A)

풀이 방법 — Who 의문문 – 사람 이름/직위/부서명으로 답하는 유형

🎧 Day 02_ P2_08.mp3

BR - US

Who is organizing the cooking demonstration at Baltimore Electronics?
(A) Twice a week.
(B) Angelina Francona.
(C) No, the oven is for professional chefs.

Baltimore 전자에서의 요리 시연을 누가 준비할 건가요?
(A) 일주일에 두 번이요.
(B) Angelina Francona요.
(C) 아뇨, 그 오븐은 전문 요리사들을 위한 거예요.

 이렇게 풀어요

1. 질문 내용 파악하기   **Who** is **organizing** the cooking demonstration at Baltimore Electronics?
   누가 / 준비하는지

2. 선택지 들으며 오답 소거하여 정답 선택하기
   (A̶) Twice a week. → 다른 의문사 답변 오답(how often)
   (B) Angelina Francona. → 정답으로 선택
   (C̶) No, the oven is for professional chefs. → 의문사 의문문에 Yes/No로 답한 오답

PART 2 What 의문문 / Who 의문문

🎧 Day 02_ P2_09.mp3

🔒 확인 문제 ❺

Mark your answer.

(A)   (B)

출제 포인트
Who로 묻는 질문에 출처나 장소 표현으로도 답할 수 있습니다.
Q. Who's responsible for the project? 누가 그 프로젝트를 책임지나요?
A. That information is in the e-mail. 그 정보는 이메일에 있습니다.

2 부정 대명사와 인칭 대명사로 답하는 유형

someone, no one, everyone, one 등 부정/부분 대명사가 쓰인 보기가 들리면 정답일 확률이 높습니다. 또한 he, she, they 등의 인칭 대명사로 답하는 문장도 정답이 될 수 있습니다.

Q. **Who**'s supposed to go to the workshop? 누가 그 워크숍에 가기로 되어 있나요?
A. **Anyone** who's interested can attend it. 관심 있는 사람은 누구나 참석할 수 있습니다.

| 인칭 대명사를 사용한 답변 | I'll send **you** the information. 제가 정보를 보내 줄게요.
He is our new manager. 그는 우리의 새로운 매니저입니다.
She will fix it tomorrow. 그녀가 내일 그것을 고칠 겁니다. |

800+

| 부정 대명사를 사용한 답변 | **Someone** in human resources. 인사부의 누군가요.
I believe **one** of the new employees will.
신입 사원들 중 한 명이 할 거예요.
Everyone in the marketing department. 마케팅부의 모든 사람들이요.
No one, for now. 지금으로선, 아무도 없어요.
Anyone who's interested can participate.
관심 있는 사람은 누구나 참석할 수 있어요. |

(A) ❺ 정답

풀이 방법   Who 의문문 – 부정 대명사/인칭 대명사로 답하는 유형

🎧 Day 02_ P2_10.mp3

[US - BR]

Who can help me apply for the reward point card?
(A) My job is very rewarding.
(B) Someone will be with you soon.
(C) The position is still open.

제가 보상 포인트 카드를 신청하도록 누가 도와주실 수 있나요?
(A) 제 일은 아주 보람 있어요.
(B) 누군가 곧 당신을 도와드릴 겁니다.
(C) 그 자리는 아직 공석입니다.

✓ 이렇게 풀어요

1. 질문 내용 파악하기 **Who can help me** apply for the reward point card?
   누가 도와줄 수 있는지

2. 선택지 들으며 오답 소거하여 정답 선택하기
   (A̶) My job is very **rewarding**. → 유사 발음 오답 (reward-rewarding)
   (B) **Someone** will be with you soon. → 정답으로 선택
   (C̶) The **position** is still open. → 연상 어휘 오답 (apply-position)

3 우회적으로 답하는 유형

구체적으로 누구인지 답변하지 않고, '모르겠다, 결정되지 않았다, ~에게 물어보세요' 등으로 답변할 수 있습니다.

Q. **Who** was assigned to our team? 누가 우리 팀으로 배정되었나요?
A. **It hasn't been decided yet.** 아직 결정되지 않았어요.

'아직 결정되지 않았다' 유형	It hasn't been decided yet. 아직 결정되지 않았어요. They are still discussing. 여전히 논의 중입니다.
'모른다' 답변 유형	I have no idea. 모르겠습니다. No one told me. 아무도 저에게 말해 주지 않았어요.

900+	
기타	How about we ask the manager? 매니저에게 물어보는 게 어때요? It's up to the board members. 임원들이 결정할 일입니다.

🎧 Day 02_ P2_11.mp3

🔒 **확인 문제 ❻**

Mark your answer.

(A)　　(B)

정답 ❻ (B)

풀이 방법　Who 의문문 – 우회적으로 답하는 유형

🎧 Day 02_ P2_12.mp3

[BR - AU]

Who should I talk to about returning this defective item?
(A) I can help you right now.
(B) The list should be itemized.
(C) No, I want a full refund.

이 결함 있는 제품을 반품하는 것에 대해 누구에게 말해야 하나요?
(A) 제가 지금 바로 도와드리겠습니다.
(B) 목록은 항목별로 적혀 있어야 해요.
(C) 아뇨, 저는 전액 환불 받고 싶어요.

> 📙 이렇게 풀어요
>
> 1. 질문 내용 파악하기　**Who should I talk to** about returning this defective item?
> 　　　　　　　　　　　　　누구에게 말해야 하는지
>
> 2. 선택지 들으며 오답 소거하여 정답 선택하기
> 　(A) I can help you right now. → 정답으로 선택
> 　(B) The list should be itemized. → 유사 발음 오답(item-itemized)
> 　(C) No, I want a full refund. → 의문사 의문문에 Yes/No로 답한 오답

따라 하면 문제가 풀리는

연습 문제

🎧 Day 02_P2_13.mp3
📍 정답 및 해석 p.11

각 질문과 보기를 들으며 빈칸을 채운 뒤 정답에는 O, 오답에는 X 표시하세요.

01. _____ do you intend to do after you retire?
　　(A) I want to _____ _____ the world. [　]
　　(B) I think his _____ was impressive. [　]

02. _____ is in charge of the annual awards banquet?
　　(A) Samuel was the award _____. [　]
　　(B) Mr. Clark will _____ _____. [　]

03. _____ should we wear to Mr. Wong's farewell party?
　　(A) No, he's _____ to London. [　]
　　(B) I heard that _____ _____ is suggested. [　]

04. _____ will notify employees of these changes?
　　(A) The _____ _____ will. [　]
　　(B) I did not _____ _____. [　]

05. _____ did the _____ say about our design proposal?
　　(A) _____ _____ to do some revisions. [　]
　　(B) Yes, this is my favorite _____. [　]

06. _____ _____ _____ call if I have a problem with the computer?
　　(A) _____, we _____ ten computers. [　]
　　(B) _____ Frank. [　]

07. _____ _____ we categorize these _____?
　　(A) It's in the file _____. [　]
　　(B) That's a _____ _____. [　]

08. _____ supposed to _____ the office today?
　　(A) _____ was supposed to _____ me here. [　]
　　(B) It's _____ _____. [　]

토익에 나올 실전 문제

🎧 Day 02_ P2_14.mp3
📍 정답 및 해설 p.12

01. Mark your answer on your answer sheet.
   (A)   (B)   (C)

02. Mark your answer on your answer sheet.
   (A)   (B)   (C)

03. Mark your answer on your answer sheet.
   (A)   (B)   (C)

04. Mark your answer on your answer sheet.
   (A)   (B)   (C)

05. Mark your answer on your answer sheet.
   (A)   (B)   (C)

06. Mark your answer on your answer sheet.
   (A)   (B)   (C)

07. Mark your answer on your answer sheet.
   (A)   (B)   (C)

08. Mark your answer on your answer sheet.
   (A)   (B)   (C)

09. Mark your answer on your answer sheet.
   (A)   (B)   (C)

10. Mark your answer on your answer sheet.
   (A)   (B)   (C)

11. Mark your answer on your answer sheet.
   (A)   (B)   (C)

12. Mark your answer on your answer sheet.
   (A)   (B)   (C)

13. Mark your answer on your answer sheet.
   (A)   (B)   (C)

14. Mark your answer on your answer sheet.
   (A)   (B)   (C)

15. Mark your answer on your answer sheet.
   (A)   (B)   (C)

16. Mark your answer on your answer sheet.
   (A)   (B)   (C)

'멋진 당신, 오늘도 화이팅'

DAY 03

오늘의 학습 포인트

PART 1. 실내 사진 (1)
1. 회의실 사진 - 긴 탁자, 원탁, 화이트보드
2. 사무실 사진 - 개인 책상, 컴퓨터, 서류
3. 상점 사진 - 쇼핑 카트, 계산대, 진열된 상품
4. 거실·침실 사진 - 소파, 테이블, 의자, 가구
5. 주방 사진 - 요리사, 조리대, 조리 도구
6. 로비·안내 데스크 사진 - 호텔 직원, 안내 데스크

PART 2. How 의문문 (1)
1. How 의문문 (1)
   1) 방법을 묻는 질문
   2) 빈도를 묻는 질문 - How often
   3) 수를 묻는 질문 - How many
   4) 가격이나 양을 묻는 질문 - How much
   5) 기간을 묻는 질문 - How long
   6) 시기를 묻는 질문 - How soon

PART 1 실내 사진 (1)

회의실, 사무실, 상점 사진의 출제 빈도가 가장 높습니다.
1~2문제가 출제되며 주로 인물이 크게 보이는 사진으로 출제됩니다.

확인 문제 ❶

(A) | (B)

출제 유형 1 회의실 사진

긴 탁자 또는 원탁이 가운데 있고, 화이트보드, 칠판, 노트북, 필기구 등이 있는 사진이 출제됩니다.
다수의 사람이 의자에 앉아 있거나 한 명이 여러 사람들 앞에 서 있는 사진이 많이 출제됩니다.

동사	point 가리키다 distribute 나누어 주다 gather 모이다 arrange 정리하다
명사	discussion 토론 meeting 회의 whiteboard 화이트보드 screen 화면 podium 연단 microphone 마이크 table 테이블 chair 의자 speaker 발표자 notepad 메모장 document 서류 chart 그래프
구	having a discussion[meeting] 토론하고[회의하고] 있다 giving a presentation 발표하고 있다 / writing on a whiteboard 화이트보드에 쓰고 있다 pointing at a screen 화면을 가리키고 있다 speaking to a group of people 한 무리의 사람들에게 말하고 있다 arranging some chairs 의자를 정리하고 있다 listening to a speaker[a presentation] 발표자의 말을[발표를] 듣고 있다 writing on a notepad[some paper] 메모장에[종이에] 필기하고 있다

800+

have gathered around a table 테이블 주위에 모여 있다
seated in a circle 둥글게 앉아 있다

 (A) ❶ 정답

풀이 방법 회의실 사진

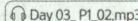 Day 03_P1_02.mp3

[BR]
(A) Some people are watching a street parade.
(B) Some people are sitting on the ground.
(C) One of the women is opening a curtain.
(D) One of the men is using a laptop computer.

이렇게 풀어요

1. **사진 파악하기** 다인 사진, 회의실, one of the women - pointing at the board(보드를 가리키고 있다), one of the men - using a laptop(노트북을 사용하고 있다)

2. **선택지 들으며 사진과 불일치하는 것 소거하여 정답 선택하기**
   (A̶) Some people are watching a street parade. 몇몇 사람들이 거리 퍼레이드를 보고 있다. → 목적어 불일치
   (B̶) Some people are sitting on the ground. 몇몇 사람들이 바닥에 앉아 있다. → 위치 불일치
   (C̶) One of the women is opening a curtain. 여자들 중 한 명이 커튼을 열고 있다. → 동사 불일치
   (D) One of the men is using a laptop computer. 남자들 중 한 명이 노트북 컴퓨터를 사용하고 있다. → 정답으로 선택

출제 유형 2 · 사무실 사진

개인의 업무를 위한 컴퓨터가 각각의 책상마다 놓여 있는 사진이 출제됩니다. 서류를 검토하거나 컴퓨터, 복사기와 같은 사무기기를 사용하고 있는 모습, 또는 전화를 받거나 사무실 서랍장을 열고 닫는 사진의 출제 빈도가 높습니다.

동사	type 타자 치다 examine 검토하다, 살펴보다 work (at/on) (~에서/~로) 일하다 hand 건네다 copy 복사하다
명사	keyboard 키보드 copy machine 복사기 (laptop) computer (노트북) 컴퓨터 printer 프린터 stationery supplies 문구용품 office furniture 사무실 가구 brochure 책자 document 서류 drawer 서랍 file folder 파일함 office equipment 사무용품 briefcase 서류가방 cabinet 캐비닛 bulletin board 게시판 locker 사물함
구	typing on a keyboard 키보드로 타자를 치고 있다 using the copy machine 복사기를 사용하고 있다 holding the machine's lid 기계의 뚜껑을 잡고 있다 sitting side by side 나란히 앉아 있다 examining some papers[document] 서류를 검토하고 있다 facing a computer screen 컴퓨터 화면을 보고 있다 working on a (laptop) computer (노트북) 컴퓨터로 일하고 있다 clipboard is placed on a desk. 책상 위에 클립보드가 놓여 있다.

900+

drawers have left open 서랍이 열려 있다
papers are scattered 종이가 흐트러져 있다

🔒 확인 문제 ❷

🎧 Day 03_ P1_03.mp3

(A) | (B)

⚠️ 주의
PART 1에서 examine은 다양한 명사와 쓰여 서로 다른 의미가 됩니다.
· examine paper/document 서류를 검토하다
· examine the machine 기계를 살펴보다
· examine a patient 환자를 진찰하다

(B) ❷ 답정

🙋 풀이 방법   사무실 사진

🎧 Day 03_ P1_04.mp3

[US]

(A) They are facing each other.
(B) They are reviewing some documents.
(C) The woman is reaching for a file folder.
(D) The man is holding a mug.

🎯 이렇게 풀어요

1. 사진 파악하기 2인 사진, 사무실, they – sitting next to each other(나란히 앉아 있다), reviewing documents(서류를 검토하고 있다), 배경 – bookshelves(책장들), file folders(파일함)

2. 선택지 들으며 사진과 불일치하는 것 소거하여 정답 선택하기
   (A̶) They are facing each other. 그들은 서로 마주 보고 있다. → 동사 불일치
   (B) They are reviewing some documents. 그들은 서류를 검토하고 있다. → 정답으로 선택
   (C̶) The woman is reaching for a file folder. 여자는 파일함에 손을 뻗고 있다. → 동사 불일치
   (D̶) The man is holding a mug. 남자는 머그잔을 들고 있다. → 목적어 불일치

🔒 확인 문제 ❸

🎧 Day 03_P1_05.mp3

(A) | (B)

출제 포인트
상점 사진에서는 사람 주어로 shop owner(상점 주인), customers/shoppers(고객들) 등이 출제되기도 합니다.

출제 유형 3 상점 사진

상점 사진은 출제 빈도가 높습니다. 물건을 고르거나 쇼핑 카트를 미는 사람의 모습이나 상품이 진열되어 있는 모습을 묘사한 표현이 정답으로 출제될 확률이 높습니다.

동사	carry 들다, 나르다 reach for ~을 향해 손을 뻗다 line 줄 서다 display 진열하다 restock 다시 채우다 try on 입어 보다 pay for 지불하다 push 밀다 pull 당기다 inspect 점검하다, 살펴보다 stack 쌓다
명사	cash register 계산대 shopping cart 쇼핑 카트 shelf 선반 counter 카운터 rack 옷걸이, 선반 price tag 가격표 product 상품 merchandise 상품 grocery 식료품 cashier 계산하는 직원 display case 진열장
구	carrying a shopping basket 쇼핑 바구니를 들고 있다 reaching for a product 상품을 향해 손을 뻗고 있다 standing at a cash register 계산대에 서 있다 trying on headphones 헤드폰을 써보고 있다 paying for some groceries[a merchandise] 식료품[상품]의 값을 지불하고 있다 pushing a shopping cart 쇼핑 카트를 밀고 있다 Garments are hanging on the racks. 의류가 옷걸이에 걸려 있다. Shopping carts have been lined up. 쇼핑 카트가 줄지어 있다. Merchandise is arranged on shelves. 상품이 선반에 진열되어 있다. Vegetables are on display. 야채가 진열되어 있다.

900+
Customers are being assisted. 고객들이 도움을 받고 있다.

정답 ❸ (A)

 풀이 방법   상점 사진

🎧 Day 03_P1_06.mp3

AU
(A) A man's making a payment at a cash register.
(B) A woman's picking up an item from the shelf.
(C) A man's loading a shopping cart with some products.
(D) They're walking down an aisle in a store.

✓ 이렇게 풀어요

1. **사진 파악하기**   다인 사진, 상점 안, they – walking down an aisle(복도를 걸어가고 있다), man – pushing a shopping cart(쇼핑 카트를 밀고 있다), 배경 – merchandise(상품), arranged(진열된), shelves(선반)

2. **선택지 들으며 사진과 불일치하는 것 소거하여 정답 선택하기**
   (A̶) A man's making a payment at a cash register. 남자가 계산대에서 돈을 지불하고 있다. → 동사 불일치
   (B̶) A woman's picking up an item from the shelf. 여자가 선반에서 물건을 꺼내고 있다. → 동사 불일치
   (C̶) A man's loading a shopping cart with some products. 남자가 쇼핑 카트에 몇몇 물건을 싣고 있다. → 동사 불일치
   (D) They're walking down an aisle in a store. 그들은 상점의 복도를 걸어가고 있다. → 정답으로 선택

출제 유형 4 거실·침실 사진

거실이나 침실 사진은 주로 사람이 없는 사진으로 출제됩니다. 따라서 소파, 테이블, 의자와 같은 가구의 상태를 묘사하거나 전등, 액자, 쿠션과 같은 장식품의 상태를 묘사하는 보기가 주로 정답으로 출제됩니다. 가구의 종류와 배치된 방식을 주의 깊게 살펴보며 보기를 들어야 합니다. 사람이 등장할 경우 서 있거나, 앉아 있는 상태 또는 청소를 하는 동작 표현이 출제됩니다.

확인 문제 ④

Day 03_P1_07.mp3

(A) | (B)

동사	prop against ~에 기대어져 있다 roll up 말리다 install 설치하다 hang 걸다 mount 고정시키다 mop 빗자루로 쓸다
명사	carpet 카펫 artwork 예술품 lamp 램프, 등 light 전등 pillow 베개 furniture 가구 curtain 커튼 (rocking) chair (흔들) 의자 decoration 장식품 ceiling 천장 wall 벽 rug 러그
구	A rug has been rolled up. 카펫이 말려 있다. changing a light bulb 전구를 교체하고 있다 vacuuming the floor 바닥을 청소기로 청소하고 있다 moving furniture 가구를 옮기고 있다 hanging up a shirt 셔츠를 걸고 있다 Flowers have been put in a vase. 꽃이 화병에 들어 있다. Pillows have been arranged on the couch. 쿠션들이 소파 위에 정리되어 있다.

900+
Curtains have been pulled open. 커튼이 걷혀 있다.

정답 (A)

풀이 방법 거실·침실 사진

Day 03_P1_08.mp3

US
(A) Some paintings are propped against the wall.
(B) A flower vase has been placed on top of a table.
(C) Some chairs have been pushed under the desk.
(D) A carpet has been rolled up in the corner.

이렇게 풀어요

1. 사진 파악하기 사물·풍경 사진, 거실, sofa(소파), cushions(쿠션), lamp on the table(테이블 위에 전등), vase(꽃병), carpet(카펫), a painting(그림), hanging on the wall(벽에 걸려 있다)

2. 선택지 들으며 사진과 불일치하는 것 소거하여 정답 선택하기
   (A) Some paintings are propped against the wall. 몇몇 그림이 벽에 기대어져 있다. → 동사 불일치
   (B) A flower vase has been placed on top of a table. 꽃병이 테이블 위에 놓여 있다. → 정답으로 선택
   (C) Some chairs have been pushed under the desk. 몇몇 의자가 책상 아래로 밀어넣어져 있다. → 위치 불일치
   (D) A carpet has been rolled up in the corner. 카펫이 모퉁이에 말려 있다. → 동사 불일치

확인 문제 ⑤

🎧 Day 03_P1_09.mp3

(A) | (B)

출제 포인트
동사 prepare가 주방 사진에 출제될 경우 '준비하다'의 의미보다는 '요리하다'의 의미로 이해하면 됩니다.

출제 유형 5 주방 사진

주방 사진에서 사람이 등장할 경우 주로 요리를 하거나 조리대에서 음식을 준비하는 모습이 출제되며, 사람이 없는 경우 조리 도구들의 상태나 위치를 묘사하는 문장이 주로 정답으로 출제됩니다.

동사	wipe 닦다 cook 요리하다 prepare (요리를) 준비하다 wash 씻다 stack 쌓다
명사	plate 접시 counter 조리대 apron 앞치마 cooking utensils 조리 도구 kitchen appliance 주방 기기 bowl 보울(그릇) sink 싱크대 container 용기
구	preparing a meal 음식을 요리하고 있다 wiping a counter 조리대를 닦고 있다 stacking some plates 접시를 쌓고 있다 cutting some food 음식을 자르고 있다 working in a kitchen 주방에서 일하고 있다 Dishes are stacked on a counter. 접시들이 조리대에 쌓여 있다. Kitchen utensils are placed on a counter. 조리 도구들이 조리대 위에 놓여 있다. An apron is hanging from a hook. 앞치마가 고리에 걸려 있다.

정답 (A) ⑤

풀이 방법   주방 사진

🎧 Day 03_P1_10.mp3

[BR]
(A) She's washing a pan in a sink.
(B) She's reaching for fruits in a basket.
(C) She's putting a plate into an oven.
(D) She's preparing some dishes.

이렇게 풀어요

1. **사진 파악하기**   1인 사진, 주방, wearing an apron(앞치마를 입고 있다), preparing dishes(요리를 하고 있다), holding a container(용기를 들고 있다), counter(조리대), fruits in a basket(바구니 안에 있는 과일)

2. **선택지 들으며 사진과 불일치하는 것 소거하여 정답 선택하기**
   (A̶) She's washing a pan in a sink. 그녀는 싱크대에서 프라이팬을 닦고 있다. → 동사 불일치
   (B̶) She's reaching for fruits in a basket. 그녀는 바구니 안에 있는 과일에 손을 뻗고 있다. → 동사 불일치
   (C̶) She's putting a plate into an oven. 그녀는 접시를 오븐에 넣고 있다. → 목적어 불일치
   (D) She's preparing some dishes. 그녀는 요리를 하고 있다. → 정답으로 선택

출제 유형 6 **로비·안내 데스크 사진**

호텔 로비나 건물의 안내 데스크 사진이 출제됩니다. 주로 손님들이 기다리고 있고 직원이 응대하고 있는 모습이 출제되는데, 손님들 전체의 공통적인 동작이 출제될 수도 있고, 손님 일부 또는 안내 데스크 직원의 동작이나 상태를 묘사할 수도 있습니다. 배경에 있는 사물에 대해 묘사하는 문장도 정답이 될 수 있으므로 사진을 전체적으로 파악해야 합니다.

🔒 확인 문제 ❻

🎧 Day 03_P1_11.mp3

(A) | (B)

동사	wait 기다리다　approach 다가가다　seat 앉다　hang 걸다　place 놓다　line 줄 서다
명사	reception area 접수처　waiting area 대기하는 장소 sitting area 앉아 있을 수 있는 장소　lobby 로비　receptionist 접수 담당자
구	loading a luggage on a cart 카트에 짐을 싣고 있다 standing at the reception desk 접수처에 서 있다 standing near a reception desk 접수처 근처에 서 있다 talking in a lobby 로비에서 대화를 나누고 있다

800+
Clocks are lined up on a wall. 벽에 시계가 줄지어 걸려 있다.

정답 ❾ (B)

풀이 방법　로비·안내 데스크 사진

🎧 Day 03_P1_12.mp3

[BR]

(A) Some people are getting off the train.
(B) Some people are waiting in a lobby.
(C) Some people are seated in a reception area.
(D) Some people are standing around the entrance.

✓ 이렇게 풀어요

1. 사진 파악하기　다인 사진, 로비, standing/waiting in a lobby(로비에 서 있다/기다리고 있다), reception desk(접수처)
2. 선택지 들으며 사진과 불일치하는 것 소거하여 정답 선택하기
   - (A) Some people are getting off the train. 몇몇 사람들이 기차에서 내리고 있다. → 동사 불일치
   - (B) Some people are waiting in a lobby. 몇몇 사람들이 로비에서 기다리고 있다. → 정답으로 선택
   - (C) Some people are seated in a reception area. 몇몇 사람들이 로비 공간에 앉아 있다. → 동사 불일치
   - (D) Some people are standing around the entrance. 몇몇 사람들이 입구 주위에 서 있다. → 위치 불일치

따라 하면 문제가 풀리는 연습 문제

Day 03_P1_13.mp3
정답 및 해석 p.15

01.

(1) 음원을 들으며 사진과 관련된 단어이면 O, 아니면 X에 표시하세요.

(A) O I X (B) O I X (C) O I X

(2) 음원을 들으며 빈칸을 채우고 정답에는 O, 오답에는 X 표시하세요.

(A) One of the men is _____ _____ a screen. [ ]
(B) One of the women is _____ documents. [ ]

02.

(1) 음원을 들으며 사진과 관련된 단어이면 O, 아니면 X에 표시하세요.

(A) O I X (B) O I X (C) O I X

(2) 음원을 들으며 빈칸을 채우고 정답에는 O, 오답에는 X 표시하세요.

(A) She is _____ on a notepad. [ ]
(B) She is talking _____ _____ _____. [ ]

03.

(1) 음원을 들으며 사진과 관련된 단어이면 O, 아니면 X에 표시하세요.

(A) O I X (B) O I X (C) O I X

(2) 음원을 들으며 빈칸을 채우고 정답에는 O, 오답에는 X 표시하세요.

(A) They are _____ in line. [ ]
(B) They are _____ _____ some items. [ ]

04.

(1) 음원을 들으며 사진과 관련된 단어이면 O, 아니면 X에 표시하세요.

(A) O I X (B) O I X (C) O I X

(2) 음원을 들으며 빈칸을 채우고 정답에는 O, 오답에는 X 표시하세요.

(A) A woman is _____ a _____. [ ]
(B) A woman is _____ a pan on a stove. [ ]

토익에 나올 실전 문제

01.

(A)　　(B)　　(C)　　(D)

02.

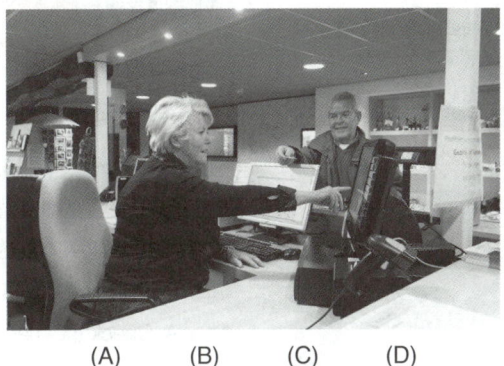

(A)　　(B)　　(C)　　(D)

03.

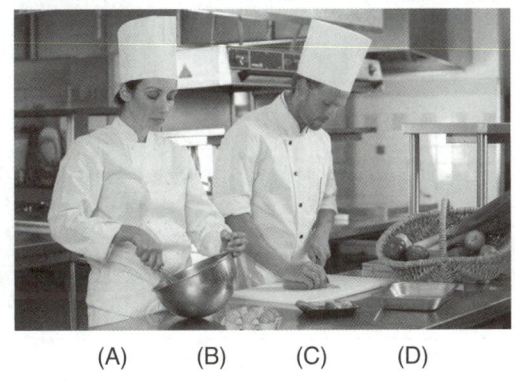

(A)　　(B)　　(C)　　(D)

04.

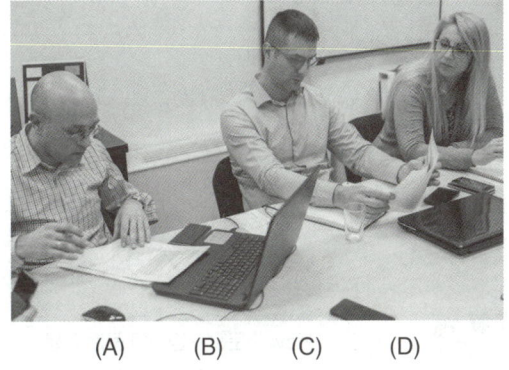

(A)　　(B)　　(C)　　(D)

05.

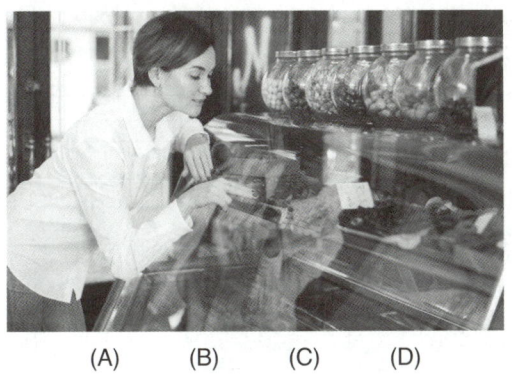

(A)　　(B)　　(C)　　(D)

06.

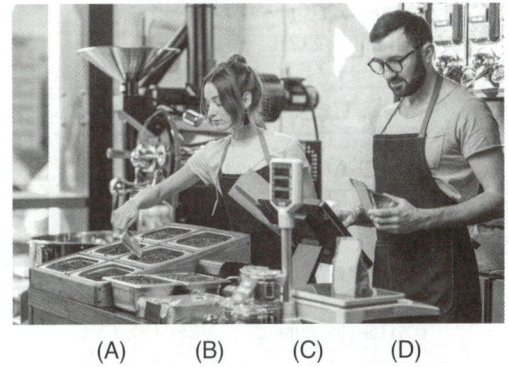

(A)　　(B)　　(C)　　(D)

PART 2 · How 의문문 (1)

How 의문문은 뒤에 오는 형용사나 부사에 따라 가격, 수량, 기간 등 다양한 내용을 물을 수 있습니다. 매회 1문제 정도 출제돼요!

적용 기술

[기적의 필기노트] 29P
LC 기술 19

🎧 Day 03_ P2_01.mp3

🔒 확인 문제 ❶

Mark your answer.

(A)   (B)

출제 포인트
수단이나 방법을 묻는 질문에 간접적인 응답도 정답으로 출제됩니다.
Q. How can we get some paper? 저희가 종이를 어떻게 얻을 수 있죠?
A. I'll give you some. 제가 좀 드릴게요.

정답 ❶ (A)

출제 유형 1

How 의문문 (1)

1. 수단이나 방법을 묻는 How 의문문

How 뒤에 동사가 나오면 주로 수단이나 방법을 묻는 질문입니다. by/through(~로/~를 통해)를 이용한 답변과 어떻게 하라고 알려 주는 명령문 형태의 답변이 대표적이지만, 최근에는 아래 풀이 방법의 예제처럼 단순히 방법이나 수단으로 답변하는 경우도 자주 출제됩니다.

Q. **How** can I operate this machine? 제가 이 기계를 어떻게 작동할 수 있죠?
A. **Check** the manual. 매뉴얼을 확인해 보세요.

by/through + 명사	by bus 버스로 by express mail 빠른 우편으로 through his help 그의 도움으로
명령문	Check the manual. 매뉴얼을 확인해 보세요. Take the bus across the street. 길 건너편에서 버스를 타세요. Fill out the application form. 신청서를 작성하세요.

풀이 방법   How 의문문 – 방법을 묻는 질문

🎧 Day 03_ P2_02.mp3

[AU - US]

How do you usually get to your office?
(A) As usual.
(B) We open at 10 every morning.
(C) I take the subway.

당신은 회사에 주로 어떻게 가나요?
(A) 평소대로요.
(B) 저희는 매일 아침 10시에 열어요.
(C) 저는 지하철을 타요.

이렇게 풀어요

1. 질문 내용 파악하기 How do you usually **get to your office**?
   어떻게   회사에 가요

2. 선택지 들으며 오답 소거하여 정답 선택하기
   (A) As **usual**. → 유사 발음 오답 (usually-usual)
   (B) We open at 10 every morning. → 다른 의문사 답변 오답 (when)
   (C) I take the subway. → 정답으로 선택

56 기적의 토익 LC

2 빈도를 묻는 How often/How frequently 의문문

How 뒤에 형용사나 부사가 나오면 정도를 묻는 질문이 되는데, How often이나 How frequently로 시작하면 빈도를 묻는 내용입니다. 따라서 이에 대한 대답은 빈도 부사나 횟수를 나타내는 표현으로 해야 합니다.

Q. **How often** do you contact the main office? 본사와 얼마나 자주 연락하세요?
A. **Sometimes** when it's an emergency. 긴급 상황일 때 가끔이요.

Q. **How frequently** do you go on business trips? 출장을 얼마나 자주 다니세요?
A. Probably, **three times a year**. 아마도, 일 년에 세 번 정도요.

빈도 부사	usually 주로 sometimes 때때로, 가끔 never 한 번도 ~않다 rarely 드물게
횟수를 나타내는 표현	once a week 일주일에 한 번 twice a month 한 달에 두 번 three times a year 일 년에 세 번 at least three hours a week 적어도 일주일에 세 시간 every day 매일 every week 매주 every year(= annually) 매년

900+
As often as I can. 제가 할 수 있는 한 자주요.

🎧 Day 03_P2_03.mp3

🔒 **확인 문제 ❷**

Mark your answer.

(A)　　(B)

정답 ❷ (B)

풀이 방법 How 의문문 – 빈도를 묻는 질문

🎧 Day 03_P2_04.mp3

[BR - BR]

How often do you take a break during your shift?
(A) At an employee lounge.
(B) Yes, I broke them.
(C) Every 50 minutes.

교대 근무 중에 얼마나 자주 휴식을 취하나요?
(A) 직원 휴게실에서요.
(B) 네, 제가 그것들을 망가뜨렸어요.
(C) 50분마다요.

이렇게 풀어요

1. 질문 내용 파악하기 How often do you take a break during your shift?
   얼마나 자주　　　휴식을 취하는지

2. 선택지 들으며 오답 소거하여 정답 선택하기
   (A) At an employee lounge. → 다른 의문사 답변 오답(where)
   (B) Yes, I broke them. → 의문사 의문문에 Yes/No로 답한 오답
   (C) Every 50 minutes. → 정답으로 선택

🎧 Day 03_P2_05.mp3

🔒 확인 문제 ❸

Mark your answer.

(A)   (B)

출제 포인트
숫자를 나타내는 아래의 표현들도 자주 출제됩니다.
a dozen 12개
a decade 10년
a couple of 두세 개의

3 수를 묻는 How many 의문문

• How many로 묻는 질문은 구체적인 수로 답변하거나, '약, 대략'이라는 의미의 부사를 사용하여 대략적인 수로 답변하는 문장이 정답이 됩니다.

Q. **How many** employees have signed up for the event?
얼마나 많은 직원들이 그 행사에 등록했나요?
A. **More than 200** so far. 지금까지 200명 이상이요.

almost(= approximately) 거의	more than(= over) ~ 이상
around/about/nearly 약/대략/거의	less than ~ 이하
at least 최소한, 적어도	

> 800+
> • How many 뒤에 times가 붙어 How many times ~?(몇 번을 ~)로 묻는 의문문은 횟수를 묻는 질문이므로 빈도 부사나 횟수를 나타내는 표현으로 답변해야 합니다.
>
> Q. **How many times** do you go out to eat per week? 한 주에 몇 번 외식하시나요?
> A. **Once a week**, regularly. 일주일에 한 번, 정기적으로요.

정답 ❸ (A)

🧑 풀이 방법   How 의문문 – 수를 묻는 질문

🎧 Day 03_P2_06.mp3

US - US

How many applications for the job opening have you received now?
(A) A marketing manager position.
(B) Almost 20.
(C) Yes, it is still open.

지금까지 공석에 몇 개의 지원서를 받았나요?
(A) 마케팅 부장 자리요.
(B) 거의 20개요.
(C) 네, 아직 모집 중입니다.

↓ 이렇게 풀어요

1. 질문 내용 파악하기   How many applications for the job opening have you received now?
   몇 개의 지원서를   받았는지

2. 선택지 들으며 오답 소거하여 정답 선택하기
   (A) A marketing manager position. → 연상 어휘 오답(applications-position)
   (B) Almost 20. → 정답으로 선택
   (C) Yes, it is still open. → 의문사 의문문에 Yes/No로 답한 오답

4 가격이나 양을 묻는 How much 의문문

How much 의문문은 가격이나 양으로 답변이 가능하며, '다시 확인해보겠다' 혹은 '다른 사람에게 물어보라' 등 우회적인 답변이 정답이 될 수도 있습니다.

Q. **How much** does the daily special cost? 일일 특선 요리가 얼마인가요?
A. It's **15 euros** on weekdays. 평일에는 15유로입니다.

Q. **How much** of our profits increased this year? 올해 우리 수익이 얼마나 증가했나요?
A. **By 20 percent.** 20퍼센트요.

가격	Ten dollars each. 하나에 10달러입니다. It's only 30 euros. 겨우 30유로예요. It comes to two hundred pounds. 200파운드입니다.
양	We offer 25 percent discount. 저희는 25퍼센트 할인해 드립니다. Twice its original price. 원래 가격의 두 배입니다.
우회적 답변	Let me check the receipt. 제가 영수증을 확인해 보겠습니다. I'll ask the manager. 매니저에게 물어보겠습니다.

🎧 Day 03_ P2_07.mp3

🔒 **확인 문제 ❹**

Mark your answer.

(A)   (B)

(B) 정답

풀이 방법 How 의문문 – 가격이나 양을 묻는 질문

🎧 Day 03_ P2_08.mp3

[AU - US]

How much do you pay for your apartment's rent?
(A) Sorry, I am past due.
(B) 750 dollars per month.
(C) On the last day of every month.

당신의 아파트 임대료로 얼마를 지불하시나요?
(A) 죄송해요, 제가 기한을 넘겼네요.
(B) 한 달에 750달러요.
(C) 매달 마지막 날에요.

✏️ 이렇게 풀어요

1. 질문 내용 파악하기   How much do you pay for your apartment's rent?

   얼마를   지불하는지

2. 선택지 들으며 오답 소거하여 정답 선택하기
   (A̶) Sorry, I am past due. → 연상 어휘 오답 (rent-past due)
   (B) 750 dollars per month. → 정답으로 선택
   (C̶) On the last day of every month. → 다른 의문사 답변 오답 (when)

🎧 Day 03_P2_09.mp3

🔒 **확인 문제** ⑤

Mark your answer.

(A)   (B)

⚠️ **주의**

How long 의문문에는 기간을 나타내는 표현으로 응답해야 하지만, How soon이나 How quickly 의문문에는 시점 또는 기간으로 모두 답변할 수 있습니다.

Q. How soon can you finish the report? 보고서를 얼마나 빨리 끝낼 수 있으세요?
A. [시점] By tomorrow morning. 내일 아침까지요.
A. [기간] It will take for a couple of weeks. 2주 정도 걸릴 거예요.

⑤ 기간을 묻는 How long 의문문

How long으로 시작하는 질문은 기간을 묻는 질문입니다. for, until, since 등 기간을 나타내는 표현을 사용하여 답하는 것이 보편적이지만 최근에는 이러한 표현들을 생략하고 바로 답하는 경우도 자주 출제됩니다.

Q. **How long** is the drive to the subway station? 지하철역까지 차로 얼마나 걸리죠?
A. It takes **about 15 minutes**. 15분 정도 걸려요.

Q. **How long** will the retirement party be? 은퇴 파티가 얼마나 오래 열릴까요?
A. (For) **Three hours**, I guess. 아마 3시간 정도요.

for + 기간	for almost a year 거의 1년 동안 for more than six months 6개월 넘게 for five hours 5시간 동안
until + 미래 시점	until next Friday 다음 주 금요일까지 until the end of the month 이번 달 말까지
since + 과거 시점	since last year 작년부터 since I was 20 내가 20살 때부터

정답 ⑤ (A)

🧑 풀이 방법   How 의문문 - 기간을 묻는 질문

🎧 Day 03_P2_10.mp3

[BR - BR]

How long will the festival last?
(A) Last Saturday.
(B) At the cultural district.
(C) For three days.

축제는 얼마나 오래 지속되나요?
(A) 지난주 토요일이요.
(B) 문화 지구에서요.
(C) 3일 동안이요.

> 💡 **이렇게 풀어요**
>
> 1. 질문 내용 파악하기 How long will the festival last?
>   얼마나 오래   축제가 지속되는지
>
> 2. 선택지 들으며 오답 소거하여 정답 선택하기
>   (A) Last Saturday. → 다른 의문사 답변 오답(when)
>   (B) At the cultural district. → 다른 의문사 답변 오답(where)
>   (C) For three days. → 정답으로 선택

`800+`

6 시기를 묻는 How soon/How quickly 의문문

How soon/How quickly로 시작하는 질문은 '얼마나 빨리'를 묻는 내용이므로 시기를 묻는 질문입니다. 따라서 When 의문문처럼 특정 시점이나 소요 시간(기간)으로 응답하는 답변이 정답입니다.

Q. **How soon** can I have the data I asked for?
  제가 요청한 자료를 얼마나 빨리 받을 수 있을까요?
A. **Before lunch.** 점심 시간 전에요.

Q. **How quickly** can you deliver the package? 얼마나 빨리 소포를 배달할 수 있으세요?
A. I'll be done **by the end of the day**. 오늘 내로 끝날 겁니다.

특정 시점을 나타내는 표현	in about two hours 약 두 시간 후에 sometime next week 다음 주 중에 before lunch 점심시간 전에 by the end of the day 오늘 내로

🎧 Day 03_P2_11.mp3

🔒 **확인 문제 ⑥**

Mark your answer.

(A)   (B)

DAY 03

정답 ⑥ (A)

풀이 방법   How 의문문 – 시기를 묻는 질문

🎧 Day 03_P2_12.mp3

[US - US]

How soon can you finish repairing my car?
(A) It'll be done by tomorrow morning.
(B) He is a car mechanic.
(C) A flat tire.

제 차의 수리를 얼마나 빨리 끝낼 수 있으신가요?
(A) 내일 아침까지는 끝날 겁니다.
(B) 그는 차 정비공입니다.
(C) 바람 빠진 타이어요.

 이렇게 풀어요

1. 질문 내용 파악하기   How soon can you finish repairing my car?
   　　　　　　　　　　얼마나 빨리　　　　수리를 끝낼 수 있는지

2. 선택지 들으며 오답 소거하여 정답 선택하기
   (A) It'll be done by tomorrow morning. → 정답으로 선택
   (B) He is a car mechanic. → 연상 어휘 오답 (repairing my car-car mechanic)
   (C) A flat tire. → 연상 어휘 오답 (repairing my car-flat tire)

PART 2 How 의문문 (1)   61

연습 문제

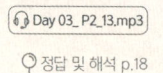

각 질문과 보기를 들으며 빈칸을 채운 뒤 정답에는 O, 오답에는 X 표시하세요.

01. _____ _____ did the transportation _____?
　　(A) I'll have to _____ the _____. [　]
　　(B) Yes, _____ is much faster. [　]

02. _____ _____ will you be staying in Tokyo?
　　(A) I'll _____ at my cousin's _____. [　]
　　(B) Only _____ _____. [　]

03. _____ did you manage to _____ so early?
　　(A) No, I _____ _____ last night. [　]
　　(B) I took a _____ _____. [　]

04. _____ _____ can you finish the work?
　　(A) Everything will be done _____ _____ _____. [　]
　　(B) Daniel will be here _____. [　]

05. _____ _____ office supplies should I order?
　　(A) We need _____ _____ _____. [　]
　　(B) The parts will be _____ this _____. [　]

06. _____ should I _____ these files?
　　(A) In an _____ _____. [　]
　　(B) He _____ a _____. [　]

07. _____ can I change the _____?
　　(A) May I have _____ _____, please? [　]
　　(B) _____, you can start now. [　]

08. _____ _____ _____ do you need to fix the machine?
　　(A) No, the _____ is over there. [　]
　　(B) _____ a couple of _____. [　]

실전 문제

🎧 Day 03_P2_14.mp3
📍 정답 및 해설 p.18

01. Mark your answer on your answer sheet.
   (A)   (B)   (C)

02. Mark your answer on your answer sheet.
   (A)   (B)   (C)

03. Mark your answer on your answer sheet.
   (A)   (B)   (C)

04. Mark your answer on your answer sheet.
   (A)   (B)   (C)

05. Mark your answer on your answer sheet.
   (A)   (B)   (C)

06. Mark your answer on your answer sheet.
   (A)   (B)   (C)

07. Mark your answer on your answer sheet.
   (A)   (B)   (C)

08. Mark your answer on your answer sheet.
   (A)   (B)   (C)

09. Mark your answer on your answer sheet.
   (A)   (B)   (C)

10. Mark your answer on your answer sheet.
   (A)   (B)   (C)

11. Mark your answer on your answer sheet.
   (A)   (B)   (C)

12. Mark your answer on your answer sheet.
   (A)   (B)   (C)

13. Mark your answer on your answer sheet.
   (A)   (B)   (C)

14. Mark your answer on your answer sheet.
   (A)   (B)   (C)

15. Mark your answer on your answer sheet.
   (A)   (B)   (C)

16. Mark your answer on your answer sheet.
   (A)   (B)   (C)

'멋진 당신, 오늘도 화이팅'

DAY
04

오늘의 학습 포인트

PART 1. 실내 사진 (2)
1. 식당 사진 - 손님과 직원의 동작이나 상태
2. 도서관 사진 - 책장, 책을 보는 사람
3. 박물관 사진 - 감상하고 있는 사람, 미술 작품 전시 상태
4. 연구실·실험실 사진 - 실험을 하고 있는 사람, 실험 기구 배치
5. 공장·창고 사진 - 유니폼/작업복을 입은 사람, 장비 작동/검사
6. 역·공항 사진 - 짐을 들고 서 있거나 기다리는 모습, 체크인, 승강장

PART 2. How 의문문 (2) / Why 의문문
1. How 의문문 (2)
   1) 의견을 묻는 질문 (1) - How + be동사
   2) 의견을 묻는 질문 (2) - How do you feel about ~?, How do you like ~?
   3) 제안하는 질문 - How about ~?

2. Why 의문문
   1) 이유나 원인을 묻는 질문 - Because (of), For, Due to
   2) 목적을 묻는 질문 - To + 동사 원형, So (that)
   3) 제안하는 질문 - Why don't you[we/I] ~?

PART 1 실내 사진 (2)

1~2문제가 출제되며 2인 이상 사진이 자주 등장해요.
식당, 연구실, 공장, 창고 등은 해당 장소에서만 쓰이는 어휘들이 있어요!

출제 유형 1 식당 사진

확인 문제 ❶

Day 04_ P1_01.mp3

(A) | (B)

식당 사진은 사람의 동작이나 상태를 묘사한 문장의 정답 비중이 높습니다. 손님과 직원의 동작/상태 묘사가 일치하는지 확인합니다.

동사	serve 서빙하다 carry 나르다 clear 치우다 wait 기다리다 pour 붓다 set 차리다
명사	(serving) tray (서빙) 쟁반 glass 유리잔 mug 머그잔 napkin 냅킨 plate 접시 bottle 병 silverware 은식기류 meal 식사 dish 요리 beverage 음료 diner 식사하는 사람 server 서빙하는 사람 cafeteria 구내식당 dining area 식사 공간
구	setting the table 테이블을 세팅하고 있다 / holding a serving tray 서빙 쟁반을 들고 있다 paying for their meal 식사를 계산하고 있다 drinking from a cup/a bottle/a mug 컵/병/머그로 마시고 있다 pouring water into a glass 유리잔에 물을 따르고 있다 looking at/studying the menu 메뉴를 살펴보고 있다 waiting on a customer 손님을 응대하고 있다 taking[placing] an order 주문을 받고[하고] 있다 customers are waiting to be seated 고객들이 앉기 위해 기다리고 있다 food is being served 음식이 제공되고 있다

출제 포인트
식당 사진에서는 주어로 server(종업원), diner(식사하는 사람) 등이 나올 수 있습니다.

800+
clearing the table 테이블을 정리하고 있다

(B) ❶ 음음

풀이 방법 식당 사진

Day 04_ P1_02.mp3

[AU]
(A) A man is taking an order from a customer.
(B) A man is standing in front of a vending machine.
(C) A woman is paying for her meal.
(D) Some diners are helping themselves to a meal.

이렇게 풀어요

1. 사진 파악하기 다인 사진, 식당[구내식당], lined up(줄 서 있다), a woman – paying(계산하고 있다)
2. 선택지 들으며 사진과 불일치하는 것 소거하여 정답 선택하기
   (A) A man is taking an order from a customer. 남자가 손님의 주문을 받고 있다. → 동사 불일치
   (B) A man is standing in front of a vending machine. 남자가 자판기 앞에 서 있다. → 위치 불일치
   (C) A woman is paying for her meal. 여자가 식사를 계산하고 있다. → 정답으로 선택
   (D) Some diners are helping themselves to a meal. 몇몇 식사하는 사람들은 식사를 하고 있다. → 동사 불일치

출제 유형 2 · 도서관 사진

🔒 **확인 문제 ❷**

 Day 04_ P1_03.mp3

도서관 사진은 책이 진열되어 있거나 사람이 책을 보고 있는 모습, 또는 전체적인 배경에 대한 문장이 정답으로 출제됩니다.

동사	reach for ~을 향해 손을 뻗다 review 검토하다 arrange 정리하다 check out 대여하다 spread 흩어져 있다 organize 정리하다
명사	book 책 magazine 잡지 (book) shelf 책장 (book) cart 책을 나르는 카트 armchair 안락의자, 팔걸이 의자
구	armchairs are occupied 팔걸이 의자에 사람이 앉아 있다 reaching for a book 책을 향해 손을 뻗고 있다 checking out some books 책을 대출하고 있다 reviewing a book 책을 보고 있다

(A) | (B)

800+
Books are spread out on a counter. 책들이 카운터에 흩어져 있다.

정답 ❷ (A)

풀이 방법 · 도서관 사진

 Day 04_ P1_04.mp3

[US]

(A) Some documents have been piled on the floor.
(B) Books have been arranged on shelves.
(C) Some chairs are occupied.
(D) All ceiling lights are being turned off.

✏️ 이렇게 풀어요

1. **사진 파악하기** 사물·풍경 사진, 도서관, shelves(책장들), books(책들), chairs are empty/unoccupied(의자가 비어 있다), lights on a ceiling(천장에 전등)

2. **선택지 들으며 사진과 불일치하는 것 소거하여 정답 선택하기**
   (A̶) Some documents have been piled on the floor. 몇몇 서류들이 바닥에 쌓여 있다. → 주어 불일치
   (B) Books have been arranged on shelves. 책들이 책장에 정리되어 있다. → 정답으로 선택
   (C̶) Some chairs are occupied. 몇몇 의자들에 사람이 앉아 있다. → 동사 불일치
   (D̶) All ceiling lights are being turned off. 모든 천장 조명들이 꺼지고 있다. → 동사 불일치

확인 문제 ❸

🎧 Day 04_ P1_05.mp3

(A) | (B)

출제 유형 3
박물관 사진

박물관이나 미술관 사진은 그림이나 작품을 감상하고 있는 사람들의 동작이나 그림과 같은 미술 작품이 전시되어 있는 상태를 묘사하는 문장이 정답으로 자주 출제됩니다.

동사	hang 걸다 display 전시하다 polish 닦다
명사	picture 그림 artwork 예술품 ticket 티켓 painting 그림
구	handing out tickets 티켓을 나누어주고 있다 displaying some artwork 예술품을 전시하고 있다 hanging up a picture 그림을 걸고 있다 Floor is being polished. 바닥이 닦이고 있다(누군가 바닥을 닦고 있다). Some artwork is hanging on the wall. 예술품이 벽에 걸려 있다.

(A) ❸ 정답

풀이 방법   박물관 사진

🎧 Day 04_ P1_06.mp3

[BR]
(A) Paintings are hanging on the wall.
(B) A woman is seated on the floor.
(C) Some people are walking down a hallway.
(D) A floor is being swept with a mop.

이렇게 풀어요

1. **사진 파악하기** 사람이 있는 사물·풍경 사진, 박물관, some people(몇몇 사람들) – standing(서 있다), a woman(여자) – sitting on a chair(의자에 앉아 있다), looking at the paintings(그림을 보고 있다), 배경 – paintings on a wall(벽에 걸린 그림)

2. **선택지 들으며 사진과 불일치하는 것 소거하여 정답 선택하기**
   (A) Paintings are hanging on the wall. 그림들이 벽에 걸려 있다. → 정답으로 선택
   (B) A woman is seated on the floor. 여자가 바닥에 앉아 있다. → 위치 불일치
   (C) Some people are walking down a hallway. 몇몇 사람들이 복도를 걷고 있다. → 동사 불일치
   (D) A floor is being swept with a mop. 바닥이 대걸레로 쓸리고 있다. → 동사 불일치

출제 유형 4 — 연구실·실험실 사진

연구실이나 실험실은 장소의 특성에 맞게 실험을 하고 있는 인물 사진이 자주 출제됩니다. 기구를 사용하고 있는 모습이나 장비를 착용하고 있는 모습에 대한 보기가 자주 출제됩니다. 하지만 인물 사진이더라도 실험 기구의 배치에 대한 문장도 답이 되는 경우가 많으므로 관련 어휘를 익혀 두어야 합니다.

🔒 확인 문제 ④

🎧 Day 04_P1_07.mp3

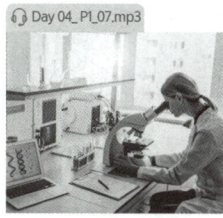

(A) | (B)

동사	wear 입다, 착용하다 examine 검사하다 clean 청소하다 use 사용하다 take off 벗다 look into ~을 들여다보다 lay 놓다, 두다 conduct 실시하다
명사	(laboratory) equipment (실험실) 장비 microscope 현미경 safety glasses 보호 안경 work surface 작업대 protective gear 보호 장비
구	wearing safety[protective] glasses 보호 안경을 착용하고 있다 wearing a pair of gloves 장갑을 끼고 있다 looking into a microscope 현미경을 들여다보고 있다 using laboratory equipment 실험실 기구를 사용하고 있다 conducting an experiment 실험을 하고 있다 opening a cabinet 캐비닛을 열고 있다

출제 포인트

도구나 기구를 사용하고 있는 사진의 경우, 해당 도구의 구체적 명칭보다 포괄적인 표현을 사용하여 묘사하는 경우가 더 많습니다.
equipment(장비),
tool(도구),
instrument(기구, 악기),
machine(기계)

(B) ④ 정답

👤 풀이 방법 — 연구실·실험실 사진

🎧 Day 04_P1_08.mp3

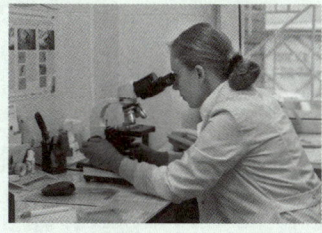

[BR]

(A) She's reading a document.
(B) Some laboratory equipment has been laid on a desk.
(C) She is taking off her gown.
(D) Protective glasses are being examined.

🔍 이렇게 풀어요

1. **사진 파악하기** 1인 사진, 실험실, a woman/she(여자) – using a microscope(현미경을 사용하고 있다), wearing a gown (가운을 입고 있다)

2. **선택지 들으며 사진과 불일치하는 것 소거하여 정답 선택하기**
   (A̶) She's reading a document. 그녀는 문서를 읽고 있다. → 동사 불일치
   (B) Some laboratory equipment has been laid on a desk. 몇몇 실험실 장비들이 책상 위에 놓여 있다. → 정답으로 선택
   (C̶) She is taking off her gown. 그녀는 가운을 벗고 있다. → 동사 불일치
   (D̶) Protective glasses are being examined. 보호 안경이 검사되고 있다. → 주어 불일치

확인 문제 ⑤

🎧 Day 04_P1_09.mp3

(A) | (B)

출제 유형 5 · 공장·창고 사진

공장이나 창고 사진에는 유니폼 또는 작업복을 입은 사람들이 주로 등장하여 그 인물들의 옷차림이나 행동을 묘사하는 문장이 출제됩니다. 장비를 작동 또는 검사하고 있는 모습과 도구를 사용하고 있는 모습의 출제 빈도가 높습니다. 또한 인물 주위에 있는 상자나 비품이 놓여 있는 모습을 묘사하는 문장도 정답으로 출제될 수 있습니다.

동사	repair 수리하다　assemble 조립하다　install 설치하다　replace 교체하다　plug 막다 close 닫다　carry 나르다　lift 들어올리다　inspect 검사하다
명사	toolbox 공구 상자　machine 기계　garage 차고　electric cord 전선　tool 도구 container 용기　shelf 선반　warehouse 창고　storage room 창고
구	boxes are stacked 박스가 쌓여 있다 picking up a carton 상자를 들고 있다 working in a warehouse 창고에서 일하고 있다 sweeping a storage room[storage area] 창고를 (빗자루로) 쓸고 있다 assembling some shelves 선반을 조립하고 있다 equipment is being inspected 장비가 점검되고 있다 working outdoors 야외에서 작업하고 있다

(B)

풀이 방법 · 공장·창고 사진

🎧 Day 04_P1_10.mp3

US
(A) A woman is wearing a vest.
(B) A woman is standing on a ladder.
(C) One of the men is inspecting a machine.
(D) One of the men is carrying a carton.

이렇게 풀어요

1. **사진 파악하기** 다인 사진, 창고, one of the men(남자들 중 한 명) – carrying a box(상자를 들고 있다), some people(몇몇 사람들) – wearing safety hats(안전모를 쓰고 있다), one of the women(여자들 중 한 명) – taking notes(무언가를 적고 있다), 배경 – ladder(사다리)

2. **선택지 들으며 사진과 불일치하는 것 소거하여 정답 선택하기**
   - (A) A woman is wearing a vest. 여자가 조끼를 입고 있다. → 목적어 불일치
   - (B) A woman is standing on a ladder. 여자가 사다리에 서 있다. → 위치 불일치
   - (C) One of the men is inspecting a machine. 남자들 중 한 명이 기계를 점검하고 있다. → 목적어 불일치
   - (D) One of the men is carrying a carton. 남자들 중 한 명이 상자를 들고 있다. → 정답으로 선택

출제 유형 6 역·공항 사진

역이나 공항의 실내 사진에서는 짐을 들고 서 있거나 기다리는 모습, 카운터에서 체크인하는 모습, 승강장에 서 있는 모습 등 승객의 동작이나 기차역 또는 공항의 실내 설비 상태에 대한 묘사가 정답으로 출제됩니다.

동사	carry 나르다 approach 접근하다 stand 서 있다
명사	suitcase 여행 가방 baggage(= luggage) 수하물, 짐 passenger 승객 platform 승강장 backpack 배낭 waiting area 대기 구역
구	seated in a waiting area 대기 구역에 앉아 있다 gathered in a waiting area 대기 구역에 모여 있다 claiming the baggage 짐을 찾고 있다 approaching a counter 카운터에 접근하고 있다 collecting tickets 표를 걷고 있다 pulling a suitcase 여행 가방을 끌고 있다

확인 문제 ⓖ

Day 04_ P1_11.mp3

(A) | (B)

출제 포인트
동사 approach는 사람이 한 장소로 다가가는 사진을 묘사하거나 기차 또는 지하철이 역으로 들어오는 모습을 묘사하는 데 모두 사용될 수 있습니다.

정답 ⓖ (A)

풀이 방법 역·공항 사진

Day 04_ P1_12.mp3

[AU]
(A) Some luggage is being loaded into a cart.
(B) Some people are boarding a plane.
(C) Some passengers are seated in a waiting area.
(D) A bus is approaching a station.

이렇게 풀어요

1. **사진 파악하기** 사람이 있는 사물·풍경 사진, 역 또는 공항, some people(몇몇 사람들) – standing(서 있다), sitting(앉아 있다), are seated(앉아 있다)

2. **선택지 들으며 사진과 불일치하는 것 소거하여 정답 선택하기**
   (A) Some luggage is being loaded into a cart. 몇몇 짐이 카트 안에 실리고 있다. → 동사 불일치
   (B) Some people are boarding a plane. 몇몇 사람들이 비행기에 탑승하고 있다. → 동사 불일치
   (C) Some passengers are seated in a waiting area. 몇몇 승객들이 대기 구역에 앉아 있다. → 정답으로 선택
   (D) A bus is approaching a station. 버스가 역에 접근하고 있다. → 주어 불일치

PART 1 실내 사진 (2)

따라 하면 문제가 풀리는 연습 문제

🎧 Day 04_ P1_13.mp3
📍 정답 및 해석 p.22

01.

(1) 음원을 들으며 사진과 관련된 단어이면 O, 아니면 X에 표시하세요.

(A) O | X　　(B) O | X　　(C) O | X

(2) 음원을 들으며 빈칸을 채우고 정답에는 O, 오답에는 X 표시하세요.

(A) They are _____ _____ to diners.　　[　]
(B) They are _____ the tables.　　[　]

02.

(1) 음원을 들으며 사진과 관련된 단어이면 O, 아니면 X에 표시하세요.

(A) O | X　　(B) O | X　　(C) O | X

(2) 음원을 들으며 빈칸을 채우고 정답에는 O, 오답에는 X 표시하세요.

(A) A chair is _____ _____.　　[　]
(B) Some armchairs are _____.　　[　]

03.

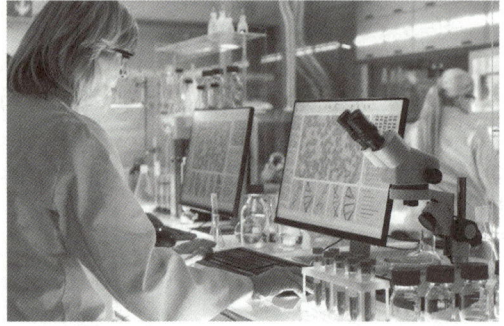

(1) 음원을 들으며 사진과 관련된 단어이면 O, 아니면 X에 표시하세요.

(A) O | X　　(B) O | X　　(C) O | X

(2) 음원을 들으며 빈칸을 채우고 정답에는 O, 오답에는 X 표시하세요.

(A) A woman is _____ _____ a drawer.　　[　]
(B) Some _____ are laid out on a workstation.　　[　]

04.

(1) 음원을 들으며 사진과 관련된 단어이면 O, 아니면 X에 표시하세요.

(A) O | X　　(B) O | X　　(C) O | X

(2) 음원을 들으며 빈칸을 채우고 정답에는 O, 오답에는 X 표시하세요.

(A) A box _____ _____ _____ on the conveyor.　　[　]
(B) An item is being put into a _____.　　[　]

토익에 나올 실전 문제

01.
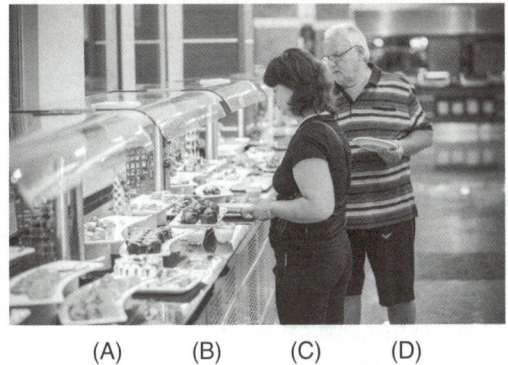
(A) (B) (C) (D)

02.

(A) (B) (C) (D)

03.
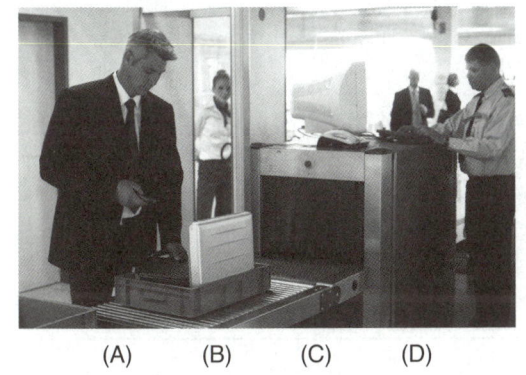
(A) (B) (C) (D)

04.

(A) (B) (C) (D)

05.

(A) (B) (C) (D)

06.

(A) (B) (C) (D)

PART 2 How 의문문 (2) / Why 의문문

의견/이유를 묻거나 제안을 하는 How 의문문은 매회 1문제 정도 출제됩니다.
Why 의문문은 매회 2문제 정도 출제돼요!

적용 기술
[기적의 필기노트] 28P
LC 기술 18

🎧 Day 04_P2_01.mp3

🔒 확인 문제 ❶

Mark your answer.

(A)　　(B)

출제 포인트
의견을 묻는 'How + be동사' 의문문은 How was ~ 의 과거 시제로 묻는 형태가 가장 많이 출제됩니다.

(B) ❶ 답정

출제 유형 1 How 의문문 (2)

1 의견을 묻는 'How + be동사' 의문문

상대방 또는 지인의 안부를 묻거나 회의, 행사, 공연, 영화 등이 어땠는지 의견을 물어볼 때 자주 사용되며 **긍정적/부정적 의미의 형용사나 동사를 이용하여 주로 답변합니다.**

Q. **How was** your business trip to Moscow? 모스크바 출장은 어땠나요?
A. It was **successful**. 성공적이었어요.

Q. **How was** the company outing? 회사 야유회는 어땠어요?
A. It **rained** all day. 하루 종일 비가 내렸어요.

긍정적 의미의 형용사	successful 성공적인 helpful 유익한 impressive 인상 깊은 worthwhile 가치 있는 promising 전도유망한 useful 유용한 effective 효과적인 informative 유익한 productive 생산적인
부정적 의미의 형용사	complicating 복잡한 difficult 어려운 disappointing 실망스러운 boring 지겨운
긍정적 의미의 동사	I really enjoyed it. 정말 즐거웠어요. Everything went smoothly. 모든 게 순조롭게 진행되었어요.
부정적 의미의 동사	It rained all day. 하루 종일 비가 내렸어요.

🧑 풀이 방법   How 의문문 – 의견을 묻는 질문 (1)

🎧 Day 04_P2_02.mp3

[BR - US]

How was the workshop you attended last Friday?
(A) To a flight attendant position.
(B) It was really informative.
(C) Fill out this form.

지난주 금요일에 참석한 워크숍은 어땠어요?
(A) 기내 승무원 직이에요.
(B) 정말 유익했어요.
(C) 이 양식을 작성하세요.

✏ 이렇게 풀어요

1. 질문 내용 파악하기   How was the workshop you attended last Friday?
　　　　　　　　　　　　어땠는지　　　워크숍이

2. 선택지 들으며 오답 소거하여 정답 선택하기
　(A̶) To a flight attendant position. → 유사 발음 오답 (attended-attendant)
　(B) It was really informative. → 정답으로 선택
　(C̶) Fill out this form. → 연상 어휘 오답 (workshop-fill out this form)

74　기적의 토익 LC

2 의견이나 이유를 묻는 How 관용 표현

상대방의 의견이나 이유를 묻는 다양한 How 관용 표현이 출제됩니다. 시험장에서 질문을 듣고 바로 의미를 파악할 수 있도록 통째로 외워 두어야 합니다.

Q. **How did you like** the seminar? 세미나는 어땠어요?
A. I found it very helpful. 매우 유익했어요.

Q. **How come** you rescheduled the workshop? 왜 워크숍 일정을 재조정했나요?
A. There were no conference rooms available. 이용 가능한 회의실이 없었어요.

How do you feel about ~? ~에 대해 어떻게 생각하나요?
How do you like ~? ~는 어떤가요?
How did ~ go? ~는 어땠어요? (행사 등이 어땠었는지 물을 때)
How is ~ coming along? ~는 어떻게 되어가고 있어요?
How come ~? 왜 ~?

🎧 Day 04_ P2_03.mp3

🔒 **확인 문제 ❷**

Mark your answer.

(A)　　　(B)

(A)

풀이 방법　How 의문문 – 의견을 묻는 질문 (2)

🎧 Day 04_ P2_04.mp3

BR – AU

How do you feel about the Thai restaurant on Mashal Street?
(A) I took a taxi.
(B) Yes, we accept any special requests.
(C) I enjoyed an exotic dish.

Mashal 가에 있는 태국 음식 레스토랑에 대해 어떻게 생각해요?
(A) 저는 택시를 탔어요.
(B) 네, 저희는 모든 특별 요청을 수락합니다.
(C) 저는 이국적인 요리를 즐겼어요.

이렇게 풀어요

1. 질문 내용 파악하기　How do you feel about the Thai restaurant on Mashal Street?
   　　　　　　　　　어떻게 생각하는지　　태국 음식 레스토랑에 대해

2. 선택지 들으며 오답 소거하여 정답 선택하기
   (A) I took a taxi. → 다른 의문사 오답 (방법을 묻는 How)
   (B) Yes, we accept any special requests. → 의문사 의문문에 Yes/No로 답한 오답
   (C) I enjoyed an exotic dish. → 정답으로 선택

🎧 Day 04_P2_05.mp3

🔒 확인 문제 ❸

Mark your answer.

(A)   (B)

800+

3 제안을 하는 How about 의문문

How about으로 묻는 질문은 제안을 하는 질문이며, 제안을 수락하거나 거절하는 답변이 출제됩니다. 직접적으로 yes나 no로 응답하기보다는 긍정적 또는 부정적 뉘앙스의 답변으로 수락이나 거절의 의미를 전달하므로 답변 내용을 유심히 들어야 합니다.

Q. **How about** we hire some part-timers? 시간제 직원들을 몇 명 채용하는 게 어때요?
A. That's what I thought. 제가 생각했던 바에요. [수락, 동의]

Q. **How about** taking the morning flight to Paris? 파리로 가는 아침 비행기를 타는 게 어때요?
A. It's too expensive. 그건 너무 비싸요. [거절]

Q. **How about** taking a short break? 잠시 쉬는 게 어때요?
A. Let's finish this section first. 먼저 이 부분부터 끝냅시다. [거절]

(B) 정답

풀이 방법 How 의문문 – 제안하는 질문

🎧 Day 04_P2_06.mp3

[BR - US]

How about volunteering to work in the Trade Fair next month?
(A) I was really eager to, but I have a prior engagement.
(B) We need more time.
(C) I don't think that's fair enough.

다음 달 무역 박람회 근무를 자원하는 게 어때요?
(A) 정말 그러고 싶었는데, 선약이 있어요.
(B) 우리는 시간이 더 필요해요.
(C) 그건 공평하지 않은 것 같아요.

✓ 이렇게 풀어요

1. 질문 내용 파악하기 How about volunteering to work in the Trade Fair next month?
                                어떤지   자원하는 것이

2. 선택지 들으며 오답 소거하여 정답 선택하기
   (A) I was really eager to, but I have a prior engagement. → 정답으로 선택
   (B̸) We need more time. → 연상 어휘 오답(next month-more time)
   (C̸) I don't think that's fair enough. → 동일 단어 반복 오답(fair)

출제 유형 2

Why 의문문

1 이유나 원인을 묻는 Why 의문문

Why 의문문은 가장 대표적으로 이유나 원인을 묻습니다. 주로 날씨가 좋지 않거나, 교통 체증이 심하거나, 다른 일정이 있는 등 **부정적인 내용의 답변이 출제**됩니다. For, Due to, Because (of) 등 이유를 나타내는 표현도 알아 두어야 합니다.

Q. **Why** was the flight to Tokyo canceled? 왜 도쿄로 가는 비행기가 취소되었나요?
A. **Due to** the mechanical problem. 기계 결함 때문에요.

교통 상황 관련	(Probably) because of the traffic jam. (아마도) 교통 체증 때문에요. The train was delayed. 기차가 연착되었어요.
날씨 관련	Because of the inclement weather condition. 악천후 때문에요. There was bad weather. 날씨가 안 좋았어요. The storm made the construction delayed. 폭풍 때문에 공사가 지연되었어요.
일정 관련	Something important came up. 갑자기 중요한 일이 생겼어요. I had no time to go. 갈 시간이 없었습니다. He has a doctor's appointment. 그는 병원 예약이 있어요.
기타	For personal business. 개인적인 사정 때문에요. Due to the mechanical problem. 기계 결함 때문에요.

적용 기술

[기적의 필기노트] 30P
LC 기술 20

Day 04_P2_07.mp3

확인 문제 ④

Mark your answer.

(A)   (B)

출제 포인트

because나 due to 등 이유를 나타내는 표현이 생략되고 바로 이유나 원인을 말하는 경우가 자주 출제됩니다.

주의

답변이 because로 시작하더라도 주어가 질문에서 묻는 것과 맞지 않을 경우 오답이므로 주의합니다.

Q. Why did you order **this projector**? 이 프로젝터를 왜 주문했나요?
A. Because **she** is well-qualified. (X) 그녀는 자격을 갖추었기 때문입니다.

(B)

 풀이 방법   Why 의문문 – 이유나 원인을 묻는 질문

Day 04_P2_08.mp3

[AU - US]

Why were you late this morning?
(A) No later than October 22.
(B) I missed the bus.
(C) I usually go to the gym after work.

오늘 아침에 왜 늦었나요?
(A) 늦어도 10월 22일까지는요.
(B) 버스를 놓쳤어요.
(C) 저는 퇴근 후에 보통 체육관에 가요.

이렇게 풀어요

1. 질문 내용 파악하기   **Why** were you **late** this morning?
                              왜   늦었는지

2. 선택지 들으며 오답 소거하여 정답 선택하기
   (A) No later than October 22. → 다른 의문사 답변 오답(How soon)
   (B) I missed the bus. → 정답으로 선택
   (C) I usually go to the gym after work. → 다른 의문사 답변 오답(What 또는 Where)

PART 2 How 의문문 (2) / Why 의문문   77

🎧 Day 04_ P2_09.mp3

🔒 **확인 문제 ❺**

Mark your answer.

(A)　　　(B)

2 목적을 묻는 Why 의문문

Why 의문문은 목적을 묻는 내용으로도 출제됩니다. 이 경우 '~하기 위해서'라는 의미를 갖는 To + 동사 원형, So (that) 등의 표현을 사용한 답변이 주로 정답이 됩니다.

Q. **Why** are you meeting with Mr. Tylor? 왜 Tylor 씨와 만나시는 거죠?
A. **To discuss** the new project. 새 프로젝트를 논의하기 위해서요.

Q. **Why** do you come to work so early these days? 요즘 왜 그렇게 일찍 출근하세요?
A. **So (that)** I can avoid the heavy traffic. 교통 체증을 피하기 위해서요.

To + 동사 원형	**To get** some information. 정보를 얻기 위해서요. **To discuss** the new project. 새 프로젝트를 논의하기 위해서요.
So (that)	**So (that)** I can confirm my reservation. 제 예약을 확인하려고요. **So (that)** I can avoid the heavy traffic. 교통 체증을 피하기 위해서요.

(A) 정답

🧑 풀이 방법　Why 의문문 – 목적을 묻는 질문

🎧 Day 04_ P2_10.mp3

[BR - BR]

Why did the manager extend the deadline?
(A) An extended vacation.
(B) To get more feedback from colleagues.
(C) No, I didn't meet her.

부장님이 왜 마감일을 연장했나요?
(A) 장기 휴가요.
(B) 동료들로부터 더 많은 의견을 받기 위해서요.
(C) 아뇨, 저는 그녀를 만나지 않았어요.

✓ **이렇게 풀어요**

1. 질문 내용 파악하기 **Why** did the manager **extend the deadline**?
　　　　　　　　　　　왜　　　　　　　마감일을 연장했는지

2. 선택지 들으며 오답 소거하여 정답 선택하기
　(A̶) An **extended** vacation. → 유사 발음 오답(extend-extended)
　(B) To get more feedback from colleagues. → 정답으로 선택
　(C̶) No, I didn't meet her. → 의문사 의문문에 Yes/No로 답한 오답

3 제안을 하는 Why don't you[we/I] 의문문

Why don't you[we/I] ~?는 '~하는 게 어때요?'라는 의미로 제안을 하는 의문문입니다. 따라서 제안을 수락하거나 거절하는 답변을 할 수 있으며, Yes/No 답변도 가능합니다.

Q. **Why don't you** come over for lunch? 점심 드시러 오시는 게 어때요?
A. Sure, why not! 좋아요, 왜 안 되겠어요!

Q. **Why don't we** go swimming tomorrow? 내일 수영 가는 게 어때요?
A. I'm much too tired. 저는 너무 피곤해요.

Q. **Why don't I** organize the warehouse today? 제가 오늘 창고를 정리해 드릴까요?
A. Yes, that would be nice. 네, 그럼 좋겠네요.

🎧 Day 04_P2_11.mp3

🔒 확인 문제 ❻

Mark your answer.

(A)　　(B)

⚠️ 주의

Why didn't[doesn't]로 묻는 질문은 제안이 아니라 이유나 목적을 묻는 Why 의문문의 부정문 형태입니다.
Q. Why didn't you come to the meeting this morning? 왜 오늘 아침에 회의에 안 오셨어요?
A. Something urgent came up. 갑자기 급한 일이 생겼어요.

(B) 정답

풀이 방법　Why 의문문 – 제안하는 질문

🎧 Day 04_P2_12.mp3

US - US

Why don't you add some visual aids to your presentation?
(A) The CEO was very impressed.
(B) Sure, that's a good idea.
(C) Because we are currently understaffed.

당신의 발표에 시각 자료를 좀 추가하는 게 어때요?
(A) 대표이사님이 매우 깊은 인상을 받았어요.
(B) 좋아요, 그거 좋은 생각이네요.
(C) 저희가 현재 인원이 부족하기 때문이에요.

이렇게 풀어요

1. 질문 내용 파악하기　Why don't you add some visual aids to your presentation?
　　　　　　　　　　　~하는 게 어떤지　　시각 자료를 추가하는 것

2. 선택지 들으며 오답 소거하여 정답 선택하기
　(A) The CEO was very impressed. → 연상 어휘 오답 (presentation-impressed)
　(B) Sure, that's a good idea. → 정답으로 선택
　(C) Because we are currently understaffed. → 주어 불일치 오답 (you-we)

따라 하면 문제가 풀리는
연습 문제

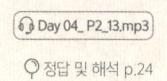

각 질문과 보기를 들으며 빈칸을 채운 뒤 정답에는 O, 오답에는 X 표시하세요.

01. _____ do you _____ the new projectors and computers?
  (A) The _____ is _____ _____ _____. [   ]
  (B) They're _____ _____ so far. [   ]

02. _____ are they _____ the office?
  (A) Yes, I'm _____. [   ]
  (B) It's our _____ _____ day. [   ]

03. _____ _____ meeting for lunch at noon?
  (A) _____, I wanted to _____ that new Italian restaurant. [   ]
  (B) I _____ her _____ _____ _____ to work. [   ]

04. _____ do you _____ the store _____ today?
  (A) They _____ _____ eight in the morning. [   ]
  (B) Because of the _____ bad _____. [   ]

05. _____ isn't Paul _____ his phone this morning?
  (A) _____, _____ _____ him yesterday. [   ]
  (B) He's taking a _____ _____. [   ]

06. _____ _____ _____ file a complaint?
  (A) _____ my order has been _____ for a week. [   ]
  (B) I think that's a _____ _____. [   ]

07. _____ _____ last night's employee award ceremony?
  (A) _____ _____ _____ the new intern. [   ]
  (B) _____ was _____. [   ]

08. _____ _____ _____ bring up this issue at the board meeting?
  (A) No, _____ _____ _____. [   ]
  (B) Sorry, we don't have this _____ _____. [   ]

🎧 Day 04_ P2_14.mp3

📍 정답 및 해설 p.25

01. Mark your answer on your answer sheet.
    (A)   (B)   (C)

02. Mark your answer on your answer sheet.
    (A)   (B)   (C)

03. Mark your answer on your answer sheet.
    (A)   (B)   (C)

04. Mark your answer on your answer sheet.
    (A)   (B)   (C)

05. Mark your answer on your answer sheet.
    (A)   (B)   (C)

06. Mark your answer on your answer sheet.
    (A)   (B)   (C)

07. Mark your answer on your answer sheet.
    (A)   (B)   (C)

08. Mark your answer on your answer sheet.
    (A)   (B)   (C)

09. Mark your answer on your answer sheet.
    (A)   (B)   (C)

10. Mark your answer on your answer sheet.
    (A)   (B)   (C)

11. Mark your answer on your answer sheet.
    (A)   (B)   (C)

12. Mark your answer on your answer sheet.
    (A)   (B)   (C)

13. Mark your answer on your answer sheet.
    (A)   (B)   (C)

14. Mark your answer on your answer sheet.
    (A)   (B)   (C)

15. Mark your answer on your answer sheet.
    (A)   (B)   (C)

16. Mark your answer on your answer sheet.
    (A)   (B)   (C)

'멋진 당신, 오늘도 화이팅'

DAY 05

오늘의 학습 포인트

PART 1. 야외 사진
 1. 거리 사진 - 보행자나 차량 신호 대기, 주차된 차, 건물, 가로등
 2. 광장·공원 사진 - 공연, 조깅, 벤치, 잔디밭
 3. 건설 현장 사진 - 각종 도구, 안전 장비
 4. 부둣가·물가 사진 - 배, 다리, 낚시
 5. 정원·마당 사진 - 잔디 깎기, 나무 손질, 도구
 6. 역·공항 외부 사진 - 야외 승강장, 활주로, 비행기, 승선

PART 2. 일반 의문문 - 긍정 - Yes/No 답변 가능, 생략도 가능
 1. Do 의문문 - 주어와 본동사 집중
 2. Have 의문문
    1) 사람 주어 - 이미 했다, 아직 안 했다 답변
    2) 사물 주어 - 완료되었다, 아직 안 되었다 답변
 3. Be 동사 의문문
    1) 현재/과거 사실
    2) 미래 계획 - be + -ing, be going to 동사 원형, be supposed to 동사 원형
 4. Can/May/Will/Should 의문문 - 부탁/허가/요청/제안, 미래 사실/계획(will)

PART 1 야외 사진

거리나 공원과 같은 야외 사진은 1문제 정도 출제됩니다.
여러 무리의 사람이 있는 배경 사진으로 주로 출제돼요!

확인 문제 ❶

Day 05_P1_01.mp3

(A) | (B)

출제 유형 1 거리 사진

거리 사진은 보행자가 길을 건너거나 신호를 기다리고 있는 모습, 자전거를 타는 모습, 자동차가 신호 대기 중이거나 주차되어 있는 모습, 건물이나 가로등의 배열 모습을 묘사한 보기가 자주 출제됩니다.

동사	block 막다 get into 타다 stand 서 있다 ride 타다 cross 건너다 surround 둘러싸다 repair 수리하다 cycle 자전거를 타다 line 일렬로 늘어서다
명사	traffic light 신호등 walkway 보도 doorway 출입구 crosswalk 횡단보도 path 길 cyclist 자전거 타는 사람 streetlamp 가로등 intersection 교차로 pedestrian 보행자 lamppost 가로등 road sign 표지판 pavement (도로의) 포장 street light 가로등 curb 연석(도로 경계석)
구	blocking a road 도로를 막고 있다 / parked near a curb 연석 근처에 주차되어 있다 stopped at an intersection 교차로에 정차해 있다 / wiping a car window 자동차 창문을 닦고 있다 crossing an intersection 교차로를 건너고 있다 / cycling on a road 도로에서 자전거를 타고 있다 descending some stairs 계단을 내려가고 있다 Trees are lining both sides of a street. 나무들이 도로 양쪽에 늘어서 있다. Vehicles are stopped at the traffic signal. 차가 교통 신호에 멈춰 있다. Walkway is divided by railing. 보도가 난간으로 분리되어 있다.

출제 포인트
거리 사진에서 사람들이 등장할 경우 일반적인 사람을 의미하는 some people 대신에 pedestrians(보행자들)가 자주 출제됩니다.

(A) ❶ 정답

풀이 방법 거리 사진

Day 05_P1_02.mp3

US

(A) Some pedestrians are crossing a street.
(B) A car is being repaired in the garage.
(C) Some workers are working on the construction site.
(D) Street lights line both sides of a road.

이렇게 풀어요

1. **사진 파악하기** 사람이 있는 사물·풍경 사진, 거리, a man(남자) – walking on the road(길을 걷고 있다), 배경 – trucks are parked(트럭이 주차되어 있다), buildings lined up(줄지어져 있는 건물들), street lights(가로등), cars/vehicles(차량들)

2. **선택지 들으며 사진과 불일치하는 것 소거하여 정답 선택하기**
   (A̶) Some pedestrians are crossing a street. 몇몇 보행자들이 길을 건너고 있다. → 동사 불일치
   (B̶) A car is being repaired in the garage. 차가 차고에서 수리되고 있다. → 위치 불일치
   (C̶) Some workers are working on the construction site. 몇몇 작업자들이 공사 현장에서 일하고 있다. → 위치 불일치
   (D) Street lights line both sides of a road. 가로등이 도로 양쪽에 늘어서 있다. → 정답으로 선택

출제 유형 2 광장·공원 사진

광장 사진은 사람들이 휴식을 취하고 있는 모습, 공연을 관람하는 모습, 광장 주위의 배경을 묘사하는 표현이 정답으로 출제됩니다. 공원 사진은 사람들이 조깅하는 모습, 벤치에 앉아 있는 모습, 나무 또는 공원의 잔디밭, 길의 모양을 묘사하는 문제가 자주 출제됩니다.

🔒 확인 문제 ❷

🎧 Day 05_ P1_03.mp3

(A) | (B)

동사	stroll 거닐다 mow 잔디를 깎다 relax 휴식을 취하다 occupy 차지하다 jog 조깅하다
명사	grass 잔디 playground 놀이터 bench 벤치 umbrella 파라솔 plaza 광장
구	tying her shoelaces 신발 끈을 묶고 있다 jogging through a park 공원에서 조깅하고 있다 resting on a bench 벤치에서 쉬고 있다 having a picnic 소풍을 하고 있다 An outdoor market is held. 야외 시장이 열리고 있다. Umbrellas have been closed. 파라솔이 접혀 있다. Benches are occupied. 벤치에 사람이 앉아 있다. Picnic tables are lined up in a row. 피크닉 테이블이 일렬로 줄지어 있다. Bicycles are leaning against a fence. 자전거들이 울타리에 기대어져 있다. Picnic tables have been set up in a plaza. 광장에 피크닉 테이블이 설치되어 있다.

정답 ❷ (B)

풀이 방법   광장·공원 사진

🎧 Day 05_ P1_04.mp3

AU

(A) A band of musicians is playing on an outdoor stage.
(B) Some people are relaxing on a bench.
(C) Picnic tables are arranged in a row.
(D) Some people are walking along the beach.

🔍 이렇게 풀어요

1. **사진 파악하기**   사람이 있는 사물·풍경 사진, 공원, some people(몇몇 사람들) – sitting on a bench(벤치에 앉아 있다), sitting on the grass(잔디에 앉아 있다), 배경 – trees are planted(나무들이 심어져 있다)

2. **선택지 들으며 사진과 불일치하는 것 소거하여 정답 선택하기**
   (A̶) A band of musicians is playing on an outdoor stage. 음악가 밴드가 야외 무대에서 공연하고 있다. → 주어 불일치
   (B) **Some people are relaxing on a bench.** 몇몇 사람들이 벤치에서 쉬고 있다. → 정답으로 선택
   (C̶) **Picnic tables** are arranged in a row. 피크닉 테이블이 일렬로 정렬되어 있다. → 주어 불일치
   (D̶) Some people are walking **along the beach**. 몇몇 사람들이 해변을 따라 걷고 있다. → 위치 불일치

PART 1 야외 사진   85

확인 문제 ❸

🔊 Day 05_P1_05.mp3

(A) | (B)

출제 포인트
야외에서 일하고 있는 사진은 인물의 구체적인 동작, 착용하고 있는 작업복, 사용하고 있는 기계와 관련된 보기 문장이 자주 출제됩니다.

출제 유형 3 — 건설 현장 사진

건설 현장이나 공사장 사진은 공사 중인 건물이나 구조물이 무엇인지 파악해야 합니다. 또한 공사 현장에 있는 각종 도구와 안전 장비를 지칭하는 표현도 알아 두어야 합니다.

동사	load 싣다 unload 내리다 move 옮기다 carry 나르다 fix 수리하다 erect 세우다 install 설치하다 hammer 망치로 치다
명사	construction worker 공사 인부 construction site 공사 현장 scaffolding 비계, 발판 dirt 먼지 shovel 삽 helmet 헬멧 ladder 사다리 wheelbarrow 손수레 bucket 양동이 soil 흙 hammer 망치
구	standing on a ladder 사다리에 서 있다 using a shovel 삽을 사용하고 있다 wearing safety helmets 안전모를 착용하고 있다 wheeling/pushing a wheelbarrow 손수레를 밀고 있다 stacked in a pile 무더기로 쌓여 있다 hammering a piece of wood 나무 조각을 망치로 치고 있다 Cart is being loaded with bricks. 수레에 벽돌이 실리고 있다. Maintenance work is being carried out. 유지보수 작업이 진행되고 있다. Rooftop is being repaired. 지붕이 수리되고 있다.

(A) 정답

풀이 방법 — 건설 현장 사진

🔊 Day 05_P1_06.mp3

[BR]

(A) A roof is being repaired.
(B) Some people are unloading some boxes.
(C) The men are installing a carpet.
(D) Some construction work is being done.

이렇게 풀어요

1. 사진 파악하기 다인 사진, 건설 현장, people/men(사람들) - working at a construction site(건설 현장에서 일하고 있다), using tools(도구를 사용하고 있다), 배경 - roof(지붕), ladder(사다리)

2. 선택지 들으며 사진과 불일치하는 것 소거하여 정답 선택하기

   (A) A roof is being repaired. 지붕이 수리되고 있다. → 동사 불일치
   (B) Some people are unloading some boxes. 몇몇 사람들이 상자를 내리고 있다. → 동사 불일치
   (C) The men are installing a carpet. 남자들이 카펫을 설치하고 있다. → 목적어 불일치
   (D) Some construction work is being done. 건설 작업이 진행되고 있다. → 정답으로 선택

출제 유형 4 **부둣가·물가 사진**

확인 문제 ❹

Day 05_P1_07.mp3

(A) | (B)

부둣가나 물가(호수, 강, 해변 등) 사진은 배가 물에 떠 있거나 정박해 있는 사진, 다리가 이어져 있는 강 사진이 자주 출제되므로 관련 표현들을 알아 두어야 합니다. 사람이 등장할 경우 물가를 산책하거나 낚시하는 모습, 해변에서 쉬는 모습의 사진이 출제될 수 있습니다.

동사	swim 수영하다 tie 묶다 lie 눕다 float 뜨다 boat 배를 타다 sail 항해하다
명사	oar 노 fishing pole 낚싯대 beach umbrella 해변 파라솔 bridge 다리 rope 밧줄 sailor 선원 lake 호수 shore 해변 pier 부두 dock 부두 waterway 수로
구	strolling along the shore 물가를 따라 산책하고 있다 holding a fishing pole 낚싯대를 잡고 있다 getting into a boat 배에 타고 있다 boating on a river 강에서 배를 타고 있다 swimming in a lake 호수에서 수영하고 있다 lying on the beach 해변에 누워 있다 sailing on the water 항해하고 있다 walking along the water 물가를 따라 걷고 있다 A boat is tied to a dock. 배가 항구에 매여 있다. A ship is approaching a pier. 배가 항구에 접근하고 있다. Houses overlook the lake. 집들이 호수를 내려다본다.

(B) ❹ 정답

풀이 방법   부둣가·물가 사진

Day 05_P1_08.mp3

[US]

(A) Some men are getting into a boat.
(B) A boat is docked at a pier.
(C) A man is tying a rope on a pole.
(D) Some people are swimming in the water.

이렇게 풀어요

1. **사진 파악하기** 사람이 있는 사물·풍경 사진, 부둣가, people(사람들) – approaching a boat(배에 다가가고 있다), 배경 – houses/buildings(집들/건물들), walkway(산책로), boat is docked(배가 정박해 있다)

2. **선택지 들으며 사진과 불일치하는 것 소거하여 정답 선택하기**

    (A) Some men are getting into a boat. 몇몇 남자들이 배를 타고 있다. → 동사 불일치
    (B) A boat is docked at a pier. 배가 항구에 정박해 있다. → 정답으로 선택
    (C) A man is tying a rope on a pole. 남자가 기둥에 끈을 묶고 있다. → 동사 불일치
    (D) Some people are swimming in the water. 몇몇 사람들이 물에서 수영하고 있다. → 동사 불일치

확인 문제 ⑤

Day 05_P1_09.mp3

(A)　|　(B)

출제 유형 5 — 정원·마당 사진

정원이나 마당이 배경이 되는 사진은 주로 정원에서 앉아서 쉬거나 정원을 가꾸는 사진이 출제됩니다. 정원 관리 도구를 사용하거나, 잔디를 깎거나 나무를 손질하는 모습, 식물에 물을 주는 모습을 묘사한 보기도 정답으로 출제돼요.

동사	water 물을 주다 trim 다듬다, 손질하다 mow 잔디를 깎다 plant 식물을 심다 surround 둘러싸다
명사	bush 관목 hose 호스 fence 울타리 patio 테라스 lawn 잔디
구	kneeling on the grass 잔디에 무릎을 꿇고 있다 watering a potted plant 화분에 물을 주고 있다 doing some gardening 정원을 가꾸고 있다 shoveling snow 눈을 삽질하고 있다 trimming the bushes 관목을 다듬고 있다 using a hose 호스를 사용하고 있다 watering the lawn 잔디에 물을 주고 있다 Balconies are being cleaned. 발코니가 청소되고 있다. A fence surrounds the garden. 울타리가 정원을 둘러싸고 있다.

(A) ⑤ 정답

풀이 방법 — 정원·마당 사진

Day 05_P1_10.mp3

US
(A) They're watering lawns with water hoses.
(B) They're trimming bushes along a driveway.
(C) They're working near each other.
(D) They're setting up a wooden fence.

이렇게 풀어요

1. **사진 파악하기** 2인 사진, 정원, they(그들) - working(일하고 있다), wearing hats(모자를 쓰고 있다), 배경 - bushes(관목), lawn(잔디)

2. **선택지 들으며 사진과 불일치하는 것 소거하여 정답 선택하기**
   - (A) They're watering lawns with water hoses. 그들은 수도 호스로 잔디에 물을 주고 있다. → 동사 불일치
   - (B) They're trimming bushes along a driveway. 그들은 진입로를 따라 있는 관목을 다듬고 있다. → 위치 불일치
   - (C) They're working near each other. 그들은 서로의 가까이에서 일하고 있다. → 정답으로 선택
   - (D) They're setting up a wooden fence. 그들은 나무 울타리를 설치하고 있다. → 목적어 불일치

출제 유형 6 — 역·공항 외부 사진

역 또는 공항의 외부 사진의 경우 야외 승강장이나 활주로의 모습이 배경이 되는 경우가 많습니다. 따라서 비행기에서 타거나 내리는 모습 또는 비행기의 상태를 묘사하는 표현이 출제됩니다. 외부 기차역 또는 버스 정거장의 경우 사람들이 기다리고 있는 모습, 타거나 내리는 모습이 가장 자주 출제되며, 기차가 서 있거나 도착하는 모습이 출제되기도 합니다.

동사	step down 내리다 get out of 내리다 take off 이륙하다 board 탑승하다 leave 출발하다 approach 다가오다, 가까이 가다
명사	passenger 승객 platform 승강장 runway 활주로
구	stepping down from a train 기차에서 내리고 있다 boarding an airplane 비행기에 탑승하고 있다 approaching the platform 승강장에 들어오고 있다 getting out of a vehicle 차량에서 내리고 있다 taking off from a runway 활주로에서 이륙하고 있다 parked side by side 나란히 주차되어 있다 A train is leaving the station. 기차가 역을 떠나고 있다. An aircraft is parked. 비행기가 세워져 있다.

🔒 확인 문제 ❻

🎧 Day 05_ P1_11.mp3

(A) | (B)

⚠️ 주의
사진에 있는 비행기나 기차 등과 관련된 연상 어휘가 오답 보기에 출제되므로 유의해야 합니다.

정답 ❻ (A)

풀이 방법 — 역·공항 외부 사진

🎧 Day 05_ P1_12.mp3

[BR]

(A) Suitcases have been placed in the overhead compartment.
(B) Some people are descending stairs.
(C) Passengers are checking in their baggage.
(D) Some people are boarding an airplane.

이렇게 풀어요

1. **사진 파악하기** 사람이 있는 사물·풍경 사진, 공항 외부, people(사람들) – boarding an airplane(비행기에 탑승하고 있다), carrying suitcases(여행 가방을 들고 있다), 배경 – airplane/aircraft(비행기), stairs(계단)

2. **선택지 들으며 사진과 불일치하는 것 소거하여 정답 선택하기**
   (A̶) Suitcases have been placed in the overhead compartment. 여행 가방들이 머리 위 짐칸에 놓여 있다. → 동사 불일치
   (B̶) Some people are descending stairs. 몇몇 사람들이 계단을 내려오고 있다. → 동사 불일치
   (C̶) Passengers are checking in their baggage. 승객들이 짐을 부치고 있다. → 동사 불일치
   (D) Some people are boarding an airplane. 몇몇 사람들이 비행기에 탑승하고 있다. → 정답으로 선택

따라 하면 문제가 풀리는 연습 문제

🎧 Day 05_P1_13.mp3
📍 정답 및 해석 p.28

01.

(1) 음원을 들으며 사진과 관련된 단어이면 O, 아니면 X에 표시하세요.

  (A) O | X   (B) O | X   (C) O | X

(2) 음원을 들으며 빈칸을 채우고 정답에는 O, 오답에는 X 표시하세요.

  (A) A _____ is _____ a street. [ ]
  (B) A _____ is being resurfaced. [ ]

02.

(1) 음원을 들으며 사진과 관련된 단어이면 O, 아니면 X에 표시하세요.

  (A) O | X   (B) O | X   (C) O | X

(2) 음원을 들으며 빈칸을 채우고 정답에는 O, 오답에는 X 표시하세요.

  (A) A crowd of people are _____ _____. [ ]
  (B) Some people are _____ performers. [ ]

03.

(1) 음원을 들으며 사진과 관련된 단어이면 O, 아니면 X에 표시하세요.

  (A) O | X   (B) O | X   (C) O | X

(2) 음원을 들으며 빈칸을 채우고 정답에는 O, 오답에는 X 표시하세요.

  (A) A _____ is being _____ with a brush. [ ]
  (B) A man is standing on a _____. [ ]

04.

(1) 음원을 들으며 사진과 관련된 단어이면 O, 아니면 X에 표시하세요.

  (A) O | X   (B) O | X   (C) O | X

(2) 음원을 들으며 빈칸을 채우고 정답에는 O, 오답에는 X 표시하세요.

  (A) Some people are _____ under umbrellas. [ ]
  (B) Some people are _____ in an _____ pool. [ ]

토익에 나올 실전 문제

01.

(A)　　(B)　　(C)　　(D)

02.

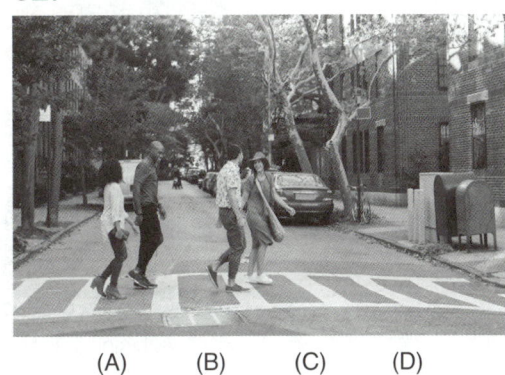

(A)　　(B)　　(C)　　(D)

03.

(A)　　(B)　　(C)　　(D)

04.

(A)　　(B)　　(C)　　(D)

05.

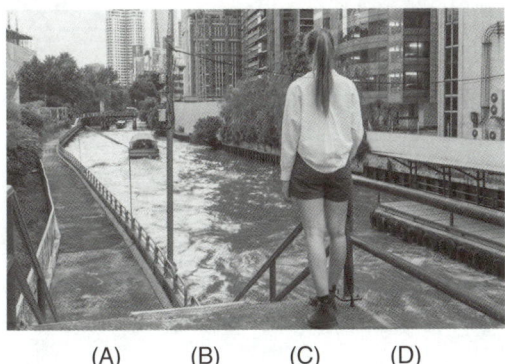

(A)　　(B)　　(C)　　(D)

06.

(A)　　(B)　　(C)　　(D)

PART 2 일반 의문문 – 긍정

일반 의문문은 다양한 정보를 물을 수 있으므로 출제되는 질문의 내용도 매우 다양합니다.
따라서 의문사 의문문에 비해 난이도가 높은 편이며 매회 2~3문제 정도 출제됩니다!

적용 기술

[기적의 필기노트] 32P~33P
LC 기술 21, 22

🎧 Day 05_P2_01.mp3

🔒 확인 문제 ❶

Mark your answer.

(A)　　(B)

⚠ 주의

질문의 주어(인칭 및 수)와 답변의 주어가 일치해야 합니다.
Q. Do **you** want to leave now?
당신 지금 갈 건가요?
A. No, **she**'s busy right now.
(X) 아니요. 그녀는 지금 바빠요.

출제 유형 1 — Do 의문문

- Do/Does/Did로 시작하는 긍정의 의문문은 과거, 현재, 미래 시제에 대한 사건, 행위, 상태 등을 묻는 질문으로 **주어와 본동사를 집중해서 들어야 하며 시제도 파악해야 합니다.**

Q. **Do** you have a key to the warehouse? 창고 열쇠 갖고 있나요?
A. No, Tim has it. 아뇨, Tim이 가지고 있어요.

Q. **Do** the contract negotiations start this afternoon? 계약 협상이 오늘 오후에 시작되나요?
A. I think they begin on Wednesday. 수요일에 시작하는 거 같습니다.

Q. **Did** you renew your driver's license? 운전 면허증 갱신했어요?
A. Haven't I told you that? 제가 말씀 안 드렸나요?

> **800+**
>
> - Do 의문문에 Yes/No로 응답할 경우, Yes/No 뒤의 내용이 질문과 전혀 무관한 내용으로 들어가 오답을 유도하는 경우가 있으므로 반드시 보기를 끝까지 들어야 합니다.
>
> Q. **Does** Jennifer Johnson still work here? Jennifer Johnson이 여전히 여기서 일하나요?
> A. **Yes**, she **resigned** two months ago. (X) 네, 그녀는 두 달 전에 그만뒀어요.
> A. **No**, she **resigned** two months ago. (O) 아뇨, 그녀는 두 달 전에 그만뒀어요.

(A) ❶ 정답

🧑 풀이 방법 — Do 의문문

🎧 Day 05_P2_02.mp3

[US - BR]

Do you have a dinner reservation with us?
(A) Just a cup of coffee.
(B) No, I just came in.
(C) The check, please.

저희에게 저녁 식사 예약하셨나요?
(A) 커피 한 잔만요.
(B) 아뇨, 저는 방금 왔어요.
(C) 계산서 주세요.

> **✓ 이렇게 풀어요**
>
> 1. 질문 내용 파악하기　Do you have a dinner reservation with us?
>   　　　　　　　　　　저녁 식사 예약을 했는지
>
> 2. 선택지 들으며 오답 소거하여 정답 선택하기
>   Just a cup of coffee. → 연상 어휘 오답(dinner-a cup of coffee)
>   (B) No, I just came in. → 정답으로 선택
>   ❌ The check, please. → 연상 어휘 오답(dinner-check)

출제 유형 2
Have 의문문

1 사람이 주어인 'Have + 주어 + p.p.' 의문문

- 'Have + 사람 주어 + p.p.' 형태로 묻는 질문은 사람 주어가 어떤 일을 완료했는지 묻는 내용입니다. 따라서, '이미 했다', '아직 안 했다'와 같은 내용의 답변이 출제됩니다.

  Q. **Has the plumber finished** fixing the faucet? 배관공이 수도꼭지를 고치는 것을 끝냈나요?
  A. **Probably not.** I'll call him again. 아마 아닐 거예요. 그에게 다시 전화하겠습니다.

  Q. **Have you completed** the employee training? 직원 연수를 마치셨어요?
  A. **Yes, a month ago.** 네, 한 달 전에요.

- Have 의문문은 과거에 대해 묻는 질문이므로 미래 시제로 답한 보기는 오답일 가능성이 높습니다.

  Q. **Has Mr. Chen submitted** his job application yet? Chen 씨가 입사 지원서를 제출했나요?
  A. I'm **planning** on going, too. (X) 저도 갈 계획이에요.
  A. Yes, I **received** it yesterday. (O) 네, 어제 받았습니다.

🎧 Day 05_ P2_03.mp3

🔒 확인 문제 ❷

Mark your answer.

(A)　　(B)

출제 포인트

Have 의문문은 Have we met before?(우리 만난 적 있나요?)와 같이 '경험'을 묻기도 하지만, 최근에는 그 비중이 줄어드는 추세이므로 '완료'의 예시를 더욱 다양하게 알아 두어야 합니다.

정답 (B)

  풀이 방법　Have 의문문 – 사람이 일을 완료했는지 묻는 질문

🎧 Day 05_ P2_04.mp3

[AU - BR]

Have they turned in the travel expense report?
(A) No, not yet.
(B) You have to report to the Human Resources.
(C) $600 a month.

그들이 출장 비용 보고서를 제출했나요?
(A) 아뇨, 아직 안 했어요.
(B) 인사부에 알리셔야 해요.
(C) 한 달에 600달러요.

✏️ 이렇게 풀어요

1. 질문 내용 파악하기   Have they turned in the travel expense report?
   　　　　　　　　　그들이 (출장 비용) 보고서를 제출했는지

2. 선택지 들으며 오답 소거하여 정답 선택하기
   (A) No, not yet. → 정답으로 선택
   (B) You have to report to the Room B. → 동일 단어 반복 오답 (report-report)
   (C) $600 a month. → 연상 어휘 오답 (expense-$600)

🎧 Day 05_P2_05.mp3

🔒 **확인 문제 ❸**

Mark your answer.

(A)　　　(B)

800+

2 사물이 주어인 'Have + 주어 + been p.p.' 의문문

'Have + 사물 주어 + been p.p.' 형태로 묻는 질문은 사건이 완료되었는지 묻는 내용입니다. 따라서 '완료되었다', '아직 안 되었다'와 같은 내용의 답변이 출제됩니다. 아래 풀이 방법에 있는 예제와 같이 Yes나 No로 답변 후 부연 설명을 붙이는 경우도 자주 출제됩니다.

Q. **Has the budget been approved** for the new campaign?
　새로운 캠페인에 대한 예산이 승인되었나요?

A. It's still being reviewed. 아직 검토 중입니다.

Q. **Have the invitations** for the grand opening ceremony **been sent out**?
　개장 기념식을 위한 초대장들이 발송되었나요?

A. Sure, by regular mail as usual. 물론이죠. 평소와 같이 보통 우편으로 보냈습니다.

(B)

🧑 풀이 방법 Have 의문문 – 사건이 완료되었는지 묻는 질문

🎧 Day 05_P2_06.mp3

[BR - US]

Have the exhibition schedules for the next quarter been posted yet?
(A) No, it's my first time to this museum.
(B) Yes, but they are tentative.
(C) You can track your package online.

다음 분기 전시 일정이 게시되었나요?
(A) 아뇨, 저는 이 박물관에 처음 와요.
(B) 네, 하지만 임시예요.
(C) 소포를 온라인상에서 추적하실 수 있어요.

✓ 이렇게 풀어요

1. 질문 내용 파악하기 Have the exhibition schedules for the next quarter been posted yet?
　　　　　　　　　　　　　　전시 일정이　　　　　　　　　　　　　게시되었는지

2. 선택지 들으며 오답 소거하여 정답 선택하기
　(A) No, it's my first time to this museum. → 연상 어휘 오답 (exhibition-museum)
　(B) Yes, but they are tentative. → 정답으로 선택
　(C) You can track your package online. → 주체가 맞지 않는 오답 (exhibition schedules-you)

출제 유형 3 Be동사 의문문

1 현재/과거의 사실을 묻는 be동사 의문문

be동사 의문문은 Is, Are, Was, Were로 시작하며, 주어의 상태나 신분을 묻거나 건물, 상점, 물건의 위치를 확인할 때 묻는 질문입니다. Yes/No 답변이 가능하고, 생략할 수도 있습니다.

Q. **Was** the vending machine repaired? 자판기가 수리되었나요?
A. (Yes.) That's what I heard. (네.) 제가 들은 바로는 그래요.

Q. **Is** there a grocery store on this street? 이 거리에 식료품점이 있나요?
A. (No.) It was relocated last month. (아니오.) 지난달에 이전했어요.

Q. **Are** you ready to go for dinner? 저녁 식사 하러 갈 준비 되었나요?
A. I just realized I have a client meeting. 고객 회의가 있다는 것을 방금 알았어요.

🎧 Day 05_P2_07.mp3

🔒 **확인 문제** ❶

Mark your answer.

(A)   (B)

⚠️ **주의**

일반 의문문은 시제 일치에 주의해야 합니다.
Q. **Is** Mr. Smith **going** to make a speech next week? Smith 씨가 다음 주에 연설하나요?
A. Yes, he **did** very well. (X)
네, 그는 아주 잘했어요.

정답 ❶

풀이 방법 Be동사 의문문 – 현재/과거

🎧 Day 05_P2_08.mp3

[US - BR]

Are you serious about transferring to the branch in Miami?
(A) A series of TV shows.
(B) Yes, I want to live with my family.
(C) I will take a train.

마이애미에 있는 지사로 전근 가려는 거 진심이에요?
(A) TV쇼 시리즈요.
(B) 네, 저는 가족과 함께 살고 싶어요.
(C) 저는 기차를 탈 거예요.

이렇게 풀어요

1. 질문 내용 파악하기 Are you serious about transferring to the branch in Miami?
   전근 가려는 게 진심인지

2. 선택지 들으며 오답 소거하여 정답 선택하기
   (A̸) A series of TV shows. → 유사 발음 오답 (serious-series)
   (B) Yes, I want to live with my family. → 정답으로 선택
   (C̸) I will take a train. → 연상 어휘 오답 (Miami-take a train)

🎧 Day 05_P2_09.mp3

🔒 **확인 문제 ❺**

Mark your answer.

(A)   (B)

2 미래의 계획을 묻는 be동사 의문문

'현재 진행형(be + -ing), be going to 동사 원형, be supposed to 동사 원형'으로 묻는 의문문은 미래의 계획 또는 일정을 묻는 질문입니다.

Q. **Are you going** to the trade fair? 무역 박람회에 가실 거예요?
A. I'm planning to. 그럴 계획입니다.

Q. **Is** Ms. Lewis **going to review** the sales figures sometime today?
   Lewis 씨가 오늘 판매 수치를 검토할까요?
A. Probably, she's free this afternoon. 아마도요, 그녀는 오늘 오후에 시간이 있어요.

Q. **Is** Jack **supposed to attend** the sales meeting today?
   Jack이 오늘 영업 회의에 참석하기로 되어 있나요?
A. He called in sick this morning. 그는 오늘 아침에 병가를 냈습니다.

(A)

🧑 풀이 방법 Be동사 의문문 – 미래

🎧 Day 05_P2_10.mp3

BR - AU

Is Mr. Harrison planning to approve the marketing proposal?
(A) Here is a floor plan.
(B) No, I need a proof of purchase.
(C) I heard he was very impressed.

Harrison 씨가 마케팅 제안서를 승인할 계획인가요?
(A) 여기 평면도가 있어요.
(B) 아뇨, 저는 구매 증빙 자료가 필요해요.
(C) 그가 아주 인상 깊게 생각했다고 들었어요.

이렇게 풀어요

1. 질문 내용 파악하기 Is Mr. Harrison planning to approve the marketing proposal?
   Harrison 씨가 승인할 계획인지

2. 선택지 들으며 오답 소거하여 정답 선택하기
   (A̶) Here is a floor plan. → 유사 발음 오답 (planning-plan)
   (B̶) No, I need a proof of purchase. → 주체가 맞지 않는 오답 (Mr. Harrison-I)
   (C) I heard he was very impressed. → 정답으로 선택

출제 유형 4 — Can/May/Will/Should 의문문

- Can/May/Will/Should로 시작하는 조동사 의문문은 주로 부탁, 허가, 요청, 제안의 의미를 갖습니다.

  Q. **Can I** suggest several changes to the presentation?
  발표에 몇 가지 수정 사항을 제안해도 될까요?
  A. I'd be glad to consider your opinions. 당신의 의견을 기꺼이 듣고 싶습니다.

부탁	Can you ~? Could you ~? Will you ~? Would you ~?
허가/요청	Can I ~? Could I ~? May I ~? Should I ~?

- Will은 단순히 미래의 사실이나 계획을 물을 때도 쓰입니다.

  Q. **Will you** be attending Mr. Baker's farewell party tomorrow?
  내일 Baker 씨의 송별회에 갈 건가요?
  A. I'll definitely be there. 당연히 가야죠.

🎧 Day 05_P2_11.mp3

🔒 확인 문제 ❻

Mark your answer.

(A)　　(B)

(B) 정답

풀이 방법 — Can/May/Will/Should 의문문

🎧 Day 05_P2_12.mp3

[BR - US]

Will our wait staff members be wearing new uniforms?
(A) Okay, I will put your name on the waiting list.
(B) Yes, probably from next month.
(C) We need to replace this worn-out part.

우리의 종업원들이 새 유니폼을 입을 건가요?
(A) 좋아요, 당신의 이름을 대기자 명단에 올릴게요.
(B) 네, 아마도 다음 달부터요.
(C) 우리는 이 닳은 부분을 교체해야 해요.

이렇게 풀어요

1. 질문 내용 파악하기 Will our wait staff members be wearing new uniforms?
   종업원들이 새 유니폼을 입을 것인지

2. 선택지 들으며 오답 소거하여 정답 선택하기
   (A̶) Okay, I will put your name on the waiting list. → 유사 발음 오답 (wait-waiting)
   (B) Yes, probably from next month. → 정답으로 선택
   (C̶) We need to replace this worn-out part. → 연상 어휘 오답 (uniforms-worn-out)

PART 2 일반 의문문 - 긍정

따라 하면 문제가 풀리는
연습 문제

🎧 Day 05_P2_13.mp3
📍 정답 및 해석 p.30

각 질문과 보기를 들으며 빈칸을 채운 뒤 정답에는 O, 오답에는 X 표시하세요.

01. _____ you _____ with this type of _____ before?
  (A) I'll _____ there _____ _____. [   ]
  (B) Yes, _____ _____ _____. [   ]

02. Do you have any _____ _____ to Los Angeles?
  (A) No, the _____ _____ is $500. [   ]
  (B) They are all _____ _____. [   ]

03. _____ _____ a discount for _____?
  (A) I'm _____ _____. Let me ask. [   ]
  (B) Yes, just _____ the street. [   ]

04. Will you _____ your _____ onto the _____?
  (A) This is a newly _____ _____. [   ]
  (B) I'll _____ it in the _____ _____. [   ]

05. Has the _____ _____ for the monthly meeting been _____ yet?
  (A) I'll leave it on your _____ _____ _____. [   ]
  (B) No, I've _____ _____ there. [   ]

06. Did you _____ on the _____ for the workshop?
  (A) _____ _____ May 20? [   ]
  (B) Yes, the _____ was well-organized. [   ]

07. Can you _____ Ben to _____ _____ my office for a minute?
  (A) He will _____ _____ the case. [   ]
  (B) _____, I'll _____ him right away. [   ]

08. Do you _____ Mr. Song's _____ _____?
  (A) He _____ _____ this morning. [   ]
  (B) I think I have it in my _____ _____. [   ]

🎧 Day 05_P2_14.mp3
정답 및 해설 p.31

01. Mark your answer on your answer sheet.
(A) (B) (C)

02. Mark your answer on your answer sheet.
(A) (B) (C)

03. Mark your answer on your answer sheet.
(A) (B) (C)

04. Mark your answer on your answer sheet.
(A) (B) (C)

05. Mark your answer on your answer sheet.
(A) (B) (C)

06. Mark your answer on your answer sheet.
(A) (B) (C)

07. Mark your answer on your answer sheet.
(A) (B) (C)

08. Mark your answer on your answer sheet.
(A) (B) (C)

09. Mark your answer on your answer sheet.
(A) (B) (C)

10. Mark your answer on your answer sheet.
(A) (B) (C)

11. Mark your answer on your answer sheet.
(A) (B) (C)

12. Mark your answer on your answer sheet.
(A) (B) (C)

13. Mark your answer on your answer sheet.
(A) (B) (C)

14. Mark your answer on your answer sheet.
(A) (B) (C)

15. Mark your answer on your answer sheet.
(A) (B) (C)

16. Mark your answer on your answer sheet.
(A) (B) (C)

'멋진 당신, 오늘도 화이팅'

DAY 06

오늘의 학습 포인트

PART 2. 일반 의문문 - 부정 - Yes/No 답변 가능, 생략도 가능
1. Don't/Didn't 의문문 - 사실 여부 확인
2. Haven't/Hasn't 의문문
3. Isn't/Aren't 의문문 - 현재 시제 / 미래 시제
   1) 현재 시제 - 일반적인 사실
   2) 미래 시제 - isn't/aren't + 주어 + -ing[going to 동사 원형]
4. Wasn't/Weren't 의문문 - 과거 사실 재확인
5. Won't/Shouldn't/Couldn't 의문문
   - 미래 사실 재확인(Won't), 제안/권유/부탁/허락(Shouldn't/Couldn't)

PART 3. 문제 유형
1. 주제·목적 문제 - 대화의 시작 부분
2. 장소·직업 문제 - 첫 대사 혹은 대화 전반, 특정 장소/직업 표현
3. 세부 사항 문제 - 걱정하는 것, 이유/방법, 특정 키워드 정보

PART 2 일반 의문문 – 부정

not이 포함된 부정문 형태의 일반 의문문은 매회 2문제 정도 출제됩니다!
의문문의 시작 부분에 익숙해져야 의미를 한번에 파악할 수 있습니다.

적용 기술

[기적의 필기노트] 33P
LC 기술 23

🎧 Day 06_ P2_01.mp3

🔒 확인 문제 ❶

Mark your answer.

(A)   (B)

⚠ 주의

부정 의문문은 긍정 의문문으로 이해하고 정답을 찾아도 됩니다. 질문이 긍정문인지 부정문인지는 답변에 영향을 주지 않기 때문입니다.

출제 유형 1 Don't/Didn't 의문문

Do 동사 부정 의문문은 Do나 Did에 not을 붙여 Don't 또는 Didn't로 묻는 질문입니다. 사실 여부를 확인하거나 상대방에게 간접적으로 재확인하는 의미를 갖습니다.

Q. **Didn't** you open a bank account last month? 당신 지난달에 계좌 개설하지 않았어요?
A. [긍정] Yes, in the downtown branch. 네, 도심 지점에서 했어요.
   [부정] No, not yet. 아니요, 아직 못했습니다.

> **800+**
> [긍정(Yes,) + 부연 설명] (Yes,) but I've never used it. (네,) 하지만 한 번도 사용하지 않았어요.
> [부정(No,) + 부연 설명] (No,) I was busy last month. (아뇨,) 지난달에 바빴습니다.
> (No,) I haven't had time yet. (아뇨,) 아직 시간이 없었어요.

👤 풀이 방법 Don't/Didn't 의문문

🎧 Day 06_ P2_02.mp3

[BR - BR]

Don't you need a security card to enter this restricted area?
(A) I don't see any guards.
(B) Yes, but I forgot to bring it.
(C) Beside the main entrance.

이 제한 구역에 들어가려면 보안 카드가 필요하지 않나요?
(A) 경비원이 없어요.
(B) 네, 그런데 가져오는 것을 잊어버렸어요.
(C) 정문 옆에요.

✓ 이렇게 풀어요

1. **질문 내용 파악하기** Don't you need a security card to enter this restricted area?
   보안 카드가 필요하지 않은지

2. **선택지 들으며 오답 소거하여 정답 선택하기**
   (A̶) I don't see any guards. → 연상 어휘 오답 (restricted area-guards)
   (B) Yes, but I forgot to bring it. → 정답으로 선택
   (C̶) Beside the main entrance. → 유사 발음 오답 (enter-entrance)

출제 유형 2
Haven't/Hasn't 의문문

동작의 완료나 경험을 묻는 'Haven't/Hasn't + 주어 + p.p.' 형태의 부정 의문문은 주어와 동사의 과거 분사 형태인 '주어 + p.p.' 부분을 잘 듣고 목적어나 전치사구 등에 유의하면서 답을 찾아야 합니다.

Q. **Haven't** all the employees been given the brochure already?
모든 직원들이 이미 안내책자를 받지 않았나요?

A. [긍정] Yes, they are going over it. 네, 그들은 그것을 검토하고 있어요.

> 800+
> [부정(No,) + 부연 설명] (No,) the research department hasn't got enough.
> (아니요,) 연구 부서는 충분히 받지 못했습니다.
>
> [긍정(Yes,) + 부연 설명] (Yes,) but some pages are missing.
> (네,) 그런데 몇몇 페이지가 없어요.

> 900+
> [반문] Who was in charge of it? 그거 담당자가 누구였나요?

🎧 Day 06_ P2_03.mp3

🔒 확인 문제 ❷

Mark your answer.

(A)   (B)

정답 ❷ (B)

풀이 방법   Haven't/Hasn't 의문문

🎧 Day 06_ P2_04.mp3

US - AU

Hasn't Mr. Shaw received his on-the-job training yet?
(A) He is seeking a full-time position.
(B) I'm sure he did last month.
(C) The delivery man arrived late.

Shaw 씨가 실무 교육을 아직 받지 않았나요?
(A) 그는 정규직을 구하고 있어요.
(B) 지난달에 받았다고 확신해요.
(C) 배달원이 늦게 도착했어요.

✏️ 이렇게 풀어요

1. 질문 내용 파악하기   Hasn't Mr. Shaw received his on-the-job training yet?
   Shaw 씨가 교육을 아직 받지 않았는지

2. 선택지 들으며 오답 소거하여 정답 선택하기
   (A̶) He is seeking a full-time position. → 시제 불일치 오답 (과거-현재)
   (B) I'm sure he did last month. → 정답으로 선택
   (C̶) The delivery man arrived late. → 연상 어휘 오답 (received-delivery man)

PART 2 일반 의문문 – 부정   103

🎧 Day 06_P2_05.mp3

🔒 확인 문제 ❸

Mark your answer.

(A)   (B)

출제 유형 3

Isn't/Aren't 의문문

1 일반적인 사실을 묻는 Isn't/Aren't 의문문

- be동사의 부정형인 Isn't/Aren't로 시작하는 의문문이며, 현재 시제는 일반적인 사실에 대해 묻는 질문입니다.

  Q. **Isn't** Ms. Peterson the keynote speaker of the event?
     Peterson 씨가 행사의 기조 연설자 아닌가요?
  A. She'll be here in a minute. 그녀가 곧 여기로 올 겁니다.

- Isn't there + 주어(명사구) + 부사/전치사구 ~?(~가 …에 있는 거 아니에요?)의 문장은 **장소나 위치를 재확인하는 의미**를 갖습니다.

  Q. **Isn't there** a parking lot across the street? 길 건너편에 주차장 있지 않아요?
  A. You are right. 맞습니다.

> **800+**
>
> - 부정 의문문도 일반 의문문과 마찬가지로 답변에서 Yes/No를 생략할 수 있습니다. Yes/No에 해당되는 대용 어구를 사용하는 답변도 출제됩니다.
>
> | Yes를 대신할 수 있는 답변 | No를 대신할 수 있는 답변 |
> | --- | --- |
> | Of course. / Certainly. 물론이죠.
You are right. 당신이 맞아요.
I'll say. 맞습니다. | Sorry, but ~ 죄송하지만, ~
I'm afraid not. 아닐 거예요.
Probably not. 아닐 거예요. |

🧑 풀이 방법 Isn't/Aren't 의문문(현재 시제)

🎧 Day 06_P2_06.mp3

[US - BR]

Isn't Hunter Ski Resort the most ideal venue for the company retreat?
(A) The record-breaking attendance.
(B) No, it's too far away from here.
(C) I bought a season ticket.

Hunter 스키 리조트가 회사 야유회를 위한 가장 이상적인 장소 아닌가요?
(A) 전례 없는 참여도예요.
(B) 아뇨, 여기서 너무 멀어요.
(C) 저는 정기권을 샀어요.

✏️ 이렇게 풀어요

1. **질문 내용 파악하기** Isn't Hunter Ski Resort the most ideal venue for the company retreat?
   Hunter 스키 리조트가 가장 이상적인 장소 아닌지

2. **선택지 들으며 오답 소거하여 정답 선택하기**
   (A̶) The record-breaking attendance. → 연상 어휘 오답(company retreat-attendance)
   (B) No, it's too far away from here. → 정답으로 선택
   (C̶) I bought a season ticket. → 연상 어휘 오답(Ski Resort-season ticket)

104 기적의 토익 LC

2 미래 사실에 대해 확인하는 Isn't/Aren't 의문문

- 'be going to 동사 원형'과 현재 진행형(be + -ing)은 가까운 미래를 나타낼 때 쓰이므로 isn't/aren't + 주어 + -ing[going to 동사 원형]로 물을 경우 미래 시제라는 것을 파악해야 합니다.

Q. **Aren't you going to** buy a new laptop computer? 새 노트북 컴퓨터를 살 거 아닌가요?
A. Mine still works fine. 제 것은 아직 잘 작동해요.

Q. **Isn't she participating** in the opening ceremony tonight?
그녀가 오늘 밤에 개막식에 참석할 거 아닌가요?
A. Yes, with her husband Mr. Lloyd. 네, 그녀의 남편인 Lloyd 씨와 함께요.

> **800+**
> - Isn't/Aren't + 주어 + expected[supposed] to ~?(하기로 되어 있지 않나요?), Isn't/Aren't + 주어 + scheduled to ~?(~할 예정이지 않나요?)도 미래 시제를 나타낼 수 있습니다.
>
> Q. **Isn't David scheduled to** go on a business trip next week?
> David이 다음 주에 출장 가기로 되어 있지 않나요?
> A. He departs on Tuesday. 그는 화요일에 출발해요.

🎧 Day 06_ P2_07.mp3

🔒 **확인 문제 ❹**

Mark your answer.

(A)　　(B)

⚠️ **주의**
부정 의문문에서는 Yes/No의 비논리적 답변에 주의해야 합니다.
Q. Aren't you going to attend the seminar? 세미나에 참석하실 거 아닌가요?
A. Yes, I'm on holiday. (X).
네, 저는 휴가 중이에요.
A. Yes, I'll be there. (O)
네, 갈 거예요.

DAY 06

정답  (A)

풀이 방법 Isn't/Aren't 의문문(미래 시제)

🎧 Day 06_ P2_08.mp3

[BR - AU]

Isn't Hirose coming to the lunch with us?
(A) At the outdoor patio.
(B) No, he has a project due tomorrow.
(C) I have a discount coupon.

Hirose는 우리와 함께 점심 식사를 하러 안 가나요?
(A) 야외 테라스에서요.
(B) 안 가요, 그는 내일 마감인 프로젝트가 있어요.
(C) 제게 할인 쿠폰이 있어요.

> **1 이렇게 풀어요**
>
> 1. 질문 내용 파악하기 Isn't Hirose coming to the lunch with us?
>   Hirose가 함께 안 가는지
>
> 2. 선택지 들으며 오답 소거하여 정답 선택하기
>   (✗) At the outdoor patio. → 다른 의문사 답변 오답(Where)
>   (B) No, he has a project due tomorrow. → 정답으로 선택
>   (✗) I have a discount coupon. → 주체가 맞지 않는 오답(Hirose-I)

PART 2 일반 의문문 - 부정

🎧 Day 06_ P2_09.mp3

🔒 **확인 문제 ⑤**

Mark your answer.

(A)　　(B)

출제 포인트

be동사 부정 의문문은 상대방의 동의를 요구하는 뉘앙스로도 자주 출제됩니다.
Q. Wasn't it great to see him dance on the stage? 그가 무대에서 춤추는 것을 보는 게 좋지 않았어요?
A. Yes, I was impressed. 네, 인상 깊었어요. (동의)

출제 유형 4
Wasn't/Weren't 의문문

Wasn't/Weren't 의문문은 과거의 사실을 재확인하며 '~ 아니었어요?'라는 의미로 묻는 질문입니다.

Q. **Weren't** you supposed to be at a conference yesterday?
어제 학회에 가셔야 했던 거 아니었어요?
A. Mr. Gonzales went instead. Gonzales 씨가 대신 갔어요.

Q. **Wasn't** this coat more expensive last weekend?
이 코트는 지난 주말에 더 비싸지 않았나요?
A. Actually, the price just went down. 사실은 가격이 막 내렸어요.

(A) ⑤

🧑 풀이 방법　Wasn't/Weren't 의문문

🎧 Day 06_ P2_10.mp3

BR - US

Wasn't that steakhouse closed for good?
(A) That's not even close.
(B) How's your steak?
(C) Yes, the chef retired.

저 스테이크 레스토랑 완전히 폐업한 거 아니었어요?
(A) 어림도 없어요.
(B) 스테이크 (맛이) 어때요?
(C) 맞아요, 요리사가 퇴직했어요.

✓ **이렇게 풀어요**

1. 질문 내용 파악하기　Wasn't that steakhouse closed for good?
　　　　　　　　　스테이크 레스토랑이 폐업하지 않았는거

2. 선택지 들으며 오답 소거하여 정답 선택하기
　(A) That's not even close. → 유사 발음 오답 (closed-close)
　(B) How's your steak? → 연상 어휘 오답 (steakhouse-steak)
　(C) Yes, the chef retired. → 정답으로 선택

106　기적의 토익 LC

출제 유형 5 **Won't/Shouldn't/Couldn't 의문문**

🎧 Day 06_ P2_11.mp3

🔒 확인 문제 ❻

Mark your answer.

(A)   (B)

800+

Won't 의문문은 미래의 사실을 재확인하는 질문이며, Shouldn't/Couldn't 의문문은 상대방에게 제안, 권유, 부탁, 허락 등을 구할 때 쓰입니다.

Q. **Won't** Mr. Choi be organizing the speech contest?
   Choi 씨가 연설 대회를 준비하지 않을까요?
A. As far as I know, he is in charge of it. 제가 아는 바로는, 그가 그것 담당이에요.

Q. **Shouldn't** we prepare materials for the workshop?
   워크숍을 위한 자료를 준비해야 하지 않을까요?
A. Let's discuss it in the meeting room. 회의실에서 논의합시다.

Q. **Couldn't** we hire some part-time workers?
   우리 파트타임 직원들을 몇 명 고용할 수 없을까요?
A. We have a limited budget. 우리는 예산이 한정되어 있어요.

정답 (B)

 **풀이 방법** Won't/Shouldn't/Couldn't 의문문

🎧 Day 06_ P2_12.mp3

US - BR

Won't Barbara be volunteering to work at the charity party this year?

(A) A non-profit organization.
(B) We need to hire more temporary workers.
(C) No, she's going on her postponed vacation.

Barbara가 올해는 자선 파티에서 일하는 것을 자원하지 않을 건가요?
(A) 비영리 단체예요.
(B) 우리는 임시 직원들을 더 고용해야 해요.
(C) 안 할 거예요, 그녀는 밀린 휴가를 갈 거예요.

이렇게 풀어요

1. 질문 내용 파악하기 Won't Barbara be volunteering to work at the charity party this year?
   Barbara가 일하는 것을 자원하지 않을 건지

2. 선택지 들으며 오답 소거하여 정답 선택하기
   (A) A non-profit organization. → 연상 어휘 오답 (charity-non-profit)
   (B) We need to hire more temporary workers. → 연상 어휘 오답 (work-hire, workers)
   (C) No, she's going on her postponed vacation. → 정답으로 선택

PART 2 일반 의문문 - 부정

따라 하면 문제가 풀리는
연습 문제

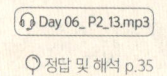

각 질문과 보기를 들으며 빈칸을 채운 뒤 정답에는 O, 오답에는 X 표시하세요.

01. Aren't the table and chairs supposed to _____ _____ _____?
   (A) _____ _____ check the _____. [   ]
   (B) _____, I think that _____ is _____ opened. [   ]

02. Don't we _____ _____ _____ some more office supplies?
   (A) Yes, I was _____. [   ]
   (B) Mr. Han _____ _____ _____ _____ it. [   ]

03. Didn't you _____ the _____ _____ at the entrance?
   (A) Sorry, I _____ _____ _____. [   ]
   (B) It's still _____ _____. [   ]

04. Can't we _____ the _____ a little _____ tomorrow?
   (A) An annual _____ of _____. [   ]
   (B) _____ have to _____. [   ]

05. Didn't Ms. Gonzales _____ _____ the _____ in person?
   (A) _____, we _____ _____ _____ the paper. [   ]
   (B) Actually, she sent it _____ _____. [   ]

06. Doesn't the _____ _____ _____ for these boxes?
   (A) No, it's _____ _____. [   ]
   (B) The room _____ $100 per night. [   ]

07. Isn't that _____ _____ _____ on the table?
   (A) Oh, _____ _____. It is. [   ]
   (B) He _____ _____ yesterday. [   ]

08. _____ _____ going to _____ to the _____ today?
   (A) I got my _____ _____. [   ]
   (B) Are these your _____ _____? [   ]

Day 06_ P2_14.mp3

정답 및 해설 p.36

01. Mark your answer on your answer sheet.
(A)　　　　(B)　　　　(C)

02. Mark your answer on your answer sheet.
(A)　　　　(B)　　　　(C)

03. Mark your answer on your answer sheet.
(A)　　　　(B)　　　　(C)

04. Mark your answer on your answer sheet.
(A)　　　　(B)　　　　(C)

05. Mark your answer on your answer sheet.
(A)　　　　(B)　　　　(C)

06. Mark your answer on your answer sheet.
(A)　　　　(B)　　　　(C)

07. Mark your answer on your answer sheet.
(A)　　　　(B)　　　　(C)

08. Mark your answer on your answer sheet.
(A)　　　　(B)　　　　(C)

09. Mark your answer on your answer sheet.
(A)　　　　(B)　　　　(C)

10. Mark your answer on your answer sheet.
(A)　　　　(B)　　　　(C)

11. Mark your answer on your answer sheet.
(A)　　　　(B)　　　　(C)

12. Mark your answer on your answer sheet.
(A)　　　　(B)　　　　(C)

13. Mark your answer on your answer sheet.
(A)　　　　(B)　　　　(C)

14. Mark your answer on your answer sheet.
(A)　　　　(B)　　　　(C)

15. Mark your answer on your answer sheet.
(A)　　　　(B)　　　　(C)

16. Mark your answer on your answer sheet.
(A)　　　　(B)　　　　(C)

PART 3 주제·목적 문제 / 장소·직업 문제 / 세부 사항 문제

주제·목적 문제와 장소·직업 문제는 매회 3~4문제 정도, 세부 사항 문제는 매회 5~12문제 정도 출제됩니다!

적용 기술
[기적의 필기노트] 47P~48P
LC 기술 35, 36

출제 포인트
대화의 주제와 목적을 묻는 문제는 선택지를 먼저 파악한 후, 대화의 시작 부분에 집중하면서 첫 1~2문장이 들릴 때 정답의 단서를 찾을 수 있어야 합니다.

⚠ 주의
대화에 언급된 특정 단어나 관련 단어를 오답 보기에 포함시키는 경우가 있으므로 주의해야 합니다.

출제 유형 1 주제·목적 문제

1 질문 유형

- 주제 문제

  What are the speakers **talking about**? 화자들은 무엇에 대해 이야기하고 있는가?
  What are the speakers **mainly discussing**? 화자들은 주로 무엇에 대해 논의하고 있는가?
  What's the **main topic** of the conversation? 대화의 주제는 무엇인가?

- 전화 목적 문제

  Why is the man[woman] **calling**? 남자[여자]는 왜 전화하고 있는가?
  Why did the woman **call** the man? 왜 여자가 남자에게 전화했는가?
  What is the **purpose** of the (phone) **call**? 전화를 건 목적은 무엇인가?

2 핵심 포인트

1. **대화의 앞부분을 잘 들어야 합니다.**
   주제나 목적 문제는 주로 첫 번째 문제로 제시되고, 단서도 대화 앞부분에서 파악할 수 있습니다. 따라서 미리 파악해 둔 선택지의 핵심 어휘와 관련된 단어나 표현이 나오는지 앞부분을 유심히 듣습니다.

2. **정답의 단서를 끌고 나오는 표현을 들어야 합니다.**
   특정 상황이나 사실, 계획, 요청, 문제점을 언급할 때 자주 쓰는 표현을 알아 두어야 합니다. 그 뒤에 대화의 주제나 목적이 언급되는 경우가 많습니다.

전화 목적을 직접 언급하는 표현	I'm calling about[regarding] ~와 관련하여 전화 드렸습니다 I'm calling to ~하기 위해 전화 드렸습니다 I'm calling because ~ 때문에 전화 드렸습니다
방문 목적을 직접 언급하는 표현	I'm here to ~하기 위해 여기 왔습니다
계획을 언급하는 표현	I'm planning to ~할 계획입니다 I'm going to ~할 것입니다
원하는 것을 직접 언급하는 표현	I'd like to ~하고 싶습니다 I'd like to see if ~인지 알고 싶습니다 I want you to 당신이 ~하기를 바랍니다 I'm looking for ~을 찾고 있습니다
상대방에게 질문하는 표현	Did you hear (that) ~? ~에 대해 들었어요? Did you know (that) ~? ~에 대해 알고 있었어요?

[단서] I'm calling regarding the workshop. 워크숍과 관련하여 전화 드렸습니다.
[정답] The upcoming event 다가오는 행사

[단서] I'd like to get a library card. 도서관 카드를 만들고 싶습니다.
[정답] Getting a membership 회원 자격을 얻는 것

주제·목적 문제

🎧 Day 06_ P3_01.mp3

[문제지]

What are the speakers **mainly talking about**?
(A) An office supply order
(B) A client meeting
(C) An ad flyer design
(D) A job opening

화자들은 주로 무엇에 대해 이야기하고 있는가?
(A) 사무용품 주문
(B) 고객 미팅
(C) 광고 전단 디자인
(D) 일자리 공석

[대화] [US - BR]

W: Barry, this is Gloria from the warehouse. **I'm reviewing the office supply order for your branch and you only asked for one box of printer paper.** That doesn't seem right.
M: That does sound like there was a mistake. We usually go through way more than that printing flyers.
W: That's what I thought. Your manager must have deleted a zero by mistake. Could you confirm that for me?
M: Actually, the manager isn't in the office at the moment. I'll call her now and confirm how much we actually need. Thanks for letting us know.

여: Barry, 저는 창고에서 근무하는 Gloria입니다. **제가 당신의 지점의 사무용품 주문을 검토하는 중인데요, 프린터용 용지를 한 박스만 요청하셨더군요.** 그게 제대로 된 것 같지 않습니다.
남: 실수가 있었던 것 같네요. 우리는 전단을 인쇄하는 데 보통 그것보다 훨씬 더 많이 사용하거든요.
여: 저도 그렇게 생각했어요. 당신의 매니저가 실수로 0을 지웠음에 틀림없습니다. 저를 위해 다시 확인해 주시겠어요?
남: 사실, 매니저님이 지금 사무실에 없습니다. 그녀에게 지금 전화해서 우리가 실제로 얼마나 필요한지 물어볼게요. 알려주셔서 감사합니다.

💡 이렇게 풀어요

문제와 선택지의 키워드는 대화가 시작되기 전에 미리 파악되어 있어야 해요!

1. **문제 파악하기**
   mainly talking about → 주제 문제임을 파악합니다.

2. **선택지 키워드 파악하기**
   (A) 사무용품 주문 (B) 고객 미팅 (C) 광고 전단 디자인 (D) 일자리 공석
   → 위의 선택지 중 무엇에 관한 내용일지 염두에 두며 대화를 듣습니다.

3. **대화 앞부분 들으며 정답 선택하기**
   I'm reviewing the office supply order for your branch and you only asked for one box of printer paper.
   → office supply order가 그대로 제시된 (A)를 정답으로 선택하고 다음 문제로 넘어갑니다.

적용 기술

[기적의 필기노트] 42P~44P
LC 기술 31, 32, 33

출제 포인트

첫 대사에서 장소가 직접적으로 언급되거나 대화 전반에 걸쳐 간접적으로 대화 장소가 드러납니다. 화자들이 사용하는 특정 어휘나 표현을 통해 장소나 직업을 유추할 수 있어야 합니다.

⚠️ **주의**

장소·직업 문제는 난이도는 높지 않지만 간혹 혼동되는 보기가 나오는 경우가 있습니다. 따라서 하나의 특정 단어만 듣고 답을 골라서는 안 되며, 확실하지 않을 경우 대화 전체를 듣고 답을 선택해야 합니다.

출제 포인트
그 밖의 빈출 대화 장소
museum 박물관
store 상점
library 도서관
bookstore 서점
hotel 호텔

그 밖의 빈출 직업
receptionist 안내원, 접수 담당자
technician 기술자
salesperson 판매 사원

출제 유형 2 — 장소·직업 문제

1 질문 유형

• **대화 장소/근무 장소 문제**
Where is the conversation **taking place**? 대화는 어디에서 일어나고 있는가?
Where does the conversation most likely **occur**? 대화는 어디에서 일어나고 있겠는가?
Where are the speakers? 화자들은 어디에 있는가?
Where do the speakers most likely **work**? 화자들은 어디에서 근무하겠는가?
What department does the **woman work in**? 여자는 어느 부서에서 일하는가?

• **직업 문제**
Who most likely is the **woman**? 여자는 누구이겠는가?
Who is the **man talking to**? 남자는 누구에게 말하고 있는가?
What type of business[company] does the **man work for**?
남자는 어떤 업종의 회사에 근무하는가?

2 핵심 포인트

1. 시험에 자주 나오는 장소와 단서가 되는 어휘들을 연결시켜 알아 두어야 합니다.

restaurant 식당 cafeteria 구내식당	table 식탁, 자리 menu 메뉴 lunch special 점심 특선 ingredients 재료 order 주문, 주문하다 server 종업원
doctor's office 병원 medical clinic 병원 pharmacy 약국	doctor 의사 appointment 진료 예약 nurse 간호사 check-up 건강 검진 patient 환자 health screening 건강 검진 dentist office 치과 take medicine 약을 복용하다
airport 공항 train station 기차역	departure 출발 boarding 탑승 take off 이륙 baggage claim 짐 찾는 곳 gate 탑승 게이트 platform 승강장

2. 직업 문제는 단서를 끌고 나오는 표현을 사용하여 직접적으로 언급하는 경우가 많습니다.

This is 이름 (calling) from 부서명/회사명	This is Angelina (calling) from accounting. 저는 회계 부서의 Angelina입니다.
This is 이름, 직업/직책	This is Eric Choi, the vice president of TW Motors. 저는 TW Motors의 부사장 Eric Choi입니다.

3. 시험에 자주 나오는 직업과 단서가 되는 어휘들을 연결시켜 알아 두어야 합니다.

real estate agent 부동산 중개인	property 부동산, 건물 studio apartment 원룸 furnished 가구를 모두 갖춘 tenant 세입자 within walking distance 걸어갈 수 있는 거리인
journalist 기자 reporter 기자 editor 편집자	article 기사 publish 출판하다 interview 인터뷰하다 revise 수정하다 publisher 출판사 edit 편집하다
architect 건축가	renovation 보수 space 공간 construct 짓다, 건설하다 blueprint 청사진

장소·직업 문제

🎧 Day 06_ P3_02.mp3

문제지

Where is the conversation **taking place**?
(A) At a park
(B) At a theater
(C) At a restaurant
(D) At a supermarket

대화는 어디에서 일어나고 있는가?
(A) 공원에서
(B) 극장에서
(C) 레스토랑에서
(D) 슈퍼마켓에서

대화 BR - AU

W: Chris, **the customers seated at the table by our restaurant's entrance** want to know about live performances in this city. I know you go to the theater quite often. Do you know of anything going on this weekend?

M: Actually, the Westbrook Drama Club is putting on a show at Hudson Park tomorrow. There's going to be an afternoon and an evening show. I think they're doing one of Shakespeare's plays.

W: Great! By the way, **after I take their food out to them**, I think I'll take my dinner break since we're not very busy right now.

여: Chris, 우리 레스토랑의 입구 옆 테이블에 앉아 있는 손님들이 이 도시의 라이브 공연에 대해 알고 싶어 해요. 당신이 극장에 꽤 자주 가는 것으로 알고 있어요. 이번 주말에 열리는 공연에 대해 좀 아나요?

남: 사실, Westbrook Drama Club이 내일 Hudson 공원에서 공연을 해요. 오후와 저녁 공연이 있을 거예요. 셰익스피어의 연극 중 하나를 할 거예요.

여: 좋네요! 그나저나, 제가 그들에게 음식을 포장해 준 뒤에, 지금 우리가 그렇게 바쁘지 않으니 저는 저녁 휴식 시간을 가질게요.

이렇게 풀어요

문제와 선택지의 키워드는 대화가 시작되기 전에 미리 파악되어 있어야 해요!

1. **문제 파악하기**
   Where, taking place → 장소 문제임을 파악합니다.

2. **선택지 키워드 파악하기**
   (A) 공원 (B) 극장 (C) 레스토랑 (D) 슈퍼마켓
   → 장소 전치사 at, on, in 등의 뒤에 나오는 명사만 빠르게 파악합니다.

3. **대화가 이루어지는 특정 장소와 관련된 단어를 토대로 정답 선택하기**
   customers seated at the table by our restaurant's entrance, take their food out
   → 레스토랑임을 알 수 있으므로 (C)를 정답으로 선택하고 다음 문제로 넘어갑니다.

적용 기술

[기적의 필기노트] 54P
LC 기술 41

출제 포인트
여자 또는 남자가 걱정하는 점을 묻는 문제, 이유/방법을 묻는 문제, 특정 키워드에 관한 정보를 묻는 문제가 매회 5~12문제 가량 출제됩니다.

출제 포인트
키워드를 제시하는 세부 사항 문제는 시간 관련 키워드(요일, 시간, today/tomorrow 등)가 가장 자주 출제됩니다.

⚠️ **주의**
단서 표현을 사용하여 직접적으로 문제점을 언급하지 않고 대화 상황이 좋지 않은 방향으로 흘러감에 따라 '비용이 증가했다', '일이 오래 걸릴 것이다'와 같이 문맥으로 파악해야 하는 경우도 있으니 주의해야 합니다.

출제 유형 3 — 세부 사항 문제

1 질문 유형

• 이유/방법을 묻는 문제

Why does the man want to **use the room today**? 남자는 왜 오늘 방을 사용하고 싶어 하는가?
According to the man, **how** can the **woman find additional information**? 남자에 따르면, 여자는 어떻게 추가 정보를 얻을 수 있는가?

• 키워드를 제시하는 세부 사항 문제

What does the **man need to do** on **Tuesday**? 남자는 화요일에 무엇을 해야 하는가?
What will take place **tomorrow**? 내일 무슨 일이 일어날 것인가?
What does the **man remind the woman to bring**? 남자는 여자에게 무엇을 가져오라고 다시 알려주는가?

> **800+**
>
> • 문제점/걱정되는 점을 묻는 문제
>
> What does the **woman** say is a **problem**? 여자는 무엇이 문제라고 말하는가?
> What **problem** does the **man** mention? 남자는 어떤 문제점을 언급하는가?
> What is the **man concerned** about? 남자는 무엇에 대해 염려하는가?

2 핵심 포인트

1. 문제점/걱정되는 점을 묻는 문제는 단서 표현 뒤에 나오는 내용을 파악합니다.

   I'm[We're] concerned because[about] 저는[우리는] ~ 때문에[~에 대해] 걱정돼요
   Unfortunately, 안타깝게도   The problem is 문제는 ~입니다
   I noticed[found out] that ~을 알았어요[발견했어요]

   [단서] **I'm concerned because** the deadline is tomorrow. 내일이 마감일이라 걱정돼요.
   [정답] Meeting a deadline 마감일을 맞추는 것

2. 방법을 묻는 문제는 주로 대화 후반부에 단서가 제시됩니다.

   주로 정보를 얻을 수 있는 방법이나 할인을 받을 수 있는 방법 등을 묻고, 대화 후반부에서 'If you have more questions, ~', 'You can find out more on our Web site'와 같은 표현이 등장하므로 비교적 수월하게 단서를 파악할 수 있습니다.

3. 키워드가 제시되는 문제의 경우, 대화에서 해당 키워드가 그대로 언급되는 경우가 많지만 패러프레이징 되는 경우도 있으므로 특히 집중해서 들어야 합니다.

   [단서] M: When are you leading your first workshop? 당신의 첫 워크숍을 언제 진행하나요?
         W: **Tuesday** afternoon. 화요일 오후에요.
   [문제] Q. What will the woman do on **Tuesday**? 여자는 화요일에 무엇을 할 것인가?

   [단서] M: Surveys are conducted **on a weekly basis**. 설문조사는 주 단위로 시행됩니다.
   [문제] Q. What does the man say happens **every week**?
         남자는 매주 무엇이 일어난다고 말하는가?

세부 사항 문제

🎧 Day 06_P3_03.mp3

[문제지]

According to the **woman**, what will be **held on Friday**?
(A) A job fair
(B) A clearance sale
(C) A graduation ceremony
(D) A grand opening celebration

여자에 따르면, 금요일에 무엇이 열릴 것인가?
(A) 채용 박람회
(B) 재고 정리 세일
(C) 졸업식
(D) 개장식

[대화] [US - AU]

W: Ricardo, I've been thinking. I don't think many young people like students know about our job fair. We should try to reach out to them by advertising on the Internet. That should get their attention.

M: That's not a bad idea, but I'm not very good with computers. Do you think you could upload pictures from last year's job fair? Maybe that would interest them.

W: Sure, I can do that. By the way, I think the Saturday we chose is the perfect date to hold the job fair. **The students at the nearby college are going to graduate on Friday.** They'll definitely be thinking about job hunting.

여: Ricardo, 제가 생각을 해 봤어요. 학생들 같은 많은 젊은 사람들은 우리의 채용 박람회에 대해 알지 못하는 것 같아요. 인터넷에 광고를 해서 그들에게 접근하는 것을 시도해야 해요. 그게 그들의 관심을 끌 거예요.

남: 나쁜 생각은 아니지만 저는 컴퓨터를 잘 못해요. 당신이 작년 채용 박람회의 사진을 업로드할 수 있을까요? 그게 그들의 흥미를 끌지도 몰라요.

여: 물론이죠, 할 수 있어요. 그나저나, 우리가 고른 토요일이 채용 박람회를 열기에 완벽한 날짜 같아요. **근처에 있는 대학의 학생들이 금요일에 졸업을 하거든요.** 그들은 분명 구직을 생각하고 있을 거예요.

이렇게 풀어요

문제와 선택지의 키워드는 대화가 시작되기 전에 미리 파악되어 있어야 해요!

1. **문제 파악하기**
   woman, held on Friday → 여자의 말에 단서가 있으며, 금요일에 무엇이 열릴지 찾는 문제임을 파악합니다.

2. **선택지 키워드 파악하기**
   (A) 채용 박람회 (B) 재고 정리 세일 (C) 졸업식 (D) 개장식

3. **문제의 키워드 주위에서 단서 캐치하여 정답 선택하기**
   The students at the nearby college are going to graduate on Friday.
   → 키워드인 Friday 앞에 언급된 graduate를 A graduation ceremony로 표현한 (C)를 정답으로 선택하고 다음 문제로 넘어갑니다.

따라 하면 문제가 풀리는
연습 문제

문제와 각 선택지의 키워드에 표시하세요. 그리고 나서 대화를 듣고 빈칸에 들어갈 말을 받아쓴 후 정답을 선택해 보세요.

01. What are the speakers talking about?

(A) A budget proposal　　　　　(B) Job application reviews

> M: I still have a lot of _____ _____ to be reviewed by this Friday. Could you help me?
> W: Sure, I have some _____ _____ this afternoon. I just finished the _____ _____ for next quarter. Can you print some of them? It will be much easier to _____ it.

02. Why is the woman calling the man?

(A) To ask for a list　　　　　(B) To schedule a meeting

> W: Hi, Chris, this is Beth from Personnel. I'm calling you to _____ the _____ of the participants who _____ the conference last week.
> M: Sure, do you need it right now? I'm _____ _____ _____ _____ to visit one of our clients.

03. Where does the woman most likely work?

(A) At a travel agency　　　　　(B) At an airport

> W: Good morning! Thank you for choosing Swedish _____. Where are you _____ to today?
> M: I'm going to Los Angeles. Here's my _____ and reservation information.

---

paraphrasing　주어진 어휘 또는 표현과 의미가 동일한 것을 연결하세요.

1. have some free time　●　　　　●　(a) available
2. request　　　　　　　●　　　　●　(b) shipping
3. delivery　　　　　　 ●　　　　●　(c) ask for

04. Who most likely is the man?

(A) An appliance salesperson   (B) A maintenance worker

> W: Hello, this is Amelia Benitez calling from the ninth floor. The _____ isn't _____ again. Could you _____ _____ and _____ a _____ at it?
>
> M: It stopped working again? I'll get my _____ and _____ _____ there as soon as I can.

05. What did the company do last week?

(A) Won an award   (B) Released a new product

> W: Did you _____ the _____ from the management? Our company _____ the Most Innovative Design Award last week.
>
> M: Yes, it was exciting news. Our team members _____ hard to _____ the new blender.

06. Why is the woman unable to enter?

(A) A device is malfunctioning.   (B) She doesn't have her security card.

> W: Hello, I'm Lucy from the marketing department. I forgot to _____ my _____ _____. Would you _____ the door please?
>
> M: Sorry, I'm not _____ to do that. I will send someone down to _____ you to the security office. A _____ card will be _____ after a verification procedure.

---

paraphrasing 주어진 어휘 또는 표현과 의미가 동일한 것을 연결하세요.

4. pick up   •   • (a) be given
5. release   •   • (b) get
6. be issued   •   • (c) launch

01. What is the conversation about?
   (A) A hotel policy
   (B) A travel fare
   (C) A bus route
   (D) A luggage limit

02. Where are the speakers?
   (A) At a vehicle repair shop
   (B) At a parking lot
   (C) At a travel agency
   (D) At a bus stop

03. What does the woman suggest doing?
   (A) Visiting a Web site
   (B) Exchanging a ticket
   (C) Presenting a form of ID
   (D) Making a formal complaint

04. What kind of project is being discussed?
   (A) Replacing a roof
   (B) Painting a house
   (C) Installing some windows
   (D) Planting a garden

05. What is scheduled to take place on Thursday?
   (A) A new regulation will go into effect.
   (B) An inspection will be carried out.
   (C) Some photographs will be taken.
   (D) Some supplies will be delivered.

06. What does the man mention about his crew members?
   (A) They took shorter breaks.
   (B) They can work on weekends.
   (C) They are highly experienced.
   (D) They will contact Ms. Fletcher.

07. What kind of business does the man work for?
   (A) A manufacturing facility
   (B) A hotel
   (C) A taxi service
   (D) An airline

08. What is the purpose of the call?
   (A) To make a payment
   (B) To inquire about a fee
   (C) To apply for a job
   (D) To change a reservation

09. What does the man suggest?
   (A) Labeling some luggage
   (B) Checking an address
   (C) Downloading a coupon
   (D) Making an advance booking

10. What is the conversation mainly about?
   (A) A schedule change
   (B) A lost ticket
   (C) A seat reservation
   (D) A music lesson

11. What does the man apologize for?
   (A) A fee has recently increased.
   (B) A group discount is not available.
   (C) Some seats will not be together.
   (D) The tickets cannot be exchanged.

12. What will the woman most likely do next?
   (A) Check a Web site
   (B) Make some phone calls
   (C) Pay for the tickets
   (D) Visit another branch

13. What problem is being discussed?
    (A) A menu has been changed.
    (B) A shipment has not arrived.
    (C) Some customers complained.
    (D) An employee is late for work.

14. Where are the speakers most likely employed?
    (A) At a restaurant
    (B) At a warehouse
    (C) At a local supermarket
    (D) At a shipping center

15. What does the man say that the woman should do?
    (A) Hire more staff
    (B) Contact the manager
    (C) Call other employees
    (D) Organize some merchandise

16. What is the purpose of the man's call?
    (A) To make a complaint
    (B) To purchase a television
    (C) To ask about local channels
    (D) To request a different room

17. Who most likely is the woman?
    (A) A construction worker
    (B) A cable technician
    (C) An electronics salesperson
    (D) A hotel front desk worker

18. What does the woman offer to do?
    (A) E-mail a bill
    (B) Send room service
    (C) Contact a supervisor
    (D) Provide a full refund

19. Where do the speakers most likely work?
    (A) At a bakery
    (B) At a grocery store
    (C) At an organic farm
    (D) At a marketing firm

20. What does the man say he likes about a new supplier?
    (A) It grows produce organically.
    (B) It provides friendly service.
    (C) It has affordable prices.
    (D) It offers free delivery.

21. What does the woman ask the man to do?
    (A) Take inventory
    (B) Create a flyer
    (C) Contact a supplier
    (D) Make an announcement

22. What did the man recently do?
    (A) He moved into a nearby neighborhood.
    (B) He transferred to a new office.
    (C) He went on a vacation.
    (D) He got a promotion.

23. According to the woman, what is a benefit of Southern California?
    (A) It is welcoming to tourists.
    (B) It is affordable to visit.
    (C) It has many tourist attractions.
    (D) It has favorable weather.

24. What will the woman most likely do next?
    (A) Contact a travel agency
    (B) Send some information
    (C) Write a blog entry
    (D) Book a flight

'멋진 당신, 오늘도 화이팅'

DAY
07

오늘의 학습 포인트

PART 2. 부가 의문문 - Yes/No 답변 가능, 생략도 가능
  1. be동사/have 동사 부가 의문문
  2. 일반 동사의 부가 의문문 - do동사 부가 의문문
  3. 조동사 부가 의문문
  4. 특수 부가 의문문

PART 3. 문제 유형
  1. 제안·요청 문제 - 대화의 중/후반부
  2. 다음 할 일 문제 - 대화의 마지막
  3. 의도 파악 문제 - 해당 문장 앞뒤에 단서

PART 2 부가 의문문

부가 의문문은 알고 있는 정보를 평서문으로 말한 후, 문장 끝에 짧은 의문문을 붙여서 묻는 형태로, 매회 2문제 정도 출제됩니다.

적용 기술

[기적의 필기노트] 33P
LC 기술 23

🎧 Day 07_P2_01.mp3

🔒 확인 문제 ❶

Mark your answer.

(A)　　(B)

출제 포인트
의문문에 not이 있든 없든 긍정적인 답변일 때는 Yes, 부정적인 답변일 때는 No로 답합니다.

⚠️ **주의**
주절의 have가 일반 동사로 쓰인 경우, 부가 의문문은 do동사를 씁니다.
Thomas **has** driver's license, **doesn't** he?
Thomas는 운전면허증을 가지고 있죠, 그렇지 않나요?

(A) ❶ 정답

출제 유형 1 be동사/have동사 부가 의문문

- 평서문의 본동사가 be동사인 경우, 평서문이 긍정문이면 'isn't/aren't/wasn't/weren't + 대명사 주어'의 부정문으로, 부정문이면 'is/are/was/were + 대명사 주어'의 긍정문 형태로 의문문이 붙습니다. 일반 의문문과 마찬가지로 Yes/No로 대답할 수 있고, 그 외 '정해지지 않았다', '모른다' 등 제3의 답변이 나올 수도 있습니다.

Q. Mr. Simpson **was** promoted as a vice president, **wasn't he**?
Simpson 씨가 부사장으로 승진됐죠, 그렇지 않나요?

A. [긍정] **Yes**, that's what I was told. 네, 제가 들은 바로는 그렇습니다.
[부정] **No**, he's not the one. 아니요, 그가 아닙니다.
[제3의 답변] **I'm not sure.** I'll ask the personnel department.
잘 모르겠어요. 인사과에 물어볼게요.

- 평서문의 본동사가 완료 형태인 경우, 평서문이 긍정문이면 'haven't/hasn't + 대명사 주어', 부정문이면 'have/has + 대명사 주어'가 붙습니다.

Q. You **have finished** the financial report, **haven't you**?
재정 보고서 끝내셨죠, 그렇지 않나요?

A. Yes, I sent it by e-mail. 네, 이메일로 보냈습니다.

👆 풀이 방법 be동사 부가 의문문

🎧 Day 07_P2_02.mp3

[BR - AU]

The overhead projector in this room is out of order, isn't it?

(A) Yes, but we have a portable one.
(B) Please close the overhead compartment.
(C) There is room for new arrivals.

이 방에 있는 오버헤드 프로젝터는 고장 났죠, 그렇지 않나요?
(A) 네, 그렇지만 우리에게 휴대용 프로젝터가 있어요.
(B) 머리 위 짐칸을 닫아주세요.
(C) 새로 도착하는 물건들을 위한 공간이 있어요.

 이렇게 풀어요

1. 질문 내용 파악하기　The **overhead projector** in this room is **out of order**, **isn't it**?
　　　　　　　　　　　　오버헤드 프로젝터가　　　　　　　　　　고장 났는지 확인

2. 선택지 들으며 오답 소거하여 정답 선택하기
　(A) Yes, but we have a portable one. → 정답으로 선택
　(B) Please close the **overhead** compartment. → 동일 단어 반복 오답(overhead)
　(C) There is **room** for new arrivals. → 동일 단어 반복 오답(room)

출제 유형 2 일반 동사의 부가 의문문

평서문에 be동사나 have동사가 아닌 일반 동사가 쓰였을 때는 꼬리에 do동사 부가 의문문이 붙습니다. 평서문이 긍정이면 'do/does + 대명사 주어', 부정이면 'don't/doesn't + 대명사 주어'가 붙습니다. 또한 평서문의 동사 시제가 현재이면 do/does/don't/doesn't, 과거이면 did/didn't가 사용됩니다.

Q. **You confirmed** the hotel reservation, **didn't you**? 호텔 예약 확인하셨죠, 그렇지 않나요?
A. [긍정] **Yes**, I just called them. 네 방금 전화했어요.
   [부정] I'll do it right now. 지금 바로 하겠습니다.
   [제3의 답변] **I totally forgot**. Thank you for reminding me.
   완전히 잊고 있었습니다. 알려 주셔서 감사합니다.

Q. **They don't accept** credit cards, **do they**? 그들은 신용카드를 받지 않죠, 그렇죠?
A. [긍정] **Yes**, you can use them. 받습니다, 신용카드를 사용할 수 있어요.
   [부정] **No**, you have to pay in cash. 받지 않아요, 현금으로 지불해야 합니다.
   [제3의 답변] **Let's ask the manager**. 매니저에게 물어봅시다.

🎧 Day 07_P2_03.mp3

🔒 확인 문제 ❷

Mark your answer.

(A)   (B)

정답 ❷ (A)

풀이 방법 do동사 부가 의문문

🎧 Day 07_P2_04.mp3

US · BR

The city has another children's hospital on Montgomery, doesn't it?
(A) All proceeds go to the hospital.
(B) They must be accompanied by their guardians.
(C) Yes, one on Oakland Street.

시가 몽고메리에 또 다른 아동 병원을 가지고 있죠, 그렇지 않나요?
(A) 모든 수익금은 병원으로 갑니다.
(B) 그들은 보호자들과 동반해야 해요.
(C) 네, Oakland 가에 하나 있어요.

이렇게 풀어요

1. 질문 내용 파악하기 The city has another children's hospital on Montgomery, doesn't it?
   몽고메리에 또 다른 아동 병원이 있는지 확인

2. 선택지 들으며 오답 소거하여 정답 선택하기
   (A) All proceeds go to the hospital. → 동일 단어 반복 오답 (hospital)
   (B) They must be accompanied by their guardians. → 연상 어휘 오답 (children, hospital-accompanied by their guardians)
   (C) Yes, one on Oakland Street. → 정답으로 선택

PART 2 부가 의문문 123

Day 07_P2_05.mp3

🔒 확인 문제 ❸

Mark your answer.

(A)   (B)

출제 유형 3
조동사 부가 의문문

평서문에 쓰이는 조동사(can, will, should)로 부가 의문문을 만들 수 있습니다. 또한 Let's로 시작되는 문장은 shall we?, 명령문은 will you?가 꼬리에 붙습니다.

Q. **We can** afford to hire more full-time employees, **can't we**?
우리 정규직 직원을 좀 더 채용할 여력이 있죠, 그렇지 않나요?

A. Probably, but I have to check the budget. 아마도요, 하지만 예산을 확인해 봐야 해요.

Q. **Let's** take a break after the meeting, **shall we**? 우리 회의 마치고 잠시 쉽시다, 그럴까요?

A. That's a good idea. 좋은 생각입니다.

Q. **Look over** the proposal before you submit it, **will you**?
제안서를 제출하기 전에 검토해 보세요, 그럴 거죠?

A. Sure, I'll do it after lunch. 물론이죠. 점심 식사 후에 하겠습니다.

 (B) ❸ 정답

풀이 방법   조동사 부가 의문문

Day 07_P2_06.mp3

BR - US

All assembly line workers will leave early this Friday, won't they?
(A) Yes, the regular inspection is scheduled.
(B) He leaves for Chicago tomorrow.
(C) It will start later in the month.

모든 조립 라인 근로자들은 금요일에 일찍 퇴근할 거예요, 그렇지 않나요?
(A) 네, 정기 검사가 예정되어 있어요.
(B) 그는 내일 시카고로 떠나요.
(C) 그건 이번 달 후반에 시작될 거예요.

이렇게 풀어요

1. 질문 내용 파악하기   All assembly line **workers will leave early** this Friday, **won't they**?
   근로자들이 일찍 퇴근할 건인지 확인

2. 선택지 들으며 오답 소거하여 정답 선택하기
   (A) Yes, the regular inspection is scheduled. → 정답으로 선택
   (B) He **leaves** for Chicago tomorrow. → 동일 단어 반복 오답(leave)
   (C) It will start later in the month. → 주체가 맞지 않는 오답(workers-It)

124 기적의 토익 LC

출제 유형 4 — 특수 부가 의문문

🎧 Day 07_P2_07.mp3

🔒 확인 문제 ❹

Mark your answer.

(A)   (B)

> 800+

평서문의 동사와 무관하게 right?/correct?/don't you think?/don't you agree? 형태의 의문문이 붙는 질문 유형도 출제됩니다.

Q. This is the book you are looking for, **right**? 이것이 당신이 찾던 책이에요, 맞죠?
A. Yes, thank you so much. 네, 정말 감사합니다.

Q. The hotel offers a shuttle service, **correct**? 호텔은 셔틀 서비스를 제공해요, 맞죠?
A. You should check it on their Web site. 웹사이트에서 확인해 보셔야 할 거예요.

Q. Mr. Miller is the best salesperson in the team, **don't you think**?
　Miller 씨는 팀에서 최고의 영업사원이에요, 그렇게 생각하지 않아요?
A. He certainly is. 확실히 그래요.

Q. The presentation was well-prepared and informative, **don't you agree**?
　그 발표는 준비가 잘 되었고 유익했어요, 그렇게 생각하지 않으세요?
A. Yeah, but it was a bit boring. 네, 하지만 약간 지루했습니다.

정답 ❹ (B)

풀이 방법 — 특수 부가 의문문

🎧 Day 07_P2_08.mp3

[BR - AU]

I need to bring the original receipt, right?
(A) At the customer service center.
(B) Yes, if you want a full refund.
(C) Cash or credit?

제가 원본 영수증을 가져와야 하죠, 그렇죠?
(A) 고객 서비스 센터에서요.
(B) 네, 전액 환불을 원하신다면요.
(C) 현금으로 하시겠어요, 카드로 하시겠어요?

↳ 이렇게 풀어요

1. 질문 내용 파악하기　I need to bring the original receipt, right?
　　　　　　　　　　　　영수증을 가져와야 하는지 확인

2. 선택지 들으며 오답 소거하여 정답 선택하기
　(A̶)̶ At the customer service center. → 다른 의문사 답변 오답 (Where)
　(B) Yes, if you want a full refund. → 정답으로 선택
　(C̶)̶ Cash or credit? → 연상 어휘 오답 (receipt-cash, credit)

따라 하면 문제가 풀리는
연습 문제

🎧 Day 07_ P2_09.mp3
📖 정답 및 해석 p.46

각 질문과 보기를 들으며 빈칸을 채운 뒤 정답에는 O, 오답에는 X 표시하세요.

01. The _____ is _____ this _____, isn't it?
    (A) You can _____ it _____ next _____. [   ]
    (B) He _____ the proposal. [   ]

02. You _____ be _____ for our annual conference, will you?
    (A) No, I'll be there _____ _____. [   ]
    (B) You are supposed to _____ a _____. [   ]

03. Ms. Curtis is _____ the workshop, isn't she?
    (A) No, she's _____ _____. [   ]
    (B) It will _____ for a _____. [   ]

04. You've _____ the latest Anthony Russo _____, haven't you?
    (A) I like to _____ _____ _____. [   ]
    (B) Not yet, I'll _____ it this _____. [   ]

05. You've already _____ the _____ to the _____, haven't you?
    (A) No, it's my first time _____ this event. [   ]
    (B) Yeah, but I _____ ten _____ of them. [   ]

06. _____ is Tina's birthday, _____ _____?
    (A) Yeah, we should _____ it together. [   ]
    (B) The _____ has been changed. [   ]

07. You _____ Carlson University, right?
    (A) _____ did you _____ that? [   ]
    (B) _____ is a _____ student. [   ]

08. We should _____ the _____ to _____ _____ next week, don't you agree?
    (A) _____ _____ I was thinking about. [   ]
    (B) I want to _____ the survey _____. [   ]

Day 07_P2_10.mp3
정답 및 해설 p.47

01. Mark your answer on your answer sheet.
(A) (B) (C)

02. Mark your answer on your answer sheet.
(A) (B) (C)

03. Mark your answer on your answer sheet.
(A) (B) (C)

04. Mark your answer on your answer sheet.
(A) (B) (C)

05. Mark your answer on your answer sheet.
(A) (B) (C)

06. Mark your answer on your answer sheet.
(A) (B) (C)

07. Mark your answer on your answer sheet.
(A) (B) (C)

08. Mark your answer on your answer sheet.
(A) (B) (C)

09. Mark your answer on your answer sheet.
(A) (B) (C)

10. Mark your answer on your answer sheet.
(A) (B) (C)

11. Mark your answer on your answer sheet.
(A) (B) (C)

12. Mark your answer on your answer sheet.
(A) (B) (C)

13. Mark your answer on your answer sheet.
(A) (B) (C)

14. Mark your answer on your answer sheet.
(A) (B) (C)

15. Mark your answer on your answer sheet.
(A) (B) (C)

16. Mark your answer on your answer sheet.
(A) (B) (C)

PART 3 제안·요청 문제 / 다음 할 일 문제 / 의도 파악 문제

제안·요청 문제는 매회 5~7문제 정도, 다음 할 일 문제는 매회 2~5문제 정도, 의도 파악 문제는 매회 2~3문제가 출제됩니다!

적용 기술
[기적의 필기노트] 50P~51P
LC 기술 38, 39

출제 포인트
상대방에게 무언가를 해주겠다고 제안하거나 요청한 것을 묻는 문제는 대화 중/후반부에 정답의 단서가 나오는 경우가 많습니다.

⚠️ **주의**
제안·요청 문제는 정답 보기가 패러프레이징 되는 경우가 많은 유형입니다. 대표적인 패러프레이징 표현을 알아 두어야 합니다.
· call/e-mail → contact
· send/mail → provide
· fill out → complete

출제 포인트
무엇을 보내달라고 요청하는지와 같이 좀 더 구체적으로 질문이 출제되는 경우도 있습니다.
What does the woman ask the man to send? 여자는 남자에게 무엇을 보내달라고 요청하는가?
→ A revised plan 수정된 계획

출제 유형 1 제안·요청 문제

1 질문 유형
What does the **woman ask the man to do**? 여자는 남자에게 무엇을 해달라고 요청하는가?
What does the **man offer to do** for the woman? 남자는 여자에게 무엇을 해주겠다고 하는가?
What is the **woman asked to do**? 여자는 무엇을 하도록 요청받는가?
What does the **man suggest[recommend]**? 남자는 무엇을 제안하는가?

2 핵심 포인트

1. 요청 문제에 대한 단서를 끌고 나오는 표현을 알아 두어야 합니다.

Can you ~해주실 수 있으세요? Would you ~해주시겠어요? Why don't you ~하는 게 어때요?	Could you ~해주실 수 있으세요? I'd like you to 당신이 ~을 해주었으면 합니다 I wonder if you can 당신이 ~해줄 수 있는지 궁금합니다

[단서] **Can you** send me the brochures containing new pictures?
　　　새로운 사진을 포함하고 있는 안내 책자를 보내 주시겠어요?
[정답] Send the updated brochure 수정된 안내 책자 보내기

2. 제안 문제에 대한 단서를 끌고 나오는 표현을 알아 두어야 합니다.

How about if I 제가 ~하면 어때요? Let me 제가 ~할게요 You should 당신은 ~하셔야 해요	Why don't I 제가 ~할까요? I suggest ~하기를 제안합니다 I can 제가 ~할게요

[단서] **Let me** check the warehouse to see if we still have one in stock.
　　　아직 재고가 남아있는지 제가 창고를 확인해 보겠습니다.
[정답] Look for a product 제품 찾아보기

3. 요청한 것을 묻는 문제인지 요청 받은 사항을 묻는 문제인지 구분해야 합니다.
What does the **woman ask** the man to do? 여자는 남자에게 무엇을 하라고 요청하는가?
→ 여자의 말에서 단서 표현이 나올 것임을 예상하며 대화를 들어야 합니다.

What is the **woman asked** to do? 여자는 무엇을 하도록 요청받는가?
→ 남자가 여자에게 무엇을 하라고 요청할 것이므로, 남자의 말에서 단서 표현이 나올 것임을 예상하며 대화를 들어야 합니다.

> **800+**
> What is the **man offer** to do? 남자는 무엇을 하겠다고 제안하는가?
> → 남자가 주체가 되므로, 남자의 말에서 단서 표현이 나올 것임을 예상하며 대화를 들어야 합니다.

제안·요청 문제

🎧 Day 07_P3_01.mp3

문제지

What does the **man offer to do** for the woman?
(A) Rearrange a schedule
(B) Reserve a venue
(C) Contact a client
(D) Plan a trip

대화 US - AU

W: Seth, you're the planner for our company's upcoming awards ceremony, aren't you? You asked me about doing a speech about the importance of insurance companies. Do you still need me to do that?
M: Yes, that would be great. Our company has a good reputation, so especially our newer employees are really proud to work here.
W: I see... The problem is, I'm going to be coming back from a business trip on the day of the event. If my flight is delayed, I might not make it on time.
M: Changing the day of the event won't work. **How about if I switch your speech to the last event that evening?**
W: Okay, that should work well.

남자는 여자에게 무엇을 해주겠다고 제안하는가?
(A) 일정 재조정하기
(B) 장소 예약하기
(C) 고객에게 연락하기
(D) 여행 계획하기

여: Seth, 당신이 우리 회사의 다가오는 시상식의 기획자죠, 그렇지 않나요? 당신이 제게 보험 회사의 중요성에 대해 강연을 해달라고 부탁했었어요. 제가 여전히 그것을 해야 하나요?
남: 네, 그럼 좋겠어요. 우리 회사는 훌륭한 명성을 갖고 있어서, 특히 신입 사원들이 여기서 일하는 것을 자랑스러워 해요.
여: 알겠어요... 문제는, 제가 행사 당일에 출장에서 돌아올 예정이에요. 비행기가 지연되면 제시간에 못 올 수도 있어요.
남: 행사일을 변경할 수는 없어요. **제가 당신의 강연을 그날 저녁의 마지막 행사로 옮기면 어때요?**
여: 좋아요, 그건 괜찮을 거예요.

🖊 이렇게 풀어요

문제와 선택지의 키워드는 대화가 시작되기 전에 미리 파악되어 있어야 해요!

1. **문제 파악하기**
   man offer to do → 남자의 말에서 단서가 제시될 것임을 예상합니다.

2. **선택지 키워드 파악하기**
   (A) 재조정하기 (B) 예약하기 (C) 연락하기 (D) 계획하기
   → 선택지의 동사가 핵심이 되므로 시간이 없을 경우 동사 위주로 빠르게 파악합니다.

3. **대화 후반부에서 단서 파악하여 정답 선택하기**
   How about if I switch your speech to the last event that evening?
   → 강연 시간을 바꾸어 주겠다고 제안한 것을 Rearrange a schedule로 표현한 (A)를 정답으로 선택합니다.

적용 기술

[기적의 필기노트] 55P~56P
LC 기술 42, 43

출제 포인트

다음 할 일을 묻는 문제는 대화가 끝난 다음에 어떤 행동을 하거나 어떤 일이 일어날지를 묻는 문제입니다. 주로 대화 마지막에 단서가 제시됩니다.

⚠ **주의**

3인 대화의 경우 문제에 화자의 이름이 제시되는 질문 유형이 출제됩니다. 따라서 문제에 이름이 있을 경우 그 사람이 누구인지 대화에서 반드시 파악해야 합니다.

M1: James, I'll show you around the factory. James 제가 공장을 구경시켜 드릴게요.
Q. What will James do next? James는 다음에 무엇을 할 것인가?
A. Take a tour of the factory 공장 견학하기

출제 유형 2 — 다음 할 일 문제

1 질문 유형

What will the **man[woman]** probably **do next**? 남자[여자]는 다음에 무엇을 하겠는가?
What will **happen next**? 다음에 무슨 일이 일어나겠는가?
What does the **woman** say she will **do next**? 여자는 다음에 무엇을 할 것이라고 말하는가?
What does the **man** say he will **do this afternoon**?
남자는 오늘 오후에 무엇을 할 것이라고 말하는가?

2 핵심 포인트

1. 다음에 할 일을 본인이 직접 말하는 경우도 있지만, 상대방이 먼저 제안하고 수락하는 것을 통해 파악해야 하는 경우도 있습니다.

   [단서] M: I'll look over the Web site. 웹사이트를 살펴볼게요.
   [문제] Q. What will the man do next? 남자는 다음에 무엇을 하겠는가?
   [정답] A. Go online 인터넷 하기

   [단서] W: **Could you send me a serial number** that I can refer to for the shipping?
   배송 관련해서 제가 참고할 수 있는 일련 번호를 보내주실 수 있나요?
   M: **Sure**. I'll do it right away. 물론이죠. 지금 바로 해드릴게요.
   [문제] Q. What does the man say he will do? 남자는 무엇을 하겠다고 말하는가?
   [정답] A. Provide the number 번호 제공하기

2. 다음 할 일에 대한 단서를 끌고 나오는 표현을 알아 두어야 합니다.

I will / I'm going to 제가 ~할 거예요 I'd better 제가 ~하는 게 좋겠네요 You'll have to 당신은 ~해야 할 거예요	Let me 제가 ~할게요 Could you ~해줄 수 있나요?

   I'll phone the real estate agent now. 제가 지금 부동산 중개인에게 전화할게요.
   Could you forward me the link? 링크를 제게 보내주시겠어요?

다음 할 일 문제

🎧 Day 07_P3_02.mp3

문제지

What will the **woman** most likely **do next**?
(A) Schedule an appointment
(B) Issue a reimbursement
(C) Transfer the man's call
(D) Take a message

여자는 다음에 무엇을 하겠는가?
(A) 약속 일정 잡기
(B) 상환하기
(C) 남자의 전화 연결해주기
(D) 메시지 받아 적기

대화 [BR - BR]

M: Hello, this is George Ludlow from Ludlow Legal Services. I use one of your Office Jet 400 printers in my office, but it keeps jamming. I need someone to come fix it.

W: I'm sorry to hear about that, sir. All of our on-duty technicians are currently out on calls. How about we send someone tomorrow?

M: That's too late. I have to print a lot of paperwork to bring to court for a hearing in the morning. I need a repairperson now.

W: **Hang on while I transfer you to my manager.** Hopefully he can work something out.

남: 안녕하세요, 저는 Ludlow 법률 사무소의 George Ludlow입니다. 제가 사무실에서 귀사의 Office Jet 400 프린터기를 사용하는데요, 계속 (종이가) 걸려 작동하지 않아요. 와서 수리해 주실 누군가가 필요합니다.

여: 죄송합니다. 근무 중인 기술자 전원이 현재 호출에 응하느라 외부에 있습니다. 내일 누군가를 보내 드려도 될까요?

남: 그러면 너무 늦어요. 아침에 공청회 때문에 법원에 가져가야 할 많은 서류를 인쇄해야 해요. 지금 수리하는 분이 필요합니다.

여: **제가 매니저를 연결해 드릴 테니 기다려 주세요.** 그가 해결해 드릴 수 있기를 바라겠습니다.

💡 이렇게 풀어요

문제와 선택지의 키워드는 대화가 시작되기 전에 미리 파악되어 있어야 해요!

1. 문제 파악하기
   woman, do next → 여자가 다음에 할 일을 묻는 문제임을 파악합니다.

2. 선택지 키워드 파악하기
   (A) 일정 잡기 (B) 상환 (C) 전화 연결 (D) 메시지

3. 대화 마지막 부분에서 단서 파악하여 정답 선택하기
   Hang on while I transfer you to my manager.
   → 여자의 마지막 대사에서 매니저를 연결해 주겠다고 했으므로 (C)를 정답으로 선택하고 다음 문제로 넘어갑니다.

적용 기술

[기적의 필기노트] 61P
LC 기술 46

출제 포인트
의도 파악 문제는 화자가 한 말의 의도를 대화의 맥락을 통해 파악하는 문제입니다. 표현 자체의 의미가 정답과 바로 연결되지 않으므로 반드시 문제를 먼저 읽어 두어야 합니다.

출제 유형 3 — 의도 파악 문제

800+

1 질문 유형

Why does the **woman[man] say**, "What a surprise"?
왜 여자[남자]는 "놀랍네요"라고 말하는가?

900+

What does the **woman[man] mean** when she[he] says, "That's not good enough"? 여자[남자]가 "그것으로 충분하지 않아요"라고 말할 때 의미하는 바는 무엇인가?

What does the **woman[man] imply** when she[he] says, "We have to change our supplier"? 여자[남자]가 "우리는 공급업체를 바꿔야 해요"라고 말할 때 암시하는 바는 무엇인가?

800+

2 핵심 포인트

1. **반드시 문제를 먼저 읽습니다.**
   대화를 듣기 전에 따옴표 안의 문장을 읽어 두고, 어떤 내용이 나올지 예측하며 들어야 합니다.

   What does the woman mean when she says, "I've never been there before"?
   여자가 "저는 전에 거기에 가 본 적이 없어요"라고 말할 때 의미하는 바는 무엇인가?

   → 대화에서 특정 장소가 언급될 것임을 예측할 수 있습니다.

2. **정답의 단서는 앞뒤 문맥과 연관**되어 있습니다.
   정답은 대부분 앞 사람의 말과 관련이 있으므로, 해당 문장의 앞뒤를 잘 파악해야 합니다.

   [단서] M: Can you stop by Dr. Shawn's office tomorrow morning?
   내일 아침에 Shawn 박사님의 사무실에 들를 수 있어요?

   W: Sure. But, I've never been there before.
   물론이죠. 그런데, 저는 전에 거기에 가 본 적이 없어요.

   [문제] Q. What does the woman mean when she says, "I've never been there before"? 여자가 "저는 전에 거기에 가 본 적이 없어요"라고 말할 때 의미하는 바는 무엇인가?

   [정답] A. She wants to get some information. 그녀는 정보를 얻고 싶어 한다.

출제 포인트
Why does the woman [man] say ~로 물을 경우 선택지는 to부정사 형태로 제시됩니다. 따라서 따옴표 안의 문장을 왜 말하는지 목적을 묻는 문제로 파악하면 됩니다.

⚠️ **주의**
의도 파악 문제의 정답은 문제로 제시된 화자의 말을 단순히 유사한 의미로 패러프레이징한 표현이 아닙니다. 보기가 의미상 문제 표현과 직접적으로 연관될수록 오답일 확률이 높습니다.

3. 화자의 **어조를 통해 긍정적인 뉘앙스인지 부정적인 뉘앙스**인지 파악할 수 있습니다.
   긍정적인 뉘앙스일 경우 높은 어조, 부정적인 뉘앙스일 경우 주로 낮은 어조로 말하므로 어조 또한 문맥을 이해하는 데 도움이 될 수 있습니다.

4. 의미가 굳어진 관용 표현을 외우기보다는 **대화의 맥락을 파악하는 것이 중요합니다.**
   'It's up in the air(아직 미정입니다)'와 같이 의미가 정해져 있는 관용 표현보다는 일반적인 문장이 주로 출제됩니다. 따라서 화자들의 어조와 대화의 맥락을 통해 의미를 파악하는 연습을 해야 합니다.

의도 파악 문제

[문제지]

What does the **woman mean** when she says, **"That was several years ago"**?
(A) The logo should be updated.
(B) The building needs renovations.
(C) The business has been successful.
(D) The client files should be digitized.

[대화] [US - US]

M: Hailey, don't you think the commercials for our store are a bit old? I'm afraid that people won't consider us a serious place to buy furniture from.
W: That's true. I think it's time for us to hire a professional advertising company.
M: **Didn't we decide that contracting an ad agency would be too expensive?**
W: **That was several years ago. We're not as small as we used to be.**
M: Good point. It would be best for us to make some higher quality commercials.
W: I'll get online and look into some possible ad companies that might be able to help us out.

여자가 "그건 몇 년 전이에요"라고 말할 때 의미하는 바는 무엇인가?
(A) 로고가 업데이트되어야 한다.
(B) 건물이 보수되어야 한다.
(C) 사업이 잘되고 있다.
(D) 고객 파일은 디지털화되어야 한다.

남: Hailey, 우리 상점의 광고가 좀 오래되었다고 생각하지 않으세요? 사람들이 우리가 가구를 구입할 중요한 장소라고 생각하지 않을까 봐 걱정이 됩니다.
여: 맞아요. 우리가 전문적인 광고 회사를 고용할 때라고 생각해요.
남: 광고 회사와 계약하는 것이 너무 비용이 많이 들 것 같다고 결정을 하지 않았었나요?
여: 그건 몇 년 전이에요. 우리는 예전의 작은 회사가 아니에요.
남: 좋은 지적입니다. 고품질의 광고를 만드는 것이 우리에게 가장 좋을 거예요.
여: 제가 인터넷으로 우리에게 도움을 줄 수 있는 광고 회사를 찾아 보겠습니다.

이렇게 풀어요

문제와 선택지의 키워드는 대화가 시작되기 전에 미리 파악되어 있어야 해요!

1. **문제 파악하기**
   woman mean, That was several years ago → 여자가 해당 문장을 말할 때 앞뒤 문맥을 파악할 준비를 합니다.

2. **선택지 키워드 파악하기**
   (A) 로고, 업데이트 (B) 건물, 보수 (C) 사업, 잘되는 (D) 파일, 디지털화

3. **대화 흐름을 파악하면서 듣고, 해당 문장이 나올 때 앞뒤 내용을 통해 단서 파악하기**
   남자가 전문 광고 회사를 고용하는 것은 너무 비싸서 안 하기로 하지 않았냐는 의도로 질문한 것에 대해 여자가 "That was several years ago"라고 말했고, 뒤이어 "우리는 예전의 작은 회사가 아니다"라고 했습니다.
   → 현재는 사업이 잘돼서 광고 회사를 고용할 형편이 된다는 뉘앙스로 말했음을 파악하여 (C)를 정답으로 선택하고 다음 문제로 넘어갑니다.

따라 하면 문제가 풀리는 연습 문제

문제와 각 선택지의 키워드에 표시하세요. 그러고 나서 대화를 듣고 빈칸에 들어갈 말을 받아쓴 후 정답을 선택해 보세요.

01. What does the man suggest the woman do?

(A) Contact the printing shop (B) Use another printer

> W: James, this printer is _____ _____ again. The papers are jammed. I will give a _____ to the board members in an hour and I need 20 _____ to be printed.
>
> M: Um... why don't you _____ the _____ _____ located at the corner and ask them to print them?

02. What does the man ask the woman to do?

(A) Schedule a meeting (B) Revise the proposal

> M: I think the _____ for the proposal is too tight. Could you call the client and _____ a _____ this week?
>
> W: Sure. _____ _____ is the most convenient for you?
>
> M: I _____ _____ _____ on Tuesday and Wednesday morning.

03. What will the man probably do next?

(A) Convert the file format (B) Fax a document

> M: Clara, did you _____ my e-mail about the price quote for the office renovation?
>
> W: Yes, but I have a _____. I downloaded the file you _____ to the e-mail, but it did not open on my computer. Could you _____ it to me _____ _____?

---

paraphrasing 주어진 어휘 또는 표현과 의미가 동일한 것을 연결하세요.

1. call •   • (a) change
2. revise •   • (b) issue
3. problem •   • (c) contact

04. What will the man probably do next?

(A) Call another branch (B) Go to the storage room

> W: I like these shoes but I'm not able to _____ _____ _____ on the shelf. Do you have the shoe in 6.5?
> M: Just give me a second to check the _____. According to our records, there are a couple _____ in the storage room. I will _____ _____ in a minute.

05. Why does the woman say, "I don't have any special plans this weekend"?

(A) To accept an offer (B) To cancel an event

> M: Jenny, will you _____ to the rock climbing club this Saturday? We will have a _____ _____ with the members at the restaurant Atkins' Table.
> W: I don't have any special plans this weekend. _____ will it be _____? It will start 4 P.M., right?

06. What does the woman mean when she says, "I'm not really surprised"?

(A) She has already read the news. (B) She expected the results.

> M: Our _____ was _____ as one of the best _____ this year!
> W: That's good news, but I'm not really surprised. We've been _____ lots of money and time on that _____.

---

paraphrasing 주어진 어휘 또는 표현과 의미가 동일한 것을 연결하세요.

4. inventory   •   • (a) suggestion
5. offer   •   • (b) stock
6. item   •   • (c) product

토익에 나올 실전 문제

01. Who most likely is the woman?
 (A) A furniture salesperson
 (B) A restaurant worker
 (C) A shop owner
 (D) A repair person

02. Why does the woman say, "The rooftop is open"?
 (A) To offer another option
 (B) To verify a design
 (C) To announce a policy change
 (D) To assign a task

03. What does the man plan to do?
 (A) Place a rush order
 (B) Check a weather report
 (C) Turn off his phone
 (D) Go to another business

04. Why is the man calling the woman?
 (A) To change a location
 (B) To extend a deadline
 (C) To cancel a meeting
 (D) To confirm a guest list

05. According to the man, what recently happened at his branch?
 (A) Some budget categories were cut.
 (B) Some clients made a complaint.
 (C) A renovation project was started.
 (D) A team hired more members.

06. What does the woman say she will do next?
 (A) E-mail the man
 (B) Reserve a room
 (C) Print an agenda
 (D) Review a report

07. Where is the conversation taking place?
 (A) At a manufacturing facility
 (B) At an advertising agency
 (C) At a grocery store
 (D) At a clothing shop

08. What problem does the woman tell the man about?
 (A) A product has been discontinued.
 (B) An employee is absent.
 (C) A shipment is late.
 (D) A machine is malfunctioning.

09. What does the woman ask the man to do?
 (A) Return some items
 (B) Adjust a work schedule
 (C) Request some samples
 (D) Post some information online

10. What does the woman plan to do next week?
 (A) Hire some new employees
 (B) Attend an industry event
 (C) Transfer to another branch
 (D) Lead a training seminar

11. What does the man mean when he says, "that's not much"?
 (A) He is surprised by a project's budget.
 (B) He is concerned about a lack of time.
 (C) He is pleased with the low price.
 (D) He is able to assist the woman.

12. What does the woman say she will do?
 (A) Make an overtime payment
 (B) Check a company policy
 (C) Speak to a manager
 (D) Give the man some instructions

13. What kind of business do the speakers most likely work at?
    (A) A computer graphic design agency
    (B) A video game company
    (C) An electronics manufacturer
    (D) A computer repair service

14. Why does the man say, "but we have plenty of people who want extra hours"?
    (A) He thinks their goal is not feasible.
    (B) He will assign more work shifts.
    (C) He wants to offer an extra service.
    (D) He plans to interview some applicants.

15. What does the man say he will do?
    (A) Hire more workers
    (B) Contact a client
    (C) Take a break
    (D) Post a memo

16. Why did the man visit the business?
    (A) To conduct an interview
    (B) To deliver a document
    (C) To take a guided tour
    (D) To inspect a facility

17. What does the woman request from the man?
    (A) A beverage
    (B) A work contract
    (C) Photo identification
    (D) The name of a contact

18. What does the woman tell the man to do?
    (A) Put on safety gear
    (B) Wait for an escort
    (C) Display a visitor's pass
    (D) Speak with a manager

19. Why is the woman calling?
    (A) To gather feedback
    (B) To request a change
    (C) To reschedule a service
    (D) To respond to a complaint

20. What problem does the woman mention?
    (A) An item was incorrect.
    (B) A shipment was delayed.
    (C) Some workers are out sick.
    (D) Some products were damaged.

21. What does the woman offer the man?
    (A) A deposit refund
    (B) A discounted charge
    (C) Free maintenance service
    (D) Some product samples

22. Where is the conversation most likely taking place?
    (A) In a bakery
    (B) In a kitchen
    (C) In a grocery store
    (D) In a home appliance store

23. What does the woman mean when she says, "This is my first time using a dough mix"?
    (A) She has to purchase a new mixer.
    (B) She is allergic to an ingredient.
    (C) She prefers a different product.
    (D) She wants to get some advice.

24. Where will the speakers most likely go next?
    (A) To a service counter
    (B) To another branch
    (C) To a cash register
    (D) To another aisle

'멋진 당신, 오늘도 화이팅'

DAY 08

오늘의 학습 포인트

PART 2. 간접 의문문 / 선택 의문문
1. 간접 의문문 - 일반 의문문 + when, where, who 등 의문사
    1) Yes/No로 답변하는 유형
    2) Yes/No를 생략하고 답변하는 유형
    3) 접속사와 결합하는 간접 의문문 - that, whether, if
2. 선택 의문문
    1) Which, Which of로 묻는 질문 - the one, none
    2) 'Which + 명사'로 묻는 선택 의문문
    3) 'A or B'로 묻는 선택 의문문 - 하나 선택, 둘 다 좋다[싫다]

PART 3. 문제 유형
1. 시각 자료 연계 문제 - 표, 평면도, 쿠폰, 차트
2. 3인 대화 문제 - 여자 2명/남자 1명, 남자 2명/여자 1명

PART 2 간접 의문문 / 선택 의문문

간접 의문문은 매회 1문제 정도 출제되는데 의문사 부분을 잘 들어야 합니다.
선택 의문문은 매회 2문제 정도 출제됩니다.

적용 기술

[기적의 필기노트] 39P
LC 기술 28

 Day 08_P2_01.mp3

확인 문제 ❶

Mark your answer.

(A)   (B)

⚠️ **주의**
간접 의문문은 '의문사 + 주어 + 동사' 부분이 내용을 파악하는 데 핵심이 되므로 이 부분을 반드시 들어야 답을 고를 수 있습니다.

출제 유형 1 — 간접 의문문

> 800+

1 Yes/No로 답변하는 유형

간접 의문문은 일반 의문문에 when, where, who 등으로 시작하는 의문사 의문문이 들어가 있는 질문 형태입니다. 의문사 의문문은 Yes/No로 답변할 수 없지만, 간접 의문문은 의문사가 아닌 조동사로 시작하므로 Yes/No로 답변할 수 있어요.

Q. **Do you know why** Mr. Smith was late this morning?
  Smith 씨가 오늘 아침에 왜 늦었는지 아세요?
A. **Yes**, I was told that there was a heavy traffic jam. 네, 교통 체증이 심했다고 들었어요.

Do you know + 의문사 + 주어 + 동사 ~?	**Do you know where** the gas station is? 주유소가 어디 있는지 아세요?
Can you tell[show] me + 의문사 + 주어 + 동사 ~?	**Can you tell me who** that man is? 저 남자가 누구인지 말해줄 수 있나요?
Did you hear + 의문사 + 주어 + 동사 ~?	**Did you hear who** is going to be promoted? 누가 승진하게 될지 들었어요?
Do you remember + 의문사 + 주어 + 동사 ~?	**Do you remember where** Patrick lives now? 지금 Patrick이 어디 사는지 기억나세요?

정답 ❶ (A)

풀이 방법 — 간접 의문문 – Yes/No로 답변하는 유형

 Day 08_P2_02.mp3

[BR - BR]

Do you know where I can find a photocopier?
(A) About 10 copies.
(B) Yes, there is one in the corner.
(C) You look fine.

복사기가 어디 있는지 아세요?
(A) 약 10부 정도요.
(B) 네, 모퉁이에 한 개 있어요.
(C) 당신 좋아 보이네요.

💡 이렇게 풀어요

1. 질문 내용 파악하기 Do you know where I can find a photocopier?
   복사기가 어디 있는지

2. 선택지 들으며 오답 소거하여 정답 선택하기
   (A̶) About 10 copies. → 연상 어휘 오답(photocopier-copies)
   (B) Yes, there is one in the corner. → 정답으로 선택
   (C̶) You look fine. → 유사 발음 오답(find-fine)

2 Yes/No를 생략하고 답변하는 유형

간접 의문문은 Yes/No를 생략하고 답변하는 경우가 훨씬 많아요. 이 경우, 문맥을 통해 적절한 응답인지 파악할 수 있어야 하므로 다양한 예시를 통해 익숙해져야 합니다.

Q. **Can you tell me why** you didn't accept the job offer?
그 일자리 제안을 왜 받아들이지 않았는지 말씀해 주실래요?

A. Actually, I wanted to work in a bigger firm. 사실, 저는 더 큰 회사에서 일하고 싶었어요.

Q. **Do you know which department** Harry works in?
Harry가 어느 부서에서 일하는지 아세요?

A. He's in accounting. 그는 회계부서에 있어요.

Q. **May I ask where** I can buy some paper cups?
제가 어디에서 종이컵을 좀 살 수 있는지 물어봐도 될까요?

A. At the shop next door. 옆 매장에서요.

🔒 **확인 문제 ❷**

Mark your answer.

(A)   (B)

풀이 방법 간접 의문문 – Yes/No를 생략하고 답변하는 유형

US - BR

Do you know when the train for Central Station departs?
(A) Maybe in 20 minutes.
(B) No, she is well-trained.
(C) $15 for the round trip?

중앙역으로 가는 기차가 언제 출발하는지 아시나요?
(A) 아마 20분 후에요.
(B) 아뇨, 그녀는 숙련되었어요.
(C) 왕복에 15달러요?

✓ 이렇게 풀어요

1. 질문 내용 파악하기 Do you know when the train for Central Station departs?
   기차가 언제 출발하는지

2. 선택지 들으며 오답 소거하여 정답 선택하기
   Maybe in 20 minutes. → 정답으로 선택
   (B) No, she is well-trained. → 주체가 맞지 않는 오답 (train-she)
   (✗) $15 for the round trip? → 연상 어휘 오답 (train-round trip)

PART 2 간접 의문문 / 선택 의문문

🎧 Day 08_P2_05.mp3

🔒 확인 문제 ❸

Mark your answer.

(A)   (B)

3 접속사와 결합하는 간접 의문문

간접 의문문 중간에 의문사 의문문이 아닌 that/whether/if절이 들어가는 질문 형태도 출제됩니다. 이 질문 형태 역시 **접속사 뒤의 내용이 질문의 핵심**이므로 끝까지 잘 들어야 해요.

Q. **Do you know whether** our company developed this software or not?
우리 회사가 이 소프트웨어를 개발했는지 아닌지를 알고 계시나요?

A. Yes, it's ours. 네, 그건 우리 회사 것입니다.

Q. **Do you think (that)** we should sign up for a tour?
우리가 투어를 신청해야 한다고 생각하시나요?

A. That depends on our schedule. 우리의 일정에 따라 달라요.

Q. **Do you know if** the boxes I ordered last week have arrived?
제가 지난주에 주문한 상자들이 도착했는지 아시나요?

A. I'll call the person in charge of it. 그것을 담당하고 있는 분에게 전화해볼게요.

풀이 방법 간접 의문문 - 접속사와 결합하는 간접 의문문

🎧 Day 08_P2_06.mp3

US - US

Do you know if human resources is hiring new employees?
(A) I'll ask Hanna.
(B) The seats higher up are already sold.
(C) Thanks for letting me know.

인사부에서 신입사원들을 채용하고 있는지를 아시나요?
(A) Hanna에게 물어볼게요.
(B) 더 높은 (등급의) 좌석은 이미 팔렸어요.
(C) 알려주셔서 감사해요.

이렇게 풀어요

1. 질문 내용 파악하기   Do you know if human resources is hiring new employees?
   인사부에서 채용하고 있는지

2. 선택지 들으며 오답 소거하여 정답 선택하기
   (A) I'll ask Hanna. → 정답으로 선택
   (B) The seats higher up are already sold. → 유사 발음 오답(hiring-higher)
   (C) Thanks for letting me know. → 동일 단어 반복 오답(know)

142 기적의 토익 LC

출제 유형 2   **선택 의문문**

1 Which, Which of로 묻는 질문

대명사 which가 쓰인 선택 의문문으로, which가 단독으로 쓰이거나 'which of + 선택 대상'으로 질문이 시작합니다. 'the one(~한 것)'을 사용한 답변이 가장 많이 출제됩니다. 아무것도 해당되지 않는다고 할 때는 none을 사용하여 대답할 수도 있습니다.

Q. **Which** is the computer that needs to be fixed? 수리되어야 하는 컴퓨터가 어떤 것인가요?
A. **The one** in the meeting room. 회의실에 있는 것이요.

Q. **Which of** you approved the proposal? 여러분 중 누가 그 제안을 승인했나요?
A. **Sam did.** Sam이 했습니다.

Q. **Which of** you can work late tomorrow? 여러분 중 누가 내일 야근할 수 있나요?
A. I guess **none** of us. 아무도 안 될 겁니다.

적용 기술
[기적의 필기노트] 35P
LC 기술 24, 25

🎧 Day 08_P2_07.mp3

🔒 **확인 문제 ❹**

Mark your answer.

(A)   (B)

⚠️ **주의**
The one in the meeting room 처럼 the one을 수식하는 말이 뒤에 올 수도 있지만, the와 one 사이에 들어갈 수도 있으니 주의해야 합니다.
Q. **Which** folder should I place this document in? 이 문서를 어느 폴더에 넣어야 할까요?
A. **The** blue **one.** 파란색 폴더요.

정답 (A)

👨 **풀이 방법**   선택 의문문 – Which, Which of로 묻는 질문

🎧 Day 08_P2_08.mp3

BR - AU

Which do you want to purchase?
(A) The yellow one.
(B) A proof of your purchase.
(C) No, I don't need it anymore.

어떤 것을 구입하고 싶으세요?
(A) 노란색이요.
(B) 당신의 구입에 대한 증빙이요.
(C) 아뇨, 저는 더 이상 그게 필요 없어요.

✔️ **이렇게 풀어요**

1. 질문 내용 파악하기   **Which** do you **want to purchase**?
   　　　　　　　　　　　어떤 것을　　　구입하고 싶은지

2. 선택지 들으며 오답 소거하여 정답 선택하기
   (A) The yellow one. → 정답으로 선택
   (B) A proof of your purchase. → 동일 단어 반복 오답(purchase)
   (C) No, I don't need it anymore. → 의문사 의문문에 Yes/No로 답한 오답

🎧 Day 08_P2_09.mp3

🔒 확인 문제 ⑤

Mark your answer.

(A)   (B)

2 'Which + 명사'로 묻는 선택 의문문

형용사 which가 쓰인 경우로, 'which + 명사'로 질문이 시작합니다. which 다음에 오는 명사를 반드시 들어야 합니다.

Q. **Which course** did you sign up for? 어떤 수업에 등록하셨어요?
A. **The one** about the time management. 시간 관리에 관한 것이요.

Q. **Which floor** is Dr. Kimberly's office on? 어느 층에 Kimberly 박사님의 사무실이 있나요?
A. I think it's on the 3rd **floor**. 3층에 있는 것 같아요.

(B)

🧑 풀이 방법   선택 의문문 – 'Which + 명사' 형태의 질문

🎧 Day 08_P2_10.mp3

US - US

Which printer would fit your office needs?
(A) I want it to be faster than the existing one.
(B) No, it was a standard room.
(C) The company dress code.

어떤 프린터가 당신의 회사의 요구에 맞나요?
(A) 저는 기존 것보다 더 빠르길 원해요.
(B) 아뇨, 그건 일반실이었어요.
(C) 회사 복장 규칙이요.

> ✏️ 이렇게 풀어요
>
> 1. 질문 내용 파악하기 **Which printer** would **fit your office needs**?
>   어떤 프린터가   회사의 요구에 맞는지
>
> 2. 선택지 들으며 오답 소거하여 정답 선택하기
>   (A) I want it to be faster than the existing one. → 정답으로 선택
>   (B) No, it was a standard room. → 의문사 의문문에 Yes/No로 답한 오답
>   (C) The company dress code. → 연상 어휘 오답(office-company dress code)

3 'A or B'로 묻는 선택 의문문

- or로 연결된 두 가지 중 하나를 선택하도록 묻는 형태입니다. A와 B 자리에는 단어, 구 또는 절 형태가 올 수 있습니다.

[단어] Q. Should we take **the bus or the subway**? 우리 버스를 탈까요, 지하철을 탈까요?

[구] Q. Do you want **to watch a movie or go shopping**?
영화를 볼래요, 아니면 쇼핑하러 갈까요?

[절] Q. **Do we have enough paper or should we buy some more**?
우리에게 종이가 충분한가요, 아니면 좀 더 사야할까요?

🎧 Day 08_P2_11.mp3

🔒 확인 문제 ❻

Mark your answer.

(A)　　　(B)

- 선택 의문문의 답변은 둘 중 하나를 선택하거나, 둘 다 괜찮다[싫다]고 하는 경우, 선택권을 다른 사람에게 넘기는 경우가 있습니다.

둘 중 하나 선택	I prefer summer. 저는 여름이 더 좋아요. I feel like going shopping. 쇼핑 가고 싶어요. A window seat, please. 창가 좌석으로 주세요.
둘 다 선택	Either will be fine. 둘 다 좋아요. I like them both. 둘 다 좋아요. I don't care. / I don't mind. / It doesn't matter. 상관없습니다. It doesn't make much difference. 별 차이가 없습니다.
둘 다 선택 안 함	Neither. 둘 다 아니에요. I don't like either of them. 둘 다 별로예요.
상대방이 결정하도록 하는 응답	It's up to you. 당신에게 달렸어요. I leave it up to you. 당신이 결정하도록 두겠습니다. Whichever you like. 당신이 좋아하는 것으로 아무거나요.

정답 ❻ (B)

풀이 방법   선택 의문문 – 'A or B' 형태의 질문

🎧 Day 08_P2_12.mp3

[BR - BR]

Do you want to go to the cafeteria or Italian restaurant for lunch?
(A) A cup of green tea, please.
(B) It will be charged to your account.
(C) Either is fine.

점심 먹으러 구내식당에 가고 싶은가요, 이탈리안 레스토랑에 가고 싶은가요?
(A) 녹차 한 잔 주세요.
(B) 당신의 계좌로 비용이 부과될 겁니다.
(C) 둘 다 좋아요.

↓ 이렇게 풀어요

1. 질문 내용 파악하기   Do you want to go to **the cafeteria or Italian restaurant** for lunch?

구내식당 또는 이탈리안 레스토랑

2. 선택지 들으며 오답 소거하여 정답 선택하기
(A̶) A cup of green tea, please. → 연상 어휘 오답 (cafeteria, restaurant-green tea)
(B̶) It will be charged to your account. → 주체가 맞지 않는 오답 (you-It)
(C) Either is fine. → 정답으로 선택

따라 하면 문제가 풀리는
연습 문제

🎧 Day 08_ P2_13.mp3

🔍 정답 및 해석 p.57

각 질문과 보기를 들으며 빈칸을 채운 뒤 정답에는 O, 오답에는 X 표시하세요.

01. _____ _____ _____ is for employees?
   (A) Approximately 100 _____. [   ]
   (B) The _____ _____ the _____. [   ]

02. Do you know _____ is working extra hours tonight?
   (A) _____ not _____. [   ]
   (B) I'll _____ the _____. [   ]

03. Do you think I should _____ _____ the _____?
   (A) _____ right at the _____. [   ]
   (B) Are you _____? [   ]

04. Are _____ going to _____ the _____ _____ or should _____ _____ it?
   (A) He said _____ was _____ in _____. [   ]
   (B) _____ _____ _____, if you are okay with it. [   ]

05. Can you tell me _____ Susan is moving into her new apartment?
   (A) It's about $800 _____ _____. [   ]
   (B) On the _____ of _____. [   ]

06. Would you like _____ to _____ out the document or will you _____ it on the _____?
   (A) Yes, we will _____ it _____. [   ]
   (B) I'd _____ a _____ _____. [   ]

07. Does your soup _____ _____ or does it need more _____?
   (A) It's _____ as it is. [   ]
   (B) Yes, I'll _____ _____. [   ]

08. Would you like a table _____ or on the _____?
   (A) _____ is _____. [   ]
   (B) _____ on the _____. [   ]

Day 08_ P2_14.mp3
정답 및 해설 p.58

01. Mark your answer on your answer sheet.
   (A)   (B)   (C)

02. Mark your answer on your answer sheet.
   (A)   (B)   (C)

03. Mark your answer on your answer sheet.
   (A)   (B)   (C)

04. Mark your answer on your answer sheet.
   (A)   (B)   (C)

05. Mark your answer on your answer sheet.
   (A)   (B)   (C)

06. Mark your answer on your answer sheet.
   (A)   (B)   (C)

07. Mark your answer on your answer sheet.
   (A)   (B)   (C)

08. Mark your answer on your answer sheet.
   (A)   (B)   (C)

09. Mark your answer on your answer sheet.
   (A)   (B)   (C)

10. Mark your answer on your answer sheet.
   (A)   (B)   (C)

11. Mark your answer on your answer sheet.
   (A)   (B)   (C)

12. Mark your answer on your answer sheet.
   (A)   (B)   (C)

13. Mark your answer on your answer sheet.
   (A)   (B)   (C)

14. Mark your answer on your answer sheet.
   (A)   (B)   (C)

15. Mark your answer on your answer sheet.
   (A)   (B)   (C)

16. Mark your answer on your answer sheet.
   (A)   (B)   (C)

PART 3 시각 자료 연계 문제 / 3인 대화

시각 자료 연계 문제는 PART 3의 후반부에 위치하며, 매회 3문항이 출제됩니다.
3인 대화는 매회 1~2개의 대화문이 출제됩니다.

적용 기술

[기적의 필기노트] 62P~64P
LC 기술 47, 48

출제 포인트
시각 자료 연계 문제는 주어진 표, 평면도, 쿠폰 등의 시각 자료와 대화 내용을 연계하여 정답을 찾는 유형입니다.

출제 포인트
일정표, 차트, 지도가 자주 출제되긴 하지만 점점 다양한 시각 자료가 나오는 추세입니다. 시각 자료 자체를 해석하는 것은 어렵지 않으므로 대화 내용과의 연결 고리만 잘 캐치하면 쉽게 풀 수 있습니다.

출제 유형 1 시각 자료 연계 문제

`800+`

1 질문 유형

Look at the graphic. Which room will the woman most likely go to?
시각 자료를 보시오. 여자는 어떤 방으로 가겠는가?

2 핵심 포인트

1. **시각 자료의 내용을 먼저 신속하게 파악**합니다.
   대화가 시작되기 전에 시각 자료와 문제를 먼저 파악하여 대화에서 어떤 내용으로 단서가 제시될지 추측하는 것이 중요합니다.

2. **대화와 시각 자료의 연결 고리를 캐치**해야 합니다.
   문제의 보기에 제시된 단어를 대화에서 직접 언급하지 않으므로 시각 자료의 정보와 대화의 정보를 연결하여 답을 찾아야 합니다.

MENU	
Lunch Set 1 (Chicken)	$20
Lunch Set 2 (Beef)	$25

[문제] Q. Look at the graphic. How much will the man pay?
　　　　시각 자료를 보시오. 남자는 얼마를 지불하겠는가?

→ 가격이 직접 언급되는 것이 아니라 Lunch Set 1, 2에 대해 언급될 것임을 예측해야 합니다.

[대화] M: I will try the one with chicken today. 저는 오늘은 치킨이 포함된 것을 먹겠어요.

→ chicken이 연결 고리 역할을 합니다. Lunch Set 1을 골랐음을 파악합니다.

[정답] $20 → Lunch Set 1의 가격인 20달러를 지불할 것임을 알 수 있습니다.

3 빈출 시각 자료 유형

1. 일정표

   행사 또는 여행 일정표가 주어지며 시간대에 따른 행사명이나 담당자 정보가 제시됩니다.

London Design Conference, June 10	
9 A.M.	Web Design, Carla Gonzales
10 A.M.	Book Design, Su-min Choi
11 A.M.	Furniture Design, Alex McMille
12 P.M.	Lunch

→ Su-min Choi가 아파서 참석하지 못한다고 하고, Min-su Kim이 대신 강연을 할 것이라고 하면 Min-su Kim이 할 강연이 어떤 것일지(Book Design) 묻는 문제가 출제됩니다.

2. 쿠폰

할인 쿠폰이나 무료 쿠폰이 출제되며, 대화를 듣기 전에 쿠폰에 기재된 정보(혜택, 사용법, 만료일 등)를 파악해야 합니다.

Discount Coupon
Gordon's Department Store
20% off on purchases of $80 – $100
25% off on purchases of $110 – $150
Discount Code: **Willis17586AD**

→ 화자가 90달러 상당의 물건을 구입했다고 했을 때 몇 퍼센트 할인을 받을 것인지(20%) 묻는 문제가 출제됩니다.

출제 포인트

쿠폰에서 나오는 어휘
valid 유효한
in-store purchases 상점에서의 구매
gift certificate 상품권
holder 소지자

3. 라벨/안내판

제품이나 기계의 정보가 명시된 라벨이나 도로 표지판이 출제됩니다. 표지판의 경우 그림이 등장하므로 어떤 정보를 나타내는 그림인지 파악해야 합니다.

Nutrition Information	
Serving Size 500g	
Calories	450kcal
Fat	15g
Protein	21g
Sugar	5g
Sodium	2g

→ 화자가 지방(fat)의 양이 잘못 표기되었다고 할 경우, 수정해야 하는 숫자가 무엇인지(15g) 묻는 문제가 출제됩니다.

출제 포인트

라벨/안내판에서 나오는 어휘
fragile 깨지기 쉬운
handle 다루다
material 소재
under construction 공사 중인
no entry 출입 금지

4. 가격표/영수증

가격표의 경우 상품별 가격표가 주어지고 화자가 어떤 것을 구입할지 물을 수 있습니다. 영수증의 경우 화자가 구입한 물건 내역에 대해 오류가 발생한 경우가 자주 출제됩니다.

Product Invoice	
1 table	$125.00
1 tablecloth	$20.00
2 chairs	$99.99
5 towels	$19.99

→ table만 주문하고 tablecloth는 주문하지 않았다고 말할 경우, 화자가 얼마를 환불 받을지 (20달러) 묻는 문제가 출제됩니다.

출제 포인트

가격표/영수증에서 나오는 어휘
invoice 송장
receipt 영수증
quantity 수량
unit price 단가

⚠️ **주의**

가격이 제시된 시각 자료는 단순히 가장 비싸거나 저렴한 것이 아니라, 예산이나 한도 기준이 함께 제시되는 경우가 많으므로 이에 주의해야 합니다.

출제 포인트
지도에서 나오는 어휘
layout 배치도
stairs 계단
hallway 통로
display area 진열 공간
intersection 교차로
entrance 입구
guide map 안내도

5. 지도/평면도

지도는 거리나 행사장의 약도, 또는 지하철 노선도가 출제될 수 있고 평면도의 경우 사무실 평면도가 자주 출제됩니다.

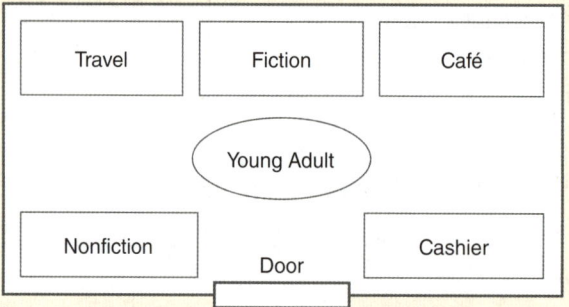

→ 화자가 특정 책의 위치를 묻고 그 책은 카페 옆에 있는 섹션에서 찾을 수 있다고 말할 경우, 화자가 갈 곳을 묻는 문제(Fiction)가 출제됩니다.

출제 포인트
차트에서 나오는 어휘
sales 매출
region 지역
market share 시장 점유율
quarterly 분기의
amount 양

`900+`

6. 차트

막대 그래프는 품목별 판매량과 직원별 계약 성사 건수 등을 나타내는 그래프가 출제될 수 있습니다.

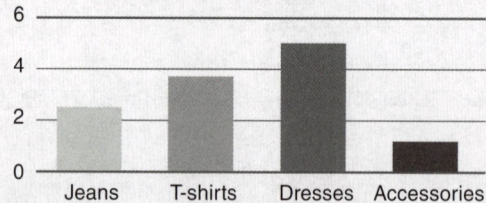

→ 매출이 가장 낮은 제품의 마케팅 전략을 세우자고 했을 때, 어떤 제품을 더 홍보할지 묻는 문제(Accessories)가 출제됩니다.

원 그래프는 각 항목에 대한 점유율을 한눈에 보기 쉽도록 작성한 그래프이고, 선 그래프는 기간에 따른 변화 추이를 보여줍니다.

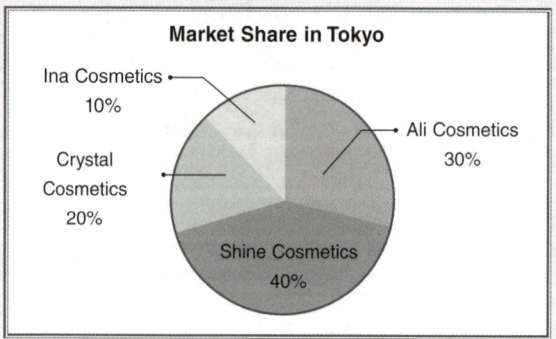

→ 도쿄에서 30퍼센트의 점유율을 가지고 있는 회사와 콜라보레이션을 할 것이라고 대화에서 언급됐을 때, 어떤 회사와 함께 일을 할지(Ali Cosmetics) 묻는 문제가 출제됩니다.

시각 자료 연계 문제

Day 08_P3_01.mp3

문제지

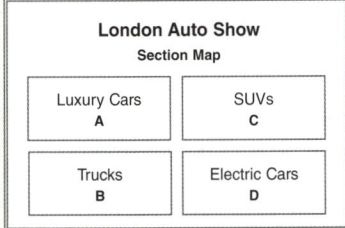

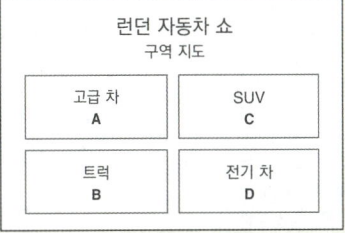

Look at the graphic. In which section will the woman meet her friends?

(A) Section A (B) Section B
(C) Section C (D) Section D

시각 자료를 보시오. 여자는 그녀의 친구들을 어느 구역에서 만날 것인가?

(A) A 구역 (B) B 구역
(C) C 구역 (D) D 구역

대화 [AU - US]

M: Welcome to the London Auto Show! Do you have a question?
W: Hi, **my friends asked me to meet them at the SUV section here.** Which section would that be?
M: Here's a map of the convention center. It shows you what's going on in each section today. Is there anything else I can help you with?
W: I saw an ad for an international food fair. When will that be?
M: We will host that in January. Here's a handout about it.
W: Great, thank you!

남: 런던 자동차 쇼에 오신 것을 환영합니다. 질문 있으신가요?
여: 안녕하세요. **제 친구들이 저에게 SUV 구역에서 만나자고 했습니다.** 그게 어느 구역인가요?
남: 여기 컨벤션 센터 지도가 있습니다. 오늘 어느 구역에서 어떤 행사가 진행 중인지 알 수 있습니다. 그 외에 다른 도와드릴 것이 더 있나요?
여: 제가 국제 음식 박람회에 대한 광고를 봤습니다. 언제 열리나요?
남: 1월에 개최할 거예요. 여기 그것에 관한 유인물이 있습니다.
여: 좋습니다. 감사합니다!

이렇게 풀어요

문제와 선택지의 키워드는 대화가 시작되기 전에 미리 파악되어 있어야 해요!

1. 시각 자료와 문제 파악하기
   - **시각 자료** 자동차 쇼의 구역 지도이고, 차의 종류별로 구역이 나뉘어져 있음.
   - **문제키워드** which section, woman meet, friends → 여자가 친구들을 만나기로 한 구역을 찾아야 함을 파악합니다.

2. 대화를 들으며 문제와 관련된 내용을 시각 자료에서 찾아 정답 선택하기
   - **대화** my friends asked me to meet them at the SUV section here.
   - **시각 자료** SUV 구역: Section C → (C)를 정답으로 선택하고 다음 문제로 넘어갑니다.

PART 3 시각 자료 연계 문제 / 3인 대화 151

적용 기술

[기적의 필기노트] 52P
LC 기술 40

출제 포인트

3인 대화는 남1-남2-여 또는 남-여1-여2의 3인이 대화를 주고 받습니다. 대화 시작에 앞서 디렉션에서 'refer to the following conversation with three speakers'라고 말해주는 부분을 통해 대화에 3인이 나올 것을 예상하고 들어야 합니다.

출제 유형 2 · 3인 대화

`800+`

1 질문 유형

- 세 명의 화자가 대화를 나누는 장소 또는 일하는 장소를 묻는 문제
  Where does the **conversation** probably **take place**? 대화는 어디에서 일어나겠는가?
  In which department do the speakers **work**? 화자들은 어느 부서에서 일하는가?

- 두 명의 동성 화자(men 또는 women)에 대해 묻는 문제
  What are the **men** concerned about? 남자들은 무엇에 대해 걱정하는가?
  Why did the **women** visit Vancouver? 여자들은 왜 밴쿠버를 방문했는가?

`900+`

- 특정 화자의 이름이 포함된 문제
  What is **Daisy**'s field of research? Daisy의 연구 분야는 무엇인가?
  What does **Paul** give to Mr. **Reed**? Paul은 Reed 씨에게 무엇을 주는가?
  What does **Jessica** ask about? Jessica는 무엇에 대해 묻는가?

`800+`

2 핵심 포인트

1. **세 명의 화자를 구별**하며 들어야 합니다.
   3인 대화는 특히 성별이 같은 두 화자를 구별해야 합니다. 이들은 목소리 외에도 다른 국적의 발음으로 구별이 가능한 경우가 많습니다. 또한 상대방의 이름을 불러주는 경우에는 이름을 기억해야 합니다. 하지만, 세 명의 화자가 아닌 제3자의 이름이 언급되기도 하므로 주의해야 합니다.

2. **화자들의 관계**를 빨리 파악할수록 대화 내용 파악이 수월합니다.
   - 3인 대화에서 자주 출제되는 화자들의 관계

     신입 직원 2명 – 상사 1명
     인턴 1명 – 기존 직원 2명
     학생 2명 – 교사 1명
     직원 2명 – 손님 1명
     회사 동료 3명

3. 3인 대화는 **턴 수가 긴 대화**도 자주 출제되므로 끝까지 흐름을 놓치지 말아야 합니다.
   3인 대화는 한 명이 짧게 말하는 대신 대화가 전환되는 턴 수가 6~8회가 되는 경우도 있습니다. 상대적으로 대화가 길게 느껴질 수 있으므로 끝까지 흐름을 놓치지 말고 집중해서 들어야 합니다.

출제 포인트

3인 대화에서는 사람 이름이 자주 등장하며, 그 인물에 대해 묻는 문제가 출제됩니다.

3인 대화

🎧 Day 08_P3_02.mp3

[문제지]

What will **Greg** most likely **receive**?
(A) A music CD
(B) A signed book
(C) A free T-shirt
(D) A concert ticket

Greg는 무엇을 받을 것 같은가?
(A) 음악 CD
(B) 사인이 된 책
(C) 무료 티셔츠
(D) 콘서트 티켓

[대화] [BR - US - AU]

M1: I'm Lester Jenkins! Welcome back to 97.7 FM. Today here in the studio with us is the great singer Paula Short. So, Paula, you're back on tour again?

W: That's right, Lester. I think my fans are really going to like the new songs I wrote.

M1: I'm sure it will be great. We've got some fans waiting on the line to speak with you here. First caller, you're on the air.

M2: **Hi, I'm Greg from LA.** I'm a huge fan of Paula's music. But, you haven't visited any cities on the West coast yet. I looked up the tour schedule, and I was disappointed again this time.

W: I know. Please be assured that my agency is still considering it. **Greg, I want to make it up to you. I'll send you an autographed copy of my new album.**

남1: 저는 Lester Jenkins입니다. 97.7 FM 청취를 환영합니다. 오늘 여기 스튜디오에서 유명한 가수인 Paula Short 씨가 우리와 함께합니다. 자 Paula 씨, 다시 투어 공연을 하신다고요?

여: 맞습니다, Lester. 저의 팬들은 제가 쓴 곡을 정말 좋아할 거예요.

남1: 성공할 것이라 확신합니다. 당신과 이야기를 나누고 싶어하는 팬들이 전화상에서 기다리고 있습니다. 첫 번째 분, 연결되셨습니다.

남2: **안녕하세요? 저는 LA에 사는 Greg입니다.** 저는 Paula의 음악의 열렬한 팬입니다. 그런데 당신은 서부 해안 지역의 어느 도시도 아직 방문하지 않았어요. 저는 투어 스케줄을 보았고, 이번에도 실망을 했습니다.

여: 알고 있습니다. 저의 기획사가 여전히 고려 중이니 안심하세요. **Greg, 당신에게 보상을 해주고 싶군요. 제가 저의 새 앨범에 사인을 해서 보내 드리겠습니다.**

🎵 이렇게 풀어요

문제와 선택지의 키워드는 대화가 시작되기 전에 미리 파악되어 있어야 해요!

1. 문제 파악하기
Want, Greg, receive → 대화에서 Greg라는 이름이 제시될 것임을 파악합니다.

2. 선택지 키워드 파악하기
(A) 음악 CD (B) 사인이 된 책 (C) 무료 티셔츠 (D) 콘서트 티켓

3. 대화 마지막 부분에서 단서 파악하여 정답 선택하기
대화 중반부에서 Greg라는 이름이 처음 언급되었고, 전화를 건 사람이라는 것을 알 수 있습니다. 이어서 대화 마지막에서 여자가 Greg에게 사인 앨범을 보내 주겠다고 한 것을 파악합니다.
→ (A)를 정답으로 선택하고 다음 문제로 넘어갑니다.

따라 하면 문제가 풀리는 연습 문제

문제와 각 선택지의 키워드에 표시하세요. 그러고 나서 대화를 듣고 빈칸에 들어갈 말을 받아쓴 후 정답을 선택해 보세요.

01. Look at the graphic. Where will the woman deliver a speech?

(A) Madrid　　　　　　　　　　(B) Barcelona

Schedule	Carl Butler
Date	**City**
October 11, Tuesday	Madrid
October 13, Thursday	Barcelona

W: The book signing event in Madrid is _____, so I will _____ the Q&A session in your book club. But, as you know, I will _____ a keynote _____ at a convention on _____ afternoon.

M: Oh, really? That's great. You will have a great time with my _____ _____ members.

02. Why did Miranda send an e-mail to the customers?

(A) To apologize for a mistake　　　(B) To request some feedback

W1: Our Web site administrator was able to find the _____ and _____ it.

M: That's good news. Miranda, have you contacted our customers yet?

W2: Yes, I sent out an e-mail this morning to _____ the _____ and tell them that we are _____ for any _____.

03. Look at the graphic. When will the woman pay for the remainder?

(A) Sep. 14th　　　　　　　　　(B) Sep. 19th

ITEM	Delivery Date
Bookshelves	Wed, Sep. 14th
Tables	Thurs, Sep. 15th
Chairs	Fri, Sep. 16th
Lamps	Mon, Sep. 19th

W: Let me check the _____ schedule. You said we already made a $5,000 _____ _____ when we placed the order. When should the _____ be paid?

M: You can make the final payment on the _____ _____ that the _____ arrive.

---

paraphrasing 주어진 어휘 또는 표현과 의미가 동일한 것을 연결하세요.

1. give a speech　　●　　　　　●　(a) the rest
2. mailing address　●　　　　　●　(b) deliver a speech
3. remainder　　　 ●　　　　　●　(c) contact information

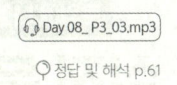

04. Look at the graphic. Which window should the man go to tomorrow?

(A) Window 1 (B) Window 4

W: Sorry, we are already closed. Here are our _____ _____ on the board.

M: Oh, okay. I came here to _____ a new business _____.

W: If so, it usually takes about 30 minutes to _____ it. You'd better come by 4:30 tomorrow at the latest. Mr. Harris will help you. His window is _____ _____ the magazine stand.

05. Who probably is the woman?

(A) A construction worker (B) A restaurant owner

W: I checked on the renovation _____ you submitted for my _____, but I'm worried that it is a little bit _____ _____. What happened?

M1: Well, some work was delayed due to the _____.

M2: But some materials arrived _____ than scheduled, so we expect all the work to be done on time.

06. What do the women agree to do?

(A) Work extra shifts (B) Postpone a meeting

M: Angela, would you mind _____ _____ _____ to your schedule this week? Olivia has a family emergency.

W1: I already knew that. I was asked if I can _____ her shifts. I can cover her Monday shift, but I have a _____ _____ with my academic advisor on Tuesday. Miranda, could you cover her Tuesday shift?

W2: _____. What time do I need to _____ _____?

paraphrasing 주어진 어휘 또는 표현과 의미가 동일한 것을 연결하세요.

4. process •   • (a) delayed
5. behind schedule •   • (b) fill in for
6. cover •   • (c) take care of

Refrigerator Model	Storage Capacity (in cubic feet)
Gourley	14
Wilkins	18
Marion	16
Abbott	20

01. Why is the business holding a sale?

    (A) To celebrate an anniversary
    (B) To introduce a new brand
    (C) To promote a relocation
    (D) To recognize a national holiday

02. Look at the graphic. Which model does the woman plan to buy?

    (A) Gourley
    (B) Wilkins
    (C) Marion
    (D) Abbott

03. What does the man offer to do?

    (A) Update a delivery address
    (B) Send a discount voucher
    (C) Check an inventory list
    (D) Hold an item for the woman

04. Who most likely is the man?

    (A) A factory supervisor
    (B) A repair shop worker
    (C) A restaurant owner
    (D) A clothing store manager

05. What does the man ask for?

    (A) Proof of purchase
    (B) Delivery details
    (C) A photo ID
    (D) A customer's signature

06. What is Tanya asked to do?

    (A) Explain a policy
    (B) Print a document
    (C) Check a storage area
    (D) Schedule a delivery

07. Where most likely do the speakers work?

    (A) At a computer store
    (B) At a moving firm
    (C) At a publishing company
    (D) At a real estate agency

08. What was changed this morning?

    (A) A project deadline
    (B) A meeting location
    (C) A price estimate
    (D) A monthly fee

09. Why does the woman say, "Lucas provided training for the software"?

    (A) To suggest adding a member to the team
    (B) To nominate Lucas for an award
    (C) To explain an absence from a meeting
    (D) To correct some outdated information

www.quickbusinessreview.net	
Cuyahoga Sporting Goods	
Service	5/5
Variety	1/5
Quality	4/5
Location	1/5

10. What is the man concerned about?

    (A) Losing market share
    (B) Canceling a contract
    (C) Failing an inspection
    (D) Having employees quit

11. Look at the graphic. What will the man discuss with Ms. Lewis?

    (A) Service
    (B) Variety
    (C) Quality
    (D) Location

12. What does the woman offer to do?

    (A) Print a product catalog
    (B) Contact a Web site owner
    (C) Create a survey
    (D) Order some supplies

13. Where is the conversation most likely taking place?

    (A) At a gym
    (B) At a park
    (C) At a school
    (D) At a stadium

14. Why should the woman present her student identification?

    (A) To reserve a spot
    (B) To get a discount
    (C) To apply for a position
    (D) To prove her date of birth

15. What will the woman most likely do next?

    (A) Input her personal information
    (B) Speak with the manager
    (C) Go to another facility
    (D) File a complaint

16. Who most likely are George and Stephanie?

    (A) Property owners
    (B) Real estate agents
    (C) Hardware store clerks
    (D) Professional gardeners

17. What are George and Stephanie concerned about?

    (A) The cost of equipment
    (B) The availability of flower seeds
    (C) The amount of work requested
    (D) The location of a client's property

18. What is said about the client?

    (A) He is available in the evenings.
    (B) He operates his own business.
    (C) He will provide equipment.
    (D) He is going out of town.

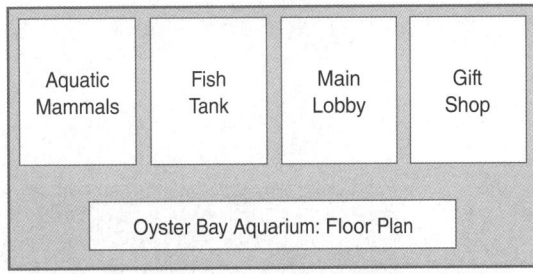

19. What does the man want to know?

    (A) Price of the ticket
    (B) Availability to join the tour
    (C) Name of the fish
    (D) Directions to the exhibit

20. Look at the graphic. Which area does the woman give directions to get to?

    (A) The Aquatic Mammals
    (B) The Fish Tank
    (C) The Main Lobby
    (D) The Gift Shop

21. What does the woman tell the man about his ticket?

    (A) It includes VIP member benefits.
    (B) It provides a discount at the shop.
    (C) It is valid throughout the weekend.
    (D) It allows admission into special events.

'멋진 당신, 오늘도 화이팅'

DAY 09

오늘의 학습 포인트

PART 2. 청유문

1. Could you/Can you/Would you/Will you
2. Why don't you[we/I]
3. Would you mind/Do you mind
   - 수락할 경우 No, 거절할 경우 Yes
4. Let's/I will/I can
5. I need to/I want to/I'd like to
6. Please + 명령문
   - 정중하게 요청하는 표현

PART 4. 문제 유형

1. 주제·목적 문제
   - 담화 초반부
2. 장소·직업 문제
   - 담화 시작 부분이나 담화 전반
3. 세부 사항 문제
   - 담화 중반부, 문제점, 이유/방법, 특정 키워드

PART 2 청유문

제안이나 권유를 하는 내용의 문장으로, 의문문과 평서문으로 모두 제시될 수 있습니다.
매회 1~2문제가 출제돼요!

적용 기술

[기적의 필기노트] 36P
LC 기술 26

🎧 Day 09_ P2_01.mp3

🔒 확인 문제 ❶

Mark your answer.

(A)   (B)

출제 포인트

제안은 보통 상대방인 you에게 하는 내용이 많으므로, he, she, they가 보기에서 들릴 경우 오답일 확률이 높습니다.
Q. Can you help me move these boxes? 이 상자 나르는 것을 도와주시겠어요?
A. Sure, I'd be happy to. (O) 물론이죠. 좋습니다.
A. Sure, she'll be there. (X) 물론이죠. 그녀는 그곳에 있을 거예요.

(A) ❶

출제 유형 1
Could you/Can you/Would you/Will you

조동사 Could/Can/Would/Will로 시작하는 제안, 제공, 요청의 의미를 가진 의문문의 형태를 알아둡시다.

Q. **Could you** show me your driver's license? 운전 면허증을 보여 주시겠어요?
A. Sure, no problem. 네, 문제없습니다.

Q. **Would you like to** come to the concert with us? 우리와 콘서트에 함께 갈래요?
A. No, thanks. I'm quite busy today. 아뇨, 괜찮아요. 제가 오늘 꽤 바빠서요.

Q. **Would you like me to** give you the analysis report today? 오늘 분석 보고서를 드릴까요?
A. I'll be in the office until 5 P.M. 저는 오후 5시까지 사무실에 있을 거예요.

Q. **Will you** give me a ride to the airport? 공항까지 저를 태워다 주시겠어요?
A. Tell me when to pick you up. 언제 태우러 가야 하는지 말해주세요.

🧑 풀이 방법 Could you/Can you/Would you/Will you

🎧 Day 09_ P2_02.mp3

BR - AU

Could you pass me the water jug, please?
(A) No, it's free.
(B) I usually water them every week.
(C) Sure, here you are.

물 주전자를 제게 건네주시겠어요?
(A) 아뇨, 무료입니다.
(B) 저는 보통 그것들에 매주 물을 줘요.
(C) 물론이죠, 여기 있습니다.

✓ 이렇게 풀어요

1. 질문 내용 파악하기 Could you pass me the water jug, please?
   물 주전자를 건네달라고 요청

2. 선택지 들으며 오답 소거하여 정답 선택하기
   (A̶) No, it's free. → 연상 어휘 오답(water-free)
   (B̶) I usually water them every week. → 동일 어휘 반복 오답(water)
   (C) Sure, here you are. → 정답으로 선택

출제 유형 2
Why don't you[we/I]

의문사 Why로 시작하는 제안, 제공, 요청의 의미를 가진 의문문의 형태를 알아 둡시다.

Q. **Why don't you** go fishing with us? 우리와 낚시 가는 거 어때요?
A. [수락] Sure, what time shall we meet? 좋아요, 몇 시에 만날까요?
　　　　 Yes, that's a great idea. 네, 좋은 생각이에요.
　[거절] I don't have time to go. 저는 갈 시간이 없어요.
　　　　 I'm not sure if I'll be available. 제가 가능할지 잘 모르겠어요.

Q. **Why don't we** ask for more office desks? 우리 사무용 책상을 더 요청하는 게 어때요?
A. [수락] Go ahead. 그렇게 하세요.
　　　　 We really need some more. 우리 정말 몇 개가 더 필요해요.
　[거절] I've never considered that. 그건 생각해 본 적이 없어요.
　　　　 I'm not sure the manager would accept it. 부장님이 승인할지 모르겠네요.

확인 문제 ❷

Mark your answer.

(A)　　(B)

⚠ **주의**
Why didn't로 물을 경우 이유를 묻는 질문이므로 듣고 구분할 수 있어야 합니다.

정답 ❷ (B)

풀이 방법　Why don't you[we/I]

[US - US]

Why don't we register for the workshop in advance for a discount?
(A) No, just one day.
(B) Yes, that's a good idea.
(C) You can pick it up at the registration desk.

할인을 위해 워크숍에 미리 등록하는 게 어때요?
(A) 아뇨, 하루 만이에요.
(B) 네, 좋은 생각이네요.
(C) 접수처에서 그것을 가져가면 돼요.

이렇게 풀어요

1. **질문 내용 파악하기** Why don't we register for the workshop in advance for a discount?
　　　　　　　　　　　　워크숍에 미리 등록하자고 제안

2. **선택지 들으며 오답 소거하여 정답 선택하기**
　(A) No, just one day. → 연상 어휘 오답(workshop-just one day)
　(B) Yes, that's a good idea. → 정답으로 선택
　(C) You can pick it up at the registration desk. → 유사 발음 오답(register-registration)

🎧 Day 09_P2_05.mp3

🔒 **확인 문제 ❸**

Mark your answer.

(A)　　(B)

출제 유형 3

Would you mind/Do you mind

900+

Would you mind/Do you mind~?는 '~해도 될까요, 제가 ~하는 게 싫은가요'의 의미로 허가를 구하거나 요청할 때 쓰이는 의문문입니다. **수락할 경우 No, 거절할 경우 Yes**라고 답변하므로 혼동하지 않도록 주의해야 합니다.

Q. **Would you mind** if I turn on the air-conditioner?
　제가 에어컨을 켜도 될까요? (제가 에어컨을 켜는 게 싫으신가요?)

A. [수락] No, not at all. 아뇨, 전혀요.
　　　　 Certainly not.(= Of course not.) 물론이죠.
　　　　 No, go ahead. 네. 그렇게 하세요.

　[거절] Actually, yes. I'm a bit cold. 사실, 그렇습니다. 저는 약간 추워요.
　　　　 Sorry, but I caught a cold. 죄송하지만 저는 감기에 걸렸어요.

(B)

🧑 풀이 방법　Would you mind/Do you mind

🎧 Day 09_P2_06.mp3

BR - US

Would you mind me opening the window?
(A) No, go ahead.
(B) Sorry, we are already closed.
(C) The window should be replaced.

제가 창문을 열어도 괜찮을까요?
(A) 네, 그러세요.
(B) 죄송합니다, 저희는 이미 영업이 종료되었습니다.
(C) 창문을 교체해야 합니다.

> ✔ 이렇게 풀어요
>
> 1. 질문 내용 파악하기　**Would you mind** me **opening the window**?
> 　　　　　　　　　　　　　　창문을 여는 게 괜찮은지 허락을 요청
>
> 2. 선택지 들으며 오답 소거하여 정답 선택하기
> 　(A) No, go ahead. → 정답으로 선택
> 　(B) Sorry, we are already closed. → 연상 어휘 오답 (window-closed)
> 　(C) The window should be replaced. → 동일 어휘 반복 오답 (window)

162　기적의 토익 LC

출제 유형 4 — Let's/I will/I can

의문문이 아닌 평서문으로 상대방에게 권유나 제안을 하는 문장도 자주 출제됩니다.

Q. **Let's** show our budget proposal to our president. 사장님께 예산 제안서를 보여드립시다.
A. That won't be necessary. 그럴 필요 없습니다.

Q. **I will** proofread this report **for you**. 제가 이 보고서를 교정 봐 드릴게요.
A. Thanks, but I can manage it. 감사하지만, 제가 할 수 있어요.

Q. **I can** make a reservation for next week **if you'd like**. 원하시면 제가 다음 주로 예약을 해 드릴게요.
A. It would be helpful. 도움이 되겠네요.

🎧 Day 09_P2_07.mp3

🔒 확인 문제 ❶

Mark your answer.

(A)   (B)

⚠️ 주의

제안, 청유는 앞으로 발생할 사실에 대해 이야기하므로, 과거 시제로 답한 보기는 오답일 확률이 높습니다.
Q. Let's meet at 10 A.M. tomorrow. 내일 오전 10시에 만나요.
A. I thought there were only seven left. (X) 저는 7개만 남아 있다고 생각했어요.

정답 ❶ (A)

풀이 방법 — Let's/I will/I can

🎧 Day 09_P2_08.mp3

BR - AU

Let's stop by a café to grab a snack.
(A) Sure, I feel hungry too.
(B) Slow down at the stop sign.
(C) Tuna sandwiches.

간식 먹으러 카페에 갑시다.
(A) 그래요, 저도 배고파요.
(B) 정지 신호에서 속도를 줄이세요.
(C) 참치 샌드위치요.

↑ 이렇게 풀어요

1. 질문 내용 파악하기   Let's stop by a café to grab a snack.
   카페에 가자고 제안

2. 선택지 들으며 오답 소거하여 정답 선택하기
    Sure, I feel hungry too. → 정답으로 선택
   (B) Slow down at the **stop** sign. → 동일 어휘 반복 오답(stop)
   (C) Tuna sandwiches. → 연상 어휘 오답(café, snack-tuna sandwiches)

🎧 Day 09_ P2_09.mp3

🔒 **확인 문제 ❺**

Mark your answer.

(A)   (B)

출제 유형 5
I need to/I want to/I'd like to

> 800+

요구, 요청, 부탁 등의 표현이 평서문으로 출제되면 난이도가 높아집니다. 고득점을 위해서 다양한 평서문 유형을 잘 익혀두어야 합니다.

Q. **I need to** register for the online training session. 저는 온라인 교육 과정에 등록해야 합니다.
A. I can help you with that. 제가 도와드리겠습니다.

Q. **I want to** exchange this coffee machine. 이 커피 기계를 교환하고 싶습니다.
A. Do you have the receipt? 영수증을 가지고 있으신가요?

Q. **I'd like to** get the information by e-mail. 저는 이메일로 정보를 받고 싶습니다.
A. Can I have your e-mail address? 이메일 주소를 알려주시겠어요?

정답 ❺ (A)

🙂 풀이 방법 I need to/I want to/I'd like to

🎧 Day 09_ P2_10.mp3

[US - BR]

I need to mail my checks for my gas and water.
(A) By express mail.
(B) You can do that online.
(C) A bottle of water, please.

저는 가스와 수도비를 위해 수표를 우편으로 보내야 해요.
(A) 속달 우편으로요.
(B) 인터넷상에서 그걸 하실 수 있어요.
(C) 물 한 병 주세요.

> **✓ 이렇게 풀어요**
>
> 1. 질문 내용 파악하기   I need to mail my checks for my gas and water.
>   수표를 우편으로 보내야 한다고 전달
>
> 2. 선택지 들으며 오답 소거하여 정답 선택하기
>   (A̶) By express mail. → 동일 어휘 반복 오답 (mail)
>   (B) You can do that online. → 정답으로 선택
>   (C̶) A bottle of water please. → 동일 어휘 반복 오답 (water)

출제 유형 6 — Please + 명령문

🎧 Day 09_ P2_11.mp3

🔒 확인 문제 ❻

Mark your answer.

(A)   (B)

800+

Please 뒤에 명령문이 오면 상대방에게 정중하게 무엇을 해 달라고 요청하는 의미입니다.

Q. **Please** remind Mr. Yamamoto of the annual meeting.
   Yamamoto 씨에게 연례 회의에 대해서 다시 한번 알려주시기 바랍니다.

A. [수락] I'll contact him right now. 지금 즉시 그에게 연락할게요.
   [거절] Sorry, but I have to leave now. 죄송하지만, 저는 지금 나가야 해요.
   [제3의 답변] What was his phone number? 그의 전화번호가 뭐였죠?

Q. **Please** let me know when you are done with the report. 보고서 끝내면 제게 알려주세요.

A. [수락] Sure, I just need a few more minutes. 물론이죠, 몇 분이면 돼요.
   [제3의 답변] Can you help me with the proofreading? 검토하는 것을 도와주실 수 있으세요?

정답 ❻ (B)

풀이 방법 — Please + 명령문

🎧 Day 09_ P2_12.mp3

[US - BR]

Please activate the security alarm when you leave.
(A) You have to keep it in a secure place.
(B) Sure, I know how to do that.
(C) He woke up late today.

나가실 때 보안 알람을 켜 주세요.
(A) 그것을 안전한 장소에 보관하셔야 해요.
(B) 물론이죠, 저는 그걸 어떻게 하는지 알아요.
(C) 그는 오늘 늦게 일어났어요.

이렇게 풀어요

1. 질문 내용 파악하기   Please activate the security alarm when you leave.
   보안 알람을 켜 달라고 요청

2. 선택지 들으며 오답 소거하여 정답 선택하기
   (A̶) You have to keep it in a secure place. → 유사 발음 오답 (security-secure)
   (B) Sure, I know how to do that. → 정답으로 선택
   (C̶) He woke up late today. → 연상 어휘 오답 (alarm-woke up late)

PART 2 청유문

따라 하면 문제가 풀리는
연습 문제

🎧 Day 09_P2_13.mp3

📍 정답 및 해석 p.68

각 질문과 보기를 들으며 빈칸을 채운 뒤 정답에는 O, 오답에는 X 표시하세요.

01. _____ take a _____ after the meeting.
    (A) The _____ was _____ again. [   ]
    (B) That _____ _____. [   ]

02. Would _____ like some _____ _____?
    (A) They're _____ _____. [   ]
    (B) I'd _____ a _____ _____. [   ]

03. _____ _____ _____ give you a tour of our gym?
    (A) _____ _____ to. [   ]
    (B) One of the _____ attractions. [   ]

04. Why don't we _____ Sophia to _____ in the meeting this afternoon?
    (A) Is _____ _____ today? [   ]
    (B) Let's go to the _____. [   ]

05. Why don't you _____ _____ a _____ in the park during the lunch break?
    (A) I'll have a burger for _____. [   ]
    (B) I will, I need some _____ _____. [   ]

06. _____ _____ going to the beach this weekend?
    (A) I _____ the subway. [   ]
    (B) I'm _____ I _____. [   ]

07. Do you _____ if I _____ _____ the volume?
    (A) I turned the _____ _____. [   ]
    (B) As a matter of fact, _____ _____. [   ]

08. I need to get a _____ _____ before the movie.
    (A) There's a _____ _____ _____ nearby. [   ]
    (B) _____ _____ that romance _____? [   ]

Day 09_ P2_14.mp3

정답 및 해설 p.69

01. Mark your answer on your answer sheet.
(A) (B) (C)

02. Mark your answer on your answer sheet.
(A) (B) (C)

03. Mark your answer on your answer sheet.
(A) (B) (C)

04. Mark your answer on your answer sheet.
(A) (B) (C)

05. Mark your answer on your answer sheet.
(A) (B) (C)

06. Mark your answer on your answer sheet.
(A) (B) (C)

07. Mark your answer on your answer sheet.
(A) (B) (C)

08. Mark your answer on your answer sheet.
(A) (B) (C)

09. Mark your answer on your answer sheet.
(A) (B) (C)

10. Mark your answer on your answer sheet.
(A) (B) (C)

11. Mark your answer on your answer sheet.
(A) (B) (C)

12. Mark your answer on your answer sheet.
(A) (B) (C)

13. Mark your answer on your answer sheet.
(A) (B) (C)

14. Mark your answer on your answer sheet.
(A) (B) (C)

15. Mark your answer on your answer sheet.
(A) (B) (C)

16. Mark your answer on your answer sheet.
(A) (B) (C)

PART 4
주제·목적 문제 / 장소·직업 문제 / 세부 사항 문제

주제·목적 문제와 장소·직업 문제는 매회 3~4문제 정도,
세부 사항 문제는 매회 15~17문제 정도 출제됩니다!

적용 기술
[기적의 필기노트] 68P
LC 기술 50

출제 유형 1 주제·목적 문제

1 질문 유형

출제 포인트
정답의 단서는 주로 담화가 시작될 때 나오는 인사말 다음에 제시되는 경우가 많으므로 초반부를 반드시 들어야 합니다.

- 주제 문제
  What is the speaker **mainly discussing**? 화자는 주로 무엇에 대해 이야기하고 있는가?
  What is the talk **mainly about**? 담화는 주로 무엇에 대한 것인가?
  What is being **announced[advertised]**? 무엇이 공지되고[광고되고] 있는가?
  What is the main **topic** of the talk? 담화의 주제는 무엇인가?

- 목적 문제
  What is the **purpose** of the message? 메시지의 목적은 무엇인가?
  Why is the speaker **calling**? 화자는 왜 전화하고 있는가?

출제 포인트
담화가 광고인 경우 상호명이나 제품명을 통해 무엇이 광고되는지 파악할 수 있습니다.

2 핵심 포인트

1. **담화의 앞부분을** 잘 들어야 합니다.
   담화의 주제 또는 목적은 주로 앞부분에서 언급되므로 반드시 첫 2~3문장을 들어야 합니다. 간혹 앞부분을 듣고 주제를 파악하기 어려운 경우, 담화 전체를 듣고 파악해야 하는 경우도 있습니다. 이때는 다른 문제를 먼저 풀고 마지막으로 주제/목적 문제의 답을 고르면 수월하게 풀 수 있습니다.

2. **주제나 목적을 끌고 나오는 표현** 다음을 주의 깊게 들어야 합니다.

출제 포인트
단서 표현 뒤에 나오는 내용이 정답 보기에 패러프레이징 되는 경우가 많습니다.
changes in our reimbursement policy 상환 정책에 있어서의 변경
→ introduce a new procedure 새로운 절차 소개

> I want to inform you that ~을 알려 드리고자 합니다
> ~ announced today 오늘 ~을 발표했습니다
> Today we are going to focus on 오늘은 ~에 대해 집중적으로 다룰 것입니다
> I'm calling to ~하기 위해 전화드립니다
> I'm calling about ~에 대해 전화드립니다
> I'd like to/I want to/I need to ~하고 싶습니다/~해야 합니다
> I'd like to remind everyone that 모두에게 ~을 상기시켜 드리고 싶습니다

[단서] The vice president **announced today** that he will leave his position next month. 부사장은 오늘 그가 다음 달에 직책에서 물러날 것이라고 발표했습니다.
[정답] To inform the retirement 퇴직을 알리기 위해

[단서] **I'm calling about** the change in your schedule for your next business trip.
    귀하의 다음 출장에 대한 일정 변경 사항에 대해 전화 드립니다.
[정답] Change in itinerary 일정 변경

[단서] **Today we are going to focus on** some complaints that we've received.
    오늘은 우리가 받은 불만 사항에 대해 집중적으로 다룰 것입니다.
[정답] To deal with the issues 문제를 다루기 위해

주제·목적 문제

🎧 Day 09_ P4_01.mp3

[문제지]

What is the speaker **mainly discussing**?
(A) Baggage fees
(B) Training sessions
(C) Complimentary food
(D) Leg room for passengers

화자는 주로 무엇에 대해 이야기하고 있는가?
(A) 수하물 요금
(B) 교육 시간
(C) 무료 음식
(D) 승객들이 다리를 뻗을 수 있는 공간

[담화] [US]

excerpt from a meeting

W: Thank you all for coming today. **Let's start off by talking about complimentary snacks.** Some airlines are charging for them, and it has really hurt their public image. Most customers expect to get some pretzels or nuts for free when they fly. I think by offering them for free to our customers, we can improve our satisfaction score. Here at Alpha Air, we strive to keep our customers happy. So, now let's take a minute to go over the most recent survey to see what the customers have to say.

회의 발췌록

여: 오늘 와 주셔서 모두 감사합니다. **무료 간식에 대한 이야기로 시작하겠습니다.** 몇몇 항공사들은 그것에 대해 요금을 부과하고 이것은 그들의 이미지에 매우 타격을 주었습니다. 대부분의 승객들은 비행할 때 프레첼이나 견과류를 무료로 받기를 기대합니다. 저는 우리의 고객들에게 무료 간식을 제공함으로써 우리의 만족 점수를 향상시킬 수 있다고 생각합니다. 이곳 Alpha Air에서, 우리는 고객들을 행복하게 하기 위하여 노력하고 있습니다. 그러니, 이제 고객들이 무엇을 말하고자 하는지 알아보기 위하여 최근 설문 조사를 검토하는 시간을 갖도록 하겠습니다.

이렇게 풀어요

문제와 선택지의 키워드는 담화가 시작되기 전에 미리 파악되어 있어야 해요!

1. **문제 파악하기**
   What, mainly discussing → 주제 문제임을 파악합니다.

2. **선택지 키워드 파악하기**
   (A) 수하물 요금 (B) 교육 시간 (C) 무료 음식 (D) 승객들이 다리를 뻗을 수 있는 공간

3. **담화 앞부분 들으며 정답 선택하기**
   Let's start off by talking about complimentary snacks.
   → Complimentary food로 패러프레이징 된 (C)를 정답으로 선택하고 다음 문제로 넘어갑니다.

적용 기술

[기적의 필기노트] 67P
LC 기술 49

출제 포인트
장소와 직업에 대한 단서는 대체로 담화의 시작 부분에 제시되지만, 특정 한 곳에서가 아니라 담화 전반에 거쳐 나올 수도 있습니다.

⚠ 주의
화자의 직업을 묻는 문제인지, 청자의 직업을 묻는 문제인지 확실히 파악한 후 담화를 들어야 합니다.

출제 유형 2 장소·직업 문제

1 질문 유형

· 장소 문제

Where is the **talk taking place**? 담화는 어디에서 일어나고 있는가?
Where most likely is the **announcement being made**?
공지는 어디에서 이루어지고 있겠는가?
Where are most likely are the **listeners**? 청자들은 어디에 있겠는가?

· 직업 문제

Who most likely is the **speaker**? 화자는 누구이겠는가?
Who most likely are the **listeners**? 청자들은 누구이겠는가?
Who is the message **intended for**? 메시지는 누구를 위한 것인가?
Where does the **speaker** probably **work**? 화자는 어디에서 일하겠는가?

2 핵심 포인트

1. 담화 유형별로 장소와 직업을 파악할 수 있는 단서 표현을 구분하여 알아 두어야 합니다.

    · announcement(공지)

    Good morning everyone, we hope you've been enjoying **the conference on** ~
    안녕하세요 여러분, ~에 대한 학회를 즐기고 계시길 바랍니다.

    Attention shoppers, today is the last day of our winter sales event.
    쇼핑객 여러분, 주목해 주세요. 오늘이 겨울 할인 행사의 마지막 날입니다.

    · telephone message(전화 메시지)

    Hi, Josh. **This is** Kim **from the management office** of Ace Apartments.
    안녕하세요, Josh. 저는 Ace 아파트 관리사무소의 Kim입니다.

    · talk(담화)

    Hello everyone, and **welcome to** our first day of beginners' guitar **lesson**.
    안녕하세요 여러분, 초급자 기타 수업의 첫날에 오신 것을 환영합니다.

    · excerpt from a meeting(회의 발췌록)

    Thank you for **having a meeting with me to discuss** our **package design**.
    우리의 포장 디자인에 대해 논의하기 위해 저와 회의를 해주셔서 감사합니다.

    As you know, **the purpose of these staff meetings is** to ensure customer satisfaction of **our restaurant**.
    아시다시피, 이 직원 회의의 목적은 우리 레스토랑의 고객 만족도를 보장하기 위한 것입니다.

2. 화자가 직접 자신의 직업이나 근무지를 밝히는 경우도 있지만, 담화 전반적으로 관련 어휘들을 조합하여 유추해야 하는 경우도 있습니다.

    upcoming building project, contract, client, construction → A construction company 다가오는 건설 프로젝트, 계약, 고객, 건설 → 건설 회사

    reserve a table, accommodate, free drink → At a restaurant
    테이블을 예약하다, 수용하다, 무료 음료 → 식당에서

장소·직업 문제

🎧 Day 09_P4_02.mp3

문제지

Who most likely is the **speaker**?
(A) A repair technician
(B) A real estate agent
(C) A service representative
(D) A restaurant manager

화자는 누구이겠는가?
(A) 수리 기술자
(B) 부동산 중개인
(C) 서비스 직원
(D) 레스토랑 지배인

담화 AU

telephone message

M: Hello, **this is Jeffrey from Homeley Appliances calling for Ms. Lincoln. You filed a complaint because you received a bill for servicing your washing machine when it broke last week.** You were sent that bill because your warranty had already expired two months before the service. Please look at the contract you signed upon purchasing the washing machine to check the expiration date. If our records are incorrect, please fax us your copy of the transcript.

전화 메시지

남: 안녕하세요? 저는 Homeley 가전제품에서 Lincoln 씨에게 전화드리는 Jeffrey입니다. 고객님은 지난주에 세탁기가 고장이 났을 때 받았던 서비스에 대해 청구서를 받으셔서 불만을 제기하셨습니다. 서비스를 받기 전에 귀하의 보증기간이 이미 만료가 되어 그 청구서를 받으신 것입니다. 만기일을 확인하기 위하여 세탁기를 구매하실 때 서명하셨던 계약서를 보시기 바랍니다. 만약 저희의 기록이 잘못 되었다면, 귀하의 복사본을 저희에게 보내주시기 바랍니다.

이렇게 풀어요

문제와 선택지의 키워드는 담화가 시작되기 전에 미리 파악되어 있어야 해요!

1. 문제 파악하기
   Who, speaker → 화자의 직업을 묻는 문제임을 파악합니다.

2. 선택지 키워드 파악하기
   (A) 수리 기술자 (B) 부동산 중개인 (C) 서비스 직원 (D) 레스토랑 지배인

3. 담화 앞부분에서 단서 파악하여 정답 선택하기
   Appliances, you filed a complaint
   → 고객의 불만에 응대하고 있음을 알 수 있으므로 (C)를 정답으로 선택하고 다음 문제로 넘어갑니다.

출제 유형 3 세부 사항 문제

1 질문 유형

- 이유/방법을 묻는 문제

  How can the **listeners get** more **information**? 청자들은 어떻게 정보를 더 얻을 수 있는가?
  Why does the **speaker apologize**? 화자는 왜 사과하는가?
  Why should the **listener come to work early** tomorrow?
  청자는 왜 내일 일찍 출근해야 하는가?

- 키워드를 제시하는 세부 사항 문제

  What is **scheduled** for **two o'clock**? 2시에 예정되어 있는 일은 무엇인가?
  According to the speaker, what can the **listeners do on a Web site**?
  화자에 따르면, 청자들은 웹사이트에서 무엇을 할 수 있는가?

> **800+**
>
> - 문제점/걱정하는 점을 묻는 문제
>
>   **What** is the **speaker concerned** about? 화자는 무엇에 대해 걱정하는가?
>   **What problem** does the speaker mention? 화자는 무슨 문제점을 언급하는가?

출제 포인트
특정 정보를 묻는 문제로 주로 담화 중반부에서 단서가 제시됩니다. 문제점/걱정하는 점을 묻는 문제, 이유/방법을 묻는 문제, 특정 키워드에 관한 정보를 묻는 문제 등이 출제되므로 질문 내용을 정확하게 파악할 수 있어야 합니다.

2 핵심 포인트

1. 세부 사항 문제는 담화에 나오는 표현이 패러프레이징 되어 보기에 제시되는 경우가 많으므로 패러프레이징에 익숙해져야 합니다.

   review the sales figures 매출 수치를 검토하다
   → go over the sales data 매출 자료를 검토하다
   prepare new work spaces 새 업무 장소 준비하기
   → set up workstations 업무 자리 준비하기

2. 세부 사항 문제는 세 문제 중 주로 두 번째 문제로 제시되므로 첫 번째 문제(주로 주제/목적/장소/직업 문제)를 빠르게 풀고 세부 사항 문제의 단서를 파악하는 데 집중하는 것이 좋습니다.

> **800+**
>
> 3. 문제점 문제는 but, unfortunately, can't, we're not able to ~ 와 같은 부정어 표현이나 It seems that, the problem is ~ 와 같은 표현 뒤에 단서가 제시됩니다.
>
>   **We're not able to** finish the budget report until the data is revised.
>   우리는 자료가 수정될 때까지 예산 보고서를 끝낼 수 없습니다.

출제 포인트
이유/방법 문제는 정보를 얻을 수 있는 방법, 할인 방법, 담당자 연락 방법 등을 묻는 문제가 자주 출제됩니다.

⚠ **주의**
세부 사항을 묻는 문제는 키워드인 의문사, 명사(시간 표현, 장소 등), 동사 등을 빠르게 파악하는 연습을 해야 합니다.
What, When, Where, Why, How long(much/many), tonight, what advice, during the meeting 등

세부 사항 문제

🎧 Day 09_ P4_03.mp3

[문제지]

According to the speaker, **what** has **decreased this year**?
(A) Business trip spending
(B) Customer complaints
(C) Office utility bills
(D) Supply expenses

화자에 따르면, 올해 무엇이 감소했는가?
(A) 출장 경비
(B) 고객 불만
(C) 사무실 공공요금
(D) 사무용품 비용

[담화] [BR]

talk

M: Good afternoon everyone, and welcome to this awards luncheon. It's my honor to present the first award to Alicia Decker for leading the company's eco-friendly initiative. Thanks to her efforts, nearly 80% of our clients have chosen to receive paperless correspondence. By greatly cutting down the amount of paper we need, **her program has significantly reduced the amount of money we spent on office supplies this year.** For those of you who are interested in environmentally friendly practices, don't forget to sign up for the workshop she will lead next month at the Denver Convention Center. Come up to receive your award, Ms. Decker.

담화

남: 안녕하세요 여러분. 시상식 오찬에 오신 것을 환영합니다. 회사의 친환경 계획을 이끌어주신 Alicia Decker 씨에게 첫 번째 상을 수여하게 되어 영광입니다. 그녀의 노력 덕분에 거의 80%의 고객들이 종이를 쓰지 않는 서신을 받는 것을 선택하였습니다. 우리가 필요로 하는 종이의 양을 크게 줄임으로써, **그녀의 프로그램은 우리는 올해 사무용품 비용을 상당히 줄였습니다**. 친환경적인 실행에 관심 있는 분들은 Denver 컨벤션 센터에서 다음 달에 그녀가 진행할 워크숍에 등록하는 것을 잊지 마세요. 올라오셔서 상을 받으시기 바랍니다, Decker 씨.

이렇게 풀어요

문제와 선택지의 키워드는 담화가 시작되기 전에 미리 파악되어 있어야 해요!

1. **문제 파악하기**
   what, decreased this year → 올해 무엇이 감소되었는지 찾는 문제임을 파악합니다.

2. **선택지 키워드 파악하기**
   (A) 출장 경비 (B) 고객 불만 (C) 사무실 공공요금 (D) 사무용품 비용

3. **문제의 키워드 주위에서 단서 캐치하여 정답 선택하기**
   her program has significantly reduced the amount of money we spent on office supplies this year
   → amount of money we spent on office supplies를 supply expenses로 표현한 (D)를 정답으로 선택하고 다음 문제로 넘어갑니다.

따라 하면 문제가 풀리는
연습 문제

문제와 각 선택지의 키워드에 표시하세요. 그러고 나서 담화를 듣고 빈칸에 들어갈 말을 받아쓴 후 정답을 선택해 보세요.

01. What is the announcement about?

(A) A new grocery store (B) A special sale

announcement

> W: Thank you for _____ at Wendy's Mart today! We'd like to _____ that we're now offering a 30% _____ on all vegetables and fruits in the _____ section. This is for Wendy's _____ _____ only.

02. What is the purpose of the call?

(A) To schedule a delivery (B) To report a faulty item

telephone message

> M: Hi, this is Tim Smith from Cedarville Construction. The wireless _____ _____ that I ordered last week _____ yesterday. I charged it for a full night and _____ it to my work site. Unfortunately, it _____ _____. The battery indicator is green. That should mean it is _____ _____.

03. Who is the intended audience for the announcement?

(A) Volunteers (B) Tourists

announcement

> M: Hello, everyone, and welcome to Delaware Nature Park. Before we _____ this year's Park Cleaning Day, thank you for _____ _____ this annual event. More and more tourists and hikers are _____ us every year. So, we need to _____ _____ _____ to preserve this park.

paraphrasing   주어진 어휘 또는 표현과 의미가 동일한 것을 연결하세요.

1. offer a discount   •   • (a) tool
2. power drill   •   • (b) price reduction
3. annual   •   • (c) once a year

04. Who most likely is the caller?

(A) A customer service agent   (B) A restaurant chef

telephone message

> M: Hello, this is Andrea Denzel from the _____ _____ Department at Happy Kitchen Supplies. I'm calling to let you know about the _____ of your order. The multi-purpose oven you ordered through our Web site is _____ _____ _____.

05. Who most likely is Emily White?

(A) A teacher   (B) A writer

talk

> W: I'm honored to _____ Emily White who will announce the _____ of this year's Dickenson Award. She also _____ this award last year. As you already know, it is awarded to the most _____ _____ of the year.

06. What can listeners do on the company's Web site?

(A) Get an application form   (B) Select a parking space

announcement

> W: I'm very pleased to announce that the _____ of the new parking _____ will be completed at the end of this month. As planned, this five-story building will _____ all of the employees' cars. The security office will take applications for _____ parking _____ next week. You can _____ the _____ from the company Web site.

---

paraphrasing 주어진 어휘 또는 표현과 의미가 동일한 것을 연결하세요.

4. through our Web Site   •   • (a) hold
5. winner   •   • (b) recipient
6. accommodate   •   • (c) online

실전 문제

01. Who is the speaker addressing?
    (A) Postal workers
    (B) Corporate accountants
    (C) Web designers
    (D) Research scientists

02. Why is the speaker giving the talk?
    (A) To gather opinions from listeners
    (B) To give an overview of a class
    (C) To recruit volunteers for a task
    (D) To explain a regulation change

03. What will the speaker most likely do next?
    (A) Pass out brochures
    (B) Write down some questions
    (C) Demonstrate some equipment
    (D) Present a video clip

04. What does the advertisement inform listeners about?
    (A) A loyalty program
    (B) A product launch
    (C) A store relocation
    (D) A clearance sale

05. What kind of business is Sierra Summit?
    (A) An auto manufacturer
    (B) A clothing designer
    (C) A camping store
    (D) A coffee shop

06. According to the speaker, what can be done on a Web site?
    (A) Downloading a coupon
    (B) Viewing a map
    (C) Placing an order
    (D) Entering a contest

07. Where does the speaker work?
    (A) At an architectural firm
    (B) At an appliance store
    (C) At a real estate agency
    (D) At a financial institution

08. According to the speaker, what is the problem?
    (A) An employee lost some documents.
    (B) A computer is not working.
    (C) A payment was received late.
    (D) A product has been discontinued.

09. Why should the listener call the speaker?
    (A) To request a refund
    (B) To get a product description
    (C) To confirm a preferred size
    (D) To provide a mailing address

10. Where most likely are the listeners?
    (A) On a train
    (B) At an airport
    (C) In a department store
    (D) At a bus stop

11. What are the listeners asked to do?
    (A) Stay in the area
    (B) Exchange a ticket
    (C) Call a helpline
    (D) Present an ID card

12. What can the listeners get at the counter?
    (A) Some refreshments
    (B) A discount coupon
    (C) An updated schedule
    (D) A sign-up form

13. What does the speaker say he is happy about?
    (A) Launching a product successfully
    (B) Opening another branch
    (C) Receiving a promotion
    (D) Reducing energy use

14. What kind of business does the speaker work at?
    (A) A law firm
    (B) An appliance manufacturer
    (C) An advertising agency
    (D) An electricity service provider

15. What is scheduled for June 9?
    (A) A company-wide training session
    (B) An international expansion
    (C) A factory inspection
    (D) A board meeting

16. What kind of service is being advertised?
    (A) Software customization
    (B) Electronics repair
    (C) Battery recycling
    (D) Mobile data

17. How can the listeners get a discount?
    (A) By joining a membership
    (B) By signing up a friend
    (C) By providing some feedback
    (D) By entering a code

18. According to the speaker, what can be found on a Web site?
    (A) A membership application
    (B) An introductory video
    (C) A business profile
    (D) A service price list

19. What is the main topic of the message?
    (A) Fashion trends
    (B) Employee training
    (C) New software
    (D) Annual inventory

20. What does the speaker say pleases him?
    (A) Friendly customer support
    (B) Increased work efficiency
    (C) Seasonal promotions
    (D) Fast service

21. What does the speaker want to discuss in more detail?
    (A) Receiving e-mail updates
    (B) Hiring more employees
    (C) Changing a supplier
    (D) Holding a training session

22. Who most likely is the speaker?
    (A) A salesperson
    (B) A building tenant
    (C) A real estate agent
    (D) A maintenance worker

23. What does the speaker say he can do tomorrow?
    (A) Repair an appliance
    (B) Make a delivery
    (C) Conduct an inspection
    (D) Review a contract

24. What does the speaker ask the listener to confirm?
    (A) A security code
    (B) An appliance brand
    (C) An appointment time
    (D) A warranty agreement

'멋진 당신, 오늘도 화이팅'

DAY 10

오늘의 학습 포인트

PART 2. 평서문
1. 정보 및 사실 전달
   - 동의, 감사, 추가 정보 전달 답변
2. 의견 전달
3. 감정 표현
   - 좋은 일: 축하와 격려, 안 좋은 일: 위로, 칭찬: 감사
4. 정보 요청
   - I'd like to ~, I'd like you to ~, I wonder ~, I was wondering ~

PART 4. 문제 유형
1. 제안·요청 문제
   - 담화 마지막 부분
2. 다음 할 일/일어날 일을 묻는 문제
   - 담화 마지막 부분
3. 의도 파악 문제
   - 문맥 파악

PART 2 평서문

평서문은 매회 1~2문제가 출제돼요!

적용 기술

[기적의 필기노트] 38P
LC 기술 27

🎧 Day 10_ P2_01.mp3

🔒 확인 문제 ❶

Mark your answer.

(A)   (B)

⚠️ 주의

평서문도 동의함을 나타낼 때는 Yes, 반대함을 나타낼 때는 No로 답변할 수 있습니다.
Q. The new secretary is very hardworking.
새 비서가 아주 열심히 일합니다.
A. **Yes**, she is also good at foreign languages.
네. 게다가 외국어도 잘 해요.

출제 유형 1 정보 및 사실 전달

800+

정보를 제공하거나 객관적인 사실을 전달하는 문장입니다. 평서문에는 Yes/No 응답, 의문문으로 되묻는 응답 등 다양한 답변이 가능하므로 예시를 알아 둡시다.

· 정보 전달에 대해 동의하는 답변

Q. Our security system needs to be inspected.
우리 보안 시스템은 점검될 필요가 있습니다.
A. You're right. It's urgent. 맞습니다. 시급합니다.

· 정보를 알려주는 것에 대해 감사를 전하는 답변

Q. The annual conference has been postponed until next month.
연례 회의가 다음 달로 연기되었어요.
A. Thanks for letting me know. 알려주셔서 감사합니다.

· 사실 전달에 대해 추가 정보를 묻는 답변

Q. I'd like to cancel my reservation for tomorrow. 내일 예약을 취소하고 싶습니다.
A. Would you like to reschedule it? 일정을 다시 잡으시겠어요?

풀이 방법 정보 및 사실 전달

🎧 Day 10_ P2_02.mp3

[BR - AU]

Hello, I have a job interview with Mr. Watson.
(A) The hotel room has a nice view.
(B) You must be Juliet Sanderson, right?
(C) Turn in the application on time.

안녕하세요, 저는 Watson 씨와 면접이 잡혀 있습니다.
(A) 그 호텔 방은 경관이 좋아요.
(B) 당신이 Juliet Sanderson 씨겠군요, 맞죠?
(C) 지원서를 제때 제출하세요.

✓ 이렇게 풀어요

1. 질문 내용 파악하기 Hello, I have a job interview with Mr. Watson.
   면접이 있다는 사실 전달

2. 선택지 들으며 오답 소거하여 정답 선택하기
   (A̶) The hotel room has a nice view. → 유사 발음 오답 (interview-view)
   (B) You must be Juliet Sanderson, right? → 정답으로 선택
   (C̶) Turn in the application on time. → 연상 어휘 오답 (job-application)

출제 유형 2 · 의견 전달

900+

'행사가 훌륭했다', '날씨가 좋다', '사람이 좋다' 등과 같은 긍정적인 의견을 말하거나, '유감이다'라는 부정적인 의견을 말하는 문장입니다.

Q. Your presentation was well-prepared. 당신의 발표는 잘 준비되었던데요.
A. It went smoother than I thought. 제가 생각했던 것보다 순조롭게 진행되었어요.

Q. I think this training program is worth taking.
이 교육 프로그램은 들을 가치가 있다고 생각합니다.
A. Why don't you register the next session as well? 다음 세션도 등록하는 게 어때요?

Q. I think we need more refreshments for the upcoming event.
곧 있을 행사를 위해서 더 많은 다과가 필요하다고 생각합니다.
A. I'll call the catering company this afternoon.
오늘 오후에 제가 출장 요리 업체에 연락하겠습니다.

🎧 Day 10_P2_03.mp3

🔒 **확인 문제 ❷**

Mark your answer.

(A)　　(B)

풀이 방법 · 의견 전달

🎧 Day 10_P2_04.mp3

[AU - US]

I thought it is easier to collect customer feedback via online.
(A) I was very satisfied.
(B) Depending on what you want to know.
(C) Fill out the blanks.

온라인을 통해 고객 의견을 수집하는 게 더 쉬울 것 같았어요.
(A) 저는 아주 만족했어요.
(B) 당신이 무엇을 알고 싶어하는지에 따라 달라요.
(C) 빈칸을 채우세요.

> **이렇게 풀어요**
>
> 1. 질문 내용 파악하기   I thought it is easier to collect customer feedback via online.
>   고객 의견을 수집하는 게 더 쉬울 줄 알았다는 의견 전달
>
> 2. 선택지 들으며 오답 소거하여 정답 선택하기
>   (A) I was very satisfied. → 연상 어휘 오답(customer feedback-satisfied)
>   (B) Depending on what you want to know. → 정답으로 선택
>   (C) Fill out the blanks. → 연상 어휘 오답(customer feedback-fill out the blanks)

🎧 Day 10_ P2_05.mp3

🔒 확인 문제 ❸

Mark your answer.

(A)　　　(B)

출제 유형 3 · 감정 표현

800+

후회, 실망, 칭찬, 놀람 등 화자의 감정을 전달하는 평서문도 자주 등장합니다. 이때 논리적으로 좋은 일에 대해서는 축하와 격려를, 안 좋은 일에 대해서는 위로를, 칭찬하는 말에 대해서는 감사의 표현을 정답으로 고르면 됩니다.

Q. You look wonderful in that suit tonight. 오늘 밤 그 양복이 잘 어울리시네요.
A. I bought it last weekend for the banquet. 연회를 위해서 지난 주말에 샀습니다.

Q. I shouldn't have taken this class. It's too difficult.
　이 수업을 듣지 말았어야 했어요. 너무 어려워요.
A. It'll get better. I can help you. 좋아질 거예요. 제가 도와드릴게요.

Q. I finally finished the project by myself. 마침내 제가 프로젝트를 스스로 마쳤어요.
A. Congratulations! Be proud of yourself. 축하합니다! 자신을 자랑스러워 하세요.

(B)  정답

풀이 방법 · 감정 표현

🎧 Day 10_ P2_06.mp3

[US - BR]

I was surprised to hear that Mr. Wilson will retire next month.
(A) She won the first prize.
(B) I had to replace both tires.
(C) Me too. Let's throw a party for him.

Wilson 씨가 다음 달에 퇴직한다는 걸 듣고 놀랐어요.
(A) 그녀는 1등을 했어요.
(B) 저는 타이어를 둘 다 교체해야 했어요.
(C) 저도요. 그를 위한 파티를 엽시다.

이렇게 풀어요

1. 질문 내용 파악하기　I was **surprised to hear** that **Mr. Wilson will retire** next month.
　　　　　　　　　　　　Wilson 씨가 퇴직한다는 걸 듣고 놀란

2. 선택지 들으며 오답 소거하여 정답 선택하기
　(A) **She** won the first prize. → 주체가 맞지 않는 응답(Mr. Wilson-She)
　(B) I had to replace both **tires**. → 유사 발음 오답(retire-tires)
　(C) Me too. Let's throw a party for him. → 정답으로 선택

출제 유형 4 — 정보 요청

'I'd like to ~', 'I'd like you to ~', 'I wonder ~', 'I was wondering ~' 구문을 이용하여 구체적인 정보를 요청하는 문장입니다.

Q. **I'd like to** know if the software on my computer has been updated while I was away. 제가 없었던 동안 제 컴퓨터에 있는 소프트웨어가 업데이트되었는지 알고 싶습니다.

A. Yes, the technical support team worked on it. 네, 기술 지원팀이 그 작업을 했어요.

Q. **I wonder** who'll be hired for the marketing manager position.
누가 마케팅 부장 자리에 채용될지 궁금합니다.

A. I heard they are still discussing. 아직 논의 중이라고 들었습니다.

Q. **I was wondering** if the deadline for the annual report was extended.
연례 보고서의 마감일이 연장되었는지 궁금합니다.

A. It's still due next Monday. 여전히 다음 주 월요일까지입니다.

Day 10_ P2_07.mp3

🔒 **확인 문제 ❹**

Mark your answer.

(A)   (B)

출제 포인트
'I wonder + 의문사' 뿐만 아니라 I wonder if/whether로 시작하는 평서문은 끝을 올려 마치 의문문인 것처럼 사실을 확인하려 할 때도 많이 쓰입니다.

정답 ❶ (A)

 **정보 요청**

Day 10_ P2_08.mp3

`AU - US`

I'd like you to fill out this form if you are new here.
(A) I already renewed my contract.
(B) Sure, I'd be happy to.
(C) No, I'm not familiar with this town.

여기 처음 오셨다면 이 양식을 작성해 주세요.
(A) 저는 이미 계약을 갱신했어요.
(B) 물론이죠, 기꺼이 할게요.
(C) 아뇨, 저는 이 동네에 익숙하지 않아요.

> ✏ **이렇게 풀어요**
>
> 1. 질문 내용 파악하기 **I'd like you to fill out this form** if you are new here.
>   양식을 작성해달라고 요청
>
> 2. 선택지 들으며 오답 소거하여 정답 선택하기
>   (A̶) I already **renewed** my contract. → 유사 발음 오답(new-renewed)
>   (B) Sure, I'd be happy to. → 정답으로 선택
>   (C̶) No, I'm **not familiar** with this town. → 연상 어휘 오답(new-not familiar)

PART 2 평서문

따라 하면 문제가 풀리는
연습 문제

🎧 Day 10_ P2_09.mp3
📍 정답 및 해석 p.79

각 질문과 보기를 들으며 빈칸을 채운 뒤 정답에는 O, 오답에는 X 표시하세요.

01. One of the _____ just _____ _____ on the floor.
   (A) I'll send someone to _____ it _____. [   ]
   (B) Did you _____ some _____ of it? [   ]

02. I _____ _____ completing the project.
   (A) I haven't been _____ _____. [   ]
   (B) You must be _____. [   ]

03. Ms. Jacobson is _____ _____ over there.
   (A) That _____ is too _____. [   ]
   (B) Thanks, I'll go _____ _____. [   ]

04. You must be _____ about the _____ of the new store.
   (A) How do I _____ _____? [   ]
   (B) I can _____ _____. [   ]

05. It _____ _____ _____ _____ to see Carla before she left.
   (A) The _____ on the _____ is better. [   ]
   (B) _____ _____, we were _____ on vacation. [   ]

06. I want to _____ this hair dryer.
   (A) Sure, please _____ _____. [   ]
   (B) Thanks, but I like my _____ _____. [   ]

07. I'd like to _____ a _____ for tonight, please.
   (A) Sorry, we're all _____ _____. [   ]
   (B) I can _____ _____ with that. [   ]

08. Your _____ _____ will be ready to _____ _____ in 20 minutes.
   (A) Okay, I'll just _____ _____. [   ]
   (B) Can you _____ them _____ _____? [   ]

01. Mark your answer on your answer sheet.
(A)　　　　(B)　　　　(C)

02. Mark your answer on your answer sheet.
(A)　　　　(B)　　　　(C)

03. Mark your answer on your answer sheet.
(A)　　　　(B)　　　　(C)

04. Mark your answer on your answer sheet.
(A)　　　　(B)　　　　(C)

05. Mark your answer on your answer sheet.
(A)　　　　(B)　　　　(C)

06. Mark your answer on your answer sheet.
(A)　　　　(B)　　　　(C)

07. Mark your answer on your answer sheet.
(A)　　　　(B)　　　　(C)

08. Mark your answer on your answer sheet.
(A)　　　　(B)　　　　(C)

09. Mark your answer on your answer sheet.
(A)　　　　(B)　　　　(C)

10. Mark your answer on your answer sheet.
(A)　　　　(B)　　　　(C)

11. Mark your answer on your answer sheet.
(A)　　　　(B)　　　　(C)

12. Mark your answer on your answer sheet.
(A)　　　　(B)　　　　(C)

13. Mark your answer on your answer sheet.
(A)　　　　(B)　　　　(C)

14. Mark your answer on your answer sheet.
(A)　　　　(B)　　　　(C)

15. Mark your answer on your answer sheet.
(A)　　　　(B)　　　　(C)

16. Mark your answer on your answer sheet.
(A)　　　　(B)　　　　(C)

PART 4

제안·요청 문제 / 다음 할 일 문제 / 의도 파악 문제

제안·요청 문제는 매회 4~6문제, 다음 할 일 문제는 매회 3~4문제,
의도 파악 문제는 매회 3문제 출제됩니다!

적용 기술

[기적의 필기노트] 69P, 76P
LC 기술 51, 57

출제 유형 1 — 제안·요청 문제

출제 포인트
화자가 청자에게 요청, 지시, 제안, 추천한 것이 무엇인지 묻는 문제입니다. 주로 세 번째 문제로 나오므로 담화 마지막 부분에 단서가 언급되는 경우가 많습니다.

1 질문 유형

What does the **speaker request** that the **listeners** do?
화자는 청자들이 무엇을 하기를 요청하는가?

What does the **speaker offer to do**? 화자는 무엇을 하겠다고 제안하는가?

What are the **listeners asked to do**? 청자들은 무엇을 하라는 요청을 받는가?

What does the **speaker suggest** that the **listeners** do?
화자는 청자들이 무엇을 할 것을 제안하는가?

What are the **listeners advised to do**? 화자들은 무엇을 하라고 권고받는가?

⚠ 주의

speaker offer to do로 묻는 문제는 상대방에게 부탁하는 것이 아니라 화자가 직접 무언가를 하겠다고 하는 부분에서 단서를 파악해야 합니다.
I'd be happy to explain the new procedure.
제가 새 절차를 설명하게 되어 기쁩니다.

2 핵심 포인트

1. 제안이나 요청을 하는 평서문, 명령문, 의문문의 형태를 알아 둡시다.

I recommend ~할 것을 권장합니다	I encourage you to ~할 것을 권장합니다
I suggest you to ~할 것을 제안합니다	Please ~해주세요
Remember to ~할 것을 잊지 마세요	Be sure to 꼭 ~하세요
Why don't you ~하는 게 어때요?	Can you ~해주실 수 있으세요?

[단서] **Can you** ask Steven about the starting date?
　　　시작 날짜에 대해 Steven에게 물어봐주시겠어요?

[정답] Contact a colleague 동료에게 연락하기

[단서] **I encourage you to** download her newest e-book.
　　　그녀의 최신 e-book을 다운로드 할 것을 권장합니다.

[정답] Download a book 책 다운로드 하기

[단서] **I recommend** leaving your bags under the desk.
　　　여러분들의 가방을 책상 아래에 두는 것을 권장합니다.

[정답] Put their belongings somewhere else 다른 곳에 소지품 두기

출제 포인트
PART 3과 마찬가지로 PART 4에서도 제안·요청을 하는 표현 뒤에 나오는 단서 내용이 보기에서 패러프레이징 되는 경우가 많습니다.
· photo ID card
　→ identification
· take pictures
　→ a photo shoot

2. 제안·요청 문제는 선택지가 동사구로 이루어져 있으므로 담화를 듣기 전에 제일 앞에 제시되는 동사 위주로 의미를 파악해 두어야 합니다.

> contact 연락하다　send 보내다　review 검토하다　submit 제출하다　sign 서명하다
> complete 작성하다, 완료하다　visit 방문하다　sign up 신청하다　watch 시청하다, 보다

제안·요청 문제

🎧 Day 10_ P4_01.mp3

[문제지]

What does the **speaker request** that the **listeners do**?
(A) Conduct a survey
(B) Review a proposal
(C) Gather some donations
(D) Submit recommendations

화자는 청자들이 무엇을 하기를 요청하는가?
(A) 설문조사 시행하기
(B) 제안서 검토하기
(C) 기부금 모으기
(D) 추천 제출하기

[담화] [BR]

excerpt from a meeting

M: That's about it for this planning meeting. I'm sure that this fundraiser will be a huge success. Our organization has made some major progress in providing educational and employment opportunities to the needy, and I'm very proud of that. We'll need to finalize the venue for this event, but I'm still waiting to hear back from one of our sponsors. I'll definitely do that by the end of this week, though. Also, we need to decide on a catering company. I'd like some input from all of you on that. **Please send me an e-mail with a place that you would recommend.**

회의 발췌록

남: 이번 기획 회의는 대략 이 정도입니다. 저는 이 모금 행사가 큰 성공을 거두리라 확신합니다. 우리 단체는 빈곤한 사람들에게 교육적인 고용 기회를 제공해 주는 것에 몇몇 주요한 발전을 이루었으며, 저는 그것을 매우 자랑스럽게 생각합니다. 우리는 이번 행사를 위한 장소를 최종 확정지어야 할 필요가 있지만, 저는 여전히 우리의 후원자들 중 한 분의 의견을 듣기 위해 기다리고 있습니다. 하지만 이번 주 말까지는 확실히 할 것입니다. 또한 우리는 출장 요리 업체를 결정해야 합니다. 그 부분에 대해 여러분들의 의견을 듣고 싶습니다. **여러분이 추천하시는 곳을 적어 저에게 이메일로 보내주시기 바랍니다.**

🔍 이렇게 풀어요

문제와 선택지의 키워드는 담화가 시작되기 전에 미리 파악되어 있어야 해요!

1. **문제 파악하기**
   What, speaker request, listeners do → 화자가 청자에게 요청한 사항을 묻고 있음을 파악합니다.

2. **선택지 키워드 파악하기**
   (A) 설문조사 (B) 제안시 (C) 기부금 (D) 추천

3. **담화 마지막 부분에서 단서 파악하여 정답 선택하기**
   Please send me an e-mail with a place that you would recommend.
   → Submit recommendations로 표현한 (D)를 정답으로 선택하고 다음 문제로 넘어갑니다.

PART 4 제안·요청 문제 / 다음 할 일 문제 / 의도 파악 문제

출제 유형 2 **다음 할 일/일어날 일을 묻는 문제**

출제 포인트
다음에 할 일이나 일어날 일을 묻는 문제의 정답 단서는 주로 담화의 마지막에서 제시됩니다.

1 질문 유형

What is the **speaker** going to **do next**? 화자는 다음에 무엇을 할 것인가?
What will the **listeners** do next? 청자들은 다음에 무엇을 할 것인가?
What will **happen next week**? 다음 주에 무슨 일이 있을 것인가?
What will the **listeners hear next**? 청자들은 다음에 무엇을 들을 것인가?

2 핵심 포인트

1. 다음 할 일/일어날 일에 대한 단서를 끌고 나오는 표현을 알아 두어야 합니다.

> Now, let's 이제, ~합시다
> Now, I'll[I'm going to] 이제, 제가 ~하겠습니다
> But first, let me 하지만 먼저 제가 ~하겠습니다
> Now, we'd like to 이제, 우리는 ~하고자 합니다
> Before I ~, I'll 제가 ~하기 전에, ~하겠습니다
> To start, let me 시작하기 위해, 제가 ~하겠습니다

[단서] **Now, I'll** give you a tour of our factory. 이제, 제가 저희 공장을 견학시켜 드리겠습니다.
[정답] Tour a facility 시설 견학하기

[단서] **Let's** take a look at some examples of the product.
제품의 견본을 몇 가지 살펴봅시다.
[정답] View sample item 샘플 상품 보기

[단서] **Let me** talk about my own experience. 저의 경험을 이야기해 드리겠습니다.
[정답] Give a personal experience 개인적인 경험 말하기

2. 미래 시간 키워드가 언급된 문제의 경우 키워드가 담화에서 그대로 언급되는 경우가 많으므로 반드시 키워드를 기억해야 합니다.

What will happen in **September**? 9월에 무엇이 일어날 것인가?
What does the speaker say will happen **in the afternoon**?
화자는 오후에 무엇이 일어날 것이라고 말하는가?

출제 포인트
자주 출제되는 미래 시간 키워드로는 tonight, next month, next week, tomorrow 등이 있습니다.

다음 할 일/일어날 일을 묻는 문제

🎧 Day 10_ P4_02.mp3

[문제지]

What is the **speaker** going to **do next**?
(A) Introduce a personal assistant
(B) Hand out registration details
(C) Reserve tickets for an event
(D) Sign some autographs

화자는 다음에 무엇을 할 것인가?
(A) 개인 비서 소개하기
(B) 등록에 관련된 세부 사항 나누어주기
(C) 행사 티켓 예약하기
(D) 사인하기

[담화] [US]

excerpt from a meeting
W: And finally, don't forget that next month the Motor City Automobile Expo will come to Daytona. It's a great way to keep up on the latest trends in our industry, so I strongly recommend going to it. Actually, I heard that the famous race car driver Tyler McCoy is going to be signing autographs at the event. If you're a fan, you won't want to miss out on this chance to see him in person. For anyone who is interested in going, **come on up here and I'll give you a pamphlet that explains how to register.** It also has more specific details about the expo.

회의 발췌록
여: 그리고 마지막으로, 다음 달 Motor City 자동차 박람회가 Daytona에 온다는 것을 잊지 마세요. 우리 업계의 최신 경향을 알 수 있는 좋은 방법이므로 저는 그곳에 갈 것을 강력히 추천합니다. 사실, 유명한 경주용 차 운전자인 Tyler McCoy 씨가 그 행사에서 사인회를 할 예정입니다. 만약 여러분이 팬이라면, 직접 그를 만날 기회를 놓치는 것을 원하지 않을 것입니다. 가기를 원하는 분들은 **여기 올라오시면 어떻게 등록하는지 설명해 놓은 팸플릿을 드리겠습니다.** 또한 박람회에 대한 구체적인 세부 사항도 수록되어 있습니다.

💡 이렇게 풀어요

문제와 선택지의 키워드는 담화가 시작되기 전에 미리 파악되어 있어야 해요!

1. **문제 파악하기**
   What, speaker, do next → 화자가 다음에 할 일을 파악해야 합니다.

2. **선택지 키워드 파악하기**
   (A) 개인 비서 소개하기
   (B) 등록에 관련된 세부 사항 나누어주기
   (C) 행사 티켓 예약하기
   (D) 사인하기

3. **담화 마지막 부분에서 단서 파악하여 정답 선택하기**
   come on up here and I'll give you a pamphlet that explains how to register.
   → Hand out registration details로 패러프레이징 된 (B)를 정답으로 선택하고 다음 문제로 넘어갑니다.

적용 기술

[기적의 필기노트] 84P
LC 기술 63

출제 포인트
화자가 언급한 말이 담화의 맥락에서 어떤 의미로 쓰였는지 파악해야 합니다.

출제 포인트
Why does the speaker say로 물을 경우 선택지는 to부정사 형태로 제시됩니다. 따라서 따옴표 안의 문장을 왜 말하는지 목적을 묻는 문제로 파악하면 됩니다.

⚠️ **주의**
화자의 의도 파악 문제의 정답은 문제로 제시된 화자의 말이 단순히 유사한 의미로 패러프레이징된 표현이 아닙니다. 보기가 문제 표현과 직접적으로 의미가 연관될수록 오답일 확률이 높습니다.

출제 유형 3 | 의도 파악 문제

800+

1 질문 유형

Why does the speaker **say**, "~"? 화자는 왜 "~"라고 말하는가?

What does the speaker **mean** when he says, "~"?
화자가 "~"라고 말할 때 의미하는 바는 무엇인가?

900+

What does the speaker **imply** when she says, "~"?
화자가 "~"라고 말할 때 암시하는 바는 무엇인가?

800+

2 핵심 포인트

1. 반드시 **문제를 먼저 읽습니다.**
   담화를 듣기 전에 따옴표 안의 문장을 읽어 두고 어떤 내용이 나올지 예측하며 들어야 합니다.

   What does the speaker mean when he says, "we've already received 60 orders"?
   화자가 "우리는 이미 60건의 주문을 받았어요"라고 말할 때 의미하는 바는 무엇인가?

   → 주문을 받는 것에 관한 내용이 전개될 것임을 예측합니다.

2. 정답의 단서는 **앞뒤 문맥과 연관**되어 있습니다.
   정답은 앞뒤 문맥과 밀접한 관련이 있으므로 전반적인 흐름을 잘 파악해야 합니다.

   [담화] M: I heard that you are worried about our new sandwich menu. Well, we've already received 60 orders. So, you should be quite satisfied.
   우리의 새 샌드위치 메뉴에 대해 걱정한다고 들었어요. 음, 우리는 이미 60개의 주문을 받았어요. 그러니, 당신은 꽤 만족하실 거예요.

   [문제] Q. What does the speaker mean when he says, "we've already received 60 orders"?
   화자가 "우리는 이미 60건의 주문을 받았어요"라고 말할 때 의미하는 바는 무엇인가?

   [정답] A. A new menu item has been successful. 새 메뉴 품목이 성공적이다.

3. 화자의 **어조를 통해 긍정적인 뉘앙스인지 부정적인 뉘앙스**인지 파악할 수 있습니다.
   긍정적인 뉘앙스일 경우 높은 어조, 부정적인 뉘앙스일 경우 낮은 어조로 주로 말하므로 문맥을 이해하는 데 도움이 될 수 있습니다.

4. 의미가 굳어진 관용 표현을 외우기보다는 **담화의 맥락을 파악하는 것이 중요합니다.**
   'It's up in the air(아직 미정입니다)'와 같이 의미가 정해져 있는 관용 표현보다는 일반적인 문장이 주로 출제됩니다. 따라서 어조와 맥락을 통해 의미를 파악하는 연습을 해야 합니다.

의도 파악 문제

🎧 Day 10_ P4_03.mp3

[문제지]

Why does the speaker **say**, **"She's scheduled to interview me from 2:30 to 3 P.M."**?
(A) To recommend cancelling an event
(B) To suggest a meeting time
(C) To designate a location
(D) To offer his assistance

화자는 왜 "그녀가 2시 30분부터 3시까지 저를 인터뷰하기로 되어 있습니다"라고 말하는가?
(A) 행사를 취소할 것을 권하기 위해
(B) 만나는 시간을 제안하기 위해
(C) 위치를 지정하기 위해
(D) 그의 도움을 제안하기 위해

[담화] [AU]

telephone message

M: Debbie, this is Allen. There's a journalist coming to our office later today to interview me about the ongoing Kennedy Tower project. Since you played a big part in it as well, she might want to speak with you while she's here. I forwarded the e-mail she sent me with questions she expects to ask. **She's scheduled to interview me from 2:30 to 3 P.M.** Let me know if you're available this afternoon to meet her. I can send her to your office.

전화 메시지

남: Debbie, 저 Allen입니다. 진행 중인 Kennedy Tower 프로젝트에 대하여 저를 인터뷰하기 위하여 오늘 늦게 우리의 사무실에 오기로 한 기자가 있습니다. 당신도 그 일에 대해 큰 역할을 했기 때문에, 그녀가 여기 있는 동안 당신과 이야기 나누기를 원할 거예요. 그녀가 묻기로 되어 있는 질문이 포함된 그녀의 이메일을 당신에게 보냈어요. 그녀가 2시 30분부터 3시까지 저를 인터뷰하기로 되어 있습니다. 오늘 오후 당신이 그녀를 만날 시간이 괜찮은지를 알려주세요. 제가 그녀를 당신의 사무실로 보내겠습니다.

🔍 이렇게 풀어요

문제와 선택지의 키워드는 담화가 시작되기 전에 미리 파악되어 있어야 해요!

1. **문제 파악하기**
   "She's scheduled to interview me from 2:30 to 3 P.M." → 이 문장의 앞뒤 문맥을 파악할 준비를 합니다.

2. **선택지 키워드 파악하기**
   (A) 행사 취소 (B) 만나는 시간 (C) 위치 지정 (D) 도움 제안

3. **문제의 키워드 주위에서 단서 캐치하여 정답 선택하기**
   She's scheduled to interview me from 2:30 to 3 P.M. Let me know if you're available this afternoon to meet her.
   → 2시 30분부터 3시까지 인터뷰하기로 되어 있으니, 시간이 괜찮은지를 알려 달라는 의미입니다. To suggest a meeting time으로 표현한 (B)를 정답으로 선택하고 다음 문제로 넘어갑니다.

PART 4 제안·요청 문제 / 다음 할 일 문제 / 의도 파악 문제 191

따라 하면 문제가 풀리는
연습 문제

문제와 각 선택지의 키워드에 표시하세요. 그러고 나서 담화를 듣고 빈칸에 들어갈 말을 받아쓴 후 정답을 선택해 보세요.

01. What are listeners advised to do?

(A) Listen to traffic updates (B) Avoid driving through an area

radio broadcast

> W: Due to recent unexpected freezing _____ _____, main water pipes burst right in front of Graham Movie Theater on South Central Boulevard. The police department is _____ the street and _____ traffic now. The Department of Energy and Water Supply expects that the repair work will be completed in two days. _____ are advised to _____ this area.

02. What will the listeners do next?

(A) Listen to weather news (B) Post their questions online

radio broadcast

> M: Hello, we are going to _____ the CEO of Cinema Plus, Morgan Smith. He will tell us how he became a successful _____. We will be right back in a few minutes after the _____ _____. Stay tuned.

03. What does the speaker suggest doing?

(A) Holding a meeting (B) Upgrading a computer

telephone message

> M: Hello, this is Min-ho from Daniel Investment. I'm afraid the printers may have been _____ too _____. Could you tell me when you are available to _____ this issue? I'm _____ this Wednesday afternoon. Someone from the _____ department will also _____ _____.

paraphrasing 주어진 어휘 또는 표현과 의미가 동일한 것을 연결하세요.

1. complete • • (a) finish
2. discuss • • (b) office equipment
3. printer • • (c) have a meeting

04. What will the listeners most likely do next?

(A) Have a Q&A session   (B) Go to a cafeteria

announcement

> W: Attention please. As I said this morning, the _____ _____ of the conveyer belts will take place this afternoon. Inspectors will _____ the inspection in 10 minutes. So, the _____ on Assembly Line A may _____ to the cafeteria now and take some rest. Inspectors will _____ some _____ about the conveyor belts when you are back _____ _____. Thanks.

05. What does the speaker mean when she says, "50 cans of light grey paint is too many"?

(A) She thinks there might be a mistake.   (B) She is happy with a large order.

telephone message

> W: Hello, Ms. Kimberly. This is Linda Yang from LY Home Improvement. I'm calling _____ your order that you _____ this morning. 50 cans of light grey paint is too many. It is _____ _____ _____. Please call me back as soon as possible to let me know if that _____ is _____. Thank you.

06. Why does the speaker say, "I really enjoyed it last time with my family"?

(A) To recommend a restaurant   (B) To give detailed information

tour information

> M: All right, everyone. We are _____ at the area called Old Town. You will _____ buildings with traditional gothic styles. You will be given two hours of free time to _____ _____ the area. If you _____ _____ _____, go to Belgian Treats & Coffee. I really enjoyed it last time with my family. Please come back to the bus by 4 P.M.

paraphrasing 주어진 어휘 또는 표현과 의미가 동일한 것을 연결하세요.

4. take some rest ●   ● (a) see
5. detailed ●   ● (b) specific
6. encounter ●   ● (c) have a break time

01. Where did the speaker meet Mr. Navarro?
    (A) At an awards banquet
    (B) At a building tour
    (C) At an industry conference
    (D) At a career fair

02. Why does the speaker say, "she has a program called Montague"?
    (A) To correct an error
    (B) To cancel an order
    (C) To give information about a product
    (D) To recommend a colleague

03. Why does the speaker encourage the listener to act quickly?
    (A) Some deliveries may take a long time.
    (B) Some supplies are likely to run out.
    (C) A deadline has been changed.
    (D) A sale event will end soon.

04. Why is the speaker giving the talk?
    (A) To provide an art critique
    (B) To give an overview to volunteers
    (C) To explain a hiring process
    (D) To promote an art exhibit

05. What does the speaker recommend?
    (A) Taking some notes
    (B) Saving a receipt
    (C) Turning off cell phones
    (D) Checking a Web site

06. What will the listeners most likely do next?
    (A) Watch a film
    (B) Submit some questions
    (C) Enjoy a meal together
    (D) Introduce themselves

07. What is the purpose of the call?
    (A) To set up a meeting time
    (B) To get approval on a design
    (C) To enroll in a career fair
    (D) To point out an error in a document

08. What does the speaker imply when he says, "they have an online option"?
    (A) He wants to make a correction to a deadline.
    (B) He thinks they should change to another business.
    (C) He found a way to reduce the cost of a project.
    (D) He is surprised that a task is not finished.

09. What does the speaker plan to do next?
    (A) Forward a form
    (B) Speak to a manager
    (C) Call a client
    (D) Review a budget

10. What is the speaker mainly talking about?
    (A) Security measures
    (B) An exchange policy
    (C) Employee training
    (D) Food options

11. What did Selby Rail do last month?
    (A) Underwent an inspection
    (B) Added more journeys
    (C) Increased its fares
    (D) Conducted a survey

12. What does the speaker ask the listeners to review?
    (A) A training manual
    (B) A work schedule
    (C) A business contract
    (D) A department budget

13. Where is the announcement being made?
    (A) In an airport
    (B) In a restaurant
    (C) In a bus terminal
    (D) In a train station

14. What does the speaker ask the listeners to do?
    (A) Show a photo ID
    (B) Listen for updates
    (C) Use a self-ticketing machine
    (D) Find another mode of transportation

15. Why should listeners see an agent?
    (A) To get a refund
    (B) To verify meal vouchers
    (C) To sign up for membership
    (D) To pick up local maps

16. What product does the talk focus on?
    (A) A sports drink
    (B) A gear bag
    (C) A camera
    (D) A bicycle

17. What does the speaker imply when she says, "It needs to be smaller"?
    (A) Their product received poor reviews.
    (B) There are too many salespeople.
    (C) Production needs to decrease.
    (D) A sales goal was not met.

18. What will the listeners most likely do next?
    (A) Read a report
    (B) Watch some ads
    (C) Review survey results
    (D) Vote on a color pattern

19. Why did the speaker call the listener?
    (A) To schedule a meeting
    (B) To request time off work
    (C) To volunteer for an event
    (D) To announce a promotion

20. What does the speaker imply when he says, "personnel reviews are coming up"?
    (A) He wants to transfer to another department.
    (B) Only a few volunteer opportunities are offered.
    (C) An event may be moved indoors due to weather.
    (D) He can improve his chances of getting promoted.

21. What will the speaker most likely do next?
    (A) Visit a local park
    (B) Update his résumé
    (C) Submit an application
    (D) Contact someone in HR

22. What section does the speaker work in?
    (A) Product development
    (B) Online marketing
    (C) Human resources
    (D) Building security

23. What does the speaker ask the listener to do?
    (A) Present some form of identification
    (B) Have an employee retrieve an item
    (C) Sign up for an orientation
    (D) Submit a lost item form

24. What does the speaker most likely mean when he says, "this already has her name and picture"?
    (A) A new policy will go into effect.
    (B) An exception can be made.
    (C) A picture should be taken.
    (D) A card has expired.

'멋진 당신, 오늘도 화이팅'

DAY 11

오늘의 학습 포인트

PART 2. 우회적 응답 모음
1. 되묻는 유형
2. I don't know 유형
   - 모르겠다
   - 기억이 나지 않는다
3. Someone knows 유형
   - 다른 사람에게 확인하라
4. It isn't decided/Sorry but 유형
   - 결정되지 않았다
   - 우회적 거절

PART 4. 문제 유형
1. 시각 자료 연계 문제
   - 표, 평면도, 쿠폰, 차트 등

PART 2 우회적 응답 모음

직접적인 답변을 하기보다는 추가 정보를 묻거나 다른 사람에게 확인하라고 하는 등 간접적으로 답변하는 유형의 출제 빈도가 높아지고 있어요!

🎧 Day 11_ P2_01.mp3

🔒 확인 문제 ❶

Mark your answer.

(A)   (B)

출제 유형 1 — 되묻는 유형

| 800+ |

우회적 응답 중에서도 난이도가 높은 유형으로, 문제의 의미를 정확히 이해해야만 어떤 내용으로 되물을 수 있을지 파악할 수 있습니다.

Q. It'll take around two hours to clean the garage.
　차고를 청소하는 데 두 시간 정도 걸릴 거예요.
A. Do you need any help? 도움이 필요하세요?

Q. If you're going downtown, I suggest avoiding Highway 13.
　만약 시내로 가시는 거면, 13번 고속도로는 피하세요.
A. Are there any heavy traffic jam? 교통 체증이 있나요?

Q. When is my car going to be ready? 언제 제 자동차가 준비될까요?
A. How soon do you need it? 얼마나 빨리 필요하신가요?

(B) ❶ 정답

풀이 방법 — 되묻는 유형

🎧 Day 11_ P2_02.mp3

[US - BR]

Who do I need to talk to about the cooling system?
(A) What problem do you have?
(B) Take a break.
(C) No, it is too hot here.

냉방 시스템과 관련해서 누구와 이야기해야 하나요?
(A) 어떤 문제가 있으세요?
(B) 휴식을 취하세요.
(C) 아뇨, 여기는 너무 덥네요.

✏️ 이렇게 풀어요

1. 질문 내용 파악하기   Who do I need to talk to about the cooling system?
　　　　　　　　　　　누구와　　　　　냉방 시스템에 대해 이야기해야 하는지

2. 선택지 들으며 오답 소거하여 정답 선택하기
　(A) What problem do you have? → 정답으로 선택
　(B) Take a break. → 유사 발음 오답 (talk-take)
　(C) No, it is too hot here. → 의문사 의문문에 Yes/No로 답한 오답

출제 유형 2: I don't know 유형

[가적의 필기노트] 40P
LC 기술 29

🎧 Day 11_ P2_03.mp3

🔒 **확인 문제 ②**

Mark your answer.

(A)   (B)

'모르겠다'는 의미로 답하는 응답은 거의 모든 질문에 대한 답이 될 수 있으므로 정답이 될 확률이 높습니다.

- **아는 바가 없어요.**
  I haven't heard. / I haven't been told. 못 들었어요.
  I haven't been notified. / I haven't been informed. 공지 못 받았어요.
  Actually, I'm not sure. 사실 저는 잘 모르겠어요.
  I wish I knew. 저도 알면 좋겠어요.
  I don't really know. 저는 정말 몰라요.
  I haven't checked it yet. 아직 확인해보지 못했어요.

- **기억이 나지 않아요.**
  I'm sorry, I forgot. 미안해요, 잊어버렸어요.
  I can't remember. 기억이 나지 않아요.
  It slipped my mind. 잊어버렸어요.
  It's on tip of my tongue. 생각이 날 듯 말 듯 해요.

정답 ❷ (A)

풀이 방법 I don't know 유형

🎧 Day 11_ P2_04.mp3

[BR - US]

Why was the weekly meeting canceled yesterday?
(A) No, it should be reported daily.
(B) You will be charged the extra.
(C) I don't know the exact reason.

어제 주간 회의가 왜 취소되었나요?
(A) 아뇨, 그건 매일 보고되어야 해요.
(B) 당신에게 추가 금액이 부과될 거예요.
(C) 정확한 이유는 모르겠어요.

📎 이렇게 풀어요

1. 질문 내용 파악하기 Why was the weekly meeting canceled yesterday?
   왜   주간 회의가 왜 취소되었는지

2. 선택지 들으며 오답 소거하여 정답 선택하기
    (A) No, it should be reported daily. → 의문사 의문문에 Yes/No로 답한 오답
   (B) You will be charged the extra. → 시제가 맞지 않는 오답(과거-미래)
   (C) I don't know the exact reason. → 정답으로 선택

PART 2 우회적 응답 모음

적용 기술

[기적의 필기노트] 40P
LC 기술 29

🎧 Day 11_ P2_05.mp3

🔒 확인 문제 ❸

Mark your answer.

(A)   (B)

⚠️ 주의
'다른 사람이 안다' 또는 '~에게 달려있다'고 답을 할 수는 있으나, 주어와 동사가 질문과 맞는지 잘 들은 후 답을 골라야 합니다.
Q. Why did you leave the office so early yesterday? 어제 왜 그렇게 일찍 퇴근했어요?
A. She didn't give me the reason. (X) 그녀가 이유를 말해주지 않았어요.

출제 유형 3
Someone knows 유형

800+

본인이 몰라서 답변해 줄 수 없으니 '다른 사람에게 확인하라'는 의미로 답하는 유형입니다.

- ~에게 확인해 볼게요.
  I'll ask the manager. 매니저에게 물어보겠습니다.
  Let me check (that for you). (당신을 위해) 제가 확인해 볼게요.
  Let me find out. 제가 알아보겠습니다.
  Amy is in charge of it. Amy가 그것을 담당하고 있어요.
  Ask Bob about that. 그것에 대해서는 Bob에게 물어보세요.
  I'll get back to you on that. 그것에 대해 나중에 알려드리겠습니다.
  I'll check with the maintenance department. 유지 관리 부서에 확인해 보겠습니다.
  I'll send you some guidelines. (제가 모르니) 지침서를 보내드릴게요.

풀이 방법   Someone knows 유형

🎧 Day 11_ P2_06.mp3

BR - AU

Where is the signed contract from Nelson Supplies?
(A) Mark might know.
(B) They offered better deals.
(C) Sign at the bottom of the form.

Nelson Supplies에서 온 서명된 계약서가 어디 있나요?
(A) Mark가 알 거예요.
(B) 그들이 더 나은 조건을 제시했어요.
(C) 양식 하단에 서명하세요.

> **이렇게 풀어요**
>
> 1. 질문 내용 파악하기   Where is the signed contract from Nelson Supplies?
>   어디 있는지   서명된 계약서가
> 2. 선택지 들으며 오답 소거하여 정답 선택하기
>   (A) Mark might know. → 정답으로 선택
>   (B) They offered better deals. → 연상 어휘 오답 (contract-better deals)
>   (C) Sign at the bottom of the form. → 유사 발음 오답 (signed-sign)

출제 유형 4 — It isn't decided/Sorry, but 유형

🎧 Day 11_ P2_07.mp3

🔒 **확인 문제 ❹**

Mark your answer.
(A)   (B)

800+

- It isn't decided 유형은 사실 확인을 하기 위해 묻는 질문에 대해 **아직 결정된 바가 없다고 답하는** 유형입니다.

  - 결정되지 않았어요.
    It hasn't been decided. 아직 결정되지 않았습니다.
    It is not confirmed yet. 아직 확정되지 않았습니다.
    They haven't decided yet. 그들이 아직 결정하지 않았습니다.
    It depends on the budget. 그건 예산에 따라 달라요.

  - 아직 논의 중입니다.
    They are still discussing[reviewing]. 여전히 논의[검토] 중입니다.
    I'm still considering it. 아직 고려 중이에요.

  - 옵션이 여러 개 있습니다.
    There are several options. 여러 옵션이 있어요.

- Sorry, but 유형은 상대방의 요청이나 제안에 대해 **우회적으로 거절할 때 쓰이는** 유형입니다.
  Sorry, but I have a prior appointment. 죄송하지만, 선약이 있습니다.
  Sorry, but I don't have much time. 죄송하지만, 제가 시간이 별로 없습니다.
  Sorry, but we have to finish this first. 죄송하지만, 이것을 먼저 마쳐야 합니다.
  I'm sorry but I'm not allowed to do that.
  죄송하지만, 저는 그것을 해드릴 수 없습니다.(저에게 권한이 없습니다.)

(B) 정답

풀이 방법 — It isn't decided 유형

🎧 Day 11_ P2_08.mp3

[BR - BR]

What gift will be given out at the company booth?
(A) I really loved it.
(B) We haven't decided yet.
(C) Yes, I've been there.

회사 부스에서 어떤 사은품을 나누어 줄 건가요?
(A) 저는 그게 정말 좋았어요.
(B) 우리는 아직 결정하지 못했어요.
(C) 네, 저는 거기 가봤어요.

📎 이렇게 풀어요

1. 질문 내용 파악하기 What gift will be given out at the company booth?
                        어떤 사은품을   나누어 줄지

2. 선택지 들으며 오답 소거하여 정답 선택하기
   (A̶) I really loved it. → 시제가 맞지 않는 오답(미래-과거)
   (B) We haven't decided yet. → 정답으로 선택
   (C̶) Yes, I've been there. → 의문사 의문문에 Yes/No로 답한 오답

PART 2 우회적 응답 모음 201

따라 하면 문제가 풀리는
연습 문제

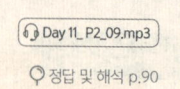

정답 및 해석 p.90

각 질문과 보기를 들으며 빈칸을 채운 뒤 정답에는 O, 오답에는 X 표시하세요.

01. _____ _____ will be sponsoring the annual banquet?
   (A) That _____ been _____ yet. [   ]
   (B) It looks like a _____ _____. [   ]

02. Which _____ did the research department _____?
   (A) I _____ the _____ _____ are left. [   ]
   (B) _____ _____ was impressive. [   ]

03. _____ isn't my last _____ _____ _____ on my statement?
   (A) I'll _____ _____ and _____ you _____. [   ]
   (B) From the _____ department. [   ]

04. Has the _____ been _____ for the company _____?
   (A) No, we don't _____ new _____. [   ]
   (B) Jason _____ _____. [   ]

05. _____ do you plan to go for the _____?
   (A) There are _____ _____ _____ I want to go. [   ]
   (B) Yes, that's the _____. [   ]

06. _____ _____ more do I need to _____ to _____ my rental car?
   (A) It _____ on which _____ you _____. [   ]
   (B) There are still plenty of _____ _____ available. [   ]

07. I have no idea _____ _____ _____ for the security training.
   (A) It's very _____. [   ]
   (B) _____ _____ Mr. Roy. [   ]

08. _____ has the workshop been _____?
   (A) They _____ _____ on Tuesday. [   ]
   (B) You _____ _____ your e-mail, have you? [   ]

🎧 Day 11_ P2_10.mp3

정답 및 해설 p.91

01. Mark your answer on your answer sheet.
(A) (B) (C)

02. Mark your answer on your answer sheet.
(A) (B) (C)

03. Mark your answer on your answer sheet.
(A) (B) (C)

04. Mark your answer on your answer sheet.
(A) (B) (C)

05. Mark your answer on your answer sheet.
(A) (B) (C)

06. Mark your answer on your answer sheet.
(A) (B) (C)

07. Mark your answer on your answer sheet.
(A) (B) (C)

08. Mark your answer on your answer sheet.
(A) (B) (C)

09. Mark your answer on your answer sheet.
(A) (B) (C)

10. Mark your answer on your answer sheet.
(A) (B) (C)

11. Mark your answer on your answer sheet.
(A) (B) (C)

12. Mark your answer on your answer sheet.
(A) (B) (C)

13. Mark your answer on your answer sheet.
(A) (B) (C)

14. Mark your answer on your answer sheet.
(A) (B) (C)

15. Mark your answer on your answer sheet.
(A) (B) (C)

16. Mark your answer on your answer sheet.
(A) (B) (C)

PART 4 시각 자료 연계 문제

시각 자료 연계 문제는 매회 2문제 출제됩니다!

적용 기술

[기적의 필기노트] 81P~83P
LC 기술 61, 62

출제 포인트
시각 자료 연계 문제는 주어진 표, 평면도, 쿠폰 등의 시각 자료와 담화 내용을 연계하여 정답을 찾는 유형입니다.

출제 포인트
일정표, 차트, 지도가 자주 출제되긴 하지만 점점 다양한 시각 자료가 나오는 추세입니다. 시각 자료 자체를 해석하는 것은 어렵지 않으므로 담화 내용과의 연결 고리만 잘 캐치하면 쉽게 풀 수 있습니다.

출제 유형 1 시각 자료 연계 문제

`800+`

1 질문 유형

Look at the graphic. Which route is closed today?
시각 자료를 보시오. 오늘 어떤 길이 폐쇄되었는가?

2 핵심 포인트

1. **시각 자료의 내용을 먼저 신속하게 파악**합니다.

   담화가 시작되기 전에 시각 자료와 문제를 먼저 파악하여 담화에서 어떤 내용으로 단서가 제시될지 추측하는 것이 중요합니다.

2. 담화와 시각 자료의 **연결 고리를 캐치**해야 합니다.

   문제의 보기에 제시된 단어를 담화에서 직접 언급하지 않으므로 시각 자료의 정보와 담화의 정보를 연결하여 답을 찾아야 합니다.

Santiago Hiking Club	
Route	Length
A	5 kilometers
B	10 kilometers
C	15 kilometers

[문제] Q. Look at the graphic. Which route is closed today?
　　　　시각 자료를 보시오. 오늘 어떤 길이 폐쇄되었는가?

[담화] M: The 10-kilometer route is not available today due to road repair work.
　　　　10킬로미터 길은 도로 보수 공사로 인해 오늘 이용할 수 없습니다.

→ 10킬로미터인 도로에 갈 수 없음을 파악합니다. 이때 10-kilometer가 담화와 시각 자료의 연결 고리 역할을 합니다.

[정답] The B Route

3 빈출 시각 자료 유형

1. 주문서(order form)

   음식 주문, 가구 주문, 사무용품 주문 내역이 담긴 양식이 제시됩니다. 주문서에 오류가 있는 부분이나 변경된 내용을 찾아야 하는 문제가 출제됩니다.

Order Form # 8910	
Name: Danny's Law Firm	
Item	**Quantity**
tuna sandwich	30
low-fat milk	50
vanilla cake	20

   → 화자가 음료 메뉴의 수량을 늘리고 싶다고 말할 경우, 어떤 수치가 변경되어야 하는지(50) 묻는 문제가 출제됩니다. 주문서에서 '음료' 메뉴인 low-fat milk(저지방 우유)를 찾아낼 수 있어야 합니다.

   출제 포인트
   주문서에서 나오는 어휘
   item 품목
   product 제품
   quantity 수량
   catering order 출장 연회 주문

2. 티켓(ticket)

   출발/도착 관련 정보가 쓰여 있으며, 변동 사항에 대해 묻는 문제가 출제됩니다.

   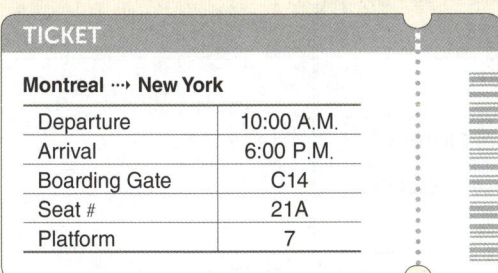

   → 플랫폼 공사가 지연되어 다른 플랫폼에서 탑승하라고 했을 때 어떤 정보가 변경되었는지(7) 묻는 문제가 출제됩니다.

   출제 포인트
   티켓에서 나오는 어휘
   departure 출발
   arrival 도착
   platform 승강장
   gate 탑승구

3. 일정표(schedule)

   한 개인의 하루 일과표, 출장 또는 여행 일정표가 제시됩니다.

Mr. Johnson's schedule – Monday, March 6th	
10:00 A.M.	board meeting
noon	lunch with branch manager
2:30 P.M.	new employee training

   → 담화에서 2시 30분 일정이 내일로 미뤄졌다고 했을 때 어떤 일정을 오늘 하지 않을 것인지 (new employee training) 묻는 문제가 출제됩니다.

PART 4 시각 자료 연계 문제   205

출제 포인트
지도/약도에서 나오는 어휘
route 길
path 길
restricted 제한된, 금지된
bike path 자전거 길
rest area 휴게소

4. 지도/약도(map)
건물의 평면도, 등산로, 거리 지도 등이 제시되며, 접근할 수 없는 길, 화자가 방문할 방의 번호 등을 묻는 문제가 출제됩니다.

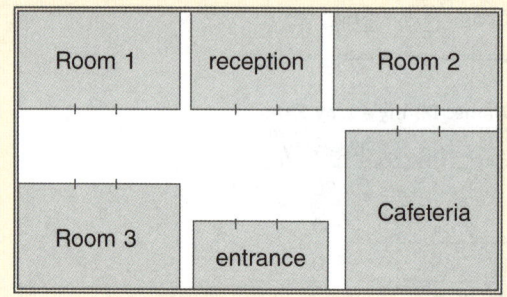

→ 화자가 자신을 방문할 청자에게 본인의 사무실 위치를 알려줄 때, 입구 바로 옆에 있는 방이라고 한다면 청자가 어디로 갈지(Room 3) 묻는 문제가 출제됩니다.

5. 빌딩 안내판(directory)
건물의 층별 안내도를 보여주는 시각 자료입니다. 청자가 어디로 가야 하는지, 이벤트를 하는 층은 어디인지, 공사를 하는 층은 어디인지 등을 묻는 문제가 출제됩니다.

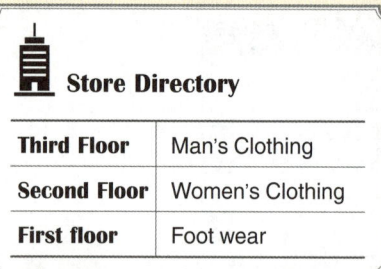

→ 신발 파는 층에서 타임 세일 행사가 진행될 것이라고 안내할 때, 어떤 층에서 할인이 진행될지(first floor) 묻는 문제가 출제됩니다.

출제 포인트
차트에서 나오는 어휘
earnings 수익
profit 수익
branch 지점, 지사
quarterly 분기의
summary 요약
per year 연간, 일년당

`900+`

6. 차트(chart)
막대 그래프는 신제품 판매량의 분기별 증감 변화를 나타내는 그래프가 출제될 수 있습니다.

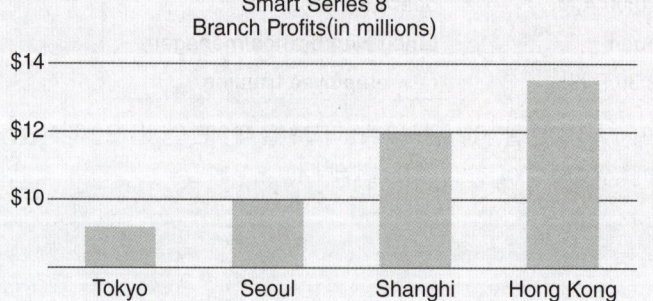

→ 매출이 가장 높았던 도시의 광고 방식을 다시 한 번 해보자고 할 때, 어느 도시(Hong Kong)의 홍보 방식을 채택할지 묻는 문제가 출제됩니다.

시각 자료 연계 문제

Day 11_P4_01.mp3

[문제지]

✈ AIR TICKET	Boarding Pass
Detroit ⋯▶ Richmond	
Departure	2:15 P.M.
Arrival	3:50 P.M.
Boarding Gate	C14
Seat	29B
Zone	3

✈ AIR TICKET	Boarding Pass
디트로이트 ⋯▶ 리치몬드	
출발	오후 2:15
도착	오후 3:50
탑승 게이트	C14
좌석	29B
구역	3

Look at the graphic. According to the speaker, which piece of information has changed?

(A) 2:15 P.M.
(B) C14
(C) 29B
(D) 3

시각 자료를 보시오. 화자에 따르면, 어떤 정보가 변경되었는가?

(A) 2:15 P.M.
(B) C14
(C) 29B
(D) 3

[담화] [US]

announcement and flight ticket

W: Attention passengers waiting to board flight VA69 to Richmond. We regret to report a problem with our computer system. **Your plane has begun pre-departure preparations at a different boarding gate. We ask that you gather your things and proceed to the new boarding gate.** In order to make up for this inconvenience, our staff can shuttle you and your luggage directly there. If you prefer to walk, you may do so, but please keep in mind that your flight should be taking off on time.

안내 방송과 비행기 티켓

여: 리치몬드행 VA69 항공편 탑승을 기다리시는 여러분께 알려드립니다. 저희 컴퓨터 시스템에 문제가 생겼다는 것을 알려드리게 되어 유감입니다. **여러분의 비행기는 다른 탑승 게이트에서 출발 전 준비를 시작했습니다. 여러분의 소지품을 챙겨 새 탑승 게이트로 가실 것을 요청 드립니다.** 이 불편함을 보상해 드리기 위하여, 저희 직원들이 여러분들과 짐을 직접 이동시켜 드리겠습니다. 걷는 것을 선호하시면 그렇게 하셔도 됩니다만, 여러분의 비행기가 정시에 이륙한다는 것을 유념해 주세요.

이렇게 풀어요

담화를 듣기 전에 먼저 시각 자료의 유형과 문제를 파악해야 해요.

1. **시각 자료와 문제 파악하기**
   - **시각 자료** 비행기 티켓이고 출발/도착 정보가 쓰여져 있음
   - **문제 키워드** which, information, changed → 변경된 정보를 찾아야 함을 파악합니다.

2. **담화를 들으며 문제와 관련된 내용을 시각 자료에서 찾아 정답 선택하기**
   - **담화** We ask that you gather your things and proceed to the new boarding gate.
   - **시각 자료** Boarding Gate: C14 → (B)를 정답으로 선택하고 다음 문제로 넘어갑니다.

따라 하면 문제가 풀리는
연습 문제

문제와 각 선택지의 키워드에 표시하세요. 그러고 나서 담화를 듣고 빈칸에 들어갈 말을 받아쓴 후 정답을 선택해 보세요.

01. Look at the graphic. Which item does the speaker want to increase?

(A) Sandwiches (B) Orange Juice

telephone message and form

Order Form # 8910	
Name: Danny's Law Firm	
Item	Quantity
Sandwiches	30
Orange Juice	50

W: Hi, I'm Linda from Danny's Law Firm. I'm calling about the _____ _____ our company placed yesterday. One of our staff members made a _____. I think we have to order more _____. Also, we need a _____ hamburgers. If you have any questions, please call me anytime.

02. Look at the graphic. In which quarter was the new product most likely released?

(A) 2nd quarter (B) 3rd quarter

talk and graph

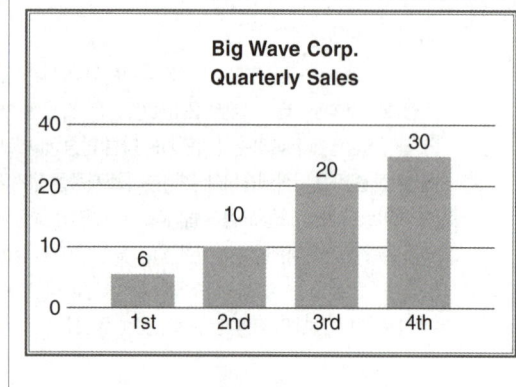

M: Thank you for attending the _____ meeting. I want to begin with good news. Our _____ _____, the Big Wave Bluetooth headset, has had _____ _____ from customers as well as industry critics. As in the report, our sales _____ in the _____ when it was _____. Give Mr. Timber and his team a round of applause and congratulate them on their _____.

---

paraphrasing 주어진 어휘 또는 표현과 의미가 동일한 것을 연결하세요.

1. made a mistake • • (a) increased
2. favorable • • (b) contains wrong information
3. doubled • • (c) positive

03. Look at the graphic. Which item in the monthly report requires additional documentation?

(A) Transportation (B) Lunch & Dinner

telephone message and report

Name: Gary Butler	
Item	Expense
Transportation	$400.00(4 days)
Accommodations	$899.19
Lunch & Dinner	$450.00
Telephone	$99.89

W: Hello. Mr. Butler. This is Sandra Peterson from accounting. I'm returning your call. I received your _____ _____ report for October. While reviewing it, I noticed that you did not _____ receipts for the expense of $450. Please make sure that you _____ itemized tables and attach all _____ for them. _____ we will be unable to _____ you.

04. Look at the graphic. What gate is not available during the construction period?

(A) East Gate (B) West Gate

broadcast and map

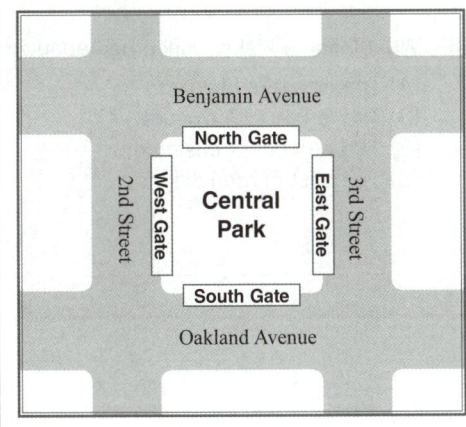

M: Yesterday the City Council announced the _____ of 3rd Street, between Benjamin Avenue and Oakland Avenue. This 4-month construction will begin at the _____ of next month, July 1st, and will _____ _____ 2 million dollars. So, during this period, be assured that you are not able to _____ Central Park _____ the parking entrance _____ the _____ area.

---

paraphrasing 주어진 어휘 또는 표현과 의미가 동일한 것을 연결하세요.

4. expense   •   • (a) pay back
5. reimburse   •   • (b) go
6. access   •   • (c) spending

Main Stage Events	
9 A.M. – 10 A.M.	Opening Ceremony
10 A.M. – Noon	Cooking Contest
1 P.M. – 3 P.M.	Dance Performance
7 P.M. – 9 P.M.	Televised Concert

Fontaine Theater	Bergman Designs	Lena's Ice Cream
Cheshire Street		
Crosby Shoes	Retro Mart	DC Apartments

01. What does the speaker warn the listeners about?
(A) A ticket shortage
(B) A lack of parking
(C) Possible bad weather
(D) Last-minute changes

02. Look at the graphic. When can festival attendees see a star from France?
(A) 9 A.M.– 10 A.M.
(B) 10 A.M.– Noon
(C) 1 P.M.– 3 P.M.
(D) 7 P.M.– 9 P.M.

03. Who is Miguel Alexander?
(A) An event planner
(B) A city official
(C) A professional singer
(D) A local businessperson

04. Who most likely is calling the listener?
(A) A real estate agent
(B) A construction worker
(C) A loan officer
(D) A clothing designer

05. Look at the graphic. Which location will be used by the listener?
(A) Fontaine Theater
(B) Bergman Designs
(C) Crosby Shoes
(D) Retro Mart

06. What is the speaker concerned about?
(A) The size of a building
(B) The length of a closure
(C) The number of customers
(D) The cost of renovations

5-Day Forecast: Chance of Snow				
WED	THU	FRI	SAT	SUN
50%	70%	40%	30%	10%

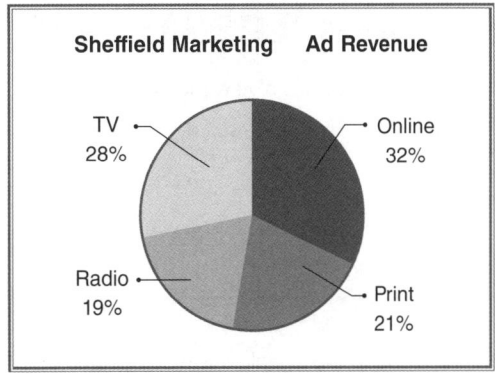

07. Who most likely are the listeners?
    (A) Tour participants
    (B) Theater critics
    (C) New employees
    (D) Bus drivers

08. Look at the graphic. On which day is the speaker making the announcement?
    (A) Wednesday
    (B) Thursday
    (C) Friday
    (D) Sunday

09. What does the speaker recommend the listeners do?
    (A) Bring a camera
    (B) Attend a performance
    (C) Lock checked luggage
    (D) Verify a ticket

10. According to the speaker, what has the company recently done?
    (A) Opened an international branch
    (B) Received publicity on a TV show
    (C) Acquired a competitor
    (D) Increased its revenue

11. Why is Ms. Moyer attending an expo?
    (A) To give a presentation
    (B) To demonstrate a product
    (C) To meet a business partner
    (D) To negotiate a business contract

12. Look at the graphic. Which type of ads does the speaker want to discuss?
    (A) Radio
    (B) Print
    (C) TV
    (D) Online

실전 문제

Jennifer's Schedule: Wednesday, April 7	
10:00 A.M.	Sales review meeting
12:00 P.M.	Lunch with author Neil Walsh
1:30 P.M.	Corporate conference call
3:00 P.M.	Seasonal hiring plan

13. What does the speaker want to speak with the listener about?

    (A) A relocation schedule
    (B) Membership benefits
    (C) A new book series
    (D) A store expansion

14. Look at the graphic. Which appointment was cancelled?

    (A) Sales review meeting
    (B) Lunch with author Neil Walsh
    (C) Corporate conference call
    (D) Seasonal hiring plan

15. What does the speaker request that the listener bring?

    (A) A company profile
    (B) A building model
    (C) A cost estimate
    (D) A writing sample

16. What event did the speaker recently participate in?

    (A) An international fashion show
    (B) A public speaking workshop
    (C) A business owners' seminar
    (D) An annual training session

17. What topic did the speaker mainly learn about?

    (A) Increasing profits
    (B) Boosting popularity
    (C) Marketing effectively
    (D) Improving customer service

18. Look at the graphic. Which section of the store will be renovated?

    (A) Children
    (B) Shoes
    (C) Men
    (D) Women

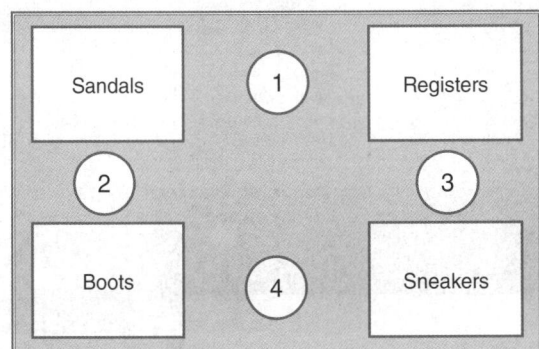

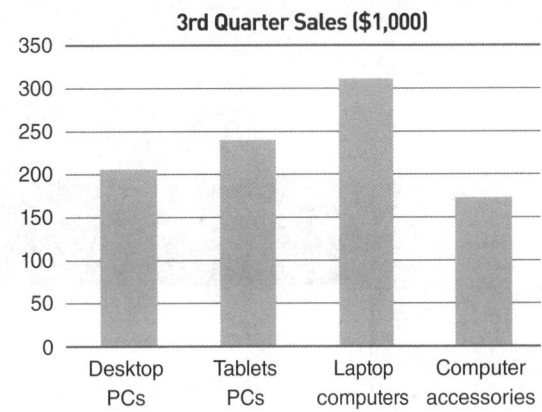

19. What is the main purpose of the change?
    (A) To improve customer satisfaction
    (B) To increase work efficiency
    (C) To reduce shipment sizes
    (D) To offer a wider variety

20. Look at the graphic. In which location were the new seats placed?
    (A) Location 1
    (B) Location 2
    (C) Location 3
    (D) Location 4

21. According to the speaker, what can be found at the registers?
    (A) A receipt
    (B) A training manual
    (C) A sign-up sheet
    (D) A coupon

22. What kind of business does the speaker work at?
    (A) A computer repair center
    (B) An electronics store
    (C) A market research firm
    (D) A computer manufacturer

23. Look at the graphic. According to the speaker, which product was featured in an ad?
    (A) Desktop PCs
    (B) Tablet PCs
    (C) Laptop computers
    (D) Computer accessories

24. What does the speaker say she will do next?
    (A) Contact a marketing agency
    (B) Show some competitors' ads
    (C) Distribute a survey
    (D) Demonstrate some products

'멋진 당신, 오늘도 화이팅'

DAY
12

오늘의 학습 포인트

PART 3. 대화 주제 - 회사

1. 업무 요청

    빈출 내용 - 타부서 업무 협조 & 자료 조사/연락 요청

    빈출 문제 - 화자들이 일하는 장소를 묻는 문제 & 다음에 할 일을 묻는 문제

2. 규정 관련

    빈출 내용 - 사내 복장 규정 & 급여 정책 & 보안 정책

    빈출 문제 - 주제/목적 문제 & 제안하는 것을 묻는 문제

PART 4. 담화 유형 - 전화 메시지(telephone message)

1. 주문·구매

    빈출 내용 - 주문 내역 & 주문/구매 관련 요청 사항

    빈출 문제 - 어떤 종류의 업체에 메시지를 남기고 있는지 묻는 질문

2. 배송·문의

    빈출 내용 - 배송 관련 정보 & 고객 문의 사항

    빈출 문제 - 문제점 문제 & 요청 문제

PART 3 회사 - 업무 요청 / 규정 관련

회사 내 업무 관련 대화나 각종 규정에 관련된 대화가 많이 출제됩니다.

출제 유형 1 업무 요청

다른 부서에 업무 협조나 자료 조사를 요청하거나 동료에게 연락해 달라고 요청하는 내용이 자주 출제됩니다.

업무 요청 대화에서 자주 나오는 문제

· 화자들이 일하는 장소를 묻는 문제
Where do the speakers most likely work?
→ a manufacturing company(제조 회사), a fitness center(피트니스 센터), an advertising agency(광고 대행사) 등 다양한 선택지가 출제되므로 공통된 키워드를 파악해 유추해야 합니다.

· 다음에 할 일을 묻는 문제
What will the man do next?
→ 대화 마지막에 업무를 요청하고 수락하는 내용이 나오므로 후반부를 집중해서 듣습니다.

· 업무 요청 관련 대화에서 자주 출제되는 어휘

favor	부탁	task	업무
feedback	피드백, 의견	on duty	근무 중인
cost estimate	견적서	urgent	긴급한
come up with	~을 생각해 내다	direction	지시(사항), 설명
workload	업무량, 작업량	assignment	업무
be in charge of	~을 담당하다	inform	알리다, 통보하다
request	요청, 요청하다	consult	상의하다
complete	완료하다	accept	받아들이다
fill in for A	A를 대신하다	postpone	연기하다
priority	우선 순위	mention	언급하다
discussion	토론, 논의	prepare	준비하다
inquire	문의하다	go over	~을 검토하다, 조사하다
meeting	회의	remind	상기시키다
review	검토하다	consent	동의하다, 합의하다
specific	구체적인, 특정한	brief	간략한
procedure	절차	set up	설치하다
supervise	관리하다, 감독하다	call off	취소하다
put off	미루다, 연기하다	resume	다시 시작하다
work overtime	초과 근무하다	still	여전히, 아직

업무 요청

US - AU

W: Martin, I have a favor to ask. I was going over some of the feedback cards from our gym's members. A lot of them say that they want a sports drink vending machine. Could you get me a cost estimate on renting a vending machine for the locker rooms?
M: I was trying to come up with promotions to attract new members. I'll get back to this later. Were there any specific requests?
W: A lot of them mentioned Thirstinator drinks.
M: Okay, I'll get online and start looking around.
W: Thanks. E-mail me any good links you find.

01. Where do the speakers most likely work?
   (A) At a cafeteria
   (B) At an ad agency
   (C) At a fitness center
   (D) At a beverage manufacturer

02. What does the man imply when he says, "I'll get back to this later"?
   (A) He needs some directions.
   (B) He is currently working on other task.
   (C) He is too busy contacting gym members.
   (D) He is planning on leaving work early.

03. What does the man say he will do?
   (A) Purchase a machine
   (B) Advertise a promotion
   (C) Review some feedback
   (D) Start some online research

이렇게 풀어요

01. 화자들은 어디에서 일하는 것 같은가?
   (A) 구내식당에서
   (B) 광고 대행사에서
   (C) 피트니스 센터에서
   (D) 음료 제조업체에서

여자가 첫 대사에서 I was going over some of the feedback cards from our gym's members라고 했어요.
→ gym을 fitness center로 패러프레이징 한 (C)가 정답입니다.

02. 남자가 "제가 나중에 이것을 처리할게요"라고 말할 때 의미하는 바는 무엇인가?
   (A) 그는 설명이 필요하다.
   (B) 그는 현재 다른 업무를 하고 있다.
   (C) 그는 체육관 회원들에게 연락하느라 너무 바쁘다.
   (D) 그는 일찍 퇴근할 계획이다.

여자가 자판기 대여 견적을 받아달라고 부탁한 것에 대해 남자가 I was trying to come up with promotions to attract new members. I'll get back to this later.라고 했어요.
→ 남자가 하고 있던 일(프로모션 생각해내기)이 있는데 그건 나중에 다시 하겠다고 한 상황이므로 (B)가 정답입니다.

03. 남자는 무엇을 할 것이라고 말하는가?
   (A) 기계를 구입하기
   (B) 판촉행사를 홍보하기
   (C) 몇몇 의견을 검토하기
   (D) 온라인 조사를 시작하기

남자가 마지막 대사에서 I'll get online and start looking around.라고 했어요.
→ look around를 research로 패러프레이징 한 (D)가 정답입니다.

출제 유형 2 — 규정 관련

사내 복장 규정, 급여 정책, 보안 정책 등 새 규정을 알리거나 변경 내용에 대해 말하는 내용이 출제됩니다.

규정 관련 대화에서 자주 나오는 문제

· 주제/목적 문제
What are the speakers discussing?
→ a policy change(정책 변경), a vacation policy(휴가 정책), a payment policy(지불 정책) 등이 정답으로 출제됩니다.

· 제안하는 것을 묻는 문제
What does the woman suggest?
→ revising/updating/changing a company policy(회사의 정책을 수정하는 것/업데이트하는 것/변경하는 것)가 정답으로 자주 출제됩니다.

· 규정 관련 대화에서 자주 출제되는 어휘

policy	정책	follow	따르다
regulation	규정	abolish	(제도를) 폐지하다
manual	설명서, 안내서	compliance	(법규의) 준수
restructure	(조직 등을) 개편하다	remind	다시 알려주다
as of	~부터	file	보관하다; 제기하다
tuition	수업, 수업료	adhere	고수하다, 지키다
reimbursement	상환, 배상	enforce	시행하다, 실시하다
strict	엄격한	obligation	의무, 책임
employee benefit	직원 복지	implement	시행하다
notice	게시, 안내문	resolve	해결하다
ban	금지하다	omit	빠뜨리다, 누락시키다
take over	인계받다, 인수하다	effect	효과, 영향
administrative	행정의	present	현재의, 제시하다
object	반대하다	fine	벌금
dress code	복장 규정	inspection	점검
personnel	인사	revise	개정하다, 수정하다
accounting	회계	retain	유지하다
public relations	홍보	officially	공식적으로
division	부서	arrangement	준비, 배치

규정 관련

US - BR

M: Good morning, Sally. I was just thinking, it seems like most of the employees that come into the Personnel Division have questions about our tuition reimbursement program.
W: Yes, I've noticed that as well. A lot of people seem to be confused about the program. Do you have any ideas on informing everyone?
M: I do, actually. We could hold a training course about employee benefits.
W: I like that idea. Let's try to organize one.
M: When do you think would be best?
W: I would have to look at our company's schedule first. I'll do that now.

01. Which division do the speakers work in?
(A) Sales
(B) Personnel
(C) Accounting
(D) Public Relations

02. What does the man recommend trying?
(A) Providing a training course
(B) Preparing pamphlets
(C) Hiring an instructor
(D) Sending an e-mail

03. What will the woman most likely do next?
(A) Send a memo
(B) Write a manual
(C) Check a schedule
(D) Contact a coworker

이렇게 풀어요

01. 화자들은 어느 부서에서 일하는가?
(A) 영업
(B) 인사
(C) 회계
(D) 홍보

남자가 첫 대사에서 it seems like most of the employees that come into the Personnel Division have questions about our tuition reimbursement program이라고 했어요.
→ personnel division을 직접 언급했으므로 (B)가 정답입니다.

02. 남자는 무엇을 해보자고 제안하는가?
(A) 교육 시간 제공하기
(B) 팸플릿 준비하기
(C) 강사 고용하기
(D) 이메일 보내기

대화 중반에서 남자가 We could hold a training course about employee benefits.라고 했어요.
→ training course가 그대로 제시된 (A)가 정답입니다.

03. 여자는 다음에 무엇을 하겠는가?
(A) 회람 보내기
(B) 설명서 작성하기
(C) 일정 확인하기
(D) 동료에게 연락하기

여자가 마지막 대사에서 I would have to look at our company's schedule first.라고 했어요.
→ look at이 check로 패러프레이징 된 (C)가 정답입니다.

따라 하면 문제가 풀리는 연습 문제

문제와 각 선택지의 키워드에 표시하세요. 그러고 나서 대화를 듣고 빈칸에 들어갈 말을 받아쓴 후 정답을 선택해 보세요.

01. What are the speakers mainly talking about?

(A) A retirement party　　　　(B) A grant proposal

> W: Andy, have you finished the _____ _____ for next year?
> M: No, I just _____ the first draft. I heard you were _____ _____ _____ last year's proposal. Could you review it and give me some _____?
> W: Sure, e-mail it to me.

02. What does the woman offer to do?

(A) Download guidelines　　　　(B) Give an application form

> M: I have a _____ _____ at Herald Investment and need to _____ a company car tomorrow. Do you know how I can _____ for one?
> W: _____ _____ a form and get a signature from your manager. And then, submit it to Mr. Jenson in the General Affairs Department. I will _____ you some copies of the form.

03. What did the company recently do?

(A) Introduced a new service　　　　(B) Changed a vendor

> W: Tom, Did you _____ _____ your monthly _____ from the Payroll Department yesterday?
> M: No. Actually, I don't need to do that anymore. The Payroll Department _____ the direct deposit service this month. You can have your paycheck deposited _____ into your bank _____.
> W: That sounds very _____.

---

paraphrasing　주어진 어휘 또는 표현과 의미가 동일한 것을 연결하세요.

1. give suggestions　　●　　　　●　(a) be approved
2. get a signature　　●　　　　●　(b) advise
3. implement　　●　　　　●　(c) introduce

04. Where does the conversation probably take place?

(A) At a manufacturing plant   (B) At a grocery store

> M: I _____ the memo from the assembly manager that any power tools should be _____ to the storage room under the team manager's _____ at the end of each shift.
>
> W: It will _____ expensive power tools from being lost and _____ from improper care. All team manager will check the returned power tools.

05. What does the woman ask the man to do?

(A) Work at the company booth   (B) Reserve flights

> W: Jason, our _____ decided to have the company _____ at Colorado Expo and I'm making travel _____. Can you _____ flights for five people to Colorado? We will depart on November 28 and return on December 2.
>
> M: Okay, are there any _____ _____? They usually want business class flights.

06. What will the woman do this afternoon?

(A) Attend a career fair   (B) Inspect a factory

> M: Hi, Amy. I received the new _____ _____ for our new office space from Rebecca's Interior. Can we go over it today sometime?
>
> W: Can we do that tomorrow morning? I need to _____ a regular factory _____ this afternoon.

---

paraphrasing 주어진 어휘 또는 표현과 의미가 동일한 것을 연결하세요.

4. supervision •   • (a) inspect
5. book •   • (b) reserve
6. conduct an inspection • • (c) control

실전 문제

01. What does the woman tell the man about?
    (A) An updated privacy policy
    (B) A meal with some coworkers
    (C) A change in an interview schedule
    (D) An upcoming awards event

02. What does the woman imply when she says, "I'm done with my monthly reports"?
    (A) She wants to request some time off.
    (B) She will visit a client this afternoon.
    (C) She can help the man with a task.
    (D) She would like to discuss some figures.

03. What will the woman probably do next?
    (A) Print some contracts
    (B) Install some software
    (C) Set up a meeting room
    (D) Check a delivery's status

04. In what industry do the speakers work?
    (A) Manufacturing
    (B) Construction
    (C) Healthcare
    (D) Transportation

05. Why is the man unavailable on Friday?
    (A) He will visit some relatives.
    (B) He will attend a training session.
    (C) He will go to a concert.
    (D) He will have a job interview.

06. What does the man suggest doing?
    (A) Calling another site
    (B) Working a late shift
    (C) Reading an employee manual
    (D) Checking a notice board

07. What is the purpose of the call?
    (A) To reserve a meeting space
    (B) To inquire about some paperwork
    (C) To inform the man of a broken device
    (D) To invite the man to an event

08. Why does the man expect a task to be delayed?
    (A) The office will close soon.
    (B) Some meeting rooms are in use.
    (C) A team is short-staffed today.
    (D) Some components must be ordered.

09. What does the woman say she wants to do?
    (A) Sign a new contract
    (B) Complete some forms
    (C) Sample some new products
    (D) Make a good impression

10. What is the conversation about?
    (A) Complying with safety regulations
    (B) Attracting more customers
    (C) Speeding up the production process
    (D) Participating in a competition

11. What does Vineet think should be changed?
    (A) A payment system
    (B) A project deadline
    (C) A training schedule
    (D) A piece of equipment

12. What does the woman offer to do?
    (A) Update a Web site
    (B) Conduct some research
    (C) Contact a client
    (D) Request more funds

13. What is scheduled to take place on April 7?
    (A) A comedy show
    (B) A theater opening
    (C) A company dinner
    (D) A product release

14. What does the woman thank the man for doing?
    (A) Meeting a client
    (B) Planning a budget
    (C) Designing a flyer
    (D) Volunteering to perform

15. What does the woman say she will do?
    (A) Ask for a discount
    (B) Contact a performer
    (C) Hold a budget meeting
    (D) Reallocate some funds

16. Where do the speakers work?
    (A) At an auto repair shop
    (B) At a manufacturing plant
    (C) At a car parts store
    (D) At a dry cleaners

17. What did the man leave at home?
    (A) A training manual
    (B) A work outfit
    (C) A tool kit
    (D) A résumé

18. According to the woman, why is the business so busy?
    (A) A special promotion has just started.
    (B) A competitor went out of business.
    (C) A manufacturer recalled a part.
    (D) A coworker did not come in.

19. What problem does the woman mention?
    (A) A manager has suddenly left the company.
    (B) A department has exceeded its budget.
    (C) Employees show up late for work.
    (D) There is too much work to do.

20. How does the man say they should solve the problem?
    (A) By changing a company policy
    (B) By recruiting more employees
    (C) By installing new equipment
    (D) By agreeing to a merger

21. What does the man tell the woman to do?
    (A) Post about a job opening
    (B) Meet with board members
    (C) Prepare a time sheet
    (D) Request overtime pay

22. What kind of business do the speakers work for?
    (A) A retail store
    (B) A university
    (C) A law firm
    (D) A bank

23. What did the speakers find surprising?
    (A) The profits from a sale
    (B) The feedback from customers
    (C) The turnout at a party
    (D) The number of intern applicants

24. What is Becky asked to do?
    (A) Create a work schedule
    (B) Conduct some training
    (C) Fill out some forms
    (D) Contact a client

PART 4 전화 메시지(telephone message)

주문/구매, 배송/문의 관련 전화 메시지가 자주 출제됩니다.

적용 기술

[기적의 필기노트] 67P~69P
LC 기술 49, 50, 51

출제 유형 1 주문·구매

업체에 전화해서 세부적인 주문 내역을 남기거나, 주문/구매와 관련한 요청 사항을 남기는 내용이 출제됩니다.

주문·구매 관련 메시지에서 자주 나오는 문제

· 화자가 어떤 종류의 업체에 메시지를 남기고 있는지 묻는 문제
What kind of business is the speaker calling?
→ 전화 메시지의 경우, 전화한 용건을 말할 때 어떤 업체에 전화했는지 파악할 수 있습니다.

· 주문·구매 관련 메시지에서 자주 출제되는 어휘

manufacturer	제조업체	specification	사양
dietary	음식물의, 식이요법의	enduring	오래 지속되는
restriction	제한, 제약	durable	내구성 있는
vegetarian	채식주의자	place an order	주문하다
associate	동료	take an order	주문을 받다
bid	입찰, 입찰하다	cancellation	취소
auction	경매, 경매로 팔다	call off	취소하다
expense	비용	make arrangements	준비하다
drop off at	~에 갖다 놓다	apply	지원하다, 적용하다
payment	지불	carefully	주의 깊게, 신중히
raffle	추첨식 판매	instruction	설명(서), 지시
toll-free	수신자 부담의	apparel	의류, 복장
pricing	가격 책정	manual	설명서
banquet	연회, 성찬	out of stock	재고가 다 떨어진
informative	유익한	original receipt	원본 영수증
contact information	연락처	run into	~을 겪다, ~를 우연히 만나다

주문·구매

[US]

M: Hello, I'm Mark Baller, and I'm calling in regards to your flower arrangement services. I work at Rumney Real Estate, and our main office has been closed recently for renovations. My boss wants to have a big special event when we reopen next week, and I've been put in charge of planning the reopening event. I think the whole thing would be better if we had someone like your company come to decorate the tables and stage. Please call me back at 555-6432 at your earliest convenience so that we can discuss what flower options you have available this season.

01. What kind of business is the speaker calling?

(A) An interior designer
(B) A construction firm
(C) A flower shop
(D) A hotel

02. What event is the speaker in charge of planning?

(A) An anniversary celebration
(B) An office relocation
(C) A grand reopening
(D) A retirement party

03. What does the speaker want to know more about?

(A) A discount
(B) Product options
(C) A job opportunity
(D) A project timeline

이렇게 풀어요

01. 화자는 어떤 종류의 업체에 전화하고 있는가? (A) 인테리어 디자인 회사 (B) 건설 회사 (C) 꽃 가게 (D) 호텔	화자가 자기 이름을 말한 뒤, I'm calling in regards to your flower arrangement services라고 했어요. → your flower arrangement services를 통해 화자가 꽃 가게에 전화했다는 것을 알 수 있으므로 (C)가 정답입니다.
02. 화자는 어떤 행사의 기획을 담당하고 있나? (A) 기념일 축하 행사 (B) 회사 이전 (C) 대규모 재개장 행사 (D) 은퇴 기념 파티	담화 중반부에 I've been put in charge of planning the reopening event라고 했어요. → 재개장 행사의 기획을 담당하고 있음을 알 수 있으므로 (C)가 정답입니다.
03. 화자가 더 알길 원하는 것은 무엇인가? (A) 할인 (B) 제품 선택 범위 (C) 취업 기회 (D) 프로젝트 일정	담화 마지막에 Please call me back at 555-6432 at your earliest convenience so that we can discuss what flower options you have available this season이라고 했어요. → 요즘 시즌에 어떤 꽃이 가능한지 논의할 수 있도록 전화 달라고 했으므로 이를 Product options라고 표현한 (B)가 정답입니다.

출제 유형 2   배송·문의

업체에서 배송 관련한 정보를 남기는 내용이 출제될 수 있고, 동료 사이, 업체와 고객 사이에서 문의 사항을 남기는 등의 다양한 내용이 나올 수 있습니다.

배송·문의 관련 메시지에서 자주 나오는 문제

· 배송 관련하여 발생한 문제점이 무엇인지 묻는 문제
What is the problem?
→ 업체 측에서 배송 지연, 오배송, 교환 및 환불 정책에 대해 전화 메시지를 남기는 담화가 출제됩니다.

· 요청 문제
What does the speaker request?
→ 배송과 관련된 추가 정보를 요청하거나, 다시 연락을 달라는 요청 사항을 주로 전달합니다.

• 배송·문의 관련 메시지에서 자주 출제되는 어휘

fragile	잘 깨지는	fundraiser	모금 행사
fuel-efficient	연료 효율이 좋은	donation	기부
waterproof	방수의	exclusive	독점적인, 전용의
claim	요구, 청구	contract	계약(서)
compensation	배상, 보상	expand	넓히다
properly	적절히, 제대로	expansion	확장
patron	단골손님	extend	연장하다
store hours	영업 시간	extension	부속 건물, 별관
charge	요금을 부과하다	pattern	양식, 패턴
full price	전액	current	현재의
adopt	채택하다	shipment	배송(품)
tentative	임시의	equipment	장비
create	만들다	malfunction	고장, 고장 나다
donate	기부하다	extensive	대규모의
charity	자선	delivery	배송
inquiry	문의	process	과정
permission	허가	repairperson	수리하는 사람
inaccessible	들어갈 수 없는	material	자료

배송·문의

BR

M: This call is for Craig Garcia. I'm Nick from Selden's Custom Clothing. You sent me an e-mail asking about making 15 work uniforms for your staff members. Normally, I charge full price for any orders under 25 items. However, since you were referred to me from someone who I regularly do business with, I will make your uniforms at the discounted rate. The only problem is that I cannot get started right away. You didn't specifically tell me the sizes that you need. Once you get back to me with that information, I can work on your order. E-mail or call me back at 555-1264 once you get this.

01. What was the speaker asked about?
 (A) Adopting a new logo
 (B) Becoming business partners
 (C) Creating some work uniforms
 (D) Donating to a charity fundraiser

02. Why does the speaker offer a discounted rate?
 (A) A donation was made to charity.
 (B) An exclusive contract was signed.
 (C) The listener was referred by a regular customer.
 (D) The listener's business has plans to expand soon.

03. Why can't the speaker start work right away?
 (A) Some sizes were not specified.
 (B) A color pattern was not selected.
 (C) A payment has not been received.
 (D) Some equipment has malfunctioned.

이렇게 풀어요

01. 화자는 무엇에 대해 문의를 받았는가?
 (A) 새로운 로고 채택하기
 (B) 사업 파트너 되기
 (C) 작업 유니폼 만들기
 (D) 자선 모금업체에 기부하기

화자가 자신을 소개한 뒤, You sent me an e-mail asking about making 15 work uniforms for your staff members라고 했어요.
→ 화자가 유니폼 제작에 대해 문의하는 메일을 받았다는 것을 알 수 있으므로 정답은 (C)입니다.

02. 화자는 왜 할인된 가격을 제공하는가?
 (A) 자선 단체에 기부를 했다.
 (B) 독점 계약을 맺었다.
 (C) 청자가 단골손님에게 소개를 받았다.
 (D) 청자의 사업이 곧 확장할 계획을 가지고 있다.

담화 중반부에서 가격에 대해 말하며 since you were referred to me from someone who I regularly do business with, ~ at the discounted rate라고 했어요.
→ 청자가 단골손님을 통해 소개를 받아서 할인을 해 준다는 것을 알 수 있으므로 정답은 (C)입니다.

03. 왜 화자는 당장 일을 시작할 수 없는가?
 (A) 몇몇 사이즈를 명시하지 않았다.
 (B) 색 패턴을 선택하지 않았다.
 (C) 금액을 지불하지 않았다.
 (D) 몇몇 장비가 고장 났다.

담화 후반부에서 You didn't specifically tell me the sizes that you need라고 했어요.
→ 사이즈를 명시하지 않아서 당장 일을 시작할 수 없다는 것을 알 수 있으므로 정답은 (A)입니다.

따라 하면 문제가 풀리는 연습 문제

문제와 각 선택지의 키워드에 표시하세요. 그러고 나서 담화를 듣고 빈칸에 들어갈 말을 받아쓴 후 정답을 선택해 보세요.

01. What is the purpose of the message?

(A) To cancel an online order   (B) To confirm the product specification

telephone message

> W: Hello, Dr. Williams. This is Sharon Gilbert from Real Scientific Instrument. I'm calling you to _____ the order you placed this morning. You ordered _____ _____ of 20 milliliter test tubes. Is this correct? According to our _____, you usually order 40 milliliter test tubes. Please call back as soon as possible and let me know if the _____ is correct. Thank you.

02. What does the speaker recommend?

(A) Visiting the store   (B) Ordering a different product

telephone message

> M: Hi, Amelia! This is Jeremy from Purchasing. The _____ you ordered for your office is _____ _____ in stock. I can _____ _____ a special order for you but it will take around 6 weeks for it to be delivered. If you need it very soon, you'd better order a _____ _____. I will e-mail a link to an online catalog. You will find _____ bookcases with _____ styles and most of them can be delivered just in two or three days.

03. Why is the speaker calling?

(A) To complain about a wrong bill   (B) To request a refund for a shipping fee

telephone message

> W: Hello, my name is Karla Smith. I'm calling about a _____ I received in the mail from your company. $220.89 was _____ for an order of desks and chairs. I placed the order on November 10, but _____ it on November 11. I also received an e-mail to confirm the order cancellation. Please pay attention to this _____ and _____ it immediately.

paraphrasing 주어진 어휘 또는 표현과 의미가 동일한 것을 연결하세요.

1. different product   •   • (a) shipped
2. delivered   •   • (b) alternative item
3. address   •   • (c) deal with

04. What caused a problem?

(A) Electricity failure (B) A defective item

telephone message

> M: This is a message from John McMillan's Buffet. Because of a _____ _____, some of the Brick City areas experienced a _____ _____ last night. I found that this spoiled most of the ice cream stored in our refrigerator. So, I want to _____ order three gallons of strawberry and chocolate flavored ice cream. I hope they can be _____ before 5 P.M. I am _____ _____ pay extra for this _____ order. Thank you.

05. What is the listener asked to do?

(A) Contact a delivery company (B) Complete a form

telephone message

> M: Hello, Mr. Grandson. This is Jonathan Clover at Sound Waves Stereos and Speakers. We are sorry to hear that one of your new XL-5300 speakers arrived _____ _____ _____. We will be happy to refund the _____ _____ or send you a replacement with the next-day delivery option. First, please fill out the return and exchange _____ _____ and mail it to us.

06. According to the speaker, what does the notice say about the package?

(A) It requires a signature. (B) It was sent to a sender.

telephone message

> W: Hello, I'm calling to find out what happened to my order. I got a _____ posted on my door and it said no one was _____ and the package _____ _____ _____ from a recipient. The second delivery will be made tomorrow. Will you _____ for the delivery to be made after 4 P.M.? Before that, there will not be anyone present. _____, is there any way to pick up my order in person?

---

paraphrasing 주어진 어휘 또는 표현과 의미가 동일한 것을 연결하세요.

4. electricity failure • • (a) power outage
5. complete • • (b) schedule
6. arrange • • (c) fill out

토익에 나올 실전 문제

01. Why is the speaker calling the listener?
    (A) To thank him for his assistance
    (B) To promote a bookstore opening
    (C) To request copies of a book
    (D) To provide a schedule update

02. What does the speaker say she has done?
    (A) Contacted a hotel
    (B) Proofread a file
    (C) E-mailed a contract
    (D) Reserved a flight

03. What is the listener asked to do?
    (A) Send some images
    (B) Approve a budget
    (C) Submit an application
    (D) Put up some posters

04. What is the purpose of the call?
    (A) To report a broken item
    (B) To inquire about shipping fees
    (C) To check the status of a delivery
    (D) To make a job offer

05. Why does the speaker expect the business to be busy this weekend?
    (A) A positive review was just printed.
    (B) A new service will be offered.
    (C) A promotional sale will be held.
    (D) A musical event is taking place.

06. What does the speaker ask the listener for?
    (A) An estimated date
    (B) A partial refund
    (C) A confirmation code
    (D) A product catalog

07. Who is the speaker?
    (A) An HR representative
    (B) A warehouse worker
    (C) A security guard
    (D) A computer technician

08. Why does the speaker say she had to work overtime?
    (A) A deadline was changed.
    (B) A delivery arrived late.
    (C) Some employees were absent.
    (D) Some equipment was not working.

09. What does the speaker imply when she says, "it looks like there are three types"?
    (A) She has found some missing items for the listener.
    (B) She does not want to place another order.
    (C) She is concerned that there is an error.
    (D) She is satisfied with the wide variety.

10. What most likely is the speaker's job?
    (A) Real estate agent
    (B) Newspaper journalist
    (C) Repair technician
    (D) Interior designer

11. What does the speaker tell the listener about?
    (A) A customer appreciation event will be held.
    (B) A contract has been terminated.
    (C) A price discount will be available.
    (D) A business is asking for customer feedback.

12. Why should the listener call the speaker back?
    (A) To book a tour
    (B) To provide an address
    (C) To arrange a payment
    (D) To claim a free gift

13. What kind of event is the speaker preparing for?
    (A) A company barbecue
    (B) A graduation ceremony
    (C) A community celebration
    (D) An educational workshop

14. According to the speaker, what is a problem?
    (A) A Web site has crashed.
    (B) An event speaker had to cancel.
    (C) The weather will be unfavorable.
    (D) People are not responding to invitations.

15. What does the speaker ask the listener to do?
    (A) Set up chairs for an event
    (B) Contact the ticket holders
    (C) Make an announcement
    (D) Check venue availability

16. What kind of business does the speaker work for?
    (A) A home delivery service
    (B) A moving company
    (C) A furniture store
    (D) A storage facility

17. What does the speaker say she has done?
    (A) Applied a member discount
    (B) Contacted a manufacturer
    (C) Placed an online order
    (D) Reserved an item

18. What does the speaker offer to the listener?
    (A) An extended sale period
    (B) A long-term warranty
    (C) Assembly assistance
    (D) Free home delivery

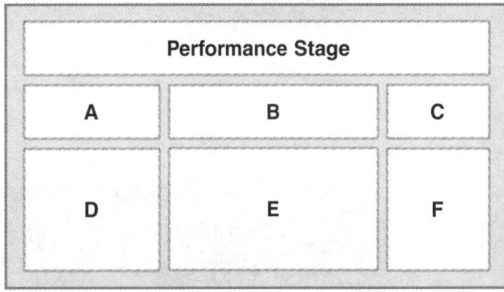

19. What is the purpose of the call?
    (A) To promote a radio show
    (B) To give directions to a theatre
    (C) To ask about a music preference
    (D) To invite the listener to a performance

20. Look at the graphic. Where are the speaker's seats located?
    (A) Section B
    (B) Section C
    (C) Section D
    (D) Section E

21. Who is Anita Florence?
    (A) An actress
    (B) A musician
    (C) A radio host
    (D) A screenplay writer

'멋진 당신, 오늘도 화이팅'

DAY 13

오늘의 학습 포인트

PART 3. 대화 주제 - 회사

1. 입사·채용
   - 빈출 내용 - 공석 채용 계획 & 신입사원 모집
   - 빈출 문제 - 주제 문제 & 다음에 할 일 문제

2. 전근·퇴임
   - 빈출 내용 - 동료 전근/퇴임 송별 파티 & 승진 축하
   - 빈출 문제 - 구체적인 정보를 묻는 문제

PART 4. 담화 유형 - 녹음 메시지(recorded message) / 설명(instructions)

1. 녹음 메시지(recorded message)
   - 빈출 내용 - 영업 시간 & 변경 사항 & 서비스 안내
   - 빈출 문제 - 화자가 근무하는 업종을 묻는 문제

2. 설명(instructions)
   - 빈출 내용 - 수업 개요 설명 & 업무 절차/주의할 점 설명
   - 빈출 문제 - 청자가 무엇을 받을지 묻는 질문

PART 3 회사 - 입사·채용 / 전근·퇴임

공석 채용 계획에 관한 대화와 전근/은퇴하는 직원을 위한 송별 파티에 대한 대화가 많이 나와요!

출제 유형 1 입사·채용

공석 채용 계획, 신입 사원 모집에 대한 대화가 가장 자주 출제됩니다.

- 입사·채용 관련 대화에서 자주 출제되는 어휘

> **입사·채용 관련 대화에서 자주 나오는 문제**
>
> · 주제 문제
> What are the speakers mainly talking about?
> → Hiring a new employee(신입 사원을 채용하는 것), A hiring plan(채용 계획) 등이 정답 보기로 출제됩니다.
>
> · 다음에 할 일을 묻는 문제
> What will the woman do next?
> → update a document (서류 업데이트 하기), make a recommendation (추천하기) 등 채용 관련하여 화자가 다음에 할 일이 정답으로 제시됩니다.

job description	업무 설명서	recruit	(신입 사원을) 모집하다
job vacancy	공석	manage	관리하다
job requirement	자격 요건	professional	직업의, 전문적인
position	직책	skilled	숙련된, 노련한
certificate	증명서, 자격증	seek	찾다, 구하다
degree	학위	highly	매우, 대단히
application	지원(서), 신청	new hire	신입 사원
candidate	지원자, 후보자	identification	신분증
résumé	이력서	adjust	조정하다, 적응하다
800+ work ethic	직업 윤리	occupation	직업
hire	고용하다	personality	성격
immediately	즉시, 바로	approval	승인
qualified	자격이 있는	opening	빈자리, 공석
recommendation	추천	exceptional	이례적인, 뛰어난
achievement	업적, 성취	**800+** probationary	수습의
full-time	정규직의	employment agency	직업 소개소
additional	추가의	meet the qualifications	자격 요건을 충족하다
consider	고려하다	expert	전문가
800+ cover letter	자기소개서	competitor	경쟁자

입사·채용

Day 13_P3_01.mp3 해석 p.116

BR - US

M: Rosalie, how is the cafeteria staff handling our company's expansion? It's not too much work for them, is it?

W: The food line is still doing alright, but we could really use an extra person on the registers. People get their food but have to wait to pay for it.

M: Okay, I'll post that we are looking for some part-time workers. Send me the job description by e-mail as soon as you get a chance.

01. Which section does the woman most likely manage?
    (A) The call center
    (B) The sales floor
    (C) The warehouse
    (D) The cafeteria

02. What are the speakers mainly talking about?
    (A) Installing registers
    (B) Hiring part-time staff
    (C) Digitizing a system
    (D) Changing a menu

03. What does the man tell the woman to do?
    (A) E-mail job requirements
    (B) Interview an applicant
    (C) Organize some files
    (D) Taste a new dish

이렇게 풀어요

01. 여자는 어느 부문을 관리하겠는가?
    (A) 콜센터
    (B) 매장
    (C) 창고
    (D) 구내식당

02. 화자들은 주로 무엇에 대해 이야기하는가?
    (A) 계산대를 설치하는 것
    (B) 시간제 직원을 고용하는 것
    (C) 시스템을 디지털화하는 것
    (D) 메뉴를 변경하는 것

03. 남자는 여자에게 무엇을 하라고 말하는가?
    (A) 자격 요건을 이메일로 보내기
    (B) 지원자 면접 보기
    (C) 파일 정리하기
    (D) 새로운 요리 맛보기

남자가 첫 대사에서 여자를 부르며 how is the cafeteria staff handling our company's expansion?이라고 물었고 여자가 구내식당의 상황에 대해 설명했습니다.
→ 구내식당을 관리하고 있음을 알 수 있으므로 (D)가 정답입니다.

여자가 but we could really use an extra person on the registers라고 했고, 남자는 I'll post that we are looking for some part-time workers라고 했습니다.
→ 시간제 직원을 고용하는 것에 대해 이야기하고 있으므로 (B)가 정답입니다.

남자가 Send me the job description by e-mail as soon as you get a chance라고 했습니다.
→ job description을 job requirements로 패러프레이징 한 (A)가 정답입니다.

출제 유형 2 — 전근·퇴임

동료가 전근 가거나 퇴임하는 상황에서 송별 파티를 계획하는 내용, 승진을 축하하는 내용 등이 출제됩니다.

전근·퇴임 관련 대화에서 자주 나오는 문제

· 구체적인 정보를 묻는 문제
What does the man say about ~?
→ about 뒤에 전근/퇴임과 관련된 키워드뿐만 아니라 대화에서 언급된 부수적인 소재가 나올 수도 있으므로 대화를 듣기 전에 질문을 먼저 파악하고 들어야 합니다.

· 전근·퇴임 관련 대화에서 자주 출제되는 어휘

relocate	전근 가다, 이전하다	supervisor	관리자, 상사
anticipate	고대하다, 예상하다	branch	지점, 지사
look forward to	~을 고대하다	encourage	장려하다, 권장하다
communicate	의사소통하다	retire	은퇴하다
on a daily basis	매일	progress	진행, 진전
appoint	임명하다, 지명하다	promote	승진시키다
competent	유능한	farewell	(작별) 인사
recommend	추천하다	replacement	후임자
transfer	전근시키다	welcome reception	환영회
opportunity	기회	going-away party	고별 파티
impressive	인상 깊게 생각하는	talented	재능이 있는
duty	직무, 의무	authority	권한
evaluate	평가하다	carry out	수행하다, 실시하다
promotion	승진	reorganize	재조직하다
inexperienced	경험이 부족한	agreement	동의(서)
overseas	해외의, 해외로	deal	거래, 협정
operation	사업, 경영	workforce	노동력
corporation	기업	asset	자산
acquisition	인수, 획득	strategy	전략

전근·퇴임

> US - US
>
> M: Tammy, are you looking forward to managing the Barcelona branch?
> W: I think so. I've never been to Spain before. I might have some problems communicating.
> M: Don't you speak Spanish well?
> W: I studied it in Mexico, but I don't use it on a daily basis.
> M: Have you heard of an app called Babel Buddy? It's supposed to be a great way to practice foreign languages. You should try downloading it before you go.
> W: Thanks, that sounds really helpful.
> M: By the way, I also have a map of famous restaurants from when I went on vacation there. Remind me to bring that in for you on Monday.

01. What does the woman mean when she says, "I've never been to Spain before"?

(A) She does not like to travel.
(B) She is worried about relocating.
(C) She needs to renew her passport.
(D) She wants to enroll in language classes.

02. According to the man, what is an app designed for?

(A) Asking directions
(B) Finding restaurants
(C) Meeting new people
(D) Learning a language

03. What does the man offer to give the woman?

(A) A map
(B) A GPS device
(C) A cultural guide
(D) A tourist handbook

이렇게 풀어요

01. 여자가 "저는 스페인에 가본 적이 없어요"라고 말할 때 의미하는 바는 무엇인가?
    (A) 여자는 여행하는 것을 좋아하지 않는다.
    (B) 여자는 전근 가는 것에 대하여 걱정한다.
    (C) 여자는 여권을 갱신할 필요가 있다.
    (D) 여자는 언어 수업에 등록하고 싶어 한다.

02. 남자에 따르면, 앱은 무엇을 위해 고안되었는가?
    (A) 길을 묻는 것
    (B) 레스토랑을 찾는 것
    (C) 새로운 사람들을 만나는 것
    (D) 언어를 학습하는 것

03. 남자는 여자에게 무엇을 주겠다고 제안하는가?
    (A) 지도
    (B) GPS 기기
    (C) 문화와 관련된 안내서
    (D) 관광 안내책자

여자가 해당 문장에 뒤이어 I might have some problems communicating.이라고 했습니다.
→ 여자는 스페인에 가 본 적이 없어 의사소통에 어려움을 겪을 것을 걱정하고 있으므로 전근 가는 것에 대해 걱정한다고 한 (B)가 정답입니다.

남자가 앱을 소개하며 Have you heard of an app called Babel Buddy? It's supposed to be a great way to practice foreign languages.라고 했습니다.
→ practice를 learn으로 패러프레이징 한 (D)가 정답입니다.

남자가 마지막 대사에서 I also have a map of famous restaurants from when I went on vacation there. Remind me to bring that in for you on Monday.라고 했습니다.
→ 지도를 가져오겠다고 했으므로 (A)가 정답입니다.

따라 하면 문제가 풀리는
연습 문제

문제와 각 선택지의 키워드에 표시하세요. 그러고 나서 대화를 듣고 빈칸에 들어갈 말을 받아쓴 후 정답을 선택해 보세요.

01. What will take place next Saturday?

(A) A conference (B) A farewell party

M: Julie is moving to New York for a new _____! So, I'm _____ her a party at Tommy's restaurant next Saturday and I was hoping you could come.
W: I _____ _____ _____ on Saturday, but thanks for letting me know. I'll make sure to _____ _____ her office before she leaves.

02. What does the woman ask the man to do?

(A) Conduct an interview (B) Review a résumé

M: Here is Sarah Phillip's _____. She's coming in at 2 P.M. for an interview.
W: Thanks, but an _____ meeting came up. If I'm not back in time, _____ _____ _____ the interview?
M: Sure, that's not a problem.

03. What caused a problem?

(A) A newly introduced policy (B) A schedule conflict

M: We are going to have _____ _____ at Mr. Harris' office this Friday.
W: Yes, I know. But we have a problem. The building _____ office says the annual _____ will fall on that day. What do you think about using Ms. Thompson's office _____?

paraphrasing 주어진 어휘 또는 표현과 의미가 동일한 것을 연결하세요.

1. won't be available   •   • (a) can't make it
2. stop by   •   • (b) visit
3. résumé   •   • (c) document

04. Why was the man surprised?

(A) A shipment was delayed. (B) A colleague will transfer.

> M: I'm surprised to hear that David applied for a _____ to Denver.
> W: Yes, I think he is doing well here and he might be _____ to a manager position soon. Why is he going to Denver?
> M: He wants to _____ more time with his family.

05. What does the woman say she will do?

(A) Visit the booth at a later time (B) Fill out a form

> W: Good morning, I'm interested in _____ _____ your assistant accountant position.
> M: Thank you for visiting our _____. Do you want to have an _____ _____ today at Wyden Job Fair? There is a _____ at 3:00. Can I book that for you?
> W: Yes, I will _____ _____ after having lunch.

06. What did the man recently do?

(A) He traveled overseas. (B) He relocated to another city.

> W: Hi, Jeff. How do you like your _____ _____ here in Atlanta so far?
> M: There are things I miss about Los Angeles, but I'm _____ _____ _____ living here. Also, I thought it would be hard to _____ from sales to marketing, but I'm handling it quite well.

paraphrasing 주어진 어휘 또는 표현과 의미가 동일한 것을 연결하세요.

4. colleague • • (a) deal with
5. switch • • (b) change
6. handle • • (c) coworker

01. What is the woman impressed with?
    (A) An industry award
    (B) A letter of recommendation
    (C) Some work experience
    (D) A portfolio of designs

02. Why does the man tell the woman about his friend?
    (A) To inquire about the status of an application
    (B) To explain how he found out about the company
    (C) To recommend an employee for a promotion
    (D) To give an example of a project he worked on

03. What is the man's specialty?
    (A) International economics
    (B) Resource management
    (C) Web site security
    (D) Architectural design

04. Why did the man visit the business?
    (A) To drop off some samples
    (B) To promote a newspaper subscription
    (C) To book a dental checkup
    (D) To inquire about an open position

05. What does the woman mention about the business?
    (A) It will extend its business hours.
    (B) It will open a second location.
    (C) It is behind schedule today.
    (D) It is highly rated by patients.

06. What does the woman recommend doing?
    (A) Checking the accuracy of a report
    (B) Filling out an online form
    (C) Updating a delivery address
    (D) Calling the business next month

07. What is the conversation mainly about?
    (A) Attending a conference
    (B) Gathering customer feedback
    (C) Hiring more employees
    (D) Improving work efficiency

08. What is the man concerned about?
    (A) Travelling alone
    (B) Giving a talk
    (C) Testing a product
    (D) Meeting with clients

09. What does Sarah plan to give to the man?
    (A) Some contact information
    (B) An updated schedule
    (C) Some survey results
    (D) Some online resources

10. What is the main purpose of the conversation?
    (A) To suggest an equipment upgrade
    (B) To talk about a job opening
    (C) To explain an investment strategy
    (D) To review a sales goal

11. What does the woman inquire about?
    (A) The number of working hours
    (B) The size of a team
    (C) The design process
    (D) The compensation system

12. What does the woman mention about herself?
    (A) She is able to learn things quickly.
    (B) She has a large professional network.
    (C) She is available to start work immediately.
    (D) She knows a lot about a product.

13. What does the man say is a problem?

    (A) A security badge does not work properly.
    (B) He cannot access the supply closet.
    (C) He is not on the office mailing list.
    (D) Some work gets deleted.

14. What will the woman have Rick do?

    (A) Conduct an inspection
    (B) Install some updates
    (C) Print a document
    (D) Give a tour

15. What does the woman say the man should do?

    (A) Complete some forms
    (B) Request special access
    (C) Restart his computer
    (D) Contact the IT department

16. Where most likely are the speakers?

    (A) At a retail store
    (B) At a medical clinic
    (C) At a publishing company
    (D) At a university library

17. What does the man say the women have to do?

    (A) Submit a proposal
    (B) Interview candidates
    (C) Attend an orientation
    (D) Complete online training

18. What does the man ask Jessica?

    (A) What time she arrives at the office
    (B) Which subject she majored in
    (C) How much experience she has
    (D) Whether she filed a form

Greensboro Public Library Management Certification Classes		
Period 1	Tuesdays	7 – 8 P.M.
Period 2	Wednesdays	8 – 9 A.M.
Period 3	Fridays	12 – 1 P.M.
Period 4	Saturdays	10 – 11 A.M.

19. What information was announced in a newsletter?

    (A) A company will open its first international branch.
    (B) A manager will transfer overseas.
    (C) A coworker will be promoted.
    (D) A merger will take place.

20. What does the man say he is worried about?

    (A) Giving a presentation to the management
    (B) Getting turned down for a promotion
    (C) Working at an international branch
    (D) Being fired due to downsizing

21. Look at the graphic. Which period will the man most likely register for?

    (A) Period 1
    (B) Period 2
    (C) Period 3
    (D) Period 4

PART 4

녹음 메시지(recorded message) / 설명(instructions)

변경 사항을 알리는 녹음 메시지와 업무 관련 설명이 자주 출제됩니다.

적용 기술

[기적의 필기노트] 67P~69P
LC 기술 49, 50, 51

출제 유형 1 — 녹음 메시지(recorded message)

업체나 회사에서 녹음해 놓은 자동 안내 메시지입니다. 영업 시간, 변경 사항, 서비스 안내에 관한 내용이 주로 출제됩니다.

녹음 메시지에서 자주 나오는 문제

· 화자가 근무하는 업종을 묻는 질문
What kind of business does the speaker work at?
→ 담화 처음의 Thank you for calling ~ 뒤에 등장하는 고유명사(업체명, 기업명 등)에서 단서를 파악할 수 있습니다.

· 녹음 메시지에서 자주 출제되는 어휘

insurance	보험, 보험업	directions	길 안내
press	누르다	settle into	~에 자리 잡다
unable	~할 수 없는	at the moment	지금
undergo	겪다, 받다	business day	영업일
renovation	수리	reach	~에 연락하다
operator	전화 교환원	get back to	~에게 다시 연락하다
currently	현재	hang up	전화를 끊다
except	~을 제외하고	drop by	~에 들르다
tone	신호음	pound key	우물 정 표시
construction	공사	star key	별표
shortly	곧	stay on the line	끊지 말고 기다리다
loan	대출	voice mail service	음성 메시지 서비스
request	요청	extension	내선 번호
redirect	다시 보내다	regular hours	정규 업무 시간
aware	알고 있는	national holiday	국경일
automatically	자동으로	leave	남기다

녹음 메시지(recorded message)

> [AU]
> M: Thank you for calling Columbus Insurance. Please be aware that our office located at 232 Echo Avenue has been moved to a new location at 810 Rosebud Boulevard. You can find a mini-map and driving directions from the highway on our Web site. As we are still settling into the new office, please leave a message with your name and contact information and we will get back to you as soon as possible.

01. What kind of business does the speaker work at?
(A) A construction company
(B) An insurance agency
(C) An Internet provider
(D) A law firm

02. What does the speaker say about the office?
(A) It is undergoing renovations.
(B) It will be closed for a holiday.
(C) It changed its business hours.
(D) It has relocated to a new building.

03. What are listeners asked to do?
(A) Leave a recording
(B) Give an address
(C) Visit a Web site
(D) Call back later

이렇게 풀어요

01. 화자는 어떤 업종에서 근무하는가?
(A) 건설회사
(B) 보험사
(C) 인터넷 공급업체
(D) 법률회사

담화 가장 처음에 Thank you for calling Columbus Insurance라고 했습니다.
→ 화자는 보험사에서 일하고 있다는 것을 알 수 있으므로 정답은 (B)입니다.

02. 화자는 사무실에 대해서 무엇을 말하고 있는가?
(A) 수리 중이다.
(B) 휴일 동안 영업을 하지 않을 것이다.
(C) 영업 시간이 변경되었다.
(D) 새로운 건물로 이전했다.

our office located at 232 Echo Avenue has been moved to a new location이라고 했습니다.
→ 새로운 위치로 이전하였다는 것을 알 수 있으므로 정답은 (D)입니다.

03. 청자들은 무엇을 할 것을 요청받는가?
(A) 녹음을 남길 것
(B) 주소를 줄 것
(C) 웹사이트를 방문할 것
(D) 나중에 전화할 것

담화 마지막에 please leave a message with your name and contact information이라고 했습니다.
→ 화자가 청자에게 이름과 연락처를 남겨 달라고 했으므로 정답은 (A)입니다.

출제 유형 2 설명(instructions)

수업에서 개요를 설명하거나, 회사에서 업무 절차나 주의해야 할 점을 설명하는 내용이 주로 출제됩니다.

설명하는 담화에서 자주 나오는 문제

· 청자가 무엇을 받을지 묻는 질문
What will the listeners receive?
→ I will distribute them to you 등과 같이 receive의 반대말인 distribute 다음에 언급되는 명사 혹은 대명사가 무엇을 의미하는지 파악하면 됩니다.

· **설명하는 담화에서 자주 출제되는 어휘**

guideline	지침	self-check register	셀프 계산대
accidentally	우연히	in the interest of	~을 위해서
issue	발행하다	device	장비, 기기
summary	요약, 개요	instructor	강사
price tag	가격표	defective	결함이 있는
assist	돕다, 보조하다	deadline	마감 기한
admit	인정하다	coordinate	조정하다, 편성하다
forward	보내다, 전달하다	leading	선도하는
conduct	수행하다, 실시하다	replace	~을 대신하다
negotiate	협상하다	in person	직접
approval	승인, 허가	volunteer	자원봉사자, 자원하다
instruct	지시하다, 가르치다	separate	분리된
challenging	도전적인, 힘든	following	다음의
assume	떠맡다, 가정하다	engage	관여하다
fulfill	이행하다	assign	할당하다
stay around	(떠나지 않고) 기다리다	add	추가하다
concern	우려, 걱정	split into groups	그룹으로 나누다

설명(instructions)

[US]
W: Thank you for coming to the meeting on such short notice. I want to talk about the online discount coupon that we issued for the sales promotion. Some customers complain that scanners at self-checkout registers cannot read it, so they couldn't get a discount. It accidentally happened at some self-checkout registers with old versions of scanners. So, I posted a sign on each register about how customers can apply coupons to their purchase. In order to get a discount, customers need to just type in the 8-digit number on the screen instead of scanning it. And, here are new coupons with bar codes that our scanners can read. I will distribute them to you. You can just scan it for the customers who have trouble following the directions.

01. What is the problem?
 (A) A device is malfunctioning.
 (B) The wrong price tag is attached.
 (C) Some merchandise is defective.
 (D) The delivery was delayed.

02. What are customers instructed to do to get a discount?
 (A) Spend a certain amount of money
 (B) Enter numbers directly on a screen
 (C) Order some items online
 (D) Mention the ads to the cashier

03. What will the listeners receive?
 (A) A new scanner
 (B) Free shipping vouchers
 (C) New coupons
 (D) A training manual

이렇게 풀어요

01. 무엇이 문제인가?
 (A) 장비가 제대로 작동하지 않는다.
 (B) 잘못된 가격표가 붙여져 있다.
 (C) 몇몇 물건에 결함이 있다.
 (D) 배송이 지연되었다.

02. 할인을 받기 위해서 고객들은 무엇을 하도록 지시 받는가?
 (A) 특정 금액을 소비하기
 (B) 화면에 직접 번호를 입력하기
 (C) 몇몇 품목을 온라인으로 주문하기
 (D) 계산원에게 광고를 언급하기

03. 청자들은 무엇을 받을 것인가?
 (A) 새로운 스캐너
 (B) 무료 배송 쿠폰
 (C) 새로운 쿠폰
 (D) 교육 매뉴얼

초반부에서 Some customers complain that scanners at self-checkout registers cannot read it, so they couldn't get a discount.라고 했습니다.
→ 셀프 계산대의 스캐너가 온라인 할인 쿠폰을 제대로 읽지 못한다고 말하고 있으므로 cannot read it이 malfunction으로 패러프레이징 된 (A)가 정답입니다.

중반부에서 In order to get a discount, customers need to just type in the 8-digit number on the screen instead of scanning it.이라고 했습니다.
→ 고객이 화면에 직접 입력을 하면 된다는 것을 알 수 있으므로 type이 enter로 패러프레이징 된 (B)가 정답입니다.

후반부에서 here are new coupons with bar codes that our scanners can read. I will distribute them to you.라고 했습니다.
→ 새로운 쿠폰을 나누어 주겠다고 했으므로 (C)가 정답입니다.

따라 하면 문제가 풀리는 연습 문제

문제와 각 선택지의 키워드에 표시하세요. 그리고 나서 담화를 듣고 빈칸에 들어갈 말을 받아쓴 후 정답을 선택해 보세요.

01. What company is the listener calling?

(A) A security agency (B) A credit card company

recorded message

> W: You have reached First Credit Card. _____ _____ of the customer service and card issuing department are from 9 A.M. to 5 P.M. So, please call again tomorrow at any time _____ our business hours. If you want to _____ a lost or stolen credit card, just press 0. Thank you.

02. What information are the listeners able to obtain from the company's Web site?

(A) New telephone numbers (B) Directions to the new location

recorded message

> M: Thank you for calling Barson Construction Company. Please note that we are _____ to a new building on Kensington Road on 3 November. You can _____ _____ to the new office on our Web site. All telephone numbers will _____ the _____. Thank you.

03. According to the speaker, what has caused a problem?

(A) A broken machine (B) Bad weather

recorded message

> W: Thank you for calling the Perkins' Ranch. We are one of the _____ ranches in the Scranton area. Due to the _____ _____ last week, all of the events and activities for tourists are _____ this week. All event schedules will go back to _____ sometime next week. We are open for business visits from 10 A.M. to 4 P.M. on weekdays. Thank you.

---

paraphrasing   주어진 어휘 또는 표현과 의미가 동일한 것을 연결하세요.

1. lost • • (a) bad weather
2. relocate • • (b) move
3. heavy snow • • (c) missing

246 기적의 토익 LC

04. What did listeners receive at the entrance?

(A) A meal voucher　　　(B) A welcome packet

instructions

> M: Attention please! I will tell you what you are going to do to _____ _____ your employee badge. You can find an application form in the _____ _____ that you received at the entrance. Would you please fill it out _____ now? I will call the name of a _____ and then they will go down to the security office in the basement.

05. What does the speaker ask the listeners to do?

(A) Give corrected price information　　(B) Distribute a discount coupon

instructions

> W: Hi, everyone. It's the first day of our seasonal _____ _____. I think today will be the _____ day of this three-day event. Before we open, I want to tell you about a _____ in the _____ on the advertisement. I will _____ _____ boards with the _____ information throughout the store. Just in case, I ask you to _____ it to every incoming customer and apologize for the mistake.

06. What are the listeners required to do?

(A) Wear protective gear　　　(B) Use basic tools

instructions

> M: Yesterday, you learned how to use the _____ _____ for woodwork. Today, we are going to use an electronic saw to _____ _____. It is the most _____ tool that we are using during the class. So, please make sure to wear these _____ _____ and goggles. They are all in the box beside the electronic saw.

paraphrasing 주어진 어휘 또는 표현과 의미가 동일한 것을 연결하세요.

4. employee badge　　•　　　　　　•　(a) gear
5. incoming　　　　　 •　　　　　　•　(b) identification
6. gloves and goggles　•　　　　　　•　(c) visiting

01. In which department does the speaker work?
    (A) Security
    (B) Sales
    (C) Finance
    (D) IT

02. What does the speaker ask the listeners to do?
    (A) Attend a workshop
    (B) Select a password
    (C) Read a user manual
    (D) Memorize a code

03. According to the speaker, why should listeners press the star key?
    (A) To search for a number
    (B) To report an error
    (C) To turn on a device
    (D) To try a process again

04. What kind of business is being called?
    (A) A law office
    (B) A department store
    (C) A utility company
    (D) An accounting firm

05. Why is an agent unavailable?
    (A) Staff members are being trained.
    (B) There are more calls than usual.
    (C) It is the weekend.
    (D) It is a national holiday.

06. Why should the listener press zero?
    (A) To make a payment by phone
    (B) To be connected to a repair person
    (C) To hear the recording again
    (D) To leave a message

07. What kind of business do the listeners work for?
    (A) A grocery store
    (B) A repair shop
    (C) A luxury hotel
    (D) A car rental agency

08. What is the speaker giving instructions about?
    (A) How to empty a vacuum
    (B) How to complete a form
    (C) How to install some software
    (D) How to operate a printer

09. What does the speaker imply when she says, "Jake will be here until six o'clock"?
    (A) A delivery will be accepted by Jake.
    (B) The speaker sent an incorrect schedule.
    (C) Jake knows how to use a device.
    (D) Jake will speak to an important client.

10. According to the speaker, what is available at the front of the room?
    (A) Towels
    (B) Gym clothes
    (C) Exercise mats
    (D) Water bottles

11. What does the speaker say about the intense class?
    (A) It is only recommended for athletic people.
    (B) It costs an extra fee to transfer into.
    (C) It requires a background in yoga.
    (D) It does not take long to fill.

12. What will the listeners do next?
    (A) Sign release forms
    (B) Visit an office
    (C) Stretch out
    (D) Make a payment

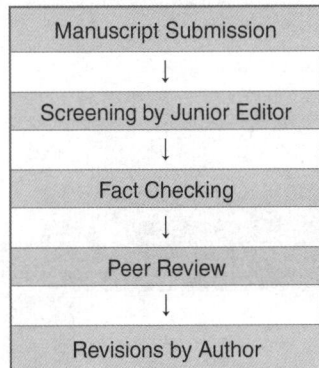

	Thursday Schedule
9:15	Summary Meeting
	– Conference Room B
9:30	Video Teleconference (Shanghai)
	– Conference Room D
10:00	Shareholder Meeting
	– CEO's Office Suite
10:45	Planning Meeting
	– Break Room

13. What does the speaker say has helped the company find new writers?
    (A) Sending messages to writing groups
    (B) Attending an industry event
    (C) Advertising on social media
    (D) Hosting writing workshops

14. Look at the graphic. According to the speaker, what is the newest step in the flowchart?
    (A) Screening by Junior Editor
    (B) Fact Checking
    (C) Peer Review
    (D) Revisions by Author

15. What concern does the speaker tell the listeners about?
    (A) A team's workload is too heavy.
    (B) Some manuscripts are not original.
    (C) A software program is difficult to use.
    (D) New competitors have entered the market.

16. According to the speaker, what happened yesterday?
    (A) Some coworkers quit.
    (B) The power went out.
    (C) New software was installed.
    (D) The company announced a merger.

17. Look at the graphic. Which room will the speaker go to first?
    (A) Conference Room B
    (B) Conference Room D
    (C) CEO's Office Suite
    (D) Break Room

18. What does the speaker say Jim Sanders will do?
    (A) Update a Web site
    (B) Test some hardware
    (C) Lead a repair team
    (D) Distribute a memo

'멋진 당신, 오늘도 화이팅'

DAY 14

오늘의 학습 포인트

PART 3. 대화 주제 - 회사

1. 사내 교육
   - 빈출 내용 - 신입 사원, 수습 직원 교육 & 특정 부서 직무 관련 교육
   - 빈출 문제 - 질문하는 것을 묻는 문제 & 방법을 묻는 문제

2. 비품·장비
   - 빈출 내용 - 비품 주문 & 고장 난 기기/장비 수리 요청
   - 빈출 문제 - 제안 문제 & 목적 문제

PART 4. 담화 유형 - 회의 발췌록(excerpt from a meeting)

1. 업무 지시
   - 빈출 내용 - 새로운 계획 & 고객 불만 & 매출 목표
   - 빈출 문제 - 화자 의도 파악 문제 & 제안·요청 문제

2. 규정 변경
   - 빈출 내용 - 정책 변경 & 기존 규정 상기
   - 빈출 문제 - 주제·목적 문제

PART 3 회사 - 사내 교육 / 비품·장비

직무 관련 교육에 관한 대화와 비품 주문, 고장 난 장비의 수리를 요청하는 대화가 많이 나와요!

출제 유형 1 사내 교육

신입 사원이나 수습 직원의 교육, 특정 부서를 대상으로 하는 직무 관련 교육에 대한 내용이 출제됩니다.

・사내 교육 관련 대화에서 자주 출제되는 어휘

사내 교육 관련 대화에서 자주 나오는 문제

・질문하는 것이 무엇인지 묻는 문제
What does the man ask about?
→ 주로 교육받는 내용에 대해 문의하는데, 대화에서 언급된 말이 정답에 패러프레이징되는 경우가 많은 문제 유형입니다. 또한 ask for로 묻는 요청 문제와 혼동하지 않도록 주의해야 합니다.

・방법을 묻는 문제
How can the man get more information?
→ 추가 정보를 얻는 방법에 대해서는 주로 대화 마지막에 언급됩니다. Contact a supervisor/coworker(상사/동료에게 연락하기), Check a Web site(웹사이트 확인하기) 등이 자주 출제됩니다.

basics	기본, 필수적인 것들	essential	필수적인
sales floor	매장	training	교육
get used to	~에 익숙해지다	workshop	워크숍
informative	유익한	attendance	출석, 참석, 참석률
inventory	물품 목록, 재고	lecture	강의, 강연
process	과정, 절차	attendee	참석자
reminder	상기시키는 것	reserve	예약하다, 보유하다
apprenticeship	수습 기간, 수습직	confidence	자신감, 확신
procedure	절차	grateful	감사하는, 고마워하는
trade show	무역 박람회	refer	참고하다, 언급하다
handle	다루다	authorize	권한을 부여하다
reception	접수처	accurate	정확한
fill out[in]	작성하다, 기입하다	commit to	~에 전념하다, 헌신하다
previous	이전의	particular	특정한, 특별한
expertise	전문성, 전문 지식	absence	부재, 결석
train	교육시키다	go smoothly	순조롭게 진행되다
trainee	교육을 받는 사람	company-wide	회사 전반의
agenda	의제, 안건	handout	유인물
draft	초안	demonstration	시연, 시범 설명

풀이 방법 — 사내 교육

🎧 Day 14_P3_01.mp3   💡 해석 p.130

[BR - AU]

W: Good morning, Phil. Welcome to your first day here at our department store. I'll show you the basics and help you get used to being on the sales floor.

M: Okay, great. The training session was very informative, but I'm still not sure what to do with newly arrived inventory. How are we supposed to handle it?

W: Just hit this button on the register to switch it to check-in mode. Then scan each item and put it out on the sales floor.

M: That sounds pretty simple.

W: It is. If you have further questions, feel free to use this radio to contact a supervisor.

---

01. What kind of business do the speakers work at?

(A) A bookstore
(B) A supermarket
(C) A department store
(D) A shipping company

02. What does the man ask about?

(A) An inventory procedure
(B) An interview schedule
(C) A commission policy
(D) A training process

03. According to the woman, how can the man get more information?

(A) By reading an employee handbook
(B) By contacting a supervisor
(C) By looking at a Web site
(D) By checking a board

🔑 이렇게 풀어요

01. 화자들은 어떤 종류의 사업체에서 근무하는가?
  (A) 서점
  (B) 슈퍼마켓
  (C) 백화점
  (D) 배송 회사

여자가 첫 대사에서 Welcome to your first day here at our department store라고 했습니다.
→ 화자들은 백화점에서 근무한다는 것을 알 수 있으므로 (C)가 정답입니다.

02. 남자는 무엇에 대해 물어보는가?
  (A) 물품 목록(을 다루는) 절차
  (B) 면접 일정
  (C) 수수료 정책
  (D) 교육 과정

남자가 but I'm still not sure what to do with newly arrived inventory. How are we supposed to handle it?이라고 물어봤습니다.
→ 물품 목록을 어떻게 다루어야 하는지 물었으므로 (A)가 정답입니다.

03. 여자에 따르면, 남자는 어떻게 정보를 더 얻을 수 있는가?
  (A) 직원 안내책자를 읽음으로써
  (B) 상사에게 연락함으로써
  (C) 웹사이트를 봄으로써
  (D) 게시판을 확인함으로써

여자가 마지막 대사에서 If you have further questions, feel free to use this radio to contact a supervisor라고 했습니다.
→ 무전기를 사용해 상사에게 연락하라고 했으므로 (B)가 정답입니다.

비품·장비

회사에서 비품을 주문하는 내용, 장비나 기기가 고장 나서 수리를 요청하는 내용이 자주 출제됩니다.

비품·장비 관련 대화에서 자주 나오는 문제

· 제안 문제
What does the woman suggest the man do?
→ 비품이나 시설에 문제가 생겼을 때 주로 Contact technical support(기술 지원 부서에 연락하기), Ask for assistance(도움 요청하기), Use a different room(다른 방 이용하기) 등이 답으로 출제됩니다.

· 목적 문제
Why is the woman calling the man?
→ To report a problem (문제를 알리기 위해), To upgrade her software (소프트웨어를 업데이트 하기 위해) 등이 출제됩니다.

· 비품·장비 관련 대화에서 자주 출제되는 어휘

in good condition	상태가 좋은	separately	따로
complex	복잡한	track	추적하다
technical	기술적인	simplify	단순화하다
prior to	~보다 앞서서	dispatch	발송하다, 보내다
soundproofed	방음 장치가 되어 있는	fragile	깨지기 쉬운
assistance	도움	freight	화물
attentive	주의를 기울이는	content	내용물
superb	훌륭한, 최고의	carton	곽, 통
thorough	철저한	quantity	양, 수량
broken part	고장 난 부품	transport	수송하다, 운반하다
rapid	빠른	stringent	(규칙이) 엄격한
uncertain	불확실한	recipient	수령인, 수취인
hazardous	위험한	exempt	면제된
business contacts	사업 거래처	faucet	수도꼭지
caution	주의를 주다, 조심	postage	우편 요금
work crew	작업반	stockroom	비품 저장실
set up	설치하다	assemble	조립하다
fix	수리하다, 해결하다	quote	견적서
warranty period	보증 기간	run out of	~이 다 떨어지다

풀이 방법 — 비품·장비

[US - US]

M: Maria, is the Internet working on your computer? I'm supposed to send an e-mail to a client, but it's not working right.
W: Really? What's wrong?
M: When I try to open the Internet browser I get an error message.
W: That's strange, mine seems to be working fine. Why don't you call the IT department? I have their phone number here if you need it.
M: Thanks. In all the time I've worked here, I've never had to ask them for help before.
W: Everyone there is really helpful. I'm sure they'll be able to fix the problem in no time.

01. What is the man trying to do?
    (A) Send an e-mail
    (B) Host a meeting
    (C) Make some copies
    (D) Update some software

02. What does the woman suggest the man do?
    (A) Use a coworker's workstation
    (B) Contact another department
    (C) Call a repairperson
    (D) File a complaint

03. What does the woman say about the people in the IT department?
    (A) They return calls quickly.
    (B) They work on another floor.
    (C) They are all highly experienced.
    (D) They are good at fixing problems.

이렇게 풀어요

01. 남자는 무엇을 하려고 하는가?
    (A) 이메일 보내기
    (B) 회의 주최하기
    (C) 복사하기
    (D) 소프트웨어 업데이트하기

    남자가 첫 대사에서 I'm supposed to send an e-mail to a client, but it's not working right이라고 했습니다.
    → 남자가 이메일을 보내야 한다고 했으므로 (A)가 정답입니다.

02. 여자는 남자에게 무엇을 하라고 제안하는가?
    (A) 동료의 자리 사용하기
    (B) 다른 부서에 연락하기
    (C) 수리하는 사람 부르기
    (D) 불만 제기하기

    여자가 대화 중반부에서 Why don't you call the IT department?라고 했습니다.
    → IT department가 another department로 패러프레이징 된 (B)가 정답입니다.

03. 여자는 IT 부서의 사람들에 대해서 뭐라고 말하는가?
    (A) 그들은 전화를 빨리 회신한다.
    (B) 그들은 다른 층에서 근무한다.
    (C) 그들은 모두 매우 경험이 많다.
    (D) 그들은 문제를 해결하는 데 능숙하다.

    여자가 마지막에 Everyone there is really helpful. I'm sure they'll be able to fix the problem in no time이라고 했습니다.
    → they'll be able to fix the problem in no time이 they are good at fixing problems로 패러프레이징 된 (D)가 정답입니다.

따라 하면 문제가 풀리는 연습 문제

문제와 각 선택지의 키워드에 표시하세요. 그러고 나서 대화를 듣고 빈칸에 들어갈 말을 받아쓴 후 정답을 선택해 보세요.

01. What will the woman most likely do next?

    (A) Scan an item   (B) Distribute books

> W: Hi, Steven. Thanks for coming in today on such _____ _____. I want to _____ a new wireless barcode scanner.
> M: It looks quite _____ to the old one.
> W: Yes. However, it has a larger display panel, so you can _____ check all information about the item, such as current stock and discounts. I'll _____ _____ user manuals.

02. Where is the conversation taking place?

    (A) In a storage room   (B) At an information desk

> W: Hi, Matthew. Ahmed said you will _____ _____ _____ ordering office supplies. I will teach you how to take the _____ of office supplies. It is required to be done before you _____ an order. Maybe this is your first time in the office supplies _____ _____.
> M: No, I came a couple of times to _____ some print paper.
> W: Okay, here is a list of current office supplies. You need to _____ each item and write the numbers on the list.

03. What problem are the speakers discussing?

    (A) The photocopier has not been delivered.   (B) The fax machine is not working.

> W: Hey, David. These _____ have to be sent to the Miami office today, but the fax machine is _____ _____.
> M: I _____ the technician but he said he wouldn't be able to come _____ next Monday.
> W: How about we call Sam in the tech department? He is really good at _____ machines.

---

paraphrasing   주어진 어휘 또는 표현과 의미가 동일한 것을 연결하세요.

1. distribute   •   • (a) give out
2. storage room   •   • (b) repair
3. fix   •   • (c) stock room

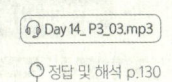

04. What should the workers do by the end of the year?

(A) Update personal information   (B) Take training sessions

> M: By the end of this year, all _____ workers are required to _____ a series of on-the-job trainings, so we need to revise some chapters in our training _____.
>
> W: Yes, right. I already _____ the personnel department to update the employee _____ chapter to include the _____ of medical insurance to our employees' family members.

05. What does the man offer to do?

(A) Install new software   (B) Help move devices

> M: Here's the key for the _____ _____. You'll find a slide projector, an overhead projector and a white board there.
>
> W: Thank you. I appreciate your help. _____ exactly is the equipment room?
>
> M: It's _____ _____ the main hall on the fourth floor. I can go with you and _____ _____ _____ _____ moving them to the meeting room.

06. What does the man suggest doing?

(A) Hiring additional workers   (B) Holding an information session

> W: Hi, Daniel. I received many _____ about the new incentive system.
>
> M: Yes, me too. I spent most of my time this morning _____ to them. _____ _____ _____ hold some information session about it?
>
> W: That sounds great. I will ask Mr. Craig about it.

paraphrasing 주어진 어휘 또는 표현과 의미가 동일한 것을 연결하세요.

4. attend a series of on-the-job trainings   •   • (a) question
5. help   •   • (b) give a hand
6. inquiry   •   • (c) take training sessions

01. What is the topic of the training session?
    (A) Labeling containers
    (B) Placing orders
    (C) Handling complaints
    (D) Reporting defects

02. What does the woman offer to do?
    (A) Rearrange the chairs
    (B) Share a manual
    (C) Take some notes
    (D) Print some documents

03. What will most likely happen next?
    (A) A sign-up sheet will be passed around.
    (B) Some sample products will be distributed.
    (C) A colleague will be introduced.
    (D) Some images will be shown.

04. In which department do the speakers work?
    (A) Information Technology
    (B) Shipping and Receiving
    (C) Accounting
    (D) Marketing

05. What does the man suggest?
    (A) Hiring a consultant
    (B) Gathering staff opinions
    (C) Adjusting team goals
    (D) Providing online training

06. What will the woman do next?
    (A) E-mail some data
    (B) Speak to a supervisor
    (C) Post a notice
    (D) Check a policy

07. What are the speakers discussing?
    (A) An employee retreat
    (B) A renovation project
    (C) A compensation package
    (D) A security plan

08. What does the woman suggest?
    (A) Posting some information online
    (B) Storing items off-site
    (C) Upgrading some equipment
    (D) Having employees share offices

09. What does the woman agree to do?
    (A) Set up an interview
    (B) Print an invoice
    (C) Adjust a budget
    (D) Contact some businesses

10. Where do the speakers most likely work?
    (A) At a warehouse
    (B) At a custom tailor
    (C) At a clothing
    (D) At a shipping center

11. What does the man ask about?
    (A) A return policy
    (B) A hiring process
    (C) A receipt format
    (D) An inventory list

12. According to the woman, how can the man get additional information?
    (A) By checking the company Web site
    (B) By referring to a handbook
    (C) By calling a supervisor
    (D) By reading a poster

13. What is the purpose of the phone call?
    (A) To request a repair
    (B) To plan a training session
    (C) To recommend a candidate
    (D) To confirm an appointment

14. What does the man mean when he says, "the teleconference starts in half an hour"?
    (A) He canceled his other appointments.
    (B) He cannot wait until the afternoon.
    (C) He intends to work through lunch.
    (D) He is focusing on another task.

15. According to the man, what is unusual about the teleconference?
    (A) It will include board members.
    (B) It will last for less than an hour.
    (C) It will be conducted in the morning.
    (D) It will be broadcasted to stockholders.

16. What are the women trying to do?
    (A) Purchase some office equipment
    (B) Prepare a room for a meeting
    (C) Print some event flyers
    (D) Place an online order

17. Who is the man?
    (A) A manufacturing plant worker
    (B) An electronics salesperson
    (C) A print shop employee
    (D) A business consultant

18. What does the man tell the women to do?
    (A) Join a membership
    (B) Write a product review
    (C) Check some product tags
    (D) Compare some options online

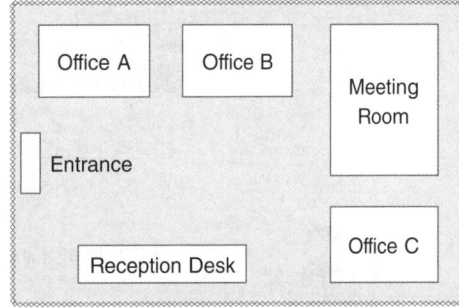

19. What is the purpose of the man's visit?
    (A) To deliver some office furniture
    (B) To interview for a position
    (C) To give a demonstration
    (D) To sign a contract

20. Look at the graphic. Which room will the man most likely go to?
    (A) Meeting Room
    (B) Office A
    (C) Office B
    (D) Office C

21. What does the man ask the woman to do?
    (A) Store an item
    (B) Copy a document
    (C) Announce an arrival
    (D) Validate a parking ticket

PART 4 회의 발췌록 (excerpt from a meeting)

각종 회의에서 새로운 계획이나 업무를 지시하는 내용과 변경된 규정에 대해 설명하는 내용이 자주 출제됩니다.

출제 유형 1 업무 지시

주간 회의나 분기별 회의에서 논의하는 형태로 제시되며, 새로운 계획이나 고객 칭찬/불만, 매출 목표에 대해 이야기하는 내용이 출제됩니다.

업무 지시 회의에서 자주 나오는 문제

· 화자의 의도 파악 문제
Why does the speaker say "~"?
→ 회의에서 논의되는 내용 중 한 문장이 발췌되므로, 논의 내용의 앞뒤 흐름 (긍정적인 내용인지, 부정적인 내용인지)을 잘 파악하며 들어야 합니다.

· 제안·요청 문제
What does the speaker ask her assistant to do?
→ 회의 참석자나 제3자에게 부탁하거나 요청하는 사항이 무엇인지 묻습니다. 주로 담화 마지막에 제시됩니다.

· 업무 지시 회의에서 자주 출제되는 어휘

initiative	(새로운) 계획	lose business	거래를 놓치다
management	경영(진)	brainstorm	브레인스토밍하다
major	주된	drop	하락, 하락하다
matter	사안	rating	등급, 순위
conclude	결론짓다	customer satisfaction	고객 만족
manageable	관리할 수 있는	average	평균의
insist	주장하다	competitor	경쟁업체
concentration	집중	run the ads	광고를 하다
sponsor	후원자, 후원하다	take notes	적다, 받아쓰다
analyst	분석가	office furniture	사무용 가구
differ	다르다	outline	개요
loyalty	충성(심)	mandatory	의무적인, 강제적인
goal	목표	accustomed	~에 익숙한
promptly	즉시, 정확히 제 시간에	routine	일상, 정해진 순서
duplicate	복사하다, 사본	acquaint	알려주다, 숙지하다
productive	생산적인	board members	임원, 이사진

업무 지시

[BR]

W: Next, let's discuss the drop in our customer satisfaction rating. At this time last year we had an average of 4.1 out of 5, but now it's down to 3.8. This is a serious problem because we could start losing business to our competitors. Let's try to brainstorm some ideas for promotions that might make our customers happy. We'll start here and go around the table. Vicky, since you're my assistant, I'd like you to write down all the ideas that we come up with and e-mail the list to us all after the meeting.

01. Why is the speaker worried?
   (A) A department exceeded its budget.
   (B) Customers are less satisfied.
   (C) There isn't enough staff.
   (D) Sales are down.

02. What are the meeting participants expected to do?
   (A) Discuss sales figures
   (B) Recommend a product
   (C) Share promotional ideas
   (D) Review customer surveys

03. What does the speaker ask her assistant to do?
   (A) Present some data
   (B) Arrange a schedule
   (C) Take meeting notes
   (D) Print some handouts

이렇게 풀어요

01. 화자는 왜 걱정을 하는가?
   (A) 부서가 예산을 초과했다.
   (B) 고객들이 덜 만족스러워 한다.
   (C) 직원이 충분하지 않다.
   (D) 판매가 감소하고 있다.

담화 초반부에 let's discuss the drop in our customer satisfaction rating라며 고객 만족도 등급 하락에 대해 이야기하자고 했습니다.
→ the drop in our customer satisfaction을 less satisfied로 패러프레이징 한 (B)가 정답입니다.

02. 회의 참석자들은 무엇을 할 것인가?
   (A) 판매 수치 논의하기
   (B) 제품 추천하기
   (C) 홍보 아이디어 공유하기
   (D) 고객 설문 검토하기

담화 중반부에서 Let's try to brainstorm some ideas for promotions that might make our customers happy라고 했습니다.
→ brainstorm을 share ideas로 패러프레이징 한 (C)가 정답입니다.

03. 화자는 그녀의 비서에게 무엇을 하라고 하는가?
   (A) 몇 가지 자료 보여주기
   (B) 일정 짜기
   (C) 회의록 작성하기
   (D) 유인물 출력하기

담화 마지막에서 Vicky, since you're my assistant, I'd like you to write down all the ideas that we come up with and e-mail the list to us all after the meeting.이라고 했습니다.
→ 비서인 Vicky에게 논의 내용을 적으라고 했으므로 (C)가 정답입니다.

출제 유형 2 — 규정 변경

사내 정책 변경에 대해 설명하거나, 기존 규정을 다시 한 번 상기시키는 내용의 담화가 출제됩니다.

규정 변경 관련 회의에서 자주 나오는 문제

· 주제·목적 문제
What is the speaker mainly talking about?
→ 주로 처음 한두 문장에서 회의 주제나 목적이 언급되는 경우가 많습니다. A company policy(회사 정책), To remind of a procedure(절차를 다시 알려주기 위해) 등의 형태로 정답이 출제됩니다.

· 규정 변경 관련 회의에서 자주 출제되는 어휘

consecutive	연속의	consultant	자문 위원
800+ overlap	겹치다	strengthen	강화하다
break room	휴게실	rule	규칙
ban	금지하다	successive	연속의
implement	이행하다	now that	~이기 때문에, ~이므로
oversee	감독하다	safety regulation	안전 규정
violate	위반하다	**800+** interact	교류하다
access	접속하다, 이용하다	prohibit	금지하다
equally	동일하게, 똑같이	restrict	제한하다
require	요구하다	warn	경고하다
importance	중요성	**800+** solicit	요청하다
800+ preliminary	예비의	incur	초래하다
put up	올리다	relevant	관련된
existing	기존의	attire	복장, 의복
destination	목적지, 장소	code	암호, 규정
disapprove	반대하다	former	이전의
800+ reassure	안심시키다	ultimately	궁극적으로

출제 포인트

What has the company changed?로 묻는 문제가 최근 출제되었습니다. 주제 문제와 동일한 전략으로 접근해서 풀면 됩니다.

규정 변경

🎧 Day 14_P4_02.mp3   해석 p.137

[US]

M: Now that you're all here, I want to go over our company's policy on using your vacation time. There are some basic rules, such as you have to apply at least two weeks in advance and you can't use any more than five consecutive days without the approval of your department head. In order to avoid any overlapping vacations among team members, you should always speak with your team leader before putting in your application. After this meeting, I'll put up a copy of this memo in the break room so that you can all refer to it.

01. What is the speaker mainly talking about?
(A) A vacation destination
(B) A company policy
(C) An open position
(D) A travel agency

02. What are the listeners instructed to do?
(A) Plan for two weeks
(B) Post their work schedules
(C) Apply five days in advance
(D) Consult with their team leader

03. What does the speaker say he is going to do after the meeting?
(A) Upload an image
(B) Print a document
(C) Send an e-mail
(D) Post a memo

이렇게 풀어요

01. 화자는 주로 무엇에 대하여 이야기하는가?
　　(A) 휴가 목적지
　　(B) 회사 정책
　　(C) 공석
　　(D) 여행사

첫 문장에서 I want to go over our company's policy on using your vacation time이라고 했습니다.
→ 회사의 정책에 대해 말하겠다고 했으므로 (B)가 정답입니다.

02. 청자들은 무엇을 할 것을 지시받는가?
　　(A) 2주 동안 계획을 세우기
　　(B) 그들의 근무 일정 게시하기
　　(C) 5일 전에 신청하기
　　(D) 팀장과 의논하기

중반부에서 you should always speak with your team leader before putting in your application이라고 했습니다.
→ speak with가 consult with로 패러프레이징 된 (D)가 정답입니다.

03. 화자는 회의 후에 무엇을 할 것이라고 말하는가?
　　(A) 사진 업로드하기
　　(B) 서류를 출력하기
　　(C) 이메일 보내기
　　(D) 회람을 게시하기

마지막에서 After this meeting, I'll put up a copy of this memo in the breakroom so that you can all refer to it이라고 했습니다.
→ put up이 post로 패러프레이징 된 (D)가 정답입니다.

따라 하면 문제가 풀리는

연습 문제

문제와 각 선택지의 키워드에 표시하세요. 그러고 나서 담화를 듣고 빈칸에 들어갈 말을 받아쓴 후 정답을 선택해 보세요.

01. What will happen next week?

(A) A client dinner will take place.   (B) Policy changes will be implemented.

excerpt from a meeting

> W: I have one _____ item on the meeting agenda. The accounting department decided to _____ a new travel expense reimbursement _____. Beginning next week, any expenses for meals should _____ original receipts and the _____ of _____ who you have meals with. In addition, business-class seats are _____ _____ except in urgent cases. Thanks in advance for your _____.

02. What did the employees complain about?

(A) Vending machines have limited beverage choices.   (B) The employee lounge is too small.

excerpt from a meeting

> M: Let's _____ _____ the next agenda. I have received many complaints about the _____ _____ in the employee lounge. People _____ that there are only a few _____ _____ of drinks and snacks. Also, the _____ are higher than in the store. So, I want you to do a _____ about what employees want.

03. Where do the listeners work?

(A) At a bank   (B) At a restaurant

excerpt from a meeting

> M: Thanks for coming a little bit earlier today. The winter holiday season is just _____ _____ _____. That means it's time to _____ our _____ for Christmas and New Year's Day. The decoration work will be _____ on the last Monday of October after we close. If you're _____, just send me an email. Those who work _____ _____ will be paid according to our policy.

paraphrasing 주어진 어휘 또는 표현과 의미가 동일한 것을 연결하세요.

1. reimbursement procedure   •   • (a) willing to do
2. complain   •   • (b) policy
3. interested   •   • (c) raise an issue

04. What will the speaker share next week?

(A) A list of sale items   (B) A new display plan

excerpt from a meeting

W: I called this meeting to _____ you that we will make some changes to the _____ _____ of our sports shoes section. Some major sports brands have contacted us and _____ us to _____ some display areas for their new basketball shoes. So, there will be a new _____ _____ for the sports shoes section next week. In _____ for this change, I ask you to make room for the old model in the _____ this week.

05. What are the listeners asked to do?

(A) Check their schedule   (B) Volunteer to work extra hours

excerpt from a meeting

W: Thank you for attending the weekly meeting. As I said in the _____ meeting, the self-check-in counters were already _____ at the both end of our airline's service area. Only _____ who travel with a carry-on bag can use those counters. Therefore, I will _____ you to work at these counters and _____ passengers on a rotating basis. Please check your _____ _____ on the board in the office.

06. What is the speaker mainly discussing?

(A) An updated hiring process   (B) A new catering company

excerpt from a meeting

M: Hello, as you know, we are going to _____ a new _____ company, Debora Foods & Service, for Ms. Kaplan's _____ _____ this Friday. This new company is well known for having professional serving staff and _____ special requests. I will send you a feedback form after the party and we will _____ _____ we will keep hiring this company for future events.

paraphrasing 주어진 어휘 또는 표현과 의미가 동일한 것을 연결하세요.

4. display   •   • (a) help
5. assist   •   • (b) showing
6. retirement party   •   • (c) event

토익에 나올 실전 문제

01. Who most likely are the listeners?
    (A) Safety inspectors
    (B) Financial planning experts
    (C) Product developers
    (D) Call center representatives

02. According to the speaker, what will happen tomorrow?
    (A) Some new equipment will be installed.
    (B) Some temporary employees will begin work.
    (C) A product line will be introduced.
    (D) A training session will be held.

03. What are the listeners asked to do?
    (A) E-mail some suggestions
    (B) Review a document
    (C) Work overtime
    (D) Check a schedule

04. What problem does the speaker mention?
    (A) A product had to be recalled.
    (B) A shipment could not be delivered.
    (C) A customer has filed a complaint.
    (D) A manufacturing plant closed temporarily.

05. What does the speaker imply when she says, "We will have a couple of very busy weeks"?
    (A) She expects that the listeners will receive shipments.
    (B) She plans to hold promotional events.
    (C) She thinks a project deadline is very tight.
    (D) She predicts the listeners will have many calls.

06. What will the speaker do next?
    (A) Meet with product development teams
    (B) Conduct job interviews
    (C) Distribute some documents
    (D) Work remotely

07. Why does the speaker think the listeners will be pleased?
    (A) A budget has been approved.
    (B) They will be moved to larger offices.
    (C) Some necessary supplies have arrived.
    (D) The staff will receive extra time off.

08. What has Ambrose Consulting offered to do?
    (A) Set up some equipment
    (B) Send a consultant
    (C) Share a meeting space
    (D) Review a proposal

09. What is Ms. Owens in charge of?
    (A) Keeping track of a schedule
    (B) Planning a staff party
    (C) Recruiting new employees
    (D) Handling incoming deliveries

10. What is the talk mainly about?
    (A) Strategies for improving a service
    (B) The launch of a new product
    (C) Changes to safety regulations
    (D) Plans for a sports competition

11. Why does the speaker say, "We're setting up the stage at the Westerville branch"?
    (A) To issue an invitation
    (B) To express a concern
    (C) To explain a delay
    (D) To clarify some information

12. Who most likely is David Brito?
    (A) A professional athlete
    (B) A marketing expert
    (C) A famous author
    (D) A research scientist

13. What is the main topic of the talk?
    (A) Decorating a garden
    (B) Upgrading some equipment
    (C) Offering a new service
    (D) Recruiting more workers

14. What problem does the speaker mention?
    (A) A delayed product launch
    (B) Insufficient workforce
    (C) Inconvenient transportation
    (D) A lack of funds

15. What does the speaker ask the listeners to do?
    (A) Recommend a contractor
    (B) Sign a document
    (C) Contact business owners
    (D) Teach a class

16. What does the speaker say about the company?
    (A) It manages many more properties than last year.
    (B) It has markedly increased its profit margin.
    (C) It will merge with another company.
    (D) It intends to downsize soon.

17. What did the speaker recently decide to do?
    (A) Update a policy
    (B) Launch a product
    (C) Relocate the office
    (D) Hire more employees

18. What does the speaker ask the listeners to do?
    (A) Complete a survey
    (B) Refer job candidates
    (C) Visit some properties
    (D) Attend a training session

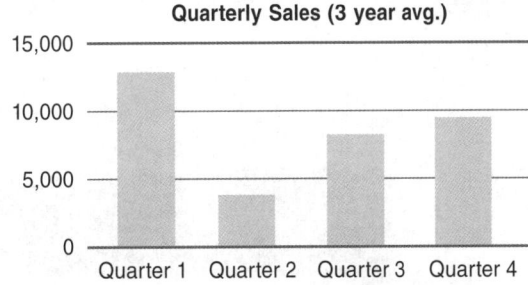

19. What kind of product does the company sell?
    (A) Tablet computers
    (B) Mobile phones
    (C) Electronics accessories
    (D) Music devices

20. Look at the graphic. Which quarter does the meeting take place in?
    (A) Quarter 1
    (B) Quarter 2
    (C) Quarter 3
    (D) Quarter 4

21. What else does the speaker want to talk about?
    (A) Web site design
    (B) Different products
    (C) Customer feedback
    (D) Head office relocation

'멋진 당신, 오늘도 화이팅'

DAY

15

오늘의 학습 포인트

PART 3. 대화 주제 - 회사/상점
1. 출장·행사
빈출 내용 - 출장 계획 & 워크숍, 콘퍼런스 등 행사 참석
빈출 문제 - 출장비 환급 관련 문제 & 행사 세부 사항 문제

2. 상품 구매·서비스
빈출 내용 - 상품/서비스 관련 문의
빈출 문제 - 업종 문제 & 요청 사항 문제

PART 4. 담화 유형 - 담화(talk)
1. 제품 시연
빈출 내용 - 신제품 출시 행사 제품 소개
빈출 문제 - 목적 문제

2. 발표
빈출 내용 - 안내 사항 & 장소 소개 & 설문 결과 설명
빈출 문제 - 다음 할 일 문제

PART 3 회사 - 출장·행사 / 상점 - 상품 구매·서비스

워크숍, 콘퍼런스 참석 등 행사 및 출장 관련 대화와 상품이나 서비스에 대해 문의하는 대화가 많이 나와요!

출제 유형 1 출장·행사

출장 계획에 대해 말하거나, 직원 연수, 워크숍, 콘퍼런스 참석 등의 사내 행사에 대해 대화하는 내용이 출제됩니다.

· 출장·행사 관련 대화에서 자주 출제되는 어휘

출장·행사 관련 대화에서 자주 나오는 문제

· 출장에 대한 환급과 관련된 문제
According to the man, what expense will be fully reimbursed?
→ 환급 관련 내용은 대화에서 reimburse, reimbursement라는 단어를 직접 언급하는 경우가 많으며 cover, pay for도 자주 등장합니다.

· 행사에 대한 세부 사항과 관련된 문제
→ 행사가 열리는 장소, 초청되는 강연자 등 세부 사항에 대해 묻는 문제가 출제됩니다.

represent	대표하다	gather	모이다, 모으다
assign	맡기다, 배치하다	conclusion	결론, 결말
depart	출발하다, 떠나다	detailed	상세한, 자세한
accommodation	숙박시설	organize	조직하다, 정리하다
arrange	준비하다	podium	연단
destination	목적지	caterer	출장 요식 업체
refreshments	다과, 간식	catering company	출장 요리 회사
expense	비용	lecturer	강사, 강연자
frequent	빈번한, 단골의	luncheon	오찬
reimburse	상환하다, 변제하다	overbooked	정원 이상으로 예약을 받은
business trip	출장	ballroom	대연회장
company outing	회사 야유회	organizer	주최측, 기획자
coworker	동료	culinary	요리의
prepare	준비하다	admission	입장
press conference	기자회견	video conference	화상 회의
equipment	장비	focus on	~에 집중하다
registration	등록	in the meantime	그 동안에
sign up for	~에 등록하다	demonstrate	시연하다
professional	전문적인	related to	~에 관련된

출장·행사

🎧 Day 15_P3_01.mp3   💬 해석 p.143

US - BR

W: Mike, I'm assigned to work at a company booth in the Mobile Technology Conference in Berlin. This is my first time to attend a conference abroad, so could you help me arrange my travel?

M: Sure, the first thing you should do is contact Chicago Travel, which usually takes care of everything related to all of our business travel. And then, they will give you a list of available flights and hotel rooms. The management is now trying to reduce travel expenses, so you'd better select the least expensive option.

W: Okay, I'll do that. By the way, can we still get reimbursed for meals?

M: Yes, but the company only covers 20 dollars for each meal unless you have a lunch or dinner with clients.

---

01. What does the woman need help with?
    (A) Making travel arrangements
    (B) Writing a report
    (C) Reviewing a proposal
    (D) Locating a file

02. What is the company trying to do?
    (A) Increase productivity
    (B) Expand its client base
    (C) Change the supplier
    (D) Cut expenses

03. According to the man, what expense will be fully reimbursed?
    (A) Meals with clients
    (B) Room services
    (C) Local transportation costs
    (D) Car rental fees

이렇게 풀어요

01. 여자는 무엇에 대한 도움이 필요한가?
    (A) 출장 준비를 하는 것
    (B) 보고서를 작성하는 것
    (C) 제안서를 검토하는 것
    (D) 파일을 찾는 것

여자가 첫 대사에서 This is my first time to attend a conference abroad, so could you help me arrange my travel?라고 했습니다.
→ 직접적으로 출장 준비 도움을 요청했으므로 (A)가 정답이다.

02. 회사는 무엇을 하려고 하는가?
    (A) 생산성 늘리기
    (B) 고객층 확장하기
    (C) 공급업체 변경하기
    (D) 비용 줄이기

남자가 The management is now trying to reduce travel expenses라고 했습니다.
→ reduce를 cut으로 패러프레이징 한 (D)가 정답입니다.

03. 남자에 따르면, 어떤 비용이 전액 변제될 것인가?
    (A) 고객과의 식사
    (B) 룸 서비스
    (C) 지역 교통비
    (D) 자동차 렌트 비용

여자가 can we still get reimbursed for meals?라고 물은 것에 대해 남자가 the company only covers 20 dollars for each meal unless you have a lunch or dinner with clients라고 했습니다.
→ 고객과 식사한 경우에만 전액 돌려받을 수 있으므로 (A)가 정답입니다.

출제 유형 2 — 상품 구매·서비스

상점에서 특정 물건을 찾고 있다고 하는 상황, 상품이나 서비스에 대해 문의하는 내용의 대화가 출제됩니다.

상품 구매·서비스 관련 대화에서 자주 나오는 문제

· 어떤 업종의 상점에서 이루어지는 대화인지 묻는 문제
What kind of business is the man visiting?
→ 대화 초반부에서 구입하고자 하는 물품을 언급할 때 알 수 있는 경우가 많지만, 전반적으로 등장하는 단어의 공통점을 찾으면 됩니다.

· 요청 사항을 묻는 문제
What does the man ask the woman to do?
→ 대화 후반부에서 단서가 등장하며 상품 구매나 서비스 이용 관련하여 무엇을 확인하거나 문의/연락해보라는 요청 사항이 자주 출제됩니다.

· 상품 구매·서비스 관련 대화에서 자주 출제되는 어휘

look for	~을 찾다	insert	삽입하다, 넣다
display case	진열장	retain	유지하다, 보유하다
express shipping	특급 배송	politely	공손하게
in stock	재고가 있는	superb	최고의, 최상의
out of stock	품절인	satisfaction	만족
find out	알아보다	basis	기준, 기초, 근거
wrap	포장하다	be willing to	기꺼이 ~하다
bill	(~에게) 청구하다	hesitate	망설이다
reach	도착하다	guarantee	보장하다, 보증하다
confuse	혼란스럽게 하다	disappoint	실망시키다
electronics store	전자기기 매장	rug	깔개
available	이용 가능한, 시간이 있는	questionnaire	설문지
weigh	무게를 재다	renewal	갱신
secondhand	중고의	merchandise	상품
business hours	영업 시간	put aside	따로 맡아 두다
newsstand	신문 가판대	payment option	지불 방법
grocery	식료품	craft	수공예품
fabric	천, 직물	appliance	전자제품
pick out	고르다	go with	~와 어울리다

상품 구매·서비스

🎧 Day 15_P3_02.mp3   📄 해석 p.144

BR - US

M: Excuse me, I'm looking for the red Ultra Man action figure. There are green and yellow ones on display, but I'd like to get the red one.
W: I'm sorry, but we sold out of the red ones this morning. It's a really popular toy. We should get more in next Monday if you could wait until then.
M: The thing is, my nephew's birthday party is tomorrow.
W: Well… Then, if you try ordering online with express shipping you might be able to get it by tomorrow.
M: Actually, could you use your computer to see if your Belford branch has one in stock? I don't mind driving out there.

---

01. What kind of business is the man visiting?

(A) A delivery service
(B) A party planner
(C) A toy store
(D) A bakery

02. What does the man imply when he says, "my nephew's birthday party is tomorrow"?

(A) He will be going out of town.
(B) He has to purchase something today.
(C) He avoids shopping for things online.
(D) He does not have free time on Wednesday.

03. What does the man ask the woman to do?

(A) Check another store's inventory
(B) Print out a gift receipt
(C) Place an online order
(D) Gift wrap an item

🎵 이렇게 풀어요

01. 남자는 어떤 종류의 업체를 방문하고 있는가? (A) 배송 서비스 업체 (B) 파티 기획 업체 (C) 장난감 가게 (D) 제과점	대화 초반부의 action figure, popular toy가 언급됐습니다. → 장난감 가게임을 알 수 있으므로 (C)가 정답입니다.
02. 남자가 "제 조카의 생일 파티가 내일입니다"라고 말할 때 암시하는 바는 무엇인가? (A) 그는 시에서 떠나 있을 것이다. (B) 그는 무언가를 오늘 구매해야 한다. (C) 그는 온라인으로 물건을 구매하는 것을 꺼린다. (D) 그는 수요일에는 시간이 없다.	주어진 문장 앞에서 상점 직원인 여자가 다음 주 월요일에 물건이 더 들어온다고 한 것에 대해 남자가 내일이 조카 생일 파티라고 한 상황입니다. → 내일 조카에게 주기 위해 오늘 구매해야 한다는 의미를 내포하므로 (B)가 정답입니다.
03. 남자는 여자에게 무엇을 할 것을 요청하는가? (A) 다른 상점의 재고를 확인하는 것 (B) 선물 영수증을 출력하는 것 (C) 온라인 주문을 하는 것 (D) 물건을 선물 포장하는 것	남자의 마지막 대사에서 could you use your computer to see if your Belford branch has one in stock?이라고 했습니다. → see를 check로, branch를 another store로 패러프레이징 한 (A)가 정답입니다.

따라 하면 문제가 풀리는
연습 문제

문제와 각 선택지의 키워드에 표시하세요. 그러고 나서 대화를 듣고 빈칸에 들어갈 말을 받아쓴 후 정답을 선택해 보세요.

01. What are the speakers mainly discussing?

(A) A company booth plan　　　(B) A client meeting

> W: Jimmy, I just reviewed the company _____ _____ plan for the culinary expo. I think the assigned booth area is not _____ enough to display all of our products.
>
> M: Actually, we were supposed to display only the new products, but the management wanted to _____ some other products. Anyway, I will _____ the conference organizer and ask whether there is a _____ _____ still available.

02. What will happen next week?

(A) A client will visit.　　　(B) A company will relocate.

> W: Jake! I haven't seen you since you _____ _____ from your trip to Egypt. How was the _____ _____ with Mohamed Apparel?
>
> M: I think our trendy shoe designs and _____ _____ prices appealed to them. They will _____ _____ next month to look around our headquarters and factory.
>
> W: That's great news!

03. What event is the woman planning to attend?

(A) A retirement party　　　(B) An industrial conference

> M: Susan, I heard you _____ _____ _____ attend the automotive conference in Chicago. When are you coming back?
>
> W: Well, the conference _____ on Wednesday, and I'm planning to _____ the _____ while I'm there.
>
> M: Oh, that's good for you. I hope you find it _____.

---

paraphrasing　주어진 어휘 또는 표현과 의미가 동일한 것을 연결하세요.

1. assigned　　　•　　　　•　(a) attract
2. appeal　　　　•　　　　•　(b) given
3. informative　 •　　　　•　(c) useful

04. What will the woman send?

(A) Detailed information　　(B) An e-mail address

> M: Hello, I saw a TV advertisement about your cable TV service and it said you are _____ a _____ period.
> W: Yes, right. _____ _____, you can receive a free upgrade to Super Channels if you _____ to Basic Channels. You can enjoy 150 TV channels instead of 100.
> M: Can you _____ me _____ information about the TV channels you are offering now?

05. What is the man invited to do?

(A) Complete an order form　　(B) Visit the store tomorrow

> W: Good evening. May I _____ you?
> M: Excuse me, do you have any more of this digital camera? I want a _____ _____.
> W: Sorry, it is currently _____ _____ _____. Another shipment will arrive tomorrow, so will you _____ _____ tomorrow afternoon? I will put a red one on hold for you.

06. What kind of business does the woman most likely work at?

(A) A restaurant　　(B) A landscaping company

> M: Hello, I'm just calling to _____ some more information about your _____ services. I have a garden at my house but I'll be _____ of the country for more than six months. Do you offer any short term _____?
> W: Sure, we can offer any contract term _____ one-time service.

---

paraphrasing 주어진 어휘 또는 표현과 의미가 동일한 것을 연결하세요.

4. further information　•　　　•　(a) provide
5. out of stock　•　　　•　(b) detailed information
6. offer　•　　　•　(c) not available

PART 3 연습 문제　275

01. What did the man forget to do?

    (A) Register for a conference
    (B) Get spending approval
    (C) Respond to an invitation
    (D) Book accommodations

02. Why does the man thank the woman?

    (A) She sent him some documents.
    (B) She completed a task for him.
    (C) She made a helpful recommendation.
    (D) She assigned more workers to his team.

03. What should the man do next week?

    (A) Lead a training session
    (B) Submit some receipts
    (C) Give a presentation
    (D) Request vacation time

04. What does the man imply when he says, "I attended last month's communication workshop"?

    (A) He has fallen behind schedule.
    (B) He can give the woman some advice.
    (C) He will be absent from a training session.
    (D) He had forgotten about an event.

05. According to the man, what has the company recently done?

    (A) Acquired more overseas clients
    (B) Added an express service
    (C) Hired some experienced workers
    (D) Installed some new software

06. What does the woman say she wants to do?

    (A) Discuss a problem later
    (B) Consult a colleague
    (C) Get a good seat
    (D) Check some figures

07. Why did the man visit the business?

    (A) To exchange an item
    (B) To get a price adjustment
    (C) To pick up an online order
    (D) To inspect some merchandise

08. What most likely is the man's occupation?

    (A) Delivery driver
    (B) Shoe salesperson
    (C) Construction worker
    (D) Laboratory technician

09. What does the woman suggest doing?

    (A) Contacting a manufacturer
    (B) Speaking with a manager
    (C) Buying another brand
    (D) Visiting a Web site

Item Description	Charge
Casserole Dish	$20
Frying Pan	$35
Stainless Steel Pot	$40
Tea Set	$60
Total	**$155**

10. What does the man ask the woman about?

    (A) A membership number
    (B) A delivery time
    (C) A customer survey
    (D) A payment preference

11. Why is the woman unable to get a discount?

    (A) The coupon that she has is expired.
    (B) Her merchandise is for the wrong brand.
    (C) She does not have enough items.
    (D) The prices were already lowered.

12. Look at the graphic. Which amount will be deleted from the invoice?

    (A) $20
    (B) $35
    (C) $40
    (D) $60

13. What is the purpose of the man's call?

    (A) To request a paper statement
    (B) To make some travel plans
    (C) To confirm his identity
    (D) To inquire about a bill

14. What did the man do last month?

    (A) He opened an account.
    (B) He went on a business trip.
    (C) He purchased a new mobile phone.
    (D) He signed up for an international phone plan.

15. According to the woman, what should the man do to avoid extra fees in the future?

    (A) Inform his service provider
    (B) Pay his bills on time
    (C) Sign a contract
    (D) Post on SNS

16. What does the man ask the woman for?

    (A) Some bags
    (B) A membership card
    (C) A receipt
    (D) Some coupons

17. What does the man imply when he says, "I can do that for you"?

    (A) The woman purchased some heavy items.
    (B) There are more products in the back.
    (C) He will help the woman install an app.
    (D) His coworker needs to approve a sale price.

18. What does the woman receive?

    (A) A free shipping
    (B) A discount
    (C) A raffle ticket
    (D) A free item

Macon Home Store Wallpaper Sale

Wallpaper Roll Size	Save
25 sq. feet	5%
50 sq. feet	10%
100 sq. feet	15%
250 sq. feet	20%

Valid in store or with online code
5WALL20

19. What will the woman do next week?

    (A) Have photos taken
    (B) Renovate her home
    (C) Reopen a restaurant
    (D) Meet an interior designer

20. What does the woman say about Playful Checkers?

    (A) She thinks it matches her current décor.
    (B) She prefers patterns with only two colors.
    (C) It is common in dining establishments.
    (D) It can be used for outdoor surfaces.

21. Look at the graphic. How much of a discount will the woman receive?

    (A) 5%
    (B) 10%
    (C) 15%
    (D) 20%

PART 4 담화(talk)

제품 사용법을 설명하는 내용과 안내 사항 발표, 장소 소개, 설문 결과 설명 등 다양한 주제에 대한 발표가 출제됩니다.

출제 유형 1 제품 시연

신제품 출시 행사에서 제품을 소개하며 사용법 등을 설명하는 내용이 출제됩니다.

제품 시연 담화에서 자주 나오는 문제

· 목적 문제
Why is the talk being given?
→ 신제품이나 새로운 서비스를 소개하는 내용이 가장 자주 출제됩니다.

· **제품 시연 담화에서 자주 출제되는 어휘**

collaboration	협동, 협력	detach	분리하다
windshield	바람막이 유리, (자동차) 전면 유리	shorten	짧게 하다
glance	훑어보다, 곁눈질	commercial	광고, 상업적인
ordinary	평범한, 보통의	devise	고안하다, 생각해내다
occur	발생하다	prove	증명하다
display	전시하다, 화면	assemble	조립하다
publicize	광고하다, 홍보하다	reliable	믿을 수 있는
operator	(기계를) 조작하는 사람	habit	습관, 취미
instrument	기구, 악기	unique	독특한, 유일무이한
equipped	장비가 갖추어진	obtain	받다, 얻다
auditorium	강당	automate	자동화하다
merger	합병	feasible	실현 가능한
reassure	재확인시키다	invent	고안하다, 발명하다
demonstration	시연	complicated	복잡한, 까다로운
spectator	관중	manufacture	제조하다, 생산하다
floor manager	현장 감독관	individual	개인의, 개개의

제품 시연

[BR]

M: Delaney Auto, in collaboration with Millenium Electronics, has created a new digital windshield for cars. At first glance, it looks like any ordinary windshield. However, from inside the car, you can see digital displays on a see-through screen. The driver can customize the display to show things such as speed, fuel, and GPS directions. People who have test driven cars equipped with it say that it makes them feel like they were in a science fiction movie. Now, the camera crew and I are going to take a turn inside the car to give you a demonstration of how it works.

01. Why is the talk being given?
(A) To announce a company merger
(B) To introduce new technology
(C) To report on driving statistics
(D) To promote a brand

02. What does the speaker say is a feature of the screen?
(A) Internet connectivity
(B) Touch screen interface
(C) Customizable displays
(D) Automatic software updates

03. What is the speaker most likely going to do next?
(A) Demonstrate a product
(B) Begin accepting orders
(C) Cut to a commercial
(D) Interview a driver

이렇게 풀어요

01. 담화는 왜 이루어지고 있는가?
    (A) 회사 합병을 발표하기 위해
    (B) 새로운 기술을 소개하기 위해
    (C) 운전 통계 자료를 보고하기 위해
    (D) 브랜드를 홍보하기 위해

02. 화자는 화면의 특징이 무엇이라고 말하는가?
    (A) 인터넷 접속 가능성
    (B) 터치 스크린 인터페이스
    (C) 원하는 대로 설정 가능한 화면
    (D) 자동 소프트웨어 업데이트

03. 화자는 다음에 무엇을 할 것인가?
    (A) 상품을 시연하기
    (B) 주문을 받기 시작하기
    (C) 광고로 바꾸기
    (D) 운전자와 인터뷰하기

첫 문장에서 Delaney Auto, in collaboration with Millenium Electronics, has created a new digital windshield for cars.라고 했습니다.
→ 첫 문장에서 신제품을 소개하고 있다는 것을 알 수 있고, 전체 내용이 a new digital windshield에 관한 내용이므로 정답은 (B)입니다.

중반부에서 The driver can customize the display to show things such as speed, fuel, and GPS directions.라고 했습니다.
→ 화면이 원하는 대로 설정될 수 있다고 했으므로 정답은 (C)입니다.

마지막에 Now, the camera crew and I are going to take a turn inside the car to give you a demonstration of how it works.라고 했습니다.
→ 화자가 어떻게 작동하는지 보여주겠다고 했으므로 정답은 (A)입니다.

출제 유형 2 발표

발표는 안내 사항 발표, 장소 소개, 설문 결과 설명 등 다양한 주제에 대해 출제됩니다.

• 발표에서 자주 출제되는 어휘

발표에서 자주 나오는 문제

• 다음 할 일을 묻는 문제
What are the listeners going to do next?
→ 발표 관련 영상이나 자료를 보거나, 관련 서류 작성하기 등이 정답 보기로 출제됩니다.

point out	지적하다	compile	편집하다
preside	사회를 보다	minutes	회의록
undertake	떠맡다	convene	소집하다
straightforward	솔직한	persuasive	설득력 있는
highlight	강조하다	oppose	반대하다
handout	유인물	take a look	살펴보다
gathering	모임	think over	숙고하다
equip	장비를 갖추다	primarily	주로
variety	다양성	paycheck	월급
rule	규칙	load	짐을 싣다
submit	제출하다	complete	완성하다
put A to the test	A를 시험해 보다	rehearsal	리허설
regularly	정기적으로	laboratory	실험실, 연구소
pass out	나누어 주다	security	안전, 보안
warehouse	창고	identify	(신원 등을) 확인하다
opinion poll	여론 조사	excuse	변명

발표

US

W: Good morning! I'm Marissa Corning, and I'm in charge of your new employee orientation. You're probably all thrilled to have been selected to work here at Tacoma Industries. As you probably know, our company primarily recruits from within, which means that as we grow, so do your opportunities. Be sure to check the company's Web page regularly for job openings that interest you. Now, before we take a tour of the facilities, I need you each to complete this form for tax purposes. It also includes your bank information so that we can deposit your paychecks directly into your account.

01. What is the main purpose of the talk?
    (A) To announce a coworker's promotion
    (B) To recruit some student interns
    (C) To discuss a company policy
    (D) To welcome new employees

02. What does the speaker say the listeners should do?
    (A) File their taxes early
    (B) Apply for tuition assistance
    (C) Recommend friends for positions
    (D) Check online for position openings

03. What are the listeners going to do next?
    (A) Fill out some paperwork
    (B) Meet the management
    (C) Watch a video
    (D) Tour a facility

이렇게 풀어요

01. 담화의 목적은 무엇인가?
    (A) 동료의 승진을 발표하는 것
    (B) 몇몇 학생 인턴을 채용하는 것
    (C) 회사 정책을 논의하는 것
    (D) 신입 직원들을 환영하는 것

담화 초반에서 I'm in charge of your new employee orientation. You're probably all thrilled to have been selected to work here at Tacoma Industries.라고 했습니다.
→ 신입 직원들을 환영하고 있음을 알 수 있으므로 정답은 (D)입니다.

02. 화자는 청자들이 무엇을 해야 한다고 말하는가?
    (A) 그들의 세금을 일찍 신고하기
    (B) 수업료 지원을 신청하기
    (C) 일자리에 친구 추천하기
    (D) 모집 직책에 대해 온라인 확인하기

담화 중반에서 사내 내부 채용 시스템을 소개하며 Be sure to check the company's Web page regularly for job openings that interest you라고 했습니다.
→ Web page는 online으로, job openings는 position openings로 패러프레이징 된 (D)가 정답입니다.

03. 청자들은 다음에 무엇을 할 것인가?
    (A) 서류 작성하기
    (B) 경영진 만나기
    (C) 영상 시청하기
    (D) 시설 둘러보기

담화 후반에서 Now, before we take a tour of the facilities, I need you each to complete this form for tax purposes.라고 했습니다.
→ complete은 fill out으로, form은 paperwork로 패러프레이징 된 (A)가 정답입니다.

따라 하면 문제가 풀리는 연습 문제

문제와 각 선택지의 키워드에 표시하세요. 그리고 나서 담화를 듣고 빈칸에 들어갈 말을 받아쓴 후 정답을 선택해 보세요.

01. What will the listeners do next?

(A) See a video   (B) Tour a house

talk

> M: Good afternoon. I'm Bob Ring, director of Wellington Valley Homes and Property. Thank you for coming to this _____ seminar about _____ _____ transactions. I will give you a clear overview of what you will _____ when buying or renting a _____. I will share with you both good and bad cases. Now, would you please _____ this short _____?

02. Where is the talk taking place?

(A) At an industry exhibition   (B) At an electronics store

talk

> W: Thank you for visiting our _____. We, Irwin Electronics, are one of the most reliable kitchen utensil _____ and we attend the Chicago Culinary Expo with _____ _____ every year. This year, we have _____ a new fryer for commercial use. It features a non-chemical auto filtering technology, so you can reduce oil use. I will show you _____ _____ _____ now.

03. What product is being discussed?

(A) Sunglasses   (B) A digital camera

talk

> M: Hello, welcome to the Optical Instrument Expo. My name is Jeff. Today, I will introduce a new _____ _____ that we just released on the _____. You have probably missed a great moment to _____ _____ _____ due to a long response time of your digital camera. That's why people _____ to take a photo with their _____. If you just _____ the shutter, it will be ready to take a photo in a second.

---

paraphrasing 주어진 어휘 또는 표현과 의미가 동일한 것을 연결하세요.

1. watch   •   • (a) see
2. show how it works   •   • (b) present
3. introduce   •   • (c) demonstrate

04. Why is Mr. Sanchez famous?

(A) He wrote a best-selling book.   (B) He created a popular product.

talk

> W: Thank you for coming to the _____ _____ of Tropical Passion at Peterson Mall. Today, we will _____ simple recipes with which you can make healthy and tasteful fruit juices in your home. Our recipe _____, Mr. Sanchez, will use only ingredients _____ _____ in your refrigerator. He is well-known for _____ the recipe for our signature juice, Sunrise Passion.

05. What will the listeners be awarded?

(A) A free product   (B) A cash bonus

talk

> W: Today, I'm going to _____ _____ _____ about the sales reports that you all submitted last quarter. I collected them and _____ to the _____. I received an e-mail saying that we _____ the sales goal and exceeded it by 20 percent. This is due largely to your _____ _____ and contribution. You will be _____ a $200 _____ and it will be reflected in your monthly pay.

06. What does the speaker ask the listeners to do?

(A) Wear a name tag   (B) Review a contract

talk

> M: Hello, everyone. I will do a final check for today's catering for Olson Real Estate. It is our first time _____ _____ _____ this agency, so I want to give them a good impression about our service. They _____ many receptions with their _____ clients. I want the waiting staff to _____ these shirts, vests, and _____ _____ on your chests. It can make us _____ more neat and professional.

---

paraphrasing 주어진 어휘 또는 표현과 의미가 동일한 것을 연결하세요.

4. signature juice   •   • (a) server
5. bonus   •   • (b) popular product
6. waiting staff   •   • (c) compensation

실전 문제

01. Who most likely are the listeners?
    (A) City officials
    (B) Hike participants
    (C) Maintenance workers
    (D) Parking attendants

02. Why is the speaker pleased?
    (A) The fee has recently decreased.
    (B) The listeners arrived on time.
    (C) A new service is available.
    (D) An area will not be crowded.

03. What advice does the speaker share with the listeners?
    (A) Walking together in groups
    (B) Reviewing a map carefully
    (C) Leaving behind unnecessary items
    (D) Taking a lot of photographs

04. According to the speaker, what has the business recently done?
    (A) Added more classes
    (B) Expanded a building
    (C) Opened a second branch
    (D) Reduced its prices

05. Who is Carol?
    (A) A tour guide
    (B) A fitness instructor
    (C) A charity founder
    (D) A business owner

06. What does the speaker mean when he says, "I always have mine with me"?
    (A) He is able to respond to listeners' needs quickly.
    (B) He wants to find a more lightweight item.
    (C) He can show an updated copy of some information.
    (D) He is encouraging the listeners to buy a product.

07. Who most likely is the speaker?
    (A) A film director
    (B) An event planner
    (C) A company founder
    (D) A board member

08. What will the quarterly profits be used for?
    (A) Funding environmental research
    (B) Setting up a scholarship fund
    (C) Investing in alternative energy
    (D) Providing training to employees

09. According to the speaker, what is available near the entrance?
    (A) Company brochures
    (B) Light refreshments
    (C) Registration forms
    (D) Presenter schedules

10. What kind of business does the speaker most likely work for?
    (A) A real estate agency
    (B) An accounting firm
    (C) A construction company
    (D) A vehicle rental firm

11. According to the speaker, what does the company plan to focus on?
    (A) Increasing worker productivity
    (B) Cutting operating costs
    (C) Protecting the environment
    (D) Keeping information private

12. Why does the speaker say, "It was prepared right before the meeting"?
    (A) To make an excuse
    (B) To thank the listeners
    (C) To update a schedule
    (D) To encourage participation

13. Where does the speaker most likely work?
    (A) At an outlet store
    (B) At a print shop
    (C) At a real estate agency
    (D) At a magazine publisher

14. What is the listener's main task for the day?
    (A) Manning a booth
    (B) Putting up posters
    (C) Handing out flyers
    (D) Greeting customers

15. What will the speaker do for the listener?
    (A) Prepare some refreshments
    (B) Revise the work schedule
    (C) Print a training manual
    (D) Make more copies

16. Where does the speaker most likely work?
    (A) At a restaurant
    (B) At a news station
    (C) At a grocery store
    (D) At a magazine company

17. Why does the speaker say, "It received a 5-star rating from food critic Allen Jones"?
    (A) To encourage critical thinking
    (B) To endorse a food critic
    (C) To recommend a dish
    (D) To praise a chef

18. According to the speaker, what is being offered this month?
    (A) Price discounts
    (B) Dessert samples
    (C) Extra reward points
    (D) Complimentary beverages

Coyote Cable Package Options		
Package	Includes	Monthly Fee
A	Local TV	$14.99
B	Local TV + Internet	$24.99
C	Local & Cable TV + Internet	$34.99
D	Local & Cable & Movie TV + Internet	$44.99

19. Where most likely are the listeners?
    (A) At a training session
    (B) At a shopping mall
    (C) At a product demonstration
    (D) At a TV show

20. Look at the graphic. According to the speaker, which package should the listeners recommend?
    (A) Package A
    (B) Package B
    (C) Package C
    (D) Package D

21. What is provided as an incentive?
    (A) Movie tickets
    (B) Cash bonuses
    (C) Equipment upgrades
    (D) Extra paid vacation days

'멋진 당신, 오늘도 화이팅'

DAY
16

오늘의 학습 포인트

PART 3. 대화 주제 - 상점
1. 멤버십·고객 의견
   - 빈출 내용 - 멤버십 가입 혜택
   - 빈출 문제 - 혜택에 대해 묻는 문제
2. 할인
   - 빈출 내용 - 할인 기간, 조건, 할인율
   - 빈출 문제 - 특정 세부 사항, 다음 할 일

PART 4. 담화 유형 - 안내(announcement)
1. 교통편 관련 안내
   - 빈출 내용 - 교통편 지연, 취소 등 변경 안내
   - 빈출 문제 - 이유/원인 문제, 제안/요청 문제
2. 콘퍼런스에서의 안내
   - 빈출 내용 - 행사 일정, 연설자 안내
   - 빈출 문제 - 안내가 어떤 행사에서 이루어지고 있는지 묻는 질문

PART 3 · 상점 – 멤버십·고객 의견 / 할인

멤버십 가입 혜택 관련 대화와 제품이나 서비스 할인에 관한 대화가 많이 나와요!

출제 유형 1 · 멤버십·고객 의견

마트나 체육관의 멤버십 가입과 혜택, 상점의 제품이나 서비스에 대해 점원과 손님이 대화를 나누는 내용이 주로 출제됩니다.

· **멤버십·고객 의견 관련 대화에서 자주 출제되는 어휘**

buyer	구매자	steady	꾸준한
recall	회수하다, 리콜	misunderstand	착각하다
have A in stock	A의 재고가 있다	periodically	주기적으로
gift wrap	선물 포장하다	keep up with	~을 따라가다
on hand	구할 수 있는, 수중에	under warranty	보증 기간 내에 있는
in that case	그런 경우에는	crack	금이 가다
trial order	샘플 주문(품)	shelf	선반
lighting fixture	조명 기구	locate	찾다
rack	걸이, 선반	checkout counter	계산대
energy efficiency	에너지 효율성	primary	주된, 주요한
mail	우편을 보내다	in preparation for	~에 대비하여
supply	공급, 공급하다	emphasize	강조하다
publication	출판(물)	verify	확인하다
renew	갱신하다	specialize in	~을 전문으로 하다
empty	비어 있는	spill	~을 쏟다, 엎지르다
unpopular	인기 없는	remaining	남아 있는
folding	접이식의	certain	특정한, 확실한
sufficient	충분한	record	기록, 기록하다

멤버십·고객 의견 관련 대화에서 자주 나오는 문제

· 멤버십 혜택에 대해 묻는 세부 사항 문제
What is a benefit of the membership?
→ 주로 대화 중반부에서 멤버십에 대해 설명하는데, you will get, we provide ~ 등의 표현 다음에 혜택이 제시됩니다.

멤버십·고객 의견

US - AU

W: Is that all you need today?
M: Yes, and I saw a banner that you introduced a new membership program for organic produce buyers. Can you tell me more about that?
W: Sure. We have made a partnership with local farms and orchards that grow vegetables and fruits without pesticides. In an effort to promote their produce, we introduced this membership program. With it, you will get 10% off any of the items with organic stickers. You will also be invited to the cooking classes and tours to the farms.
M: Awesome. I'm moving to a townhouse with a garden in August. Visiting organic farms gives me helpful tips for how to raise a garden without pesticides.

01. How did the man hear about the new membership program?
(A) From a TV commercial
(B) From a store banner
(C) From a magazine
(D) From a colleague

02. According to the woman, what is a benefit of the membership?
(A) It comes with free items.
(B) It offers free deliveries.
(C) It gives double reward points.
(D) It provides a chance to visit farms.

03. What will the man do in August?
(A) Hold a retirement party
(B) Lead a seminar
(C) Relocate to a new location
(D) Open a restaurant

이렇게 풀어요

01. 남자는 어떻게 새 멤버십 프로그램에 대해 들었는가?
(A) TV 광고에서
(B) 매장 배너에서
(C) 잡지에서
(D) 동료로부터

남자의 첫 대사에서 I saw a banner that you introduced a new membership program ~이라고 했습니다.
→ 배너를 봤다고 했으므로 (B)가 정답입니다.

02. 여자에 따르면, 멤버십의 혜택은 무엇인가?
(A) 무료 품목이 딸려 온다.
(B) 무료 배송을 제공한다.
(C) 두 배의 보상 포인트를 준다.
(D) 농장을 방문할 기회를 제공한다.

멤버십에 대해 설명하는 여자의 대사에서 You will also be invited to the cooking classes and tours to the farms라고 했습니다.
→ tours를 chance to visit으로 패러프레이징 한 (D)가 정답입니다.

03. 남자는 8월에 무엇을 할 것인가?
(A) 은퇴 파티 개최하기
(B) 세미나 진행하기
(C) 새로운 장소로 이사하기
(D) 레스토랑 개점하기

남자의 마지막 대사에서 I'm moving to a townhouse with a garden in August라고 했습니다.
→ move를 relocate로 패러프레이징 한 (C)가 정답입니다.

출제 유형 2 **할인**

제품이나 서비스의 할인 기간, 할인 조건, 할인율에 대해 대화를 나누는 내용이 주로 출제됩니다.

· **할인 관련 대화에서 자주 출제되는 어휘**

reasonable	(가격이) 합리적인	affordable	(가격이) 알맞은
promotion	홍보, 판촉 행사	take a moment	잠시 시간을 내다
voucher	상품권, 할인권, 쿠폰	qualify	자격을 주다
unsure	확신하지 못하는	patronage	단골, 애용
accompany	동행하다, 동반하다	fit	(크기 등이) 맞다
prefer	선호하다	offer a discount	할인을 제공하다
purchase	구매하다	for free	무료로
relatively	상대적으로	in bulk	대량으로
retail	소매	overpriced	가격이 비싸게 매겨진
on sale	할인 중인, 판매되는	cashier	계산원
shopper	쇼핑객	storeroom	창고
display case	진열장	cash register	계산대
make a purchase	구매하다	half price	절반 가격
enroll in	~에 등록하다	regular price	정가
add	추가하다	mark down	가격을 인하하다
prize drawing	경품 추첨	common	일반적인, 공통의
a wide selection of	다양한	pick out	고르다
cost	비용, 비용이 들다	good rate	적절한 가격
flyer	전단	ad	광고

할인 관련 대화에서 자주 나오는 문제

· 특정 세부 사항 문제
What does the woman want to know?
→ I'd like to know if ~와 같은 단서 표현을 캐치합니다.
What does the man say about the coffee machine?
→ 질문의 키워드 coffee machine이 언급되는 부분에서 단서를 파악합니다.

· 다음 할 일을 묻는 문제
What will the man most likely do next?
→ 대화 후반부에서 명령문이나 제안하는 문장으로 단서가 제시됩니다.

할인

Day 16_P3_02.mp3 해석 p.157

BR - US

M: Hi, could you help me? I'm trying to find a pair of running shoes in size 10. This ad shows these Lightfeather shoes on sale for half price.

W: I'm sorry, but I actually just sold our last pair of those in size 10. We won't get another shipment until this weekend.

M: Oh, really? The ad says that it's a one-day sale, and I was really hoping to get them at that price.

W: If you go to the register and give them your name and number, we can call you once we do get another pair of size 10 Lightfeather shoes in. You can also get a voucher to get them at the sale price.

---

01. What does the man need assistance with?

(A) Applying for a job
(B) Locating a product
(C) Making a payment
(D) Choosing some shoes

02. What caused a problem?

(A) An item is out of stock.
(B) A manager is unavailable.
(C) A sale period has already ended.
(D) An advertisement was misprinted.

03. Where does the woman tell the man to go?

(A) To the storeroom
(B) To another department
(C) To the manager's office
(D) To the checkout register

이렇게 풀어요

01. 남자는 무엇에 대해 도움을 필요로 하는가?
(A) 일자리에 지원하는 것
(B) 제품을 찾는 것
(C) 돈을 지불하는 것
(D) 신발을 고르는 것

02. 무엇이 문제를 야기했는가?
(A) 제품이 품절이다.
(B) 매니저가 없다.
(C) 할인 기간이 이미 끝났다.
(D) 광고가 잘못 인쇄되었다.

03. 여자는 남자에게 어디로 가라고 말하는가?
(A) 창고로
(B) 다른 부서로
(C) 매니저의 사무실로
(D) 계산대로

남자가 첫 대사에서 I'm trying to find a pair of running shoes in size 10이라고 했습니다.
→ try to find가 locate로, a pair of running shoes가 product로 패러프레이징 된 (B)가 정답입니다.

여자가 I actually just sold our last pair of those in size 10이라고 하여 남자가 원하는 신발을 현재 구입할 수 없음을 알리고 있습니다.
→ sold our last pair ~가 out of stock으로, pair of those in size 10이 an item으로 패러프레이징 된 (A)가 정답입니다.

여자가 마지막 대사에서 If you go to the register ~ 라고 했습니다.
→ register가 checkout register로 패러프레이징 된 (D)가 정답입니다.

따라 하면 문제가 풀리는 연습 문제

문제와 각 선택지의 키워드에 표시하세요. 그러고 나서 대화를 듣고 빈칸에 들어갈 말을 받아쓴 후 정답을 선택해 보세요.

01. What is given out to new members?

(A) An assigned locker   (B) Free items

> M: Hello, I'm here to _____ _____ your facility and exercise equipment.
>
> W: Welcome to Stay Fit. We are a nationwide chain. You can visit and _____ _____ at one of more than 200 _____ locations. In addition, if you become a member today, you will _____ _____ a _____ towel and bags.

02. What is the woman asked to do?

(A) Print out a discount coupon   (B) Come at later time

> W: Hello, I'm looking for the strawberry cheesecakes in this _____. I read your ad in the local newspaper and they are 30% off the _____ _____.
>
> M: I'm sorry. They all _____ _____ in the morning. If you don't mind, would you _____ _____ in about two hours? Our bakers are baking new cakes now and they will be _____ at that time.

03. What is the man planning to do?

(A) Go on a vacation   (B) Participate in a race

> M: Well, I'd like to _____ _____ _____ for my vacation, and I've been told that this is the best place in town. I'll be _____ to Black Mountain to ski with some of my friends, so we'd like _____ a minivan or SUV.
>
> W: Okay, that shouldn't be a _____. And we're offering one free day to _____ who rent any car for more than three days.

paraphrasing 주어진 어휘 또는 표현과 의미가 동일한 것을 연결하세요.

1. be given out   •   • (a) be offered
2. coupon   •   • (b) take part in
3. participate   •   • (c) voucher

🎧 Day 16_P3_03.mp3

정답 및 해석 p.158

04. Where is the conversation taking place?
(A) At a hotel lobby
(B) At a restaurant

> W: How's your _____? Your satisfaction is always our _____, so we are now soliciting feedback about your _____ at Tampa Bed & Breakfast. Do you have time to fill out this _____?
> M: Sorry, we are supposed to take a _____ _____ to the airport in 10 minutes.
> W: That's fine. You are able to do this online on our Web site. Once you _____ it, you will be _____ a 10% discount voucher for your next visit.

05. Who most likely is the woman?
(A) A tailor
(B) A sales representative

> M: Excuse me. I like this t-shirt, but do you have one in _____ _____? I want a white one instead of blue.
> W: I'm sorry. Unfortunately, that is the _____ _____ that we have in stock. If you _____ it, I can offer you a 30% discount.

06. What does the woman want to do?
(A) Buy a computer
(B) Advertise a new TV

> W: I'd like to _____ a desktop computer for my office. I saw a TV advertisement yesterday that said your store is _____ a clearance sale.
> M: Sorry. Unfortunately, all _____ items were already sold out. How about this model? This _____ _____ a monitor, keyboard, and mouse that you need to purchase _____.

paraphrasing 주어진 어휘 또는 표현과 의미가 동일한 것을 연결하세요.

4. solicit •   • (a) at a reduced price
5. offer a discount •   • (b) purchase
6. buy •   • (c) request

01. What is the man's problem?

    (A) His colleague has not arrived.
    (B) His membership card is damaged.
    (C) He lost some of his golf equipment.
    (D) He forgot to pay his membership fees.

02. What does the woman imply when she says, "this is my first day"?

    (A) She is unfamiliar with some equipment.
    (B) She cannot authorize discounts.
    (C) She is excited about an opportunity.
    (D) She plans to work later than usual.

03. What does the woman tell the man to do?

    (A) E-mail a manager
    (B) Come back tomorrow
    (C) Wait in the lobby
    (D) Complete a form

04. Where most likely is the conversation taking place?

    (A) At a movie theater
    (B) At a public library
    (C) At a fitness facility
    (D) At a post office

05. What does Ivan ask the woman for?

    (A) Her membership number
    (B) Her mailing address
    (C) Her friend's name
    (D) Her phone number

06. What will the woman probably do next?

    (A) Show an ID card
    (B) Make a payment
    (C) Sign a contract
    (D) Go on a tour

07. Where most likely does the woman work?

    (A) At a newsstand
    (B) At an electronics store
    (C) At a clothing shop
    (D) At a bookstore

08. What does the woman ask the man to do?

    (A) Enroll in a loyalty program
    (B) Select the size of a product
    (C) View a demonstration
    (D) Take part in a survey

09. According to the woman, what will the business do next week?

    (A) Hold a storewide sale
    (B) Open a second branch
    (C) Introduce a new product
    (D) Distribute some prizes

10. What is the purpose of the man's visit?

    (A) To get a coupon
    (B) To request a refund
    (C) To make a purchase
    (D) To get a price adjustment

11. What does the woman ask for?

    (A) A receipt
    (B) A photo ID
    (C) A credit card
    (D) An order invoice

12. What does the woman offer to do for the man?

    (A) Call another branch
    (B) Put an item on hold
    (C) Place an online order
    (D) Register him for a service

13. How did the woman learn about Hamilton Book Club?
    (A) From a news article
    (B) From a coworker
    (C) From a radio ad
    (D) From a flyer

14. According to the man, what makes Hamilton Book Club unique?
    (A) It has a café area that sells snacks.
    (B) It focuses on a new book every month.
    (C) It provides discounts on all store purchases.
    (D) It buys books back from members after reading them.

15. What will the woman do in September?
    (A) Join a book club
    (B) Publish an article
    (C) Complete her degree
    (D) Begin graduate school

16. Why is the woman calling?
    (A) To confirm a shipment
    (B) To schedule a paint job
    (C) To respond to a complaint
    (D) To request some feedback

17. What kinds of goods does the woman's company carry?
    (A) Home improvement products
    (B) Art and craft materials
    (C) Household furniture
    (D) Cleaning supplies

18. What does the woman offer to do for the man?
    (A) Schedule a consultation
    (B) Send a representative
    (C) Give a cost estimate
    (D) Provide a discount

AUDRA'S COFFEE SHOP	
Baked Goods Made Fresh Daily	
Monday	Classic Donut
Tuesday	Almond Croissant
Wednesday	Cinnamon Roll
Thursday	Banana Nut Bread
Friday	Blueberry Scone

19. Look at the graphic. On what day are the speakers having a conversation?
    (A) Monday
    (B) Tuesday
    (C) Wednesday
    (D) Friday

20. What does the woman recommend that the man do?
    (A) Save a receipt
    (B) Join a mailing list
    (C) Read a menu carefully
    (D) Try a new food

21. What does the man inquire about?
    (A) Parking in a nearby lot
    (B) Taking food off-site
    (C) Hosting a private party
    (D) Accessing the Internet

PART 4 안내(announcement)

교통편의 지연이나 취소 등 변경 사항 관련 안내와 행사 일정이나 연설자 관련 안내가 주로 출제됩니다.

적용 기술

[기적의 필기노트] 71P
LC 기술 52

교통편 관련 안내에서 자주 나오는 문제

· 제안·요청 문제
What are the listeners asked to do?
→ 교통편 관련 안내에서는 우회로를 이용하거나, 다른 교통 수단을 이용하라고 제안하는 내용이 자주 출제됩니다.

출제 유형 1 교통편 관련 안내

역이나 공항에서 교통편의 지연이나 취소 등 변경 사항에 관련된 안내가 주로 출제됩니다.

· 교통편 관련 안내에서 자주 출제되는 어휘

intercity	도시 간의	block	막다, 차단하다
manner	방식, 태도	impose	부과하다
feasible	실현 가능한	crew	팀, 승무원
local	지역의	fleet	(차량, 선박) 무리
alternative	대안의, 양자 택일의	ahead of	~에 앞서
transportation	교통(수단), 운송	ongoing	진행 중인
temporary	일시적인, 임시의	pave	(도로를) 포장하다
tend to	~하는 경향이 있다	tow	견인하다
obstruct	방해하다	tolerate	참다, 용인하다
official	공식적인, 공무원	pedestrian	보행자
fuel	연료	sidewalk	인도
detour	우회, 우회하다	intersection	교차로
convey	운반하다, 전달하다	separate	별개의
strictly	엄격하게	pavement	(도로) 포장
prohibit	금지하다	transit	운송, 수송
determine	알아내다, 결정하다	passenger	승객

교통편 관련 안내

🎧 Day 16_P4_01.mp3   해석 p.164

[BR]

M: Attention, travelers. This intercity bus terminal will be closed on Wednesday, June 14th due to a TV show filming. Anyone without a security pass for the filming crew will not be allowed into the area. We recommend that you use the local bus and train networks for any travel that you need to do on that day. Please refer to the City of San Antonio Web site for more details and local public transportation schedules. If you have already purchased a ticket to travel through our intercity bus terminal on that day, please report to a customer service counter so that you can be issued a refund.

---

01. Why will the intercity terminal be closed on June 14th?
 (A) A construction work will be carried out.
 (B) A new electrical board will be installed.
 (C) A TV show will do filming there.
 (D) Government officials will inspect its facilities.

02. What are the listeners advised to do?
 (A) Use local transportation
 (B) Upgrade their tickets
 (C) Book the tickets in advance
 (D) Avoid travelling

03. According to the speaker, why should certain listeners go to the customer service counter?
 (A) To look at a map
 (B) To retrieve a lost item
 (C) To get a transportation schedule
 (D) To be refunded for a reservation

🔎 이렇게 풀어요

01. 왜 6월 14일에 시외 버스 터미널이 폐쇄되는가?
 (A) 공사가 시행될 것이다.
 (B) 새로운 전광판이 설치될 것이다.
 (C) TV 쇼가 그곳에서 촬영을 할 것이다.
 (D) 정부 공무원들이 시설들을 점검할 것이다.

02. 청자들은 무엇을 하도록 권고받는가?
 (A) 지역 교통을 이용할 것
 (B) 그들의 표를 업그레이드 할 것
 (C) 티켓을 미리 예매할 것
 (D) 여행을 피할 것

03. 화자에 따르면, 왜 특정 청자들은 고객 서비스 카운터로 가야 하는가?
 (A) 지도를 보기 위해
 (B) 잃어버린 물건을 찾기 위해
 (C) 교통편 스케줄을 받기 위해
 (D) 예약에 대해 환불받기 위해

담화 초반부에 This intercity bus terminal will be closed on Wednesday, June 14th due to a TV show filming.이라고 했습니다.
→ TV 쇼 촬영 때문에 시외 버스 터미널이 폐쇄된다고 하였으므로 정답은 (C)입니다.

시외 버스 터미널의 폐쇄를 알린 후, We recommend that you use the local bus and train networks ~ on that day.라고 했습니다.
→ 지역 버스와 기차 노선을 이용할 것을 권장하므로 local bus and train networks가 local transportation으로 패러프레이징 된 (A)가 정답입니다.

담화 마지막에서 If you have already purchased a ticket ~ please report to a customer service counter so that you can be issued a refund.라고 했습니다.
→ 이미 표를 구매했다면 환불받을 수 있도록 고객 서비스 카운터에 알리라고 했으므로 already purchased a ticket이 reservation으로 패러프레이징 된 (D)가 정답입니다.

PART 4 안내(announcement)   297

출제 유형 2 — 콘퍼런스에서의 안내

학회나 콘퍼런스에서 참석자들에게 행사 일정이나 프로그램, 연설자에 대해 말하는 담화가 출제됩니다.

• 콘퍼런스에서의 안내에서 자주 출제되는 어휘

express	표현하다, 속달의	convene	소집하다, 모으다
breakthrough	큰 발전, 새 발견	notable	유명한, 주목할 만한
medicine	의학, 약물	placement	배치
frequently	자주	guest speaker	초청 연사
gathering	모임	keynote speaker	기조 연설자
fairground	축제 마당, 박람회장	keynote address	기조 연설
auditorium	강당	knowledge	지식
charity	자선 단체	financial plan	재정 계획
fundraiser	모금 행사	agriculture	농업
contest	대회, 시합	nutrition	영양
book signing	책 사인회	investor	투자자
on time	정시에	annual	연례의
take part in	~에 참석하다	developer	개발자
participate in	~에 참석하다	patron	고객
instrumental	중요한	limitation	제한

콘퍼런스에서의 안내에서 자주 나오는 문제

• 안내가 어떤 행사에서 이루어지고 있는지 묻는 질문
What kind of event is the announcement being made at?
→ 처음 인사말 다음에 어디에서 안내가 이루어지고 있는지 파악할 수 있습니다. conference, expo, seminar 등의 어휘가 등장하고 어떤 분야인지 (automotive, medical 등)도 함께 언급되는 경우가 많습니다.

콘퍼런스에서의 안내

US

W: Hello folks, I hope you're all enjoying this conference on breakthroughs in medicine. Most of you have already signed up for the seminars and workshops tomorrow, but if you haven't, you should come out to Springfield Hall to participate in a contest of medical knowledge. It will be run quite like a game show, and all of you are welcome to join. The gathering point will be the fairground right in front of Springfield Hall at 2 P.M. Please remember that you have to be on time, or you won't be allowed into the auditorium.

01. What kind of event is the announcement being made at?
    (A) A charity fundraiser
    (B) A student orientation
    (C) A medical conference
    (D) A graduation ceremony

02. What does the speaker say some listeners can do tomorrow?
    (A) Take part in a contest
    (B) Attend a book signing
    (C) Go on a campus tour
    (D) Meet a professor

03. What are the listeners encouraged to do?
    (A) Register in advance
    (B) Arrive on schedule
    (C) Complete a survey
    (D) Show a photo ID

이렇게 풀어요

01. 안내는 어떤 종류의 행사에서 이루어지고 있는가?
    (A) 자선 모금 행사
    (B) 학생 오리엔테이션
    (C) 의학 콘퍼런스
    (D) 졸업식

담화 처음에서 I hope you're all enjoying this conference on breakthroughs in medicine.이라고 했습니다.
→ 의학에 대한 콘퍼런스임을 알 수 있으므로 정답은 (C)입니다.

02. 화자는 몇몇 청자들이 내일 무엇을 할 수 있다고 하는가?
    (A) 대회에 참석하기
    (B) 책 사인회에 참석하기
    (C) 캠퍼스 투어 하기
    (D) 교수님 만나기

키워드 tomorrow가 언급된 부분에서 Most of you have already ~ tomorrow, but if you haven't, ~ to participate in a contest of medical knowledge.라고 했습니다.
→ participate in이 take part in으로 패러프레이징 되었습니다. 내일 대회에 참석할 수 있다는 것을 알 수 있으므로 정답은 (A)입니다.

03. 청자들은 무엇을 하도록 권장받는가?
    (A) 미리 등록하기
    (B) 정시에 도착하기
    (C) 설문지 작성하기
    (D) 사진이 부착된 신분증 보여주기

마지막 문장에서 Please remember that you have to be on time, or you won't be allowed into the auditorium.이라고 했습니다.
→ be on time이 arrive on schedule로 패러프레이징 된 (B)가 정답입니다.

따라 하면 문제가 풀리는
연습 문제

문제와 각 선택지의 키워드에 표시하세요. 그러고 나서 담화를 듣고 빈칸에 들어갈 말을 받아쓴 후 정답을 선택해 보세요.

01. What is the cause of the delay?

(A) The engine was malfunctioning.   (B) A tree blocked the track.

announcement

> M: Attention, passengers for Train 345 to Cleveland. The train was _____ scheduled to depart at Platform 7. There will be a 30 minute delay due to a _____ tree on the _____. If you plan to _____ to other trains in Cleveland, please come to the ticketing desk and make sure that this delay will not affect your _____ train. Thank you for your understanding.

02. What are the listeners reminded to do?

(A) Pick up a welcome packet   (B) Validate their parking

announcement

> M: Welcome to the Highland _____ Conference for computer software developers. We will begin with the opening ceremony at 10 A.M. All _____ sessions are _____ on the second floor in the East Wing. You will have a one and a half hour _____ _____. And don't forget to _____ your _____ at the reception desk. Thank you.

03. What will be sent to the listeners?

(A) Text messages   (B) Meal vouchers

announcement

> W: Attention, all passengers leaving on the 9 P.M. _____ _____ to Queensland. Due to heavy snowfall around the Dutch County area, this bus has been _____. The Department of Transportation decided to stop _____ express buses until tomorrow morning. All cancelled buses are _____ for tomorrow. We will keep you posted about your bus schedules _____ _____.

paraphrasing 주어진 어휘 또는 표현과 의미가 동일한 것을 연결하세요.

1. railroad   •   • (a) depart
2. validate   •   • (b) track
3. leave   •   • (c) confirm

04. Where is the announcement being made?

(A) In an airplane (B) At a bus terminal

announcement

> M: Attention passengers, this is your _____ speaking. Our _____ will depart in 20 minutes. It is 30 minutes _____ _____ scheduled. We are waiting for other passengers who _____ to our flight. We will depart as soon as they are _____ _____. Our flight attendant will _____ you a beverage while you are waiting. Thank you.

05. Who most likely are the listeners?

(A) Job seekers (B) Local business owners

announcement

> W: Hello, thank you for coming to the fifth Butler County _____ _____. I'm very honored to _____ this event. We have produced outstanding and _____ graduates to our county since its foundation. This year, more than 200 local _____ will participate and set up booths. Most of them are offering on-site _____ _____. I hope you all find _____ during this three-day event.

06. How can listeners enter in a raffle?

(A) By becoming a member (B) By turning in a feedback form

announcement

> M: Hello, folks, I hope you've enjoyed the second day of this year's Sports Broadcasting Technology Exposition. Today, many popular _____ in our industry will _____ their expertise and various pieces of the _____ broadcasting _____ will be introduced. When you join a seminar, you will be asked to _____ feedback forms and _____ them in this box. You will be _____ entered in a raffle for various items.

---

paraphrasing 주어진 어휘 또는 표현과 의미가 동일한 것을 연결하세요.

4. serve •   • (a) provide
5. find employment •   • (b) turn in
6. submit •   • (c) get a job

PART 4 연습 문제   301

01. What kind of business does the speaker work at?
    (A) An art supply store
    (B) A camera shop
    (C) A museum
    (D) A travel agency

02. What does the speaker imply when she says, "The amount is up to you"?
    (A) Some artwork will be sold at an auction.
    (B) The listeners are encouraged to donate.
    (C) Some items are currently on sale.
    (D) The listeners should return later.

03. What are some listeners reminded to do?
    (A) Update their contact information
    (B) Register for regular updates
    (C) Change their camera settings
    (D) Join a membership

04. What is the purpose of the new program?
    (A) To collect donations
    (B) To attract more members
    (C) To renovate the classrooms
    (D) To promote class attendance

05. What are the listeners asked to do?
    (A) Fill out surveys
    (B) Join a book club
    (C) Post class reviews
    (D) Borrow more books

06. Who is Randall?
    (A) A teacher
    (B) A librarian
    (C) An electrician
    (D) A software designer

07. Where is the announcement being made?
    (A) At a tea shop
    (B) At a furniture store
    (C) At a hardware store
    (D) At a theater

08. What are the listeners encouraged to do?
    (A) Join a membership
    (B) Pick up a coupon
    (C) Buy a teapot
    (D) Try a sample

09. According to the speaker, why are Tea Tree products healthier than others on the market?
    (A) They are all organic.
    (B) They are carefully blended.
    (C) They are harvested by hand.
    (D) They are selected by dieticians.

10. Who most likely are the listeners?
    (A) Actors
    (B) Writers
    (C) Teachers
    (D) Publishers

11. What does the speaker mean when he says, "this conference room is only reserved until 3 P.M."?
    (A) He will not wait to begin.
    (B) He has another appointment.
    (C) The room must be cleaned afterwards.
    (D) Late arrivals will not be allowed into the room.

12. What will be passed around to the listeners?
    (A) A sign-in sheet
    (B) A training manual
    (C) Parking validations
    (D) The workshop schedule

13. What does the speaker mention about the work?

    (A) It will be paid at a higher rate.
    (B) It is expected to take an hour.
    (C) It will be done at a different location.
    (D) It is made up of three phases.

14. In which department do the listeners most likely work?

    (A) Maintenance
    (B) Finance
    (C) Research and development
    (D) Human resources

15. What will the listeners do next?

    (A) Form small groups
    (B) Complete a survey
    (C) Share some suggestions
    (D) Watch a demonstration

16. What kind of business does the speaker most likely work for?

    (A) A bookstore
    (B) A supermarket
    (C) A clothing shop
    (D) A restaurant

17. Why is the business making a special offer?

    (A) To promote a new brand
    (B) To advertise a relocation
    (C) To celebrate an anniversary
    (D) To get rid of excess stock

18. What does the speaker say the listeners should do to get a discount?

    (A) Recommend a product
    (B) Show a membership card
    (C) Present a coupon
    (D) Join a mailing list

Session Plan	Presenter
Session A	Paul Vance
Session B	Tammy Finnigan
Session C	Joan Carlyle
session D	Herman Lester

19. Why does the speaker apologize?

    (A) A room is not available.
    (B) An event is starting late.
    (C) There are not enough seats.
    (D) A name is misspelled.

20. Look at the graphic. Which session has been changed?

    (A) Session A
    (B) Session B
    (C) Session C
    (D) Session D

21. According to the speaker, how can the listeners provide feedback?

    (A) By completing a card
    (B) By attending a group session
    (C) By contacting the speaker
    (D) By commenting on a Web site

'멋진 당신, 오늘도 화이팅'

DAY
17

오늘의 학습 포인트

PART 3. 대화 주제 - 상점 / 병원·약국

1. 환불·고객 불만

   빈출 내용 - 결함 제품 환불/교환

   빈출 문제 - 목적 문제 & 문제 상황을 묻는 문제

2. 병원·약국

   빈출 내용 - 진료 예약/확인, 처방전

   빈출 문제 - 장소를 묻는 문제

PART 4. 담화 유형 - 광고(advertisement)

1. 제품 광고

   빈출 내용 - 가전제품, 전자기기, 가구

   빈출 문제 - 광고되는 제품이 무엇인지를 묻는 문제 & 제품의 혜택을 묻는 문제

2. 서비스 광고

   빈출 내용 - 무료 배송 서비스, 방문 수리 서비스, 정원 관리 서비스

   빈출 문제 - 업체의 웹사이트를 왜 방문해야 하는지 묻는 문제

PART 3 상점 – 환불·고객 불만 / 병원·약국

상품의 교환이나 환불 관련된 대화와 병원 진료 예약과 관련된 대화가 많이 나와요!

적용 기술
[기적의 필기노트] 49P
LC 기술 37

출제 유형 1
환불·고객 불만

상점에서 결함이 있는 상품에 대해 환불이나 교환을 요청하는 상황이 출제됩니다.

· 환불·고객 불만 관련 대화에서 자주 출제되는 어휘

accidentally	뜻하지 않게, 잘못하여	customer service	고객 서비스
insurance	보험	shut off	멈추다
defect	결함	defective	결함이 있는
complaint	불평, 불만	representative	상담원, 직원
specify	명시하다	in particular	특히
thoroughly	철저하게	component	(구성) 요소, 부품
instant	즉각적인, 순간의	on delivery	배달 시에
carry	취급하다	urgently	급하게
exchange	교환, 교환하다	refund	환불, 환불하다
face	직면하다	repair	수리, 수리하다
apology	사과	transform	변형시키다
needs	요구	desired	희망하는
inquire	문의하다	overcharge	과다 청구하다
dissatisfied	불만스러워하는	price quote	견적서
receipt	영수증	replace	대신하다, 대체하다
tracking number	추적 번호	malfunction	오작동하다
order status	주문 상태	decline	거절하다; 감소하다
broken	고장 난	incorrect	부정확한
process one's request	~의 요청을 처리하다	for no reason	아무 이유 없이

환불·고객 불만 관련 대화에서 자주 나오는 문제

· 목적을 묻는 문제
Why is the man calling the woman?
→ 주로 To complain about 으로 시작하는 보기가 정답일 확률이 높습니다.

· 문제 상황이 무엇인지 묻는 문제
What is the woman's problem?
→ I noticed that ~, have difficulty[trouble] ~ 등의 표현 뒤에 정답의 단서가 나옵니다.

환불·고객 불만

[US - US]

W: Hello, this is Maria with Dudley's Kitchen Appliances' customer service.
M: Hi, I bought your professional coffee maker for my coffee shop last week, and I'm already having problems with it.
W: The professional coffee maker is one of our top products. What's wrong?
M: I brew a lot of coffee for my customers. That means I need to have coffee ready at the right temperature. Instead of maintaining drinking temperature, it gets too hot or shuts off.
W: That shouldn't happen if you program your desired temperature. Have you done that?
M: Um, I don't think so. Where is that button?
W: You have to use the digital display. You can specify the temperature using that.

01. Where does the man work?
(A) At a coffee shop
(B) At a university
(C) At a warehouse
(D) At an appliance store

02. What does the man say is wrong with a coffee maker?
(A) It is difficult to clean.
(B) It uses too much electricity.
(C) It has a cracked display screen.
(D) It does not keep a steady temperature.

03. What does the woman tell the man to do?
(A) Read a manual
(B) Program a setting
(C) Unplug the device
(D) Confirm the model number

이렇게 풀어요

01. 남자는 어디에서 일하는가?
    (A) 커피숍에서
    (B) 대학교에서
    (C) 창고에서
    (D) 가전제품 가게에서

남자가 첫 대사에서 I bought your professional coffee maker for my coffee shop이라고 했습니다.
→ 남자가 my coffee shop이라고 했으므로 (A)가 정답입니다.

02. 남자는 커피 메이커가 무엇이 문제라고 말하는가?
    (A) 세척하기 어렵다.
    (B) 전력 소모가 너무 크다.
    (C) 표시 화면에 금이 갔다.
    (D) 안정적인 온도가 유지되지 않는다.

여자가 What's wrong이라고 물은 것에 대해 남자는 Instead of maintaining drinking temperature, it gets too hot or shuts off라고 했습니다.
→ drinking temperature가 steady temperature로, maintain이 keep으로 패러프레이징 된 (D)가 정답입니다.

03. 여자는 남자에게 무엇을 하라고 하는가?
    (A) 설명서를 읽기
    (B) 설정을 하기
    (C) 기기의 플러그를 뽑기
    (D) 모델 번호를 확인하기

대화 후반부에서 여자가 That shouldn't happen if you program your desired temperature라고 했고 마지막에 You can specify the temperature using that이라고 했습니다.
→ program a setting으로 패러프레이징 된 (B)가 정답입니다.

출제 유형 2 병원·약국

병원에서의 진료 예약 및 확인, 약국에서 처방전을 주며 약을 받는 상황 등이 출제됩니다.

병원·약국 대화에서 자주 나오는 문제

· 대화 장소를 묻는 문제
Where most likely are the speakers?
→ doctor(의사), prescription(처방전), checkup(검진) 등 병원이나 약국 관련 단어는 정해져 있으므로 키워드를 통해 쉽게 파악할 수 있습니다.

· **병원·약국 대화에서 자주 출제되는 어휘**

treatment	치료, 대우, 처우	diagnosis	진단
pill	알약	prescription	처방전
slip	(작은 종이) 조각, 쪽지	medication	약물
medical	의학의	confidential	기밀의, 비밀의
symptom	증상	cancelation	취소
dose	1회 복용량	disease	질병, 질환
recovery	회복	cautiously	조심스럽게, 신중하게
examine	검진하다	ingredient	재료, 성분
checkup	건강 검진	fatigue	피로
condition	상태, 조건	refrain	삼가다
treat	치료하다	relieve	덜어주다, 완화시키다
concern	우려, 관심사	prescribe	처방하다
physical	신체의	periodically	주기적으로
pharmacist	약사	urgent	긴급한
patient	환자; 인내심 있는	care	돌보다, 관심을 가지다
first aid	응급 치료	sore	아픈, 쓰린
injury	부상	recover	회복하다
medical insurance	의료 보험	surgery	수술

병원·약국

BR - AU

W: Hello, I'm Stephanie Coors. Dr. Burns sent me here to pick up my prescription.
M: Hello, Ms. Coors. I haven't received a call from his office about you yet. Did he give you a slip to bring here?
W: Oh, I almost forgot. Here it is.
M: Thank you. I'll prepare your pill bottle in just a moment. Will you be paying by cash or credit?

01. Where most likely are the speakers?
  (A) At a restaurant
  (B) At a pharmacy
  (C) At a hospital
  (D) At a law firm

02. What did the woman bring with her?
  (A) An appointment slip
  (B) A medicine bottle
  (C) A medical record
  (D) A prescription

03. What does the man ask the woman about?
  (A) How she intends to pay
  (B) How much time she has
  (C) How satisfied she was
  (D) How she feels

이렇게 풀어요

01. 화자들은 어디에 있겠는가?
  (A) 레스토랑에
  (B) 약국에
  (C) 병원에
  (D) 법률 사무소에

여자가 pick up my prescription을, 남자가 prepare your pill bottle 등을 언급했습니다.
→ 약국임을 알 수 있으므로 (B)가 정답입니다.

02. 여자는 무엇을 가져왔는가?
  (A) 예약증
  (B) 약병
  (C) 의료 기록
  (D) 처방전

남자가 의사가 준 종이를 가지고 왔는지 물었고, 여자가 그것을 건네자 남자가 약을 주겠다고 했습니다.
→ slip을 prescription으로 패러프레이징 한 (D)가 정답입니다.

03. 남자는 여자에게 무엇에 대해 묻는가?
  (A) 그녀가 어떻게 돈을 지불할 것인지
  (B) 그녀가 시간이 얼마나 있는지
  (C) 그녀가 어느 정도 만족했는지
  (D) 그녀의 기분이 어떤지

대화 마지막에서 남자가 Will you be paying by cash or credit?이라고 물었습니다.
→ 현금 또는 신용카드 중 무엇으로 돈을 지불할지를 묻고 있으므로 (A)가 정답입니다.

따라 하면 문제가 풀리는 연습 문제

문제와 각 선택지의 키워드에 표시하세요. 그러고 나서 대화를 듣고 빈칸에 들어갈 말을 받아쓴 후 정답을 선택해 보세요.

01. What is the man encouraged to do?

(A) Come to the office earlier   (B) Visit a Web site

> W: Dr. Grant's office, how may I help you?
> M: Hello, this is Mark Perkins. I'd like to _____ my _____ for a checkup on Tuesday.
> W: Sure, I'll _____ you _____ there. But as you may already know, we _____ to a building on Franklin Avenue. Please _____ to the directions on our Web site.

02. What does the man ask for?

(A) An order number   (B) A name of product

> W: Hi, my name is Sarah Green. I'm _____ _____ ask about my order. I expected it to be _____ yesterday. I already _____ for two-day shipping.
> M: Wait a second. Let me _____ our records. What is your _____ _____? It's on your _____.

03. What day will the woman most likely visit?

(A) Tuesday   (B) Wednesday

> M: This is John calling from Indiana _____ _____. Our records say you have an appointment with Dr. Anderson next Monday. Unfortunately, he will be _____ of the office that day due to a _____ _____. He will be back to the office _____ _____. Can you come on Tuesday afternoon or Wednesday morning?
> M: Hmm... Actually, I will not be _____ for next Tuesday afternoon since I am _____ to have a client meeting.

---

paraphrasing 주어진 어휘 또는 표현과 의미가 동일한 것을 연결하세요.

1. make appointment   •   • (a) proof or purchase
2. receipt   •   • (b) personal matter
3. family emergency   •   • (c) set a schedule

04. What department does the woman work in?

(A) Customer service   (B) Employee training

W: Can I help you with anything, sir?
M: Yes, I'd like to _____ this hot pot that I _____ here last week. There is a _____ on the lid after just one use. Can I return and _____ it with a new one of another brand?
W: That shouldn't be a problem. Do you have the _____ _____?

05. What problem does the man mention?

(A) He received a wrong item.   (B) A device is not working properly.

M: Hello, I'm _____ _____ the computer that I bought two days ago. It takes a while when I _____ certain software. Much _____ than I expected.
W: Oh, I can help you with that. _____ _____ _____ _____ the serial number? It's a seven-digit number. You will _____ it on the left side of the computer.

06. What will the man most likely do next?

(A) Reschedule an appointment   (B) Go to a waiting area

M: Hello. I'm here for an _____ _____ Dr. Douglas at 3 P.M.
W: Here is your name on the schedule. But he is busy now, so your appointment will be _____ _____. He can see you at 3:15 P.M. _____ _____ _____ taking a seat in the waiting area and helping yourself to some tea or coffee?

paraphrasing 주어진 어휘 또는 표현과 의미가 동일한 것을 연결하세요.

4. hot pot   •   • (a) device
5. computer   •   • (b) postpone
6. delay   •   • (c) cooking utensil

토익에 나올 실전 문제

01. Who most likely is the woman?
    (A) A car mechanic
    (B) A taxi driver
    (C) A doctor
    (D) A pharmacist

02. Why does the man say, "I have to drive for work"?
    (A) To list his qualities
    (B) To emphasize a problem
    (C) To apologize for a mistake
    (D) To request time off from work

03. What does the woman tell the man he should do?
    (A) Look for other work
    (B) Register at a pharmacy
    (C) Purchase an insurance plan
    (D) Take a different medication

04. What are the speakers talking about?
    (A) A medical procedure
    (B) A doctor's schedule
    (C) A prescription
    (D) An illness

05. Why is the woman running behind schedule?
    (A) A large order was just received.
    (B) A computer network is down.
    (C) An item was misplaced.
    (D) A coworker is out sick.

06. What does the man say he will do?
    (A) Fill out some forms
    (B) Make a phone call
    (C) Order some food
    (D) Take a pill

07. Where does the man work?
    (A) At a hotel
    (B) At a candy store
    (C) At a medical clinic
    (D) At a real estate agency

08. What does the woman say has become a problem?
    (A) A lack of clients
    (B) Working late
    (C) Painful teeth
    (D) Giving presentations

09. What does the woman imply when she says, "I get off at 5 P.M. on Wednesdays"?
    (A) She recently started a full-time position.
    (B) She cannot make an appointment time.
    (C) She only has time on weekends.
    (D) She has to attend a meeting.

10. Who most likely is the man?
    (A) A lab technician
    (B) A business client
    (C) A patient
    (D) A receptionist

11. What is the purpose of the woman's call?
    (A) To schedule a meeting
    (B) To offer some feedback
    (C) To change an appointment
    (D) To make a monetary donation

12. What will the woman do on Friday?
    (A) Meet a client
    (B) Open an account
    (C) Get a physical checkup
    (D) Donate blood

13. Where is the conversation taking place?

    (A) At camping shop
    (B) At a construction company
    (C) At a hardware store
    (D) At an electricity company

14. What problem does the woman mention?

    (A) A product is malfunctioning.
    (B) Some merchandise is sold out.
    (C) She was overcharged for a purchase.
    (D) Some items were mislabeled.

15. What will the man most likely do next?

    (A) Contact a manufacturer
    (B) Look for a replacement
    (C) Speak to a manager
    (D) Issue a refund

16. What kind of business is the woman calling?

    (A) A nail salon
    (B) A financial institution
    (C) A computer shop
    (D) A medical clinic

17. What did the woman do this month?

    (A) Moved to a new city
    (B) Took a vacation
    (C) Signed up for a program
    (D) Attended a conference

18. What does the man imply when he says, "I'd give it half an hour"?

    (A) There is a lot of paperwork to complete.
    (B) The business has changed its opening hours.
    (C) He wants the woman to call back later.
    (D) He thinks a problem will be resolved soon.

String of Lights	£30
Pack of Metallic Balloons	£10
Banner	£15
Centerpiece Vase	£20

19. What kind of event does the man mention?

    (A) A design contest
    (B) A birthday party
    (C) A company celebration
    (D) A product launch

20. Look at the graphic. Which amount will the woman change?

    (A) £30
    (B) £10
    (C) £15
    (D) £20

21. What can the man receive from a supervisor?

    (A) A product catalog
    (B) A new receipt
    (C) A free sample
    (D) A store coupon

PART 4 광고(advertisement)

가전제품, 전자기기 등 제품 광고와 무료 배송 서비스, 방문 서비스 등의 서비스 광고가 주로 출제됩니다.

적용 기술
[기적의 필기노트] 78P, 79P
LC 기술 58, 59

출제 유형 1 제품 광고

가전제품, 전자기기, 가구에 관한 광고가 최근 자주 출제됩니다.

- 제품 광고에서 자주 출제되는 어휘

제품 광고에서 자주 나오는 문제

· 광고되는 제품 또는 서비스가 무엇인지를 묻는 문제
What is the advertisement for?
→ 담화 초반부에서 제품 명을 말하고 그것의 가장 큰 장점이나 특징이 언급됩니다.

· 제품의 혜택을 묻는 문제
What benefit does the speaker mention?
→ offer, this week only, savings, complimentary, free 등의 단어와 함께 혜택이 언급됩니다.

decision	결정	design	고안하다
immediately	즉시	complimentary	무료의
have a hard time -ing	~하는 데 어려움을 겪다	service representative	서비스 직원
efficient	효율적인	sales representative	판매원
efficiency	효율성	early bird	일찍 오는 사람
affordability	적절한 가격	first-ever	최초의
compatibility	호환성	competitive	경쟁력 있는
durability	내구성	provider	공급 업체
tax filing	세금 신고	especially	특별히
tax exemption	세금 면제(공제)	proof of purchase	구매 증거
portable	휴대용의	revolutionary	혁신적인
compensate	보상하다	comfort	편안함
outdated	시대에 뒤떨어진	regarding	~에 관한
promotional	홍보의	loyal customer	단골 고객
browse	둘러보다, 훑어보다	downtown	시내, 도심

제품 광고

[AU]

M: Tax season is around the corner again, and you might be wasting a lot of money by using a tax filing service. Instead, download Tax Time, the easy-to-use software that helps you to file your taxes without expensive service fees. Simply download the program and follow the prompts. Tax Time won the Simple Software award last year for being so efficient. If you have used our service before, you know how great it is. Also, Tax Time offers complimentary updates to all of its customers, so you don't have to pay again every year. Visit our Web site to download either the program or the annual update.

01. What is the advertisement for?
(A) A sports complex
(B) A software program
(C) A phone charger
(D) An online game

02. What has Tax Time received an award for?
(A) Its efficiency
(B) Its affordability
(C) Its compatibility
(D) Its customer service

03. What benefit does the speaker mention?
(A) Customer support
(B) Tax exemption
(C) Free updates
(D) Newsletters

이렇게 풀어요

01. 무엇을 위한 광고인가?
(A) 스포츠 복합시설
(B) 소프트웨어 프로그램
(C) 휴대전화 충전기
(D) 온라인 게임

담화 초반부에서 download Tax Time, the easy-to-use software that helps you to file your taxes without expensive service fees라고 했습니다.
→ Tax Time은 세금 신고를 돕는 소프트웨어라는 것을 알 수 있으므로 정답은 (B)입니다.

02. Tax Time은 무엇에 대해 상을 받았는가?
(A) 효율성
(B) 적절한 가격
(C) 호환성
(D) 고객 서비스

담화 중반부에서 Tax Time won the Simple Software award last year for being so efficient라고 했습니다.
→ 효율성으로 수상했다는 것을 알 수 있으므로 정답은 (A)입니다.

03. 화자는 어떤 혜택을 언급하는가?
(A) 고객 지원
(B) 세금 면제
(C) 무료 업데이트
(D) 소식지

담화 후반부에서 Tax Time offers complimentary updates to all of its customers라고 했습니다.
→ complimentary를 free로 패러프레이징 한 (C)가 정답입니다.

출제 유형 2 | 서비스 광고

무료 배송 서비스, 방문 수리 서비스, 정원 관리 서비스에 관한 광고가 최근 자주 출제됩니다.

서비스 광고에서 자주 나오는 문제

· 업체의 웹사이트를 왜 방문해야 하는지 묻는 문제
Why should the listeners visit a Web site?
→ 할인 정보, 행사 정보, 카탈로그를 보기 위해 업체의 웹사이트에 방문하라는 내용이 자주 출제됩니다.

· 서비스 광고에서 자주 출제되는 어휘

grocery	식료품	flea market	벼룩 시장
be bound to	~하려고 하다	mark down	할인하다
daytime	낮 동안의	charger	충전기
expert	전문가	basically	기본적으로
nutritionist	영양사	disposable product	일회용품
interrupt	방해하다	gladly	기쁘게
produce	농산물	in need of	~을 필요로 하는
make a payment	결제하다	in installments	할부로
look over	검토하다	as of	~부터
for free	무료로	wearable	착용할 수 있는
debut	첫 출시, 데뷔	at no extra charge	추가 요금 없이
normal	보통의	instructional	교육용의
be on display	전시 중이다	save	절약하다, 아끼다
purse	지갑	cosmetics	화장품
take effort	힘이 들다, 노력을 필요로 하다	security system	보안 시스템
shorten	짧아지다, 단축하다	narrow	좁은
stick to	방침을 고수하다	mere	겨우 ~의
hassle	귀찮은 일	sync with	~와 동시에 움직이다

풀이방법: 서비스 광고

🎧 Day 17_P4_02.mp3   해석 p.177

[US]
W: If you need to go grocery shopping, then Tammy's Market is the place! We offer the freshest meats and produce, and even have an in-house bakery to provide fresh bread options. Also, as of next month, there will be several tasting stations set up throughout our store so that you can sample some of the foods we sell for free. In order to help you prepare a shopping list, we have posted our weekly sales flyer on our Web site. Be sure to look there so that you can plan your meals for the week!

01. What kind of business is the advertisement for?
(A) A catering service
(B) A grocery store
(C) A restaurant
(D) A café

02. What will members be able to do as of next month?
(A) Try free samples
(B) Place orders online
(C) Consult a nutritionist
(D) Purchase organic foods

03. Why should the listeners visit a Web site?
(A) To get recipes
(B) To give feedback
(C) To check a location
(D) To view an online flyer

이렇게 풀어요

01. 광고는 어떤 종류의 사업체를 위한 것인가?
(A) 출장 요리 서비스
(B) 식료품점
(C) 레스토랑
(D) 카페

첫 문장에서 If you're need to go grocery shopping, then Tammy's Market is the place!라고 했습니다.
→ 식료품점을 광고하고 있다는 것을 알 수 있으므로 정답은 (B)입니다.

02. 다음 달부터 회원들은 무엇을 할 수 있는가?
(A) 무료 시식하기
(B) 온라인으로 주문하기
(C) 영양사와 상담하기
(D) 유기농 음식 구매하기

중반부에 키워드인 다음 달이 언급되면서 as of next month, there will be several tasting stations set up throughout our store so that you can sample some of the foods we sell for free라고 했습니다.
→ 다음 달부터 무료 시식을 할 수 있으므로 정답은 (A)입니다.

03. 청자들은 왜 웹사이트를 방문해야 하는가?
(A) 요리법을 얻기 위해
(B) 피드백을 주기 위해
(C) 위치를 확인하기 위해
(D) 온라인 전단을 보기 위해

웹사이트가 언급된 후반부에서 we have posted our weekly sales flyer on our Web site. Be sure to look there ~ 라고 했습니다.
→ look이 view로 패러프레이징 된 (D)가 정답입니다.

따라 하면 문제가 풀리는 연습 문제

문제와 각 선택지의 키워드에 표시하세요. 그러고 나서 담화를 듣고 빈칸에 들어갈 말을 받아쓴 후 정답을 선택해 보세요.

01. What is the advertisement for?

(A) A washing machine　　　　　　(B) A vacuum cleaner

advertisement

> W: Are you satisfied with your _____ _____? Our vacuum cleaner, Power Sweeper, is cord-free and _____ with a long-lasting battery. Its new, innovative, powerful motor system will _____ 30% more dust and dirt than our previous model. It can deeply _____ both carpets and floors. It comes with various _____ accessories. Visit one of your nearest _____ stores and buy one today. You will get a free battery _____ station.

02. Why are items on sale?

(A) A store is moving to another location.　　(B) New products will arrive soon.

advertisement

> M: After over 20 years _____ _____ downtown, Bed & Beddings is about to _____ to Lloyd Mall. All of the items currently in stock will _____ _____ at 20% off. All displayed items in the showroom are drastically _____ for clearance. Come today and check their _____. Hurry up! Don't miss this _____ opportunity.

03. What will be given to those who renew membership early?

(A) Free admissions　　　　　　(B) A free gift

advertisement

> M: The winter season is _____. This means your museum membership _____ soon and it's the perfect time to _____ it. We offer early bird discounts to those who renew it _____ November 30. You will get 20% off and _____ T-shirts. Membership holders can _____ all regular exhibitions at a discounted price and 10% off all _____ in the gift shop.

---

paraphrasing　주어진 어휘 또는 표현과 의미가 동일한 것을 연결하세요.

1. remove　　　●　　　　　　●　(a) clear out
2. drastically　●　　　　　　●　(b) come to an end
3. expire　　　●　　　　　　●　(c) greatly

04. How can listeners get a discount?

(A) By referring to an advertisement   (B) By registering for a newsletter

advertisement

> W: Do you want to avoid _____ of _____ work such as tree trimming and grass mowing? That's why Dominguez Landscaping is here at Centerville. Call us today to get a free _____ _____. One of our experienced _____ will visit your home or building. _____ this ad when you _____ our service, and you will get 20% off.

05. Where does the speaker most likely work?

(A) At a delivery company   (B) At a supermarket

advertisement

> W: Are you _____ _____ to go grocery shopping every day? We will _____ _____ the Pick-up Grocery service. Just _____ your groceries online at our Web site and _____ a time for you to pick them up. Our workers will bag the _____ you ordered. All you have to do is _____ _____ one of the counters and pick up your order. We will open a drive-through window soon.

06. What is required to get a discount?

(A) Show a student ID   (B) Present a coupon

advertisement

> M: Back-to-School is coming! Reynolds Furniture is offering a _____ _____ to the students of Grand Hill College. We have the _____ _____ of desks, chairs, bookshelves, and so on. Just _____ your _____ ID to a cashier, and you will get 15% off from the total of your _____. Don't miss this special deal.

---

paraphrasing 주어진 어휘 또는 표현과 의미가 동일한 것을 연결하세요.

4. refer to   •   • (a) show
5. introduce   •   • (b) mention
6. present   •   • (c) launch

01. What kind of business is the ad promoting?

    (A) A fitness center
    (B) A cleaning company
    (C) A real estate agency
    (D) A business consultant

02. According to the speaker, what is the business known for?

    (A) Its quick service
    (B) Its satisfaction scores
    (C) Its competitive prices
    (D) Its use of natural products

03. What kind of offer is mentioned by the speaker?

    (A) Weekend service
    (B) A free trial period
    (C) A satisfaction guarantee
    (D) Customer appreciation discounts

04. What is the advertisement for?

    (A) Driving lessons
    (B) An upcoming job fair
    (C) Budget planning sessions
    (D) An online marketing seminar

05. What benefit does the speaker mention?

    (A) A new parking lot
    (B) A convenient schedule
    (C) An easy-to-find location
    (D) An affordable registration fee

06. What does the speaker say is a contest prize?

    (A) A car
    (B) Event tickets
    (C) A tablet device
    (D) Business consultation

07. What kind of product does the company sell?

    (A) Cash registers
    (B) Inventory software
    (C) Packaging materials
    (D) Security systems

08. What feature does the speaker emphasize?

    (A) The product is affordable.
    (B) It is an all-in-one product.
    (C) Customers have written positive reviews.
    (D) Updates are given automatically.

09. What is being offered for free for a limited time?

    (A) An extended warranty
    (B) Delivery
    (C) A trial period
    (D) Installation

10. What is Deals on Meals?

    (A) A restaurant
    (B) A food delivery app
    (C) A grocery store
    (D) A catering company

11. Why does the speaker say, "Type in the name of a food you want"?

    (A) To stress a service's easiness to use
    (B) To give some instructions
    (C) To ask for more information
    (D) To solicit feedback

12. Why should listeners act quickly?

    (A) It may take a long time to make a delivery.
    (B) Some menu items are only seasonal.
    (C) A discount will expire soon.
    (D) Seating is limited.

13. What is the advertisement about?
    (A) A hair salon
    (B) A fashion studio
    (C) A dental clinic
    (D) A fitness facility

14. What has the business recently done?
    (A) Extended its hours
    (B) Opened another branch
    (C) Changed its location
    (D) Received an award

15. Why are the listeners invited to visit a Web site?
    (A) To read about the staff
    (B) To download a coupon
    (C) To view some images
    (D) To book an appointment

16. What is being advertised?
    (A) An online service
    (B) A digital camera
    (C) A smartphone app
    (D) A laptop computer

17. What does the speaker highlight about the product?
    (A) Its long-lasting battery
    (B) Its affordable price
    (C) Its extended warranty
    (D) Its compatibility

18. According to the speaker, what is available for members?
    (A) Support forums
    (B) Software updates
    (C) Monthly newsletters
    (D) Instructional videos

Brand: Valencia	
Item	Special Offer
Ski Boots	~~$460~~ → $325
Ski Goggles	~~$220~~ → $105
Ski Helmet	~~$100~~ → $85
Ski Bag	~~$45~~ → $35

19. Look at the graphic. Which price is for the item the speaker mentions?
    (A) $325
    (B) $105
    (C) $85
    (D) $35

20. What does the speaker say about the Valencia brand?
    (A) It is HB Sports' newest line of products.
    (B) It is preferred by sales representatives.
    (C) It is recommended by professional skiers.
    (D) It is rarely offered at reduced prices.

21. How can customers get free delivery?
    (A) By presenting a loyalty card
    (B) By spending more than a certain amount
    (C) By ordering three or more items
    (D) By signing up for a mailing list

'멋진 당신, 오늘도 화이팅'

DAY
18

오늘의 학습 포인트

PART 3. 대화 주제 - 호텔/식당

1. 예약
   - 빈출 내용 - 예약 시간, 인원 수, 선호하는 방/좌석
   - 빈출 문제 - 예약 또는 예약 변경과 관련된 세부 사항

2. 요청 사항
   - 빈출 내용 - 메뉴나 서비스에 대한 요청
   - 빈출 문제 - 요청 사항을 묻는 문제 & 직업을 묻는 문제

PART 4. 담화 유형 - 관광 정보(tour information) / 소개(introduction)

1. 관광 정보(tour information)
   - 빈출 내용 - 특정 지역, 동물원, 생산 공장 견학
   - 빈출 문제 - 장소를 묻는 문제 & 제안/요청 문제

2. 소개(introduction)
   - 빈출 내용 - 강연자 소개
   - 빈출 문제 - 인물이 어떤 분야에서 일을 하고 있는지 묻는 문제

PART 3 호텔/식당 - 예약/요청 사항

예약 시간 및 인원 수 등 예약에 관한 대화와 메뉴나 서비스 관련 특별 요청 사항에 관한 대화가 많이 나와요!

출제 유형 1 예약

주로 전화 통화를 하는 대화로 출제되며, 예약 시간 및 인원 수, 선호하는 방/좌석에 대한 대화를 나눕니다.

• **호텔/식당에서의 예약 관련 대화에서 자주 출제되는 어휘**

예약 관련 대화에서 자주 나오는 문제

• 예약 관련하여 어디에 전화하는지 묻는 문제
What kind of business is the woman calling?
→ 주로 대화의 전반부에서 restaurant, hotel, table, room 등의 키워드를 통해 파악할 수 있습니다.

• 예약 또는 예약 변경과 관련한 세부 사항 문제
→ 주로 대화 중반부에서 단서가 제시되며 it was supposed to ~, but ~ 등의 표현이 사용됩니다.

book	예약하다	accommodate	수용하다
reserve	예약하다	travel agency	여행사
reservation	예약	suitable	적합한
recipe	요리법	chef	주방장
lack	부족	pay off	성공하다, 성과를 올리다
gather	모으다, 모이다	packed	(사람들이) 꽉 들어찬
serve	제공하다, 대접하다	process	과정, 진행
taste	맛보다	itinerary	여행 일정(표)
up to	(수·정도) ~까지	beforehand	미리
brochure	안내 책자	expenditure	지출
suitcase	여행 가방	assure	보장하다, 장담하다
broaden	넓히다	outgoing	떠나는, 출발하는
souvenir	기념품	overseas	해외로, 해외의
comfortably	편안하게	rush	혼잡, 번잡
tourist attraction	관광지	dine	식사하다
outing	야유회	plug in	플러그를 꽂다
help oneself to	마음껏 먹다	room rate	객실 요금
diner	식당 손님	vacant	비어 있는
ahead of schedule	예정보다 먼저	go on a business trip	출장 가다

예약

BR - US

W: Hello, I'm Lisa O'Connor. I have a dinner reservation for six at your restaurant this Friday evening.
M: Hello, Ms. O'Connor. Do you need to change the reservation?
W: Yes, it was supposed to be a company outing, but two of my associates will have to leave town urgently on business. They won't be back from their trip until the 21, so we'll have to have the dinner on that day.
M: Okay, I can do that for you. By the way, did you know that we now have an online reservation system? You can also browse the menu on our Web site.

01. What kind of business is the woman calling?

(A) A travel agency
(B) A restaurant
(C) An airline
(D) A hotel

02. What does the woman mention about her associates?

(A) Their family will join the trip.
(B) Their work hours have been changed.
(C) They have to go on a business trip.
(D) They requested vegetarian meal.

03. What does the man say can be done online?

(A) Reserve a table
(B) Select a seat
(C) Place an order
(D) View a recipe

이렇게 풀어요

01. 여자는 어떤 종류의 업체에 전화하고 있는가?
    (A) 여행사
    (B) 레스토랑
    (C) 항공사
    (D) 호텔

02. 여자는 그녀의 동료들에 대해 무엇을 언급하는가?
    (A) 그들의 가족이 여행에 합류할 것이다.
    (B) 그들의 업무 시간이 변경되었다.
    (C) 그들은 출장을 가야 한다.
    (D) 그들은 채식 요리를 요청했다.

03. 남자는 온라인으로 무엇을 할 수 있다고 말하는가?
    (A) 테이블을 예약하는 것
    (B) 좌석을 선택하는 것
    (C) 주문하는 것
    (D) 요리법을 보는 것

여자의 첫 대사에서 dinner reservation at your restaurant라고 했습니다.
→ 레스토랑에 전화하고 있음을 알 수 있으므로 (B)가 정답입니다.

여자가 my associates라고 언급되는 부분에서 leave town urgently on business라고 했습니다.
→ leave town urgently on business를 go on a business trip으로 패러프레이징 한 (C)가 정답입니다.

남자가 마지막 대사에서 we now have an online reservation system이라고 했습니다.
→ have an online reservation system을 reserve a table로 패러프레이징 한 (A)가 정답입니다.

출제 유형 2 — 요청 사항

주문한 메뉴에 대한 특별 요청 사항이나 호텔 룸 또는 서비스에 대해 특정 사항을 요구하는 내용이 출제됩니다.

호텔·식당에서 요청 관련 대화에서 자주 나오는 문제

· 요청 사항을 묻는 문제
What does the man ask the woman to do?
→ 요청하는 사람의 말에서 Could you, Would you, Please ~ 뒤에 주로 정답의 단서가 제시됩니다.

· 직업을 묻는 문제
Who is 사람 이름?
→ 대화에서 이름이 언급되는 주변에 직업(chef, manager 등)이 직접적으로 언급되거나, 대화 장소를 통해 직업을 유추할 수 있습니다.

• 호텔/식당에서 요청하는 대화에서 자주 출제되는 어휘

bistro	식당	make requests	요청하다
authentic	정통의, 진짜의	amount	양, 액수
seasoned	양념을 한	sample	시식하다, 시음하다
unattended	주인이 없는, 내버려 둔	extensive use	광범위한 사용
moderate	보통의, 적당한	go along with	~에 동의하다, 찬성하다
apparently	듣자 하니, 보아 하니	get back	돌아오다
means	수단, 방법	ahead of time	예정보다 빨리
astonish	놀라게 하다	eatery	식당
be about to	~하려는 참이다	dine out	외식하다
accident	사고	keep records of	기록을 남기다
luggage	짐, 수하물	take time off	시간을 내다
tentative	잠정적인, 임시의	turn in	제출하다
secondhand	중고의	double check	재차 확인하다
outdoor	야외의	lost and found	분실물 취급소
leave behind	두고 가다	selection	선택, 선정
be set	준비가 되다	vegetarian	채식주의자
organize	준비하다	dish	음식, 요리
If I'm not mistaken	제가 틀리지 않다면	stick with	~을 고수하다

풀이 방법 — 요청 사항

AU - US

M: Welcome to Miami Beach Hotel. How can I help you? Are you here to check in?

W: No, I had a lunch meeting with my client at your business lounge on the 10th floor. On the way back to my office, I realized I left my fountain pen on the chair. I talked with a waitress about it but she said all lost items are reported immediately to the front desk when they are found. So I'm here now.

M: Okay, I see. Give me a second... There is only one pen on the list of the lost-and-found items. Could you take a seat in the lobby and wait for me to bring it from the office?

---

01. Why did the woman initially visit the Miami Beach Hotel?
   (A) To reserve an event venue
   (B) To lead a seminar
   (C) To meet a client
   (D) To attend a conference

02. What does the woman need help with?
   (A) Finding a lost item
   (B) Setting up audio equipment
   (C) Adding vegetarian options
   (D) Ordering more beverages

03. What does the man ask the woman to do?
   (A) Come back at a later time
   (B) Call front desk
   (C) Sign a contract
   (D) Wait in the lobby

이렇게 풀어요

01. 여자는 처음에 왜 Miami Beach 호텔에 방문했는가?
   (A) 행사 장소를 예약하기 위해
   (B) 세미나를 진행하기 위해
   (C) 고객을 만나기 위해
   (D) 회의에 참석하기 위해

여자가 첫 대사에서 I had a lunch meeting with my client at your business lounge ~라고 했습니다.
→ 고객을 만났다는 의미이므로 (C)가 정답입니다.

02. 여자는 어떤 도움을 필요로 하는가?
   (A) 잃어버린 물건을 찾는 것
   (B) 오디오 장비를 설치하는 것
   (C) 채식주의자 옵션을 추가하는 것
   (D) 음료를 더 주문하는 것

여자가 I realized I left my fountain pen on the chair. ~ she said all lost items are reported immediately to the front desk라고 했습니다.
→ 여자가 두고 온 만년필을 찾으려 한다는 것을 알 수 있으므로 (A)가 정답입니다.

03. 남자는 여자에게 무엇을 하라고 요청하는가?
   (A) 나중에 다시 돌아오기
   (B) 프런트 데스크에 전화하기
   (C) 계약서에 서명하기
   (D) 로비에서 기다리기

남자가 마지막 대사에서 Could you take a seat in the lobby and wait for me to bring it from the office?라고 했습니다.
→ 로비에서 기다리라고 한 것이므로 (D)가 정답입니다.

따라 하면 문제가 풀리는
연습 문제

문제와 각 선택지의 키워드에 표시하세요. 그러고 나서 대화를 듣고 빈칸에 들어갈 말을 받아쓴 후 정답을 선택해 보세요.

01. Where does the conversation take place?

(A) At a hospital   (B) At a restaurant

> W: Would you like a _____ for two?
> M: Actually, we will have more people _____ us soon, so we'll need a table for six.
> W: Certainly. We _____ _____ a table for six people available now, but if you'd like to _____ _____ _____ at the bar I can offer you a drink.

02. Where does the woman most likely work?

(A) At a museum   (B) At a hotel

> M: I have a _____ under the name of Mark Smith.
> W: Okay, you _____ a standard room for three nights from today. You have been a _____ _____ for more than five years. Would you like to _____ _____ _____ to an ocean-view executive room?

03. What are the speakers mainly discussing?

(A) An annual event   (B) A summer vacation

> M: Hi Darlene, this is Joseph. I'm excited to hear that you decided to _____ your _____ company dinner at our conference center.
> W: Most of our _____ were very _____ with your facilities and foods. And I just want to know whether you can _____ more meat options to the dinner menu because there will be clients from _____ in the Middle East.

---

paraphrasing 주어진 어휘 또는 표현과 의미가 동일한 것을 연결하세요.

1. have a reservation   •   • (a) yearly event
2. regular customer   •   • (b) booked
3. annual company dinner •   • (c) frequent visitor

328 기적의 토익 LC

04. What does the woman request?

(A) A group discount　　　　(B) A private space

> W: Hi. I'm calling to make a reservation for eight people at 6:00 this Thursday.
> M: Wait a second while I _____ the _____. Do you have any other _____?
> W: Well, actually it will be a dinner with a client, so do you have a _____ _____ for us?

05. What will the woman probably do next?

(A) Have a snack　　　　(B) Visit business center

> W: Nice to meet you, Dr. Smith. I think this hotel is very _____ _____ the conference.
> M: Yes, it is. It has a spacious business center with _____ equipment.
> W: Anyway, I will _____ _____ _____ before reviewing the slideshows for my presentation.

06. Who most likely is the man?

(A) A wait staff member　　　　(B) A general manager

> M: Good evening. I'm Benjamin, your _____ today. Are you ready to order or do you need more time?
> W: I'm ready to order. I _____ a Caesar salad with Italian dressing, and seafood pasta with grilled squid. _____ _____ _____ serve the salad dressing on the side?
> M: Sure, any drink for you?

paraphrasing　주어진 어휘 또는 표현과 의미가 동일한 것을 연결하세요.

4. room　　　　　　　　　　　(a) space
5. grab a bite　　　　　　　　(b) wait staff member
6. server　　　　　　　　　　(c) have a snack

토익에 나올 실전 문제

01. What problem does the woman have?
    (A) Her team members need her help.
    (B) Her laptop battery is low.
    (C) She needs a power cord.
    (D) She lost a receipt.

02. Where is the conversation taking place?
    (A) At a computer repair shop
    (B) At an electronics store
    (C) At a bookstore
    (D) At a café

03. What does the man say the woman should do?
    (A) Ask for a refund
    (B) Return at a later time
    (C) Try a new coffee blend
    (D) Go to another business

04. What kind of event is being planned?
    (A) A company anniversary
    (B) A wedding ceremony
    (C) A training seminar
    (D) A trade show

05. What does the woman ask about?
    (A) Room availability
    (B) Internet access
    (C) Transportation
    (D) Hosting fees

06. What does the hotel provide for free?
    (A) Event seating
    (B) Food options
    (C) Guest parking
    (D) Entertainment

07. Where do the speakers most likely work?
    (A) At a theater
    (B) At a restaurant
    (C) At a supermarket
    (D) At a music store

08. What does the man not like doing?
    (A) Organizing band schedules
    (B) Signing business contracts
    (C) Interviewing candidates
    (D) Performing on stage

09. What does the woman say she will bring tomorrow?
    (A) A microphone
    (B) A software program
    (C) Some recipe books
    (D) Some food samples

10. What does the man want to do?
    (A) Eat at a restaurant
    (B) Use valet parking
    (C) Prepare a meal
    (D) Visit a park

11. What information does the man tell the woman?
    (A) His car is parked out front.
    (B) His group is on the way.
    (C) He prefers booth seating.
    (D) He has a reservation.

12. What does the woman inform the man about?
    (A) A daily special
    (B) A membership discount
    (C) A change in business hours
    (D) An updated company policy

13. Who most likely is the man?
    (A) A restaurant worker
    (B) A hotel owner
    (C) A call center employee
    (D) A department store manager

14. What does Kimberly apologize for?
    (A) Overcharging a customer
    (B) Arriving for work later than scheduled
    (C) Bringing the wrong order
    (D) Forgetting to record a reservation

15. What does the man ask Ms. Sherman to do?
    (A) Accept a refund
    (B) Wait in the area
    (C) Speak to Kimberly
    (D) Settle a bill

16. Why does the man thank the woman?
    (A) She recommended a nearby business.
    (B) She moved him to a larger room.
    (C) She waived a fee on his bill.
    (D) She extended his checkout time.

17. What does the man plan to do in Melbourne next month?
    (A) Conduct an inspection
    (B) Negotiate a contract
    (C) Visit a family member
    (D) Interview for a job

18. What does the woman give to the man?
    (A) A room key
    (B) An application form
    (C) A shuttle schedule
    (D) A city map

Receiver : Roberta Tandy
- Zip Code: 53039
- Weight (pounds): 6.2
- Standard Fee: $49.75
- Tracking Fee: $8.25

19. Look at the graphic. What information does the man inquire about?
    (A) The zip code
    (B) The weight
    (C) The standard fee
    (D) The tracking fee

20. What does the man mention about the package?
    (A) It will require a signature.
    (B) It needs to arrive in a hurry.
    (C) It contains fragile items.
    (D) It will be sent overseas.

21. What does the woman remind the man to do?
    (A) Take some promotional materials
    (B) Review some regulations
    (C) Visit the business's Web site
    (D) Keep a receipt for his records

PART 4

관광 정보(tour information)/소개(introduction)

박물관, 생산 공장 등의 견학을 안내하는 관광 정보와 세미나나 콘퍼런스에서 강연자를 소개하는 내용이 주로 출제됩니다.

출제 유형 1   관광 정보(tour information)

특정 지역, 박물관, 동물원, 생산 공장 등의 견학을 안내하는 가이드 담화가 출제됩니다.

· 관광 정보에서 자주 출제되는 어휘

관광 정보에서 자주 나오는 문제

· 담화가 이루어지는 장소를 묻는 문제
Where is the talk being given?
→ 관광 가이드 담화에서는 welcome to 다음에 등장하는 장소 표현이 정답입니다.

· 제안·요청 문제
What does the speaker suggest doing?
→ recommend, suggest, please 다음에 단서가 제시되며, 특정 장소를 방문하기, 몇 시까지 다시 모이기 등이 정답으로 주로 출제됩니다.

wander	거닐다, 돌아다니다	artifact	공예품
tourist attraction	관광 명소	site	부지, 장소
facility	시설	preference	선호, 애호
souvenir	기념품	recipe	요리법
800+ silence	(휴대전화 등의) 소리가 나지 않게 하다	exit through	~을 통해 나가다
variety	다양성, 여러 가지	organization	단체, 기구, 조직
pavilion	전시관, 가설 건물	comparison	비유, 비교
floor	층, 작업장	institution	기관, 협회
attract	(주의를) 끌다	**800+** concierge	(호텔 등의) 안내인
belongings	소지품	gift-wrapping	선물 포장
flavor	맛, 풍미	wait on	시중 들다
delighted	아주 기뻐하는	sightseeing	관광
decorate	장식하다, 꾸미다	scenery	경치, 풍경
patience	참을성, 인내	landscape	풍경
ceramics	도자기	**800+** landmark	주요 지형지물
artist	예술가	be made out of	~로 만들어지다
recreate	되살리다, 재현하다	feed	먹이를 주다

관광 정보(tour information)

[BR]
W: Hello everyone, and welcome to this tour of Pennington Candy Factory! My name is Lucy, and I'll be your tour guide today. As you follow me throughout the facility, you will get to watch and learn all about how the delicious treats you enjoy are made. At the end, I highly recommend going to our gift shop. Candies that come out in unusual shapes are sold there. When you're purchasing something, don't forget to show them you tour ticket stub for a 10% discount. Now, before we enter the production floor, please put on one of these masks to avoid spreading germs.

01. Where is the talk being given?
(A) At a factory
(B) At a hospital
(C) At a restaurant
(D) At a laboratory

02. What does the speaker suggest doing?
(A) Ordering a dish
(B) Trying a sample
(C) Riding a shuttle
(D) Visiting a gift shop

03. What are the listeners asked to do?
(A) Wear masks
(B) Fill out a survey
(C) Turn off their phones
(D) Return some equipment

이렇게 풀어요

01. 담화는 어디에서 이루어지는가?
(A) 공장에서
(B) 병원에서
(C) 레스토랑에서
(D) 실험실에서

첫 문장에서 welcome to this tour of Pennington Candy Factory!라고 했습니다.
→ 사탕 공장이므로 정답은 (A)입니다.

02. 화자는 무엇을 할 것을 제안하는가?
(A) 음식 주문하기
(B) 샘플 시식하기
(C) 셔틀버스 타기
(D) 기념품점 방문하기

담화 중반부에서 I highly recommend going to our gift shop이라고 했습니다.
→ recommend는 suggest로, go to는 visit로 패러프레이징 된 (D)가 정답입니다.

03. 청자들은 무엇을 하라고 요청받는가?
(A) 마스크 착용하기
(B) 설문지 작성하기
(C) 휴대전화 끄기
(D) 장비 반납하기

담화 후반부에서 before we enter the production floor, please put on one of these masks라고 했습니다.
→ put on이 wear로 패러프레이징 된 (A)가 정답입니다.

적용 기술

[기적의 필기노트] 80P
LC 기술 60

소개에서 자주 나오는 문제

· 특정 인물이 어떤 분야에서 일을 하고 있는지 묻는 문제
Which field does Robert Cantu work in?
→ 특정 인물의 직업, 업적에 대해 직접 알려 주기도 하지만, 어떤 종류의 conference, seminar, workshop인지 등을 파악한 후 전체 내용을 듣고 정답을 찾아야 하는 경우도 있으니 주의합니다.

출제 유형 2 — 소개(introduction)

세미나나 콘퍼런스에서 강연자를 소개하는 내용이 출제됩니다. 강연자의 전문 분야, 업적 등에 대해 이야기합니다.

· 소개에서 자주 출제되는 어휘

introduce	소개하다	founder	설립자
speech	연설, 강연	with no further ado	지체 없이
dedication	헌신	present	소개하다, 발표하다, 수여하다
prominent	중요한, 유명한	scheme	계획, 배합, 구성
producer	제작자	accomplish	성취하다, 해내다
set aside	챙겨 두다, 확보하다	direct	지휘하다, 총괄하다
give a lecture	강연하다	split	나누다, 나뉘다
afterwards	나중에	involve	수반하다, 관련되다
succeed	성공하다	growth	성장
persuasive	설득력 있는	unanimously	만장일치로
preview	시사회, 미리 보기	archive	기록 보관소
appeal	관심을 끌다	manuscript	원고
interpret	설명하다, 통역하다	transcript	글로 옮긴 글
prevalent	널리 퍼진, 일반적인	supplement	보충(물), 보충하다
subsequent	다음의	method	방법
switch off	~을 끄다	distraction	방해
minimize	최소화하다	award winning	상을 받은

소개(introduction)

[US]

M: Good morning everyone, and thank you all for coming to the Mayfield Heights Marketing Conference. I'm sure you're all just as excited as I am to meet our first speaker of the day, Robert Cantu. He's been a prominent producer of commercials for over twenty years. Today, he's going to present a lecture on the importance of colors and patterns, and how to use them effectively when creating advertisements. His speech should last about an hour, which leaves some time set aside for questions and answers afterwards. So, if there is anything you would like to ask Mr. Cantu, please save it for after he finishes speaking. With no further ado, I present to you Mr. Robert Cantu!

01. Which field does Robert Cantu work in?
  (A) Tourism
  (B) Marketing
  (C) Accounting
  (D) Customer service

02. What will Robert Cantu talk about?
  (A) Using color schemes
  (B) Directing commercials
  (C) Attracting customers
  (D) Providing quick services

03. What are the listeners asked to do?
  (A) Refer to a pamphlet
  (B) Wait to ask questions
  (C) Split into discussion groups
  (D) Move to empty seats in front

이렇게 풀어요

01. Robert Cantu는 어떤 분야에서 일하는가?
  (A) 관광
  (B) 마케팅
  (C) 회계
  (D) 고객 서비스

02. Robert Cantu는 무엇에 대하여 이야기할 것인가?
  (A) 색채의 배합을 사용하는 것
  (B) 광고를 감독하는 것
  (C) 고객을 끌어당기는 것
  (D) 빠른 서비스를 제공하는 것

03. 청자들은 무엇을 하도록 요청받는가?
  (A) 팸플릿 참고하기
  (B) 질문하는 것을 기다리기
  (C) 토론 그룹으로 나뉘기
  (D) 앞의 빈 좌석으로 이동하기

첫 문장에서 Mayfield Heights Marketing Conference라고 했고, Robert Cantu 씨는 광고 업계에서 중요한 제작자였다고 소개했습니다.
→ 마케팅 콘퍼런스에 강연하러 온 광고 제작자이므로 정답은 (B)입니다.

담화 중반에서 he's going to present a lecture on the importance of colors and patterns, and how to use them effectively when creating advertisements라고 했습니다.
→ 색과 패턴의 중요성과 광고를 만들 때 어떻게 그것들을 효과적으로 이용하는지에 대해 강연한다고 하였으므로 정답은 (A)입니다.

담화 마지막에서 if there is anything you would like to ask Mr. Cantu, please save it for after he finishes speaking이라고 했습니다.
→ save it for after를 wait으로 패러프레이징 한 (B)가 정답입니다.

따라 하면 문제가 풀리는
연습 문제

문제와 각 선택지의 키워드에 표시하세요. 그리고 나서 담화를 듣고 빈칸에 들어갈 말을 받아쓴 후 정답을 선택해 보세요.

01. What does the speaker recommend?

(A) Taking a taxi (B) Wearing comfortable shoes

tour information

> W: Hello, everyone. I will briefly talk about today's _____. We are going to _____ downtown Milan and spend the whole afternoon, _____ one hour of free time. We will move around _____ _____ mostly by foot, so I suggest that you _____ _____ or running shoes and _____ your hats and sunglasses.

02. Where is the talk taking place?

(A) On a bus (B) On a boat

tour information

> M: Welcome _____ _____ Tiger City Bus Tour. I'm your driver and guide. Our company operates two city tour _____ _____. This is line A. We are _____ _____ the city from north to south. The other one is from east to west. This tour is three hours _____. We will stop at the famous café, Wong's Tea Café, to _____ _____ _____.

03. What will the listeners do next?

(A) Go to the testing room (B) Watch a performance

tour information

> W: Welcome to Vernon Coffee Factory. First, I wanted to _____ you a _____ _____ about how the coffee beans are turned into a _____ from harvest to packaging. But there is a _____ with the screen now and it will _____ _____ in 15 minutes. _____ _____ _____ taste a cup of freshly brewed coffee at our taste _____ room? Let's move upstairs.

---

paraphrasing 주어진 어휘 또는 표현과 의미가 동일한 것을 연결하세요.

1. by foot •   • (a) well-known
2. famous •   • (b) walk
3. turn into •   • (c) become

04. Who is Dr. Hopkins?

(A) A yoga instructor (B) A nutritionist

introduction

> M: Welcome to What's New in Finance on TNBC Radio. Today, we will meet Dr. Emilia Hopkins, professor of _____ science at Johnstown College, and she will share _____ _____ on easy ways to manage your daily _____. If you want to have a brief _____ on your _____ _____, please call us at 234-872-4569.

05. What will happen after the presentation?

(A) Mr. Haywood will answer questions. (B) A reception will be held.

introduction

> W: Thanks for coming to the tax seminar. Before we start, I want to introduce our _____, Mark Haywood. He is a chief tax _____ at Jonathan Accounting Firm. He will present how new business _____ _____ are different and how they _____ your business. _____ the presentation, we will have a Q&A session. Now, let's welcome Mr. Haywood to the podium.

06. Where do the listeners most likely work?

(A) At a product design company (B) At a marketing agency

introduction

> M: Good morning. We have Jason Peterson here today who will lead the online _____ training for all Pennington _____ _____ employees. He will share his personal _____ about what just a tiny careless _____ can bring to the company. In addition, he will give clear _____ of what you have to do and what you _____ _____ do.

paraphrasing 주어진 어휘 또는 표현과 의미가 동일한 것을 연결하세요.

4. have a consultation • • (a) influence
5. affect • • (b) get advice
6. firm • • (c) agency

01. Where is the talk taking place?
    (A) At a historical home
    (B) At a museum
    (C) At a garden
    (D) At a market

02. What does the speaker recommend doing?
    (A) Breaking into two groups
    (B) Watching a demonstration
    (C) Taking a lot of photographs
    (D) Making a donation

03. What will the speaker give to the listeners?
    (A) An event schedule
    (B) An entry ticket
    (C) A visitor badge
    (D) A site map

04. What is the purpose of the event?
    (A) To celebrate a company anniversary
    (B) To honor a retiring executive
    (C) To recognize outstanding staff
    (D) To provide some training

05. What does the speaker say the company has focused on?
    (A) Offering better customer service
    (B) Launching a new product
    (C) Attracting more customers
    (D) Meeting a sales goal

06. What will most likely happen next?
    (A) An award will be presented.
    (B) A speech will be given.
    (C) A meal will be served.
    (D) A photo will be taken.

07. Where does the speaker work?
    (A) At a design institute
    (B) At a manufacturing facility
    (C) At a national park
    (D) At an art museum

08. What does the speaker mention about the next phase of the tour?
    (A) It requires safety gear.
    (B) It includes a video.
    (C) It is very popular.
    (D) It will be noisy.

09. Why does the speaker say, "Douglas, the on-duty supervisor, will be there"?
    (A) To suggest directing questions to her colleague
    (B) To encourage listeners to take another tour
    (C) To recommend a way to resolve complaints
    (D) To explain why a schedule was changed

10. In what industry does Ann Rodriguez work?
    (A) Construction
    (B) Manufacturing
    (C) Insurance
    (D) Real estate

11. What will be the topic of Ms. Rodriquez's talk?
    (A) Developing new products
    (B) Keeping employees motivated
    (C) Reducing operating costs
    (D) Attracting new customers

12. What are the listeners asked to do?
    (A) Save questions for the end
    (B) Turn off their cell phones
    (C) Take notes during the talk
    (D) Complete a survey form

13. Where is the tour most likely taking place?
    (A) At a zoo
    (B) At a bottling factory
    (C) At a fitness center
    (D) At a train station

14. What does the speaker say is new about the tour?
    (A) The gift shop discount
    (B) The ending point
    (C) The duration
    (D) The rules

15. What does the speaker offer to the listeners?
    (A) Some free samples
    (B) Discount coupons
    (C) Parking passes
    (D) Safety gear

16. Where is the talk most likely being given?
    (A) At a historical village
    (B) At an indoor museum
    (C) At a theater
    (D) At a grocery store

17. What is the purpose of the talk?
    (A) To introduce a guide
    (B) To outline a tour plan
    (C) To explain a lifestyle
    (D) To review a policy

18. What does the speaker encourage the listeners to do?
    (A) Ask questions
    (B) Buy souvenirs
    (C) Read handouts
    (D) Take pictures

19. Where do the listeners most likely work?
    (A) At a manufacturing plant
    (B) At a bookstore
    (C) At a research firm
    (D) At an electronics store

20. Who is Steven Jones?
    (A) An electrician
    (B) A motivational speaker
    (C) A computer programmer
    (D) An author

21. What does the speaker ask the listeners to do?
    (A) Sign a form
    (B) Discuss their ideas
    (C) Practice a technique
    (D) Attend an event

22. Where does the speaker most likely work?
    (A) At a magazine company
    (B) At a research laboratory
    (C) At a public library
    (D) At a television station

23. What does the speaker say about Michael Wagner?
    (A) He recently won an award.
    (B) He is a world-renowned photographer.
    (C) He travels to speak about climate change.
    (D) He was first published in This, Our Planet.

24. What are listeners encouraged to do?
    (A) Join a subscription
    (B) Text in questions
    (C) Sign a petition
    (D) Take notes

'멋진 당신, 오늘도 화이팅'

DAY
19

오늘의 학습 포인트

PART 3. 대화 주제 - 공항/역
  1. 체크인
      빈출 내용 - 표 구매, 체크인, 탑승 대기
      빈출 문제 - 문제점을 묻는 문제
  2. 변경 요청
      빈출 내용 - 티켓 날짜/시간 변경, 좌석 변경
      빈출 문제 - 시각 자료 연계 문제

PART 4. 담화 유형 - 라디오 방송(radio broadcast)
  1. 지역 행사 안내 방송
      빈출 내용 - 지역 사회 행사
      빈출 문제 - 세부 사항 문제 & 의도 파악 문제
  2. 기업 소개 관련 방송
      빈출 내용 - 새로 개업한 레스토랑, 사업체 소개
      빈출 문제 - 인물의 직업을 묻는 문제 & 다음에 할 일을 묻는 문제

PART 3 공항/역 – 체크인/변경 요청

공항/역에서 표 구매, 체크인 등에 관한 대화와 시간대 및 좌석 변경에 대한 대화가 많이 나와요!

출제 유형 1 체크인

표 구매, 체크인, 탑승 대기 등의 상황에서 할 수 있는 대화가 출제됩니다.

공항/역에서의 체크인 관련 대화에서 자주 나오는 문제

· 문제의 원인이 무엇인지 묻는 문제
According to the woman, what caused the problem?
→ 직원 부족(understaffed), 좋지 않은 날씨(bad weather), 기계적 문제(technical issues) 등이 출제됩니다.

· **공항/역에서의 체크인 관련 대화에서 자주 출제되는 어휘**

backpack	배낭	miss	놓치다
distant	먼, 떨어져 있는	on schedule	일정에 맞춰서
aircraft	비행기	get to	~에 도착하다
location	위치	leave for	~로 떠나다
passport	여권	go on a vacation	휴가를 떠나다
on time	시간을 어기지 않고	stopover(= layover)	경유
solve	해결하다	bound for	~로 향하는
airfare	항공 요금	on board	기내에
pack	짐을 싸다	schedule board	일정 안내판
one way	편도	round trip	왕복
sightseeing	관광	head to	~로 가다, 향하다
customs	세관, 관세	understaffed	직원이 부족한
declare	(세관 등에) 신고하다	load	짐을 싣다
otherwise	그렇지 않다면	transfer	갈아타다
attempt	시도하다, 시도	via	~을 통해, ~을 거쳐
land	착륙하다, 내리다	gate	게이트, 탑승구
takeoff	이륙	flight attendant	승무원
captain	기장	crew	승무원
return flight	돌아오는 항공편	overhead compartment	(비행기의) 머리 위 짐칸

풀이방법 체크인

🎧 Day 19_P3_01.mp3 💡 해석 p.196

[AU - US]

M: Excuse me, I'm travelling to Detroit and I was supposed to depart at 3 P.M. The problem is, my boarding time is now, but the gate is still not open yet. So, I was just wondering if I am at the right gate.
W: I apologize for your inconvenience. What's your flight number?
M: Alliance Airlines 58.
W: Well, you are at the right gate. Our luggage team is understaffed today and there is an unusually large amount to be loaded. Bags are being loaded now, so it shouldn't be long. Please stay in this area so that you don't miss the boarding announcement.

---

01. What is the man asking about?
 (A) Meal options
 (B) Lost luggage
 (C) A departure gate
 (D) An online check-in

02. According to the woman, what caused the problem?
 (A) A lack of staff
 (B) A gate change
 (C) Severe weather
 (D) A malfunctioning device

03. What does the woman ask the man to do?
 (A) Have his ticket ready
 (B) Fill out the form
 (C) Proceed to a different gate
 (D) Wait for an announcement

이렇게 풀어요

01. 남자는 무엇에 대하여 묻고 있는가?
 (A) 식사 옵션
 (B) 잃어버린 짐
 (C) 출발 게이트
 (D) 온라인 체크인

02. 여자에 따르면, 무엇이 문제를 야기했는가?
 (A) 직원 부족
 (B) 게이트 변경
 (C) 험한 날씨
 (D) 고장 난 장비

03. 여자는 남자에게 무엇을 하라고 요청하는가?
 (A) 티켓을 준비해 놓기
 (B) 양식을 작성하기
 (C) 다른 게이트로 가기
 (D) 안내 방송 기다리기

남자가 첫 대사에서 I was just wondering if I am at the right gate라고 했습니다.
→ 게이트가 맞는지 묻고 있는 것이므로 (C)가 정답입니다.

여자가 Our luggage team is understaffed today and there is an unusually large amount to be loaded라고 했습니다.
→ understaffed를 lack of staff로 패러프레이징 한 (A)가 정답입니다.

여자가 마지막에 Please stay in this area so that you don't miss the boarding announcement라고 했습니다.
→ stay를 wait for로 패러프레이징 한 (D)가 정답입니다.

출제 유형 2 — 변경 요청

티켓을 다른 날짜로 교환하거나 좌석을 변경하는 상황 등이 출제됩니다.

변경 요청 관련 대화에서 자주 나오는 문제

• 시각 자료 연계 문제
Look at the graphic. What is the new departure time for the delayed train?
→ 항공 티켓이나 기차 티켓이 시각 자료로 제시되고 변경되는 정보에 대해 이야기하는 대화가 출제됩니다.

• 공항/역에서의 변경 요청 대화에서 자주 출제되는 어휘

transaction	거래	be supposed to V	~하기로 되어 있다
formal	공식적인	scheduling conflict	일정이 겹치는 것
cancel	취소하다	timetable	시간표
route	길, 노선	confirmation number	확인 번호
current	현재의	plan to V	~할 계획이다
through	~을 통하여	catch a bus	버스를 타다
retry	다시 시도하다	rearrange	재조정하다
renew	갱신하다	outage	정전
invoice	청구서	connecting flight	연결 항공편
approach	다가오다	track	선로
deadline	마감일	full	꽉 찬, 만석인
ship	배송하다	within walking distance	도보 거리에 있는
reschedule	다시 일정을 잡다	time zone	시간대
apply	신청하다	ask[do] a favor	부탁하다
inclement weather	악천후	cooperation	협조
assist	돕다	status	상황
alternative	대안의	notify	알리다
permit	허용하다	empty seat	빈 좌석
suspend	연기하다, 보류하다	unavailable	(사용이) 불가능한

풀이 방법 — 변경 요청

🎧 Day 19_P3_02.mp3   💡 해석 p.197

BR - US

M: Hi, I just purchased some plane tickets online through your Web site, but you didn't e-mail the receipt. The transaction number is KA-474. I normally get an e-mail right away when I buy tickets online.

W: Okay, let me see... Here's the problem. Since you used an overseas card, the payment cannot be confirmed until the next business day in both countries. Today is Saturday, so that could take a few days. Would you like me to cancel your purchase so that you can retry with a domestic card? Then it would be processed right away.

M: Yes, definitely. I'm attending an award banquet in my honor this weekend, so I need to reserve my tickets right away.

---

01. According to the woman, what couldn't her company do?
(A) Confirm a payment
(B) Open an account
(C) Apply a discount
(D) Ship an order

02. What does the woman offer to do?
(A) Give a refund
(B) Change a flight
(C) Send an e-mail
(D) Cancel a transaction

03. Why does the man have to make a reservation soon?
(A) He is going out of town for business.
(B) He plans to attend a formal event.
(C) An airline lost his luggage.
(D) A deadline is approaching.

이렇게 풀어요

01. 여자에 따르면, 그녀의 회사는 무엇을 할 수 없었는가?
(A) 지불 승인하기
(B) 계좌 개설하기
(C) 할인 적용하기
(D) 주문품 배송하기

여자가 Since you used an overseas card, the payment cannot be confirmed until the next business day in both countries라고 했습니다.
→ 해외 카드를 사용해서 지불 승인이 즉시 안 된다는 것을 알 수 있으므로 (A)가 정답입니다.

02. 여자는 무엇을 해 주겠다고 제안하는가?
(A) 환불해 주기
(B) 항공편 변경하기
(C) 이메일 보내기
(D) 거래 취소하기

여자가 Would you like me to cancel your purchase so that you can retry with a domestic card?라고 제안했습니다.
→ purchase를 transaction으로 패러프레이징 한 (D)가 정답입니다.

03. 남자는 왜 빨리 예약을 해야 하는가?
(A) 그는 업무차 출장을 갈 것이다.
(B) 그는 공식적인 행사에 참석할 계획이다.
(C) 항공사가 그의 짐을 분실했다.
(D) 마감일이 다가오고 있다.

남자가 마지막 대사에서 I'm attending an award banquet in my honor this weekend, so I need to reserve my tickets right away라고 했습니다.
→ award banquet을 formal event로 패러프레이징 한 (B)가 정답입니다.

따라 하면 문제가 풀리는
연습 문제

문제와 각 선택지의 키워드에 표시하세요. 그리고 나서 대화를 듣고 빈칸에 들어갈 말을 받아쓴 후 정답을 선택해 보세요.

01. What will the speakers do next?

(A) Go to a self-kiosk   (B) Claim their luggage

> M: There are long lines at the _____ _____. We should have arrived at the airport _____ than usual.
> W: Yes, you know, it's the _____ _____ for summer vacations. _____ _____ _____ use the self-check-in kiosk since we just have _____ bags?
> M: That sounds great.

02. What caused a problem?

(A) Heavy traffic   (B) An engine failure

> W: Excuse me, can I get a _____ _____ for Middleborough that departs at 9:30?
> M: Yes, but unfortunately due to the _____ engine, it will depart 50 minutes _____ than scheduled, and at Platform 10 _____ _____ Platform 5.

03. Where does this conversation take place?

(A) At a subway station   (B) At an airport

> W: Mike, I'm Jennifer at Gate 5. There are some _____ here who are going to _____ to a flight for Beijing, but it will _____ _____ just in a half an hour. Can you _____ me a cart since some of them are seniors and kids?
> M: Sure, and can you call to International Terminal and _____ _____ _____ the passengers will be at the boarding gate in 15 minutes?

---

paraphrasing 주어진 어휘 또는 표현과 의미가 동일한 것을 연결하세요.

1. luggage •   • (a) depart
2. malfunctioning engine •   • (b) bag
3. take off •   • (c) engine failure

346 기적의 토익 LC

04. Why will the woman visit New York City?

(A) To attend an awards ceremony (B) To present some information

> W: Hello, I _____ my connecting flight to New York City. Is there _____ _____ _____ available today? I have to give a _____ tomorrow morning at 9.
>
> M: Let me check... I'm looking it up... and there is only one option you have. The flight will depart in an hour but you have a _____ in Detroit for two hours.

05. What does the woman recommend the man do?

(A) Take a taxi (B) Use a company car

> M: I saw the schedule on the Web site and it said that buses _____ every 15 minutes. But I've been _____ _____ one for more than 30 minutes. What happened? I have to _____ a client meeting in 30 minutes.
>
> W: There is _____ _____ downtown, so the buses are getting delayed. Why don't you _____ _____ _____? If you do, you can make on time.

06. What caused the delay?

(A) Bad weather (B) A malfunctioning engine

> M: Hello, has flight KE621 arrived _____ _____? It was expected to land 20 minutes ago.
>
> W: Actually, no. It was _____ 30 minutes at Chicago Airport due to _____ _____. It will arrive in 15 minutes.
>
> M: Oh, that's great. I thought I was late to _____ _____ my client.

---

paraphrasing 주어진 어휘 또는 표현과 의미가 동일한 것을 연결하세요.

- 4. give a presentation •
- 5. operate •
- 6. stormy •

- • (a) bad weather
- • (b) present some information
- • (c) run

토익에 나올 실전 문제

01. Where is the conversation most likely taking place?
    (A) At a travel agency
    (B) At a bus station
    (C) At an airport
    (D) At a hotel

02. Why will the man be charged a fee?
    (A) He brought an extra bag.
    (B) He purchased a meal.
    (C) He asked for an upgrade to first class.
    (D) He wanted to depart earlier.

03. What does the man plan to do in Los Angeles?
    (A) Tour a property
    (B) Conduct an inspection
    (C) Attend an interview
    (D) Give a demonstration

04. What is the woman trying to do?
    (A) Change a seat
    (B) Purchase a ticket
    (C) Find a platform
    (D) Receive a refund

05. What does the woman mean when she says, "there are so many"?
    (A) She is disappointed with a high price.
    (B) She thinks the train station is too crowded.
    (C) She needs some help making a decision.
    (D) She will require assistance with her bags.

06. What benefit of the 3:40 train does the man mention?
    (A) It includes free refreshments.
    (B) It has more comfortable seats.
    (C) It is the next train to depart.
    (D) It does not make multiple stops.

07. How did the man find out about the flight cancelation?
    (A) By speaking to another passenger
    (B) By listening to an announcement
    (C) By reading a text message alert
    (D) By looking at the departures board

08. According to the woman, what has caused a problem?
    (A) A ticketing error
    (B) Bad weather conditions
    (C) Some faulty equipment
    (D) An absent employee

09. What does the woman ask the man to do?
    (A) Show his passport
    (B) Move to the back of the line
    (C) Stay in the area
    (D) Keep his boarding pass

DEPARTURES INFORMATION		
Airline	Destination	Gate
Starway	Shanghai	G7
Olvera	Tokyo	B22
Toth Air	Istanbul	F9
Lemax	Delhi	A16

10. Why is the man calling the woman?
    (A) To request a repair
    (B) To announce a cancelation
    (C) To report missing luggage
    (D) To check a flight's status

11. Look at the graphic. Which airline is affected?
    (A) Starway
    (B) Olvera
    (C) Toth Air
    (D) Lemax

12. What does the man plan to do?
    (A) Check some tickets
    (B) Move to a new gate
    (C) Post a notice
    (D) Ask passengers to board

13. What does the man say has caused a problem?

    (A) Engine failures
    (B) An incoming storm
    (C) Increased fuel prices
    (D) A renovation project

14. What is the woman supposed to do tomorrow?

    (A) Speak at a conference
    (B) Participate in a meeting
    (C) Attend a training session
    (D) Interview for a job opening

15. Why does the man say, "There is one at 7:30 P.M. if that would work for you"?

    (A) To recommend a different mode of transportation
    (B) To inform the woman of a security procedure
    (C) To provide another option
    (D) To apologize for a delay

16. What problem does the man mention?

    (A) He lost his wallet.
    (B) He missed his bus.
    (C) His rental car is not ready.
    (D) His luggage was damaged.

17. What does the woman ask for?

    (A) A reservation number
    (B) A departure station
    (C) A baggage receipt
    (D) A ticket stub

18. Where will the man most likely go next?

    (A) To a baggage claim area
    (B) To a passenger lounge
    (C) To a station office
    (D) To a ticket booth

Train Schedule				
	East Hampton	Amityville	Hartford	Brentwood
Red Line	5:05	5:15		5:45
Blue Line	5:10	5:20	5:35	

19. What problem does the woman have?

    (A) She took the wrong train.
    (B) A concert has been sold out.
    (C) Her ticket does not allow transfers.
    (D) A location was changed at the last minute.

20. Look at the graphic. Where will the woman transfer to another train?

    (A) East Hampton
    (B) Amityville
    (C) Hartford
    (D) Brentwood

21. Why is the woman in a rush?

    (A) She has to take part in a photo shoot.
    (B) She is on her way to see a live show.
    (C) She is running late for a meeting.
    (D) She needs time to practice.

PART 4 라디오 방송(radio broadcast)

각종 지역 사회 행사를 알리는 라디오 방송과 새로 개업한 업체를 소개하는 방송이 자주 출제됩니다.

출제 유형 1 지역 행사 안내 방송

지역 사회에서 열리는 각종 행사에 대한 세부 정보를 안내하는 방송이 출제됩니다.

지역 행사 안내 방송에서 자주 나오는 문제

· 세부 사항 문제
According to the speaker, why/what ~?
→ 방송에서 안내하는 행사의 구체적인 정보에 대해 묻는데, 주로 담화 중반부에서 단서가 제시됩니다.

· 의도 파악 문제
Why does the speaker say, "~"?
→ 라디오에서 지역 소식을 전하면서 어딘가를 가보기를 추천하거나 계획에 대해 말할 때 화자의 의도를 파악할 수 있어야 합니다.

• 지역 행사 안내 방송에서 자주 출제되는 어휘

public service announcement	공공 서비스 안내	thought	생각
fundamental	핵심적인, 기본 원칙	professional	전문적인
election	선거	feature	~을 특색으로 하다, 특별히 포함하다
afterwards	그 후에, 나중에	secure	확실히 하다, 확보하다
radio station	라디오 방송국	obtain	획득하다, 얻다
profile	개요	hourly	1시간마다
stay tuned	채널 고정하다	in response	이에 대응하여
profession	직업	broadcast	방송하다, 방송
host	(TV나 라디오의) 진행자	region	지역
unique	독특한	hold	열다, 개최하다
approximately	대략, 거의	release	발표하다, 출시하다
amenity	편의 시설	indicate	나타내다, 보여 주다
encounter	맞닥뜨리다, 만나다	independent	독립적인, 독자적인
integrate	통합시키다	closely	면밀하게, 철저하게
report	보도하다	compare	비교하다

풀이 방법 — 지역 행사 안내 방송

> Day 19_P4_01.mp3   해석 p.203

[BR]

W: This is a Radio 9 public service announcement. The Copperhead Community Center will be holding a special cooking workshop on April 9th from 2 to 5 P.M. This course will include basic cooking fundamentals, professional tips, and even a few quick and easy recipes for you to try at home. The 'Try it yourself' part of the workshop will give participants a chance to cook some of the featured dishes. Afterwards, feel free to bring home whatever dishes you made. Seats are limited and reservations are only available online, so go online to reserve yours!

01. What will be taught at the workshop?
 (A) Cooking tips
 (B) Creative thinking
 (C) Interview strategies
 (D) Basic computer skills

02. What can attendees do after the workshop?
 (A) Meet a chef
 (B) Take food home
 (C) Purchase a cookbook
 (D) Receive a coupon

03. Why does the speaker ask the listeners to visit the Web site?
 (A) To read a profile
 (B) To write feedback
 (C) To make a payment
 (D) To secure a seat

이렇게 풀어요

01. 워크숍에서 무엇을 배울 것인가?
 (A) 요리법
 (B) 창의적 사고
 (C) 면접 전략
 (D) 기본적인 컴퓨터 기술

담화 초반부에서 요리 워크숍이 열릴 것이라고 안내한 뒤, This course will include basic cooking fundamentals, ~ quick and easy recipes for you라고 했습니다.
→ 요리법을 배운다는 것을 알 수 있으므로 정답은 (A)입니다.

02. 워크숍 후에 참석자들은 무엇을 할 수 있는가?
 (A) 요리사 만나기
 (B) 음식을 집으로 가져가기
 (C) 요리책 구매하기
 (D) 쿠폰 받기

담화 후반부에서 Afterwards, feel free to bring home whatever dishes you made라고 했습니다.
→ dishes you made는 food로, bring은 take로 패러프레이징 된 (B)가 정답입니다.

03. 왜 화자는 청자들에게 웹사이트를 방문하라고 요청하는가?
 (A) 개요를 읽기 위해
 (B) 피드백을 쓰기 위해
 (C) 돈을 지불하기 위해
 (D) 자리를 확보하기 위해

담화 마지막에서 Seats are limited and reservations are only available online, so go online to reserve yours라고 했습니다.
→ 온라인으로 자리를 확보할 것을 요청하고 있으므로 정답은 (D)입니다.

출제 유형 2 — 기업 소개 관련 방송

새로 개업한 레스토랑, 지역 사회의 유명한 사업체 등을 소개하는 방송이 출제됩니다.

기업 소개 관련 방송에서 자주 나오는 문제

· 인물의 직업을 묻는 문제
According to the speaker, who is Juan Trujillo?
→ 방송에서 언급된 사람의 직업을 묻습니다.

· 다음에 할 일을 묻는 문제
What will the speaker most likely do next?/ What will the listeners hear next?
→ 화자가 할 일이나 청자가 할 일에 대해 묻습니다. 방송 내용에 대해 더 설명한다고 하거나, 다음에 들을 방송(날씨, 교통 방송 등)을 소개하는 내용이 자주 출제됩니다.

· 기업 소개 관련 방송에서 자주 출제되는 어휘

contradict	반박하다	favorable	호의적인
ordinance	법령, 조례	acquisition	인수, 획득, 습득
used to V	(과거에) ~했었다	phase	단계, 국면
typical	전형적인	constant	끊임없는
reputation	명성, 평판	established	평판이 좋은
competition	경쟁, 시합	prospective	잠재적인
agreement	합의, 동의	finalize	마무리 짓다
period	기간, 시기	merge	합병하다
persuade	설득하다	reveal	밝히다, 드러내다
approach	다가가다	settle	해결하다, 정착하다
perform	공연하다, 실행하다	bid	입찰하다
expire	만료되다	reject	거부하다
proceed	진행하다	talented	재능 있는
roadwork	도로 공사	convert	전환시키다
fraud	사기(죄)	top-rated	최고 등급의

기업 소개 관련 방송

Day 19_P4_02.mp3 해석 p.203

[US]

M: In local business news, a new Mexican restaurant will open on Sunset Avenue next week. The owner, Juan Trujillo, has over 20 years of experience working in the food industry. He used to operate a food truck, but thanks to the recent decrease in rent prices, he decided to move his business into a building. The restaurant, called Juan's Upon A Time, will specialize in dishes from Mr. Trujillo's hometown. The interior was designed to give the feel of being in a typical restaurant in Mexico. As of next month, Juan's Upon A Time will begin offering a delivery service as well.

01. What is the main topic of the broadcast?
   (A) A new city ordinance
   (B) A cooking contest
   (C) An international festival
   (D) A business opening

02. According to the speaker, who is Juan Trujillo?
   (A) A delivery driver
   (B) A radio show host
   (C) A restaurant owner
   (D) An interior designer

03. What does Juan's Upon A Time plan to do next month?
   (A) Introduce a delivery service
   (B) Offer seasonal menu items
   (C) Hold a grand opening event
   (D) Host live music performances

이렇게 풀어요

01. 방송의 주제는 무엇인가?
   (A) 새로운 도시 법령
   (B) 요리 대회
   (C) 국제적인 축제
   (D) 사업체의 개업

담화 첫 문장에서 a new Mexican restaurant will open on Sunset Avenue next week라고 했습니다.
→ 레스토랑이 개업한다는 사실을 알 수 있으므로 정답은 (D)입니다.

02. 화자에 따르면, Juan Trujillo는 누구인가?
   (A) 배달 기사
   (B) 라디오 방송 진행자
   (C) 레스토랑 주인
   (D) 인테리어 디자이너

개업 소식에 바로 이어서 The owner, Juan Trujillo라고 언급되었습니다.
→ 레스토랑 주인임을 알 수 있으므로 정답은 (C)입니다.

03. Juan's Upon A Time은 다음 달에 무엇을 할 계획인가?
   (A) 배달 서비스를 시작하기
   (B) 계절 메뉴를 제공하기
   (C) 개업 행사 열기
   (D) 라이브 음악 공연을 주최하기

담화 마지막에서 As of next month, Juan's Upon A Time will begin offering a delivery service as well이라고 했습니다.
→ 다음 달에 배달 서비스를 한다는 것을 알 수 있으므로 정답은 (A)입니다.

따라 하면 문제가 풀리는

연습 문제

문제와 각 선택지의 키워드에 표시하세요. 그러고 나서 담화를 듣고 빈칸에 들어갈 말을 받아쓴 후 정답을 선택해 보세요.

01. What information can the listeners get from the city's Web site?

(A) Detours (B) Event schedules

radio broadcast

> W: Thanks for listening to HBS Radio. We are only one week _____ _____ the annual Iron Valley Festival. It _____ a talent competition, a night market, and many _____ activities for children. The detailed _____ _____ are _____ on the city's Web site. Traditionally, it begins with a street parade. So, there will be some _____ downtown on the first day of the festival.

02. What event will be taking place next week?

(A) A book signing event (B) A job fair

radio broadcast

> M: Welcome to the show. The Summer _____ _____ will be _____ next week. Over 120 companies have _____ to set up booths at the fair, and want to fill over 2,000 full-time and summer intern _____. Approximately 10,000 students and _____ are expected to _____ it. This _____ turnout is almost double the _____ year's.

03. Who is Patrick Hans?

(A) A worker at the hotel (B) A radio program host

radio broadcast

> W: Good evening WUNB Radio listeners, and welcome to the Redding Local news. Last Saturday, over 300 people _____ at Riverside Park to clean the Sacramento River Trail. The Seaside Redding Hotel sponsored this _____ event and 56 employees _____ this big cause. Patrick Hans, _____ of the hotel's public relations, said that this shows how we can _____ _____ the community for this beautiful nature.

paraphrasing 주어진 어휘 또는 표현과 의미가 동일한 것을 연결하세요.

1. detour •   • (a) worker
2. career fair •   • (b) job fair
3. manager •   • (c) take alternative routes

04. What is Cedarville Builders known for?

(A) Short construction periods   (B) Ecofriendly building methods

radio broadcast

> M: Welcome to CBN radio's weekly news. Yesterday, Cedarville Builders officially announced that it _____ a three-million-dollar _____ contract with the city government for a new _____ _____. Cedarville Builders was _____ just three years ago, but it became one of the most _____ construction companies with _____ _____ construction methods.

05. What will the listeners likely hear next?

(A) A game prediction   (B) A weather update

radio broadcast

> W: And now for the Bedford City News. Today, the _____ _____ of the national college ice hockey league championship will be held at Oliver Ice Rink. It is the first time in the team's _____ that the Hornets _____ _____ the final. We invite Mr. Palmer, _____ professional ice hockey player, to _____ both teams and _____ the game. Mr. Palmer, which team do you think is _____ to the championship trophy?

06. What event was held yesterday?

(A) A hospital opening   (B) A music festival

radio broadcast

> M: This is Paul Brown with the news updates. The grand _____ _____ of a children's _____ was held at Harrington Medical Center yesterday. After a _____ _____ of construction, the seven-story building has 30 wards with 200 beds for _____ and state-of-the-art equipment for accurate _____.

paraphrasing 주어진 어휘 또는 표현과 의미가 동일한 것을 연결하세요.

4. ecofriendly
5. closer to the championship trophy
6. accurate

(a) likely to win
(b) precise
(c) environmentally friendly

실전 문제

01. Who is Angelina Braxton?
    (A) A news reporter
    (B) A pharmacist
    (C) A doctor
    (D) An actress

02. What kind of project is Angelina Braxton working on?
    (A) Visiting hospital patients
    (B) Singing at a concert
    (C) Shooting a new film
    (D) Curing a disease

03. What does the speaker say Angelina Braxton is going to do?
    (A) Test a vaccine
    (B) Hold an audition
    (C) Interview patients
    (D) Request donations

04. What kind of business does Mr. Harding own?
    (A) A software design company
    (B) An employment agency
    (C) An engineering firm
    (D) A retail store

05. What kind of software will Mr. Harding talk about?
    (A) Security
    (B) Inventory
    (C) Scheduling
    (D) Data tracking

06. What does the speaker ask the listeners to do?
    (A) Submit personal information
    (B) Call in with questions
    (C) Download a demo
    (D) Apply for a job

07. What is the main topic of the talk?
    (A) A music concert
    (B) An awards show
    (C) A sports game
    (D) A new menu

08. What does the speaker imply when she says, "Unfortunately, the Stadium does not allow outside food or beverages"?
    (A) Attendees must make meal reservations in advance.
    (B) Refreshments must be purchased at the event venue.
    (C) All kinds of dietary restrictions will be catered to.
    (D) People should avoid exercising right after eating.

09. Why does the speaker tell the listeners to visit a Web site?
    (A) To reserve their seats
    (B) To apply for a parking pass
    (C) To read a performer's profile
    (D) To view a performance lineup

10. Who is the show intended for?
    (A) Small business owners
    (B) Human resources workers
    (C) Sales representatives
    (D) Computer technicians

11. What does Ms. Cohen specialize in?
    (A) Language skills
    (B) Training methods
    (C) Personal finance
    (D) Social media

12. What are the listeners asked to do?
    (A) Attend an event
    (B) Submit their questions
    (C) Send a payment
    (D) Review a product

13. What kind of event is the broadcast about?
    (A) A grand opening
    (B) A long-distance race
    (C) A community picnic
    (D) A musical performance

14. What will the donations be used for?
    (A) Conducting a study
    (B) Renovating a stadium
    (C) Planting a garden
    (D) Holding some classes

15. According to the speaker, what can listeners do on the Web site?
    (A) Purchase some tickets
    (B) Share their opinions
    (C) Sign up for updates
    (D) View some pictures

16. What is the main topic of the broadcast?
    (A) Selecting locations
    (B) Attracting investors
    (C) Negotiating contracts
    (D) Recruiting good workers

17. What does the speaker imply when she says, "Since then, the number of interested investors has more than doubled"?
    (A) A business had to agree to a merger.
    (B) An audience is easy to target.
    (C) An advertising cost may be too high.
    (D) A method has worked well.

18. What does the speaker say will happen next?
    (A) A specialist will share her thoughts.
    (B) They will return after commercials.
    (C) A contest will be announced.
    (D) They will play some music.

19. What is the speaker discussing in the broadcast?
    (A) A bicycle race
    (B) A subway system
    (C) Exercise trails
    (D) Park closures

20. What has a local charity done?
    (A) Raised funds for improvements
    (B) Been nominated for an award
    (C) Taken extensive measurements
    (D) Launched a new Web site

21. Why does the speaker say, "It'll be on my phone by the end of the day"?
    (A) To explain setup steps
    (B) To endorse a service
    (C) To apologize for a delay
    (D) To highlight an event

22. What is the broadcast about?
    (A) A dry cleaner
    (B) A fashion magazine
    (C) A clothing store
    (D) A fabric manufacturer

23. According to the speaker, what is unique about the business?
    (A) It has the area's lowest prices.
    (B) It is open around the clock.
    (C) It offers free delivery.
    (D) It is environmentally friendly.

24. What will be given to people who visit the business today?
    (A) Some catalogs
    (B) Some refreshments
    (C) A free sample
    (D) A discount coupon

'멋진 당신, 오늘도 화이팅'

DAY
20

오늘의 학습 포인트

PART 3. 대화 주제 - 박물관·공연장/교통수단

1. 박물관·공연장

   빈출 내용 - 진행 중인 전시 & 공연 관람

   빈출 문제 - 주제 문제 & 제안하는 것을 묻는 문제

2. 교통수단

   빈출 내용 - 셔틀 버스, 카풀, 택시

   빈출 문제 - 장소 문제

PART 4. 담화 유형 - 뉴스 보도(news report)

1. 업계 소식 보도

   빈출 내용 - 신제품 출시 & 합병

   빈출 문제 - 어떤 종류의 회사인지 묻는 문제 & 어떤 일이 발생했는지 묻는 문제

2. 연구 결과 보도

   빈출 내용 - 소비자 조사 결과 & 최근 연구 결과

   빈출 문제 - 무엇에 대한 방송인지 묻는 문제

PART 3 박물관·공연장/교통수단

전시 및 공연 관련 대화와 다양한 교통수단에서 이루어지는 대화가 많이 나와요!

출제 유형 1 : 박물관·공연장

진행 중인 전시 관련 대화나 공연 관람 후 공연에 대해 의견을 나누는 내용이 출제됩니다.

- 박물관·공연장에서의 대화에서 자주 출제되는 어휘

박물관·공연장에서의 대화에서 자주 나오는 문제

• 주제 문제
What are the speakers talking about?
→ 박물관이나 공연장에서 티켓을 구입하거나 공연 관람 후기에 대해 이야기하는 대화가 자주 나옵니다.

• 제안하는 것을 묻는 문제
What does the man recommend the woman do?
→ You can ~, Don't forget to ~, Why don't you ~ 와 같은 표현 뒤에 정답의 단서가 제시됩니다.

play	연극, 공연	fair	박람회
availability	가능성, 유효성	floor plan	도면
cast	출연진	exhibition room	전시실
performance	공연; 업무 성과	seating arrangement	좌석 배치
community	지역 사회	raffle	추첨
admission	입장	show one's interest	관심을 보이다
rehearsal	리허설	stage	무대
audience	청중, 관객	opening performance	개막식
entertain	즐겁게 하다	entitled	~라는 제목의
collection	수집(물)	allow	허락하다
playhouse	극장	intermission	중간 휴식 시간
fundraising	자금 조달	masterpiece	걸작, 명작
passion	열정	instrument	악기, 도구
portrait	초상화	sculpture	조각(품)
theater	극장	renowned	유명한, 명성 있는
release	개봉하다	critic	평론가
lighting	조명	impress	깊은 인상을 주다
exchange A for B	A를 B로 교환하다	anniversary	기념일

박물관·공연장

> [US - AU]
>
> W: Hi, I already have two tickets for this theater's play on Saturday afternoon, but some other friends would like to join. Can I get four more?
> M: I apologize, but there are no more tickets left for that show. However, there are plenty of seats left for the Sunday evening one.
> W: So, could I exchange these tickets for that show instead of having to pay for six tickets for us to all see it together? And can we all get seated next to each other?
> M: No problem. By the way, after the evening shows, you can get your picture taken with the cast. Don't forget to bring a camera!

01. What are the speakers talking about?
(A) Ticket availability
(B) A floor plan of exhibition room
(C) A meal preference
(D) A seating arrangement

02. Why does the man say he is sorry?
(A) A coupon has expired.
(B) A location has changed.
(C) A parking pass is invalid.
(D) An event is already sold out.

03. What does the man recommend the woman do?
(A) Take a shuttle
(B) Call back later
(C) Bring a camera
(D) Purchase a souvenir

이렇게 풀어요

01. 화자들은 무엇에 대해 이야기하고 있는가?
(A) 티켓 구매 가능 여부
(B) 전시실의 도면
(C) 선호 음식
(D) 좌석 배치

get four more, no more tickets left, seats left for Sunday, exchange 등의 키워드를 파악합니다.
→ 티켓을 더 구매할 수 있는지에 대한 대화를 나누고 있으므로 (A)가 정답입니다.

02. 남자는 왜 미안하다고 말하는가?
(A) 쿠폰이 만기되었다.
(B) 장소가 변경되었다.
(C) 주차증이 유효하지 않다.
(D) 행사가 이미 매진이다.

남자가 I apologize, but there are no more tickets left for that show라고 했습니다.
→ no more tickets를 sold out으로, show를 event로 패러프레이징 한 (D)가 정답입니다.

03. 남자는 여자에게 무엇을 할 것을 제안하는가?
(A) 셔틀버스 타기
(B) 나중에 다시 전화하기
(C) 카메라 가져오기
(D) 기념품 구매하기

남자가 대화 마지막에서 By the way, after the evening shows, you can get your picture taken with the cast. Don't forget to bring a camera!라고 했습니다.
→ 카메라를 가져오라는 말이므로 (C)가 정답입니다.

출제 유형 2 · 교통수단

셔틀 버스, 카풀, 택시 등 다양한 교통수단을 이용하는 상황에서 이루어지는 대화가 출제된다.

・ 교통수단 관련 대화에서 자주 출제되는 어휘

교통수단 관련 대화에서 자주 나오는 문제

・장소 문제
Where is the conversation taking place?
→ 교통수단 관련 대화에서 대화가 이루어지는 장소로 자주 등장하는 곳은 버스 정류장, 승강장(플랫폼), 공항, 기차역입니다.

fix a car	차를 수리하다	platform	승강장
stop for fuel	주유소에 들르다	railway	철로
bus route	버스 노선	bypass	우회 도로, 우회하다
pass	탑승권	cabin	기내
give A a ride	A를 태워주다	mist	안개
miss a connection	(열차, 비행기 등의) 연결편을 놓치다	runway	활주로
walk over to	~로 걸어가다	cab	택시
highway	고속도로	commute	통근하다, 통근
board	타다, 탑승하다	fare	교통 요금
direct flight	직항 항공편	fee	요금
get out of	~에서 내리다	fine	벌금
exit	출구, 나가다	vehicle	차량, 탈것
make a stop	정차하다	timely	시기적절하게
driving direction	운전 경로 정보	closure	폐쇄
be backed up	차가 막히는	congestion	(교통의) 혼잡, 정체
ferry dock	선착장	stroll	산책하다
cross the street	길을 건너다	intersection	교차로

교통수단

🎧 Day 20_P3_02.mp3   해석 p.211

BR - US

W: Good morning, Jason. I'm glad to see you here. It means I'm not too late to get a shuttle to the office.
M: Good morning, Olivia. It's unusual for the shuttle bus to not arrive by 8. <mark>It should have been here ten minutes ago.</mark> I'm a little bit worried that I will be late for the weekly meeting starting at 8:40.
W: I heard a traffic update before I left my home and there was a car accident on the route of our bus. I think that probably caused the delay.
M: Really? If so, I will call Minsu and ask him to give us a ride today. I hope he is still home now.

---

01. Where is the conversation taking place?
 (A) At an office
 (B) At a bus stop
 (C) On a train
 (D) At an airport

02. What does the man imply when he says,
 "It should have been here ten minutes ago"?
 (A) He could be late for a meeting.
 (B) He might miss a connection.
 (C) He will buy a car.
 (D) He was waiting at the wrong bus stop.

03. What will the man do next?
 (A) Refer to an e-mail
 (B) Change a ticket
 (C) Contact another colleague
 (D) Go to the information center

이렇게 풀어요

01. 대화가 이루어지는 곳은 어디인가?
 (A) 사무실에서
 (B) 버스 정류장에서
 (C) 기차에서
 (D) 공항에서

02. 남자가 "10분 전에 여기 왔어야 해요"라고 말할 때 암시하는 바는 무엇인가?
 (A) 회의에 늦을 수도 있다.
 (B) 연결편을 놓칠 수도 있다.
 (C) 그는 자동차를 살 것이다.
 (D) 그는 잘못된 버스 정류장에서 기다리고 있었다.

03. 남자는 다음에 무엇을 할 것인가?
 (A) 이메일을 참고하기
 (B) 티켓을 바꾸기
 (C) 다른 동료에게 연락하기
 (D) 안내 센터로 가기

여자가 It means I'm not too late to get a shuttle to the office라고 했고, 남자가 It's unusual for the shuttle bus to not arrive by 8. It should have been here ten minutes ago라고 했습니다.
→ 셔틀 버스를 타려고 하고 있으므로 (B)가 정답입니다.

남자가 It should have been here ten minutes ago. I'm a little bit worried that I will be late for the weekly meeting starting at 8:40이라고 했습니다.
→ 8시 40분에 시작하는 회의에 늦을 것을 걱정하면서 10분 전에는 여기 버스가 왔어야 했다고 말하는 것을 알 수 있으므로 (A)가 정답입니다.

남자가 대화 마지막에서 If so, I will call Minsu and ask him to give us a ride today라고 했습니다.
→ call을 contact로, Minsu는 colleague로 패러프레이징 한 (C)가 정답입니다.

따라 하면 문제가 풀리는 연습 문제

문제와 각 선택지의 키워드에 표시하세요. 그리고 나서 대화를 듣고 빈칸에 들어갈 말을 받아쓴 후 정답을 선택해 보세요.

01. What caused the detour?

(A) Construction work   (B) A car accident

> W: Good morning, Jason. How was your _____ to the office today? There was an unexpected _____ on Main Street. I was _____ this morning.
> M: I listened to the _____ _____ and it said that _____ work started this morning. It won't be _____ until next month. I commuted to the office _____ _____ this morning. It will be good for my health.

02. Where is the conversation most likely taking place?

(A) At a post office   (B) At a theater

> W: Excuse me, I booked a _____ _____ for the 6:30 show. The _____ e-mail said that I need to _____ it _____ at the box office.
> M: Okay. What's your last name? And would you please _____ a photo ID?

03. What does the man offer to do?

(A) Give a discount coupon   (B) Sign the woman up for a tour

> M: Welcome to Bologna Museum. Here is your ticket and a _____ _____. Do you need anything else?
> W: Yes, I want to _____ more about Angela Russo's artwork. Do you have any _____ guide services?
> M: _____, we don't because it is a special exhibition. But we do _____ a guided tour instead. You need to _____ for it first. Shall I do that for you?

---

paraphrasing 주어진 어휘 또는 표현과 의미가 동일한 것을 연결하세요.

1. resurfacing   •   • (a) sign up
2. present   •   • (b) show
3. register   •   • (c) construction

04. What does the woman suggest doing?

(A) Renting a car (B) Using a shuttle bus

> M: Jaime, do you think we need to _____ a car _____ the conference?
> W: That would be more _____ if we have something to be handled urgently. But we have a _____ _____, so why don't we just _____ the hotel _____? During the conference, it _____ every 30 minutes from our hotel to the conference center.

05. What will the man do next?

(A) Take some photos (B) Buy some souvenirs

> M: The Centerville Ball Park is one of the _____ sports stadiums that I have ever visited.
> W: Yes, I read on the board that it was _____ in 1922 and maintained with minimum renovations.
> M: Wow, amazing. I'm going to go to the player's locker room and _____ _____ _____ before I stop by the gift shop.

06. What will the speakers take to the airport?

(A) Airport bus (B) Subway

> W: We are supposed to _____ _____ the airport in an hour to pick up Mr. Kim. Do you think we need to _____ _____ _____?
> M: I don't think so. The airport expressway is fine but there might be _____ _____ downtown. Therefore, we'd better take the _____ to arrive on time.

---

paraphrasing 주어진 어휘 또는 표현과 의미가 동일한 것을 연결하세요.

4. limited budget • • (a) traffic congestion
5. construct • • (b) not enough money
6. heavy traffic • • (c) build

01. Who most likely is the man?
    (A) A theater owner
    (B) A film director
    (C) A singer
    (D) A reporter

02. What does the man ask the woman about?
    (A) The available equipment
    (B) The expected attendance
    (C) The lighting arrangement
    (D) The rehearsal times

03. What does the woman say the theater did for the first time?
    (A) Offered discounted rates for groups
    (B) Broadcasted a show on its Web site
    (C) Advertised exclusively online
    (D) Extended the box office hours

04. Why is the woman calling the business?
    (A) To report a lost item
    (B) To request a refund
    (C) To change her flight
    (D) To sign up for a program

05. What does the man ask the woman for?
    (A) A confirmation code
    (B) A passport number
    (C) A seat preference
    (D) A credit card number

06. Why does the man say, "There's one departing at 6 A.M."?
    (A) To suggest a solution
    (B) To correct a scheduling error
    (C) To apologize for a delay
    (D) To explain when to call back

07. What kind of event are the speakers discussing?
    (A) A film festival
    (B) A sales workshop
    (C) A musical performance
    (D) A gallery opening

08. What do the men decide to do?
    (A) Read some reviews
    (B) Leave the office early
    (C) Have a meal together
    (D) Make a booking online

09. What does Leon ask the woman to do?
    (A) Practice a presentation
    (B) Update a schedule
    (C) Print a receipt
    (D) Contact a client

10. What do the speakers plan to do next week?
    (A) Host a client appreciation banquet
    (B) Go on a business trip together
    (C) Train some newly hired staff members
    (D) Tour a potential building site

11. According to the woman, what has the company recently done?
    (A) Changed a reimbursement policy
    (B) Canceled a car rental contract
    (C) Finalized some service agreements
    (D) Paid bonuses to employees

12. Why does the man say, "the 408 bus runs every half hour"?
    (A) To correct some outdated details
    (B) To encourage the woman to hurry
    (C) To confirm an itinerary
    (D) To suggest a change of plans

13. What does the woman offer the man?
    (A) A role in an upcoming show
    (B) Tickets to a performance
    (C) Some meal vouchers
    (D) A ride to the office

14. What does the man imply when he says, "I live close to Brookshire Theater"?
    (A) He needs driving directions.
    (B) He is interested in the offer.
    (C) He does not like theater shows.
    (D) He cannot afford to purchase tickets.

15. What does the woman agree to do?
    (A) Take some pictures
    (B) Reserve some seats
    (C) Have a meal with the man
    (D) Work from another office for a day

16. Why did the man call the woman?
    (A) To propose holding a sale
    (B) To introduce a business associate
    (C) To confirm an appointment time
    (D) To remind her of an upcoming event

17. What does the woman suggest doing?
    (A) Making an announcement
    (B) Creating some posters
    (C) Postponing a meeting
    (D) Issuing a refund

18. What does the man say he will do?
    (A) Contact a customer
    (B) Send out a memo
    (C) Adjust some prices
    (D) Apologize for a mistake

Stamford Museum of History

HISTORY MUSICAL (AGES 6~13)	$5.25
LECTURE: LOCAL HISTORICAL FIGURES	$7.75
MOVIE: FIRST SETTLERS	$8.50
GUIDED ARTIFACT TOUR	$9.90

19. Look at the graphic. How much will the man pay to attend a special event?
    (A) $5.25
    (B) $7.75
    (C) $8.50
    (D) $9.90

20. What does the woman say about the noon showing?
    (A) It is popular among visitors.
    (B) Seating is assigned in advance.
    (C) The museum is offering a discount.
    (D) It might be hard to find a seat.

21. What does the woman say the man will have to provide?
    (A) A membership card
    (B) A photo ID
    (C) A ticket
    (D) A receipt

PART 4 뉴스 보도(news report)

신제품 출시 및 합병 등 업계 소식이나 연구 결과를 알리는 내용이 자주 출제됩니다.

출제 유형 1 업계 소식 보도

기업의 신제품 출시, 프로모션 행사, 합병 등 다양한 내용이 뉴스 형태로 출제됩니다.

· 업계 소식 보도에서 자주 출제되는 어휘

cover	보도하다, 취재하다	press	언론
subscribe	구독하다	media coverage	취재 범위
shockwave	충격적인 여파	reveal	밝히다, 드러내다
nationwide	전국적으로	association	협회
consume	섭취하다, 소비하다	mobile device	휴대용 단말기
exposition	전시회	power source	전원
subsidiary	자회사	wage	임금
benefit	이익, 복지 혜택	motivate	동기를 부여하다
assess	평가, 평가하다	boost	촉진하다
advance	발전, 진보	allowance	수당, 비용
compensation	보상(금), 배상	reflect	반영하다
recognize	인정하다	oversee	감독하다
comprehensive	포괄적인	anticipate	예상하다
regard	여기다, 간주하다	advantage	이점, 장점
reward	보상(금), 보상하다	much-needed	매우 필요한

업계 소식 보도에서 자주 나오는 문제

· 어떤 종류의 회사인지 묻는 문제
What kind of business is OverSurge?
→ 회사명인 고유명사 앞이나 뒤에 어떤 업종인지 제시됩니다. 첫 문장에서 방송 소개를 하고 바로 뒤이어 나오는 경우가 많으므로 초반부에서 파악할 수 있습니다.

· 특정 시점에 어떤 일이 발생할지 묻는 세부 정보 문제
According to the speaker, what is scheduled to be held in July?
→ 업계 소식을 알리면서 담화 초반에 나오는 경우도 있고, 마지막에 나오는 경우도 있습니다. 질문에 언급된 시간 표현 키워드가 그대로 언급되는 경우가 많으므로 키워드 주변에서 정답을 파악할 수 있습니다.

풀이 방법 — 업계 소식 보도

🎧 Day 20_P4_01.mp3   📍 해석 p.217

[US]

M: Good morning, this is Joshua Young. You're watching Business Update from the number one TV channel, BNF America. The electronics company OverSurge is sending shockwaves throughout the mobile device industry. It has just created a battery that can be charged remotely without any wires. One power source can charge up to 50 batteries at the same time. According to the company's spokesperson, Jessie Vaughn, the battery will be used in the company's mobile phones. The first mobile phone with this breakthrough battery is scheduled to be released in July.

---

01. What kind of business is OverSurge?
 (A) A mobile phone service provider
 (B) An electronics manufacturer
 (C) A software company
 (D) A department store

02. What does the speaker say is special about a new product?
 (A) It lasts longer than others of its kind.
 (B) It features a high connection speed.
 (C) It can fit into a person's pocket.
 (D) It does not require any wires.

03. According to the speaker, what is scheduled to be held in July?
 (A) A product release
 (B) An opening party
 (C) An ad campaign
 (D) An exposition

이렇게 풀어요

01. OverSurge는 어떤 종류의 회사인가?
 (A) 휴대폰 서비스 제공업체
 (B) 전자 제품 제조 업체
 (C) 소프트웨어 회사
 (D) 백화점

방송 소개에 이어 The electronics company OverSurge라고 했습니다.
→ 전자 제품 업체라는 사실을 알 수 있으므로 정답은 (B)입니다.

02. 화자는 신제품에 대하여 무엇이 특별하다고 하는가?
 (A) 그 종류의 다른 제품들보다 오래 유지된다.
 (B) 빠른 연결 속도가 특징이다.
 (C) 사람의 주머니 속에 딱 맞게 들어간다.
 (D) 어떠한 선도 필요 없다.

기업 소개에 이어서 It has just created a battery that can be charged remotely without any wires라고 했습니다.
→ 선(wires)이 필요 없다는 것을 알 수 있으므로 정답은 (D)입니다.

03. 화자에 따르면, 7월에 무엇이 열릴 예정인가?
 (A) 제품 출시
 (B) 개업 파티
 (C) 광고 캠페인
 (D) 전시회

담화 마지막에서 The first mobile phone with this breakthrough battery is scheduled to be released in July라고 했습니다.
→ 7월에 휴대폰이 출시될 예정이라고 했으므로 정답은 (A)입니다.

출제 유형 2   연구 결과 보도

소비자 조사 결과에 대해 보도하거나 최근 연구 결과에 대해 알리는 내용이 뉴스 형태로 출제됩니다.

연구 결과 보도에서 자주 나오는 문제

· 무엇에 대한 방송인지 묻는 문제
What is the broadcast about?
→ 방송이나 뉴스는 처음 소개 이후에 바로 어떤 주제에 대해 다룰지 언급됩니다. Today ~ 이후를 잘 들어야 합니다.

· **연구 결과 보도에서 자주 출제되는 어휘**

consultant	상담가, 자문위원	pattern	양식, 패턴
findings	연구 결과	cost-effective	비용 효율적인
reliability	신뢰도	corporate	기업의, 법인의
lending	대출	immensely	엄청나게, 대단히
family-run	가족 경영의	corporation	기업, 법인
start-up	신규 업체, 착수의	analyze	분석하다
public	대중	analysis	분석
theory	이론	analyst	분석가
summarize	요약하다	side effect	부작용
trigger	계기, 촉발시키다	chronic	만성적인
substance	물질	point out	설명하다, 지적하다
segment	단편, 조각, 부분	underestimate	과소평가하다
propose	제안하다	journal	학술지
pharmaceutical	약학의, 제약의	factor	요인
scientific	과학의	massive	거대한

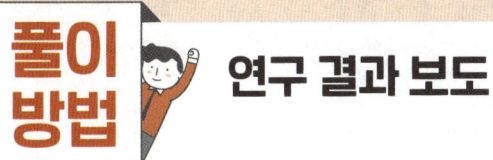 ## 연구 결과 보도

[BR]

M: Welcome back to Economy Eagle. This is Jonathan Glavine with TFW TV. Today, our show focuses on the spending patterns of consumers. Although there are some highly successful startup companies, most consumers are worried about the reliability of their products or services. They should be. Just because a company has a flashy name and an innovative CEO does not mean that it cannot fail. Let's consider now some reports from businesses that were not successful and I'll point out why. Sometimes the smallest factor can lead a business to ruin.

01. What is the broadcast about?

(A) Contract negotiation
(B) Corporate investments
(C) Consumer spending
(D) Commercial lending

02. According to the speaker, what are the consumers worried about?

(A) International corporations
(B) Family-run businesses
(C) Startup companies
(D) Private firms

03. What does the speaker say he will do?

(A) Test products
(B) Analyze reports
(C) Speak with listeners
(D) Review a business plan

이렇게 풀어요

01. 무엇에 대한 방송인가?
(A) 계약 협상
(B) 기업 투자
(C) 소비자 지출
(D) 상업 대출

화자가 인사말을 한 뒤, Today, our show focuses on the spending patterns of consumers라고 했습니다.
→ 소비자 지출에 대해 다루겠다고 했으므로 정답은 (C)입니다.

02. 화자에 따르면, 소비자들은 무엇에 대해 걱정하는가?
(A) 국제 기업
(B) 가족 경영 기업
(C) 신생 회사
(D) 개인 회사

Although there have some highly successful startup companies, most consumers are worried about the reliability of their products or services라고 했습니다.
→ 소비자들이 신생 회사의 신뢰도에 대해 걱정한다고 했으므로 정답은 (C)입니다.

03. 화자는 무엇을 할 것이라고 하는가?
(A) 제품 테스트하기
(B) 보고서 분석하기
(C) 청자들과 대화하기
(D) 사업 계획 검토하기

후반부에서 Let's consider now some reports from businesses that were not successful and I'll point out why라고 했습니다.
→ 보고서를 살펴보고 이유를 설명하겠다고 했으므로 정답은 (B)입니다.

따라 하면 문제가 풀리는 연습 문제

문제와 각 선택지의 키워드에 표시하세요. 그러고 나서 담화를 듣고 빈칸에 들어갈 말을 받아쓴 후 정답을 선택해 보세요.

01. What is the news report about?

(A) A new bookstore opening　　(B) A change in management

news report

> W: Welcome to Business World Today. This is Emilia Williams. Last Wednesday, the nationwide _____ _____ Owl's Nest announced that Maria Perez will start working as _____ executive _____ beginning September 20. Her extensive _____ and valuable insight will _____ to bouncing up Owl's Nest's lagging sales.

02. What did Toys' Land experience in December?

(A) Relocation of its headquarters　　(B) A drop in sales

news report

> M: Good morning. In today's business news, the city's largest toy _____, Toys' Land, released its monthly sales _____ and reported a significant sales _____ of December compared to the same month of the _____ year. Most industry experts are surprised by the almost 30% decrease _____ the fact that December is the _____ _____ for the toy industry.

03. What is the news report about?

(A) A corporate merger　　(B) A marketing campaign

news report

> M: And now for business news. There is a _____ rumor that DFO Digital and Lamington Electronics have been _____ a merger deal. According to Mr. Smithson, an _____ analyst, the _____ would be expected to produce more than two billion dollars overall in annual _____ gains and cost savings. However, both companies officially denied it.

paraphrasing 주어진 어휘 또는 표현과 의미가 동일한 것을 연결하세요.

1. extensive　　•　　　　　•　(a) considerable
2. decline　　　•　　　　　•　(b) generate
3. produce　　•　　　　　•　(c) drop

04. What can the listeners do on Dr. Adams' Web site?

(A) Watch a video (B) Download a survey result

news report

> W: Welcome to HBS's Health News. In a recent study _____ by Dr. Carol Adams, she indicates that an only 10-minute _____ every day is effective enough to _____ body fat. 70% of the participants showed a fat reduction after one month of _____. Dr. Adams suggests that all participants _____ to do this after completion of the research. You can get more information about the 10-minute workout and _____ a short _____ on her Web site.

05. What are people encouraged to do?

(A) Use more efficient electronics (B) Turn off unnecessary lights

news report

> M: Good afternoon. Tonight, I'll be talking about a new _____ by the city government. According to recent statistics on _____ _____, the amount of reserve power dropped by almost 7% on July 28. At that time, the energy department was taking measures in case of a _____. Since summer is getting hotter, the government will draw up a _____ to give a grant to those who _____ their _____ air conditioner with more energy-efficient one.

06. What is the news report about?

(A) A construction project for a new apartment (B) A recent increase in housing rent

news report

> M: In local news, a city official reported that the City of Battleston has experienced a large _____ of newcomers over the past 18 months. This has caused monthly rent to _____ up to 50%. A _____ at Height Hill Apartment said that the landlord wants to _____ the monthly _____ to $600. His current monthly rental is $450. Most residents are worried about their _____ next year.

paraphrasing 주어진 어휘 또는 표현과 의미가 동일한 것을 연결하세요.

4. workout •   • (a) increase
5. air conditioner •   • (b) electronics
6. soar •   • (c) exercise

실전 문제

01. What kind of business is Chardon Corporation?

    (A) An online DIY forum administrator
    (B) A power tool manufacturer
    (C) A construction company
    (D) A news broadcaster

02. What does the speaker say is special about a new product line?

    (A) It will be easily affordable.
    (B) It has been advertised online.
    (C) It is designed for amateur use.
    (D) It features long-lasting batteries.

03. According to the speaker, what will happen on May 4th?

    (A) A product line will be available for purchase.
    (B) A massive construction project will begin.
    (C) A hardware store will change ownership.
    (D) A public demonstration will be given.

04. What kind of facility is the speaker reporting on?

    (A) A theater
    (B) A museum
    (C) A community center
    (D) A government office

05. According to the speaker, what is the purpose of the class?

    (A) To raise interest in art programs
    (B) To promote local artists
    (C) To help beautify the city
    (D) To support a charity auction

06. What does the speaker imply when she says, "and they are expected to be the hottest items"?

    (A) Artwork sells for high prices at auctions.
    (B) A public space needs an air conditioner.
    (C) The event has been successful in the past.
    (D) Many people have volunteered to help out.

07. What is the main topic of the news report?

    (A) A public transportation system
    (B) An upcoming election
    (C) A garbage facility
    (D) A recycling law

08. According to the speaker, what will be given out to the listeners?

    (A) A new train ticket
    (B) An annual expense report
    (C) Recycling bins
    (D) A parking permit

09. What does the speaker invite the listeners to do?

    (A) Post their opinions
    (B) Make a donation
    (C) Look at the map
    (D) Cast a vote

10. According to the news report, what will happen by the end of next year?

    (A) A major airport will be expanded.
    (B) An airline will offer new VIP services.
    (C) A new subway line will be completed.
    (D) A tourist agency will begin offering more packages.

11. What does Mr. Marsh say will be a benefit of the project?

    (A) Comfortable seating
    (B) Reduced travel time
    (C) Automated service
    (D) Cheaper fares

12. According to the speaker, who is most excited by the news?

    (A) Construction companies
    (B) Airline club members
    (C) Airline employees
    (D) Travel agents

13. What will the city of Engleburg do next year?

    (A) Construct a new library
    (B) Hold a sports tournament
    (C) Launch a tourism campaign
    (D) Host an international conference

14. What problem with the project does the speaker mention?

    (A) Price increases are expected.
    (B) There is not enough funding.
    (C) The staff is not large enough.
    (D) Most residents oppose it.

15. What will the speaker do next?

    (A) Provide some contact information
    (B) Interview a city official
    (C) Attend an opening ceremony
    (D) Take a tour of a site

16. What has changed about the festival this year?

    (A) It will include special guests.
    (B) It will implement new technology.
    (C) It will last for one week.
    (D) It will use multiple screens.

17. According to the speaker, how can listeners get tickets?

    (A) By e-mailing the event planners
    (B) By calling the theater's box office
    (C) By logging on to the theater's Web site
    (D) By visiting the theater in person

18. Why does the speaker say, "The doors for the first film open at 6 P.M."?

    (A) To point out an error in a program
    (B) To encourage listeners to arrive early
    (C) To suggest watching a different film
    (D) To emphasize a deadline for buying tickets

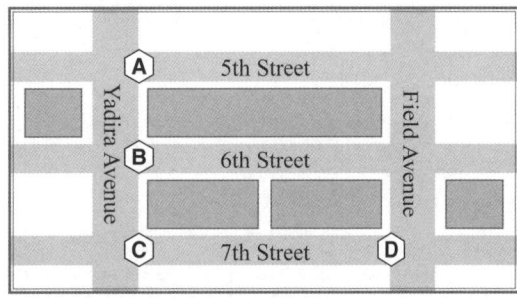

19. What has caused a problem?

    (A) A missing signal
    (B) A broken pipe
    (C) A power outage
    (D) A traffic accident

20. Look at the graphic. Which location does the speaker refer to?

    (A) Location A
    (B) Location B
    (C) Location C
    (D) Location D

21. What will the listeners hear in fifteen minutes?

    (A) Another traffic report
    (B) A sports update
    (C) A weather report
    (D) International news

eng.conects.com
영단기

영단기 토익 교재

입문서

| 영단기 토익 왕기초 LC | 영단기 토익 왕기초 RC | 영단기 신토익 스타트 LC | 영단기 신토익 스타트 RC | 영단기 영문법 스타트 |

기본서

 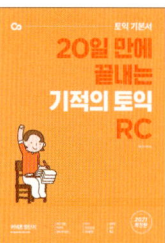   

기적의 토익 LC | 기적의 토익 RC | 영단기 토익 LC | 영단기 토익 RC | 영단기 토익 기출보카

필기노트

영단기 700+ 기적의 필기노트 | 영단기 토익 만점자 필기노트 PART 5 문법

LC+RC 통합 기본서

영단기 토익 LC+RC 700+한 달에 끝내기 | 정재현 토익 똑똑한 기본서 LC+RC

기술서/요약서

영단기 토익 기술 LC | 영단기 토익 기술 실전문제집 LC | 영단기 토익 기술 RC | 영단기 토익 기술 실전문제집 RC | 영단기 신토익 LC 20일 속성 | 영단기 신토익 RC 20일 속성

토익 기본서

20일 만에 끝내는 기적의 토익 LC

영단기 연구소

해설집

영단기
eng.conects.com

토익 기본서

20일 만에 끝내는 기적의 토익 LC

해설집

DAY 01

PART 1 · 1인 사진 / 2인 사진

확인 문제

❶ [BR]

(A) A woman is using her phone.
(B) A woman is working on a computer.

(A) 여자가 전화기를 사용하고 있다.
(B) 여자가 컴퓨터로 일을 하고 있다.

❷ [US]

(A) A man is sitting on a bench.
(B) A man is running along the beach.

along ~을 따라

(A) 남자가 벤치에 앉아 있다.
(B) 남자가 해변을 따라 달리고 있다.

❸ [AU]

(A) They are facing each other.
(B) They are standing in front of the audience.

face each other 서로 마주 보다   audience 청중

(A) 그들은 서로 마주 보고 있다.
(B) 그들은 청중 앞에 서 있다.

❹ [US]

(A) One of the women is typing on a keyboard.
(B) One of the women is writing on a notepad.

type 타자 치다   notepad 노트, 메모지

(A) 여자들 중 한 명이 키보드로 타자를 치고 있다.
(B) 여자들 중 한 명이 노트에 적고 있다.

❺ [BR]

(A) Flowers have been arranged in a vase.
(B) A woman is wiping a counter with a cloth.

arrange 정리하다   vase 꽃병   wipe 닦다   cloth 천

(A) 꽃들이 꽃병에 정리되어 있다.
(B) 여자가 천으로 작업대를 닦고 있다.

❻ [US]

(A) A kitchen appliance is on a table.
(B) A man is wearing an apron.

kitchen appliance 주방 기기   apron 앞치마

(A) 주방 기기가 테이블 위에 있다.
(B) 남자가 앞치마를 입고 있다.

연습 문제

01. [US]

(1) (A) a wheelbarrow (O)   (B) a woman (X)   (C) grass (O)
(2)
(A) He is pushing a wheelbarrow. [O]
(B) He is holding a potted plant. [X]

wheelbarrow 손수레   grass 잔디

(A) 그는 손수레를 밀고 있다.
(B) 그는 화분을 들고 있다.

02. [AU]

(1) (A) a bicycle (O)   (B) leaning against (O)   (C) walking (X)
(2)
(A) They're strolling along the river. [X]
(B) A bicycle is leaning against a fence. [O]

lean against ~에 기대다

(A) 그들은 강을 따라 산책하고 있다.
(B) 자전거가 울타리에 기대어져 있다.

03. [BR]

(1) (A) boarding (X)   (B) a train (O)   (C) suitcases (O)
(2)
(A) They are pulling suitcases. [O]
(B) They are boarding a train. [X]

board 탑승하다

(A) 그들은 여행 가방을 끌고 있다.
(B) 그들은 기차에 탑승하고 있다.

04. [BR]

(1) (A) pouring coffee (O)   (B) a sink (X)
    (C) a laptop computer (O)
(2)
(A) A man is pouring coffee into a mug. [O]
(B) A woman is washing dishes in a sink. [X]

pour 따르다, 붓다

(A) 남자가 머그잔에 커피를 따르고 있다.
(B) 여자가 싱크대에서 접시를 닦고 있다.

실전 문제

01. (C)   02. (D)   03. (D)   04. (A)   05. (C)   06. (C)

01. US

(A) The woman is placing a dish on a table.
(B) The woman is turning on a light.
(C) The woman is drinking from a cup.
(D) The woman is opening a door.

place 놓다, 두다 turn on 켜다

(A) 여자가 탁자 위에 접시를 놓고 있다.
(B) 여자가 전등을 켜고 있다.
(C) 여자가 잔으로 (음료를) 마시고 있다.
(D) 여자가 문을 열고 있다.

[해설] 여자가 잔에 든 무언가를 마시고 있는 사진으로, 인물의 동작이나 상태에 집중해서 들어야 한다.
(A) 사진에 접시와 탁자가 등장하긴 하지만 여자가 접시를 놓는(placing) 동작을 하고 있지 않다.
(B) 사진에 전등(light)이 보이기는 하지만 여자가 전등을 켜고(turning on) 있지 않다.
(C) 여자가 잔에 든 음료를 마시고 있는 모습을 정확히 묘사한 정답이다.
(D) 여자가 문을 여는(opening a door) 동작을 하고 있지 않다.

02. AU

(A) They're entering into a building.
(B) They're cleaning a garage with a mop.
(C) They're seated in a car.
(D) They're loading an item into a vehicle.

enter into ~에 들어가다 garage 차고, 주차장 mop 대걸레 load 싣다 item 물건 vehicle 차량, 탈것

(A) 그들은 건물에 들어가고 있다.
(B) 그들은 대걸레로 차고를 청소하고 있다.
(C) 그들은 자동차 안에 앉아 있다.
(D) 그들은 차에 물건을 싣고 있다.

[해설] 두 사람이 차의 트렁크를 열어 놓고 물건을 들고 있는 사진으로, 두 사람 각각의 동작 및 공통 동작을 잘 살펴야 한다.
(A) 두 사람은 건물 안에 들어가고(entering into) 있지 않다.
(B) 두 사람이 있는 곳이 차고로 보이긴 하지만 청소하고(cleaning) 있지는 않다.
(C) 두 사람은 자동차 안에 앉아 있는(seated in a car) 것이 아니라 밖에 나와 있다.
(D) 두 사람이 차량 트렁크에 물건을 싣는 모습을 정확히 묘사한 정답이다.

03. BR

(A) The woman is taking off her jacket.
(B) The woman is typing on a keyboard.
(C) The man is turning on the computer monitor.
(D) The man is handing a key to the woman.

take off (옷 등을) 벗다 type (타자기·컴퓨터로) 타자 치다, 입력하다 hand 건네주다, 넘겨주다

(A) 여자가 재킷을 벗고 있다.
(B) 여자가 키보드로 타자를 치고 있다.
(C) 남자가 컴퓨터 모니터를 켜고 있다.
(D) 남자가 여자에게 열쇠를 건네고 있다.

[해설] 테이블을 사이에 두고 두 사람이 마주 앉아 있는 모습으로, 두 사람의 공통 동작이나 상태를 잘 살펴야 한다.
(A) 재킷을 벗는(taking off her jacket) 동작은 사진과 전혀 무관한 묘사이다.
(B) 테이블 위에 컴퓨터 키보드가 있지만 여자가 타자를 치고 있지는(typing) 않다.
(C) 테이블 위에 컴퓨터 모니터가 있지만 남자가 이것을 켜는(turning on) 동작을 하고 있지는 않다.
(D) 남자가 여자에게 열쇠를 건네는 동작을 정확히 묘사한 정답이다.

04. US

(A) The men are shoveling some soil.
(B) A line is being drawn on a road.
(C) A fence is being set up.
(D) One of the men is driving a car.

shovel 삽으로 파다 soil 토양, 흙 fence 울타리 set up 설치하다

(A) 남자들이 삽으로 흙을 파고 있다.
(B) 도로에 선이 그려지고 있다.
(C) 울타리가 설치되고 있다.
(D) 남자들 중 한 명이 차를 운전하고 있다.

[해설] 두 사람이 야외에서 일을 하고 있는 사진으로, 두 사람의 동작이나 주변의 상황에 모두 집중하면서 들어야 한다.
(A) 두 남자가 흙더미에서 삽으로 작업하는 모습을 정확히 묘사한 정답이다.
(B) 두 남자 옆쪽으로 길이 보이기는 하지만 선을 그리는(being drawn) 작업을 하는 사람은 없다.
(C) 울타리(fence)를 설치하는(set up) 사람은 보이지 않는다.
(D) 사진에 차를 운전하는(driving a car) 사람은 보이지 않는다.

05. BR

(A) She's wiping her desk with a cloth.
(B) She's looking into a microscope.
(C) She's wearing protective gloves.
(D) She's pushing a button on a machine.

wipe 닦다 cloth 옷감, 직물 look into ~의 속을 들여다보다, 조사하다 microscope 현미경 protective 보호하는, 보호용의

(A) 그녀는 헝겊으로 자신의 책상을 닦고 있다.
(B) 그녀는 현미경 안을 들여다보고 있다.
(C) 그녀는 보호용 장갑을 끼고 있다.
(D) 그녀는 기계의 버튼을 누르고 있다.

[해설] 한 여자가 실험실에서 작업을 하고 있는 모습으로, 여자와 주변 사물의 관계에 집중하면서 들어야 한다.
(A) 여자는 책상을 닦는(wiping her desk) 동작을 하고 있지 않다.
(B) 실험 장비 중 현미경이 보이기는 하지만 여자가 현미경을 들여다보고(looking into) 있지는 않다.
(C) 여자가 보호용 장갑을 낀 채 실험 기구를 만지고 있으므로 정답이다.
(D) 여자는 시험관 등의 실험용 용기를 들고 있을 뿐 기계(machine)를 조작하고 있지는 않다.

06. [AU]

(A) An awning is being opened.
(B) The stairs are being painted.
(C) A woman is holding onto a handrail.
(D) A woman is carrying her bag on her shoulder.

awning 차양, 가리개   stairs 계단   hold onto ~을 꼭 잡다
handrail 난간   carry 들고 있다, 나르다

(A) (누군가가) 차양을 걷고 있다.
(B) (누군가가) 계단에 페인트칠을 하고 있다.
(C) 여자가 난간을 잡고 있다.
(D) 여자가 어깨에 가방을 메고 있다.

[해설] 한 여자가 난간을 잡고 있는 사진으로, 인물의 동작이나 상태에 집중하면서 들어야 한다.
(A) 사진에서 창이나 문에 드리우는 차양(awning)은 보이지 않는다.
(B) 계단에 페인트칠을 하고 있는(being painted) 사람은 보이지 않는다.
(C) 여자가 난간을 잡고 있는 모습을 정확히 묘사한 정답이다.
(D) 여자의 가방은 보이지 않으므로 오답이다.

PART 2 When 의문문 / Where 의문문

확인 문제

① [US-BR]

When does your train depart?
(A) To Paris.
(B) At three.

depart 출발하다

당신의 기차는 언제 출발하나요?
(A) 파리로요.
(B) 3시에요.

② [AU-BR]

When can I get the shipping code?
(A) As soon as the order is confirmed.
(B) I packed your items.

shipping code 주문 번호

제가 주문 번호를 언제 받을 수 있나요?
(A) 주문이 확인되자마자요.
(B) 제가 당신의 물건들을 포장했습니다.

③ [US-AU]

When is your final presentation?
(A) It's my present.
(B) They didn't tell me an exact date.

exact 정확한

당신의 최종 발표는 언제입니까?
(A) 저의 선물이에요.
(B) 그들은 저에게 정확한 날짜를 알려주지 않았어요.

④ [BR-US]

Where did you leave your key?
(A) On the table.
(B) At noon.

당신의 열쇠를 어디에 두셨나요?
(A) 테이블 위에요.
(B) 정오에요.

⑤ [BR-AU]

Where did you put the sales report?
(A) About the sales figures.
(B) The vice president should have it.

vice president 부사장

판매 보고서를 어디에 두셨나요?
(A) 매출 수치에 대해서요.
(B) 그거 부사장님이 가지고 있을 거예요.

⑥ [BR-US]

Where did you hear the news?
(A) Actually, everybody is talking about it.
(B) It is newly released.

release 출시하다

그 소식은 어디서 들으셨나요?
(A) 사실, 모든 사람이 그 이야기를 하고 있어요.
(B) 그거 새로 출시되었어요.

연습 문제

01. (B) 02. (A) 03. (A) 04. (A) 05. (A) 06. (A)
07. (B) 08. (B)

01. [US-AU]

Where can I find Ms. Timber in the accounting department?
(A) She is a senior accountant. [×]
(B) Go through the fifth door on the right. [○]

accounting department 회계부서   accountant 회계사

제가 회계부서에 있는 Timber 씨를 어디서 찾을 수 있나요?
(A) 그녀는 선임 회계사입니다.
(B) 오른쪽 다섯 번째 문으로 들어가세요.

02. [US-BR]

Where can I submit my job application?
(A) Put it here. [○]
(B) Probably around 4 P.M. [×]

제가 입사 지원서를 어디에 제출하면 되나요?
(A) 여기에 놔두세요.
(B) 아마 오후 4시 정도에요.

03. US-BR

> When is Bernard going to meet with the new clients?
> (A) He met with them yesterday. [O]
> (B) They are open until ten. [X]

Bernard는 언제 새로운 고객들을 만나러 갈 건가요?
(A) 그는 어제 그들을 만났습니다.
(B) 그들은 10시까지 문을 엽니다.

04. BR-AU

> When are we announcing the company merger?
> (A) As soon as the president returns from the seminar. [O]
> (B) It will be held in the auditorium. [X]
>
> merger 합병   auditorium 강당

저희는 언제 회사 합병에 대해 발표하나요?
(A) 세미나에서 사장님이 돌아오시자마자요.
(B) 강당에서 열릴 거에요.

05. US-BR

> Where can I get this document photocopied?
> (A) There's a machine on the third floor. [O]
> (B) Two copies per person should be sufficient. [X]

이 서류를 어디서 복사할 수 있죠?
(A) 3층에 기계가 있습니다.
(B) 한 사람당 두 장이면 충분합니다.

06. AU-US

> When are you taking a coffee break?
> (A) Not for another hour. [O]
> (B) I want to take a walk. [X]

언제 휴식을 가질 건가요?
(A) 앞으로 한 시간 동안은 못 쉽니다.
(B) 저는 산책을 하고 싶어요.

07. BR-AU

> Where can I find the notice about the personnel?
> (A) Yes, go straight and turn left. [X]
> (B) It will be posted on our Web site. [O]
>
> personnel 인사

인사에 대한 공고를 어디서 찾을 수 있죠?
(A) 네, 곧장 가서 왼쪽으로 도세요.
(B) 우리의 웹사이트에 공지될 거예요.

08. US-US

> When can I come in for my regular check-up?
> (A) Sorry, that book has already been checked out. [X]
> (B) Can you spare some time around three tomorrow afternoon? [O]
>
> check-up 건강 검진   spare (시간·돈 등을) 할애하다

제가 언제 정기 건강 검진을 받으러 갈 수 있나요?
(A) 죄송합니다만, 그 책은 이미 대출되었습니다.
(B) 내일 오후 3시쯤에 시간 되시나요?

실전 문제

01. (C)	02. (C)	03. (B)	04. (C)	05. (C)	06. (A)
07. (C)	08. (C)	09. (A)	10. (B)	11. (B)	12. (C)
13. (A)	14. (A)	15. (C)	16. (A)		

01. US-BR

> Where will your new office be?
> (A) No, not yet.
> (B) Fourteen stories.
> **(C) In the downtown area.**
>
> story (건물의) 층   downtown area 도심 지역

당신의 새 사무실은 어디에 있게 되나요?
(A) 아니요, 아직이에요.
(B) 14층이에요.
(C) 도심 지역이에요.

[해설] 새 사무실의 위치를 묻는 Where 의문이다.
(A) 의문사 의문문에는 Yes/No로 응답하지 않으며, not yet 또한 주로 무언가를 완료했는지 묻는 질문에 대한 응답으로 쓰이므로 오답이다.
(B) 이때의 story는 '건물의 층'을 뜻하는 단어로, 건물의 층수를 물었을 때 어울리는 답변이므로 오답이다.
(C) 장소 부사구를 써서 특정 장소를 알려주는 정답이다.

02. BR-US

> Where's the nearest ATM?
> (A) I'd rather pay in cash.
> (B) A seminar about investing.
> **(C) On the other side of Main Street.**
>
> nearest 가장 가까운   I'd rather 차라리 ~하겠다   invest 투자하다   on the other side of ~의 반대편에

가장 가까운 현금 자동 입출금기는 어디에 있나요?
(A) 차라리 현금으로 지불하겠어요.
(B) 투자에 관한 세미나예요.
(C) Main가 반대편에요.

[해설] 현금 자동 입출금기의 위치를 묻는 Where 의문문이다.
(A) ATM에서 연상되는 cash를 이용하여 혼동을 유도한 오답으로, 지불 수단을 묻는 How 의문문에 어울리는 응답이다.
(B) ATM과 직접적 관련이 있는 '돈'에서 연상되는 investing을 이용하여 혼동을 유도한 오답이다.

(C) 구체적인 위치로 답한 정답이다.

03. AU-US

> When will you get your certificate?
> (A) She is a certified dealer.
> **(B) Right after I pass the final test.**
> (C) From a private institution.
>
> certificate 자격증, 증명서   certified 보증[증명]된, 공인의
> dealer (상품을 사고파는) 딜러, 중개인   private institution 사설 기관, 민간 단체

당신은 자격증을 언제 취득하나요?
(A) 그녀는 공인된 중개인이에요.
(B) 제가 최종 시험을 통과한 직후예요.
(C) 사설 기관으로부터요.
[해설] 자격증을 취득하는 시점을 묻는 When 의문문이다.
(A) 질문의 certificate에서 연상 가능한 certified를 이용하여 혼동을 유도한 오답이다. 또한 질문에서 she로 지칭할 만한 인물이 언급되지도 않았다.
(B) 언제 자격증을 취득하는지 묻는 질문에 '최종 시험을 통과한 직후'라고 구체적인 시점으로 답했으므로 정답이다.
(C) 자격증을 어디서 받는지 묻는 Where 의문문에 적합한 응답이므로 오답이다.

04. AU-BR

> Where should I set up the new display?
> (A) Because the price tags aren't attached.
> (B) That's too expensive.
> **(C) Here's the latest floor plan.**
>
> set up 설치하다, 세우다   display 전시(품), 진열(품)   price tag 가격표   attach 붙이다, 첨부하다   latest 최근의, 최신의   floor plan 평면도

새 진열품을 어디에 설치해야 하나요?
(A) 가격표가 붙어 있지 않기 때문입니다.
(B) 그건 너무 비싸요.
(C) 여기 가장 최근의 평면도입니다.
[해설] 새 진열품을 설치할 장소를 묻는 Where 의문문이다.
(A) Because로 시작하여 이유를 설명하는 응답이므로 Why 의문문에 적합하다.
(B) 가격이나 요금 같은 비용에 관련된 응답으로 적합하므로 오답이다.
(C) 평면도를 보여줌으로써 질문자가 직접 위치를 확인하도록 유도하는 응답이므로 정답이다.

05. US-US

> Where is your organic milk?
> (A) From Dakota Farms.
> (B) That should do it.
> **(C) Sorry, but we're all sold out.**
>
> That should do it. 확실하다.

유기농 우유는 어디에 있나요?
(A) Dakota 농장으로부터요.
(B) 확실해요.
(C) 죄송하지만 다 팔렸어요.
[해설] 상점에서 특정 제품의 위치를 묻는 Where 의문문이다.
(A) milk에서 연상 가능한 farm을 이용한 오답으로, 우유가 어디에서 나온 제품인지 물었다면 정답이 될 수 있다.
(B) That should do it은 I'm sure 또는 I guarantee it처럼 '확실하다'는 의미로, 유기농 우유가 맞는지 묻는 질문에 적합한 응답이므로 오답이다.
(C) 다 팔렸다는 말로 현재 유기농 우유가 없다고 응답한 정답이다.

06. BR-AU

> Where can I get a new name badge?
> **(A) You have to go to Human Resources.**
> (B) A security background check.
> (C) Please show it to a security guard.
>
> name badge 명찰   background (사람의) 배경
> security guard 경비원, 보안 요원

새 명찰은 어디에서 받을 수 있나요?
(A) 인사부로 가셔야 합니다.
(B) 보안 목적의 배경 조사입니다.
(C) 보안 요원에게 그것을 보여주세요.
[해설] 명찰을 받을 수 있는 곳을 묻는 Where 의문문이다.
(A) 인사부로 가라고 구체적인 장소를 알려준 정답이다.
(B) name badge에서 연상되는 신원 확인의 용도를 묻는 질문에 적절한 응답이므로 오답이다.
(C) name badge를 누구에게 보여줘야 하는지 묻는 Who 질문에 적절한 응답이므로 오답이다.

07. BR-US

> When will I get my reimbursement check?
> (A) The full $500.
> (B) Let's put it on the company card.
> **(C) Try asking Wilfred.**
>
> reimbursement 상환, 배상   put it on one's card ~의 신용카드로 계산하다   full 가득 찬, 전부의

제가 환급 수표를 언제 받게 되나요?
(A) 500달러 전액이요.
(B) 그것을 회사 카드로 계산합시다.
(C) Wilfred에게 물어보세요.
[해설] 자신에게 언제 환급 수표가 지급되는지 묻는 When 의문문이다.
(A) 구체적인 금액을 제시하였으므로 가격이나 비용을 묻는 How much 의문문에 적합한 오답이다.
(B) check에서 연상되는 대금 결제 상황에서 나올 수 있는 표현으로 혼동을 유도한 오답이다.
(C) 언제 환급 수표가 지급되는지 묻는 질문에 제3자에게 물어보라고 응답함으로써 자신은 알지 못한다는 것을 우회적으로 드러낸 정답이다.

08. BR-US

> Where is the extra safety gear?
> (A) Yes, in the storage room.

(B) After the inspection.
(C) **Ms. Chang will tell you.**

extra 추가의, 여분의   safety gear 안전 장치   storage room 창고
inspection 점검, 검사

여분의 안전 장치는 어디 있나요?
(A) 네, 창고예요.
(B) 점검 후에요.
(C) Chang 씨가 말해 줄 거예요.

[해설] 안전 장치의 위치를 묻는 Where 의문문이다.
(A) 의문사 의문문에는 Yes/No로 응답할 수 없으므로 오답이다.
(B) 시점을 나타내는 표현은 When 의문문에 적합하므로 오답이다.
(C) 보관함의 위치를 묻는 질문에 구체적 장소로 대답하는 대신 특정 인물이 말해 줄 거라고 우회적으로 응답하고 있으므로 정답이다.

09. US-AU

Where should I take my clients for lunch?
(A) **Ms. Brenner knows this area well.**
(B) Try the daily special.
(C) 9 dollars per person.

try 먹어보다, 써보다, 해보다   per person 1인당

점심 식사를 위해서 제 고객들을 어디로 모시고 가야 할까요?
(A) Brenner 씨가 이 지역을 잘 알아요.
(B) 오늘의 특별 요리를 드셔보세요.
(C) 한 사람당 9달러입니다.

[해설] 고객에게 점심 식사를 대접할 장소를 묻는 Where 의문문이다.
(A) 식사 장소를 묻는 질문에 Brenner 씨가 이 지역을 잘 안다고 말함으로써 자신은 잘 모르니 Brenner 씨에게 물어볼 것을 우회적으로 권하는 정답이다.
(B) 어떤 음식을 먹는 것이 좋을지 묻는 What 의문문에 적합한 응답이다.
(C) 음식의 가격을 묻는 How much 의문문에 적합한 응답이다.

10. BR-BR

When should I expect my order to arrive?
(A) In your mailbox.
(B) **Usually in three business days.**
(C) Express shipping options.

expect 기대[예상]하다   order 주문(품)   mailbox 우편함
business day 영업일, 평일   express 급행의, 신속한   shipping 운송, 수송

제 주문품이 언제 도착할 것으로 예상하세요?
(A) 당신의 우편함에요.
(B) 보통 영업일로 3일 후에요.
(C) 급송 옵션입니다.

[해설] 주문품의 도착 시점을 묻는 When 의문문이다.
(A) 장소 부사구(in)을 사용했으므로 Where 의문문에 적합한 응답이다.
(B) 주문품이 도착하는 시점을 묻는 질문에 '영업일로 3일 후'라는 구체적인 시점을 제시했으므로 정답이다.
(C) 주문품이 배송되는 상황에서 연상할 수 있는 배송 옵션의 하나인 express shipping으로 혼동을 유도한 오답이다.

11. US-AU

Where can I find a quiet place to read?
(A) Here's my library card.
(B) **There is a lot of construction noise around here.**
(C) In the table of contents.

construction 건설, 공사   noise 소음   table of contents 목차

책을 읽을 만한 조용한 장소가 어디 있나요?
(A) 여기 제 도서 대출 카드입니다.
(B) 이 주변에는 공사 소음이 너무 큽니다.
(C) 목차에서요.

[해설] 책 읽기에 조용한 장소를 묻는 Where 의문문이다.
(A) read에서 연상되는 library card를 이용하여 혼동을 유도하는 오답이다.
(B) 조용한 곳의 위치를 묻는 말에 이 근처에는 공사 소음이 심하다고 말함으로써 가까운 곳에는 조용한 장소가 없음을 돌려서 말한 정답이다.
(C) read에서 쉽게 연상되는 책이나 잡지의 table of contents를 이용해 혼동을 유도하는 오답이다.

12. US-US

When should we put up the sale banners?
(A) Our annual customer appreciation event.
(B) Is there space in the front window?
(C) **As soon as they are delivered.**

put up 달다, 게시하다   banner 현수막, 배너   annual 연례의
customer 고객   appreciation 감사   space 공간

세일 현수막을 언제 내걸어야 할까요?
(A) 우리의 연례 고객 감사 행사요.
(B) 앞창에 공간이 있나요?
(C) 그것들이 도착하자마자요.

[해설] 현수막을 내걸어야 하는 시기를 묻는 When 의문문이다.
(A) 질문과 상관없는 답변이므로 오답이다.
(B) 장소 부사구(in the front window)를 사용했으므로 Where 의문문에 적합한 응답이다.
(C) 시간 접속사 as soon as를 이용하여 '그것들이 도착하자마자'라고 구체적 시점을 제시했으므로 정답이다.

13. US-BR

When will the new dress code be implemented?
(A) **It's posted on the message board.**
(B) A white shirt with black pants.
(C) The system was effective.

dress code 복장 규정   implement 시행하다   effective 효과적인

새 복장 규정은 언제 시행될 것인가요?
(A) 게시판에 공고되어 있어요.
(B) 흰색 셔츠와 검정색 바지입니다.
(C) 그 시스템은 효과적이었어요.

[해설] 새 복장 규정이 시행되는 시점을 묻는 When 의문문이다.
(A) 새 복장 규정이 언제 시행되는지 묻는 질문에 게시판에 공고되어 있다고 답함으로써 직접 구체적인 시기를 제시하기보다는 질문자가 게시판

을 통해 직접 확인할 것을 우회적으로 제안하고 있으므로 정답이다.
(B) dress code에서 연상 가능한 white shirt with black pants를 이용하여 혼동을 유도한 오답이다.
(C) dress code와 implemented에서 연상 가능한 system을 이용해 혼동을 유도하는 오답으로, 질문의 시제는 미래인데 과거로 답했으므로 시제 역시 불일치한다.

14. US-BR

Where can I go to submit this request form?
(A) Mr. Jefferson will be right with you.
(B) Sure, we accept special requests.
(C) She is not a former manager.

submit 제출하다   request form 신청서   accept 받아들이다, 접수하다   former 이전의

이 신청서를 제출하러 어디로 가면 되나요?
(A) Jefferson 씨가 곧 당신을 도와줄 겁니다.
(B) 물론이죠, 저희는 특별 요청을 받습니다.
(C) 그녀는 이전 매니저가 아니에요.

[해설] 신청서 제출 장소를 묻는 Where 의문문이다.
(A) 신청서를 어디에 가서 제출하면 되는지 묻는 질문에 Jefferson 씨가 도와줄 것이라고 했으므로 정답이다. Where 의문문에 직접적인 장소로 답하는 대신 이렇게 도와줄 누군가를 알려주는 간접적인 응답도 가능하다.
(B) 질문의 request를 반복 사용하여 혼동을 유도한 오답이다.
(C) 질문에서 대명사 she로 지칭할 만한 사람이 언급되지 않았으므로 오답이다.

15. AU-BR

When will the Finance Department release the new budget?
(A) No, I haven't read the e-mail yet.
(B) About a thousand dollars.
(C) It's not due until the end of the month.

release 공개[발표]하다   budget 예산   due ~하기로 되어 있는, 예정된

회계부는 새 예산을 언제 발표할 건가요?
(A) 아니요, 저는 아직 이메일을 읽지 않았어요.
(B) 약 1천 달러요.
(C) 이달 말은 되어야 합니다.

[해설] 새 예산이 발표되는 시점을 묻는 When 의문문이다.
(A) 의문사 의문문에는 Yes/No로 응답할 수 없으므로 오답이다.
(B) 구체적 금액으로 답변했으므로 How much 의문문에 적합한 오답이다.
(C) 회계부에서 새 예산을 발표하는 시기를 묻는 질문에 '이달 말'이라는 구체적인 시점을 제시했으므로 정답이다.

16. US-US

When did the clearance sale start?
(A) Didn't you receive a newsletter from us?
(B) I would prefer to start working early.
(C) To give a clear explanation.

clearance sale 재고 정리 세일   newsletter 소식지   prefer 선호하다   give an explanation 설명하다

재고 정리 세일이 언제 시작했나요?
(A) 저희에게서 소식지를 받지 않으셨나요?
(B) 저는 일찍 일을 시작하는 것을 선호합니다.
(C) 명확히 설명하기 위해서요.

[해설] 재고 정리 세일이 시작된 시점을 묻는 When 의문문이다.
(A) 세일이 언제 시작됐는지 묻는 질문에 소식지를 받지 못했냐고 되물음으로써 소식지에 나와 있다고 간접적으로 전하고 있으므로 정답이다.
(B) 질문의 start를 반복 사용하여 혼동을 유도한 오답이다.
(C) 질문의 clearance와 발음이 비슷한 clear를 사용하여 혼동을 유도한 오답이다.

DAY 02

PART 1 다인 사진/사물·풍경 사진

확인 문제

❶ US

(A) They are setting up tents.
(B) They have gathered beside the sea.

set up 설치하다   gather 모이다, 모으다

(A) 그들은 텐트를 설치하고 있다.
(B) 그들은 바다 옆에 모여 있다.

❷ AU

(A) Some people are sitting on stools.
(B) One of the women is paying for an item.

stool (등받이와 팔걸이가 없는) 의자, 스툴

(A) 몇몇 사람들이 의자에 앉아 있다.
(B) 여자들 중 한 명이 상품에 대한 돈을 지불하고 있다.

❸ US

(A) Some people are pulling some cakes out of an oven.
(B) A piece of dough is being weighed on a scale.

weigh 무게를 재다   scale 저울

(A) 몇몇 사람들이 오븐에서 케이크를 꺼내고 있다.
(B) 밀가루 반죽이 저울에서 무게가 재어지고 있다.

❹ BR

(A) There is a table on a carpet.
(B) A chair is being assembled in a room.

assemble 조립하다

(A) 카펫 위에 탁자가 있다.
(B) 의자가 방에서 조립되고 있다.

❺ BR

(A) A road is blocked by a barricade.
(B) Some cars are parked along the street.

block 막다   barricade 바리케이드, 방어벽

(A) 도로가 바리케이드에 의해 막혀 있다.
(B) 몇몇 차량이 거리를 따라 주차되어 있다.

❻ US

(A) Stairs lead to the upper floor.
(B) Some people are watching a performance.

upper floor 위층

(A) 계단이 위층으로 이어진다.
(B) 몇몇 사람들이 공연을 보고 있다.

연습 문제

01. AU

(1) (A) working (O) (B) sitting on a bench (✗)
    (C) a road (O)
(2)
(A) Some people are working at a construction site. [O]
(B) Some people are standing on the scaffoldings. [✗]

scaffolding 비계, 발판

(A) 몇몇 사람들이 건설 현장에서 일하고 있다.
(B) 몇몇 사람들이 발판에 서 있다.

02. US

(1) (A) people (O) (B) a tent (O) (C) fishing (✗)
(2)
(A) They're fishing on a riverbank. [✗]
(B) A tent is being set up on the grass. [O]

riverbank 강둑

(A) 그들은 강둑에서 낚시를 하고 있다.
(B) 텐트가 잔디 위에 설치되고 있다.

03. US

(1) (A) a bed (O) (B) curtains (O) (C) a man (✗)
(2)
(A) There are cushions on a bed. [O]
(B) Some curtains are pulled closed. [✗]

(A) 침대 위에 쿠션이 있다.
(B) 몇몇 커튼이 닫혀 있다.

04. BR

(1) (A) a car (✗) (B) some boats (O) (C) a bridge (✗)
(2)
(A) A car is driving on a bridge. [✗]
(B) Some boats are floating on a river. [O]

bridge 다리   float 뜨다

(A) 자동차가 다리 위를 달리고 있다.
(B) 몇몇 배들이 강에 떠 있다.

실전 문제

01. (B)   02. (B)   03. (D)   04. (C)   05. (D)   06. (B)

01. US

(A) One of the men is setting up a board.
(B) One of the men is standing behind a counter.
(C) Some dishes are being prepared on a stove.
(D) One of the women is cutting a loaf of bread.

set up 설치하다, 세우다   counter 계산대, 판매대   prepare 준비하다   stove (요리용) 레인지, 난로

(A) 남자들 중 한 명이 판자를 세우고 있다.
(B) 남자들 중 한 명이 판매대 뒤에 서 있다.
(C) 레인지 위에서 음식이 조리되고 있다.
(D) 여자들 중 한 명이 빵을 자르고 있다.

[해설] 다수의 인물과 사물이 섞여 있는 사진으로, 음식을 판매/구매하는 사람과 주변 사물 모두에 집중하면서 들어야 한다.
(A) 사진에서 판자(board)를 세우는 사람은 보이지 않는다.
(B) 판매대 뒤에 남자와 여자가 서 있으므로 바르게 묘사한 정답이다.
(C) 음식 판매대인 것은 맞지만 불 위에서 조리 중인(being prepared) 음식은 보이지 않는다.
(D) 빵을 자르는(cutting a loaf of bread) 사람은 보이지 않는다.

02. BR

(A) One of the women is purchasing a ticket at a booth.
(B) One of the women is boarding a bus.
(C) One of the men is talking on the phone.
(D) One of the men is coming up the stairs.

purchase 구매하다   booth (칸막이를 한) 작은 공간, 부스   board 승선[승차/탑승]하다   stairs 계단

(A) 여자들 중 한 명이 부스에서 표를 구입하고 있다.
(B) 여자들 중 한 명이 버스에 타고 있다.
(C) 남자들 중 한 명이 전화 통화를 하고 있다.
(D) 남자들 중 한 명이 계단을 오르고 있다.

[해설] 버스에 타려고 하는 다수의 인물이 등장하는 사진으로, 각 인물의 동작을 잘 살펴야 한다.
(A) 표를 파는 곳(booth)이나 표를 구매하는(purchasing a ticket) 사람이 보이지 않는다.
(B) 맨 앞의 여자가 막 버스에 승차하고 있는 것을 정확히 묘사한 정답이다.

(C) 전화를 하고 있는(talking on the phone) 사람은 보이지 않는다.
(D) 계단을 오르고 있는(coming up the stairs) 남자는 없다.

03. [AU]

(A) Some guests are reading a menu together.
(B) Some food trays are set up in a corner.
(C) A waiter is pouring water from a pitcher.
(D) A server is writing on a notepad.

food tray 식판   set up 세우다, 놓다   pour 붓다, 따르다
pitcher 손 잡이가 달린 물병   server (식당에서) 서빙하는 사람
notepad 메모지

(A) 손님들이 함께 메뉴를 읽고 있다.
(B) 식판들이 한구석에 놓여 있다.
(C) 웨이터가 물병에서 물을 따르고 있다.
(D) 식당 종업원이 메모지에 무언가를 적고 있다.
[해설] 식당 종업원 1인과 식당 손님 3인의 모습으로, 모든 등장 인물의 동작을 잘 살펴야 한다.
(A) 남자 손님들이 한 남자가 손에 든 무언가를 보고 있긴 하지만 메뉴인지 알 수 없다.
(B) 한구석에 놓여 있는 식판(food trays)은 보이지 않는다.
(C) 물을 따르고 있는(pouring water) 웨이터(waiter)는 보이지 않는다.
(D) 식당 종업원으로 보이는 여자가 메모를 하면서 주문을 받는 모습을 묘사한 정답이다.

04. [BR]

(A) A table is being placed on the carpet.
(B) Some decorations are set on the windowsill.
(C) Some books have been arranged on the table.
(D) A sofa is being moved to the entrance.

place 놓다, 두다   decoration 장식(물)   set 놓다   windowsill 창턱   arrange 정리하다, 배열하다   entrance (출)입구

(A) 탁자가 카펫 위에 놓이고 있다.
(B) 창턱에 장식물들이 놓여 있다.
(C) 책들이 테이블 위에 놓여 있다.
(D) 소파가 출입구로 옮겨지고 있다.
[해설] 사람이 등장하지 않는 실내 사진으로, 사진 속 모든 사물의 위치나 상태를 잘 살펴야 한다.
(A) 사람이 등장하지 않는 사진에서 수동태 진행형(is being placed)은 오답이다.
(B) 사진에서 창턱(windowsill)은 보이지 않는다.
(C) 테이블 위에 책들이 잘 정리되어 놓여 있는 모습을 정확히 묘사한 정답이다.
(D) 사람이 등장하지 않는 사진에서 수동태 진행형(is being moved)은 오답이다.

05. [US]

(A) A tree is being planted in a pot.
(B) A dining table has been set up on an outdoor patio.
(C) A driveway is being swept with a broom.
(D) Benches are lined along a walkway.

pot 화분   outdoor 야외의   patio 파티오(집 뒤의 테라스)
driveway (도로에서 집·차고까지의) 진입로   sweep (빗자루로) 쓸다   broom 빗자루   walkway 통로, 보도

(A) 나무가 화분에 심어지고 있다.
(B) 야외 파티오에 식탁이 차려져 있다.
(C) 진입로를 빗자루로 쓸고 있다.
(D) 벤치들이 보도를 따라 늘어서 있다.
[해설] 사람이 등장하지 않는 야외의 풍경 사진으로, 사진 속 모든 사물의 위치나 상태에 주목해야 한다.
(A) 사람이 등장하지 않는 사진에서 수동태 진행형(is being planted)은 오답이다.
(B) 사진 속 장소는 야외 파티오(patio)가 아니라 공원이며, 식탁(dining table)도 보이지 않는다.
(C) 사람이 등장하지 않는 사진에서 수동태 진행형(is being swept)은 오답이다.
(D) 보도 양쪽에 벤치가 늘어서 있는 모습을 정확히 묘사한 정답이다.

06. [AU]

(A) Some people are sitting in an airplane.
(B) Some people are gathered in a baggage claim area.
(C) Some people are passing through an entrance.
(D) Some people are checking their luggage in at the counter.

be gathered 모이다   baggage claim area 수하물 찾는 곳
pass through ~을 통과해 지나가다

(A) 몇몇 사람들이 비행기 안에 앉아 있다.
(B) 몇몇 사람들이 수하물 찾는 곳에 모여 있다.
(C) 몇몇 사람들이 출입구를 통과해 지나가고 있다.
(D) 몇몇 사람들이 카운터에서 짐을 부치고 있다.
[해설] 다수의 인물이 공항의 수하물 찾는 곳에 있는 사진으로, 각 인물들의 개별 동작과 공통 동작에 집중하며 들어야 한다.
(A) 사람들은 비행기 안(in an airplane)이 아니라 공항 내 수하물 찾는 곳에 있다.
(B) 사람들이 수하물이 나오기를 기다리고 있는 모습을 정확히 묘사한 정답이다.
(C) 출입구를 통과하는(passing through an entrance) 사람들은 보이지 않는다.
(D) 사람들은 짐을 부치고 있는(checking their luggage) 것이 아니라 짐을 찾으려고 기다리고 있고 카운터도 보이지 않으므로 오답이다.

PART 2   What 의문문 / Who 의문문

확인 문제

❶ [US-BR]

What time do you usually get up?
(A) Between 6 and 7.
(B) It was yesterday.

주로 몇 시에 일어나세요?
(A) 6시에서 7시 사이에요.
(B) 어제였습니다.

② US-US

What should I do if I'm late?
(A) I've been there lately.
(B) Just let your supervisor know.

제가 늦으면 어떻게 해야 하죠?
(A) 저는 최근에 그곳에 다녀왔습니다.
(B) 상사에게 알리시기만 하면 돼요.

③ AU-BR

What do you think of the new parking policy?
(A) You aren't allowed to park here.
(B) I'm quite satisfied.

새 주차 정책에 대해 어떻게 생각해요?
(A) 여기에 주차하시면 안 됩니다.
(B) 저는 꽤 만족해요.

④ US-US

Who's Mr. Johnson meeting with?
(A) The new interns.
(B) I have met him before.

Johnson 씨가 누구를 만나고 있나요?
(A) 새 인턴들이요.
(B) 저는 전에 그를 만난 적이 있어요.

⑤ BR-US

Who do you recommend for the department head?
(A) I need to think of someone, too.
(B) It is a newly established department.

부서장으로 누구를 추천하시나요?
(A) 저도 누군가를 생각해봐야 해요.
(B) 그건 새로 생긴 부서예요.

⑥ US-AU

Who is supposed to give a speech tomorrow?
(A) Mr. Lee is our regular customer.
(B) How about we ask Jamie?

누가 내일 연설하기로 되어 있나요?
(A) Lee 씨는 우리의 단골 고객입니다.
(B) 우리 Jamie에게 물어보는 게 어때요?

연습 문제

01. (A) 02. (B) 03. (B) 04. (A) 05. (B) 06. (B)
07. (B) 08. (B)

---

01. AU-BR

What do you intend to do after you retire?
(A) I want to travel throughout the world. [○]
(B) I think his performance was impressive. [×]

intend to ~하려고 하다   retire 은퇴하다

당신은 은퇴 후에 무엇을 할 계획인가요?
(A) 저는 전 세계를 여행하고 싶어요.
(B) 저는 그의 공연이 인상 깊었다고 생각해요.

02. US-AU

Who is in charge of the annual awards banquet?
(A) Samuel was the award winner. [×]
(B) Mr. Clark will manage it. [○]

awards banquet 시상식   manage 관리하다

연례 시상식을 누가 담당하고 있나요?
(A) Samuel이 수상자였어요.
(B) Clark 씨가 관리할 것입니다.

03. BR-US

What should we wear to Mr. Wong's farewell party?
(A) No, he's transferring to London. [×]
(B) I heard that formal clothing is suggested. [○]

transfer 전근 가다

Wong 씨의 송별 파티에 무엇을 입고 가야 할까요?
(A) 아뇨, 그는 런던으로 전근 갑니다.
(B) 저는 정장을 입는 것이 권장된다고 들었습니다.

04. US-US

Who will notify employees of these changes?
(A) The personnel department will. [○]
(B) I did not notice him. [×]

notify A of B A에게 B를 알려주다   notice 알아채다

누가 이러한 변경 사항들을 직원들에게 알릴 건가요?
(A) 인사부에서요.
(B) 저는 그를 알아보지 못했습니다.

05. BR-AU

What did the client say about our design proposal?
(A) He suggested to do some revisions. [○]
(B) Yes, this is my favorite painting. [×]

proposal 제안서   revision 수정

고객이 우리의 디자인 제안서에 대해서 뭐라고 했나요?
(A) 그는 몇 가지 수정할 것을 제안했어요.
(B) 네, 이게 제가 가장 좋아하는 그림입니다.

06. US-AU

> Who can I call if I have a problem with the computer?
> (A) Yes, we need ten computers. [×]
> **(B) Call Frank.** [○]

컴퓨터에 문제가 있으면 누구에게 전화해야 하나요?
(A) 네, 우리는 컴퓨터 10대가 필요해요.
(B) Frank에게 전화하세요.

07. BR-BR

> What if we categorize these files?
> (A) It's in the file drawer. [×]
> **(B) That's a good idea.** [○]

drawer 서랍

우리가 이 파일들을 분류하면 어때요?
(A) 그건 파일 서랍에 있어요.
(B) 좋은 생각이에요.

08. BR-US

> Who's supposed to clean the office today?
> (A) She was supposed to meet me here. [×]
> **(B) It's my turn.** [○]

turn 차례

누가 오늘 사무실 청소를 하기로 되어 있나요?
(A) 그녀는 저를 여기서 만나기로 했었습니다.
(B) 제가 할 차례입니다.

실전 문제

01. (A)	02. (C)	03. (C)	04. (C)	05. (A)	06. (C)
07. (B)	08. (B)	09. (A)	10. (B)	11. (A)	12. (C)
13. (B)	14. (C)	15. (A)	16. (A)		

01. US-US

> Who should I contact about lost and found items?
> **(A) The security department.**
> (B) Be careful not to lose it.
> (C) Yesterday around noon.

lost and found items 분실물

분실물에 관해서는 누구한테 연락해야 하나요?
(A) 보안팀이요.
(B) 그것을 잃어버리지 않도록 주의하세요.
(C) 어제 정오쯤에요.

[해설] 분실물에 관해 알아보려면 누구에게 연락해야 하는지 묻는 Who 의문문이다.
(A) 분실물 담당자가 누구인지 묻는 질문에 특정 부서명으로 답한 정답이다.
(B) lost and found items에서 연상되는 lose를 이용하여 혼동을 유도한 오답이다.

(C) 시간 부사구로 답변했으므로 When 의문문에 적합한 응답이다.

02. US-BR

> What will we cover in the annual training session?
> (A) We'll interview some candidates.
> (B) There will be more people than usual.
> **(C) Mostly providing good service.**

cover 다루다, 포함시키다   annual 연례의, 매년의
mostly 주로, 일반적으로

우리는 연례 교육에서 무엇을 다룰 것인가요?
(A) 몇몇 지원자들의 면접을 볼 거예요.
(B) 평소보다 사람들이 많을 거예요.
(C) 주로 좋은 서비스를 제공하는 것이요.

[해설] 연례 교육에서 다룰 주제를 묻는 What 의문문이다.
(A) 질문의 training session에서 연상되는 직장이나 취업과 관련된 interview나 candidate를 이용해 혼동을 유도한 오답이다.
(B) 교육에 얼마나 많은 인원이 참석하는지 물어보는 질문에 적합한 응답이므로 오답이다.
(C) 연례 교육에서 다루게 될 주제로 답변했으므로 정답이다.

03. BR-US

> Who will give the presentation to the board?
> (A) On slide 4.
> (B) Any staff member can post on the bulletin board.
> **(C) Sophie from Public Relations usually does that.**

give a presentation 발표하다, 프레젠테이션하다   board 이사회
post 게시하다   bulletin board 게시판   usually 보통

누가 이사회에 프레젠테이션을 할 건가요?
(A) 4번째 슬라이드에요.
(B) 어느 직원이든지 게시판에 게시할 수 있어요.
(C) 보통 홍보 부서의 Sophie가 그것을 합니다.

[해설] 프레젠테이션을 누가 할 것인지 묻는 Who 의문문이다.
(A) presentation에서 연상할 수 있는 slide를 사용하여 혼동을 유도한 오답이다.
(B) 질문의 board를 다른 의미로 반복 사용하여 혼동을 유도한 오답이다.
(C) 구체적인 인물로 답하고 정답이다.

04. US-BR

> What plans do you have for your summer vacation this year?
> (A) An event calendar.
> (B) We'll have a full week off.
> **(C) I'd like to go on an Alaskan cruise.**

have ~ off ~동안 쉬다   go on a cruise 크루즈 여행을 가다

올해 여름 휴가 동안 무슨 계획이 있나요?
(A) 행사 일정표예요.
(B) 우리는 꼬박 일주일 휴가를 낼 거예요.
(C) 저는 알래스카 크루즈 여행을 가고 싶어요.

[해설] 여름 휴가 계획을 묻는 What 의문문이다.

(A) 질문의 plan에서 연상 가능한 calendar를 이용하여 혼동을 유도하는 오답이다.
(B) 질문의 vacation에서 연상되는 휴가 기간(a full week off)을 이용하여 혼동을 유도하는 오답이다. 얼마 동안 휴가를 갈 계획인지 묻는 질문에 어울리는 응답이다.
(C) 알래스카 크루즈 여행을 가고 싶다고 희망 사항을 구체적으로 제시한 정답이다.

05. BR-US

Who should I talk to about my computer running slowly?
(A) Someone from IT could help you.
(B) The system requirements.
(C) Ever since Ms. Taylor retired.

run 작동하다 slowly 천천히 requirements 필요(한 것)
ever since ~이후로 줄곧[계속]

제 컴퓨터가 느리게 작동하는 것에 대해 누구에게 말해야 하나요?
(A) IT 부서의 누군가가 당신을 도와줄 수 있어요.
(B) 시스템 요구 사항이요.
(C) Taylor 씨가 퇴직한 이후로 줄곧이요.
[해설] 컴퓨터 관련 문제의 담당자가 누구인지 묻는 Who 의문문이다.
(A) 특정 부서를 제시하여 답변했으므로 정답이다.
(B) 질문의 computer에서 연상 가능한 system을 이용하여 혼동을 유도한 오답이다.
(C) 특정 시점이나 지속 기간을 묻는 질문에 적합한 응답이다. 특정 인물(Ms. Taylor)이 언급되었다고 무조건 정답으로 고르지 않도록 주의해야 한다.

06. BR-AU

Who is in charge of calling customers today?
(A) A plan with unlimited talk and text included.
(B) From 11 A.M.
(C) The department schedule is on the desk.

be in charge of ~을 담당하다

오늘 누가 고객들에게 전화하는 일을 담당하나요?
(A) 무제한 통화와 문자가 포함된 상품이요.
(B) 오전 11시부터요.
(C) 부서 일정표가 책상 위에 있습니다.
[해설] 고객들에게 전화하는 업무를 담당하는 사람을 묻는 Who 의문문이다.
(A) 질문의 calling에서 연상 가능한 휴대폰으로 이용 가능한 서비스인 talk(통화)과 text(문자)를 이용하여 혼동을 유도하는 오답이다.
(B) 시점을 묻는 When 의문문에 적합한 응답이므로 오답이다.
(C) 부서 일정이 책상 위에 있다는 말로 담당자에 대한 정보를 간접적으로 제시하고 있으므로 정답이다.

07. US-US

Who are we supposed to interview with tomorrow?
(A) About half an hour long.
(B) Here is the list of candidates.
(C) First thing in the morning.

candidate 지원자

우리는 내일 누구와 면접을 하기로 되어 있나요?
(A) 약 30분간 진행됩니다.
(B) 여기 지원자 명단이 있습니다.
(C) 아침 제일 먼저요.
[해설] 면접 대상을 묻는 Who 의문문이다.
(A) 약 30분간 진행된다고 했으므로 지속 시간을 묻는 How long 의문문에 적합한 응답이다.
(B) 지원자 명단을 제시함으로써 질문자가 면접 대상을 직접 확인하도록 유도하고 있으므로 정답이다.
(C) 구체적인 시점을 제시했으므로 When 의문문에 적합한 응답이다.

08. US-BR

What ingredients go into that dish?
(A) A Chinese tradition.
(B) Let me check the recipe.
(C) It tastes delicious.

ingredient (요리 등의) 재료 dish 요리

저 요리에는 어떤 재료가 들어가나요?
(A) 중국의 전통입니다.
(B) 제가 조리법을 확인해 볼게요.
(C) 맛있어요.
[해설] 요리에 들어가는 재료를 묻는 What 의문문이다.
(A) dish에서 연상 가능한 Chinese를 이용하여 혼동을 유도한 오답이다.
(B) 요리에 어떤 재료가 들어가는지 묻는 질문에 조리법을 확인해보겠다는 말로 '나도 잘 모른다'는 의미를 우회적으로 전달하는 정답이다.
(C) 질문의 dish에서 연상되는 tastes delicious를 이용해 혼동을 유도하는 오답이다.

09. US-BR

Who will be representing our company at the conference?
(A) Mr. Hamilton, our regional manager.
(B) Lunch will not be provided.
(C) At the West Hampton Conference Center.

represent 대표하다 regional 지방[지역]의

학회에서 누가 우리 회사를 대표할 건가요?
(A) 우리 지역 매니저인 Hamilton 씨요.
(B) 점심 식사는 제공되지 않을 겁니다.
(C) West Hampton 학회장에서요.
[해설] 누가 회사를 대표할 예정인지 묻는 Who 의문문이다.
(A) 구체적인 인물(Mr. Hamilton)을 제시하여 응답했으므로 정답이다.
(B) 점심 식사 제공 여부에 대해 묻지 않았으므로 질문과 무관한 내용의 오답이다.
(C) 구체적인 장소를 언급했으므로 Where 의문문에 적합한 응답이다.

10. BR-BR

What happened at the factory last night?
(A) Some assembly line workers.

(B) I had a day-off yesterday.
(C) I think we can meet the quota.

assembly line (공장의) 조립 라인   day-off 쉬는 날   meet 충족시키다   quota 할당량

어젯밤에 공장에서 무슨 일이 있었어요?
(A) 몇몇의 조립 라인 근로자들이요.
(B) 저는 어제 쉬었어요.
(C) 저는 우리가 할당량을 채울 수 있다고 생각해요.
[해설] 어제 공장에서 있었던 일을 묻는 What 의문문이다.
(A) 질문의 factory에서 연상되는 assembly line을 이용해 혼동을 유도하는 오답이다. 특정 업무 작업자들로 답변했으므로 Who 의문문에 적합한 응답이다.
(B) 어제 쉬었다는 말로 어제 무슨 일이 있었는지 모른다는 것을 우회적으로 표현한 정답이다.
(C) 질문의 factory에서 연상되는 meet the quota(할당량을 채우다)를 이용하여 혼동을 유도하는 오답이다.

11. AU-BR

What room should I prepare for the meeting?
(A) Conference Room B.
(B) About last year's sales figures.
(C) During lunch tomorrow.

sales figures 매출액

회의를 위해서 제가 어느 방을 준비해야 하나요?
(A) B 회의실이요.
(B) 작년 매출액에 대해서요.
(C) 내일 점심 시간 동안이요.
[해설] 어느 방을 준비해야 하는지 묻는 What 의문문이다.
(A) 'B 회의실'이라며 특정 회의실을 분명하게 제시했으므로 정답이다.
(B) 질문의 meeting에서 연상 가능한 sales figures로 혼동을 유도하는 오답이다. 회의의 안건을 묻는 What 의문문에 적합한 응답이다.
(C) 구체적인 시간으로 답했으므로 When 의문문에 적합한 응답이다.

12. US-BR

Who drew this poster design?
(A) I need 50 copies.
(B) Here are some markers.
(C) One of the sales team's interns.

copy (책·신문 등의) 한 부

누가 이 포스터 디자인을 그렸나요?
(A) 저는 50부가 필요합니다.
(B) 여기 마커펜이 좀 있습니다.
(C) 영업팀의 인턴 사원들 중 한 명이요.
[해설] 포스터 디자인을 그린 사람이 누구인지 묻는 Who 의문문이다.
(A) 질문의 poster에서 연상할 수 있는 copies를 이용하여 혼동을 유도한 오답이다. 수량(50 copies)으로 답했으므로 How many 의문문에 적합하다.
(B) 질문의 drew에서 연상되는 그림 도구인 marker를 이용해 혼동을 유도한 오답이다.

(C) 구체적인 부서명과 직위로 답변한 정답이다.

13. US-US

What kind of research are you working on?
(A) Thanks to a reliable source.
(B) Renewable energy.
(C) Yes, everyone is very nice here.

thanks to ~ 덕분에   reliable 믿을 수 있는   source (연구) 자료, (자료의) 출처, 정보원[소식통]   renewable energy 재생 가능 에너지

당신은 어떤 종류의 연구를 하고 있나요?
(A) 믿을 수 있는 소식통 덕분에요.
(B) 재생 가능 에너지요.
(C) 네, 이곳의 모든 사람들이 아주 괜찮아요.
[해설] 무엇에 대해 연구하고 있는지 묻는 What 의문문이다.
(A) 질문의 research에서 연상 가능한 source를 이용해 혼동을 유도한 오답이다.
(B) '재생 가능 에너지'라고 구체적인 연구 분야를 밝혔으므로 정답이다.
(C) 의문사 의문문에는 Yes/No로 답변할 수 없으므로 오답이다.

14. BR-BR

What time will the orientation be over?
(A) The new transfer students.
(B) Yes, I completed the training.
(C) It won't run past noon.

transfer student 전학생   complete 완료하다, 끝마치다   run (얼마의 기간동안) 계속되다

오리엔테이션은 몇 시에 끝날 예정인가요?
(A) 새로 온 전학생들이에요.
(B) 네, 저는 교육을 이수했습니다.
(C) 정오 전에는 끝날 거예요.
[해설] 오리엔테이션이 끝나는 시간을 묻는 What 의문문이다.
(A) 질문의 orientation에서 연상 가능한 new transfer students를 이용해 혼동을 유도하는 오답이다.
(B) 의문사 의문문에는 Yes/No로 응답할 수 없으므로 오답이다.
(C) 정오 전에는 끝날 것이라고 구체적 시점을 제시하여 답변했으므로 정답이다.

15. US-BR

What's on the daily special menu for today?
(A) A vegetarian pasta dish.
(B) I'd like to sit outside.
(C) This restaurant has great reviews.

vegetarian 채식주의자; 채식주의(자)의

오늘의 특별 요리 메뉴에는 무엇이 있나요?
(A) 채식주의자를 위한 파스타 요리입니다.
(B) 저는 밖에 앉고 싶어요.
(C) 이 식당은 후기가 훌륭해요.
[해설] 오늘의 특별 요리 메뉴를 묻는 What 의문문이다.

(A) 오늘의 특별 요리 메뉴를 묻는 질문에 구체적인 음식 메뉴로 답변했으므로 정답이다.
(B) 식당 등에서 어떤 자리에 앉길 원하는지 묻는 질문에 적합한 응답이므로 오답이다.
(C) daily special menu에서 연상되는 restaurant를 이용해 혼동을 유도한 오답이다.

16. BR-US

What logo design will we be using for the new package?
(A) It's still under review.
(B) Yes, we made a new company logo.
(C) You have to put in enough time.

under review 검토 중인 put in (시간·노력을) 들이다

우리가 새 포장 상자에 어떤 로고 디자인을 사용할 것인가요?
(A) 아직 검토 중이에요.
(B) 네, 우리는 새로운 회사 로고를 만들었어요.
(C) 당신은 충분한 시간을 들여야 해요.

[해설] 포장 상자에 어떤 로고 디자인을 사용할지 묻는 What 의문문이다.
(A) 어떤 디자인을 사용할지 묻는 질문에 아직 검토 중이라는 말로, 아직 디자인을 결정하지 못한 상황임을 우회적으로 드러낸 정답이다.
(B) 의문사 의문문에는 Yes/No 답변을 할 수 없을 뿐만 아니라 미래 시제 질문에 과거 시제로 답변했으므로 시제도 일치하지 않는다.
(C) 어떤 디자인을 사용할 것인지 묻는 사람에게 충분한 시간을 들이라고 충고하는 것은 부자연스러우므로 오답이다.

DAY 03

PART 1 실내 사진 (1)

확인 문제

❶ AU

(A) One of the women is speaking to a group of people.
(B) One of the women is writing on a whiteboard.

(A) 여자들 중 한 명이 한 무리의 사람들에게 말하고 있다.
(B) 여자들 중 한 명이 화이트보드에 쓰고 있다.

❷ US

(A) A man is playing a musical instrument.
(B) A man is typing on a keyboard.

musical instrument 악기

(A) 남자가 악기를 연주하고 있다.
(B) 남자가 키보드로 타자를 치고 있다.

❸ BR

(A) A woman is carrying a basket.
(B) A woman is reaching for an item.

reach for ~을 향해 손을 뻗다

(A) 여자가 바구니를 들고 있다.
(B) 여자가 물건을 향해 손을 뻗고 있다.

❹ BR

(A) Some cushions are arranged on a couch.
(B) A light bulb is being replaced.

arrange 정돈하다   couch 소파   light bulb 전구

(A) 소파에 쿠션 몇 개가 정돈되어 있다.
(B) 전구가 교체되고 있다.

❺ US

(A) A man is washing a dish in a sink.
(B) A man is using a mobile phone.

(A) 남자가 싱크대에서 접시를 닦고 있다.
(B) 남자가 휴대전화를 사용하고 있다.

❻ AU

(A) A man is carrying his suitcase.
(B) A woman is standing behind a counter.

(A) 남자가 그의 짐을 나르고 있다.
(B) 여자가 카운터 뒤에 서 있다.

연습 문제

01. US

(1) (A) computers (✗) (B) a screen (○) (C) pointing at (○)
(2)
(A) One of the men is pointing at a screen. [○]
(B) One of the women is distributing documents. [✗]

point at ~을 가리키다   distribute 나누어주다

(A) 남자들 중 한 명이 화면을 가리키고 있다.
(B) 여자들 중 한 명이 서류를 나누어주고 있다.

02. US

(1) (A) a telephone (○) (B) talking (○) (C) writing (✗)
(2)
(A) She is writing on a notepad. [✗]
(B) She is talking on the phone. [○]

(A) 여자가 노트에 (무언가를) 쓰고 있다.
(B) 여자가 전화 통화를 하고 있다.

03. [AU]

(1) (A) a shopping cart (○) (B) picking up (○)
    (C) running (✗)
(2)
(A) They are waiting in line. [✗]
(B) They are picking up some items. [○]

(A) 그들은 줄을 서서 기다리고 있다.
(B) 그들은 몇몇 물건을 고르고 있다.

04. [BR]

(1) (A) a reception area (✗) (B) wiping (○) (C) counter (○)
(2)
(A) A woman is wiping a counter. [○]
(B) A woman is placing a pan on a stove. [✗]

wipe 닦다   counter 작업대

(A) 여자가 작업대를 닦고 있다.
(B) 여자가 가스 레인지에 팬을 놓고 있다.

실전 문제

01. (B)   02. (C)   03. (B)   04. (C)   05. (B)   06. (D)

01. [US]

(A) Some books are being stored in a box.
(B) The workstations are all unoccupied.
(C) The tables have been stacked at a corner.
(D) Some lights are being turned off.

store 저장[보관]하다   workstation 1명의 작업자가 작업하기 위한 자리   unoccupied 비어 있는   stack 쌓다, 포개다   turn off 끄다

(A) 책들이 상자 안에 보관되고 있다.
(B) 자리가 모두 비어 있다.
(C) 테이블들이 구석에 쌓여 있다.
(D) 전등을 끄고 있다.

[해설] 컴퓨터 작업이 가능한 공간의 사진으로, 사람이 등장하지 않는다. 사진 속 모든 사물의 위치나 상태에 집중한다.
(A) 책(books)이나 상자(box)는 보이지 않는다.
(B) 모든 자리가 비어 있는 상태를 정확히 묘사한 정답이다.
(C) 테이블은 쌓여 있지(have been stacked) 않고 잘 배열되어 있다.
(D) 사람이 없는 사진에서 사물을 주어로 하는 수동태 진행(are being turned off)은 오답이다.

02. [BR]

(A) Some items are being placed into a bag.
(B) A shelf is being restocked with items.
(C) A cash register has been mounted on the counter.
(D) A chair is being pushed into a desk.

shelf 선반   restock 다시 채우다   cash register 금전 등록기

mount 고정시키다, 올려 놓다   counter 카운터, 계산대

(A) 몇몇 제품들이 가방에 담기고 있다.
(B) 선반이 제품들로 채워지고 있다.
(C) 금전 등록기가 카운터 위에 놓여 있다.
(D) 의자를 책상 밑으로 밀어 넣고 있다.

[해설] 여자와 남자가 상점 계산대에 있는 모습으로, 인물의 동작이나 상태는 물론 주변 사물의 위치와 상태에도 주목해야 한다.
(A) 가방(bag)은 보이지 않는다.
(B) 선반이 보이기는 하지만 현재 다시 채워지고 있는 중(being restocked)은 아니다.
(C) 여자 앞의 카운터 위에 놓여 있는 금전 등록기를 바르게 묘사한 정답이다.
(D) 여자가 의자에 앉아 있으나 의자를 책상 밑으로 밀어 넣고 있는 모습은 아니다.

03. [US]

(A) Some bread is being pulled out of an oven.
(B) Vegetables have been put in a basket.
(C) There are some dishes on a kitchen sink.
(D) A pot is boiling on a gas stove.

pull out of ~에서 꺼내다   vegetable 채소   pot 냄비, 솥   boil 끓다, 끓이다   gas stove 가스 레인지

(A) 빵을 오븐에서 꺼내고 있다.
(B) 채소가 바구니에 담겨 있다.
(C) 주방 싱크대에 접시들이 있다.
(D) 냄비가 가스 레인지 위에서 끓고 있다.

[해설] 두 명의 요리사가 음식을 준비하고 있는 사진으로, 두 사람의 개별 동작은 물론 주변 사물의 위치와 상태를 파악해야 한다.
(A) 사진에서 빵(bread)이나 오븐(oven)은 보이지 않는다.
(B) 남자 옆의 바구니에 채소가 담겨 있는 것을 정확히 묘사한 정답이다.
(C) 싱크대(kitchen sink)는 보이지 않는다.
(D) 가스 레인지(gas stove) 위에 올려진 냄비(pot)는 보이지 않는다.

04. [BR]

(A) One of the men is distributing a handout.
(B) A woman is working on a computer.
(C) Some people are looking at documents.
(D) Some people are writing on a board.

distribute 나누어 주다   handout 인쇄물, 유인물

(A) 남자들 중 한 명이 인쇄물을 나누어 주고 있다.
(B) 여자가 컴퓨터로 작업하고 있다.
(C) 사람들이 문서를 보고 있다.
(D) 사람들이 보드에 무언가를 적고 있다.

[해설] 3명의 사람이 사무실에 있는 사진으로, 각 인물의 개별 동작이나 공통 동작에 초점을 맞추고 들어야 한다.
(A) 인쇄물이 보이기는 하지만 인쇄물을 나누어 주는(distributing) 사람은 없다.
(B) 여자는 컴퓨터로 작업하고 있지(working on a computer) 않다.
(C) 사진 속의 두 남자가 각자 앞에 있는 문서를 보고 있는 모습을 묘사한 정답이다.

(D) 사람들 뒤쪽으로 보드가 보이기는 하지만 무언가를 적고 있는 (writing) 사람은 없다.

05. BR

(A) A woman is wiping a display window.
(B) Some containers have been filled with items.
(C) A woman is carrying a tray.
(D) A sign board is next to a door.

wipe 닦다   display window 진열창   container 그릇, 용기
be filled with ~로 채워지다   carry 나르다   tray 쟁반
sign board 간판

(A) 여자가 진열창을 닦고 있다.
(B) 몇몇 용기들이 상품으로 채워져 있다.
(C) 여자가 쟁반을 나르고 있다.
(D) 간판이 문 옆에 있다.

[해설] 여자가 진열창 안을 들여다보고 있는 사진으로, 인물의 동작 및 주변 사물의 위치/상태를 잘 살펴야 한다.
(A) 여자는 진열창을 닦고 있는(wiping) 것이 아니라 진열창 안의 무언가를 들여다보고 있다.
(B) 진열대 위에 가지런히 정리된 용기들 안에 상품이 담겨 있는 것을 묘사한 정답이다.
(C) 쟁반을 나르는(carrying a tray) 사람은 보이지 않는다.
(D) 사진에서 간판(sign board)은 보이지 않는다.

06. AU

(A) The woman is paying for a purchase.
(B) The man is removing his apron.
(C) The woman is operating a machine.
(D) The man is weighing a bag on a scale.

remove (옷 등을) 벗다   apron 앞치마   operate 가동[조작]하다
weigh 무게를 달다   scale 저울

(A) 여자가 물건 값을 지불하고 있다.
(B) 남자가 앞치마를 벗고 있다.
(C) 여자가 기계를 조작하고 있다.
(D) 남자가 저울로 봉지의 무게를 재고 있다.

[해설] 앞치마를 입고 작업 중인 두 사람의 사진으로, 두 사람의 개별 동작에 주목해서 들어야 한다.
(A) 여자는 앞에 놓인 무언가를 퍼서 담고 있을 뿐 돈을 지불하고(paying) 있지는 않다.
(B) 남자는 앞치마를 착용한 상태이고 앞치마를 벗고 있는(removing his apron) 중은 아니다.
(C) 여자 뒤로 기계가 보이기는 하지만 여자가 이것을 조작하고 (operating) 있지는 않다.
(D) 남자가 앞에 놓인 저울로 봉지에 든 것의 무게를 재는 모습을 묘사한 정답이다.

PART 2   How 의문문 (1)

확인 문제

❶ US-BR

How do you turn this coffee maker on?
(A) Push the button here.
(B) A cup of water, please.

이 커피 메이커를 어떻게 켜요?
(A) 여기 있는 버튼을 누르세요.
(B) 물 한 잔 부탁합니다.

❷ BR-US

How often do you attend the seminar?
(A) For three hours.
(B) Once a month.

그 세미나에 얼마나 자주 참석하시나요?
(A) 3시간 동안이요.
(B) 한 달에 한 번이요.

❸ BR-BR

How many brochures do you need for the show?
(A) Thirty would be enough.
(B) Sure, I'd be happy to.

그 쇼에 얼마나 많은 책자가 필요한가요?
(A) 30개면 충분할 거예요.
(B) 물론이죠, 기꺼이 할게요.

❹ AU-BR

How much is the ticket for the concert?
(A) Yes, it's expensive.
(B) About 50 dollars.

그 콘서트 표는 얼마인가요?
(A) 네, 비싸요.
(B) 50달러 정도예요.

❺ US-US

How long have you been living in New York?
(A) Since I was twenty.
(B) Three years ago.

뉴욕에 사신 지는 얼마나 되셨나요?
(A) 제가 20살일 때부터요.
(B) 3년 전에요.

❻ US-AU

How quickly will the weekly report be done?
(A) I'll finish it by tomorrow.
(B) It's valid only for this week.

주간 보고서가 얼마나 빨리 마무리될까요?
(A) 내일까지 끝내겠습니다.
(B) 이번 주 동안만 유효합니다.

연습 문제

01. (A) 02. (B) 03. (B) 04. (A) 05. (A) 06. (A)
07. (A) 08. (B)

01. US-BR

How much did the transportation cost?
(A) I'll have to check the receipt. [O]
(B) Yes, subway is much faster. [x]

교통편이 얼마가 들었나요?
(A) 영수증을 확인해봐야 해요.
(B) 네, 지하철이 훨씬 더 빨라요.

02. US-BR

How long will you be staying in Tokyo?
(A) I'll stay at my cousin's place. [x]
(B) Only three days. [O]

도쿄에 얼마나 오래 머무르실 건가요?
(A) 저는 제 사촌 집에서 머무를 거예요.
(B) 3일 동안만요.

03. US-AU

How did you manage to arrive so early?
(A) No, I worked late last night. [x]
(B) I took a different route. [O]

어떻게 그렇게 일찍 도착하실 수 있었어요?
(A) 아니요, 저는 어젯밤에 늦게까지 일했어요.
(B) 저는 다른 길로 왔어요.

04. BR-US

How soon can you finish the work?
(A) Everything will be done by next Monday. [O]
(B) Daniel will be here soon. [x]

그 일을 얼마나 빨리 끝낼 수 있나요?
(A) 다음 주 월요일까지 다 끝날 거예요.
(B) Daniel이 곧 여기 올 거예요.

05. AU-BR

How many office supplies should I order?
(A) We need quite a few. [O]
(B) The parts will be ordered this afternoon. [x]

제가 얼마나 많은 사무용품을 주문해야 하죠?
(A) 우리는 꽤 많이 필요합니다.
(B) 부품들은 오늘 오후에 주문될 것입니다.

06. BR-BR

How should I organize these files?
(A) In an alphabetical order. [O]
(B) He filed a lawsuit. [x]

이 파일들을 어떻게 정리해야 하나요?
(A) 알파벳 순으로요.
(B) 그는 소송을 제기했어요.

07. US-BR

How can I change the reservation?
(A) May I have your name, please? [O]
(B) Yes, you can start now. [x]

예약을 어떻게 변경할 수 있나요?
(A) 성함을 알려주시겠어요?
(B) 네, 지금 시작하셔도 됩니다.

08. US-AU

How much longer do you need to fix the machine?
(A) No, the printer is over there. [x]
(B) Just a couple of hours. [O]

기계를 수리하는 데 시간이 얼마나 더 오래 필요하시나요?
(A) 아뇨, 프린터는 저기 있어요.
(B) 몇 시간이면 됩니다.

실전 문제

01. (B) 02. (C) 03. (B) 04. (C) 05. (B) 06. (A)
07. (C) 08. (B) 09. (A) 10. (C) 11. (A) 12. (A)
13. (B) 14. (C) 15. (B) 16. (B)

01. BR-US

How do you set the timer on this unit?
(A) I don't know what time it is.
(B) Use the remote control.
(C) Yes, it will arrive on schedule.

set the timer 타이머를 설정하다   unit 기구, 장치
remote control 리모컨   on schedule 예정된 시간에

이 장치의 타이머를 어떻게 설정하나요?
(A) 몇 시인지 모르겠어요.
(B) 리모컨을 사용하세요.
(C) 네, 그것은 예정된 시간에 도착할 거예요.

[해설] 장치의 타이머 설정 방법을 묻는 How 의문문이다.
(A) 질문의 timer에서 연상되는 time을 이용해 혼동을 유도하는 오답이다.
(B) 리모컨을 사용하라며 구체적인 방법을 제시한 정답이다.
(C) 의문사 의문문에는 Yes/No로 응답할 수 없으므로 오답이다.

02. US-US

How are we going to get to New York for the conference?
(A) Before the registration deadline.
(B) It seems like it will be informative.
(C) HR will reserve plane tickets for us.

registration 등록   deadline 마감일   informative 유익한

우리는 콘퍼런스를 위해서 뉴욕에 어떻게 갈 예정인가요?

(A) 등록 마감일 전에요.
(B) 유용할 것 같아요.
(C) 인사부에서 우리를 위해 비행기 티켓을 예약해줄 거예요.

[해설] 콘퍼런스를 위해서 뉴욕에 가는 방법을 묻는 How 의문문이다.
(A) 질문의 conference에서 연상 가능한 registration을 이용해 혼동을 유도하는 오답으로, 시간 표현 before가 있으므로 When 의문문에 적합한 응답이다.
(B) 질문의 conference에서 연상 가능한 informative를 이용해 혼동을 유도하는 오답으로, 콘퍼런스가 어떨 것 같은지 묻는 질문에 어울리는 응답이다.
(C) 인사부에서 비행기 티켓을 예약해줄 거라는 말로 항공편을 이용할 것임을 우회적으로 전달하고 있으므로 정답이다.

03. US-AU

How do you enter information into the new database?
(A) Yes, I was able to learn a lot.
(B) I haven't installed that software yet.
(C) We should use the back entrance.

install 설치하다 back entrance 뒷문

어떻게 새로운 데이터베이스에 정보를 입력하나요?
(A) 네, 저는 많이 배울 수 있었어요.
(B) 저는 아직 그 소프트웨어를 설치하지 않았어요.
(C) 우리는 뒷문을 이용해야 해요.

[해설] 새로운 데이터베이스에 정보를 입력하는 방법을 묻는 How 의문문이다.
(A) 의문사 의문문에는 Yes/No로 답할 수 없으므로 오답이다.
(B) 정보 입력과 관련된 소프트웨어를 설치하지 않아 정보 입력 방법을 잘 모른다는 뜻이므로 정답이다.
(C) 질문의 enter와 발음이 유사한 entrance를 이용해 혼동을 유도하는 오답이다.

04. BR-BR

How many guests will we be serving?
(A) A highly-rated caterer.
(B) Sure, I'll take a look at the menu.
(C) Around fifty.

serve (식당에서 음식을) 제공하다, (상점에서 손님) 시중을 들다
highly-rated 높이 평가받는 caterer (행사의) 음식 공급 업체

우리는 얼마나 많은 손님을 응대할 것인가요?
(A) 높이 평가받는 음식 공급 업체입니다.
(B) 물론이죠, 제가 메뉴를 볼게요.
(C) 약 50명이요.

[해설] 응대하게 될 손님의 인원수를 묻는 How many 의문문이다.
(A) 질문의 guest와 serving에서 연상 가능한 caterer를 이용해 혼동을 유도하는 오답이다.
(B) Yes/No 응답과 마찬가지로 Sure도 의문사 의문문에 대한 응답이 될 수 없으므로 오답이다.
(C) '약 50명'이라고 구체적인 수치를 제시했으므로 정답이다.

05. US-US

How many volunteers signed up for the cleanup project?
(A) I'll finish writing a proposal for the project.
(B) 20 so far.
(C) It looks clean to me.

volunteer 자원봉사자 sign up for ~에 등록하다, ~을 신청하다
cleanup (대)청소 proposal 제안(서)

대청소 프로젝트에 얼마나 많은 자원봉사자들이 등록했나요?
(A) 저는 그 프로젝트의 제안서 작성을 마칠 거예요.
(B) 지금까지 20명이요.
(C) 제가 보기엔 깨끗하네요.

[해설] 몇 명의 자원봉사자들이 등록했는지 묻는 How many 의문문이다.
(A) 질문의 project를 반복 사용하여 혼동을 유도한 오답이다.
(B) 20명이라는 정확한 숫자로 답변했으므로 정답이다.
(C) 질문의 cleanup과 발음이 유사한 clean을 사용하여 혼동을 유도한 오답이다.

06. US-BR

How often do you go out to eat?
(A) Almost every day for lunch.
(B) How much would you like?
(C) My favorite restaurant.

얼마나 자주 외식을 하나요?
(A) 점심은 거의 매일이요.
(B) 얼마나 원하세요?
(C) 제가 가장 좋아하는 식당이요.

[해설] 얼마나 자주 외식을 하는지 빈도를 묻는 How often 의문문이다.
(A) 점심은 거의 '매일' 외식을 한다고 구체적인 빈도로 답변했으므로 정답이다.
(B) 외식 빈도를 묻는 질문에 '얼마나 원하세요?'라고 되묻는 것은 어색하므로 오답이다.
(C) 질문의 go out to eat에서 연상 가능한 restaurant를 이용해 혼동을 유도하는 오답이다.

07. BR-US

How much will the renovations cost?
(A) Yes, it looks much better.
(B) By the end of the summer.
(C) I will send the quote to your e-mail.

renovation 수리, 수선, 보수 cost (값·비용이) ~ 들다
quote(= quotation) 견적

수리 비용이 얼마나 들까요?
(A) 네, 그게 훨씬 더 보기 좋아요.
(B) 여름이 끝날 때까지요.
(C) 견적을 당신의 이메일로 보내줄게요.

[해설] 수리 비용이 얼마나 들지 비용을 묻는 How much 의문문이다.
(A) 의문사 의문문에는 Yes/No 답변을 할 수 없으므로 오답이다.
(B) 시간 부사구로 답변했으므로 When 의문문에 적합한 응답이다.
(C) 직접적으로 구체적인 금액을 제시하는 대신 이메일로 견적을 보내주겠

다고 답변한 것은 견적서를 보고 직접 확인하라는 의도이므로 정답이다.

08. AU-BR

How long are you waiting for your pizza order?
(A) Our cheese is imported from France.
(B) Approximately 30 minutes.
(C) What toppings would you like?

order 주문(하다)   import 수입하다   approximately 거의

얼마 동안 피자 주문을 기다리고 있는 중인가요?
(A) 우리 치즈는 프랑스에서 수입한 것이에요.
(B) 거의 30분이요.
(C) 어떤 토핑을 원하세요?

[해설] 피자를 얼마나 오래 기다리고 있는지 소요 시간을 묻는 How long 의문문이다.
(A) 질문의 pizza에서 연상되는 cheese를 이용해 혼동을 유도하는 오답이다.
(B) '거의 30분'이라는 구체적인 소요 시간으로 답변했으므로 정답이다.
(C) 질문의 pizza에서 연상되는 toppings를 이용해 혼동을 유도하는 오답이다.

09. US-BR

How soon can you start working at this branch?
(A) Right from next Monday.
(B) Many tall trees.
(C) In my cover letter.

branch 지사, 지점; 나뭇가지   cover letter 자기소개서

이 지점에서 얼마나 빨리 근무를 시작할 수 있나요?
(A) 다음 주 월요일부터 바로요.
(B) 많은 키가 큰 나무들이요.
(C) 제 자기소개서에요.

[해설] 얼마나 빨리 근무를 시작할 수 있는지, 즉 언제부터 근무가 가능한지 묻는 How soon 의문문이다.
(A) '다음 주 월요일부터 바로'라며 구체적 시점으로 답변했으므로 정답이다.
(B) 질문의 branch를 '나뭇가지'로 이해할 경우 연상되는 tree를 이용하여 혼동을 유도하는 오답이다.
(C) 보통 취업 면접 시 지원자에게 근무 시작 가능일을 물을 때 하는 질문인 점을 고려하여, 입사 지원과 연관된 어휘인 cover letter로 혼동을 유도하는 오답이다.

10. BR-BR

How long was the episode you watched last night?
(A) Yes, the critics loved it.
(B) A new movie theater.
(C) Just one hour.

critic 비평가, 평론가

당신이 어젯밤에 본 에피소드는 얼마나 길었나요?
(A) 네, 비평가들이 그것을 좋아했어요.
(B) 새로운 영화관이에요.
(C) 겨우 한 시간이요.

[해설] 어젯밤 시청한 에피소드의 길이, 즉 소요 시간을 묻는 How long 의문문이다.
(A) 의문사 의문문에는 Yes/No로 답변할 수 없으므로 오답이다.
(B) 질문의 watched에서 연상되는 movie를 이용해 혼동을 유도하는 오답이다.
(C) '겨우 한 시간'이라며 구체적인 소요 시간으로 답변했으므로 정답이다.

11. BR-AU

How long is the orientation supposed to last?
(A) It depends on how many questions there are.
(B) We'll be welcoming the new employees.
(C) There should be enough handbooks.

last 계속하다, 지속하다   depend on ~에 달려 있다, 좌우되다
handbook 안내서

오리엔테이션은 얼마 동안 지속될 예정인가요?
(A) 질문이 얼마나 많은지에 달려 있어요.
(B) 우리가 새로운 직원들을 맞이할 거예요.
(C) 안내서가 충분히 있어야 해요.

[해설] 오리엔테이션 지속 시간을 묻는 How long 의문문이다.
(A) 질문이 얼마나 많은지에 따라 다르다는 말로 오리엔테이션 지속 시간이 정해져 있지 않음을 나타내고 있으므로 정답이다.
(B) 질문의 orientation에서 연상 가능한 new employees를 이용하여 혼동을 유도하는 오답이다.
(C) 질문의 orientation에서 연상 가능한 handbook을 이용하여 혼동을 유도하는 오답이다.

12. US-BR

How much did we spend on office supplies last quarter?
(A) Nearly four thousand dollars.
(B) In the supply closet.
(C) Usually by the next day.

office supplies 사무용품   quarter 분기   nearly 거의
supply closet 비품 창고

우리가 지난 분기에 사무용품에 얼마나 많이 지출했나요?
(A) 거의 4천 달러요.
(B) 비품 창고 안에요.
(C) 보통 다음 날까지요.

[해설] 사무용품에 쓴 돈이 얼마인지 금액을 묻는 How much 의문문이다.
(A) '거의 4천 달러'라는 구체적 금액으로 답변했으므로 정답이다.
(B) 장소 부사구로 답변했으므로 사무용품이 어디 있는지 묻는 Where 의문문에 적합한 응답이다.
(C) 시간 부사구로 답변했으므로 When 의문문에 적합한 응답이다.

13. BR-US

How often do you take a flight?
(A) You can upgrade to business class.
(B) A couple times a year.
(C) May I see your boarding pass?

당신은 얼마나 자주 비행기를 타나요?
(A) 당신은 비즈니스석으로 업그레이드하실 수 있습니다.

(B) 일 년에 두어 번이요.
(C) 탑승권을 보여주시겠습니까?

[해설] 얼마나 자주 비행기를 타는지 빈도를 묻는 How often 의문문이다.
(A) 질문의 flight에서 연상되는 upgrade to business class를 이용한 오답이다.
(B) '일 년에 두어 번'이라는 빈도로 답변했으므로 정답이다.
(C) 질문의 flight에서 연상되는 boarding pass를 이용한 오답이다.

14. US-US

How old is your bookstore?
(A) An anniversary promotion.
(B) Our customers are highly satisfied.
(C) We've been in business for 20 years.

highly 매우   be in business 영업을 하고 있다

당신의 서점은 얼마나 오래되었나요?
(A) 기념일 판촉 행사입니다.
(B) 저희 고객들이 매우 만족해 합니다.
(C) 저희는 20년 동안 운영해오고 있습니다.

[해설] 서점이 얼마나 오래되었는지, 즉 서점이 얼마나 오랫동안 운영되어 왔는지 묻는 How old 의문문이다.
(A) 의문사 What을 사용해 서점에서 어떤 행사를 열고 있는지 물어보는 질문에 할 수 있는 응답이다.
(B) 질문의 bookstore에서 연상되는 customers를 이용해 혼동을 유도하는 오답이다.
(C) '20년 동안 운영해오고 있다'며 구체적인 기간을 제시했으므로 정답이다.

15. BR-US

How long will it take to repaint the office?
(A) Okay, see you this afternoon.
(B) Probably a day or two.
(C) It's a very popular app.

repaint 페인트를 다시 칠하다   popular 인기 있는

사무실에 페인트를 다시 칠하는 데 얼마나 걸릴까요?
(A) 좋아요, 오늘 오후에 봬요.
(B) 아마 하루나 이틀이요.
(C) 그건 매우 인기 있는 앱이에요.

[해설] 페인트를 다시 칠하는 데 걸리는 시간을 묻는 How long 의문문이다.
(A) 의문사 의문문에는 Yes와 비슷한 의미인 Okay로 답변할 수 없으므로 오답이다.
(B) '하루나 이틀'이라며 소요 시간으로 답변했으므로 정답이다.
(C) 질문과 상관없는 답변이므로 오답이다.

16. US-AU

How soon can you complete the digitization project?
(A) This is a very useful database.
(B) I should be finished by the end of the week.
(C) Please check the file cabinet.

complete 완료하다   digitization 디지털화   useful 유용한

얼마나 빨리 디지털화 프로젝트를 완료할 수 있나요?
(A) 이것은 아주 유용한 데이터베이스입니다.
(B) 저는 이번 주말까지는 끝낼 겁니다.
(C) 서류 캐비닛을 확인하시기 바랍니다.

[해설] 얼마나 빨리 디지털화 프로젝트를 완료할 수 있는지, 즉, 완료 시점을 묻는 How soon 의문문이다.
(A) 질문의 digitization처럼 정보 기술 관련 어휘인 database를 이용해 혼동을 유도하는 오답이다.
(B) 주말까지 끝내겠다고 구체적 시점을 제시하여 답변했으므로 정답이다.
(C) 특정 공간을 확인하라는 응답은 Where 의문문에 적합하다.

DAY 04

PART 1 실내 사진 (2)

확인 문제

① AU

(A) A man is looking at a menu.
(B) A woman is holding a serving tray.

(A) 남자가 메뉴를 보고 있다.
(B) 여자가 서빙 쟁반을 들고 있다.

② US

(A) A woman is reaching for a book on a shelf.
(B) Some books are being stacked on a cart.

reach for ~을 향해 손을 뻗다   shelf 선반, 책장   stack 쌓다

(A) 여자가 책장에 있는 책을 향해 손을 뻗고 있다.
(B) 책들이 카트 위에 쌓이고 있다. (책을 카트 위에 쌓고 있다.)

③ US

(A) There are some artifacts on display.
(B) The display glass is being wiped.

artifact 공예품

(A) 몇몇 공예품들이 전시되어 있다.
(B) 진열 유리가 닦이고 있다.

④ BR

(A) A woman is turning on a computer.
(B) A woman is looking into a microscope.

turn on ~을 켜다

(A) 여자가 컴퓨터를 켜고 있다.
(B) 여자가 현미경을 들여다보고 있다.

❺ [AU]

(A) Some cartons are being loaded into a truck.
(B) People are wearing safety vests.

carton 상자   safety vest 안전 조끼

(A) 몇몇 상자들이 트럭에 실리고 있다.
(B) 사람들이 안전 조끼를 입고 있다.

❻ [BR]

(A) A man is pulling a suitcase.
(B) A man is claiming his baggage.

(A) 남자가 여행 가방을 끌고 있다.
(B) 남자가 수하물을 찾고 있다.

연습 문제

01. [AU]

(1) (A) servers (O) (B) tables (O) (C) food (X)
(2)
(A) They are serving food to diners. [X]
(B) They are setting the tables. [O]

(A) 그들은 식사하는 사람들에게 음식을 서빙하고 있다.
(B) 그들은 테이블을 차리고 있다.

02. [US]

(1) (A) bookshelves (O) (B) reading books (X)
    (C) armchairs (O)
(2)
(A) A chair is being assembled. [X]
(B) Some armchairs are unoccupied. [O]

(A) 의자가 조립되고 있다.
(B) 몇몇 팔걸이 의자가 비어 있다.

03. [AU]

(1) (A) containers (O) (B) looking into (X)
    (C) a drawer (X)
(2)
(A) A woman is looking into a drawer. [X]
(B) Some containers are laid out on a workstation.
    [O]

(A) 여자가 서랍을 들여다보고 있다.
(B) 몇몇 용기가 자리에 놓여 있다.

04. [BR]

(1) (A) conveyor (O) (B) sweeping (X) (C) a box (O)
(2)
(A) A box has been opened on the conveyor. [O]
(B) An item is being put into a carton. [X]

(A) 상자가 컨베이어 위에 열려 있다.
(B) 물건이 상자 안에 넣어지고 있다.

실전 문제

01. (C)   **02.** (D)   **03.** (D)   **04.** (C)   **05.** (B)   **06.** (B)

01. [US]

(A) The woman is waiting in line.
(B) The man is standing in front of an audience.
(C) They are holding dishes.
(D) They are facing each other.

audience 청중, 관중   face each other 마주 보다

(A) 여자가 줄을 서서 기다리고 있다.
(B) 남자가 청중들 앞에 서 있다.
(C) 그들은 접시를 들고 있다.
(D) 그들은 마주 보고 있다.

[해설] 뷔페 식당에서 음식을 담고 있는 사람들의 사진으로, 두 사람의 개별 동작 및 공통 동작을 잘 살펴야 한다.
(A) 식당에 사람이 별로 없으므로 여자는 줄을 서서 기다리고(waiting in line) 있지 않다.
(B) 사진에서 '청중(audience)'이라고 할 만한 사람들은 보이지 않는다.
(C) 음식을 담기 위해 접시를 들고 있는 두 사람을 바르게 묘사한 정답이다.
(D) 두 사람은 모두 음식을 보고 있지 마주 보고(facing each other) 있지 않다.

02. [AU]

(A) There are water jars on the table.
(B) One of the men is approaching a cashier.
(C) A group of people is dining outside.
(D) Some food is being served.

jar 병, 단지   approach 다가가다   cashier 계산원   dine 식사를 하다   serve (음식을) 차려 주다, 내다

(A) 테이블 위에 물병들이 있다.
(B) 남자들 중 한 명이 계산원에게 다가가고 있다.
(C) 한 무리의 사람들이 야외에서 식사하고 있다.
(D) 음식이 서빙되고 있다.

[해설] 다수의 사람들이 식당에 있는 모습으로, 등장 인물의 동작/상태와 주변 사물의 위치에 주의하며 들어야 한다.
(A) 사람들이 앉아 있는 테이블이 여러 개 보이지만 테이블 위의 물병들(water jars)은 확인되지 않는다.
(B) 사진에서 계산원(cashier)은 보이지 않는다.
(C) 사람들이 식사하고 있는 곳은 실내이지 야외(outside)가 아니다.
(D) 사진 중앙에 서 있는 남자가 음식을 테이블에 내려놓고 있는 모습을 묘사한 정답이다.

03. [BR]

(A) One of the men is talking on the phone.
(B) One of the men is writing on a notepad.
(C) One of the men is folding a coat.
(D) One of the men is typing on a keyboard.

notepad 메모지　fold 접다, 개키다

(A) 남자들 중 한 명이 전화 통화를 하고 있다.
(B) 남자들 중 한 명이 메모지에 뭔가를 쓰고 있다.
(C) 남자들 중 한 명이 코트를 접고 있다.
(D) 남자들 중 한 명이 키보드로 타자를 치고 있다.

[해설] 공항 검색대를 배경으로 여러 인물들이 등장하는 사진으로, 각 인물의 동작에 집중한다.
(A) 전화 통화를 하는(talking on the phone) 사람은 보이지 않는다.
(B) 메모를 하고 있는(writing on a notepad) 사람은 보이지 않는다.
(C) 코트를 접는(folding a coat) 사람은 보이지 않는다.
(D) 사진 우측의 검색관이 키보드로 무언가를 입력하는 모습을 묘사한 정답이다.

04. [BR]

(A) Passengers are reading an information board.
(B) People are checking in their baggage.
(C) The train is stopped at the platform.
(D) Some suitcases are loaded on a train.

passenger 승객　check in (비행기 등을 탈 때) ~을 부치다
baggage (여행용) 짐, 수하물　platform 승강장

(A) 승객들이 안내판을 읽고 있다.
(B) 사람들이 짐을 부치고 있다.
(C) 열차가 승강장에 멈춰 있다.
(D) 여행 가방들이 열차에 실려 있다.

[해설] 열차 승강장을 배경으로 한 사진으로, 사진 속 모든 요소들을 꼼꼼히 확인하면서 들어야 한다.
(A) 멀리 사람들이 보이기는 하지만 안내판을 읽고 있는지(reading an information board)는 알 수 없다.
(B) 짐을 부치는(checking in their baggage) 사람들은 보이지 않는다.
(C) 승강장에 멈춰 서 있는 기차의 모습을 바르게 묘사한 정답이다.
(D) 열차에 여행 가방이 실려 있는(loaded on a train) 모습은 보이지 않는다.

05. [US]

(A) Some people are leaning against the wall.
(B) A man is pointing to a statue.
(C) The men are hanging a painting.
(D) Some people are sitting on a floor.

lean against ~에 기대다　statue 조각상　hang 걸다

(A) 몇몇 사람들이 벽에 기대어 있다.
(B) 한 남자가 조각상을 가리키고 있다.
(C) 남자들이 그림을 걸고 있다.
(D) 몇몇 사람들이 바닥에 앉아 있다.

[해설] 미술관의 작품들을 관람하고 있는 사람들의 모습으로, 각 인물들의 개별 동작 및 공통 동작을 모두 잘 파악해야 한다.
(A) 사람들이 벽에 기대어(leaning against the wall) 있지 않다.
(B) 안내원으로 보이는 중앙의 남자가 조각상을 가리키고 있는 모습을 정확히 묘사한 정답이다.
(C) 그림을 걸고 있는(hanging a painting) 사람은 보이지 않는다.

(D) 사람들은 바닥에 앉아 있지(sitting on a floor) 않고 모두 서 있다.

06. [AU]

(A) One of the men is writing on a board.
(B) Some documents are spread out on a desk.
(C) One of the men is seated on a chair.
(D) Chairs have been arranged in a circle.

spread out 넓게 펼치다　arrange 정리하다, 배열하다

(A) 남자들 중 한 명이 보드에 뭔가를 쓰고 있다.
(B) 서류들이 책상 위에 펼쳐져 있다.
(C) 남자 중 한 명이 의자에 앉아 있다.
(D) 의자들이 둥글게 배치되어 있다.

[해설] 여러 사람들이 테이블 주위에 모여 있는 사진으로, 각 인물의 동작과 주변 사물의 위치/상태에 주의하며 들어야 한다.
(A) 보드에 뭔가를 쓰고 있는(writing on a board) 사람은 없다.
(B) 책상 위에 서류가 펼쳐져 있는 것을 묘사한 정답이다.
(C) 모든 사람들이 서 있으므로 앉아 있는(is seated) 남자는 없다.
(D) 사람들 뒤로 의자가 보이긴 하지만 둥글게(in a circle) 놓여 있지는 않다.

PART 2　How 의문문 (2) / Why 의문문

확인 문제

① [BR-US]

How was the movie you saw yesterday?
(A) I am very tired at the moment.
(B) It was disappointing.

당신이 어제 봤던 영화는 어땠나요?
(A) 저는 지금 매우 피곤해요.
(B) 실망스러웠어요.

② [US-US]

How do you like your new company?
(A) I like how flexible they are.
(B) You look great.

당신의 새 회사는 어떤가요?
(A) 그들이 융통성이 있어서 좋아요.
(B) 당신 아주 좋아 보여요.

③ [AU-BR]

How about we stop by a coffee shop?
(A) I have been working here for two years.
(B) I know a nice place not far from here.

우리 커피숍에 들르는 게 어때요?
(A) 저는 이곳에서 2년 동안 근무하고 있어요.
(B) 제가 여기서 멀지 않은 좋은 곳을 알아요.

④ US-AU

Why was everyone so busy in the warehouse?
(A) Yes, I read about it.
(B) A shipment arrived late due to the storm.

창고에서 다들 왜 그렇게 바빴나요?
(A) 네, 그것에 대해 읽었어요.
(B) 폭풍 때문에 물건이 늦게 왔어요.

⑤ US-US

Why did you call the technician?
(A) To ask him to check some wiring.
(B) It's cold this morning.

왜 기술자에게 연락하셨나요?
(A) 배선 점검을 요청하기 위해서요.
(B) 오늘 아침 춥네요.

⑥ US-BR

Why don't we order some more sandwiches for attendees?
(A) Once your order is confirmed.
(B) Okay. That sounds good.

참석자들을 위해서 샌드위치를 좀 더 주문하는 게 어떨까요?
(A) 당신의 주문이 승인되면요.
(B) 그래요. 좋을 것 같아요.

 연습 문제

01. (B) 02. (B) 03. (A) 04. (B) 05. (B) 06. (A)
07. (B) 08. (A)

01. BR-BR

How do you like the new projectors and computers?
(A) The project is ahead of schedule. [×]
(B) They're working well so far. [○]

ahead of schedule 예정보다 앞서

새 프로젝터와 컴퓨터들은 어때요?
(A) 그 프로젝트는 예정보다 앞서 있어요.
(B) 지금까지는 잘 작동하고 있습니다.

02. US-US

Why are they vacuuming the office?
(A) Yes, I'm available. [×]
(B) It's our regular cleaning day. [○]

vacuum 청소기로 청소하다

왜 그들이 사무실을 청소기로 청소하고 있나요?
(A) 네, 저는 가능해요.
(B) 우리의 정기적인 청소 날이에요.

03. BR-US

How about meeting for lunch at noon?
(A) Sure, I wanted to try that new Italian restaurant. [○]
(B) I met her on my way to work. [×]

on one's way to ~로 가는 길에

우리 점심 먹으러 12시에 만나는 거 어때요?
(A) 좋아요, 저는 그 새로 생긴 이탈리안 레스토랑에 가보고 싶었어요.
(B) 저는 출근하는 길에 그녀를 만났어요.

04. AU-BR

Why do you close the store early today?
(A) They open at eight in the morning. [×]
(B) Because of the unexpected bad weather. [○]

unexpected 예상치 못한

오늘은 왜 상점을 일찍 닫으시나요?
(A) 그들은 아침 8시에 문을 열어요.
(B) 예상치 못한 나쁜 날씨 때문에요.

05. BR-AU

Why isn't Paul answering his phone this morning?
(A) No, I phoned him yesterday. [×]
(B) He's taking a sick leave. [○]

sick leave 병가

Paul이 오늘 아침에 왜 전화를 받지 않나요?
(A) 아뇨, 저는 어제 그에게 전화했어요.
(B) 그는 병가를 냈어요.

06. US-AU

Why did you file a complaint?
(A) Because my order has been delayed for a week. [○]
(B) I think that's a great idea. [×]

file a complaint 불만을 제기하다

왜 불만을 제기하셨나요?
(A) 제 주문이 일주일 동안 지연되었어요.
(B) 그거 좋은 생각 같아요.

07. US-BR

How was last night's employee award ceremony?
(A) Let me introduce the new intern. [×]
(B) Everything was nice. [○]

어젯밤의 직원 시상식 어땠어요?
(A) 새 인턴을 소개해 드릴게요.
(B) 모든 게 좋았어요.

08. BR-US

Why don't you bring up this issue at the board meeting?
(A) No, I'd rather not. [O]
(B) Sorry, we don't have this month's issue. [×]

issue 사안, (잡지 등의) 호

이 사안을 이사진 회의에서 제기하는 게 어때요?
(A) 아뇨, 안 할래요.
(B) 죄송합니다, 이번 달 호는 없어요.

실전 문제

01. (A)	02. (B)	03. (C)	04. (A)	05. (C)	06. (C)
07. (A)	08. (B)	09. (C)	10. (B)	11. (C)	12. (B)
13. (A)	14. (C)	15. (B)	16. (B)		

01. AU-US

Why don't you pack some warm clothes?
(A) Thanks for reminding me.
(B) This fits nicely.
(C) A cold winter.

따뜻한 옷을 좀 챙기는 게 어때요?
(A) 알려줘서 고마워요.
(B) 이것이 잘 어울려요.
(C) 추운 겨울입니다.

[해설] 짐을 쌀 때 따뜻한 옷을 챙겨 넣으라고 권하는 권유/제안 의문문이다.
(A) 따뜻한 옷을 좀 챙겨 넣으라는 권유에 알려줘서 고맙다는 말로 상대방의 제안을 수락하는 답변이므로 정답이다.
(B) 질문의 clothes만 듣고 옷을 입어보는 상황을 연상할 경우 고를 수 있는 오답이다.
(C) 질문의 warm clothes에서 연상되는 cold winter를 이용해 혼동을 유도하는 오답이다.

02. BR-BR

Why has my order been delayed?
(A) One of those, please.
(B) Because it had to be rerouted.
(C) An electronic receipt.

reroute 다른 길로 수송하다

왜 제 주문이 지연되었나요?
(A) 그것들 중 하나를 주세요.
(B) 다른 길로 수송되어야 했기 때문이에요.
(C) 전자 영수증이에요.

[해설] 주문이 지연되는 이유를 묻는 Why 의문문이다.
(A) 질문의 order만 듣고 무언가를 주문하는 상황으로 잘못 이해했을 경우 선택할 수 있는 오답이다.
(B) 다른 길로 수송되어야 했기 때문이라며 구체적 이유를 제시한 정답이다.
(C) 질문의 order에서 연상할 수 있는 receipt를 이용해 혼동을 유도하는 오답이다.

03. BR-US

How's the food at Philly Steakhouse?
(A) Yes, I made a reservation.
(B) What did you order?
(C) You'd better try other places.

Philly Steakhouse의 음식은 어땠나요?
(A) 네, 제가 예약을 했어요.
(B) 무엇을 주문했나요?
(C) 다른 곳을 가보는 게 좋겠어요.

[해설] 식당의 음식이 어땠는지 의견을 묻는 How 의문문이다.
(A) 의문사 의문문에는 Yes/No로 응답하지 않으므로 오답이다.
(B) '특정 식당의 음식'에서 연상 가능한 표현인 order(주문하다)를 이용해 혼동을 유도하는 오답이다.
(C) 다른 곳에 가볼 것을 권함으로써 그 식당의 음식이 만족스럽지 않았다는 의견을 우회적으로 전달하고 있는 정답이다.

04. US-US

Why is the Becker Street entrance closed?
(A) For some road repairs.
(B) The downtown area.
(C) No, I don't go that way.

road repair 도로 보수   downtown area 도심 지역

Becker 가 입구가 왜 폐쇄되었나요?
(A) 도로 보수 때문에요.
(B) 도심 지역이요.
(C) 아니요, 저는 그 길로 가지 않아요.

[해설] 특정 도로로 들어가는 입구가 폐쇄된 이유를 묻는 Why 의문문이다.
(A) 도로 보수 때문이라며 이유를 제시하였으므로 정답이다.
(B) 질문의 Becker Street처럼 특정 거리나 지역에 대해 얘기할 때 종종 나오는 downtown area를 이용하여 혼동을 유도한 오답이다.
(C) 의문사 의문문에는 Yes/No로 응답할 수 없으므로 오답이다.

05. US-AU

How was the concert last weekend?
(A) I already bought a ticket.
(B) Over three hours.
(C) My friends and I had a great time.

지난 주말 콘서트는 어땠어요?
(A) 저는 이미 티켓을 샀어요.
(B) 3시간 넘게요.
(C) 제 친구들과 저는 즐거운 시간을 보냈어요.

[해설] 지난 주말 콘서트에 대한 의견을 묻는 How 의문문이다.
(A) 질문의 concert에서 연상되는 ticket을 이용해 혼동을 유도하는 오답이다.
(B) 소요 시간으로 답변했으므로 How long 의문문에 적합한 응답이다.
(C) 친구들과 즐거운 시간을 보냈다며 콘서트에 대한 느낌/소감을 전달했으므로 정답이다.

06. US-US

Why don't we continue this budget meeting tomorrow?
(A) She works in the marketing department.
(B) For the finance team.
(C) I'm leaving on a business trip tonight.

budget 예산 finance 재정, 재무

이 예산 회의를 내일 계속하는 게 어때요?
(A) 그녀는 마케팅 부서에서 일합니다.
(B) 재무팀을 위해서요.
(C) 저는 오늘 밤에 출장을 떠나요.
[해설] 내일 예산 회의를 계속할 것을 제안하는 권유/제안 의문문이다.
(A) 질문의 budget meeting처럼 업무 상황과 연관된 marketing department를 이용해 혼동을 유도하는 오답이다.
(B) 질문의 budget에서 연상되는 finance를 이용해 혼동을 유도하는 오답이다.
(C) 내일 이어서 예산 회의를 하자는 제안에 오늘 밤 출장을 떠난다는 구체적인 이유를 들어 거절의 의사를 표현하고 있으므로 정답이다.

07. BR-US

Why don't I print some extra pamphlets for the job fair?
(A) We'll probably need them.
(B) I used an original design.
(C) They describe our ideal candidates.

job fair 취업 박람회 ideal 이상적인 candidate 지원자

제가 취업 박람회를 위해 책자를 추가로 인쇄하는 게 어떨까요?
(A) 아마도 우리에게 그것들이 필요할 거예요.
(B) 저는 원본 디자인을 사용했어요.
(C) 그것들이 우리의 이상적인 지원자들을 설명해줘요.
[해설] 추가로 책자를 인쇄할 것을 제안하는 권유/제안 의문문이다.
(A) 취업 박람회를 위해 추가로 책자를 인쇄하는 게 어떠냐는 제안에 그것들이 필요할 것이라고 답변함으로써 간접적으로 제안에 동의하고 있으므로 정답이다.
(B) 질문의 pamphlets에서 연상되는 design을 이용해 혼동을 유도하는 오답이다.
(C) 질문의 job fair에서 연상되는 candidates를 이용해 혼동을 유도하는 오답이다.

08. US-AU

Why is today's shipment still on the loading dock?
(A) They're made of steel.
(B) Because we've been so busy.
(C) Earlier this morning.

shipment 수송, 수송품, 적하물 loading dock (건물의) 짐 싣는 곳

오늘 선적분이 왜 아직도 하역장에 있는 거죠?
(A) 그것들은 강철로 만들어졌어요.
(B) 우리가 너무 바빴기 때문이에요.
(C) 오늘 아침 일찍이요.
[해설] 오늘 선적분이 여전히 하역장에 있는 이유를 묻는 Why 의문문이다.
(A) 질문의 still과 발음이 비슷한 steel을 사용하여 혼동을 유도한 오답이다.
(B) 우리가 매우 바빴기 때문이라며 이유를 제시했으므로 정답이다.
(C) 시간 부사구로 답변했으므로 When 의문에 적합한 응답이다.

09. BR-US

How do you like your new office?
(A) Yes, on the third floor.
(B) Right after the relocation.
(C) It has a nice view.

relocation 이전, 전근 view 전망, 경관

새 사무실은 어떤가요?
(A) 네, 3층에요.
(B) 전근 직후에요.
(C) 전망이 좋아요.
[해설] 새 사무실이 어떤지 의견을 묻는 How 의문문이다.
(A) 의문사 의문문에는 Yes/No로 답변할 수 없으므로 오답이다.
(B) 시점을 나타내는 표현이므로 When 의문에 어울리는 답변이다.
(C) 전망이 좋다는 말로 긍정적인 의견을 제시한 정답이다.

10. AU-US

How does your customer survey go?
(A) It can be customized.
(B) The response rate is very low.
(C) I'm going to turn it in shortly.

customer survey 고객 설문 조사 customize 주문 제작하다
response rate 응답률 turn in 제출하다, 반납하다 shortly 곧

당신의 고객 설문 조사는 어떻게 되어 가나요?
(A) 주문 제작될 수 있어요.
(B) 응답률이 매우 저조해요.
(C) 곧 제출할게요.
[해설] 고객 설문 조사의 진행 상황을 묻는 How 의문문이다.
(A) 질문의 customer와 발음이 유사한 customized를 이용해 혼동을 유도하는 오답이다.
(B) 응답률이 저조하다는 말로 설문 조사가 순조롭게 진행되지 못하고 있음을 알리는 정답이다.
(C) 질문의 customer survey에서 연상되는 turn in을 이용해 혼동을 유도하는 오답이다.

11. US-BR

How come you missed the train?
(A) We would miss her so much.
(B) He is well-trained.
(C) I was confused about the departure time.

well-trained 잘 훈련된 be confused about ~에 대해 혼선을 겪다

어쩌다 기차를 놓친 거예요?
(A) 우리는 그녀가 몹시 그리울 거예요.
(B) 그는 잘 훈련되었어요.

(C) 출발 시간이 헷갈렸어요.

[해설] 기차를 놓친 이유를 묻는 How come 의문문이다.
(A) 질문의 miss(놓치다)와 동음이의어인 miss(그리워하다)를 사용하여 혼동을 유도하는 오답이다.
(B) 질문의 train(기차)과 동음이의어인 train(훈련시키다)을 사용하여 혼동을 유도하는 오답이다.
(C) 출발 시간이 헷갈렸다며 구체적인 이유를 제시하였으므로 정답이다.

12. US-AU

Why are you leaving early tomorrow?
(A) At 2 P.M.
(B) To see a dentist.
(C) I'll see you then.

당신은 내일 왜 일찍 떠나나요?
(A) 오후 2시에요.
(B) 치과 진료를 받기 위해서요.
(C) 그때 봅시다.

[해설] 상대방에게 내일 일찍 떠나는 이유를 묻는 Why 의문문이다.
(A) 특정 시간으로 답변했으므로 When 의문문에 적합한 응답이다.
(B) '치과 진료를 받기 위해서'라는 구체적 이유를 제시했으므로 정답이다.
(C) 질문의 tomorrow를 then으로 받을 수는 있지만 내일 일찍 떠나는 이유를 묻는 질문에 내일 보자는 답변은 어색하므로 오답이다.

13. AU-BR

How was the holiday sale event?
(A) We broke a sales record.
(B) Happy holidays to you, too.
(C) An impressive buffet spread.

break a record 기록을 경신하다   impressive 인상적인, 인상 깊은   spread 진수성찬

휴일 할인 행사는 어땠어요?
(A) 우리가 매출 기록을 경신했어요.
(B) 당신도 즐거운 연휴 되세요.
(C) 인상적인 뷔페식 성찬이었어요.

[해설] 휴일 할인 행사에 대한 의견을 묻는 How 의문문이다.
(A) 매출 기록을 경신했다는 말로 행사가 아주 성공적이었다는 의견을 제시했으므로 정답이다.
(B) 질문의 holiday를 반복 사용한 오답이다.
(C) 행사(event)에서 뷔페식 식사(buffet)가 제공되는 상황을 연상하도록 유도한 오답으로, 행사의 음식이 어땠냐는 질문에 적합한 응답이다.

14. AU-BR

Why won't the remote control work?
(A) No, it doesn't.
(B) Which button should I press?
(C) You probably need to replace the batteries.

probably 아마도   replace 교체하다

왜 리모컨이 작동하지 않나요?
(A) 아니요, 그렇지 않아요.
(B) 어떤 버튼을 눌러야 하나요?

(C) 아마도 배터리를 교체해야 할 거예요.

[해설] 리모컨이 작동하지 않는 이유를 묻는 Why 의문문이다.
(A) 의문사 의문문에는 Yes/No로 응답할 수 없으므로 오답이다.
(B) 질문의 remote control에서 연상 가능한 press를 이용하여 혼동을 유도하는 오답이다.
(C) 배터리를 교체해야 한다는 말로 배터리가 방전되었기 때문임을 간접적으로 전달하고 있으므로 정답이다.

15. US-US

How do you feel about the advertising proposal from Yang Marketing?
(A) The newly created TV commercial.
(B) It is very impressive but I'm concerned about the budget.
(C) Farmer's Market might carry them.

proposal 제안   commercial 광고 (방송)   impressive 인상적인
be concerned about ~에 대해 걱정하다   carry 취급하다

Yang Marketing의 광고 제안에 대해 어떻게 생각하시나요?
(A) 새로 제작된 TV 광고입니다.
(B) 매우 인상적이지만 예산이 걱정돼요.
(C) Farmer's Market에서 그것들을 취급할지도 몰라요.

[해설] 특정 업체의 광고 제안에 대한 의견을 묻는 How 의문문이다.
(A) 질문의 advertising에서 연상 가능한 commercial을 이용하여 혼동을 유도하는 오답이다.
(B) 자신의 의견을 제시하고 있으므로 정답이다.
(C) 질문의 업체명(~ Marketing)과 응답의 업체명(~ Market)을 유사하게 만들어 서로 관련된 내용으로 혼동하도록 유도하는 오답이다.

16. US-AU

How about looking for a new apartment close to your office?
(A) Yes, they're already closed.
(B) I'm not affordable for that.
(C) On the moving day.

look for ~을 찾다   close to ~에 가까운   affordable 감당할 수 있는   moving day 이사하는 날

당신의 사무실과 가까운 새 아파트를 찾는 게 어때요?
(A) 네, 벌써 문을 닫았어요.
(B) 저는 그럴 여유가 없어요.
(C) 이사하는 날에요.

[해설] 사무실과 가까운 새 아파트를 찾는 게 어떠냐고 제안하는 권유/제안 의문문이다.
(A) 질문의 close와 발음이 유사한 closed를 이용해 혼동을 유도하는 오답이다.
(B) 그럴 여유가 없다며 상대방의 제안을 거절하고 있으므로 정답이다.
(C) 시간 표현으로 답변했으므로 When 의문문에 적합한 응답이다.

DAY 05

PART 1 야외 사진

확인 문제

❶ US

(A) Pedestrians are crossing the street.
(B) Some people are cycling on a road.

(A) 보행자들이 거리를 건너고 있다.
(B) 몇몇 사람들이 도로에서 자전거를 타고 있다.

❷ AU

(A) Some people are seated on the grass.
(B) A bench is occupied.

occupied (자리를) 차지한

(A) 몇몇 사람들이 잔디에 앉아 있다.
(B) 벤치를 (사람들이) 차지하고 있다.

❸ US

(A) They are wearing protective helmets.
(B) One of the men is using a tool.

(A) 그들은 안전모를 착용하고 있다.
(B) 남자들 중 한 명은 도구를 사용하고 있다.

❹ BR

(A) A woman is fixing a tire.
(B) A boat is floating on the water.

tire 타이어 float 뜨다

(A) 여자가 타이어를 수리하고 있다.
(B) 배가 물 위에 떠 있다.

❺ BR

(A) A woman is watering plants.
(B) A woman is shoveling dirt.

shovel 삽질하다   dirt 흙

(A) 여자가 식물에 물을 주고 있다.
(B) 여자가 흙을 삽질하고 있다.

❻ US

(A) A train is approaching the platform.
(B) Some people are boarding a train.

(A) 기차가 승강장에 들어오고 있다.
(B) 몇몇 사람들이 기차에 탑승하고 있다.

연습 문제

01. AU

(1) (A) a man (✗) (B) a barrier (○)
    (C) crossing the street (✗)
(2)
(A) A barrier is blocking a street. [○]
(B) A street is being resurfaced. [✗]

barrier 장벽   resurface 표면을 보수하다

(A) 장벽이 거리를 막고 있다.
(B) 거리의 표면이 보수되고 있다.

02. US

(1) (A) people (○) (B) outdoors (○)
    (C) standing in line (✗)
(2)
(A) A crowd of people are gathered outdoors. [○]
(B) Some people are applauding performers. [✗]

applaud 박수를 치다

(A) 많은 사람들이 야외에 모여 있다.
(B) 몇몇 사람들이 공연자들에게 박수를 치고 있다.

03. BR

(1) (A) a ladder (○) (B) a wall (✗) (C) standing (○)
(2)
(A) A wall is being painted with a brush. [✗]
(B) A man is standing on a ladder. [○]

(A) 벽이 붓으로 페인트칠되고 있다.
(B) 남자가 사다리에 서 있다.

04. US

(1) (A) umbrellas (○) (B) swimming (✗) (C) boarding (✗)
(2)
(A) Some people are relaxing under umbrellas. [○]
(B) Some people are swimming in an indoor pool. [✗]

indoor 실내의

(A) 몇몇 사람들이 파라솔 아래에서 휴식을 취하고 있다.
(B) 몇몇 사람들이 실내 수영장에서 수영하고 있다.

실전 문제

01. (B)   02. (D)   03. (A)   04. (B)   05. (C)   06. (A)

01. US

(A) They are posing for a photo.
(B) They are descending a mountain trail.
(C) They are resting on a rock.
(D) They are having a snack.

pose for ~을 위해 포즈를 취하다   descend 내려오다, 내려가다
trail 오솔길, 시골길

(A) 그들은 사진을 찍기 위해 포즈를 취하고 있다.
(B) 그들은 산길을 내려가고 있다.
(C) 그들은 바위에서 쉬고 있다.
(D) 그들은 간식을 먹고 있다.

[해설] 산길을 걷고 있는 사람들의 사진으로, 등장 인물들의 공통 동작에 초점을 맞춰 듣는다.
(A) 카메라를 들고 있거나 사진 찍을 포즈를 취하는(posing for a photo) 사람은 보이지 않는다.
(B) 산길을 내려가고 있는 사람들의 모습을 바르게 묘사한 정답이다.
(C) 사진에 등장하는 인물들은 모두 아래쪽으로 걸어가고 있을 뿐 쉬고 있는(resting) 사람은 없다.
(D) 무언가를 먹고 있는(having a snack) 사람은 보이지 않는다.

02. BR

(A) One of the women is looking at her mobile phone.
(B) A car is stopped at a traffic signal.
(C) Some people are boarding a bus.
(D) Some people are crossing at a crosswalk.

traffic signal 교통 신호

(A) 여자들 중 한 명이 휴대 전화를 보고 있다.
(B) 자동차 한 대가 신호등 앞에 멈춰 있다.
(C) 몇몇 사람들이 버스에 타고 있다.
(D) 몇몇 사람들이 횡단보도를 건너고 있다.

[해설] 다수의 사람들이 길을 건너는 사진으로, 등장 인물의 동작은 물론 사진 속 사물의 위치/상태에도 주목해야 한다.
(A) 사진에서 휴대 전화는 보이지 않는다.
(B) 일부 차량들이 보이기는 하지만 신호등(traffic signal) 앞에 멈춰 있는 것이 아니라 도로를 따라 주차되어 있다.
(C) 버스에 오르고 있는(boarding a bus) 사람들은 보이지 않는다.
(D) 횡단보도에서 길을 건너고 있는 사람들의 모습을 바르게 묘사한 정답이다.

03. AU

(A) Some people are riding bicycles along the water.
(B) Some people are gathered on a boat.
(C) Some people are sitting on the grass.
(D) Some people are examining a piece of equipment.

ride 타다   grass 풀, 잔디   examine 조사[검토]하다
equipment 장비, 용품

(A) 몇몇 사람들이 물가를 따라 자전거를 타고 있다.
(B) 몇몇 사람들이 보트 위에 모여 있다.
(C) 몇몇 사람들이 잔디 위에 앉아 있다.
(D) 몇몇 사람들이 장비 하나를 살펴보고 있다.

[해설] 야외를 배경으로 다수의 인물이 등장하는 사진으로, 사람들의 공통 동작을 잘 살펴야 한다.
(A) 물 옆으로 난 길을 따라 자전거를 타고 있는 사람들을 묘사한 정답이다.
(B) 보트(boat)를 타고 있는 사람들은 보이지 않는다.
(C) 사진 우측에 잔디가 보이기는 하지만 그 위에 앉아 있는(sitting) 사람은 없다.
(D) 장비를 살펴보고 있는(examining a piece of equipment) 사람은 보이지 않는다.

04. US

(A) A tree is being planted.
(B) Some wood is being loaded onto a truck.
(C) A man is repairing a vehicle.
(D) A man is sawing some wood.

plant 심다   load 싣다   repair 수리하다   vehicle 차량, 탈것
saw 톱질하다

(A) 나무가 심기고 있다.
(B) 나무가 트럭에 실리고 있다.
(C) 남자가 차량을 수리하고 있다.
(D) 남자가 나무에 톱질을 하고 있다.

[해설] 남자가 트럭에 나무를 싣는 모습으로, 남자의 동작 및 주변 사물의 상태에 초점을 맞추고 들어야 한다.
(A) 나무가 보이기는 하지만 심기고 있는(being planted) 모습은 아니다.
(B) 남자가 나무를 트럭에 싣고 있는 모습을 나무를 주어로 묘사한 정답이다.
(C) 차량을 수리하는(repairing) 모습은 보이지 않는다.
(D) 톱질하는(sawing) 모습은 보이지 않는다.

05. BR

(A) Some people are walking on a bridge.
(B) The stairs lead to the building entrance.
(C) A boat is floating on the river.
(D) A road is being repaved.

stairs 계단   lead to ~로 이어지다   repave (도로를) 재포장하다

(A) 사람들이 다리 위를 걷고 있다.
(B) 계단이 건물 입구로 이어진다.
(C) 배가 강 위에 떠 있다.
(D) 도로를 재포장하고 있다.

[해설] 사람과 사물/배경이 섞여 있는 사진으로, 사람은 물론 사물/배경 등 사진 속 모든 요소를 잘 살펴야 한다.
(A) 사진에 사람이 여자 한 명뿐이므로 오답이다.
(B) 여자 앞으로 계단이 놓여 있긴 하지만 건물 입구로 이어지는지는(lead to the building entrance) 알 수 없다.
(C) 강 위에 떠 있는 배를 바르게 묘사한 정답이다.
(D) 도로(road)를 재포장하고(repaved) 있는 사람들은 보이지 않는다.

06. US

(A) Some people are shopping at an outdoor market.
(B) One of the women is paying for her purchase.
(C) One of the women is sampling some pie.
(D) Some people are entering a building.

enter 들어가다

(A) 사람들이 야외 시장에서 쇼핑을 하고 있다.

(B) 여자들 중 한 명이 구입한 물건의 값을 치르고 있다.
(C) 여자들 중 한 명이 파이를 시식하고 있다.
(D) 사람들이 건물로 들어가고 있다.

[해설] 야외 시장을 배경으로 다수의 인물이 등장하는 사진으로, 각 인물의 개별 동작과 공통 동작 모두 잘 살펴야 한다.
(A) 야외의 파이 판매대 앞에 파이를 고르고 있는 사람들의 모습을 묘사한 정답이다.
(B) 돈을 지불하고 있는(paying for her purchase) 사람의 모습은 보이지 않는다.
(C) 파이들이 많이 진열되어 있긴 하지만 이를 시식하는(sampling) 사람은 없다.
(D) 배경에 건물이 보이긴 하지만 건물에 들어가는(entering) 사람은 보이지 않는다.

PART 2 일반 의문문 - 긍정

확인 문제

❶ US-BR

Did you contact the client?
(A) Yes, I called him this morning.
(B) The contract is already renewed.

그 고객에게 연락하셨나요?
(A) 네, 오늘 아침에 그에게 전화했습니다.
(B) 그 계약은 이미 갱신되었습니다.

❷ BR-US

Have you finished reviewing the article for the company newsletter?
(A) No, I sent it by express mail.
(B) Yes, I've already reviewed it twice.

사보를 위한 기사 검토를 마치셨나요?
(A) 아뇨, 특급 배송으로 보냈어요.
(B) 네, 이미 두 번 검토했어요.

❸ AU-BR

Has the copy machine been fixed?
(A) There is some heavy machinery.
(B) It's still being repaired now.

복사기가 고쳐졌나요?
(A) 중장비가 있습니다.
(B) 현재 아직 수리 중입니다.

❹ US-US

Is there a bus to the city hall from here?
(A) No, nothing is left.
(B) There's one every 20 minutes.

여기에서 시청으로 가는 버스가 있나요?
(A) 아니요, 아무것도 남지 않았어요.
(B) 20분마다 한 대씩 있어요.

❺ BR-US

Is your sister coming to visit you tomorrow?
(A) Yes, she'll stay for a week.
(B) It's right across the street.

당신의 여동생이 내일 당신을 보러 오나요?
(A) 네, 그녀는 일주일 동안 머무를 거예요.
(B) 바로 길 건너편에 있어요.

❻ BR-AU

Can I bring you a drink menu?
(A) It's 10 euros.
(B) I'll just have water, thanks.

음료 메뉴판을 가져다 드릴까요?
(A) 10유로입니다.
(B) 저는 그냥 물 마실게요, 감사합니다.

연습 문제

01. (B) 02. (B) 03. (A) 04. (B) 05. (A) 06. (A)
07. (B) 08. (B)

01. BR-US

Have you worked with this type of machinery before?
(A) I'll go there after work. [×]
(B) Yes, for several years. [○]

예전에 이런 종류의 기계류를 사용해 보신 적이 있으세요?
(A) 퇴근 후에 제가 그곳에 가겠습니다.
(B) 네, 몇 년 동안이요.

02. AU-BR

Do you have any direct flights to Los Angeles?
(A) No, the cheapest flight is $500. [×]
(B) They are all sold out. [○]

로스엔젤레스까지 직항 비행편이 있나요?
(A) 아뇨, 가장 싼 항공편은 500달러입니다.
(B) 그건 다 팔렸습니다.

03. US-BR

Is there a discount for students?
(A) I'm not sure. Let me ask. [○]
(B) Yes, just across the street. [×]

학생들을 위한 할인이 있나요?
(A) 확실하지 않아요. 물어볼게요.
(B) 네, 바로 길 건너에요.

04. US-US

Will you take your baggage onto the plane?
(A) This is a newly purchased bag. [×]
(B) I'll put it in the overhead compartment. [○]

overhead compartment (기차·비행기의) 머리 위 짐칸

짐을 비행기 내로 가지고 갈 건가요?
(A) 이것은 새로 구입한 가방입니다.
(B) 비행기 머리 위 짐칸에 둘 거예요.

05. US-AU

Has the sales report for the monthly meeting been prepared yet?
(A) I'll leave it on your desk by noon. [○]
(B) No, I've never been there. [×]

월간 회의를 위한 매출 보고서가 준비되었나요?
(A) 정오까지 책상 위에 두겠습니다.
(B) 아니요, 저는 거기 가 본 적이 없습니다.

06. AU-BR

Did you decide on the dates for the workshop?
(A) How about May 20? [○]
(B) Yes, the program was well-organized. [×]

date 날짜

워크숍 날짜 정하셨나요?
(A) 5월 20일 어때요?
(B) 네, 프로그램은 잘 구성되었어요.

07. US-BR

Can you ask Ben to come into my office for a minute?
(A) He will look into the case. [×]
(B) Sure, I'll contact him right away. [○]

Ben에게 잠시 제 사무실로 오라고 해줄래요?
(A) 그가 그 사건을 조사할 겁니다.
(B) 물론이죠. 당장 그에게 연락하겠습니다.

08. BR-US

Do you know Mr. Song's phone number?
(A) He called you this morning. [×]
(B) I think I have it in my contact list. [○]

Song 씨의 전화번호를 아세요?
(A) 그가 오늘 아침에 전화했었어요.
(B) 제 연락처에 있을 거예요.

실전 문제

01. (A)	02. (A)	03. (B)	04. (A)	05. (C)	06. (B)
07. (C)	08. (B)	09. (A)	10. (A)	11. (C)	12. (A)
13. (B)	14. (C)	15. (B)	16. (A)		

01. BR-AU

Do you accept credit cards?
(A) We only take cash.
(B) It should be on the receipt.
(C) Sign here, please.

accept 받다   receipt 영수증

신용카드를 받으시나요?
(A) 저희는 현금만 받아요.
(B) 영수증에 적혀 있습니다.
(C) 여기에 서명해주십시오.

[해설] 계산을 할 때 신용카드를 받는지 묻는 일반 의문문이다.
(A) 현금만 받는다는 말로 신용카드를 받지 않는다고 우회적으로 답변한 정답이다.
(B) 질문의 상황과 같은 계산할 때 받는 receipt을 이용해 혼동을 유도하는 오답이다.
(C) 질문의 credit card에서 서명하는(sign) 상황이 연상되도록 유도하는 오답이다.

02. US-US

Has the new vacation policy been implemented yet?
(A) No, we do that in November.
(B) Great, the resort couldn't be better.
(C) You will need prior approval from your supervisor.

implement 시행하다   couldn't be better 더 좋을 수 없다
prior approval 사전 승인   supervisor 감독관, 관리자

새로운 휴가 정책이 벌써 시행되었나요?
(A) 아니요, 11월에 해요.
(B) 좋아요. 리조트가 더 없이 좋아요.
(C) 상사로부터의 사전 승인이 필요할 거예요.

[해설] 새로운 휴가 정책이 시행되었는지 묻는 일반 의문문이다.
(A) 부정의 No로 응답한 후 11월에 시행한다고 부연 설명하고 있으므로 정답이다.
(B) 질문의 vacation에서 연상 가능한 resort를 이용해 혼동을 유도하는 오답이다.
(C) 정책(policy)을 시행할(implemented) 때 보통 상사(supervisor)의 승인(approval)이 필요하다는 점을 이용해 혼동을 유도하는 오답이다.

03. BR-AU

Do you normally commute by subway?
(A) Yes, this bus goes there.
(B) No, but my car's in the shop.
(C) At a community center.

normally 보통, 보통 때는   commute 통근하다

당신은 보통 지하철로 통근하나요?
(A) 네, 이 버스는 그곳에 가요.
(B) 아니요, 하지만 제 차가 정비소에 있어요.
(C) 지역 문화 센터에서요.

[해설] 보통 지하철로 출근하는지 묻는 일반 의문문이다.
(A) 긍정의 Yes로 응답했으나 질문과 무관한 버스에 대한 내용이 이어지므로 오답이다.
(B) 부정의 No로 응답한 후 지금은 차가 정비소에 있다는 말을 덧붙임으로써 평소에는 자동차로 출근하지만 오늘은 차가 정비소에 있어 지하철을 이용했음을 우회적으로 전달하는 정답이다.
(C) 질문의 commute와 유사한 발음의 community를 사용하여 혼동을 유도하는 오답이다.

04. [BR-AU]

Are we flying business class on our next trip?
(A) The company reduced the budget.
(B) It's going to be held in Berlin, right?
(C) Plenty of frequent flyer miles.

reduce 줄이다, 축소하다   plenty of 많은   frequent flyer (항공편) 단골 고객

우리는 다음 출장 때 비즈니스석으로 항공편을 이용하나요?
(A) 회사에서 예산을 삭감했어요.
(B) 베를린에서 열릴 예정이에요, 맞죠?
(C) 항공편 마일리지가 많아요.

[해설] 다음 출장 시 항공편 비즈니스석을 이용할 것인지 묻는 Be동사 의문문이다.
(A) 회사가 예산을 삭감했다는 말로 비즈니스석을 이용하지 못할 것임을 우회적으로 드러내고 있으므로 정답이다.
(B) 질문의 trip에서 특정 목적지 또는 여행지(Berlin)를 연상하도록 유도한 오답이다.
(C) 질문의 flying과 business class에서 연상 가능한 frequent flyer(항공편 단골 이용 고객)를 이용하여 혼동을 유도하는 오답이다.

05. [BR-US]

Did you apply for some time off?
(A) A national holiday.
(B) Did you have a certain place in mind?
(C) I'm waiting for approval.

apply for ~을 신청하다   time off 휴식, 휴가   national holiday 국경일   certain 특정한   approval 승인

휴가를 신청했나요?
(A) 국경일이요.
(B) 염두에 두신 특정한 장소가 있나요?
(C) 승인을 기다리고 있어요.

[해설] 휴가를 신청했는지 묻는 일반 의문문이다.
(A) 질문의 time off에서 연상 가능한 holiday를 사용하여 혼동을 유도한 오답이다.
(B) 질문의 time off에서 연상 가능한 certain place를 사용하여 혼동을 유도한 오답이다.
(C) 승인을 기다리고 있다는 말로 신청을 했다는 의미를 전달하고 있으므로 정답이다.

06. [US-BR]

Have you completed the online training?
(A) No, my computer is working fine.
(B) Yes, it didn't take long.
(C) A stable wifi connection.

complete 완료하다, 끝마치다   stable 안정적인

온라인 교육을 이수했나요?
(A) 아니요, 제 컴퓨터는 작동이 잘 돼요.
(B) 네, 오래 걸리지 않았어요.
(C) 안정적인 와이파이 연결이요.

[해설] 온라인 교육을 이수했는지 묻는 일반 의문문이다.
(A) 질문에 No로 응답했으므로 컴퓨터가 잘 작동하고 있다는 내용보다는 온라인 교육을 이수하지 못한 이유가 이어지는 것이 자연스럽다.
(B) 긍정의 Yes로 응답한 후, 교육을 이수하는 데 오랜 시간이 걸리지 않았다고 부연 설명하고 있는 정답이다.
(C) 질문의 online에서 연상 가능한 wifi connection을 이용해 혼동을 유도하는 오답이다.

07. [BR-US]

Have you selected your vacation destination?
(A) I visited there last year.
(B) I like the design.
(C) No, where would you recommend?

select 선택하다   vacation destination 휴가지

당신의 휴가지를 골랐나요?
(A) 저는 거기에 작년에 갔었어요.
(B) 디자인이 좋아요.
(C) 아니요, 어디를 추천하시겠어요?

[해설] 휴가지를 골랐는지 묻는 일반 의문문이다.
(A) 질문의 vacation destination에서 연상 가능한 visited를 이용해 혼동을 유도하는 오답이다.
(B) 특정 물건을 선택한 이유를 묻는 질문이었다면 가능한 응답이다.
(C) 부정의 No로 응답한 후, 상대방에게 휴가지 추천을 부탁하고 있으므로 정답이다.

08. [US-AU]

Has the order for printer cartridges been placed with our office supplier yet?
(A) No, there's a different form for that.
(B) They will be delivered tomorrow.
(C) It was more spacious than ours.

place an order with ~에 주문을 하다   office supplier 사무용품 공급업체   spacious 널찍한

우리 사무용품 공급 업체에게 프린터 카트리지 주문을 이미 했나요?
(A) 아니요, 그것을 위한 다른 서식이 있어요.
(B) 내일 배달될 거예요.
(C) 그것이 우리 것보다 더 넓었어요.

[해설] 프린터 카트리지 주문을 했는지 확인하는 일반 의문문이다.
(A) 질문의 order에서 주문 서식을 떠올리도록 form을 이용하여 혼동을 유도하는 오답이다.
(B) 내일 배달될 거라고 Yes의 의미로 답변하고 추가 정보를 전달하고 있으므로 정답이다.

(C) 질문의 동사 placed를 '장소, 위치'를 뜻하는 place로 잘못 이해했을 경우 연상 가능한 spacious를 이용하여 혼동을 유도하는 오답이다.

09. US-US

Does your department hold a meeting every Wednesday?
(A) Oh, on Thursdays.
(B) The production department.
(C) Do you have plans next week?

department 부서   hold 열다, 개최하다   production 생산

당신의 부서는 매주 수요일에 회의를 하나요?
(A) 아, 목요일마다 합니다.
(B) 생산부서요.
(C) 다음 주에 계획 있어요?

[해설] 수요일마다 부서에서 회의를 하는지 묻는 일반 의문문이다.
(A) '목요일마다'라고 상대방의 정보를 정정함으로써 우회적으로 부정의 답변을 하는 정답이다.
(B) 질문의 department를 반복 사용한 오답이다.
(C) 질문의 weekly에서 연상할 수 있는 어휘인 week를 이용해 혼동을 유도하는 오답이다.

10. BR-AU

Are your staff members paid based on their performance?
(A) It was a very entertaining show.
(B) No, the annual bonus.
(C) The sales team earns commission.

staff members 직원들   be paid 보수를 받다   based on ~에 근거하여   performance 성과, 실적   annual 매년의, 연례의   earn (이자·수익 등을) 받다   commission 수수료, 커미션

당신의 직원들은 업무 실적에 근거하여 급여를 받나요?
(A) 아주 재미있는 공연이었어요.
(B) 아니요, 연례 보너스입니다.
(C) 판매팀은 수수료를 받아요.

[해설] 직원들이 업무 실적에 근거해 급여를 받는지 묻는 Be동사 의문문이다.
(A) performance는 질문에서 쓰인 '실적, 성과'라는 뜻 외에 '공연'을 뜻하기도 하는데 이 뜻에서 연상 가능한 show를 이용해 혼동을 유도하는 오답이다.
(B) Be동사 의문문에는 Yes/No 응답이 가능하지만 No라는 응답과 뒤에 이어지는 '연례 보너스'의 연결이 부자연스러우므로 오답이다.
(C) 판매팀은 수수료를 받는다는 말로 판매팀의 경우 실적에 근거해 급여를 받고 있음을 우회적으로 전달하고 있는 정답이다.

11. US-BR

Was your team's quarterly sales goal changed recently?
(A) The company soccer team.
(B) Sure, I can handle that.
(C) Not that I know of.

quarterly 분기별의   sales goal 매출 목표   handle 처리하다, 다루다

당신 팀의 분기별 매출 목표가 최근에 변경되었나요?
(A) 회사의 축구팀이요.
(B) 물론입니다, 제가 처리할 수 있어요.
(C) 제가 알기로는 그렇지 않아요.

[해설] 분기별 매출 목표가 변경되었는지 묻는 Be동사 의문문이다.
(A) 질문의 team을 반복 사용하고 질문의 goal을 축구 용어로 혼동하도록 유도하는 오답이다.
(B) 긍정의 Sure로 응답한 후 이어지는 내용이 질문과 무관한 내용이므로 오답이다.
(C) 자신이 아는 바로는 그렇지 않다고 말함으로써 변경되지 않았다고 확인해주고 있는 정답이다.

12. US-BR

Are you going to present our budget proposal?
(A) Mr. Chung is a much better speaker.
(B) From the meeting minutes.
(C) There was a five thousand dollar increase.

present 발표하다, 제출하다   budget proposal 예산안   minutes 회의록   increase 증가, 인상

당신이 우리의 예산안을 발표할 것인가요?
(A) Chung 씨가 훨씬 더 우수한 발표자입니다.
(B) 회의록에서요.
(C) 5천 달러가 증가했어요.

[해설] 상대방에게 예산안을 발표할 것인지 묻는 Be동사 의문문이다.
(A) Mr. Chung이 훨씬 더 우수한 발표자라고 말함으로써 자신이 발표하지 않을 것임을 우회적으로 드러내고 있으므로 정답이다.
(B) 질문의 budget proposal이 보통 회의(meeting)에서 다뤄지는 안건임을 이용하여 혼동을 유도하는 오답이다.
(C) 질문의 budget에서 연상되는 구체적인 수치를 이용해 혼동을 유도하는 오답이다.

13. US-US

Did you finish checking our inventory?
(A) A call from the warehouse.
(B) No, I'm still working on that.
(C) The next shipment is on schedule.

inventory 재고   warehouse 창고   shipment 배송

재고 조사는 끝내셨나요?
(A) 창고에서 온 전화요.
(B) 아니요, 아직 작업하고 있어요.
(C) 다음 배송은 예정대로 진행됩니다.

[해설] 재고 조사를 끝냈는지 묻는 일반 의문문이다.
(A) 질문의 inventory에서 연상할 수 있는 warehouse를 사용하여 혼동을 유도한 오답이다.
(B) 아니라고(No) 대답하고 아직 하고 있다고 설명하고 있으므로 정답이다.
(C) 질문과 상관없는 답변이므로 오답이다.

14. US-US

Are the new hires going to join us for lunch today?
(A) I have a takeout menu in my desk.

DAY 05 33

(B) Right, the first round of interviews.
(C) Well, they will have a luncheon with the directors.

new hire 신입 사원   the first round 1차   luncheon 오찬
director (회사의) 임원, (부서의) 책임자

신입 사원들이 오늘 우리와 같이 점심식사를 하나요?
(A) 제 책상에 테이크아웃 음식 메뉴가 있어요.
(B) 맞아요. 1차 면접이에요.
(C) 음, 그들은 임원들과 오찬을 가질 거예요.

[해설] 신입 직원들과 같이 점심을 먹을 예정인지 묻는 Be동사 의문문이다.
(A) 질문의 lunch에서 연상 가능한 takeout menu를 이용해 혼동을 유도하는 오답이다.
(B) 질문의 new hires에서 연상 가능한 interviews를 이용해 혼동을 유도하는 오답이다.
(C) 신입 직원들이 임원들과 오찬을 할 예정이라고 답함으로써 우회적으로 부정의 답변을 하고 있으므로 정답이다.

15. BR-BR

Will this speech be immediately followed by the panel discussion?
(A) No, from the immediate supervisor.
(B) The updated schedule's in the welcome packet.
(C) Follow me, please.

immediately 즉시, 즉각   A be followed by B A 뒤에 B가 오다
panel discussion 공개 토론회   immediate 직속의

이 연설 직후에 공개 토론회가 이어지나요?
(A) 아니요, 직속 상사로부터요.
(B) 최신 일정이 환영 패키지에 있어요.
(C) 저를 따라오세요.

[해설] 연설 직후에 공개 토론회가 이어지는지 묻는 조동사 의문문이다.
(A) 부정의 No로 답변한 것은 자연스러우나 뒤에 이어지는 내용이 어색하다. 질문의 immediately와 발음이 유사한 immediate를 이용해 혼동을 유도하는 오답이다.
(B) 연설 직후에 공개 토론회가 이어지는지 묻는 질문에 최신 일정이 환영 패키지에 있다는 말로 '환영 패키지에서 일정을 직접 확인해보라'는 의미를 우회적으로 전달하는 정답이다.
(C) 질문의 follow를 반복 사용하여 혼동을 유도하는 오답이다.

16. US-BR

Can you pick me up from the airport?
(A) Sorry, but I'm hosting an open house event all day.
(B) I prefer to sit in an aisle seat.
(C) Don't forget to pick up your laundry.

pick up ~를 (차에) 태우러 가다, ~을 찾아오다   host 주최하다, 열다   open house 공개일, 손님을 환대하는 집   aisle 통로
laundry 세탁물

저를 공항으로 데리러 와주시겠어요?
(A) 미안하지만 저는 하루 종일 오픈 하우스 행사를 진행할 거예요.
(B) 저는 통로 쪽 좌석에 앉는 것을 선호해요.
(C) 세탁물 찾아오는 것 잊지 말아요.

[해설] 공항으로 데리러 와줄 것을 부탁하는 조동사 의문문이다.
(A) 공항으로 데리러 와달라는 부탁에 미안하다며 부탁을 거절하고 하루 종일 오픈 하우스 행사를 진행한다는 말로 그 이유를 제시하고 있으므로 정답이다.
(B) 질문의 airport에서 기내 좌석(aisle seat) 선택 상황을 연상하도록 유도하는 오답이다.
(C) 질문의 pick up을 반복 사용하여 혼동을 유도하는 오답이다.

DAY 06

PART 2 일반 의문문 - 부정

확인 문제

❶ US-BR

Don't you have baggage to check in?
(A) Yes, I have two.
(B) I'll be there tomorrow.

부칠 짐이 있지 않으세요?
(A) 네, 두 개가 있어요.
(B) 내일 거기에 갈 거예요.

❷ US-US

Haven't you received Michael's application yet?
(A) No, I won't apply for it.
(B) When did he send it?

apply 지원하다, 적용하다, 바르다

Michael의 지원서 아직 못 받으셨나요?
(A) 아니요, 거기 지원하지 않을 거예요.
(B) 그가 언제 그걸 보냈나요?

❸ AU-BR

Isn't the road still closed?
(A) I believe the repair work is completed.
(B) We close at five today.

그 도로가 여전히 폐쇄되어 있지 않나요?
(A) 보수 작업이 끝났을 거예요.
(B) 저희는 오늘 5시에 문을 닫습니다.

❹ BR-BR

Aren't you leaving for Europe tomorrow?
(A) Yes, I'm looking forward to it.
(B) You are right. He's planning to.

내일 유럽으로 떠나시는 거 아닌가요?
(A) 네, 저는 기대하고 있어요.
(B) 맞습니다. 그는 그럴 계획입니다.

❺ BR-US

Weren't you expected to hand in the sales report this morning?
(A) I'm sorry, but it's not ready yet.
(B) He is expecting us soon.

오늘 아침에 매출 보고서를 제출하기로 되어 있었던 거 아니었나요?
(A) 죄송하지만, 아직 준비가 안 되었어요.
(B) 그는 우리가 곧 올 거라고 기대하고 있어요.

❻ US-US

Couldn't we change the venue to Charles Hall?
(A) Go ahead and turn right at the corner.
(B) I'll see if it's possible.

우리 장소를 Charles 홀로 변경할 수 없나요?
(A) 앞으로 쭉 가서 모퉁이에서 오른쪽으로 도세요.
(B) 가능할지 알아볼게요.

연습 문제

01. (A) 02. (B) 03. (A) 04. (B) 05. (B) 06. (A)
07. (A) 08. (A)

01. US-AU

Aren't the table and chairs supposed to be delivered today?
(A) Let me check the status. [O]
(B) Yes, I think that store is newly opened. [×]

status 상황, 상태   newly 새로

테이블과 의자들이 오늘 배송되기로 예정되어 있지 않나요?
(A) 상황을 확인해 볼게요.
(B) 네, 저 상점은 새로 문을 연 것 같아요.

02. AU-BR

Don't we need to order some more office supplies?
(A) Yes, I was surprised. [×]
(B) Mr. Han will take care of it. [O]

take care of ~을 처리하다

우리 사무용품을 더 주문해야 하지 않나요?
(A) 네, 저는 놀랐어요.
(B) Han 씨가 그것을 처리할 거예요.

03. BR-US

Didn't you see the warning sign at the entrance?
(A) Sorry, I didn't notice it. [O]
(B) It's still pretty warm. [×]

당신은 출입구에 있는 경고 안내판을 못 보셨나요?
(A) 죄송해요, 알아차리지 못했어요.
(B) 여전히 꽤 따뜻하네요.

04. BR-AU

Can't we leave the office a little earlier tomorrow?
(A) An annual gathering of managers. [×]
(B) I'll have to ask. [O]

gathering 모임

우리 내일 조금 일찍 퇴근할 수 없나요?
(A) 부장들의 연례 모임이요.
(B) 물어봐야 해요.

05. US-BR

Didn't Ms. Gonzales turn in the paperwork in person?
(A) No, we ran out of the paper. [×]
(B) Actually, she sent it by e-mail. [O]

turn in 제출하다   paperwork 서류, 문서 작업   in person 직접
run out of ~을 다 쓰다

Gonzales 씨가 서류를 직접 제출하지 않았나요?
(A) 아뇨, 우리는 종이가 다 떨어졌어요.
(B) 사실, 그녀는 이메일로 그것을 보냈어요.

06. US-US

Doesn't the closet have room for these boxes?
(A) No, it's completely full. [O]
(B) The room costs $100 per night. [×]

벽장에 이 상자들이 들어갈 자리가 없나요?
(A) 아니요, 완전히 가득 찼습니다.
(B) 그 방은 하룻밤에 100달러입니다.

07. US-BR

Isn't that your phone ringing on the table?
(A) Oh, you're right. It is. [O]
(B) He called me yesterday. [×]

테이블 위에서 벨이 울리는 게 당신 전화기 아니에요?
(A) 네, 맞아요. 그렇습니다.
(B) 그는 어제 제게 전화했습니다.

08. AU-BR

Weren't you going to go to the gym today?
(A) I got my arm injured. [O]
(B) Are these your running shoes? [×]

got injured 다치다, 부상을 입다

당신 오늘 체육관에 갈 거 아니었어요?
(A) 팔을 다쳤어요.

(B) 이거 당신 운동화인가요?

실전 문제

01. (A)	02. (A)	03. (A)	04. (C)	05. (A)	06. (B)
07. (C)	08. (B)	09. (C)	10. (B)	11. (B)	12. (B)
13. (A)	14. (B)	15. (B)	16. (C)		

01. US-US

Wasn't that an exciting movie?
(A) Yes, that whole series is great.
(B) The next showing is in half an hour.
(C) No, that one will be shown in Theater 8.

whole 전체의   series (라디오·텔레비전의) 시리즈   showing (영화) 상영

그 영화 흥미롭지 않았어요?
(A) 네, 전체 시리즈가 훌륭해요.
(B) 다음 상영은 30분 뒤에 있어요.
(C) 아니요, 그것은 8관에서 상영될 거예요.

[해설] 영화가 재미있었는지 확인하는 부정 의문문이다.
(A) Yes로 응답한 후 전체 시리즈가 훌륭하다고 부연 설명하는 정답이다.
(B) 질문의 movie에서 연상할 수 있는 showing을 이용해 혼동을 유도하는 오답이다.
(C) 질문의 movie에서 연상되는 theater를 이용해 혼동을 유도한 오답으로, 과거로 묻는 질문에 미래로 답변하고 있으므로 시제 역시 불일치한다.

02. BR-BR

Doesn't Samuel work at this laboratory?
(A) Yes, but he is out of office for vacation.
(B) Actually, we have met before.
(C) It's quite far from here.

laboratory 실험실   quite 꽤, 상당히

Samuel이 이 실험실에서 일하지 않나요?
(A) 네, 하지만 그는 휴가 중이라 자리에 없어요.
(B) 사실 우리는 전에 만난 적이 있어요.
(C) 여기서 꽤 멀어요.

[해설] Samuel이 이 실험실에서 일하는지 확인하는 부정 의문문이다.
(A) Yes라고 한 후, 현재는 휴가 중이라 자리에 없다고 부연 설명하고 있으므로 정답이다.
(B) Samuel에 대해 묻는 질문에 we로 답변하여 대명사가 맞지 않는 오답이다.
(C) 질문과 무관한 응답으로, 실험실의 위치를 묻는 Where 의문문에 적합하다.

03. US-AU

Don't you have a membership for the Central Gym?
(A) Yes, and it is open 24 hours.
(B) It's already shipped.
(C) No, I don't play sports.

ship 수송[운송]하다

Central Gym의 회원권을 가지고 계시지 않나요?
(A) 네, 그리고 그곳은 24시간 운영해요.
(B) 그것은 이미 수송되었어요.
(C) 아니요, 저는 스포츠를 하지 않아요.

[해설] Central Gym의 회원인지 여부를 확인하는 부정 의문문이다.
(A) 긍정의 Yes로 응답한 후 Central Gym이 24시간 운영된다고 부연 설명하고 있으므로 정답이다.
(B) 질문의 membership과 발음이 비슷한 ship을 사용한 오답이다.
(C) 질문의 gym에서 연상 가능한 sports를 이용하여 혼동을 유도하는 오답이다.

04. AU-BR

Haven't the sale posters been put up yet?
(A) That sounds efficient.
(B) Okay, I'll print some more copies.
(C) No, I found some discounted prices misprinted.

put up 내붙이다[게시하다]   yet 아직   efficient 효율적인   misprint ~을 잘못 인쇄하다

세일 포스터를 아직 붙이지 않았나요?
(A) 그거 효율적이겠네요.
(B) 좋아요, 제가 몇 부 더 인쇄할게요.
(C) 아니요, 제가 할인 가격이 잘못 인쇄된 것을 발견했어요.

[해설] 세일 포스터를 아직 붙이지 않았는지 확인하는 부정 의문문이다.
(A) 질문과 무관한 내용으로, 세일 포스터를 붙이자고 제안하거나 의견을 묻는 의문문에 적합한 응답이다.
(B) 질문의 poster에서 연상할 수 있는 print를 이용해 혼동을 유도하는 오답이다.
(C) 부정의 No로 응답한 후 포스터를 붙이지 않은 이유를 덧붙인 정답이다.

05. BR-US

Isn't it convenient that a new subway line opened up?
(A) Definitely. It cut my commute time in half.
(B) A detour along Tower Street.
(C) I usually drive this way.

convenient 편리한   open up ~이 이용 가능해지다   definitely 분명히, 틀림없이   commute time 통근 시간   detour 우회로

새 지하철 노선이 개통되니 편리하지 않나요?
(A) 정말 그래요. 제 통근 시간이 절반으로 줄었어요.
(B) Tower 가 쪽 우회로요.
(C) 저는 보통 이 길을 운전해서 다녀요.

[해설] 새 지하철 노선이 개통되니 편리하지 않은지 확인하는 부정 의문문이다.
(A) Definitely로 강한 긍정의 응답을 한 후 통근 시간이 절반으로 줄었다며 그 이유를 덧붙인 정답이다.
(B) 질문의 new subway line에서 지하철 공사로 인해 우회(detour)해야 하는 상황을 연상하도록 유도하는 오답이다.
(C) 어떤 교통 수단을 이용하는지 묻는 질문에 적합한 응답이다.

06. [BR-US]

Hasn't your manager released next month's work schedule?
(A) I'll be there on time.
(B) It is posted in the lounge.
(C) Only two sick days left.

release 발표하다, 공개하다   on time 시간을 어기지 않고, 정각에
post 게시[공고]하다

당신의 매니저가 다음 달 근무 일정표를 발표하지 않았나요?
(A) 제가 시간에 맞춰 그곳에 갈게요.
(B) 그것은 휴게실에 게시되어 있어요.
(C) 병가가 겨우 이틀 남았어요.

[해설] 다음 달 근무 일정표를 공개했는지 확인하는 부정 의문문이다.
(A) 질문의 schedule에서 연상할 수 있는 on time을 이용해 혼동을 유도하는 오답이다.
(B) 현재 휴게실에 게시되어 있다고 Yes의 의미로 답하는 정답이다.
(C) 질문의 work schedule에 영향을 미치는 요소인 sick days(병가)를 이용해 혼동을 유도하는 오답이다.

07. [AU-BR]

Haven't the VIP coupons been mailed out yet?
(A) That's a great price.
(B) An anniversary sale.
(C) They just arrived from the print shop.

mail out 발송하다

VIP 쿠폰이 아직 발송되지 않았나요?
(A) 그거 괜찮은 가격이네요.
(B) 기념일 세일이에요.
(C) 방금 인쇄소에서 도착했어요.

[해설] VIP 쿠폰이 발송되었는지 확인하는 부정 의문문이다.
(A) 질문의 coupons에서 연상할 수 있는 price를 이용해 혼동을 유도하는 오답이다.
(B) 질문의 coupons에서 연상할 수 있는 sale을 이용해 혼동을 유도하는 오답이다.
(C) 쿠폰들이 인쇄소에서 방금 도착했다고 답변함으로써 발송되지 않았다는 부정의 No를 우회적으로 말한 정답이다.

08. [US-US]

Isn't Mark Brown your most senior staff member?
(A) Several other supervisors.
(B) No, he just recently started here.
(C) An opening on the marketing team.

senior 고위의   supervisor 감독관, 관리자

Mark Brown이 가장 직위가 높은 직원 아닌가요?
(A) 여러 다른 관리자들이요.
(B) 아니요, 그는 최근에 막 이곳에서 근무를 시작했어요.
(C) 마케팅 팀에 공석이 있어요.

[해설] Mark Brown이 가장 직위가 높은 직원인지 확인하는 부정 의문문이다.
(A) 질문의 senior staff member에서 연상할 수 있는 supervisors를 이용해 혼동을 유도하는 오답이다.
(B) No로 응답한 후 이곳에서 근무를 시작한 지 얼마 안 되었다고 부연 설명하고 있는 정답이다.
(C) 질문의 staff member에서 직원 충원과 관련된 상황, 즉 공석(opening)이 생긴 상황을 연상하도록 유도하는 오답이다.

09. [BR-AU]

Aren't you glad you joined the fitness program?
(A) This shirt doesn't fit me.
(B) One hour every day.
(C) Yes, I feel so healthy.

join 가입하다   fit (옷 등이) 맞다

신체 단련 프로그램에 가입하니 기분이 좋지 않나요?
(A) 이 셔츠는 제게 맞지 않아요.
(B) 매일 한 시간이요.
(C) 네, 아주 건강해지는 느낌이에요.

[해설] 신체 단련 프로그램에 가입하니 기분이 좋지 않냐며 확인하는 부정 의문문이다.
(A) 질문의 fitness와 발음이 유사한 fit을 이용해 혼동을 유도하는 오답이다.
(B) 소요 시간을 묻는 How long 의문문에 적합한 응답이다.
(C) Yes로 응답한 후 건강해지는 느낌이라는 말을 덧붙인 정답이다.

10. [US-BR]

Haven't you already renewed your certificates this year?
(A) These are newly released.
(B) No, they are valid until next year.
(C) It's not a certification program.

renew 갱신[연장]하다   certificate 자격증, 증명서   release 공개[발표]하다   valid 유효한   certification 증명, 인증

올해 당신의 자격증을 이미 갱신하지 않았나요?
(A) 이것들은 새롭게 공개되었어요.
(B) 아니요, 그것들은 내년까지 유효해요.
(C) 그것은 인증 프로그램이 아니에요.

[해설] 자격증을 갱신했는지 여부를 확인하는 부정 의문문이다.
(A) 질문의 renewed와 비슷한 발음의 newly를 사용하여 혼동을 유도한 오답이다.
(B) 부정의 No로 응답한 후 내년까지 유효하다며 갱신하지 않은 이유를 덧붙인 정답이다.
(C) 질문의 certificates와 관련된 단어인 certification을 사용하여 혼동을 유도한 오답이다.

11. [AU-US]

Isn't the HR Department going to the workshop next week?
(A) A few more interviews.
(B) That is rescheduled for this week.
(C) The event was packed.

packed (사람들이) 꽉 들어찬

다음 주에 인사부가 워크숍에 가지 않나요?
(A) 면접이 몇 개 더 있어요.
(B) 이번 주로 일정이 변경되었어요.
(C) 그 행사에는 사람들이 많았어요.

[해설] 다음 주에 인사부가 워크숍에 가지 않는지 확인하는 부정 의문문이다.
(A) 질문의 HR Department의 주요 업무인 interviews(면접)를 이용해 혼동을 유도하는 오답이다.
(B) 이번 주로 일정이 바뀌었다며 질문자의 정보를 정정해줌으로써 부정의 No를 우회적으로 말한 정답이다.
(C) 질문의 workshop에서 연상 가능한 event를 이용해 혼동을 유도하는 오답이다.

12. US-BR

Aren't you joining a tennis club after work today?
(A) It was a good game.
(B) No, I have a report to review.
(C) Four tickets, please.

join 가입하다, 함께 ~하다 review 검토하다

오늘 근무 후에 테니스 클럽에 가입하지 않으실래요?
(A) 좋은 경기였어요.
(B) 아니요, 저는 검토해야 할 보고서가 있어요.
(C) 입장권 4장 주세요.

[해설] 테니스 클럽에 가입하지 않을지 확인하는 부정 의문문이다.
(A) 질문의 tennis에서 연상할 수 있는 game을 사용하여 혼동을 유도한 오답이다.
(B) No로 응답한 후 보고서를 검토해야 한다고 이유를 설명하고 있으므로 정답이다.
(C) 질문의 tennis에서 연상할 수 있는 tickets를 사용하여 혼동을 유도한 오답이다.

13. BR-AU

Didn't you want me to buy 10 tickets for this game?
(A) Mike and Julia have a family emergency.
(B) I'd like to go there.
(C) Yes, the game was exciting.

family emergency 급한 집안일

제가 이 경기 티켓 10장을 사기를 바라지 않았나요?
(A) Mike와 Julia에게 급한 집안일이 있어요.
(B) 저는 그곳에 가고 싶어요.
(C) 네, 그 경기는 흥미진진했어요.

[해설] 자신이 경기 티켓 10장을 사기를 바라지 않았는지 확인하는 부정 의문문이다.
(A) Mike와 Julia에게 급한 집안일이 생겼다고 말함으로써 함께 경기를 보려고 했었던 사람들 중 일부가 사정상 함께할 수 없어 티켓 10장 모두가 필요하지 않은 상황임을 우회적으로 설명하는 정답이다.
(B) 질문과 무관한 내용의 응답으로, 경기를 관람하고 싶은지 묻는 질문에 적합하다.
(C) 질문의 game을 반복해 혼동을 유도한 오답이다.

14. BR-BR

Weren't you getting a new office chair?
(A) A comfortable seat.
(B) It's temporarily out of stock now.
(C) Yes, I like the new office.

temporarily 일시적으로, 임시로 out of stock 품절된

당신은 새 사무실 의자를 마련할 예정 아니었나요?
(A) 편안한 좌석입니다.
(B) 그것은 지금 일시적으로 품절이에요.
(C) 네, 저는 새 사무실이 마음에 들어요.

[해설] 새 사무실 의자를 마련할 것 아니었는지 확인하는 부정 의문문이다.
(A) 질문의 chair에서 연상할 수 있는 seat을 이용하여 혼동을 유도하는 오답이다.
(B) 지금 일시적으로 품절 상태라고 답함으로써, 구하지 못했음을 우회적으로 말하고 있으므로 정답이다.
(C) Yes로 답했으나 이어지는 내용이 어색하다. 질문의 office를 반복 사용한 오답이다.

15. BR-US

Shouldn't we send out a group text message?
(A) An online notification system.
(B) That's a good idea.
(C) I prefer this font.

notification 알림, 통지 font 서체, 폰트

우리가 단체 문자 메시지를 발송해야 하지 않을까요?
(A) 온라인 통보 시스템입니다.
(B) 그거 좋은 생각이에요.
(C) 저는 이 서체가 더 좋아요.

[해설] 단체 문자 메시지를 발송하자고 제안하는 부정 의문문이다.
(A) 질문의 text message에서 연상할 수 있는 online notification(온라인 통보)을 이용해 혼동을 유도하는 오답이다.
(B) 좋은 생각이라며 질문자의 제안에 찬성하는 정답이다.
(C) 질문의 text에서 연상할 수 있는 font를 이용해 혼동을 유도하는 오답이다.

16. US-AU

Won't you stay for the appreciation dinner tonight?
(A) A delicious spread.
(B) I appreciate your concern.
(C) No, I have to take a 6 P.M. flight back.

spread 진수 성찬 concern 우려, 걱정

오늘 밤 감사 만찬 동안 머무르실 것 아닌가요?
(A) 맛있는 진수 성찬입니다.
(B) 걱정해주셔서 감사해요.
(C) 아니요, 저는 저녁 6시 항공편을 타고 돌아가야 해요.

[해설] 감사 만찬 동안 머무를 건지 확인하는 부정 의문문이다.
(A) 질문의 dinner에서 연상할 수 있는 delicious spread(맛있는 진수 성찬)를 이용해 혼동을 유도하는 오답이다.
(B) 질문의 appreciation의 동사형인 appreciate를 이용해 혼동을 유

도하는 응답이다.
(C) No로 응답한 후 6시 항공편을 타고 돌아가야 한다는 이유를 덧붙인 정답이다.

PART 3　주제·목적 문제 / 장소·직업 문제 / 세부 사항 문제

 연습 문제

01. (B)　02. (A)　03. (B)　04. (B)　05. (A)　06. (B)

01. [AU-BR]

What are the speakers **talking about**?
(A) A **budget** proposal　(B) **Job application** reviews

M: I still have a lot of job applications to be reviewed by this Friday. Could you help me?
W: Sure, I have some free time this afternoon. I just finished the budget proposal for next quarter. Can you print some of them? It will be much easier to review it.

job application 입사 지원서

화자들은 무엇에 대해 이야기하는가?
(A) 예산안　**(B) 입사 지원서 검토**

남: 저는 이번 주 금요일까지 검토해야 할 입사 지원서가 아직도 많아요. 저를 도와줄 수 있으세요?
여: 물론이죠. 제가 오늘 오후에 시간이 좀 있어요. 다음 분기를 위한 예산안을 지금 막 끝냈거든요. 그것들을 프린트해서 줄 수 있나요? 검토하기에 훨씬 더 수월할 거예요.

02. [BR-US]

Why is the **woman calling** the man?
(A) To **ask for** a list　(B) To **schedule** a meeting

W: Hi, Chris, this is Beth from Personnel. I'm calling you to request the list of the participants who attended the conference last week.
M: Sure, do you need it right now? I'm out of the office to visit one of our clients.

request 요청하다　participant 참석자

여자는 왜 남자에게 전화하는가?
(A) 목록을 요청하기 위해서　(B) 회의 일정을 잡기 위해서

여: 안녕하세요, Chris, 저는 인사부의 Beth예요. 지난주에 학회에 참가한 참석자들의 목록을 요청하려고 전화했어요.
남: 물론이죠, 지금 바로 필요하신가요? 제가 우리 고객들 중 한 명을 만나기 위해 사무실 밖에 나와 있어요.

03. [US-US]

Where does the **woman** most likely **work**?
(A) At a **travel agency**　(B) At an **airport**

W: Good morning! Thank you for choosing Swedish Airlines. Where are you flying to today?
M: I'm going to Los Angeles. Here's my passport and reservation information.

airline 항공사　passport 여권　reservation 예약

여자는 어디에서 일하겠는가?
(A) 여행사에서　**(B) 공항에서**

여: 안녕하세요! Swedish 항공을 선택해 주셔서 감사합니다. 오늘 어디로 가실 건가요?
남: 로스앤젤레스로 갈 거예요. 여기 제 여권과 예약 정보가 있어요.

04. [BR-US]

Who most likely is the **man**?
(A) An **appliance salesperson**
(B) A **maintenance worker**

W: Hello, this is Amelia Benitez calling from the ninth floor. The heater isn't working again. Could you come up and take a look at it?
M: It stopped working again? I'll get my toolbox and head up there as soon as I can.

toolbox 공구함　head 가다, 향하다

남자는 누구이겠는가?
(A) 가전제품 판매원　**(B) 유지 보수 직원**

여: 안녕하세요. 저는 9층에서 전화 드리는 Amelia Benitez입니다. 히터가 또 작동하지 않아요. 오셔서 봐 주실 수 있으신가요?
남: 또 작동하지 않는다고요? 제 공구함을 챙겨서 가능한 한 빨리 그곳으로 올라갈게요.

05. [BR-US]

What did the **company** do **last week**?
(A) **Won** an **award**　(B) **Released** a new **product**

W: Did you read the memo from the management? Our company won the Most Innovative Design Award last week.
M: Yes, it was exciting news. Our team members worked hard to develop the new blender.

management 경영진

회사는 지난주에 무엇을 했는가?
(A) 상을 받았다　(B) 신상품을 출시했다

여: 경영진에서 보낸 회람을 읽으셨어요? 우리 회사가 지난주에 가장 혁신적인 디자인 상을 받았대요.
남: 네, 좋은 소식이었어요. 우리 팀원들이 그 새 믹서기를 개발하기 위해 열심히 일했어요.

06. (BR-AU)

Why is the **woman unable to enter**?
(A) A **device** is **malfunctioning**.
(B) She **doesn't have** her **security card**.

> W: Hello, I'm Lucy from the marketing department. I forgot to bring my security card. Would you open the door please?
> M: Sorry, I'm not allowed to do that. I will send someone down to escort you to the security office. A temporary card will be issued after a verification procedure.

escort 바래다주다　temporary 임시의　issue 발급하다
verification 확인

여자는 왜 들어갈 수 없는가?
(A) 기기가 제대로 작동하지 않는다.
(B) 그녀는 보안 카드가 없다.

여: 안녕하세요, 저는 마케팅 부서의 Lucy입니다. 제가 보안 카드를 가지고 오는 것을 잊어버렸어요. 문을 열어주시겠어요?
남: 죄송합니다, 제가 그렇게 하도록 허용되지 않아요. 보안 사무실까지 당신을 바래다줄 사람이 내려오도록 할게요. 확인 절차 후에 임시 카드가 발급될 거예요.

paraphrasing 정답　1. (a)　2. (c)　3. (b)　4. (b)　5. (c)　6. (a)

실전 문제

01. (C)	02. (D)	03. (A)	04. (A)	05. (C)	06. (A)
07. (C)	08. (B)	09. (D)	10. (C)	11. (C)	12. (B)
13. (C)	14. (A)	15. (C)	16. (A)	17. (D)	18. (A)
19. (B)	20. (A)	21. (C)	22. (C)	23. (D)	24. (B)

[01-03] (US-US)

Questions 01-03 refer to the following conversation.

> M: Excuse me. Are you familiar with the ⁰¹**bus system**? **I'm wondering about the best way to get to the Eastdale neighborhood.**
> W: ⁰²**The 304 departs from here about every half hour.** ⁰¹**It has stops near major sites** like the Valley Mall and the Klein Hotel. But you just missed it.
> M: What a shame! That's the one I needed. Do you know if there are ⁰²**any other routes from here?**
> W: I'm not sure, but ⁰³**there is a complete list of routes on the Department of Transportation's Web site.** You can just check it from your phone.

be familiar with ~에 대해 잘 알다　neighborhood 근처, 인근, 이웃　depart from ~에서 출발하다　site 위치, 장소
route (버스·기차 등의) 노선　complete 모든 것이 갖춰진, 완전한
transportation 교통, 수송

01-03은 다음 대화에 관한 문제입니다.
남: 실례합니다. ⁰¹**버스 체계**에 대해 잘 아시나요? ⁰¹**Eastdale 근처에 가는 가장 좋은 방법**이 궁금해서요.
여: ⁰²**304번이 약 30분마다 여기서 출발해요.** Valley 쇼핑몰과 Klein 호텔 같은 ⁰¹**주요 장소 근처에 정류장**이 있어요. 하지만 방금 놓치셨어요.
남: 이런! 제가 타야 했던 게 바로 그거예요. ⁰²**여기서 가는 다른 노선**이 있는지 아시나요?
여: 잘 모르겠어요, 하지만 ⁰³**교통부 웹사이트에 노선 전체 목록이 있어요.** 휴대폰에서도 간단히 확인하실 수 있어요.

01.

무엇에 관한 대화인가?
(A) 호텔 정책
(B) 이동 요금
(C) 버스 노선
(D) 수하물 한도

[해설] 주제를 묻는 문제의 단서는 주로 대화의 전반부에 나온다. 대화 초반, 남자가 버스 체계(bus system)를 언급하며 Eastdale 근처에 가는 방법(the best way to get to the Eastdale neighborhood)을 묻자, 여자가 구체적인 버스 번호와 배차 간격 및 정류장 등 버스 노선에 대한 정보를 알려주고 있는 것으로 보아 두 사람은 버스 노선에 대해 이야기하고 있음을 알 수 있으므로 정답은 (C)이다.

[어휘] fare (교통) 요금

02.

화자들은 어디에 있는가?
(A) 자동차 정비소에
(B) 주차장에
(C) 여행사에
(D) 버스 정류장에

[해설] 대화가 이루어지는 장소를 묻는 문제로, 304번이 30분마다 여기서 출발한다는(The 304 departs from here about every half hour) 여자의 말과 여기서 출발하는 다른 노선(any other routes from here)이 있는지 묻는 남자의 말에서 버스 정류장에서 이루어지는 대화임을 알 수 있으므로 정답은 (D)이다.

03.

여자는 무엇을 하라고 제안하는가?
(A) 웹사이트 방문하기
(B) 티켓 교환하기
(C) 신분증 제시하기
(D) 공식적인 불만 제기하기

[해설] 여자가 제안하는 것을 묻는 문제로, 여자의 대사에서 정답의 근거를 찾는다. 다른 버스 노선에 대해 궁금해하는 남자에게 여자가 교통부 웹사이트에 노선 전체 목록이 있다고(there is a complete list of routes on the Department of Transportation's Web site) 했으므로 정답은 (A)이다.

paraphrasing　there is a complete list of routes on the Department of Transportation's Web site 교통부 웹사이트에 노선 전체 목록이 있다 → Visiting a Web site 웹사이트 방문하기

[어휘] present 제시하다, 보여주다　make a complaint 불만을 제기하다　formal 공식적인

[04-06] BR-AU

Questions 04-06 refer to the following conversation.

W: Hi, Carl. It's Rochelle. I wanted to check on **04how things are going with putting the new roof on Ms. Fletcher's house.**
M: We're making steady progress.
W: Wonderful! As you know, Ms. Fletcher is getting ready to put her home on the market. **05She plans to have a professional photographer come by on Thursday to do a shoot for the real estate listing.** Will that be a problem?
M: Not at all. **06My crew members have been cutting their breaks short so that we can be done by tomorrow afternoon.**
W: Thanks. I'll let Ms. Fletcher know.

make steady progress 착착 진행되다   professional 전문적인, 직업의   come by 잠깐 들르다   real estate 부동산   crew (함께 일을 하는) 팀, 반, 조   cut A short A를 갑자기 끝내다, 삭감하다

04-06은 다음 대화에 관한 문제입니다.
여: 안녕하세요, Carl. Rochelle이에요. **04Fletcher 씨 집의 지붕을 새로 놓는 작업이 어떻게 되어가고 있는지** 확인하고 싶었어요.
남: 착착 진행되고 있어요.
여: 좋아요! 아시다시피 Fletcher 씨가 집을 내놓으려고 하잖아요. **05그녀가 목요일에 전문 사진사를 불러서 부동산 매물 목록용 촬영을 할 계획이에요.** 그게 문제가 될까요?
남: 전혀요. **06저희 팀원들이 내일 오후까지 완료하기 위해 휴식 시간도 줄여가며 일하고 있어요.**
여: 고마워요. Fletcher 씨에게 전해줄게요.

04.
어떤 종류의 프로젝트에 대해 이야기하고 있는가?
(A) 지붕 교체하기
(B) 주택에 페인트칠하기
(C) 창문 설치하기
(D) 정원에 나무 심기

[해설] 대화의 주제는 대화 전반부에서 확인할 수 있다. 여자의 첫 번째 대사에서 Fletcher 씨 집의 지붕을 새로 놓는(putting the new roof) 일이 어떻게 되어가고 있는지 확인하고 싶다고 했고, 뒤이어 작업 일정에 대해 이야기하는 것으로 보아 주택의 지붕을 교체하는 작업에 관해 논의하고 있음을 알 수 있으므로 정답은 (A)이다.

paraphrasing putting the new roof 지붕 새로 놓기 → Replacing a roof 지붕 교체하기

[어휘] replace 교체하다   plant a garden 정원에 나무를 심다

05.
목요일에 무슨 일이 예정되어 있는가?
(A) 새로운 규정이 발효될 것이다.
(B) 검사가 실시될 것이다.
(C) 사진을 촬영할 것이다.
(D) 일부 비품이 배송될 것이다.

[해설] 핵심 키워드인 Thursday가 언급된 곳에 정답의 단서가 있다. 대화 중반부에서 의뢰인으로 보이는 Fletcher 씨가 집을 부동산 매물로 내놓기 위해 목요일에 전문 사진사를 불러 촬영을 진행할 계획이라고(She plans to have a professional photographer come by on Thursday to do a shoot) 했으므로 목요일에 사진 촬영이 있을 것임을 알 수 있다. 따라서 정답은 (C)이다.

paraphrasing have a professional photographer come by on Thursday to do a shoot 목요일에 전문 사진사를 불러서 촬영을 하게 하다 → Some photographs will be taken. 사진을 촬영할 것이다.

[어휘] regulation 규정   go into effect 발효하다, 실시되다   inspection 점검, 검사   carry out ~을 실시하다   supplies 비품

06.
남자는 자신의 팀원들에 대해서 무엇이라고 언급하는가?
(A) 휴식 시간을 줄였다.
(B) 주말에도 일할 수 있다.
(C) 경험이 풍부하다.
(D) Fletcher 씨에게 연락할 것이다.

[해설] 남자의 마지막 말에 crew members, 즉 자신의 팀원들에 대한 언급이 나온다. 내일 오후까지 작업을 마치기 위해 팀원들이 휴식 시간까지 줄였다고(My crew members have been cutting their breaks short) 했으므로 (A)가 정답이다.

paraphrasing My crew members have been cutting their breaks short 팀원들이 휴식 시간을 줄여가며 일하고 있다. → They took shorter breaks. 휴식 시간을 줄였다.

[어휘] take a break 잠시 휴식을 취하다   highly 대단히, 매우

[07-09] AU-US

Questions 07-09 refer to the following conversation.

M: **07You've reached Henderson Taxi Service.** This is Todd. How may I help you?
W: Good morning. My team and I are coming to Vancouver to inspect a manufacturing facility next week, and my hotel doesn't have a shuttle. **08I'm wondering how much it would cost for a trip from the airport to downtown.**
M: Will you be able to use one of our standard cars?
W: Probably not. There will be five of us as well as five bags.
M: In that case, you'll need one of our larger cabs. We only have a few of those, **09so I strongly suggest that you book ahead of time** so you're not disappointed.

inspect 점검하다   manufacturing facility 생산 시설   standard 일반적인, 보통의, 표준의   in that case 그런 경우라면, 그렇다면   ahead of time 미리, 사전에

07-09는 다음 대화에 관한 문제입니다.
남: **07Henderson 택시 서비스입니다.** 저는 Todd입니다. 어떻게 도와드릴까요?
여: 안녕하세요. 저희 팀이 다음 주에 밴쿠버에 가서 생산 시설을 점검할 예정인데 호텔에 셔틀 서비스가 없네요. **08공항에서 시내까지 이동하는 데 비용이 얼마나 들지 궁금합니다.**

남: 저희 표준 차량 중 하나를 이용하시면 될까요?
여: 그건 안 될 거예요. 저희 인원이 다섯 명이고 가방도 다섯 개예요.
남: 그렇다면, 저희의 대형 택시 중 한 대가 필요하시겠네요. 그런 차량은 몇 대밖에 보유하고 있지 않으니 **09미리 예약하실 것을 강력히 제안드립니다.** 그래야 실망하시는 일이 없을 거예요.

07.

남자는 어떤 종류의 업체에서 근무하는가?
(A) 생산 시설
(B) 호텔
(C) 택시 회사
(D) 항공사

[해설] 화자의 직업을 묻는 문제는 대화 초반부에 정답의 근거가 언급될 가능성이 크다. 대화 시작 부분에서 남자가 소속 회사를 'Henderson 택시 서비스(Henderson Taxi Service)'라고 명확히 밝혔으므로 남자가 택시 회사에서 근무함을 알 수 있다. 따라서 정답은 (C)이다.

08.

전화의 목적은 무엇인가?
(A) 대금을 지불하기 위해
(B) 요금에 대해 문의하기 위해
(C) 입사 지원을 하기 위해
(D) 예약을 변경하기 위해

[해설] 무엇을 도와줄지 묻는 남자의 말에 여자는 공항에서 시내까지 이동하는 데 비용이 얼마나 드는지 궁금하다며(I'm wondering how much it would cost for a trip from the airport to downtown) 용건을 구체적으로 밝혔다. 따라서 택시 요금 문의가 전화의 목적임을 알 수 있으므로 정답은 (B)이다.

[어휘] make a payment 대금을 지불하다 inquire about ~에 대해 문의하다 apply for ~에 지원하다

09.

남자가 제안하는 것은 무엇인가?
(A) 수하물에 라벨 붙이기
(B) 주소 확인하기
(C) 쿠폰 다운로드하기
(D) 사전 예약 하기

[해설] 남자가 제안하는 것을 묻는 문제로, 후반부 남자의 말에 집중한다. 여자의 일행에게 대형 택시를 제안하면서 해당 차량의 보유 수량이 적으니 미리 예약할 것을 권하고(so I strongly suggest that you book ahead of time) 있다. 즉, 사전 예약을 제안하고 있으므로 (D)가 정답이다.

paraphrasing book ahead of time 미리 예약하기 → Making an advance booking 사전 예약 하기

[어휘] label 라벨을 붙이다, 딱지를 붙이다 advance booking 사전 예약

[10-12] BR-BR

Questions 10-12 refer to the following conversation.

W: Hello. **10I'd like to reserve six tickets for the orchestra concert** on June 4.
M: That show is very popular, so let me see what's available. Hmm... we do have six seats still open, but **11three of them are in Row K and the other three are in Row M. I'm sorry about that.** Do you still want them?
W: Well, I don't think that will be a problem, but **12I'd better call my friends to make sure.**
M: I understand. I can hold this reservation for you for up to thirty minutes while you work out the details. Just come back to the counter when you're ready.

reserve 예약하다   make sure ~을 확실히 하다

10-12는 다음 대화에 관한 문제입니다.

여: 안녕하세요. 6월 4일에 있을 **10오케스트라 콘서트 티켓 6장을 예약하고 싶습니다.**
남: 그 공연은 인기가 매우 많아서, 표가 있는지 한번 볼게요. 음... 아직 여섯 좌석이 있긴 한데 **11그중 셋은 K열이고 나머지 셋은 M열이에요. 죄송합니다.** 그래도 구매하시겠어요?
여: 음, 그건 문제가 될 것 같지 않지만 **12확실하게 하기 위해서 친구들에게 전화해보는 게 좋겠어요.**
남: 알겠습니다. 세부적인 것들을 결정하시는 동안 최대 30분 동안 예약을 보류해 놓겠습니다. 준비되시면 카운터로 다시 오세요.

10.

대화는 주로 무엇에 관한 것인가?
(A) 일정 변경
(B) 티켓 분실
(C) 좌석 예약
(D) 음악 수업

[해설] 여자가 첫 번째 대사에서 오케스트라 콘서트의 티켓을 예약하겠다고(I'd like to reserve six tickets for the orchestra concert) 했고, 이어지는 대화에서 해당 공연의 잔여 좌석 수 및 좌석 위치 등에 대해 이야기하고 있다. 따라서 공연 좌석 예약에 대한 대화임을 알 수 있으므로 정답은 (C)이다.

[어휘] lost 잃어버린

11.

남자는 무엇에 대해 사과하는가?
(A) 최근에 요금이 인상되었다.
(B) 단체 할인을 이용할 수 없다.
(C) 일부 좌석이 붙어 있지 않을 것이다.
(D) 티켓이 교환되지 않는다.

[해설] 질문의 apologize가 핵심 키워드로, 남자의 대사 중 I'm sorry가 언급된 부분에 단서가 있다. 여자가 구매하고자 하는 좌석들이 따로 떨어져 있음을(three of them are in Row K and the other three are in Row M) 알린 후 미안하다고(I'm sorry about that) 덧붙이고 있으므로 일부 좌석이 붙어 있지 않을 것이라고 한 (C)가 정답이다.

[어휘] recently 최근에 increase 인상되다, 증가하다 exchange 교환하다

12.

여자는 다음에 무엇을 할 것 같은가?
(A) 웹사이트를 확인하기
(B) 전화하기
(C) 티켓 값을 지불하기

(D) 다른 지점을 방문하기

[해설] 여자의 후반부 대사에 단서가 있다. 좌석이 떨어져 있는데도 구매하겠냐는 남자의 질문에 여자는 확실하게 하기 위해서 친구들에게 전화해보는 게 좋겠다고(I'd better call my friends to make sure) 했으므로 여자가 전화를 할 것임을 알 수 있다. 따라서 정답은 (B)이다.

paraphrasing call 전화하다 → Make some phone calls 전화하기

[어휘] branch 지점, 지사

[13-15] US-BR

Questions 13-15 refer to the following conversation.

> M: Good morning, Anna. ¹³**I heard that we had some complaints about slow service last night.** Were you working at that time?
> W: I was. ¹⁴**One of our servers and a kitchen assistant** both called in sick right before they were supposed to come in to work.
> M: I see. Well, next time that happens, ¹⁵**try calling some of our other staff to ask them to come in.** Several of them have been asking for more work hours.

at that time 그때에 server (식당에서) 서빙하는 사람 assistant 조수, 보조원 call in sick 전화로 병결을 알리다 ask for ~를 요구하다

13-15는 다음 대화에 관한 문제입니다.

남: 안녕하세요, Anna. ¹³지난밤 서비스가 느려서 불평한 분들이 있었다고 들었어요. 그때 당신도 근무하고 있었나요?
여: 그랬어요. ¹⁴우리 서빙 직원 중 한 명과 주방 보조 직원이 둘 다 출근 직전에 전화를 해서 병가를 냈어요.
남: 그렇군요. 음, 다음번에 그런 일이 발생하면 ¹⁵다른 직원들에게 전화해서 나와 달라고 요청하세요. 근무 시간을 늘려 달라고 요청한 직원들이 여러 명 있었어요.

13.

어떤 문제가 논의되고 있는가?
(A) 메뉴가 변경되었다.
(B) 배송품이 도착하지 않았다.
(C) 일부 고객들이 불만을 제기했다.
(D) 직원 한 명이 지각했다.

[해설] 대화 초반, 남자가 여자에게 지난밤 서비스가 느려 불평이 있었다고(we had some complaints about slow service last night) 했고, 이어지는 대화에서 서비스가 느렸던 이유와 다음번에 같은 문제가 발생할 경우의 대책 등을 논의하고 있다. 따라서 정답은 (C)이다.

paraphrasing we had some complaints 불만을 들었다 → Some customers complained. 일부 고객들이 불만을 제기했다.

[어휘] shipment 배송품

14.

화자들은 어디에 고용되어 있는 것 같은가?
(A) 식당에
(B) 창고에
(C) 지역 슈퍼마켓에
(D) 배송 센터에

[해설] 지난밤에 서비스가 느렸던 이유는 서빙 직원(servers) 한 명과 주방 보조 직원(kitchen assistant) 한 명이 아파서 결근했기 때문이라고 했으므로 화자들이 일하는 곳은 식당임을 알 수 있다. 따라서 정답은 (A)이다.

15.

남자는 여자에게 무엇을 하라고 말하는가?
(A) 직원을 더 고용하기
(B) 매니저에게 연락하기
(C) 다른 직원들에게 전화하기
(D) 상품을 정리하기

[해설] 남자가 여자에게 요청한 일을 묻는 문제이다. 대화 마지막에서 남자는 다음번에 그런 일이 발생하면 다른 직원들에게 전화해서 나와 달라고 요청하라고(try calling some of our other staff to ask them to come in) 했다. 따라서 정답은 (C)이다.

paraphrasing other staff 다른 직원들 → other employees 다른 직원들

[어휘] hire 고용하다 organize 준비하다, 정리하다 merchandise 상품

[16-18] AU-US

Questions 16-18 refer to the following conversation.

> M: Hello, ¹⁷**I'm staying in room 214** and ¹⁶**the TV isn't working right.** I can only get one channel.
> W: ¹⁷**I'm sorry to hear about that. We received the same complaint from another guest,** and a technician is on his way here now.
> M: Okay, but since I paid for a room with cable TV, can I get reimbursed for the extra charge? It only seems fair.
> W: Yes, of course. ¹⁸**If you would like, I can send your updated invoice by e-mail.**

receive 받다   technician 기술자, 기사   pay for 대금을 지불하다   get reimbursed 환급 받다   extra charge 초과 요금   fair 타당한, 온당한   invoice 송장, 청구서

16-18은 다음 대화에 관한 문제입니다.

남: 여보세요, ¹⁷저는 **214호**에 묵고 있는데요, ¹⁶TV가 제대로 나오지 않습니다. 한 채널만 볼 수 있어요.
여: ¹⁷그렇다니 죄송합니다. 다른 손님으로부터 같은 불만을 접수해서, 기술자가 지금 오고 있는 중입니다.
남: 알겠습니다. 그런데 제가 케이블 TV가 포함된 객실의 요금을 지불했으니 초과 요금을 환급 받을 수 있는 건가요? 그렇게 되어야 마땅할 것 같은데요.
여: 네, 물론입니다. ¹⁸원하시면 수정된 청구서를 이메일로 보내드릴 수 있습니다.

16.

남자가 전화한 목적은 무엇인가?
(A) 불만을 제기하는 것
(B) 텔레비전을 구매하는 것

(C) 지역 채널에 대해 문의하는 것
(D) 다른 방을 요청하는 것

[해설] 남자가 첫 대사에서 객실 번호를 밝히며 TV가 제대로 나오지 않아 한 채널만 볼 수 있다고(the TV isn't working right. I can only get one channel.) 했으므로 불만을 제기하기 위해서 전화했음을 알 수 있다. 따라서 정답은 (A)이다.

[어휘] complaint 불만 purchase 구매하다

17.
여자는 누구일 것 같은가?
(A) 건설 노동자
(B) 케이블 기술자
(C) 전자제품 판매원
(D) 호텔 안내 데스크 직원

[해설] 여자의 직업을 묻는 문제이다. 호텔 숙박객으로 보이는(I'm staying in room 214) 남자의 전화를 응대하고 있는(I'm sorry to hear about that. We received the same complaint from another guest ~) 것으로 보아 여자는 호텔 안내 데스크 직원임을 알 수 있으므로 정답은 (D)이다.

[어휘] construction 건설, 공사 electronics 전자제품 salesperson 판매원, 영업사원

18.
여자는 무엇을 해주겠다고 하는가?
(A) 청구서를 이메일로 보내기
(B) 룸서비스 보내주기
(C) 관리자에게 연락하기
(D) 전액 환불 해주기

[해설] 여자가 제안한 일이 무엇인지 묻는 문제로, 후반부 여자의 대사에 단서가 있다. 일부 요금 환불을 원하는 남자에게 여자가 수정된 청구서를 이메일로 보내줄 수 있다고(If you would like, I can send your updated invoice by e-mail.) 했으므로 정답은 (A)이다.

[paraphrasing] I can send your updated invoice by e-mail 수정된 청구서를 이메일로 보내드릴 수 있다 → e-mail a bill 청구서를 이메일로 보내다

[어휘] bill 청구서 supervisor 감독관, 관리자 full refund 전액 환불

[19-21] US-BR
Questions 19-21 refer to the following conversation.

> M: Heidy, I wanted to talk to you. ¹⁹**We've been getting most of our produce from Lewis Farms,** but maybe we should try Tanner Farms as a ¹⁹**supplier.**
> W: Really? Why do you think so?
> M: ²⁰**All of their produce is organic,** and organic foods are becoming popular these days.
> W: That's not a bad idea. But I think it's important to get the word out. ²¹**Could you make a flyer that we could distribute to attract more shoppers?**

> produce 농산물 try 써보다, 해보다 supplier 공급자, 공급 회사 get the word out 말을 퍼트리다 flyer (광고·안내용) 전단 distribute 배포하다

19-21은 다음 대화에 관한 문제입니다.
남: Heidy, 당신과 얘기하고 싶었어요. ¹⁹우리가 Lewis Farms에서 대부분의 농산물을 구해왔잖아요, 그런데 아마도 ¹⁹공급업체로 Tanner Farms를 이용해봐야겠어요.
여: 정말이요? 왜 그렇게 생각하세요?
남: ²⁰그들의 농산물은 모두 유기농인데, 요즘 유기농 식품이 인기가 많아지고 있어요.
여: 괜찮은 생각이에요. 하지만 입소문이 나게 하는 것이 중요한 것 같아요. ²¹우리가 더 많은 고객을 끌어모을 수 있도록 배포할 전단을 만들어주시겠어요?

19.
화자들은 어디서 일할 것 같은가?
(A) 빵집에서
(B) 식료품점에서
(C) 유기농 농장에서
(D) 마케팅 회사에서

[해설] 남자가 Lewis Farms에서 대부분의 농산물을 구해왔다고(We've been getting most of our produce from Lewis Farms) 한 것과 '공급업체(supplier)', '유기농 식품(organic foods)' 등을 언급한 것으로 보아 화자들은 공급업체로부터 식품을 납품 받아 일반 소비자에게 판매하는 식료품점에서 일함을 알 수 있다. 따라서 정답은 (B)이다.

20.
남자는 새 공급업체의 어떤 점이 마음에 든다고 말하는가?
(A) 농산물을 유기농으로 재배한다.
(B) 친절한 서비스를 제공한다.
(C) 가격이 적당하다.
(D) 무료 배송을 해준다.

[해설] 질문의 핵심 키워드 a new supplier는 남자가 새로운 공급업체로 고려하고 있는 Tanner Farms를 가리킨다. 대화 중반, 남자는 이들의 장점으로 모든 농산물이 유기농이라는(All of their produce is organic) 점을 언급했으므로 정답은 (A)이다.

[paraphrasing] all of their produce is organic 그들의 농산물은 모두 유기농이다 → It grows produce organically. 농산물을 유기농으로 재배한다.

[어휘] affordable (가격이) 알맞은 free delivery 무료 배송

21.
여자는 남자에게 무엇을 하라고 요청하는가?
(A) 재고 조사 하기
(B) 전단 만들기
(C) 공급업체에 연락하기
(D) 발표하기

[해설] 여자가 남자에게 부탁한 것을 묻는 문제로, 대화 후반 여자의 대사에 단서가 있다. 여자는 더 많은 고객을 끌어모을 수 있도록 배포할 전단을 만들어달라고(Could you make a flyer ~) 부탁한다. 따라서 정답은 (B)이다.

[paraphrasing] make a flyer 전단 만들기 → create a flyer 전단 만들기

[어휘] take inventory 재고 조사를 하다

[22-24] BR-US

Questions 22-24 refer to the following conversation.

W: Hi, Luke. **22How was your trip to Seattle?** It's been a while since you took such a long vacation.
M: It was nice to relax, but the weather was cold and rainy the whole time I was there.
W: If you want to enjoy sunny, warm weather then you should go to Southern California. **23That region is known for its favorable weather throughout the year.**
M: Who doesn't know that? I have to visit my younger sister there. Actually I'll take a business trip to LA next month, so I'll have a chance to enjoy the favorable weather.
W: Great. I've actually been looking at some travel blogs about the southwest. **24I'll send you the links so you can check them out.**

region 지역, 지방   be known for ~로 알려져 있다   favorable (기후가) 양호한

22-24는 다음 대화에 관한 문제입니다.

여: 안녕하세요, Luke. **22시애틀 여행은 어땠어요?** 당신이 그렇게 긴 휴가를 떠난 게 한참 만이네요.
남: 느긋하게 쉬니까 좋았지만, 그곳에 있는 내내 날씨가 너무 춥고 비가 왔어요.
여: 화창하고 따뜻한 날씨를 즐기고 싶다면 남부 캘리포니아로 가야 해요. **23그 지역은 연중 온화한 날씨로 알려져 있어요.**
남: 모르는 사람이 어디 있겠어요. 전 그곳에 있는 제 여동생을 방문해야 해요. 실은 다음 달에 LA로 출장을 가요. 그러니 좋은 날씨를 즐길 기회가 있을 거예요.
여: 잘됐네요. 사실 제가 남서부에 대한 여행 블로그들을 구독하고 있어요. **24당신이 확인해볼 수 있도록 링크를 보내줄게요.**

22.

남자는 최근에 무엇을 했는가?
(A) 근처 동네로 이사했다.
(B) 새로운 사무실로 옮겼다.
(C) 휴가를 갔다.
(D) 승진을 했다.

[해설] 대화 시작 부분, 여자의 말에 정답의 단서가 있다. 여자는 남자에게 시애틀 여행이 어땠는지(How was your trip to Seattle?) 물었으며, 이어서 남자가 장기 휴가를 떠난 지(since you took such a long vacation) 한참이 되었다고 덧붙였다. 따라서 남자는 최근 시애틀로 휴가를 갔다가 돌아왔음을 알 수 있으므로 정답은 (C)이다.

paraphrasing   took such a long vacation 장기 휴가를 떠났다 → went on a vacation 휴가를 갔다

[어휘] nearby 인근의, 가까운 곳의   neighborhood 근처, 이웃   transfer to ~로 옮기다   promotion 승진

23.

여자에 따르면, 남부 캘리포니아의 이점은 무엇인가?
(A) 관광객들을 환대한다.
(B) 방문하는 데 비용이 많이 들지 않는다.
(C) 관광 명소가 많다.
(D) 날씨가 온화하다.

[해설] 질문의 키워드인 Southern California가 언급된 대화 중반, 여자는 화창하고 따뜻한 날씨를 즐기고 싶다면 남부 캘리포니아로 가야 한다면서, 그 지역은 연중 온화한 날씨로 알려져 있다고(That region is known for its favorable weather throughout the year.) 덧붙였다. 즉, 남부 캘리포니아 지역의 온화한 날씨를 언급했으므로 정답은 (D)이다.

[어휘] affordable (가격이) 적당한

24.

여자는 다음에 무엇을 할 것 같은가?
(A) 여행사에 연락하기
(B) 정보를 보내기
(C) 블로그 항목을 작성하기
(D) 항공편 예약하기

[해설] 앞으로 일어날 일에 관한 내용은 대화의 후반부에 언급된다. 여자가 남서부에 관한 여행 블로그를 언급하면서, 남자가 확인해보도록 링크를 보내주겠다고(I'll send you the links so you can check them out) 했다. '링크'를 '정보'로 바꿔 표현할 수 있으므로 (B)가 정답이다.

paraphrasing   send you the links 링크를 보내다 → send some information 정보를 보내다

[어휘] entry (장부·일기 등의 개별) 항목

DAY 07

PART 2   부가 의문문

확인 문제

❶ US-US

The new model is much more expensive, isn't it?
(A) Well, the price is almost the same.
(B) Mine works fine.

새로운 모델이 훨씬 더 비싸죠, 그렇지 않나요?
(A) 음, 가격은 거의 비슷합니다.
(B) 제 것은 잘 작동해요.

❷ BR-AU

You called the technical support team, didn't you?
(A) Actually, Claire did.
(B) No, it's broken.

당신이 기술 지원팀에 전화하셨죠, 그렇지 않나요?
(A) 사실, Claire가 했어요.
(B) 아뇨, 그건 고장 났어요.

❸ US-BR

I can park here on weekends, can't I?
(A) I'm available on Monday.
(B) You need to present the permit.

주말에는 여기에 주차해도 되죠, 그렇지 않나요?
(A) 저는 월요일에 시간이 있어요.
(B) 허가증을 제시하셔야 해요.

❹ AU-BR

You came here by train, right?
(A) The airport is located close to downtown.
(B) No, I drove my car.

당신은 여기에 기차를 타고 오셨죠, 맞죠?
(A) 공항은 시내 가까이에 있어요.
(B) 아뇨, 제 차를 운전해서 왔어요.

 연습 문제

01. (A) 02. (A) 03. (A) 04. (B) 05. (B) 06. (A)
07. (A) 08. (A)

01. US-BR

The proposal is due this Friday, isn't it?
(A) You can turn it in next Monday. [O]
(B) He accepted the proposal. [X]

proposal 제안서

그 제안서는 이번 주 금요일까지죠, 그렇지 않나요?
(A) 다음 주 월요일에 제출하셔도 됩니다.
(B) 그가 제안을 받아들였어요.

02. US-US

You won't be late for our annual conference, will you?
(A) No, I'll be there on time. [O]
(B) You are supposed to deliver a speech. [X]

연례 콘퍼런스에 늦지 않을 거죠, 그렇죠?
(A) 안 늦을 거예요. 정시에 가겠습니다.
(B) 당신은 연설을 하기로 되어 있어요.

03. BR-US

Ms. Curtis is leading the workshop, isn't she?
(A) No, she's on vacation. [O]
(B) It will last for a week. [X]

Curtis 씨가 워크숍을 진행할 거죠, 그렇지 않나요?
(A) 아뇨, 그녀는 휴가를 갔어요.
(B) 일주일 동안 진행될 거예요.

04. US-AU

You've seen the latest Anthony Russo movie, haven't you?
(A) I like to read movie reviews. [X]
(B) Not yet, I'll watch it this weekend. [O]

Anthony Russo의 최신 영화 보셨죠, 그렇지 않나요?
(A) 저는 영화 비평을 읽는 것을 좋아합니다.
(B) 아직 안 봤어요, 이번 주말에 볼 거예요.

05. AU-BR

You've already distributed the booklets to the participants, haven't you?
(A) No, it's my first time attending this event. [X]
(B) Yeah, but I need ten more of them. [O]

distribute 배포하다   booklet 소책자

소책자를 참석자들에게 이미 배포하셨죠, 그렇지 않나요?
(A) 아뇨, 저는 이 행사에 참석하는 게 이번이 처음이에요.
(B) 네, 그런데 10부가 더 필요해요.

06. US-US

Tomorrow is Tina's birthday, isn't it?
(A) Yeah, we should celebrate it together. [O]
(B) The date has been changed. [X]

내일이 Tina의 생일이죠, 그렇지 않나요?
(A) 네, 우리 함께 축하해야 해요.
(B) 날짜가 변경되었어요.

07. BR-BR

You graduated Carlson University, right?
(A) How did you know that? [O]
(B) She is a college student. [X]

당신 Carlson 대학교를 졸업했죠, 맞죠?
(A) 어떻게 아셨어요?
(B) 그녀는 대학생이에요.

08. US-BR

We should ask the committee to conduct surveys next week, don't you agree?
(A) That's what I was thinking about. [O]
(B) I want to know the survey results. [X]

다음 주에 설문조사를 시행하자고 위원회에 요청해야 해요, 그렇게 생각하지 않으세요?
(A) 저도 그렇게 생각하고 있었어요.
(B) 설문조사 결과를 알고 싶어요.

실전 문제

01. (B) 02. (C) 03. (B) 04. (B) 05. (A) 06. (C)
07. (B) 08. (B) 09. (A) 10. (A) 11. (C) 12. (C)
13. (B) 14. (C) 15. (B) 16. (B)

01. [BR-US]

There aren't any seats left in Economy Class, are there?
(A) There is one layover.
(B) No, but you can fly in Business Class.
(C) The economy is in deep recession.

economy class 일반석   economy 경기, 경제   recession 경기 침체

일반석에는 남은 좌석이 없어요, 그렇죠?
(A) 경유하는 것이 하나 있어요.
(B) 없어요, 하지만 비즈니스 클래스를 타실 수는 있어요.
(C) 경제가 극심한 침체 상태입니다.

[해설] 일반석 좌석이 남아 있지 않는지 확인하는 부가 의문문이다.
(A) 질문의 Economy Class에서 연상할 수 있는 layover를 이용해 혼동을 유도하는 오답이다.
(B) No로 응답한 후 비즈니스 클래스를 탈 것을 제안하는 정답이다.
(C) 질문의 economy를 반복 사용하여 혼동을 유도하는 오답이다.

02. [US-US]

You can't just give me a cash refund, can you?
(A) Don't forget your change.
(B) These have been selling well.
(C) No, not without a receipt.

refund 환불   change 거스름돈, 잔돈   sell well 잘 팔리다
receipt 영수증

그냥 현금으로 환불해 주실 수 없지요, 그렇죠?
(A) 거스름돈 잊지 마세요.
(B) 이것들은 잘 팔리고 있어요.
(C) 환불해 드릴 수 없어요, 영수증 없이는 안 돼요.

[해설] 현금으로 환불이 가능한지 확인하는 부가 의문문이다.
(A) 질문의 cash에서 연상할 수 있는 change(거스름돈, 잔돈)를 이용해 혼동을 유도하는 오답이다.
(B) 물건을 사고 파는 상황에서 나올 수 있는 표현이지만 질문과는 무관한 응답이다.
(C) No로 응답한 후 환불이 불가능한 이유(영수증이 없음)를 덧붙이고 있으므로 정답이다.

03. [AU-US]

All the merchandise was put on display last night, wasn't it?
(A) Click the play button at the bottom.
(B) No, we were too understaffed.
(C) On the delivery truck.

merchandise 상품   be put on display 전시[진열]되다
understaffed 인원이 부족한

어젯밤에 모든 상품이 진열된 거죠, 그렇지 않나요?
(A) 아래쪽의 재생 버튼을 클릭하세요.
(B) 아니요, 우리 일손이 너무 부족했어요.
(C) 배달 트럭이에요.

[해설] 어젯밤에 모든 상품이 진열되었는지 확인하는 부가 의문문이다.
(A) 질문의 display와 발음이 유사한 play를 이용해 혼동을 유도하는 오답이다.
(B) No로 대답한 후 일손이 너무 부족했다고 그 이유를 덧붙이고 있으므로 정답이다.
(C) 질문의 merchandise에서 연상 가능한 delivery를 이용한 오답으로 상품들이 어디 있는지 묻는 Where 의문문에 적합한 응답이다.

04. [US-BR]

You haven't signed a rent contract yet, have you?
(A) I need your contact information.
(B) No, I haven't.
(C) A two-story townhouse.

sign 서명하다   rent contract 임대 계약서   contact information 연락처   two-story 2층짜리의   townhouse 연립 주택

임대 계약서에 서명하지 않으셨죠, 그렇죠?
(A) 당신의 연락처가 필요해요.
(B) 아니요, 안 했어요.
(C) 2층짜리 연립 주택이에요.

[해설] 임대 계약서에 서명하지 않았는지 확인하는 부가 의문문이다.
(A) 질문의 contract와 발음이 유사한 contact를 이용하여 혼동을 유도하는 오답이다.
(B) 서명을 안 했다고 응답하고 있으므로 정답이다.
(C) 질문의 rent contract에서 주택이나 건물 등을 연상할 경우 고를 수 있는 오답이다.

05. [BR-BR]

The register's scanner has been fixed, hasn't it?
(A) No, it will be replaced with a new one.
(B) I registered in advance.
(C) That store has good offers.

register 등록, 현금 등록기; 등록하다   scanner 판독 장치, 스캐너
fix 수리하다   replace 교체하다   in advance 미리, 사전에
offer 할인, 제안

현금 등록기의 스캐너가 고쳐졌지요, 그렇지 않나요?
(A) 안 고쳐졌어요, 새것으로 교체될 거예요.
(B) 제가 미리 등록했어요.
(C) 그 가게는 할인을 많이 해줘요.

[해설] 현금 등록기의 스캐너가 고쳐졌는지 확인하는 부가 의문문이다.
(A) No로 응답한 후 새것으로 교체할 거라고 부연 설명을 하는 정답이다.
(B) 질문의 register를 반복 사용하여 혼동을 유도하는 오답이다.
(C) 질문의 register's scanner에서 연상되는 store를 이용해 혼동을 유도하는 오답이다.

06. [BR-AU]

We should start offering a delivery service, don't you think?

(A) I got lunch from a food truck today.
(B) A reliable source.
(C) Many other restaurants do.

offer 제공하다   reliable source 믿을 만한 소식통

우리는 배달 서비스 제공을 시작해야 해요, 그렇게 생각하지 않아요?
(A) 저는 오늘 푸드트럭에서 점심을 사다 먹었어요.
(B) 믿을 만한 소식통이에요.
(C) 많은 다른 식당들이 그렇게 해요.

[해설] 배달 서비스를 제공해야 한다고 제안하는 부가 의문문이다.
(A) 질문의 delivery에서 연상 가능한 lunch와 food를 이용하여 혼동을 유도하는 오답이다.
(B) 질문과 무관한 내용의 응답으로, 정보의 출처를 묻는 질문에 적합하다.
(C) 다른 식당들도 많이 그렇게 한다는 말로 상대방의 제안에 동의하고 있으므로 정답이다.

07. AU-BR

We don't have to attend the seminar, do we?
(A) It will be held at Lakeland Center.
(B) No, that's only for new hires.
(C) I learned a lot.

우리는 세미나에 참석할 필요가 없어요, 그렇죠?
(A) 그것은 Lakeland Center에서 열릴 예정이에요.
(B) 참석할 필요 없어요, 그건 신입사원들만을 위한 거예요.
(C) 많이 배웠어요.

[해설] 세미나에 참석할 필요가 없는지 확인하는 부가 의문문이다.
(A) 질문의 seminar에서 세미나 개최 장소를 연상할 경우 고를 수 있는 오답으로, Where 의문에 적합한 응답이다.
(B) No(참석할 필요가 없다)로 응답한 후 해당 세미나는 신입사원들만을 위한 것이라고 부연 설명을 하고 있는 정답이다.
(C) 질문의 seminar에서 연상할 수 있는 learned를 이용해 혼동을 유도하는 오답이다.

08. BR-AU

Ms. Smithers works for our competitor now, doesn't she?
(A) It is a highly competitive product.
(B) Yes, they made her a very generous offer.
(C) Check the working hours.

competitor 경쟁자, 경쟁 업체   highly 대단히, 매우
competitive 경쟁력 있는   product 상품   make an offer 제안하다   generous 후한, 너그러운

Smithers 씨가 지금 우리 경쟁사에서 근무하죠, 그렇지 않나요?
(A) 그것은 대단히 경쟁력 있는 상품이에요.
(B) 네, 그들이 그녀에게 아주 후한 제안을 했어요.
(C) 근무 시간을 확인하세요.

[해설] Smithers 씨가 경쟁사에서 근무하는지 확인하는 부가 의문문이다.
(A) 질문의 competitor와 발음이 유사한 competitive를 이용해 혼동을 유도하는 오답이다.
(B) Yes로 응답한 후 그녀가 경쟁사로 가게 된 이유를 덧붙이고 있는 정답이다.
(C) 질문의 work을 반복 사용하여 혼동을 유도하는 오답이다.

09. BR-BR

You processed all reimbursement requests for the last month's seminar, didn't you?
(A) No, they are under review now.
(B) I'd rather pay in cash.
(C) The registration fee.

process 처리하다   reimbursement 변제, 상환   request 요청, 신청   under review 조사[검토]를 받고 있는   pay in cash 현금으로 지불하다   registration fee 등록비

지난달 세미나에 대한 모든 비용 상환 요청서를 처리하셨죠, 그렇지 않나요?
(A) 아니요, 현재 검토 중입니다.
(B) 차라리 현금으로 지불하겠습니다.
(C) 등록비입니다.

[해설] 지난달에 있었던 세미나의 비용 상환 요청서를 처리했는지 확인하는 부가 의문문이다.
(A) No로 대답한 후 현재 검토하고 있는 중이라며 그 이유를 덧붙였으므로 정답이다.
(B) 질문의 reimbursement에서 지불 수단에 관한 표현인 pay in cash를 연상하도록 유도하는 오답이다.
(C) 질문의 seminar에서 연상할 수 있는 registration fee를 이용하여 혼동을 유도하는 오답이다.

10. US-US

There weren't a lot of mechanics at the training, were there?
(A) Most of them attended the one last month.
(B) It will be held in Conference Room 2.
(C) From 1 to 3 P.M. this Saturday.

mechanic 정비공

교육에 정비공들이 많지 않았어요, 그렇죠?
(A) 그들 중 대부분이 지난달 교육에 참석했어요.
(B) 2번 회의실에서 열릴 예정입니다.
(C) 이번 주 토요일 오후 1시부터 3시까지입니다.

[해설] 교육에 참석한 정비공들이 많지 않았음을 확인하는 부가 의문문이다.
(A) 대부분이 지난달에 참석했다고 답변함으로써 긍정의 Yes를 대신한 정답이다.
(B) 질문의 training이 이루어지는 장소로 Conference Room을 연상하도록 유도하는 오답으로, Where 의문문에 적합하다.
(C) 질문의 training이 이루어지는 시간을 연상하도록 유도하는 오답으로, When 의문문에 적합하다.

11. AU-BR

We should prepare coffee and doughnuts for the morning meeting, shouldn't we?
(A) Mondays at 9 A.M.
(B) A coffee shop on the corner.
(C) Yes, everyone would appreciate that.

우리가 아침 회의를 위해 커피와 도넛을 준비해야 해요, 그렇지 않나요?
(A) 매주 월요일 오전 9시요.
(B) 모퉁이에 있는 커피숍이요.
(C) 네, 모두들 고마워할 거예요.

[해설] 아침 회의를 위해 커피와 도넛을 준비해야 하는지 확인하는 부가 의문문이다.
(A) 질문의 morning에서 연상 가능한 시간대인 9 A.M.을 이용하여 혼동을 유도하는 오답으로, When 의문문에 적합한 응답이다.
(B) 질문의 coffee를 반복 사용하여 혼동을 유도하는 오답이다.
(C) Yes로 응답한 후, 모든 사람들이 고마워할 것이라고 답변하고 있으므로 정답이다.

12. US-US

Let's move to a larger meeting room with an overhead projector and screen, shall we?
(A) It was more than we projected.
(B) This two-bedroom apartment is fully furnished.
(C) I will check whether I can reserve it now.

project 예상[추정]하다 fully furnished 가구가 완비된

오버헤드 프로젝터와 스크린이 있는 더 넓은 회의실로 옮길까요?
(A) 우리가 예상한 것보다 더 많았어요.
(B) 침실이 두 개인 이 아파트는 가구가 완비되어 있어요.
(C) 지금 예약할 수 있는지 확인해볼게요.

[해설] 더 넓은 회의실로 옮기자고 제안하는 부가 의문문이다.
(A) 질문의 projector와 발음이 비슷한 projected를 이용하여 혼동을 유도하는 오답이다.
(B) 질문의 room을 반복 사용하여 혼동을 유도하는 오답이다.
(C) 지금 예약할 수 있는지 확인하겠다고 답함으로써, 상대의 제안을 수락하고 있으므로 정답이다.

13. BR-BR

Please present any kind of photo identification, will you?
(A) She is kind and thoughtful.
(B) Sure, here it is.
(C) Someone should be present at your home.

present 제시[제출]하다; 있는, 참석한 photo identification 사진이 부착된 신분증 thoughtful 사려 깊은

사진이 부착된 신분증이면 어떤 종류든 제시해주세요, 그러시겠어요?
(A) 그녀는 친절하고 사려 깊어요.
(B) 물론입니다. 여기 있어요.
(C) 누군가 당신의 집에 있어야 해요.

[해설] 신분증을 제시해달라고 부탁하는 부가 의문문이다.
(A) 질문의 kind(종류)의 동음이의어인 kind(친절한)를 반복 사용하여 혼동을 유도하는 오답이다.
(B) 여기 있다고 하므로 정답이다.
(C) 질문의 present(제시하다)와 발음이 유사한 present(있는, 참석한)를 사용하여 혼동을 유도하는 오답이다.

14. AU-BR

The engineering conference is being held in Amsterdam this year, right?
(A) I believe he's majoring in physics.
(B) Which engine model?
(C) Yes, and I'll be leading a session there.

engineering 공학 기술 major in ~을 전공하다 physics 물리학 lead 이끌다

올해 공학 기술 학회가 암스테르담에서 열릴 예정이에요, 맞죠?
(A) 제가 알기로는 그는 물리학을 전공하고 있어요.
(B) 어떤 엔진 모델이요?
(C) 네, 그리고 제가 그곳에서 한 세션을 이끌 거예요.

[해설] 공학 기술 학회가 암스테르담에서 열리는지 확인하는 부가 의문문이다.
(A) 질문의 engineering conference와 같은 학문과 관련된 내용 (majoring in physics)으로 혼동을 유도하는 오답이다.
(B) 질문의 engineering과 발음이 유사한 engine을 이용하여 혼동을 유도하는 오답이다.
(C) Yes로 응답한 후 자신이 한 세션을 이끈다고 부연 설명을 하고 있으므로 정답이다.

15. US-BR

We've been business partners for a year already, haven't we?
(A) I'm on my way.
(B) Yes, and it's going great.
(C) A long-term contract.

business partner 동업자 on one's way 가는[오는] 중인 long-term 장기의 contract 계약

우리가 벌써 1년간 동업자 관계를 유지해왔어요, 그렇지 않나요?
(A) 저는 가는 중이에요.
(B) 네, 그리고 잘 해내고 있어요.
(C) 장기 계약이요.

[해설] 1년간 동업자 관계를 유지해온 것을 확인하는 부가 의문문이다.
(A) 질문의 내용과 무관한 응답으로, we에 대해 물었는데 I로 답하고 있으므로 주어 불일치 오답이다.
(B) 긍정의 Yes로 응답한 후 긍정적인 평가를 덧붙이고 있으므로 정답이다.
(C) 질문의 business에서 연상할 수 있는 contract를 이용해 혼동을 유도하는 오답이다.

16. US-US

We need a new TV commercial, don't you think?
(A) Another movie is coming out soon.
(B) Yes, but our marketing budget is limited.
(C) That's not for commercial use.

commercial 광고; 상업의 budget 예산 limited 제한된

우리는 새로운 TV 광고가 필요해요, 그렇게 생각하지 않나요?
(A) 다른 영화가 곧 개봉할 거예요.
(B) 네, 하지만 우리 마케팅 예산이 제한되어 있어요.

(C) 그건 상업용이 아니에요.

[해설] TV 광고가 필요하지 않냐고 묻는 부가 의문문이다.
(A) TV에서 연상할 수 있는 movie를 사용하여 혼동을 유도한 오답이다.
(B) Yes로 동의를 표한 후, 하지만 예산이 제한되어 있다고 추가 설명한 정답이다.
(C) 질문의 commercial을 반복 사용하여 혼동을 유도한 오답이다.

PART 3 제안·요청 문제 / 다음 할 일 문제 / 의도 파악 문제

 연습 문제

01. (A) 02. (A) 03. (B) 04. (B) 05. (A) 06. (B)

01. [US-BR]
What does the **man suggest the woman do**?
(A) **Contact** the **printing shop**   (B) **Use another printer**

> W: James, this printer is not working again. The papers are jammed. I will give a presentation to the board members in an hour and I need 20 copies to be printed.
> M: Um... why don't you call the printing shop located at the corner and ask them to print them?

남자는 여자에게 무엇을 하라고 제안하는가?
(A) 인쇄소에 연락하기
(B) 다른 프린터 사용하기

여: James, 이 프린터가 또 작동하지 않아요. 종이가 걸렸어요. 제가 한 시간 후에 이사진들에게 발표를 해야 하고 20부를 복사해야 해요.
남: 음... 모퉁이에 있는 인쇄소에 전화해서 그것들을 프린트 해달라고 하는 게 어때요?

02. [US-US]
What does the **man ask the woman to do**?
(A) **Schedule** a **meeting**   (B) **Revise** the **proposal**

> M: I think the deadline for the proposal is too tight. Could you call the client and hold a meeting this week?
> W: Sure. What day is the most convenient for you?
> M: I have free time on Tuesday and Wednesday morning.

남자는 여자에게 무엇을 하라고 부탁하는가?
(A) 회의 일정 잡기
(B) 제안서 수정하기

남: 제안서의 마감일이 너무 빠듯한 것 같아요. 고객에게 전화해서 이번 주에 회의를 잡을 수 있어요?
여: 물론이죠. 어느 요일이 편하세요?
남: 저는 화요일과 수요일 아침에 비는 시간이 있어요.

03. [BR-US]
What will the **man** probably **do next**?
(A) **Convert** the file **format**   (B) **Fax** a **document**

> M: Clara, did you receive my e-mail about the price quote for the office renovation?
> W: Yes, but I have a problem. I downloaded the file you attached to the e-mail, but it did not open on my computer. Could you send it to me by fax?

남자는 다음에 무엇을 하겠는가?
(A) 파일 형식 변경하기
(B) 서류를 팩스로 보내기

남: Clara, 사무실 개조를 위한 가격 견적서에 대한 제 이메일 받으셨어요?
여: 네, 그런데 문제가 있어요. 당신이 이메일에 첨부한 파일을 다운로드 받았는데 제 컴퓨터에서 열리지 않아요. 팩스로 보내주시겠어요?

04. [US-US]
What will the **man** probably **do next**?
(A) **Call** another branch   (B) **Go to** the storage room

> W: I like these shoes but I'm not able to find my size on the shelf. Do you have the shoe in 6.5?
> M: Just give me a second to check the inventory. According to our records, there are a couple pairs in the storage room. I will come back in a minute.

남자는 다음에 무엇을 하겠는가?
(A) 다른 지점에 전화하기
(B) 창고로 가기

여: 저는 이 신발이 좋은데 선반에서 제 사이즈를 찾을 수가 없어요. 이 신발로 6.5 사이즈가 있나요?
남: 재고를 확인하도록 잠시만 시간을 주세요. 저희 기록에 따르면, 창고에 몇 켤레가 있네요. 곧 돌아올게요.

05. [AU-BR]
Why does the **woman say**, "**I don't have any special plans this weekend**"?
(A) To **accept** an **offer**   (B) To **cancel** an **event**

> M: Jenny, will you come to the rock climbing club this Saturday? We will have a late dinner with the members at the restaurant Atkins' Table.
> W: I don't have any special plans this weekend. Where will it be held? It will start 4 P.M., right?

여자는 왜 "저는 이번 주말에 특별한 계획이 없어요"라고 말하는가?
(A) 제안을 수락하기 위해
(B) 행사를 취소하기 위해

남: Jenny, 이번 주 토요일에 암벽 등반 동호회에 올래요? 회원들과 Atkins' Table 레스토랑에서 늦은 저녁을 먹을 거예요.
여: 저는 이번 주말에 특별한 계획이 없어요. 어디서 열리나요? 오후 4시에 시작할 거죠, 맞죠?

06. US-BR

What does the **woman mean** when she says, "**I'm not really surprised**"?
(A) She has **already read** the **news**.
(B) She **expected** the **results**.

> M: Our item was chosen as one of the best products this year!
> W: That's good news, but I'm not really surprised. We've been spending lots of money and time on that product.

여자가 "저는 그다지 놀랍지 않아요"라고 말할 때 의미하는 바는 무엇인가?
(A) 그녀는 이미 뉴스를 읽었다.
(B) 그녀는 결과를 예상했다.

남: 우리 제품이 올해의 베스트 제품 중 하나로 선정되었어요!
여: 좋은 소식이네요. 하지만 저는 그다지 놀랍지 않아요. 우리는 많은 돈과 시간을 그 제품에 들였어요.

paraphrasing 정답 1. (c) 2. (a) 3. (b) 4. (b) 5. (a) 6. (c)

실전 문제

01. (B)	02. (A)	03. (B)	04. (A)	05. (C)	06. (B)
07. (A)	08. (C)	09. (C)	10. (B)	11. (D)	12. (C)
13. (C)	14. (B)	15. (D)	16. (D)	17. (C)	18. (A)
19. (C)	20. (D)	21. (B)	22. (C)	23. (C)	24. (A)

[01-03] US-BR

Questions 01-03 refer to the following conversation.

> W: ⁰¹Welcome to Berkeley Bistro. Would you like to sit at a table or a booth?
> M: A table would be best, and there will be six of us. It seems quite noisy in the main dining area. ⁰²Do you have any private rooms?
> W: The rooftop is open.
> M: Hmm... isn't it supposed to rain today?
> W: Not until later in the day, I heard.
> M: Well, ⁰³I'd better look up the weather forecast on my phone first before deciding to sit outside.

bistro 작은 식당 rooftop (건물의) 옥상 look up (정보를) 찾아보다 weather forecast 일기 예보

01-03은 다음 대화에 관한 문제입니다.
여: ⁰¹Berkeley Bistro에 오신 것을 환영합니다. 테이블 좌석과 칸막이가 있는 좌석 중 어디에 앉으시겠어요?
남: 테이블 좌석이 좋겠어요. 그리고 저희 일행은 여섯 명이에요. 중앙의 식사 공간은 좀 시끄러울 것 같아요. ⁰²개별 공간이 있나요?
여: 옥상 공간이 이용 가능해요.
남: 흠... 오늘 비가 오기로 되어 있지 않나요?
여: 오늘 늦게까지는 안 온다고 들었어요.
남: 그럼, 바깥에 앉을지 결정하기 전에 ⁰³우선 전화로 일기 예보를 찾아보는 게 좋겠어요.

01.
여자는 누구일 것 같은가?
(A) 가구 판매원
(B) 식당 직원
(C) 상점 주인
(D) 수리공

[해설] 화자의 직업이나 신분은 주로 대화 전반부에서 드러난다. 여자가 첫 번째 대사에서 Berkeley Bistro에 온 것을 환영한다고 했는데, bistro는 '작은 식당'을 의미하므로 Berkeley Bistro는 식당 이름임을 유추할 수 있으며, 뒤이어 어느 자리에 앉을 것인지(Would you like to sit at a table or a booth?) 묻는 것으로 보아 여자는 식당에서 일하는 사람임을 알 수 있다. 따라서 정답은 (B)이다.

paraphrasing bistro 작은 식당 → restaurant 식당

02.
여자는 왜 "옥상 공간이 이용 가능해요"라고 말하는가?
(A) 또 다른 옵션을 제시하기 위해
(B) 디자인을 확인하기 위해
(C) 정책 변경을 알리기 위해
(D) 업무를 배정하기 위해

[해설] 화자의 의도 파악 문제는 해당 문장과 앞뒤 문맥을 종합하여 답을 찾아야 한다. 앞서 남자가 중앙의 공간이 아닌 개별 공간이 있는지(Do you have any private rooms?) 물었고, 이에 대해 여자가 "옥상 공간이 이용 가능하다"고 말한 것은 남자에게 일행이 앉을 만한 곳을 추가로 제시하기 위한 의도임을 알 수 있다. 따라서 정답은 (A)이다.

[어휘] verify 확인하다 policy 정책 assign 맡기다, 배정하다

03.
남자는 무엇을 할 계획인가?
(A) 서둘러 주문하기
(B) 일기 예보 확인하기
(C) 전화기 끄기
(D) 다른 업소에 가기

[해설] 남자가 할 일을 묻는 문제로, 남자의 후반부 대사에 집중한다. 옥상의 좌석을 제안하는 여자의 말에 혹시 비가 오지 않을지 염려하던 남자가 전화기로 일기 예보를 확인하겠다고(I'd better look up the weather forecast on my phone) 했으므로 정답은 (B)이다.

paraphrasing look up the weather forecast 일기 예보를 찾아보다 → Check a weather report 일기 예보를 확인하기

[어휘] place an order 주문하다 business 사업체(회사, 가게, 공장 등)

[04-06] BR-BR

Questions 04-06 refer to the following conversation.

> M: Hi, Emma. It's Tony. Our design teams are supposed to meet at my branch tomorrow at two o'clock, but I don't think that will be possible. ⁰⁴Could we hold the meeting at your branch instead?
> W: Of course. It's less convenient for your team, though.
> M: That's not an issue. You see, ⁰⁵our branch is being renovated, and the work started yesterday. The room I was planning to use is off limits.

W: I see. ⁰⁶**I'll book a conference room now** so that we have space for everyone. See you tomorrow.

---

branch 지점, 지사   convenient 편리한   issue 문제   off limits 출입 금지 구역

04-06은 다음 대화에 관한 문제입니다.

남: 안녕하세요, Emma. Tony예요. 우리 디자인 팀들이 내일 2시에 우리 지점에서 만나기로 했는데 가능할 것 같지 않아요. ⁰⁴**그 회의를 대신 당신의 지점에서 열 수 있을까요?**

여: 물론이죠. 당신 팀에게는 좀 불편하겠지만요.

남: 그건 별 문제 아니에요. 있잖아요, ⁰⁵**우리 지점이 보수 중인데, 작업이 어제 시작됐어요.** 제가 사용하려고 계획했던 방이 출입 금지되었어요.

여: 그렇군요. ⁰⁶**지금 회의실을 예약해서** 모두를 수용할 수 있는 공간을 확보할게요. 내일 봐요.

04.

남자는 왜 여자에게 전화하는가?
(A) 장소를 변경하기 위해
(B) 마감일을 연장하기 위해
(C) 회의를 취소하기 위해
(D) 손님 명단을 확인하기 위해

[해설] 남자가 전화한 이유를 묻는 문제로, 남자의 첫 번째 대사에서 단서를 찾을 수 있다. 내일 남자의 지점에서 회의를 열 예정이었으나 불가능할 것 같다며 상대방, 즉 여자의 지점에서 회의를 여는 것이 가능한지(Could we hold the meeting at your branch instead?) 묻고 있다. 즉, 회의 장소를 변경하기 위해 전화한 것임을 알 수 있으므로 (A)가 정답이다.

[어휘] extend 연장하다, 확장하다   deadline 마감일   confirm 확인하다

05.

남자에 따르면, 최근에 그의 지점에서 무슨 일이 있었는가?
(A) 일부 예산 범주가 삭감되었다.
(B) 일부 고객이 불만을 제기했다.
(C) 보수 작업이 시작되었다.
(D) 한 팀에서 팀원을 더 고용했다.

[해설] 핵심 키워드 recently가 대화에서는 yesterday로 언급되었다. 대화 중반부에 남자가 원래 계획했던 장소에서 회의를 진행할 수 없는 이유를 자신의 지점이 보수 중이고, 그 작업이 어제 시작됐다(our branch is being renovated, and the work started yesterday) 때문이라고 밝혔다. 따라서 (C)가 정답이다.

[어휘] budget 예산   category 범주   make a complaint 불만을 제기하다   hire 고용하다

06.

여자는 다음에 무엇을 하겠다고 말하는가?
(A) 남자에게 이메일 보내기
(B) 방을 예약하기
(C) 안건을 인쇄하기
(D) 보고서를 검토하기

[해설] 여자가 다음에 할 일을 묻는 문제로, 여자의 마지막 대사에서 단서를 찾는다. 지금 회의실을 예약하겠다고(I'll book a conference room now) 했으므로 정답은 (B)이다.

paraphrasing book 예약하다 → reserve 예약하다

[어휘] agenda 의제, 안건

[07-09] US-AU

Questions 07-09 refer to the following conversation.

W: Dennis, I wanted to talk to you about ⁰⁷**an issue that we're having here at the factory.**

M: What's the problem?

W: Well, ⁰⁸**we were supposed to receive a shipment of fabric two days ago, but it still hasn't arrived.**

M: This has happened several times. We should consider changing our supplier to Garcia Textiles. That company has received excellent reviews online.

W: Hmm... ⁰⁹**why don't you contact the company and ask them for some fabric samples?** Then we can check the quality before making a decision.

---

shipment 수송품, 적하물   fabric 직물, 천   consider -ing ~하는 것을 고려하다   supplier 공급자, 공급 회사   excellent 훌륭한, 탁월한   quality 질, 품질   make a decision 결정하다

07-09는 다음 대화에 관한 문제입니다.

여: Dennis, ⁰⁷**이곳 공장에서 발생하고 있는 문제점**에 관해 당신과 얘기하고 싶었어요.

남: 문제가 뭐죠?

여: 음, ⁰⁸**이틀 전에 직물을 배송 받기로 되어 있었는데 아직 도착하지 않았어요.**

남: 여러 번 그런 일이 있었죠. 우리 공급처를 Garcia Textiles로 변경하는 것을 고려해봐야 해요. 그 회사는 온라인 이용 후기가 아주 좋아요.

여: 흠... ⁰⁹**그 회사에 연락해서 직물 샘플을 좀 요청하시는 게 어때요?** 그러면 우리가 결정하기 전에 품질을 확인해볼 수 있어요.

07.

대화는 어디에서 이루어지고 있는가?
(A) 생산 시설에서
(B) 광고 회사에서
(C) 식료품점에서
(D) 옷가게에서

[해설] 화자들이 대화를 하고 있는 장소를 묻는 문제로, 대화 시작 부분에서 여자가 '이곳 공장에서(here at the factory)'라고 언급한 것으로 보아 두 사람이 현재 공장과 같은 생산 시설에서 대화를 나누고 있는 것을 알 수 있으므로 정답은 (A)이다.

paraphrasing factory 공장 → manufacturing facility 생산 시설

08.

여자는 남자에게 무슨 문제에 대해 말하는가?
(A) 제품 생산이 중단되었다.
(B) 직원 한 명이 결근했다.
(C) 배송이 늦어지고 있다.
(D) 기계가 제대로 작동하지 않는다.

[해설] 여자가 언급한 문제점을 묻는 질문이므로 여자의 말에서 단서를 찾는다. 이틀 전에 받았어야 할 직물이 아직 도착하지 않았다는(we were supposed to receive a shipment of fabric two days ago, but it still hasn't arrived) 말로 배송 지연에 대한 문제점을 지적하고 있으므

로 정답은 (C)이다.

[어휘] discontinue 중단하다 employee 직원 absent 결근한, 결석한 malfunction 제대로 작동하지 않다

09.

여자는 남자에게 무엇을 하라고 요청하는가?
(A) 일부 물품 반품하기
(B) 작업 일정 조정하기
(C) 일부 샘플 요청하기
(D) 일부 정보를 온라인에 게시하기

[해설] 여자가 남자에게 부탁한 일을 묻는 문제로, 후반부 여자의 대사 중 부탁이나 요청을 하는 표현에서 정답의 단서를 찾는다. 그 회사, 즉 앞서 언급한 Garcia Textiles에 연락해서 직물 샘플을 요청할 것을 제안하고 있으므로(why don't you contact the company and ask them for some fabric samples?) 정답은 (C)이다.

paraphrasing ask 요청하다 → request 요청하다

[어휘] adjust 조정하다

[10-12] BR-AU

Questions 10-12 refer to the following conversation.

> W: Diego, could you do me a favor? ¹⁰**I'm going to the National Conference of Banking Professionals next week.** I need to have all of my duties covered.
> M: My schedule is pretty full these days, but ¹¹**I'll help if I can.** What do you need done?
> W: I've assigned most of my tasks to other people, but ¹¹**I still need someone to post the new exchange rates in the lobby every morning.**
> M: Oh, that's not much.
> W: I really appreciate it. ¹²**I'll let the department manager know** that you'll be taking care of that.

do A a favor A의 부탁을 들어주다 duty 직무, 임무 assign (일·책임 등을) 맡기다 task 일 exchange rate 환율

10-12은 다음 대화에 관한 문제입니다.

여: Diego, 부탁 하나 들어줄 수 있어요? ¹⁰제가 다음 주에 전국 금융 전문가 콘퍼런스에 가요. 제 모든 업무에 공백이 생기지 않아야 해요.
남: 요즘 제 일정이 꽉 차 있긴 하지만 ¹¹가능하면 도울게요. 무엇을 처리해야 하죠?
여: 대부분의 제 업무는 다른 사람들에게 맡겼는데, ¹¹매일 아침 로비에 새 환율을 게시해줄 사람이 아직 필요해요.
남: 아, 그건 별거 아니에요.
여: 정말 고마워요. 당신이 그 일을 처리해줄 거라고 ¹²부서장에게 알릴게요.

10.

여자는 다음 주에 무엇을 할 계획인가?
(A) 신입 직원들을 고용하기
(B) 업계 행사에 참석하기
(C) 다른 지점으로 근무지를 옮기기
(D) 교육 세미나를 이끌기

[해설] 여자가 다음 주에 할 일을 묻는 문제로, 핵심 키워드 next week가 언급된 곳에 단서가 있다. 여자가 다음 주에 전국 금융 전문가 콘퍼런스에 간다고(I'm going to the National Conference of Banking Professionals next week.) 한 것으로 보아 여자가 자신이 종사하는 업계의 행사에 참석할 예정임을 알 수 있다. 따라서 정답은 (B)이다.

paraphrasing National Conference of Banking Professionals 전국 금융 전문가 콘퍼런스 → an industry event 업계 행사

[어휘] hire 고용하다 attend 참석하다 transfer 이동하다, 전근 가다

11.

남자가 "그건 별거 아니에요"라고 말할 때 의미하는 것은 무엇인가?
(A) 프로젝트의 예산에 놀랐다.
(B) 시간이 부족해 걱정이다.
(C) 가격이 저렴해 기쁘다.
(D) 여자를 도와줄 수 있다.

[해설] 해당 표현의 앞뒤 문맥을 파악해 화자의 의도를 파악하는 문제이다. 여자가 콘퍼런스 참석 때문에 회사를 비우는 동안 매일 아침 로비에 새 환율을 게시해줄 사람이 필요하다는(I still need someone to post the new exchange rates in the lobby every morning) 말에 남자가 "그건 별거 아니에요"라고 한 것은 자신이 대신 해주겠다, 즉 여자를 도와줄 수 있다는 말이므로 (D)가 정답이다.

[어휘] budget 예산 be concerned about ~에 대해 걱정하다 be pleased with ~에 대해 기뻐하다 assist 돕다

12.

여자는 무엇을 하겠다고 말하는가?
(A) 초과 근무 수당을 지급하기
(B) 회사 정책을 확인하기
(C) 관리자에게 말하기
(D) 남자에게 지시 사항을 전달하기

[해설] 여자가 할 일을 묻는 문제로, 후반부 여자의 대사에서 정답의 단서를 찾는다. 앞서 남자가 여자의 일을 대신해 줄 것을 수락하자 남자가 그 일을 처리할 것임을 부서장에게 알리겠다고(I'll let the department manager know) 했으므로 정답은 (C)이다.

paraphrasing let the department manager know 부서장에게 알리다 → speak to a manager 관리자에게 말하다

[어휘] make (a) payment 지불하다 overtime 초과 근무 policy 정책, 방침 instructions 지시, 명령

[13-15] US-US

Questions 13-15 refer to the following conversation.

> W: Hey, Lamar. I just got off the phone with one of our clients, Lakeland Computer Repair. They said that ¹³**they want another 200 graphics cards by next week.** Do you think we could produce that many in such a short time?
> M: ¹⁴**Not on our current schedule, but we have plenty of people who want extra hours.** ¹⁴**I think it sounds like a feasible goal.**
> W: That's great news. I'll call them back now.
> M: Alright, and ¹⁵**I'll put a memo up in the break room.**
> W: Thanks for your help!

DAY 07 53

get off the phone 전화 통화를 끝내다   client 고객, 의뢰인
produce 생산하다   current 현재의   plenty of 많은   feasible
실현 가능한   goal 목표   break room 휴게실

13-15는 다음 대화에 관한 문제입니다.
여: 있잖아요, Lamar 씨. 제가 방금 고객사 중 한 곳인 Lakeland Computer Repair와 전화 통화를 했어요. 다음 주까지 **13그래픽 카드 200개를 추가로 원한다고 하네요.** 우리가 그렇게 짧은 시간에 그 정도로 많이 생산할 수 있다고 생각하세요?
남: **14현재의 일정으로는 안 돼요. 하지만 초과 근무를 하는 사람들이 많이 있어요. 14실현 가능한 목표인 것 같아요.**
여: 좋은 소식이네요. 제가 그들에게 다시 전화할게요.
남: 좋아요, 그러면 **15제가 휴게실에 메모를 붙일게요.**
여: 도와줘서 고마워요!

13.
화자들은 어떤 업종에서 근무하는 것 같은가?
(A) 컴퓨터 그래픽 디자인 회사
(B) 비디오 게임 회사
(C) 전자 장치 제조업체
(D) 컴퓨터 수리 서비스

[해설] 대화 초반, 여자의 대사 중 고객사에서 추가로 그래픽 카드 200개(another 200 graphics cards)를 원한다는 말과, 남자에게 짧은 시간에 그 정도의 양을 생산할 수 있는지(Do you think we could produce that many in such a short time?) 묻는 것으로 보아 이들은 그래픽 카드 같은 전자 장치를 제조하는 업체에서 일함을 알 수 있다. 따라서 정답은 (C)이다.

paraphrasing graphics cards 그래픽 카드 → electronics 전자 장치
[어휘] electronics 전자 장치   manufacturer 제조업체

14.
남자는 왜 "하지만 초과 근무를 원하는 사람들이 많이 있어요"라고 말하는가?
(A) 그들의 목표가 실현 불가능하다고 생각한다.
(B) 근무 시간을 더 많이 배정할 것이다.
(C) 추가 서비스를 제공하고 싶어 한다.
(D) 몇몇 지원자들을 인터뷰할 것이다.

[해설] 화자의 말의 의도를 파악하는 문제는 앞뒤 문맥을 잘 살펴야 한다. 앞서 여자가 고객사의 추가 주문을 수용할 수 있는 상황인지 묻자, 남자가 현재 일정으로는 불가능하다고(Not on our current schedule) 한 뒤 해당 표현을 언급했고, 이어서 실현 가능한 목표(a feasible goal)라고 덧붙였다. 즉, 더 많이 일하고 싶어하는 사람들이 있기 때문에 근무 시간을 더 많이 배정하면 가능하다는 의미로 해당 표현을 쓴 것이므로 정답은 (B)이다.

[어휘] assign 맡기다, 배정하다   work shift 근무 교대(제)   applicant 지원자, 신청자

15.
남자는 무엇을 할 것이라고 말하는가?
(A) 직원들을 더 채용하기
(B) 고객에게 연락하기
(C) 휴식을 취하기
(D) 메모를 게시하기

[해설] 대화 후반부, 남자가 휴게실에 메모를 붙이겠다고(I'll put a memo up in the break room) 했으므로 정답은 (D)이다. 바로 앞에서, 고객에게 다시 전화하겠다는 여자의 말을 남자의 말로 착각하여 (B)를 정답으로 고르지 않도록 주의해야 한다.

paraphrasing put a memo up 메모를 붙이다 → post a memo 메모를 게시하다

[16-18] AU-US
Questions 16-18 refer to the following conversation.

M: Hello, I'm Craig Jennings. **16I'm here to inspect your factory's bottling line.**
W: Oh, hello. Ms. Bryce said to be expecting you. **17I'll just need an ID with your picture on it.**
M: Sure, here it is. So, where is your bottling line? Should I just go through those large doors over there?
W: **18Everyone inside has to wear gloves, goggles, and a mask at all times for safety reasons.** You can get them through that door. The next door leads to the bottling plant.

inspect 점검[검사]하다   bottling 병에 채워 넣는 것   line (공장의) 작업 라인, 조립 공정   at all times 항상   lead to ~로 이어지다   plant 공장

16-18은 다음 대화에 관한 문제입니다.
남: 안녕하세요, 저는 Craig Jennings입니다. **16당신의 공장의 보틀링 라인을 점검하러 왔어요.**
여: 아, 안녕하세요. Bryce 씨가 당신을 기다리고 있다고 했어요. **17사진이 있는 신분증만 보여주세요.**
남: 물론이죠, 여기 있습니다. 그럼, 보틀링 라인은 어디 있나요? 저쪽에 있는 큰 문들을 통해서 가면 되나요?
여: **18안전상의 이유로 내부에서는 모두 항상 장갑, 고글, 마스크를 착용해야 해요.** 저 문을 통해서 그것들을 받으시면 돼요. 그 다음에 있는 문이 보틀링 공장으로 이어져 있어요.

16.
남자는 왜 업체를 방문했는가?
(A) 면접을 진행하기 위해서
(B) 서류를 전달하기 위해서
(C) 안내원이 있는 견학을 하기 위해서
(D) 시설을 점검하기 위해서

[해설] 남자의 방문 목적을 묻는 문제이다. 대화 초반, 남자는 공장의 보틀링 라인을 점검하러 왔다고(I'm here to inspect your factory's bottling line.) 방문 목적을 밝혔다. 보틀링 라인은 일종의 생산 시설이라고 할 수 있으므로 정답은 (D)이다.

paraphrasing factory's bottling line 공장의 보틀링 라인 → a facility 시설

[어휘] conduct (특정한 활동을) 하다   document 서류, 문서   facility 시설

17.
여자는 남자에게 무엇을 요청하는가?
(A) 음료

(B) 작업 계약서
(C) 사진이 부착된 신분증
(D) 연락을 받을 사람의 이름

[해설] 앞서 공장을 방문한 남자가 자신의 이름과 방문 목적을 밝히자 여자가 Bryce 씨로부터 얘기를 들었다며 사진이 있는 신분증이 필요하다고(I'll just need an ID with your picture on it.) 했다. 따라서 정답은 (C)이다.

paraphrasing ID with your picture on it 사진이 있는 당신의 신분증 → photo identification 사진이 부착된 신분증

[어휘] beverage 음료 contract 계약(서) identification 신분증

18.

여자는 남자에게 무엇을 하라고 말하는가?
(A) 안전 장비를 착용하기
(B) 안내해줄 사람을 기다리기
(C) 출입증을 보여주기
(D) 관리자와 얘기하기

[해설] 여자의 마지막 대사에서 안전상의 이유로 내부에서는 항상 장갑, 고글, 마스크를 착용해야 하니(Everyone inside has to wear gloves, goggles, and a mask at all times for safety reasons.) 그것들을 받은 다음에 보틀링 공장으로 들어가라고 했다. 즉, 남자에게 안전 장비를 착용하라는 것이므로 정답은 (A)이다.

paraphrasing wear gloves, goggles, and a mask 장갑, 고글, 마스크를 착용하다 → put on safety gear 안전 장비를 착용하다

[어휘] safety gear 안전 장비 display 내보이다, 보여주다

[19-21] BR-AU

Questions 19-21 refer to the following conversation.

W: Hello, I'm Nancy with Houston Interior Design. [19]**We were scheduled to retile your bathroom tomorrow morning, but unfortunately we won't be able to do so until later in the week.**
M: Really? That's inconvenient. I already told my supervisor that I needed to take off from work tomorrow because I'm remodeling my house.
W: I apologize for the inconvenience. [20]**There was an accident and the tiles you wanted us to use were cracked while in transit to us.**
M: Well, when can you do the installation? How about Thursday?
W: Yes, that should be possible. [21]**As an apology, we'll take 5% off your total.**

retile 타일을 다시 깔다 inconvenient 불편한, 곤란한
supervisor 감독관, 관리자 take off from work 직장에서 휴가를 내다 crack 갈라지다, 금이 가다 in transit 수송 중에
installation 설치

19-21은 다음 대화에 관한 문제입니다.

여: 여보세요, Houston Interior Design의 Nancy입니다. [19]저희가 내일 아침에 당신의 욕실 타일을 다시 깔 예정이었는데, 안타깝게도 이번 주 후반에나 가능할 것 같아요.
남: 정말요? 그건 곤란한데요. 집 리모델링 때문에 내일 휴가를 내야 한다고 상사에게 이미 말했거든요.
여: 불편을 드려 죄송합니다. [20]사고가 좀 발생해서 저희가 사용하기 원하셨던 타일들이 저희에게 운송되는 동안 금이 갔어요.
남: 음, 언제 설치하실 수 있나요? 목요일은 어떤가요?
여: 네, 그건 가능할 거예요. [21]사과의 의미로, 저희가 총액에서 5퍼센트 할인해 드릴게요.

19.

여자는 왜 전화를 하고 있는가?
(A) 의견을 모으기 위해서
(B) 변경을 요청하기 위해서
(C) 서비스 일정을 변경하기 위해서
(D) 불평에 응대하기 위해서

[해설] 전화의 목적은 주로 대화 초반에 드러난다. 대화 초반, 여자가 내일 아침에 예정되어 있던 욕실 타일 공사 작업이 이번 주 후반이 되어야 가능하다고(We were scheduled to retile your bathroom tomorrow morning, but unfortunately we won't be able to do so until later in the week.) 알리는 말로 보아 작업 일정을 변경하기 위해 전화했음을 알 수 있으므로 정답은 (C)이다.

[어휘] gather 모으다 feedback 의견, 반응 respond to ~에 대응하다

20.

여자는 어떤 문제를 언급하는가?
(A) 물품이 잘못되었다.
(B) 배송이 지연되었다.
(C) 일부 작업자들이 아파서 나오지 않았다.
(D) 일부 제품이 손상되었다.

[해설] 여자는 리모델링 공사가 지연되는 이유로 남자가 원했던 타일들이 운송 중에 금이 갔다는(the tiles you wanted us to use were cracked while in transit to us) 사실을 언급했다. 즉, 작업에 필요한 일부 제품이 손상된 것이 문제점이므로 정답은 (D)이다.

paraphrasing tiles 타일 → product 제품, cracked 금이 간 → damaged 손상

[어휘] item 물품, 품목 incorrect 부정확한, 맞지 않는 shipment 수송(품) delay 지연시키다 be out sick 아파서 결석[결근]하다 damage 손상을 주다

21.

여자는 남자에게 무엇을 제안하는가?
(A) 보증금 환불
(B) 할인된 요금
(C) 무료 유지보수 서비스
(D) 제품 샘플

[해설] 제안이나 요청 사항은 주로 대화 후반에 제시된다. 대화 마지막, 여자는 리모델링 공사 지연에 대해 사과하는 의미로 총액에서 5퍼센트 할인해주겠다고(As an apology, we'll take 5% off your total.) 제안했다. 따라서 정답은 (B)이다.

paraphrasing we'll take 5% off your total 총액에서 5퍼센트 할인해줄 것이다 → a discounted charge 할인된 요금

[어휘] deposit 보증금, 착수금 refund 환불(금) charge 요금 maintenance 유지, 보수 관리

[22-24] BR-US

Questions 22-24 refer to the following conversation.

> W: Excuse me, **²²I'm trying to find Doe Nut brand cookie dough mix.** I thought it would be in this aisle, but I don't see it.
> M: It's there, right behind you.
> W: Oh! Thank you! Umm... This is my first time using a dough mix.
> M: ²³It's really simple. Just follow the directions on the back of the box.
> W: Oh, great! ²²And is this on sale?
> M: Yes, but only people with membership cards qualify for sale prices. If you don't have one yet, ²⁴I could bring you to the service counter and help you do so.
> W: ²⁴I would really appreciate that.

dough 밀가루 반죽   aisle 통로   follow (충고·지시 등을) 따르다
direction 지시, 명령   qualify for ~의 자격을 얻다

22-24는 다음 대화에 관한 문제입니다.
여: 실례합니다, ²²Doe Nut 브랜드의 쿠키 반죽 믹스를 찾고 있어요. 이쪽 통로에 있었던 것 같은데 보이질 않네요.
남: 저쪽에 있어요, 당신 바로 뒤에요.
여: 아! 감사합니다! 음... 반죽 믹스를 사용하는 건 이번이 처음이에요.
남: ²³정말 간단해요. 그냥 상자 뒷면의 지시를 따라하면 돼요.
여: 아, 좋네요! ²²그리고 이것이 지금 세일 중인가요?
남: 네, 하지만 회원 카드를 가지고 계신 분들에게만 할인 가격이 적용돼요. 아직 가지고 계시지 않다면 ²⁴서비스 카운터로 안내해드리고 회원 카드를 만드시는 걸 도와 드릴게요.
여: ²⁴그래 주시면 정말 고맙죠.

22.

어디서 이루어지는 대화인 것 같은가?
(A) 제과점에서
(B) 부엌에서
(C) 식료품점에서
(D) 가전제품 상점에서

[해설] 화자들이 있는 장소를 묻는 문제이다. 손님으로 보이는 여자가 직원으로 보이는 남자에게 쿠키 반죽 믹스(cookie dough mix)의 위치를 물어보고, 제품의 세일 여부(And is this on sale?) 등을 확인하는 것으로 보아 두 사람이 식료품점에서 대화를 나누고 있음을 알 수 있다. 따라서 정답은 (C)이다.

[어휘] home appliance 가전제품

23.

여자가 "반죽 믹스를 사용하는 건 이번이 처음이에요"라고 말할 때 의미하는 것은 무엇인가?
(A) 새로운 믹서기를 구매해야 한다.
(B) 한 재료에 알레르기가 있다.
(C) 다른 제품을 선호한다.
(D) 조언을 받고 싶다.

[해설] 화자의 의도 파악 문제는 해당 문장의 앞뒤 문맥을 파악해야 한다.

여자는 쿠키 반죽 믹스 찾는 것을 도와준 남자에게 감사 인사를 전한 후 "반죽 믹스를 사용하는 건 이번이 처음이에요"라고 말했고, 이에 남자가 그냥 상자 뒷면의 지시를 따라하면 된다고(Just follow the directions on the back of the box.) 말해주었다. 즉, 이 제품을 처음 사용하는 여자가 남자에게 이용법에 대한 조언을 구하려는 의도로 해당 문장을 언급한 것으로 볼 수 있으므로 정답은 (D)이다.

24.

화자들은 다음에 어디로 갈 것 같은가?
(A) 서비스 카운터로
(B) 다른 지점으로
(C) 계산대로
(D) 다른 통로로

[해설] 앞으로 일어날 일을 묻는 문제의 단서는 주로 대화 후반부에 나온다. 대화 마지막, 남자는 여자에게 회원 카드가 없다면 서비스 카운터로 안내해주겠다고(I could bring you to the service counter) 했고, 이에 여자가 고맙다고(I would really appreciate that.) 했다. 따라서 이들은 대화 후에 서비스 카운터로 갈 것임을 알 수 있으므로 정답은 (A)이다.

DAY 08

PART 2 간접 의문문 / 선택 의문문

확인 문제

❶ US-US

Can you tell me when the meeting starts?
(A) Yeah, it begins at 10 o'clock.
(B) I met Sam yesterday.

언제 회의가 시작하는지 말해줄 수 있나요?
(A) 네, 10시에 시작합니다.
(B) 저는 어제 Sam을 만났어요.

❷ AU-US

May I ask why Mr. Johnson is canceling the event?
(A) You'd better ask Jenny, his assistant.
(B) I got up late this morning.

왜 Johnson 씨가 행사를 취소하는지 여쭤봐도 될까요?
(A) 그의 비서인 Jenny에게 물어보는 게 좋을 것 같아요.
(B) 저는 오늘 아침에 늦게 일어났습니다.

❸ US-BR

Do you think that we should renovate the office?
(A) Yes, they will re-open today.
(B) Let's do an employee survey.

우리가 사무실을 개조해야 한다고 생각하시나요?
(A) 네, 그들은 오늘 다시 문을 열 거예요.
(B) 직원 설문조사를 합시다.

❹ BR-US

Which of these sweaters do you prefer to buy?
(A) I want the blue one.
(B) It's a birthday gift.

이 스웨터들 중 무엇을 사고 싶으신가요?
(A) 파란색을 원합니다.
(B) 생일 선물입니다.

❺ AU-BR

Which parking area is for the residents?
(A) I don't have any.
(B) The one next to the gym.

어느 주차 공간이 주민들을 위한 것입니까?
(A) 저는 아무것도 가지고 있지 않아요.
(B) 체육관 옆에 있는 거요.

❻ BR-AU

Do you want to have lunch delivered or go to a restaurant?
(A) That would be nice.
(B) It doesn't matter.

점심 식사를 배달시킬까요, 아니면 레스토랑에 가시겠어요?
(A) 그게 좋겠네요.
(B) 상관 없어요.

 연습 문제

01. (B) 02. (B) 03. (B) 04. (B) 05. (B) 06. (B)
07. (A) 08. (A)

01. US-BR

Which parking area is for employees?
(A) Approximately 100 workers. [×]
(B) The one behind the building. [○]

어느 주차장이 직원들을 위한 것입니까?
(A) 대략 100명의 직원들입니다.
(B) 건물 뒤에 있는 것입니다.

02. BR-US

Do you know who is working extra hours tonight?
(A) They're not yours. [×]
(B) I'll ask the manager. [○]

누가 오늘 밤에 추가 근무 하는지 아세요?
(A) 당신 것이 아닙니다.
(B) 제가 매니저에게 물어보겠습니다.

03. US-AU

Do you think I should turn on the heat?
(A) Go right at the intersection. [×]
(B) Are you cold? [○]

난방을 틀어야 한다고 생각하시나요?
(A) 교차로에서 오른쪽으로 가세요(우회전 하세요).
(B) 추우세요?

04. US-US

Are you going to give the sales presentation or should I do it?
(A) He said he was interested in sales. [×]
(B) I'll do it, if you are okay with it. [○]

매출 발표를 당신이 하시겠어요, 아니면 제가 해야 하나요?
(A) 그는 판매에 관심이 있다고 말했어요.
(B) 당신이 괜찮으시다면 제가 하겠습니다.

05. AU-BR

Can you tell me when Susan is moving into her new apartment?
(A) It's about $800 a month. [×]
(B) On the first of March. [○]

언제 Susan이 새 아파트로 이사하는지 말씀해 주시겠어요?
(A) 한 달에 약 800달러입니다.
(B) 3월 1일에요.

06. US-BR

Would you like me to print out the document or will you read it on the screen?
(A) Yes, we will read it tomorrow. [×]
(B) I'd like a paper copy. [○]

문서를 제가 출력해 드리기를 원하시나요, 아니면 화면으로 읽으시겠어요?
(A) 네, 우리는 내일 그것을 읽을 것입니다.
(B) 저는 종이에 인쇄된 것을 (읽는 것을) 좋아합니다.

07. BR-US

Does your soup taste alright or does it need more salt?
(A) It's perfect as it is. [○]
(B) Yes, I'll have dessert. [×]

수프의 맛이 괜찮으세요, 아니면 소금이 더 필요하세요?
(A) 있는 그대로 완벽한 맛이에요.
(B) 네, 저는 디저트를 먹을 거예요.

08. US-BR

Would you like a table inside or on the patio?
(A) Anywhere is fine. [○]
(B) Turn on the radio. [×]

실내 테이블이 좋으세요, 테라스가 좋으세요?
(A) 어느 곳이든 좋습니다.
(B) 라디오를 켜세요.

실전 문제

01. (A) 02. (A) 03. (B) 04. (B) 05. (A) 06. (B)
07. (B) 08. (C) 09. (B) 10. (C) 11. (B) 12. (C)
13. (A) 14. (B) 15. (A) 16. (C)

01. [BR-US]

Do you know how to remove shipping fees for customers?
(A) No, you'd better ask a manager.
(B) It will take more than three days.
(C) Items ship directly from our warehouse.

remove 제거하다   fee 요금, 수수료   customer 고객
directly 바로, 곧장   warehouse 창고

고객의 배송 요금을 없애는 방법을 아시나요?
(A) 아니요, 매니저에게 물어보는 게 좋겠어요.
(B) 3일 이상 걸릴 거예요.
(C) 제품들은 창고에서 바로 배송됩니다.

[해설] 배송 요금을 없애는 방법을 아는지 묻는 의문사 how가 포함된 간접 의문문이다.
(A) No로 응답한 후, 매니저에게 물어보라고 조언하고 있으므로 정답이다.
(B) 기간 답변이므로 how long 의문문에 어울리는 답변이다.
(C) 질문의 shipping과 발음이 비슷한 ship을 사용하여 혼동을 유도한 오답이다.

02. [AU-BR]

Do you know where Ms. Orwell's office is?
(A) Yes, it's the third door on the left.
(B) I saw her earlier.
(C) It's an official meeting.

earlier 앞서, 전에

Orwell 씨의 사무실이 어디인지 아시나요?
(A) 네, 왼쪽 세 번째 문이에요.
(B) 저는 전에 그녀를 봤어요.
(C) 공식적인 모임입니다.

[해설] Orwell 씨의 사무실 위치를 묻는 의문사 where가 포함된 간접 의문문이다.
(A) Yes로 응답한 후 구체적인 위치를 추가로 알려주고 있는 정답이다.
(B) 질문의 Ms. Orwell을 가리키는 대명사 her를 이용하여 혼동을 유도한 오답으로, 내용이 질문과 무관하다.
(C) 질문의 office와 발음이 유사한 official을 이용해 혼동을 유도하는 오답이다.

03. [US-BR]

Will you use public transportation again, or did you decide to rent a car?
(A) Here's your itinerary.
(B) I'll go around by bus.
(C) Yes, I've been there before.

public transportation 대중교통   itinerary 여행 일정표
go around 돌아다니다

또 대중교통을 이용하실 건가요, 아니면 차를 빌리기로 결정했나요?
(A) 여기 당신의 여행 일정표입니다.
(B) 버스를 타고 돌아다닐 거예요.
(C) 네, 전에 거기 가본 적이 있어요.

[해설] 대중교통을 이용할 건지, 아니면 차를 빌릴 건지 묻는 선택 의문문이다.
(A) 질문의 public transportation과 car 같은 교통 수단에서 연상할 수 있는 '여행'과 관련된 단어인 itinerary를 이용해 혼동을 유도하는 오답이다.
(B) 버스로 돌아다닐 것이라고 답변함으로써 대중교통을 이용할 것임을 우회적으로 말하고 있는 정답이다.
(C) 선택 의문문에는 Yes/No로 응답할 수 없으므로 오답이다.

04. [US-BR]

Which flavor did you like the most?
(A) No, for take-out.
(B) The second one I sampled.
(C) My compliments to the chef.

compliment 칭찬(의 말), 찬사

당신은 어떤 맛이 가장 좋았나요?
(A) 아니요, 포장해주세요.
(B) 제가 두 번째로 맛본 것이요.
(C) 주방장님께 찬사를 보냅니다.

[해설] 어떤 맛이 가장 좋았는지 묻는 선택 의문문이다.
(A) 의문사 which로 질문했으므로 Yes/No 응답은 불가능하며, 식당에서 주문할 때 먹고 갈 것인지 묻는 질문에 어울리는 응답이다.
(B) 두 번째로 맛본 것이라고 구체적으로 지목하여 답변했으므로 정답이다.
(C) 질문의 flavor에서 연상할 수 있는 chef를 이용해 혼동을 유도하는 응답이다.

05. [BR-US]

Do you know when Bunny's Ice Cream Shop opens?
(A) Usually at 11 A.M.
(B) Yes, I love the strawberry flavor.
(C) You can shop and make a purchase online.

Bunny의 아이스크림 가게가 언제 문을 여는지 아세요?
(A) 보통 오전 11시에요.
(B) 네, 저는 딸기 맛을 아주 좋아해요.
(C) 온라인으로 쇼핑하고 물건을 구입할 수 있어요.

[해설] 특정 상점이 문을 여는 시간을 아는지 묻는 의문사 when이 포함된 간접 의문문이다.
(A) '오전 11시'라는 구체적인 시간으로 응답하고 있으므로 정답이다.
(B) 간접 의문문에 Yes/No 응답은 가능하나 뒤에 이어지는 내용이 질문과 무관하므로 오답이다.
(C) 질문의 shop를 반복 사용하여 혼동을 유도하는 오답이다.

06. US-US

Could you tell me who you submitted your application to?
(A) The reserved parking permit.
(B) Actually, I did it online.
(C) Apply three times a day.

submit 제출하다   application 지원[신청](서)   reserved 지정된   permit 허가증   apply (페인트·크림 등을) 바르다

당신이 누구에게 지원서를 제출했는지 알려주시겠어요?
(A) 지정 주차 허가증입니다.
(B) 실은, 온라인으로 했어요.
(C) 하루에 세 번 바르세요.

[해설] 누구에게 지원서를 제출했는지 알려줄 것을 요청하는 의문사 who를 포함한 간접 의문문이다.
(A) 질문의 submit와 발음이 비슷한 permit을 이용하여 혼동을 유도하는 오답이다.
(B) 특정 인물이 아닌 온라인으로 제출했다고 답변한 정답이다.
(C) 질문의 application에서 연상 가능한 apply(지원하다)와 동음이의어인 apply(바르다)를 이용하여 혼동을 유도하는 오답이다.

07. AU-BR

Have you heard that our company will merge with Johnson Chemical next month?
(A) Be careful. It's toxic.
(B) Oh, are you sure?
(C) Right after long negotiations.

merge with ~와 합병하다   toxic 유독성의   negotiation 협상

다음 달에 우리 회사가 Johnson Chemical과 합병할 것이라는 거 들었어요?
(A) 조심해요. 그건 독성이 있어요.
(B) 아, 확실해요?
(C) 오랜 협상 직후에요.

[해설] 다음 달에 회사가 Johnson Chemical과 합병할 것이라는 얘기를 들었는지 확인하는 간접 의문문이다.
(A) 질문에 나온 회사명의 일부인 chemical에서 연상 가능한 toxic을 이용해 혼동을 유도하는 오답이다.
(B) 확실한 것인지 되물음으로써 소식을 듣지 못했음을 우회적으로 드러내는 정답이다.
(C) 질문의 merge에서 연상 가능한 negotiations(협상)를 이용해 혼동을 유도하는 오답이다.

08. US-AU

Which of these suitcases do you think I should bring?
(A) Just in case it rains.
(B) It's such a long flight.
(C) You'll want a lot of packing space.

suitcase 여행 가방   bring 가져오다   just in case ~한 경우에

이 여행 가방들 중 제가 어떤 것을 가져와야 한다고 생각해요?
(A) 비가 올 경우에 대비해서요.
(B) 아주 긴 비행이에요.
(C) 짐을 넣을 공간이 많이 필요할 거예요.

[해설] 어떤 여행 가방을 가져와야 하는지 상대방의 의견을 묻는 선택 의문문이다.
(A) 질문의 suitcases와 발음이 유사한 case를 이용해 혼동을 유도하는 오답이다.
(B) 질문의 suitcases에서 연상할 수 있는 flight(비행)를 이용해 혼동을 유도하는 오답이다.
(C) 짐을 넣을 공간이 많이 필요할 거라는 말로 큰 가방을 가져갈 것을 제안하고 있으므로 정답이다.

09. BR-US

Which class would you recommend for a beginner photograph?
(A) This is the beginning of the film.
(B) The Saturday morning one Ms. Porter teaches.
(C) Yeah, I liked that class.

사진을 처음 배우는 사람에게 어떤 수업을 추천하시겠어요?
(A) 이것은 영화의 시작 부분이에요.
(B) Porter 씨가 가르치는 토요일 아침 수업이요.
(C) 네, 저는 그 수업이 좋았어요.

[해설] 사진을 처음 배우는 사람에게 어떤 수업을 추천할지 묻는 선택 의문문이다.
(A) 질문의 beginner에서 연상되는 beginning을 이용해 혼동을 유도하는 오답이다.
(B) 'Porter 씨가 가르치는 토요일 아침 수업'이라고 특정 시간대의 수업을 제시하는 정답이다.
(C) 의문사 which가 포함되어 있으므로 Yes/No로 응답할 수 없으며, that class가 무엇을 지칭하는지 알 수 없으므로 오답이다.

10. US-BR

Do you know where Sunnyfield Bank is?
(A) Their tellers are very friendly.
(B) A great investment opportunity.
(C) It's on Laker Street.

teller (은행의) 창구 직원   investment 투자   opportunity 기회

Sunnyfield 은행이 어디 있는지 아시나요?
(A) 그곳의 창구 직원들은 매우 친절해요.
(B) 굉장한 투자 기회입니다.
(C) Laker 가에 있어요.

[해설] Sunnyfield 은행의 위치를 아는지 묻는 의문사 where가 포함된 간접 의문문이다.
(A) 질문의 bank에서 연상 가능한 tellers(은행의 창구 직원)를 이용해 혼동을 유도하는 오답이다.
(B) 질문의 bank에서 연상 가능한 investment(투자)를 이용해 혼동을 유도하는 오답이다.
(C) Laker 가에 있다고 구체적 위치를 제시하고 있으므로 정답이다.

11. US-US

Which pattern do you like, the striped one or the solid one?

(A) These fit perfectly.
(B) I think the striped one looks good on me.
(C) Do you have a cup lid?

pattern 양식, 패턴   striped 줄무늬가 있는   solid 단색의, 무늬가 없는   fit (모양·크기가) 맞다   look good on ~와 잘 어울리다

어떤 패턴이 마음에 드시나요, 줄무늬가 있는 것이요, 아니면 무늬가 없는 것이요?
(A) 이것들이 딱 맞아요.
(B) 줄무늬가 있는 것이 제게 잘 어울리는 것 같아요.
(C) 컵 뚜껑이 있나요?

[해설] 줄무늬가 있는 것과 무늬가 없는 것 중 어떤 패턴이 마음에 드는지 묻는 선택 의문문이다.
(A) these가 질문에서 제시한 두 가지 선택 사항, 즉 줄무늬가 있는 것과 무늬가 없는 것 중 무엇을 가리키는지 알 수 없으므로 오답이다.
(B) 줄무늬가 있는 것이 자신에게 잘 어울린다는 말로 둘 중 하나를 고른 정답이다.
(C) 질문의 solid와 발음이 비슷한 lid를 이용해 혼동을 유도하는 오답이다.

12. [BR-BR]

Would you rather rent a small-sized or medium-sized vehicle?
(A) They're more spacious than I expected.
(B) We have in-house mechanics.
(C) A small-sized one should be fine.

vehicle 차량, 탈것   spacious 널찍한   expect 기대하다, 예상하다   in-house (회사·조직) 내부의   mechanic 정비공

소형차를 빌리고 싶으세요, 아니면 중형차를 빌리고 싶으세요?
(A) 그것들은 제가 예상했던 것보다 더 널찍해요.
(B) 저희는 내부 정비공들을 보유하고 있습니다.
(C) 소형차가 좋겠어요.

[해설] 소형차와 중형차 중 어떤 차량을 빌리고 싶은지 묻는 선택 의문문이다.
(A) They가 질문에서 제시한 소형차와 중형차 중 무엇을 지칭하는지 모호하므로 오답이다.
(B) 질문의 vehicle을 수리하는 상황에서 연상 가능한 mechanics를 이용해 혼동을 유도하는 오답이다.
(C) 소형차를 선택하고 있으므로 정답이다.

13. [US-AU]

Do you prefer watching the final game on TV or going to the stadium?
(A) Tickets are already sold out.
(B) 50 euros per month.
(C) Enjoy the game.

결승전을 TV로 보는 것을 선호하시나요, 아니면 경기장에 가는 것을 선호하시나요?
(A) 티켓이 이미 매진되었어요.
(B) 한 달에 50유로예요.
(C) 경기 즐겁게 관람하세요.

[해설] 결승전을 TV로 보고 싶은지, 아니면 경기장에 직접 가고 싶은지 묻는 선택 의문문이다.
(A) 티켓이 다 팔렸다고 답함으로써 어쩔 수 없이 TV로 봐야 하는 상황임을 우회적으로 전달하고 있는 정답이다.
(B) 가격을 묻는 How much 의문문 또는 What is the price of ~ 유형의 의문문에 적합한 응답이다.
(C) 질문의 game를 반복 사용하여 혼동을 유도하는 오답이다.

14. [AU-BR]

Are you going to travel somewhere or stay at home during the break?
(A) It has beautiful scenery.
(B) I plan to travel overseas.
(C) Over the holiday season.

scenery 경치, 풍경   overseas 해외에, 해외로

휴가 동안 어디로 여행을 갈 건가요, 아니면 집에 있을 건가요?
(A) 그곳은 경치가 아름다워요.
(B) 해외로 여행 갈 계획이에요.
(C) 휴가철 동안이요.

[해설] 휴가 동안 여행을 갈 건지, 아니면 집에 있을 건지 묻는 선택 의문문이다.
(A) 질문에 대명사 it으로 가리킬 만한 특정 장소가 언급되지 않았으므로 오답이다.
(B) 해외 여행을 계획하고 있다고 답변함으로써 여행을 가는 쪽을 선택한 정답이다.
(C) 질문의 travel과 break에서 연상할 수 있는 holiday를 이용하여 혼동을 유도하는 오답이다.

15. [US-BR]

Do you know when Mr. Marx is coming in for an interview?
(A) Sometime tomorrow, I think.
(B) I'll review his résumé.
(C) There are several open positions.

résumé 이력서   position (일)자리, 직위

언제 Marx 씨가 면접을 위해 오는지 아세요?
(A) 제 생각으로는 내일일 거예요.
(B) 제가 그의 이력서를 검토할 거예요.
(C) 공석이 여러 개 있어요.

[해설] 언제 Marx 씨가 면접을 위해 오는지를 알고 있는지 묻는 의문사 when이 포함된 간접 의문문이다.
(A) 특정 시간 표현으로 답변하고 있으므로 정답이다.
(B) 질문의 interview에서 연상 가능한 résumé를 이용해 혼동을 유도하는 오답이다.
(C) 질문의 interview에서 연상 가능한 positions를 이용해 혼동을 유도하는 오답이다.

16. [US-US]

Would you like to use your points to upgrade your seat or stay in economy?
(A) Yes, I appreciate it.
(B) I'm on my way to a business meeting.

(C) I'll stay in economy this time.

appreciate 감사하다

포인트를 사용하여 좌석을 업그레이드하시겠어요, 아니면 이코노미석에 계시겠어요?
(A) 네, 감사합니다.
(B) 저는 업무 회의에 가는 길이에요.
(C) 이번에는 이코노미석에 있을게요.

[해설] 좌석을 업그레이드하길 원하는지 이코노미석에 있을 것인지 묻는 선택 의문문이다.
(A) 선택 의문문에는 Yes/No로 답변할 수 없다.
(B) economy 다음 등급인 business를 사용하여 혼동을 유도한 오답이다.
(C) 이코노미석에 있는 걸 선택하는 정답이다.

PART 3 — 시각 자료 연계 문제 / 3인 대화

 연습 문제

01. (B)　02. (A)　03. (B)　04. (B)　05. (B)　06. (A)

01. US-BR

Look at the graphic. **Where** will the **woman** deliver a **speech**?
(A) **Madrid**　(B) **Barcelona**

Schedule	
	Carl Butler
Date	**City**
October 11, Tuesday	Madrid
October 13, Thursday	Barcelona

W: The book signing event in Madrid is cancelled, so I will lead the Q&A session in your book club. But, as you know, I will give a keynote speech at a convention on Thursday afternoon.
M: Oh, really? That's great. You will have a great time with my book club members.

시각 자료를 보시오. 여자는 어디에서 강연을 할 것인가?
(A) 마드리드　**(B) 바르셀로나**

일정표	
	Carl Butler
날짜	**도시**
10월 11일, 화요일	마드리드
10월 13일, 목요일	바르셀로나

W: 마드리드에서의 책 사인회가 취소돼서, 당신의 책 동호회에서 Q&A 시간을 가질 거예요. 하지만, 아시다시피, 목요일 오후에는 제가 컨벤션에서 강연을 해야 해요.
M: 오, 정말요? 잘됐네요. 저의 책 동호회 회원들과 좋은 시간을 가질 거예요.

02. US-US-BR

Why did **Miranda** send an **e-mail** to the customers?
(A) To **apologize** for a **mistake**
(B) To **request** some **feedback**

W1: Our Web site administrator was able to find the error and correct it.
M: That's good news. Miranda, have you contacted our customers yet?
W2: Yes, I sent out an e-mail this morning to explain the situation and tell them that we are sorry for any confusion.

administrator 관리자　correct 수정하다, 바로잡다
contact 연락하다　situation 상황　confusion 혼란, 혼동

Miranda는 왜 고객들에게 이메일을 보냈는가?
(A) 실수를 사과하기 위해
(B) 피드백을 요청하기 위해

W1: 우리 웹사이트 관리자가 오류를 찾아서 바로잡을 수 있었어요.
M: 좋은 소식이네요. Miranda, 고객들께 연락은 했나요?
W2: 네, 오늘 아침에 이메일을 보내서 상황을 설명하고 혼란을 드려 죄송하다고 했어요.

03. BR-US

Look at the graphic. **When** will the **woman pay** for the **remainder**?
(A) **Sep. 14th**　(B) **Sep. 19th**

ITEM	Delivery Date
Bookshelves	Wed, Sep. 14th
Tables	Thurs, Sep. 15th
Chairs	Fri, Sep. 16th
Lamps	Mon, Sep 19th

W: Let me check the delivery schedule. You said we already made a $5,000 down payment when we placed the order. When should the remainder be paid?
M: You can make the final payment on the same day that the lamps arrive.

시각 자료를 보시오. 여자는 남은 금액을 언제 지불할 것인가?
(A) 9월 14일　**(B) 9월 19일**

품목	배달 날짜
책장	수요일, 9월 14일
테이블	목요일, 9월 15일
의자	금요일, 9월 16일
전등	월요일, 9월 19일

W: 배달 일정을 확인해볼게요. 당신은 우리가 주문할 때 5천 달러를 선금으로 지불했다고 하셨죠. 잔금이 언제 지불되어야 하나요?
M: 당신은 전등이 도착하는 당일에 최종 지불을 하시면 됩니다.

04. US-US

Look at the graphic. **Which window** should the **man go to tomorrow**?
(A) Window **1**   (B) Window **4**

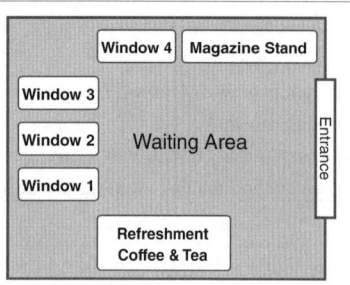

W: Sorry, we are already closed. Here are our business hours on the board.
M: Oh, okay. I came here to open a new business account.
W: If so, it usually takes about 30 minutes to process it. You'd better come by 4:30 tomorrow at the latest. Mr. Harris will help you. His window is right beside the magazine stand.

시각 자료를 보시오. 남자는 내일 어느 창구로 가야 하는가?
(A) 창구 1   **(B) 창구 4**

W: 죄송합니다, 저희는 이미 문을 닫았어요. 여기 게시판에 저희 영업 시간이 있습니다.
M: 아, 알겠습니다. 저는 사업 계좌를 개설하러 왔어요.
W: 그러시다면, 그것을 처리하는 데 보통 30분이 걸립니다. 내일 늦어도 4시 30분까지 오시는 게 좋을 거예요. Harris 씨가 도와줄 겁니다. 그의 창구는 잡지 매대 바로 옆이에요.

05. US-AU-BR

Who probably is the **woman**?
(A) A **construction worker**   (B) A **restaurant owner**

W: I checked on the renovation status you submitted for my restaurant, but I'm worried that it is a little bit behind schedule. What happened?
M1: Well, some work was delayed due to the rain.
M2: But some materials arrived earlier than scheduled, so we expect all the work to be done on time.

여자는 아마도 누구이겠는가?
(A) 공사 작업자   **(B) 레스토랑 주인**

W: 제 레스토랑을 위해 당신이 제출한 개조 공사 현황을 확인해 봤는데, 일정보다 약간 뒤처진 것 같아 걱정입니다. 무슨 일이 있나요?
M1: 음, 비 때문에 일부 작업이 지연되었어요.
M2: 하지만 몇몇 자재는 일정보다 빨리 도착해서, 모든 작업은 제시간에 끝날 것으로 예상합니다.

06. AU-US-BR

What do the **women agree** to do?
(A) **Work extra** shifts   (B) **Postpone** a meeting

M: Angela, would you mind adding extra shifts to your schedule this week? Olivia has a family emergency.
W1: I already knew that. I was asked if I can cover her shifts. I can cover her Monday shift, but I have a prior appointment with my academic advisor on Tuesday. Miranda, could you cover her Tuesday shift?
W2: Sure. What time do I need to come in?

여자들은 무엇을 하는 데 동의하는가?
(A) 추가 근무를 하는 것
(B) 회의를 미루는 것

M: Angela, 이번 주에 추가 근무를 해도 괜찮아요? Olivia가 급한 집안 일이 있어요.
W: 저는 이미 알고 있었어요. 제가 그녀의 작업 시간을 대신해줄 수 있는지 요청받았어요. 그녀의 월요일 근무는 대신할 수 있는데, 화요일에는 저의 지도 교수님과 선약이 있어요. Miranda, 그녀의 화요일 근무를 대신할 수 있어요?
W2: 물론이죠. 제가 몇 시에 와야 하나요?

paraphrasing 정답   1. (b) 2.(c) 3. (a) 4. (c) 5. (a) 6. (b)

실전 문제

01. (C)	02. (D)	03. (D)	04. (D)	05. (A)	06. (C)
07. (C)	08. (A)	09. (A)	10. (A)	11. (B)	12. (C)
13. (A)	14. (B)	15. (A)	16. (D)	17. (C)	18. (A)
19. (D)	20. (A)	21. (B)			

[01-03] US-AU

Questions 01-03 refer to the following conversation and list.

Refrigerator Model	Storage Capacity (in cubic feet)
Gourley	14
Wilkins	18
Marion	16
[02]Abbott	[02]20

W: Hi, I read in the newspaper that [01]**your store is having a big sale because you've relocated to the Lakewood neighborhood.**
M: That's right. We are offering special deals all week.
W: I'm interested in purchasing a refrigerator.

M: May I recommend the Marion model? It has 16 cubic feet of storage space, and it's half off.
W: Hmm... I'm not sure that will be large enough.
M: [02]**We've got one with 20 cubic feet of space.**
W: [02]**Perfect!** I'll stop by the store later this week.
M: Well, that model's selling out fast. [03]**I'd be happy to set one aside for you,** though, as long as you're here within three days.

neighborhood 근처, 인근   cubic feet 입방피트   storage 보관(소), 저장(고)   sell out 다 팔리다, 매진되다   set A aside A를 챙겨놓다   capacity 용량, 수용력

01-03은 다음 대화와 목록에 관한 문제입니다.

냉장고 모델	보관 용량 (입방피트)
Gourley	14
Wilkins	18
Marion	16
[02]**Abbott**	[02]**20**

여: 안녕하세요. [01]당신의 매장이 레이크우드 인근으로 이전하게 되어서 대규모 세일을 한다고 신문에서 읽었어요.
남: 맞아요. 일주일 내내 특가 상품들이 있어요.
여: 저는 냉장고 구매에 관심이 있어요.
남: Marion 모델을 추천해드려도 될까요? 보관 가능한 공간이 16입방피트인데 반값이에요.
여: 흠... 저는 그게 충분히 넓은 건지 잘 모르겠어요.
남: [02]공간이 20입방피트인 것도 있어요.
여: [02]딱 좋아요! 이번 주 후반에 매장에 들를게요.
남: 음, 그 모델은 빨리 나가는 제품이에요. 하지만 [03]당신을 위해서 기꺼이 한 대를 따로 챙겨 놓을게요. 3일 안에만 오신다면요.

01.

이 업체는 왜 세일을 하는가?
(A) 기념일을 축하하기 위해서
(B) 새로운 브랜드를 소개하기 위해서
(C) 이전을 홍보하기 위해서
(D) 국경일을 상기하기 위해서

[해설] 핵심 키워드 sale이 언급되는 곳에서 단서를 찾는다. 대화 초반에, 레이크우드 인근으로 이전하게 되어서 대규모 세일을 한다고(having a big sale because you've relocated to the Lakewood neighborhood) 신문에서 읽었다는 여자의 말이 나온다. 즉, 매장 이전을 홍보하기 위해 세일을 하는 것이므로 정답은 (C)이다.

paraphrasing   having a big sale 대규모 세일을 하다 → holding a sale 세일을 하다

[어휘] promote 홍보하다, 증진하다   relocation 이전, 재배치   recognize 인지하다, 상기하다

02.

시각 자료를 보시오. 여자는 어느 모델을 살 계획인가?
(A) Gourley
(B) Wilkins
(C) Marion
(D) Abbott

[해설] 시각 자료 연계 문제로, 대화에서 여자가 원하는 제품의 특징을 잘 듣고 시각 자료에서 해당 모델을 찾아야 한다. 20입방피트의 제품이 있다(We've got one with 20 cubic feet of space.)는 남자의 말에 여자가 딱 좋다고(Perfect!) 답했으므로 시각 자료의 Abbott이 여자가 구매할 모델이다. 정답은 (D)이다.

paraphrasing   storage space 저장 공간 → storage capacity 저장 용량

03.

남자는 무엇을 해주겠다고 하는가?
(A) 배송 주소를 업데이트하기
(B) 할인 쿠폰을 보내주기
(C) 재고 목록을 확인하기
(D) 여자를 위해 품목을 확보해 두기

[해설] 남자가 제안한 것을 묻는 문제로, 후반부 남자의 대사에 나오는 제안 표현에서 단서가 있다. 여자를 위해 기꺼이 하나를 따로 챙겨 두겠다고(I'd be happy to set one aside for you) 했으므로 정답은 (D)이다.

paraphrasing   set one aside 챙겨 두다 → Hold an item 품목을 확보해 두다

[어휘] voucher 할인권, 쿠폰   inventory 재고(품), 물품 목록

[04-06] BR-US-US

Questions 04-06 refer to the following conversation with three speakers.

W1: Excuse me. [04]**I'd like to speak to the manager.**
M: [04]**That's me.** How can I help?
W1: [04]**I bought this dress here yesterday,** but when I got it home, I noticed that it's torn. Could I get a refund?
M: [05]**I'll need the original receipt.** Do you have it with you?
W1: Unfortunately, I threw it away.
M: Don't worry. You can still exchange it for the same item. [06]**Tanya, could you check the stockroom** to see if we have more of these?
W2: Certainly. We just got a shipment in today.
M: Feel free to look around while you wait, ma'am.

torn 찢어진   refund 환불(금)   stockroom 창고, 물품 보관소   shipment 수송품, 적하물

04-06은 다음 세 명의 대화에 관한 문제입니다.

여1: 실례합니다. [04]매니저와 얘기하고 싶은데요.
남: [04]접니다. 무엇을 도와드릴까요?
여1: [04]제가 여기서 어제 이 드레스를 샀는데, 집에 가서 보니 찢어졌더라고요. 환불할 수 있을까요?
남: [05]원본 영수증이 있어야 해요. 가지고 계신가요?
여1: 유감스럽게도 버렸어요.
남: 걱정 마세요. 그래도 같은 품목으로 교환하실 수는 있어요. [06]**Tanya, 창고를 확인해서** 이 제품들이 더 있는지 알아봐줄래요?
여2: 물론이죠. 오늘 막 입고가 되었어요.
남: 기다리시는 동안 편하게 둘러보세요, 손님.

04.

남자는 누구일 것 같은가?
(A) 공장 감독관
(B) 수리점 직원
(C) 식당 주인
(D) 옷가게 매니저

[해설] 남자의 직업을 묻는 문제로, 화자의 직업이나 신분은 주로 대화 전반부에서 알 수 있다. 매니저와 얘기하고 싶다는(I'd like to speak to the manager) 여자1의 말에 남자가 본인이 매니저라고 밝히자, 여자1이 여기서 어제 드레스를 구매했다고(I bought this dress here yesterday) 했다. 따라서 남자는 옷가게의 매니저임을 알 수 있으므로 정답은 (D)이다.

[어휘] supervisor 감독관 repair 수리(하다) clothing 옷, 의복

05.

남자는 무엇을 요청하는가?
(A) 구매 증거
(B) 배송 세부 사항
(C) 사진이 부착된 신분증
(D) 고객의 서명

[해설] 남자의 요청 사항을 묻는 문제이므로 남자의 대사에 나오는 요청 표현에서 정답의 단서를 찾는다. 대화 중반부에서 여자가 환불이 가능한지 묻자 남자가 원본 영수증이 필요하다고(I'll need the original receipt.) 했다. 영수증은 일종의 구매 증거이므로 (A)가 정답이다.

paraphrasing the original receipt 원본 영수증 → proof of purchase 구매 증거

[어휘] proof 증거(물) purchase 구매

06.

Tanya는 무엇을 하라고 요청받는가?
(A) 정책 설명하기
(B) 문서 인쇄하기
(C) 보관 구역 확인하기
(D) 배달 일정 잡기

[해설] Tanya가 요청받은 일을 묻는 문제로, 핵심 키워드이자 특정 인물인 Tanya가 언급되는 곳에 단서가 있다. 대화 중반부에서 남자가 Tanya의 이름을 부르며 창고를 확인해달라고(Tanya, could you check the stockroom) 요청하고 있으므로 정답은 (C)이다.

paraphrasing stockroom 창고 → storage area 보관 구역

[어휘] policy 정책, 방침 document 서류, 문서 storage 저장

[07-09] ⟨AU-US-BR⟩

Questions 07-09 refer to the following conversation with three speakers.

M1: I wanted to meet with you both so we could check the progress of our new assignment.
W: ⁰⁷**The photographer has supplied the images for the magazine's cover, but we still need to arrange the text and layout.**
M1: That'll be difficult. ⁰⁸**This was supposed to be due on Friday, but the lead editor said this morning that he wants it by tomorrow afternoon.** I need more time than that because ⁰⁹**I'm not very familiar with using the design software.**
W: Hmm... Lucas provided training for the software.
M2: Right. I'm sure he'd be willing to give us a hand.

assignment 업무, 과제   progress 진전, 진척, 진행   arrange 정리하다, 배열하다   layout 레이아웃, 배치   due ~하기로 예정되어 있는, 예정된   lead editor 수석 편집자   be willing to V 기꺼이 ~하다   give a hand 도와주다

07-09는 다음 세 명의 대화에 관한 문제입니다.

남1: 새로운 업무의 진행 상황을 확인하기 위해서 두 분과 만나고 싶었어요.
여: ⁰⁷사진작가가 잡지 표지에 쓸 이미지를 보냈지만, 글과 레이아웃은 아직 정리해야 해요.
남1: 그거 힘들겠네요. ⁰⁸이 작업을 금요일까지 마무리하기로 되어 있었지만, 오늘 아침에 수석 편집자께서 내일 오후까지 마무리되기를 원한다고 말씀하셨어요. ⁰⁹제가 디자인 소프트웨어 사용에 그다지 익숙하지 않기 때문에 그것보다 시간이 더 필요해요.
여: 흠... Lucas가 소프트웨어 교육을 해줬어요.
남2: 맞아요. 그가 기꺼이 도와줄 거라고 확신해요.

07.

화자들은 어디에서 일할 것 같은가?
(A) 컴퓨터 상점에서
(B) 이사 업체에서
(C) 출판사에서
(D) 부동산 중개소에서

[해설] 화자의 직업이나 근무처에 대한 정보는 주로 대화 전반부에 나온다. 여자가 '잡지 표지를 위한 이미지(images for the magazine's cover)'를 언급하고, 아직 글과 레이아웃을 정리해야 한다고(we still need to arrange the text and layout) 말한 것으로 보아 화자들이 출판사에서 일하고 있음을 알 수 있으므로 (C)가 정답이다.

[어휘] publishing 출판 real estate 부동산

08.

오늘 아침에 무엇이 바뀌었는가?
(A) 프로젝트 마감일
(B) 회의 장소
(C) 가격 견적
(D) 월 이용료

[해설] 핵심 키워드 this morning이 언급된 곳에서 단서를 찾는다. 남자1의 대사에서, 이 작업이 금요일로 예정되어 있으나 오늘 아침 수석 편집자가 내일 오후까지 작업물을 원한다고(the lead editor said this morning that he wants it by tomorrow afternoon) 했다. 따라서 오늘 아침에 작업 마감 기한이 변경되었음을 알 수 있으므로 정답은 (A)이다.

[어휘] deadline 마감 기한 location 장소, 위치 estimate 견적(서) fee 요금, 수수료

09.

여자가 "Lucas가 소프트웨어 교육을 해줬어요"라고 말하는 이유는 무엇인가?
(A) 팀에 구성원을 추가할 것을 제안하기 위해
(B) Lucas를 수상 후보자로 지명하기 위해

(C) 회의 불참을 해명하기 위해
(D) 일부 낡은 정보를 수정하기 위해

[해설] 해당 표현의 전후 맥락을 살펴서 화자의 의도를 파악하는 문제이다. 남자1이 작업 완료 기한이 당겨졌음을 언급한 후 자신이 디자인 소프트웨어 사용에 익숙하지 않아(I'm not very familiar with using the design software) 시간이 더 필요하다고 하자 여자가 "Lucas가 소프트웨어 교육을 해줬어요"라고 말한 것은 소프트웨어에 대해 잘 아는 Lucas의 도움을 받거나 Lucas를 작업에 합류시키자는 의미이다. 따라서 '팀에 한 명을 추가한다'고 표현한 (A)가 정답이다.

[어휘] add A to B B에 A를 추가하다 nominate 지명[추천]하다 absence 결석, 결근 correct 수정하다, 고치다 outdated 낡은, 구식인

[10-12] BR-AU

Questions 10-12 refer to the following conversation and review.

---

www.quickbusinessreview.net

Cuyahoga Sporting Goods

Service	5/5
¹¹Variety	¹¹1/5
Quality	4/5
Location	1/5

W: Keith, I came across a number of bad reviews for our store online. A lot of them had similar ratings. Here's one as an example.

M: Oh, no! If we don't resolve these issues, ¹⁰I'm worried that customers may start buying their sports gear from our competitors.

W: Exactly. Now, ¹¹we can't do anything about our location.

M: Right. ¹¹But we could focus on the other poorly rated category. I'll discuss this with Ms. Lewis.

W: Okay, thanks. In the meantime, ¹²I can make a short questionnaire for our mailing list customers to find out what changes they would like to see.

---

come across ~을 우연히 발견하다 rating 순위, 평가, 등급 resolve (문제 등을) 해결하다 issue 문제점, 쟁점 gear (특정 활동에 필요한) 장비, 복장 focus on ~에 집중하다 category 범주 in the meantime 그동안 questionnaire 설문 mailing list 우편물 수신자 명단 variety 다양성

10-12는 다음 대화와 후기에 관한 문제입니다.

---

www.quickbusinessreview.net

Cuyahoga 스포츠용품

서비스	5/5
¹¹다양성	¹¹1/5
품질	4/5
위치	1/5

여: Keith, 온라인상에서 우리 상점에 대한 나쁜 후기 여러 개를 우연히 발견했어요. 많은 후기들의 평가가 비슷했어요. 여기 한 가지 예를 보세요.
남: 오, 이런! 우리가 이 문제점들을 해결하지 않으면 ¹⁰고객들이 우리 경쟁사에서 스포츠용품을 구매하기 시작할지도 모르니 걱정이네요.
여: 맞아요. 자, ¹¹우리 위치에 대해서는 우리가 할 수 있는 게 없어요.
남: 맞아요. ¹¹하지만 나쁜 등급을 받은 나머지 다른 분야에 집중할 수 있겠죠. 이 문제에 대해서 Lewis 씨와 얘기해볼게요.
여: 좋아요, 고마워요. 그러는 동안에 그들이 어떤 점이 바뀌길 바라는지 알아보기 위해 제가 우편물 수신 고객들을 대상으로 ¹²간단한 설문지를 만들면 되겠어요.

10.
남자는 무엇에 대해서 우려하는가?
(A) 시장 점유율을 잃는 것
(B) 계약을 취소하는 것
(C) 검사에서 불합격하는 것
(D) 직원들을 내보내는 것

[해설] 질문의 핵심 키워드 concerned가 대화에서는 worried로 표현되었다. 여자가 고객들의 온라인 후기가 좋지 않음을 지적하자 남자는 고객들이 경쟁사에서 스포츠용품을 구매할까 봐 걱정이라고(I'm worried that customers may start buying their sports gear from our competitors.) 말한다. 경쟁사에게 고객을 빼앗기는 것은 곧 시장 점유율을 잃는 것이므로 정답은 (A)이다.

paraphrasing I'm worried that ~이 걱정이다 → concerned about ~에 대해서 걱정하는

[어휘] be concerned about ~에 대해 걱정하다 market share 시장 점유율 contract 계약 inspection 검사, 조사

11.
시각 자료를 보시오. 남자는 Lewis 씨와 무엇에 대해 논의하겠는가?
(A) 서비스
(B) 다양성
(C) 품질
(D) 위치

[해설] 시각 자료 연계 문제로, 남자가 Lewis 씨와 논의하겠다고 한 내용을 듣고 시각 자료에서 해당 항목을 찾아야 한다. 남자가 장소(our location)에 대해서는 할 수 있는 일이 없다며, 나쁜 평가를 받은 나머지 분야(the other poorly rated category)에 대해 Lewis 씨와 논의하겠다고(I'll discuss this with Ms. Lewis) 했다. 시각 자료에서 안 좋은 평가를 받은 항목인 Variety(다양성)와 Location(위치) 중 Location을 제외하면 나머지는 Variety이므로 정답은 (B)이다.

12.
여자가 하겠다고 제안하는 것은 무엇인가?
(A) 제품 카탈로그 인쇄하기
(B) 웹사이트 소유주에게 연락하기
(C) 설문 조사 만들기
(D) 물품 주문하기

[해설] 대화 마지막 부분에 여자가 자신이 하겠다고 제안하는 내용이 나온다. 앞서 남자가 안 좋은 평가를 받은 범주에 대해 Lewis 씨와 논의하겠다고 하자 여자가 그러면 자신은 우편물 수신 고객들을 위한 간단한 설문지를 만들겠다고(I can make a short questionnaire) 했으므로 정답은 (C)이다.

paraphrasing make a short questionnaire 간단한 설문지를 만들다 → create a survey 설문 조사를 만들다

[어휘] survey (설문) 조사 supplies 공급품

[13-15] US AU US

Questions 13-15 refer to the following conversation with three speakers.

> W: Hi, **[13]I would like to join an exercise class.** What activities does your center offer?
> M1: We have several programs. **[13]Our group activities include spinning, yoga, and water aerobics.** Each one costs $50 per month to register for.
> W: That's pretty expensive. Is there a student discount?
> M1: Let me check. Hey, Lance, do we give discounts to students?
> M2: Yes, **[14]if someone has a valid college student ID then they get 10% off.**
> W: Really? I brought my ID with me. I'd like to sign up for the spinning class, please.
> M1: Okay, **[15]I'll just need you to put your contact information into this computer here.**

spinning 스피닝(운동용 자전거 타기)   aerobics 에어로빅
register for ~에 등록하다   pretty 꽤, 상당히   expensive 비싼
valid 유효한   sign up for ~을 신청[가입]하다   contact information 연락처

13-15는 다음 세 명의 대화에 관한 문제입니다.
여: 안녕하세요, **[13]저는 운동 수업에 가입하고 싶은데요.** 여기 센터는 어떤 활동들을 제공하나요?
남1: 여러 프로그램들이 있습니다. **[13]그룹 활동에는 스피닝, 요가, 수중 에어로빅이 있어요.** 등록하는 데 각각 한 달에 50달러입니다.
여: 꽤 비싸네요. 학생 할인이 있나요?
남1: 확인해볼게요. 저기요, Lance 씨, 우리가 학생들에게 할인을 제공하나요?
남2: 네, **[14]유효한 대학교 학생증이 있으면 10퍼센트 할인을 받아요.**
여: 정말이요? 제 학생증을 가지고 왔어요. 스피닝 교실에 등록할게요.
남1: 알겠습니다. **[15]당신이 여기 있는 이 컴퓨터에 연락처를 입력해주시기만 하세요.**

13.

대화는 어디에서 이루어지는 것 같은가?
(A) 체육관에서
(B) 공원에서
(C) 학교에서
(D) 경기장에서

[해설] 운동 교실에 가입하고 싶다는(I would like to join an exercise class) 여자의 말과, 스피닝, 요가, 수중 에어로빅(spinning, yoga, and water aerobics) 같은 그룹 활동이 있다는 남자의 말로 보아 헬스클럽 같은 운동 시설을 방문한 여자와 그곳의 직원인 남자의 대화임을 알 수 있다. 따라서 정답은 (A)이다.

14.

여자는 왜 자신의 학생증을 제시해야 하는가?
(A) 자리를 맡기 위해서
(B) 할인을 받기 위해서
(C) 일자리에 지원하기 위해서
(D) 자신의 생년월일을 증명하기 위해서

[해설] 운동 교실 등록 비용에 대해 문의하면서 여자가 학생 할인이 있냐고 물었고 남자2가 학생증이 있으면 10퍼센트 할인을 받는다고(if someone has a valid college student ID then they get 10% off) 했다. 즉, 할인을 받기 위해서는 학생증을 제시해야 하므로 정답은 (B)이다.

paraphrasing get 10% off 10퍼센트를 할인 받다 → get a discount 할인을 받다

[어휘] reserve (자리 등을) 따로 잡아 두다   spot 장소, 자리   apply for ~에 지원하다

15.

여자는 다음에 무엇을 할 것 같은가?
(A) 자신의 개인 정보를 입력하기
(B) 매니저와 얘기하기
(C) 다른 시설에 가기
(D) 불만을 제기하기

[해설] 앞으로 일어날 일에 대한 문제의 단서는 대화 후반에 제시된다. 대화 후반, 스피닝 교실에 등록하고 싶다는 여자의 말에, 남자가 컴퓨터에 연락처를 입력해달라고(I'll just need you to put your contact information into this computer here) 했으므로, 대화 후 여자가 자신의 개인 정보를 컴퓨터에 입력할 것임을 알 수 있다. 정답은 (A)이다.

paraphrasing put your contact information 연락처를 입력하다 → input her personal information 개인 정보를 입력하다

[어휘] input 입력하다   personal information 개인 정보   facility 시설   file a complaint 불만을 제기하다

[16-18] BR-AU-US

Questions 16-18 refer to the following conversation with three speakers.

> W1: **[16]George, Stephanie,** thanks for coming. **[16]I'd like to assign you two to maintain the garden for this client.**
> M: We'll take on the project, but **[17]we are a bit concerned.**
> W2: **[17]The client is asking for a lot more work than usual.** Do we have a timeline to refer to?
> W1: He said that it's flexible, but you can contact him directly about that.
> W2: Alright, did he say when the best time to reach him would be?
> W1: **[18]He's busy in the mornings and afternoons, but could talk with you after that.**

assign A to V A를 ~하는 일에 배정하다   maintain 관리하다
take on (일 등을) 맡다   ask for ~을 부탁하다, 요청하다
than usual 평소보다   timeline 시각표, 연대표   refer to ~을 보다, ~에게 문의하다   flexible 융통성 있는, 탄력적인   directly 곧장, 똑바로   reach (전화로) 연락하다

16-18은 다음 세 명의 대화에 관한 문제입니다.
여1: **[16]George, Stephanie,** 와줘서 고마워요. **[16]두 사람에게 이 의뢰인의 정원을 관리하는 일을 배정하려고 해요.**
남: 저희가 그 작업을 맡을게요. 그런데 **[17]조금 걱정이 되네요.**

여2: ¹⁷그 의뢰인이 평소보다 훨씬 많은 작업을 요청하고 있어요. 우리에게 참고할 만한 일정표가 있나요?
여1: 그건 유동적이라고 그가 말했어요. 하지만 그 부분에 대해서는 당신이 그에게 직접 연락하면 돼요.
여2: 알겠어요, 그가 연락을 받기에 가장 좋은 시간이 언제인지 말해주었나요?
여1: ¹⁸그는 오전과 오후 시간에는 바쁘대요. 하지만 그 이후에는 통화할 수 있을 거예요.

16.

George와 Stephanie는 누구일 것 같은가?
(A) 건물주들
(B) 부동산 중개인들
(C) 철물점 직원들
(D) 전문 정원사들

[해설] 여자1은 대화 시작 부분에서, George와 Stephanie의 이름을 부르며, 이들에게 특정 의뢰인의 정원을 관리하는 일을 배정하고자 한다고(I'd like to assign you two to maintain the garden for this client) 했다. 따라서 George와 Stephanie는 전문 정원사들임을 유추할 수 있으므로 정답은 (D)이다.

[어휘] property 재산, 부동산, 건물 real estate 부동산 agent 대리인, 중개상 hardware 철물 professional 전문적인, 직업적인 gardener 정원사

17.

George와 Stephanie는 무엇에 대해서 걱정하는가?
(A) 장비의 가격
(B) 꽃씨의 이용 가능성
(C) 요청받은 작업의 양
(D) 고객의 집의 위치

[해설] George와 Stephanie는 여자1로부터 작업을 배정받은 남자와 여자2이다. 작업을 배정받은 후 남자가 조금 걱정스럽다고(we are a bit concerned) 하자 이어서 여자가 그 의뢰인이 평소보다 훨씬 많은 작업을 요청한다며(The client is asking for a lot more work than usual) 걱정하는 이유를 덧붙였다. 즉, 두 사람은 요청받은 작업의 양이 너무 많아 걱정하고 있으므로 정답은 (C)이다.

[어휘] equipment 장비, 용품 availability 유효성, (입수) 가능성 amount 양 location 위치, 장소

18.

고객에 대해 언급된 것은 무엇인가?
(A) 저녁에 시간이 있다.
(B) 자신의 사업체를 운영한다.
(C) 장비를 제공할 것이다.
(D) 도시를 떠날 것이다.

[해설] 질문의 client는 정원 관리 작업을 요청한 의뢰인을 가리킨다. 대화 마지막에 여자2가 의뢰인에게 연락하기 좋은 시간이 언제인지 묻자, 여자1이 오전과 오후 시간에는 바쁘지만 그 이후에는 통화할 수 있다고(He's busy in the mornings and afternoons, but could talk with you after that) 했다. 즉, 의뢰인이 저녁에는 시간 여유가 있다는 뜻이므로 정답은 (A)이다.

paraphrasing He's busy in the mornings and afternoons, but could talk with you after that. 오전과 오후 시간에는 바쁘지만 그 이후에는 통화할 수 있다. → He is available in the evenings. 저녁에 시간이 있다.

[어휘] operate 운영하다 go out of town (출장 등으로) 도시를 떠나다

[19-21] US-US

Questions 19-21 refer to the following conversation and floor plan.

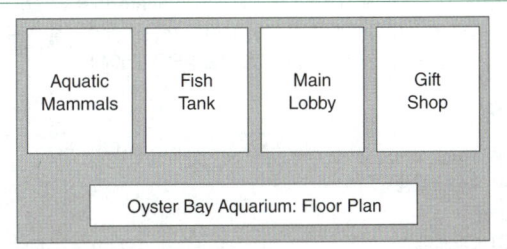

Oyster Bay Aquarium: Floor Plan

W: Hello, and welcome to the Oyster Bay Aquarium. How can I help you?
M: Hi, ¹⁹**I heard that you have a new exhibit,** so you don't just feature fish here. ¹⁹**Where is that?**
W: Well, we're in the Main Lobby right now. That door leads to the Fish Tank, and if you go straight through that area, ²⁰**you'll find the new exhibit right past the Fish Tank.**
M: Thanks. I was wondering, ²¹**this pass** lasts the whole day, right?
W: Yes, it does. ²¹**Be sure to hold onto it because it gives you 15% off anything in the gift shop.**

floor plan 평면도 aquarium 수족관 exhibit 전시, 전시품 feature ~의 특색을 이루다 lead to ~로 이어지다 fish tank 어류 탱크 wonder 궁금해하다 last 계속하다, 지속하다 hold onto 계속 보유하다 aquatic 수생의 mammal 포유동물

19-21은 다음 대화와 평면도에 관한 문제입니다.

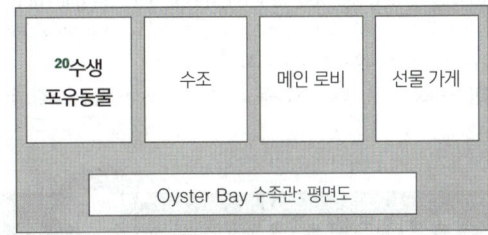

Oyster Bay 수족관: 평면도

여: 안녕하세요, Oyster Bay 수족관에 오신 것을 환영합니다. 무엇을 도와드릴까요?
남: 안녕하세요, ¹⁹새로운 전시가 있다고 들었어요. 그럼 이곳에서 어류만 전시하는 것은 아니죠? ¹⁹그곳은 어디인가요?
여: 음, 지금 이곳은 메인 로비예요. 저 문이 수조로 이어져 있어요. 저쪽 구역을 통과해서 직진하시면 ²⁰수조를 지나자마자 새로운 전시물이 보이실 거예요.
남: 감사합니다. 궁금한 것이 있는데요. ²¹이 패스는 하루 종일 지속되는 것이죠, 맞죠?
여: 네, 맞습니다. ²¹선물 가게에서 무엇을 사시든 15퍼센트 할인해드리니 꼭 가지고 다니세요.

19.

남자는 무엇을 알고 싶어 하는가?
(A) 티켓의 가격
(B) 투어에 합류할 수 있는지 여부
(C) 어류의 이름
(D) 전시관으로 가는 길

[해설] 남자는 새로운 전시가 있다고 들었다며(I heard that you have a new exhibit), 그곳이 어디인지(Where is that?) 물었다. 즉, 새로운 전시가 있는 곳으로 가는 길을 묻고 있으므로 정답은 (D)이다.

20.

시각 자료를 보시오. 여자는 어느 구역으로 가는 길을 안내하는가?
(A) 수생 포유동물
(B) 수조
(C) 메인 로비
(D) 선물 가게

[해설] 남자가 새로운 전시물이 어디에 있는지 묻자, 여자는 현재의 위치가 메인 로비(Main Lobby)이고, 수조를 지나자마자 새로운 전시가 보일 거라고(you'll find the new exhibit right past the Fish Tank) 했다. 시각 자료로 제공된 평면도에서 메인 로비에서 출발해 수조를 지나자마자 도착하는 곳은 수생 포유동물 구역이므로 정답은 (A)이다.

21.

여자는 남자에게 티켓에 대해 무엇이라고 말하는가?
(A) VIP 회원 혜택이 포함되어 있다.
(B) 상점에서 할인을 받게 해준다.
(C) 주말 내내 유효하다.
(D) 특별 행사에 입장하게 해준다.

[해설] 질문의 키워드 ticket은 대화 후반 남자가 언급한 pass를 가리킨다. 이때의 pass는 '출입증, 통행증'이라는 뜻이다. 남자가 자신의 패스가 하루 종일 유효한지 묻자 여자가 그렇다며, 그것이 있으면 선물 가게에서 15퍼센트 할인을 해준다고(it gives you 15% off anything in the gift shop.) 덧붙였다. 따라서 정답은 (B)이다.

paraphrasing it gives you 15% off anything in the gift shop 선물 가게의 모든 물건에 대해 15퍼센트 할인을 해준다 → It provides a discount at the shop. 상점에서 할인을 제공한다.

[어휘] benefit 이익, 혜택 valid 유효한, 타당한 admission 입장, 입학

DAY 09

PART 2 청유문

확인 문제

❶ US-US

Would you like to have some coffee?
(A) I was planning to go get one.
(B) I'm not sure I can help you.

커피 좀 마시겠어요?
(A) 한 잔 사러 가려고 했어요.
(B) 당신을 도와 드릴 수 있을지 잘 모르겠네요.

❷ AU-BR

Why don't we continue the discussion after lunch?
(A) I'm the last speaker.
(B) I'll be out of the office in the afternoon.

우리 점심식사 후에 계속 논의하는 게 어때요?
(A) 저는 마지막 연사입니다.
(B) 저는 오후에 회사에 없을 거예요.

❸ BR-US

Would you mind taking messages for me while I'm not here?
(A) She's not in the office.
(B) No, not at all.

제가 여기 없는 동안 메시지 좀 받아 주시겠어요?
(A) 그녀는 사무실에 없습니다.
(B) 물론이죠.

❹ BR-BR

I can print out a copy of the schedule if you'd like.
(A) Thank you for your help.
(B) Let's reschedule the meeting.

원하시면 제가 일정표 한 부를 출력해 드릴 수 있어요.
(A) 도와주셔서 감사합니다.
(B) 회의 일정을 다시 잡읍시다.

❺ AU-US

I'd like to see Dr. Choi for my regular check-up.
(A) He is out at the moment.
(B) Why don't you check your invoice?

정기 검진을 위해 Choi 박사님을 뵙고 싶어요.
(A) 그는 지금 외출 중이에요.
(B) 당신의 송장을 확인해 보는 게 어때요?

❻ US-AU

Please send me the information about the total expense.
(A) The less expensive one.
(B) Sure, no problem. I'll do it now.

총 비용에 대한 정보를 제게 보내주세요.
(A) 덜 비싼 거요.
(B) 네, 문제없습니다. 지금 해 드릴게요.

 연습 문제

01. (B) 02. (B) 03. (A) 04. (A) 05. (B) 06. (B)
07. (B) 08. (A)

01. US-BR

> Let's take a break after the meeting.
> (A) The computer was broken again. [×]
> (B) That sounds great. [○]

회의 후에 휴식을 취합시다.
(A) 컴퓨터가 또 고장 났어요.
(B) 좋은 생각이에요.

02. BR-US

> Would you like some ice cream?
> (A) They're her favorite. [×]
> (B) I'd prefer a hot drink. [○]

아이스크림 드시겠어요?
(A) 그건 그녀가 제일 좋아하는 겁니다.
(B) 저는 따뜻한 음료가 더 좋습니다.

03. BR-BR

> Why don't I give you a tour of our gym?
> (A) I'd love to. [○]
> (B) One of the tourist attractions. [×]

제가 저희 헬스클럽을 안내해 드릴까요?
(A) 좋아요.
(B) 관광 명소 중 한 곳이요.

04. US-BR

> Why don't we ask Sophia to participate in the meeting this afternoon?
> (A) Is she here today? [○]
> (B) Let's go to the party. [×]

Sophia에게 오늘 오후 회의에 참석하라고 하는 게 어때요?
(A) 그녀가 오늘 여기 있나요?
(B) 파티에 갑시다.

05. BR-US

> Why don't you go for a walk in the park during the lunch break?
> (A) I'll have a burger for lunch. [×]
> (B) I will, I need some fresh air. [○]

점심 시간 동안 공원을 산책하는 게 어때요?
(A) 저는 점심 식사로 햄버거를 먹겠습니다.
(B) 그럴 거예요, 저는 좀 신선한 공기가 필요해요.

06. US-AU

> How about going to the beach this weekend?
> (A) I took the subway. [×]
> (B) I'm afraid I can't. [○]

이번 주말에 해변에 가는 거 어때요?
(A) 저는 지하철을 탔어요.
(B) 죄송하지만 저는 못 가요.

07. AU-BR

> Do you mind if I turn up the volume?
> (A) I turned the lights off. [×]
> (B) As a matter of fact, I do. [○]

소리를 키워도 괜찮을까요?
(A) 제가 전등을 껐어요.
(B) 사실, 안 그러시면 좋겠습니다.

08. US-BR

> I need to get a quick bite before the movie.
> (A) There's a fast food restaurant nearby. [○]
> (B) How about that romance movie? [×]

저는 영화 전에 잠깐 뭐 좀 먹어야겠어요.
(A) 근처에 패스트푸드점이 있어요.
(B) 저 로맨스 영화 어때요?

실전 문제

01. (C)	02. (A)	03. (B)	04. (B)	05. (A)	06. (B)
07. (B)	08. (C)	09. (A)	10. (A)	11. (C)	12. (C)
13. (C)	14. (A)	15. (C)	16. (C)		

01. AU-BR

> Could you help me assist these customers?
> (A) You can customize your suits.
> (B) I saw an ad for this product.
> (C) Sure, I'll be right there.

assist 돕다 customize 주문 제작하다 suit 정장
ad 광고(= advertisement)

제가 이 고객들을 돕는 것을 도와주시겠어요?
(A) 당신의 정장을 주문 제작하실 수 있어요.
(B) 이 제품의 광고를 봤어요.
(C) 물론입니다, 제가 바로 갈게요.

[해설] 고객들을 돕는 것을 도와달라고 부탁하는 청유문이다.
(A) 질문의 customers와 발음이 비슷한 customize를 이용해 혼동을 유도하는 오답이다.
(B) 질문의 customers에서 연상 가능한 product를 이용해 혼동을 유도하는 오답이다.
(C) 지금 바로 가겠다는 말로 부탁을 수락하고 있으므로 정답이다.

02. US-AU

> Would you mind changing your seat with mine so we can sit together?
> (A) Of course not.
> (B) How long did it last?
> (C) No, I haven't ordered yet.

last 계속하다, 지속하다 order 주문하다

저희가 같이 앉을 수 있도록 저와 자리를 바꿔 주시겠습니까?
(A) 물론이죠.
(B) 얼마나 오래 지속되었나요?
(C) 아니요, 아직 주문하지 않았어요.

[해설] 자리를 바꿔 달라고 부탁하는 청유문이다.
(A) 자리를 바꿔 달라는 부탁에 부정의 not을 써서 수락하고 있으므로 정답이다. Would/Do you mind ~? 표현으로 부탁을 하는 경우 수락할 때는 부정의 표현, 거절할 때는 긍정의 표현을 쓴다는 것을 알아두자.
(B) 자리를 바꿔 달라는 부탁에 얼마나 지속되었냐고 되묻고 있으므로 질문의 내용과 무관한 오답이다.
(C) 부정의 No로 상대방의 부탁을 수락했으나 뒤에 이어지는 내용이 질문과 무관하므로 오답이다.

03. BR-US

Please prepare for the dinner rush now.
(A) The kitchen staff.
(B) I'll slice the vegetables.
(C) A table for 6 diners.

rush 혼잡, 북적거림   slice (얇게) 썰다   vegetable 채소
diner 식사하는 손님

이제 저녁식사 손님이 몰릴 것에 대비해주세요.
(A) 주방 직원입니다.
(B) 제가 채소를 썰게요.
(C) 6명의 손님을 위한 테이블이요.

[해설] 저녁식사 손님이 몰릴 것에 대비해달라고 요청하는 명령문이다.
(A) 질문의 dinner에서 연상할 수 있는 kitchen을 이용해 혼동을 유도하는 오답이다.
(B) 식사 손님이 몰릴 것에 대비해 달라는 말에 채소를 썰겠다고 구체적인 대비 방법을 설명함으로써 우회적으로 상대방의 요청을 수락하고 있으므로 정답이다.
(C) 질문의 dinner rush에서 연상할 수 있는 diners를 이용해 혼동을 유도하는 오답이다.

04. US-US

Would you like me to prepare some charts?
(A) I want a pair of hiking boots.
(B) I'm still receiving the data from the branches.
(C) Let's turn to page 9.

prepare 준비하다   a pair of 한 쌍의   hiking boots 등산화
branch 지점, 지사   turn to page ~ ~쪽을 펴다

제가 도표를 준비해드릴까요?
(A) 저는 등산화 한 켤레를 원합니다.
(B) 제가 아직 지점들로부터 자료를 받는 중이에요.
(C) 9쪽을 펩시다.

[해설] 도표를 준비해주겠다고 제안하는 의문문이다.
(A) 질문의 prepare와 발음이 유사한 pair를 이용하여 혼동을 유도하는 오답이다.
(B) 도표를 준비해주겠다는 제안에 아직 지점들로부터 자료를 받고 있다는 말로 아직 자료를 취합하는 중이니 당장 도표를 준비하지 않아도 된다고 상대방의 제안을 우회적으로 거절하고 있는 정답이다.
(C) 질문의 chart를 듣고 도표가 실려 있는 보고서의 어느 페이지를 연상

할 경우 고를 수 있는 오답이다.

05. BR-US

Will you submit your time sheet today?
(A) Yes, since I will have a day-off tomorrow.
(B) Can I change my seat?
(C) It's half past 2.

submit 제출하다   time sheet 근무 시간 기록표   day-off 휴일

오늘 당신의 근무 시간 기록표를 제출하시겠어요?
(A) 네, 내일은 제가 휴가니까요.
(B) 제 좌석을 바꿔도 될까요?
(C) 2시 30분입니다.

[해설] 오늘 근무 시간 기록표를 제출해 달라고 부탁하는 청유문이다.
(A) Yes로 상대방의 부탁을 수락한 후 오늘 제출해야만 하는 이유를 덧붙이고 있으므로 정답이다.
(B) 질문의 sheet와 발음이 유사한 seat를 이용하여 혼동을 유도하는 오답이다.
(C) 질문의 time에서 연상 가능한 시간 표현을 이용하여 혼동을 유도하는 오답이다.

06. US-US

Why don't you join us for lunch today?
(A) The menu should be posted online.
(B) Sure, see you soon at the building entrance.
(C) Yes, could you bring me a chicken salad?

join 함께 ~하다   post 게시하다   entrance 입구

오늘 저희와 점심 식사를 함께 하시는 게 어때요?
(A) 메뉴가 온라인에 올라가 있어야 해요.
(B) 좋아요, 건물 입구 앞에서 봬요.
(C) 네, 치킨 샐러드 좀 가져다 주시겠어요?

[해설] 같이 점심을 먹자고 제안하는 의문문이다.
(A) 질문의 lunch에서 연상할 수 있는 menu를 사용하여 혼동을 유도한 오답이다.
(B) 제안에 sure로 수락한 후 건물 입구에서 보자고 덧붙이고 있으므로 정답이다.
(C) Yes로 수락하고 있으나 어울리지 않는 질문이 이어지고 있다. 질문의 lunch에서 연상할 수 있는 chicken salad를 사용하여 혼동을 유도한 오답이다.

07. BR-US

Would you mind waiting in the car for a minute?
(A) It has very low mileage.
(B) Did you forget something?
(C) Yes, it runs fine.

for a minute 잠시 동안   mileage 주행 거리, 마일 수

잠시 차에서 기다려줄래요?
(A) 그건 주행 거리가 얼마 되지 않아요.
(B) 뭘 잊어버렸나요?
(C) 네, 잘 작동돼요.

[해설] 잠시 동안 차에서 기다려달라고 부탁하는 청유문이다.
(A) 질문의 car에서 연상할 수 있는 mileage를 이용해 혼동을 유도하는 오답이다.
(B) 잠시 차에서 기다려달라는 부탁에 그런 부탁을 하는 이유를 묻고 있으므로 정답이다. 부탁하는 의문문에 수락 또는 거절하는 표현 이외에 다양한 방법으로 답변할 수 있음을 알아두자.
(C) 질문의 car에서 연상할 수 있는 run을 이용해 혼동을 유도하는 오답이다.

08. US-BR

Could I be moved to an aisle seat?
(A) It's not removable.
(B) A ferry to North Island departs once every hour.
(C) Wait a second. I'll check on that for you.

aisle 통로   removable 제거할 수 있는, 이동식의   ferry 배, 페리   depart 출발하다

통로 쪽 자리로 옮길 수 있을까요?
(A) 그건 이동식이 아닙니다.
(B) North Island로 가는 페리는 한 시간에 한 번씩 출발합니다.
(C) 잠시만요. 확인해 보겠습니다.

[해설] 통로 쪽 자리로 옮기는 것을 요청하는 의문문이다.
(A) 질문의 move에서 연상할 수 있는 removable을 사용하여 혼동을 유도한 오답이다.
(B) 질문의 aisle과 발음이 비슷한 Island를 사용하여 혼동을 유도한 오답이다.
(C) 잠시만 기다리라며 확인해 보겠다고 하였으므로 정답이다.

09. US-US

Do you mind if I videotape your speech?
(A) Recording devices are not allowed.
(B) It was very informative.
(C) Yes, you can.

videotape 비디오테이프에 녹화하다   recording device 기록 장치   allowed 허용되는   informative 유익한

제가 당신의 연설을 비디오테이프에 녹화해도 괜찮을까요?
(A) 기록 장치는 허용되지 않습니다.
(B) 그것은 매우 유익했어요.
(C) 네, 그러셔도 됩니다.

[해설] 상대방의 연설을 녹화해도 괜찮을지 묻는 요청/부탁 의문문이다.
(A) 기록 장치는 허용되지 않는다고 답변함으로써 우회적으로 상대방의 부탁을 거절하고 있으므로 정답이다.
(B) 질문의 speech를 가리키는 대명사 it을 이용해 혼동을 유도한 오답으로, speech에 대한 소감을 묻는 질문에 어울리는 응답이다.
(C) you로 묻는 질문에 I나 we가 아닌 you로 답변했으므로 대명사 불일치 오답이다.

10. BR-AU

Let's go to the movies this weekend.
(A) Sure, that should be fun.
(B) Based on a true story.
(C) Yes, it's a sequel.

based on ~에 근거하여   sequel 속편

이번 주말에 영화 보러 갑시다.
(A) 그래요. 그거 재미있겠네요.
(B) 실화에 근거했어요.
(C) 네, 그것은 속편이에요.

[해설] 이번 주말에 영화를 보러 가자고 제안하는 청유문이다.
(A) 긍정의 Sure로 상대방의 제안을 수락한 뒤 재미있겠다며 기대감을 드러내고 있는 정답이다.
(B) 질문의 movie만 듣고 특정 영화의 내용이나 특징에 대해 묻는 질문으로 잘못 이해했을 경우 고를 수 있는 오답이다.
(C) 영화를 보러 가자는 제안에 긍정의 Yes로 수락했으나 대명사 it으로 가리킬 만한 특정 영화가 질문에서 언급되지 않았으므로 오답이다.

11. US-AU

I want to return these pants.
(A) We accept cash and credit.
(B) Our dressing room is over there.
(C) Sorry, but we don't carry that brand any more.

return 돌려주다, 반납하다   accept 받아들이다   dressing room 탈의실   carry 취급하다

이 바지를 반품하고 싶어요.
(A) 저희는 현금과 신용카드를 받습니다.
(B) 저희 탈의실은 저쪽에 있습니다.
(C) 죄송합니다만, 저희는 더 이상 그 브랜드를 취급하지 않아요.

[해설] 바지를 반품하고 싶다고 요청하는 평서문이다.
(A) 상점에서 벌어지는 상황임을 이용하여 cash나 credit card 같은 결제 수단을 연상하도록 유도하는 오답이다.
(B) 질문의 pants로 보아 옷 가게에서 벌어지는 상황임을 유추할 수 있는데, 옷 가게에서 연상되는 dressing room을 이용해 혼동을 유도하는 오답이다.
(C) 죄송하다고 요청을 거절한 후 그 브랜드를 더 이상 취급하지 않는다며 거절의 이유를 설명하고 있으므로 정답이다.

12. BR-BR

I can ask the chef to cook your steak a bit more if you'd like.
(A) I really enjoyed it, thank you.
(B) It didn't take that long.
(C) No, this looks just right.

just right 적당히, 딱 알맞게

원하시면 제가 주방장에게 스테이크를 좀 더 익혀 달라고 할게요.
(A) 정말 맛있게 먹었어요, 감사해요.
(B) 그렇게 오래 걸리지 않았어요.
(C) 아니요, 이게 딱 알맞은 것 같아요.

[해설] 원한다면 주방장에게 스테이크를 좀 더 익혀 달라고 하겠다고 제안하는 평서문이다.
(A) 스테이크를 좀 더 익혀 달라고 해주겠다는 제안에 맛있게 먹었다는 답변은 어색하다. 오히려 오늘 음식이 어땠는지 묻는 질문에 적합한 응답이다.
(B) 질문의 steak와 발음이 유사한 take를 이용해 혼동을 유도하는 오답

DAY 09   71

이다.
(C) No로 거절한 후 지금이 딱 좋다고 거절의 이유를 덧붙이고 있는 정답이다.

13. US-US

I need the latest version of our service contract.
(A) Please sign on the bottom.
(B) We have an outstanding service rating.
(C) There are extra copies in the file cabinet.

latest 가장 최근의, 최신의   contract 계약(서)   outstanding 뛰어난, 걸출한   rating 순위, 평가, 등급   extra copy 여분의 사본   file cabinet 서류 캐비닛

우리 서비스 계약서의 가장 최근 버전이 필요합니다.
(A) 맨 아래에 서명해 주세요.
(B) 우리는 우수한 서비스 등급을 받았습니다.
(C) 서류 캐비닛에 여분의 사본들이 있습니다.

[해설] 서비스 계약서의 가장 최근 버전이 필요하다고 요청하는 평서문이다.
(A) 질문의 contract에서 연상 가능한 sign을 이용해 혼동을 유도하는 오답이다.
(B) 질문의 service를 반복 사용하여 혼동을 유도하는 오답이다.
(C) 서류 캐비닛에 여분의 사본들이 있다며 계약서가 있는 구체적인 위치를 알려주고 있으므로 정답이다.

14. AU-BR

Let's take our clients to Luke's Diner for dinner tomorrow.
(A) I'll make a reservation for four people.
(B) Here are your menus.
(C) No, I'm not familiar with that dish.

client 고객, 의뢰인   make a reservation 예약을 하다
be familiar with ~를 잘 알다, ~에 정통하다   dish 요리

내일 저녁식사를 위해 우리 고객들을 Luke's Diner로 모시고 가요.
(A) 제가 4명으로 예약할게요.
(B) 여기 메뉴가 있습니다.
(C) 아니요, 저는 그 요리에 대해서 잘 몰라요.

[해설] 고객들을 특정 식당에 데리고 가자고 제안하는 청유문이다.
(A) 4명으로 예약하겠다고 답변함으로써 상대방의 제안을 우회적으로 수락하고 있는 정답이다.
(B) dinner에서 연상 가능한 menu를 이용해 혼동을 유도하는 오답이다.
(C) dinner에서 연상 가능한 dish를 이용해 혼동을 유도하는 오답이다.

15. BR-AU

Please be sure to have your photo ID ready when boarding the ship.
(A) A 9:15 A.M. arrival.
(B) The board of directors will be there.
(C) Thanks for reminding me.

board of directors 경영진, 이사회   remind 상기시키다

배에 탈 때 반드시 사진이 부착된 신분증을 준비하시기 바랍니다.
(A) 9시 15분 도착입니다.
(B) 경영진이 거기 갈 것입니다.
(C) 상기시켜 주셔서 고마워요.

[해설] 배에 탈 때 반드시 사진이 부착된 신분증을 준비하라고 요청하는 명령문이다.
(A) 질문의 boarding the ship(배에 타기)에서 배가 도착하는(arrival) 시간을 연상하도록 유도하는 오답이다.
(B) 질문의 boarding과 발음이 비슷한 board를 이용해 혼동을 유도하는 오답이다.
(C) 배에 탈 때 반드시 사진이 부착된 신분증을 준비하라는 말에 생각나게 해줘서 고맙다는 인사를 하고 있으므로 정답이다.

16. BR-US

Would you like to join our car pool group?
(A) My car is in good condition.
(B) Be sure to drive safely.
(C) Actually, I take the subway.

join 함께 하다, 합류하다   car pool 카풀, 승용차 함께 타기
in good condition 상태가 좋은

저희 카풀 팀에 합류하시겠어요?
(A) 제 차는 상태가 좋아요.
(B) 반드시 안전 운전 하세요.
(C) 사실, 저는 지하철을 타요.

[해설] 함께 카풀할 것을 제안하는 의문문이다.
(A) 질문의 car를 반복 사용하여 혼동을 유도하는 오답이다.
(B) 질문의 car에서 연상할 수 있는 drive를 이용하여 혼동을 유도하는 오답이다.
(C) 함께 카풀을 하겠냐는 질문에 지하철을 탄다고 답변함으로써 상대방의 제안을 우회적으로 거절하고 있으므로 정답이다.

PART 4 — 주제·목적 문제 / 장소·직업 문제 / 세부 사항 문제

연습 문제

01. (B) 02. (B) 03. (A) 04. (A) 05. (B) 06. (A)

01. US

What is the announcement **about**?
(A) A new **grocery store**   (B) A special **sale**

안내

W: Thank you for underlined shopping at Wendy's Mart today! We'd like to announce that we're now offering a 30% discount on all vegetables and fruits in the produce section. This is for Wendy's reward members only.

produce 농산물

안내는 무엇에 대한 것인가?

(A) 새로운 식료품점 (B) 특별 할인

여: 오늘 Wendy's Mart에서 쇼핑해주셔서 감사합니다! 저희가 지금 농산물 섹션의 모든 채소와 과일에 대해 30퍼센트의 할인을 제공한다는 점을 알려드리고자 합니다. 이것은 Wendy's 리워드 회원들에게만 해당됩니다.

02. [US]
What is the **purpose** of the **call**?
(A) To **schedule** a **delivery**   (B) To **report** a **faulty item**

전화 메시지

> M: Hi, this is Tim Smith from Cedarville Construction. The wireless power drill that I ordered last week arrived yesterday. I charged it for a full night and brought it to my work site. Unfortunately, it doesn't work. The battery indicator is green. That should mean it is fully charged.

work site 작업 현장, 일터

전화의 목적은 무엇인가?
(A) 배송 일정을 잡기 위해 **(B) 결함이 있는 물품을 알리기 위해**

남: 안녕하세요, 저는 Cedarville Construction의 Tim Smith입니다. 제가 지난주에 주문한 무선 전기 드릴이 어제 도착했습니다. 저는 밤새 그것을 충전했고 제 작업 현장에 가지고 왔습니다. 안타깝게도, 그것이 작동하지 않습니다. 배터리 표시 장치가 초록색이에요. 그럼 완전히 충전되었다는 뜻일텐데요.

03. [AU]
Who is the **intended audience** for the announcement?
(A) **Volunteers**   (B) **Tourists**

안내

> M: Hello, everyone, and welcome to Delaware Nature Park. Before we begin this year's Park Cleaning Day, thank you for participating in this annual event. More and more tourists and hikers are visiting us every year. So, we need to make an effort to preserve this park.

preserve 보존하다

공지가 대상으로 하는 청자는 누구인가?
(A) 자원봉사자들   (B) 여행객들

남: 안녕하세요, 여러분, Delaware Nature Park에 오신 것을 환영합니다. 올해 공원 청소의 날을 시작하기 전에, 이 연례 행사에 참가해 주셔서 감사합니다. 더 많은 여행객들과 등산객들이 매해 저희를 방문하고 있습니다. 그래서, 저희는 이 공원을 보존하기 위해 노력해야 합니다.

04. [BR]
Who most likely is the **caller**?
(A) A **customer service agent**   (B) A restaurant **chef**

전화 메시지

> M: Hello, this is Andrea Denzel from the Customer Relations Department at Happy Kitchen Supplies. I'm calling to let you know about the status of your order. The multi-purpose oven you ordered through our Web site is out of stock.

전화한 사람은 누구이겠는가?
(A) 고객 서비스 직원   (B) 레스토랑 셰프

남: 안녕하세요, 저는 Happy 주방 용품의 고객 상담 부서에 있는 Andrea Denzel입니다. 고객님의 주문 상황에 대해 알려드리려고 전화했습니다. 당신이 저희 웹사이트를 통해 주문하신 다용도 오븐은 품절입니다.

05. [US]
Who most likely is **Emily White**?
(A) A **teacher**   (B) A **writer**

담화

> W: I'm honored to introduce Emily White who will announce the winner of this year's Dickenson Award. She also received this award last year. As you already know, it is awarded to the most promising author of the year.

promising 유망한, 저명한

Emily White는 누구이겠는가?
(A) 교사   **(B) 작가**

여: 올해의 Dickenson 상의 수상자를 발표할 Emily White를 소개하게 되어 영광입니다. 그녀 역시 작년에 이 상을 수상하셨죠. 여러분이 이미 알고 있겠지만, 이것은 그 해의 가장 유망한 작가에게 수여됩니다.

06. [US]
What can **listeners do** on the company's **Web site**?
(A) **Get** an application **form**   (B) **Select** a **parking space**

안내

> W: I'm very pleased to announce that the construction of the new parking garage will be completed at the end of this month. As planned, this five-story building will accommodate all of the employees' cars. The security office will take applications for reserved parking spaces next week. You can download the form from the company Web site.

청자들은 회사의 웹사이트에서 무엇을 할 수 있는가?
(A) 신청서 받기   (B) 주차 공간 선택하기

여: 새 주차장의 공사가 이번 달 말에 완료될 것이라는 것을 공지하게 되어 기쁩니다. 계획한 대로, 그 5층짜리 건물은 모든 직원들의 차량을 수용할 것입니다. 경비실은 다음 주에 지정된 주차 공간을 위한 신청서를 받을 것입니다. 여러분은 회사 웹사이트에서 그것을 다운로드 받을 수 있습니다.

paraphrasing 정답 1. (b) 2. (a) 3. (c) 4. (c) 5. (b) 6. (a)

실전 문제

01. (C)	02. (B)	03. (A)	04. (C)	05. (C)	06. (B)
07. (B)	08. (D)	09. (B)	10. (B)	11. (A)	12. (D)
13. (A)	14. (B)	15. (D)	16. (B)	17. (A)	18. (D)
19. (C)	20. (B)	21. (D)	22. (D)	23. (A)	24. (C)

[01-03] BR
Questions 01-03 refer to the following talk.

> W: Good afternoon, everyone. My name is Clara Simms, and I'm an instructor at the Prospect Technology Institute. Thank you for inviting me to ^{01}**your Web design firm** today. ^{02}**I would like to tell you a little bit about our upcoming class in animation.** It is held three evenings a week throughout the month of June, and it will teach you how to use various animation programs. You'll also learn how to decrease loading times for animated elements, and you'll have plenty of hands-on practice. ^{03}**I've got some brochures that provide more information about this, so I'd like to distribute those now.**
>
> instructor 강사, 교사 prospect 가망, 가능성 throughout ~ 동안 죽, 내내 decrease 줄다, 감소하다 load (데이터나 프로그램을) 로딩하다 animated 동영상으로 된, 만화영화로 된 element 요소, 성분 plenty of 많은 hands-on 직접 해보는 practice 실습, 연습 distribute 나눠주다, 분배하다

01-03은 다음 담화에 관한 문제입니다.

여: 여러분, 안녕하세요. 제 이름은 Clara Simms이고, Prospect Technology Institute의 강사입니다. 오늘 저를 ^{01}여러분의 웹디자인 회사에 초대해주셔서 감사합니다. ^{02}곧 있을 애니메이션 강좌에 대해 조금 말씀드리고자 합니다. 6월 내내 주 3회 저녁에 열리며, 다양한 애니메이션 프로그램을 사용하는 법에 대해 가르쳐드릴 것입니다. 또한 여러분들은 동영상으로 된 요소들의 로딩 시간을 줄이는 법도 배우게 될 것이며, 상당한 양의 실습을 직접 하시게 됩니다. ^{03}이에 대한 더 많은 정보가 담긴 책자를 가져왔으니 지금 나눠드리겠습니다.

01.

화자는 누구에게 말하고 있는가?
(A) 우편 배달원들
(B) 기업의 회계사들
(C) 웹디자이너들
(D) 연구원들

[해설] 화자가 누구를 대상으로 이야기하고 있는지 묻고 있으므로 결국 청자의 직업을 묻는 문제이다. 담화 전반부에 화자가 오늘 자신을 '여러분의 웹디자인 회사(your Web design firm)'에 초대해주어 감사하다고 했고, 이어지는 내용에서 웹디자인과 관련된 애니메이션 강좌에 대해서 설명하는 것으로 보아 청자들은 웹디자인 회사에서 근무하는 웹디자이너들임을 알 수 있으므로 정답은 (C)이다.

[어휘] address 말하다, 연설하다 postal 우편의 corporate 기업[회사]의 accountant 회계원, 회계사

02.

화자는 왜 강연을 하고 있는가?
(A) 청자들로부터 의견을 취합하기 위해서
(B) 수업의 개요를 설명하기 위해
(C) 어떤 일에 대한 자원자들을 모집하기 위해
(D) 규정 변경을 설명하기 위해

[해설] 담화 전반부에 곧 있을 애니메이션 강좌에 대해 조금 이야기하고

자 한다고(I would like to tell you a little bit about our upcoming class in animation) 담화의 목적을 분명히 밝혔다. 따라서 정답은 (B)이다.

paraphrasing tell you a little bit about our upcoming class 곧 있을 강좌에 대해 조금 얘기하다 → give an overview of a class 수업의 개요를 설명하다

[어휘] give a talk 강연하다 gather 모으다, 모이다 opinion 의견 give an overview of ~의 개요를 설명하다 recruit (신입 사원 등을) 모집하다 volunteer 자원봉사자, 자원해서 하는 사람 task 일, 과업 regulation 규정, 규제

03.

화자는 다음에 무엇을 하겠는가?
(A) 책자를 배포하기
(B) 질문을 적기
(C) 일부 장치를 시연하기
(D) 비디오 클립을 보여주기

[해설] 담화 마지막 부분에 단서가 있다. 화자가 앞서 설명한 강좌에 대한 더 많은 정보가 담긴 책자를 가져왔으니 지금 나눠주겠다고(I've got some brochures that provide more information about this, so I'd like to distribute those now.) 했으므로 정답은 (A)이다.

paraphrasing distribute 나눠주다 → pass out 배포하다

[어휘] pass out ~을 나눠주다 demonstrate 보여주다, 설명하다 equipment 장비, 용품 present 제시하다, 보여주다

[04-06] AU
Questions 04-06 refer to the following advertisement.

> M: Sierra Summit has always been dedicated to bringing our loyal customers the best products at great prices, and we've got great news for you. ^{04}**On June 1, we're moving to 495 Cambridge Avenue, right across from the Remington Theater.** ^{05}**There you'll find all of the tents, sleeping bags, and other outdoor equipment that Sierra Summit is famous for.** But what's more, our new store will have an even wider variety of brands. ^{06}**Visit our Web site to see a map of the new site and directions for how to get there.**
>
> dedicated to ~에 전념하는, 헌신하는 bring A B A에게 B를 가져다주다 loyal customer 단골 고객 across from ~의 바로 맞은편에 sleeping bag 침낭 outdoor 옥외[야외]의 equipment 장비, 용품

04-06은 다음 광고에 관한 문제입니다.

남: Sierra Summit은 항상 저희의 단골 고객들에게 최적의 가격에 최고의 제품을 제공하고자 최선을 다해왔는데요, 여러분에게 전할 좋은 소식이 있습니다. ^{04}6월 1일에, 저희는 Remington 극장 바로 건너편인 Cambridge 가 495번지로 이전할 예정입니다. ^{05}여러분은 그곳에서 그 유명한 Sierra Summit의 모든 종류의 텐트, 침낭, 기타 아웃도어 용품들을 찾으실 수 있습니다. 더욱이, 저희의 새로운 매장은 훨씬 더 다양한 브랜드의 제품들을 갖추게 될 것입니다. ^{06}저희 웹사이트를 방문하셔서 새로운 장소의 지도와 찾아오시는 법을 확인해보세요.

04.

광고에서 청자들에게 무엇에 대해 알리는가?
(A) 고객 보상 프로그램
(B) 제품 출시
(C) 매장 이전
(D) 창고 정리 세일

[해설] 담화는 Sierra Summit이라는 업체의 광고로, 전반부에서 6월 1일에, Remington 극장 바로 건너편 Cambridge 가 495번지로 이전할 예정이라고(On June 1, we're moving to 495 Cambridge Avenue, right across from the Remington Theater.) 알리고 있다. 즉, 영업장의 이전을 공지하는 광고이므로 정답은 (C)이다.

> paraphrasing moving 이전하는 것 → relocation 이전

[어휘] launch 출시; 출시하다 relocation 이전, 재배치 clearance sale 창고 정리 세일

05.

Sierra Summit은 어떤 종류의 업체인가?
(A) 자동차 제조사
(B) 의류 디자인 업체
(C) 캠핑 용품 매장
(D) 커피숍

[해설] 매장을 이전할 예정임을 알린 후 새로운 매장에서 모든 종류의 텐트, 침낭, 기타 아웃도어 용품들을 찾을 수 있다고(you'll find all of the tents, sleeping bags, and other outdoor equipment) 언급했다. 이로 보아 Sierra Summit은 텐트, 침낭을 비롯한 아웃도어 용품, 즉 캠핑 용품을 취급하는 곳임을 알 수 있으므로 정답은 (C)이다.

[어휘] manufacturer 제조사, 생산회사

06.

화자의 말에 따르면, 웹사이트에서 무엇을 할 수 있는가?
(A) 쿠폰 다운받기
(B) 지도 보기
(C) 주문하기
(D) 경연 참가하기

[해설] 화자는 광고 마지막 부분에서 웹사이트에서 새로운 장소의 지도와 찾아오는 법을 확인하라고(Visit our Web site to see a map of the new site and directions for how to get there) 했다. 따라서 정답은 (B)이다.

> paraphrasing see a map 지도 보기 → viewing a map 지도 보기

[어휘] view 보다 enter (대회 등에) 출전[참가]하다

[07-09] US
Questions 07-09 refer to the following telephone message.

M: Hello, this message is for Charlotte McDaniel. ⁰⁷**This is Tony calling from Ace Domestic Goods.** We received your request for a Tyler brand ⁰⁷**washing machine**... um... model R90. Well, I'm afraid ⁰⁸**there's an issue with your order.** I think you must have been looking at an old catalog because ⁰⁸**the company is no longer making that machine.** I'm sure you understand that we had no choice but to cancel your order. However, there's a very similar one made by another company that you might be interested in. ⁰⁹**I can tell you about the features if you call me back** at 555-7902. I hope to hear from you soon. Thanks.

domestic 국내의, 가정용의   goods 상품, 제품   request 요청, 신청   washing machine 세탁기   issue (걱정거리가 되는) 문제   order 주문   have no choice but to V ~할 수밖에 없다   similar 비슷한   be interested in ~에 관심이 있다   feature 특징, 특성

07-09는 다음 전화 메시지에 관한 문제입니다.
남: 여보세요, Charlotte McDaniel 씨에게 전하는 메시지입니다. 저는 ⁰⁷**Ace 가정용품의 Tony**입니다. 저희에게 Tyler 브랜드의 ⁰⁷**세탁기**를 요청하셨는데요... 음... 모델 번호는 R90이고요. 그런데, 안타깝게도 ⁰⁸**당신의 주문에 문제가 있습니다.** 예전 카탈로그를 보신 게 틀림없는 것 같아요. 왜냐하면 ⁰⁸**그 회사는 더 이상 그 세탁기를 제조하지 않거든요.** 저희가 당신의 주문을 취소할 수밖에 없었음을 이해해주시리라 믿습니다. 하지만 당신이 관심 있어 하실만한, 다른 업체에서 제조한 아주 비슷한 제품이 있습니다. 555-7902로 ⁰⁹**다시 전화 주시면 제가 사양에 대해 설명해 드리겠습니다.** 곧 연락주시기를 바랍니다. 감사합니다.

07.

화자는 어디에서 일하는가?
(A) 건축 회사에서
(B) 가전제품 매장에서
(C) 부동산 중개업소에서
(D) 금융 기관에서

[해설] 고객의 주문을 받은 업체의 직원으로 보이는 화자가 해당 고객에게 남기는 전화 메시지 내용이다. 메시지 초반 화자가 자신을 Ace Domestic Goods의 Tony라고 소개한 점과 고객이 세탁기(washing machine)를 주문했다고 한 점 등으로 보아 화자는 가전제품 매장에서 근무하고 있음을 유추할 수 있으므로 정답은 (B)이다.

> paraphrasing Domestic Goods 가정용품/washing machine 세탁기 → appliance 가전제품

[어휘] architectural 건축학의 appliance 가전제품 real estate 부동산 financial institution 금융 기관

08.

화자에 따르면, 무엇이 문제인가?
(A) 직원이 일부 문서를 잃어버렸다.
(B) 컴퓨터가 작동하지 않는다.
(C) 대금을 늦게 받았다.
(D) 제품의 생산이 중단되었다.

[해설] 질문의 핵심 키워드 problem이 전화 메시지에서는 issue로 언급되었다. 메시지 중반에 당신의 주문에 문제가 있다며(there's an issue with your order), 그 회사는 더 이상 그 세탁기를 제조하지 않는다고(the company is no longer making that machine) 했다. 즉, 고객이 주문한 제품의 생산이 중단되었다는 뜻이므로 정답은 (D)이다.

> paraphrasing the company is no longer making that machine 그 회사는 더 이상 그 세탁기를 제조하지 않는다 → A product has been discontinued 제품의 생산이 중단되었다

[어휘] payment 지불, 지급 discontinue (생산을) 중단하다

09.

청자는 왜 화자에게 전화해야 하는가?
(A) 환불을 요청하기 위해서
(B) 제품 설명을 듣기 위해서
(C) 선호하는 크기를 확인하기 위해서
(D) 우편 주소를 제공하기 위해서

[해설] 메시지 후반에 화자는 청자가 관심을 가질만한 비슷한 다른 제품이 있다면서 자신에게 다시 전화를 하면 그 제품의 사양에 대해 설명해주겠다고(I can tell you about the features if you call me back) 했다. 즉, 청자는 제품 설명을 듣기 위해 전화해야 하므로 정답은 (B)이다.

paraphrasing features 특징 → a product description 제품 설명

[어휘] refund 환불 description 설명 confirm 확인하다 preferred 선호하는

[10-12] BR

Questions 10-12 refer to the following announcement.

> W: Attention, ¹⁰travelers on Flight 791 to Santiago. We regret to inform you that this flight has been postponed due to severe weather. We appreciate your patience while we await further instructions from the ¹⁰air traffic control team. We don't know when the ¹⁰boarding procedures will begin, so ¹¹please stay here near Gate 56 for further announcements. By way of apology, we'd like to offer all frequent flyer members five thousand bonus miles. ¹²If you are not a member of the program yet, you can visit the ticketing counter to pick up a registration form from.

inform 알리다 postpone 연기하다, 미루다 await 기다리다 instructions 지시, 명령 air traffic control 항공 교통 관제 boarding procedure 탑승 절차 by way of apology 사과의 의미로 registration form 등록 양식

10-12는 다음 안내 방송에 관한 문제입니다.
여: ¹⁰산티아고 행 791 항공편에 탑승하실 여행객들은 주목해주십시오. 이 항공편이 기상 악화로 인해 지연되었음을 알려드리게 되어 유감입니다. 저희가 ¹⁰항공 교통 관제 팀의 추후 지시를 기다리는 동안 양해해주시면 감사하겠습니다. ¹⁰탑승 수속 절차가 언제 시작될지 모르므로 추후 공지가 있을 때까지 ¹¹이곳 56번 탑승구 근처에 머물러 주시기 바랍니다. 사과의 의미로 저희 항공사의 단골 고객 회원 전원에게 보너스 5,000마일을 지급해드리고자 합니다. ¹²아직 이 프로그램의 회원이 아니시라면 발권 카운터에 방문하셔서 등록 양식을 받아가시면 됩니다.

10.

청자들은 어디에 있는 것 같은가?
(A) 기차에
(B) 공항에
(C) 백화점에
(D) 버스 정류장에

[해설] 공항 내에서 이뤄지는 안내 방송으로, 항공사 측에서 탑승객들에게 항공편 지연에 대해 알리고 있으므로 청자들이 있는 곳은 공항이므로 정답은 (B)이다. 화자가 언급한 내용 중 '산티아고 행 791 항공편(Flight 791 to Santiago)', '항공 교통 관제 팀(air traffic control team)', '탑승 수속 절차(boarding procedures)' 같은 표현을 들었다면 쉽게 정답을 알 수 있는 문제다.

11.

청자들은 무엇을 하라고 요청받는가?
(A) 그곳에서 머물기
(B) 티켓 교환하기
(C) 전화 상담 서비스에 전화하기
(D) 신분증 제시하기

[해설] 대화 중반에 단서가 있다. 탑승 수속 절차가 언제 시작될지 모르니 추후 공지가 있을 때까지 이곳 56번 탑승구 근처에 머물러 달라고(please stay here near Gate 56) 했다. 즉, 청자들에게 지금 그 위치에 그대로 있으라고 요청한 것이므로 정답은 (A)이다.

[어휘] area (특정 건물·공간 내의) 구역 exchange 교환하다 helpline 전화 상담 서비스 present 제시하다, 보여주다

12.

청자들은 카운터에서 무엇을 받을 수 있는가?
(A) 다과
(B) 할인 쿠폰
(C) 업데이트된 일정표
(D) 등록 양식

[해설] 안내 방송 마지막 부분에 정답의 단서가 있다. 앞서 항공편 지연에 대한 사과의 의미로 이 항공사를 자주 이용하는 회원으로 가입되어 있는 이용객들에게는 보너스 마일리지를 지급하겠다고 한 후, 아직 회원이 아니라면 발권 카운터에 방문하여 등록 양식을 받아가라고(you can visit the ticketing counter to pick up a registration form) 했으므로 정답은 (D)이다.

paraphrasing a registration form 등록 양식 → a sign-up form 등록 양식

[어휘] refreshments 다과 sign-up 등록, 가입

[13-15] AU

Questions 13-15 refer to the following announcement.

> M: I'm happy to start our meeting off with some good news. ¹³,¹⁴I am very pleased to hear that our newly launched product, the NV Air Conditioner has been quite successful in the market. Customers have responded favorably to our new product and our sales have been higher than ever. Our development team did a great job of putting together a unit that greatly reduces energy use. They're trying to apply the same technology to the other home appliances that we make as well. ¹⁵Their team leader will give a presentation about it at the board meeting on June 9.

launch 출시하다 quite 꽤, 상당히 respond 응답하다, 반응을 보이다 favorably 호의적으로, 호의를 가지고 development 개발 put together 조립하다, 만들다 unit 장치, 설비, 도구 greatly 대단히, 크게 reduce 줄이다, 축소하다 apply 적용하다, 쓰다 home appliances 가전제품 as well 또한, 역시 board meeting 이사회

13-15는 다음 공지에 관한 문제입니다.
남: 몇 가지 좋은 소식으로 회의를 시작하게 되어 기분이 좋습니다. ¹³,¹⁴우리가 새롭게 출시한 제품인 NV 에어컨이 시장에서 상당히 성공적이라는 소식에 매우 기쁩니다. 고객들은 우리의 신제품에 우호적인 반응을 보이고 있고, 우리 매출은 여느 때보다도 높습니다. 우리 개발팀은 에너지 사용을 크게 감소시키는 장치를 아주 잘 만들어냈습니다. 그들은 똑같은 기술을 우리가 만드는 다른 가전제품들에도 적용시키려고 노력하고 있습니다. ¹⁵그 팀의 팀장이 6월 9일 이사회에서 그에 대해 발표할 예정입니다.

13.
화자는 무엇에 대해 기쁘다고 말하는가?
(A) 성공적으로 제품을 출시한 것
(B) 또 다른 지점을 연 것
(C) 승진한 것
(D) 에너지 사용을 줄인 것

[해설] 담화 초반, 화자는 새롭게 출시한 제품인 NV 에어컨이 시장에서 상당히 성공적이라는 소식을 듣게 되어 매우 기쁘다고(I am very pleased to hear that our newly launched product, the NV Air Conditioner has been quite successful in the market.) 했다. 즉, 성공적으로 제품 출시하여 기쁘다는 말이므로 정답은 (A)이다.

paraphrasing our newly launched product ~ has been quite successful in the market 우리가 새롭게 출시한 제품이 시장에서 상당히 성공적이다 → launching a product successfully 성공적으로 제품을 출시한 것

[어휘] branch 지점, 지사 promotion 승진

14.
화자는 어떤 종류의 업체에 근무하는가?
(A) 법률 사무소
(B) 전자제품 제조사
(C) 광고 대행사
(D) 전력 서비스 공급업체

[해설] 화자가 근무하고 있는 업체의 종류를 묻는 문제로, 담화 전반부에서 단서를 찾는다. '우리가 새롭게 출시한 제품인 NV 에어컨(our newly launched product, the NV Air Conditioner)'이라는 말로 보아 화자의 회사는 전자제품 제조사임을 알 수 있으므로 정답은 (B)이다.

[어휘] law firm 법률 사무소 manufacturer 제조사, 생산 회사 advertising agency 광고 대행사 electricity 전기, 전력

15.
6월 9일에는 무엇이 예정되어 있는가?
(A) 전사 차원의 교육
(B) 해외 진출
(C) 공장 시찰
(D) 이사회

[해설] 질문의 핵심 키워드 June 9는 담화 마지막에 언급된다. 팀장이 6월 9일 이사회에서 발표할 예정이라고(Their team leader will give a presentation about it at the board meeting on June 9.) 말했으므로 6월 9일에 이사회가 열릴 것임을 알 수 있으므로 정답은 (D)이다.

[어휘] company-wide 회사 전반의 expansion 확대, 확장 inspection 점검, 검사, 시찰

[16-18] US

Questions 16-18 refer to the following advertisement.

W: Are your computers, tablets, or other electronic devices not working as well as they used to? Bring them to Trenton's Tinkers! ¹⁶**We can repair and upgrade your electronics so that they are as good as new.** ¹⁷**Become a member to get 20% off your first service.** ¹⁸**Visit us at Trenton's Tinkers Web site to see a list of how much our services cost.**

electronic device 전자기기 repair 수리하다 electronics 전자기기 as good as new 새것 같은 cost (비용이) ~이다

16-18은 다음 광고에 관한 문제입니다.
여: 여러분의 컴퓨터, 태블릿 PC 또는 그 밖의 다른 전자기기들이 예전만큼 잘 작동하지 않나요? Trenton's Tinkers에 가져오세요! ¹⁶여러분의 전자기기들을 새것처럼 수리해드리고 업그레이드시켜 드릴 수 있습니다. ¹⁷최초 서비스에 대하여 20퍼센트 할인을 받기 위해 회원이 되세요. ¹⁸저희 서비스에 드는 비용을 확인하시려면 저희 Trenton's Tinkers의 웹사이트를 방문해주세요.

16.
어떤 종류의 서비스가 광고되고 있는가?
(A) 소프트웨어 주문 제작
(B) 전자기기 수리
(C) 배터리 재활용
(D) 모바일 데이터

[해설] 담화 초반 전자기기들이 예전만큼 잘 작동하지 않는지 물은 후 전자기기들을 새것처럼 수리하고 업그레이드시켜 줄 수 있다는(We can repair and upgrade your electronics so that they are as good as new.) 말로 보아 전자기기 수리 서비스를 광고하고 있음을 알 수 있으므로 정답은 (B)이다.

[어휘] customization 주문에 따라 만듦 recycling 재활용

17.
청자들은 어떻게 할인을 받을 수 있는가?
(A) 회원 가입을 함으로써
(B) 친구를 가입시킴으로써
(C) 피드백을 제공함으로써
(D) 암호를 입력함으로써

[해설] 담화 중반, 최초 서비스에 대하여 20퍼센트 할인을 받기 위해 회원이 되라는(Become a member to get 20% off your first service.) 내용이 언급된다. 즉, 회원 가입을 하면 할인을 받을 수 있다는 말이므로 정답은 (A)이다.

paraphrasing become a member 회원이 되다 → joining a membership 회원 가입하기

[어휘] sign up 가입하다, 등록하다 enter 입력하다 code 부호, 암호

18.
화자에 따르면, 웹사이트에서 무엇을 찾을 수 있는가?
(A) 회원 가입 신청서
(B) 소개 영상
(C) 사업 개요

(D) 서비스 가격표

[해설] 담화 마지막에서 서비스에 드는 비용의 목록을 확인하면 웹사이트를 방문하라고(Visit us at Trenton's Tinkers Web site to see a list of how much our services cost.) 했으므로 웹사이트에서는 서비스 가격표를 찾을 수 있다. 정답은 (D)이다.

paraphrasing a list of how much our services cost 우리 서비스에 드는 비용의 목록 → a service price list 서비스 가격표

[어휘] application 지원(서), 신청(서) introductory 소개용의 profile 개요(서)

[19-21] BR

Questions 19-21 refer to the following telephone message.

> M: Hi, this is Ken Sato from Fashion Outfit Outlet. ¹⁹I'm calling about the software that you made for my business. It has really simplified inventory. ²⁰I'm really pleased about how much more efficiently my people can work thanks to it. In fact, it has been so helpful that ²¹I want to hold a regular training session for our newly hired store managers and workers. I'd like to speak with you in more detail about it. Please call me back as soon as you get a chance. Thanks.

simplify 간소화하다 inventory 물품 목록, 재고(품), 재고 조사 efficiently 능률[효율]적으로 thanks to ~ 덕분에 in fact 사실은, 실은 newly hired 새로 채용된

19-21은 다음 전화 메시지에 관한 문제입니다.

남: 안녕하세요, Fashion Outfit Outlet의 Ken Sato입니다. ¹⁹저희 회사를 위해 만들어주신 소프트웨어와 관련하여 전화 드립니다. 그것이 재고 조사를 정말로 간소화시켰어요. ²⁰그것 덕분에 저희 직원들이 얼마나 더 효율적으로 근무할 수 있는지 정말 기쁩니다. 실은 그것이 매우 도움이 되어서 ²¹새로 채용된 매장 매니저들과 직원들을 대상으로 정기적인 교육을 진행하고 싶습니다. 이에 대해 당신과 더욱 상세히 얘기를 나누고 싶습니다. 시간 나시는 대로 제게 다시 전화 주시기 바랍니다. 감사합니다.

19.

메시지의 주제는 무엇인가?
(A) 패션 경향
(B) 직원 교육
(C) 새로운 소프트웨어
(D) 연간 재고 조사

[해설] 담화 초반에 메시지의 주제가 드러난다. 화자는 자신의 회사를 위해 청자가 만들어준 소프트웨어와 관련하여 전화했다고(I'm calling about the software that you made for my business) 밝혔으며, 이어서 이 소프트웨어의 장점 및 관련 계획을 언급하고 있다. 따라서 정답은 (C)이다.

[어휘] trend 동향, 추세 annual 연간의, 연례의

20.

화자는 무엇이 자신을 기쁘게 한다고 말하는가?
(A) 친절한 고객 지원 서비스
(B) 증가한 업무 효율성

(C) 시즌별 홍보
(D) 빠른 서비스

[해설] 화자는 청자가 만들어준 소프트웨어로 인해 재고 조사가 매우 간소화되었다면서, 그것 덕분에 직원들이 얼마나 더 효율적으로 근무할 수 있는지 정말 기쁘다고(I'm really pleased about how much more efficiently my people can work thanks to it.) 했다. 즉, 소프트웨어 덕분에 업무 효율성이 증대되어 기쁘다는 말이므로 정답은 (B)이다.

paraphrasing how much more efficiently my people can work 우리 직원들이 얼마나 더 효율적으로 근무할 수 있는지 → increased work efficiency 증가한 업무 효율성

[어휘] customer support 고객 지원 서비스 increased 증가한 work efficiency 업무 효율성 seasonal 계절적인, 계절의, 주기적인 promotion 홍보, 판촉

21.

화자는 무엇에 대해 더욱 자세하게 논의하고 싶어 하는가?
(A) 이메일로 최신 정보를 받는 것
(B) 직원을 더 고용하는 것
(C) 공급업체를 바꾸는 것
(D) 교육을 진행하는 것

[해설] 담화 후반, 화자는 새로 채용된 매장 매니저들과 직원들을 대상으로 정기 교육을 진행하고 싶다고(I want to hold a regular training session for our newly hired store managers and workers.) 한 후, 이에 대해 청자와 더욱 상세히 얘기 나누고 싶다고 했다. 따라서 정답은 (D)이다.

[어휘] supplier 공급업체

[22-24] US

Questions 22-24 refer to the following telephone message.

> M: Hello, Ms. Jenkins. This is Roger Smith returning ²², ²³your call about the broken Blenz Café brand coffee machine in your office. Unfortunately, I'm completely booked today, but ²², ²³I can be there tomorrow to fix it. Would 10 A.M. be a good time for you? ²⁴Please get back to me to confirm if that time works for you or not. If I don't answer, just leave a message. Thank you, goodbye.

broken 고장 난 completely 완전히, 전적으로 booked 예약된, 선약이 있는 fix 고치다 confirm 확인하다 work (계획 등이) 잘 되어가다

22-24는 다음 전화 메시지에 관한 문제입니다.

남: 여보세요, Jenkins 씨. 저는 Roger Smith이고 ²²당신의 사무실에 있는 **Blenz Café** 브랜드의 커피 머신이 고장 났다는 전화에 회신 드립니다. 안타깝게도 오늘은 예약이 완전히 꽉 찼어요. 하지만 ²², ²³내일 방문해서 고쳐드릴 수 있습니다. 오전 10시면 괜찮을까요? ²⁴제게 다시 연락 주셔서 그 시간이 괜찮은지 확인해주시기 바랍니다. 제가 전화를 받지 않으면 그냥 메시지를 남겨주세요. 고맙습니다. 안녕히 계세요.

22.

화자는 누구일 것 같은가?
(A) 판매원

(B) 건물 세입자
(C) 부동산 중개인
(D) 보수 관리 직원

[해설] 화자의 직업을 묻는 문제로, 메시지 초반 전화의 용건을 밝힌 부분에 정답의 단서가 있다. 화자는 커피 머신이 고장 났다는(the broken ~ coffee machine) 청자의 전화에 답신 전화를 한 것임을 밝힌 후, 오늘은 예약이 꽉 찼으니 내일 방문해서 고쳐주겠다고(I can be there tomorrow to fix it) 했다. 따라서 화자가 건물이나 기계 등을 점검하고 보수하는 일을 한다는 것을 알 수 있으므로 정답은 (D)이다.

[어휘] salesperson 판매원 tenant 세입자 real estate agent 부동산 중개인 maintenance 보수 관리

23.
화자는 내일 무엇을 할 수 있다고 말하는가?
(A) 가전제품을 고치기
(B) 배달하기
(C) 점검을 실시하기
(D) 계약서를 검토하기

[해설] 질문의 핵심 키워드 tomorrow가 언급되는 부분에 단서가 있다. 화자는 오늘은 예약이 꽉 찼지만 내일은 방문해서 그것을 고칠 수 있다고 했다(I can be there tomorrow to fix it.). 여기서 it은 앞서 언급한 '고장 난 커피 머신'을 의미하므로 정답은 (A)이다.

`paraphrasing` fix 고치다 → repair 고치다

[어휘] repair 수리[보수]하다 appliance 가전제품 make a delivery 배달하다 conduct (특정한 활동을) 하다 inspection 점검, 조사 review 검토하다 contract 계약(서)

23.
화자는 청자에게 무엇을 확인하라고 요청하는가?
(A) 보안 코드
(B) 가전제품 브랜드
(C) 약속 시간
(D) 보증서

[해설] 메시지 후반, 화자는 청자에게 내일 방문하여 커피 머신을 수리할 시간으로 오전 10시를 제안하며, 자신에게 다시 연락해서 그 시간이 괜찮은지 확인해 달라고(Please get back to me to confirm if that time works for you or not.) 했다. 즉, 약속 시간에 대한 확인을 요청하고 있으므로 정답은 (C)이다.

[어휘] security 보안, 경비 appointment (업무 관련) 약속 warranty agreement 보증서

PART 2 평서문

확인 문제

❶ `US-AU`

The renovation work costs more than we planned.
(A) Isn't it still within the budget?
(B) The construction site is dangerous.

보수 작업이 우리가 예상했던 것보다 비용이 더 듭니다.
(A) 여전히 예산 범위 이내 아닌가요?
(B) 그 공사 현장은 위험합니다.

❷ `BR-BR`

I think this new office chair is comfortable.
(A) I prefer the old one.
(B) It's a furnished apartment.

저는 이 새로운 사무실 의자가 편하다고 생각해요.
(A) 저는 예전 의자가 더 좋습니다.
(B) 가구가 갖추어진 아파트입니다.

❸ `US-US`

I expected the apartment to be more spacious.
(A) I'm moving in next Friday.
(B) How about you rearrange the furniture?

저는 아파트가 더 넓길 기대했어요.
(A) 저는 다음 주 금요일에 이사 가요.
(B) 당신이 가구를 재배치하면 어때요?

❹ `AU-BR`

I wonder if I can afford this car.
(A) We're offering discounts now.
(B) Taking the bus will be faster.

제가 이 차를 살 형편이 될지 의문이네요.
(A) 저희는 지금 할인을 해드리고 있어요.
(B) 버스를 타는 게 더 빠를 거예요.

연습 문제

| 01. (A) | 02. (B) | 03. (B) | 04. (B) | 05. (B) | 06. (A) |
| 07. (B) | 08. (A) |

01. `US-BR`

One of the guests just spilled coffee on the floor.
(A) I'll send someone to clean it up. [O]
(B) Did you make some copies of it? [×]

손님들 중 한 분이 바닥에 커피를 엎질렀어요.
(A) 제가 사람을 보내서 치우도록 하겠습니다.
(B) 그거 복사하셨나요?

02. `BR-US`

I worked late completing the project.
(A) I haven't been there lately. [×]
(B) You must be exhausted. [O]

프로젝트를 완료하느라 늦게까지 일했어요.

(A) 저는 최근에 거기 간 적이 없어요.
(B) 피곤하시겠어요.

03. (AU-BR)

Ms. Jacobson is standing right over there.
(A) That light is too bright. [×]
(B) Thanks, I'll go introduce myself. [○]

Jacobson 씨가 바로 저기 서 계십니다.
(A) 저 불이 너무 밝습니다.
(B) 감사합니다. 제가 가서 제 소개를 하겠습니다.

04. (US-US)

You must be excited about the opening of the new store.
(A) How do I open this? [×]
(B) I can hardly wait. [○]

새 가게를 여는 것에 대해서 무척 흥분되시겠어요.
(A) 이것을 어떻게 여나요?
(B) 네, 기다릴 수가 없습니다.

05. (BR-US)

It would have been nice to see Carla before she left.
(A) The one on the right is better. [×]
(B) Too bad, we were away on vacation. [○]

Carla가 떠나기 전에 만났더라면 좋았을 텐데요.
(A) 오른쪽에 있는 것이 더 낫네요.
(B) 아쉽게도, 우리는 휴가 중이었습니다.

06. (US-AU)

I want to exchange this hair dryer.
(A) Sure, please follow me. [○]
(B) Thanks, but I like my hair color. [×]

이 헤어 드라이어를 교환하고 싶어요.
(A) 물론이죠, 저를 따라오세요.
(B) 고맙지만, 저는 제 머리 색깔이 좋아요.

07. (AU-BR)

I'd like to cancel a reservation for tonight, please.
(A) Sorry, we're all sold out. [×]
(B) I can help you with that. [○]

오늘 밤 예약을 취소하고 싶습니다.
(A) 죄송합니다만, 모두 팔렸습니다.
(B) 제가 그것을 도와드리겠습니다.

08. (US-BR)

Your meal order will be ready to pick up in 20 minutes.
(A) Okay, I'll just wait here. [○]
(B) Can you order them by date? [×]

당신의 식사 주문은 20분 후에 가지고 가실 수 있을 거예요.
(A) 알겠습니다, 그냥 여기서 기다릴게요.
(B) 그것들을 날짜별로 정리해주시겠어요?

실전 문제

01. (C)	02. (C)	03. (C)	04. (A)	05. (C)	06. (A)
07. (B)	08. (C)	09. (B)	10. (C)	11. (B)	12. (C)
13. (C)	14. (B)	15. (B)	16. (C)		

01. (BR-US)

This bed cover is incredibly soft.
(A) It covers all information needed.
(B) No, I don't make children's clothes.
(C) We use the finest linen.

incredibly 믿을 수 없을 정도로, 엄청나게 cover 다루다, 포함시키다 fine 질 높은, 좋은

이 침대 커버는 엄청나게 부드러워요.
(A) 그것은 필요한 모든 정보를 다룹니다.
(B) 아니요, 저는 아동복을 만들지 않아요.
(C) 저희는 가장 좋은 리넨을 사용해요.

[해설] 침대 커버가 부드럽다는 내용의 평서문이다.
(A) 질문의 cover를 반복 사용하여 혼동을 유도하는 오답이다.
(B) 질문의 soft가 섬유의 부드러움을 나타낼 때 쓰이므로 clothes를 이용해 혼동을 유도하는 오답이다.
(C) 가장 좋은 리넨을 사용한다며 그 이유를 말하고 있으므로 정답이다.

02. (US-US)

I was surprised that Mr. Adams is retiring soon.
(A) The price will remain the same.
(B) Yes, you look very tired.
(C) He wants to run his own business.

retire 은퇴하다 run a business 사업을 하다

Adams 씨가 곧 은퇴할 거라니 놀랐어요.
(A) 가격은 동일하게 유지될 거예요.
(B) 네, 당신은 아주 피곤해 보여요.
(C) 그는 자기 사업을 하고 싶어 해요.

[해설] Adams 씨가 은퇴할 거라는 소식을 듣고 놀랐다는 내용의 평서문이다.
(A) 질문의 surprised와 발음이 유사한 the price를 이용하여 혼동을 유도하는 오답이다.
(B) 질문의 retiring과 발음이 유사한 tired를 이용하여 혼동을 유도하는 오답이다.
(C) Mr. Adams를 대명사 he로 받아 그가 자기 사업을 하고 싶어한다며 은퇴 이유를 덧붙이고 있는 정답이다.

03. (BR-AU)

Western Cape University received millions in donations.
(A) She's a professor.
(B) Isn't Timothy returning to college?
(C) Now they can provide more scholarships.

millions 수백만   donation 기부, 기증   professor 교수
return 돌아오다[가다]   provide 제공하다   scholarship 장학금

Western Cape 대학교가 기부금으로 수백만 달러를 받았어요.
(A) 그녀는 교수입니다.
(B) Timothy가 대학으로 돌아가지 않나요?
(C) 이제 그들은 장학금을 더 많이 줄 수 있어요.

[해설] Western Cape 대학교가 기부금으로 수백만 달러를 받았다고 말하는 평서문이다.
(A) 질문의 university에서 연상할 수 있는 professor를 이용하여 혼동을 유도한 오답으로, 질문에서 대명사 she로 받을 만한 특정 인물이 언급되지 않았다.
(B) 질문의 university에서 연상할 수 있는 college를 이용하여 혼동을 유도한 오답이다.
(C) 이제 장학금을 더 많이 줄 수 있게 되었다며 기부금의 사용처를 언급하고 있으므로 정답이다.

04. [AU-US]

I got a flat tire on Mohawk Highway.
(A) We'll send someone to help.
(B) The speed limit is 60 miles per hour.
(C) I don't feel tired.

flat tire 펑크 난 타이어

Mohawk 고속도로에서 타이어가 펑크 났어요.
(A) 도와드릴 사람을 보내드리겠습니다.
(B) 속도 제한은 시속 60마일입니다.
(C) 저는 피곤하지 않아요.

[해설] 고속도로에서 타이어가 펑크 났다고 말하는 평서문이다.
(A) 도와줄 사람을 보내주겠다는 말로 처리 방법을 제시하고 있으므로 정답이다.
(B) 질문의 highway에서 연상 가능한 speed limit을 이용하여 혼동을 유도하는 오답이다.
(C) 질문의 tire와 발음이 유사한 tired를 이용해 혼동을 유도하는 오답이다.

05. [US-AU]

Ms. White's room has been double-booked.
(A) At the lost and found department.
(B) No, I don't have a reservation.
(C) I'll call the hotel's manager.

double-booked 이중으로 예약된   lost and found 분실물 취급소

White 씨의 방이 이중으로 예약되었어요.
(A) 분실물 센터에서요.
(B) 아니요, 저는 예약을 하지 않았어요.
(C) 제가 호텔 매니저에게 전화할게요.

[해설] 방이 이중으로 예약되었다며 문제점을 알리는 평서문이다.
(A) 방이 이중으로 예약되었다는 사실과 분실물 센터는 전혀 상관없는 내용이므로 오답이다.
(B) 질문의 booked에서 연상할 수 있는 reservation을 이용해 혼동을 유도하는 오답이다.
(C) 자신이 호텔 매니저에게 전화하겠다고 응답함으로써 문제 해결 방법을 제시하고 있으므로 정답이다.

06. [BR-US]

I think there's a mistake on my bill.
(A) Okay, I'll have a look at it.
(B) With a manager's approval.
(C) At the bottom of the receipt.

mistake 실수   bill 청구서, 계산서   look up 찾아보다   approval 승인   receipt 영수증

제 청구서에 실수가 있는 것 같아요.
(A) 그래요, 한번 볼게요.
(B) 매니저의 승인으로요.
(C) 영수증 아래 부분에요.

[해설] 청구서에 실수가 있는 것 같다고 말하는 평서문이다.
(A) 한번 보겠다는 말로 상대방의 문제점을 해결해 주려는 의사를 보여 주고 있는 정답이다.
(B) 질문과 상관없는 답변이므로 오답이다.
(C) bill에서 연상할 수 있는 receipt를 사용하여 혼동을 유도하는 오답이다.

07. [US-US]

This new TV commercial has been remarkably successful.
(A) The names of successful candidates.
(B) Yes, it is endorsed by a famous actress.
(C) In commercial district.

commercial (TV나 라디오의) 광고, 상업의   remarkably 두드러지게, 현저하게   candidate 지원자, 후보자   endorse (유명인이 광고에 나와서 상품을) 홍보하다

이 새로운 TV 광고는 크게 성공했어요.
(A) 합격한 지원자들의 이름입니다.
(B) 네, 그것은 유명한 여배우에 의해 홍보되고 있습니다.
(C) 상업 지구에요.

[해설] 새로운 TV 광고가 크게 성공했다고 말하는 평서문이다.
(A) 질문의 successful을 반복 사용하여 혼동을 유도하는 오답이다.
(B) Yes로 동의한 후 유명한 여배우가 홍보하고 있다며 성공의 이유를 덧붙이고 있으므로 정답이다.
(C) 질문의 commercial을 반복 사용하여 혼동을 유도하는 오답이다.

08. [BR-AU]

I need to see the latest customer survey results.
(A) The online survey.
(B) It only takes a minute to fill out.
(C) I'll get them to you later today.

latest (가장) 최근의, 최신의   customer survey 고객 여론 조사   result 결과   fill out 작성하다, 기입하다

저는 가장 최근의 고객 여론 조사 결과를 봐야 합니다.
(A) 온라인 설문 조사입니다.
(B) 작성하는 데 잠깐이면 됩니다.
(C) 오늘 늦게 갖다 드릴게요.

[해설] 가장 최근의 고객 여론 조사 결과를 봐야 한다고 말하는 평서문이다.
(A) 질문의 survey를 반복 사용하여 혼동을 유도하는 오답이다.
(B) 질문의 survey에서 연상할 수 있는 fill out(작성하다)을 이용하여 혼동을 유도하는 오답이다.
(C) customer survey results를 대명사 them으로 받아 오늘 늦게 가져다주겠다며 상대의 요청을 수락하고 있는 정답이다.

09. AU-US

I learned a lot at the workshop earlier.
(A) Please present a photo ID.
(B) Ms. Dalton is knowledgeable about our products.
(C) Welcome to our university.

present 제시하다   knowledgeable 아는 것이 많은

저는 앞서 워크숍에서 많은 것을 배웠어요.
(A) 사진이 부착된 신분증을 보여주세요.
(B) Dalton 씨는 저희 제품에 대해 잘 알고 있어요.
(C) 저희 대학에 오신 것을 환영합니다.

[해설] 워크숍에서 많은 것을 배웠다고 말하는 평서문이다.
(A) 질문의 workshop에서 연상되는 present(발표하다)와 동음이의어인 present(제시하다)를 이용해 혼동을 유도하는 오답이다.
(B) Dalton 씨가 우리 제품에 대해 많이 알고 있다고 응답함으로써 워크숍에서 Dalton 씨가 참석자들에게 제품에 대한 정보를 잘 전달해주었음을 우회적으로 말하는 정답이다.
(C) 질문의 learned에서 연상할 수 있는 university를 이용해 혼동을 유도하는 오답이다.

10. US-BR

I was very happy to hear that Mr. Hunt was selected Employee of the Month.
(A) Don't forget to include your performance review.
(B) The position might still be open.
(C) I think he deserves it.

select 선택하다   include 포함하다   performance review 업무 평가, 인사 고과   deserve 받을 만하다

Hunt 씨가 이 달의 직원으로 선정되었다는 소식을 듣고 기뻤어요.
(A) 당신의 업무 평가를 포함하는 걸 잊지 마세요.
(B) 그 자리는 아직 공석일 거예요.
(C) 그는 받을 만하다고 생각해요.

[해설] Hunt 씨가 이 달의 직원으로 선정되었다는 소식을 듣고 기뻤다는 내용의 평서문이다.
(A) Employee of the Month에서 연상할 수 있는 performance review를 사용하여 혼동을 유도하는 오답이다.
(B) 평서문의 내용과 상관없는 답변이므로 오답이다.
(C) 그가 받을 만하다며 내용에 동의하는 답변을 하였으므로 정답이다.

11. US-BR

Our dishwasher made record sales in England.
(A) Do you need help washing the dishes?
(B) We thought people would like it.
(C) That should be effective.

dishwasher 식기 세척기   made sales 매출을 내다
record 기록적인   effective 효과적인

우리의 식기 세척기가 영국에서 기록적인 매출을 올렸어요.
(A) 설거지를 도와드릴까요?
(B) 우리는 사람들이 좋아할 거라고 생각했어요.
(C) 그건 효과적일 거예요.

[해설] 식기 세척기가 영국에서 매우 많이 팔렸다는 내용의 평서문이다.
(A) 질문의 dishwasher에서 연상할 수 있는 washing the dishes를 이용해 혼동을 유도하는 오답이다.
(B) 사람들이 좋아할 거라고 생각했다고 말함으로써 이 제품이 잘 팔릴 것을 예상했음을 표현하고 있는 정답이다.
(C) 질문의 dishwasher의 특성을 나타내는 표현으로 연상 가능한 effective를 이용해 혼동을 유도하는 오답이다.

12. BR-US

The board of directors was disappointed with the low sales.
(A) You will find the directions to the clinic.
(B) It should be lowered.
(C) Yes, they are worse than we expected.

board of directors 이사회   be disappointed with ~에 실망하다   directions to ~로 찾아가는 길   clinic 병원   lower ~을 내리다, 낮추다   expect 예상[기대]하다

이사회가 저조한 매출에 실망했어요.
(A) 당신은 그 병원으로 가는 길을 찾을 거예요.
(B) 그것을 내려야 해요.
(C) 네, 우리가 예상했던 것보다 더 나빠요.

[해설] 이사회가 저조한 매출에 실망했다고 말하는 평서문이다.
(A) 질문의 directors와 발음이 유사한 directions를 이용해 혼동을 유도하는 오답이다.
(B) 질문의 low에서 연상할 수 있는 lowered를 이용해 혼동을 유도하는 오답이다.
(C) Yes로 응답한 후 the low sales를 대명사 they로 받아 예상했던 것보다 매출이 더 나빴다고 부연 설명하는 정답이다.

13. US-AU

I'm very sorry for the delivery delay.
(A) You can track the delivery status online.
(B) It's out of stock now.
(C) Can you refund it?

delivery 배달   delay 지연, 지체   track 추적하다   status (진행 과정의) 상황   out of stock 품절[매진]이 되어   refund 환불하다

배송이 지연되어 대단히 죄송합니다.
(A) 온라인으로 배송 상황을 추적할 수 있습니다.
(B) 현재 품절입니다.
(C) 환불해주시겠어요?

[해설] 배송이 지연되어 미안하다는 평서문이다.
(A) 질문의 delivery를 반복 사용하여 혼동을 유도하는 오답이다.
(B) 질문의 delivery delay(배송 지연)의 이유로 연상 가능한 out of stock(품절된)을 이용해 혼동을 유도하는 오답으로, 오히려 배달하는

(C) 배송이 지연되어 미안하다는 말에 환불해줄 수 있는지 되묻고 있는 정답이다.

14. BR-BR

Please send me last quarter's sales figures by the end of the week.
(A) We will figure it out.
(B) Okay, that won't be a problem.
(C) Yes, I met my goal.

quarter 분기   figure out 생각해 내다, 이해하다, 해결하다
meet a goal 목표를 달성하다

이번 주 말까지 제게 지난 분기의 매출 수치를 보내주세요.
(A) 저희가 해결할게요.
(B) 알겠어요, 그건 별 문제 아니에요.
(C) 네, 저는 목표를 달성했어요.

[해설] 매출 수치를 보내달라고 요청하는 평서문이다.
(A) 질문의 figure를 반복 사용하여 혼동을 유도하는 오답이다.
(B) Okay라고 수락한 뒤 별로 어려운 일이 아니니 기꺼이 해줄 수 있다는 의미로 별 문제 아니라고 덧붙인 정답이다.
(C) 질문의 sales figures에서 매출 목표를 연상하도록 유도하는 goal을 이용한 오답이다.

15. BR-US

This place has the best Mexican food around.
(A) Mr. Gonzalez is away on business.
(B) That's why I recommended it.
(C) The beef burrito, please.

place 위치, 장소   away 자리에 없는   on business 볼일이 있어, 업무로

이곳의 멕시코 음식이 이 주위에서 가장 맛있어요.
(A) Gonzalez 씨는 업무차 자리를 비웠어요.
(B) 그래서 제가 추천한 거예요.
(C) 소고기 브리또로 주세요.

[해설] 화자들이 있는 장소의 멕시코 음식이 가장 맛있다고 말하는 평서문이다.
(A) 질문의 Mexican에서 연상할 수 있는 멕시코 사람의 이름 Mr. Gonzalez를 이용하여 혼동을 유도하는 오답이다.
(B) 그래서 자신이 이곳을 추천한 거라며 상대방의 말에 강한 동의를 표하고 있으므로 정답이다.
(C) 질문의 Mexican food에서 연상할 수 있는 beef burrito를 이용해 혼동을 유도하는 오답이다.

16. US-US

Charles asked us to submit our article proposal by tomorrow.
(A) I'd like to renew my subscription.
(B) Yes, it's a very interesting article.
(C) I'm leaving on a business trip this afternoon.

submit 제출하다   article 기사   proposal 제안, 제의
renew 갱신하다   subscription 구독   business trip 출장

Charles가 우리에게 내일까지 기사 기획안을 제출하라고 했어요.
(A) 저는 구독을 갱신하고 싶습니다.
(B) 네, 그것은 매우 흥미로운 기사였어요.
(C) 저는 오늘 오후에 출장을 떠나요.

[해설] Charles가 내일까지 기사 기획안을 제출하라고 했다는 내용의 평서문이다.
(A) 질문의 article에서 연상할 수 있는 잡지나 신문의 '구독'을 뜻하는 subscription을 이용해 혼동을 유도하는 오답이다.
(B) 질문의 article을 반복 사용하여 혼동을 유도하는 오답이다.
(C) 자신은 오늘 오후 출장을 떠난다고 말함으로써 내일까지 제출하는 것이 불가능함을 간접적으로 전하고 있으므로 정답이다.

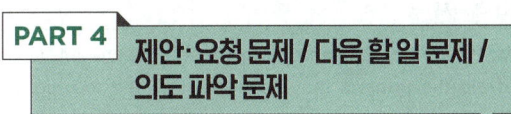

PART 4 제안·요청 문제 / 다음 할 일 문제 / 의도 파악 문제

 연습 문제

01. (B)   02. (A)   03. (A)   04. (B)   05. (A)   06. (A)

01. US

What are **listeners advised to do**?
(A) **Listen** to **traffic updates**
(B) **Avoid driving** through an **area**

라디오 방송

W: Due to recent unexpected freezing cold weather, main water pipes burst right in front of Graham Movie Theater on South Central Boulevard. The police department is blocking the street and redirecting traffic now. The Department of Energy and Water Supply expects that the repair work will be completed in two days. Motorists are advised to avoid this area.

burst 터지다, 파열하다   redirect ~의 방향을 바꾸다

청자들은 무엇을 하도록 조언 받는가?
(A) 최신 교통 방송 듣기   **(B) 어떤 지역을 운전하는 것 피하기**

여: 최근의 예기치 않은 아주 추운 날씨로 인해, South Central 대로의 Graham 영화관 바로 앞의 주요 수도관이 터졌습니다. 경찰은 거리를 폐쇄하고 교통을 재정리하고 있습니다. 에너지와 수도 공급 부서는 수리 공사가 이틀 후에 완료될 것이라고 알렸습니다. 운전자들은 이 지역을 피할 것이 권고됩니다.

02. BR

What will the **listeners do next**?
(A) **Listen** to **weather** news
(B) **Post** their **questions** online

라디오 방송

> M: Hello, we are going to meet the CEO of Cinema Plus, Morgan Smith. He will tell us how he became a successful businessperson. We will be right back in a few minutes after the weather update. Stay tuned.

청자들은 다음에 무엇을 할 것인가?
(A) 날씨 뉴스 듣기   (B) 온라인에 질문 올리기

남: 안녕하세요, 우리는 Cinema Plus의 CEO인 Morgan Smith를 만날 것입니다. 그는 그가 어떻게 성공적인 사업가가 되었는지 말해줄 거예요. 날씨 소식 뒤에 몇 분 후에 바로 돌아오겠습니다. 채널 고정해 주세요.

03. [AU]

What does the **speaker suggest doing**?
(A) **Holding** a **meeting**   (B) **Upgrading** a **computer**

전화 메시지

> M: Hello, this is Min-ho from Daniel Investment. I'm afraid the printers may have been priced too high. Could you tell me when you are available to discuss this issue? I'm free this Wednesday afternoon. Someone from the purchasing department will also join in.

화자는 무엇을 할 것을 제안하는가?
(A) 회의 열기   (B) 컴퓨터 업그레이드 하기

남: 안녕하세요, 저는 Daniel Investment의 Min-ho입니다. 프린터의 가격이 너무 높게 측정된 것 같아 우려됩니다. 이 사안에 대해 언제 논의 가능하신지 알려주시겠어요? 저는 이번 주 수요일 오후에 시간이 됩니다. 구매 부서의 직원 분도 함께 하실 거예요.

04. [US]

What will the **listeners** most likely **do next**?
(A) Have a **Q&A session**   (B) **Go** to a **cafeteria**

안내

> W: Attention please. As I said this morning, the regular inspection of the conveyer belts will take place this afternoon. Inspectors will begin the inspection in 10 minutes. So, the workers on Assembly Line A may go to the cafeteria now and take some rest. Inspectors will ask some questions about the conveyor belts when you are back on duty. Thanks.

on duty 일하고 있는, 근무 중인

청자들은 다음에 무엇을 하겠는가?
(A) 질의응답 시간 갖기   **(B) 구내식당으로 가기**

여: 주목해 주세요. 제가 오늘 아침에 말한 것처럼, 컨베이어 벨트의 정기 점검이 오늘 오후에 진행될 것입니다. 조사관들은 10분 후에 점검을 시작하실 거예요. 그러므로, 조립 라인 A의 직원들은 지금 구내식당으로 가서 좀 쉬도록 하세요. 다시 일하러 오시면 조사관들이 컨베이어 벨트에 대한 질문을 몇 개 하실 겁니다. 감사합니다.

05. [BR]

What does the speaker **mean** when she says, "**50 cans of light grey paint is too many**"?
(A) She thinks there might be a **mistake**.
(B) She is **happy** with a **large order**.

전화 메시지

> W: Hello, Ms. Kimberly. This is Linda Yang from LY Home Improvement. I'm calling regarding your order that you placed this morning. 50 cans of light grey paint is too many. It is larger than usual. Please call me back as soon as possible to let me know if that number is correct. Thank you.

화자가 "연한 회색 페인트 50통은 너무 많아요"라고 말할 때 의미하는 바는 무엇인가?
(A) 실수가 있다고 생각한다.   (B) 대량 주문에 만족한다.

여: 안녕하세요, Kimberly 씨. 저는 LY Home Improvement의 Linda Yang입니다. 당신이 오늘 아침에 주문하신 것과 관련하여 전화드렸습니다. 연한 회색 페인트 50통은 너무 많아요. 평소보다 더 많습니다. 가능한 한 빨리 제게 다시 전화주셔서 그 숫자가 맞는지 알려주세요. 감사합니다.

06. [US]

Why does the speaker **say**, "**I really enjoyed it last time with my family**"?
(A) To **recommend** a **restaurant**
(B) To **give** detailed **information**

여행 안내

> M: All right, everyone. We are arriving at the area called Old Town. You will encounter buildings with traditional gothic styles. You will be given two hours of free time to look around the area. If you need to rest, go to Belgian Treats & Coffee. I really enjoyed it last time with my family. Please come back to the bus by 4 P.M.

화자는 왜 "저는 지난 번에 저의 가족과 그곳을 정말 즐겼어요"라고 말하는가?
(A) 레스토랑을 추천하기 위해   (B) 세부 정보를 주기 위해

남: 좋아요, 여러분. 저희는 올드 타운이라고 불리는 지역에 도착하고 있습니다. 여러분은 전통적인 고딕 스타일의 건물을 마주할 거예요. 이 지역을 둘러보는 데 2시간의 자유 시간이 주어질 겁니다. 휴식이 필요하시면, Belgian Treats & Coffee로 가세요. 저는 지난번에 저의 가족과 그곳을 정말 즐겼어요. 버스로 오후 4시까지 돌아오시기 바랍니다.

paraphrasing 정답   1. (a) 2. (c) 3. (b) 4. (c) 5. (b) 6. (a)

실전 문제

01. (C)	02. (C)	03. (D)	04. (B)	05. (A)	06. (D)
07. (B)	08. (A)	09. (D)	10. (D)	11. (D)	12. (B)
13. (D)	14. (B)	15. (A)	16. (B)	17. (A)	18. (B)
19. (C)	20. (D)	21. (C)	22. (D)	23. (B)	24. (B)

[01-03] AU

Questions 01-03 refer to the following telephone message.

M: Hi, Mr. Navarro. This is Robert Hollis. **01I hope you remember me from the National Advertising Conference** earlier this month. I'm pleased that you were impressed with my colleague's designs, and I recall that you were wondering what kind of software she uses, since **02you're looking to upgrade your technology.** I checked with my colleague, and she has a program called Montague. It's the perfect time to purchase it online, because **03it's currently being offered at half off the usual price. So, if you're interested, you'll want to take care of this as soon as possible.**

pleased 기뻐하는, 만족해하는   be impressed with ~에 감동받다   colleague 동료   recall 기억해 내다, 상기하다   usual price 통상 가격

01-03은 다음 전화 메시지에 관한 문제입니다.
남: 안녕하세요, Navarro 씨. 저는 Robert Hollis입니다. 01이달 초 전국 광고 콘퍼런스에서 저를 만나셨던 것을 기억하시길 바랍니다. 당신이 제 동료의 디자인에 대해 깊은 인상을 받았다니 기뻐요. 그리고 02당신이 당신의 기술 업그레이드를 생각하고 있어서 그녀가 어떤 종류의 소프트웨어를 사용하는지 궁금해하셨던 것이 생각나요. 제 동료에게 확인해봤는데 그녀는 Montague라는 프로그램을 가지고 있어요. 그것을 온라인으로 구입하기에 지금이 최적의 시기입니다. 03왜냐하면 현재 평소의 절반 가격에 제공되고 있거든요. 그러니 관심이 있으시다면 가능한 한 빨리 처리하셔야 할 거예요.

01.

화자는 Navarro 씨를 어디에서 만났는가?
(A) 시상식 연회에서
(B) 건물 투어에서
(C) 업계 콘퍼런스에서
(D) 취업 박람회에서

[해설] 핵심 키워드 Mr. Navarro는 이 전화 메시지의 수신인이므로 화자와 청자가 만난 장소를 묻는 문제이다. 메시지 초반 화자가 이달 초 전국 광고 콘퍼런스에서 저를 만나셨던 것을 기억하길 바란다고(I hope you remember me from the National Advertising Conference) 말했으므로 이를 '업계 콘퍼런스'로 바꿔 표현한 (C)가 정답이다.

paraphrasing the National Advertising Conference 전국 광고 콘퍼런스 → an industry conference 업계 콘퍼런스

[어휘] banquet 연회, 만찬   industry 산업, 업계   career fair 취업 박람회

02.

화자는 왜 "그녀는 Montague라는 프로그램을 가지고 있어요"라고 말하는가?
(A) 오류를 정정하기 위해서
(B) 주문을 취소하기 위해서
(C) 상품에 대한 정보를 전달하기 위해서
(D) 동료를 추천하기 위해서

[해설] 해당 표현의 앞뒤 문맥을 파악하여 화자의 의도를 파악하는 문제이다. 해당 표현에 앞서 메시지 수신인이 기술 업그레이드를 위한 제품의 구입에 관심이 있어(you're looking to upgrade your technology) 화자의 동료가 사용하는 프로그램의 종류를 궁금해했다는 내용이 나오고, 해당 표현 뒤에는 지금이 온라인으로 그것을 구입하기에 최적의 시기이니 서두르라는 내용이 나온다. 즉, 화자가 "그녀는 Montague라는 프로그램을 가지고 있어요"라고 특정 제품의 이름을 말한 것은 제품에 대한 정보를 제공하기 위한 것이므로 정답은 (C)이다.

[어휘] correct 바로잡다, 정정하다

03.

화자는 왜 청자에게 빨리 행동을 취할 것을 권장하는가?
(A) 배송에 시간이 오래 걸릴지도 모른다.
(B) 몇몇 물품이 다 떨어질 것 같다.
(C) 마감일이 변경되었다.
(D) 세일 행사가 곧 종료될 것이다.

[해설] 대화 마지막 부분에서, 화자는 그것이 현재 평소의 절반 가격에 제공되고 있으니(it's currently being offered at half off the usual price) 관심이 있으면 가능한 한 빨리(as soon as possible) 서두르라고 말한다. 여기서 말하는 그것(it)은 앞서 언급한, 화자의 동료가 사용하는 프로그램인 Montague를 가리키는데, 이것이 현재 할인 판매 중이니 빨리 사라는 것은 곧 할인 행사가 종료될 것임을 암시하므로 정답은 (D)이다.

[어휘] encourage 권장[장려]하다   supplies 용품, 비품   run out 다 떨어지다

[04-06] US

Questions 04-06 refer to the following talk.

W: Good morning. My name is Jodie Coborn, and **04I'd like to summarize what we'll be doing today** at the Hattiesburg Museum of Art. First, you'll learn about our mission and our daily operations. **04As volunteers here at the museum**, your role is vital in helping us to make art available to the public. Next, we'll cover the museum's policies. These are very important, so **05I recommend writing down the important points.** After that, you'll be assigned to your teams. **06Before we go any further, I'd like to go around the room and have each of you tell your name and a little bit about yourself.**

summarize 간략히 말하다, 요약하다   mission 임무   operation 작업   volunteer 자원봉사자   role 역할   vital 필수적인   public 일반 사람들   cover 다루다, 포함시키다   policy 정책, 방침   assign A to B A를 B에 배정하다   go further (말하는 내용과 관련하여) 더 나아가다   go around 돌다

04-06은 다음 담화에 관한 문제입니다.
여: 안녕하세요. 제 이름은 Jodie Coborn이고요, Hattiesburg 미술관에서 04오늘 우리가 무엇을 하게 될지에 대해 간략히 말씀드리려고 합니다. 우선, 여러분은 우리의 임무와 일과 작업에 대해 알게 되실 겁니다. 04이곳 미술관의 자원봉사자로서, 여러분의 역할은 우리가 미술품을 일반 대중이 이용 가능하도록 하는 것이 필수적입니다. 다음으로, 우리는 미술관의 방침을 다룰 것입니다. 이것들은 매우 중요하므로 05중요한 내용들은 필기하실 것을 권합니다. 그 후에 여러분들은 팀에 배정될 것입니다. 06더

진행하기에 앞서 방을 돌면서 여러분 각자가 이름을 비롯하여 자신에 대해 간단히 얘기하는 시간을 갖도록 하겠습니다.

04.
화자는 왜 이야기를 하고 있는가?
(A) 미술 비평을 제공하기 위하여
(B) 자원봉사자들에게 개요를 설명하기 위하여
(C) 채용 과정을 설명하기 위하여
(D) 미술 전시회를 홍보하기 위하여

[해설] 담화 초반 화자가 자신을 소개한 후 미술관에서 오늘 우리가 무엇을 하게 될지에 대해 간략히 말하겠다고(I'd like to summarize what we'll be doing today.) 했고, 이후에 언급한 이곳 미술관의 자원봉사자로서(As volunteers here at the museum)라는 표현으로 보아 미술관 자원봉사자들에게 오늘 할 일의 개요를 설명하기 위한 담화임을 알 수 있으므로 정답은 (B)이다.

paraphrasing summarize 간략히 말하다 → give an overview 개요를 설명하다

[어휘] critique 비평, 평론 overview 개관, 개요 hiring process 채용 과정 promote 홍보하다 exhibit 전시

05.
화자는 무엇을 권하는가?
(A) 메모하기
(B) 영수증 모으기
(C) 휴대폰 끄기
(D) 웹사이트 확인하기

[해설] 질문의 핵심 키워드 recommend가 담화 중반에 언급된다. 화자는 미술관의 방침을 다룰 것인데, 이것들은 매우 중요하니 중요한 점들은 필기할 것을 권했다(I recommend writing down the important points). 따라서 정답은 (A)이다.

paraphrasing writing down 필기하다 → taking some notes 메모하기

[어휘] take a note 메모를 하다 receipt 영수증

06.
청자들은 다음에 무엇을 할 것 같은가?
(A) 영화 보기
(B) 몇몇 질문 제출하기
(C) 함께 식사하기
(D) 자기소개 하기

[해설] 다음 할 일을 묻는 문제의 단서는 주로 담화 마지막 부분에 나온다. 화자는 담화를 이어나가기 전에 방을 돌아다니면서 청자들 각자가 이름을 비롯하여 자신에 대하여 간단히 얘기하게 시키겠다고(have each of you tell your name and a little bit about yourself) 했다. 다시 말해 담화 직후에 청자들이 자기소개를 하는 시간을 가질 것임을 알 수 있으므로 정답은 (D)이다.

paraphrasing each of you tell your name and a little bit about yourself 각자가 자신의 이름과 자신에 대해 간단히 말한다 → introduce themselves 자기 자신을 소개하다

[07-09] BR
Questions 07-09 refer to the following telephone message.

M: Hi, Ms. Kasey. It's Henry. Have you had a chance to look at ⁰⁷the design for the career fair banner? I need to get that approved before sending it to the printer. ⁰⁸I told you earlier that it had to be done by four, because that's when the shop closes. But don't worry, they have an online option. Also, ⁰⁹I'll look over the event budget now to see if we have enough money for two banners. Thanks.

career fair 취업 박람회 banner 현수막 approve 승인하다 look over 훑어보다, 살펴보다 budget 예산

07-09는 다음 전화 메시지에 관한 문제입니다.
남: 안녕하세요, Kasey 씨. Henry예요. ⁰⁷취업 박람회 현수막 디자인을 혹시 보셨나요? 그것을 인쇄소에 보내기 전에 승인을 받아야 해요. ⁰⁸4시까지 끝내야 한다고 제가 전에 말씀드렸는데 그때가 인쇄소가 문을 닫는 시간이거든요. 하지만 걱정하지 마세요. 온라인으로 하는 방법이 있어요. 또한, ⁰⁹제가 지금 행사 예산을 훑어보고 현수막을 두 개 제작할 만큼 돈이 충분한지 확인할게요. 고마워요.

07.
전화의 목적은 무엇인가?
(A) 회의 시간을 잡기 위해
(B) 디자인을 승인받기 위해
(C) 취업 박람회에 등록하기 위해
(D) 문서의 오류를 지적하기 위해

[해설] 메시지를 남긴 목적을 묻는 문제로, 메시지 전반부에서 단서를 찾는다. 화자는 메시지 수신인에게 취업 박람회 현수막 디자인(the design for the career fair banner)을 봤는지 물어본 후, 인쇄소에 보내기 전 승인을 받아야 한다고(I need to get that approved) 덧붙였다. 즉, 현수막 디자인에 대한 승인을 받기 위해 전화를 건 것이므로 정답은 (B)이다.

[어휘] set up 정하다, 결정하다 get approval 승인을 받다 enroll in ~에 등록하다 point out 지적[언급]하다

08.
화자가 "온라인으로 하는 방법이 있어요"라고 말할 때 암시하는 것은 무엇인가?
(A) 마감 시간을 정정하고 싶다.
(B) 다른 업체로 바꾸어야 한다고 생각한다.
(C) 프로젝트 비용을 줄일 방법을 찾았다.
(D) 업무가 끝나지 않아서 놀랐다.

[해설] 화자는 인쇄소 문을 닫는 4시까지 디자인 승인이 완료되어야 한다고(it had to be done by 4, because that's when the shop closes) 말했었지만 걱정하지 말라고 한 후 "온라인으로 하는 방법이 있어요"라고 덧붙였다. 이 말은 원래는 4시까지 디자인이 완료되어야 했지만 온라인으로 인쇄소에 전달할 수 있으니 굳이 4시까지 작업을 완료할 필요가 없다는 뜻이다. 즉, 당초 언급했던 작업 마감 시간을 정정하고자 하는 화자의 의도가 읽히므로 정답은 (A)이다.

[어휘] make a correction 정정하다, 고치다 reduce 줄이다, (가격 등을) 낮추다

09.

화자는 다음에 무엇을 할 계획인가?
(A) 양식 전달하기
(B) 관리자에게 얘기하기
(C) 고객에게 전화하기
(D) 예산을 검토하기

[해설] 메시지 후반부에서, 화자가 지금 행사 예산을 훑어보고(I'll look over the event budget now) 현수막을 두 개 제작할 만큼 돈이 충분한지 확인하겠다고 했다. 따라서 화자가 메시지를 남긴 직후에 예산을 검토할 계획임을 알 수 있으므로 정답은 (D)이다.

`paraphrasing` look over 검토하다 → review 검토하다

[어휘] forward 보내다, 전달하다 review 검토하다

[10-12] AU

Questions 10-12 refer to the following excerpt from a meeting.

M: To wrap up today's staff meeting, I'd like to give you an update on Selby Rail's on-board food service. **¹⁰In addition to the usual sandwiches and drinks, we're going to start serving some hot dishes as well.** This is something that a lot of passengers requested in **¹¹the customer survey that we carried out last month.** Now, this does mean that the buffet car will be busier, so your regular work shifts will change. **¹²I've created a revised schedule of your shifts. Please review it carefully now.**

wrap up (회의 등을) 마무리 짓다   on-board 기내의, 차내의
in addition to ~에 더하여   usual 평상시의   passenger 승객
carry out 수행[이행]하다   buffet car (기차의) 식당차   regular 규칙적인, 정기적인   work shift 근무 시간, 근무 조

10-12는 다음 회의 발췌록에 관한 문제입니다.

남: Selby 철도의 열차 내 음식 서비스에 대한 최신 정보를 전달하는 것으로 오늘 직원 회의를 마무리 짓고자 합니다. ¹⁰평상시의 샌드위치와 음료에 더하여 우리는 따뜻한 음식의 서빙을 시작할 예정입니다. 이것은 ¹¹우리가 지난달에 실시한 고객 설문 조사에서 많은 승객들이 요청한 것입니다. 자, 이것은 식당차가 더욱 혼잡해지게 될 것임을 의미하므로 여러분의 정규 근무 시간이 바뀔 것입니다. ¹²제가 수정된 근무 시간표를 작성했습니다. 지금 주의 깊게 살펴봐주세요.

10.

화자는 주로 무엇에 대해 이야기하고 있는가?
(A) 보안 조치
(B) 교환 정책
(C) 직원 교육
(D) 음식 옵션

[해설] 담화 초반 화자는 열차 내에서 제공되는 음식 서비스에 대한 최신 정보를 전달하겠다고 했고, 구체적으로 평상시의 샌드위치와 음료에 더하여 따뜻한 음식을 서빙할 예정이라고(In addition to the usual sandwiches and drinks, we're going to start serving some hot dishes as well.) 했다. 즉, 승객들이 선택할 수 있는 음식의 메뉴가 다양해졌음을 알리고 있으므로 정답은 (D)이다.

[어휘] measure 조치, 정책 exchange 교환 policy 정책, 방침 option 선택(권), 옵션

11.

Selby 철도는 지난달에 무엇을 했는가?
(A) 점검을 받았다.
(B) 더 많은 여정을 추가했다.
(C) 요금을 인상했다.
(D) 설문조사를 시행했다.

[해설] 질문의 핵심 키워드인 Selby Rail과 last month에 집중한다. Selby Rail은 화자와 청자들이 소속된 철도 회사이고, 담화 중반 '우리가 지난달 실시한 고객 설문조사(the customer survey that we carried out last month)'라는 표현이 나온다. 즉, Selby Rail은 지난달에 설문 조사를 시행했음을 알 수 있으므로 (D)가 정답이다.

`paraphrasing` carry out 실시하다 → conduct 하다

[어휘] undergo 겪다, 받다 inspection 점검, 사찰 journey 여행, 여정 fare (교통) 요금 conduct (특정한 활동을) 하다

12.

화자는 청자들에게 무엇을 검토하라고 요청하는가?
(A) 교육 설명서
(B) 작업 일정표
(C) 사업 계약서
(D) 부서 예산

[해설] 제안·요청 문제에 대한 단서는 주로 담화 후반부에 나온다. 담화 마지막 부분에서, 화자는 수정된 근무 시간표를 작성했으니 지금 주의 깊게 살펴봐 달라고(I've created a revised schedule of your shifts. Please review it carefully now.) 청자들에게 요청했다. 따라서 정답은 (B)이다.

`paraphrasing` a revised schedule of your shifts 수정된 근무 시간표 → a work schedule 작업 일정표

[어휘] manual 설명서 contract 계약(서) department 부서 budget 예산

[13-15] BR

Questions 13-15 refer to the following announcement.

W: **¹³Attention passengers waiting for the train WE 76 to Cleveland.** Due to problems in the engine car, your train has been delayed indefinitely. We are trying to fix the problem, but you will most likely have to wait until another train arrives to take its place. **¹⁴Updates will be announced as soon as they become available, so please continue listening for them.** If you decide to take another mode of transportation, **¹⁵you need to see a ticketing agent to have your current ticket fully refunded.** We deeply apologize for the inconvenience.

indefinitely 무기한으로   fix 고치다   take one's place ~를 대신하다   mode 방식, 유형   transportation 수송, 운송   ticketing agent 매표직원   current 현재의   fully refunded 전액 환불된   deeply 대단히, 몹시

13-15는 다음 안내에 관한 문제입니다.

여: **13클리블랜드 행 WE 76 열차**를 기다리고 계신 승객 여러분은 주목해주시기 바랍니다. 기관 차량의 문제로 인해 열차가 무기한 연기되었습니다. 저희가 문제를 해결하려고 노력 중이지만 대신할 다른 열차가 도착할 때까지 기다리셔야 할 것 같습니다. **14새로운 소식이 들어오는 대로 공지해드릴 예정이니 계속해서 귀 기울여주시기 바랍니다.** 다른 교통수단을 이용하기로 결정하신 경우에는 **15매표 직원을 방문하시어 현재의 티켓을 전액 환불 받으셔야 합니다.** 불편을 끼쳐드려 대단히 죄송합니다.

13.
안내는 어디에서 이루어지고 있는가?
(A) 공항에서
(B) 식당에서
(C) 버스 터미널에서
(D) 기차역에서

[해설] 클리블랜드 행 WE 76 열차를 기다리고 계신 승객들은 주목해 주기 바란다는(Attention passengers waiting for train WE 76 to Cleveland.) 내용으로 담화가 시작되는 것으로 보아 기차역에서 들을 수 있는 안내 방송이다. 따라서 정답은 (D)이다.

14.
화자는 청자들에게 무엇을 하라고 요청하는가?
(A) 사진이 부착된 신분증을 보여줄 것
(B) 새로운 소식에 귀 기울일 것
(C) 셀프 발권기를 이용할 것
(D) 다른 교통수단을 찾을 것

[해설] 부탁 또는 요청을 할 때 흔히 쓰는 표현인 please 이후에 제시되는 내용에 주목한다. 화자는 열차의 지연을 알린 후 새로운 소식이 들어오는 대로 공지할 예정이니 계속해서 귀 기울여달라고(Updates will be announced as they become available, so please continue listening for them.) 요청했다. 따라서 정답은 (B)이다.

15.
청자들은 왜 직원을 만나야 하는가?
(A) 환불을 받기 위해서
(B) 식권을 확인하기 위해서
(C) 회원 가입을 하기 위해서
(D) 지역 지도를 얻기 위해서

[해설] 질문의 핵심 키워드 agent는 담화의 ticketing agent를 가리킨다. 즉, 청자들이 매표 직원을 만나야 하는 이유를 묻는 문제로, 담화 후반에서 다른 교통수단을 이용하기로 결정한 경우에는 매표 직원을 만나 현재의 티켓을 전액 환불 받으라고(you need to see a ticketing agent to have your current ticket fully refunded) 했으므로 정답은 (A)이다.

[어휘] get a refund 환불받다 verify 확인하다 meal voucher 식권 sign up for ~을 신청[가입]하다

[16-18] US

Questions 16-18 refer to the following excerpt from a meeting.

W: Welcome to today's product design team meeting. **16Let's begin by talking about our travel and exercise gear bag for cyclists. 17I've received some feedback from our customers about its design. It needs to be smaller.** These days, people use their cell phones as cameras, so there's no more need for the large camera pocket. **18Now, let's take a look at how some of our competitors are advertising their versions of similar products.** I'll play them on the projector.

gear (특정한 용도의) 장비, 복장 cyclist 자전거 타는 사람 take a look at ~을 한번 보다 competitor 경쟁사

16-18은 다음 회의 발췌록에 관한 문제입니다.

여: 오늘 상품 디자인 팀 회의에 오신 것을 환영합니다. **16자전거 이용자들을 위한 여행 및 운동 용품 가방에 대한 얘기로 시작하겠습니다. 17제가 우리 고객들로부터 디자인에 대한 의견을 좀 받았습니다. 더 작아야 합니다.** 요즘에는, 사람들은 휴대폰을 카메라로 사용합니다. 따라서 큰 카메라 주머니는 더 이상 필요하지 않습니다. **18이제, 우리 경쟁사들이 비슷한 유형의 제품을 어떻게 광고하는지 한번 봅시다.** 제가 영사기로 틀어드리겠습니다.

16.
담화는 어떤 제품에 초점을 맞추는가?
(A) 스포츠 음료
(B) 운동 용품 가방
(C) 카메라
(D) 자전거

[해설] 회의에서 다루고 있는 제품이 무엇인지 묻는 문제로, 담화 초반 회의 안건을 소개하는 부분에 단서가 있다. 자전거 이용자들을 위한 여행 및 운동 용품 가방(our travel and exercise gear bag for cyclists)에 대해 얘기하겠다고 했으므로 정답은 (B)이다.

17.
화자가 "더 작아야 합니다"라고 말할 때 암시하는 것은 무엇인가?
(A) 그들의 제품이 낮은 평가를 받았다.
(B) 판매원이 너무 많다.
(C) 생산을 줄여야 한다.
(D) 판매 목표를 달성하지 못했다.

[해설] 화자의 의도를 파악하는 문제로 해당 문장의 앞뒤 맥락을 잘 살펴야 한다. 앞서 고객들로부터 디자인에 대한 의견을 받았다고(I've received some feedback from our customers about its design.) 한 직후에 "더 작아야 합니다"라고 한 것으로 보아 고객들이 가방의 크기에 대해 불만을 제기했음을 짐작할 수 있다. 즉, 고객들이 제품에 대해 좋지 않은 평가를 한 것으로 보이므로 정답은 (A)이다.

[어휘] production 생산 decrease 줄이다, 감소시키다 goal 목표 meet 충족시키다

18.
청자들은 다음에 무엇을 할 것 같은가?
(A) 보고서 읽기
(B) 광고 보기
(C) 설문 조사 결과를 검토하기
(D) 색조 무늬에 대해 투표하기

[해설] 앞으로 일어날 일을 묻는 문제의 단서는 담화 후반에서 찾는다. 화자가 경쟁사들이 비슷한 유형의 제품을 어떻게 광고하는지 한번 보

자고(let's take a look at how some of our competitors are advertising their versions of similar products.) 한 후 영기로 틀겠다고 한 것으로 보아 담화 직후 청자들은 광고를 볼 것임을 알 수 있다. 정답은 (B)이다.

paraphrasing advertising 광고하다 → ad 광고

[어휘] ad 광고 vote on ~에 대해 투표하다

[19-21] AU

Questions 19-21 refer to the following telephone message.

M: Hi, this is Phil. ¹⁹I heard about the volunteer opportunity at the annual summer festival that will be held in Orange Park next month, and I'd like to sign up for it. I'm sure you know, but personnel reviews are coming up. ²⁰Usually the people selected to move up into supervisor positions participate in events like these. ²¹I'll send my application to HR right away. I just wanted to call you first to make sure that there are still openings.

volunteer 자원 봉사자; 자원 봉사를 하다 opportunity 기회
personnel (조직의) 인원, 직원들, 인사과 come up (행사나 때가) 다가오다 move up into ~로 승진하다 supervisor 감독관, 관리자 position 직위 participate in ~에 참가하다
application 신청(서), 지원(서) opening 빈자리, 공석

19-21은 다음 전화 메시지에 관한 문제입니다.

남: 안녕하세요, Phil이에요. ¹⁹다음 달 Orange 공원에서 열리는 연례 여름 축제의 자원 봉사 기회에 관해서 들었는데 신청하고 싶어요. 당신도 분명히 알겠지만 인사 평가가 다가와요. ²⁰보통은 관리자 직위로 승진을 위해 선발되는 사람들이 이런 행사에 참가해요. ²¹제가 즉시 신청서를 인사부로 보낼게요. 일단 당신에게 전화해서 아직 자리가 남아 있는지 확인하고 싶었어요.

19.

화자는 왜 청자에게 전화했는가?
(A) 회의 일정을 잡기 위해서
(B) 휴가를 신청하기 위해서
(C) 행사에서 자원 봉사를 하기 위해서
(D) 승진을 발표하기 위해서

[해설] 전화의 목적을 묻는 문제로, 메시지 초반에 단서가 있다. 다음 달에 열리는 연례 여름 축제의 자원 봉사 기회에 관해서 들었는데 신청하고 싶다고(I heard about the volunteer opportunity at the annual summer festival that will be held in Orange Park next month, and I'd like to sign up for it.) 했으므로 정답은 (C)이다.

[어휘] time off work 휴가 promotion 승진

20.

화자가 "인사 평가가 다가와요"라고 말할 때 암시하는 것은 무엇인가?
(A) 다른 부서로 옮기고 싶다.
(B) 겨우 몇 가지의 자원 봉사 기회만 제공된다.
(C) 날씨 때문에 행사가 실내로 옮겨질지도 모른다.
(D) 자신이 승진될 가능성을 높이고 싶다.

[해설] 화자는 "인사 평가가 다가와요"라고 한 뒤 관리자 직위로 승진을 위해 선발되는 사람들이 이런 행사에 참가한다며(Usually the people selected to move up into supervisor positions participate in events like these) 즉시 신청서를 인사부로 보내겠다고 했다. 즉, 이번 행사에서 자원 봉사를 함으로써 자신이 승진 대상자가 될 가능성을 높이고 싶다는 의미이므로 정답은 (D)이다.

[어휘] transfer to ~로 옮기다, 전근 가다 only a few 몇 안 되는, 근소한 indoors 실내에서, 실내로 due to ~ 때문에

21.

화자는 다음에 무엇을 할 것 같은가?
(A) 지역 공원을 방문하기
(B) 이력서를 업데이트하기
(C) 신청서를 제출하기
(D) 인사부의 누군가에게 연락하기

[해설] 화자가 담화 직후 할 일을 묻는 문제로, 메시지 후반부에서 단서를 찾는다. 앞서 여름 축제에서 자원봉사를 하고 싶다는 의사와 그 이유를 밝힌 후 즉시 신청서를 인사부로 보내겠다고(I'll send my application to HR right away.) 했으므로 정답은 (C)이다.

paraphrasing I'll send my application to HR 신청서를 인사부로 보내겠다 → submit an application 신청서를 제출하다

[22-24] BR

Questions 22-24 refer to the following telephone message.

M: Hello, ²²this is Brian calling from the building's security office. An employee badge was turned into our lost and found, and it belongs to one of your employees, Ms. Janice Brown. She won't be able to get in or out of the building without this, ²³so you should tell her to pick it up right away. ²⁴Normally we require ID to claim lost and found items, but this already has her name and picture. Thanks in advance.

security office 경비실, 보안과 employee badge 사원증
lost and found 분실물 취급소 belong to ~에 속하다, ~소유이다
normally 보통 때는 require 필요[요구]하다 claim (권리나 재산을) 요구[요청]하다 in advance 미리, 사전에

22-24는 다음 전화 메시지에 관한 문제입니다.

남: 여보세요, ²²저는 Brian이고요, 건물 보안실에서 전화 드립니다. 사원증 하나가 저희 분실물 취급소로 들어왔는데 당신의 직원인 Janice Brown 씨 것입니다. 이것 없이는 건물 출입이 불가능할 테니 ²³그녀에게 즉시 이것을 찾아가라고 말해주세요. ²⁴보통은 분실물을 찾으려면 저희가 신분증을 요구하지만 이것에 이미 그녀의 이름과 사진이 있네요. 미리 감사드립니다.

22.

화자는 어느 분야에서 근무하는가?
(A) 상품 개발
(B) 온라인 마케팅
(C) 인사
(D) 건물 보안

[해설] 화자의 직종을 묻는 문제로, 메시지 초반에 단서가 있다. 화자는 자신의 이름을 밝힌 후 건물 보안실에서 전화한다며(calling from the building's security office) 소속 부서를 밝혔다. 따라서 정답은 (D)이다.

[어휘] section 부분, 부문   development 개발   human resources 인사

23.
화자는 청자에게 무엇을 하라고 요청하는가?
(A) 신분증을 제시할 것
(B) 직원이 물품을 되찾아가게 할 것
(C) 오리엔테이션을 신청할 것
(D) 분실물 양식을 제출할 것

[해설] 메시지 중반에 화자의 요청 사항이 제시된다. 앞서 청자의 직원 중 한 사람의 신분증을 분실물 취급소에서 보관하고 있다고 밝힌 후, 그녀, 즉 신분증을 잃어버린 직원에게 즉시 신분증을 찾아가라고 얘기해달라고(you should tell her to pick it up right away) 했다. 따라서 정답은 (B)이다.

paraphrasing   pick up 찾아가다 → retrieve 되찾아가다

[어휘] present 제시[제출]하다   identification 신원 확인, 신분 증명   retrieve 되찾아오다   sign up for ~을 신청[가입]하다   submit 제출하다

24.
화자가 "이것에 이미 그녀의 이름과 사진이 있네요"라고 말할 때 의미하는 것은 무엇이겠는가?
(A) 새 정책이 시행될 것이다.
(B) 예외가 허용될 수 있다.
(C) 사진이 촬영되어야 한다.
(D) 카드가 만료되었다.

[해설] 화자는 보통은 분실물을 찾으려면 신분증을 요구하지만(Normally we require ID to claim lost and found items), "이것에 이미 그녀의 이름과 사진이 있습니다"라고 말했다. 즉, 신분증을 잃어버린 Janice Brown이 분실물 취급소에 신분증을 찾으러 올 때는 예외가 허용되어 별도의 신분 확인이 필요하지 않을 것임을 의미하므로 정답은 (B)이다.

[어휘] policy 정책, 방침   go into effect 발효하다, 실시되다   make an exception 예외를 허락하다   expire 만료되다, 만기가 되다

DAY 11

PART 2   우회적 응답 모음

확인 문제

❶ [US-AU]

Can you take these boxes up to my office room?
(A) An accounting department.
(B) On what floor is your office?

이 상자들을 제 사무실로 올려다 주실 수 있으세요?
(A) 회계 부서요.
(B) 당신의 사무실이 몇 층에 있나요?

❷ [BR-US]

Who's in charge of the project?
(A) I haven't been told.
(B) It's a new projector.

누가 그 프로젝트 책임자입니까?
(A) 저는 못 들었어요.
(B) 새 영사기예요.

❸ [BR-AU]

Is there a new version of this program?
(A) I'll get back to you on that.
(B) Yes, they are going to launch a new product.

이 프로그램의 새 버전이 있나요?
(A) 그것에 대해 나중에 알려드리겠습니다.
(B) 네, 그들은 신제품을 출시할 거예요.

❹ [AU-US]

Who will be promoted to replace Mr. Parker?
(A) I need some replacement parts.
(B) It hasn't been decided yet.

Parker 씨 후임자로 누가 승진될까요?
(A) 교체 부품이 필요합니다.
(B) 아직 결정된 바가 없습니다.

 연습 문제

01. (A)   02. (A)   03. (A)   04. (B)   05. (A)   06. (A)
07. (B)   08. (B)

01. [US-BR]

Which division will be sponsoring the annual banquet?
(A) That hasn't been announced yet. [○]
(B) It looks like a good plan. [×]

어느 부서가 연례 연회를 후원할 건가요?
(A) 그건 아직 발표되지 않았습니다.
(B) 좋은 계획인 것 같습니다.

02. [US-AU]

Which applicant did the research department hire?
(A) I heard the final interviews are left. [○]
(B) His presentation was impressive. [×]

연구 부서가 어떤 지원자를 채용했나요?
(A) 최종 면접이 남았다고 들었어요.
(B) 그의 발표는 인상 깊었어요.

03. [BR-US]

Why isn't my last payment showing up on my statement?

(A) I'll find out and call you back. [O]
(B) From the accounting department. [X]

왜 저의 지난번 납입 금액이 내역서에서 보이지 않는 거죠?
(A) 제가 알아보고 다시 연락드리겠습니다.
(B) 회계 부서에서요.

04. BR-BR

Has the date been set for the company outing?
(A) No, we don't need new outfit. [X]
(B) Jason might know. [O]

회사 야유회의 날짜가 잡혔나요?
(A) 아니요, 우리는 새 옷이 필요 없습니다.
(B) Jason이 알 거예요.

05. US-AU

Where do you plan to go for the holidays?
(A) There are so many places I want to go. [O]
(B) Yes, that's the plan. [X]

휴가로 어디에 갈 계획이세요?
(A) 가고 싶은 곳이 너무 많아요.
(B) 네, 그것이 계획입니다.

06. BR-US

How much more do I need to pay to upgrade my rental car?
(A) It depends on which car you want. [O]
(B) There are still plenty of software updates available. [X]

제 렌터카의 등급을 올리려면 돈을 얼마나 더 내야 하나요?
(A) 어떤 차를 원하시는지에 따라 달라요.
(B) 아직 이용할 수 있는 소프트웨어 업데이트가 많아요.

07. US-US

I have no idea where to go for the security training.
(A) It's very fragile. [X]
(B) Check with Mr. Roy. [O]

보안 교육을 위해 어디로 가야 하는지 모르겠어요.
(A) 그건 깨지기 쉬워요.
(B) Roy 씨에게 확인해 보세요.

08. AU-US

Why has the workshop been canceled?
(A) They will arrive on Tuesday. [X]
(B) You haven't read your e-mail, have you? [O]

왜 워크숍이 취소되었나요?
(A) 그들은 화요일에 도착할 거예요.
(B) 당신 이메일을 안 읽으셨죠, 그렇죠?

실전 문제

01. (B)	02. (A)	03. (B)	04. (B)	05. (A)	06. (C)
07. (A)	08. (A)	09. (B)	10. (C)	11. (A)	12. (C)
13. (A)	14. (C)	15. (B)	16. (B)		

01. AU-US

Jennifer, what are you still doing at the office?
(A) Okay, I can come in early.
(B) Why, what's the time?
(C) Sorry, I totally forgot.

totally 완전히, 전적으로

Jennifer, 아직 사무실에서 뭐하고 있는 거예요?
(A) 알겠어요, 저는 일찍 나올 수 있어요.
(B) 왜요, 몇 신데요?
(C) 미안해요, 완전히 잊어버렸어요.

[해설] 왜 이렇게 늦게까지 사무실에 남아 있는지 궁금하다는 뉘앙스의 질문이다.
(A) Okay는 수락/동의를 나타내는 표현이므로 의문사 의문문에 대한 응답으로는 어색하다.
(B) 왜 그러냐고 되물으며 지금이 몇 시인지 질문함으로써 시간이 늦은 줄 몰랐다는 것을 우회적으로 드러내고 있으므로 정답이다.
(C) 미안하다고 응답할 만한 내용이 질문에서 언급되지 않았으므로 어색하다.

02. US-US

I want you to cover the upcoming soccer tournament.
(A) Sorry, but I'm working on another story.
(B) Some items are covered with a white cloth.
(C) Two VIP tickets.

cover 다루다, 포함시키다   be covered with ~로 덮이다

당신이 다가오는 축구 토너먼트를 다뤘으면 좋겠어요.
(A) 죄송하지만 저는 다른 이야기를 작업 중이에요.
(B) 몇몇 물품들은 흰 천으로 덮여 있어요.
(C) VIP 티켓 두 장이요.

[해설] 다가오는 축구 토너먼트에 대해 다뤄 달라고 요청하는 평서문이다.
(A) 다가오는 축구 토너먼트에 대해 다뤄 달라는 말에 미안하다는 사과로 우회적으로 거절 의사를 밝힌 후 거절의 이유를 덧붙이고 있는 정답이다.
(B) 질문의 cover(다루다)와 다른 의미로 쓰인 be covered with(덮여 있다)를 이용하여 혼동을 유도하는 오답이다.
(C) 질문의 soccer tournament에서 연상할 수 있는 ticket을 이용해 혼동을 유도하는 오답이다.

03. BR-AU

How often does Ms. Kim change her mobile phone?
(A) A two-year contract.
(B) Did she get a new one?
(C) I have an extra battery in my locker.

Kim 씨는 얼마나 자주 휴대폰을 바꾸나요?

(A) 2년짜리 계약입니다.
(B) 그녀가 새것을 샀나요?
(C) 제 사물함에 여분의 배터리가 있습니다.

[해설] Kim 씨가 얼마나 자주 휴대폰을 바꾸는지 빈도를 묻는 How often 의문문이다.
(A) 기간을 묻는 How long 의문문에 적합한 응답이므로 오답이다.
(B) Kim 씨가 얼마나 자주 휴대폰을 바꾸는지 묻는 질문에 그녀가 새 휴대폰을 사기라도 했냐고 되물음으로써 우회적으로 질문의 의도를 다시 확인하고 있으므로 정답이다.
(C) 질문의 mobile phone에서 연상 가능한 battery를 이용하여 혼동을 유도하는 오답이다.

04. US-US

Did you hear which room we have to go to for the reception?
(A) Here is the original receipt.
(B) It hasn't been announced yet.
(C) The train schedule is posted online.

receipt 영수증

우리가 환영회를 위해 어떤 방으로 가야 하는지 들었나요?
(A) 여기 원본 영수증이 있습니다.
(B) 아직 발표되지 않았어요.
(C) 열차 시간표는 온라인에 게시되어 있어요.

[해설] 환영회를 위해 어떤 방으로 가야 하는지 묻는 의문사 which를 포함한 간접 의문문이다.
(A) 질문의 reception과 발음이 유사한 receipt를 이용해 혼동을 유도하는 오답이다.
(B) 환영회를 위해 어떤 방으로 가야 하는지 들었냐고 묻는 질문에 아직 발표되지 않았다고 답함으로써 부정의 No를 대신하고 있으므로 정답이다.
(C) 열차가 출발하는 시간을 묻는 질문에 대한 우회적 응답으로 가능한 답변이므로 오답이다.

05. BR-US

You have receipts for everything, don't you?
(A) Can't I just show the electronic statement?
(B) He would like to make some returns.
(C) I want to receive it by express mail.

statement 명세표, 입출금 내역서   make a return 반납하다
by express mail 빠른 우편으로

모든 것에 대해 영수증을 가지고 계시죠, 그렇죠?
(A) 그냥 전자 명세표를 보여드리면 안 될까요?
(B) 그는 몇 가지를 반납하고 싶어 합니다.
(C) 저는 그것을 빠른 우편으로 받고 싶어요.

[해설] 영수증을 가지고 있는지 확인하는 부가 의문문이다.
(A) 영수증을 가지고 있는지 묻는 질문에 그냥 전자 명세표를 제시하면 안 되는지 되물음으로써 영수증을 가지고 있지 않다고 우회적으로 말하고 있는 정답이다.
(B) 보통 반품(returns)이나 환불을 할 때 영수증(receipt) 제시하도록 요구받는 점을 이용한 오답으로, 질문에서 대명사 he로 지칭할 만한 특정

인물이 언급되지 않았다.
(C) 질문의 receipt와 발음이 유사한 receive를 이용해 혼동을 유도하는 오답이다.

06. US-BR

The travel reimbursements will be included in this paycheck, right?
(A) I'm not sure which form you need.
(B) A business trip.
(C) I don't think so.

reimbursement 변제, 상환   include 포함시키다   paycheck 급료, 봉급   form 서식, 양식   business trip 출장

출장 경비 환급은 이번 급여에 포함되겠지요, 맞죠?
(A) 당신이 어떤 서식을 필요로 하는지 잘 모르겠어요.
(B) 출장입니다.
(C) 그럴 것 같지 않아요.

[해설] 출장 경비 환급이 이번 급여에 포함되는지 확인하는 부가 의문문이다.
(A) 출장 경비 환급(travel reimbursements)을 요청할 때 관련 양식(form)을 작성하는 상황을 연상하도록 유도하는 오답이다.
(B) 질문의 travel에서 연상 가능한 trip을 이용하여 혼동을 유도하는 오답이다.
(C) 출장 경비 환급이 이번 급여에 포함되는지 묻는 질문에 그럴 것 같지 않다고 상대방의 의견에 부정하는 정답이다.

07. BR-US

What restaurant should I bring the new clients to for lunch?
(A) I forgot its exact name, but I have a business card.
(B) These are our daily specials.
(C) No thanks, I already ate.

점심식사를 위해 새 고객들을 어떤 식당으로 모셔야 할까요?
(A) 제가 그것의 정확한 이름은 잊어버렸지만, 명함을 가지고 있어요.
(B) 이것들은 저희의 오늘의 특별 요리입니다.
(C) 괜찮습니다. 이미 먹었습니다.

[해설] 점심식사를 위해 새 고객들을 어떤 식당으로 데리고 가야 할지 상대방의 의견을 묻는 What 의문문이다.
(A) 점심식사 때 고객들을 어떤 식당으로 데리고 가야 할지 묻는 질문에 식당의 이름은 잊어버렸지만 명함을 가지고 있다고 답함으로써 괜찮은 식당을 알고 있음을 우회적으로 드러내고 있으므로 정답이다.
(B) 질문의 restaurant에서 연상 가능한 daily specials를 이용해 혼동을 유도하는 오답이다.
(C) 질문의 restaurant와 lunch에서 연상 가능한 동사 ate를 이용한 오답으로, 음식을 권하거나 무엇을 먹겠냐고 묻는 질문에 어울리는 응답이다.

08. US-AU

Should I rent a car when I go to Sydney?
(A) I don't know your driver's license is valid there.
(B) It's a beautiful city.
(C) You should use this app to find parking.

valid 유효한, 타당한

제가 시드니에 가면 차를 빌려야 할까요?
(A) 당신의 운전면허증이 그곳에서도 유효한지 모르겠어요.
(B) 그곳은 아름다운 도시예요.
(C) 주차장을 찾으려면 이 앱을 사용하세요.

[해설] 시드니에 가면 차를 빌려야 하는지 상대방의 의견을 묻는 조동사 의문이다.
(A) 시드니에 가면 차를 빌려야 하는지 묻는 질문에 시드니에서 상대방의 운전면허증이 유효한지 모르겠다고 답변하는 '나도 모른다' 류의 응답이므로 정답이다.
(B) 질문의 Sydney에서 연상 가능한 city를 이용해 혼동을 유도하는 오답이다.
(C) 질문의 car에서 연상 가능한 parking을 이용해 혼동을 유도하는 오답이다.

09. US-BR

We have collected enough data from the survey, right?
(A) It will take a few minutes to complete it.
(B) You'd better ask Jimmy.
(C) We have a wide collection of cheese and butter.

collect 모으다, 수집하다   complete 완성하다, 작성하다

우리는 그 조사에서 충분한 자료를 모았어요, 맞지요?
(A) 완료하는 데 몇 분 정도 걸릴 거예요.
(B) Jimmy에게 물어보는 게 좋겠어요.
(C) 우리는 다양한 치즈와 버터를 보유하고 있습니다.

[해설] 충분한 자료를 모았는지 확인하는 부가 의문문이다.
(A) 소요 기간으로 답했으므로 How long 의문문에 어울리는 답변이다.
(B) Jimmy에게 물어보라고 답변하는 것은 나는 잘 모르니 다른 사람인 Jimmy에게 물어보라는 의미의 응답이므로 정답이다.
(C) 질문의 collected와 발음이 비슷한 collection을 사용하여 혼동을 유도한 오답이다.

10. AU-US

There are still available seats, aren't there?
(A) That was a comfortable seat.
(B) Thanks, in the front, please.
(C) Let me check it for you.

아직 좌석이 남아 있지요, 그렇지 않나요?
(A) 그 좌석은 편안했어요.
(B) 고맙습니다. 앞쪽으로 주세요.
(C) 제가 확인해드릴게요.

[해설] 아직 좌석이 남아 있는지 확인하는 부가 의문문이다.
(A) 질문의 seat를 반복 사용하여 혼동을 유도하는 오답이다.
(B) 질문의 seat에서 '앞 열의 좌석'을 연상하도록 유도하는 front를 이용한 오답이다.
(C) 아직 좌석이 남아 있는지 묻는 질문에 확인해주겠다고 답변하는 것은 '나도 모른다'고 우회적으로 말하는 것이므로 정답이다.

11. BR-BR

Has the new merchandise arrived at the store?
(A) Why don't you check with George?
(B) On a weekly basis.
(C) Thanks, I appreciate your help.

merchandise 상품, 물품   on a weekly basis 매주, 주 단위로

새 상품들이 매장에 도착했나요?
(A) George에게 확인해 보는 게 어때요?
(B) 주 단위로요.
(C) 고마워요, 도와주셔서 감사해요.

[해설] 새 상품이 매장에 도착했는지 묻는 조동사 의문문이다.
(A) 새 상품이 매장에 도착했는지 묻는 질문에 George에게 확인해 보라고 답변하는 것은 '자신은 모르니 George한테 물어보라'는 의미의 응답이므로 정답이다.
(B) 질문의 내용과 무관한 응답으로, 빈도를 묻는 How often 의문문에 어울린다.
(C) 질문에서 상대방이 감사 인사를 할 만한 내용이 언급되지 않았으므로 어색한 응답이다.

12. AU-US

You sent the package to our clients, right?
(A) Several delivery options.
(B) We're running low on packing material.
(C) Didn't they get it by now?

run low on ~이 모자라게 되다, 떨어져 가다   packing material 포장 재료

우리 고객들에게 소포를 보내셨죠, 맞죠?
(A) 몇몇 배달 옵션이요.
(B) 포장 재료가 떨어져 가요.
(C) 그들이 지금까지 받지 못했나요?

[해설] 고객들에게 소포를 보냈는지 확인하는 부가 의문문이다.
(A) 질문의 sent the package에서 연상 가능한 delivery를 이용해 혼동을 유도하는 오답이다.
(B) 질문의 package에서 연상되는 packing material을 이용해 혼동을 유도하는 오답이다.
(C) 고객들에게 소포를 보냈는지 묻는 질문에 고객들이 지금까지 받지 못했냐고 되물음으로써 자신이 이미 소포를 보냈다고 우회적으로 말하고 있는 정답이다.

13. US-AU

Where will Mr. Smith's retirement dinner be held?
(A) We are still deciding.
(B) After 30 years with the company.
(C) Yes, I plan on attending.

Smith 씨의 은퇴 기념식이 어디서 열리나요?
(A) 우리가 아직 결정하는 중이에요.
(B) 이 회사에서 근무한 지 30년 만에요.
(C) 네, 저는 참석할 계획이에요.

[해설] Smith 씨의 은퇴 기념식이 열리는 장소를 묻는 Where 의문문이다.
(A) Smith 씨의 은퇴 기념식이 어디에서 열리는지 묻는 질문에 아직 결정하는 중이라고 말한 우회/회피성 응답이므로 정답이다.
(B) 은퇴 기념식 장소를 묻는 질문에 근무 기간으로 답했으므로 오답이다.
(C) 의문사 의문문에는 Yes/No로 응답하지 않으므로 오답이다.

14. [BR-US]

Who's in charge of the next ad campaign?
(A) I'll show it to you.
(B) On TV and radio.
(C) It hasn't been decided yet.

in charge of ~을 맡아서, 담당해서 ad 광고(= advertisement)

누가 다음 광고 캠페인을 담당합니까?
(A) 제가 그것을 보여줄게요.
(B) TV와 라디오에서요.
(C) 아직 결정되지 않았습니다.

[해설] 누가 다음 광고 캠페인을 담당하는지 묻는 Who 의문문이다.
(A) 질문의 핵심은 다음 광고를 담당할 '사람'인데, 사람을 대명사 it으로 지칭할 수 없으므로 오답이다.
(B) 질문의 ad에서 TV와 라디오 광고를 연상하도록 유도하는 오답이다.
(C) 누가 다음 광고 캠페인을 담당하는지 묻는 질문에 아직 결정되지 않았다고 답변함으로써 '나도 모른다'는 의미를 우회적으로 전달하고 있으므로 정답이다.

15. [US-BR]

Have you seen next month's schedule yet?
(A) Several new staff members.
(B) Has it been released already?
(C) On Mondays and Fridays.

staff member 직원 release 공개하다, 발표하다

다음 달 일정표를 보셨나요?
(A) 몇몇 새 직원들이요.
(B) 벌써 발표가 되었나요?
(C) 월요일과 금요일마다요.

[해설] 다음 달 일정을 보았는지 확인하는 조동사 의문문이다.
(A) 질문의 next month's schedule의 영향을 받을 만한 대상인 staff members를 이용해 혼동을 유도하는 오답으로, Who 의문문에 적합하다.
(B) 다음 달 일정을 보았는지 묻는 질문에 벌써 발표가 되었냐고 되물음으로써 아직 보지 못했다고 우회적으로 말하고 있으므로 정답이다.
(C) 질문의 schedule에서 연상되는 시간과 관련된 표현인 Mondays와 Fridays를 이용하여 혼동을 유도하는 오답으로 When 또는 How often 의문문에 적합한 응답이다.

16. [BR-BR]

I can't seem to find your expense report from the trip.
(A) Yes, it was quite expensive.
(B) Sorry, but I didn't submit it yet.
(C) I plan on spending a week there.

expense report 비용 보고서

당신의 여행 경비 보고서를 못 찾겠어요.
(A) 네, 그것은 꽤 비쌌어요.
(B) 미안하지만, 제가 아직 제출하지 않았어요.
(C) 그곳에서 일주일을 보낼 계획이에요.

[해설] 상대방의 여행 경비 보고서를 못 찾겠다는 내용의 평서문이다.

(A) 질문의 expense와 발음이 유사한 expensive를 이용해 혼동을 유도하는 오답이다.
(B) 상대방의 여행 경비 보고서를 못 찾겠다는 말에 미안하다고 한 후 자신이 제출하지 않았다고 말함으로써 보고서가 없는 이유를 덧붙이고 있으므로 정답이다.
(C) 질문의 expense에서 연상 가능한 spending을 이용해 혼동을 유도하는 오답이다.

PART 4 시각 자료 연계 문제

연습 문제

01. (B) 02. (B) 03. (B) 04. (A)

01. [BR]

Look at the **graphic**. **Which item** does the speaker want to **increase**?
(A) **Sandwiches** **(B) Orange Juice**

W: Hi, I'm Linda from Danny's Law Firm. I'm calling about the catering order our company placed yesterday. One of our staff members made a mistake. I think we have to order more beverages. Also, we need a dozen hamburgers. If you have any questions, please call me anytime.

시각 자료를 보시오. 화자는 어떤 품목을 늘리고 싶어 하는가?
(A) 샌드위치 **(B) 오렌지 주스**

전화 메시지와 양식

주문번호 # 8910	
이름: Danny's 법률 사무소	
품목	수량
샌드위치	30
오렌지 주스	50

여: 안녕하세요, 저는 Danny's 법률 사무소의 Linda입니다. 저희 회사가 어제 주문한 출장 음식 관련해서 전화드렸습니다. 저희 직원들 중 한 명이 실수를 했어요. 저희가 음료 주문을 더 해야 할 것 같습니다. 또한, 햄버거 12개도 필요합니다. 질문이 있으시면, 제게 언제든 전화해 주세요.

02. [BR]

Look at the **graphic**. In **which quarter** was the **new product** most likely **released**?
(A) **2nd** quarter **(B) 3rd** quarter

M: Thank you for attending the weekly meeting. I want to begin with good news. Our new product, the Big wave Bluetooth headset, has had favorable responses from customers as well as industry critics. As in the report, our sales doubled in the quarter when it was released. Give Mr. Timber and his team a round of applause and congratulate them on their accomplishment.

favorable 좋은, 호의적인

시각 자료를 보시오. 어떤 분기에 신제품이 출시되었겠는가?
(A) 2분기 **(B) 3분기**

담화와 그래프

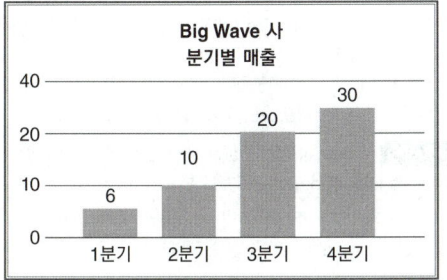

남: 주간 회의에 참석해주셔서 감사합니다. 좋은 소식으로 시작하고 싶습니다. 우리의 신제품인 Big Wave 블루투스 헤드셋이 업계 비평가들뿐만 아니라 고객들에게도 좋은 반응을 얻었습니다. 보고서에서 보이는 것처럼, 우리 매출이 그것이 출시되던 분기에 두 배가 되었어요. Timber 씨와 그의 팀에게 그들의 성취에 대해 큰 박수를 보내고 축하를 해주시기 바랍니다.

03. US

Look at the **graphic**. **Which item** in the monthly report **requires** additional **documentation**?
(A) **Transportation**   (B) **Lunch & Dinner**

W: Hello. Mr. Butler. This is Sandra Peterson from accounting. I'm returning your call. I received your monthly expense report for October. While reviewing it, I noticed that you did not attach receipts for the expense of $450. Please make sure that you provide itemized tables and attach all receipts for them. Otherwise we will be unable to reimburse you.

expense 비용   reimburse 상환하다

시각 자료를 보시오. 월간 보고서의 어떤 항목이 추가 서류를 필요로 하는가?
(A) 교통 **(B) 점심식사와 저녁식사**

전화 메시지와 보고서

	이름: Gary Butler
항목	비용
교통	400달러(4일)
숙박	899.19달러
점심식사와 저녁식사	450.00달러
전화	99.89달러

여: 안녕하세요, Butler 씨. 저는 회계팀의 Sandra Peterson입니다. 당신의 전화에 대해 회신합니다. 당신의 10월 비용 보고서를 받았어요. 검토하다가, 450달러에 대한 영수증을 첨부하지 않은 것을 발견했습니다. 항목화된 표와 모든 영수증을 첨부하셔야 합니다. 그렇지 않으면 상환을 해 드릴 수 없을 것입니다.

04. AU
Look at the **graphic**. **What gate** is **not available** during the construction period?
(A) **East** Gate   (B) **West** Gate

M: Yesterday the City Council announced the repair of 3rd Street, between Benjamin Avenue and Oakland Avenue. This 4-month construction will begin at the beginning of next month, July 1st, and will cost approximately 2 million dollars. So, during this period, be assured that you are not able to access Central park through the parking entrance facing the construction area.

시각 자료를 보시오. 공사 기간 동안 어떤 출입구를 이용할 수 없는가?
(A) 동쪽 출입구 (B) 서쪽 출입구

방송과 지도

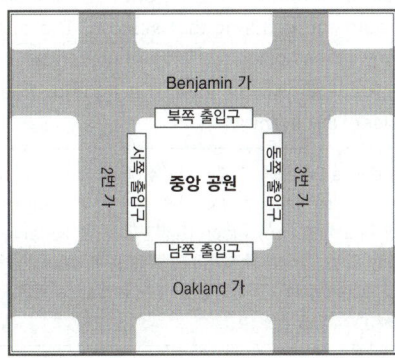

남: 어제 시 의회는 Benjamin 가와 Oakland 가 사이에 있는 3번 가의 수리를 알렸습니다. 이 네 달 간의 공사는 다음 달 초인 7월 1일에 시작할 것이고 거의 200만 달러가 들 것입니다. 그러므로 이 기간 동안, 공사 지역을 마주하고 있는 주차장 출입구를 통해 Central 공원에 들어가실 수 없다는 것을 알아두시기 바랍니다.

| paraphrasing 정답 | 1. (b) | 2. (c) | 3. (a) | 4. (c) | 5. (a) | 6. (b) |

실전 문제

01. (B)	02. (B)	03. (D)	04. (C)	05. (D)	06. (B)
07. (A)	08. (D)	09. (B)	10. (B)	11. (A)	12. (B)
13. (D)	14. (D)	15. (C)	16. (B)	17. (A)	18. (B)
19. (A)	20. (D)	21. (C)	22. (B)	23. (C)	24. (C)

[01-03] BR
Questions 01-03 refer to the following news report and event schedule.

Main Stage Events	
9 A.M. – 10 A.M.	Opening Ceremony
02 10 A.M. – Noon	**Cooking Contest**
1 P.M. – 3 P.M.	Dance Performance
7 P.M. – 9 P.M.	Televised Concert

M: You're listening to the local news report on KRT Radio. The big event this weekend is the annual Independence Day Festival. You don't need a ticket to attend this event. However, since it is taking place at Collins Park, **01 you're going to want to get there very early. There aren't many places to park.** Event planners are excited to announce that **02 famous French chef Sebastian Leclair will be one of the judges for this year's cooking competition.** Fans will be able to get autographs during that session. The opening ceremony will be hosted by **03 Miguel Alexander, owner of the local shopping mall** and a major financial supporter of this event.

Independence Day 독립 기념일 take place 개최되다, 일어나다 chef 요리사 judge 판사, 심판, 심사위원 competition 경쟁, 경연대회, 시합 autograph (유명인의) 사인 opening ceremony 개막식 host 주최하다, 진행하다 financial 금융 [재정]의 supporter 지지자, 후원자 performance 공연 televised TV로 방송되는

01-03은 다음 뉴스 보도와 행사 일정표에 관한 문제입니다.

본 무대 행사	
오전 9시 – 10시	개막식
02 오전 10시 – 정오	요리 경연대회
오후 1시 – 3시	댄스 공연
오후 7시 – 9시	TV 방송용 콘서트

남: 여러분은 KRT 라디오의 지역 뉴스 보도를 듣고 계십니다. 이번 주말에 있을 큰 행사는 연례 독립기념일 축제입니다. 이 행사에 참가하기 위해 티켓이 필요하지는 않습니다. 하지만 행사가 Collins Park에서 열릴 예정이므로 **01 여러분은 아주 일찍 도착하셔야 할 겁니다. 주차할 곳이 많지 않거든요.** 행사 기획자들이 신나서 전하는 바에 의하면, **02 유명한 프랑스 셰프 Sebastian Leclair가 올해의 요리 경연대회의 심사위원 중 한 명이 될 거라고 합니다.** 팬들은 그 시간 동안 사인을 받을 수 있을 것입니다.

개막식은 **03 지역 쇼핑몰의 소유주이자 이번 행사의 주요 재정 후원자인 Miguel Alexander** 씨가 진행할 예정입니다.

01.

화자는 청자들에게 무엇에 대하여 경고하는가?
(A) 티켓 부족
(B) 주차장 부족
(C) 나쁠 수도 있는 날씨
(D) 마지막 순간의 변경

[해설] 행사 장소가 Collins Park라고 언급한 다음 청자들이 아주 일찍 도착하고 싶을 거라며 그 이유로 주차할 곳이 많지 않다고(There aren't many places to park.) 덧붙인다. 이는 주차 공간이 부족하니 행사 장소에 일찍 도착하라고 주의를 주는 것이므로 정답은 (B)이다.

paraphrasing There aren't many places to park. 주차할 곳이 많지 않다. → a lack of parking 주차장 부족

[어휘] warn 경고하다, 주의를 주다 shortage 부족 a lack of ~의 부족, 결핍 last-minute 마지막 순간의, 막바지의

02.

시각 자료를 보시오. 축제 참석자들은 언제 프랑스에서 온 스타를 볼 수 있는가?
(A) 오전 9시 – 10시
(B) 오전 10시 – 정오
(C) 오후 1시 – 3시
(D) 오후 7시 – 9시

[해설] 먼저 질문의 a star from France는 뉴스 보도에서 언급한 유명한 프랑스 셰프(famous French chef) Sebastian Leclair를 가리킨다. 뉴스 보도 중반부에 유명한 프랑스 셰프 Sebastian Leclair가 올해의 요리 경연대회의 심사위원(one of the judges for this year's cooking competition)이 될 것이라고 했으므로 시각 자료에서 요리 경연대회가 열리는 시간을 확인하면 오전 10시에서 정오까지다. 따라서 축제 참석자들이 프랑스에서 온 스타, 즉 유명한 프랑스 셰프를 만날 수 있는 시간은 오전 10시부터 정오 사이이므로 정답은 (B)이다.

paraphrasing famous French chef 유명한 프랑스 셰프 → a star from France 프랑스에서 온 스타 / competition 경연대회 → contest 경연대회

03.

Miguel Alexander는 누구인가?
(A) 행사 기획자
(B) 시 공무원
(C) 프로 가수
(D) 지역 사업가

[해설] 질문의 키워드 Miguel Alexander는 뉴스 보도 마지막 부분에 언급되는데, 이번 행사의 개막식을 진행하는 사람의 이름으로, 지역 쇼핑몰의 소유주(owner of the local shopping mall)이자 이번 행사의 주요 재정 후원자로 소개되고 있다. 즉, Miguel Alexander는 지역의 사업가임을 알 수 있으므로 정답은 (D)이다.

paraphrasing owner of the local shopping mall 지역 쇼핑몰의 소유주 → a local businessperson 지역 사업가

[어휘] official 공무원, 관리 professional 전문적인 businessperson 사업가

[04-06] US

Questions 04-06 refer to the following telephone message and map.

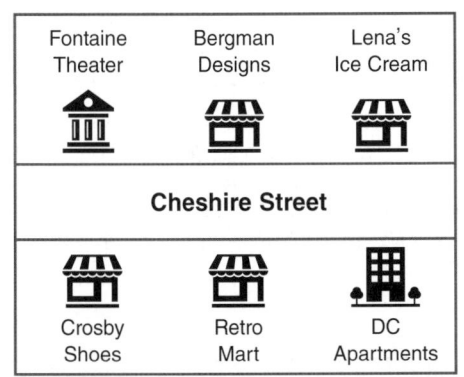

M: Hello. ⁰⁴**This is Jeffrey Duncan calling from Hampton Bank. I'm looking over your application for a business loan** for your donut shop. ⁰⁵**You indicated that you will be relocating to Cheshire Street, right across from Bergman Designs.** This is an excellent location, because it is a lively neighborhood. And because there are many events at Fontaine Theater, you'll have a steady supply of customers. The only thing I'm worried about is that you wrote on your application that ⁰⁶**you'll be closed for four months** to do some redecorating at the new site. ⁰⁶**I'm worried that might be too long.** Please call me back so we can discuss this further. I'm at 555-7810. Thanks.

look over 훑어보다, 살펴보다 application 신청(서) business loan 기업 대출(금) indicate (글로) 명시하다 relocate 이전 [이동]하다 neighborhood 근처, 인근, 이웃 steady 꾸준한 supply 공급 redecorate 실내 장식을 새로 하다 site (건물이 들어설) 위치, 장소, 현장, 부지

04-06은 다음 전화 메시지와 지도에 관한 문제입니다.

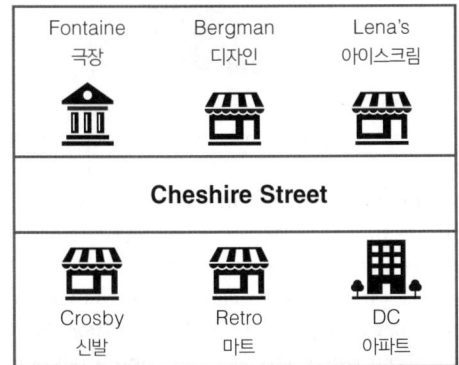

남: 여보세요. ⁰⁴저는 Hampton 은행의 Jeffrey Duncan입니다. 당신의 도넛 가게를 위한 ⁰⁴사업자 대출 신청서를 검토하고 있는 중입니다. ⁰⁵Cheshire 가의 Bergman 디자인 바로 맞은편으로 이전할 예정이라고 명시하셨습니다. 그곳은 활기찬 동네이기 때문에 아주 좋은 위치예요. 그리고 Fontaine 극장에서 많은 행사가 열리기 때문에 고객들이 꾸준히 유입될 겁니다. 제가 우려하는 단 하나는 새로운 장소에 내부 장식을 새로 하기 위해 ⁰⁶4개월간 문을 닫을 예정이라고 신청서에 기입하신 점입니다. ⁰⁶그건 너무 긴 기간인 것 같아 걱정스럽습니다. 이 문제에 대해 더 상의할 수 있도록 제게 다시 전화 주세요. 제 번호는 555-7810입니다. 감사합니다.

04.

누가 청자에게 전화하는 것 같은가?
(A) 부동산 중개인
(B) 건설 노동자
(C) 대출 담당 직원
(D) 의류 디자이너

[해설] 화자의 직업을 묻는 문제다. 메시지 초반에 화자는 자신의 소속을 Hampton Bank라고 밝혔으며, 이어서 청자, 즉 메시지 수신인이 제출한 사업자 대출 신청서를 검토하고 있다고(I'm looking over your application for a business loan) 언급했다. 따라서 화자는 은행에서 대출 업무를 담당하고 있음을 알 수 있으므로 정답은 (C)이다.

[어휘] real estate 부동산 construction 건설, 공사 loan officer 대출 담당 직원

05.

시각 자료를 보시오. 청자가 이용하게 될 위치는 어느 곳인가?
(A) Fontaine 극장
(B) Bergman 디자인
(C) Crosby 신발
(D) Retro 마트

[해설] 청자가 도넛 가게를 이전할 예정이라는 내용이 언급되었으므로 문제에서 말한 '청자가 이용하게 될 장소'는 결국 청자가 새 도넛 가게를 열 위치를 가리킨다. 담화에서 Cheshire Street의 Bergman Designs 바로 맞은편이라고(right across from Bergman Designs) 했으므로 지도에서 이 위치를 찾으면 Retro Mart임을 알 수 있다. 따라서 정답은 (D)이다.

06.

화자는 무엇에 대해 우려하는가?
(A) 건물의 크기
(B) 폐점 기간
(C) 고객의 수
(D) 수리 비용

[해설] 질문의 키워드 concerned가 담화에서는 worried로 표현되었다. 담화 중반에 화자가 우려하는 바가 구체적으로 언급되는데, 청자가 내부 장식 때문에 새로운 매장을 4개월 동안 문을 닫을 예정이라고(you'll be closed for four months) 한 점을 지적하면서 기간이 너무 길어 걱정스럽다고(I'm worried that might be too long) 했다. 즉, 화자는 상점이 문을 닫는 기간에 대해 우려하고 있으므로 정답은 (B)이다.

[어휘] be concerned about ~에 대해 우려하다 length 길이 closure 폐점

[07-09] US

Questions 07-09 refer to the following announcement and weather report.

5-Day Forecast: Chance of Snow				
WED	THURS	FRI	SAT	⁰⁸Sun
50%	70%	40%	30%	10%

W: All right, everyone, ⁰⁷**I hope you enjoyed the tourist sites we visited yesterday, and there's more to see today.** We'll wait here in the lobby for our bus to arrive. Our first stop will be the Toledo Aquarium, which has the area's largest collection of marine species. After that, we'll go to the famous Township Market. The market closes ⁰⁸**in case of snow, but there's only a ten percent chance of that happening today,** so we should be fine. After that, we'll come back to the hotel, and you'll have free time for the rest of the day. ⁰⁹**There's a dance show** at the Ritter Theater tonight at 7, right across the street. ⁰⁹**I suggest checking that out.**

collection 수집품, 소장품   in case of ~의 경우   chance 확률
rest of the day 하루의 나머지 시간

07-09는 다음 안내 방송과 일기예보에 관한 문제입니다.

5일간 일기예보: 눈이 올 확률				
수요일	목요일	금요일	토요일	⁰⁸일요일
50%	70%	40%	30%	10%

여: 자, 여러분, ⁰⁷어제 우리가 방문했던 관광지에서 즐거운 시간 보내셨기를 바랍니다. 오늘은 볼 것들이 더 많답니다. 이곳 로비에서 버스가 도착하는 것을 기다리겠습니다. 우리가 첫 번째로 들를 곳은 Toledo Aquarium인데요, 이곳은 이 지역에서 해양 생물들을 가장 많이 보유하고 있습니다. 그 후에, 그 유명한 Township Market으로 이동하겠습니다. 이 시장은 ⁰⁸눈이 올 경우 폐장하지만 오늘 그러한 일이 발생할 확률은 겨우 **10퍼센트이니** 우리는 괜찮을 거예요. 그 후에는 호텔로 돌아와서 남은 하루 동안 자유 시간을 가지겠습니다. 오늘 밤 7시에 길 바로 건너편 Ritter Theater에서 ⁰⁹댄스 공연이 있습니다. 그것을 확인해 보시길 권합니다.

07.

청자들은 누구일 것 같은가?
(A) 여행 참가자들
(B) 연극 평론가들
(C) 신입사원들
(D) 버스 기사들

[해설] 화자가 어제 우리가 방문했던 관광지에서 즐거운 시간 보냈기를 바라며, 오늘은 볼 것들이 더 많다(I hope you enjoyed the tourist sites we visited yesterday, and there's more to see today.) 말로 담화를 시작한 후 이어서 추후 일정들을 소개하는 것으로 보아 화자는 여행 가이드이고 청자들은 여행 프로그램의 참가자임을 알 수 있으므로 정답은 (A)이다.

08.

시각 자료를 보시오. 화자는 무슨 요일에 공지를 하고 있는가?
(A) 수요일
(B) 목요일
(C) 금요일
(D) 일요일

[해설] 오늘 일정 중 Township Market 방문이 포함되어 있는데, 이곳은 눈이 올 경우 폐장하지만 오늘 그러한 일이 발생할 확률은 겨우 10퍼센트라는(in case of snow, but there's only a ten percent chance of that happening today) 말은 오늘 눈이 올 확률이 10퍼센트라는 뜻이다. 시각 자료에서 이에 해당하는 요일을 찾으면 일요일이므로 정답은 (D)이다.

09.

화자는 청자들에게 무엇을 하라고 권장하는가?
(A) 카메라 가져오기
(B) 공연에 참석하기
(C) 부칠 짐을 자물쇠로 채우기
(D) 티켓을 확인하기

[해설] 제안이나 요청 사항은 주로 담화 후반부에 제시된다. 화자는 오늘의 일정 안내를 마무리하며 오늘 저녁 호텔 건너편 극장에서 댄스 공연이 있으니 확인해보라고(There's a dance show ~ I suggest checking that out.) 했다. 따라서 정답은 (B)이다.

[어휘] verify 확인하다

[10-12] BR

Questions 10-12 refer to the following excerpt from a meeting and pie chart.

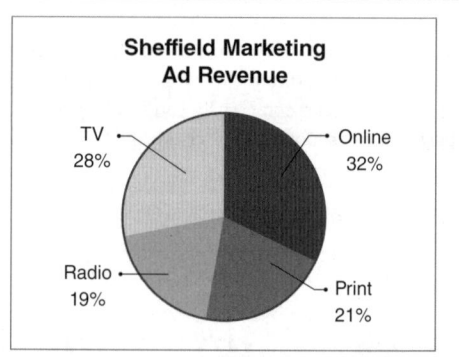

W: The next thing on today's agenda is our marketing company's recent success. You must know that ¹⁰**we were recently featured on Business Time, a TV program** that focuses on innovative businesses. The host praised our approach to marketing and the companies that chose to hire us. Unfortunately, Ms. Moyer is unable to join us today. ¹¹**She is attending the Essex Expo where she will be giving a talk about modern advertising.** For now, let's discuss one of our marketing types. ¹²**If you look at this chart, you can see that it accounts for 21%** of our ad revenue.

agenda 안건   recent 최근   success 성공   feature (잡지 등) 특집으로 싣다   focus on ~에 초점을 맞추다   innovative 혁신적인   host 진행자   praise 칭찬하다   approach 접근   unfortunately 안타깝게도   account for (비율을) 차지하다   revenue 수입

10-12는 다음 회의 발췌록과 원 그래프에 관한 문제입니다.

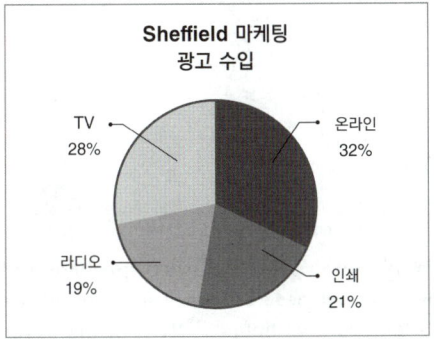

여: 오늘의 다음 안건은 우리 마케팅 회사의 최근 성공입니다. 혁신적인 기업들에 초점을 맞춘 [10]TV 프로그램인 <비즈니스 타임>에 최근 우리가 특집으로 다뤄진 것을 아실 겁니다. 진행자는 우리의 마케팅 접근과 우리를 고용한 회사들을 칭찬했습니다. 안타깝게도 Moyer 씨는 오늘 우리와 함께할 수 없습니다. [11]그녀는 Essex 엑스포에 참석하여 현대 광고에 대해서 강연할 것입니다. 우선 지금은 우리 마케팅 유형 중 하나에 대해서 이야기합시다. [12]이 차트를 보시면 이것이 우리 수익의 21%를 차지한다는 것을 보실 수 있습니다.

10.
화자에 따르면, 회사는 최근 무엇을 했는가?
(A) 해외 지사를 개설했다.
(B) TV 쇼에서 주목을 받았다.
(C) 경쟁사를 인수했다.
(D) 수익을 올렸다.

[해설] 담화 초반에 회사가 TV 프로그램에서 특집으로 다뤄졌다는(we were recently featured on Business Time, a TV program) 내용이 언급되어 있으므로 (B)가 정답이다.

paraphrasing   featured on Business Time, a TV program → sReceived publicity on a TV show

[어휘] international 해외의   branch 지점, 지사   publicity 매스컴[언론]의 주목[관심]   acquire 인수하다, 획득하다   competitor 경쟁사, 경쟁자   increase 올리다   revenue 수익, 수입

11.
Moyer 씨는 왜 엑스포에 참석하고 있는가?
(A) 발표를 하기 위해
(B) 제품을 시연하기 위해
(C) 사업 파트너를 만나기 위해
(D) 업체 계약을 협상하기 위해

[해설] 질문의 핵심 키워드인 Ms. Moyer는 담화 중반부에 언급된다. Moyer 씨는 오늘 함께할 수 없다며, Essex 엑스포에 참석하여 현대 광고에 대해서 강연할 것이라고(She is attending the Essex Expo where she will be giving a talk about modern advertising) 했으므로 (A)가 정답이다.

paraphrasing   will be giving a talk 강연을 할 것이다 → give a presentation 발표를 하다

[어휘] demonstrate 시연하다   negotiate 협상하다   contract 계약

12.
시각 자료를 보시오. 화자는 어떤 유형의 광고에 대해서 이야기하길 원하는가?
(A) 라디오
(B) 인쇄
(C) TV
(D) 온라인

[해설] 보기로 광고 유형이 제시되어 있으므로 담화에서 %가 언급될 것을 예상할 수 있다. 담화 후반부에 마케팅 유형 중 하나에 대해서 이야기하자며, 차트에서 이것이 21%를 차지한다고(If you look at this chart, you can see that it accounts for 21%) 했으므로 시각 자료에서 21%를 차지하는 것을 찾으면 (B)가 정답이다.

[13-15] US

Questions 13-15 refer to the following telephone message and schedule.

Jennifer's Schedule: Wednesday, April 7	
10:00 A.M.	Sales review meeting
12:00 P.M.	Lunch with author Neil Walsh
1:30 P.M.	Corporate conference call
[14]3:00 P.M.	Seasonal hiring plan

W: Hello, this is Jennifer from Atlas Bookstore. [13]I would like to go ahead with the expansion of my store, but I want to talk about it with you in more detail. You said that Wednesday works well for you, and [14]my 3 o'clock meeting this Wednesday was just cancelled. [15]Hopefully you can come to my office with a projected expense report. I look forward to seeing you.

go ahead with ~을 추진하다   expansion 확대, 확장   projected 예상된   expense report 경비 보고서   corporate 기업[회사]의   conference call 전화 회의   seasonal 계절적인, 정기의   hiring 고용

13-15는 다음 전화 메시지와 일정표에 관한 문제입니다.

Jennifer의 일정: 4월 7일 수요일	
오전 10:00	매출 검토 회의
정오	작가 Neil Walsh와 점심식사
오후 1:30	회사 전화 회의
[14]오후 3:00	정기 채용 계획

여: 여보세요, 저는 Atlas 서점의 Jennifer입니다. [13]저희 가게의 확장을 추진하려고 하는데 그에 대해 당신과 좀더 상세하게 얘기 나누고 싶어

요. 수요일이 괜찮다고 하셨죠. **¹⁴저의 이번 주 수요일 3시 회의가 방금 취소되었어요. ¹⁵당신이 예상 경비 보고서를 가지고 제 사무실에 와주셨으면 좋겠어요.** 뵙기를 기대합니다.

13.
화자는 무엇에 대해 청자와 얘기하고 싶어 하는가?
(A) 이전 일정
(B) 회원 가입 혜택
(C) 새로운 도서 시리즈
(D) 매장 확장

[해설] 메시지 초반 전화의 용건을 밝힌 부분에서 정답을 찾을 수 있다. 화자는 가게를 확장할 계획인데 그에 대해 청자와 얘기 나누고 싶다고(I would like to go ahead with the expansion of my store, but I want to talk about it with you in more detail.) 했으므로 정답은 (D)이다.

[어휘] relocation 재배치, 이전   benefit 혜택, 이득

14.
시각 자료를 보시오. 어떤 약속이 취소되었는가?
(A) 매출 검토 회의
(B) 작가 Neil Walsh와의 점심식사
(C) 회사 전화 회의
(D) 정기 채용 계획

[해설] 담화에 언급된 정보와 시각 자료를 종합하여 정답을 찾는다. 메시지 중반 이번 주 수요일 3시 회의가 방금 취소되었다고(my 3 o'clock meeting this Wednesday was just cancelled) 했으므로 일정표에서 이 시간의 일정을 살펴보면 '정기 채용 계획'임을 알 수 있다. 따라서 정답은 (D)이다.

15.
화자는 청자가 무엇을 가져올 것을 요청하는가?
(A) 회사 소개서
(B) 건물 모델
(C) 비용 견적서
(D) 작문 샘플

[해설] 메시지 후반에 화자는 청자에게 예상 경비 보고서를 가지고 자신의 사무실에 오기 바란다고(Hopefully you can come to my office with a projected expense report.) 했다. 즉, 비용 견적서를 가져올 것을 요청한 것이므로 정답은 (C)이다.

paraphrasing a projected expense report 예상 경비 보고서 → a cost estimate 비용 견적서

[어휘] profile 개요(서)   estimate 추정(치), 견적서

[16-18] AU
Questions 16-18 refer to the following excerpt from a meeting and chart.

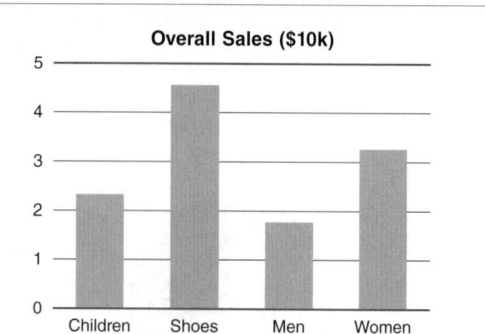

M: As you all may know, ¹⁶**I just got back from a seminar for business owners.** It was very informative, and I learned a lot from it. ¹⁷**Most of the sessions focused on how a small business like ours can earn a bigger profit.** ¹⁸**They suggested renovating the section with the highest sales.** This quarterly sales chart clearly shows which one that is. Also, the men's section will be reduced since it doesn't bring in nearly as many customers as the other departments.

business owner 경영주, 사업주   informative 유용한 정보를 주는, 유익한   earn (수익을) 올리다, 받다   profit 이익, 수익   suggest 제안하다   renovate 개조[보수]하다, 쇄신[혁신]하다   sales 매출   quarterly 분기별의   clearly 분명하게   reduce 줄이다, 낮추다   bring in (이익을) 가져오다   nearly 거의

16-18은 다음 회의 발췌록과 도표에 관한 문제입니다.

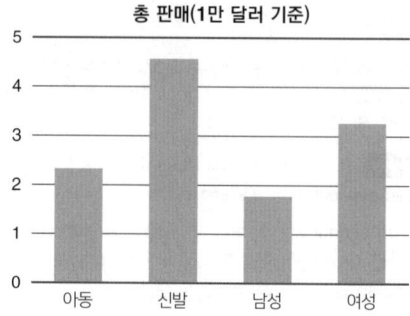

남: 여러분 모두 아시다시피 ¹⁶**저는 사업주들을 위한 세미나에서 막 돌아왔습니다.** 매우 유익했고, 그곳에서 많은 것을 배웠습니다. ¹⁷**대부분의 시간들이 어떻게 하면 우리 같은 작은 기업들이 더 큰 수익을 낼 수 있는지에 초점을 맞췄습니다.** ¹⁸**그들은 매출이 가장 높은 부문을 혁신할 것을 제안했습니다.** 이 분기별 매출 기록표는 어느 부문이 이에 해당하는지 분명히 보여줍니다. 또한 남성 부문은 나머지 매장만큼 많은 고객을 유치하지 못하므로 축소될 것입니다.

16.
화자는 최근 어떤 행사에 참가했는가?
(A) 국제 패션쇼
(B) 대중 연설 워크숍

(C) 사업주들의 세미나
(D) 연례 교육

[해설] 담화 초반 화자는 사업주들을 위한 세미나에서 막 돌아왔다고(I just got back from a seminar for business owners.) 언급했다. 따라서 정답은 (C)이다.

17.
화자는 주로 무슨 주제에 대해 배웠는가?
(A) 수익 증대시키기
(B) 인기 늘리기
(C) 효율적으로 마케팅하기
(D) 고객 서비스 개선하기

[해설] 화자는 자신이 참석한 워크숍에서 많은 것을 배웠다고 언급한 후, 대부분의 시간이 어떻게 하면 작은 기업들이 더 큰 수익을 낼 수 있는지에 초점을 맞췄다고(Most of the sessions focused on how a small business like ours can earn a bigger profit.) 했다. 이를 통해 주로 수익 증대에 대해 배웠음을 유추할 수 있으므로 정답은 (A)이다.

paraphrasing earn a bigger profit 더 큰 수익을 내다 → increasing profits 수익 증대시키기

[어휘] boost 신장시키다, 북돋우다 effectively 효과적으로 improve 개선하다, 향상시키다

18.
시각 자료를 보시오. 상점의 어떤 부문이 혁신될 것인가?
(A) 아동
(B) 신발
(C) 남성
(D) 여성

[해설] 담화 중반, 세미나에서 매출이 가장 높은 부문을 혁신할 것을 제안했다고(They suggested renovating the section with the highest sales.) 했으므로 주어진 도표에서 매출이 가장 높은 신발 부문이 혁신될 것임을 알 수 있다. 따라서 정답은 (B)이다.

[19-21] US

Questions 19-21 refer to the following instructions and floor plan.

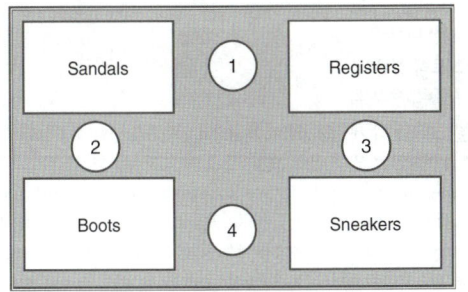

W: Good morning. Before we open for business today, I just wanted to point out one minor change. I have heard several customers complain that they don't have a place to sit while trying on shoes or waiting for whoever they're shopping with. So ¹⁹I added some extra seats to satisfy them. ²⁰They're located between the boots and sneakers sections. Also, we have a big shipment coming in next Monday. The new line of Orin shoes are coming in and we'll need some extra help that day. ²¹Put your name on the sign-up sheet at the registers if you're interested.

instructions 지시, 명령 floor plan 평면도 point out 지적[언급]하다 minor 작은, 가벼운 try on 입어[신어]보다 add 추가하다 satisfy 만족시키다 shipment 수송, 수송품 come in (상품 등이) 들어오다 sign-up sheet 참가 신청서 register (금전) 등록기

19-21은 다음 설명과 도면에 관한 문제입니다.

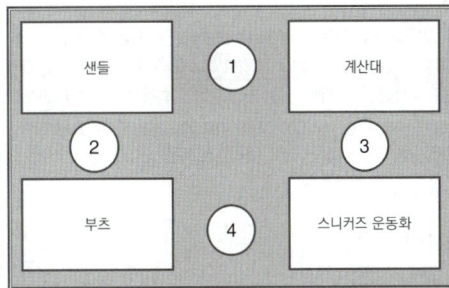

여: 안녕하세요. 오늘 영업을 시작하기 전에 한 가지 작은 변화를 언급하고 싶었습니다. 저는 여러 고객들이 불만을 제기하는 것을 들었는데 신발을 신어보거나 함께 쇼핑할 사람을 기다리는 동안 앉을 곳이 없다는 것입니다. 그래서 ¹⁹그런 분들을 만족시키기 위해 여분의 좌석을 추가했습니다. ²⁰그것들은 부츠와 스니커즈 운동화 섹션 사이에 위치합니다. 또한 다음 주 월요일에 많은 양의 화물이 입고됩니다. Orin 신발의 신제품 라인이 들어오므로 그날 도움이 더 필요할 것입니다. ²¹관심이 있으시면 계산대에 있는 신청서에 이름을 적어주세요.

19.
변화의 주요 목적은 무엇인가?
(A) 고객 만족도를 높이기 위해서
(B) 작업 효율성을 증대시키기 위해서
(C) 화물 규모를 줄이기 위해서
(D) 더 다양한 종류를 제공하기 위해서

[해설] 담화 초반, 화자는 작은 변화(one minor change)를 언급하고 싶다고 한 후, 여러 고객들이 신발을 신어보거나 함께 쇼핑할 사람을 기다리는 동안 앉을 곳이 없어 불만을 제기한다면서 이들을 만족시키기 위해 여분의 좌석을 추가했다고(I added some extra seats to satisfy them) 했다. 즉, 화자가 언급한 '변화'는 '좌석 추가'를 가리키며, 이는 고객들을 만족시키기 위한 것이므로 정답은 (A)이다.

paraphrasing satisfy them 그들을 만족시키다 → improve customer satisfaction 고객 만족도를 높이다

[어휘] improve 개선시키다, 향상시키다 customer satisfaction 고객 만족 work efficiency 작업 효율

20.
시각 자료를 보시오. 어느 위치에 새로운 좌석이 배치되었는가?
(A) 위치 1
(B) 위치 2
(C) 위치 3

DAY 11 101

(D) 위치 4

[해설] 평면도에서 좌석을 새로 배치한 위치를 찾는 문제이다. 담화 중반, 화자는 좌석을 추가했다며, 그 위치가 부츠와 스니커즈 운동화 섹션 사이라고(They're located between the boots and sneakers sections.) 했다. 시각 자료로 제시된 평면도에서 해당 장소를 찾으면 위치 4임을 알 수 있으므로 정답은 (D)이다.

21.

화자의 말에 따르면, 계산대에서 무엇을 찾을 수 있는가?
(A) 영수증
(B) 교육 안내서
(C) 신청서
(D) 쿠폰

[해설] 질문의 핵심 키워드 registers는 담화 마지막에 언급된다. 앞서 다음 주 월요일에 많은 양의 화물이 입고되니 도움이 더 필요할 것이라며, 관심이 있는 사람은 계산대에 있는 신청서에 이름을 적어 달라고(Put your name on the sign-up sheet at the registers) 했다. 따라서 계산대에서 신청서를 찾을 수 있으므로 정답은 (C)이다.

[어휘] manual 설명서, 안내서

[22-24] BR
Questions 22-24 refer to the following excerpt from a meeting and graph.

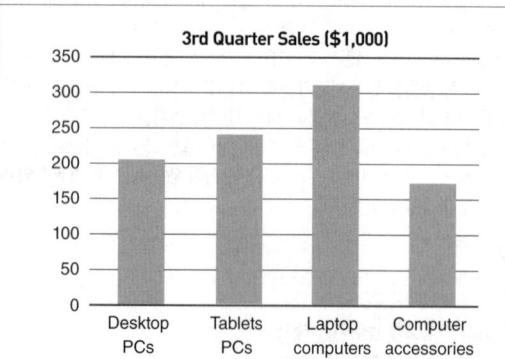

W: ²²**I've been looking over our electronics store's sales from the third quarter.** ²³**I wanted to focus specifically on our computers section. You can see by this chart that we sold over 300 thousand dollars in a single category.** That's probably because that type of product was featured in our last ad campaign. Now, ²⁴**I'm going to pass these forms around. I want each of you to give some feedback about what you like most about each type of product.** That might help us develop better ads for the other categories.

electronics 전자 제품   quarter 분기   focus on ~에 초점을 맞추다   specifically 특별히   section 섹션, 부문, 구역   category 카테고리, 범주, 부문   feature 특징으로 하다, 특집으로 실리다

22-24는 다음 회의 발췌록과 그래프에 관한 문제입니다.

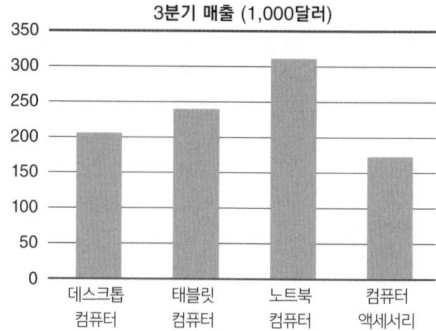

여: ²²우리 전자 제품 매장의 3분기 매출을 살펴보았습니다. 저는 특별히 우리의 컴퓨터 섹션에 초점을 맞추고 싶어요. ²³우리가 하나의 카테고리에서 **30만 달러 이상**을 판매한 것을 이 차트에서 확인하실 수 있습니다. 그건 아마도 이런 유형의 제품이 우리 최근 광고에서 특별히 다루어졌기 때문일 것입니다. 이제, ²⁴저는 이 양식을 돌리겠습니다. 여러분 각자가 각 유형의 제품에 대해서 무엇을 가장 좋아하는지 피드백을 주시기 바랍니다. 다른 카테고리의 광고를 더 좋게 만드는 데 도움이 될 것입니다.

22.

화자는 어떤 종류의 업체에서 일하는가?
(A) 컴퓨터 수리점
(B) 전자제품 매장
(C) 시장 조사 기관
(D) 컴퓨터 생산 회사

[해설] 화자가 일하는 업체의 종류는 초반부에 언급된다. 도입부에 우리 전자 제품 매장의 3분기 매출을 살펴보았다고(I've been looking over our electronics store's sales from the third quarter) 했으므로 (B)가 정답이다.

[어휘] manufacturer 생산 회사

23.

시각 자료를 보시오. 화자에 따르면 어떤 제품이 광고에서 특별히 다루어졌는가?
(A) 데스크톱 컴퓨터
(B) 태블릿 컴퓨터
(C) 노트북 컴퓨터
(D) 컴퓨터 액세서리

[해설] 보기에 각 제품의 종류가 제시되어 있으므로 담화에서 수치가 언급될 것을 예상할 수 있다. 담화 초반부에 30만 달러 이상 판매된 유형을(You can see by this chart that we sold over 300 thousand dollars in a single category) 언급하며, 그건 아마도 이런 유형의 제품이 최근 광고에서 특별히 다루어졌기 때문일 것이라고(That's probably because that type of product was featured in our last ad campaign) 했으므로 시각 자료에서 매출이 30만 달러 이상인 것을 찾으면 (C)가 정답이다.

24.

화자는 다음에 무엇을 할 것이라고 말하는가?
(A) 마케팅 대행사에 연락하기
(B) 경쟁사 광고 보여 주기

(C) 설문지 나누어 주기
(D) 일부 제품 시연하기

[해설] 다음에 할 일은 담화 후반부에서 확인할 수 있다. 담화 후반부에 양식을 돌리겠다고(I'm going to pass these forms around) 한 후, 각자 각 유형의 제품에 대해서 무엇을 가장 좋아하는지 피드백을 주기 바란다고(I want each of you to give some feedback about what you like most about each type of product) 했으므로 설문지를 나누어 줄 것임을 알 수 있다. 따라서 (C)가 정답이다.

paraphrasing pass these forms around 양식을 돌리다 → Distribute a survey 설문지 나누어 주기

[어휘] contact 연락하다 agency 대행사 competitor 경쟁사 distribute 배포하다, 나누어 주다 demonstrate 시연하다

DAY 12

PART 3 회사 - 업무 요청/규정 관련

출제 유형 01 업무 요청

| 풀이 방법 해석 |

여: Martin, 부탁 드릴 게 있어요. 우리 체육관의 회원분들에게 받은 피드백 카드를 검토하고 있습니다. 많은 사람들이 스포츠 음료 자판기를 원한다고 했어요. 탈의실에 자판기를 대여하는 견적서를 저에게 가져다 주시겠어요?
남: 새로운 회원을 모집할 수 있는 홍보 방안을 생각하던 중이었어요. 이건 제가 나중에 알려드릴게요. 다른 특별한 요청 사항들도 있었나요?
여: 많은 사람들이 Thirstinator 음료에 대해서 언급했어요.
남: 알겠습니다. 제가 온라인으로 살펴보겠습니다.
여: 감사해요. 당신이 찾은 좋은 링크가 있으면 이메일로 보내주세요.

출제 유형 02 규정 관련

| 풀이 방법 해석 |

남: 좋은 아침입니다, Sally. 제가 생각 중이었는데, 인사부로 들어오는 대부분의 직원들이 우리의 수업료 환급 프로그램에 대해서 질문이 있는 것 같아 보여요.
여: 네. 저도 그걸 알아챘어요. 많은 사람들이 그 프로그램에 대해 혼란스러워 하는 것 같아요. 모든 사람들에게 알려줄 수 있는 아이디어가 있으신가요?
남: 사실 있어요. 직원 혜택에 대한 교육 시간을 가지면 좋겠어요.
여: 그거 좋네요. 교육을 준비해보기로 하죠.
남: 언제가 가장 좋을까요?
여: 우선 회사 스케줄을 확인해 봐야 합니다. 지금 할게요.

연습 문제

01. (B) 02. (B) 03. (A) 04. (A) 05. (B) 06. (B)

 01. US-BR

What are the speakers **mainly talking about**?
(A) A **retirement party** (B) A **grant proposal**

W: Andy, have you finished the grant proposal for next year?
M: No, I just finished the first draft. I heard you were in charge of last year's proposal. Could you review it and give me some suggestions?
W: Sure, e-mail it to me.

화자들은 주로 무엇에 대해 이야기하는가?
(A) 퇴직 파티 **(B) 보조금 지원서**

여: Andy, 내년 보조금 지원서 끝내셨어요?
남: 아뇨, 이제 막 초안을 끝냈어요. 당신이 작년 지원서를 담당했었다고 들었어요. 이걸 검토하시고 제게 몇 가지 제안을 해주실 수 있으세요?
여: 물론이죠, 제게 이메일로 보내주세요.

02. AU-US

What does the **woman offer** to do?
(A) **Download guidelines** (B) **Give** an **application form**

M: I have a client meeting at Herald Investment and need to use a company car tomorrow. Do you know how I can apply for one?
W: Fill out a form and get a signature from your manager. And then, submit it to Mr. Jenson in the General Affairs Department. I will bring you some copies of the form.

여자는 무엇을 하겠다고 제안하는가?
(A) 설명서 다운로드 하기 **(B) 신청서 주기**

남: 제가 Herald 투자에서 고객 미팅이 있어서 내일 회사 차를 사용해야 해요. 어떻게 신청할 수 있는지 아세요?
여: 양식을 작성하셔서 부장님에게 서명을 받으세요. 그러고 나서, 총무부의 Jenson 씨에게 제출하세요. 제가 양식 사본 몇 부를 가져다 드릴게요.

03. US-US

What did the **company** recently **do**?
(A) **Introduced** a new **service** (B) **Changed a vendor**

W: Tom, did you pick up your monthly paycheck from the Payroll Department yesterday?
M: No. Actually, I don't need to do that anymore. The Payroll Department implemented the direct deposit service this month. You can have your paycheck deposited directly into your bank account.
W: That sounds very convenient.

회사는 최근에 무엇을 했는가?
(A) 새로운 서비스를 도입했다. (B) 판매 회사를 변경했다.

여: Tom, 어제 급여 지급 부서에서 월급 받아 갔어요?
남: 아뇨. 사실, 저는 이제 그렇게 하지 않아도 돼요. 급여 지급 부서가 이번 달에 직접 송금하는 서비스를 시행했거든요. 당신의 월급을 은행 계좌로 바로 받을 수 있어요.
여: 그거 매우 편리하게 들리네요.

04. AU-BR

Where does the **conversation** probably **take place**?
(A) At a **manufacturing plant**   (B) At a **grocery store**

> M: I received the memo from the assembly manager that any power tools should be returned to the storage room under the team manager's supervision at the end of each shift.
> W: It will prevent expensive power tools from being lost and malfunctioning from improper care. All team manager will check the returned power tools.

대화는 아마도 어디에서 이루어지고 있겠는가?
(A) 제조 공장   (B) 식료품점

남: 조립 부서 부장님께 회람을 받았는데 각 교대 근무 작업이 끝나면 팀 매니저의 감독 하에 모든 공구들이 창고로 반납되어야 한대요.
여: 그건 비싼 공구들이 분실되고 부적절한 관리로 인해 오작동하는 것을 방지할 거예요. 모든 팀 매니저가 반납된 공구들을 확인할 거예요.

05. US-BR

What does the **woman** ask the **man** to **do**?
(A) Work at the **company booth**   (B) **Reserve flights**

> W: Jason, our management decided to have the company booth at Colorado Expo and I'm making travel arrangements. Can you book flights for five people to Colorado? We will depart on November 28 and return on December 2.
> M: Okay, are there any board members? They usually want business class flights.

여자는 남자에게 무엇을 하라고 요청하는가?
(A) 회사 부스에서 일하기   **(B) 항공편 예약하기**

여: Jason, 우리 경영진이 콜로라도 박람회에서 회사 부스를 열기로 결정했고 제가 출장 계획을 세우고 있어요. 콜로라도로 가는 5명을 위한 항공편을 예약해줄 수 있어요? 우리는 11월 28일에 떠나서 12월 2일에 돌아올 거예요.
남: 알겠어요, 임원들도 있나요? 그들은 보통 비즈니스석 항공편을 원하거든요.

06. AU-US

What will the **woman** do this **afternoon**?
(A) **Attend** a **career fair**   (B) **Inspect** a **factory**

> M: Hi, Amy. I received the new floor plan for our new office space from Rebecca's Interior. Can we go over it today sometime?
> W: Can we do that tomorrow morning? I need to conduct a regular factory inspection this afternoon.

여자는 오늘 오후에 무엇을 할 것인가?
(A) 직업 박람회에 참석하기   **(B) 공장 점검하기**

남: 안녕하세요, Amy. 제가 Rebecca's 인테리어로부터 우리 새로운 사무실 공간을 위한 새 평면도를 받았어요. 오늘 언젠가 우리가 그것을 검토할 수 있을까요?
여: 그것을 내일 아침에 해도 될까요? 제가 오늘 오후에 공장 정기 점검을 해야 해요.

paraphrasing 정답   1. (b)   2. (a)   3. (c)   4. (c)   5. (b)   6. (a)

실전 문제

01. (C)	02. (C)	03. (D)	04. (C)	05. (A)	06. (D)
07. (C)	08. (D)	09. (D)	10. (A)	11. (C)	12. (D)
13. (A)	14. (C)	15. (D)	16. (A)	17. (B)	18. (C)
19. (D)	20. (A)	21. (C)	22. (C)	23. (D)	24. (B)

[01-03] US-US

Questions 01-03 refer to the following conversation.

> W: Hi, Tomo. Did you read the memo from Mr. Bradford? **01**The group interviews will start at 1 P.M. today instead of 4.
> M: Yes, I saw that. I had planned on having some time after lunch to prepare everything. **02**I don't know how I'll get it all done.
> W: Well, I'm done with my monthly reports. What's left on your To Do list?
> M: Oh, thanks! **03**I'm waiting for some company brochures from Henson Printing. They were supposed to be here yesterday. I need to hand those out this afternoon.
> W: **03**Don't worry. I'm on it.

get ~ done ~을 마치다   be done with ~을 끝내다   hand out ~을 나누어 주다

01-03은 다음 대화에 관한 문제입니다.
여: 안녕하세요, Tomo. Bradford 씨가 보낸 메모 읽으셨어요? **01**집단 면접이 오늘 오후 4시가 아니라 1시에 시작할 거예요.
남: 네, 봤어요. 점심식사 후에 시간을 좀 내서 모든 걸 준비하려고 했거든요. **02**제가 어떻게 모든 걸 마칠지 모르겠어요.
여: 음, 전 월간 보고서를 다 끝냈어요. 당신이 해야 할 일 중 뭐가 남았어요?
남: 아, 고마워요! **03**Henson 인쇄소에서 올 회사 브로슈어를 기다리고 있어요. 어제 도착하기로 되어 있었거든요. 오늘 오후에 그것들을 배포해야 해요.
여: 걱정 말아요. 제가 할게요.

01.

여자는 남자에게 무엇에 대해 말하는가?
(A) 최신 개인 정보 보호 정책
(B) 몇몇 동료 직원들과의 식사
(C) 면접 일정 변경
(D) 곧 있을 시상식

[해설] 대화 초반부에 여자가 남자에게 집단 면접이 4시가 아니라 1시에 시작한다고(The group interviews will start at 1 P.M. today instead of 4.) 언급했고, 뒤이어 일정 변경으로 생긴 문제점을 해결하기 위한 대화가 이어지고 있다. 따라서 정답은 (C)이다.

paraphrasing   The group interviews will start at 1 P.M. today

instead of 4. 집단 면접이 오늘 오후 4시 대신 1시에 시작할 것이다.
→ A change in an interview schedule 면접 일정 변경

02.
여자가 "전 월간 보고서를 다 끝냈어요"라고 말할 때 암시하는 것은 무엇인가?
(A) 휴가를 요청하고 싶다.
(B) 오늘 오후에 의뢰인을 방문할 것이다.
(C) 남자의 일을 도와줄 수 있다.
(D) 일부 수치에 대해 논의하고 싶다.

[해설] 해당 표현의 주변 문장을 파악하여 화자의 의도를 찾는 문제이다. 해당 표현에 앞서 집단 면접 일정이 당겨져 준비 시간이 부족해진 남자의 상황이 제시되었고, 다 끝낼 수 있을지 모르겠다는(I don't know how I'll get it all done.) 남자의 말에 여자가 "전 월간 보고서를 다 끝냈어요"라고 말한 것은 결국 남자의 일을 도와주겠다는 것이므로 정답은 (C)이다.

[어휘] request 요청[신청]하다 time off 휴식, 휴가 task 일, 과업 figure (자료의) 수치

03.
여자는 아마도 다음에 무엇을 할 것인가?
(A) 계약서 인쇄하기
(B) 소프트웨어 설치하기
(C) 회의실 준비하기
(D) 배송 상황 확인하기

[해설] 여자가 다음에 할 일을 묻는 문제로, 대화 후반부에서 단서를 찾는다. 앞서 남자의 일을 도와주기로 한 여자가 남자에게 해야 할 일이 무엇인지 묻자, 남자는 인쇄소로부터 회사 브로슈어를 기다리고 있다며(I'm waiting for some company brochures from Henson Printing.) 어제 도착해야 한다고(They were supposed to be here yesterday.) 덧붙인다. 이에 여자가 걱정 말라며 자신이 하겠다고(Don't worry. I'm on it.) 한 것으로 보아 대화 후에 여자는 브로슈어가 언제 도착하는지 배송 상황을 확인할 것임을 유추할 수 있다. 따라서 정답은 (D)이다.

[어휘] contract 계약서 install 설치하다 set up 설치하다, 준비하다 status (진행 과정상의) 상황

[04-06] BR-AU
Questions 04-06 refer to the following conversation.

> W: Eric, could you cover my shift on **⁰⁵Friday?** I saw that you have the day off, and there's **⁰⁴a training workshop for nurses** that I want to attend.
> M: I'd love to help you out, but **⁰⁵I'm going to Houston to see my cousins that day.**
> W: Oh, have a good time. I'll keep looking. I just need **⁰⁴someone who can look after my patients** for a few hours.
> M: **⁰⁶Sometimes people put up messages on the notice board when they want to pick up shifts. Try looking there.**

04-06은 다음 대화에 관한 문제입니다.
여: Eric, ⁰⁵금요일에 제 근무를 대신해줄 수 있나요? 그날 당신이 쉬는 날이란 걸 봤고, 그런데 제가 참석하고 싶은 ⁰⁴간호사 교육 워크숍이 있거든요.
남: 도와주고 싶지만 ⁰⁵그날 사촌들을 만나러 휴스턴에 가요.
여: 아, 재미있는 시간 보내요. 계속 알아볼게요. 몇 시간 동안만 ⁰⁴제 환자들을 돌봐줄 수 있는 사람이 필요해요.
남: ⁰⁶종종 사람들이 교대 근무를 잡고 싶을 때 게시판에 메시지를 올려요. 거길 한번 보도록 해요.

04.
화자들은 어떤 업계에서 일하는가?
(A) 제조
(B) 건설
(C) 보건 의료
(D) 운송

[해설] 화자의 직업을 묻는 문제로, 여자의 대사에서 근무 분야를 알 수 있는 단서가 나온다. 여자가 언급한 간호사 교육 워크숍(a training workshop for nurses)과 자신의 환자를 돌볼 사람(someone who can look after my patients)이 필요하다는 말에서 두 사람이 보건 의료 업계에 종사함을 알 수 있으므로 정답은 (C)이다.

05.
남자는 왜 금요일에 시간이 되지 않는가?
(A) 친척을 방문할 것이다.
(B) 교육 과정에 참석할 것이다.
(C) 콘서트에 갈 것이다.
(D) 취업 면접을 볼 것이다.

[해설] 핵심 키워드인 Friday가 언급되는 곳에 집중하여 대화를 듣는다. 여자가 남자에게 금요일에 자신의 근무를 대신 해줄 수 있는지(could you cover my shift on Friday) 묻자 남자는 그날 사촌들을 만나러 휴스턴에 간다며(I'm going to Houston to see my cousins that day) 거절했다. 즉, 남자는 금요일에 친척을 방문할 예정이므로 정답은 (A)이다.

paraphrasing see my cousins 사촌들을 만나다 → visit some relatives 친척을 방문하다

[어휘] relative 친척, 친지 training session 교육 (과정)

06.
남자는 무엇을 할 것을 제안하는가?
(A) 다른 장소에 전화하기
(B) 야간 교대 근무 하기
(C) 직원 안내서 읽기
(D) 게시판 확인하기

[해설] 남자가 제안하는 것을 묻는 문제로, 후반부 남자의 대사에 정답의 단서가 있다. 교대 근무를 잡고 싶을 때 게시판에 메시지를 올리는 사람들이 있으니 그곳을 보라고(Sometimes people put up messages on the notice board when they want to pick up shifts. Try looking there.) 한 것은 게시판을 확인하라는 말이므로 (D)가 정답이다.

[어휘] site 장소, 현장 manual 설명서

[07-09] US-BR
Questions 07-09 refer to the following conversation.

> W: Hi, Adrian. It's Scarlett Alston from the 3rd floor. **⁰⁷I wanted to tell you that there's a problem with the ceiling fan in Conference Room B. Even when the switch is turned on, it doesn't move.**

M: All right, but I won't be able to make the repairs until later this week.
W: Oh, really? I was hoping it could be done today.
M: ⁰⁸**We don't keep any of those parts on hand, so I'll have to request them from the supplier.**
W: That's too bad. I'm meeting a client for the first time today, so ⁰⁹**I want him to have a favorable view of our company.** I'll have to see if any of the other rooms are available.

> ceiling fan 천장 선풍기 make a repair 수리하다 on hand 구할 [얻을] 수 있는, 수중에 supplier 공급자, 공급회사 favorable 호의적인 view 견해, 생각, 의견

07-09는 다음 대화에 관한 문제입니다.
여: 안녕하세요, Adrian. 3층의 Scarlett Alston이에요. ⁰⁷B 회의실의 천장 선풍기에 문제가 있다고 말씀드리려고요. 스위치를 켜도 작동하지 않아요.
남: 알겠습니다, 그런데 이번 주 후반까지는 수리를 할 수 없을 거예요.
여: 아, 정말요? 오늘 중으로 고칠 수 있었으면 했어요.
남: ⁰⁸그 부품들을 하나도 가지고 있지 않아서, 공급처에 그것들을 요청해야 해요.
여: 그거 유감이네요. 오늘 한 고객을 처음으로 만나는데, ⁰⁹그분이 우리 회사에 대해 호감을 갖기를 바라거든요. 다른 회의실을 사용할 수 있는지 알아봐야겠어요.

07.
전화의 목적은 무엇인가?
(A) 회의 공간을 예약하기 위해서
(B) 일부 서류 작업에 대해 문의하기 위해서
(C) 남자에게 고장 난 장비를 알리기 위해서
(D) 남자를 행사에 초대하기 위해서

[해설] 전화의 목적은 주로 대화 전반부에 단서가 나온다. 대화 초반에 여자가 회의실 천장의 선풍기에 문제가 있다고(there's a problem with the ceiling fan in Conference Room B) 알린 후 스위치를 켜도 움직이지 않는다며(Even when the switch is turned on, it doesn't move.) 작동 이상에 대해 구체적으로 덧붙이고 있으므로 (C)가 정답이다.

paraphrasing tell you that there's a problem with the ceiling fan 천장 선풍기에 문제가 있다고 말하다 → inform the man of a broken device 고장 난 장비를 알리다

[어휘] reserve 예약하다 inquire about ~에 대해서 문의하다 paperwork 서류 작업 inform A of B A에게 B를 알리다 broken 고장 난 device 장치

08.
남자는 왜 작업이 지연될 것이라고 예상하는가?
(A) 사무실이 곧 문을 닫을 것이다.
(B) 일부 회의실이 사용 중이다.
(C) 오늘 팀의 인력이 부족하다.
(D) 일부 부품을 주문해야 한다.

[해설] 우선 질문의 키워드 task가 가리키는 것이 여자가 남자에게 요청한 회의실 천장 선풍기의 수리 작업임을 파악해야 한다. 남자는 수리 작업을 오늘 끝낼 수 없다고 했는데, 그 이유가 가지고 있는 부품이 없어서 공급처에 요청해야 하기(We don't keep any of those parts on hand, so I'll have to request them from the supplier.) 때문이라고 했으므로 정답은 (D)이다.

paraphrasing request them from the supplier 공급처에 그것들을 요청하다 → Some components must be ordered. 일부 부품을 주문해야 한다.

[어휘] in use 사용 중인 short-staffed 일손이 모자란 component (구성) 요소, 부품 order 주문하다

09.
여자는 무엇을 하고 싶다고 말하는가?
(A) 신규 계약 체결하기
(B) 양식 기입하기
(C) 신제품 시험 사용해보기
(D) 좋은 인상 주기

[해설] 여자가 하고 싶어 하는 것을 묻는 문제로, 여자의 마지막 대사에 단서가 있다. 오늘 처음 만나기로 되어 있는 고객이 회사에 대해 호감을 갖게 하고 싶다고(I want him to have a favorable view of our company) 한 것으로 보아 좋은 인상을 주고 싶어 함을 알 수 있으므로 정답은 (D)이다.

paraphrasing I want him to have a favorable view of our company 그가 우리 회사에 대해 호감을 갖기를 바란다. → Make a good impression 좋은 인상 주기

[어휘] contract 계약(서) complete 기입하다, 완료하다 sample 시식[시음]하다, (경험 삼아) 시도해 보다 make a good impression 좋은 인상을 주다

[10-12] US-US-BR

Questions 10-12 refer to the following conversation with three speakers.

> W: Stanley, Vineet, I appreciate your stopping by my office. ¹⁰**I wanted to discuss ways that our factory can meet the new government regulations for safety.**
> M1: I know that we had a low score on the last inspection, so we need to do something about that to make the working conditions safer.
> M2: ¹¹**It would be a good idea to adjust how often we train the employees.** They only get retrained on their equipment once a year.
> W: Good point, ¹¹**Vineet.** We could make that training more frequent.
> M2: Yes, but that'll cost more than we currently have in the budget.
> W: ¹²**Let me talk to the site manager to see if the budget can be increased.**

> stop by ~에 들르다 meet 충족시키다, 지키다 government regulations 정부 규정 safety 안전 inspection 조사, 점검 working condition 작업 환경 adjust 조정[조절]하다 get retrained 재훈련을 받다 equipment 장비, 용품 frequent 잦은, 빈번한 currently 현재, 지금 budget 예산, (지출 예상) 비용

10-12은 다음 세 명의 대화에 관한 문제입니다.
여: Stanley, Vineet, 제 사무실에 들러줘서 고마워요. **¹⁰우리 공장이 새로운 정부 안전 규정을 지킬 수 있는 방안에 대해 논의하고 싶었어요.**
남1: 우리가 지난 검사에서 낮은 점수를 받은 걸 알고 있어요, 그러니 작업 환경을 보다 안전하게 하기 위해 그 문제에 관해 뭐든 해야 해요.
남2: **¹¹직원들을 교육시키는 빈도를 조정하는 것도 좋은 생각이 될 거예요.** 겨우 일 년에 한 번만 장비에 대해 재교육을 받잖아요.
여: 좋은 지적이에요, **¹¹Vineet.** 그 교육을 좀 더 자주 하면 되겠어요.
남2: 네, 하지만 현재 확보된 예산보다 더 많은 비용이 들 거예요.
여: **¹²제가 현장 관리자와 얘기해서 예산을 증액할 수 있는지 알아볼게요.**

10.
무엇에 관한 대화인가?
(A) 안전 규정 준수하기
(B) 더 많은 고객 유치하기
(C) 생산 과정 속도 높이기
(D) 대회에 참가하기

[해설] 주제 문제의 단서는 주로 대화의 전반부에서 찾을 수 있다. 대화 초반에 여자가 다른 화자들에게 공장에서 새로운 정부 안전 규정을 지킬 수 있는 방안에 대해 논의하고 싶었다고(I wanted to discuss ways that our factory can meet the new government regulations for safety.) 밝혔고, 이어지는 대화에서 이를 위한 구체적인 방법이 제시되고 있으므로 정답은 (A)이다.

paraphrasing meet the new government regulations for safety 새로운 정부 안전 규정을 지키다 → Complying with safety regulations 안전 규정 준수하기

[어휘] comply with 지키다, 준수하다 competition 대회, 시합

11.
Vineet이 바꿔야 한다고 생각한 것은 무엇인가?
(A) 지불 시스템
(B) 프로젝트 마감 시한
(C) 교육 일정
(D) 장비

[해설] 3인의 화자 중 한 사람의 의견을 묻는 문제로, 일단 Vineet이 누구인지 파악해야 한다. 여자가 Vineet의 이름을 부르며 좋은 지적이라고 한 것으로 보아 바로 앞에서 말한 남자2가 Vineet임을 알 수 있다. 남자2는 직원들을 교육시키는 빈도를 조정하는 것이 좋겠다고(It would be a good idea to adjust how often we train the employees.) 제안했으므로 직원 교육 일정을 변경해야 한다고 생각한다고 볼 수 있다. 따라서 정답은 (C)이다.

12.
여자는 무엇을 하겠다고 제안하는가?
(A) 웹사이트를 갱신하기
(B) 조사를 실시하기
(C) 의뢰인에게 연락하기
(D) 더 많은 자금을 요청하기

[해설] 대화 후반부 여자의 말 중 대표적인 제안 표현인 Let me ~ 이하에서 정답의 단서를 찾을 수 있다. 현장 관리자와 얘기해서 예산을 증액할 수 있는지 알아보겠다는(Let me talk to the site manager to see if the budget can be increased.) 말에서 여자가 자금을 더 요청할 것임을 알 수 있으므로 정답은 (D)이다.

paraphrasing see if the budget can be increased 예산을 증액할 수 있는지 알아보다 → Request more funds 더 많은 자금을 요청하다

[어휘] conduct (특정한 활동을) 수행하다 fund 기금, 자금

[13-15] BR-US

Questions 13-15 refer to the following conversation.

W: Hey, Simon. Guess what? **¹³I got the standup comedian Tony Mills to perform here on April 7!**
M: Well done! I'll add him to the lineup on the **¹⁴flyers.**
W: **¹⁴Thank you for creating the design for them,** it looks really nice. Don't you think it would be better to print them in color, though?
M: I didn't think our budget would allow that, so I just went with a black and white design.
W: **¹⁵I'll reallocate some money so that we can afford the color prints.**

standup comedian 무대에서 단독 연기하는 코미디언 add A to B A를 B에 추가하다 lineup (행사 등의) 예정표 flyer (광고·안내용) 전단 budget 예산 allow 허용하다, 가능하게 하다 reallocate 재분배하다 afford 여유[형편]가 되다

13-15는 다음 대화에 관한 문제입니다.
여: 저기요, Simon. 있잖아요. **¹³제가 스탠드업 코미디언 Tony Mills가 4월 7일에 이곳에서 공연을 하게 만들었어요!**
남: 잘됐네요! 제가 **¹⁴전단**의 공연 예정표에 그를 추가할게요.
여: **¹⁴전단 디자인을 만들어줘서 고마워요,** 정말 멋져요. 그래도, 컬러로 인쇄하는 것이 더 낫겠죠?
남: 우리 예산상 그건 불가능하다고 생각해서, 제가 그냥 흑백 디자인으로 갔던 거예요.
여: **¹⁵컬러 인쇄를 할 여유가 되도록 돈을 재분배할게요.**

13.
4월 7일에 무슨 일이 예정되어 있는가?
(A) 코미디 공연
(B) 극장 개관
(C) 회사 회식
(D) 상품 출시

[해설] 질문의 키워드 April 7은 대화 초반 여자의 대사에 언급된다. 스탠드업 코미디언 Tony Mills가 4월 7일에 이곳에서 공연을 하게 만들었다는(I got the standup comedian Tony Mills to perform here on April 7!) 말로 보아 4월 7일에 코미디 공연이 열릴 예정임을 유추할 수 있다. 따라서 정답은 (A)이다.

[어휘] release 출시, 발표, 개봉

14.
여자는 남자가 무엇을 해줘서 고맙다고 하는가?
(A) 고객을 만나기
(B) 예산을 기획하기
(C) 전단을 디자인하기
(D) 자진해서 공연을 하기

[해설] 대화 중반, 여자는 남자에게 그것들을 위해 디자인을 만들어줘서 고

말다고(Thank you for creating the design for them) 말한다. 여기서 '그것들(them)'은 앞서 남자가 언급한 '전단(flyers)'을 가리키므로 결국 여자는 남자가 전단을 디자인해주어 고맙다고 한 것이다. 따라서 정답은 (C)이다.

paraphrasing creating the design for them 전단지를 위한 디자인을 만들기 → designing a flyer 전단 디자인하기

[어휘] volunteer to V 자진해서 ~하다

15.

여자는 무엇을 할 것이라고 말하는가?
(A) 할인을 요청하기
(B) 공연자에게 연락하기
(C) 예산 회의를 열기
(D) 자금을 재분배하기

[해설] 여자가 앞으로 할 일을 묻는 문제이므로 대화 후반부에 단서가 있다. 예산상 컬러 인쇄가 어렵다는 남자의 말에 여자가 컬러 인쇄를 할 수 있도록 돈을 재분배할 것이라고(I'll reallocate some money) 했다. 따라서 정답은 (D)이다.

paraphrasing reallocate some money 돈을 재분배하다 → reallocate some funds 자금을 재분배하기

[16-18] US-AU

Questions 16-18 refer to the following conversation.

W: Hi, Jeff. I'm glad you were able to come in. **16**I never expected so many customers to come in on the same day to get their cars worked on.
M: Actually, I was already out and came straight here, so **17**my work uniform is at home.
W: That's fine. There are some extra uniforms in the office closet that you can use.
M: Okay, thanks. By the way, **18**why are there so many customers today?
W: **18**There was a recall on a part for last year's Carmen model. Everyone that has one is trying to get the part replaced.

straight 곧장, 곧바로   closet 벽장   by the way 그런데
recall (하자가 있는 제품을) 회수[리콜]하다; 회수, 리콜   part 부품
replace 교체하다

16-18은 다음 대화에 관한 문제입니다.

여: 안녕하세요, Jeff. 당신이 올 수 있어서 다행이에요. **16**이렇게 많은 손님들이 같은 날 와서 자동차 작업을 맡길 거라고는 전혀 예상하지 못했어요.
남: 실은, 제가 이미 외출을 한 상태에서 바로 이곳으로 와서 **17**제 작업용 유니폼이 집에 있어요.
여: 그건 괜찮아요. 사무실 벽장에 당신이 사용해도 되는 여벌의 유니폼이 좀 있어요.
남: 잘됐네요, 고마워요. 그런데, **18**오늘 왜 저렇게 손님이 많은 거죠?
여: **18**작년에 나온 Carmen 모델 부품에 대해 리콜이 있었어요. 그 모델을 가지고 있는 모든 사람들이 부품을 교체받으려고 하는 중이에요.

16.

화자들은 어디에서 일하는가?
(A) 자동차 정비소에서
(B) 제조 공장에서
(C) 자동차 부품 가게에서
(D) 세탁소에서

[해설] 화자들의 근무 장소를 묻는 문제로, 대화 초반 여자의 대사에서 단서를 찾을 수 있다. 이렇게 많은 손님들이 같은 날 자동차 작업을 맡길(to get their cars worked on) 것을 예상하지 못했다는 것으로 보아 이들은 자동차를 수리하는 자동차 정비소에서 일함을 알 수 있으므로 정답은 (A)이다.

[어휘] auto repair 자동차 수리 manufacturing plant 제조 공장 dry cleaners 세탁소

17.

남자는 무엇을 집에 두고 왔는가?
(A) 교육 자료
(B) 작업복
(C) 공구 키트
(D) 이력서

[해설] 남자가 집에 두고 온 것을 묻는 문제로, 질문의 핵심 키워드 at home이 대화 전반부 남자의 대사에 그대로 나온다. 외출했다가 바로 오는 바람에 작업용 유니폼이 집에 있다고(my work uniform is at home) 했으므로 정답은 (B)이다.

paraphrasing my work uniform 내 작업용 유니폼 → a work outfit 작업복

[어휘] outfit 옷, 복장 kit (특정한 목적용 도구·장비) 세트

18.

여자의 말에 따르면, 업체는 왜 그토록 바쁜가?
(A) 특별 판촉행사가 막 시작되었다.
(B) 경쟁업체가 폐업했다.
(C) 제조사가 부품을 리콜했다.
(D) 동료가 나오지 않았다.

[해설] 대화 후반, 남자가 오늘 손님이 그렇게 많은 이유를 물었고, 이에 대해 여자가 작년에 나온 Carmen 모델 부품에 대해 리콜이 있었는데(There was a recall on a part for last year's Carmen model.) 그 모델을 소유한 사람들이 부품을 교체받으려고 하기 때문이라고 말했다. 따라서 정답은 (C)이다.

paraphrasing There was a recall on a part for last year's Carmen model. 작년에 나온 Carmen 모델 부품에 대해 리콜이 있었다. → A manufacturer recalled a part. 제조사가 부품을 리콜했다.

[어휘] promotion 홍보[판촉] (활동) competitor 경쟁자, 경쟁사 go out of business 폐업하다 manufacturer 제조사, 생산 회사 coworker 동료

[19-21] BR-AU

Questions 19-21 refer to the following conversation.

W: Hello, Mr. Yang. I've been wanting to talk with you about **19**the workload that my department has lately. It's way too much for us to handle.

M: I've heard that some of you have been staying late.
W: Yes, we have. And we've been coming in early, too. Just overtime pay isn't enough; we need to hire more people in order to keep going.
M: [20]Normally our policy is to only hire at the end of the year, but perhaps we can try to change that. I'll speak with the board.
W: Thanks. Is there anything I can do to help?
M: Actually, yes. [21]I need you to get a time sheet ready. One that shows the hours your department has been putting in lately.

workload 업무량, 작업량   department 부서   lately 최근에
handle 다루다, 처리하다   overtime pay 초과 근무 수당
hire 고용하다   keep going 계속하다[견디다]   policy 정책, 방침
board 이사회   time sheet 근무 시간 기록표   put in (많은 시간·노력을) 쏟다[들이다]

19-21은 다음 대화에 관한 문제입니다.
여: 안녕하세요, Yang 씨. [19]최근 저희 부서의 업무량에 대해 당신과 얘기하고 싶었어요. [19]저희가 처리하기에는 지나치게 많아요.
남: 여러분들 중 몇몇은 늦게까지 일한다고 저도 들었어요.
여: 네, 그래요. 그리고 저희는 일찍 출근하고 있기도 해요. 초과 근무 수당만으로는 충분하지 않아요. 계속 유지하려면 더 많은 사람을 고용해야 해요.
남: [20]보통은 우리 정책상 연말에만 채용을 하지만, 바꾸려고 해볼 수 있을 거예요. 제가 이사회와 얘기해볼게요.
여: 고마워요. 제가 도와드릴 일이 있을까요?
남: 실은, 있어요. [21]근무 시간 기록표를 준비해주세요. 당신의 부서가 최근 작업한 근무 시간을 보여주는 것으로요.

19.

여자는 어떤 문제를 언급하는가?
(A) 관리자가 갑자기 회사를 떠났다.
(B) 부서가 예산을 초과했다.
(C) 직원들이 늦게 출근한다.
(D) 할 일이 너무 많다.

[해설] 여자가 제기한 문제점을 묻는 문제이다. 대화 초반, 여자는 최근 자신의 부서 업무량(the workload that my department has lately)이 지나치게 많다(It's way too much for us to handle.) 점을 지적했다. 따라서 정답은 (D)이다.

paraphrasing It's way too much for us to handle. 우리가 처리하기에는 지나치게 많다. → There is too much work to do. 할 일이 너무 많다.

[어휘] exceed 넘다, 초과하다   budget 예산   employee 직원   show up (예정된 곳에) 나타나다

20.

남자는 어떻게 문제를 해결해야 한다고 말하는가?
(A) 회사 정책을 바꿈으로써
(B) 더 많은 직원을 채용함으로써
(C) 새로운 장비를 설치함으로써
(D) 합병에 합의함으로써

[해설] 업무량 과다 문제를 해결하기 위해 여자가 직원 채용을 제안했고, 이에 대해 남자는 회사 정책상 연말에만 채용을 하지만(our policy is to only hire at the end of the year) 이를 바꾸려고 해볼 수 있다고(we can try to change that) 말했다. 즉, 남자가 제시한 해결책은 회사 정책을 바꾸는 것이므로 정답은 (A)이다. 더 많은 직원을 고용하는 것은 여자가 제시한 해결책이므로 (B)는 오답이다.

[어휘] recruit 모집하다, 뽑다   install 설치하다   equipment 장비, 용품   agree to ~에 대해 합의하다   merger 합병

21.

남자는 여자에게 무엇을 하라고 말하는가?
(A) 구인 공고를 내기
(B) 이사회 임원들과 만나기
(C) 근무 시간 기록표를 준비하기
(D) 초과 근무 수당을 요청하기

[해설] 남자가 여자에게 요청한 일을 묻는 문제로, 부탁/제안/요청 사항은 주로 대화 후반부에 나타난다. 대화 마지막, 남자가 여자에게 근무 시간 기록표를 준비해 달라고(I need you to get a time sheet ready.) 했으므로 정답은 (C)이다.

paraphrasing get a time sheet ready 근무 시간 기록표를 준비하다 → prepare a time sheet 근무 시간 기록표를 준비하기

[어휘] job opening (직장의) 공석

[22-24] US-AU-BR

Questions 22-24 refer to the following conversation with three speakers.

W1: Marcus, Becky, thanks for your help with interviewing [22]the applicants for the internship position here at our law firm. [23]There were so many more than last year.
M: [23]That surprised me, too. It's no wonder you couldn't handle it on your own.
W2: Since none of them have office experience, we'll have to come up with a training program.
W1: That's true. [24]Becky, I would like you to lead this training session. You did so well last time.

applicant 지원자   law firm 법률 회사   no wonder 당연하다
handle 처리하다, 다루다   on one's own 혼자, 혼자 힘으로
office experience 사무직 경험   come up with 찾아내다, 내놓다
lead 이끌다, 안내하다

22-24는 다음 세 명의 대화에 관한 문제입니다.
여1: Marcus, Becky, [22]우리 법률 회사의 인턴 사원 자리 지원자 면접을 도와줘서 고마워요. [23]작년보다 더 많은 사람들이 왔어요.
남: [23]그래서 저도 놀랐어요. 당신 혼자서 처리하지 못했던 것도 당연해요.
여2: 그들 중에 사무직 경험이 있는 사람이 아무도 없어서 우리가 교육 프로그램을 짜야 할 거예요.
여1: 맞아요. [24]Becky, 당신이 이번 교육을 진행하면 좋겠어요. 지난번에도 아주 잘했잖아요.

22.

화자들은 어떤 종류의 업체에서 근무하는가?
(A) 소매점

(B) 대학교
(C) 법률 회사
(D) 은행

[해설] 여자1의 첫 대사에 화자들이 근무하는 업종에 대한 단서가 있다. 우리 법률 회사의 인턴 사원 자리 지원자(the applicants for the internship position here at our law firm) 면접을 도와줘서 고맙다는 말에서 이들이 법률 회사에서 근무함을 알 수 있으므로 정답은 (C)이다.

[어휘] retail 소매

23.

화자들은 무엇이 놀랍다고 생각했는가?
(A) 판매 수익
(B) 고객들의 의견
(C) 파티의 참석자
(D) 인턴 지원자들의 수

[해설] 여자1이 인턴 지원자를 언급한 후 작년보다 더 많은 사람들이 왔다고(There were so many more than last year.) 하자 남자가 자신도 놀랐다고(That surprised me, too.) 했다. 즉, 화자들은 인턴 지원자들의 수가 많아 놀라워하고 있으므로 정답은 (D)이다.

[어휘] profit 이익, 수익 feedback 피드백, 의견 turnout 참가자의 수

24.

Becky는 무엇을 하라고 요청받는가?
(A) 작업 일정표 만들기
(B) 교육을 실시하기
(C) 양식을 작성하기
(D) 고객에게 연락하기

[해설] 질문의 핵심 키워드인 Becky라는 이름이 언급되는 곳에 집중해 들어야 한다. 대화 마지막, 여자1은 Becky를 부르며, 그녀가 이번 교육을 진행하면 좋겠다고(I would like you to lead this training session.) 말했다. 즉, Becky는 교육 진행을 요청받았으므로 정답은 (B)이다.

`paraphrasing` lead this training session 이번 교육을 이끌다 → conduct some training 교육을 실시하기

[어휘] conduct (특정한 활동을) 하다 fill out 작성하다, 기입하다

PART 4 전화 메시지(telephone message)

출제 유형 01 주문·구매

| 풀이 방법 해석 |

남: 안녕하세요. Mark Baller입니다. 귀하의 꽃꽂이 서비스 관련해서 전화드려요. 저는 Rumney 부동산에서 일하는데 저희 본사는 최근 보수 공사로 문을 닫고 있어요. 사장님이 다음 주에 문을 다시 열 때 크게 특별 이벤트를 하길 원하는데 제가 그 재개장 이벤트의 기획을 담당하게 되었어요. 귀사와 같은 곳에서 오셔서 테이블과 무대를 꾸며 주시면 모든 게 훨씬 좋을 것 같아요. 요즘 시즌에 어떤 꽃들이 가능한지 논의할 수 있도록 가급적 빨리 555-6432로 제게 전화해 주세요.

출제 유형 02 배송·문의

| 풀이 방법 해석 |

남: 이 전화는 Craig Garcia를 위한 것입니다. 저는 Selden's 맞춤 의류의 Nick입니다. 당신이 직원들을 위한 유니폼 15벌 제작에 관해 문의하는 메일을 보내셨죠. 일반적으로, 저는 25벌 이하의 품목 주문에 대해서는 전액을 청구합니다. 하지만, 당신이 제가 정기적으로 거래를 진행하는 분에게 추천을 받으셨으니, 할인된 가격에 유니폼을 제작해 드리겠습니다. 유일한 문제점은 제가 바로 시작할 수 없다는 것입니다. 당신이 제게 필요한 사이즈를 구체적으로 말해주지 않으셨어요. 그 정보를 제게 알려 주시면, 그 주문품에 대해 작업을 하겠습니다. 이 메시지를 받으시면 제게 이메일을 보내시거나 555-1264로 전화 주세요.

 연습 문제

01. (B) 02. (B) 03. (A) 04. (A) 05. (B) 06. (A)

01. US

What is the **purpose** of the message?
(A) To **cancel** an online **order**
(B) To **confirm** the product **specification**

W: Hello, Dr. Williams. This is Sharon Gilbert from Real Scientific Instrument. I'm calling you to confirm the order you placed this morning. You ordered three boxes of 20 milliliter test tubes. Is this correct? According to our record, you usually order 40 milliliter test tubes. Please call back as soon as possible and let me know if the order is correct. Thank you.

메시지의 목적은 무엇인가?
(A) 온라인 주문을 취소하기 위해 (B) 제품 사양을 확인하기 위해

전화 메시지
여: 안녕하세요, Williams 선생님. 저는 Real Scientific Instrument의 Sharon Gilbert입니다. 오늘 아침에 당신이 주문하신 것에 대해 확인하려고 전화드렸습니다. 20밀리미터 시험관을 세 박스 주문하셨습니다. 이게 맞나요? 저희 기록에 따르면, 당신은 보통 40밀리미터 시험관을 주문하시거든요. 가능한 한 빨리 제게 다시 전화 주셔서 이 주문이 정확한지 알려주세요. 감사합니다.

02. AU

What does the speaker **recommend**?
(A) **Visiting** the **store** (B) **Ordering** a different **product**

M: Hi, Amelia! This is Jeremy from Purchasing. The bookcase you ordered for your office is no longer in stock. I can put in a special order for you but it will take around 6 weeks for it to be delivered. If you need it very soon, you'd better order a different product. I will e-mail a link to an online catalog. You will find various bookcases with similar styles and most of them can be delivered just in two or three days.

화자는 무엇을 제안하는가?
(A) 상점을 방문하기 (B) 다른 제품 주문하기

전화 메시지
남: 안녕하세요, Amelia! 저는 구매팀의 Jeremy입니다. 당신이 사무실을 위해 주문하신 책장의 재고가 없습니다. 특별 주문을 해 드릴 수 있지만 배송되는 데 대략 6주가 걸릴 거예요. 정말 빨리 필요하시다면, 다른 제품을 주문하시는 게 좋을 것 같아요. 온라인 카탈로그의 링크를 보내드릴게요. 비슷한 스타일의 다양한 책장을 보실 수 있고 그것들 중 대부분은 이틀이나 3일 안에 배송될 수 있어요.

03. [BR]
Why is the speaker calling?
(A) To complain about a wrong bill
(B) To request a refund for a shipping fee

W: Hello, my name is Karla Smith. I'm calling about a bill I received in the mail from your company. $220.89 was charged for an order of desks and chairs. I placed the order on November 10, but canceled it on November 11. I also received an e-mail to confirm the order cancellation. Please pay attention to this issue and address it immediately.

화자는 왜 전화하는가?
(A) 잘못된 청구서에 대해 불만을 제기하기 위해
(B) 배송비 환불을 요구하기 위해

전화 메시지
여: 안녕하세요, 제 이름은 Karla Smith입니다. 당신의 회사에서 받은 우편물에 들어 있던 청구서에 대해 전화 드립니다. 책상과 의자 주문에 대해 220.89달러가 청구되었습니다. 그 주문을 11월 10일에 했는데, 11월 11일에 취소했어요. 주문 취소에 대해 확인하라는 이메일도 받았습니다. 이 사안에 대해 신경을 써주시고 즉시 해결해 주세요.

04. [US]
What caused a problem?
(A) Electricity failure   (B) A defective item

M: This is a message from John McMillan's Buffet. Because of a severe thunderstorm, some of the Brick City areas experienced a power outage last night. I found that this spoiled most of the ice cream stored in our refrigerator. So, I want to urgently order three gallons of strawberry and chocolate flavored ice cream. I hope they can be delivered before 5 P.M. I am willing to pay extra for this rush order. Thank you.

무엇이 문제를 야기했는가?
(A) 정전   (B) 결함 있는 제품

전화 메시지
남: 이 메시지는 John McMillan의 뷔페에서 남기는 것입니다. 심한 뇌우 때문에, Brick City의 일부 지역에 어젯밤에 정전이 발생했습니다. 이것이 저희 냉장고에 보관되어 있던 아이스크림 대부분에 피해를 준 것을 발견했습니다. 그래서, 급하게 딸기와 초콜릿 맛 아이스크림 3갤런을 주문하고 싶습니다. 오후 5시 전에 배송될 수 있기를 바랍니다. 이 긴급 주문에 대해 추가 비용을 지불할 의향이 있습니다. 감사합니다.

05. [BR]
What is the listener asked to do?
(A) Contact a delivery company   (B) Complete a form

M: Hello, Mr. Grandson. This is Jonathan Clover at Sound Waves Stereos and Speakers. We are sorry to hear that one of your new XL-5300 speakers arrived in poor condition. We will be happy to refund the full amount or send you a replacement with the next-day delivery option. First, please fill out the return and exchange request form and mail it to us.

청자는 무엇을 하도록 요청 받는가?
(A) 배송 회사에 연락하기   **(B)** 양식 작성하기

전화 메시지
남: 안녕하세요, Grandson 씨. 저는 Sound Waves Stereos and Speakers의 Jonathan Clover입니다. 당신의 새 XL-5300 스피커 중 하나가 안 좋은 상태로 배송되었다는 것을 들어서 유감입니다. 저희는 기꺼이 전액을 환불해 드리거나 익일 배송 옵션으로 대체품을 보내드리겠습니다. 우선, 반품과 교환 요청 양식을 작성하셔서 저희에게 우편으로 보내주세요.

06. [US]
According to the speaker, what does the notice say about the package?
(A) It requires a signature.   (B) It was sent to a sender.

W: Hello, I'm calling to find out what happened to my order. I got a notice posted on my door and it said no one was present and the package needs a signature from a recipient. The second delivery will be made tomorrow. Will you arrange for the delivery to be made after 4 P.M.? Before that, there will not be anyone present. Otherwise, is there any way to pick up my order in person?

화자에 따르면, 소포에 대해 공지에 무엇이라고 쓰여 있는가?
(A) 서명이 필요하다.   (B) 보낸 사람에게 발송되었다.

전화 메시지
여: 안녕하세요, 제 주문에 무슨 일이 발생했는지 알아보려고 전화했습니다. 제 문에 붙여있는 공지를 봤는데 아무도 없었고 소포는 수령인의 서명이 필요하다고 써 있었어요. 내일 두 번째 배송이 될 겁니다. 배송이 오후 4시 이후에 오도록 해 주실래요? 그 전에는 아무도 없을 거예요. 아니면, 제 주문품을 직접 가지러 갈 수 있는 방법이 있을까요?

paraphrasing 정답   1. (b) 2. (a) 3. (c) 4. (a) 5. (c) 6. (b)

실전 문제

01. (D)	02. (A)	03. (A)	04. (C)	05. (D)	06. (A)
07. (B)	08. (C)	09. (C)	10. (A)	11. (B)	12. (A)
13. (B)	14. (C)	15. (D)	16. (C)	17. (D)	18. (A)
19. (D)	20. (A)	21. (A)			

[01-03] BR
Questions 01-03 refer to the following telephone message.

W: Hi, Mr. Connors. It's Sadie. I'm calling about your upcoming book-signing event at Tustin Bookstore. ⁰¹**It was originally scheduled for April 9,** but there's a conflict with another major event. ⁰¹**Because of that, we've moved it to April 16,** which will most likely result in better attendance. ⁰²**I've already called the hotel** to change your room booking, and since you plan to drive to Toronto, we don't have to worry about flights. I still need to print the posters, so ⁰³**please send me the photographs you want included** on that. I remember that you had a few that you thought would work well. Thanks!

conflict with ~와의 충돌   result in (결과적으로) ~을 낳다[야기하다]   attendance 참석, 출석   booking 예약

01-03은 다음 전화 메시지에 관한 문제입니다.
여: 안녕하세요, Connors 씨. Sadie예요. Tustin 서점에서 곧 있을 당신의 도서 사인회 행사와 관련해서 전화 드렸어요. ⁰¹원래는 4월 9일로 예정되어 있었으나 다른 중요한 행사와 일정이 겹쳤어요. ⁰¹그 때문에 4월 16일로 옮겼는데요, 이렇게 하면 결과적으로 더 많은 분들이 참석하시게 될 거 같아요. ⁰²제가 이미 호텔에 전화해서 객실 예약을 변경했고, 토론토까지 운전해서 가실 계획이니 항공편에 대해서는 걱정할 필요 없고요. 아직 포스터를 인쇄해야 하니 ⁰³포스터에 넣고 싶으신 사진들을 제게 보내주세요. 잘 어울릴 거라고 생각하셨던 몇 장을 갖고 계셨던 걸로 기억해요. 고맙습니다!

01.
화자는 왜 청자에게 전화하는가?
(A) 도와준 것에 대해 감사하기 위해
(B) 서점 개장을 홍보하기 위해
(C) 책의 사본을 요청하기 위해
(D) 최신 일정을 알려주기 위해

[해설] 전화의 목적은 주로 담화 전반부에 드러난다. 화자는 청자의 책 사인회를 언급하면서 원래는 4월 9일로 예정되어 있었으나(It was originally scheduled for April 9) 다른 중요한 행사와 일정이 겹친 탓에 4월 16일로 옮겼다고(we've moved it to April 16) 했다. 즉, 새롭게 바뀐 일정을 알려주기 위해 전화한 것이므로 정답은 (D)이다.

[어휘] assistance 도움, 지원   promote 홍보하다   request 요청하다   copy (책, 신문 등의) 한 부   provide 제공하다

02.
화자는 자신이 무엇을 했다고 말하는가?
(A) 호텔에 연락했다.
(B) 파일의 교정을 봤다.
(C) 계약서를 이메일로 보냈다.
(D) 항공편을 예약했다.

[해설] 화자가 한 일을 묻는 문제이다. 사인회 일정이 변경되었음을 알린 후 자신이 이미 호텔에 전화해서(I've already called the hotel) 객실 예약을 변경했다고 했으므로 정답은 (A)이다. 항공편(flight)에 대한 언급이 있기는 하지만 자동차를 이용할 계획이니 항공편에 대해서는 걱정할 필요 없다는 내용이므로 flight만 듣고 (D)를 고르지 않도록 한다.

paraphrasing I've already called the hotel 내가 이미 호텔에 전화했다 → Contacted a hotel 호텔에 연락했다

[어휘] proofread 교정을 보다   reserve 예약하다

03.
청자는 무엇을 하도록 요청받는가?
(A) 이미지 보내기
(B) 예산 승인하기
(C) 신청서 제출하기
(D) 포스터 게시하기

[해설] 제안이나 요청하는 내용은 주로 담화 후반부에 제시된다. 담화 후반부에서, 화자는 아직 포스터를 인쇄해야 하니 포스터에 넣고 싶은 사진들을 보내달라고(please send me the photographs you want included) 요청했다. 따라서 photographs를 images로 바꿔 표현한 (A)가 정답이다.

paraphrasing please send me the photographs 제게 사진을 보내주세요 → Send some images 이미지 보내기

[어휘] approve 승인하다   budget 예산   submit 제출하다   application 신청서   put up 게시하다

[04-06] US
Questions 04-06 refer to the following telephone message.

M: Hi, my name is Jeff Enright. I work for Burke Hotel, and we placed an order with your company for some new bed linens. It's been over a week since ordering, so ⁰⁴**I'm wondering if these items have been shipped yet.** ⁰⁵**Due to a large music festival in town this weekend, we are fully booked,** so we're going to need those items. ⁰⁶**Please call me back to let me know approximately which date we could expect to receive them.** If it's too late, we might have to make other arrangements with another supplier. My number is 555-0467. Thanks.

place an order with ~에 주문을 하다   item 물품, 품목   ship 수송[운송]하다   approximately 대략, 거의   make an arrangement with ~와의 합의에 이르다   supplier 공급자, 공급 회사

04-06은 다음 전화 메시지에 관한 문제입니다.
남: 안녕하세요, 제 이름은 Jeff Enright입니다. 저는 Burke Hotel에서 근무하는데요, 저희가 당신의 회사에 몇 가지 새 침구를 주문했습니다. 주문한 지 일주일이 넘어서 ⁰⁴이 품목들이 배송되었는지 궁금합니다. ⁰⁵이번 주말에 도심에서 있을 대규모 음악 축제 때문에 예약이 모두 되어서 그 품목들이 필요할 것입니다. ⁰⁶제게 다시 전화 주셔서 대략 몇 일쯤 저희가 그것들을 받을 수 있을지 알려주세요. 만약 너무 늦는다면 다른 업체와 진행해야 할 것 같습니다. 제 번호는 555-0467입니다. 감사합니다.

04.
전화의 목적은 무엇인가?
(A) 고장 난 품목에 대해 알리기 위해서
(B) 배송비에 대해 문의하기 위해서
(C) 배송 상황을 확인하기 위해서

(D) 일자리를 제안하기 위해서

[해설] 전화의 목적은 주로 메시지 전반부에 드러난다. 화자는 호텔의 직원으로, 청자의 회사에 침구를 주문한 지 일주일이 넘었다고 언급하면서 이 품목들의 배송되었는지 궁금하다고(I'm wondering if these items have been shipped yet) 했다. 즉, 화자는 물품의 배송 상황을 확인하기 위해 전화한 것이므로 정답은 (C)이다.

paraphrasing I'm wondering if these items have been shipped yet 이 품목들이 배송되었는지 궁금하다. → check the status of a delivery 배송 상황을 확인하기

[어휘] broken 고장 난 inquire about ~에 대해 문의하다 shipping fee 배송비 status (진행 과정상의) 상황

05.

화자는 왜 업체가 이번 주말에 바쁠 것이라고 예상하는가?
(A) 인쇄물에 호평이 실렸다.
(B) 새로운 서비스가 제공될 것이다.
(C) 판촉 세일이 열릴 것이다.
(D) 음악 행사가 열릴 것이다.

[해설] 질문의 핵심 키워드 this weekend가 언급되는 곳에 정답의 단서가 있다. 메시지 중반, 이번 주말에 도심에서 있을 대규모 음악 축제 때문에 호텔 예약이 꽉 찼다는(Due to a large music festival in town this weekend, we are fully booked) 말로 보아 이 호텔은 이번 주말에 있을 음악 행사 때문에 매우 바쁠 것임을 예상할 수 있으므로 정답은 (D)이다.

paraphrasing a large music festival in town this weekend 이번 주말에 도심에서 있을 대규모 음악 축제 → A musical event is taking place. 음악 행사가 열릴 것이다.

[어휘] review 비평, 검토 promotional 홍보[판촉]의 take place 개최되다, 일어나다

06.

화자는 청자에게 무엇을 요청하는가?
(A) 예상되는 날짜
(B) 부분적인 환불
(C) 확인 번호
(D) 제품 카탈로그

[해설] 요청 또는 제안 사항은 주로 메시지 후반부에 언급된다. 화자는 주문한 물품의 배송 상황을 문의한 후, 대략 며칠이면 물품을 받을 수 있을지 전화로 알려달라고(Please call me back to let me know approximately which date we could expect to receive them.) 했다. 즉, 화자가 청자에게 요청하는 것은 물품 도착 예상 날짜이므로 정답은 (A)이다.

paraphrasing approximately which date we could expect to receive them 대략 며칠쯤 우리가 받을 수 있을지 → an estimated date 예상되는 날짜

[어휘] estimated 견적의, 추측의 partial 부분적인, 불완전한 refund 환불 confirmation 확인

[07-09] US

Questions 07-09 refer to the following telephone message.

W: Hi, Evan. ⁰⁷**This is Sarah, a member of the warehouse team.** ⁰⁸**I'm working late today because three people called in sick,** so we didn't get all of our tasks done during the shift. Anyway, I'm organizing the cosmetics sent from Oneil Incorporated. ⁰⁹**I have a crate here labeled as three hundred bottles of nighttime moisturizer.** I opened it up, but... um... **it looks like there are three types.** Could you call me back? I'm not sure whether this needs to be sent back. Thanks.

warehouse 창고 call in sick 전화로 병결을 알리다 get ~ done ~을 마치다 task 일, 과업 shift 교대 근무 (시간) organize 정리하다 cosmetics 화장품 crate (물품 운송용 대형 나무) 상자 label as ~라고 딱지를 붙이다

07-09는 다음 전화 메시지에 관한 문제입니다.

여: 안녕하세요, Evan. ⁰⁷**저는 창고팀의 일원인 Sarah입니다.** ⁰⁸세 사람이 병가를 내서 저희가 근무 시간 내에 모든 작업을 완료하지 못했기 때문에 ⁰⁸**제가 오늘 늦게까지 근무하고 있어요.** 그건 그렇고, 제가 Oneil Incorporated에서 보내온 화장품을 정리하고 있는 중이에요. ⁰⁹'**야간용 보습제 300병**'이라고 라벨이 붙은 상자가 여기 하나 있어요. 제가 열어봤더니, 그런데... 음... **세 종류가 있는 것 같아요.** 제게 다시 전화 주시겠어요? 이것을 되돌려 보내야 하는 건지 아닌지 잘 모르겠어요. 감사해요.

07.

화자는 누구인가?
(A) 인사부 직원
(B) 창고 직원
(C) 보안 요원
(D) 컴퓨터 기술자

[해설] 화자의 직업을 묻는 문제로, 메시지 초반 창고팀의 일원인 Sarah라며(This is Sarah, a member of the warehouse team.) 자신의 이름과 소속을 밝혔다. 즉, 화자는 창고 직원임을 알 수 있으므로 정답은 (B)이다.

paraphrasing a member of the warehouse team 창고팀 일원 → a warehouse worker 창고 직원

[어휘] representative 대표, 대리인, 직원 security guard 경비원, 보안 요원 technician 기술자

08.

화자는 왜 자신이 초과 근무를 해야 했다고 말하는가?
(A) 마감일이 변경되었다.
(B) 배송품이 늦게 도착했다.
(C) 일부 직원이 결근했다.
(D) 일부 장비가 작동하지 않고 있었다.

[해설] 화자가 초과 근무를 하는 이유를 묻는 문제로, 화자는 세 사람이 병가를 내서(three people called in sick) 근무 시간 내에 작업을 완료하지 못했기 때문에 자신이 오늘 늦게까지 근무하고 있다고(I'm working late today) 언급했다. 즉, 일부 직원이 결근했기 때문에 화자가 초과 근무 중인 것이므로 정답은 (C)이다.

paraphrasing three people called in sick 세 사람이 병가를 냈다 → Some employees were absent. 일부 직원이 결근했다.

[어휘] absent 결근한, 결석한 equipment 장비, 용품

09.

화자가 "세 종류가 있는 것 같아요"라고 말할 때 암시하는 것은 무엇인가?
(A) 청자를 위해 분실품을 찾았다.
(B) 또 주문하고 싶지 않다.
(C) 오류가 있을 것으로 우려된다.
(D) 다양한 종류에 만족한다.

[해설] 화자의 의도 파악 문제는 앞뒤 상황을 포괄적으로 설명한 보기가 정답이다. '야간용 보습제 300병'이라는 라벨이 붙은 상자(a crate here labeled as three hundred bottles of nighttime moisturizer)를 열어봤다는 말에 바로 이어 "세 종류가 있는 것 같아요"라고 한 것은 상자의 라벨과 내용물이 일치하지 않는다는 의미다. 즉, 오류가 있는 것 같다는 우려를 드러내고 있으므로 정답은 (C)이다.

[어휘] missing items 분실품 place an order 주문하다
be concerned (about/that) (~에 대해) 걱정하다

[10-12] BR

Questions 10-12 refer to the following telephone message.

> W: Good afternoon. This message is for Kyle Shelton. **¹⁰This is Marie calling from Kenwood Realty. I showed you a few apartments in the Brookview neighborhood.** I know you really wanted to be in the Warren Building but the units were all rented. Well, I have some good news. **¹¹One of the tenants canceled his lease early** so there's a two-bedroom apartment available. **¹²Please call me back at 555-3462 to arrange a tour of this site.** Thanks!
>
> realty 부동산 neighborhood 근처, 인근, 지역, 지방 unit (아파트 같은 공동 주택 내의) 한 가구 tenant 세입자 cancel 취소하다 lease 임대차 계약 arrange 마련하다, (일을) 처리하다 site 현장, 부지

10-12는 다음 전화 메시지에 관한 문제입니다.
여: 안녕하세요. Kyle Shelton 씨에게 보내는 메시지입니다. ¹⁰저는 **Kenwood 부동산의 Marie**입니다. 제가 당신에게 **Brookview** 인근의 아파트 몇 곳을 보여드렸었죠. 당신이 정말로 Warren Building에 거주하고 싶어 하셨던 건 알고 있지만 그 세대들은 모두 임대되었었지요. 음, 제게 좋은 소식이 있어요. ¹¹세입자들 중 한 명이 임대 계약을 일찍 취소해서 침실 두 개짜리 아파트가 비어 있어요. ¹²이곳을 둘러볼 일정을 잡도록 555-3462로 제게 다시 전화 주세요. 감사합니다!

10.

화자의 직업은 무엇일 것 같은가?
(A) 부동산 중개인
(B) 신문 기자
(C) 수리 기술자
(D) 인테리어 디자이너

[해설] 전화 메시지에서 화자의 직업에 대한 정보는 주로 메시지 초반에 제시된다. 화자는 자신의 소속을 Kenwood 부동산이라고 밝혔으며, 이어서 청자에게 아파트 몇 곳을 보여주었다고(I showed you a few apartments) 덧붙였다. 따라서 화자의 직업은 부동산 중개인임을 알 수 있으므로 정답은 (A)이다.

[어휘] real estate 부동산 agent 대리인, 중개상 journalist 저널리스트, 기자 repair 수리, 수선 technician 기술자 interior 내부

11.

화자는 청자에게 무엇에 대해 말하는가?
(A) 고객 감사 행사가 열릴 것이다.
(B) 계약 한 건이 종료되었다.
(C) 가격 할인을 받을 수 있을 것이다.
(D) 업체가 고객 의견을 요청하고 있다.

[해설] 메시지 중반, 화자가 청자에게 부동산을 소개하는 부분에 정답의 단서가 있다. 화자는 Warren Building의 세입자들 중 한 명이 일찍 임대 계약을 취소했다고(One of the tenants canceled his lease early) 했는데, 이 말은 화자가 소개하고 있는 아파트의 임대 계약이 종료되었다는 말이므로 정답은 (B)이다.

paraphrasing One of the tenants canceled his lease early 세입자들 중 한 명이 임대 계약을 일찍 취소했다 → A contract has been terminated. 계약 한 건이 종료되었다.

[어휘] terminate 끝내다, 종료하다

12.

청자는 화자에게 왜 다시 전화해야 하는가?
(A) 둘러보는 일정을 예약하기 위해
(B) 주소를 알려주기 위해
(C) 대금 지불을 협의하기 위해
(D) 사은품을 요구하기 위해

[해설] 메시지 마지막 부분에서, 화자는 앞서 소개한 아파트를 둘러볼 일정을 잡도록 자신에게 다시 전화를 달라고 (Please call me back at 555-3462 to arrange a tour of this site.) 했으므로 정답은 (A)이다.

paraphrasing arrange a tour 둘러볼 일정을 잡다 → book a tour 둘러보는 일정을 예약하다

[어휘] book 예약하다 payment 지불, 지급 claim 요구[요청]하다 free gift 경품, 사은품

[13-15] AU

Questions 13-15 refer to the following telephone message.

> M: Hi Cecilia, it's Theo. **¹³I really appreciate your help getting ready for the upcoming graduation ceremony** here at Sayville University. Everything has been fine so far. Something has come up, though. As we discussed, we are going to set a stage and seats at University Garden. I was looking at the weather report, and **¹⁴it's supposed to rain all next week.** I don't think we'll be able to hold it outdoors as we originally wanted to. **¹⁵Could you do me a favor and look into which event halls will be available that day?** We need to find a space for at least 500 guests. Thanks again.
>
> so far 지금까지 hold 주최하다, 열다 outdoors 야외에서 originally 원래, 본래 do ~ a favor ~의 부탁을 들어주다 look into ~을 조사하다

13-15는 다음 전화 메시지에 관한 문제입니다.
남: 안녕하세요, Cecilia. Theo예요. ¹³이곳 **Sayville** 대학교에서 곧

있을 졸업식 준비를 도와주셔서 정말 감사해요. 지금까지는 모든 것이 좋습니다. 일이 좀 생기긴 했지만요. 우리가 얘기했던 대로 대학교 정원에 무대와 좌석을 설치할 예정입니다. 제가 일기 예보를 봤는데 **14다음 주 내내 비가 올 것이라고 합니다.** 우리가 처음에 원했던 대로 야외에서 진행할 수 없을 것 같아요. **15저의 부탁을 좀 들어 주셔서 그날 어떤 행사장이 이용 가능한지 알아봐 주시겠어요?** 적어도 500명의 내빈을 수용할 공간을 찾아야 합니다. 다시 한 번 감사드려요.

13.

화자는 어떤 종류의 행사를 준비하고 있는가?
(A) 회사 바비큐 파티
(B) 졸업식
(C) 지역사회 축하 행사
(D) 교육 워크숍

[해설] 메시지 초반, 화자가 청자에게 곧 있을 졸업식 준비를 도와주셔서 정말 감사하다고(I really appreciate your help getting ready for the upcoming graduation ceremony) 한 것으로 보아 화자는 졸업식을 준비하고 있음을 알 수 있으므로 정답은 (B)이다.

14.

화자에 따르면, 무엇이 문제인가?
(A) 웹사이트가 멈췄다.
(B) 행사 발표자가 취소해야 했다.
(C) 날씨가 좋지 않을 것이다.
(D) 사람들이 초대에 응하지 않는다.

[해설] 메시지 중반, 화자는 일기 예보를 확인했는데 다음 주 내내 비가 올 것이라고 했다며(it's supposed to rain all next week) 처음 얘기했던 대로 야외에서 행사를 준비할 수 없을 것 같다고 전했다. 즉, 나쁜 날씨가 예상되어 야외 행사 준비에 차질이 생긴 상황이므로 정답은 (C)이다.

paraphrasing it's supposed to rain all next week 다음 주 내내 비가 올 것이다 → The weather will be unfavorable. 날씨가 좋지 않을 것이다.

[어휘] crash (컴퓨터가) 갑자기 서버리다 cancel 취소하다 unfavorable 호의적이 아닌, 불리한 respond to ~에 대응하다 invitation 초대, 초대장

15.

화자는 청자에게 무엇을 해달라고 부탁하는가?
(A) 행사를 위해 의자를 놓기
(B) 티켓 소지자에게 연락하기
(C) 공지하기
(D) 장소의 이용 가능성 확인하기

[해설] 메시지 후반에 나오는 Could you do me a favor?는 대표적인 부탁 표현이다. 이 표현 뒤에 화자는 그날 어떤 행사장이 이용 가능한지 알아봐 줄 것을(look into which event halls will be available that day) 부탁했다. 따라서 정답은 (D)이다.

[어휘] set up 놓다, 설치하다 ticket holder 티켓 소지자 make an announcement 발표를 하다, 공지하다 venue (행사의) 장소 availability 이용 가능성

[16-18] US

Questions 16-18 refer to the following telephone message.

W: Hello, this message is for Tim Watters. This is Sarah from Colorado Corner, **16returning your call about the Hanson armchair in blue.** I looked up our records and found that the branch store on Franklin Avenue does have one left in stock, so **17I put it on hold for you.** This means you have to come in and purchase it within only 24 hours. After that, anyone can buy it. Also, the promotion you asked about was over yesterday, but **18if you call us and place an order today, we will still honor the sale price.** And the item will be shipped directly from the branch store.

return a call 답례 전화를 하다 armchair 안락의자 look up (정보를) 찾아보다 branch 지사, 지점 in stock 재고가 있는 put on hold ~을 보류[연기]하다 purchase 구매하다 within ~ 이내에 promotion 홍보, 판촉 be over 끝나다 place an order 주문하다 honor 유효로 인정해서 그 요구에 따르다 ship 수송[운송]하다 directly 곧장, 똑바로

16-18은 다음 전화 메시지에 관한 문제입니다.
여: 안녕하세요, 이 메시지는 Tim Watters에게 보내는 것입니다. 저는 Colorado Corner의 Sarah이고요, **16파란색 Hanson 안락의자에 관해 주신 전화에 답신 드립니다.** 저희 기록을 살펴보니 Franklin Avenue 지점에 재고가 하나 남아 있어서, **17당신을 위해 제가 그것을 맡아 두었습니다.** 이 말은 24시간 이내에 방문하셔서 그것을 구매하셔야 한다는 뜻입니다. 그 시간 이후에는 다른 사람이 구매할 수 있습니다. 또한, 문의하셨던 홍보 행사는 어제 종료되었습니다만 **18저희에게 전화하셔서 오늘 주문하시면 세일 가격을 적용해드리겠습니다.** 그러면 해당 품목이 지점에서 바로 배송될 것입니다.

16.

화자는 어떤 종류의 업체에서 근무하는가?
(A) 가정 배달 서비스
(B) 이사 회사
(C) 가구점
(D) 저장 시설

[해설] 화자가 일하는 곳을 묻는 문제이다. 메시지 전반부를 보면, 화자는 안락의자에 대해 문의한 고객에게 답신 전화를 하고 있음을(returning your call about the Hanson armchair in blue) 알 수 있으므로 화자가 가구를 취급하는 곳에서 근무함을 유추할 수 있다. 따라서 정답은 (C)이다.

paraphrasing armchair 안락의자 → furniture 가구

[어휘] storage 저장, 보관 facility 시설

17.

화자는 자신이 무엇을 했다고 말하는가?
(A) 회원 할인을 적용했다.
(B) 제조사에 연락했다.
(C) 온라인으로 주문했다.
(D) 물품을 예약해 두었다.

[해설] 화자는 청자가 문의한 제품이 Franklin Avenue 지점에 하나 남아 있다고 한 후 그것을 맡아 두었다고(I put it on hold for you) 했다. 즉, 다른 사람들이 구매하지 못하도록 예약해 두었다는 말이므로 정답은 (D)이다.

DAY 12 115

paraphrasing I put it on hold for you 당신을 위해 그것을 맡아 두었다 → Reserved an item 물품을 예약해 두었다

[어휘] apply 적용하다 manufacturer 제조업체 reserve 예약하다, 따로 잡아 두다

18.
화자는 청자에게 무엇을 제공하는가?
(A) 연장된 세일 기간
(B) 장기적인 품질 보증
(C) 조립 지원
(D) 무료 가정 배달

[해설] 메시지 후반, 청자가 문의했던 홍보 행사가 어제 종료되었지만 오늘 전화로 주문을 하면 세일 가격을 적용해주겠다고(if you call us and place an order today, we will still honor the sale price) 했다. 즉, 일단 오늘 전화로 구매 의사를 밝히면 세일 기간과 같은 조건으로 처리해주겠다는 말이므로 정답은 (A)이다.

[어휘] extended 연장된 period 기간 long-term 장기적인 warranty 품질 보증 assembly 조립 assistance 지원, 도움

[19-21] US
Questions 19-21 refer to the following telephone message and seating chart.

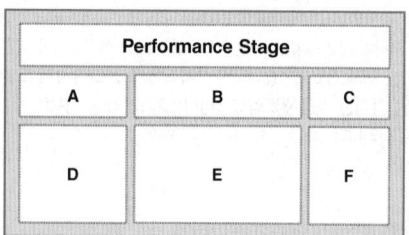

M: Hey Steve, it's Eric. I want to thank you first for helping me writing a sales proposal. Without your assistance, I couldn't have met the deadline. I wanted to show my appreciation in some way. Fortunately ¹⁹**I just won two tickets to go see the musical Tiger Queen at East Hampton Theatre next Saturday evening!** ¹⁹**I thought you might be interested in seeing it with me** since you said you're a big fan of musicals. ²⁰**The seats are great; they're in the center right in front of the stage.** Also, I know you'll be excited about the cast. ²¹**Anita Florence will be playing the lead role!** Call me back as soon as you get this message.

sales proposal 판매 제안서 assistance 도움, 지원 meet the deadline 마감 일자에 맞추다 in some way 어떻게 해서든 win 획득하다, 얻다 be interested in ~에 관심이 있다 cast (연극이나 영화의) 출연진 play the lead role 주인공을 연기하다, 주역을 맡다

19-21은 다음 전화 메시지와 좌석 안내도에 관한 문제입니다.

남: 안녕하세요, Steve. Eric이에요. 우선 제가 판매 제안서를 작성하는 걸 도와줘서 고맙다는 말을 하고 싶어요. 당신의 도움이 없었다면 마감 일자를 맞추지 못했을 거예요. 어떻게 해서든 감사의 마음을 표하고 싶었어요. 운 좋게도 방금 다음 주 토요일 저녁 East Hampton 극장에서 하는 ¹⁹뮤지컬 <Tiger Queen>을 보러 갈 수 있는 티켓 두 장이 생겼어요! 당신이 열렬한 뮤지컬 팬이라고 얘기했으니 ¹⁹저와 함께 이것을 보는 데 관심이 있을 것 같았어요. ²⁰자리도 좋고, 무대 바로 앞 중앙이에요. 게다가, 있잖아요, 출연진도 기대될 거예요. ²¹Anita Florence가 주인공을 연기할 예정이에요! 이 메시지를 듣는 대로 제게 다시 전화 주세요.

19.
전화의 목적은 무엇인가?
(A) 라디오 프로그램을 홍보하기 위해서
(B) 극장으로 가는 길을 안내해주기 위해서
(C) 음악 선호도에 대해 묻기 위해서
(D) 청자를 공연에 초대하기 위해서

[해설] 화자는 메시지 중반에 뮤지컬 티켓 두 장이 생겼다며(I just won two tickets to go see the musical Tiger Queen) 청자가 함께 보러 가는 데 관심이 있을 것 같다는(I thought you might be interested in seeing it with me) 말로 함께 뮤지컬을 보러 가자고 청하고 있다. 따라서 정답은 (D)이다.

[어휘] promote 홍보하다 directions to ~로 찾아가는 길 안내 preference 선호(도) performance 공연, 연주회

20.
시각 자료를 보시오. 화자의 좌석은 어디에 위치하는가?
(A) B 구역
(B) C 구역
(C) D 구역
(D) E 구역

[해설] 메시지 후반, 화자는 티켓의 자리가 좋다며, 무대 바로 앞 중앙(they're in the center right in front of the stage)이라고 좌석의 위치를 구체적으로 설명했다. 이에 해당하는 위치를 시각 자료에 찾으면 B구역이므로 정답은 (A)이다.

21.
Anita Florence는 누구인가?
(A) 배우
(B) 음악가
(C) 라디오 진행자
(D) 시나리오 작가

[해설] 질문의 핵심 키워드 Anita Florence는 담화 마지막 부분에 언급된다. Anita Florence가 주인공을 연기할 예정이라고(Anita Florence will be playing the lead role!) 했으므로 Anita Florence는 화자가 보러 갈 뮤지컬에 출연하는 배우임을 알 수 있다. 따라서 정답은 (A)이다.

DAY 13

PART 3 회사 – 입사·채용 / 전근·퇴임

출제 유형 01 입사·채용
| 풀이 방법 해석 |

남: Rosalie, 식당 직원들이 우리 회사의 확장을 어떻게 감당하고 있나요? 그들에게 일이 너무 많은 것은 아니죠, 그렇죠?
여: 음식 라인은 여전히 제대로 하고 있지만, 계산대에는 추가로 한 사람을 더 써야 할 것 같습니다. 사람들이 그들의 음식은 받지만 돈을 지불하기 위해서 기다려야 하거든요.
남: 알겠어요. 시간제로 일할 사람을 찾는 공고를 내겠습니다. 당신이 시간이 될 때 직무 설명서를 제게 이메일로 보내주세요.

출제 유형 02 전근·퇴임
| 풀이 방법 해석 |

남: Tammy, 바르셀로나 지점을 관리하는 것이 기대되나요?
여: 그런 것 같아요. 저는 스페인을 가본 적이 없어요. 의사소통 하는 데 문제가 좀 있을 것 같아요.
남: 스페인어를 잘하지 않나요?
여: 멕시코에서 공부를 했지만, 매일 스페인어를 사용하지 않으니까요.
남: 'Babel Buddy'라는 앱 들어보셨어요? 외국어를 연습할 수 있는 좋은 방법일 거예요. 가기 전에 그 앱을 다운로드해 보세요.
여: 감사합니다. 정말 도움이 될 것 같아요.
남: 그건 그렇고, 제게 거기 휴가 갔을 때의 유명 레스토랑들의 지도도 있어요. 월요일에 당신을 위해 그것을 가지고 와야 한다는 것을 제게 다시 알려주세요.

연습 문제

01. (B) 02. (A) 03. (B) 04. (B) 05. (A) 06. (B)

01. AU-BR
What will **take place** next **Saturday**?
(A) A **conference**   (B) A **farewell party**

M: Julie is moving to New York for a new job! So, I'm throwing her a party at Tommy's restaurant next Saturday and I was hoping you could come.
W: I won't be available on Saturday, but thanks for letting me know. I'll make sure to stop by her office before she leaves.

다음 주 토요일에 무엇이 열릴 것인가?
(A) 학회 **(B) 송별 파티**

남: Julile가 새 직장을 위해 뉴욕으로 가요! 그래서 다음 주 토요일에 Tommy's 레스토랑에서 파티를 열어주려고 하는데 나는 당신이 오기를 바라고 있었어요.
여: 저는 토요일에 안 될 것 같아요, 하지만 알려줘서 고마워요. 그녀가 떠나기 전에 그녀의 사무실에 꼭 들를게요.

02. BR-US
What does the woman ask the **man** to **do**?
(A) **Conduct** an **interview**   (B) **Review** a **résumé**

M: Here is Sarah Phillip's résumé. She's coming in at 2 P.M. for an interview.
W: Thanks, but an urgent meeting came up. If I'm not back in time, can you begin the interview?
M: Sure, that's not a problem.

여자는 남자에게 무엇을 하라고 요청하는가?
(A) 인터뷰하기   (B) 이력서 검토하기

남: 여기 Sarah Phillip의 이력서가 있어요. 오후 2시에 면접을 보러 올 거예요.
여: 고마워요, 하지만 제게 급한 회의가 잡혔어요. 제가 제시간에 돌아오지 않으면, 면접을 시작해 주시겠어요?
남: 물론이죠, 문제 될 거 없어요.

03. AU-BR
What caused a **problem**?
(A) A **newly introduced policy**   (B) A **schedule conflict**

M: We are going to have job interviews at Mr. Harris' office this Friday.
W: Yes, I know. But we have a problem. The building maintenance office says the annual inspection will fall on that day. What do you think about using Ms. Thompson's office instead?

무엇이 문제를 야기했는가?
(A) 새로 도입된 정책 **(B) 일정의 겹침**

남: 우리 이번 주 금요일에 Harris 씨의 사무실에서 구직 면접이 있을 거예요.
여: 네, 알아요. 그런데 우리 문제가 있어요. 건물 관리 사무소에서 연례 점검이 그날 이루어질 거래요. 대신에 Thompson 씨의 사무실을 쓰는 게 어때요?

04. US-US
Why was the **man surprised**?
(A) A **shipment** was **delayed**.
(B) A **colleague** will **transfer**.

M: I'm surprised to hear that David applied for a transfer to Denver.
W: Yes, I think he is doing well here and he might be promoted to a manager position soon. Why is he going to Denver?
M: He wants to spend more time with his family.

남자는 왜 놀랐었는가?
(A) 배송이 지연되었다. **(B) 동료가 전근 갈 것이다.**

남: David이 덴버로 전근을 신청했다는 걸 듣고 놀랐어요.
여: 네, 그는 여기서 잘하고 있는 것 같고 곧 매니저 직으로 승진할 것 같아요. 그가 왜 덴버로 가는 건가요?

남: 그의 가족과 더 많은 시간을 보내고 싶어 해요.

05. BR-BR

What does the **woman** say she will **do**?
(A) **Visit** the **booth** at a later time   (B) **Fill out** a **form**

> W: Good morning, I'm interested in applying for your assistant accountant position.
> M: Thank you for visiting our booth. Do you want to have an on-site interview today at Wyden Job Fair? There is a spot at 3:00. Can I book that for you?
> W: Yes, I will come back after having lunch.

여자는 그녀가 무엇을 할 거라고 말하는가?
(A) 나중에 부스 방문하기   (B) 양식 작성하기

여: 좋은 아침입니다, 저는 귀사의 보조 회계사 직에 지원하는 것에 관심이 있어요.
남: 우리 부스를 방문해 주셔서 감사합니다. 오늘 Wyden 취업 박람회에서 현장 면접을 보고 싶으세요? 3시에 자리가 있어요. 예약해 드릴까요?
여: 네, 점심 식사를 하고 돌아오겠습니다.

06. US-BR

What did the **man** recently **do**?
(A) He **traveled overseas**.
(B) He **relocated** to another city.

> W: Hi, Jeff. How do you like your new job here in Atlanta so far?
> M: There are things I miss about Los Angeles, but I'm getting used to living here. Also, I thought it would be hard to switch from sales to marketing, but I'm handling it quite well.

남자는 최근에 무엇을 했는가?
(A) 해외 여행을 했다.   **(B) 다른 도시로 이전했다.**

여: 안녕하세요, Jeff. 이곳 애틀랜타에서의 새 직장은 지금까지 어때요?
남: 로스엔젤레스에 대해 그리운 것들이 있지만, 여기 사는 것에 익숙해지고 있어요. 또한, 영업에서 마케팅으로 전환하는 게 어려울 것 같았는데 꽤 잘 해내고 있어요.

paraphrasing 정답   1. (a)   2. (b)   3. (c)   4. (c)   5. (b)   6. (a)

실전 문제

01. (C)	02. (B)	03. (C)	04. (D)	05. (A)	06. (B)
07. (A)	08. (B)	09. (D)	10. (B)	11. (D)	12. (A)
13. (D)	14. (B)	15. (C)	16. (C)	17. (A)	18. (D)
19. (B)	20. (B)	21. (A)			

[01-03] BR-US

Questions 01-03 refer to the following conversation.

> W: Thanks for attending this interview on such short notice, Mr. Bailey. I wanted to make sure that you were considered for this role because ⁰¹**I thought your work history was very impressive. You have a lot of experience.**
> M: Thanks. When ⁰²**I heard about your company from my friend, Rosa Esposito,** I knew it would be a great opportunity for me.
> W: Wonderful. Now, according to your résumé, you're currently working at Larimore Incorporated. Why are you looking for a change?
> M: In that position, my daily tasks mainly include Web design. However, ⁰³**I specialize in Web site security,** so I'm looking for a job that will use those skills.

short notice 촉박한 통보   work history 경력   impressive 인상적인   opportunity 기회   currently 현재, 지금   position (일)자리, 직위   daily task 매일의 업무   specialize in ~을 전문으로 하다

01-03은 다음 대화에 관한 문제입니다.
여: 촉박하게 통보했는데도 이 인터뷰에 참석해 주셔서 감사합니다, Bailey 씨. ⁰¹**당신의 이력이 매우 인상적이라고 생각했기 때문에** 이 자리에 당신을 꼭 고려하고 싶었어요. ⁰¹경력이 풍부하시더군요.
남: 고맙습니다. ⁰²**제 친구 Rosa Esposito로부터 당신의 회사에 대해 들었을 때** 제가 굉장히 기회가 될 거라는 걸 알았어요.
여: 정말 잘됐네요. 자, 당신의 이력서에 따르면 현재 Larimore Incorporated에서 근무하고 있군요. 왜 다른 일을 찾고 있는 거죠?
남: 그 자리에서, 일상적인 제 업무는 주로 웹디자인이 포함돼요. 그런데 ⁰³**저는 웹사이트 보안 전문이어서**, 그 기술을 활용할 자리를 찾고 있어요.

01.

여자는 무엇에 대해 깊은 인상을 받았는가?
(A) 업계에서 주는 상
(B) 추천서
(C) 업무 경력
(D) 디자인 포트폴리오

[해설] 여자가 어떤 점에 깊은 인상을 받았는지 묻는 문제이다. 핵심 키워드 impressed가 대화에서는 impressive로 언급되었다. 여자가 남자에게 이력이 매우 인상적이라며(I thought your work history was very impressive) 경력이 많다고(You have a lot of experience.) 덧붙였으므로 정답은 (C)이다.

paraphrasing   work history 이력 → work experience 업무 경력 / very impressive 매우 인상적인 → impressed with ~에 대해 깊은 인상을 받은

[어휘] be impressed with ~에 깊은 인상을 받다   industry 산업   recommendation 추천, 권고   portfolio (대표 작품을 모은) 선집

02.

남자는 여자에게 자신의 친구에 대해서 얘기하는 이유는 무엇인가?
(A) 지원 상황에 대해 문의하기 위해
(B) 그가 어떻게 이 회사에 대해 알게 되었는지 설명하기 위해
(C) 승진 대상 직원을 추천하기 위해
(D) 그가 작업한 프로젝트의 예를 들기 위해

[해설] 남자가 자신의 친구에 대해 언급한 이유를 묻는 문제이다. 입사

면접 중인 남자는 자신의 친구로부터 이 회사에 대해 들었다는(I heard about your company from my friend, Rosa Esposito) 말로 입사 지원한 회사에 대해 알게 된 계기를 설명하고 있으므로 정답은 (B)이다.

paraphrasing I heard about your company from my friend 친구로부터 당신의 회사에 대해 들었다 → how he found out about the company 그가 그 회사에 대해 어떻게 알게 되었는지

[어휘] status (진행 과정상의) 상황 application 지원[신청](서) promotion 승진, 진급 work on ~에 대한 작업을 하다

03.

남자의 전문 분야는 무엇인가?
(A) 국제 경제학
(B) 자원 관리
(C) 웹사이트 보안
(D) 건축 설계

[해설] 남자의 전문 분야가 무엇인지 묻는 문제이다. 핵심 키워드 specialty(전문, 전공)가 대화에서는 specialize in(~을 전문으로 하다)으로 표현되었다. 남자가 대화 마지막 부분에서 자신이 웹사이트 보안을 전문으로 한다고(I specialize in Web site security) 밝혔으므로 정답은 (C)이다.

[어휘] specialty 전문, 전공 economics 경제학 resource 자원 architectural 건축의

[04-06] US-BR

Questions 04-06 refer to the following conversation.

W: Good afternoon. Welcome to Woodridge Dental Clinic. How can I help you?
M: Hello. **04I read your job posting in the newspaper, so I stopped by to find out if you're still accepting applications.**
W: Yes, we are. We need another receptionist here at the welcome desk to work part-time in the evenings. **05From next month, we plan to stay open later, until 8 P.M.,** so that our patients can book appointments after work.
M: I go to school in the mornings, so part-time hours would be perfect for me. Do you have an application that I could fill out?
W: Actually, **06we have the application form posted online. You should complete that** by June 13 in order to be eligible.

job posting 구인 공고 stop by (~에) 잠시 들르다 accept 받아들이다 application 지원[신청](서) receptionist 접수원 part-time 시간제의 fill out 작성하다 complete 기입하다, 작성하다 eligible ~을 할 수 있는

04-06은 다음 대화에 관한 문제입니다.
여: 안녕하세요. Woodridge 치과에 오신 것을 환영합니다. 어떻게 도와드릴까요?
남: 안녕하세요. 04신문에서 구인 공고를 읽어서, 아직 지원서를 받고 계신지 알아보려고 들렀어요.
여: 네, 받고 있어요. 이곳 접수처에서 저녁에 시간제로 일할 접수원이 한 명 더 필요해서요. 저희 환자들이 퇴근 후로 예약을 하실 수 있도록 05다음 달부터 저녁 8시까지 진료 시간을 연장할 계획이거든요.
남: 제가 오전에는 학교에 다녀요, 그래서 시간제 근무가 제게 딱이에요. 제가 작성할 지원서를 가지고 계신가요?
여: 실은, 06지원 양식은 온라인으로 게시해 두었어요. 6월 13일까지 06그 양식에 기입해야 지원하실 수 있어요.

04.

남자는 왜 이 업체를 방문했는가?
(A) 샘플을 갖다 주기 위해서
(B) 신문 구독을 홍보하기 위해서
(C) 치과 검진을 예약하기 위해서
(D) 공석인 자리에 대해 문의하기 위해서

[해설] 남자의 방문 목적을 묻는 문제이다. 대화 초반 남자가 신문에서 구인 공고를 읽었다며 아직 지원서를 받고 있는지 알아보려고 왔다고(I stopped by to find out if you're still accepting applications) 방문 이유를 밝혔으므로 정답은 (D)이다. 대화 시작 부분에서 장소가 치과인 것만 듣고 남자를 병원을 찾은 환자로 착각하면 안 된다.

paraphrasing find out if you're still accepting applications 아직 지원서를 받는지 알아보다 → inquire about an open position 공석인 자리에 대해 문의하다

[어휘] drop ~ off 을 내려 주다, 갖다 주다 promote 촉진하다, 홍보하다 subscription 구독 dental checkup 치과 검진 inquire about ~에 대해 문의하다

05.

여자는 이 업체에 대해 무엇이라고 말하는가?
(A) 영업 시간을 연장할 것이다.
(B) 두 번째 지점을 열 것이다.
(C) 오늘 일정이 밀려 있다.
(D) 환자들로부터 높은 평가를 받는다.

[해설] 현재 접수원을 채용 중인 치과에서 직원과 입사 희망자 사이에 이루어지는 대화로, 대화 중반 치과 직원으로 보이는 여자가 직원을 추가로 채용하는 이유를 설명하는 부분에 정답의 단서가 있다. 다음부터 저녁 8시까지 진료 시간을 연장할 계획이라는(From next month, we plan to stay open later, until 8 P.M.) 것으로 보아 이 업체, 즉 이 치과가 영업 시간을 늘릴 것임을 알 수 있으므로 정답은 (A)이다.

paraphrasing stay open later 더 늦게까지 문을 열다 → extend its business hours 영업 시간을 연장하다

[어휘] extend 연장하다, 늘리다 business hours 영업 시간 behind schedule 일정이 뒤쳐진 highly 몹시, 매우 rate 평가하다, 등급을 매기다

06.

여자는 무엇을 하라고 추천하는가?
(A) 보고서의 정확성을 확인하기
(B) 온라인 양식에 기입하기
(C) 배송 주소를 갱신하기
(D) 다음 달에 이 업체에 전화하기

[해설] 여자의 제안 사항을 묻는 문제로, 대화 마지막에 정답의 단서가 있다. 입사 지원서가 있는지 묻는 남자에게 여자는 지원 양식은 온라인으로 게시해 두었으니 그것을 작성하라고(we have the application form posted online. You should complete that) 답했다. 따라서 정답은

(B)이다.

paraphrasing the application form posted online 온라인에 게시한 지원 양식 → an online form 온라인 양식 / complete 기입하다 → fill out 기입하다

[어휘] accuracy 정확성 fill out 기입하다, 작성하다

[07-09] US-US-BR

Questions 07-09 refer to the following conversation with three speakers.

W1: Paul, ⁰⁷I heard that you'll be going to the Green Energy Conference.
M: Yes, I am! It's early next month, so HR already made my travel reservations.
W2: It's taking place in Seattle, right? I would love to go. There's so much to do there.
M: Well, I've never been there, but I don't think I'll be able to explore the city. ⁰⁸This will be my first time giving a speech as a company representative, so I'm pretty nervous.
W2: You shouldn't worry, I'm sure you'll do fine.
M: Sarah, haven't you done this sort of thing before? Could you give me some advice?
W1: Actually, ⁰⁹there are some very helpful Web sites on public speaking that I referred to. I will e-mail their links to you this morning.

reservation 예약 explore 탐험하다, 답사하다 representative 대표, 대리인 nervous 긴장한 advice 조언 public speaking 공개 연설 refer to 참고하다

07-09는 다음 세 명의 대화에 관한 문제입니다.
여1: Paul, ⁰⁷그린 에너지 학회에 갈 거라고 들었어요.
남: 네, 맞아요. 다음 달 초라서, HR에서 이미 제 여행편을 예약해 주었어요.
여2: 시애틀에서 열리는 거지요, 맞죠? 저도 정말 가고 싶어요. 거기는 할 수 있는 게 정말 많아요.
남: 흠, 저는 아직 거기 가 본 적이 없지만 도시를 다니지는 못할 것 같아요. ⁰⁸회사를 대표해서 강연을 하는 게 이번이 처음이라 상당히 긴장되거든요.
여2: 걱정 마세요. 분명 잘하실 거예요.
남: Sarah, 전에 이런 종류의 일을 해보신 적이 있죠? 제게 조언을 좀 해 주시겠어요?
여1: 실은 ⁰⁹제가 참고했던 대중 연설에 관한 아주 유용한 웹사이트들이 있어요. 오늘 아침에 그 링크들을 이메일로 보내 드릴게요.

07.

대화는 주로 무엇에 관한 것인가?
(A) 학회 참석
(B) 고객 피드백 수집
(C) 추가 직원 고용
(D) 업무 효율 증진

[해설] 주제를 묻는 문제의 단서는 주로 대화 전반부에 나온다. 대화 초반 여자1이 남자의 학회 참석에 대해 들었다며(I heard that you'll be going to the Green Energy Conference) 대화를 시작했고, 학회 장

소 등에 대해서 이야기하고 있으므로 정답은 (A)이다.

paraphrasing going to the Green Energy Conference 그린 에너지 학회에 가다 → Attending a conference 학회 참석

[어휘] gather 모으다, 모이다 improve 증진시키다, 향상시키다 efficiency 효율

08.

남자는 무엇을 걱정하는가?
(A) 혼자 여행하는 것
(B) 강연하는 것
(C) 제품을 테스트하는 것
(D) 고객과 만나는 것

[해설] 중반부 남자가 회사를 대표해서 강연을 하는 게 이번이 처음이라 상당히 긴장된다고(This will be my first time giving a speech as a company representative, so I'm pretty nervous) 했으므로 (B)가 정답이다.

paraphrasing giving a speech 강연하는 것 → Giving a talk 강연하는 것

09.

Sarah는 남자에게 무엇을 줄 계획인가?
(A) 연락처
(B) 최신 일정
(C) 조사 결과
(D) 온라인 출처

[해설] 담화 후반부에 남자가 Sarah를 부르며 조언을 구하자, 여자1이 참고했던 대중 연설에 관한 아주 유용한 웹사이트들이 있다며(there are some very helpful Web sites on public speaking that I referred to), 그 링크들을 이메일로 보내 주겠다고(I will e-mail their links to you this morning) 했으므로 (D)가 정답이다.

paraphrasing links 링크 → online resources 온라인 출처

[어휘] contact information 연락처 resources 원천, 자원

[10-12] AU-BR

Questions 10-12 refer to the following conversation.

M: Ms. Costello, ¹⁰I think you have the right experience for our firm, and we've covered everything I wanted to discuss in this interview. Are there any questions I can answer?
W: I'm still a bit confused about ¹¹the commission rate paid to salespeople. Is it a flat rate, or does it increase as you get into higher tiers?
M: It's a flat rate, but there are regular performance bonuses as well. You'll have to learn about the products in detail in order to explain their features to customers.
W: That's not a problem. ¹²I'm a very fast learner.

cover 다루다, 포함시키다 confused 혼란스러워하는 commission 수수료[커미션] flat rate 정액제 tier (조직·시스템에서) 단계 regular 정기적인, 규칙적인 in detail 자세하게 feature 특징

10-12는 다음 대화에 관한 문제입니다.
남: Costello 씨, ¹⁰당신은 우리 회사에 딱 맞는 경력을 갖고 있는 것 같아요. 그리고 우리가 이번 면접에서 얘기 나누고 싶었던 건 모두 다 다루었어요. 제가 답변해드릴 질문이 있으신가요?
여: ¹¹판매원에게 지급되는 수수료율에 대해서 아직도 조금 헷갈려요. 고정제인가요, 아니면 단계가 높아지면 더 많아지나요?
남: 고정제이긴 하지만 정기적인 성과 보너스도 있어요. 고객들에게 제품 특징을 설명하기 위해서 상품들에 대해서 자세하게 익혀야 할 거예요.
여: 그건 문제없어요. ¹²저는 아주 빨리 배우거든요.

10.
대화의 주요 목적은 무엇인가?
(A) 장비 업그레이드를 제안하기 위해
(B) 구인 중인 자리에 대해 얘기하기 위해
(C) 투자 전략을 설명하기 위해
(D) 판매 목표를 검토하기 위해

[해설] 대화의 목적을 묻는 문제로, 대화 초반부에서 단서를 찾는다. 초반부에 여자가 언급한 남자의 경력(experience), 우리 회사(our firm), 이번 면접(interview) 같은 어휘와 질문이 있냐는(Are there any questions I can answer?) 부분 등으로 보아 남자는 채용을 진행하는 회사 측의 면접관, 여자는 면접 응시자임을 알 수 있으므로 정답은 (B)이다.

[어휘] equipment 장비, 용품 job opening (직장의) 빈 자리 investment 투자 strategy 전략 goal 목표

11.
여자는 무엇에 대해 문의하는가?
(A) 근무 시간
(B) 팀의 규모
(C) 디자인 과정
(D) 보상 체계

[해설] 입사 지원자인 여자가 면접관으로 보이는 남자에게 한 질문 내용에 정답의 단서가 있다. 여자는 판매원에게 지급되는 수수료율(the commission rate paid to salespeople)이 헷갈린다며, 고정제인지, 아니면 단계가 높아지면 더 많아지는지(Is it a flat rate, or does it increase as you get into higher tiers?) 묻고 있다. 즉, 판매 실적에 따라 어떻게 보상이 이뤄지는지 문의하고 있으므로 정답은 (D)이다.

`paraphrasing` the commission rate paid to salespeople 판매원에게 지급되는 수수료율 → The compensation system 보상 체계

[어휘] compensation 보상(금)

12.
여자는 자신에 대해서 무엇이라고 말하는가?
(A) 빨리 배울 수 있다.
(B) 광범위한 전문 네트워크를 확보하고 있다.
(C) 일을 당장 시작할 수 있다.
(D) 제품에 대해 많이 안다.

[해설] 여자가 자신에 대해 어떻게 말했는지 묻는 문제이다. 대화 후반부에 남자가 고객들에게 제품에 대해 설명하려면 제품에 대해 자세하게 배워야 한다고 하자 여자가 문제없다며 자신을 빨리 배우는 사람(fast learner)이라고 표현했다. 따라서 (A)가 정답이다.

`paraphrasing` I'm a very fast learner. 나는 아주 빨리 배운다. → She is able to learn things quickly. 그녀는 빨리 배울 수 있다.

[어휘] professional 전문적인 immediately 즉시, 당장

[13-15] US-US
Questions 13-15 refer to the following conversation.

W: Hi, Martin. How are you adjusting to this office? Have you been having any trouble at all?
M: Well, ¹³there is a problem with my computer. Sometimes when I come into the office in the morning, ¹³all the work I did the previous day got deleted.
W: Really? That shouldn't happen. ¹⁴I'll have Rick update the software on your computer. That should fix the problem.
M: Thank you.
W: By the way, ¹⁵you should try turning your computer off and on again. That's usually the most basic way to fix a problem.

adjust to ~에 적응하다 previous 이전의 fix 수리하다, 바로잡다 try -ing ~해보다

13-15는 다음 대화에 관한 문제입니다.
여: 안녕하세요, Martin. 이 사무실에 잘 적응하고 있어요? 조금이라도 곤란했던 것이 있나요?
남: 음, ¹³컴퓨터에 문제가 있어요. 제가 아침에 사무실에 오면 가끔씩 ¹³전날 했던 모든 작업이 지워져 있어요.
여: 정말요? 그런 일이 있어서는 안 돼요. ¹⁴Rick에게 당신 컴퓨터의 소프트웨어를 업데이트하라고 할게요. 그러면 그 문제가 해결될 거예요.
남: 고마워요.
여: 그런데, ¹⁵컴퓨터를 껐다가 다시 켜보세요. 그게 일반적으로 문제를 해결하는 가장 기본적인 방법이에요.

13.
남자는 무엇이 문제라고 하는가?
(A) 보안 신분증이 제대로 작동하지 않는다.
(B) 비품 창고를 이용할 수 없다.
(C) 사무실 우편물 수신자 명단에 본인이 없다.
(D) 일부 작업이 삭제된다.

[해설] 질문의 핵심 키워드 problem은 남자의 대사에서 언급된다. 남자는 컴퓨터에 문제가 있다며(there is a problem with my computer), 가끔씩 전날 했던 모든 작업이 지워진다고(all the work I did the previous day got deleted) 했다. 따라서 (D)가 정답이다.

[어휘] security 보안, 안보 badge 배지, 신분 증명서 properly 제대로, 적절히 access 접근; 접근하다; 들어가다; 이용하다 supply closet 비품 창고 mailing list 우편물 수신자 명단

14.
여자는 Rick이 무엇을 하게 할 것인가?
(A) 점검 실시하기
(B) 업데이트 설치하기
(C) 문서 인쇄하기
(D) 구경시켜 주기

[해설] 질문의 핵심 키워드 Rick은 대화 중반 여자의 대사에 등장한다. 앞서 남자가 컴퓨터 파일이 삭제되는 문제점을 언급하자, 여자는 Rick에게 남자의 컴퓨터의 소프트웨어를 업데이트하게 하겠다고(I'll have Rick update the software on your computer.) 했다. 따라서 정답은 (B)이다.

paraphrasing update the software 소프트웨어를 업데이트하다 → install some updates 업데이트를 설치하다

[어휘] conduct (특정한 행동을) 하다 inspection 조사, 점검 install 설치하다 document 문서

15.

여자는 남자가 무엇을 해야 한다고 말하는가?
(A) 양식 작성하기
(B) 특별 접속 요청하기
(C) 컴퓨터를 다시 시작하기
(D) IT 부서에 연락하기

[해설] 대화 마지막, 여자는 컴퓨터를 껐다가 다시 켜보라며(you should try turning your computer off and on again), 이것이 가장 기본적인 문제 해결 방법이라고 덧붙이고 있다. 따라서 정답은 (C)이다.

paraphrasing try turning your computer off and on again 컴퓨터를 껐다가 다시 켜보다 → Restart his computer 컴퓨터를 다시 시작하다

[어휘] complete 기입하다, 작성하다 restart 다시 시작하다

[16-18] US-BR-US

Questions 16-18 refer to the following conversation with three speakers.

M: Jessica, do you have a minute? This is Anna Bower. You'll be sharing your office with her from now on.
W1: ¹⁶You must be the new columnist. Welcome to Green Garden Monthly.
W2: Thanks! I really admire your work, Jessica.
M: I guess you've read some of Jessica's articles? That's good. ¹⁷Jessica can help you turn in your first proposal for our next issue while she's doing her own. By the way, ¹⁸Jessica, did you file your expense report for this month?
W1: Not yet, I plan on doing that later today.
M: Maybe you should show Anna how to fill out the form when you get around to it.
W2: I would really appreciate that.

share 함께 쓰다, 공유하다 from now on 이제부터 columnist 정기 기고가, 칼럼니스트 monthly 한 달에 한 번의, 매월의 admire 감탄하다, 동경하다 article 기사 turn in 제출하다 proposal 제안, 제의, 안 issue (정기 간행물의) 호 file (문서 등을 정리하여) 보관하다, 제출하다 expense 비용 get around to ~할 시간을 내다, ~까지도 하다

16-18은 다음 세 명의 대화에 관한 문제입니다.

남: Jessica 씨, 시간 좀 있어요? 이쪽은 Anna Bower 씨예요. 지금부터 당신의 사무실을 이분과 같이 쓸 거예요.
여1: ¹⁶새 칼럼니스트시군요. <월간 Green Garden>에 오신 것을 환영해요.
여2: 감사해요! 당신의 글은 정말 경탄할 만해요, Jessica 씨.

남: Jessica 씨의 기사들을 읽어보신 것 같군요. 잘됐네요. ¹⁷Jessica 씨가 자신의 작업을 하면서 다음 호를 위해 당신이 처음으로 안을 제출하는 걸 도와줄 수 있어요. 그런데, ¹⁸Jessica 씨, 이번 달 비용 보고서를 제출했나요?
여1: 아직이요, 오늘 늦게 할 계획인데요.
남: 당신이 그 작업을 할 때 Anna 씨에게 양식 작성 방법을 알려주는 게 좋겠어요.
여2: 그래 주시면 정말 감사하겠어요.

16.

화자들은 어디에 있는 것 같은가?
(A) 소매점에
(B) 병원에
(C) 출판사에
(D) 대학교 도서관에

[해설] 화자들이 현재 있는 장소이자 종사하는 직종을 묻는 문제이다. 남자가 여자1에게 오늘부터 함께 근무하게 된 여자2를 소개하는 대화로, 이들의 대화 중 언급되는 columnist(칼럼니스트), Green Garden Monthly(<월간 Green Garden>), articles(기사), next issue(다음 호) 등의 어휘로 보아 이들은 현재 출판사에 있음을 알 수 있다. 따라서 정답은 (C)이다.

[어휘] retail 소매 medical 의학[의료]의 clinic 병원 publishing 출판

17.

남자는 여자들이 무엇을 해야 한다고 말하는가?
(A) 제안서 제출하기
(B) 후보자 면접하기
(C) 오리엔테이션 참석하기
(D) 온라인 교육 이수하기

[해설] 대화 중반, 남자는 Jessica가 자신의 작업도 하면서 다음 호를 위해 Anna Bower가 처음으로 안을 제출하는 걸 도와줄 것이라고(Jessica can help you turn in your first proposal for our next issue while she's doing her own.) 했다. 이는 Jessica와 Anna 두 사람 모두 다음 호를 위한 제안서를 제출해야 한다는 말이므로 정답은 (A)이다.

paraphrasing turn in your first proposal 첫 번째 안을 제출하다 → Submit a proposal 제안서를 제출하다

18.

남자는 Jessica에게 무엇을 물어보는가?
(A) 몇 시에 사무실에 도착하는지
(B) 어떤 과목을 전공했는지
(C) 경력이 얼마나 많은지
(D) 양식을 제출했는지

[해설] 대화 중반, 남자는 Jessica의 이름을 부르며 이번 달 비용 보고서를 제출했는지(Jessica, did you file your expense report for this month?) 물었으므로 정답은 (D)이다.

paraphrasing Did you file your expense report? 비용 보고서를 정리했는가? → whether she filed a form 양식을 제출했는지 안 했는지

[어휘] subject 학과, 과목 major in ~을 전공하다 file (문서 등을) 보관하다[철하다]; 제출하다

[19-21] US-BR

Questions 19-21 refer to the following conversation and list.

Greensboro Public Library Management Certification Classes		
[21]Period 1	Tuesdays	7 – 8 P.M.
Period 2	Wednesdays	8 – 9 A.M.
Period 3	Fridays	12 – 1 P.M.
Period 4	Saturdays	10 – 11 A.M.

W: [19]Did you hear that our branch manager, Ms. Thompson, is transferring to our Madrid branch next year? I just found out from our company newsletter.
M: Yeah, I saw that earlier. As much as [20]I would like to take over her position here, but I'm worried that the company will turn me down because I lack a management background.
W: Why don't you try taking some management classes at Greensboro Public Library?
M: [21]I work in the mornings Monday through Saturday, so I wouldn't be able to attend anything before 6 P.M.
W: They have several different class periods. One of them is bound to work for you.

branch 지점, 지사 transfer to ~로 옮기다 newsletter 소식지
take over ~을 인계받다 turn down ~을 거절[거부]하다
lack ~이 없다[부족하다] management 경영, 운영, 관리
period (학교의 일과를 나눠 놓은) 시간 bound to V 꼭 ~할 것 같은, ~할 가능성이 큰

19-21은 다음 대화와 목록에 관한 문제입니다.

Greensboro 공립도서관 경영 인증 수업		
[21]1기	매주 화요일	오후 7 – 8시
2기	매주 수요일	오전 8 – 9시
3기	매주 금요일	오후 12 – 1시
4기	매주 토요일	오전 10 – 11시

여: [19]우리 지점 매니저 Thompson 씨가 내년에 마드리드 지점으로 옮긴다는 소식 들었어요? 방금 우리 회사 사보에서 알았어요.
남: 맞아요, 저도 아까 봤어요. 이곳에서 [20]그녀의 자리를 인계받고 싶지만 제가 관리 경험이 부족해서 회사에서 거부할까 봐 걱정이에요.
여: Greensboro 공립도서관에서 경영 수업을 좀 듣는 게 어때요?
남: [21]월요일부터 토요일까지 매일 아침에는 일을 해서, 저녁 6시 이전에는 어떤 수업도 들을 수 없을 거예요.
여: 다양한 수업 시간이 있어요. 그중 하나는 반드시 당신에게 맞을 거예요.

19.

어떤 정보가 사보에서 발표되었는가?
(A) 회사가 첫 번째 해외 지사를 열 것이다.
(B) 매니저가 해외로 전근 갈 것이다.
(C) 동료가 승진할 것이다.
(D) 합병이 이루어질 것이다.

[해설] 질문의 핵심 키워드 newsletter는 여자의 첫 대사에 언급된다. 우리 지점 매니저(our branch manager)가 내년에 마드리드 지점으로 옮긴다는(is transferring to our Madrid branch) 소식을 들었냐며 사보에서 알게 되었다고(I just found out from our company newsletter.) 한 것으로 보아, 매니저가 해외로 전근 간다는 사실이 사보를 통해 발표되었음을 알 수 있으므로 정답은 (B)이다.

paraphrasing our branch manager is transferring to our Madrid branch 우리 지점 매니저가 마드리드 지점으로 옮긴다 → A manager will transfer overseas. 매니저가 해외로 전근 갈 것이다.

[어휘] overseas 해외에, 외국에 promote 승진시키다 merger 합병 take place 일어나다, 개최되다

20.

남자는 무엇에 대해 걱정이 된다고 말하는가?
(A) 경영진들 앞에서 발표하기
(B) 승진 거부당하기
(C) 해외 지사에서 일하기
(D) 인원 감축으로 인해 해고되기

[해설] 남자가 걱정하는 것을 묻는 문제이다. 남자는 해외로 전근을 가는 Ms. Thompson의 자리를 인계받고 싶지만 관리 경험이 부족한 탓에 회사에서 거부할까 봐 걱정이라고(I'm worried that the company will turn me down because I lack a management background.) 했다. 즉, 자신의 승진이 거부될까 봐 걱정하고 있으므로 정답은 (B)이다.

[어휘] give a presentation 발표를 하다 promotion 승진, 진급 be fired 해고되다 due to ~ 때문에 downsizing 인원 삭감

21.

시각 자료를 보시오. 남자가 어느 시간에 등록할 것 같은가?
(A) 1기
(B) 2기
(C) 3기
(D) 4기

[해설] 남자는 월요일부터 토요일까지 매일 오전에 일을 하므로 저녁 6시 이전에는 어떤 수업도 들을 수 없다고(I work in the mornings Monday through Saturday, so I wouldn't be able to attend anything before 6 P.M.) 했다. 시각 자료에서 남자의 근무 시간대에 해당하지 않는 것은 매주 화요일 오후 7-8시 수업뿐이므로 정답은 (A)이다.

[어휘] register for ~에 등록하다

PART 4 녹음 메시지(recorded message) / 설명(instructions)

출제 유형 01 녹음 메시지(recorded message)

| 풀이 방법 해석 |

남: Columbus 보험사에 전화해주셔서 감사합니다. Echo 가 232번지에 위치하고 있던 저희 사무실이 새 위치인 Rosebud 대로 810번지로 옮겼다는 것을 알아두세요. 저희 웹사이트에서 미니 지도와 고속도로에서부터의 운전 방향을 찾아보실 수 있습니다. 저희가 아직 새 사무실에 맞추어 정리 중이니 귀하의 이름과 연락처를 남겨주시면 가능한 한 빨리 다시 연락드리겠습니다.

출제 유형 02 설명(instructions)

| 풀이 방법 해석 |

여: 갑작스러운 공지에도 회의에 와주셔서 감사합니다. 우리가 판촉을 위해 발행했던 온라인 할인 쿠폰에 대해 말하고자 합니다. 몇몇 고객들이 셀프 계산대에 있는 스캐너에서 그것이 읽히지 않아서 할인을 받지 못했다고 불평합니다. 그것은 옛날 버전의 스캐너가 있는 몇몇 셀프 계산대에서 우연히 발생했습니다. 그래서 저는 각각의 계산대에 고객들이 그들의 구매품에 대해 어떻게 쿠폰을 사용할 수 있는지에 대한 게시물을 붙여 놓았습니다. 할인을 받기 위해, 고객들은 스캔을 하는 대신 화면에 8자리 숫자를 입력하면 됩니다. 그리고 여기 우리 스캐너가 읽을 수 있는 바코드가 찍힌 새 쿠폰이 있습니다. 이것들을 여러분들께 나누어 드릴게요. 설명을 따라하는 데 어려움을 겪는 고객들에게 그냥 스캔해 주시면 됩니다.

 연습 문제

01. (B)　02. (B)　03. (B)　04. (B)　05. (A)　06. (A)

01. [BR]

What company is the listener **calling**?
(A) A **security agency**　(B) A **credit card company**

W: You have reached First Credit Card. <u>Business hours</u> of the customer service and card issuing department are from 9 A.M. to 5 P.M. So, please call again tomorrow at any time <u>within</u> our business hours. If you want to <u>report</u> a lost or stolen credit card, just press 0. Thank you.

청자는 어떤 회사에 전화하고 있는가?
(A) 보안 회사　**(B) 신용카드 회사**

녹음 메시지
여: First Credit Card에 전화하셨습니다. 고객 서비스와 카드 발급 부서의 영업 시간은 오전 9시에서 오후 5시까지입니다. 그러므로 내일 영업 시간 내에 아무때나 다시 전화해 주시기 바랍니다. 분실이나 도난 카드에 대해 신고하시려면, 0번만 누르시면 됩니다. 감사합니다.

02. [US]

What information are the listeners able to **obtain** from the company's **Web site**?
(A) New **telephone numbers**
(B) **Directions** to the new location

M: Thank you for calling Barson Construction Company. Please note that we are <u>relocating</u> to a new building on Kensington Road on 3 November. You can <u>get directions</u> to the new office on our Web site. All telephone numbers will <u>remain</u> the <u>same</u>. Thank you.

청자들은 회사의 웹사이트에서 어떤 정보를 얻을 수 있는가?
(A) 새 전화번호　**(B) 새 위치로 가는 방법**

녹음 메시지
남: Barson Construction Company에 전화해 주셔서 감사합니다. 저희가 11월 3일에 Kensington 가의 새 건물로 이전할 것이라는 점을 유념해 주세요. 저희 웹사이트에서 새 사무실로 가는 길을 확인할 수 있습니다. 모든 전화번호는 동일하게 유지될 겁니다. 감사합니다.

03. [US]

According to the speaker, **what** has **caused** a **problem**?
(A) A **broken machine**　(B) **Bad weather**

W: Thank you for calling the Perkins' Ranch. We are one of the <u>largest</u> ranches in the Scranton area. Due to the <u>heavy snow</u> last week, all of the events and activities for tourists are <u>canceled</u> this week. All event schedules will go back to <u>normal</u> sometime next week. We are open for business visits from 10 A.M. to 4 P.M. on weekdays. Thank you.

화자에 따르면, 무엇이 문제를 야기했는가?
(A) 고장 난 기계　**(B) 안 좋은 날씨**

녹음 메시지
여: Perkins' 목장에 전화해 주셔서 감사합니다. 저희는 Scranton 지역에서 가장 큰 목장 중 하나입니다. 지난주 폭설로 인해, 이번 주 관광객들을 위한 모든 행사와 활동이 취소되었습니다. 모든 행사 일정은 다음 주 중에 정상으로 돌아갈 것입니다. 사업상의 방문을 위해서는 평일 오전 10시부터 오후 4시까지 열려 있습니다. 감사합니다.

04. [AU]

What did listeners **receive** at the entrance?
(A) A **meal voucher**　(B) A **welcome packet**

M: Attention please! I will tell you what you are going to do to <u>apply for</u> your employee badge. You can find an application form in the <u>welcoming packet</u> that you received at the entrance. Would you please fill it out <u>completely</u> now? I will call the name of a <u>department</u> and then they will go down to the security office in the basement.

청자들은 입구에서 무엇을 받았는가?
(A) 식사 쿠폰　**(B) 환영 꾸러미**

설명
남: 주목해 주세요! 여러분이 사원증을 신청하기 위해 무엇을 해야 할지 알려 드릴게요. 입구에서 받은 환영 꾸러미에 신청서 양식이 있을 겁니다. 그것을 지금 완전히 작성해 주시겠어요? 제가 부서 이름을 부르면 그분들은 지하에 있는 보안실로 내려갈 겁니다.

05. US

What does the speaker ask the **listeners** to **do**?
(A) **Give** corrected **price information**
(B) **Distribute** a discount **coupon**

> W: Hi, everyone. It's the first day of our seasonal <u>clearance sale</u>. I think today will be the <u>busiest</u> day of this three-day event. Before we open, I want to tell you about a <u>typo</u> in the <u>price</u> on the advertisement. I will <u>set up</u> boards with the <u>correct</u> information throughout the store. Just in case, I ask you to <u>mention</u> it to every incoming customer and apologize for the mistake.

화자는 청자들에게 무엇을 하라고 요청하는가?
(A) 수정된 가격 정보를 주기   (B) 할인 쿠폰을 나누어주기

설명
여: 안녕하세요, 여러분. 시즌 정리 세일의 첫날이네요. 오늘이 이 3일간의 행사 중 가장 바쁜 날이 될 것 같아요. 문을 열기 전에, 광고에 있는 가격 오타에 대해 말씀 드리고 싶어요. 제가 매장 전체에 정확한 정보가 쓰여 있는 안내판을 설치할 겁니다. 만약에 대비해서, 방문하는 모든 고객들에게 그것을 언급해주시고 실수에 대해 사과해 주시길 부탁합니다.

06. BR

What are the **listeners** required to **do**?
(A) **Wear protective gear**   (B) **Use basic tools**

> M: Yesterday, you learned how to use the <u>basic tools</u> for woodwork. Today, we are going to use an electronic saw to <u>cut boards</u>. It is the most <u>dangerous</u> tool that we are using during the class. So, please make sure to wear these <u>protective gloves</u> and goggles. They are all in the box beside the electronic saw.

청자들은 무엇을 하도록 요청받는가?
(A) 보호 장비 착용하기   (B) 기본적인 도구 사용하기

설명
남: 어제, 우리는 목공예를 위한 기본적인 도구를 어떻게 사용하는지 배웠습니다. 오늘은 판자를 자르기 위해 전기톱을 사용할 겁니다. 이건 우리가 수업에서 사용하는 가장 위험한 도구입니다. 그러므로 이 보호 장갑과 고글을 반드시 착용하세요. 전기톱 옆에 있는 상자에 모두 들어 있습니다.

paraphrasing 정답 1. (c) 2. (b) 3. (a) 4. (b) 5. (c) 6. (a)

실전 문제

01. (A)	02. (D)	03. (D)	04. (C)	05. (A)	06. (B)
07. (D)	08. (A)	09. (C)	10. (A)	11. (D)	12. (C)
13. (B)	14. (B)	15. (A)	16. (B)	17. (C)	18. (D)

[01-03] BR
Questions 01-03 refer to the following instructions.

> W: As I'm sure you've heard by now, **01my security team** will install new card readers at all entrances in the building over the weekend. Your manager should have given you **02a five-digit code** for your department. **02Please memorize this**, because it should not be written down. To use the device, simply type in the code and then hold your ID badge against the card reader for a few seconds. The door should then open. If the light turns red, it means that you don't have access to that room. If you think this happened in error, **03you can press the star key to start over**.

by now 지금쯤은 이미   install 설치하다   card reader 카드 판독기   entrance 출입구   digit 숫자   code 암호, 부호   memorize 암기하다   device 장치, 기구   type in 입력하다   have access to ~에 출입할 수 있다   in error 잘못하여   start over 다시 시작하다

01-03은 다음 설명에 관한 문제입니다.
여: 지금쯤이면 여러분도 들으셨을 거라 믿는데요, **01저희 보안팀**이 주말 동안 건물 내의 모든 출입구에 새로운 카드 판독기를 설치할 예정입니다. 여러분의 관리자가 여러분의 부서에 배당된 **02다섯 자리 암호**를 알려주셨을 겁니다. **02이것을 외워두시기 바랍니다**. 적어 두시면 안 되기 때문입니다. 장치를 이용하시려면, 그저 비밀번호를 입력한 다음 카드 판독기에 몇 초간 신분증을 갖다 대세요. 그러면 문이 열립니다. 빨간색 불이 들어오면 그 방에 들어갈 수 없다는 뜻입니다. 오류로 이러한 상황이 발생했다고 생각되시면 **03별표를 눌러서 다시 시작하시면 됩니다**.

01.
화자는 어느 부서에서 근무하는가?
(A) 보안
(B) 영업
(C) 재무
(D) 정보기술

[해설] 화자의 직업이나 업종과 관련된 정보는 주로 담화 초반에 제시된다. 담화 초반, 저희 보안팀(my security team)이라는 말로 소속 부서를 밝혔으므로 화자는 보안팀에서 근무함을 알 수 있다. 따라서 정답은 (A)이다.

02.
화자는 청자들에게 무엇을 하라고 요청하는가?
(A) 워크숍에 참석하기
(B) 비밀번호 고르기
(C) 사용자 설명서 읽기
(D) 암호 외우기

[해설] 화자는 건물 내 모든 출입구에 카드 판독기를 새로 설치할 예정이라면서, 관리자가 부서에 배당된 다섯 자리 암호(a five-digit code)를 알려주었을 거라고 한 후 이것을 외워두라고(Please memorize this) 요청한다. 따라서 정답은 (D)이다.

03.
화자의 말에 따르면, 청자들은 왜 별표를 눌러야 하는가?
(A) 숫자를 찾기 위해서
(B) 오류를 보고하기 위해서
(C) 장치를 켜기 위해서
(D) 과정을 다시 시도하기 위해서

[해설] 질문의 키워드 star key는 담화 마지막 부분에 언급된다. 화자가 새로 설치될 예정인 카드 판독기의 이용 방법을 설명하면서, 오류가 났다고

생각되면 별표를 눌러서 다시 시작하면 된다고(you can press the star key to start over) 했다. 즉, 카드 판독기에 신분증을 인식시키는 과정을 다시 시도하려면 별표를 눌러야 함을 알 수 있으므로 정답은 (D)이다.

paraphrasing start over 다시 시작하다 → try a process again 과정을 다시 시도하다

[어휘] search for ~를 찾다 process 과정, 절차

[04-06] BR

Questions 04-06 refer to the following recorded message.

> M: You've reached the offices of ⁰⁴**Berkshire, the region's largest supplier of energy** for residential properties. ⁰⁵**Our agents are unable to take your call at this time, as we are holding our annual company-wide training day.** We apologize for any inconvenience this may cause. For general inquiries, you can visit our Web site for more information. ⁰⁶**If you are calling about an emergency repair and need to speak to a repair technician immediately, please press zero,** and we will transfer your call. Thank you.

reach (특히 전화로) 연락하다 region 지방, 지역 supplier 공급자, 공급 회사 residential 주택지의 property 부동산, 건물 agent 대리인, 직원 company-wide 회사 전반의 inconvenience 불편 cause ~을 야기하다 general 일반적인 inquiry 문의 repair 수리 technician 기술자 immediately 즉시 transfer 옮기다, 건네주다

04-06은 다음 녹음 메시지에 관한 문제입니다.
남: 주거용 건물을 위한 ⁰⁴지역 최대의 에너지 공급회사인 **Berkshire** 사무소에 연결되셨습니다. ⁰⁵매해 있는 전사적인 교육을 진행하는 날이므로 저희 직원들이 지금 전화를 받을 수 없습니다. 이로 인해 불편을 드려 죄송합니다. 일반 문의는 저희 웹사이트를 방문하시면 더 많은 정보를 얻으실 수 있습니다. ⁰⁶긴급 수리와 관련해 전화하셨고 즉시 수리 기술자와의 상담이 필요하시면 0번을 눌러주세요. 그러면 전화를 연결해드리겠습니다. 감사합니다.

04.

어떤 종류의 업체가 전화를 받고 있는가?
(A) 법률 사무소
(B) 백화점
(C) 공익 기업
(D) 회계 법인

[해설] 고객이 특정 업체에 전화했을 경우 들을 수 있는 녹음 메시지의 일종이다. 이런 경우 대개 회사를 소개하는 말로 메시지를 시작하는데, 여기서도 주거용 건물을 위한 지역 최대의 에너지 공급회사(the region's largest supplier of energy)라는 말로 회사를 소개했다. 전기, 가스, 수도 같은 공익 사업을 utility로 표현하므로 정답은 (C)이다.

paraphrasing the region's largest supplier of energy 지역 최대의 에너지 공급회사 → a utility company 공익 기업

[어휘] utility company (전기, 가스, 상·하수도, 교통 기관 등의) 공익 기업 accounting firm 회계 법인, 회계사무소

05.

왜 직원과 통화할 수 없는가?
(A) 직원들이 교육을 받고 있는 중이다.
(B) 평소보다 전화가 더 많이 온다.
(C) 주말이다.
(D) 국경일이다.

[해설] 직원들이 전화를 받을 수 없는 이유를 묻는 문제이다. 화자는 매해 있는 전사적인 교육을 진행하는 날이므로 직원들이 지금 전화를 받을 수 없다고(Our agents are unable to take your call at this time, as we are holding our annual company-wide training day.) 밝혔다. 이로 보아 현재 전 직원들이 교육을 받고 있기 때문에 전화를 받지 못함을 알 수 있으므로 정답은 (A)이다.

paraphrasing we are holding our annual company-wide training day 매해 있는 전사적인 교육을 진행하고 있다 → Staff members are being trained. 직원들이 교육을 받고 있는 중이다.

[어휘] train 교육[훈련]시키다 than usual 평상시보다

06.

청자는 왜 0번을 눌러야 하는가?
(A) 전화로 대금을 결제하기 위해서
(B) 수리 담당자와 연결되기 위해서
(C) 녹음 내용을 다시 듣기 위해서
(D) 메시지를 남기기 위해서

[해설] 질문의 키워드 press zero가 언급되는 대화 후반부에 정답의 단서가 있다. 긴급 수리(an emergency repair)와 관련해 전화했고 즉시 수리 기술자와의 상담이 필요하다면(need to speak to a repair technician immediately) 0번을 누르라고(please press zero) 했다. 즉, 수리 담당자와의 통화를 하기 위해서는 0번을 눌러야 하므로 정답은 (B)이다.

paraphrasing need to speak to a repair technician 수리 기술자와 상담이 필요하다 → be connected to a repair person 수리 담당자와 연결되다

[어휘] make a payment 대금을 결제하다 be connected to ~와 연결되다

[07-09] US

Questions 07-09 refer to the following instructions.

> W: All right, everyone, we've recently received some complaints from customers saying that ⁰⁷**the cars they rent from our agency** are not very clean. We've purchased some ⁰⁸**handheld vacuums** to make the cleaning process easier, and each car should be double-checked before giving it to the customer. ⁰⁸**When the vacuum gets full, simply press the "Release" button on the side.** Then pull the container out gently and ⁰⁸**dump the contents into a trash bin.** Next, push the container back in until you hear a click. ⁰⁹**You probably won't have any issues, but if you do, Jake will be here until six o'clock.**

agency 대리점, 대행사 purchase 구매하다 handheld 손에 들고 쓰는 vacuum 진공청소기(= vacuum cleaner) process

절차, 과정   double-check 재확인하다   release 방출하다
pull out 빼내다   container 용기   gently 부드럽게   dump 버리
다   contents 내용물   trash bin 쓰레기통   issue 문제, 거리

07-09는 다음 설명에 관한 문제입니다.
여: 자, 여러분, 최근 고객들로부터 불만을 접수했는데요, **07우리 대리점에서 빌린 차량들**이 그리 깨끗하지 않다고 하는군요. 청소 과정이 보다 간편해지도록 **08손에 들고 쓰는 소형 진공청소기**를 구매했으니 각 차량을 고객들에게 인도하기 전에 재확인하시기 바랍니다. **08진공청소기가 가득 차**면 간단히 옆쪽에 있는 "내보내기" 버튼을 누르세요. 그런 다음 용기를 부드럽게 빼내어 **08내용물을 쓰레기통에 버리세요**. 다음으로, "딸각" 소리가 날 때까지 용기를 다시 밀어 넣으세요. **09아마도 별 문제가 생기지는 않겠지만 만약 문제가 생긴다면 Jake가 6시까지 이곳에 있을 겁니다.**

07.
청자들은 어떤 업체에서 일하는가?
(A) 식료품점
(B) 수리점
(C) 고급 호텔
(D) 자동차 대여소

[해설] 담화 초반 화자가 최근 고객들로부터 불만을 접수했다면서 고객들이 우리 대리점에서 빌린 차량들(the cars they rent from our agency)이 그리 깨끗하지 않다고 했다는 말로 보아 이들이 자동차를 빌려주는 곳에서 근무함을 알 수 있으므로 정답은 (D)이다.

[어휘] luxury 사치(품)의, 고급(품)의   rental 임대, 임차, 대여

08.
화자는 무엇에 관해 지시 사항을 전달하고 있는가?
(A) 진공청소기를 비우는 법
(B) 양식을 기입하는 법
(C) 소프트웨어를 설치하는 법
(D) 프린터를 조작하는 법

[해설] 화자는 대여용 차량의 청소를 위해 손에 들고 쓰는 소형 진공청소기(handheld vacuums)를 구매했다고 한 후, 청소기가 가득 차면(When the vacuum gets full) 옆쪽의 버튼을 눌러 용기를 빼내어 내용물을 쓰레기통에 버리라고(dump the contents into a trash bin) 했다. 즉, 청소기 먼지 통을 비우는 방법을 자세히 설명하고 있으므로 정답은 (A)이다.

paraphrasing   dump the contents into a trash bin 내용물을 쓰레기통에 버리다 → empty a vacuum 진공청소기를 비우다

[어휘] empty 비우다   complete 작성하다, 기입하다   install 설치하다   operate 가동[조작]하다

09.
화자가 "Jake가 6시까지 이곳에 있을 겁니다"라고 말할 때 암시하는 것은 무엇인가?
(A) Jake가 배달물을 받을 것이다.
(B) 화자가 잘못된 일정을 보냈다.
(C) Jake가 장치 사용법을 알고 있다.
(D) Jake가 중요한 고객과 이야기할 것이다.

[해설] 화자의 의도 파악 문제는 앞뒤 문맥을 종합적으로 파악하여 정답을 찾아야 한다. 앞서 청소기를 비우는 방법을 자세히 설명한 후, 만약 문제가 생긴다면(You probably won't have any issues, but if you do) "Jake가 6시까지 이곳에 있을 겁니다"라고 한 것으로 보아 Jake가 청소기 작동법을 잘 알고 있으니 문제가 생기면 Jake에게 연락하라는 의도로

해당 표현을 사용한 것임을 알 수 있다. 따라서 정답은 (C)이다.

[어휘] accept 받다   incorrect 잘못된   device 장치, 기구

[10-12] [BR]
Questions 10-12 refer to the following instructions.

W: Hello, my name is Yvonne and I'll be leading this yoga class. If you didn't bring your own mat, **10there are extras available up here at the front of the classroom.** Also, there's a vending machine in the hallway that sells bottles of water or sports drinks. After today's session, if you would like to switch to a more intense class, you can do so at the main office. **11Be aware that the intense class usually fills up quickly, though.** Okay, **12let's get started with some stretches!**

lead 안내하다, 이끌다   vending machine 자동 판매기
hallway 복도   switch to ~으로 바뀌다   intense 극심한, 강렬한
be aware that ~을 인지하다   fill up 가득 차다

10-12는 다음 설명에 관한 문제입니다.
여: 안녕하세요, 제 이름은 Yvonne이고, 이 요가 수업을 지도할 예정입니다. 자신의 매트를 가져오지 않으셨다면, **10교실 앞쪽 여기에 이용하실 수 있는 여분의 매트들이 있습니다.** 또한, 복도에 물과 스포츠 음료를 판매하는 자판기가 있습니다. 오늘 시간 이후에 좀더 난도가 높은 수업으로 옮기고 싶다면 중앙 사무실에서 하시면 됩니다. **11하지만 심화 수업은 보통 빨리 마감된다는 것을 알아두시기 바랍니다.** 좋습니다, **12스트레칭으로 시작해보죠!**

10.
화자의 말에 따르면, 방의 앞쪽에서 무엇을 이용할 수 있는가?
(A) 수건
(B) 운동복
(C) 운동 매트
(D) 물병

[해설] 질문의 키워드인 room은 담화에서 언급한 classroom을 가리킨다. 화자는 교실 앞쪽에 여분의 매트들이 있다고(there are extras available up here at the front of the classroom) 했는데, 이 매트들은 요가를 위한 것이다. 따라서 요가 매트를 '운동 매트'로 표현한 (C)가 정답이다.

11.
화자는 심화 수업에 대해 무엇이라고 말하는가?
(A) 운동 선수들에게만 권장된다.
(B) 옮겨 가려면 추가 요금이 든다.
(C) 요가를 해본 경험을 요구한다.
(D) 채워지는 데 오래 걸리지 않는다.

[해설] 담화 후반 intense class가 언급되는 부분에 정답의 단서가 있다. 심화 수업은 보통 빨리 마감된다는 것을 알아두라는(Be aware that the intense class usually fills up quickly) 말로 보아 심화 수업의 인원은 오래 걸리지 않아 모두 채워짐을 알 수 있으므로 정답은 (D)이다.

paraphrasing   the intense class usually fills up quickly 심화 수업은 보통 빨리 마감된다 → It does not take long to fill. 채워지는 데 오

래 걸리지 않는다.

[어휘] recommend 추천하다 athletic people 운동을 잘하는 사람 extra fee 추가 요금 transfer into ~로 옮기다 require 요구하다, 필요로 하다 background 배경, 경력, 경험

12.

청자들은 다음에 무엇을 할 것인가?
(A) 양도 계약서에 서명하기
(B) 사무실을 방문하기
(C) 스트레칭을 하기
(D) 대금을 지불하기

[해설] 담화 마지막 부분에서 화자가 청자들에게 스트레칭으로 시작해보자고(let's get started with some stretches) 한 것으로 보아 담화 직후 청자들이 스트레칭을 할 것임을 알 수 있으므로 정답은 (C)이다.

[어휘] release form 양도 계약서 stretch out 쭉 펴다 make a payment 대금을 납부하다

[13-15] AU

Questions 13-15 refer to the following instructions and flowchart.

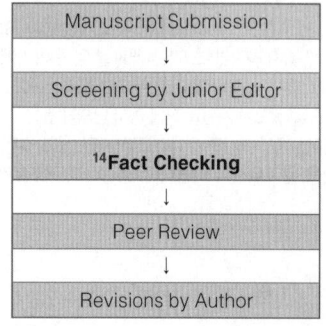

M: I'd like to take a moment to discuss what happens when a new manuscript is submitted to our publishing company. **¹³In the past few weeks, we've received a lot more manuscripts than usual. That's thanks to our booth at the recent National Convention of Publishers.** It really raised our profile among writers. To make the process go more smoothly, ¹⁴**we've added an extra step between the screening by the junior editor and the peer review.** ¹⁵**A few people have mentioned concerns that the peer review team is extremely busy these days,** so we're looking for a way to relieve some pressure. We hope this new process will help with that.

manuscript 원고   publishing company 출판사   thanks to ~ 덕분에   booth (칸막이를 한) 작은 공간, 부스   publisher 출판인, 출판사   raise one's profile ~의 인지도를 높이다   smoothly 부드럽게, 순조롭게   screening 검사[심사]   junior 하급의, 부하의   editor 편집자   peer review 동료 검토, 동업자의 평가   concern 우려, 걱정   extremely 극도로, 극히   relieve 없애다, 덜어주다   pressure 압박, 압력   submission 제출   fact checking 사실 확인   revision 수정, 정정   author 작가, 저자

13-15는 다음 설명과 순서도에 관한 문제입니다.

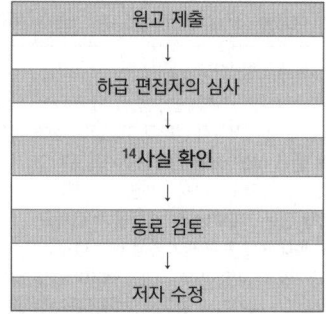

남: 잠시 시간을 내어 우리 출판사에 새로운 원고가 투고되면 어떻게 처리되는지에 대해 얘기하고자 합니다. ¹³지난 몇 주간 우리는 평상시보다 훨씬 많은 원고를 받았습니다. 이것은 최근 전국 출판사 총회에서 우리 부스가 설치된 덕분입니다. 그로 인해 작가들 사이에서 우리의 인지도가 정말 높아졌습니다. 절차가 보다 원활하게 진행되도록 ¹⁴하급 편집자의 심사와 동료 검토 사이에 한 단계를 더 추가했습니다. ¹⁵몇몇 분들이 동료 검토 팀이 요즘 극도로 바쁘다는 우려를 표명하였기에 우리는 부담을 경감시킬 방법을 찾는 중입니다. 이 새로운 절차가 도움이 되기를 희망합니다.

13.

화자는 무엇이 회사가 새로운 작가들을 찾는 데 도움이 되었다고 말하는가?
(A) 글쓰기 모임에 메시지를 보낸 것
(B) 업계 행사에 참석한 것
(C) 소셜미디어에 광고한 것
(D) 글쓰기 워크숍을 주최한 것

[해설] 새로운 작가들을 찾았다는 것은 지난 몇 주간 평상시보다 훨씬 많은 원고를 받은(we've received a lot more manuscripts than usual) 것을 달리 표현한 것이다. 화자는 그 이유를 최근 전국 출판사 총회에서 부스가 설치된 덕분이라고(That's thanks to our booth ~ National Convention of Publishers.) 했다. 즉, 업계의 행사에 참석함으로써 새로운 작가들을 발굴하게 되었으므로 정답은 (B)이다.

paraphrasing the recent National Convention of Publishers 최근 전국 출판사 총회 → an industry event 업계 행사

14.

시각 자료를 보시오. 화자에 따르면, 순서도에 새로 생긴 단계는 무엇인가?
(A) 하급 편집자의 심사
(B) 사실 확인
(C) 동료 검토
(D) 저자 수정

[해설] 화자는 담화 중반, 하급 편집자의 심사와 동료 검토 사이에 한 단계를 더 추가했다고(we've added an extra step between the screening by the junior editor and the peer review) 했다. 시각 자료에서 '하급 편집자의 심사'와 '동료 검토' 사이의 절차는 Fact Checking이므로 정답은 (B)이다.

15.

화자는 청자들에게 어떤 우려에 대해 말하는가?
(A) 한 팀의 업무량이 너무 많다.
(B) 일부 원고가 독창적이지 않다.

(C) 소프트웨어 프로그램이 사용하기 어렵다.
(D) 시장에 새로운 경쟁업체들이 등장했다.

[해설] 담화 후반부에 몇몇 사람들이 동료 검토 팀이 요즘 너무 바쁜 것을 우려했다는(A few people have mentioned concerns that the peer review team is extremely busy these days) 말로 보아 특정 팀의 업무량이 과도한 것에 대한 우려가 있음을 알 수 있으므로 정답은 (A)이다.

paraphrasing the peer review team is extremely busy 동료 검토 팀이 극도로 바쁘다 → A team's workload is too heavy. 한 팀의 업무량이 너무 많다.

[어휘] workload 업무량, 작업량 competitor 경쟁자, 경쟁업체

[16-18] US
Questions 16-18 refer to the following instructions and schedule.

Thursday Schedule	
9:15	Summary Meeting - Conference Room B
9:30	Video Teleconference (Shanghai) - Conference Room D
10:00	¹⁷Shareholder Meeting - CEO's Office Suite
10:45	Planning Meeting - Break Room

M: Good morning. Today will be extra busy because of ¹⁶yesterday's blackout. We have to help everyone get back online and restore the settings for our automated systems. ¹⁷Since the shareholder meeting attendees tend to show up early, I'm going to go to where they will meet first. The rest of you try to go around to each department and help them out before any of their meetings start. ¹⁸Jim Sanders has volunteered to go visit each department this morning to pass out a copy of this memo explaining the current situation.

blackout 정전 restore 회복시키다 setting 설정, 세팅 automated system 자동화 시스템 shareholder 주주 attendee 참석자 tend to V ~하는 경향이 있다 show up 나타나다 go around 돌다 volunteer to V 자원해서 ~하다 pass out 나누어 주다 current situation 현재 상황 summary 요약, 개요; 간략한 video teleconference (원격) 화상 회의 office suite 사무실 break room 휴게실

16-18은 다음 지시와 일정표에 관한 문제입니다.

목요일 일정	
9:15	요약 회의 - B 회의실
9:30	화상 회의 (상하이) - D 회의실
10:00	¹⁷주주총회 - CEO 사무실
10:45	기획 회의 - 휴게실

남: 안녕하세요. ¹⁶어제의 정전 때문에 오늘은 더 바쁠 것입니다. 우리는 모든 사람들이 다시 온라인에 접속하여 우리 자동화 시스템을 위한 설정을 복구하는 것을 도와야 합니다. ¹⁷주주총회 참석자들이 일찍 모습을 드러내는 경향이 있기 때문에 저는 우선 그들이 만날 예정인 곳으로 갈 것입니다. 남은 사람들은 모든 회의가 시작되기 전에 각 부서를 돌면서 그들을 도와주세요. ¹⁸Jim Sanders가 오늘 아침 각 부서를 방문하여 현재 상황을 설명하는 이 메모의 사본을 나눠주겠다고 자원했습니다.

16.
화자의 말에 따르면, 어제 무슨 일이 있었는가?
(A) 일부 직원들이 그만뒀다.
(B) 전기가 나갔다.
(C) 새로운 소프트웨어가 설치되었다.
(D) 회사에서 합병을 발표했다.

[해설] 담화 초반, 화자는 어제의 정전(yesterday's blackout) 때문에 오늘 특별히 바쁠 것이라고 했다. 따라서 어제 전기가 나갔음을 알 수 있으므로 정답은 (B)이다.

paraphrasing blackout 정전 → The power went out. 전기가 나갔다.

[어휘] quit (직장, 학교 등을) 그만두다 go out (전깃불이) 꺼지다, 나가다 install 설치하다 announce 발표하다 merger 합병

17.
시각 자료를 보시오. 화자는 우선 어느 방으로 갈 것인가?
(A) B 회의실
(B) D 회의실
(C) CEO의 사무실
(D) 휴게실

[해설] 담화의 내용과 시각 자료의 정보를 종합하여 정답을 찾는 문제이다. 화자는 주주총회 참석자들(shareholder meeting attendees)이 일찍 모습을 드러내는 경향이 있기 때문에 우선 그들이 만날 예정인 곳으로 가겠다고(I'm going to go to where they will meet first) 했다. 일정표에서 주주총회가 있는 장소를 찾으면 CEO의 사무실이므로 정답은 (C)이다.

18.
화자는 Jim Sanders가 무엇을 할 것이라고 말하는가?
(A) 웹사이트를 업데이트하기
(B) 일부 하드웨어를 테스트하기
(C) 수리 팀을 이끌기
(D) 메모를 배포하기

[해설] Jim Sanders는 담화 후반에 언급되는 인물로, 그가 오늘 아침 각 부서를 방문하여 현재 상황을 설명하는 메모의 사본을 나눠주기로 자원했다고(Jim Sanders has volunteered to go visit each department this morning to pass out a copy of this memo) 했으므로 정답은 (D)이다.

paraphrasing pass out a copy of this memo 이 메모의 사본을 나눠주다 → Distribute a memo 메모를 배포하다

[어휘] lead 이끌다, 안내하다 repair 수리 distribute 나누어 주다, 배부하다

DAY 13 129

DAY 14

PART 3 회사 - 사내 교육 / 비품·장비

출제 유형 01 사내 교육
| 풀이 방법 해석 |

여: 좋은 아침입니다. Phil. 우리 백화점에서의 첫날을 환영합니다. 당신에게 기본적인 것들을 보여드리고, 매장에서 근무하는 것에 익숙해지도록 돕겠습니다.
남: 네, 좋습니다. 교육 시간은 매우 유익했지만, 새로 도착한 물품 목록으로 무엇을 해야 할지 여전히 잘 모르겠습니다. 어떻게 다루어야 하나요?
여: 체크인 모드로 전환하기 위해서 계산대에서 이 버튼을 누르기만 하면 됩니다. 그러고 나서 각 상품을 스캔하고 매장에 내놓으면 됩니다.
남: 아주 간단한 것 같습니다.
여: 네, 맞아요. 추가 질문이 있으시면, 이 무전기를 사용해 상사에게 연락하세요.

출제 유형 02 비품·장비
| 풀이 방법 해석 |

남: Maria, 당신 컴퓨터에서 인터넷이 되나요? 제가 고객에게 이메일을 보내야 하는데, 제대로 작동하지 않아요.
여: 정말이에요? 뭐가 문제인 거죠?
남: 인터넷 브라우저를 열려고 하면, 저는 에러 메시지가 떠요.
여: 이상하네요. 제 것은 잘 작동됩니다. IT 부서에 전화해 보는 게 어때요? 만약 당신이 필요하시다면, 여기 그들의 전화번호가 있습니다.
남: 감사합니다. 여기서 제가 일을 하는 동안, 전에 도움을 요청해 본 적이 없습니다.
여: 그곳의 모든 사람들이 정말 도움을 많이 주십니다. 그들이 곧 문제를 해결해 줄 수 있을 거라 확신해요.

 연습 문제

01. (B) 02. (A) 03. (B) 04. (B) 05. (B) 06. (B)

01. US-US
What will the **woman** most likely **do next**?
(A) **Scan** an **item**   (B) **Distribute books**

W: Hi, Steven. Thanks for coming in today on such short notice. I want to introduce a new wireless barcode scanner.
M: It looks quite similar to the old one.
W: Yes. However, it has a larger display panel, so you can easily check all information about the item, such as current stock and discounts. I'll give out user manuals.

여자는 다음에 무엇을 하겠는가?
(A) 물건을 스캔하기   **(B) 안내 책자 나누어 주기**

여: 안녕하세요, Steven. 오늘 갑작스러운 연락에도 와 주셔서 감사해요. 새로운 무선 바코드 스캐너를 소개시켜 드리고 싶어요.
남: 예전 것과 꽤 비슷해 보이네요.
여: 네. 하지만, 이건 더 큰 화면이 있어서 현재 재고와 할인 같은 물건에 대한 모든 정보를 쉽게 확인할 수 있어요. 사용자 설명서를 나누어 줄게요.

02. US-US
Where is the conversation **taking place**?
(A) In a **storage room**   (B) At an **information desk**

W: Hi, Matthew. Ahmed said you will take care of ordering office supplies. I will teach you how to take the inventory of office supplies. It is required to be done before you place an order. Maybe this is your first time in the office supplies stock room.
M: No, I came a couple of times to get some print paper.
W: Okay, here is a list of current office supplies. You need to count each item and write the numbers on the list.

대화는 어디에서 이루어지고 있는가?
(A) 창고에서   (B) 안내 데스크에서

여: 안녕하세요, Matthew. Ahmed가 당신이 사무용품 주문하는 것을 담당할 거라고 말했어요. 사무용품 재고를 어떻게 파악하는지 알려 드릴게요. 주문을 하기 전에 완료되어야 해요. 아마 이번이 당신이 사무용품 창고에 있는 게 처음이겠군요.
남: 아뇨, 인쇄용지를 가지러 몇 번 왔었어요.
여: 알겠어요, 여기 현재 사무용품 목록이 있어요. 각 품목을 세서 목록에 숫자를 적으셔야 해요.

03. BR-AU
What problem are the speakers **discussing**?
(A) The **photocopier** has **not** been **delivered**.
(B) The **fax machine** is not **working**.

W: Hey, David. These documents have to be sent to the Miami office today, but the fax machine is still down.
M: I called the technician but he said he wouldn't be able to come until next Monday.
W: How about we call Sam in the tech department? He is really good at fixing machines.

화자들은 어떤 문제점을 논의하고 있는가?
(A) 복사기가 배달되지 않았다.   **(B) 팩스가 작동하지 않는다.**

여: 안녕하세요, David. 이 서류들을 오늘 마이애미 사무실로 보내야 하는데, 팩스가 여전히 작동하지 않아요.
남: 기술자를 불렀는데 다음 주 월요일에나 올 수 있다고 하네요.
여: 기술 부서의 Sam에게 전화해 보면 어때요? 그가 기계를 고치는 것을 정말 잘하잖아요.

04. US-BR

What should the **workers** do by the end of the year?
(A) **Update** personal **information**
(B) **Take training** sessions

> M: By the end of this year, all current workers are required to attend a series of on-the-job trainings, so we need to revise some chapters in our training handbook.
> W: Yes, right. I already requested the personnel department to update the employee benefits chapter to include the extension of medical insurance to our employees' family members.

직원들은 올해 말까지 무엇을 해야 하는가?
(A) 개인 정보 업데이트하기 (B) 교육 듣기

남: 올해 말까지, 모든 현재 직원들은 일련의 직무 교육을 들어야 해서, 우리 교육 안내 책자의 몇몇 챕터를 수정해야 해요.
여: 네, 맞아요. 제가 이미 인사부에 직원들의 가족을 위한 의료 보험 확대를 포함하도록 직원 혜택 챕터를 업데이트하라고 요청했어요.

05. BR-BR

What does the **man offer to do**?
(A) **Install** new **software**   (B) Help **move devices**

> M: Here's the key for the equipment room. You'll find a slide projector, an overhead projector and a white board there.
> W: Thank you. I appreciate your help. Where exactly is the equipment room?
> M: It's next to the main hall on the fourth floor. I can go with you and give you a hand moving them to the meeting room.

남자는 무엇을 해주겠다고 하는가?
(A) 새 소프트웨어 설치하기 (B) 장비 옮기는 것 돕기

남: 여기 장비실 열쇠가 있어요. 슬라이드 프로젝터, 오버헤드 프로젝터, 그리고 화이트 보드를 거기서 찾을 수 있을 거예요.
여: 감사합니다. 도움 주셔서 감사해요. 장비실이 정확히 어디에 있나요?
남: 4층의 대강당 옆에 있어요. 제가 같이 가서 그것들을 회의실로 옮기는 것을 도와줄게요.

06. US-AU

What does the **man suggest doing**?
(A) **Hiring** additional **workers**
(B) **Holding** an **information session**

> W: Hi, Daniel. I received many inquiries about the new incentive system.
> M: Yes, me too. I spent most of my time this morning responding to them. Why don't we hold some information session about it?
> W: That sounds great. I will ask Mr. Craig about it.

남자는 무엇을 할 것을 제안하는가?
(A) 추가 직원 채용하기 (B) 정보 교육 시간 열기

여: 안녕하세요, Daniel. 새 인센티브 시스템에 대한 질문을 많이 받았어요.
남: 네, 저도요. 오늘 아침 대부분을 그것에 응대하느라 썼네요. 그것에 대한 정보 교육 시간을 여는 게 어때요?
여: 좋아요. Craig 씨에게 그것에 대해 물어볼게요.

paraphrasing 정답 1. (a) 2. (c) 3. (b) 4. (c) 5. (b) 6. (a)

실전 문제

01. (A)	02. (B)	03. (D)	04. (C)	05. (D)	06. (B)
07. (B)	08. (B)	09. (D)	10. (C)	11. (A)	12. (B)
13. (A)	14. (B)	15. (C)	16. (A)	17. (B)	18. (C)
19. (B)	20. (C)	21. (A)			

[01-03] AU-US-BR

Questions 01-03 refer to the following conversation with three speakers.

> M1: Everyone did a great job on the first day of the orientation yesterday. **01Today, our session will be about how to label the boxes and crates that arrive at our warehouse.** Before we get started, does anyone have any questions for me?
> M2: Yes, I'm really sorry, but I forgot to bring **02my employee handbook** with me today.
> W: Don't worry. **02You can look on with me, Tony.**
> M1: Thanks, Veronica. **03Now, I've got some slides that feature pictures of some incorrect information attached to the boxes.** Let's see if you can spot the problems in each one.

crate (물품 운송용 대형 나무) 상자   employee handbook 직원 안내서   feature (~의) 특징을 이루다   incorrect 부정확한, 맞지 않는   attach to ~에 붙이다   spot 발견하다, 찾다, 알아채다

01-03은 다음 세 명의 대화에 관한 문제입니다.

남1: 모든 분들이 어제 오리엔테이션 첫날에 잘 해내셨어요. **01오늘 이 시간은 우리 창고에 도착하는 상자와 대형 나무 상자에 라벨을 붙이는 방법에 관한 것이 될 거예요.** 시작하기 전에 제게 질문이 있으신 분 계신가요?
남2: 네, 정말 죄송하지만 제가 오늘 **02제 직원 안내서를** 가져오는 것을 잊었어요.
여: 걱정 마세요. **02저랑 같이 보시면 돼요, Tony.**
남1: 고마워요, Veronica. **03자, 제게 상자에 부착된 잘못된 정보의 사진들로 이루어진 슬라이드가 있어요.** 여러분이 각 상자에서 문제를 찾아낼 수 있는지 봅시다.

01.

이 교육 과정의 주제는 무엇인가?
(A) 용기에 라벨 붙이기
(B) 주문하기
(C) 불만 처리하기

(D) 결함 보고하기

[해설] 대화 초반 남자1의 말에서 이 대화가 직무 관련 교육 중에 이뤄지는 것임을 알 수 있는데, 특히 오늘 이 시간은 우리 창고에 도착하는 상자에 라벨을 붙이는 방법(how to label the boxes and crates)에 관한 것이라고 했으므로 정답은 (A)이다.

paraphrasing boxes and crates 상자와 대형 나무 상자 → containers 용기

[어휘] training session 교육 (과정)　container 용기, 컨테이너　handle 다스리다, 처리하다　complaint 불만, 불평　defect 결함

02.

여자가 하겠다고 제안한 것은 무엇인가?
(A) 의자를 재배열하기
(B) 설명서를 같이 보기
(C) 메모하기
(D) 문서 인쇄하기

[해설] 여자가 해주겠다고 제안한 것을 묻는 문제로, 대화 중반 여자는 걱정 말라며, Tony에게 자신과 같이 보면 된다고(You can look on with me, Tony) 말했는데, 여자의 이 말은 바로 앞에서 남자2가 자신의 직원 안내서(my employee handbook)를 가지고 오지 않았다는 말에 이어서 한 것이다. 즉, 여자가 남자2에게 직원 안내서를 같이 보자고 제안한 것이므로 정답은 (B)이다.

paraphrasing employee handbook 직원 안내서 → manual 설명서

[어휘] rearrange 재배열하다　share 공유하다　manual 설명서

03.

다음에 무슨 일이 있을 것 같은가?
(A) 참가 신청서를 돌릴 것이다.
(B) 견본 제품이 배포될 것이다.
(C) 동료가 소개될 것이다.
(D) 이미지가 보여질 것이다.

[해설] 남자1은 직무 교육을 진행하는 사람, 남자2와 여자는 직무 교육을 받는 사람들이다. 대화 후반에서 남자1이 상자에 부착된 잘못된 정보의 사진들로 이루어진 슬라이드(some slides that feature pictures of some incorrect information attached to the boxes)를 언급했고, 문제를 찾아낼 수 있는지 보자고 했으므로 대화 이후에 남자1이 나머지 사람들에게 슬라이드의 이미지들을 보여줄 것임을 알 수 있다. 따라서 정답은 (D)이다.

paraphrasing some slides that feature pictures 사진으로 이루어진 슬라이드 → some images 일부 이미지들

[어휘] sign-up sheet 참가 신청서　pass around (여러 사람이 보도록) ~을 돌리다　distribute 나누어 주다　colleague 동료

[04-06] BR-US

Questions 04-06 refer to the following conversation.

M: Hi, Leslie. It seems that most of the employees **04here in the accounting department** are having difficulty with the new tax codes. There's so much to learn.
W: I thought so, too. But because some of our team members work from home, it's difficult to hold a meeting about this.
M: **05Maybe we could offer a training session online.** Then people could complete it in their spare time.
W: That's a good idea.
M: Do you think we have room in the budget for that?
W: **06I'll talk to the department head about this now** to see what our options are.

accounting 회계 (업무)　tax code 세법　work from home 재택 근무를 하다　training session 교육 (과정)　complete 완료하다, 끝마치다　spare 남는, 여분의　room 여지, 여유　budget 예산　department head 부서장

04-06은 다음 대화에 관한 문제입니다.

남: 안녕하세요, Leslie. 04이곳 회계부의 우리 직원들 대부분이 새로운 세법에 어려움을 느끼고 있어요. 배워야 할 게 너무 많아요.
여: 저도 그렇게 생각했어요. 하지만 우리 팀원 중 일부가 재택 근무를 하기 때문에 이 문제에 관해 회의를 열기가 어려워요.
남: 05아마도 우리가 온라인으로 교육을 제공할 수 있을 거예요. 그러면 사람들이 여유 시간에 이수할 수 있어요.
여: 좋은 생각이에요.
남: 그렇게 할 만큼 예산에 여유가 있을까요?
여: 06지금 이걸 부서장님께 말씀드려서 어떤 선택 방안이 있는지 알아볼게요.

04.

화자들은 어느 부서에서 일하는가?
(A) 정보 기술
(B) 출하 및 반품(물류 관리)
(C) 회계
(D) 마케팅

[해설] 화자들의 근무 부서를 묻는 문제로, 화자들의 직장이나 직무에 관련된 정보는 주로 대화 초반에 나온다. 대화 초반 남자가 이곳 회계부(here in the accounting department)의 대부분의 직원들이라고 소속 부서를 직접적으로 언급했으므로 정답은 (C)이다.

05.

남자는 무엇을 제안하는가?
(A) 자문가 고용하기
(B) 직원 의견 취합하기
(C) 팀의 목표 조정하기
(D) 온라인 교육 제공하기

[해설] 남자가 제안한 것을 묻는 문제로, 대화 중반 남자의 대사에서 단서를 찾는다. 앞서 새로운 세법 때문에 직원들이 어려움을 겪고 있으나 재택 근무 직원들이 있어서 이 문제에 대해 회의를 하기도 힘든 상황이라는 문제점이 제기되었다. 이에 대한 해결책으로 남자가 온라인 교육을 제공하면 된다고(Maybe we could offer a training session online.) 했으므로 정답은 (D)이다.

paraphrasing offer a training session online 온라인으로 교육을 제공하다 → Providing online training 온라인 교육 제공하기

[어휘] consultant 상담가, 자문 위원　gather 모으다　adjust 조정[조절]하다　provide 제공하다

06.

여자는 다음에 무엇을 할 것인가?

(A) 자료를 이메일로 보내기
(B) 관리자에게 이야기하기
(C) 공지를 게시하기
(D) 정책을 확인하기

[해설] 대화 이후 여자가 할 일을 묻는 문제로, 후반부 여자의 대사에 정답의 근거가 있다. 온라인 교육을 위한 예산이 있는지 궁금해하는 남자의 말에 여자가 지금 부서장과 얘기해 보겠다고(I'll talk to the department head about this now) 했으므로 정답은 (B)이다.

paraphrasing talk to the department head 부서장에게 얘기하다 → Speak to a supervisor 관리자에게 이야기하기

[어휘] supervisor 감독관, 관리자 post 게시하다 notice 공지 policy 정책, 방침

[07-09] BR-AU

Questions 07-09 refer to the following conversation.

W: Mr. Griffin, I just heard that the budget committee approved ⁰⁷**plans to renovate the offices on the third floor.** What will happen to the employees working there?
M: During the work, most of those employees will be moved to the fifth floor. But our main storage room is on the third floor. We're still trying to figure out what to do with all of that equipment.
W: ⁰⁸**There are a number of self-storage businesses in town. We could rent one of those units and keep our equipment there temporarily.**
M: That's a good idea. ⁰⁹**Could you call a few companies to find out how much they charge?**
W: ⁰⁹**Sure, I can take care of that.**

budget committee 예산 위원회 approve 승인하다 renovate 개조[보수]하다 storage room 저장고 figure out 이해하다, 알아내다 self-storage 개인 창고 rent 임대하다 equipment 장비, 용품 temporarily 임시로 charge (요금·값을) 청구하다

07-09는 다음 대화에 관한 문제입니다.
여: Griffin 씨, 방금 예산 위원회에서 ⁰⁷3층의 사무실들을 개조하는 계획을 승인했다고 들었어요. 거기서 근무하는 직원들은 어떻게 되는 건가요?
남: 공사 작업 동안 그 직원들 대부분은 5층으로 이동하게 될 거예요. 하지만 중앙 창고가 3층에 있잖아요. 장비 전부를 어떻게 해야 할지를 알아내려고 아직 애쓰고 있어요.
여: ⁰⁸시내에 개인 창고 업체들이 많이 있어요. 그런 시설 중 하나를 임대해서 그곳에 임시로 장비를 보관할 수 있어요.
남: 좋은 생각이에요. ⁰⁹몇 군데 업체에 전화해서 비용이 얼마나 드는지 알아봐 주시겠어요?
여: ⁰⁹물론이죠, 제가 처리할게요.

07.
화자들은 무엇에 관해 논의하고 있는가?
(A) 직원 야유회
(B) 개조 작업
(C) 보수
(D) 보안 계획

[해설] 대화의 주제를 묻는 문제의 단서는 주로 대화 초반에 나온다. 대화 초반 여자가 3층 사무실 개조 계획(plans to renovate the offices on the third floor)을 언급했고, 뒤이어 개조 공사 중 3층에서 근무하던 직원들과 창고의 장비들은 어떻게 되는지에 대한 논의가 이루어지고 있으므로 화자들은 개조 작업에 대해 논의하고 있음을 알 수 있다. 따라서 정답은 (B)이다.

paraphrasing plans to renovate 개조하는 계획 → A renovation project 개조 작업

[어휘] retreat 야유회 renovation 개조, 보수 compensation package (급여와 복리후생을 포함한) 보수 security 보안

08.
여자는 무엇을 제안하는가?
(A) 일부 정보를 온라인에 게시하기
(B) 물품들을 회사 밖에 보관하기
(C) 일부 장비 개선하기
(D) 직원들이 사무실을 함께 쓰게 하기

[해설] 개조 공사 동안 중앙 창고의 장비들의 처리 방안을 놓고 고민 중이라는 남자의 말에 여자가 시내에 개인 창고 업체들이 많이 있으니 그런 시설 중 하나를 임대해서 임시로 장비를 보관할 수 있다고(There are a number of self-storage businesses in town. We could rent one of those units and keep our equipment there temporarily.) 했다. 즉, 회사가 아닌 곳에 장비를 보관하자고 제안한 것이므로 정답은 (B)이다.

paraphrasing self-storage businesses 개인 창고 업체들 → Storing items off-site 물품들을 회사 밖에 보관하기

[어휘] store 저장[보관]하다 off-site 부지[용지] 밖의 upgrade 개선하다 share 공유하다

09.
여자는 무엇을 하는 것에 동의하는가?
(A) 면접 일정 잡기
(B) 송장 인쇄하기
(C) 예산 조정하기
(D) 몇몇 업체에 연락하기

[해설] 대화 후반부 남자가 몇 군데 업체에 전화해서 비용이 얼마나 드는지 알아봐 달라고(Could you call a few companies to find out how much they charge?) 하자 여자가 이를 수락했으므로(Sure, I can take care of that.) 정답은 (D)이다.

paraphrasing call a few companies 몇 군데 업체에 전화하기 → Contact some businesses 몇몇 업체에 연락하기

[어휘] set up (어떤 일이 있도록) 마련하다 invoice 송장, 청구서 adjust 조정[조절]하다 budget 예산

[10-12] US-BR

Questions 10-12 refer to the following conversation.

W: Hi, Dennis. ¹⁰**I know it's only been a few days since you started working at our clothing store.** Do you have any questions so far?
M: Ringing up sales seems pretty simple. However, ¹¹**I'm still not completely clear on what we do and don't accept as returns.**

W: If it's not a brand we carry, we only offer store credit for returned items. A supervisor could approve exceptions, though.
M: Okay, that sounds pretty standard.
W: Cool. **¹²If you're ever unsure, feel free to look at one of the handbooks that we keep at each register.**

so far 지금까지, 이 시점까지   ring up (상점에서 금전 등록기에 상품 가격을) 입력하다   completely 완전히, 전적으로   accept 받아들이다   return 반품   carry (가게에서 품목을) 취급하다   store credit 반환하는 물건 값이 적힌 표   supervisor 감독관, 관리자   approve 승인하다   exception 예외   standard 일반적인, 보통의   unsure 확신하지 못하는   handbook 안내서   register 금전 등록기

10-12는 다음 대화에 관한 문제입니다.
여: 안녕하세요, Dennis. **¹⁰당신이 우리 옷 가게에서 일을 시작한 지 며칠 안 됐잖아요.** 지금까지 무슨 질문이라도 있나요?
남: 매출을 입력하는 것은 매우 쉬워 보여요. 그런데 **¹¹어떤 건 반품으로 접수하고 어떤 건 접수하지 않는 건지 아직도 완전히 이해되지 않아요.**
여: 우리가 취급하지 않는 브랜드인 경우에는 반환된 물건에 대해 물건 값이 적힌 표만 제공해요. 관리자가 예외를 인정하는 경우도 있겠지만요.
남: 알겠습니다, 그건 매우 일반적인 것 같네요.
여: 좋아요. **¹²언제든 잘 모르는 것이 있으면 각 금전 등록기 앞에 보관해둔 안내서들 중 하나를 자유롭게 살펴보도록 하세요.**

10.
화자들은 어디에서 일하는 것 같은가?
(A) 창고에서
(B) 맞춤 양복점에서
(C) 옷 가게에서
(D) 배송 센터에서

[해설] 대화 시작 부분, 여자는 남자에게 우리 옷 가게에서 일을 시작한 지 며칠 안 됐는데(I know it's only been a few days since you started working at our clothing store.) 질문하고 싶은 것은 없는지 물었다. 이로 보아 두 사람이 옷 가게에서 근무함을 알 수 있으므로 정답은 (C)이다.

[어휘] custom tailor 맞춤 양복점

11.
남자는 무엇에 대해 묻는가?
(A) 반품 정책
(B) 채용 과정
(C) 영수증 서식
(D) 재고 목록

[해설] 여자가 질문이 있냐고 묻자, 남자는 무엇을 반품으로 접수하고 무엇은 접수하지 않는지 아직도 완전히 이해되지 않는다고(I'm still not completely clear on what we do and don't accept as returns.) 했다. 즉, 이 옷 가게의 반품 정책에 대해 묻고 있으므로 정답은 (A)이다.

[어휘] policy 정책, 방침   hiring 고용   receipt 영수증   format 형식, 형태   inventory 재고(품)

12.
여자에 따르면, 남자는 어떻게 추가 정보를 얻을 수 있는가?
(A) 회사 웹사이트를 확인함으로써
(B) 안내서를 참고함으로써
(C) 관리자에게 전화함으로써
(D) 포스터를 읽음으로써

[해설] 대화 마지막에 여자는 남자에게 모르는 것이 있으면 금전 등록기 앞에 있는 안내서를 보라고(feel free to look at one of the handbooks that we keep at each register) 했다. 따라서 안내서를 참고해서 추가 정보를 얻을 수 있으므로 정답은 (B)이다.

paraphrasing   look at one of the handbooks 안내서들 중 하나를 보다 → refer to a handbook 안내서를 참고하다

[어휘] additional 추가적인   refer to ~을 보다, 참고하다

[13-15] US-US
Questions 13-15 refer to the following conversation.

M: Hi, Lisa? This is Ryan from R&D. **¹³Could you come and fix the camera in Conference Room C?** It won't turn on.
W: Sure, **¹⁴I should have plenty of time after lunch today.**
M: After lunch? The thing is, the teleconference starts in half an hour.
W: Oh, in that case, I'll head up there now. Is there anything else you need done?
M: No, thank you. Actually, **¹⁵I'm surprised they want to do it so early this time. Because of the time difference, it's normally after noon here by the time we start.**

fix 수리하다, 바로잡다   conference room 회의실   in that case 그런 경우에는, 그렇다면   turn on 켜다, 켜지다   plenty of 많은   the thing is 실은, 문제는   teleconference (원격) 화상 회의   head (특정 방향으로) 가다   up there 저기서, 저기에   time difference 시차   by the time ~할 때까지는

13-15는 다음 대화에 관한 문제입니다.
남: 안녕하세요, Lisa? 연구개발 부서의 Ryan이에요. **¹³오셔서 C 회의실의 카메라를 고쳐 주시겠어요?** 켜지지 않아요.
여: 물론이죠, **¹⁴오늘 점심시간 이후에는 시간이 여유로워요.**
남: 점심시간 이후라고요? 실은 화상 회의가 30분 후에 시작해요.
여: 아, 그렇다면 제가 지금 거기로 갈게요. 그 밖에 처리되어야 하는 것이 더 있나요?
남: 없어요, 감사해요. 실은, **¹⁵이번에 그들이 아주 일찍 회의를 하고 싶어 해서 뜻밖이었어요.** 시차 때문에 여긴 보통은 정오 이후에 시작하거든요.

13.
전화의 목적은 무엇인가?
(A) 수리를 요청하기 위해
(B) 교육을 기획하기 위해
(C) 후보자를 추천하기 위해
(D) 예약을 확인하기 위해

[해설] 전화의 목적을 묻는 문제에 대한 단서는 대화 초반에 제시된다. 남자가 여자에게 회의실 카메라를 고치러 와줄 수 있는지(Could you come and fix the camera in Conference Room C?) 묻는 것으로 보아 수리를 요청하기 위해 전화했음을 알 수 있다. 따라서 정답은 (A)이다.

paraphrasing Could you come and fix the camera ~? 와서 카메라를 고쳐 주시겠어요? → request a repair 수리를 요청하다

[어휘] request 요청하다 repair 수리, 수선 training session 교육(과정) candidate 후보자 confirm 확인해 주다 appointment (업무 관련) 약속

14.

남자가 "화상 회의가 30분 후에 시작해요"라고 말할 때 의미하는 것은 무엇인가?
(A) 다른 약속을 취소했다.
(B) 오후까지 기다릴 수 없다.
(C) 점심시간 내내 일할 생각이다.
(D) 다른 업무에 집중할 것이다.

[해설] 주어진 문장의 앞뒤 문맥을 파악해서 화자의 의도를 찾는 문제이다. 앞서 남자는 여자에게 회의실 카메라 수리를 요청했는데, 여자가 점심시간 이후에 시간이 난다는(I should have plenty of time after lunch today) 말로 오후에 고치겠다는 의사를 드러내자, 남자가 "화상 회의가 30분 후에 시작해요"라고 했다. 이것은 오후까지 기다릴 수 없으니 더 빨리 와 달라는 의도이므로 정답은 (B)이다.

[어휘] intend to V ~할 작정이다 focus on ~에 집중하다

15.

남자에 따르면, 화상 회의의 어떤 점이 색다른가?
(A) 이사회 임원들이 포함될 것이다.
(B) 한 시간 미만 동안 지속될 것이다.
(C) 오전에 실시될 것이다.
(D) 주주들에게 방송될 것이다.

[해설] 대화 후반 남자의 말에 단서가 있다. 아주 일찍 회의를 하고 싶어 해서 놀랐다며(I'm surprised they want to do it so early this time.), 보통은 정오 이후에 시작한다는(it's normally after noon here by the time we start) 말로 보아 이번 화상 회의가 오전에 실시되는 것이 평소와 다른 점임을 알 수 있으므로 정답은 (C)이다.

[어휘] unusual 특이한, 색다른 board member 이사 last 지속하다, 계속하다 conduct 실시하다 broadcast 방송하다 stockholder 주주

[16-18] US-BR-US

Questions 16-18 refer to the following conversation with three speakers.

W1: There are a lot of printers at this electronics store. Which one should we get?
W2: I'm not sure which one would be best for our office. [17]**Maybe we should ask a salesperson.**
W1: That's a good idea. Excuse me, sir. [16]**We're trying to pick out a printer for our office.** We usually print 500 pages per day. [17]**Which one would be best?**
M: Actually, [18]**all you need to do is look at the tags.** They recommend daily print counts.
W1: Oh, really? Thanks for letting us know.
M: By the way, this brand's products are all on sale right now. It gets great customer reviews.

electronics 전자제품 salesperson 판매원 pick out 선택하다 tag 꼬리표, 태그 print count 인쇄 매수 product 제품 on sale 할인[세일] 중인 customer review 고객 후기

16-18은 다음 세 명의 대화에 관한 문제입니다.

여1: 이 전자제품 매장에는 프린터가 많네요. 어떤 것을 구매해야 할까요?
여2: 어떤 것이 우리 사무실에 가장 적합할지 잘 모르겠어요. [17]아마도 판매원에게 물어봐야 할 거 같아요.
여1: 좋은 생각이에요. 실례합니다, 선생님. [16]저희 사무실에서 쓸 프린터를 고르려고 하는데요. 저희는 보통 하루에 500페이지를 인쇄해요. [17]어떤 것이 가장 좋을까요?
남: 사실, [18]꼬리표를 보시기만 하면 됩니다. 권장하는 일일 인쇄 매수가 나와 있어요.
여1: 아, 그래요? 알려주셔서 감사해요.
남: 그나저나 이 브랜드의 제품이 현재 전부 세일 중이에요. 고객 후기도 좋고요.

16.

여자들은 무엇을 하려고 하는 중인가?
(A) 사무실 장비를 구매하기
(B) 회의실을 준비하기
(C) 행사 전단을 인쇄하기
(D) 온라인으로 주문하기

[해설] 전자제품 매장에서 나누는 대화이다. 여자1이 여자2와 어떤 것을 구매할지 고민하다가 사무실에서 쓸 프린터를 고려한다며(We're trying to pick out a printer for our office.) 남자에게 도움을 요청하는 것으로 보아 이들은 사무실 장비를 구매하려는 중이다. 따라서 정답은 (A)이다.

paraphrasing pick out a printer for our office 우리 사무실에서 쓸 프린터를 고르다 → purchase some office equipment 사무실 장비를 구매하기

[어휘] purchase 구매하다 equipment 장비, 용품 prepare 준비하다 flyer 전단 place an order 주문하다

17.

남자는 누구인가?
(A) 제조 공장 근로자
(B) 전자제품 판매원
(C) 인쇄소 직원
(D) 사업 컨설턴트

[해설] 여자2가 어떤 프린터가 사무실에 적합할지 모르겠다며 판매원에게 물어봐야겠다고(Maybe we should ask a salesperson.) 하자, 여자1이 남자에게 어떤 것이 가장 좋을지 묻고, 남자가 이에 대해 답한다. 이로 보아 남자는 전자제품 판매원임을 알 수 있으므로 (B)가 정답이다.

[어휘] manufacturing plant 제조 공장 print shop 인쇄소 consultant 상담가, 자문 위원, 컨설턴트

18.

남자는 여자들에게 무엇을 하라고 말하는가?
(A) 회원 가입을 하기
(B) 제품 후기를 작성하기

(C) 제품 꼬리표를 확인하기
(D) 온라인으로 선택 사항을 비교하기

[해설] 사무실에서 쓸 프린터로 어떤 것이 좋을지 묻는 여자1의 질문에 대한 남자의 대답에 단서가 있다. 남자는 꼬리표를 보기만 하면 된다며(all you need to do is look at the tags), 권장 일일 인쇄 매수가 나와 있다고 덧붙였다. 따라서 정답은 (C)이다.

paraphrasing look at the tags 꼬리표를 보다 → check some product tags 제품 꼬리표를 확인하다

[어휘] compare 비교하다

[19-21] BR-BR

Questions 19-21 refer to the following conversation and floor plan.

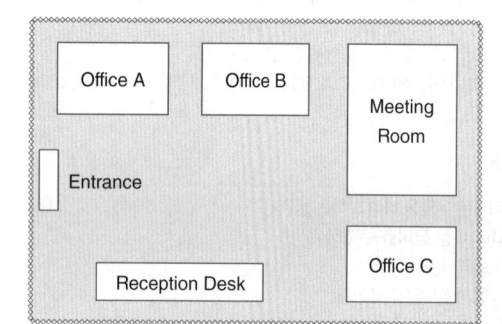

M: Hello, ¹⁹I applied for the intern opening and was asked to come in for an interview.
W: Oh, hello. You must be Kevin Jordan, right?
M: Yes, that's me. Do I need to sign in?
W: No, ²⁰you can go right into Mr. Cobain's office. It's the one between Office A and the meeting room.
M: Great, thank you. Also, ²¹could you do me a favor and hold onto my bicycle helmet? I rode a city bicycle here, so I don't have anywhere to put it.
W: Of course. I'll put it right here for you.

apply for ~에 지원하다 opening 빈자리, 공석 sign in ~의 이름을 기록하다, 도착 시 서명하다 do ~ a favor ~의 부탁을 들어주다 hold onto ~을 맡아 주다, 보관하다 ride (자전거나 오토바이 등을) 타다 right here 바로 이곳에 reception desk 접수처, 프런트, 안내 데스크

19-21은 다음 대화와 평면도에 관한 문제입니다.

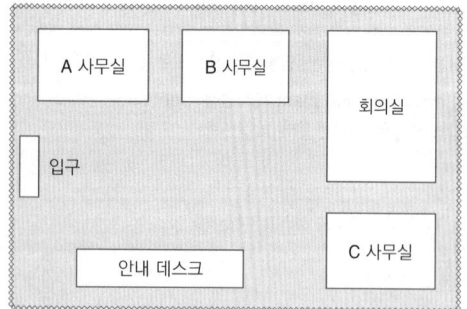

남: 안녕하세요, ¹⁹제가 인턴 자리에 지원했는데, 면접을 보러 오라고 하셨어요.
여: 아, 안녕하세요. 당신이 Kevin Jordan 씨군요, 맞으시죠?
남: 네, 저예요. 이름을 적어야 하나요?
여: 아니요, ²⁰바로 Cobain 씨의 사무실로 가시면 됩니다. A 사무실과 회의실 사이에 있어요.
남: 좋아요, 감사합니다. 또, ²¹부탁이 한 가지 있는데요, 제 자전거 헬멧을 맡아 주시겠어요? 도시 자전거를 타고 왔는데, 헬멧을 둘 곳이 없네요.
여: 물론이죠. 여기에 놓아 둘게요.

19.

남자가 방문한 목적은 무엇인가?
(A) 사무용 가구를 배달하기 위해서
(B) 일자리의 면접을 보기 위해서
(C) 시연을 하기 위해서
(D) 계약서에 서명하기 위해서

[해설] 남자의 방문 목적은 대화 초반에 드러난다. 남자는 인턴 자리에 지원했는데 면접을 보러 오라고 했다며(was asked to come in for an interview) 채용 면접을 보기 위해 방문했음을 밝혔다. 따라서 정답은 (B)이다.

[어휘] demonstration (작동 과정 또는 사용법에 대한) 설명 contract 계약(서)

20.

시각 자료를 보시오. 남자는 어느 방으로 갈 것 같은가?
(A) 회의실
(B) A 사무실
(C) B 사무실
(D) C 사무실

[해설] 대화 중반, 여자가 남자에게 바로 Cobain 씨의 사무실로 가면 된다고 하면서, A 사무실과 회의실 사이에 있다고(It's the one between Office A and the meeting room) 구체적인 위치를 설명했다. 시각 자료로 주어진 평면도에서 이 위치를 확인하면 B 사무실이므로 정답은 (C)이다.

21.

남자는 여자에게 무엇을 해달라고 요청하는가?
(A) 물품을 보관하기
(B) 서류를 복사하기
(C) 도착을 알리기
(D) 주차권을 확인하기

[해설] 요청/제안 사항은 주로 대화 후반부에 제시된다. 대화 후반, 남자는 여자에게 부탁이 있다며, 자전거 헬멧을 맡아 달라고(could you do me a favor and hold onto my bicycle helmet?) 했다. 즉, 헬멧을 보관해 달라는 말이므로 정답은 (A)이다.

paraphrasing hold onto my bicycle helmet 자전거 헬멧을 맡아 주다 → store an item 물품을 보관하다

[어휘] store 보관하다, 저장하다 document 서류, 문서 arrival 도착 validate 확인하다, 인증하다

PART 4 회의 발췌록 (excerpt from a meeting)

출제 유형 01 업무 지시
| 풀이 방법 해석 |

여: 다음으로, 우리의 고객 만족도 등급 하락에 대해 논의해 봅시다. 작년 이 시기에 우리는 5점 만점에 평균 4.1을 받았는데, 지금은 3.8로 내려갔습니다. 우리가 경쟁사들에게 사업을 빼앗기기 시작할 수 있기 때문에 이것은 심각한 문제입니다. 우리의 고객들을 만족시킬 수 있는 홍보 방안을 위한 아이디어를 브레인스토밍 해 봅시다. 우리는 여기부터 시작해서 테이블을 돌아갈 것입니다. Vicky, 당신이 제 비서이니, 제안되는 모든 아이디어들을 적어서 회의 후에 저희 모두에게 이메일로 보내주실 것을 부탁드립니다.

출제 유형 02 규정 변경
| 풀이 방법 해석 |

남: 이제 여러분 모두가 여기 있으니, 우리의 휴가 시간을 사용하는 것에 대한 회사 정책을 검토하고자 합니다. 2주 전에 미리 신청해야 하고 부서장의 승인 없이 5일 연속 사용할 수 없다는 기본적인 규칙이 있습니다. 팀들간의 휴가가 겹치는 것을 피하기 위해, 신청서를 쓰기 전에 팀장과 논의해야 합니다. 이 회의 후에, 이 회람의 복사본을 휴게실에 게시해서 여러분 모두가 참고할 수 있도록 할게요.

연습 문제
01. (B) 02. (A) 03. (A) 04. (B) 05. (A) 06. (B)

01. US
What will **happen next week**?
(A) A **client dinner** will **take place**.
(B) **Policy changes** will be **implemented**.

W: I have one last item on the meeting agenda. The accounting department decided to introduce a new travel expense reimbursement procedure. Beginning next week, any expenses for meals should include original receipts and the names of clients who you have meals with. In addition, business-class seats are not allowed except in urgent cases. Thanks in advance for your cooperation.

다음 주에 무슨 일이 있을 것인가?
(A) 고객과의 저녁 식사가 있을 것이다.
(B) 정책 변경이 시행될 것이다.

회의 발췌록
여: 회의 안건에 한 가지 마지막 항목이 있습니다. 회계 부서는 새로운 출장 비용 환급 절차를 도입하기로 결정했습니다. 다음 주부터, 식사에 대한 모든 비용은 원본 영수증과 당신이 식사를 함께한 고객의 이름이 포함되어야 합니다. 게다가, 급한 경우를 제외하고는 비즈니스 등급 좌석은 허용되지 않습니다. 여러분의 협조에 미리 감사 드립니다.

02. BR
What did the **employees complain** about?
(A) **Vending machines** have **limited beverage** choices.
(B) The **employee lounge** is too **small**.

M: Let's move onto the next agenda. I have received many complaints about the vending machines in the employee lounge. People complained that there are only a few limited choices of drinks and snacks. Also, the prices are higher than in the store. So, I want you to do a survey about what employees want.

직원들은 무엇에 대해 불만을 제기했는가?
(A) 자판기의 음료 선택권이 제한적이다.   (B) 직원 휴게실이 너무 좁다.

회의 발췌록
남: 다음 안건으로 넘어갑시다. 직원 휴게실에 있는 자판기에 대해 많은 불만을 접수했습니다. 사람들은 음료와 간식에 몇 개밖에 되지 않는 제한된 선택권만 있다고 불평했습니다. 또한, 가격이 상점에서 파는 것보다 더 쌉니다. 그래서, 여러분들이 직원들이 원하는 것이 무엇인지에 대해 설문조사를 해 주시길 바랍니다.

03. AU
Where do the **listeners work**?
(A) At a **bank**   (B) At a **restaurant**

M: Thanks for coming a little bit earlier today. The winter holiday season is just around the corner. That means it's time to decorate our bank for Christmas and New Year's Day. The decoration work will be done on the last Monday of October after we close. If you're interested, just send me an email. Those who work extra hours will be paid according to our policy.

청자들은 어디에서 일하는가?
(A) 은행에서   (B) 레스토랑에서

회의 발췌록
남: 오늘 조금 일찍 와주셔서 감사합니다. 겨울 휴가 시즌이 다가오고 있습니다. 우리가 우리 은행을 크리스마스와 새해 장식으로 꾸며야 할 때라는 의미죠. 장식 업무는 10월의 마지막 월요일에 우리가 문을 닫은 후 진행될 것입니다. 관심이 있으시면, 제게 이메일을 보내주세요. 추가 근무를 하는 사람들은 우리 정책에 따라 돈이 지급될 것입니다.

04. BR
What will the **speaker share next week**?
(A) A **list** of **sale items**   (B) A new **display plan**

W: I called this meeting to inform you that we will make some changes to the display area of our sports shoes section. Some major sports brands have contacted us and asked us to arrange some display areas for their new basketball shoes. So, there will be a new floor plan for the sports shoes section next week. In preparation for this change, I ask you to make room for the old model in the stockroom this week.

화자는 다음 주에 무엇을 공유할 것인가?
(A) 할인 품목의 목록   (B) 새로운 진열 배치도

회의 발췌록
여: 저희의 스포츠 신발 섹션의 진열 구역에 변화를 줄 것이라는 점을 알리기 위해 이 회의를 소집했습니다. 몇몇의 주요 스포츠 브랜드가 저희에게 연락해서 그들의 새로운 농구화를 위한 진열 구역을 배정해 줄 것을 요청했습니다. 그래서 다음 주에 스포츠 신발 구역을 위한 새로운 배치도가 나올 것입니다. 이 변화를 준비하기 위해, 이번 주에 창고에 구식 모델을 위한 공간을 마련해 주시길 부탁 드립니다.

05. US

What are the **listeners asked to do**?
(A) **Check** their **schedule**
(B) **Volunteer to work** extra hours

> W: Thank you for attending the weekly meeting. As I said in the **previous** meeting, the self-check-in counters were already **installed** at both end of our airline's service area. Only **passengers** who travel with a carry-on bag can use those counters. Therefore, I will **assign** you to work at these counters and **assist** passengers on a rotating basis. Please check your **working schedule** on the board in the office.

청자들은 무엇을 하도록 요청받는가?
(A) 그들의 일정 확인하기   (B) 추가 근무 자원하기

회의 발췌록
여: 주간 회의에 참석해 주셔서 감사합니다. 제가 이전 회의에서 말씀 드린 것처럼, 셀프 체크인 카운터가 우리 항공사 서비스 구역의 양쪽 끝에 이미 설치되었습니다. 기내 수하물을 가지고 여행하는 승객들만 그 카운터를 이용할 수 있습니다. 그러므로 여러분들이 돌아가면서 이 카운터들에서 일하고 승객들을 도와주도록 배정할 것입니다. 사무실에 있는 게시판에서 여러분의 업무 일정을 확인해 주세요.

06. US

What is the speaker **mainly discussing**?
(A) An **updated hiring process**
(B) A **new catering company**

> M: Hello, as you know, we are going to **hire** a new **catering** company, Debora Foods & Service, for Ms. Kaplan's **retirement party** this Friday. This new company is well known for having professional serving staff and **accepting** special requests. I will send you a feedback form after the party and we will **decide whether** we will keep hiring this company for future events.

화자는 주로 무엇에 대해 이야기하는가?
(A) 업데이트된 채용 과정   **(B)** 새로운 출장 연회 업체

회의 발췌록
남: 안녕하세요, 아시다시피, 우리는 이번 주 금요일 Kaplan 씨의 퇴직 파티를 위해 새로운 출장 연회 업체인 Debora Foods & Service를 고용할 것입니다. 이 새로운 회사는 전문적인 종업원들을 보유하고 특별 요청을 받아주는 것으로 잘 알려져 있습니다. 파티 후에 제가 여러분들에게 피드백

양식을 보내서 향후의 행사에서 이 회사를 계속 고용할지 결정할 것입니다.

paraphrasing 정답   1. (b)   2. (c)   3. (a)   4. (b)   5. (a)   6. (c)

실전 문제

01. (D)	02. (B)	03. (B)	04. (A)	05. (D)	06. (C)
07. (A)	08. (C)	09. (A)	10. (B)	11. (D)	12. (A)
13. (B)	14. (D)	15. (C)	16. (A)	17. (D)	18. (B)
19. (A)	20. (B)	21. (A)			

[01-03] US

Questions 01-03 refer to the following excerpt from a meeting.

> W: Next on the agenda, there's been a product recall on one of our toaster ovens. As a result, many customers will be contacting us ⁰¹**here at the call center.** ⁰²**We're bringing in some short-term staff members starting from tomorrow** to help handle the increased call volume. ⁰³**I've passed out a three-page script to everyone. Please look it over** to get familiar with the recall process.

> agenda 안건, 의제   recall 회수, 리콜   as a result 결과적으로   bring ~ in ~를 관여[참여]하게 하다   short-term 단기의, 단기적인   staff member 직원   handle 처리하다   increased 증가한   volume (~의) 양   pass out 나눠주다   script 대본, 원고   look over 훑어보다, 살펴보다   get familiar with ~에 익숙해지다   process 절차, 과정

01-03은 다음 회의 발췌록에 관한 문제입니다.
여: 다음 안건으로 넘어가자면, 우리 토스터 오븐들 중 하나에 대해 제품 리콜이 있었습니다. 그 결과, 많은 고객들이 ⁰¹**이곳 콜센터로** 저희에게 연락을 해올 것입니다. 증가한 통화량을 처리하는 것을 돕기 위해 ⁰²**내일부터 단기 직원들을 투입시킬 것입니다.** ⁰³제가 모든 분들에게 3장짜리 대본을 나누어 드렸습니다. 리콜 절차에 익숙해지도록 ⁰³잘 살펴보시기 바랍니다.

01.

청자들은 누구일 것 같은가?
(A) 안전 검사관들
(B) 재정 계획 전문가들
(C) 상품 개발자들
(D) 콜센터 직원들

[해설] 화자가 이야기하는 대상의 직업을 묻는 문제이다. 상품 리콜 문제로 인해 많은 고객들이 이곳 콜센터로(here at the call center) 우리에게 연락해올 것이라는 말로 보아 화자와 청자는 모두 고객 문의를 처리하는 콜센터 직원들임을 알 수 있으므로 정답은 (D)이다.

[어휘] inspector 조사관, 감독관   financial 재정의   expert 전문가   developer 개발자   representative 대표자, 대리인

02.

화자에 따르면, 내일 무슨 일이 있을 것인가?
(A) 새 장비가 설치될 것이다.
(B) 임시 직원들이 업무를 시작할 것이다.

(C) 제품 라인이 소개될 것이다.
(D) 교육 과정이 열릴 것이다.

[해설] 질문의 핵심 키워드 tomorrow는 담화 중반에 언급된다. 앞서 고객들의 전화가 증가할 것이라며, 이에 대처하기 위해 내일부터 단기 직원들을 투입시킬 것이라고(We're bringing in some short-term staff members starting from tomorrow) 했다. 즉, 내일 임시 직원들이 일을 시작할 것이므로 정답은 (B)이다.

paraphrasing We're bringing in some short-term staff members 단기 직원들을 투입시킬 것이다 → Some temporary employees will begin work. 임시 직원들이 업무를 시작할 것이다.

[어휘] equipment 장비, 용품 install 설치하다 temporary 임시의, 일시적인 product line 제품 라인(일련의 생산 과정으로 생산되는 제품군)

03.

청자들은 무엇을 하라고 요청받는가?
(A) 이메일로 제안 사항 보내기
(B) 문서 검토하기
(C) 초과 근무 하기
(D) 일정 확인하기

[해설] 제안이나 요청 사항은 주로 담화 후반부에 제시된다. 화자는 3장짜리 대본(a three-page script)을 나누어 주었으니 리콜 절차에 익숙해지도록 살펴볼(Please look it over) 것을 부탁했다. 즉, 청자들에게 문서 검토를 요청하고 있으므로 정답은 (B)이다.

paraphrasing a three-page script 3장짜리 대본 / look it over 그것을 살펴보다 → review a document 문서 검토하기

[04-06] BR

Questions 04-06 refer to the following excerpt from a meeting.

W: Good afternoon. Some of you may have already heard about this problem, since it was reported on the news this morning. **04We have had to issue a product recall on our latest dishwasher model, the Sparkle 500.** There is a problem where the water line leaks onto the power cord, which can cause serious problems, including power outages or fires. I spoke with the head of our technical support team, and he told me how they would handle this issue. **05Customers will contact us through the hotline and we need to arrange the service visit. We will have a couple of very busy weeks. 06I will give you some training scripts about how you should respond to the calls.**

issue 발표하다, 발행하다; 문제 recall 리콜, 회수 dishwasher 식기세척기 leak 새다 power outage 정전 handle 처리하다, 다루다 arrange 마련하다, 준비하다, 주선하다 script 대본 respond 대응하다

04-06은 다음 회의 발췌록에 관한 문제입니다.
여: 안녕하세요. 오늘 오전에 뉴스에서 보도가 되어서 여러분 중 일부는 이미 이 문제에 대해서 들으셨을 수도 있겠네요. **04우리의 최신 식기세척기 모델인 the Sparkle 500을 제품 리콜을 진행해야 했습니다.** 수도관에서 전원 코드로 물이 새는 문제가 있었고, 그것은 정전이나 화재 같은 심각한 문제를 초래할 수 있어요. 저는 기술 지원팀의 팀장과 대화를 나누었고, 그는 그들이 이 사안을 어떻게 처리할 것인지 말해 주었습니다. **05고객들이 상담 전화로 저희에게 연락을 해 올 것이고, 우리는 서비스 방문 준비를 해야 합니다. 우리는 약 두 주간 아주 바쁠 거예요. 06전화에 어떻게 응대해야 하는지에 관한 훈련용 대본을 드리겠습니다.**

04.

화자는 어떤 문제를 언급하는가?
(A) 제품이 리콜되어야 했다.
(B) 배송품이 배달되지 않았다.
(C) 고객이 항의를 제기했다.
(D) 제조 공장이 일시적으로 문을 닫았다.

[해설] 담화 초반에 최신 식기세척기 모델인 the Sparkle 500을 제품 리콜을 진행해야 했다고(We have had to issue a product recall on our latest dishwasher model, the Sparkle 500) 했으므로 (A)가 정답이다.

paraphrasing We have had to issue a product recall 제품 리콜을 진행해야 했다 → A product had to be recalled. 제품이 리콜되어야 했다.

[어휘] shipment 배송(품) file a complaint 고소하다, 항의를 제기하다 temporarily 일시적으로, 임시로

05.

화자가 "우리는 약 두 주간 아주 바쁠 거예요"라고 말할 때 암시하는 것은 무엇인가?
(A) 청자들이 배송품을 받을 것으로 예상한다.
(B) 판촉 행사를 열 계획이다.
(C) 프로젝트 마감이 너무 빡빡하다고 생각한다.
(D) 청자들이 많은 전화를 받을 것으로 예상한다.

[해설] 해당 표현의 앞뒤 맥락을 잘 살펴서 정답을 고른다. 화자는 리콜 진행에 대해서 설명한 후 고객들이 상담 전화로 연락을 해 올 것이고, 서비스 방문 준비를 해야 한다고(Customers will contact us through the hotline and we need to arrange the service visit) 한 후 아주 바쁠 거라고 말한 것이다. 이는 고객들로부터 전화가 많이 걸려 올 것이라는 의미임을 알 수 있으므로 (D)가 정답이다.

[어휘] promotional 홍보의, 판촉의 deadline 마감 tight 빡빡한 predict 예상하다

06.

화자는 다음에 무엇을 할 것인가?
(A) 제품 개발팀들 만나기
(B) 면접 진행하기
(C) 서류 나누어 주기
(D) 원격으로 근무하기

[해설] 다음에 할 일은 주로 담화 후반부에서 확인할 수 있다. 후반부에 전화에 어떻게 응대해야 하는지에 관한 훈련용 대본을 주겠다고(I will give you some training scripts about how you should respond to the calls) 했으므로 (C)가 정답이다.

paraphrasing give you some training scripts 훈련용 대본을 주다 → Distribute some documents 서류 나누어 주기

[어휘] development 개발 conduct 하다, 수행하다

[07-09] AU

Questions 07-09 refer to the following excerpt from a meeting.

> M: Next on today's meeting agenda, **07I have some news that I think you'll like. We finally got approval for our renovation budget.** That means the second floor will be undergoing changes for about six weeks, during which time there will be no access to the two conference rooms. Fortunately, **08Ambrose Consulting, on the fifth floor of this building, has offered to let us use its conference room** on Tuesday mornings and Thursday afternoons. Since the time is so limited, **09Patricia Owens will handle the scheduling of meetings,** so please talk to her to get a time slot.
>
> agenda 안건, 의제   get approval for ~에 대해 승인을 얻다
> budget 예산   undergo 겪다, 받다   access to ~에의 접근[출입]
> handle 다루다, 처리하다   time slot 시간대

07-09는 다음 회의 발췌록에 관한 문제입니다.

남: 오늘 회의의 다음 안건으로, 07여러분이 좋아하실 만한 소식이 있습니다. 드디어 수리 예산에 대해 승인을 받았습니다. 이것은 약 6주간 2층에 변화가 있을 것임을 의미하며, 그 기간 동안 두 개의 회의실을 이용할 수 없게 됩니다. 다행스럽게도, 08이 건물 5층의 Ambrose 컨설팅에서 우리가 화요일 오전과 목요일 오후에 그들의 회의실을 이용하게 해주었습니다. 시간이 매우 제한되어 있으므로 09Patricia Owens가 회의 일정을 조율할 것이니 시간대를 정하시려면 그녀에게 얘기하시기 바랍니다.

07.

화자는 왜 청자들이 기뻐할 것이라고 생각하는가?
(A) 예산이 승인되었다.
(B) 더 큰 사무실로 이사 갈 것이다.
(C) 필요한 비품들이 도착했다.
(D) 직원들이 휴가를 더 받을 것이다.

[해설] 담화 초반 화자는 청자들이 좋아할 만한 소식이 있다며(I have some news that I think you'll like) 드디어 수리 예산에 대해 승인을 받았다고(We finally got approval for our renovation budget) 덧붙였다. 따라서 정답은 (A)이다.

paraphrasing   got approval for our renovation budget 수리 예산에 대해 승인을 받았다 → A budget has been approved. 예산이 승인되었다.

[어휘] approve 승인하다   supplies 비품   time off 휴가

08.

Ambrose 컨설팅은 무엇을 해주겠다고 제안했는가?
(A) 일부 장비를 설치하기
(B) 컨설턴트를 보내기
(C) 회의 공간을 함께 쓰기
(D) 제안을 검토하기

[해설] 질문의 키워드 Ambrose Consulting이 언급되는 곳에서 단서를 찾는다. 앞서 화자는 건물 보수로 인해 회의실 이용이 불가능하다는 정보를 전했고, 이어서 5층의 Ambrose Consulting에서 화요일 오전과 목요일 오후에 그들의 회의실을 이용하게 해주었다고(has offered to let us use its conference room) 알렸다. 따라서 정답은 (C)이다.

paraphrasing   let us use its conference room 회의실을 이용하게 해주다 → share a meeting space 회의 공간을 함께 쓰기

[어휘] set up 설치하다, 세우다   equipment 장비, 용품   consultant 상담가, 자문 위원, 컨설턴트   share 함께 쓰다, 공유하다   proposal 제안, 제의

09.

Owens 씨는 무엇을 담당하는가?
(A) 일정 파악하기
(B) 직원 파티 계획하기
(C) 신규 직원 채용하기
(D) 들어오는 배달 물품 처리하기

[해설] 질문의 핵심 키워드 Ms. Owens는 담화 마지막 부분에 언급된다. 회의실 사용과 관련하여 Patricia Owens가 회의 일정을 조율할 것이라고(Patricia Owens will handle the scheduling of meetings) 했으므로 Owens 씨는 회의 시간이 겹치지 않도록 회의 일정을 잘 파악하여 조정하는 일을 담당한다. 따라서 정답은 (A)이다.

paraphrasing   handle the scheduling of meetings 회의 일정을 조율하다 → keeping track of a schedule 일정 파악하기

[어휘] be in charge of ~을 담당하다   keep track of ~에 대해 계속 알고[파악하고] 있다   recruit 모집하다, 뽑다   incoming 도착하는, 들어오는

[10-12] US

Questions 10-12 refer to the following excerpt from a meeting.

> M: I'd like to give you all an update on **10the plans for our launch of the new Oswego Energy Drink.** We expect **10this newest addition to our product line** to be very popular. The drink will be on sale at all of our stores, but **11some of you have been asking whether there will be a big event at each store. We're setting up the stage at the Westerville branch.** Large crowds are expected there, as **12David Brito, a basketball player for the Longview Eagles,** has agreed to endorse our product and sign autographs. We're expecting that to give us a big boost.
>
> launch 출시, 개시   expect 예상하다, 기대하다   addition 추가된 것, 부가물   product line 제품 라인   on sale 판매되는, 구입할 수 있는   set up 세우다, 설치하다   branch 지점   crowd 사람들, 군중   endorse (유명인이 특정 상품을) 홍보하다, 광고하다   sign autographs 서명하다   give ~ a boost ~을 후원하다, ~에 활력을 불어넣다

10-12는 다음 회의 발췌록에 관한 문제입니다.

남: 여러분 모두에게 10신제품인 Oswego 에너지 드링크의 출시 계획에 대한 최신 정보를 말씀드리려고 합니다. 우리 제품 라인에 새롭게 추가되는 이것이 많은 인기를 끌 것으로 예상됩니다. 이 음료가 모든 우리 매장에서 판매될 예정인데요, 11여러분 중 일부가 각 매장에서 대규모 행사를 열 것인지 아닌지를 물어보셨습니다. 우리는 Westerville 지

점에 무대를 설치할 예정입니다. **¹²Longview Eagles**의 농구 선수인 **David Brito**가 우리 제품을 광고하고 사인을 해주기로 했기 때문에 많은 사람들이 몰려들 것으로 예상됩니다. 그것이 우리에게 큰 동력이 될 것으로 기대합니다.

10.

주로 무엇에 관한 담화인가?
(A) 서비스 개선을 위한 전략
(B) 신제품 출시
(C) 안전 규정 변경
(D) 스포츠 경기 계획

[해설] 담화의 주제를 묻는 문제이다. 회의 발췌록이므로 회의 안건이 곧 담화의 주제다. 담화 초반 화자는 새로운 Oswego Energy Drink의 출시 계획(the plans our launch of the new Oswego Energy Drink.)에 대한 최신 정보를 전하겠다는 말로 안건을 밝혔으며, 이어지는 내용에서 Oswego Energy Drink를 우리 제품 라인에 새롭게 추가된 것(this newest addition to our product line)으로 표현했다. 즉, '신제품 출시'에 관한 담화이므로 정답은 (B)이다.

paraphrasing this newest addition to our product line 우리 제품 라인에 새롭게 추가된 이것 → a new product 신제품

[어휘] strategy 전략 improve 개선하다, 향상시키다 safety regulations 안전 규정 competition 경쟁, 대회

11.

화자는 왜 "우리는 Westerville 지점에 무대를 설치할 예정입니다"라고 말하는가?
(A) 초대장을 보내기 위해서
(B) 우려를 나타내기 위해서
(C) 지연에 대해 설명하기 위해서
(D) 일부 정보를 명확히 하기 위해서

[해설] 화자의 의도를 파악하는 문제는 해당 표현 앞뒤 내용을 종합해서 정답을 찾아야 한다. 화자는 청자들 중 일부가 각 매장에서 신제품 출시와 관련하여 큰 행사가 열리는지 여부를 문의했다고(some of you have been asking whether there will be a big event at each store) 한 후에 "우리는 Westerville 지점에서 무대를 설치할 예정입니다"라고 말했다. 즉, 특정 지점에서 큰 행사를 열 예정임을 분명히 밝힌 것이므로 정답은 (D)이다.

[어휘] issue an invitation 초대장을 보내다 concern 우려, 걱정 delay 지연, 지체 clarify 명확하게 하다, 분명히 말하다

12.

David Brito는 누구일 것 같은가?
(A) 프로 운동선수
(B) 마케팅 전문가
(C) 유명한 작가
(D) 연구원

[해설] 질문의 핵심 키워드 David Brito는 담화 후반부에 언급된다. 신제품을 광고하기로 한 인물로 David Brito를 언급하면서 Longview Eagles의 농구 선수(a basketball player for the Longview Eagles)라고 소개하고 있으므로 정답은 (A)이다.

paraphrasing a basketball player for the Longview Eagles Longview Eagles의 농구 선수 → a professional athlete 프로 운동선수

[어휘] professional 직업의, 전문적인 expert 전문가 author 작가

[13-15] US

Questions 13-15 refer to the following excerpt from a meeting.

> M: Thank you all for coming to this meeting. Today, **¹³I'd like to focus on upgrading our library's computers and other equipment.** As you know, we are a public library funded by the city, so it's not easy to obtain additional funds. **¹⁴The main problem is that we don't have enough resources to help our community members use our library more conveniently.** That's where you come in. I'd like each of you to take a section of this local business list. **¹⁵There might be some business owners willing to donate to our cause. Call them and ask if they could help us.**

focus on ~에 초점을 맞추다 equipment 장비 fund 자금; 자금을 대다 obtain 얻다, 획득하다 additional 추가의 resource 자원, 재원 conveniently 편리하게 section 부문, 구획 local 지역의 donate 기부하다 cause 명분, 대의

13-15는 다음 회의 발췌록에 관한 문제입니다.

남: 모두 이번 회의에 와 주셔서 감사합니다. 오늘 ¹³저는 우리 도서관의 컴퓨터와 장비를 업그레이드하는 것에 초점을 맞추고 싶어요. 아시다시피 우리는 시의 보조를 받고 있어서 자금을 추가로 받는 것이 쉽지 않아요. ¹⁴우리의 주된 문제는 지역 주민들이 도서관을 더 편리하게 이용하도록 돕기 위한 자원이 부족하다는 거예요. 그 부분에서 여러분의 역할이 필요합니다. 여러분 각자 이 지역 업체 리스트에서 한 부분이 맡아 주시면 좋겠습니다. ¹⁵우리의 대의를 위해 기꺼이 돈을 기부해 주실 사업주들이 있을 수도 있어요. 그들에게 전화해서 우리를 도와주실 수 있는지 물어봐 주세요.

13.

담화의 주제는 무엇인가?
(A) 정원 장식하기
(B) 장비 업그레이드하기
(C) 새로운 서비스 제공하기
(D) 추가 직원 채용하기

[해설] 주제는 담화 초반부에서 확인할 수 있다. 초반부에 도서관의 컴퓨터와 장비를 업그레이드하는 것에 초점을 맞추고 싶다고(I'd like to focus on upgrading our library's computers and other equipment) 했으므로 (B)가 정답이다.

[어휘] decorate 장식하다 garden 정원 recruit 채용하다

14.

화자는 어떤 문제를 언급하는가?
(A) 제품 출시 지연
(B) 불충분한 노동력
(C) 불편한 교통
(D) 자금 부족

[해설] 담화 중반부에 주된 문제는 지역 주민들이 도서관을 더 편리하게 이용하도록 돕기 위한 자원이 부족하다는 거라고(The main problem is

DAY 14 141

that we don't have enough resources to help our community members use our library more conveniently) 했으므로 (D)가 정답이다.

paraphrasing we don't have enough resources 자원이 부족하다 → A lack of funds 자금 부족

[어휘] delayed 지연된 launch 출시, 출간 insufficient 불충분한 workforce 직원, 노동력 inconvenient 불편한 lack 부족

15.
화자는 청자들에게 무엇을 요청하는가?
(A) 하청 업체 추천
(B) 문서 서명
(C) 사업주 연락
(D) 수업

[해설] 제안/요청 문제의 단서는 담화 후반부에 등장한다. 후반부에 기꺼이 돈을 기부해 줄 사업주들이 있을 거라며(There might be some business owners willing to donate to our cause), 그들에게 전화해서 도와줄 수 있는지 물어보라고(Call them and ask if they could help us) 했으므로 (C)가 정답이다.

paraphrasing call 전화하다 → contact 연락하다

[어휘] contractor 하청업자, 계약자

[16-18] [AU]
Questions 16-18 refer to the following excerpt from a meeting.

M: The next thing I'd like to talk about is your workload. I've been hearing a lot of complaints that there's just too much to handle. ¹⁶**Over the past year, we have significantly increased the number of properties that we manage.** To help with the extra work, ¹⁷**I decided to hire three additional full-time agents.** I posted the job details on our Web site, but ¹⁸**if you know anyone with real estate certifications, please refer them to me.** The sooner we can hire and train people, the more reasonable each of your workloads will become.

workload 업무량, 작업량 handle 처리하다, 다루다 significantly 상당히 property 건물 manage 운영[관리]하다 additional 추가의 full-time 상의, 정규직의 agent 대리인, 중개상 real estate 부동산 certification 증명, 증명서 refer A to B (도움을 받을 수 있도록) A를 B에게 보내다 reasonable 합리적인

16-18은 다음 회의 발췌록에 관한 문제입니다.
남: 다음으로 얘기 나누고 싶은 것은 여러분의 작업량입니다. 처리해야 할 것들이 너무 많다는 불만을 많이 듣고 있습니다. ¹⁶지난 1년 동안 우리가 관리하는 건물의 수가 상당히 많이 늘었습니다. 시간 외 근무를 돕기 위해 ¹⁷세 명의 상근 중개인을 추가로 고용하기로 결정했습니다. 우리 웹 사이트에 상세 직무를 올렸습니다만 ¹⁸부동산 자격증을 가지고 있는 사람을 알고 계시다면 누구라도 제게 알려 주세요. 우리가 빨리 사람을 채용해서 교육시킬수록 여러분 각자의 업무량이 보다 적절해질 것입니다.

16.
화자는 이 회사에 대해 무엇이라고 말하는가?
(A) 작년보다 더 많은 건물들을 관리한다.
(B) 이익이 현저하게 늘었다.
(C) 다른 회사와 합병할 것이다.
(D) 곧 인원을 감축할 것이다.

[해설] 화자는 지난 1년 동안 그들이 관리하는 건물의 수가 상당히 많이 늘어(Over the past year, we have significantly increased the number of properties that we manage.) 작업량이 너무 많아진 점을 지적했다. 따라서 정답은 (A)이다.

paraphrasing Over the past year, we have significantly increased the number of properties that we manage. 지난 1년 동안 우리가 관리하는 건물의 수가 상당히 많이 늘었다. → It manages many more properties than last year. 작년보다 더 많은 건물들을 관리한다.

[어휘] markedly 현저하게, 두드러지게 profit margin 이윤, 이익 merge with ~와 합병하다 downsize (인원을) 줄이다, 축소하다

17.
화자는 최근 무엇을 하기로 결정했는가?
(A) 정책을 업데이트하기
(B) 상품을 출시하기
(C) 사무실을 이전하기
(D) 직원을 더 고용하기

[해설] 앞서 관리해야 하는 건물의 수가 늘어 업무량이 많아졌다는 점을 언급한 후, 이로 인한 시간 외 근무를 돕기 위해 세 명의 상근 중개인을 추가로 고용하기로 결정했다고(I decided to hire three additional full-time agents.) 밝혔다. 따라서 정답은 (D)이다.

paraphrasing hire three additional full-time agents 세 명의 상근 중개인을 추가로 고용하다 → hire more employees 직원을 더 고용하기

[어휘] policy 정책, 방침 launch 출시하다 relocate 이전하다

18.
화자는 청자들에게 무엇을 할 것을 요청하는가?
(A) 설문조사 작성하기
(B) 입사 지원자 추천하기
(C) 일부 건물들에 방문하기
(D) 교육에 참석하기

[해설] 화자는 업무량 과다 문제를 해결하기 위해 추가 고용을 결정하고 채용 공고를 냈다며, 부동산 자격증을 가지고 있는 사람을 알고 있다면 누구라도 자신에게 알려 달라고(if you know anyone with real estate certifications, please refer them to me) 했다. 즉, 청자들에게 입사 지원자를 추천해 달라고 부탁하고 있으므로 정답은 (B)이다.

[어휘] complete 작성하다, 기입하다 job candidate 입사 지원자

[19-21] BR
Questions 19-21 refer to the following excerpt from a meeting and graph.

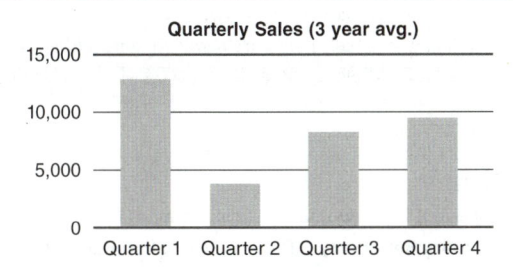

M: Hello, and welcome to our quarterly meeting. [19, 20] **We are starting the quarter in which our tablet computer sales are generally at their lowest.** This graph shows our average figures from the past three years. In order to increase our sales during this quarter, [21]**I want to give our Web site a big makeover to draw more attention to our brand.** Let's discuss how we can go about doing that.

quarterly 분기별의   quarter 4분의 1, 사분기   sales 매출
generally 일반적으로   average 평균   figures 수치   increase 늘리다   makeover 변모, 변신, 수리, 수선   draw 끌어내다
attention 관심, 주의   go about ~을 시작하다, ~에 착수하다

19-21은 다음 회의 발췌록과 그래프에 관한 문제입니다.

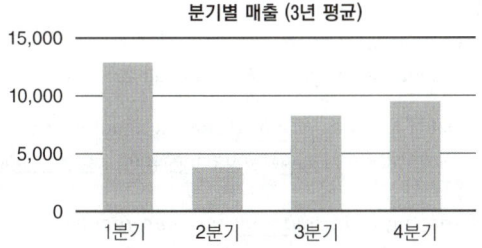

남: 안녕하세요, 분기별 회의에 오신 것을 환영합니다. [19, 20]우리는 우리 태블릿 컴퓨터의 매출이 일반적으로 가장 저조한 분기를 시작하고 있습니다. 이 그래프는 지난 3년간의 평균 수치를 보여줍니다. 이번 분기의 매출을 늘리기 위해서, [21]저는 우리 웹사이트에 대대적인 변화를 주어 우리 브랜드에 대한 더 많은 관심을 끌어내고 싶습니다. 어떻게 하면 그렇게 할 수 있는지 논의해봅시다.

19.
이 회사는 어떤 종류의 제품을 판매하는가?
(A) 태블릿 컴퓨터
(B) 휴대폰
(C) 전자기기 부속품
(D) 음악 장치

[해설] 매출 실적에 관한 회의에서 발췌한 담화로, 초반부에, 이번 분기의 태블릿 컴퓨터 매출(our tablet computer sales)이 저조하다는 내용이 언급된다. 이로 보아 태블릿 컴퓨터를 판매하는 회사임을 알 수 있으므로 정답은 (A)이다.

[어휘] mobile 이동하는, 이동식의   electronics 전자제품

accessories 장신구, 액세서리   device 장치

20.
시각 자료를 보시오. 이 회의는 어느 분기에 이루어지고 있는가?
(A) 1분기
(B) 2분기
(C) 3분기
(D) 4분기

[해설] 시각 자료의 정보와 담화의 내용을 연계하여 푸는 문제이다. 화자는 태블릿 컴퓨터의 매출이 일반적으로 가장 저조한 분기를 시작하고 있다고(We are starting the quarter in which our tablet computer sales are generally at their lowest.) 했는데, 그래프에서 매출이 가장 저조한 분기를 찾으면 2분기이므로 회의를 하고 있는 시점은 2분기임을 알 수 있다. 따라서 정답은 (B)이다.

21.
화자는 그 밖에 무엇에 대해 논의하고 싶어하는가?
(A) 웹사이트 디자인
(B) 다른 제품
(C) 고객 의견
(D) 본사 이전

[해설] 담화 후반, 화자는 매출 증대 방안의 하나로 웹사이트에 대대적인 변화를 주어 자사의 브랜드에 대한 더 많은 관심을 끌어내고 싶다고 (I want to give our Web site a big makeover to draw more attention to our brand.) 했다. 즉, 웹사이트 디자인 개편에 대해 논의하고 싶다는 의미이므로 정답은 (A)이다.

paraphrasing   give our Web site a big makeover 웹사이트에 대대적인 변화를 주다 → Web site design 웹사이트 디자인

[어휘] head office 본사   relocation 이전

DAY 15

PART 3 회사/상점

출제 유형 01 출장·행사

| 풀이 방법 해석 |

여: Mike, 제가 베를린의 모바일 기술 학회에서 회사 부스에서 근무하는 일을 맡았어요. 저는 해외 학회에 참석하는 것이 이번이 처음이라, 제가 출장 준비하는 것을 도와주실 수 있으신가요?
남: 물론이죠. 당신이 해야 하는 첫 번째 일은 우리의 출장과 관련된 모든 일을 주로 담당하는 Chicago Travel에 연락하는 거예요. 그럼 그들이 당신에게 가능한 항공편과 호텔방의 목록을 줄 거예요. 경영진이 현재 출장 경비를 줄이려고 하고 있으니, 가장 저렴한 옵션을 선택하는 게 좋을 거예요.
여: 알겠습니다, 그렇게 하겠습니다. 그런데 식사에 대해서는 환급을 받을 수 있나요?
남: 네. 하지만 당신이 고객과 점심 식사나 저녁 식사를 하는 경우가 아니라면, 회사는 각 식사에 대해 20달러만 대줍니다.

출제 유형 02 상품 구매·서비스

풀이 방법 해석

남: 실례합니다만, 저는 빨간색 울트라 맨 액션 피규어(인형)를 찾고 있습니다. 초록색과 노란색은 있는 것 같은데, 저는 빨간색을 구매하고 싶습니다.
여: 죄송하지만, 오늘 아침에 빨간색이 모두 판매되었습니다. 정말 인기 있는 장난감이거든요. 만약 그때까지 기다려 주실 수 있다면, 다음 주 월요일에 더 들어올 예정입니다.
남: 문제는, 제 조카의 생일 파티가 내일입니다.
여: 음.... 그렇다면, 특급 배송으로 온라인으로 주문하시면, 내일까지 받으실 수 있을 거예요.
남: 사실, 귀사의 벨포드 지점에 재고가 있는지 당신의 컴퓨터로 알아봐 주실 수 있나요? 제가 거기까지 기꺼이 운전해서 가겠습니다.

 연습 문제

01. (A) 02. (A) 03. (B) 04. (A) 05. (B) 06. (B)

01. BR-US

What are the speakers **mainly discussing**?
(A) A company **booth plan** (B) A **client meeting**

W: Jimmy, I just reviewed the company booth arrangement plan for the culinary expo. I think the assigned booth area is not spacious enough to display all of our products.
M: Actually, we were supposed to display only the new products, but the management wanted to include some other products. Anyway, I will contact the conference organizer and ask whether there is a larger space still available.

화자들은 주로 무엇을 논의하는가?
(A) 회사 부스 배치도 (B) 고객 미팅

여: Jimmy, 제가 막 요리 박람회의 회사 부스 배치도를 검토했어요. 배정된 부스 구역이 우리의 모든 제품을 진열하기에 충분히 넓지 않은 것 같아요.
남: 사실, 우리는 신제품만 진열하기로 되어 있었는데, 경영진이 다른 상품도 포함시키길 원했어요. 어쨌든, 제가 학회 기획자에게 연락해서 더 큰 공간이 가능할지 물어볼게요.

02. BR-AU

What will **happen next week**?
(A) A **client** will **visit**. (B) A **company** will **relocate**.

W: Jake! I haven't seen you since you got back from your trip to Egypt. How was the client meeting with Mohamed Apparel?
M: I think our trendy shoe designs and competitive prices appealed to them. They will visit us next month to look around our headquarters and factory.
W: That's great news!

다음 주에 무슨 일이 일어날 것인가?
(A) 고객이 방문할 것이다. (B) 회사가 이전할 것이다.

여: Jake! 당신이 이집트 여행에서 돌아온 이후로 보지 못했네요. Mohamed 의류와의 고객 미팅은 어땠나요?
남: 우리의 최신 유행 신발 디자인과 경쟁력 있는 가격이 그들의 관심을 끈 것 같아요. 그들이 우리 본사와 공장을 둘러보기 위해 다음 달에 방문할 거예요.
여: 그거 좋은 소식이네요!

03. US-US

What event is the **woman** planning to **attend**?
(A) A **retirement party** (B) An **industrial conference**

M: Susan, I heard you are supposed to attend the automotive conference in Chicago. When are you coming back?
W: Well, the conference ends on Wednesday, and I'm planning to visit the headquarters while I'm there.
M: Oh, that's good for you. I hope you find it informative.

여자는 어떤 행사에 참석할 계획인가?
(A) 퇴직 파티 **(B) 산업 학회**

남: Susan, 당신이 시카고에서 열리는 자동차 학회에 참석할 거라고 들었어요. 언제 돌아오나요?
여: 음, 학회가 수요일에 끝나고 제가 거기 있는 동안 본사에 방문할 계획이에요.
남: 오, 잘됐네요. 유익하길 바랄게요.

04. BR-US

What will the **woman send**?
(A) **Detailed information** (B) An **e-mail address**

M: Hello, I saw a TV advertisement about your cable TV service and it said you are offering a promotional period.
W: Yes, right. In addition, you can receive a free upgrade to Super Channels if you subscribe to Basic Channels. You can enjoy 150 TV channels instead of 100.
M: Can you send me further information about the TV channels you are offering now?

여자는 무엇을 보낼 것인가?
(A) 세부 정보 (B) 이메일 주소

남: 안녕하세요, 당신의 케이블 TV 서비스에 대한 TV 광고를 봤고, 홍보 기간을 제공 중이라고 하던데요.
여: 네, 맞습니다. 게다가, 기본 채널을 구독하시면 슈퍼 채널로 무료 업그레이드를 받으실 수 있어요. 100개 채널 대신 150개 채널을 즐기실 수 있습니다.
남: 지금 제공하시는 TV 채널에 대한 추가 정보를 제게 보내주실 수 있나요?

05. US-US

What is the **man invited to do**?
(A) **Complete** an order **form**

(B) **Visit** the **store tomorrow**

W: Good evening. May I help you?
M: Excuse me, do you have any more of this digital camera? I want a red one.
W: Sorry, it is currently out of stock. Another shipment will arrive tomorrow, so will you come again tomorrow afternoon? I will put a red one on hold for you.

남자는 무엇을 하도록 요청받는가?
(A) 주문 양식 작성하기   (B) 내일 상점 방문하기

여: 안녕하세요. 무엇을 도와드릴까요?
남: 실례합니다. 이 디지털 카메라를 더 보유하고 계신가요? 저는 빨간색을 원해요.
여: 죄송합니다. 현재 품절입니다. 내일 추가 배송품이 도착할 것이니, 내일 오후에 다시 오시겠어요? 빨간색을 맡아 두겠습니다.

06. BR-BR

What kind of **business** does the **woman** most likely **work at**?
(A) A **restaurant**   (B) A **landscaping company**

M: Hello, I'm just calling to get some more information about your landscaping services. I have a garden at my house but I'll be out of the country for more than six months. Do you offer any short term contracts?
W: Sure, we can offer any contract term including one-time service.

여자는 어떤 사업체에서 일하는 것 같은가?
(A) 레스토랑   **(B) 조경 회사**

남: 안녕하세요, 조경 서비스에 대해 정보를 더 얻으려고 전화드립니다. 제 집에 정원이 있는데 제가 6개월 이상 해외에 있을 예정입니다. 단기 계약도 제공하시나요?
여: 물론이죠, 한 번의 서비스를 포함한 어떤 계약 기간도 제공해 드립니다.

paraphrasing 정답   1. (b) 2. (a) 3. (c) 4. (b) 5. (c) 6. (a)

실전 문제

01. (D)	02. (C)	03. (B)	04. (C)	05. (A)	06. (C)
07. (A)	08. (C)	09. (A)	10. (D)	11. (A)	12. (B)
13. (D)	14. (B)	15. (A)	16. (B)	17. (C)	18. (B)
19. (C)	20. (A)	21. (B)			

[01-03] US-AU

Questions 01-03 refer to the following conversation.

W: William, you said you wanted to talk to me about something?
M: Yes. I'm attending the Annual Technology Convention in Seattle this weekend, and **⁰¹I forgot to reserve a hotel room.** Now the conference hall doesn't have any vacancies.
W: Don't worry. **⁰²There's another good hotel right across the street, the Nashua Inn.** I'm sure they'll have space.
M: Oh, **⁰²thanks.** I didn't know about that.
W: No problem. And remember that you'll be reimbursed for all of your business expenses, so **⁰³please turn in your receipts when you get back next week.**
M: Okay.

reserve 예약하다   vacancy (호텔 등의) 빈 방[객실]
reimburse 배상[변제]하다   expense 돈, 비용   turn in ~을 제출하다   receipt 영수증

01-03은 다음 대화에 관한 문제입니다.
여: William, 저와 하고 싶은 얘기가 있다고 하셨죠?
남: 네. 제가 이번 주말에 시애틀에서 열리는 연례 기술 컨벤션에 참석할 예정인데 ⁰¹호텔 방 예약하는 걸 잊었어요. 이제 콘퍼런스홀에는 빈 방이 없어요.
여: 걱정 말아요. ⁰²길 건너에 다른 괜찮은 호텔이 있어요. Nashua Inn이라고요. 거기엔 분명히 방이 있을 거예요.
남: 아, ⁰²고마워요. 그건 몰랐어요.
여: 별일 아닌 걸요. 모든 업무 경비는 상환된다는 걸 기억하세요. 그러니 ⁰³다음 주에 돌아오시면 영수증을 제출해주세요.
남: 알겠어요.

01.

남자는 무엇을 하는 것을 잊었는가?
(A) 콘퍼런스에 등록하기
(B) 지출 승인을 받기
(C) 초대에 응하기
(D) 숙박시설 예약하기

[해설] 남자가 잊어버려서 못한 일을 묻는 문제이다. 남자는 주말에 있을 컨벤션에 참석할 예정인데 호텔 방 예약하는 걸 잊었다고(I forgot to reserve a hotel room.) 했으므로 정답은 (D)이다.

paraphrasing   reserve a hotel room 호텔 방을 예약하다 → Book accommodations 숙박시설 예약하기

[어휘] register for ~에 등록하다   spending 지출   approval 승인   respond to an invitation ~에 대응하다   accommodations 숙박시설

02.

남자는 왜 여자에게 고마워하는가?
(A) 그에게 서류를 보냈다.
(B) 그를 위해 일을 완료했다.
(C) 도움이 되는 추천을 해주었다.
(D) 그의 팀에게 더 많은 직원을 배정했다.

[해설] 호텔을 예약하는 것을 잊어버렸다는 남자에게 여자가 걱정 말라며 길 건너에 Nashua Inn이라는 다른 괜찮은 호텔이 있다고(There's another good hotel right across the street, the Nashua Inn) 말해주자 남자가 여자에게 고맙다는(thanks) 인사를 한다. 즉, 호텔을 추천해준 것에 대해 고맙다고 한 것이므로 정답은 (C)이다.

[어휘] document 서류, 문서   complete 완료하다, 끝마치다   task 일, 과제   make a recommendation 추천하다   assign 맡기다, 배정하다

03.

남자가 다음 주에 해야 하는 것은 무엇인가?
(A) 교육을 이끌기
(B) 영수증을 제출하기
(C) 발표를 하기
(D) 휴가를 요청하기

[해설] 남자가 다음 주에 할 일을 묻는 문제이다. 대화 후반에 여자가 출장에서 돌아오면 영수증을 제출하라고(please turn in our receipts when you get back next week) 하자 이에 대해 남자가 알겠다고 했으므로 남자는 다음 주에 영수증을 제출할 것임을 알 수 있다. 따라서 정답은 (B)이다.

▶paraphrasing turn in your receipts 영수증을 제출하다 → Submit some receipts 영수증을 제출하기

[어휘] lead 이끌다, 안내하다 training session 교육 (과정) submit 제출하다 presentation 발표 request 요청하다

[04-06] [BR-US]

Questions 04-06 refer to the following conversation.

W: Leonard, do you still think you can get the monthly report done by the end of the day? ⁰⁴**Aren't you going to the session this afternoon?**
M: Well, I attended last month's communication workshop. I heard that today will cover the same topics.
W: Oh, I see. Did you find it useful?
M: Definitely. I picked up a lot of helpful tips. And ⁰⁵**now that our company has signed up with twenty new international clients,** those kinds of skills are even more important, since we'll mostly be communicating by e-mail.
W: That's true. Anyway, I'm headed to the conference room now. ⁰⁶**I want to be near the front so I have an unobstructed view of the screen.**

monthly 매월의 get ~ done ~을 마치다 session (특정 활동을 위한) 시간, 회의, 수업 attend 참석하다 cover 다루다 definitely 분명히, 확실히 now that ~이므로, ~이기 때문에 sign up with ~와 계약하다 mostly 주로, 일반적으로 communicate 의사소통하다 be headed to ~로 향하다 front 맨 앞쪽 unobstructed 가로막히지 않은

04-06은 다음 대화에 관한 문제입니다.
여: Leonard, 여전히 오늘 안으로 월간 보고서를 끝맡칠 수 있을 것 같아요? ⁰⁴오늘 오후에 그 교육에 가지 않나요?
남: 음, 전 지난달에 커뮤니케이션 워크숍에 참석했어요. 오늘 똑같은 주제를 다룬다고 들었어요.
여: 아, 그렇군요. 그것이 유용했나요?
남: 확실히요. 도움이 될 만한 조언을 많이 얻었어요. 그리고 ⁰⁵우리 회사가 20명의 새로운 해외 고객과 계약을 맺었기 때문에 그런 종류의 능력은 훨씬 더 중요해요. 우리는 대부분 이메일로 소통할 거니까요.
여: 사실이에요. 어쨌든 저는 지금 회의실로 가는 중이에요. ⁰⁶가려서 화면이 잘 보이지 않는 일이 없도록 앞쪽 가까이 앉고 싶어요.

04.

남자가 "전 지난달에 커뮤니케이션 워크숍에 참석했어요"라고 말할 때 의미하는 것은 무엇인가?
(A) 계획보다 늦어졌다.
(B) 여자에게 조언을 줄 수 있다.
(C) 교육에 참석하지 않을 것이다.
(D) 행사에 대해 잊어버렸다.

[해설] 여자가 오늘 오후에 그 교육에 가지 않는지(Aren't you going to the session this afternoon?) 참석 여부를 묻자 남자가 해당 문장으로 "지난달에 커뮤니케이션 워크숍에 참석했다"고 말하며, 오늘 같은 주제를 다룬다고 들었다고 덧붙인다. 즉, 남자는 이미 같은 주제의 교육에 참석한 적이 있으므로 이번 교육에는 참석하지 않겠다는 의사를 밝힌 것이므로 정답은 (C)이다.

[어휘] fall behind schedule 계획이 늦어지다 advice 조언, 충고 be absent from ~에 결석하다 training session 교육 (과정)

05.

남자에 의하면, 이 회사는 최근에 무엇을 했는가?
(A) 더 많은 해외 고객을 확보했다.
(B) 속달 서비스를 추가했다.
(C) 경험이 풍부한 직원들을 고용했다.
(D) 새로운 소프트웨어를 설치했다.

[해설] 화자들의 회사가 최근에 한 일을 남자의 말에서 찾아야 한다. 대화 중반 남자가 커뮤니케이션 워크숍이 도움이 되었다며, 그 같은 커뮤니케이션 기술이 중요한 이유로 회사에서 20명의 새로운 해외 고객과 계약을 맺었다는(now that our company has signed up with twenty new international clients) 사실을 언급한다. 즉, 이 회사는 최근에 해외 고객을 더 많이 확보했음을 알 수 있으므로 정답은 (A)이다.

▶paraphrasing our company has signed up with twenty new international clients 우리 회사가 20명의 새로운 해외 고객들과 계약을 맺었다 → Acquired more overseas clients 더 많은 해외 고객을 확보했다.

[어휘] acquire 취득[획득]하다 overseas 해외의 express service 속달 서비스 experienced 경험이 많은 install 설치하다

06.

여자가 하고 싶다고 말한 것은 무엇인가?
(A) 나중에 문제에 대해 논의하기
(B) 동료와 상담하기
(C) 좋은 좌석 확보하기
(D) 일부 수치 확인하기

[해설] 여자의 후반부 대사에 정답의 단서가 있다. 마지막 대사에서 여자는 지금 회의실로 가는 중이라며 가려서 화면이 잘 보이지 않는 일이 없도록 앞쪽 가까이 앉고 싶다고(I want to be near the front so I have an unobstructed view of the screen.) 말했다. 즉, 시야를 막지 않는 좋은 좌석에 앉고 싶다는 말이므로 정답은 (C)이다.

▶paraphrasing be near the front so I have an unobstructed view of the screen. 가려서 화면이 잘 보이지 않는 일이 없도록 앞쪽 가까이 가다 → Get a good seat 좋은 좌석 확보하기

[어휘] discuss 논의하다 consult ~와 상담하다 figures 수치

[07-09] US-BR

Questions 07-09 refer to the following conversation.

> M: Hi, I'm here because of these steel-tipped boots. **07I just bought them last month, but they're already falling apart. 08Protective gear like this is really important on construction sites.**
> W: Let me see your receipt... Wow, these shouldn't wear out so quickly. Unfortunately, I can't give you cash back because it was a final sale.
> M: There must be something you can do for me, right?
> W: I can issue store credit for them. Also, **09here's the phone number of the manufacturer. They should be able to help you.**

steel-tipped boots 안전화   fall apart 떨어지다, 무너지다
protective gear 보호 장비   construction site 건설 현장
wear out 마모되다, 닳다   a final sale 교환/환불 불가 상품
manufacturer 제조사

07-09는 다음 대화에 관한 문제입니다.

남: 안녕하세요. 저는 이 안전화 때문에 왔어요. **07바로 지난달에 이걸 샀는데 이미 부서지기 시작했어요. 08이런 보호 장비는 건설 현장에서 정말 중요해요.**
여: 영수증을 볼게요… 와우, 이건 이렇게 빨리 마모되면 안 돼요. 안타깝게도, 그건 교환/환불 불가 상품이어서 환불은 해 드릴 수가 없어요.
남: 그래도 뭔가 해 주실 수 있는 게 있겠죠, 그렇죠?
여: 제가 매장 포인트를 발행해 드릴게요. 그리고 **09여기 제조사 전화번호가 있어요. 그들이 도와 드릴 수 있을 거예요.**

07.

남자는 왜 업체를 방문했는가?
(A) 제품을 교환하기 위해
(B) 가격 조정을 하기 위해
(C) 온라인으로 주문한 것을 가져가기 위해
(D) 상품을 검사하기 위해

[해설] 업체를 방문한 이유는 대화 초반에 언급된다. 초반에 남자가 지난달에 안전화를 샀는데 벌써 부서지고 있다고(I just bought them last month, but they're already falling apart) 했으므로 구입한 물건을 교환하기 위해 온 것임을 알 수 있다. 따라서 (A)가 정답이다.

[어휘] exchange 교환하다   price adjustment 가격 조정   inspect 검사하다, 점검하다   merchandise 상품, 물품

08.

남자의 직업은 무엇일 것 같은가?
(A) 배송 기사
(B) 신발 판매원
(C) 건설 노동자
(D) 실험실 기술자

[해설] 남자의 직업은 대화 초반부에 알 수 있다. 초반부에 남자가 안전화 얘기를 하면서 이런 보호 장비는 건설 현장에서 정말 중요하다고(Protective gear like this is really important on construction sites) 했으므로 건설 현장에서 일하고 있음을 유추할 수 있다. 따라서 (C)가 정답이다.

[어휘] occupation 직업   laboratory 실험실

09.

여자는 무엇을 할 것을 제안하는가?
(A) 제조사에 연락하기
(B) 매니저와 이야기하기
(C) 다른 브랜드를 구입하기
(D) 웹사이트 방문하기

[해설] 제안/요청 문제의 단서는 대화 후반부에 언급된다. 후반부에 여자가 제조사의 전화번호를 건네며(here's the phone number of the manufacturer) 그들이 도와줄 수 있을 거라고(They should be able to help you) 했으므로 제조사에 연락해 볼 것을 제안하고 있음을 알 수 있다. 따라서 (A)가 정답이다.

[10-12] US-BR

Questions 10-12 refer to the following conversation and invoice.

Item Description	Charge
Casserole Dish	$20
17Frying Pan	$35
Stainless Steel Pot	$40
Tea Set	$60
Total	**$155**

> M: I'm glad you found everything you were looking for today, ma'am. Your total is one fifty-five. **10Would you prefer to pay by cash or credit card?**
> W: By credit card, please. And I almost forgot ...um... I've got **11a coupon for ten percent off.** Here it is.
> M: I'm really sorry, but you won't be able to use this. **11It was only valid until April 30,** so the computer will not allow me to input the code.
> W: Oh, I didn't realize that. In that case, **12I don't think I'll get the frying pan today. Could you please take that charge off the invoice?**
> M: Certainly. Just a moment.

prefer ~을 더 좋아하다   valid 유효한   input 입력하다   in that case 그런 경우에는   charge 요금, 청구액   invoice 청구서   certainly 틀림없이, 분명히   description 서술, 묘사   casserole 캐서롤(오븐에 넣어 만든 찜 비슷한 요리)용 냄비

10-12는 다음 대화와 청구서에 관한 문제입니다.

품목 내역	청구액
캐서롤용 냄비	20달러
11프라이팬	35달러
스테인리스강 냄비	40달러
찻잔 세트	60달러
합계	155달러

남: 오늘 찾고 계시던 것을 모두 찾으셨다니 기쁘네요, 손님. 모두 155달러입니다. **¹⁰현금으로 지불하시겠어요, 아니면 신용카드로 지불하시겠어요?**

여: 신용카드로 하겠습니다. 그리고 잊어버릴 뻔했는데요... 음... 제게 **¹¹10퍼센트 할인 쿠폰**이 있어요. 여기요.

남: 정말 죄송하지만 이건 사용하실 수 없어요. **¹¹4월 30일까지만 유효해요.** 그래서 컴퓨터로 코드 입력이 안 될 거예요.

여: 아, 그건 몰랐어요. 그렇다면 **¹²프라이팬은 오늘 못 살 것 같아요. 청구서에서 그 금액을 빼주시겠어요?**

남: 물론이죠. 잠깐만요.

10.
남자는 여자에게 무엇에 대해 물어보는가?
(A) 회원 번호
(B) 배송 시간
(C) 고객 조사
(D) 선호하는 지불 방법

[해설] 상점 계산대에서 손님과 직원이 나누는 대화로, 대화 초반 직원인 남자가 고객인 여자에게 현금과 신용카드 중 무엇으로 지불하고 싶은지(Would you prefer to pay by cash or credit card?) 묻는다. 즉, 선호하는 지불 방법에 대해 물었으므로 정답은 (D)이다.

11.
여자가 할인을 받을 수 없는 이유는 무엇인가?
(A) 그녀에게 있는 쿠폰이 만료되었다.
(B) 그녀의 상품의 브랜드가 잘못된 것이다.
(C) 상품이 충분하지 않다.
(D) 가격이 이미 인하되었다.

[해설] 신용카드 지불을 선택한 여자가 10퍼센트 할인 쿠폰(a coupon for ten percent off)이 있다고 했고, 이에 남자가 이용할 수 없는 쿠폰이라며 4월 30일까지만 유효하다고(It was only valid until April 30) 덧붙였다. 즉, 여자가 가지고 있는 쿠폰의 기한이 만료되어 할인을 받을 수 없다는 의미이므로 정답은 (A)이다.

paraphrasing It was only valid until April 30 4월 30일까지만 유효하다 → The coupon that she has is expired. 그녀에게 있는 쿠폰이 만료되었다.

[어휘] expire 만료되다, 만기가 되다 merchandise (상점에서 파는) 상품 lower ~을 내리다, 낮추다

12.
시각 자료를 보시오. 어떤 금액이 청구서에서 삭제될 것인가?
(A) 20달러
(B) 35달러
(C) 40달러
(D) 60달러

[해설] 시각 자료로 주어진 청구서에서 삭제될 금액을 묻는 문제로, 보기에 금액이 제시되어 있으므로 대화에서는 청구서의 품목들 중 하나가 언급될 것임을 예상해야 한다. 대화 후반부에서 여자가 프라이팬은 오늘 못 살 것 같다며 청구서에서 그 금액을 빼달라고(I don't think I'll get the frying pan today. Could you please take that charge off the invoice?) 요청했다. 청구서에서 프라이팬에 해당하는 금액이 35달러이므로 정답은 (B)이다.

paraphrasing take that charge off the invoice 청구서에서 그 금액을 빼다 → be deleted from the invoice 청구서에서 삭제되다

[13-15] BR-US
Questions 13-15 refer to the following conversation.

M: Hello, **¹³I'm calling about my cell phone bill.** I'm Dale Chaney and my number is 619-9774. Why am I being charged so much more than usual?

W: Okay, I see you have some international roaming fees. Did you travel abroad?

M: Yes, **¹⁴I went to Australia for business last month.** I didn't make any calls while I was there, though.

W: According to our records, you didn't sign up for an international plan before leaving. Therefore, you were charged for all the data that you used while you were overseas. I can remove the charge this time, but **¹⁵in the future, you have to let us know before you go abroad.**

M: Oh, I see. Thanks for your help. I'll be sure to do that next time.

bill 고지서, 청구서 charge 요금; (요금을) 청구하다 roaming (휴대전화의) 로밍(일반적인 계약 지역 외에서의 사용) fee 수수료, 요금 abroad 해외에, 해외로 sign up for ~을 신청하다 overseas 해외에, 외국에 remove 없애다, 제거하다

13-15는 다음 대화에 관한 문제입니다.

남: 안녕하세요, **¹³제 휴대폰 청구서 때문에 전화드렸어요.** 저는 Dale Chaney라고 하고요, 제 번호는 619-9774입니다. 평소보다 왜 이렇게 많은 요금이 청구된 것인가요?

여: 알겠습니다, 해외 로밍 요금이 있으시네요. 해외 여행을 다녀오셨나요?

남: 네, **¹⁴지난달에 업무 차 호주에 갔었어요.** 하지만 그곳에 있는 동안 전혀 전화를 걸지 않았는데요.

여: 저희 기록에 따르면, 떠나시기 전에 국제 요금제를 신청하지 않으셨어요. 그래서 해외에 계신 동안 사용하신 모든 데이터에 대해 요금이 청구되었어요. 이번에는 제가 요금을 빼드리면 되지만 **¹⁵앞으로 해외에 나가시기 전에는 저희한테 알려주셔야 해요.**

남: 아, 그렇군요. 도와주셔서 감사합니다. 다음 번에는 꼭 그렇게 할게요.

13.
남자가 전화한 목적은 무엇인가?
(A) 종이로 된 명세서를 요청하기 위해서
(B) 여행 계획을 세우기 위해서
(C) 신원을 확인하기 위해서
(D) 청구서에 대해 문의하기 위해서

[해설] 전화를 한 목적을 묻는 문제로, 주로 대화 초반에 단서가 제시된다. 남자는 휴대폰 청구서 때문에 전화했다고(I'm calling about my cell phone bill) 말한 뒤 평소보다 많은 요금이 청구된 이유를 묻고 있다. 따라서 정답은 (D)이다.

[어휘] statement 명세서 confirm 확인하다 identity 신원, 신분, 정체 inquire 문의하다

14.

남자는 지난달에 무엇을 했는가?
(A) 계좌를 개설했다.
(B) 출장을 갔다.
(C) 새로운 휴대폰을 샀다.
(D) 국제 전화 요금제를 신청했다.

[해설] 질문의 핵심 키워드 last month는 대화 중반에 그대로 나온다. 해외 여행을 다녀왔냐는 여자의 물음에 남자가 지난달에 업무 차 호주에 갔다고(I went to Australia for business last month) 했다. 즉, 남자가 지난달 해외 출장을 다녀왔음을 알 수 있으므로 정답은 (B)이다.

paraphrasing I went to Australia for business 업무 차 호주에 갔다 → He went on a business trip. 출장을 갔다.

[어휘] open an account 계좌를 개설하다 purchase 구매하다

15.

여자에 따르면, 남자는 앞으로 추가 요금을 피하려면 무엇을 해야 하는가?
(A) 서비스 제공업체에 알리기
(B) 청구 요금을 제때 지불하기
(C) 계약서에 서명하기
(D) SNS에 게시하기

[해설] 앞서 남자에게 전화요금이 많이 청구된 이유로, 해외에 나가기 전에 국제 요금제를 신청하지 않았기 때문이라고 여자가 설명했다. 이어서 앞으로 해외에 나가기 전에는 자신들에게 알려달라고(in the future, you have to let us know before you go abroad) 한 것으로 보아 앞으로 남자가 해외에 나갈 때 추가 요금을 내지 않으려면 통신 서비스 회사에 통보해야 함을 알 수 있다. 따라서 정답은 (A)이다.

paraphrasing let us know 우리에게 통보하라 → inform 알리기

[어휘] extra fee 추가 요금 inform 알리다, 통지하다 service provider 서비스 제공 업체 on time 정각에 contract 계약(서) post 게시하다, 공고하다

[16-18] US-BR

Questions 16-18 refer to the following conversation.

> M: Good afternoon! ¹⁶**Do you have your store membership card?**
> W: No, I forgot it at home.
> M: That happens all the time. But if you install our store app, you wouldn't need to bring it.
> W: Oh, really? That's convenient. ¹⁷**I should do that later because I can't connect to the Wi-Fi here.**
> M: **I can do that for you.** Also, ¹⁸**you can use a 10% welcome coupon today.** Your total comes to 34 dollars and 50 cents. That means you saved more than $3.

forget 잊다, 잊어버리다 happen 발생하다, 일어나다 install 설치하다 convenient 편리한 connect 연결하다, 접속하다 total 총; 총액 save 모으다, 아끼다

16-18은 다음 대화에 관한 문제입니다.
남: 안녕하세요! ¹⁶매장 회원 카드를 가지고 계신가요?
여: 아니요, 잊어버리고 집에 안 가져왔어요.
남: 그런 일은 항상 있지요. 그러나 저희 매장 앱을 설치하신다면 가져오실 필요가 없어요.
여: 오, 정말이요? 그거 참 편리하네요. ¹⁷여기는 와이파이가 연결이 안 되니 다음에 그렇게 해야겠어요.
남: 제가 해 드릴 수 있어요. 또한, ¹⁸오늘 10% 할인 환영 쿠폰도 사용하실 수 있어요. 초 34달러 50센트입니다. 3달러 이상 절약했다는 말이지요.

16.

남자는 여자에게 무엇을 요청하는가?
(A) 가방
(B) 회원 카드
(C) 영수증
(D) 쿠폰

[해설] 대화 초반에 남자가 여자에게 매장 회원 카드를 가지고 왔는지(Do you have your store membership card) 물었으므로 (B)가 정답이다.

[어휘] receipt 영수증

17.

남자가 "제가 해 드릴 수 있어요"라고 말할 때 의미하는 것은 무엇인가?
(A) 여자가 무거운 제품을 구입했다.
(B) 더 많은 제품들이 뒤쪽에 있다.
(C) 그는 여자가 앱을 설치하는 것을 도울 것이다.
(D) 그는 여자가 앱을 설치하는 것을 도울 것이다.

[해설] 화자의 의도 파악 문제는 주어진 문장의 앞뒤 문맥을 잘 살펴야 한다. 앞서 여자가 여기는 와이파이가 안 되니 다음에 앱을 설치해야겠다고(I should do that later because I can't connect to the Wi-Fi here) 하자, 남자가 "제가 해 드릴 수 있어요"라고 말한 것이다. 이는 여자가 앱 설치하는 것을 도와줄 수 있다는 말이므로 (C)가 정답이다.

[어휘] coworker 동료 approve 승인하다

18.

여자는 무엇을 받는가?
(A) 무료 배송
(B) 할인
(C) 응모권
(D) 무료 제품

[해설] 대화 마지막 부분에 남자가 오늘 10% 할인 환영 쿠폰도 사용하실 수 있다며(you can use a 10% welcome coupon today) 추가 할인을 언급했으므로 (B)가 정답이다.

paraphrasing a 10% welcome coupon 10% 할인 환영 쿠폰 → A discount 추가 할인

[어휘] raffle ticket 응모권

[19-21] US-US

Questions 19-21 refer to the following conversation and coupon.

Macon Home Store Wallpaper Sale

Wallpaper Roll Size	Save
25 sq. feet	5%
²¹50 sq. feet	10%
100 sq. feet	15%
250 sq. feet	20%

Valid in store or with online code
5WALL20

W: Hello, ¹⁹**my restaurant is scheduled to reopen next week,** but I need some new wallpaper.
M: Okay, here are the patterns that we carry. Which one do you prefer?
W: This one here, Playful Checkers. ²⁰**I think it will pair really well with the rest of the interior.**
M: Hopefully it does. By the way, our wallpaper is currently on sale. Check out this coupon.
W: Honestly, the new area isn't extremely large. ²¹**I'm sure that 50 square feet will be plenty to cover it all.**

reopen 다시 문을 열다 wallpaper 벽지 pattern (옷감이나 벽지 등의) 견본 carry 취급하다 prefer 선호하다 pair with ~와 짝을 이루다 rest 나머지, 다른 것들 interior 내부 hopefully 바라건대 currently 현재 on sale 세일 중인 check out 확인하다 honestly 솔직히 extremely 극도로, 극히 square feet 평방피트 plenty 풍부함, 충분함 cover 바르다, 뒤덮다 valid 유효한, 정당한 code 암호, 부호

19-21은 다음 대화와 쿠폰에 관한 문제입니다.

Macon Home Store 벽지 세일

벽지 두루마리 크기	할인
25평방피트	5퍼센트
²¹50평방피트	10퍼센트
100평방피트	15퍼센트
250평방피트	20퍼센트

매장에서 또는 온라인 코드
5WALL20으로 이용 가능

여: 안녕하세요, ¹⁹저희 식당이 다음 주에 재개점할 예정인데, 새로운 벽지가 필요합니다.
남: 알겠습니다. 여기 저희가 취급하는 견본들을 보세요. 어떤 것이 마음에 드세요?
여: 여기 있는 이거요. Playful Checkers요. ²⁰나머지 실내 공간과 아주 잘 어울릴 것 같아요.
남: 그랬으면 좋겠네요. 그건 그렇고, 저희 벽지가 현재 세일 중입니다. 이 쿠폰을 확인해보세요.
여: 솔직히, 새로 벽지를 바를 공간이 그렇게 넓지 않아요. ²¹모든 부분을 바르는 데 50평방피트면 충분할 거라고 확신해요.

19.

여자는 다음 주에 무엇을 할 것인가?
(A) 사진을 찍기
(B) 집을 개조하기
(C) 식당을 재개점하기
(D) 인테리어 디자이너를 만나기

[해설] 질문의 핵심 키워드 next week은 대화 초반에 언급된다. 여자는 다음 주에 자신의 식당을 재개점할 예정이라고(my restaurant is scheduled to reopen next week) 했으므로 정답은 (C)이다.

[어휘] renovate 개조[보수]하다

20.

여자는 Playful Checkers에 대해 무엇이라고 말하는가?
(A) 현재의 인테리어와 잘 맞는다.
(B) 두 가지 색상만 있는 패턴을 선호한다.
(C) 식당 시설에 일반적이다.
(D) 야외 표면에 사용될 수 있다.

[해설] Playful Checkers는 대화 중반에 언급되는데, 여자가 맘에 들어 한 벽지 견본의 이름이다. 여자는 이것이 다른 실내 공간과 아주 잘 어울릴 것 같다고(it will pair really well with the rest of the interior) 했으므로 여자의 식당의 현재 인테리어와 잘 맞는다는 의미이다. 따라서 정답은 (A)이다.

paraphrasing it will pair really well with the rest of the interior. 다른 실내 공간과 아주 잘 어울릴 것이다 → it matches her current décor 현재의 인테리어와 잘 맞는다

[어휘] match (색깔이나 스타일이 서로) 맞다 current 현재의 décor 실내장식, 인테리어 common 일반적인 establishment 시설, 영업소, 점포 surface 표면

21.

시각 자료를 보시오. 여자는 할인을 얼마나 받게 될 것인가?
(A) 5퍼센트
(B) 10퍼센트
(C) 15퍼센트
(D) 20퍼센트

[해설] 시각 자료로 주어진 쿠폰의 할인율이 보기로 제시되었으므로 대화에서는 쿠폰의 벽지 사이즈가 언급될 것임을 예상하고 들어야 한다. 대화 마지막, 여자가 모든 부분을 바르는 데 50평방피트면 충분하다고(I'm sure that 50 square feet will be plenty to cover it all.) 했으므로 쿠폰에서 이 크기의 벽지에 해당하는 할인율을 찾으면 10퍼센트이다. 따라서 정답은 (B)이다.

PART 4 담화(talk)

출제 유형 01 제품 시연
| 풀이 방법 해석 |

남: Delaney 자동차는 Millenium 전자와 협력하여 새로운 자동차 디지털 전면 유리를 만들었습니다. 처음 보기에는, 일반 전면 유리와 같아 보입니다. 하지만 차 안에서는 밖이 보이는 화면을 통해 디지털 화면을 볼 수 있습니다. 운전자는 속도, 연료, 그리고 GPS 방향을 보여주도록 화면을 원하는 대로 설정할 수 있습니다. 그것이 장착되어 있는 차량을 시험 운전해 본 사람들은 그들이 공상 과학 영화 속에 있는 것 같다고 말합니다. 이제, 카메라 팀과 제가 차 안으로 들어가 어떻게 작동하는지 보여 드리겠습니다.

출제 유형 02 발표
| 풀이 방법 해석 |

여: 좋은 아침입니다! 저는 Marissa Corning이고 신입 직원 오리엔테이션의 책임자입니다. 여러분들은 모두 이곳 Tacoma 산업에서 일하도록 선정된 것에 대해 신이 날 것입니다. 아시다시피, 우리 회사는 내부 채용을 주로 하는데, 여러분이 성장할수록 기회도 많아진다는 것입니다. 회사 웹페이지를 정기적으로 확인해서 관심을 끄는 직책이 있는지 확인하세요. 이제, 시설을 돌아보기 전에, 세금에 대한 이 양식을 각자 작성해 주시길 부탁드립니다. 그것은 매달 월급이 여러분의 계좌로 입금될 수 있도록 은행 정보도 포함하고 있습니다.

연습 문제
01. (A) 02. (A) 03. (B) 04. (B) 05. (B) 06. (A)

01.
What will the listeners do next?
(A) **See** a **video**   (B) **Tour** a **house**

M: Good afternoon. I'm Bob Ring, director of Wellington Valley Homes and Property. Thank you for coming to this informative seminar about real estate transactions. I will give you a clear overview of what you will encounter when buying or renting a property. I will share with you both good and bad cases. Now, would you please watch this short video?

청자들은 다음에 무엇을 할 것인가?
(A) 영상 보기   (B) 집을 둘러 보기

담화
남: 안녕하세요. 저는 Wellington Valley Homes and Property의 책임자인 Bob Ring입니다. 부동산 거래에 대한 이 유익한 세미나에 와 주셔서 감사합니다. 당신이 집을 사거나 빌릴 때 맞닥뜨릴 것에 대한 명확한 개요를 설명해 드리겠습니다. 좋은 경우와 나쁜 경우를 모두 공유해 드리겠습니다. 이제, 이 짧은 영상을 봐주시겠어요?

02. BR
Where is the talk **taking place**?
(A) At an **industry exhibition**
(B) At an **electronics store**

W: Thank you for visiting our booth. We, Irwin Electronics, are one of the most reliable kitchen utensil providers and we attend the Chicago Culinary Expo with new products every year. This year, we have developed a new fryer for commercial use. It features a non-chemical auto filtering technology, so you can reduce oil use. I will show you how it works now.

담화는 어디에서 이루어지고 있는가?
(A) 산업 박람회에서   (B) 전자기기 매장에서

담화
여: 저희 부스를 방문해 주셔서 감사합니다. 저희 Irwin 전자는 가장 신뢰할 수 있는 주방 기구 공급업체 중 하나이고 매해 신제품을 가지고 시카고 요리 박람회에 참석합니다. 올해, 저희는 새로운 상업용 프라이어를 개발했습니다. 화학 제품이 없는 자동 필터링 기술을 특징으로 하고 있어, 여러분은 기름의 사용을 줄일 수 있습니다. 이제 그것이 어떻게 작동하는지 보여 드리겠습니다.

03. AU
What product is being **discussed**?
(A) **Sunglasses**   (B) A **digital camera**

M: Hello, welcome to the Optical Instrument Expo. My name is Jeff. Today, I will introduce a new digital camera that we just released on the market. You have probably missed a great moment to take a photo due to a long response time of your digital camera. That's why people prefer to take a photo with their cellphone. If you just press the shutter, it will be ready to take a photo in a second.

어떤 제품이 논의되고 있는가?
(A) 선글라스   (B) 디지털 카메라

담화
남: 안녕하세요, 시각 기기 박람회에 오신 것을 환영합니다. 제 이름은 Jeff입니다. 오늘, 저는 저희가 막 시장에 출시한 새로운 디지털 카메라를 소개할 것입니다. 여러분은 아마도 여러분의 디지털 카메라의 긴 반응 시간 때문에 사진을 찍을 훌륭한 순간을 놓쳤던 때가 있을 겁니다. 그게 사람들이 휴대전화로 사진 찍는 것을 선호하는 이유죠. 셔터를 누르시기만 하면, 순식간에 사진 찍을 준비가 될 것입니다.

04. US
Why is **Mr. Sanchez famous**?
(A) He **wrote** a best-selling **book**.
(B) He **created** a popular **product**.

W: Thank you for coming to the grand opening of Tropical Passion at Peterson Mall. Today, we will share simple recipes with which you can make healthy and tasteful fruit juices in your home. Our recipe developer, Mr. Sanchez, will use only ingredients easily found in your refrigerator. He is well-known for creating the recipe for our signature juice, Sunrise Passion.

Sanchez 씨는 왜 유명한가?
(A) 베스트셀러 책을 썼다. (B) 인기 있는 제품을 만들었다.

담화
여: Peterson 쇼핑몰에 있는 Tropical Passion의 개점 행사에 와주셔서 감사합니다. 오늘, 저희는 여러분의 집에서 건강하고 맛있는 과일 주스를 만들 수 있는 간단한 레시피를 공유할 것입니다. 저희 레시피 개발자인 Sanchez 씨는 당신의 냉장고에서 쉽게 찾을 수 있는 재료들만 사용할 것입니다. 그는 저희의 대표 주스인 Sunrise Passion의 레시피를 개발한 것으로도 유명합니다.

05. [BR]

What will the listeners be awarded?
(A) A free product   (B) A cash bonus

W: Today, I'm going to let you know about the sales reports that you all submitted last quarter. I collected them and reported to the headquarters. I received an e-mail saying that we achieved the sales goal and exceeded it by 20 percent. This is due largely to your hard work and contribution. You will be given a $200 bonus and it will be reflected in your monthly pay.

청자들은 무엇을 받을 것인가?
(A) 무료 제품 (B) 현금 보너스

담화
여: 오늘, 저는 여러분 모두가 지난 분기에 제출한 매출 보고서에 대해 알려 드릴 것입니다. 저는 그것들을 모아서 본사에 보고했습니다. 저는 우리가 매출 목표를 달성했고 20퍼센트 초과했다고 알리는 이메일을 받았습니다. 이것은 여러분이 열심히 일하고 헌신한 덕분입니다. 여러분은 200달러의 보너스를 받을 것이고 월급에 반영될 것입니다.

06. [BR]

What does the speaker ask the listeners to do?
(A) Wear a name tag (B) Review a contract

M: Hello, everyone. I will do a final check for today's catering for Olson Real Estate. It is our first time doing business with this agency, so I want to give them a good impression about our service. They hold many receptions with their potential clients. I want the waiting staff to wear these shirts, vests, and name tags on your chests. It can make us look more neat and professional.

화자는 청자들에게 무엇을 하라고 요청하는가?
(A) 이름표 착용하기   (B) 계약서 검토하기

담화
남: 안녕하세요, 여러분. 오늘 Olson 부동산으로의 출장 연회를 위한 마지막 확인을 할 것입니다. 이 회사와 일을 하는 것은 이번이 처음이어서, 우리 서비스에 대해 좋은 인상을 주고 싶습니다. 그들은 그들의 잠재 고객과 많은 연회를 엽니다. 저는 종업원들이 이 셔츠, 조끼를 입고 가슴에 이름표를 착용하길 원합니다. 그건 우리가 더 깔끔하고 전문적으로 보이게 할 수 있습니다.

---

paraphrasing 정답 1. (a) 2. (c) 3. (b) 4. (b) 5. (c) 6. (a)

실전 문제

01. (B)	02. (D)	03. (C)	04. (D)	05. (B)	06. (D)
07. (D)	08. (C)	09. (A)	10. (B)	11. (D)	12. (A)
13. (A)	14. (C)	15. (D)	16. (A)	17. (C)	18. (C)
19. (A)	20. (C)	21. (A)			

[01-03] [BR]
Questions 01-03 refer to the following talk.

M: Good morning, everyone. ⁰¹I hope you all have a great time today as we hike the famous Goldmine Trail here at Willow Park. Now, it's quite cold today, but that's actually good news for us. ⁰²It means there will be hardly any people using the trail, so I'm glad about that. Before we begin, ⁰³if you have anything in your bags that you don't plan to specifically use on the trail, you'd better put it in the lockers so you don't have to carry it around.

hike 하이킹, 하이킹[도보 여행]을 가다 trail 오솔길, 시골길, 루트, 코스 quite 꽤, 상당히 hardly 거의 ~ 아니다 specifically 분명히, 특별히 locker 물품 보관함 carry around 휴대하다, 들고 다니다

01-03은 다음 담화에 관한 문제입니다.
남: 여러분, 안녕하세요. 이곳 Willow 공원의 ⁰¹유명한 Goldmine Trail을 하이킹하면서 오늘 여러분 모두 즐거운 시간 보내시길 바랍니다. 자, 오늘 꽤 춥긴 하지만요, 사실은 그게 우리에겐 좋은 소식이에요. ⁰²그 코스를 이용하는 사람들이 거의 없을 거라는 뜻이니 저는 그 점 때문에 기쁩니다. 시작하기에 앞서서, ⁰³코스 도중에 특별히 사용할 계획이 아닌 물건이 가방에 있는 분들은 물품 보관함에 넣어 두시는 게 좋겠습니다. 그러면 가지고 다니지 않아도 되니까요.

01.

청자들은 누구일 것 같은가?
(A) 시 공무원들
(B) 하이킹 참가자들
(C) 유지 보수 직원들
(D) 주차 단속 요원들

[해설] 화자가 인사와 함께 Goldmine Trail을 하이킹하면서 여러분 모두 즐거운 시간 보내길 바란다는(I hope you all have a great time today as we hike the famous Goldmine Trail) 말로 담화를 시작한 후, 하이킹 코스와 관련한 추가 정보 등을 제공하는 것으로 보아 하이킹 참가자를 대상으로 하고 있음을 알 수 있으므로 정답은 (B)이다.

[어휘] official 공무원, 관리 participant 참가자 maintenance 유지, 관리 parking attendant 주차 단속 요원

02.

화자는 왜 기뻐하는가?
(A) 최근에 요금이 인하되었다.
(B) 청자들이 제시간에 도착했다.
(C) 새로운 서비스를 이용할 수 있다.

(D) 지역이 혼잡하지 않을 것이다.

[해설] 화자는 오늘 날씨가 꽤 추운 탓에 코스를 이용하는 사람들이 거의 없을 것이라서 기쁘다고(It means there will be hardly any people using the trail, so I'm glad about that.) 언급했다. 즉, 하이킹 코스가 혼잡하지 않을 것이 예상되어 기분이 좋다는 의미이므로 정답은 (D)이다.

paraphrasing there will be hardly any people using the trail 그 코스를 이용하는 사람들이 거의 없을 것이다 → An area will not be crowded. 어떤 지역이 혼잡하지 않을 것이다.

[어휘] recently 최근에 decrease 줄다, 감소하다 on time 제시간에 area 지역, 구역 crowded 붐비는, 혼잡한

03.

화자는 청자들과 어떤 충고를 공유하는가?
(A) 무리 지어 함께 걷기
(B) 지도를 주의 깊게 살펴보기
(C) 불필요한 물품을 두고 가기
(D) 사진을 많이 찍기

[해설] 담화 후반부에, 코스 도중에 특별히 사용할 계획이 아닌 물건이 가방에 있다면 물품 보관함에 넣어 두라고(if you have anything in your bags that you don't plan to specifically use on the trail, you'd better put it in the lockers) 조언했으므로 정답은 (C)이다.

paraphrasing if you have anything in your bags that you don't plan to specifically use on the trail, you'd better put it in the lockers 코스 도중에 특별히 사용할 계획이 아닌 물건이 가방에 있다면 물품 보관함에 넣어 두는 게 좋겠다 → leaving behind unnecessary items 불필요한 물품을 두고 가기

[어휘] in groups 무리 지어 leave behind 두고 가다 unnecessary 불필요한

[04-06] AU

Questions 04-06 refer to the following talk.

> M: It's great to see so many people here for Timber Gym's open house event. As you may know, [04]**we've just cut our membership fees by thirty percent** so that more people can enjoy our facility. After the tour, you can try one of our exercise classes for free. For example, [05]**there's a yoga class at two o'clock that is taught by Carol.** As you leave today, make sure you check out the sports equipment we sell at the front desk. [06]**Our best-selling item is a step counter.** It can be used for people of any level. In fact, I always have mine with me.

> open house (모든 방문객을 환영하는) 개방 파티, 공개일 membership fee 회비 facility 시설 try 시험 삼아 해보다 for free 무료로 check out 확인하다 equipment 장비, 용품 best-selling 가장 많이 팔리는 step counter 만보기 in fact 사실

04-06은 다음 담화에 관한 문제입니다.

남: Timber 체육관 공개 행사를 위한 이 자리에서 이렇게 많은 분들을 뵙게 되어 영광입니다. 아시다시피 저희는 더욱 많은 분들이 저희 시설을 이용하실 수 있도록 [04]**회비를 30퍼센트 인하했습니다.** 둘러보신 후 저희 운동 강좌 중 하나를 무료로 들어 보실 수 있습니다. 예를 들어, [05]**Carol이 강의하는 요가 강좌가 2시에 있습니다.** 오늘 나가실 때 안내 데스크에서 판매중인 운동용품들을 꼭 확인해보시기 바랍니다. [06]**가장 잘 팔리는 품목은 만보기입니다.** 모든 수준의 사람들이 이용할 수 있습니다. 사실 저는 항상 제 것을 지니고 다닙니다.

04.

화자에 따르면, 이 업체는 최근에 무엇을 했는가?
(A) 더 많은 강좌를 추가했다.
(B) 건물을 확장했다.
(C) 두 번째 지점을 열었다.
(D) 가격을 낮췄다.

[해설] 피트니스 센터를 공개하는 행사에 참석한 잠재 고객들을 대상으로 하는 담화이다. 담화 초반, 화자는 많은 사람들이 시설을 이용할 수 있도록 회비를 30퍼센트 인하했다고(we've just cut our membership fees by thirty percent) 했다. 즉, 이용 가격을 낮춘 것이므로 정답은 (D)이다.

paraphrasing we've just cut our membership fees by thirty percent 회비를 30퍼센트 인하했다 → reduced its prices 가격을 낮췄다.

[어휘] add 추가하다 expand 확장시키다 reduce 낮추다, 인하하다

05.

Carol은 누구인가?
(A) 관광 안내원
(B) 운동 강사
(C) 자선 단체 설립자
(D) 사업주

[해설] 질문의 핵심 키워드인 Carol이라는 인물은 담화 중반에 언급된다. Carol이 강의하는 요가 강좌가 2시에 있다는(there's a yoga class at two o'clock that is taught by Carol) 말로 보아 Carol은 운동 강사임을 알 수 있으므로 정답은 (B)이다.

[어휘] fitness instructor 운동 강사 charity 자선 단체 founder 창립자, 설립자

06.

화자가 "저는 항상 제 것을 지니고 다닙니다"라고 말할 때 의미하는 것은 무엇인가?
(A) 청자들의 요구에 빨리 대응할 수 있다.
(B) 더 가벼운 물품을 찾고 싶다.
(C) 일부 정보의 최신 복사본을 보여줄 수 있다.
(D) 청자들이 제품을 구입할 것을 권장한다.

[해설] 담화 후반부, 화자는 안내 데스크에서 판매하는 운동용품들을 확인해보라며, 가장 잘 팔리는 품목은 만보기라고(Our best-selling item is a step counter) 한 뒤에 "저는 항상 제 것을 지니고 다닙니다"라고 했다. 즉, 자신이 항상 가지고 다닐 정도로 좋은 제품이니 만보기를 구입하라고 권하기 위해 해당 표현을 썼으므로 정답은 (D)이다.

[어휘] respond to ~에 대응하다 lightweight 가벼운, 경량의 encourage 권장[장려]하다

[07-09] US

Questions 07-09 refer to the following speech.

> W: Ladies and gentlemen, we'd like to get this press conference started. My name is Marilyn DeBoer, and

07I'm a member of GB Manufacturing's board of directors. We are constantly looking for ways to be an industry leader. Therefore, we are pleased to announce that **08**our profits from the third quarter will be used to purchase solar panels for all of our facilities. By using **08**alternative sources of electricity, we can reduce our company's impact on the environment. You can find out more about this project in **09**the brochures that we have provided on the table near the entrance. I hope you pick one up.

press conference 기자회견 board of directors 이사회 constantly 끊임없이 industry 산업, ~업 announce 발표하다, 알리다 profit 이익, 수익 quarter 사분기 purchase 구매하다 solar panel 태양 전지판 facilities 설비, 시설 alternative 대안, 선택 가능한 것 source 원천, 근원 electricity 전기 reduce 줄이다, 낮추다 impact 충격, 영향 provide 제공하다, 주다 entrance (출)입구

07-09는 다음 연설에 관한 문제입니다.
여: 신사숙녀 여러분, 이번 기자회견을 시작하도록 하겠습니다. 제 이름은 Marilyn DeBoer이고, **07**GB 제조사 이사회 임원입니다. 저희는 업계의 선두주자가 되기 위한 방법들을 끊임없이 찾고 있습니다. 따라서, **08**3분기 이익이 우리의 모든 시설을 위한 태양 전지판을 구입하는 데 사용될 예정임을 알려드리게 되어 기쁩니다. **08**전기의 대체 공급원을 이용함으로써 우리 회사가 환경에 끼치는 영향을 줄일 수 있습니다. **09**저희가 입구 근처 테이블에 준비해둔 안내책자를 보시면 이 작업에 대해 더 많이 아실 수 있습니다. 한 부씩 가져가시기 바랍니다.

07.
화자는 누구일 것 같은가?
(A) 영화 감독
(B) 행사 기획자
(C) 회사 설립자
(D) 이사회 임원

[해설] 화자의 신분이나 직업을 묻는 문제의 단서는 주로 담화 초반부에 나온다. 화자는 기자회견의 시작을 알리면서 자신을 GB Manufacturing 이사회 임원(I'm a member of GB Manufacturing's board of directors)이라고 소개하고 있다. 즉, 화자는 이사회 임원임을 알 수 있으므로 정답은 (D)이다.

paraphrasing a member of GB Manufacturing's board of directors GB Manufacturing 이사회 임원 → a board member 이사회 임원

08.
분기 이익이 무엇을 위해 사용될 예정인가?
(A) 환경 연구에 자금을 대기
(B) 장학 재단을 설립하기
(C) 대체 에너지에 투자하기
(D) 직원들에게 교육을 제공하기

[해설] 질문의 핵심 키워드 the quarterly profits가 담화 중반의 our profits from the third quarter에 해당한다는 것을 알 수 있어야 한다. 3분기 이익이 태양 전지판을 구입하는 데 사용될 것이고(our profits from the third quarter will be used to purchase solar panels) 이어서 전기의 대체 공급원(alternative sources of electricity)을 이용할 거라는 말은 곧 해당 분기의 이익을 대체 에너지에 투자할 것이라는 뜻이므로 정답은 (C)이다.

paraphrasing our profits from the third quarter 3분기 이익 → the quarterly profits 분기의 이익 / alternative sources of electricity 전기의 대체 공급원 → alternative energy 대체 에너지

[어휘] quarterly 분기별의 fund 기금, 자금; 자금[기금]을 대다 environmental 환경 set up ~을 세우다, 놓다 scholarship 장학금 invest in ~에 투자하다 alternative energy 대체 에너지

09.
화자에 따르면, 입구 근처에서 무엇을 이용할 수 있는가?
(A) 회사 안내책자
(B) 가벼운 다과
(C) 등록 양식
(D) 발표자 일정

[해설] 담화 후반부에서, 화자는 입구 근처 테이블에 준비해둔 안내책자 (the brochures that we have provided on the table near the entrance)에 자세한 설명이 있다고 했으므로 정답은 (A)이다.

[어휘] refreshments 다과 registration 등록 presenter 발표자, 진행자

[10-12] BR
Questions 10-12 refer to the following talk.

W: Last month, we conducted a customer survey. This is one way that our company, **10**Prime Accounting, can show continual improvement. Based on the responses, it seems that the most common concern is about how **11**customers' information is treated. **11**They want more protections in place to ensure confidentiality, so that is what we will focus on for the next few months. I've prepared a handout of some of the points that we'd like you to keep in mind. **12**I noticed a few typos in this handout. It was prepared right before the meeting.

conduct (특정한 활동을) 하다 customer survey 고객 여론 조사 continual 끊임없는, 부단한 improvement 개선, 호전 based on ~에 근거하여 response 응답 common 공동의, 공통의 concern 우려, 걱정 treat 다루다, 취급하다 protection 보호, 보호물[책] in place ~을 위한 준비가 되어 있는 ensure 반드시 ~하게 하다, 보장하다 confidentiality 비밀 keep in mind 명심하다 notice 의식하다, 알다 typo 오자

10-12는 다음 담화에 관한 문제입니다.
여: 지난달, 우리는 고객 설문 조사를 진행했습니다. 이것은 우리 회사 **10**Prime 회계가 지속적인 발전을 보여줄 수 있는 한 방법입니다. 응답에 기초하면, 가장 공통적인 우려는 **11**고객 정보가 어떻게 취급되는지인 것으로 보입니다. **11**고객들은 비밀을 보장하기 위해 더 많은 보호 장치가 준비되길 원합니다. 따라서 우리는 다음 몇 달간 그것에 집중하게 될 것입니다. 여러분들이 명심하시기 바라는 주요 내용들을 유인물로 준비했습니다. **12**이 유인물에 오자가 몇 개 있다는 걸 알게 되었습니다. 회의 직전에 준비가 되었습니다.

10.
화자는 어떤 종류의 업체에서 일하는 것 같은가?
(A) 부동산 중개소
(B) 회계 법인
(C) 건설 회사
(D) 차량 대여 회사

[해설] 화자의 직종이나 직업에 대한 단서는 대부분 담화 초반에 제시된다. 담화 초반, 화자는 우리 회사 Prime Accounting이라는 말로 자신의 소속 회사를 밝혔다. 회사 이름에 '회계'를 뜻하는 accounting이 포함되어 있는 것으로 보아 화자는 회계 법인에서 일함을 알 수 있으므로 정답은 (B)이다.

[어휘] real estate 부동산 accounting 회계 vehicle rental 차량 대여

11.
화자에 따르면, 이 회사는 무엇에 집중할 계획인가?
(A) 직원의 생산성 향상하기
(B) 운영비 삭감하기
(C) 환경 보호하기
(D) 개인 정보 보호하기

[해설] 질문의 핵심 키워드 focus on이 언급되는 곳에 집중한다. 앞서 화자는 설문 조사의 결과, 고객들이 고객 정보(customers' information)가 어떻게 처리되는지 우려했다면서, 고객들이 비밀 보장(ensure confidentiality)을 위해 더 많은 보호 장치가 준비되길 원하므로 다음 몇 달간 그것에 집중하게 될 거라고 했다. 즉, 회사는 개인 정보 보호에 집중할 계획임을 알 수 있으므로 정답은 (D)이다.

paraphrasing customers' information 고객 정보 / ensure confidentiality 비밀을 보장하다 → keeping information private 개인 정보 보호

[어휘] increase 증가시키다 productivity 생산성 operating cost 운영비 protect 보호하다 environment 환경

12.
화자는 왜 "회의 직전에 준비가 되었습니다"라고 말하는가?
(A) 변명을 하기 위해
(B) 청자들에게 감사하기 위해
(C) 최신 일정을 알려주기 위해
(D) 참가를 권장하기 위해

[해설] 담화 후반 화자는 주요 내용이 담긴 유인물을 준비했다면서 유인물에 오자가 있음을 알린(I noticed a few typos in this handout.) 직후 "회의 직전에 준비가 되었습니다"라고 했다. 즉, 회의 직전 급하게 준비한 것이 유인물에 오자가 몇 개 생긴 이유라고 해당 표현을 이용해 설명 또는 변명하고 있으므로 정답은 (A)이다.

[어휘] make an excuse 변명하다 participation 참가, 참여

[13-15] [AU]
Questions 13-15 refer to the following talk.

M: [13]**Welcome to your first day working here at our outlet store.** I know that you don't have any prior work experience, so I'm going to give you a really easy task for the day. At the front entrance of our store, there are stacks of our current sale flyers. [14]**What I want you to do is to walk around the outlet and distribute them to shoppers.** When you run out, just come back for more. Let me know if we start to run low. [15]**I'll photocopy more for you.** Go ahead and get started. Report back at 2 o'clock to take your break.

prior 사전의, 이전의 work experience 근무 경력 task 일, 과업, 과제 front entrance 정문, 현관 stacks of 많은 current 현재의, 지금의 flyer 전단 distribute 나누어 주다, 배부하다 run out (공급품이) 다 떨어지다 run low 고갈되다, 떨어져 가다 photocopy 복사하다 go ahead 시작하다 report back (근무 장소로) 돌아가다 take a break 잠시 휴식을 취하다

13-15는 다음 담화에 관한 문제입니다.

남: [13]이곳 우리 아울렛 매장에서의 첫 근무를 환영합니다. 당신에게 이전 근무 경력이 전혀 없다는 것을 알고 있습니다. 따라서 오늘은 아주 쉬운 일을 드리겠습니다. 우리 매장 정문에 현재의 판매 전단이 쌓여 있습니다. [14]당신이 해주길 바라는 일은 아울렛을 걸어 다니면서 쇼핑객들에게 전단을 나눠 주는 것입니다. 전단이 다 떨어지면 더 가지러 돌아오시면 됩니다. 다 떨어지기 시작하면 제게 알려 주세요. [15]더 복사해 드리겠습니다. 가서 시작하세요. 2시 정각에 돌아와서 잠시 휴식을 취하시기 바랍니다.

13.
화자는 어디서 일하는 것 같은가?
(A) 아울렛 매장에서
(B) 인쇄소에서
(C) 부동산 중개소에서
(D) 잡지 출판사에서

[해설] 화자는 청자에게 이곳 우리 아울렛 매장에서의 첫 근무를 환영한다고(Welcome to your first day working here at our outlet store.) 말하는 것으로 담화를 시작했다. 따라서 화자가 아울렛 매장에서 근무함을 알 수 있으므로 정답은 (A)이다.

[어휘] real estate 부동산 publisher 출판인, 출판사

14.
오늘 청자의 주요 업무는 무엇인가?
(A) 부스 담당하기
(B) 포스터 붙이기
(C) 전단 배포하기
(D) 고객 맞이하기

[해설] 화자는 청자에게 오늘은 아주 쉬운 일을 맡기겠다며 업무 내용을 자세히 설명했는데, 아울렛을 걸어 다니면서 쇼핑객들에게 전단을 나눠 주는(to walk around the outlet and distribute them to shoppers) 일이라고 했다. 따라서 정답은 (C)이다.

paraphrasing sale flyers 판매 전단 / distribute them to shoppers 쇼핑객들에게 나눠 주다 → handing out flyers 전단 배포하기

[어휘] man ~에 인력을 배치하다, ~을 담당하다 put up 내붙이다, 게시하다 hand out 나누어 주다 greet 맞다, 환영하다

15.
화자는 청자를 위해서 무엇을 할 것인가?
(A) 다과를 준비하기
(B) 업무 일정을 수정하기
(C) 교육 자료를 인쇄하기

(D) 복사를 더 해주기

[해설] 앞서 청자에게 전단 배포 업무를 할당한 화자는 전단이 다 떨어지면 자신에게 알려 달라며 더 복사해주겠다고(I'll photocopy more for you.) 했다. 따라서 정답은 (D)이다.

> paraphrasing   I'll photocopy more for you 더 복사해 드리겠습니다 → make more copies 복사를 더 해주기

[어휘] prepare 준비하다   refreshments 다과   revise 변경[수정]하다   training manual 교육 자료   make a copy 복사하다

[16-18] US

Questions 16-18 refer to the following talk.

> M: Good evening, and ¹⁶welcome to Gordon's Steakhouse! I'm Isaac and I'll be taking care of you this evening. ¹⁶Here in the middle of the menu is our list of entrees. ¹⁶, ¹⁷Note our 3-course T-bone steak dinner with garlic mashed potatoes on top. It received a 5-star rating from food critic Allen Jones. Also, if you're not already a member, you should sign up now. ¹⁸In celebration of our anniversary, members get double reward points throughout the month.

take care of ~을 돌보다   in the middle of ~의 중앙에   entrée 앙트레(주요리 또는 주요리 앞에 나오는 요리)   note ~에 주목[주의]하다   garlic 마늘   mashed potatoes 매시트 포테이토(삶은 감자에 우유와 버터를 넣고 으깬 음식)   rating 순위, 평가, 등급   critic 비평가   sign up 가입하다, 등록하다   in celebration of ~을 축하하여   reward 보상   throughout ~동안 쭉, 내내

16-18은 다음 담화에 관한 문제입니다.

남: 안녕하세요, ¹⁶Gordon's Steakhouse에 오신 것을 환영합니다! 저는 Isaac이고요, 제가 오늘 저녁 여러분을 모시겠습니다. ¹⁶여기 메뉴 중앙에 주요리 목록이 있습니다. ¹⁶, ¹⁷맨 위에 갈릭 매시트 포테이토를 곁들인 3코스 티본 스테이크 저녁식사를 주목해 주세요. 그것은 음식 비평가 Allen Jones로부터 별 다섯 개 평가를 받았습니다. 또한 아직 회원이 아니시라면 지금 가입하세요. ¹⁸저희 기념일을 축하하는 의미로 이달 내내 회원들은 두 배의 보상 포인트를 받습니다.

16.

화자는 어디서 일할 것 같은가?

(A) 식당에서
(B) 뉴스 방송국에서
(C) 식료품점에서
(D) 잡지 회사에서

[해설] 담화 초반, 화자가 Gordon's Steakhouse에 오신 것을 환영한다고(welcome to Gordon's Steakhouse!) 한 점과 이후에 나오는 menu, entrees, 3-course T-bone steak dinner 같은 표현들로 보아 화자는 식당에서 일함을 알 수 있다. 따라서 정답은 (A)이다.

[어휘] station 방송국

17.

화자는 왜 "그것은 음식 비평가 Allen Jones로부터 별 다섯 개 평가를 받았습니다"라고 말하는가?

(A) 비판적 사고를 권장하기 위해서

(B) 음식 비평가를 지지하기 위해서
(C) 요리를 추천하기 위해서
(D) 주방장을 칭찬하기 위해서

[해설] 해당 표현 주변의 문장을 확인하여 화자의 의도를 파악하는 문제이다. 3코스 티본 스테이크 저녁식사를 주목해 달라는(Note our 3-course T-bone steak dinner) 말 뒤에 "그것은 음식 비평가 Allen Jones로부터 별 다섯 개 평가를 받았습니다"라고 덧붙인 것은 이 메뉴가 비평가로부터 좋은 평가를 받을 만큼 훌륭한 음식이니 먹어볼 것을 권하기 위한 의도이다. 따라서 정답은 (C)이다.

[어휘] encourage 격려하다, 고무하다   critical 비판적인   endorse (공개적으로) 지지하다   praise 칭찬하다

18.

화자에 따르면, 이번 달에 무엇이 제공되는가?

(A) 가격 할인
(B) 디저트 샘플
(C) 추가적인 보상 포인트
(D) 무료 음료

[해설] 담화 마지막, 기념일을 축하하기 위해서 이 달 내내 회원들에게 두 배의 보상 포인트를 지급한다는(In celebration of our anniversary, members get double reward points throughout the month.) 내용이 언급된다. 즉, 이번 달에는 보상 포인트가 추가적으로 제공된다는 의미이므로 정답은 (C)이다.

> paraphrasing   double reward points 두 배의 보상 포인트 → extra reward points 추가적인 보상 포인트

[19-21] US

Questions 19-21 refer to the following talk and chart.

Coyote Cable Package Options		
Package	Includes	Monthly Fee
A	Local TV	$14.99
B	Local TV + Internet	$24.99
²⁰C	Local & Cable TV + Internet	$34.99
D	Local & Cable & Movie TV + Internet	$44.99

> W: ¹⁹Please keep in mind that you are representing Coyote Cable when speaking with customers on the phone regarding the services we provide. ¹⁹If you turn to page 10 in your manuals, you will see a list of our updated package options. A lot of our customers currently have the local TV and Internet package, but ²⁰we want to encourage them to upgrade to the one that includes local and cable TV along with Internet. ¹⁹Please remember to say that they will only pay $24.99 for the next three months. ²¹Whoever gets the most customers to upgrade each week will get this voucher good for two adult tickets to any film playing at SuperBox Theater.

keep in mind 명심하다   represent 대표[대신]하다   regarding ~에 관하여   manual 설명서, 안내서   currently 현재, 지금   encourage 격려[고무]하다   include 포함하다   along with ~와 함께   voucher 상품권   good 유효한

19-21은 다음 담화와 도표에 관한 문제입니다.

Coyote 케이블 패키지 사양		
패키지	포함 내용	월 이용료
A	지역 TV	14.99달러
B	지역 TV + 인터넷	24.99달러
[20]C	지역 & 케이블 TV + 인터넷	34.99달러
D	지역 & 케이블 & 영화 TV + 인터넷	44.99달러

여: 우리가 제공하는 서비스에 관하여 고객들과 전화로 상담할 때 [19]여러분이 Coyote Cable을 대표하고 있음을 명심하시기 바랍니다. 설명서 10페이지를 펼치면 최신 패키지 사양 목록이 보이실 겁니다. 많은 고객들이 현재 지역 TV와 인터넷 결합 패키지를 이용합니다. 하지만 [20]우리는 그들에게 인터넷과 함께 지역 및 케이블 TV를 포함하는 상품으로 업그레이드하도록 장려하고자 합니다. [19]다음 3개월간 24.99달러만 내게 된다고 얘기하는 것을 기억하시기 바랍니다. [21]매주 가장 많은 고객을 업그레이드하게 한 사람에게는 SuperBox 극장에서 상영하는 어느 영화든 성인 2인이 볼 수 있는 이 상품권이 지급됩니다.

19.
청자들은 어디에 있는 것 같은가?
(A) 교육 과정에
(B) 쇼핑몰에
(C) 제품 시연회에
(D) TV 프로그램에

[해설] 케이블 TV 서비스 업체가 자사의 고객 상담원들에게 업무 관련 사항을 전달하는 담화이다. 청자들이 Coyote Cable을 대표함을 명심하라고 했고, 설명서를 보라고 했다. 이어서 지역 및 케이블 TV와 인터넷 결합 상품으로의 업그레이드를 장려하고 3개월간 24.99달러만 낸다고 얘기할 것 등을 지시하는 것으로 보아 청자들에게 일종의 서비스 교육을 시행하고 있는 것으로 볼 수 있으므로 정답은 (A)이다.

20.
시각 자료를 보시오. 화자에 따르면, 청자들은 어떤 패키지를 추천해야 하는가?
(A) A 패키지
(B) B 패키지
(C) C 패키지
(D) D 패키지

[해설] 담화 중반, 화자는 고객들에게 인터넷과 함께 지역 및 케이블 TV를 포함하는 상품으로 업그레이드하도록 장려하고자 한다고(we want to encourage them to upgrade to the one that includes local and cable TV along with Internet) 했는데, 도표에서 인터넷과 지역 및 케이블 TV 결합 상품을 찾으면 C 패키지이므로 정답은 (C)이다. 이어서 이 상품을 이용하면 3개월간 24.99달러만 내면 된다는 내용이 이어지는데 이것만 듣고 B를 고르지 않도록 주의해야 한다. 원래는 이용료가 월 34.99달러이지만 3개월간 24.99달러로 할인해준다는 의미이다.

21.
인센티브로 무엇이 제공되는가?
(A) 영화 티켓
(B) 현금 보너스
(C) 장비 업그레이드
(D) 추가 유급 휴가

[해설] 담화 후반, 매주 가장 많은 고객을 업그레이드시킨 사람에게는 SuperBox 극장에서 상영하는 영화를 볼 수 있는 상품권(this voucher good for two adult tickets to any film playing at SuperBox Theater)이 지급된다고 했다. 즉, 인센티브로 영화 티켓이 제공된다는 것이므로 정답은 (A)이다.

[어휘] equipment 장비, 용품   paid vacation 유급 휴가

출제 유형 01 멤버십·고객 의견
| 풀이 방법 해석 |

여: 그게 오늘 필요하신 전부인가요?
남: 네, 그리고 제가 유기농 농산물 구매자들을 위한 새 멤버십 프로그램을 도입했다는 배너를 봤어요. 그것에 대해 더 말해 주실 수 있으세요?
여: 물론이죠. 저희는 채소와 과일을 살충제 없이 재배하는 지역 농장 및 과수원과 제휴를 맺었어요. 그들의 농산물을 홍보하기 위해, 이 멤버십 프로그램을 도입했어요. 이것으로, 당신은 유기농 스티커가 붙어 있는 모든 품목에 대해 10퍼센트 할인을 받으실 거예요. 요리 수업과 농장 투어에도 초대받으실 겁니다.
남: 아주 좋네요. 저는 8월에 정원이 있는 집으로 이사 가요. 유기농 농장들을 방문하는 것은 살충제 없이 정원을 가꾸는 것에 대해 유용한 정보를 줘요.

출제 유형 02 할인
| 풀이 방법 해석 |

남: 안녕하세요, 저를 도와주시겠어요? 사이즈 10의 운동화를 찾고 있습니다. 이 광고에서 이 Lightfeather 신발을 절반 가격에 할인한다고 해서요.
여: 죄송하지만, 사실은 제가 10 사이즈의 마지막 신발 한 켤레를 방금 막 판매했습니다. 이번 주말이 되어야 또 다른 배송품이 들어올 겁니다.
남: 그래요? 이 광고가 하루만 할인한다고 해서 저는 그 가격에 구입을 정말 하고 싶었습니다.
여: 계산대로 가셔서 당신의 이름과 전화번호를 알려주시면, 사이즈 10의 Lightfeather 신발이 입고되자마자 전화드리겠습니다. 또한 할인 가격에 구매할 수 있는 쿠폰을 받으실 수 있습니다.

연습 문제

01. (B) 02. (B) 03. (A) 04. (A) 05. (B) 06. (A)

01. BR-US
What is **given out** to **new members**?
(A) An assigned **locker**   (B) **Free items**

> M: Hello, I'm here to look around your facility and exercise equipment.
> W: Welcome to Stay Fit. We are a nationwide chain. You can visit and work out at one of more than 200 gym locations. In addition, if you become a member today, you will be offered a free towel and bags.

신규 회원들에게 무엇이 제공되는가?
(A) 배정된 사물함   **(B) 무료 물품들**

남: 안녕하세요, 시설과 운동 기구를 둘러보려고 왔습니다.
여: Stay Fit에 오신 것을 환영합니다. 저희는 전국적인 체인이에요. 200개가 넘는 체육관 지점 중 한 곳에 방문하셔서 운동하실 수 있습니다. 게다가, 오늘 회원이 되시면, 무료 수건과 가방을 받으실 겁니다.

02. US-US
What is the **woman asked to do**?
(A) **Print out** a discount **coupon**   (B) **Come** at **later** time

> W: Hello, I'm looking for the strawberry cheesecakes in this flyer. I read your ad in the local newspaper and they are 30% off the regular price.
> M: I'm sorry. They all sold out in the morning. If you don't mind, would you come back in about two hours? Our bakers are baking new cakes now and they will be ready at that time.

여자는 무엇을 하도록 요청받는가?
(A) 할인 쿠폰 인쇄하기   **(B) 나중에 오기**

여: 안녕하세요, 이 전단에 있는 딸기 치즈 케이크를 찾고 있습니다. 지역 신문에서 광고를 봤는데 정가에서 30퍼센트 할인한다고 하더라고요.
남: 죄송합니다. 오늘 아침에 모두 팔렸습니다. 괜찮으시다면, 2시간 정도 후에 다시 오시겠어요? 저희 제빵사들이 지금 새 케이크를 굽고 있고 그때쯤이면 준비될 거예요.

03. AU-BR
What is the **man planning to do**?
(A) **Go** on a **vacation**   (B) **Participate** in a **race**

> M: Well, I'd like to rent a car for my vacation, and I've been told that this is the best place in town. I'll be traveling to Black Mountain to ski with some of my friends, so we'd like either a minivan or SUV.
> W: Okay, that shouldn't be a problem. And we're offering one free day to those who rent any car for more than three days.

남자는 무엇을 할 계획인가?
(A) 휴가 가기   (B) 경주에 참가하기

남: 음, 제가 휴가를 위해 차를 빌리고 싶은데, 이곳이 시내에서 제일 좋은 곳이라고 들었어요. 제 친구들과 스키를 타러 Black Mountain에 갈 거라, 미니밴이나 SUV를 빌리고 싶습니다.
여: 알겠습니다, 문제될 거 없습니다. 그리고 저희는 3일 이상 차를 렌트하신 분들께 하루를 무료로 드리고 있습니다.

04. US-US
Where is the conversation **taking place**?
(A) At a **hotel lobby**   (B) At a **restaurant**

> W: How's your stay? Your satisfaction is always our priority, so we are now soliciting feedback about your experience at Tampa Bed & Breakfast. Do you have time to fill out this survey?
> M: Sorry, we are supposed to take a shuttle bus to the airport in 10 minutes.
> W: That's fine. You are able to do this online on our Web site. Once you complete it, you will be issued a 10% discount voucher for your next visit.

대화는 어디에서 이루어지고 있는가?
(A) 호텔 로비에서   (B) 레스토랑에서

여: 숙박은 어떠셨나요? 당신의 만족이 저희의 최우선 사항이므로, Tampa Bed & Breakfast에서의 당신의 경험에 대한 의견을 요청드리려고 합니다. 이 설문 조사를 작성하실 시간이 있으신가요?
남: 죄송해요, 저희는 10분 후에 공항으로 가는 셔틀버스를 타야 해요.
여: 괜찮습니다. 저희 웹사이트에서 온라인으로 하실 수 있습니다. 작성하시면, 다음 방문에 사용하실 수 있는 10퍼센트 할인 쿠폰이 발행될 거예요.

05. BR-US
Who most likely is the **woman**?
(A) A **tailor**   (B) A **sales representative**

> M: Excuse me. I like this t-shirt, but do you have one in other colors? I want a white one instead of blue.
> W: I'm sorry. Unfortunately, that is the last one that we have in stock. If you purchase it, I can offer you a 30% discount.

여자는 누구이겠는가?
(A) 재단사   **(B) 판매 직원**

남: 실례합니다. 이 티셔츠가 마음에 드는데요, 다른 색이 있나요? 파란색 대신 흰색을 원합니다.
여: 죄송합니다. 안타깝지만, 이게 저희 재고에 있는 마지막이에요. 그것을 구매하시면, 30퍼센트 할인해 드릴 수 있어요.

06. US-AU
What does the **woman want to do**?
(A) Buy a **computer**   (B) **Advertise** a new **TV**

> W: I'd like to purchase a desktop computer for my office. I saw a TV advertisement yesterday that said your

store is holding a clearance sale.

M: Sorry. Unfortunately, all clearance items were already sold out. How about this model? This comes with a monitor, keyboard, and mouse that you need to purchase separately.

여자는 무엇을 하고 싶어 하는가?
(A) 컴퓨터 구매하기   (B) 새 TV 광고하기

여: 제 사무실을 위한 데스크톱 컴퓨터를 구입하고 싶습니다. 어제 TV 광고를 봤는데 당신의 매장이 재고 정리 할인을 한다고 하더라고요.
남: 죄송합니다. 안타깝지만, 모든 재고 정리 제품들은 이미 다 팔렸습니다. 이 모델은 어떠세요? 이건 별도로 구매하셔야 하는 모니터, 키보드, 그리고 마우스가 딸려 옵니다.

paraphrasing 정답 1. (a) 2. (c) 3. (b) 4. (c) 5. (a) 6. (b)

실전 문제

01. (B)	02. (A)	03. (D)	04. (C)	05. (C)	06. (D)
07. (B)	08. (D)	09. (D)	10. (D)	11. (A)	12. (D)
13. (D)	14. (C)	15. (D)	16. (D)	17. (A)	18. (A)
19. (C)	20. (B)	21. (D)			

[01-03] (BR-US)

Questions 01-03 refer to the following conversation.

M: Excuse me, ⁰¹I accidentally bent my golf membership card, and now it won't slide through the card reader. I need a new one.
W: ⁰²We have a special machine that prints those cards, but... um... this is my first day.
M: Then, would you be able to let me in today anyway?
W: Of course. And my manager will be back soon. ⁰³Could you fill out this membership application form? Then we'll have a new card ready by the time you leave.

accidentally 우연히, 뜻하지 않게   bend 굽히다, 구부리다
slide 미끄러뜨리다, 미끄러지듯이 움직이다   card reader 카드 판독기   fill out 작성하다, 기입하다   application form 신청서

01-03은 다음 대화에 관한 문제입니다.
남: 실례합니다. ⁰¹실수로 제 골프 회원 카드를 구부러뜨렸어요. 그래서 이제는 카드 리더기에 밀어 넣어지지 않아요. 새 카드가 필요합니다.
여: ⁰²그런 카드를 인쇄하는 특별한 기계가 있기는 한데요... 음... 오늘 제가 첫날이어서요.
남: 그러면, 어쨌든 오늘 입장하게 해주실 수는 있는 건가요?
여: 물론입니다. 그리고 제 매니저가 곧 돌아올 거예요. ⁰³이 회원 가입 신청서를 작성해 주시겠어요? 그러면 떠나실 때까지 저희가 새 카드를 준비해 드릴게요.

01.
남자의 문제는 무엇인가?
(A) 그의 동료가 도착하지 않았다.
(B) 그의 회원 카드가 손상되었다.
(C) 그의 골프 장비 일부를 잃어버렸다.
(D) 회비를 납부하는 것을 잊었다.

[해설] 대화 초반 남자가 실수로 골프 회원 카드를 구부러뜨려서(I accidentally bent my golf membership card) 카드 리더기에 밀어 넣어지지 않는다고 했다. 즉, 회원 카드가 손상된 상황이므로 정답은 (B)이다.

paraphrasing I accidentally bent my golf membership card 실수로 내 골프 회원 카드를 구부러뜨렸다 → His membership card is damaged. 그의 회원 카드가 손상되었다.

[어휘] damaged 손상된   equipment 장비, 용품   membership fee 회비

02.
여자가 "오늘 제가 첫날이어서요"라고 말할 때 암시하는 것은 무엇인가?
(A) 일부 장비에 익숙하지 않다.
(B) 할인을 허가해줄 수 없다.
(C) 기회에 대해 들떠 있다.
(D) 평소보다 늦게까지 일할 계획이다.

[해설] 회원 카드가 구부러져 리더기 통과가 안 된다는 남자의 말에 여자가 그런 카드를 인쇄하는 특별한 기계가 있다고(We have a special machine that prints those cards) 한 후 머뭇거리면서 해당 문장을 덧붙였다. 다시 말해, 오늘이 자신의 근무 첫날이라 문제가 있는 카드를 인쇄하는 기계를 사용하는 것에 익숙하지 않다는 의미이므로 정답은 (A)이다.

[어휘] unfamiliar with ~에 익숙하지 않은   authorize 허가하다, 권한을 부여하다

03.
여자가 남자에게 하라고 말하는 것은 무엇인가?
(A) 매니저에게 이메일 보내기
(B) 내일 다시 오기
(C) 로비에서 기다리기
(D) 양식 작성하기

[해설] 대화 마지막 부분 여자가 남자에게 회원 가입 신청서를 작성해 달라고(Could you fill out this membership application form?) 하면서 그러면 떠날 때까지 새 카드를 준비해 놓겠다고 했다. 따라서 정답은 (D)이다.

paraphrasing fill out 작성하다 → Complete 작성하기

[어휘] complete 기입하다, 작성하다

[04-06] (US-BR-US)

Questions 04-06 refer to the following conversation with three speakers.

W: Good morning. I'm thinking about becoming a member of ⁰⁴your gym.
M1: All right, ma'am. There's the standard package, which gives you access to ⁰⁴the pool and all workout equipment, or the premium package, which includes all of that and daily ⁰⁴exercise classes.
W: I think I'll start out with the standard package. And do I get a discount because my friend is a member here and she referred me?

M1: Let me check. ⁰⁵**Ivan**, do we give discounts for friend referrals?
M2: Yes, it's thirty percent off the first month. ⁰⁵**What's your friend's name**, ma'am?
W: It's Karen Schaeffer.
M2: All right. Let me look up her account information ⁰⁶**while my colleague here shows you around our site**.

---

standard 일반적인, 보통의   access 입장, 접근   workout equipment 운동 장비   refer 소개하다, 언급하다   referral 소개, 위탁   look up (정보를) 찾아보다   account 고객; 계좌, 계정   show around 둘러보게 해주다, 구경시켜 주다

04-06은 다음 세 사람의 대화에 관한 문제입니다.
여: 안녕하세요, 저는 ⁰⁴이곳 체육관의 회원이 될까 생각 중이에요.
남1: 좋습니다, 손님. ⁰⁴수영장과 모든 운동 장비를 이용하실 수 있는 기본 회원권이 있고요, 이것들 모두와 매일의 ⁰⁴운동 강습까지 포함되는 프리미엄 회원권이 있습니다.
여: 기본 회원권으로 시작하는 게 좋을 것 같아요. 그리고 제 친구가 이곳 회원인데 그녀에게 소개를 받은 거면 할인이 되나요?
남: 확인해볼게요. ⁰⁵Ivan, 우리에게 친구 소개 할인 제도가 있나요?
남2: 네, 첫 달에 30퍼센트 할인이 돼요. ⁰⁵친구분 성함이 어떻게 되시죠, 손님?
여: Karen Schaeffer예요.
남2: 알겠습니다. ⁰⁶제 동료가 저희 시설을 둘러보시도록 안내해 드리는 동안 제가 그분의 고객 정보를 확인해볼게요.

04.

대화가 이루어지는 곳은 어디일 것 같은가?
(A) 영화관에서
(B) 공공 도서관에서
(C) 운동 시설에서
(D) 우체국에서

[해설] 대화 초반 여자가 언급한 체육관(your gym)과 남자1이 언급한 수영장(pool), 운동 장비(workout equipment), 운동 강습(exercise classes) 등의 표현을 통해 헬스클럽 같은 운동 시설에서 나누는 대화임을 유추할 수 있으므로 정답은 (C)이다.

paraphrasing   gym 체육관, pool 수영장, workout equipment 운동 장비, exercise classes 운동 강좌 → a fitness facility 운동 시설

05.

Ivan이 여자에게 요청하는 것은 무엇인가?
(A) 회원 번호
(B) 우편 주소
(C) 친구의 이름
(D) 전화번호

[해설] 일단 세 명의 화자 중에서 Ivan이 누구인지 파악해야 한다. 전체 대화를 보면 여자는 헬스클럽을 찾은 손님, 남자들은 헬스클럽의 직원임을 알 수 있는데, 대화 중반 남자1이 동료로 보이는 Ivan의 이름을 부르며 친구 추천 할인 정책이 있는지 묻고, 이에 대해 남자2가 답을 했으므로 남자2가 Ivan임을 알 수 있다. 뒤이어 남자2가 여자에게 친구의 이름이 무엇인지 (What's your friend's name) 물었으므로 정답은 (C)이다.

06.

여자는 아마도 다음에 무엇을 할 것인가?
(A) 신분증을 보여주기
(B) 돈을 지불하기
(C) 계약서에 서명하기
(D) 둘러보기

[해설] 대화 후반부 남자2의 말에 정답의 단서가 있다. 앞서 여자가 친구 추천을 통해 할인을 받고 싶다는 의사를 밝혔고, 대화 마지막 남자2는 자신의 동료가 여자에게 시설을 둘러보도록 안내해주는 동안(while my colleague here shows you around our site.) 자신이 여자의 친구의 회원 정보를 확인하겠다고 했다. 즉, 여자는 대화 직후 헬스클럽을 둘러볼 것임을 알 수 있으므로 정답은 (D)이다.

paraphrasing   my colleague here shows you around our site 내 동료가 당신에게 우리 시설을 구경시켜 주다 → Go on a tour 둘러보기

[07-09] BR-AU

Questions 07-09 refer to the following conversation.

W: Excuse me, sir. Can I help you find anything today?
M: Yes, ⁰⁷**I'm looking for a flat-screen television** with a curved screen.
W: I can show you where those are. And if you have a few minutes, ⁰⁸**would you fill out this customer feedback survey?** It'll give us a chance to find out where we can make improvements.
M: Sure, do I just give it back to you?
W: Yes, me or any other member of staff. And to thank you for sharing your opinions, you will be entered into ⁰⁹**a prize drawing for one of three fifty-dollar vouchers. We'll be giving those out to the winners next week.**

---

curved 곡선의, 약간 굽은   fill out 기입하다, 작성하다
make an improvement 개선하다   enter into ~에 들어가다
prize drawing 경품 추첨   give out ~을 나누어 주다

07-09은 다음 대화에 관한 문제입니다.
여: 실례합니다. 찾는 것을 도와 드릴까요?
남: 네, 곡선형 화면이 있는 ⁰⁷평면 텔레비전을 찾고 있어요.
여: 제가 그것들이 있는 곳으로 안내해 드릴게요. 그리고 시간이 좀 있으시면 ⁰⁸이 고객 의견 설문지를 작성해 주시겠어요? 저희가 어떤 부분을 개선시키면 되는지 알 수 있게 해줄 거예요.
남: 물론입니다. 당신에게 다시 돌려 드리면 되나요?
여: 네, 저나 다른 직원에게요. 그리고 의견을 나눠주신 데 대해 감사하는 의미로 ⁰⁹50달러 상당의 상품권 3개 중 1개를 받는 경품 추첨에 응모 되십니다. ⁰⁹다음 주에 당첨자들에게 나눠 드릴 예정이에요.

07.

여자는 어디에서 일하는 것 같은가?
(A) 신문 잡지 판매대에서
(B) 전자제품 매장에서
(C) 옷가게에서
(D) 서점에서

[해설] 대화 초반 여자가 남자에게 찾는 것을 도와줄지 묻자 남자가 평면

텔레비전을 찾고 있다고(I'm looking for a flat-screen television) 답했다. 즉, 여자는 전자제품 매장의 직원, 남자는 손님임을 알 수 있으므로 정답은 (B)이다.

paraphrasing a flat-screen television 평면 텔레비전 → electronics 전자제품

[어휘] newsstand 신문 잡지 판매대[가판대] electronics 전자제품

08.

여자는 남자에게 무엇을 할 것을 요청하는가?
(A) 로열티 프로그램에 등록하기
(B) 제품의 크기 선택하기
(C) 시연 보기
(D) 설문 조사에 참여하기

[해설] 대화 중반 여자의 말에 정답의 단서가 있다. 전자제품 매장의 직원으로 보이는 여자가 고객으로 보이는 남자에게 고객 의견 설문지를 작성해 달라는(would you fill out this customer feedback survey?) 부탁을 한다. 따라서 정답은 (D)이다.

paraphrasing fill out this customer feedback survey 이 고객 의견 설문지를 작성하다 → Take part in a survey 설문 조사에 참여하기

[어휘] enroll in ~에 등록하다 loyalty 충실, 충성(심) demonstration 시연, 시범 설명 take part in ~에 참여하다

09.

여자에 따르면, 이 업체는 다음 주에 무엇을 할 것인가?
(A) 점포 전체 세일 열기
(B) 두 번째 지점을 열기
(C) 신상품을 소개하기
(D) 상품을 나누어 주기

[해설] 대화의 장소인 전자제품 매장에서 다음 주에 할 일을 묻는 문제로, 대화 마지막 여자의 말에 단서가 있다. 설문 조사에 참가하면 경품 추첨(a prize drawing for one of three fifty-dollar vouchers)에 응모가 되며, 다음 주에 당첨자들에게 상품을 나눠 준다고(We'll be giving those out to the winners next week) 했으므로 정답은 (D)이다.

paraphrasing We'll be giving those out to the winners 당첨자들에게 나눠줄 것이다 → Distribute some prizes 상품을 나누어 주기

[어휘] storewide 점포 전체의 branch 지점, 지사 distribute 나누어 주다

[10-12] US-BR

Questions 10-12 refer to the following conversation.

M: Hi, I was here yesterday and made a purchase, but after I got home I found this coupon. ¹⁰I was wondering if you would adjust the price for me.
W: Yes, I can help you with that. ¹¹Do you have the receipt?
M: Sure, here it is.
W: Okay, this will just take a moment. While you're here, ¹²would you like me to add you to our digital mailing list? That way you can get coupons sent to your phone.
M: Yes, please. That sounds very convenient.

make a purchase 물건을 사다 wonder 궁금하다, 궁금해하다 adjust 조정[조절]하다 take a moment 시간을 내다 add 추가하다 mailing list 우편물 수신자 명단 convenient 편리한, 간편한

10-12는 다음 대화에 관한 문제입니다.

남: 안녕하세요, 제가 어제 여기서 물건을 샀는데 집에 가서 보니 이 쿠폰이 있더라고요. ¹⁰가격을 조정해 주실 수 있는지 궁금합니다.
여: 네, 도와 드릴게요. ¹¹영수증을 가지고 계신가요?
남: 물론입니다, 여기 있어요.
여: 알겠습니다, 잠깐이면 됩니다. 여기 계신 동안 ¹²저희의 디지털 우편물 수신자 명단에 올려 드릴까요? 그렇게 하면 당신의 휴대전화로 쿠폰이 전송되게 하실 수 있어요.
남: 네, 그렇게 해주세요. 아주 편리하겠네요.

10.

남자가 방문한 목적이 무엇인가?
(A) 쿠폰을 받기 위해서
(B) 환불을 요청하기 위해서
(C) 물건을 사기 위해서
(D) 가격 조정을 받기 위해서

[해설] 남자의 방문 목적을 묻는 문제로, 대화 초반에 단서가 있다. 남자는 어제 산 물건의 쿠폰이 있다는 걸 집에 가서야 알았다며 가격을 조정해 줄 수 있는지 궁금하다고(I was wondering if you would adjust the price for me) 했다. 즉, 가격을 조정해 달라고 요청하기 위해 방문한 것이므로 정답은 (D)이다.

[어휘] refund 환불 adjustment 조정, 적응

11.

여자는 무엇을 요청하는가?
(A) 영수증
(B) 사진이 있는 신분증
(C) 신용카드
(D) 주문 송장

[해설] 남자는 어제 물건을 구매한 손님, 여자는 상점의 직원이다. 남자가 뒤늦게 쿠폰이 적용된 가격으로 조정해 달라고 하자 여자가 이를 수락하면서, 영수증을 가지고 있냐고(Do you have the receipt?) 물었다. 즉, 여자는 영수증을 요청하고 있으므로 정답은 (A)이다.

[어휘] order invoice 주문 송장

12.

여자는 남자를 위해 무엇을 해주겠다고 제안하는가?
(A) 다른 지점에 전화하기
(B) 물품을 맡아 두기
(C) 온라인 주문하기
(D) 남자를 서비스에 등록시키기

[해설] 대화 후반, 여자가 남자에게 디지털 우편물 수신자 명단에 올려줄지를(would you like me to add you to our digital mailing list?) 묻는다. 즉, 남자가 원한다면 온라인으로 이 상점이 보내는 소식을 받는 서비스에 등록시켜 주겠다고 제안하는 상황이므로 정답은 (D)이다.

paraphrasing add you to our digital mailing list 디지털 우편물 수신자 명단에 올리다 → register him for a service 남자를 서비스에 등록시키기

[어휘] put A on hold A를 맡아 두다   place an order 주문하다
register for ~에 등록하다

[13-15] US-US

Questions 13-15 refer to the following conversation.

> W: Hi, ¹³I saw a flyer about your bookstore's book club. It seems really interesting. Would I have to pay membership fees to join?
> M: Yes, but as a member of ¹³Hamilton Book Club, you get a free book every month, ¹⁴along with discounts on all purchases here, including our café area. That's a deal you can't find anywhere else.
> W: That sounds really helpful. ¹⁵I start grad school in September, and I'm sure I'll need to buy a lot of books since my major is literature.

pay (돈을) 내다, 지불하다   deal 거래, 합의   grad school 대학원   major 전공   literature 문학

13-15는 다음 대화에 관한 문제입니다.
여: 안녕하세요, ¹³제가 이 서점의 북클럽에 관한 전단을 봤어요. 정말 흥미로워 보여요. 가입하려면 회비를 내야 하나요?
남: 네, 하지만 ¹³Hamilton 북클럽의 회원이 되시면, 카페 구역을 포함해서 ¹⁴이곳에서 구매하신 모든 제품에 대해 할인을 받으실 수 있고, 이에 더불어 매달 책 한 권을 무료로 받으실 수 있어요. 다른 어디에서도 찾아보실 수 없는 조건이에요.
여: 그러면 정말 도움이 되겠어요. ¹⁵9월에 대학원을 다니기 시작하는데 제 전공이 문학이라서 분명히 책을 많이 사야 할 거예요.

13.
여자는 Hamilton 북클럽에 대해서 어떻게 알게 되었는가?
(A) 뉴스 기사에서
(B) 동료에게서
(C) 라디오 광고에서
(D) 전단에서

[해설] 여자가 남자에게 서점의 북클럽에 관해 문의하는 내용으로, 남자의 대사 중 언급되는 Hamilton Book Club이 북클럽의 이름이다. 대화 초반, 여자가 서점의 북클럽에 관한 전단을 봤다고(I saw a flyer about your bookstore's book club) 했으므로 정답은 (D)이다.

14.
남자에 따르면, 무엇이 Hamilton 북클럽을 특별하게 만드는가?
(A) 간식을 판매하는 카페 구역이 있다.
(B) 매달 새 책에 집중한다.
(C) 모든 상점 구매품에 대해 할인을 해준다.
(D) 책을 읽은 후에 회원들로부터 책을 되산다.

[해설] 남자가 언급한 Hamilton 북클럽의 특징은 매월 책 한 권을 무료로 받고, 카페를 포함하여 모든 구매품에 대해 할인을 받을 수 있다는(discounts on all purchases here) 점이다. 따라서 정답은 (C)이다.

15.
여자는 9월에 무엇을 할 것인가?
(A) 북클럽에 가입하기
(B) 기사를 게재하기

(C) 학위를 마치기
(D) 대학원을 다니기 시작하기

[해설] 질문의 핵심 키워드 September는 여자의 마지막 말에 언급된다. 여자는 9월에 대학원을 다니기 시작한다고(I start grad school in September) 했으므로 정답은 (D)이다.

> paraphrasing   I start grad school 대학원에 다니기 시작한다 → begin graduate school 대학원을 다니기 시작하기

[어휘] publish (기사 등을) 게재하다, 싣다   complete 완료하다, 끝마치다   graduate school 대학원

[16-18] BR-BR

Questions 16-18 refer to the following conversation.

> W: Hi, this is Amanda from Lockland Hardware. ¹⁶, ¹⁷I'm calling because you recently purchased some custom paints from us, and we would like to hear your experience with us.
> M: I'm really happy with it. The color matches my deck perfectly. I was thinking of ¹⁷buying some tiles from your store for a bathroom renovation project soon.
> W: Really? If you would like, ¹⁸I could schedule you for a free consultation with one of our tile specialists.

purchase 구매하다   custom 맞춘, 주문하여 만든(= custom-made)   experience 경험, 경력   match 어울리다, 맞다   deck (집에 딸린) 목제 테라스   consultation 상담, 자문   specialist 전문가

16-18은 다음 대화에 관한 문제입니다.
여: 안녕하세요, Lockland 철물점의 Amanda입니다. ¹⁶, ¹⁷최근에 저희에게 맞춤 페인트를 구입하셨기 때문에 전화드렸어요. 저희 제품을 이용한 경험이 어떠셨는지 듣고 싶어요.
남: 정말 마음에 들어요. 색상이 저희 테라스와 완벽하게 어울려요. ¹⁷곧 욕실 보수 공사 작업을 위해 당신의 상점에서 타일을 구매하려고 생각하고 있었어요.
여: 정말요? 괜찮으시다면 ¹⁸저희 타일 전문가들 중 한 사람과 무료 상담을 받으시도록 일정을 잡아드릴 수 있어요.

16.
여자는 왜 전화하는가?
(A) 배송을 확인하기 위해서
(B) 페인트 작업 일정을 잡기 위해서
(C) 불평에 응대하기 위해서
(D) 의견을 요청하기 위해서

[해설] 대화 초반, 여자는 남자에게 최근 자신의 회사에서 맞춤 페인트를 구매한 경험에 대해 묻고 싶어 전화했다고(I'm calling because you recently purchased some custom paints from us, and we would like to hear your experience with us.) 밝혔다. 즉, 고객의 의견을 요청하기 위해 전화한 것이므로 정답은 (D)이다.

> paraphrasing   we would like to hear your experience with us 저희 제품을 이용한 경험이 어떠셨는지 듣고 싶다 → request some feedback 의견을 요청하다

[어휘] confirm 확인하다 shipment 선적, 수송 respond to ~에 대응하다 request 요청하다 feedback 의견

17.

여자의 회사는 어떤 종류의 제품을 취급하는가?

(A) 주택 개조 제품
(B) 미술 공예 재료
(C) 가정용 가구
(D) 청소용품

[해설] 남자가 여자의 회사에서 페인트를 구매한 점, 욕실 보수 공사 작업을 위해 타일을 구매하려고(buying some tiles from your store for a bathroom renovation project) 하는 점 등으로 보아 여자의 회사는 주택 보수나 개조에 관련된 제품을 취급함을 알 수 있다. 따라서 정답은 (A)이다.

[어휘] carry 취급하다 home improvement 주택 개조 craft 공예 material 재료 household 가정 cleaning supplies 청소용품

18.

여자는 남자를 위해 무엇을 해주겠다고 제안하는가?

(A) 상담 일정을 잡기
(B) 직원을 보내기
(C) 비용 견적서를 주기
(D) 할인을 해주기

[해설] 제안/요청 사항은 주로 대화 후반부에 나온다. 타일 구매를 생각하고 있다는 남자에게 여자가 타일 전문가들 중 한 사람과 무료 상담 일정을 잡아줄 수 있다고(I could schedule you for a free consultation with one of our tile specialists) 했으므로 정답은 (A)이다.

[어휘] representative 대리인, 대표 estimate 견적서 discount 할인

[19-21] US-BR

Questions 19-21 refer to the following conversation and menu.

W: If you're finished with that plate, I can clear it away for you. **[19]Did you enjoy the cinnamon roll?**
M: Yes, it was delicious. I wish you served it every day.
W: It's a very popular item. We're thinking of adding it to our menu permanently. If you want to find out news about our menu changes, **[20]you should sign up for our customer mailing list.**

M: Thanks, I'll do that. Oh, and **[21]I'd like to log on to your coffee shop's Wi-Fi connection. Could you please tell me the password?**
W: Of course. It's "coffee123", all one word. If you have any trouble with it, just let me know.

plate 요리; 접시, 그릇 clear away 청소하다; ~을 치우다
serve (식당 등에서 음식을) 제공하다 permanently 영구히, 불변으로 sign up for ~을 신청[가입]하다

19-21은 다음 대화와 메뉴에 관한 문제입니다.

여: 음식을 다 드셨으면 치워 드리겠습니다. **[19]시나몬롤은 맛있게 드셨나요?**
남: 네, 맛있었어요. 매일 나왔으면 좋겠어요.
여: 아주 인기 있는 메뉴예요. 메뉴에 영구적으로 추가할지에 대해 생각 중이에요. 저희 메뉴 변경에 대한 소식을 알고 싶으시면 **[20]저희 고객 우편물 수신자 명단에 등록해 주시면 됩니다.**
남: 고마워요, 그렇게 할게요. 아, 그리고 **[21]여기 커피숍의 와이파이에 접속하고 싶어요. 비밀번호를 알려 주시겠어요?**
여: 물론입니다. 'coffee123'이고요, 모두 한 단어예요. 문제 있으시면 바로 제게 알려주세요.

19.

시각 자료를 보시오. 화자들은 무슨 요일에 대화를 하고 있는가?

(A) 월요일
(B) 화요일
(C) 수요일
(D) 금요일

[해설] 화자들이 대화를 하고 있는 요일을 묻는 문제로, 시각 자료의 메뉴가 대화 중에 언급될 것임을 예상해야 한다. 대화 초반 식당 직원으로 보이는 여자가 손님으로 보이는 남자에게 시나몬롤을 맛있게 먹었는지(Did you enjoy the cinnamon roll?) 물었는데, 시각 자료를 보면 시나몬롤이 나오는 요일은 수요일임을 알 수 있다. 즉, 화자들이 대화하는 요일은 수요일이므로 정답은 (C)이다.

20.

여자는 남자에게 무엇을 하라고 권하는가?

(A) 영수증 모으기
(B) 우편물 수신자 명단에 가입하기
(C) 메뉴를 주의 깊게 읽기

(D) 새로운 음식을 먹어보기

[해설] 대화 중반 여자가 남자에게 하는 말에 정답의 단서가 있다. 여자는 메뉴 변경에 대한 소식을 알고 싶으면 우편물 수신 고객 명단에 등록하면 된다고(you should sign up for our customer mailing list) 했다. 따라서 정답은 (B)이다.

paraphrasing sign up for our customer mailing list 우리 고객 우편물 수신자 명단에 등록하다 → Join a mailing list 우편물 수신자 명단에 가입하기

21.

남자는 무엇에 대해 문의하는가?
(A) 근처 부지에 주차하기
(B) 음식을 밖으로 가지고 나가기
(C) 사적인 파티 열기
(D) 인터넷에 접속하기

[해설] 남자의 문의 사항을 묻는 문제로, 대화 후반부 남자의 말에 집중한다. 커피숍의 와이파이에 접속하고 싶다며(I'd like to log on to your coffee shop's Wi-Fi connection) 비밀번호를 알려 달라고 하는 것으로 보아 남자는 인터넷 접속에 대해 문의하고 있으므로 정답은 (D)이다.

paraphrasing log on to your coffee shop's Wi-Fi connection 여기 커피숍의 와이파이에 접속하다 → Accessing the Internet 인터넷에 접속하기

[어휘] nearby 근처의, 인근의 lot (특정 용도용) 지역[부지] off-site 부지[용지] 밖의[에서] private 개인의, 사적인 access (컴퓨터에) 접속하다, 접근하다

PART 4 안내(announcement)

출제 유형 01 교통편 관련 안내

| 풀이 방법 해석 |

남: 여행객 여러분들, 주목해 주세요. TV 쇼 촬영 때문에 6월 14일 수요일에 시외 버스 터미널이 폐쇄될 것입니다. 촬영 팀을 위한 보안 패스가 없는 사람들은 누구도 그 지역에 접근할 수 없습니다. 그날 이동을 하셔야 하는 분들은 지역 버스와 기차 노선을 이용하실 것을 권장합니다. 구체적인 사항과 지역 대중교통 스케줄은 샌앤토니오 시 웹사이트를 참고해 주세요. 이미 그날 시외 버스 터미널을 통해 가는 표를 구매하셨다면, 환불받으실 수 있도록 고객 서비스 카운터에 알리시기 바랍니다.

출제 유형 02 콘퍼런스에서의 안내

| 풀이 방법 해석 |

여: 안녕하세요, 여러분. 의학계의 큰 발전에 대한 이 콘퍼런스를 모두 즐기고 계시길 바랍니다. 여러분 대부분이 내일의 세미나와 워크숍을 이미 신청하셨지만, 아직 안 하셨다면 의학 지식 대회에 참여하기 위해 Springfield Hall로 나오셔야 합니다. 게임 쇼와 꽤 비슷하게 진행될 것이고 여러분 모두의 참석을 환영합니다. 만남 장소는 Springfield Hall 바로 앞 박람회장에서 오후 2시가 될 것입니다. 정시에 오셔야 한다는 것을 기억해 주세요, 그렇지 않으면 강당에 들어오실 수 없을 겁니다.

 연습 문제

01. (B) 02. (B) 03. (A) 04. (A) 05. (A) 06. (B)

01. [US]

What is the **cause** of the **delay**?
(A) The **engine** was **malfunctioning**.
(B) A **tree blocked** the track.

M: Attention, passengers for Train 345 to Cleveland. The train was originally scheduled to depart at Platform 7. There will be a 30 minute delay due to a fallen tree on the railroad. If you plan to transfer to other trains in Cleveland, please come to the ticketing desk and make sure that this delay will not affect your connecting train. Thank you for your understanding.

지연의 원인은 무엇인가?
(A) 엔진이 오작동했다. **(B) 나무가 선로를 막았다.**

안내
남: 클리블랜드로 가는 345번 열차 승객들께 알립니다. 기차는 원래 7번 승강장에서 출발할 예정이었습니다. 기차 선로에 쓰러진 나무로 인해 30분 지연될 것입니다. 클리블랜드에서 다른 기차로 갈아탈 계획이셨다면, 매표 창구로 오셔서 이 지연이 연결편 열차에 영향을 주지 않도록 해주세요. 양해해 주셔서 감사합니다.

02. [AU]

What are the **listeners reminded to do**?
(A) **Pick up** a welcome **packet**   (B) **Validate** their **parking**

M: Welcome to the Highland Career Conference for computer software developers. We will begin with the opening ceremony at 10 A.M. All afternoon sessions are held on the second floor in the East Wing. You will have a one and a half hour lunch break. And don't forget to validate your parking at the reception desk. Thank you.

청자들은 무엇을 하도록 상기되는가?
(A) 환영 꾸러미 가져가기 **(B) 주차 확인 받기**

안내
남: 컴퓨터 소프트웨어 개발자들을 위한 Highland 직업 콘퍼런스에 오신 것을 환영합니다. 오전 10시에 오프닝 행사로 시작할 것입니다. 모든 오후 세션들은 동쪽 건물의 2층에서 열릴 것입니다. 여러분은 한 시간 반 동안의 점심 식사 시간을 가질 것입니다. 그리고 안내 데스크에서 주차 확인 받는 것을 잊지 마세요. 감사합니다.

03. [US]

What will be **sent to** the **listeners**?
(A) **Text messages**   (B) **Meal vouchers**

W: Attention, all passengers leaving on the 9 P.M. express bus to Queensland. Due to heavy snowfall around the Dutch County area, this bus has been canceled. The Department of Transportation decided to stop operating express buses until tomorrow morning. All canceled buses are rescheduled for tomorrow. We will keep you posted about your bus schedules by text.

청자들에게 무엇이 보내질 것인가?
(A) 문자 메시지   (B) 식사 쿠폰

안내
여: 오후 9시 고속버스를 타고 퀸즈랜드로 가는 승객 여러분들 주목해 주세요. 더치 카운티 지역의 폭설로 인해 이 버스는 취소되었습니다. 교통부가 내일 아침까지 고속버스를 운행하는 것을 중지하기로 결정했습니다. 취소된 모든 버스들은 내일로 운행 일정이 변경되었습니다. 여러분의 버스 스케줄에 대해 문자 메시지로 계속 알려 드리겠습니다.

04. BR
Where is the **announcement** being **made**?
(A) In an **airplane**   (B) At a **bus terminal**

M: Attention passengers, this is your captain speaking. Our flight will depart in 20 minutes. It is 30 minutes later than scheduled. We are waiting for other passengers who transfer to our flight. We will depart as soon as they are on board. Our flight attendant will serve you a beverage while you are waiting. Thank you.

안내는 어디에서 이루어지고 있는가?
(A) 비행기에서   (B) 버스 터미널에서

안내
남: 승객 여러분 주목해 주세요, 저는 기장입니다. 우리 비행기는 20분 후에 출발할 것입니다. 예정보다 30분 늦은 것입니다. 우리는 우리 비행기로 환승하는 다른 승객들을 기다리고 있습니다. 그들이 탑승하자마자 출발할 것입니다. 기다리시는 동안 저희 승무원이 음료를 제공하겠습니다. 감사합니다.

05. BR
Who most likely are the **listeners**?
(A) Job **seekers**   (B) Local **business owners**

W: Hello, thank you for coming to the fifth Butler County Job Fair. I'm very honored to host this event. We have produced outstanding and competent graduates to our county since its foundation. This year, more than 200 local businesses will participate and set up booths. Most of them are offering on-site job interviews. I hope you all find employment during this three-day event.

청자들은 누구이겠는가?
(A) 구직자들   (B) 지역 사업체 소유주들

안내
여: 안녕하세요, 다섯 번째 Butler County 직업 박람회에 와주셔서 감사합니다. 이 행사를 진행하게 되어 매우 영광입니다. 저희는 설립 때부터 우리 주에 뛰어나고 능력 있는 졸업생들을 배출했습니다. 올해에는, 200개가 넘는 지역 사업체가 참석하고 부스를 설치할 것입니다. 그들 대부분은 현장 면접을 진행합니다. 여러분 모두가 이 3일간의 행사 동안 직업을 찾기를 바랍니다.

06. US
How can **listeners enter** in a **raffle**?
(A) By **becoming** a **member**
(B) By **turning in** a **feedback** form

M: Hello, folks, I hope you've enjoyed the second day of this year's Sports Broadcasting Technology Exposition. Today, many popular professionals in our industry will share their expertise and various pieces of the latest broadcasting equipment will be introduced. When you join a seminar, you will be asked to complete feedback forms and submit them in this box. You will be automatically entered in a raffle for various items.

청자들은 어떻게 추첨에 응모할 수 있는가?
(A) 회원이 됨으로써   **(B)** 피드백 양식을 제출함으로써

안내
남: 안녕하세요, 여러분. 올해의 스포츠 방송 기술 박람회의 두 번째 날을 즐기셨기를 바랍니다. 오늘, 우리 업계에서 인기 있는 많은 전문가들이 그들의 전문 지식을 나누고 다양한 최신 방송 장비가 소개될 것입니다. 세미나에 참석하실 때, 피드백 양식을 작성하셔서 이 상자에 제출할 것을 요청받으실 겁니다. 여러분은 자동적으로 다양한 상품이 걸려 있는 추첨에 응모하실 겁니다.

paraphrasing 정답   1. (b)   2. (c)   3. (a)   4. (a)   5. (c)   6. (b)

실전 문제

01. (C)	02. (B)	03. (C)	04. (D)	05. (C)	06. (B)
07. (A)	08. (B)	09. (A)	10. (C)	11. (A)	12. (A)
13. (A)	14. (C)	15. (C)	16. (B)	17. (A)	18. (D)
19. (B)	20. (B)	21. (D)			

[01-03] BR
Questions 01-03 refer to the following announcement.

W: Hello, and **01**welcome to the Fitzgerald Museum of Art. If you'd like to wait for a tour, the next one will begin at noon. One thing that makes our establishment special is that we do not charge entrance fees. Instead, **02**we rely on a combination of large donations from benefactors and smaller ones from like visitors like you. The amount is up to you. Before entering our exhibits, please check your cameras. **03**Flash photography is not allowed, so you need to turn off the flash setting before entering. Thank you in advance.

establishment 기관, 시설   charge 부과하다   entrance 입장
fee 요금, 수수료   rely on ~에 의지하다   a combination of 여러
donation 기부   benefactor 후원자   visitor 방문자   amount
양, 총액   enter 들어가다   exhibit 전시(회)   allow 허용하다

01-03은 다음 안내에 관한 문제입니다.
여: 안녕하세요. **01Fitzgerald** 미술관에 오신 것을 환영합니다. 투어를 위해 기다리길 원하시면 다음 투어는 정오에 시작합니다. 저희 시설을 특별하게 만드는 한 가지는 입장료를 부과하지 않는다는 것입니다. 대신 **02저희는 여러 후원자들의 큰 기부와 여러분 같은 방문객들의 작은 기부에 의존합니다. 금액은 여러분께 달려 있습니다.** 전시실에 들어가기 전에 카메라를 확인해 주세요. **03플래시 촬영은 허용되지 않으니 입장하시기 전에 플래시 설정을 꺼 주시기 바랍니다.** 미리 감사드립니다.

01.
화자는 어떤 종류의 업체에서 일하는가?
(A) 미술용품 매장
(B) 카메라 가게
(C) 미술관
(D) 여행사

[해설] 담화 초반에 인사와 함께 Fitzgerald 미술관에 온 것을 환영한다고(welcome to the Fitzgerald Museum of Art) 했으므로 미술관에 근무하고 있음을 알 수 있다. 따라서 (C)가 정답이다.

02.
화자가 "금액은 여러분께 달려 있습니다"라고 말할 때 암시하는 것은 무엇인가?
(A) 일부 미술품은 경매에서 팔릴 것이다.
(B) 청자들에게 기부를 권유한다.
(C) 일부 품목들은 현재 할인 중이다.
(D) 청자들은 다음에 다시 와야 한다.

[해설] 앞서 입장료를 받지 않는 대신 여러 후원자들의 큰 기부와 방문객들의 작은 기부에 의존한다고(we rely on a combination of large donations from benefactors and smaller ones from like visitors like you) 한 후 "금액은 여러분께 달려 있습니다"라고 말했으므로 기부를 권하기 위해 한 말임을 알 수 있다. 따라서 (B)가 정답이다.

[어휘] auction 경매 currently 현재

03.
청자들에게 무엇을 할 것을 상기시키는가?
(A) 연락처 업데이트하기
(B) 정기 업데이트 신청하기
(C) 카메라 설정 변경하기
(D) 회원 가입하기

[해설] 담화 후반부에 플래시 촬영은 허용되지 않으니 입장하기 전에 플래시 설정을 꺼 달라고(Flash photography is not allowed, so you need to turn off the flash setting before entering) 했으므로 (C)가 정답이다.

paraphrasing turn off the flash setting 플래시 설정을 끄다 → Change their camera settings 카메라 설정 변경하기

[어휘] register for ~에 등록하다 regular 정기적인

[04-06] US
Questions 04-06 refer to the following announcement.

W: Douglass Library has started a new online program. **04We would like to get more people to attend classes here, so we added an extra section to our library's Web site.** It's a review section for each of the public classes that we offer. **05If you take a class, we ask that you go online and leave comments about what you learned from it.** For those of you who are not comfortable with computers, simply ask **06Randall, our head librarian**, for assistance with posting your comments.

add 추가하다 review 검토, 비평 public 공공의, 공개적인
comment 논평, 언급 comfortable 편안한 simply 그냥, 그저
head librarian 수석 사서 assistance with ~에 대한 도움
post 게시하다, 공고하다

04-06은 다음 안내에 관한 문제입니다.
여: Douglass 도서관이 새로운 온라인 프로그램을 시작했습니다. **04저희는 더 많은 사람들이 이곳의 강좌에 참석하게 하고 싶어서, 우리 도서관 웹사이트에 섹션을 하나 더 추가했습니다.** 저희가 제공하는 각 공개 강좌에 대한 후기 섹션입니다. **05강좌를 수강하시면 온라인에 접속하시어 강좌에서 배운 내용에 대한 의견을 남겨주실 것을 부탁드립니다.** 컴퓨터 사용이 익숙하지 않은 분들의 경우에는 그냥 **06저희 수석 사서인 Randall 씨에게** 여러분의 의견을 올리는 것을 도와 달라고 하시면 됩니다.

04.
새로운 프로그램의 목적은 무엇인가?
(A) 기부금을 모으는 것
(B) 더 많은 회원을 유치하는 것
(C) 교실을 보수하는 것
(D) 강좌 참석률을 높이는 것

[해설] 담화 초반, 새로운 온라인 프로그램을 시작했다고 하면서, 더 많은 사람들이 이 도서관의 강좌에 참석하게 하기 위해(We would like to get more people to attend classes here) 웹사이트에 강좌 후기 섹션을 추가했다고 했으므로 정답은 (D)이다.

paraphrasing get more people to attend classes 더 많은 사람들이 강좌에 참석하게 하다 → promote class attendance 강좌 참석률을 높이다

[어휘] collect 모으다, 수집하다 donation 기부, 기증 renovate 개조[보수]하다 promote 촉진하다, 고취하다 attendance 출석, 참석, 참석자 수, 출석률

05.
청자들은 무엇을 하도록 요청받는가?
(A) 설문조사 작성하기
(B) 독서 클럽에 가입하기
(C) 강좌 후기를 올리기
(D) 책을 더 빌리기

[해설] 담화 중반에 나오는 부탁/요청 표현 we ask ~ 이후의 내용에 집중한다. 강좌를 수강하면 온라인에 접속해 배운 내용에 대한 의견을 남겨줄 것을 부탁하고(If you take a class, we ask that you go online and leave comments about what you learned from it) 있으므로 정답은 (C)이다.

paraphrasing go online and leave comments about what you learned from it 온라인에 접속하여 배운 내용에 대한 의견을 남기다 → post class reviews 강좌 후기를 올리기

[어휘] fill out 기입하다, 작성하다 survey 설문조사 borrow 빌리다

06.
Randall은 누구인가?
(A) 교사
(B) 사서
(C) 전기 기사
(D) 소프트웨어 디자이너

[해설] Randall은 담화 마지막에 언급되는 인물의 이름이다. 컴퓨터 사용이 익숙하지 않은 사람들은 수석 사서인 Randall 씨(Randall, our head librarian)에게 요청하라는 내용으로 보아 정답은 (B)이다.

[07-09] BR
Questions 07-09 refer to the following announcement.

> W: Attention customers. ⁰⁷**Have you tried the new blended teas from Tea Tree?** ⁰⁸**Feel free to take a coupon from the display** to save on this delicious and healthy product. ⁰⁹**Tea Tree organically grows its roots and leaves to provide you with the healthiest choice on the market.** Try some today!

> blended (차·담배·술 등) 혼합된, 블렌드된 display 전시, 진열 save on ~를 절약하다 grow 재배하다 provide A with B A에게 B를 제공하다 on the market (상품이) 시장[시중]에 나와 있는

07-09는 다음 안내에 관한 문제입니다.
여: 고객 여러분 주목해 주세요. ⁰⁷Tea Tree의 새로운 혼합 차를 드셔 보셨나요? ⁰⁸진열대에서 자유롭게 쿠폰을 가져가셔서 이 맛있고 건강에 좋은 제품을 할인 받으세요. ⁰⁹Tea Tree는 여러분께 시중에서 가장 건강에 좋은 제품을 제공할 수 있도록 그 뿌리와 잎을 유기농으로 재배합니다. 오늘 드셔 보세요!

07.
어디서 이루어지는 안내인가?
(A) 찻집에서
(B) 가구점에서
(C) 철물점에서
(D) 극장에서

[해설] 화자가 고객들의 주의를 집중시킨 후, Tea Tree의 새로운 혼합 차를 마셔 보았는지(Have you tried the new blended teas from Tea Tree?) 묻는 것으로 보아 차를 취급하는 상점에서 고객들을 대상으로 안내하는 담화임을 알 수 있으므로 정답은 (A)이다.

08.
청자들은 무엇을 하라고 권장받는가?
(A) 회원 가입하기
(B) 쿠폰 가져가기
(C) 찻주전자 사기
(D) 시음하기

[해설] 진열대에서 자유롭게 쿠폰을 가져가서 할인을 받으라고(Feel free to take a coupon from the display) 했으므로 정답은 (B)이다.

paraphrasing take a coupon 쿠폰을 가져가다 → pick up a coupon 쿠폰 가져가기

09.
화자의 말에 따르면, Tea Tree 제품이 시중의 다른 제품들보다 더 건강에 좋은 이유는 무엇인가?
(A) 모두 유기농이다.
(B) 주의 깊게 혼합된다.
(C) 손으로 수확된다.
(D) 영양사에 의해 선별된다.

[해설] 담화 후반 Tea Tree 제품의 특징이 언급되는 부분에 단서가 있다. Tea Tree는 시중에서 가장 건강에 좋은 제품을 제공할 수 있도록 그 뿌리와 잎을 유기농으로 재배한다고(Tea Tree organically grows its roots and leaves to provide you with the healthiest choice on the market.) 했으므로 Tea Tree 제품은 유기농임을 알 수 있다. 따라서 정답은 (A)이다.

paraphrasing organically grows its roots and leaves 뿌리와 잎을 유기농으로 재배한다 → They are all organic. 그것들은 모두 유기농이다.

[어휘] harvest 수확하다, 거둬들이다 dietician 영양사

[10-12] BR
Questions 10-12 refer to the following announcement.

> M: ¹⁰**Welcome to this workshop for writing teachers.** This afternoon we will focus on helping students write their ideas in an organized manner. ¹¹**It seems like some people are running late,** but this conference room is only reserved until 3 P.M. Now, ¹²I'm going to send this sign-in sheet around. Please sign your name next to where it is printed. If you don't see your name, please write it in on the bottom so that we can give you credit for attending.

> focus on ~에 주력하다, 초점을 맞추다 organized 조직화된, 정리된 manner 방식, 태도 run late 늦다 conference room 회의실 reserved 예약된 send around (여기저기) 보내다, 돌리다 sign-in sheet 참가 신청서, 출석 명부 sign 서명하다 credit 수료 증명, 이수 단위, 학점

10-12는 다음 안내에 관한 문제입니다.
남: ¹⁰작문 교사를 위한 이번 워크숍에 오신 것을 환영합니다. 오늘 오후에는 학생들이 체계적인 방식으로 자신의 생각을 쓰는 것을 돕는 데 초점을 맞출 것입니다. ¹¹몇몇 분들이 늦을 것 같지만 이 회의실은 오후 3시까지만 예약이 되어 있습니다. 이제 ¹²제가 이 출석 명부를 돌리겠습니다. 이름이 인쇄된 곳 옆에 서명해주시기 바랍니다. 만약 자신의 이름이 없다면 저희가 출석 인정 점수를 드릴 수 있도록 맨 아래에 적어 주세요.

10.
청자들은 누구일 것 같은가?
(A) 배우들
(B) 작가들
(C) 교사들
(D) 출판인들

[해설] 담화 첫 부분에서 작문 교사를 위한 이번 워크숍에 온 것을 환영한다는(Welcome to this workshop for writing teachers.) 말로 보아 청자들이 교사임을 알 수 있으므로 정답은 (C)이다.

11.
화자가 "이 회의실은 오후 3시까지만 예약이 되어 있습니다"라고 말할 때 의미하는 것은 무엇인가?
(A) 기다리지 않고 시작할 것이다.
(B) 그는 다른 약속이 있다.
(C) 나중에 방을 청소해야 한다.
(D) 늦게 도착하는 사람들은 방에 들어올 수 없다.

[해설] 몇몇 사람들이 늦을 것 같지만(It seems like some people are running late) "이 회의실은 오후 3시까지만 예약이 되어 있습니다"라고 한 것으로 보아 회의실 이용 가능 시간이 한정되어 있으니 늦는 사람들을 기다리지 않고 바로 워크숍을 시작하겠다는 의미로 해당 문장을 말했음을 알 수 있다. 따라서 정답은 (A)이다.

[어휘] appointment (업무 관련) 약속 afterwards 나중에, 그 뒤에 arrival 도착; 도착한 사람 allow 허용하다

12.
청자들에게 무엇이 돌려질 것인가?
(A) 출석 명부
(B) 교육 안내서
(C) 주차 확인증
(D) 워크숍 일정

[해설] 질문의 핵심 키워드 pass around(돌리다)는 담화의 send around와 같은 의미이다. 담화 후반, 화자가 출석 명부를 돌리겠다(I'm going to send this sign-in sheet around) 했으므로 정답은 (A)이다.

paraphrasing send around (여기저기) 돌리다 → pass around (여러 사람이 보도록) ~을 돌리다

[어휘] manual 설명서 validation 확인

[13-15] US
Questions 13-15 refer to the following announcement.

W: Thanks for coming to work on the weekend, everyone. Because it is outside your usual schedule, ¹³**you'll all be paid time-and-a-half instead of your usual hourly wage.** Our goal today is to prepare some preliminary examples for ¹⁴**the new product line that our team is developing.** We need to narrow it down to some clear ideas that can be presented to the board on Monday. ¹⁵**First, I'd like to have everyone tell a few ideas**, which I'll write on the board. We'll then discuss ¹⁵**these suggestions** to determine which ones are feasible.

usual 평상시의, 보통의 time-and-a-half 1배 반[1.5배]의 지급 instead of ~ 대신에 hourly wage 시간당 임금 goal 목표 prepare 준비하다 preliminary 예비의, 예비적인 product line 제품 라인 narrow down 좁히다, 줄이다 clear 분명한, 확실한 present 제출하다, 제시하다 board 판자, 이사회 discuss 논의하다 suggestion 제안, 제의 determine 확정[결정]하다 feasible 실현 가능한

13-15는 다음 안내에 관한 문제입니다.
여: 주말인데도 출근해 주신 여러분 모두에게 감사드립니다. 평소 일정 이외의 업무이므로 ¹³여러분 모두에게는 평소의 시급 대신 1.5배의 금액이 지급될 것입니다. 오늘 우리의 목표는 ¹⁴우리 팀이 개발 중인 신제품 라인의 예비 견본을 준비하는 것입니다. 우리는 그것을 월요일에 이사회에 보여 줄 수 있는 몇 가지 명확한 아이디어로 좁혀야 합니다. ¹⁵우선, 모든 분들이 몇 가지 아이디어를 내 주시길 바랍니다. 그것을 제가 보드에 적겠습니다. 그런 다음 ¹⁵이 제안들에 대해 논의하여 어떤 것들이 실현 가능할지 결정하겠습니다.

13.
화자는 업무에 대해 무엇이라고 말하는가?
(A) 더 많은 급료가 지불될 것이다.
(B) 한 시간이 걸릴 것으로 예상된다.
(C) 다른 장소에서 이뤄질 것이다.
(D) 3단계로 구성된다.

[해설] 정규 업무와 별도로 주말에 출근한 직원들을 대상으로 하는 담화이다. 담화 초반, 화자는 평소 일정 이외의 업무이므로 평소 시급의 1.5배의 금액이 지급될 것이라고(you'll all be paid time-and-a-half instead of your usual hourly wage) 알렸다. 즉, 오늘 업무에 대해서는 평소보다 더 많은 급료가 지불될 것이라는 말이므로 정답은 (A)이다.

paraphrasing you'll all be paid time-and-a-half instead of your usual hourly wage 여러분 모두에게는 평소의 시급 대신 1.5배의 금액이 지급될 것이다 → It will be paid at a higher rate. 더 많은 급료가 지불될 것이다.

[어휘] rate 비율, 요금 expect 기대[예상]하다 phase 단계

14.
청자들은 아마도 어떤 부서에서 근무하겠는가?
(A) 유지 보수
(B) 재무
(C) 연구 개발
(D) 인사 관리

[해설] 담화 중반에서 화자는 오늘 할 업무에 대해 설명하면서 우리 팀이 개발 중인 신제품 라인(the new product line that our team is developing)이라고 언급했다. 이로 보아 화자와 청자들은 제품을 개발하는 부서에 근무하고 있음을 알 수 있으므로 정답은 (C)이다.

15.
청자들은 다음에 무엇을 할 것인가?
(A) 작은 그룹을 만들기
(B) 설문조사를 작성하기
(C) 제안을 공유하기
(D) 시연을 보기

[해설] 담화 후반부 화자가 청자에게 요구하는 내용에 정답의 단서가 있다. 화자는 모든 사람들이 아이디어를 내면(I'd like to have everyone tell a few ideas) 그것을 보드에 적은 후 그 제안들(these suggestions)에 대해 논의하겠다고 했다. 즉, 담화 직후 청자들 각자가 제안을 하고 서로의 제안을 공유할 것임을 알 수 있으므로 정답은 (C)이다.

paraphrasing have everyone tell a few ideas 모든 사람들이 몇 가지 아이디어를 내게 하다 → share some suggestions 제안을 공유한다

[어휘] form 구성하다   share 공유하다   demonstration 시연, 시범

[16-18] [BR]

Questions 16-18 refer to the following announcement.

M: Attention, ¹⁶**Fresh Mart shoppers. While you're picking up your weekly staples such as bread, meat, and vegetables, why not head over to the dairy section** to try some free samples? ¹⁷**We're pleased to introduce a new brand of yogurt, Three Lakes,** which comes in six delicious flavors. Whether you're a Fresh Mart loyalty club member or not, ¹⁷,¹⁸**you can get half off your purchase of any Three Lakes yogurt today simply by signing up for the monthly newsletter.** More information is available from our friendly and helpful staff.

staples 기본 식료품, 중요 상품   head over to ~로 가다, ~로 향하다   dairy 유제품의   sign up for ~을 신청[가입]하다   monthly newsletter 월간 소식지

16-18은 다음 안내에 관한 문제입니다.

남: ¹⁶Fresh Mart의 쇼핑객들은 주목해 주십시오. ¹⁶여러분이 빵, 육류, 채소 같은 매주 이용하는 기본 식료품을 고르시는 동안 유제품 코너로 오셔서 무료 시식을 해보시는 게 어떠세요? ¹⁷저희는 새로 나온 요구르트 브랜드인 Three Lakes를 소개하게 되어 기쁩니다. 이것은 여섯 가지 맛으로 나옵니다. Fresh Mart의 단골 회원이건 아니건 간에 ¹⁷,¹⁸ 여러분이 월간 소식지를 신청하시기만 하면 오늘 Three Lakes 요구르트를 반값에 구매하실 수 있습니다. 친절하고 도움이 되는 저희 직원들을 찾으시면 더 많은 정보를 이용하실 수 있습니다.

16.

화자는 어떤 종류의 업체에 근무하는 것 같은가?
(A) 서점
(B) 슈퍼마켓
(C) 옷가게
(D) 식당

[해설] Fresh Mart의 쇼핑객들(Fresh Mart shoppers)은 주목해 달라는 말로 담화를 시작한 점과 이어지는 내용에서 빵, 육류, 채소 같은 기본 식료품(staples such as bread, meat, and vegetables) 및 유제품 코너(the dairy section) 등의 언급으로 보아 슈퍼마켓에서 하는 고객 대상 공지임을 알 수 있다. 따라서 화자는 슈퍼마켓 직원으로 보이므로 정답은 (B)이다.

17.

이 업체는 왜 특가 판매를 하고 있는가?
(A) 새로운 브랜드를 홍보하기 위해
(B) 이전을 광고하기 위해
(C) 기념일을 축하하기 위해
(D) 남은 재고를 처분하기 위해

[해설] 담화 후반부에서, 월간 소식지를 신청하면 반값에 구매할 수 있다고(you can get half off your purchase of any Three Lakes yogurt today) 했다. 이에 앞서 새로 나온 요구르트 브랜드를 소개하게 되어 기쁘다고(We're pleased to introduce a new brand of yogurt) 한 것으로 보아 새로운 제품을 홍보하기 위해 할인 행사를 하고 있음을 알 수 있으므로 정답은 (A)이다.

paraphrasing We're pleased to introduce a new brand of yogurt 새로 나온 요구르트 브랜드를 소개하게 되어 기쁘다 → promote a new brand 새로운 브랜드를 홍보하다

[어휘] promote 홍보하다   advertise 광고하다   relocation 재배치, 이전   celebrate 축하하다   anniversary 기념일   get rid of ~을 처리하다[없애다]   excess stock 초과 재고품

18.

화자는 청자들이 할인을 받으려면 무엇을 해야 한다고 말하는가?
(A) 상품을 추천하기
(B) 회원증을 보여주기
(C) 쿠폰을 제시하기
(D) 우편물 수신자 명단에 가입하기

[해설] 담화 후반에서 화자는 청자들이 월간 소식지를 신청함으로써(by signing up for the monthly newsletter) 요구르트를 반값에 구매할 수 있다고(you can get half off your purchase) 했으므로 정답은 (D)이다.

paraphrasing signing up for the monthly newsletter 월간 소식지를 신청하기 → join a mailing list 우편물 수신자 명단에 가입하기

[19-21] [BR]

Questions 19-21 refer to the following announcement and schedule.

Session Plan	Presenter
Session A	Paul Vance
²⁰Session B	Tammy Finnigan
Session C	Joan Carlyle
Session D	Herman Lester

W: Good morning, ladies and gentlemen, and welcome to the National Journalism Convention. ¹⁹**I'm very sorry that we're starting about ten minutes behind schedule.** We had some difficulty with the sound system, but everything is working fine now. There is a change in your program that I would like to make you aware of. Owing to a missed flight, ²⁰**Tammy Finnigan will not be able to give her talk. That session will be replaced** by a panel discussion among several prominent newspaper journalists. We hope you all learn a lot today, and we'd appreciate your feedback. ²¹**You can share your opinions by visiting our Web site and leaving a comment on the main page.** Thank you.

journalism 저널리즘, 신문 잡지 편집   convention (대규모) 대회, 협의회   aware of ~을 깨닫은   owing to ~ 때문에   replace 대신[대체]하다   panel discussion 공개 토론회   prominent 중요한; 유명한   newspaper journalist 신문 기자   share 함께 나누다   comment 논평, 언급; 견해를 밝히다

19-21은 다음 안내와 일정표에 관한 문제입니다.

세션 계획	발표자
A 세션	Paul Vance
[20]B 세션	**Tammy Finnigan**
C 세션	Joan Carlyle
D 세션	Herman Lester

여: 신사숙녀 여러분, 안녕하세요. 전국 저널리즘 컨벤션에 오신 것을 환영합니다. [19]예정보다 약 10분 늦게 시작하게 되어 대단히 죄송합니다. 음향 시스템에 문제가 좀 있었지만 지금은 모든 것이 잘 작동하고 있습니다. 프로그램에 변경 사항이 있어 여러분에게 알려 드리려고 합니다. 항공편을 놓친 탓에 [20]Tammy Finnigan 씨가 강연을 할 수 없게 되었습니다. 그 세션은 여러 저명한 신문기자들의 공개 토론회로 [20]대체될 예정입니다. 여러분 모두 오늘 많은 것을 배워 가시길 바라며, 여러분의 의견을 주시면 감사하겠습니다. [21]저희 웹사이트를 방문하셔서 메인 페이지에 의견을 남김으로써 여러분의 의견을 공유하실 수 있습니다. 감사합니다.

19.

화자는 왜 사과하는가?
(A) 어떤 방을 이용할 수 없다.
(B) 행사가 늦게 시작하고 있다.
(C) 좌석이 충분하지 않다.
(D) 이름의 철자가 틀렸다.

[해설] 담화 초반, 화자는 환영 인사를 한 후에 예정보다 약 10분 늦게 시작하게 되어 죄송하다고(I'm very sorry that we're starting about ten minutes behind schedule.) 덧붙였다. 즉, 행사 지연에 대해 사과하고 있으므로 정답은 (B)이다.

paraphrasing starting about ten minutes behind schedule. 예정보다 약 10분 늦게 시작하다. → An event is starting late. 행사가 늦게 시작한다.

20.

시각 자료를 보시오. 어느 세션이 변경되었는가?
(A) A 세션
(B) B 세션
(C) C 세션
(D) D 세션

[해설] 시각 자료의 각 세션이 보기로 제시되었으므로 각 세션의 발표자 중 한 명이 담화에서 언급될 것임을 예상하고 들어야 한다. 담화 중반, Tammy Finnigan 씨가 강연을 할 수 없게 되어(Tammy Finnigan will not be able to give her talk) 해당 세션이 신문기자들의 공개 토론회로 대체될 예정이라고(That session will be replaced) 밝혔다. 시각 자료에서 발표자가 Tammy Finnigan으로 되어 있는 세션을 찾으면 정답은 (B)이다.

21.

화자의 말에 따르면, 청자들은 어떻게 의견을 전달할 수 있는가?
(A) 카드를 작성함으로써
(B) 그룹 세션에 참여함으로써
(C) 화자에게 연락함으로써
(D) 웹사이트에 의견을 남김으로써

[해설] 담화 후반, 청자들이 의견을 제시하는 방법에 대해 안내하고 있다.

웹사이트를 방문하여 메인 페이지에 의견을 남김으로써 의견을 공유할 수 있다고(You can share your opinions by visiting our Web site and leaving a comment on the main page.) 했으므로 정답은 (D)이다.

paraphrasing visiting our Web site and leaving a comment on the main page 우리 웹사이트를 방문하여 메인 페이지에 의견을 남기기 → commenting on a Web site 웹사이트에 의견을 남기기

DAY 17

PART 3 상점/병원·약국

출제 유형 01 환불·고객 불만

| 풀이 방법 해석 |

여: 안녕하세요, 저는 Dudley's 주방 기기의 고객 서비스에 있는 Maria입니다.
남: 안녕하세요, 저는 지난주에 제 커피숍에서 사용할 전문 커피 메이커를 구매했는데요, 벌써 문제가 발생했어요.
여: 그 전문 커피 메이커는 저희의 가장 잘 팔리는 상품들 중 하나입니다. 무엇이 문제인가요?
남: 저는 제 고객들을 위해 많은 커피를 내립니다. 그건 제가 알맞은 온도에 커피가 준비되게 해야 한다는 거예요. 마실 온도로 유지되지 않고 너무 뜨거워지거나 멈춰 버립니다.
여: 희망 온도를 설정하시면 그런 일이 일어나지 않을 거예요. 그렇게 해 보셨나요?
남: 음, 안 해 본 것 같아요. 그 버튼이 어디 있나요?
여: 디지털 표시 장치를 이용하셔야 합니다. 그걸 사용해서 온도를 구체적으로 설정할 수 있어요.

출제 유형 02 병원·약국

| 풀이 방법 해석 |

여: 안녕하세요, 저는 Stephanie Coors입니다. Burns 박사님께서 여기서 처방 약을 받으라고 보내셨습니다.
남: 안녕하세요, Coors 씨. 아직 그의 병원에서 전화를 받지 못했어요. 그가 당신이 여기 가지고 올 종이를 주셨나요?
여: 아, 잊어버릴 뻔 했네요. 여기 있습니다.
남: 감사합니다. 약병을 곧 준비해 드릴게요. 현금으로 지불하시겠어요, 신용카드로 지불하시겠어요?

 연습 문제

01. (B) 02. (A) 03. (B) 04. (A) 05. (B) 06. (B)

01. US-AU
What is the **man encouraged to do**?
(A) **Come** to the office **earlier**   (B) **Visit** a **Web site**

W: Dr. Grant's office, how may I help you?
M: Hello, this is Mark Perkins. I'd like to make my appointment for a checkup on Tuesday.
W: Sure, I'll put you in there. But as you may already know, we moved to a building on Franklin Avenue. Please refer to the directions on our Web site.

남자는 무엇을 하도록 권장받는가?
(A) 사무실에 일찍 오기 (B) 웹사이트 방문하기

여: Grant 선생님 병원입니다, 어떻게 도와드릴까요?
남: 안녕하세요, 저는 Mark Perkins입니다. 화요일에 검진을 위해 예약하고 싶어요.
여: 물론이죠, 그날로 예약해 드리겠습니다. 하지만 아마 이미 아시다시피, 저희는 Franklin 가의 건물로 이전했어요. 저희 웹사이트에서 오시는 길을 참고해 주세요.

02. BR-US
What does the man ask for?
(A) An **order number** (B) A **name** of **product**

W: Hi, my name is Sarah Green. I'm calling to ask about my order. I expected it to be delivered yesterday. I already paid for two-day shipping.
M: Wait a second. Let me check our records. What is your order number? It's on your receipt.

남자는 무엇을 요청하는가?
(A) 주문 번호 (B) 상품의 이름

여: 안녕하세요, 제 이름은 Sarah Green입니다. 제 주문에 대해 문의드리려고 전화했어요. 어제 배송될 것을 예상했거든요. 저는 이미 이틀 배송으로 돈을 지불했어요.
남: 잠시만 기다려 주세요. 저희 기록을 확인해 보겠습니다. 당신의 주문 번호가 무엇인가요? 영수증에 있습니다.

03. BR-US
What day will the **woman** most likely **visit**?
(A) **Tuesday** (B) **Wednesday**

M: This is John calling from Indiana Dental Clinic. Our records say you have an appointment with Dr. Anderson next Monday. Unfortunately, he will be out of the office that day due to a family emergency. He will be back to the office next Tuesday. Can you come on Tuesday afternoon or Wednesday morning?
W: Hmm... Actually, I will not be available for next Tuesday afternoon since I am scheduled to have a client meeting.

여자는 어떤 날에 방문하겠는가?
(A) 화요일 **(B) 수요일**

남: 저는 Indiana 치과의 John입니다. 저희 기록에 의하면 다음 주 월요일에 Anderson 박사님과 예약이 되어 있으시네요. 안타깝지만, 그는 그날 집안 사정으로 병원에 안 계실 거예요. 다음 주 화요일에 다시 출근하실 겁니다. 화요일 오후나 수요일 오전에 오실 수 있나요?
여: 음... 사실, 다음 주 화요일 오후에는 고객 미팅이 있어서 안 됩니다.

04. US-US
What department does the **woman work** in?
(A) **Customer service** (B) **Employee training**

W: Can I help you with anything, sir?
M: Yes, I'd like to return this hot pot that I purchased here last week. There is a crack on the lid after just one use. Can I return and exchange it with a new one of another brand?
W: That shouldn't be a problem. Do you have the original receipt?

여자는 어떤 부서에서 일하는가?
(A) 고객 서비스 (B) 직원 교육

여: 도와 드릴까요, 손님?
남: 네, 여기서 지난주에 구매한 이 전기냄비를 반품하고 싶어요. 단 한 번 사용한 후로 뚜껑에 금이 갔어요. 반품하고 다른 브랜드의 새 것으로 교환할 수 있나요?
여: 문제 될 것 없습니다. 영수증 원본 가지고 계신가요?

05. BR-BR
What problem does the **man mention**?
(A) He received a **wrong item**.
(B) A **device** is **not working properly**.

M: Hello, I'm calling about the computer that I bought two days ago. It takes a while when I run certain software. Much longer than I expected.
W: Oh, I can help you with that. Could you tell me the serial number? It's a seven-digit number. You will find it on the left side of the computer.

남자는 어떤 문제점을 언급하는가?
(A) 잘못된 물품을 받았다.. **(B) 기기가 제대로 작동하지 않는다.**

남: 안녕하세요, 이틀 전에 산 컴퓨터에 대해 전화드립니다. 특정 소프트웨어를 작동하면 시간이 걸립니다. 제가 예상했던 것보다 훨씬 더 오래 걸려요.
여: 아, 제가 도와 드릴 수 있습니다. 시리얼 번호를 말해 주시겠어요? 7자리 숫자입니다. 컴퓨터의 왼편에 보이실 거예요.

06. AU-BR
What will the **man** most likely **do next**?
(A) **Reschedule** an appointment
(B) **Go** to a **waiting area**

M: Hello. I'm here for an appointment with Dr. Douglas at 3 P.M.
W: Here is your name on the schedule. But he is busy now, so your appointment will be slightly delayed. He can see you at 3:15 P.M. Would you mind taking a seat in the waiting area and helping yourself to some tea or coffee?

남자는 다음에 무엇을 하겠는가?
(A) 예약 다시 잡기 (B) 대기실로 가기

남: 안녕하세요. 저는 오후 3시 Douglas 선생님과의 진료를 위해 왔습니다.
여: 일정에 당신 이름이 있네요. 하지만 그는 지금 바쁘셔서 진료가 약간 지연될 거예요. 그는 3시 15분에 당신을 진료하실 수 있습니다. 대기실에 앉아 차나 커피를 드시겠어요?

| paraphrasing 정답 | 1. (c) | 2. (a) | 3. (b) | 4. (c) | 5. (a) | 6. (b) |

실전 문제

01. (C)	02. (B)	03. (D)	04. (C)	05. (D)	06. (B)
07. (C)	08. (C)	09. (B)	10. (D)	11. (C)	12. (D)
13. (C)	14. (A)	15. (B)	16. (D)	17. (A)	18. (A)
19. (C)	20. (D)	21. (D)			

[01-03] BR-US

Questions 01-03 refer to the following conversation.

W: Hello, Mr. Kent. **01, 02 I heard that the medication I prescribed to you last time makes you drowsy.**
M: Yes, and **I have to drive for work**.
W: In that case, **03 I'm going to try prescribing a different medication for you.** It might not be quite as effective, but it shouldn't make you drowsy at all.
M: Is it very expensive?
W: No, it's about the same price as the one you were taking. Besides, your insurance will cover it.

medication 약, 약물   prescribe (의사가) 처방을 내리다   drowsy 졸리는, 나른하게 만드는   in that case 그런 경우에는   quite 아주, 정말로   effective 효과적인   besides 게다가, 뿐만 아니라   insurance 보험   cover 보장하다

01-03은 다음 대화에 관한 문제입니다.

여: 안녕하세요, Kent 씨. **01, 02제가 지난번에 처방해 드린 약 때문에 졸음이 오신다고요.**
남: 네, 그리고 **저는 운전해서 출근해야 해요.**
여: 그렇다면, **03다른 약을 처방해 드려 볼게요.** 그만큼 약효가 있지는 않을 수도 있지만 더 이상 졸음이 오지는 않을 거예요.
남: 많이 비싼가요?
여: 아니요, 복용하시던 것과 거의 같은 가격이에요. 뿐만 아니라 가입하신 보험으로 보장되고요.

01.

여자는 누구일 것 같은가?
(A) 자동차 정비공
(B) 택시 기사
(C) 의사
(D) 약사

[해설] 대화 초반 여자는 지난번에 자신이 처방해준 약을(the medication I prescribed to you last time) 언급했다. 따라서 의사인 여자와 환자인 남자의 대화임을 알 수 있으므로 정답은 (C)이다.

[어휘] mechanic 정비공   pharmacist 약사

02.

남자는 왜 "저는 운전해서 출근해야 해요"라고 말하는가?
(A) 자신의 자질을 열거하기 위해서
(B) 문제점을 강조하기 위해서
(C) 실수에 대해 사과하기 위해서
(D) 직장에서 휴가를 요청하기 위해서

[해설] 처방해준 약이 졸음을 유발한다는 사실을 확인하는(the medication I prescribed to you last time makes you drowsy) 여자의 말 뒤에 남자가 "저는 운전해서 출근해야 해요"라고 한 것은 처방약으로 인해 졸음이 오는 증상이 운전할 때 영향을 미쳐서는 절대 안 된다는 것을 강조하기 위해 한 말이다. 즉, 여자가 처방해준 약의 문제점을 강조하기 위한 의도이므로 정답은 (B)이다.

[어휘] list 열거하다   qualities (사람의) 자질   emphasize 강조하다   time off 휴식

03.

여자는 남자가 무엇을 해야 한다고 말하는가?
(A) 다른 일을 찾기
(B) 약국에 등록하기
(C) 의료 보험에 가입하기
(D) 다른 약을 복용하기

[해설] 처방해준 약이 졸음을 유발한다는 남자에게 여자가 다른 약을 처방해주겠다고(I'm going to try prescribing a different medication) 했다. 즉, 남자에게 다른 약을 복용할 것을 권하는 말이므로 정답은 (D)이다.

[어휘] register 등록하다   pharmacy 약국   insurance plan 의료 보험

[04-06] BR-US

Questions 04-06 refer to the following conversation.

M: Hello, my name is Richard Moore. **04My doctor said to come here to pick up my prescription.** I just came from his office though, so it might not be ready yet.
W: Let's see… Here it is. **05My coworker called in sick, so I'm the only pharmacist here right now. 04Could you wait for a few minutes while I fill this for you?**
M: Sure thing. In the meantime, **06I'll call my office to let them know that I won't be going back this afternoon.**

prescription 처방전, 처방된 약   coworker 동료   call in sick 전화로 병결을 알리다   pharmacist 약사   fill a prescription 약을 조제하다

04-06은 다음 대화에 관한 문제입니다.

남: 안녕하세요, 제 이름은 Richard Moore입니다. **04의사 선생님이 여기에 와서 처방 약을 찾아가라고 하셨어요.** 제가 방금 그분의 진료실에서 온 터라 아직 준비되지 않았을 수도 있겠네요.
여: 한번 볼게요… 여기 있네요. **05제 동료가 아파서 안 나와서 지금 여긴 약사가 저뿐이에요. 04조제하는 동안 잠깐 기다려 주시겠어요?**
남: 그럼요. 그러는 동안 **06제 사무실에 전화해서 오늘 오후에 들어가지 않는다고 전해야겠어요.**

04.

화자들은 무엇에 대해 얘기하는가?
(A) 의료 수술
(B) 의사의 일정
(C) 처방된 약
(D) 질환

[해설] 남자는 의사가 처방해준 약을 찾으러 왔다고(come here to pick up my prescription) 했고, 이에 여자가 조제하는 동안 기다려 달라고 (Could you wait for a few minutes while I fill this for you) 한 것으로 보아 환자인 남자와 약사인 여자가 처방된 약에 대해 나누는 대화임을 알 수 있다. 따라서 정답은 (C)이다.

[어휘] medical 의학[의료]의 procedure 절차, 수술 illness 병, 질환

05.

여자는 왜 예정보다 업무가 늦어지는가?
(A) 방금 많은 양의 주문을 받았다.
(B) 컴퓨터 네트워크가 다운되었다.
(C) 물품을 제자리에 두지 않았다.
(D) 동료가 아파서 안 나왔다.

[해설] 여자는 동료가 아파서 출근하지 않은(My coworker called in sick) 탓에 지금은 약사가 자신뿐이라며, 조금만 기다려 달라고 양해를 구하고 있다. 즉, 동료의 병가 때문에 현재 일이 많이 밀려 있음을 알 수 있으므로 정답은 (D)이다.

paraphrasing My coworker called in sick 내 동료가 병가를 냈다 → A coworker is out sick. 동료가 아파서 안 나왔다.

[어휘] behind schedule 예정보다 늦게 order 주문, 지시 misplace 제자리에 두지 않다

06.

남자는 무엇을 할 것이라고 말하는가?
(A) 양식을 작성하기
(B) 전화를 하기
(C) 음식을 주문하기
(D) 알약을 먹기

[해설] 앞으로 일어날 일을 묻는 문제의 단서는 주로 대화 후반에 나온다. 남자는 약이 조제되길 기다리는 동안 사무실에 전화해서(I'll call my office) 오후에 복귀하지 않는다고 알리겠다고 했다. 따라서 정답은 (B)이다.

paraphrasing call 전화하다 → make a phone call 전화를 걸기

[어휘] fill out 작성하다, 기입하다 pill 알약, 정제

[07-09] AU-BR

Questions 07-09 refer to the following conversation.

M: ⁰⁷This is Michael with Northbrook Dental Clinic. How may I direct your call?
W: Hi, I'm Angela Burris. It's been a while since I've seen a dentist, and ⁰⁸I've been getting toothaches recently. When is your next available appointment?
M: ⁰⁹We have an opening at 4 P.M. on Wednesday. Shall I put you down for that time?
W: I get off at 5 P.M. on Wednesdays.
M: We're only open until 6 P.M. on weekdays. Could you make it by 5:30?
W: Okay, that sounds good. I'll see you then.

direct ~로 보내다 toothache 치통 recently 최근에 available 이용할 수 있는 appointment 약속, 예약 put down 적다, 적어 두다 get off (직장에서) 퇴근하다 weekday 평일 make it 시간 맞춰 가다

07-09는 다음 대화에 관한 문제입니다.

남: ⁰⁷Northbrook 치과의 Michael입니다. 전화를 어디로 돌려 드릴까요?
여: 안녕하세요, 저는 Angela Burris라고 해요. 치과 진료를 받은 지 한참 지났는데, ⁰⁸최근 치통이 있어요. 다음에 예약 가능한 때가 언제인가요?
남: ⁰⁹수요일 오후 4시에 시간이 비어요. 그때로 예약해 드릴까요?
여: 제가 수요일에는 5시에 퇴근해요.
남: 저희는 주중에는 오후 6시까지만 진료를 합니다. 5시 30분까지 오실 수 있나요?
여: 네, 괜찮습니다. 그때 뵐게요.

07.

남자는 어디서 일하는가?
(A) 호텔에서
(B) 사탕 가게에서
(C) 병원에서
(D) 부동산 중개소에서

[해설] 대화 시작 부분에서 남자는 자신의 소속을 Northbrook Dental Clinic이라고 밝혔다. 즉, 남자는 치과에서 근무하므로 정답은 (C)이다.

paraphrasing Dental Clinic 치과 → medical clinic 병원

[어휘] medical clinic 병원 real estate agency 부동산 중개소

08.

여자는 무엇이 문제가 되었다고 말하는가?
(A) 고객 부족
(B) 늦게까지 일하는 것
(C) 아픈 치아
(D) 발표하는 것

[해설] 여자의 문제가 무엇인지 묻는 문제로, 치과 예약을 위해 전화한 여자가 증상을 설명하는 부분을 잘 듣는다. 여자는 치과 진료를 받은 지 한참 지났는데, 최근 들어 치통이 있다고(I've been getting toothaches recently) 했다. 즉, 치아가 아프다는 말이므로 정답은 (C)이다.

paraphrasing I've been getting toothaches recently. 최근 치통이 있다. → painful teeth 아픈 치아

[어휘] lack 부족 painful 아픈, 고통스러운

09.

여자가 "제가 수요일에는 5시에 퇴근해요"라고 말할 때 암시하는 것은 무엇인가?
(A) 최근 정규직으로 일하기 시작했다.
(B) 예약 시간에 맞출 수 없다.
(C) 주말에만 시간이 있다.
(D) 회의에 참석해야 한다.

[해설] 남자가 수요일 오후 4시로 진료 시간을 예약하면 되는지(We have an opening at 4 P.M. on Wednesday. Shall I put you down for that time) 묻는 말에 여자가 "제가 수요일에는 5시에 퇴근해요"라고 답했다. 즉, 수요일 오후 4시는 퇴근 시간보다 이른 시각이므로 그 시간에 맞춰 병원에 올 수 없다는 뜻으로 한 말이므로 정답은 (B)이다.

[어휘] a full-time position 정규직 attend 참석하다

[10-12] US-US

Questions 10-12 refer to the following conversation.

> M: Hello, ¹⁰you've reached Dayton Central Hospital.
> W: Hi, I'm Rachel Banks. ¹⁰, ¹¹I have an appointment at 2:30 this afternoon, but I don't think I'll be able to make it because an urgent client meeting just came up.
> M: I understand, Ms. Banks. ¹²Would you like to reschedule your blood donation for another day?
> W: Yes, ¹²Friday should work well for me.

reach (전화로) 연락하다   urgent 긴급한   come up 생기다, 발생하다   reschedule 일정을 변경하다   blood donation 헌혈

10-12는 다음 대화에 관한 문제입니다.

남: 안녕하세요, ¹⁰Dayton Central 병원에 연결되셨습니다.
여: 안녕하세요, 저는 Rachel Banks라고 합니다. ¹⁰, ¹¹오늘 오후 2시 30분에 예약되어 있는데, 고객과의 긴급한 회의가 막 잡혀서 ¹¹시간에 맞춰 갈 수 없을 것 같아요.
남: 알겠습니다, Banks 씨. ¹²다른 날로 헌혈 일정을 다시 잡아드릴까요?
여: 네, ¹²금요일이면 좋겠어요.

10.

남자는 누구일 것 같은가?
(A) 실험실 기술자
(B) 사업상의 고객
(C) 환자
(D) 접수 담당자

[해설] 대화 초반, 남자가 Dayton Central Hospital이라고 소속을 밝혔고, 이어서 여자가 이름과 예약 시간 등을 언급한 것으로 보아 남자는 병원에서 환자들의 진료 예약 등의 접수 업무를 담당하는 사람임을 알 수 있다. 따라서 정답은 (D)이다.

[어휘] lab 실험실(= laboratory) technician 기술자 receptionist 접수 담당자

11.

여자가 전화한 목적은 무엇인가?
(A) 회의 일정을 잡는 것
(B) 의견을 제시하는 것
(C) 예약을 변경하는 것
(D) 돈을 기부하는 것

[해설] 전화의 목적은 주로 대화 전반부에서 드러난다. 여자는 오늘 오후 2시 30분으로 예약을 했으나 긴급한 회의 때문에 시간에 맞춰 병원에 갈 수 없다고(I have an appointment at 2:30 this afternoon, but I don't think I'll be able to make it) 했다. 이로 보아 예약 시간을 변경하기 위해 전화한 것임을 알 수 있으므로 정답은 (C)이다.

[어휘] monetary 금전의 donation 기부, 기증

12.

여자는 금요일에 무엇을 할 것인가?
(A) 고객을 만나기
(B) 계좌를 개설하기
(C) 건강 검진을 받기
(D) 헌혈을 하기

[해설] 질문의 핵심 키워드 Friday는 대화 마지막에 언급되는데, 바로 앞에서 남자가 헌혈 일정을 다시 잡을지(reschedule your blood donation for another day) 묻는 말에 여자가 금요일이 좋겠다고(Friday should work well for me) 했다. 이로 보아 여자는 금요일에 헌혈을 할 예정임을 알 수 있으므로 (D)가 정답이다.

paraphrasing blood donation 헌혈 → donate blood 헌혈하다

[어휘] account 계좌, 계정 physical checkup 건강 검진 donate 기부[기증]하다

[13-15] AU-US

Questions 13-15 refer to the following conversation.

> M: Thanks for stopping by ¹³Bryce Hardware. Can I help you with anything?
> W: Yes. I'm having an issue with an ¹³electric drill that I bought here a few days ago.
> M: We always try to provide the best quality. What seems to be wrong with the drill?
> W: Well, ¹⁴when I turn it on, sometimes it speeds up or slows down for no reason. And then other times, it doesn't turn on at all.
> M: Hmm... That sounds like a problem with the motor. It shouldn't be doing that.
> W: ¹⁵Do you happen to have another one in stock?
> M: I believe so. Please wait here while ¹⁵I go and see if I can find it for you.

stop by (~에) 잠시 들르다   hardware 철물, (컴퓨터) 하드웨어
have an issue with ~와 문제가 있다   electric drill 전기 드릴
quality 질, 우수함, 양질   speed up 속도를 더 내다[높이다]
for no reason 아무 이유 없이   happen to V 우연히 ~하다
in stock 비축되어, 재고로

13-15 다음 대화에 관한 문제입니다.

남: ¹³Bryce 철물점을 찾아주셔서 감사합니다. 제가 좀 도와 드릴까요?
여: 네. 며칠 전에 제가 여기서 산 ¹³전기 드릴에 문제가 있습니다.
남: 저희는 항상 최고의 품질을 제공하려고 노력합니다. 드릴에 어떤 문제가 있어 보이시나요?
여: 음, ¹⁴전원을 켜면 가끔씩 아무 이유 없이 속도가 빨라지거나 느려져요. 그리고 어떤 때는 아예 켜지지도 않아요.
남: 음... 모터에 문제가 있는 것 같아요. 그러면 안 되거든요.
여: ¹⁵혹시 다른 재고가 있나요?
남: 있을 거예요. ¹⁵제가 가서 찾아봐 드리는 동안 여기서 기다려 주세요.

13.

어디에서 대화가 이루어지고 있는가?

(A) 캠핑용품점에서
(B) 건설 회사에서
(C) 철물점에서
(D) 전기 회사에서

[해설] 대화 초반에 두 사람이 대화를 나누는 장소에 대한 단서가 나온다. 남자는 상점의 직원, 여자는 손님으로 보이는데, 남자가 언급한 상점 이름 Bryce Hardware와 여자가 언급한 전기 드릴(electric drill) 같은 어휘로 보아 두 사람이 있는 곳은 철물이나 장비 등을 취급하는 곳임을 알 수 있으므로 정답은 (C)이다.

14.
여자는 어떤 문제점을 언급하는가?
(A) 제품이 제대로 작동하지 않는다.
(B) 일부 상품이 품절되었다.
(C) 여자가 구입한 것에 금액이 너무 많이 청구되었다.
(D) 일부 품목에 라벨이 잘못 붙여졌다.

[해설] 대화 초반에 여자는 자신이 구매한 전기 드릴에 문제가 있다고 했고, 대화 중반에서, 전원을 켜면 가끔씩 아무 이유 없이 속도가 빨라지거나 느려지고, 어떤 때는 아예 켜지지 않는다며(when I turn it on, sometimes it speeds up or slows down for no reason. And then other times, it doesn't turn on at all) 제품의 오작동 현상을 상세히 설명한다. 따라서 정답은 (A)이다.

paraphrasing it speeds up or slows down for no reason 아무 이유 없이 속도가 빨라지거나 느려진다 / it doesn't turn on at all 아예 켜지지 않는다 → A product is malfunctioning 제품이 제대로 작동하지 않는다.

[어휘] malfunction 제대로 작동하지 않다 merchandise 상품 overcharge 너무 많이 청구하다, 바가지를 씌우다 mislabel ~에 라벨을 잘못 붙이다

15.
남자는 다음에 무엇을 할 것 같은가?
(A) 제조업체에 연락하기
(B) 대체품을 찾기
(C) 매니저에게 얘기하기
(D) 환불해 주기

[해설] 남자가 다음에 할 일을 묻는 문제로 대화 후반부에서 단서를 찾는다. 문제가 있는 전기 드릴을 구매한 여자가 대화 후반에 다른 재고가 있는지(Do you happen to have another one in stock?) 묻자 남자가 가서 찾아보는(I go and see if I can find it for you) 동안 여기서 기다려 달라고 말한다. 즉, 남자는 대화 직후 여자에게 바꿔줄 다른 전기 드릴을 찾으러 갈 것임을 알 수 있으므로 정답은 (B)이다.

paraphrasing go and see if I can find 찾을 수 있는지 가서 알아본다 → Look for 찾다

[어휘] manufacturer 제조업체 replacement 교체[대체]품

[16-18] US-BR
Questions 16-18 refer to the following conversation.

M: Good morning. You've reached the [16]**Ferguson Clinic**. How may I help you?
W: Hi. I would like to make an appointment for [16]a **checkup**. Do you have any available on Friday morning?
M: Yes, there's an open time slot at 10:30. Could I get your full name, please?
W: Yes, it's Bethany Torres. But I won't be in your computer system because I'm a new patient. [17]**I just moved to Boston from Atlanta this month.**
M: No problem. I'll book you in for 10:30, but [18]**you should come in early to complete several new patient forms.** I'd give it half an hour.
W: All right. Thanks.

time slot 시간대 patient 환자 book ~ in 고객이나 환자 등을 접수시키다 complete 작성하다, 기입하다 form 양식

16-18은 다음 대화에 관한 문제입니다.
남: 안녕하세요. [16]Ferguson 의원입니다. 어떻게 도와 드릴까요?
여: 안녕하세요. [16]검진 예약을 하려고요. 금요일 오전에 가능할까요?
남: 네, 10시 30분 시간이 비어 있어요. 성함을 알려 주시겠어요?
여: 네, Bethany Torres예요. 하지만 제가 이 병원이 처음이라서 컴퓨터 시스템에는 없을 거예요. [17]이번 달에 애틀랜타에서 보스턴으로 막 이사 왔거든요.
남: 문제없습니다. 10시 30분으로 접수해 드릴게요. 하지만 [18]일찍 오셔서 여러 개의 신규 환자 양식을 작성하셔야 해요. 30분 걸릴 거예요.
여: 알겠습니다. 감사합니다.

16.
여자는 어떤 종류의 업체에 전화하고 있는가?
(A) 네일숍
(B) 금융 기관
(C) 컴퓨터 상점
(D) 의원

[해설] 대화 시작 부분 남자가 전화를 받으면서 Ferguson 의원(Ferguson Clinic)이라고 언급했고, 여자가 검진(checkup)을 예약하고 싶다고 전화 용건을 밝혔다. 따라서 여자는 의원에 전화하고 있음을 알 수 있으므로 정답은 (D)이다.

[어휘] financial 금융[재정]의 institution 기관, 단체, 협회 medical 의학의

17.
여자는 이번 달에 무엇을 했는가?
(A) 새로운 도시로 이사했다.
(B) 휴가를 갔다.
(C) 프로그램에 등록했다.
(D) 콘퍼런스에 참석했다.

[해설] 여자가 이번 달에 한 일을 묻는 문제로, 질문의 핵심 키워드 this month가 언급된 곳에 단서가 있다. 대화 중반, 여자가 이번 달에 애틀랜타에서 보스턴으로 막 이사 왔다고(I just moved to Boston from Atlanta this month.) 했으므로 정답은 (A)이다.

paraphrasing I just moved to Boston from Atlanta 애틀랜타에서 보스턴으로 막 이사 왔다 → Moved to a new city 새로운 도시로 이사했다.

18.
남자가 "30분 걸릴 거예요"라고 말할 때 암시하는 것은 무엇인가?
(A) 작성할 서류가 많다.

DAY 17 175

(B) 업체가 영업 시간을 변경했다.
(C) 여자가 나중에 다시 전화하기를 바란다.
(D) 문제가 곧 해결될 것이라고 생각한다.

[해설] 대화 후반부, 남자가 여자에게 일찍 와서 여러 개의 신규 환자 양식을 작성해야 한다고(you should come in early to complete several new patient forms) 한 다음에 "30분 걸릴 거예요"라고 덧붙였다. 즉, 서류 작성에 30분이 소요된다는 의미이고, 이것은 이 병원에서 처음 진료를 받는 환자의 경우에는 작성할 서류가 꽤 많다는 것을 암시하므로 정답은 (A)이다.

[어휘] paperwork 서류 작업 opening hours 영업 시간 resolve (문제 등을) 해결하다

[19-21] US-BR

Questions 19-21 refer to the following conversation and receipt.

String of Lights	£30
Pack of Metallic Balloons	£10
Banner	£15
[20]Centerpiece Vase	£20

W: Is there anything I can help you find, sir?
M: Actually, I just bought these supplies for [19]**my company's anniversary party**, but I think I was charged too much. [20]**I saw a sign that says all vases are thirty percent off.**
W: I'm sorry about that. Could I see your receipt, please?
M: Yes, I have it right here.
W: Hmm… you're right. [20]**I'll change that on your receipt now** and refund the difference with cash.
M: Thank you very much.
W: And to apologize, [21]**I'll ask my manager to give you a coupon for ten percent off your next purchase.**

supplies 용품, 비품 charge 청구하다 sign 표지판, 간판 receipt 영수증 string 끈, 줄 pack 묶음, 꾸러미 metallic 금속성의 banner 플래카드, 현수막 centerpiece 중앙부 장식

19-21은 다음 대화와 영수증에 관한 문제입니다.

줄 전구	30파운드
금속성 풍선 묶음	10파운드
현수막	15파운드
[20]장식용 꽃병	20파운드

여: 찾으시는 걸 제가 도와 드릴까요, 손님?
남: 실은 제가 방금 [19]**저희 회사 기념일 파티**에 쓸 이 용품들을 샀는데 제게 너무 많이 청구된 것 같아요. [20]**모든 꽃병을 30퍼센트 할인한다는 안내판을 봤거든요.**

여: 그 점은 죄송합니다. 영수증을 보여 주시겠어요?
남: 네, 지금 여기 가지고 있어요.
여: 흠... 손님 말씀이 맞네요. [20]**제가 지금 영수증에서 그 내용을 고치고** 차액을 현금으로 환불해 드릴게요.
남: 정말 고맙습니다.
여: 그리고 사과의 의미로, [21]**제가 매니저에게 요청해서 다음 번 구매 시 쓸 수 있는 10퍼센트 할인 쿠폰을 드리도록 하겠습니다.**

19.

남자는 어떤 종류의 행사를 언급하는가?
(A) 디자인 경연 대회
(B) 생일 파티
(C) 기업 축하 행사
(D) 상품 출시

[해설] 상점의 직원과 손님이 나누는 대화로, 대화 초반 남자가 여자에게 회사 기념일 파티(my company's anniversary party)에 쓰기 위해 용품들을 샀는데, 너무 많은 금액이 청구된 것 같다고 말한다. 즉, 남자가 언급한 행사의 종류는 기업의 축하 행사이므로 정답은 (C)이다.

paraphrasing my company's anniversary party 우리 회사의 기념일 파티 → A company celebration 기업 축하 행사

[어휘] celebration 기념[축하] 행사 launch 출시(하다)

20.

시각 자료를 보시오. 여자는 어떤 금액을 고칠 것인가?
(A) 30파운드
(B) 10파운드
(C) 15파운드
(D) 20파운드

[해설] 품목과 금액이 적힌 영수증이 제시되었고, 보기가 금액으로 구성되어 있으므로 대화에서 특정 품목의 상품이 언급될 것임을 예상하고 들어야 한다. 남자가 너무 많은 금액이 청구되었다면서 모든 꽃병을 30퍼센트 할인한다는 안내판을 봤다고(I saw a sign that says all vases are thirty percent off.) 했고, 이에 여자가 그것을 영수증에서 고치고(I'll change that on your receipt now) 차액을 환불해 주겠다고 했으므로 영수증에서 꽃병의 가격이 잘못되었음을 알 수 있다. 따라서 여자는 꽃병의 금액인 20파운드를 고칠 것이므로 정답은 (D)이다.

21.

남자는 관리자로부터 무엇을 받을 수 있는가?
(A) 제품 카탈로그
(B) 새 영수증
(C) 무료 샘플
(D) 상점 쿠폰

[해설] 문제의 핵심 키워드 supervisor(관리자, 감독관)가 대화에서는 manager로 표현되었다. 대화 마지막 부분에서 여자가 manager를 언급하는데, 매니저에게 요청해서 남자에게 다음 번 구매 시 쓸 수 있는 10퍼센트 할인 쿠폰을 주겠다고(I'll ask my manager to give you a coupon for ten percent off your next purchase) 했다. 즉, 남자는 여자의 관리자로부터 상점에서 사용할 수 있는 쿠폰을 받게 되므로 정답은 (D)이다.

paraphrasing manager 매니저 → supervisor 관리자

PART 4 광고(advertisement)

출제 유형 01 제품 광고
| 풀이 방법 해석 |

남: 세금 납부 기간이 다시 돌아왔고, 당신은 세금 신고 서비스를 사용하는 데 많은 돈을 쓰고 있을지도 모릅니다. 그 대신, 비싼 서비스 수수료 없이 여러분의 세금을 신고하는 데 도움을 줄 사용하기 쉬운 Tax Time을 다운로드하세요. 프로그램을 다운로드하기만 하셔서 설명을 따라 하세요. Tax Time은 아주 효율적인 것에 대해 작년에 Simple Software 상을 수상했습니다. 저희의 서비스를 이전에 사용해 보신 적이 있다면, 얼마나 좋은지 아실 겁니다. 또한, Tax Time은 모든 고객들에게 무료 업데이트를 제공하므로 매해 또 다시 돈을 지불하지 않으셔도 됩니다. 프로그램 또는 연간 업데이트를 다운로드 받기 위해 저희 웹사이트를 방문해 주세요.

출제 유형 02 서비스 광고
| 풀이 방법 해석 |

여: 만약 식료품 쇼핑을 가셔야 한다면, Tammy's Market이 그 장소입니다! 저희는 가장 신선한 고기와 농산물을 제공하고, 신선한 빵을 제공하기 위해 매장 내 베이커리도 있습니다. 또한, 다음 달부터 저희가 판매하는 음식들을 무료로 시식해 보실 수 있도록 저희 매장 여기 저기에 시식할 수 있는 장소를 설치해 놓을 것입니다. 당신이 쇼핑 목록을 준비하실 것을 돕기 위해, 저희는 웹사이트에 주간 판매 전단을 게시해 두었습니다. 한 주 동안 여러분의 식사를 계획하실 수 있도록 그곳에서 확인해 보시기 바랍니다!

 연습 문제

01. (B)　02. (A)　03. (B)　04. (A)　05. (B)　06. (A)

01. [BR]
What is the **advertisement** for?
(A) A **washing machine**　(B) A **vacuum cleaner**

W: Are you satisfied with your vacuum cleaner? Our vacuum cleaner, Power Sweeper, is cord-free and lightweight with a long-lasting battery. Its new, innovative, powerful motor system will remove 30% more dust than our previous model. It can deeply clean both carpets and floors. It comes with various detachable accessories. Visit one of your nearest electronic stores and buy one today. You will get a free battery charging station.

무엇에 대한 광고인가?
(A) 세탁기　**(B) 진공 청소기**

광고
여: 당신의 진공 청소기에 만족하시나요? 저희의 진공 청소기 Power Sweeper는 코드가 없고 오래 지속되는 배터리가 있고 가볍습니다. 그것의 새롭고, 혁신적이고, 강력한 모터 시스템은 저희의 이전 모델보다 먼지를 30퍼센트 더 제거할 것입니다. 그것은 카펫과 바닥 모두 깊은 곳까지 청소할 수 있습니다. 그것은 분리 가능한 다양한 액세서리가 딸려 옵니다. 가장 가까운 전자기기 매장 중 한 곳에 방문하셔서 오늘 구매하세요. 무료 배터리 충전기를 받으실 겁니다.

02. [AU]
Why are items **on sale**?
(A) A **store** is **moving** to another location.
(B) **New products** will **arrive** soon.

M: After over 20 years in business downtown, Bed & Beddings is about to relocate to Lloyd Mall. All of the items currently in stock will be sold at 20% off. All displayed items in the showroom are drastically reduced for clearance. Come today and check their price. Hurry up! Don't miss this saving opportunity.

제품들은 왜 할인을 하는가?
(A) 상점이 다른 곳으로 이전한다.　(B) 새 제품들이 곧 도착할 것이다.

광고
남: 시내에서 20년 이상의 사업 후에, Bed & Beddings가 Lloyd Mall로 이전하려고 합니다. 현재 재고가 있는 모든 제품들은 20퍼센트 할인된 가격에 판매될 것입니다. 쇼룸에 있는 모든 진열 제품들은 재고 정리를 위해 엄청나게 할인될 것입니다. 오늘 오셔서 가격을 확인해 보세요. 서두르세요! 이 절약할 수 있는 기회를 놓치지 마세요.

03. [BR]
What will be **given** to those **who renew membership** early?
(A) **Free admissions**　(B) A **free gift**

M: The winter season is approaching. This means your museum membership expires soon and it's the perfect time to renew it. We offer early bird discounts to those who renew it before November 30. You will get 20% off and complimentary T-shirts. Membership holders can access all regular exhibitions at a discounted price and 10% off all merchandise in the gift shop.

멤버십을 일찍 갱신하는 사람들에게 무엇이 제공될 것인가?
(A) 무료 입장　**(B) 무료 사은품**

광고
남: 겨울 시즌이 다가오고 있습니다. 이것은 여러분의 박물관 멤버십이 곧 만료되고 갱신하기에 최적의 시기라는 것입니다. 11월 30일 전에 갱신하는 분들에게는 얼리버드 할인을 제공합니다. 20퍼센트 할인과 무료 티셔츠를 받으실 것입니다. 멤버십 소지자는 할인된 가격에 모든 일반 전시에 입장할 수 있고 기념품점에서 모든 상품을 10퍼센트 할인된 가격에 살 수 있습니다.

04. [US]
How can listeners **get** a **discount**?
(A) By **referring** to an **advertisement**
(B) By **registering** for a **newsletter**

W: Do you want to avoid hassles of gardening work such as tree trimming and grass mowing? That's why Dominguez Landscaping is here at Centerville. Call us today to get a free cost estimate. One of our experienced landscapers will visit your home or building. Mention this ad when you reserve our service, and you will get 20% off.

청자들은 어떻게 할인을 받을 수 있는가?
(A) 광고를 언급함으로써 (B) 소식지를 신청함으로써

광고
여: 나무 다듬기와 잔디 깎는 것과 같은 귀찮은 정원 손질 일을 피하고 싶으신가요? 그래서 이곳 센터빌에 Dominguez 조경이 있습니다. 오늘 저희에게 전화 주셔서 무료 비용 견적을 받으세요. 저희의 숙련된 조경사 중 한 명이 당신의 집 또는 건물을 방문할 것입니다. 서비스를 예약하실 때 이 광고를 언급하시면 20퍼센트 할인을 받으실 겁니다.

05. [BR]

Where does the **speaker** most likely **work**?
(A) At a **delivery company** (B) At a **supermarket**

W: Are you too busy to go grocery shopping every day? We will introduce the Pick-up Grocery service. Just order your groceries online at our Web site and book a time for you to pick them up. Our workers will bag the groceries you ordered. All you have to do is come to one of the counters and pick up your order. We will open a drive-through window soon.

화자는 어디에서 일하겠는가?
(A) 배송 회사에서 **(B) 슈퍼마켓에서**

광고
여: 매일 식료품을 사러 가기에 너무 바쁘신가요? Pick-up Grocery 서비스를 소개해 드리겠습니다. 저희 웹사이트에서 온라인으로 식료품을 주문하고 그것을 가지러 올 시간을 예약하기만 하세요. 저희의 직원들이 당신이 주문한 식료품을 포장할 것입니다. 여러분은 계산대 중 한 곳으로 오셔서 주문품을 가져가기만 하면 됩니다. 저희는 곧 드라이브 스루 창구도 열 것입니다.

06. [AU]

What is **required** to **get a discount**?
(A) **Show** a **student ID** (B) **Present** a **coupon**

M: Back-to-School is coming! Reynolds Furniture is offering a special deal to the students of Grand Hill College. We have the largest selection of desks, chairs, bookshelves, and so on. Just present your student ID to a cashier, and you will get 15% off from the total of your purchase. Don't miss this special deal.

할인을 받기 위해 무엇을 해야 하는가?
(A) 학생증 보여주기 (B) 쿠폰 제시하기

광고
남: 새 학기가 다가오고 있습니다! Reynolds 가구는 Grand Hill 대학교 학생들에게 특별 할인을 제공하고 있습니다. 저희는 가장 다양한 책상, 의자, 책장 등을 보유하고 있습니다. 계산원에게 여러분의 학생증을 보여주기만 하면 구매품 총액에서 15퍼센트 할인을 받으실 것입니다. 이 특별 할인을 놓치지 마세요.

paraphrasing 정답 1. (a) 2. (c) 3. (b) 4. (b) 5. (c) 6. (a)

실전 문제

01. (B)	02. (A)	03. (C)	04. (C)	05. (D)	06. (A)
07. (B)	08. (D)	09. (C)	10. (B)	11. (A)	12. (C)
13. (A)	14. (D)	15. (C)	16. (B)	17. (D)	18. (C)
19. (B)	20. (D)	21. (B)			

[01-03] [US]
Questions 01-03 refer to the following advertisement.

M: If you feel overwhelmed by work and chores around the house or at your office, you're not alone. **01**Home Shine sends people to your home or office to take care of all your cleaning needs. Home Shine even has a mobile app that can be used to call one of our employees at any time during weekdays. **02**We are known for showing up earlier and getting the job done faster than any of our competitors. This month we are offering a special promotion. **03**If you aren't completely satisfied with our Super Shine package, we will give you a full refund!

overwhelmed 압도된   chores 잡일, 허드렛일   take care of ~을 처리하다   weekday 평일   be known for ~로 알려져 있다   show up 나타나다   competitor 경쟁자, 경쟁 업체   completely 완전히, 전적으로   full refund 전액 환불

01-03은 다음 광고에 관한 문제입니다.
남: 집이나 사무실에서 업무와 집안일로 스트레스를 받는다면 당신은 혼자가 아닙니다. **01**Home Shine이 당신의 집이나 사무실로 사람을 보내 당신의 모든 청소 요구를 처리해 드립니다. Home Shine은 심지어 주중 언제라도 저희 직원을 부르는 데 사용할 수 있는 모바일 앱도 있습니다. **02**저희는 어떤 경쟁업체보다도 더 일찍 도착하여 더 빠르게 작업을 끝내는 것으로 알려져 있습니다. 이번 달에는 특별 판촉 행사를 진행합니다. **03**저희의 Super Shine 패키지 상품에 완전히 만족하지 못하신다면 전액을 환불해 드리겠습니다!

01.

광고는 어떤 종류의 업체를 홍보하고 있는가?
(A) 피트니스 센터
(B) 청소 회사
(C) 부동산 중개소
(D) 사업 컨설턴트

[해설] Home Shine이 집이나 사무실로 사람을 보내 모든 청소 요구를 처리해 준다는(Home Shine sends people to your home or office to take care of all your cleaning needs) 내용으로 보아 청소 서비스를 제공하는 회사를 홍보하는 광고임을 알 수 있으므로 정답은

(B)이다.

[어휘] promote 홍보하다 fitness center 피트니스 센터, 헬스클럽 real estate 부동산 consultant 상담자, 자문 위원

02.

화자에 따르면, 이 업체는 무엇으로 알려져 있는가?
(A) 신속한 서비스
(B) 만족도 점수
(C) 경쟁력 있는 가격
(D) 천연 제품 사용

[해설] 담화 중반, 자사의 서비스의 특장점을 언급한 곳에 정답의 단서가 있다. 어떤 경쟁업체보다도 더 일찍 도착하여 더 빠르게 작업을 끝내는 것으로 알려져 있다고(We are known for showing up earlier and getting the job done faster than any of our competitors.) 했다. 즉, 신속한 서비스로 알려져 있다는 말이므로 정답은 (A)이다.

paraphrasing showing up earlier and getting the job done faster 더 일찍 도착하여 더 빠르게 작업을 끝내는 것 → Its quick service 신속한 서비스

[어휘] competitive 경쟁적인

03.

화자에 의해 어떤 종류의 제안이 언급되는가?
(A) 주말 서비스
(B) 무료 체험 기간
(C) 만족 보장
(D) 고객 감사 할인

[해설] 담화 마지막에 제안 사항이 제시된다. 자사의 Super Shine 상품에 완전히 만족하지 못한다면 전액을 환불해 주겠다고(If you aren't completely satisfied with our Super Shine package, we will give you a full refund!) 했으므로 정답은 (C)이다.

[어휘] period 기간 guarantee 보장

[04-06] BR
Questions 04-06 refer to the following advertisement.

W: Do you struggle with balancing your personal or business budget? It's a more common problem than you might think. **04That's why Roswell Community Center is offering classes to help you plan and stick to your budget.** The great thing about these classes is that they are sponsored by the local business council, so **05they are much cheaper than you would expect.** Register for **05a mere $5 per session** and be automatically entered into **06a drawing for a new car** from Roswell Auto!

struggle with ~로 고생하다 balance 균형을 유지하다 personal 개인의, 개인적인 budget 예산 common 흔한 stick to ~을 굳게 지키다, 방침을 고수하다 business council 기업 협의회 mere 겨우 ~의 enter into ~을 시작하다, ~에 들어가다 drawing 제비뽑기, 추첨

04-06은 다음 광고에 관한 문제입니다.
여: 개인적으로나 업무적으로 예산의 균형을 유지하느라 고생하고 계신가요? 그것은 여러분이 생각하는 것보다 더욱 흔한 문제입니다. **04그러한 이유로 Roswell 커뮤니티 센터가 여러분이 예산을 계획하고 지키도록 돕는 강좌들을 제공합니다.** 이러한 강좌들의 좋은 점은 지역 기업 협의회의 후원을 받는다는 것입니다. 따라서 **05여러분이 예상하는 것보다 훨씬 저렴합니다.** 한 과정당 단 5달러로 등록하시고 Roswell 자동차의 **06신차가 걸린 추첨 행사에 자동으로 응모하세요!**

04.

무엇을 위한 광고인가?
(A) 운전 강습
(B) 다가오는 취업 박람회
(C) 예산 계획 강좌
(D) 온라인 마케팅 세미나

[해설] 광고하는 제품이나 서비스에 대한 정보는 대개 광고문 전반부에 드러난다. 예산의 균형을 유지하느라 고생하고 있는지 묻는 것으로 시작한 이 광고문은 Roswell Community Center가 예산을 계획하고 지키도록 돕는 강좌들을 제공한다는(Roswell Community Center is offering classes to help you plan and stick to your budget.) 말로 광고하는 대상이 예산 계획과 관련한 강좌임을 밝혔다. 따라서 정답은 (C)이다.

[어휘] job fair 취업 박람회

05.

화자는 어떤 이점을 언급하는가?
(A) 새로운 주차장
(B) 편리한 일정
(C) 찾기 쉬운 위치
(D) 저렴한 등록비

[해설] 담화 중반, 지역 기업 협의회의 후원을 받아서 예상보다 훨씬 저렴하다고(they are much cheaper than you would expect) 한 후 구체적인 등록비를 제시했다. 즉, 저렴한 등록비가 이점이라는 말이므로 정답은 (D)이다.

paraphrasing they are much cheaper than you would expect. 여러분이 예상하는 것보다 훨씬 저렴하다 → an affordable registration fee 저렴한 등록비

[어휘] convenient 편리한 affordable (가격이) 알맞은 registration fee 등록비

06.

화자는 무엇이 콘테스트의 경품이라고 말하는가?
(A) 자동차
(B) 행사 티켓
(C) 태블릿 기기
(D) 경영 자문

[해설] 행사의 경품이 무엇인지 묻는 문제이다. 담화 마지막, 강좌에 등록하고 Roswell Auto의 신차가 걸린 경품 행사(a drawing for a new car)에 자동으로 응모하라고 한 것으로 보아 자동차가 경품으로 주어짐을 알 수 있으므로 정답은 (A)이다.

[어휘] consultation 상담, 자문

[07-09] AU

Questions 07-09 refer to the following advertisement.

M: If you own a business, then you must know the hassle of ⁰⁷**keeping track of your inventory**. You and your employees have to check inventory at the end of the business day. Sometimes it does not match your sales with the remaining inventory. Let go of the trouble and get Item Tracker! ⁰⁷, ⁰⁸**This revolutionary new software will sync with your registers and send you automatic updates on what you need to order.** ⁰⁹**For a limited time only, we are offering a free test trial.** Call today to experience the convenience of Item Tracker!

own 소유하다   hassle 귀찮은 일, 번거로운 상황   keep track of ~에 대해 계속 파악하다   inventory 재고(품), 재고 조사   business day 영업일   match ~와 맞다   remaining 남아 있는, 남은   let go of ~에서 손을 놓다   revolutionary 혁명의, 혁명적인   sync with ~와 동시에 움직이다   register (금전) 등록기   trial (최종 결정 전의) 시험, 실험   convenience 편리함

07-09는 다음 광고에 관한 문제입니다.

남: 당신이 사업체를 소유하고 있다면, ⁰⁷재고를 계속 파악하는 것의 번거로움을 틀림없이 알 것입니다. 당신과 직원들은 그날의 영업이 끝날 때 재고를 확인해야 합니다. 가끔은 매출과 남아 있는 재고가 맞지 않기도 합니다. 그런 번거로움에서 벗어나 Item Tracker를 구매하세요! ⁰⁷, ⁰⁸이 혁명적인 새 소프트웨어는 당신의 금전 등록기와 동기화되어 주문해야 하는 것을 자동으로 업데이트하여 보내 줍니다. ⁰⁹한정된 시간 동안만 무료 시험판을 제공합니다. 오늘 전화하셔서 Item Tracker의 편리함을 경험해 보세요!

07.

이 회사는 어떤 종류의 상품을 판매하는가?
(A) 금전 등록기
(B) 재고 관리 소프트웨어
(C) 포장 재료
(D) 보안 시스템

[해설] 앞서 재고 파악의 번거로움을 언급한 후, 이 혁명적인 새로운 소프트웨어가 금전 등록기와 동기화되어 주문해야 하는 것들을 자동으로 업데이트하여 보내 준다고(This revolutionary new software will sync with your registers and send you automatic updates on what you need to order.) 했습니다. 즉, 재고 관리 소프트웨어를 광고하고 있으므로 정답은 (B)이다.

08.

화자는 어떤 특징을 강조하는가?
(A) 제품의 가격이 저렴하다.
(B) 일체형 제품이다.
(C) 고객들이 긍정적인 후기를 작성했다.
(D) 최신 정보가 자동으로 제공된다.

[해설] 광고하고 있는 소프트웨어를 이용하면 주문해야 하는 것을 자동으로 업데이트하여 보내 준다는(This revolutionary new software will sync with your registers and send you automatic updates on what you need to order.) 내용으로 보아 정답은 (D)이다.

paraphrasing   send you automatic updates 자동으로 업데이트하여 보내 준다 → Updates are given automatically. 최신 정보가 자동으로 제공된다.

[어휘] feature 특징   emphasize 강조하다   affordable (가격이) 알맞은   all-in-one 일체형의   positive 긍정적인

09.

한정된 기간 동안 무엇이 무료로 제공될 예정인가?
(A) 연장된 보증 기간
(B) 배송
(C) 시험 사용 기간
(D) 설치

[해설] 담화 후반에 무료로 제공되는 서비스가 언급된다. 한정된 시간 동안 무료 시험판을 제공한다고(For a limited time only, we are offering a free test trial.) 했으므로 정답은 (C)이다.

[어휘] extended (기간 등을) 연장한   warranty 품질 보증   installation 설치

[10-12] US

Questions 10-12 refer to the following advertisement.

M: Everyone is so busy these days, and it's hard to find time to go out to restaurants. ¹⁰**You can enjoy high quality meals from places that you love with the Deals on Meals mobile app!** We have partnered with hundreds of local food establishments, so you can choose one from all kinds of food options. Type in the name of a food you want ¹¹and we will list restaurants in order of distance or price. ¹²All new members receive a 10% discount on their first order until the end of this week, so download Deals on Meals today and place an order while this offer still lasts!

quality 품질   partner 제휴하다   local 지역의   establishment 시설, 회사   choose 선택하다   type in 입력하다   in order of ~순으로   distance 거리

10-12는 다음 광고에 관한 문제입니다.

남: 요즘은 모두들 너무 바쁘고, 외식하러 갈 시간을 내기가 어렵습니다. ¹⁰**Deals on Meals 모바일 앱과 함께라면 여러분이 좋아하는 장소에서 높은 품질의 음식을 즐기실 수 있습니다!** 우리는 수백 개의 지역 음식점들과 제휴를 맺어서 모든 종류 중에서 원하시는 것을 선택하실 수 있습니다. 원하시는 음식의 이름을 입력하세요. ¹¹그러면 가격이나 거리순으로 음식점 목록을 제공합니다. ¹²모든 신규 회원은 이번 주까지 첫 주문 시 10% 할인을 받으실 수 있으니 Deals on Meals를 오늘 다운로드하셔서 혜택이 지속되는 동안 주문을 하세요!

10.

Deals on Meals는 무엇인가?
(A) 음식점
(B) 음식 배달 앱
(C) 식품점
(D) 출장 요리 회사

[해설] Deals on Meals는 광고되는 것의 이름인데 Deals on Meals

모바일 앱과 함께라면 좋아하는 장소에서 높은 품질의 음식을 즐길 수 있다고(You can enjoy high quality meals from places that you love with the Deals on Meals mobile app) 했으므로 음식 배달 앱인 것을 알 수 있다. 따라서 (B)가 정답이다.

11.

화자는 왜 "원하시는 음식의 이름을 입력하세요"라고 말하는가?
(A) 서비스 이용이 쉽다는 것을 강조하기 위해
(B) 지시를 하기 위해
(C) 더 많은 정보를 요청하기 위해
(D) 피드백을 요청하기 위해

[해설] 음식 배달 앱을 소개하며 "원하시는 음식의 이름을 입력하세요"라고 한 후 그러면 가격이나 거리순으로 음식점 목록을 제공한다고(Type in the name of a food you want and we will list restaurants in order of distance or price) 덧붙였다. 이는 이 어플이 사용하기 쉽다는 것을 말하기 위해 한 말임을 알 수 있으므로 (A)가 정답이다.

[어휘] stress 강조하다 easiness 쉬움 instruction 지시, 설명
solicit 요청하다

12.

청자들은 왜 빠르게 행동해야 하는가?
(A) 배달 시간이 오래 걸릴 수 있다.
(B) 일부 메뉴는 특정 시즌에만 가능하다.
(C) 할인이 곧 만료될 것이다.
(D) 좌석이 제한적이다.

[해설] 담화 후반부에 모든 신규 회원은 이번 주까지 첫 주문 시 10% 할인을 받을 수 있으니 Deals on Meals를 오늘 다운로드하여 혜택이 지속되는 동안 주문을 하라고(All new members receive a 10% discount on their first order until the end of this week, so download Deals on Meals today and place an order while this offer still lasts) 했다. 할인이 이번 주까지이니 서두르라는 의미이므로 (C)가 정답이다.

[어휘] aquickly 빠르게 seasonal 계절적인, 시즌 특유의 expire 만료되다 limited 제한된

[13-15] US

Questions 13-15 refer to the following advertisement.

M: Look and feel your best with help from **¹³Primrose Style**, located in the Scottsdale Mall. We provide a wide variety of services such as **¹³haircuts, hair straightening, dyeing**, and more. We have an experienced staff, and, **¹⁴just last month, we won the Chamber of Commerce's Best Business Award** in our category. Call us today at 555-4663 to book an appointment. **¹⁵You can save time by selecting a look in advance from our comprehensive photo gallery. You can find it on our Web site.**

dyeing 염색 experienced 경험이 있는, 능숙한 Chamber of Commerce 상공 회의소 book 예약하다 save 절약하다, 아끼다 in advance 사전에, 미리 comprehensive 포괄적인, 종합적인

13-15는 다음 광고에 관한 문제입니다.
남: Scottsdale Mall에 위치한 **¹³Primrose Style**의 도움으로 당신의 최고의 모습을 직접 보고 느껴 보세요. 저희는 **¹³커트, 스트레이트 파마, 염색** 등의 매우 다양한 서비스를 제공합니다. 숙련된 직원을 보유하고 있으며 **¹⁴지난달에는 우리 분야에서 상공 회의소의 최우수 기업 상을 받았습니다.** 오늘 555-4663으로 전화하셔서 예약하세요. **¹⁵저희의 통합 사진 갤러리에서 미리 머리 모양을 고르시면 시간을 절약하실 수 있습니다. 저희 웹사이트에서 찾아보시면 됩니다.**

13.

무엇에 관한 광고인가?
(A) 미용실
(B) 패션 스튜디오
(C) 치과
(D) 운동 시설

[해설] 화자가 언급한 상호명 Primrose Style과 커트, 스트레이트 파마, 염색(haircuts, hair straightening, dyeing) 등의 서비스를 제공한다는 말로 보아 미용실 광고임을 알 수 있으므로 정답은 (A)이다.

[어휘] facility 시설

14.

이 업체는 최근에 무엇을 했는가?
(A) 영업시간을 연장했다.
(B) 다른 지점을 열었다.
(C) 위치를 옮겼다.
(D) 상을 받았다.

[해설] 질문의 핵심 키워드 recently(최근에)가 담화 중반의 just last month(바로 지난달)를 바꿔 표현한 것임을 파악해야 한다. 지난달에 상공 회의소에서 주는 최우수 기업 상을 받았다고(just last month, we won the Chamber of Commerce's Best Business Award) 했으므로 정답은 (D)이다.

paraphrasing won the Chamber of Commerce's Best Business Award 상공 회의소 최우수 기업 상을 받았다 → received an award 상을 받았다

[어휘] extend 연장하다, 확대하다

15.

청자들은 왜 웹사이트를 방문할 것을 요청받는가?
(A) 직원들에 대해서 읽어보기 위해서
(B) 쿠폰을 다운받기 위해서
(C) 이미지를 보기 위해서
(D) 예약을 하기 위해서

[해설] 담화 후반 통합 사진 갤러리에서 미리 머리 모양을 고르면 시간을 절약할 수 있으니(You can save time by selecting a look in advance from our comprehensive photo gallery) 웹사이트에서 찾아보라고 했다. 즉, 웹사이트에서 다양한 머리 모양을 이미지로 확인할 수 있으므로 정답은 (C)이다.

paraphrasing selecting a look in advance from our comprehensive photo gallery 우리의 통합 사진 갤러리에서 미리 머리 모양을 고르기 → view some images 이미지를 보다

[16-18] US

Questions 16-18 refer to the following advertisement.

> W: Nothing captures a great memory like a good picture. For the best pictures, **[16]professionals and amateurs around the world agree that the CP Series digital camera is number one!** Not only is the CP Series easy to use, **[17]it is compatible with all kinds of accessories from all top-brand manufacturers.** **[18]Sign up for a free membership when you register your CP Series and get free access to monthly newsletters about the product and its many uses!**

capture 잡다, 표현하다 professional 전문가 agree 동의하다 compatible with ~와 호환이 되는 manufacturer 제조사 register 등록하다

16-18은 다음 광고에 관한 문제입니다.

여: 좋은 사진처럼 멋진 기억을 포착할 수 있는 것은 어느 것도 없습니다. 최고의 사진을 위해서 **[16]전세계의 전문가와 아마추어들은 CP 시리즈 디지털 카메라가 최고라는 것에 동의합니다.** CP 시리즈는 사용하기 쉬울 뿐만 아니라 **[17]모든 유명 제조사의 모든 액세서리들과 호환이 됩니다.** **[18]CP 시리즈를 등록하실 때 무료 회원에 가입하셔서 제품과 많은 사용에 관한 월간 소식지를 무료로 이용하세요.**

16.

무엇이 광고되고 있는가?
(A) 온라인 서비스
(B) 디지털 카메라
(C) 스마트폰 앱
(D) 노트북 컴퓨터

[해설] 광고되는 것은 담화의 초반부에서 확인할 수 있다. 전세계의 전문가와 아마추어들은 CP 시리즈 디지털 카메라가 최고라는 것에 동의한다며(professionals and amateurs around the world agree that the CP Series digital camera is number one) CP 시리즈 디지털 카메라에 대해 광고하고 있으므로 (B)가 정답이다.

17.

화자는 제품의 어떤 점을 강조하는가?
(A) 오래 지속되는 배터리
(B) 알맞은 가격
(C) 연장된 품질 보증 기간
(D) 호환성

[해설] 담화 중반부에 CP 시리즈는 사용하기 쉬울 뿐만 아니라 모든 유명 제조사의 모든 액세서리들과 호환이 된다고(it is compatible with all kinds of accessories from all top-brand manufacturers) 했으므로 (D)가 정답이다.

[paraphrasing] it is compatible with all kinds of accessories 모든 액세서리들과 호환이 된다 → Its compatibility 호환성

[어휘] highlight 강조하다 long-lasting 오래 지속되는 affordable (가격이) 알맞은 extended 연장된 warranty 품질 보증 compatibility 호환성

18.

화자에 따르면 회원은 무엇을 이용할 수 있는가?
(A) 지원 포럼
(B) 소프트웨어 업데이트
(C) 월간 소식지
(D) 교육용 비디오

[해설] 담화 후반부에 무료 회원에 가입하여 제품과 많은 사용에 관한 월간 소식지를 무료로 이용하라고(Sign up for a free membership when you register your CP Series and get free access to monthly newsletters about the product and its many uses) 했으므로 (C)가 정답이다.

[어휘] available 이용 가능한 instructional 교육의

[19-21] BR

Questions 19-21 refer to the following advertisement and price list.

Brand: Valencia	
Item	Special Offer
Ski Boots	$460 → $325
[19]Ski Goggles	$220 → **$105**
Ski Helmet	$100 → $85
Ski Bag	$45 → $35

> M: HB Sports has the area's widest selection of sporting goods for a variety of activities. This week, we're having a huge sale on Valencia ski equipment. For example, **[19]we've got plenty of goggles in stock**, and these are specially tinted to make it easier to see obstacles while you are skiing. **[20]Valencia only holds sales once every few years**, so you won't want to miss this opportunity. And, **[21]if you order at least two hundred dollars or more worth of HB Sports merchandise, you'll get delivery absolutely free.**

equipment 장비, 용품 plenty of 많은 goggle 보호 안경 in stock 비축되어, 재고로 specially 특별히 tint (약간의) 색깔을 넣다 obstacle 장애물 opportunity 기회 worth 가치 merchandise 물품, 상품 absolutely 전적으로, 틀림없이

19-21은 다음 광고와 가격표에 관한 문제입니다.

브랜드: Valencia	
품목	특별 가격
스키 부츠	460달러 → 325달러
[19]스키 고글	220달러 → **105달러**
스키 헬멧	100달러 → 85달러
스키 가방	45달러 → 35달러

남: HB Sports는 여러 가지 활동을 위한 스포츠 용품들을 이 지역에서 가장 다양하게 갖추고 있습니다. 이번 주, 저희는 Valencia 스키 용품을 크게 할인합니다. 예를 들면, **[19]상당히 많은 양의 고글을 확보해 두었는데**, 이것들은 스키를 타면서 장애물을 알아보기 쉽도록 특별히 색깔을 넣은 것들입니다. **[20]Valencia는 고작해야 몇 년에 한 번 세일 행사를 하므로** 이

번 기회를 놓치고 않으실 겁니다. 그리고, **²¹HB Sports**의 상품을 최소 **2백 달러 이상** 주문하시면 완전히 무료로 배송해 드립니다.

19.

시각 자료를 보시오. 화자가 언급한 품목의 가격은 얼마인가?
(A) 325달러
(B) 105달러
(C) 85달러
(D) 35달러

[해설] 스포츠 용품점에서 특정 브랜드의 스키 용품 할인 판매 행사를 광고하는 담화이다. 할인 판매 중인 상품의 한 예로, 상당히 많은 양의 고글을 확보해 두었다고(we've got plenty of goggles in stock) 했고, 이어서 해당 제품의 특징을 설명하고 있다. 시각 자료로 제공된 가격표에서 고글의 가격을 확인하면, 원래는 220달러였으나 105달러로 할인하여 판매되고 있음을 알 수 있으므로 정답은 (B)이다.

20.

화자는 Valencia 브랜드에 대해 무엇이라고 말하는가?
(A) HB Sports의 최신 상품이다.
(B) 판매 직원들이 선호한다.
(C) 전문적으로 스키를 타는 사람들이 추천한다.
(D) 좀처럼 가격을 할인하지 않는다.

[해설] 질문의 핵심 키워드 Valencia는 광고에서 할인 행사를 하는 제품의 브랜드 이름으로 언급되었다. 담화 후반부에서, Valencia는 고작해야 몇 년에 한 번 세일 행사를 한다고(only holds sales once every few years) 한 것으로 보아 이 브랜드는 좀처럼 가격을 할인하지 않음을 알 수 있으므로 정답은 (D)이다.

paraphrasing only holds sales once every few years 고작해야 몇 년에 한 번 세일 행사를 한다. → It is rarely offered at reduced prices. 좀처럼 가격을 할인하지 않는다.

[어휘] sales representative 판매 직원 professional 전문적인, 직업의 rarely 드물게, 좀처럼 ~하지 않는

21.

고객들은 어떻게 무료 배송을 받을 수 있는가?
(A) 고객 카드를 제시함으로써
(B) 일정 금액 이상 소비함으로써
(C) 세 가지 이상의 품목을 주문함으로써
(D) 우편물 수신자 명단에 등록함으로써

[해설] 무료 배송을 받는 방법은 광고 마지막에 나온다. HB Sports의 상품을 최소 2백 달러 이상 주문하면 완전히 무료로 배송해 준다고(if you order at least two hundred dollars or more worth of HB Sports merchandise, you'll get delivery absolutely free) 했으므로 일정 금액 이상 소비하면 무료로 배송됨을 알 수 있다. 따라서 정답은 (B)이다.

paraphrasing if you order at least two hundred dollars or more worth 최소 2백 달러치 이상 주문하면 → by spending more than a certain amount 특정 금액 이상 소비함으로써

[어휘] present 제시하다, 보여주다 loyalty card (상점의) 고객[포인트 적립] 카드 certain 특정한, 일정한 amount 금액

DAY 18

PART 3 호텔/식당 - 예약/요청 사항

출제 유형 01 예약

| 풀이 방법 해석 |

여: 안녕하세요, 저는 Lisa O'Connor입니다. 이번 주 금요일 저녁에 당신의 레스토랑에 6명 저녁 식사를 예약했습니다.
남: 안녕하세요, O'Connor 씨. 예약을 변경하셔야 하나요?
여: 네, 회사 회식을 위한 거였는데, 제 동료들 중 두 명이 급하게 업무차 출장을 가야 합니다. 그들은 21일이 되어야 돌아올 거라서, 그날에 저녁 식사를 해야 해요.
남: 알겠습니다. 그렇게 해 드리겠습니다. 그건 그렇고, 저희가 이제 온라인 예약 시스템이 있다는 것을 아셨나요? 저희 웹사이트에서 메뉴도 둘러보실 수 있습니다.

출제 유형 02 요청 사항

| 풀이 방법 해석 |

남: Miami Beach 호텔에 오신 것을 환영합니다. 무엇을 도와 드릴까요? 체크인을 하기 위해 오셨나요?
여: 아뇨, 저는 10층에 있는 비즈니스 라운지에서 저의 고객과 점심 식사를 하며 회의를 했습니다. 제 사무실로 돌아가는 길에, 제가 의자에 제 만년필을 두고 온 것을 알았습니다. 그것에 대해 종업원과 이야기를 했는데 모든 분실물은 발견되면 프런트 데스크로 바로 보내진다고 해서요. 그래서 왔습니다.
남: 알겠습니다. 잠시만요... 분실물 목록에 한 개의 펜만 있네요. 제가 사무실에서 그것을 가져올 테니 로비에 앉아서 기다려 주시겠어요?

연습 문제

01. (B) 02. (B) 03. (A) 04. (B) 05. (A) 06. (A)

01. BR-US

Where does the conversation **take place**?
(A) At a **hospital**   (B) At a **restaurant**

W: Would you like a table for two?
M: Actually, we will have more people join us soon, so we'll need a table for six.
W: Certainly. We don't have a table for six people available now, but if you'd like to have a seat at the bar I can offer you a drink.

대화는 어디서 이루어지는가?
(A) 병원에서   **(B) 레스토랑에서**

여: 두 명을 위한 자리를 원하시나요?
남: 사실, 곧 사람들이 더 합류할 거라서, 6명을 위한 테이블이 필요해요.
여: 알겠습니다. 지금은 6명을 위한 테이블이 없지만, 바에 앉길 원하시면 음료를 제공해 드리겠습니다.

02. (AU-BR)

Where does the **woman** most likely **work**?
(A) At a **museum** (B) At a **hotel**

> M: I have a reservation under the name of Mark Smith.
> W: Okay, you booked a standard room for three nights from today. You have been a regular customer for more than five years. Would you like to upgrade your room to an ocean-view executive room?

여자는 어디에서 일하겠는가?
(A) 박물관에서 **(B) 호텔에서**

남: 저는 Mark Smith 이름으로 예약을 했습니다.
여: 알겠습니다, 일반실을 오늘부터 3박 예약하셨네요. 5년 넘게 단골 고객이시군요. 바다가 보이는 고급 룸으로 업그레이드 하시겠어요?

03. (AU-US)

What are the speakers mainly **discussing**?
(A) An **annual event** (B) A summer **vacation**

> M: Hi Darlene, this is Joseph. I'm excited to hear that you decided to hold your annual company dinner at our conference center.
> W: Most of our employees were very satisfied with your facilities and foods. And I just want to know whether you can add more meat options to the dinner menu because there will be clients from countries in the Middle East.

화자들은 주로 무엇에 대해 이야기하는가?
(A) 연례 행사 (B) 여름 휴가

남: 안녕하세요 Darlene, 저 Joseph입니다. 우리 콘퍼런스 센터에서 당신의 연례 회사 저녁 만찬을 개최하기로 결정했다고 한 걸 듣고 기뻤어요.
여: 저희 직원들의 대부분이 당신의 시설과 음식에 매우 만족했어요. 그리고 중동 국가에서 오는 고객들이 있을 것이기 때문에 저녁 식사 메뉴에 고기 옵션을 더 추가해줄 수 있는지 알고 싶어요.

04. (US-US)

What does the **woman request**?
(A) A **group discount** (B) A **private space**

> W: Hi. I'm calling to make a reservation for eight people at 6:00 this Thursday.
> M: Wait a second while I check the availability. Do you have any other requests?
> W: Well, actually it will be a dinner with a client, so do you have a private room for us?

여자는 무엇을 요청하는가?
(A) 그룹 할인 **(B) 독립된 공간**

여: 안녕하세요. 이번 주 목요일 6시에 8명 예약하려고 전화했습니다.
남: 가능할지 확인해보는 동안 잠시만 기다려주세요. 다른 요청 사항이 있으신가요?
여: 음, 사실 고객과의 저녁 식사라서요, 저희를 위한 독립된 방이 있으신가요?

05. (US-AU)

What will the **woman** probably **do** next?
(A) **Have a snack** (B) **Visit business center**

> W: Nice to meet you, Dr. Smith. I think this hotel is very suitable for the conference.
> M: Yes, it is. It has a spacious business center with up-to-date equipment.
> W: Anyway, I will grab a bite before reviewing the slideshows for my presentation.

여자는 다음에 무엇을 하겠는가?
(A) 간식 먹기 (B) 비즈니스 센터 방문하기

여: 만나서 반갑습니다, Smith 박사님. 이 호텔은 학회에 매우 적합한 것 같아요.
남: 네, 그렇습니다. 최신 장비가 있는 넓은 비즈니스 센터가 있어요.
여: 그나저나, 저는 제 발표를 위한 슬라이드 쇼를 검토하기 전에 간단히 뭘 좀 먹을 거예요.

06. (US-BR)

Who most likely is the **man**?
(A) A **wait staff** member (B) A **general manager**

> M: Good evening. I'm Benjamin, your server today. Are you ready to order or do you need more time?
> W: I'm ready to order. I want a Caesar salad with Italian dressing, and seafood pasta with grilled squid. Would you please serve the salad dressing on the side?
> M: Sure, any drink for you?

남자는 누구이겠는가?
(A) 종업원 (B) 총 지배인

남: 좋은 저녁입니다. 저는 오늘 여러분의 서버인 Benjamin입니다. 주문할 준비가 되셨나요, 아니면 시간이 더 필요하신가요?
여: 저는 주문할 준비가 되었습니다. 저는 이탈리안 드레싱을 뿌린 시저 샐러드와 구운 오징어가 있는 해산물 파스타로 할게요. 샐러드 드레싱은 옆에 따로 가져다 주시겠어요?
남: 물론입니다. 음료는 어떤 걸로 하시겠어요?

paraphrasing 정답 1. (b) 2. (c) 3. (a) 4. (a) 5. (c) 6. (b)

실전 문제

01. (B)	02. (D)	03. (D)	04. (B)	05. (A)	06. (C)
07. (B)	08. (A)	09. (D)	10. (A)	11. (B)	12. (C)
13. (A)	14. (D)	15. (B)	16. (D)	17. (A)	18. (B)
19. (D)	20. (C)	21. (A)			

[01-03] US-BR

Questions 01-03 refer to the following conversation.

W: Excuse me, I wanted to get some work done on my laptop, but **⁰¹the battery is almost dead**. Do you have any seats near power outlets?
M: Sorry, but **⁰²our coffee shop only has a few outlets** and it looks like people are already using them.
W: I see... Is there any place nearby where I can plug in my laptop? I'm trying to work on an urgent project.
M: There's **⁰³a bookstore called Lines** about a block from here with seating and outlets. **⁰³You should try going there.**

dead (기계 등이) 작동을 안 하는   power outlet 전원 콘센트   nearby 인근에, 가까운 곳에   plug in 전원을 연결하다, ~의 플러그를 꽂다   urgent 긴급한   seating 좌석, 자리

01-03은 다음 대화에 관한 문제입니다.

여: 실례합니다, 제 노트북으로 작업을 좀 마치고 싶은데 ⁰¹배터리가 거의 다 되었어요. 전원 콘센트와 가까운 좌석이 있나요?
남: 죄송합니다만 ⁰²저희 커피숍은 콘센트가 몇 개밖에 없는데 이미 사람들이 사용 중인 것 같아요.
여: 그렇군요... 근처에 노트북을 전원에 연결할 수 있는 장소가 있나요? 급한 작업을 하려는 중이에요.
남: 여기서 한 블록 떨어진 곳에 ⁰³Lines라는 서점이 있는데 좌석과 콘센트가 있어요. ⁰³그곳으로 가보세요.

01.

여자에게는 어떤 문제가 있는가?
(A) 팀원들이 그녀의 도움을 필요로 한다.
(B) 노트북 컴퓨터의 배터리 잔량이 적다.
(C) 전원 코드가 필요하다.
(D) 영수증을 잃어버렸다.

[해설] 여자의 문제를 묻는 문제로, 대화 초반 여자가 노트북으로 작업을 하고 싶은데 배터리가 거의 다 되었다며(the battery is almost dead) 전원 콘센트와 가까운 좌석을 찾고 있는 것으로 보아 정답은 (B)이다.

paraphrasing   battery is almost dead 배터리가 거의 다 되었다 → battery is low 배터리 잔량이 적다

02.

어디에서 이루어지는 대화인가?
(A) 컴퓨터 수리점에서
(B) 전자제품 매장에서
(C) 서점에서
(D) 카페에서

[해설] 대화의 장소를 묻는 문제로, 전원 콘센트와 가까운 좌석이 있냐는 여자의 물음에 남자가 자신의 커피숍은 콘센트가 몇 개밖에 없는데(our coffee shop only has a few outlets) 이미 사람들이 사용 중인 것 같다고 말했다. 즉, 커피숍에서 노트북을 이용하려는 여자와 커피숍 직원인 남자의 대화이므로 정답은 (D)이다.

paraphrasing   coffee shop 커피숍 → a café 카페

[어휘] repair 수리, 수선   electronics 전자제품

03.

남자는 여자에게 무엇을 하라고 말하는가?
(A) 환불을 요청하기
(B) 나중에 다시 오기
(C) 새로운 커피 조합을 맛보기
(D) 다른 업체로 가기

[해설] 남자가 여자에게 제안한 것을 묻는 문제로, 대화 후반에 단서가 제시된다. 남자는 Lines라는 서점(a bookstore called Lines)에 좌석과 콘센트가 갖춰져 있다고 그곳에 가보라고(You should try going there) 했다. 즉, 다른 가게에 가보라는 말이므로 정답은 (D)이다.

[어휘] ask for ~를 요청하다

[04-06] US-BR-AU

Questions 04-06 refer to the following conversation with three speakers.

M1: Hello, thanks for coming to the Woodbridge Hotel. I'm the head manager, and this is my assistant, Mike. So, you'd like to hold an event here?
W: That's right. **⁰⁴I think your conference room would be the perfect place for my clients' wedding on May 9**. They expect about 200 people to come.
M2: As you may know, **⁰⁴we have a lot of experience hosting wedding parties.** Our conference room is quite lovely.
W: Good. A lot of the people will be coming from far away and will probably need a place to stay. **⁰⁵Do you have available rooms?**
M1: I'll double check, but we usually have plenty of empty rooms at that time of year.
M2: Also, **⁰⁶we don't charge our guests to park here.**

assistant 조수, 보조원   hold an event 행사를 치르다   expect 기대하다, 예상하다   experience 경험   host (행사를) 주최하다   far away 멀리 떨어져   double check 재확인하다   plenty of 많은   empty 비어 있는, 빈   charge (요금을) 청구하다

04-06은 다음 세 명의 대화에 관한 문제입니다.

남1: 안녕하세요, Woodbridge 호텔에 와주셔서 감사합니다. 저는 수석 매니저이고, 이쪽은 제 비서인 Mike입니다. 그러니까, 여기서 행사를 치르시려고요?
여: 맞습니다. ⁰⁴이곳 콘퍼런스룸이 5월 9일 제 고객의 결혼식을 위한 최적의 장소라고 생각해요. 약 200명이 올 것으로 예상됩니다.
남2: 아시다시피 ⁰⁴저희는 결혼식 파티를 주최한 경험이 많습니다. 저희 콘퍼런스룸은 매우 아름다워요.
여: 좋네요. 많은 사람들이 멀리서 올 예정이어서 아마도 머무를 장소가 필요할 거예요. ⁰⁵이용 가능한 객실이 있나요?
남1: 제가 재확인하겠지만 저희는 보통 이맘때 빈 방이 많아요.
남2: 또한 ⁰⁶투숙객들에게 주차 요금을 받지 않아요.

04.

어떤 종류의 행사가 기획되고 있는가?
(A) 회사 기념일

DAY 18   185

(B) 결혼식
(C) 교육 세미나
(D) 무역 박람회

[해설] 화자들의 대화 중에 언급되는 행사에 집중하며 들어야 한다. 호텔의 시설을 이용하려는 여자와 호텔 측 직원으로 보이는 두 남자의 대화로, 여자가 고객의 결혼식(my clients' wedding)을 언급한 점과 남자가 결혼식 파티를 주최한 경험이 많다고(we have a lot of experience hosting wedding parties) 말한 점 등으로 볼 때 결혼식을 기획하고 있음을 알 수 있으므로 (B)가 정답이다.

05.

여자는 무엇에 대해 물어보는가?
(A) 객실 이용 가능 여부
(B) 인터넷 접속
(C) 교통편
(D) 주최 비용

[해설] 대화 후반에 여자의 질문이 나온다. 앞서 여자는 이 호텔의 콘퍼런스룸에서 고객의 결혼식을 진행하고자 하는 의사를 밝혔고, 그 세부 사항으로 하객의 인원수 및 숙박 장소의 필요성을 언급하면서 이용 가능한 객실이 있는지(Do you have available rooms?) 물었다. 따라서 정답은 (A)이다.

[어휘] availability 이용 가능성   access 접속, 접근   fee 수수료

06.

이 호텔은 무엇을 무료로 제공하는가?
(A) 행사 좌석
(B) 음식 선택 사항
(C) 투숙객 주차
(D) 오락거리

[해설] 질문의 핵심 키워드는 for free(무료로)다. 따라서 대화에서 무료로 제공되는 서비스가 언급된 곳을 찾아보면, 대화 마지막 남자2가 투숙객들에게 주차 요금을 받지 않는다고(we don't charge our guests to park here) 했다. 따라서 정답은 (C)이다.

paraphrasing don't charge 요금을 받지 않는다 → for free 무료로

[07-09] US-AU

Questions 07-09 refer to the following conversation.

W: Your idea to hold a karaoke hour after the dinner rush really seems to be paying off. **⁰⁷Our sales are up, especially for beverages and desserts.**
M: Yeah, it's really convenient just letting people sign up. **⁰⁸I don't like having to work out schedules and contracts with bands.**
W: **⁰⁷I was also thinking of expanding our appetizer menu**. I can think of ⁰⁹several dishes that would probably sell really well during the karaoke hour.
M: That could be a good idea. I'd like to try them before adding them to the menu.
W: Okay, ⁰⁹I'll bring in some samples tomorrow.

rush 혼잡, 북적거림   pay off 성공하다, 성과를 올리다   especially 특별히   convenient 편리한, 간편한   sign up 참가

하다, 가입하다   work out ~을 해결하다, ~을 계획해 내다   contract 계약   expand 확대하다   appetizer 전채 요리   dish 요리   add 추가하다   bring in 들여오다, 가져오다

07-09는 다음 대화에 관한 문제입니다.

여: 바쁜 저녁 식사 시간대 이후에 노래방 시간을 열자는 당신의 아이디어가 결실을 보이는 것 같아요. ⁰⁷특히 음료와 디저트의 매출이 상승했어요.
남: 맞아요, 그냥 사람들이 참가하게만 하면 되니 정말 편리해요. ⁰⁸저는 밴드와 일정을 잡고 계약을 조율해야 하는 걸 안 좋아해요.
여: ⁰⁷저는 우리 에피타이저 메뉴를 확대하는 것도 생각하고 있었어요. 아마도 노래방 시간 동안 아주 잘 팔릴 ⁰⁹요리 몇 가지를 생각해낼 수 있어요.
남: 그거 좋은 생각이에요. 그것들을 메뉴에 추가하기 전에 한번 먹어보고 싶어요.
여: 알겠어요, ⁰⁹내일 샘플을 가져올게요.

07.

화자들은 어디에서 일할 것 같은가?
(A) 극장에서
(B) 식당에서
(C) 슈퍼마켓에서
(D) 음반 가게에서

[해설] 주로 여자의 대사에 두 사람의 근무 장소를 유추할 수 있는 단서들이 나온다. 음료와 디저트의 매출이 상승했다는(Our sales are up, especially for beverages and desserts.) 말과 에피타이저 메뉴 확대를 생각하고 있다는(I was also thinking of expanding our appetizer menu) 말에서 화자들이 식당에서 일함을 알 수 있으므로 정답은 (B)이다.

08.

남자는 무엇을 하는 것을 좋아하지 않는가?
(A) 밴드의 일정을 짜기
(B) 사업 계약을 맺기
(C) 후보자들을 면접하기
(D) 무대에서 공연하기

[해설] 남자는 노래방 시간에는 그냥 사람들이 참가하게만 하면 되니 편리하다며, 자신은 밴드와 일정을 잡고 계약을 조율해야 하는 걸 안 좋아한다고(I don't like having to work out schedules and contracts with bands.) 했다. 따라서 (A)가 정답이다.

paraphrasing work out schedules and contracts with bands 밴드와 일정을 세우고 계약을 조율하다 → organizing band schedules 밴드의 일정을 짜기

[어휘] organize 조직하다, 준비하다   candidate 후보자   perform 공연하다

09.

여자는 내일 무엇을 가져오겠다고 말하는가?
(A) 마이크
(B) 소프트웨어 프로그램
(C) 요리책
(D) 음식 샘플

[해설] 대화에서 질문의 키워드 tomorrow가 언급되는 부분에 집중한다. 대화 마지막, 여자가 내일 샘플을 가져오겠다고(I'll bring in some samples tomorrow) 했는데, 이 샘플은 앞서 언급한 아주 잘 팔릴 요리 몇 가지(several dishes)의 샘플을 의미하므로 정답은 (D)이다.

[어휘] recipe 조리[요리]법

[10-12] US-US

Questions 10-12 refer to the following conversation.

> M: Wow, ¹⁰your restaurant is really packed. I should have made a reservation. ¹⁰Can we get a table for four?
> W: Yes, but you'll have to wait a bit. ¹⁰It could take up to a half an hour before we can seat you.
> M: That's okay, ¹¹we're still waiting for two of our friends. I guess we should eat quickly so you can close on time.
> W: There's no need to worry about that. ¹²Now that we're under new management, we don't close until 11 P.M., so you have plenty of time to enjoy your meal.

packed (특히 사람들이) 꽉 들어찬   up to (수, 정도) ~까지   seat 앉히다   I guess ~일 것 같다   on time 정각에   now that ~이므로, ~이기 때문에   management 경영진   plenty of 많은   meal 식사

10-12는 다음 대화에 관한 문제입니다.

남: 우와, ¹⁰식당에 정말 사람이 많군요. 예약을 할 걸 그랬어요. ¹⁰네 명이 앉을 테이블이 있나요?
여: 네, 하지만 조금 기다리셔야 해요. ¹⁰자리를 안내해 드리기 전까지 최대 30분이 걸릴 수 있어요.
남: 그 정도는 괜찮아요. ¹¹아직 친구 두 명을 기다리고 있는 중이거든요. 제시간에 문을 닫으실 수 있도록 저희가 빨리 먹어야 할 것 같네요.
여: 그 점은 걱정 안 하셔도 돼요. ¹²경영진이 새로 바뀌었기 때문에 밤 11시까지 영업을 해요. 그러니 식사를 즐기실 시간은 충분하답니다.

10.

남자는 무엇을 하기를 원하는가?
(A) 식당에서 식사하기
(B) 발레파킹 이용하기
(C) 식사 준비하기
(D) 공원 방문하기

[해설] 식당에 사람이 아주 많다며 네 명이 앉을 테이블이 있는지(Can we get a table for four?) 묻는 남자의 질문과 최대 30분까지 기다려야 한다는(It could take up to a half an hour before we can seat you) 여자의 답변으로 보아 남자는 식사를 위해 식당에 온 것이므로 정답은 (A)이다.

11.

남자는 여자에게 어떤 정보를 말하는가?
(A) 차가 입구 쪽에 주차되어 있다.
(B) 일행이 오고 있는 중이다.
(C) 칸막이 있는 좌석을 선호한다.
(D) 예약을 했다.

[해설] 남자가 여자에게 하는 말에 집중한다. 자리를 안내받기까지 최대 30분이 소요된다는 여자의 말에 남자가 괜찮다며 아직 친구 두 명을 기다리고 있다고(we're still waiting for two of our friends) 했다. 즉, 일행 중 일부가 지금 오고 있는 중이라는 말이므로 정답은 (B)이다.

paraphrasing we're still waiting for two of our friends 아직 친구 두 명을 기다리고 있는 중이다 → His group is on the way. 일행이 오고 있는 중이다.

[어휘] out front (건물의) 입구 쪽에   on the way 도중에, 오는 중인   prefer 선호하다   booth (칸막이를 한) 작은 공간, 부스

12.

여자는 남자에게 무엇에 대해 알리는가?
(A) 오늘의 특별 요리
(B) 회원 할인
(C) 영업 시간 변경
(D) 업데이트된 회사 정책

[해설] 여자가 남자에게 하는 말에 집중한다. 대화 후반, 여자는 경영진이 새로 바뀌었기 때문에 밤 11시까지 영업을 한다고(Now that we're under new management, we don't close until 11 P.M.) 했다. 즉, 변경된 영업 시간에 대해 알리고 있으므로 정답은 (C)이다.

[13-15] US-AU-BR

Questions 13-15 refer to the following conversation with three speakers.

> W1: Hello, ¹³I have a reservation for six people.
> M: What name would it be listed under?
> W1: It's under Paula Sherman, and it's for seven o'clock.
> M: I don't see your name on our reservation list, Ms. Sherman.
> W1: Oh, really? I called today right after lunch.
> M: Hmm... Kimberly probably took the call. ¹⁴Kimberly, Ms. Sherman ¹³booked a table this afternoon, but ¹⁴it isn't on our reservation list.
> W2: Oh, ¹⁴I must have forgotten to write it down. I'm very sorry.
> M: ¹⁵If you can wait here for a while, Ms. Sherman, I'll seat you at the next available table.

list 명단에 포함시키다   probably 아마   forget 잊다

13-15은 다음 세 명의 대화에 관한 문제입니다.

여1: 안녕하세요. ¹³6명 자리를 예약을 했는데요.
남: 어느 분 성함으로 예약하셨나요?
여1: Paula Sherman으로요. 그리고 7시로 예약했어요.
남: 예약자 명단에 당신의 이름이 보이지 않네요, Sherman 씨.
여1: 아, 정말요? 제가 오늘 점심시간 직후에 전화했어요.
남: 음... 아마도 Kimberly가 전화를 받은 것 같네요. ¹⁴Kimberly, Sherman 씨가 오늘 오후에 ¹³테이블을 예약했는데 ¹⁴우리 예약자 명단에 없어요.
여2: 아, ¹⁴제가 적어 두는 걸 잊은 게 분명해요. 정말 죄송합니다.
남: ¹⁵Sherman 씨, 여기서 잠시 기다리시면 다음 테이블이 준비되는 대로 안내해 드리겠습니다.

13.
남자는 누구일 것 같은가?
(A) 식당 직원
(B) 호텔 소유주
(C) 콜센터 직원
(D) 백화점 매니저

[해설] 여자가 6명 자리를 예약했다는(I have a reservation for six people) 말로 대화가 시작된 후 남자가 예약자 명단에서 여자의 이름을 찾지 못하는 상황이 이어지고, 대화 중반에 테이블을 예약했다는(booked a table) 표현으로 보아 식당에서 손님과 직원이 나누는 대화임을 알 수 있다. 즉, 남자는 식당의 직원이므로 정답은 (A)이다.

14.
Kimberly는 무엇에 대해 사과하는가?
(A) 고객에게 금액을 많이 청구한 것
(B) 일정보다 직장에 늦게 도착한 것
(C) 주문한 음식을 잘못 가져온 것
(D) 예약 내용을 기록하는 것을 잊은 것

[해설] 3인의 화자 중 한 명이 사과한 이유를 묻는 문제로, 일단 Kimberly가 누구인지 파악해야 한다. 대화 중반 남자가 동료 직원으로 보이는 Kimberly의 이름을 부르며 여자 손님의 이름이 예약자 명단에 없다고(it isn't on our reservation list) 하자 이에 여자2가 대답했으므로 여자2가 Kimberly이다. 여자2가 자신이 적어 두는 걸 잊은 게 분명하다며 사과하는(I must have forgotten to write it down. I'm very sorry.) 것으로 보아 정답은 (D)이다.

`paraphrasing` write it down 적어 두다 → record 기록하다

[어휘] overcharge (금액을) 많이 청구하다

15.
남자는 Sherman 씨에게 무엇을 하라고 하는가?
(A) 환불 받기
(B) 그곳에서 기다리기
(C) Kimberly에게 얘기하기
(D) 계산하기

[해설] 대화 마지막에서 남자는 Ms. Sherman에게 여기서 잠시 기다리면(If you can wait here for a while) 자리가 나는 대로 안내해 주겠다고 했다. 따라서 정답은 (B)이다.

[16-18] BR-US
Questions 16-18 refer to the following conversation.

W: Did you enjoy your stay here at the Burton Hotel, Mr. Palos?
M: Yes, and ¹⁶**I wanted to thank you again for changing my checkout time from 11 A.M. to noon.**
W: I was happy to help. I hope you'll stay with us again soon.
M: I will. ¹⁷**My company is purchasing a new manufacturing facility here in Melbourne, so I'll be back to inspect it next month.**
W: In that case, you should sign up for our loyalty program. It takes only a few minutes to apply.
M: That's a good idea, since I'll probably stay here whenever I'm in Melbourne.
W: ¹⁸**Here's the form to fill out.** If you have any questions, just let me know.
M: All right.

manufacturing facility 생산 시설 inspect 점검[검사]하다
in that case 그런 경우에는, 그렇다면 apply 신청하다, 지원하다
fill out 기입하다, 작성하다

16-18은 다음 대화에 관한 문제입니다.
여: 저희 Burton 호텔에서 즐거운 시간 보내셨나요, Palos 씨?
남: 네, 그리고 ¹⁶제 체크아웃 시간을 오전 11시에서 정오로 바꿔 주신 것 다시 한번 감사드려요.
여: 도움 드릴 수 있어서 기뻤어요. 조만간 또 여기서 머물게 되시길 바랍니다.
남: 그러려고요. ¹⁷저희 회사가 여기 멜버른의 생산 시설을 새로 매입하려고 해요. 그래서 다음 달에 그곳을 조사하러 다시 올 거예요.
여: 그렇다면, 저희 고객 보상 프로그램에 가입하세요. 신청하는 데 몇 분 안 걸려요.
남: 좋은 생각이에요. 제가 멜버른에 올 때마다 아마도 여기서 묵을 테니까요.
여: ¹⁸여기 작성하실 양식입니다. 질문 있으시면 제게 알려주세요.
남: 알겠어요.

16.
남자는 왜 여자에게 고마워하는가?
(A) 근처의 업체를 추천해 주었다.
(B) 자신을 더 큰 방으로 옮겨 주었다.
(C) 청구서의 요금을 면제해 주었다.
(D) 체크아웃 시간을 연장해 주었다.

[해설] 호텔에서 체크아웃하는 남자 손님과 여자 직원의 대화이다. 대화 전반부 남자가 여자에게 체크아웃 시간을 오전 11시에서 정오로 바꿔 주어서 고맙다는(I wanted to thank you again for changing my checkout time from 11 A.M. to noon.) 인사를 하는 것으로 보아 여자가 남자의 체크아웃 시간을 늦춰 주었음을 알 수 있으므로 정답은 (D)이다.

`paraphrasing` changing my checkout time from 11 A.M. to noon. 나의 체크아웃 시간을 오전 11시에서 정오로 바꿔 준 것 → extended his checkout time 체크아웃 시간을 연장해 주었다

[어휘] nearby 근처의, 인근의 business (회사, 가게, 공장 같은) 사업체 waive (권리 등을) 포기하다 fee 요금, 수수료 bill 청구서 extend 연장하다

17.
남자는 다음 달에 멜버른에서 무엇을 할 계획인가?
(A) 조사를 실시하기
(B) 계약을 협상하기
(C) 가족을 방문하기
(D) 취업 면접을 하기

[해설] 핵심 키워드 next month는 대화 중반 남자의 말에서 언급된다. 남자의 회사가 이 지역의 생산 시설을 새로 매입할 예정이어서 다음 달에 조사차 다시 온다고(My company is purchasing a new manufacturing facility here in Melbourne, so I'll be back to inspect it next month.) 했다. 즉, 남자는 다음 달에 조사를 실시할 계획이므로 정답은 (A)이다.

paraphrasing inspect 조사하다 → Conduct an inspection 조사를 실시하기

[어휘] conduct (특정한 활동을) 하다 inspection 점검, 검사 negotiate 협상하다

18.

여자는 남자에게 무엇을 주는가?
(A) 방 열쇠
(B) 신청서
(C) 셔틀버스 시간표
(D) 시내 지도

[해설] 대화 마지막에 정답의 단서가 있다. 앞으로도 이 호텔을 이용할 의사가 있다는 것을 밝힌 남자에게 여자가 호텔의 고객 보상 프로그램에 가입할 것을 권하고, 남자가 이를 수락하자 여자가 작성할 양식을 건넨다(Here's the form to fill out). 즉, 여자가 남자에게 해당 프로그램 등록을 위한 신청서를 준 것이므로 정답은 (B)이다.

[19-21] US-BR

Questions 19-21 refer to the following conversation and form.

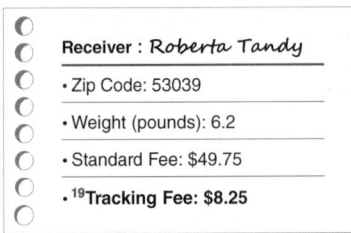

M: Good afternoon. I'd like to send this package domestically.
W: All right. It looks like you've already filled out the form.
M: Yes. ¹⁹**And I just want to make sure that eight twenty-five is correct.**
W: Yes, as we've recently raised the price for that.
M: All right. Now, ²⁰**the package contains some glassware, which could break easily.**
W: That's fine. I'll put a special sticker on it so that people know that they should handle it carefully.
M: Thank you. I guess that's everything I need.
W: Okay, and on your way out, you'll see a table with ²¹**some brochures outlining our new services. Don't forget to take some with you.**

domestically 국내에서 fill out 기입하다, 작성하다 form 서식 correct 맞는, 정확한 recently 최근에 raise 올리다, 인상하다 contain 포함하다 glassware 유리 제품 handle 처리하다, 다루다 outline 개요를 서술하다 zip code 우편번호 standard 일반적인, 보통의 fee 수수료 tracking 추적

19-21은 다음 대화와 서식에 관한 문제입니다.

> 수신자 : *Roberta Tandy*
> • 우편번호: 53039
> • 무게 (파운드): 6.2
> • 일반 요금: 49.75달러
> • ¹⁹추적 요금: 8.25달러

남: 안녕하세요. 이 소포를 국내에 보내고 싶습니다.
여: 알겠습니다. 이미 서식을 작성하신 것 같군요.
남: 네. ¹⁹**그리고 8달러 25센트가 맞는지 확인하고 싶어요.**
여: 네, 저희가 최근에 가격을 인상한 대로네요.
남: 좋습니다. 그런데, ²⁰**이 소포에 유리 제품이 들어 있어서 쉽게 깨질 수 있어요.**
여: 괜찮습니다. 사람들이 그것을 주의 깊게 취급해야 한다는 것을 알 수 있도록 거기에 특별 스티커를 붙이겠습니다.
남: 고맙습니다. 제게 필요한 건 그게 다인 것 같아요.
여: 알겠습니다. 그리고 나가시는 길에 테이블을 보시면 ²¹**저희의 새 서비스를 간략히 설명해놓은 브로셔가 있어요. 잊지 말고 가져가세요.**

19.

시각 자료를 보시오. 남자는 어떤 정보에 대해 문의하는가?
(A) 우편번호
(B) 무게
(C) 일반 요금
(D) 추적 요금

[해설] 소포를 부치려고 하는 남자와 직원인 여자가 나누는 대화이다. 시각 자료에는 받는 사람의 이름과 우편번호 및 소포의 무게와 요금 등이 제시되어 있으므로 이와 관련한 내용이 대화에 언급될 것임을 예상할 수 있다. 대화 전반부에 남자가 8달러 25센트가 맞는지 확인하고 싶다(I just want to make sure that eight twenty-five is correct) 했는데 이 금액은 서식의 마지막 항목인 Tracking fee(추적 요금)의 금액과 일치한다. 따라서 남자가 문의하는 정보는 추적 요금이므로 정답은 (D)이다.

20.

남자는 소포에 대해 무엇이라고 언급하는가?
(A) 서명이 필요할 것이다.
(B) 서둘러 도착해야 한다.
(C) 깨지기 쉬운 물건이 들어 있다.
(D) 해외로 보내질 것이다.

[해설] 대화 중반 남자는 자신이 부치려고 하는 소포에 유리 제품이 들어 있어서 쉽게 깨질 수 있다고(the package contains some glassware, which could break easily) 말했다. 이를 fragile items(깨지기 쉬운 물건)로 바꿔 표현한 (C)가 정답이다.

paraphrasing some glassware, which could break easily 쉽게 깨질 수 있는 유리 제품 → fragile items 깨지기 쉬운 물건

[어휘] signature 사인, 서명 in a hurry 서둘러, 급히 fragile 깨지기 쉬운 overseas 해외로, 국외로

21.

여자는 남자에게 무엇을 할 것을 상기시키는가?
(A) 홍보 자료를 가져가기

(B) 규정을 검토하기
(C) 이 업체의 웹사이트를 방문하기
(D) 기록을 위해 영수증을 보관하기

[해설] 여자가 남자에게 상기시키는 것을 묻는 문제로, 대화 마지막 여자의 말에 정답의 단서가 있다. 여자가 용무를 마친 남자에게 나가는 길에 테이블을 보면 새 서비스를 소개하는 브로셔(some brochures outlining our new services)가 있으니 잊지 말고 가져가라고(Don't forget to take some with you.) 당부하는데, 이는 새로운 서비스를 홍보하는 자료를 가져가라는 것이므로 정답은 (A)이다.

`paraphrasing` brochures outlining our new services 우리의 새 서비스를 간략히 설명하는 브로셔 → promotional materials 홍보 자료

[어휘] promotional 홍보의, 판촉의 material 자료 regulations 규정

PART 4 관광 정보(tour information) / 소개(introduction)

출제 유형 01 관광 정보(tour information)
| 풀이 방법 해석 |

여: 안녕하세요 여러분. Pennington 사탕 공장 견학에 오신 것을 환영합니다! 제 이름은 Lucy이고 오늘 여러분의 투어 가이드가 될 것입니다. 저를 따라 시설 곳곳을 다니면서, 여러분이 즐기는 맛있는 사탕이 어떻게 만들어지는지 보고 배울 수 있을 겁니다. 마지막에는, 기념품점에 가실 것을 매우 추천합니다. 흔하지 않은 모양으로 나오는 사탕을 그곳에서 판매합니다. 무언가를 사시면, 10퍼센트 할인을 위해 투어 티켓의 일부를 보여주는 것을 잊지 마세요. 이제, 생산 작업장에 들어가기 전에, 세균이 퍼지는 것을 막기 위하여 이 마스크를 착용해 주세요.

출제 유형 02 소개(introduction)
| 풀이 방법 해석 |

남: 안녕하세요, Mayfield Heights 마케팅 콘퍼런스에 와주셔서 감사합니다. 저희의 첫 번째 연사인 Robert Cantu 씨를 만나는 것에 대해 여러분들도 저만큼 흥분될 것이라 확신합니다. 그는 20년 넘게 유명한 광고 제작자였습니다. 오늘, 그는 색과 패턴의 중요성과 광고를 만들 때 어떻게 그것들을 효과적으로 이용하는지에 대해 강연을 할 겁니다. 그의 강연은 한 시간 가량 진행될 것인데, 이후 질의응답을 위해 시간을 조금 남겨둘 것입니다. 그러므로, 만약 Cantu 씨에게 질문이 있으시면, 그의 강연이 끝난 후를 위해서 남겨 두세요. 더 이상 지체하지 않고, Robert Cantu 씨를 소개합니다!

연습 문제
01. (B)　02. (A)　03. (A)　04. (B)　05. (A)　06. (B)

01. US
What does the **speaker recommend**?
(A) **Taking** a **taxi**　(B) **Wearing comfortable shoes**

W: Hello, everyone. I will briefly talk about today's schedule. We are going to visit downtown Milan and spend the whole afternoon, including one hour of free time. We will move around tourist attractions mostly by foot, so I suggest that you wear sneakers or running shoes and bring your hats and sunglasses.

화자는 무엇을 제안하는가?
(A) 택시를 타기　**(B) 편한 신발을 신기**

관광 정보
여: 안녕하세요, 여러분. 오늘 일정에 대해 간략히 말씀드리겠습니다. 우리는 밀라노의 시내를 방문하여 한 시간의 자유 시간을 포함해서 오후 전체를 보낼 것입니다. 관광 명소를 주로 걸어서 돌아다닐 것이므로, 운동화나 러닝화를 신고 모자와 선글라스를 가지고 올 것을 제안드립니다.

02. BR
Where is the talk **taking place**?
(A) On a **bus**　(B) On a **boat**

M: Welcome on board Tiger City Bus Tour. I'm your driver and guide. Our company operates two city tour bus lines. This is line A. We are going through the city from north to south. The other one is from east to west. This tour is three hours long. We will stop at the famous cafe, Wong's Tea Café, to take a break.

담화는 어디에서 이루어지고 있는가?
(A) 버스에서　(B) 배에서

관광 정보
남: Tiger 시티 버스 투어에 탑승하신 것을 환영합니다. 저는 여러분의 운전기사이자 가이드입니다. 저희 회사는 두 개의 시티 투어 버스 노선을 운영합니다. 이건 A노선입니다. 우리는 도시를 북쪽에서 남쪽으로 통과해 갈 것입니다. 또 다른 노선은 동쪽에서 서쪽으로 가는 것입니다. 이 투어는 세 시간이 걸립니다. 우리는 유명한 카페인 Wong's Tea Café에 휴식을 취하기 위해 정차할 것입니다.

03. BR
What will the **listeners do next**?
(A) **Go** to the **testing room**　(B) **Watch** a **performance**

W: Welcome to Vernon Coffee Factory. First, I wanted to show you a short video about how the coffee beans are turned into a product from harvest to packaging. But there is a problem with the screen now and it will be ready in 15 minutes. Why don't we taste a cup of freshly brewed coffee at our taste testing room? Let's move upstairs.

청자들은 다음에 무엇을 할 것인가?
(A) 시음실로 가기　(B) 공연 보기

관광 정보
여: Vernon 커피 공장에 오신 것을 환영합니다. 우선, 커피콩이 수확에서부터 포장까지 어떻게 제품이 되는지를 보여주는 짧은 영상을 보여드리고 싶습니다. 하지만 지금 스크린에 문제가 있어서 15분 후에 준비될 것입니다. 저희의 맛 시음실에서 신선하게 내린 커피 한잔을 맛보는 게 어떨까요? 위층으로 올라가시죠.

04. AU

Who is Dr. **Hopkins**?
(A) A **yoga instructor**   (B) A **nutritionist**

> M: Welcome to What's New in Finance on TNBC Radio. Today, we will meet Dr. Emilia Hopkins, professor of nutritional science at Johnstown College, and she will share useful tips on easy ways to manage your daily diets. If you want to have a brief consultation on your eating habits, please call us at 234-872-4569.

Hopkins 박사는 누구인가?
(A) 요가 강사   **(B)** 영양사

관광 정보
남: TNBC 라디오의 What's New in Finance에 오신 것을 환영합니다. 오늘, 우리는 Johnstown 대학의 영양 과학 교수인 Emilia Hopkins 박사를 만날 것이고, 그녀는 여러분의 매일의 식단을 관리하는 쉬운 방법에 대한 유용한 조언을 해주실 것입니다. 여러분의 식습관에 대한 간단한 상담을 원하시면, 234-872-4569로 저희에게 전화해 주세요.

05. US

What will **happen after** the **presentation**?
(A) Mr. **Haywood** will **answer questions**.
(B) A **reception** will be held.

> W: Thanks for coming to the tax seminar. Before we start, I want to introduce our instructor, Mark Haywood. He is a chief tax accountant at Jonathan Accounting Firm. He will present how new business tax laws are different and how they affect your business. After the presentation, we will have a Q&A session. Now, let's welcome Mr. Haywood to the podium.

발표 후에 무슨 일이 있을 것인가?
(A) Haywood 씨가 질문에 답할 것이다.   (B) 연회가 열릴 것이다.

관광 정보
여: 세금 세미나에 와주셔서 감사합니다. 시작하기 전에, 우리의 강사인 Mark Haywood 씨를 소개하고 싶습니다. 그는 Jonathan 회계 사무소의 수석 세금 회계사입니다. 그는 새로운 사업 세법이 어떻게 다르고 여러분의 사업에 어떻게 영향을 미칠지 알려주실 겁니다. 발표 후에는, 질의응답 시간을 가질 것입니다. 이제, Haywood 씨를 연단으로 모셔보죠.

06. US

Where do the **listeners** most likely **work**?
(A) At a product **design company**
(B) At a **marketing agency**

> M: Good morning. We have Jason Peterson here today who will lead the online security training for all Pennington Marketing Firm employees. He will share his personal experience about what just a tiny careless behavior can bring to the company. In addition, he will give clear guidelines of what you have to do and what you should not do.

청자들은 어디에서 일하겠는가?
(A) 제품 디자인 회사에서에서   **(B)** 마케팅 회사에서

관광 정보
남: 안녕하세요. Pennington 마케팅 회사 전 직원들에게 온라인 보안 교육을 해주실 Jason Peterson 씨가 오늘 여기 와 있습니다. 그는 하나의 사소한 부주의한 행동이 회사에 어떻게 영향을 미칠지에 대한 그의 개인적인 경험을 말해주실 겁니다. 게다가, 여러분이 해야 할 것과 하지 말아야 할 것에 대한 명확한 가이드라인을 주실 겁니다.

paraphrasing 정답   1. (b)   2. (a)   3. (c)   4. (b)   5. (a)   6. (c)

실전 문제

01. (C)	02. (B)	03. (D)	04. (A)	05. (A)	06. (C)
07. (B)	08. (D)	09. (A)	10. (C)	11. (D)	12. (A)
13. (B)	14. (C)	15. (A)	16. (A)	17. (B)	18. (A)
19. (D)	20. (B)	21. (A)	22. (D)	23. (A)	24. (B)

[01-03] US

Questions 01-03 refer to the following tour information.

> W: Good afternoon, and ⁰¹welcome to the San Diego Botanical Garden. My name is Lydia, and I'll be showing you around our famous collection of rose plants. Following that, you'll be free to wander the site on your own. At three o'clock at the central pavilion, ⁰²one of our staff members will be demonstrating how to get rid of unwanted pests naturally. I highly recommend that. Now, ⁰³I'll pass out maps to each of you that show the various sections and trails. You may need to refer to these throughout your visit. If everyone's ready, let's get started.

botanical 식물의   wander 거닐다, 돌아다니다   site 위치, 장소   on one's own 혼자서, 단독으로   pavilion 전시관   staff member 직원   demonstrate (작동 과정이나 사용법을) 보여주다   get rid of ~을 제거하다   unwanted 원치 않는, 반갑지 않은   pest 해충, 유해 동물   pass out 나누어 주다   trail 산책로, 오솔길   refer to ~을 보다, ~에게 문의하다   throughout ~ 동안 죽, 내내

01-03은 다음 관광 정보에 관한 문제입니다.
여: 안녕하세요, ⁰¹샌디에이고 식물원에 오신 것을 환영합니다. 제 이름은 Lydia이고, 제가 여러분들에게 저희의 유명한 장미 나무 콜렉션을 안내해 드리겠습니다. 그 이후에 여러분은 각자 자유롭게 둘러보시게 됩니다. 3시에 중앙 전시관에서 ⁰²저희 직원 중 한 명이 원치 않는 해충을 자연적으로 제거하는 방법을 보여 드릴 예정입니다. 저는 그것을 강력히 추천합니다. 자, 여러분 모두에게 다양한 구역과 산책로를 보여주는 ⁰³지도를 나누어 드리겠습니다. 방문하시는 동안 이것들을 봐야 할 수도 있습니다. 모두 준비되셨으면, 시작하겠습니다.

01.

담화는 어디에서 이루어지고 있는가?
(A) 역사와 관련된 집에서
(B) 박물관에서
(C) 정원에서

(D) 시장에서

[해설] 담화가 이루어지는 장소를 묻는 문제로, 담화 초반의 샌디에이고 식물원에 오신 것을 환영한다는(welcome to the San Diego Botanical Garden) 말로 보아 정답은 (C)이다.

02.

화자는 무엇을 할 것을 추천하는가?
(A) 두 그룹으로 나누기
(B) 설명 보기
(C) 사진 많이 찍기
(D) 기부하기

[해설] 질문의 키워드 recommend가 담화 중반부에 그대로 언급된다. 직원 중 한 명이 원치 않는 해충을 자연적으로 제거하는 방법을 보여줄 예정이라며(one of our staff members will be demonstrating how to get rid of unwanted pests naturally), 강력히 추천한다고 (I highly recommend that.) 덧붙였다. 즉, 직원의 해충 제거 설명을 볼 것을 추천하고 있으므로 정답은 (B)이다.

[어휘] break into 나누다, 쪼개다 demonstration 시범, 설명 make a donation 기부하다

03.

화자는 청자들에게 무엇을 줄 것인가?
(A) 행사 일정
(B) 입장권
(C) 방문증
(D) 현장 지도

[해설] 담화 후반, 화자가 다양한 구역과 산책로를 보여주는 지도를 나눠 주겠다고(I'll pass out maps) 했으므로 정답은 (D)이다.

> **paraphrasing** pass out 나눠 주다 → give 주다

[어휘] entry 입장, 출입 badge (신분 등을 나타내는) 표, 배지

[04-06] AU

Questions 04-06 refer to the following introduction.

> W: Good afternoon everyone, and welcome to this special event. **04Today we celebrate the 50th anniversary of our company.** During half a century in business, we have grown from a family-owned jewelry shop into a nationwide brand. **05We have focused on providing better service to our customers.** Well, **06it looks like lunch is all ready, so the servers will bring out our food now.** While you eat, we will play a slideshow put together by our marketing and personnel departments. It's compiled of pictures from our company's previous events. You will see what we have achieved and what we are doing.

celebrate 축하하다, 기념하다 anniversary 기념일 century 세기 nationwide 전국적인 put together 합치다, 만들다, 준비하다 compile 편집하다, 엮다 previous 이전의 achieve 달성하다, 성취하다

04-06은 다음 소개에 관한 문제입니다.
여: 안녕하세요, 여러분. 이번 특별 행사에 오신 것을 환영합니다. 04오늘은 우리는 회사의 50주년을 기념합니다. 반 세기 동안 영업을 하면서 우리는 가족 소유의 보석 매장에서 전국적인 규모의 브랜드로 성장했습니다. 05우리는 우리 고객들에게 더 나은 서비스를 제공하는 것에 초점을 맞춰 왔습니다. 음, 06점심이 모두 준비된 것 같군요. 종업원들이 지금 우리의 음식을 가져올 겁니다. 드시는 동안 우리 마케팅 부서와 인사 부서가 준비한 슬라이드 쇼를 틀어 드릴 겁니다. 우리 회사의 이전 행사 사진들이 편집된 것입니다. 우리가 달성한 것들과 우리가 하고 있는 것들을 보실 수 있습니다.

04.

행사의 목적은 무엇인가?
(A) 회사 기념일을 축하하는 것
(B) 은퇴하는 경영진을 예우하는 것
(C) 뛰어난 직원을 인정하는 것
(D) 교육을 제공하는 것

[해설] 행사의 목적은 담화 초반부에 언급된다. 환영 인사에 이어 오늘은 우리는 회사의 50주년을 기념한다고(Today we celebrate the 50th anniversary of our company) 했으므로 (A)가 정답이다.

[어휘] honor 예우하다 retire 은퇴하다, 퇴직하다 executive 경영진 recognize 인정하다 outstanding 뛰어난

05.

화자는 회사가 무엇에 초점을 맞춰 왔다고 말하는가?
(A) 더 나은 고객 서비스를 제공하는 것
(B) 신제품을 출시하는 것
(C) 더 많은 고객들을 유치하는 것
(D) 매출 목표를 달성하는 것

[해설] 중반부에 고객들에게 더 나은 서비스를 제공하는 것에 초점을 맞춰 왔다고(We have focused on providing better service to our customers) 했으므로 (A)가 정답이다.

> **paraphrasing** providing better service to our customers 고객들에게 더 나은 서비스를 제공하는 것 → Offering better customer service 더 나은 고객 서비스를 제공하는 것

[어휘] launch 출시하다, 착수하다 attract 끌다, 유치하다 goal 목표

06.

다음에 무슨 일이 있을 것 같은가?
(A) 상이 수여될 것이다.
(B) 강연이 있을 것이다.
(C) 식사가 제공될 것이다.
(D) 사진이 촬영될 것이다.

[해설] 중반부 이후에 점심이 모두 준비된 것 같다며 종업원들이 지금 음식을 가져올 거라고(it looks like lunch is all ready, so the servers will bring out our food now) 했으므로 (C)가 정답이다.

> **paraphrasing** the servers will bring out our food 종업원들이 음식을 가져올 것이다 → A meal will be served. 식사가 제공될 것이다.

[어휘] happen 일어나다, 발생하다 award 상 present 주다, 수여하다

[07-09] BR
Questions 07-09 refer to the following tour information.

W: I hope you are all enjoying today's tour of the ⁰⁷Brogan Inc. furniture factory. ⁰⁸In this next phase of the tour, there are numerous machines running on the production floor, so ⁰⁸it will be too loud for us to talk to each other. However, after this, we'll go to a quiet area ⁰⁹so you can learn more about what you saw. Douglas, the on-duty supervisor, will be there.

phase 단계, 시기, 국면 numerous 많은 run 작동하다, 기능하다 floor (건물 내에서 특정한 활동이 벌어지는) 작업장 on-duty 근무 중인, 당번인 supervisor 감독관, 관리자

07-09는 다음 견학 정보에 관한 문제입니다.
여: 여러분 모두 오늘 ⁰⁷Brogan 사 가구 공장 견학에서 즐거운 시간 보내시기 바랍니다. ⁰⁸이 견학의 다음 순서에서는, 생산 작업장에서 여러 기계들이 가동되고 있기 때문에 우리가 서로 얘기를 나누기에는 ⁰⁸몹시 시끄러울 것입니다. 하지만 그 다음에는 조용한 구역으로 이동하여 ⁰⁹여러분이 보신 것에 대해 더 많이 배울 수 있을 것입니다. 근무 중인 감독관 Douglas 씨가 그곳에 계실 겁니다.

07.
화자는 어디에서 근무하는가?
(A) 디자인 기관에서
(B) 생산 시설에서
(C) 국립 공원에서
(D) 미술관에서

[해설] 화자의 직업/직종에 관한 단서는 대부분 담화 초반부에 나온다. 여러분 모두 오늘 Brogan 사 가구 공장(Brogan Inc. furniture factory) 견학에서 즐거운 시간 보내기 바란다는 말로 보아 화자가 근무하는 곳이 가구를 제작하는 곳, 즉 가구 생산 시설임을 알 수 있으므로 정답은 (B)이다.

paraphrasing furniture factory 가구 공장 → a manufacturing facility 생산 시설

[어휘] institute 기관, 협회

08.
화자는 견학의 다음 단계에 대해서 무엇이라고 말하는가?
(A) 안전 장비가 필요하다.
(B) 영상물이 포함되어 있다.
(C) 아주 인기가 많다.
(D) 시끄러울 것이다.

[해설] 질문의 핵심 키워드 next phase of the tour는 담화 전반부에 그대로 언급된다. 견학의 다음 단계에 대해(In this next phase of the tour) 설명하면서, 생산 작업장에서 가동되는 여러 기계들 때문에 너무 시끄러울 것이라고(it will be too loud) 했다. 따라서 정답은 (D)이다.

paraphrasing it will be too loud 너무 시끄러울 것이다 → It will be noisy. 시끄러울 것이다.

09.
화자는 왜 "근무 중인 감독관 Douglas 씨가 그곳에 계실 겁니다"라고 말하는가?
(A) 그녀의 동료에게 질문을 하라고 제안하기 위해서
(B) 청자들에게 견학을 더 하라고 독려하기 위해서
(C) 불만을 해결할 방법을 추천하기 위해서
(D) 일정이 왜 변경되었는지 설명하기 위해서

[해설] 화자는 해당 표현 바로 앞에서, 조용한 구역으로 이동하여 여러분이 본 것에 대해 더 많이 배울 수 있을 것이라고(so you can learn more about what you saw) 했다. 그곳에 감독관이 참석할 예정이니 그와의 대화를 통해 더 많은 정보를 얻으라는 의미로 해당 표현을 사용한 것이므로 따라서 감독관(supervisor)을 동료(colleague)로 지칭한 (A)가 정답이다.

[어휘] direct ~(에게)로 보내다 encourage 격려[고무]하다 resolve 해결하다

[10-12] US
Questions 10-12 refer to the following introduction.

W: It's wonderful to see so many people here for our monthly Business Entrepreneurs Luncheon. I hope you all learn a lot of useful information today. Our speaker is ¹⁰Ann Rodriguez, the owner of Shelter Insurance. Her company has been in business for over three decades, and Ms. Rodriguez has worked hard to develop its reputation. ¹¹Her presentation today will be about how to get new clients interested in your business. She'll offer a number of techniques that may help your own business. ¹²There will be a question-and-answer session at the end of the presentation, so please hold your inquiries until then. Without further ado, let's welcome Ms. Rodriguez to the stage.

monthly 매달의 entrepreneur 사업가, 기업가 luncheon 오찬 owner 주인, 소유주 insurance 보험 in business 사업을 하는 develop a reputation 명성을 쌓다 interested in ~에 관심이 있는 technique 기법, 기술 question-and-answer session 질의 응답 시간 inquiry 문의, 질문 without further ado 지체 없이

10-12는 다음 소개에 관한 문제입니다.
여: 이렇게 많은 분들을 이곳 월례 기업인 오찬에서 뵙게 되어 기쁩니다. 여러분 모두 오늘 유용한 정보를 많이 얻어 가시기를 바랍니다. 연사는 ¹⁰Shelter 보험사의 소유주인 Ann Rodriguez 씨입니다. 그녀의 회사는 30년이 넘는 기간 동안 운영되어 왔으며, Rodriguez 씨는 회사의 명성을 쌓기 위해 열심히 노력했습니다. ¹¹오늘 그녀가 할 발표는 새로운 고객들을 여러분의 사업에 관심을 갖게 만드는 방법에 관한 것입니다. 그녀가 여러분의 사업에 도움이 될 수 있는 많은 기법들을 알려 드릴 것입니다. ¹²발표 마지막에 질의 응답 시간이 있을 예정이니 그때까지는 질문을 보류해 주시기 바랍니다. 더 이상 지체하지 않고 Rodriguez 씨를 무대로 모시겠습니다.

10.
Ann Rodriguez는 어떤 산업에 종사하는가?
(A) 건설
(B) 제조
(C) 보험
(D) 부동산

[해설] 강연에 앞서 연사를 소개하는 담화이다. Ann Rodriguez는 오

늘 강연을 할 연사의 이름으로 Shelter 보험사의 소유주(the owner of Shelter Insurance)로 소개되었으므로 정답은 (C)이다.

[어휘] construction 건설 manufacturing 제조, 생산 real estate 부동산

11.

Rodriquez 씨의 강연 주제는 무엇이 될 것인가?
(A) 신제품 개발하기
(B) 직원들의 동기를 부여하기
(C) 운영비 줄이기
(D) 신규 고객 유치하기

[해설] 담화 중반, Rodriquez 씨가 발표할 내용에 대한 설명이 나온다. 오늘 그녀가 할 발표는 새로운 고객들을 여러분의 사업에 관심을 갖게 만드는 방법에 관한 것이라는(Her presentation today will be about how to get new clients interested in your business) 말에서 '신규 고객 유치하기'가 강연의 주제임을 알 수 있다. 따라서 정답은 (D)이다.

[어휘] motivated 동기가 부여된 reduce (가격 등을) 인하하다, 낮추다 operating cost 운영비

12.

청자들은 무엇을 하라고 요청받는가?
(A) 마지막을 위해 질문을 남겨 두기
(B) 휴대폰을 끄기
(C) 강연 중에 메모하기
(D) 설문지를 작성하기

[해설] Please 다음에는 대부분 청자에게 요청하는 사항이 제시되니 이 표현이 나오면 이어지는 내용을 주의 깊게 들어야 한다. 담화 후반부, 발표 마지막에 질의 응답 시간이 있을 예정이니 그때까지는 질문을 보류해 주기 바란다고(There will be a question-and-answer session at the end of the presentation, so please hold your inquiries until then) 했으므로 정답은 (A)이다.

paraphrasing hold your inquiries 질문을 보류하기 → save questions 질문을 남겨두기

[어휘] take notes 메모하다

[13-15] BR

Questions 13-15 refer to the following tour information.

M: Good afternoon, and [13]**welcome to this tour of Owens Bottling Plant**. This particular factory mainly produces sports drinks, which have been in very high demand lately. You'll get to see how we go from empty plastic bottles to labeled products ready for sale. [14]**Thanks to some new equipment, the whole process is even faster. That means that the tour will finish about ten minutes earlier.** [15]**We'll use that extra time to let you sample some for yourself in our product testing area**. Shall we get started?

bottling 병에 채워 넣기 plant 공장 particular 특정한 mainly 주로, 대부분 produce 생산하다 in demand 수요가 많은 lately 최근에, 얼마 전에 empty 비어 있는, 빈 labeled 표를 붙인 thanks to ~ 덕분에 equipment 장비, 용품 whole 전체의 process 과정 sample 시식[시음]하다 for oneself 스스로

13-15는 다음 견학 정보에 관한 문제입니다.

남: 안녕하세요, [13]이번 Owens 음료 공장 견학에 오신 것을 환영합니다. 이 특별한 공장은 주로 스포츠 음료를 생산하는데, 최근 수요가 매우 많습니다. 여러분은 저희가 어떻게 빈 플라스틱 병들을 판매 준비가 된 라벨이 붙은 제품으로 변화시키는지 보게 될 겁니다. [14]일부 새 장비 덕분에 전체 과정이 훨씬 더 빨라졌습니다. 이는 견학이 약 10분 더 일찍 끝날 것이라는 의미입니다. [15]저희가 남는 시간을 이용하여 여러분이 저희의 제품 테스트 구역에서 직접 시음할 수 있도록 하겠습니다. 출발하실까요?

13.

어디서 이루어지고 있는 견학이겠는가?
(A) 동물원에서
(B) 음료 공장에서
(C) 헬스클럽에서
(D) 기차역에서

[해설] 담화 초반 Owens 음료 공장 견학에 온 것을 환영한다는(welcome to this tour of Owens Bottling Plant) 말에서 음료 공장임을 알 수 있다. 따라서 정답은 (B)이다.

paraphrasing Plant 공장 → factory 공장

14.

화자는 견학에 대해 무엇이 새롭다고 말하는가?
(A) 선물 가게 할인
(B) 종료 지점
(C) 지속 시간
(D) 규칙

[해설] 담화 중반, 새 장비 덕분에 전체 과정이 빨라져 견학이 약 10분 더 일찍 끝날 것이라고(Thanks to some new equipment, the whole process is even faster. That means that the tour will finish about ten minutes earlier.) 언급했다. 즉, 견학에 소요되는 시간이 줄었다는 말이므로 정답은 (C)이다.

[어휘] ending point 종료점, 종점 duration 지속; (지속되는) 기간 rule 규칙

15.

화자는 청자들에게 무엇을 제공하는가?
(A) 무료 샘플
(B) 할인 쿠폰
(C) 주차권
(D) 안전 장비

[해설] 담화 마지막, 남는 견학 시간을 이용하여 청자들이 직접 시음을 해볼 수 있도록 하겠다는(We'll use that extra time to let you sample some for yourself in our product testing area.) 말은 무료 샘플을 제공하겠다는 의미이므로 정답은 (A)이다.

[16-18] AU

Questions 16-18 refer to the following talk.

M: [16]**Welcome to Mohawk Historical Village**. On today's tour, you will get a chance to see how the natives of the Mohawk area lived before Europeans came to the region. [17]**We will start with the houses they lived in, and proceed on to the sites they used for important gatherings**. Then we will visit a farm to see the kinds of crops they grew and how they cultivated them. Everyone working here is demonstrating the lifestyle of that period, so ¹⁸**feel free to ask them about their way of life.**

native 토착민, 현지인, 원주민 region 지역 proceed on to ~을 향하여 나아가다[이동하다] site 현장, 부지 gathering 모임 crops 농작물 cultivate 경작하다, 일구다 lifestyle 생활 방식 period 기간

16-18은 다음 담화에 관한 문제입니다.

남: ¹⁶Mohawk 역사 마을에 오신 것을 환영합니다. 오늘 투어에서, 여러분은 유럽인들이 이 지역에 오기 전에 Mohawk 지역 원주민들이 어떻게 살았는지 보실 기회를 가지게 됩니다. ¹⁷그들이 살았던 집으로 시작하여 그들이 중요한 모임을 위해 이용했던 현장들로 이동합니다. 그런 다음 농장에 방문하여 그들이 길렀던 작물의 종류들과 그것들을 어떻게 경작했는지 보시게 됩니다. 여기서 일하는 모든 사람들이 그 시대의 생활 양식을 실제로 보여주고 있으니 ¹⁸자유롭게 그들의 생활 방식에 대해 물어보십시오.

16.
어디서 이루어지고 있는 담화인 것 같은가?
(A) 역사 마을에서
(B) 실내 박물관에서
(C) 극장에서
(D) 식료품점에서

[해설] Mohawk 역사 마을에 온 것을 환영한다는(Welcome to Mohawk Historical Village.) 말과 이후 관람 세부 일정이 이어지는 것으로 보아 역사 마을을 방문한 관람객들을 대상으로 한 담화임을 알 수 있다. 따라서 정답은 (A)이다.

[어휘] indoor 실내의

17.
담화의 목적은 무엇인가?
(A) 가이드를 소개하기 위해
(B) 관람 계획을 요약 설명하기 위해
(C) 생활 방식을 설명하기 위해
(D) 정책을 검토하기 위해

[해설] Mohawk 역사 마을의 관람객들을 대상으로 한 담화로, Mohawk 지역 원주민들이 살았던 집(the houses they lived in), 그들이 중요한 모임을 위해 사용했던 현장(the sites they used for important gatherings) 및 농작물을 경작했던 농장(farm) 등 관람할 곳에 대해 순서대로 소개하고 있다. 즉, 관람 일정을 요약 설명하기 위한 담화이므로 정답은 (B)이다.

18.
화자는 청자들에게 무엇을 하라고 권장하는가?
(A) 질문하기
(B) 기념품 사기
(C) 유인물 읽기
(D) 사진 찍기

[해설] 담화 후반, 여기서 일하는 모든 사람들이 그 시대의 생활 양식을 실제로 보여주고 있으니 자유롭게 그들의 생활 방식에 대해 물어보라고(feel free to ask them about their way of life) 했다. 따라서 정답은 (A)이다.

[어휘] souvenir 기념품 handout 인쇄물, 유인물

[19-21] US

Questions 19-21 refer to the following introduction.

W: It's my honor today to introduce you to Steven Jones, ¹⁹**who will be sharing strategies to help you increase your sales here at McCall's Electronics.** ²⁰**Steven has been giving speeches to motivate salespeople for nearly a decade.** Most stores that he visits report an increase of at least 15% in their sales, largely thanks to the improved attitudes of the employees. ²¹**After his speech, I'll need each of your signatures on one of these forms to show that you attended this session.**

share 공유하다, 함께 쓰다 strategy 전략 sales 매출 salespeople 판매원 nearly 거의 at least 적어도 largely 주로 thanks to ~ 덕분에 improved 향상된, 개선된 attitude 태도, 자세

19-21은 다음 소개에 관한 문제입니다.

여: 오늘 여러분에게 Steven Jones 씨를 소개하게 되어 영광입니다. ¹⁹그가 이곳 McCall's 전자에서 여러분의 매출을 높이도록 도와줄 전략들을 공유할 것입니다. ²⁰Steven 씨는 거의 10년 동안 판매 사원들에게 동기를 부여하기 위한 강연을 해왔습니다. 그가 방문하는 대부분의 상점들은 매출이 최소 15퍼센트는 상승했다고 전하는데요, 주로 직원들의 개선된 태도 덕분입니다. ²¹그의 강연 후에, 여러분이 이 시간에 참석했음을 보여주기 위해 제가 이 서식들 중 하나에 여러분 각자의 서명을 받아야 합니다.

19.
청자들은 어디에서 일할 것 같은가?
(A) 제조 공장에서
(B) 서점에서
(C) 조사 회사에서
(D) 전자 제품 상점에서

[해설] 담화 초반, 오늘의 강연자인 Steven Jones를 소개하며, 그가 이곳 McCall's 전자에서 청자들이 매출을 높이도록 도와줄 전략들을 공유할 것이라고(will be sharing strategies to help you increase your sales here at McCall's Electronics) 했다. 이로 보아 청자들은 McCall's 전자 소속의 판매 사원들임을 알 수 있으므로 정답은 (D)이다.

[어휘] manufacturing plant 제조 공장 research firm 조사 회사 electronics 전자 제품

20.
Steven Jones는 누구인가?
(A) 전기 기사
(B) 동기 부여 연설가
(C) 컴퓨터 프로그래머
(D) 작가

[해설] Steven 씨는 거의 10년 동안 판매 사원들의 동기를 부여하기 위한 강연을 해왔다는(Steven has been giving speeches to motivate salespeople for nearly a decade.) 말로 보아 그가 동기

부여 전문 연설가임을 알 수 있으므로 정답은 (B)이다.

[어휘] motivational 동기 부여의

21.
화자는 청자들에게 무엇을 하라고 요청하는가?
(A) 서식에 서명하기
(B) 그들의 의견 논의하기
(C) 기법 연습하기
(D) 행사에 참석하기

[해설] 요청 사항은 주로 담화 후반부에 제시된다. 강연에 참석했다는 것을 보여주기 위해, 강연 후에 청자 각자의 서명을 받아야 한다며(I'll need each of your signatures on one of these forms to show that you attended this session) 청자들에게 서명해줄 것을 요청하고 있으므로 정답은 (A)이다.

paraphrasing I'll need each of your signatures on one of these forms 이 서식에 여러분 각자의 서명을 받아야 한다 → sign a form 서식에 서명하기

[어휘] practice 연습하다 technique 기법, 기술

[22-24] US

Questions 22-24 refer to the following introduction.

M: ²²Thanks for tuning in, folks! You are now watching Friday Night Cameras. Our special guest tonight is Michael Wagner, a senior writer for the magazine *This, Our Planet*. As you may know, ²³Mr. Wagner was recently named Journalist of the Year for his work covering global climate change. As always, ²⁴feel free to text your questions to us throughout the interview at 555-0134. I'll check some of them and ask him your questions during the interview.

tune in (라디오, TV의) 주파수[채널]에 맞춰 듣다, 청취[시청]하다
senior writer 선임 작가 planet 행성 recently 최근에
name 지명[임명]하다 journalist 저널리스트, 기자 cover 다루다, 포함시키다 climate change 기후 변화 throughout ~ 동안 쭉, 내내

22-24는 다음 소개에 관한 문제입니다.

남: ²²시청해 주셔서 감사합니다, 여러분! 여러분은 지금 <Friday Night Cameras>를 시청하고 계십니다. 오늘 밤 특별 초대 손님은 잡지 <This, Our Planet>의 선임 필자인 Michael Wagner 씨입니다. 여러분도 아시다시피 ²³Wagner 씨는 지구 기후 변화를 다룬 글로 최근 올해의 저널리스트로 지명되었습니다. 늘 그렇듯이 555-0134로 ²⁴인터뷰 내내 자유롭게 문자로 질문을 보내주세요. 제가 질문 중 일부를 확인하고 인터뷰 동안 그에게 여러분의 질문을 물어보겠습니다.

22.
화자는 어디에서 일하겠는가?
(A) 잡지 회사에서
(B) 연구소에서
(C) 공립 도서관에서
(D) 텔레비전 방송국에서

[해설] <Friday Night Cameras>라는 TV 프로그램에서 초대 손님을 소개하는 내용의 담화로, 화자는 이 프로그램의 진행자이다. 따라서 화자가 근무하는 곳은 방송국임을 유추할 수 있으므로 정답은 (D)이다.

23.
화자는 Michael Wagner에 대해 무엇이라고 말하는가?
(A) 최근에 상을 받았다.
(B) 세계적으로 유명한 사진작가이다.
(C) 여행을 다니며 기후 변화에 대해 얘기한다.
(D) <This, Our Planet>에 처음으로 실렸다.

[해설] Michael Wagner는 이 프로그램에 출연하는 초대 손님의 이름으로, 담화 중반에서 지구 기후 변화를 다룬 글로 최근 올해의 저널리스트로 지명되었다고(Mr. Wagner was recently named Journalist of the Year) 소개되었다. 즉, Wagner 씨가 상을 받았다는 말이므로 정답은 (A)이다.

paraphrasing was recently named Journalist of the Year 최근 올해의 저널리스트로 지명되었다 → recently won an award 최근에 상을 받았다.

[어휘] win an award 상을 받다 world-renowned 세계적으로 유명한 publish 게재하다, 싣다

24.
청자들은 무엇을 하라고 권장받는가?
(A) 정기 구독에 가입하기
(B) 문자로 질문 보내기
(C) 탄원서에 서명하기
(D) 메모하기

[해설] 담화 후반, 인터뷰하는 동안 청자들이 자유롭게 문자로 질문을 보내주면(feel free to text your questions to us throughout the interview) 화자가 초대 손님에게 질문을 해주겠다고 했으므로 정답은 (B)이다.

[어휘] subscription 구독 petition 진정[탄원](서)

DAY 19

PART 3 공항/역

출제 유형 01 체크인

| 풀이 방법 해석 |

남: 실례합니다. 저는 디트로이트로 가는데 오후 3시에 출발하기로 되어 있어요. 문제는 제 탑승 시간이 지금인데 게이트가 아직 안 열려서요. 제가 맞는 게이트에 있는지 궁금합니다.
여: 불편함에 대해 사과드립니다. 항공편 번호가 무엇인가요?
남: Aliance 항공 58입니다.
여: 음, 맞는 게이트에 있으십니다. 오늘 저희 수하물 팀 직원이 부족한데 실어야 할 짐들이 특히 많습니다. 지금 가방이 실리고 있으므로, 오래 걸리지 않을 겁니다. 탑승 안내 방송을 놓치지 않도록 이곳에 계시기 바랍니다.

출제 유형 02 변경 요청

| 풀이 방법 해석 |

남: 안녕하세요, 제가 귀사의 웹사이트를 통해 방금 비행기 표를 구매했는데, 제게 영수증을 이메일로 보내 주시지 않았습니다. 거래 번호는 KA-474예요. 보통은 온라인에서 티켓을 구매하면 바로 이메일을 받거든요.

여: 알겠습니다. 확인해 보겠습니다... 여기 문제점이 있네요. 당신이 해외 카드를 사용해서 지불이 두 나라에서 모두 영업일 기준으로 익일이 되어야 승인될 수 있습니다. 오늘이 토요일이니, 며칠 걸릴 수도 있습니다. 국내 카드로 다시 시도하실 수 있도록 구매를 취소해 드릴까요? 그러면 바로 처리될 것입니다.

남: 네, 물론이죠. 이번 주말에 저를 위한 시상식 연회에 참석해야 해서 지금 바로 티켓을 예약해야 해요.

 연습 문제

01. (A) 02. (B) 03. (B) 04. (B) 05. (A) 06. (A)

01. BR-BR
What will the **speakers** do next?
(A) **Go** to a **self-kiosk**   (B) **Claim** their **luggage**

M: There are long lines at the check-in counters. We should have arrived at the airport earlier than usual.
W: Yes, you know, it's the peak season for summer vacations. Why don't we use the self-check-in kiosk since we just have carry-on bags?
M: That sounds great.

화자들은 다음에 무엇을 할 것인가?
(A) 셀프 단말기로 가기   (B) 수하물 찾기

남: 체크인 카운터에 줄이 기네요. 우리 평상시보다 공항에 더 일찍 도착했어야 해요.
여: 맞아요, 여름 휴가 성수기잖아요. 우리는 기내용 가방만 있으니 셀프 체크인 단말기를 사용하는 게 어때요?
남: 좋아요.

02. US-US
What caused a **problem**?
(A) **Heavy traffic**   (B) An **engine failure**

W: Excuse me, can I get a train ticket for Middleborough that departs at 9:30?
M: Yes, but unfortunately due to the malfunctioning engine, it will depart 50 minutes later than scheduled, and at Platform 10 instead of Platform 5.

무엇이 문제를 야기했는가?
(A) 교통 체증   **(B)** 엔진 결함

여: 실례합니다. 미들버러로 가는 9시 30분에 출발하는 기차표를 살 수 있을까요?
남: 네, 하지만 안타깝게도 엔진 오작동으로 인해 예정보다 50분 늦게 출발할 거고, 5번 플랫폼이 아닌 10번 플랫폼에서 출발할 거예요.

03. BR-AU
Where does this conversation **take place**?
(A) At a **subway station**   (B) At an **airport**

W: Mike, I'm Jennifer at Gate 5. There are some passengers here who are going to transfer to a flight for Beijing, but it will take off just in a half an hour. Can you send me a cart since some of them are seniors and kids?
M: Sure, and can you call to International Terminal and let them know the passengers will be at the boarding gate in 15 minutes?

대화는 어디에서 일어나고 있는가?
(A) 지하철역에서   **(B)** 공항에서

여: Mike, 저 5번 게이트의 Jennifer예요. 여기 베이징으로 가는 항공편으로 갈아탈 승객들이 있는데, 30분이면 이륙할 거예요. 몇몇 분들이 노인과 아이들이니 카트를 보내 주시겠어요?
남: 물론이죠. 그리고 국제선 터미널에 전화해서 15분 후에 승객들이 도착할 거라고 알려 주시겠어요?

04. US-BR
Why will the **woman visit New York City**?
(A) To **attend** an **awards ceremony**
(B) To **present** some **information**

W: Hello, I missed my connecting flight to New York City. Is there any other flight available today? I have to give a presentation tomorrow morning at 9.
M: Let me check... I'm looking it up... and there is only one option you have. The flight will depart in an hour but you have a layover in Detroit for two hours.

여자는 왜 뉴욕 시를 방문할 것인가?
(A) 시상식에 참석하기 위해   **(B)** 어떤 정보를 발표하기 위해

여: 안녕하세요, 저는 뉴욕 시로 가는 연결 항공편을 놓쳤어요. 오늘 탈 수 있는 다른 항공편이 있나요? 제가 내일 아침 9시에 발표를 해야 해서요.
남: 확인해 보겠습니다... 보고 있습니다... 옵션이 한 개 밖에 없네요. 한 시간 후에 항공편이 출발할 것이지만 디트로이트에서 2시간 동안 경유하셔야 합니다.

05. US-BR
What does the **woman recommend the man do**?
(A) **Take** a **taxi**   (B) **Use** a **company car**

M: I saw the schedule on the Web site and it said that buses operate every 15 minutes. But I've been waiting for one for more than 30 minutes. What happened? I have to attend a client meeting in 30 minutes.
W: There is construction work downtown, so the buses are getting delayed. Why don't you take a taxi? If you do, you can make on time.

여자는 남자에게 무엇을 할 것을 권장하는가?
(A) 택시를 타기   (B) 회사 차 사용하기

남: 웹사이트에서 스케줄을 봤는데 버스가 15분마다 운행한다고 써 있었어요. 그런데 저는 30분 넘게 기다렸어요. 무슨 일 있나요? 저는 30분 후에 고객 미팅에 참석해야 해요.
여: 시내에서 공사 작업이 있어서, 버스가 지연되고 있어요. 택시를 타시는 게 어때요? 그러면 시간에 맞춰 갈 수 있을 거예요.

06. BR-US
What caused the delay?
(A) **Bad weather**   (B) A **malfunctioning engine**

M: Hello, has flight KE621 arrived on time? It was expected to land 20 minutes ago.
W: Actually, no. It was delayed 30 minutes at Chicago Airport due to stormy weather. It will arrive in 15 minutes.
M: Oh, that's great. I thought I was late to pick up my client.

무엇이 지연을 야기했는가?
(A) 안 좋은 날씨   (B) 오작동하는 엔진

남: 안녕하세요, KE621 항공편이 정시에 도착했나요? 20분 전에 착륙하기로 되어 있었어요.
여: 사실, 도착하지 않았습니다. 폭풍우가 치는 날씨 때문에 시카고 공항에서 30분 지연되었어요. 15분 후에 도착할 겁니다.
남: 아, 잘 됐네요. 저는 고객을 모시러 왔는데 늦은 줄 알았어요.

paraphrasing 정답 1. (b) 2. (c) 3. (a) 4. (b) 5. (c) 6. (a)

실전 문제

01. (C)	02. (A)	03. (D)	04. (B)	05. (C)	06. (D)
07. (B)	08. (B)	09. (C)	10. (A)	11. (B)	12. (C)
13. (D)	14. (B)	15. (C)	16. (A)	17. (D)	18. (C)
19. (A)	20. (B)	21. (D)

[01-03] BR-US
Questions 01-03 refer to the following conversation.

M: Good morning. **⁰¹I'm checking in for Flight 464** to Los Angeles. I've printed a copy of my itinerary, and here is my passport. I'm planning to have my laptop bag as my carry-on, but **⁰²I've got two other big suitcases.**
W: All right, sir. Now, according to our policy for economy-class passengers, **⁰²the first checked bag is free. However, there will be a charge of thirty-five dollars for your second bag.** This should be paid here at the counter.
M: I was expecting that. **⁰³I'm bringing along my company's new products to demonstrate them to some investors in Los Angeles.** So, I couldn't avoid bringing so many things with me on this trip.

itinerary 여행 일정표   suitcase 여행 가방   policy 정책
charge 요금, (요금을) 청구하다   expect 예상하다, 기대하다
demonstrate 보여주다, 설명하다   investor 투자자

01-03은 다음 대화에 관한 문제입니다.

남: 안녕하세요. 로스앤젤레스 행 ⁰¹464 항공편 탑승 수속을 하려고 합니다. 제 일정표 한 부를 인쇄해 왔고 여기 제 여권도 있어요. 노트북 컴퓨터 가방은 기내에 반입할 계획이지만 ⁰²다른 큰 여행 가방이 두 개 더 있습니다.
여: 알겠습니다, 손님. 자, 저희 이코노믹스 승객 정책에 따르면, ⁰²첫 번째로 부치는 가방은 무료예요. 하지만 두 번째 가방부터는 35달러의 요금이 부과될 겁니다. 이것은 이곳 카운터에서 납부하셔야 합니다.
남: 그럴 거라고 예상했어요. ⁰³제가 로스앤젤레스에서 몇몇 투자자들에게 시연을 하기 위해 저희 회사의 신제품을 가지고 갑니다. 그러는 바람에 어쩔 수 없이 이번 여행에 물건을 아주 많이 가져가게 되었어요.

01.
어디에서 대화가 이루어지고 있겠는가?
(A) 여행사에서
(B) 버스 정류장에서
(C) 공항에서
(D) 호텔에서

[해설] 대화 장소에 대한 정보는 주로 대화 초반부에 나온다. 대화 시작 부분에서 남자가 464 항공편 탑승 수속을 하려고 한다고(I'm checking in for Flight 464) 말하는 것으로 보아 공항에서 이루어지는 대화임을 알 수 있으므로 정답은 (C)이다.

02.
남자에게 왜 요금이 부과될 것인가?
(A) 가방을 추가로 더 가져왔다.
(B) 식사를 구매했다.
(C) 일등석으로 업그레이드를 요청했다.
(D) 더 일찍 출발하기를 원했다.

[해설] 대화 중반 가방을 부치려는 남자에게 여자가 수하물 정책에 대해 설명하는데, 처음 하나는 무료이지만 그 다음부터는 요금이 부과된다고(the first checked bag is free. However, there will be a charge of thirty-five dollars for your second bag) 말한다. 앞서 남자가 여행 가방이 두 개 더 있다고(I've got two other big suitcases) 했으므로 남자는 무료로 부칠 수 있는 수량보다 가방을 더 많이 가져왔기 때문에 요금을 지불해야 함을 알 수 있다. 따라서 정답은 (A)이다.

03.
남자는 로스앤젤레스에서 무엇을 할 계획인가?
(A) 부동산을 둘러보기
(B) 조사를 실시하기
(C) 인터뷰에 참석하기
(D) 시연을 하기

[해설] 대화 후반부 로스앤젤레스에서 몇몇 투자자들에게 시연을 하기 위해 자신의 회사의 신제품을 가지고 가는 중이라는(I'm bringing along my company's new products to demonstrate them to some investors in Los Angeles) 남자의 말에서 로스앤젤레스에서 제품 관련 시연을 할 것임을 알 수 있으므로 정답은 (D)이다.

paraphrasing demonstrate 시연하다 → Give a demonstration 시연을 하기

[어휘] property 부동산 conduct (특정한) 활동을 하다, 실시하다 inspection 조사, 검사

[04-06] BR-AU

Questions 04-06 refer to the following conversation.

W: Hello. ⁰⁴**I need to buy one ticket to Manchester** for today, please.
M: Certainly, ma'am. The next train is boarding now, so I don't think you'll make it to the platform in time, but we have others leaving at 3:15, 3:40, 4:05, and 4:30.
W: Well, ⁰⁵**I know that some trains make more stops than others, depending on the route.** Hmm... there are so many.
M: Well, in my opinion, ⁰⁶**your best option would be the 3:40 train.** It's a little more expensive than the others, but ⁰⁶**it's the only one that is a direct journey to Manchester.**
W: Oh, that sounds perfect. I'll go with that.

board 승차[탑승]하다   make it 시간 맞춰 가다   platform 승강장   in time 제시간에   depending on ~에 따라   route 길, 경로   in my opinion 내 생각에는   direct 직행[직통]의   journey 여행, 여정

04-06은 다음 대화에 관한 문제입니다.
여: 안녕하세요. 오늘 ⁰⁴맨체스터로 가는 티켓 한 장을 사려고 해요, 부탁드립니다.
남: 물론이지요, 손님. 다음 기차는 지금 탑승 중이에요. 그래서 제시간에 승강장까지 못 가실 것 같네요. 하지만 3시 15분, 3시 40분, 4시 5분, 4시 30분에 출발하는 다른 열차가 있습니다.
여: 음, ⁰⁵경로에 따라서 어떤 열차들은 다른 열차보다 더 많이 정차한다고 알고 있어요. 음... 아주 많이 있네요.
남: 음, 제 생각에는 ⁰⁶3시 40분 열차가 최상의 선택인 것 같아요. 나머지 열차보다 조금 더 비싸긴 하지만 ⁰⁶맨체스터까지 직행인 유일한 열차편이에요.
여: 아, 그게 딱 좋겠네요. 그것으로 할게요.

04.

여자는 무엇을 하려고 하는가?
(A) 좌석 변경하기
(B) 티켓 구매하기
(C) 승강장 찾기
(D) 환불 받기

[해설] 대화 초반 여자가 맨체스터로 가는 티켓 한 장을 사려고 한다고(I need to buy one ticket to Manchester) 했으므로 정답은 (B)이다.

paraphrasing buy 사다 → Purchase 구매하기

05.

여자가 "아주 많이 있네요"라고 말할 때 의미하는 것은 무엇인가?
(A) 가격이 비싸서 실망스럽다.
(B) 기차역이 너무 혼잡하다고 생각한다.
(C) 결정을 하는 데 도움이 필요하다.
(D) 가방 때문에 도움이 필요할 것이다.

[해설] 앞서 남자가 열차 출발 시간을 쭉 나열했고 여자는 이 중에서 원하는 열차편을 선택해야 하는 상황임을 알 수 있다. 여자가 경로에 따라서 어떤 열차들은 더 많이 정차한다고 알고 있다고(I know that some trains make more stops than others, depending on the route.) 한 뒤에 "아주 많이 있네요"라고 덧붙인 것으로 보아 여자는 열차편 중에서 어떤 것을 선택해야 할지 결정하지 못해 망설이고 있음을 알 수 있다. 즉, 열차편 결정에 도움이 필요한 상황임을 우회적으로 드러낸 것으로 볼 수 있으므로 정답은 (C)이다.

[어휘] be disappointed with ~에 실망하다   make a decision 결정하다   require 요구하다, 필요로 하다   assistance with ~에 대한 도움, 지원

06.

남자는 3시 40분 열차의 이점으로 무엇을 언급하는가?
(A) 무료 다과가 포함되어 있다.
(B) 편안한 좌석이 더 많이 있다.
(C) 다음으로 출발하는 열차이다.
(D) 여러 번 정차하지 않는다.

[해설] 질문의 핵심 키워드 3:40 train에 집중한다. 대화 후반부 남자가 3시 40분 열차가 여자에게 최상의 선택이라며(your best option would be the 3:40 train) 맨체스터까지 직행인 유일한 열차편이라고(it's the only one that is a direct journey to Manchester.) 덧붙였다. 즉, 중간에 정차하지 않고 맨체스터까지 바로 간다는 뜻이므로 정답은 (D)이다.

paraphrasing a direct journey 직항 → does not make multiple stops 여러 번 정차하지 않는다

[07-09] AU-BR

Questions 07-09 refer to the following conversation.

M: Hi. ⁰⁷**I just heard the announcement you made about the cancelation of Flight 610 to Winnipeg.**
W: Yes, we're very sorry for the inconvenience. ⁰⁸**There is a severe snowstorm in Winnipeg right now**, so we were not able to take off. Unfortunately, there was nothing we could do.
M: I understand, but I still need to get to Winnipeg. Am I able to book tickets on a new flight now?
W: We will begin rebooking everyone on this flight shortly, once we have more accurate information. We'll be calling people up by their boarding zones, so ⁰⁹**please don't leave the gate area.**

cancelation 취소   inconvenience 불편   severe 심각한, 극심한   snowstorm 눈보라   take off 이륙하다   rebook 다시 예약하다   shortly 곧   accurate 정확한   boarding zone 탑승 구역

07-09는 다음 대화에 관한 문제입니다.
남: 안녕하세요, ⁰⁷방금 위니펙 행 610 항공편 취소에 관한 안내 방송을 들었습니다.
여: 네, 불편을 드려 대단히 죄송합니다. ⁰⁸지금 위니펙에 심각한 눈보라가 발생해서 이륙할 수가 없었어요. 안타깝지만 저희가 어떻게 할 수가 없네요.
남: 알겠습니다. 하지만 그래도 저는 위니펙에 가야 해요. 지금 다른 항공편의 티켓을 예약할 수 있을까요?

DAY 19 199

여: 일단 좀 더 정확한 정보가 입수되면, 잠시 후에 이 항공편의 모든 분들에 대한 재예약을 시작할 예정입니다. 저희가 탑승 구역 옆에서 승객들을 부를 테니 ⁰⁹탑승구 주변을 떠나지 마시기 바랍니다.

07.

남자는 항공편 취소에 대해 어떻게 알았는가?
(A) 다른 승객과 얘기함으로써
(B) 안내 방송을 들음으로써
(C) 긴급 문자 메시지를 읽음으로써
(D) 출발 안내 전광판을 봄으로써

[해설] 항공사의 직원으로 보이는 여자와 항공편을 이용하려는 남자의 대화로, 질문의 핵심 키워드 flight cancelation(항공편 취소)은 대화 초반 남자의 대사에서 언급된다. 남자가 방금 610 항공편 취소에 관한 안내 방송을 들었다고(I just heard the announcement you made about the cancelation of Flight 610) 했으므로 정답은 (B)이다.

[어휘] passenger 승객 departures board 출발 안내 전광판

08.

여자에 따르면, 무엇으로 인해 문제가 발생했는가?
(A) 발권 오류
(B) 나쁜 기상 조건
(C) 장비의 결함
(D) 부재중인 직원

[해설] 우선 질문의 핵심 키워드 a problem이 무엇을 가리키는지 파악해야 하는데, 대화의 흐름으로 보아 이것은 앞서 남자가 언급한 '항공편 취소'를 가리키므로 여자의 말에서 항공편 취소의 이유를 찾아야 한다. 여자는 지금 위니펙에 심각한 눈보라가 발생해서(There is a severe snowstorm in Winnipeg right now) 이륙할 수가 없다고 했으므로 항공편이 취소된 것은 나쁜 날씨 때문이다. 따라서 정답은 (B)이다.

paraphrasing a severe snowstorm 심각한 눈보라 → Bad weather conditions 나쁜 기상 조건

[어휘] faulty 결함이 있는 equipment 장비, 용품 absent 결석한, 결근한

09.

여자는 남자에게 무엇을 하라고 요청하는가?
(A) 여권 보여주기
(B) 뒤쪽으로 가서 줄 서기
(C) 이 구역에 머물기
(D) 탑승권을 소지하기

[해설] 요청/제안 문제의 단서는 주로 대화 후반부에 나온다. 대화 마지막에 여자는 탑승구 주변을 떠나지 말라고(please don't leave the gate area) 했다. 즉, 멀리 가지 말고 지금 이 장소에 계속 있으라는 말이므로 정답은 (C)이다.

paraphrasing don't leave the gate area 탑승구 주변을 떠나지 말 것 → Stay in the area 이 구역에 머물기

[10-12] US·BR

Questions 10-12 refer to the following conversation and table.

DEPARTURES INFORMATION		
Airline	Destination	Gate
Starway	Shanghai	G7
¹¹**Olvera**	**Tokyo**	**B22**
Toth Air	Istanbul	F9
Lemax	Delhi	A16

M: Hello, ¹⁰**I'm calling about some urgent maintenance work that is needed in Terminal 3.** The door to the walkway won't open, so we cannot begin boarding procedures.
W: All right, sir. I'll send someone over right away. Which gate are you using?
M: ¹¹**We're at Gate B22**, and we're supposed to begin boarding now. ¹²**I'll put a notice on the door** so that no one tries to force it open. That might make the problem even worse.
W: Good idea. The technician will be there as soon as possible.

urgent 긴급한, 시급한 maintenance (건물, 기계 등의) 유지, 보수 walkway 통로, 보도 boarding procedures 탑승 절차 force 억지[강제]로 ~하다 worse 더 심한, 심각한 technician 기술자, 기사 departure 출발 airline 항공사 destination 목적지, 도착지

10-12는 다음 대화와 표에 관한 문제입니다.

출발 정보		
항공사	도착지	탑승구
Starway	상하이	G7
¹¹**Olvera**	**도쿄**	**B22**
Toth Air	이스탄불	F9
Lemax	델리	A16

남: 여보세요, ¹⁰3번 터미널에 긴급 보수 작업이 필요해서 전화드렸어요. 통로로 가는 문이 열리지 않아서 탑승 절차를 시작하지 못하고 있어요.
여: 알겠습니다. 지금 바로 사람을 보낼게요. 몇 번 탑승구를 이용하고 계신가요?
남: ¹¹B22 탑승구에 있어요. 지금 탑승을 시작하기로 되어 있어요. ¹²제가 문에 공지문을 붙일게요. 억지로 열려 하는 사람이 없도록요. 그러면 문제가 훨씬 더 심각해질지도 모르니까요.
여: 좋은 생각이에요. 최대한 빨리 기술자가 거기로 갈 거예요.

10.

남자는 왜 여자에게 전화하고 있는가?
(A) 수리를 요청하기 위해
(B) 취소를 알리기 위해
(C) 수하물 분실 신고를 하기 위해

(D) 항공편 상황을 확인하기 위해

[해설] 대화 초반에 단서가 나온다. 남자가 3번 터미널에 긴급 보수 작업이 필요해서 전화한다고(I'm calling about some urgent maintenance work that is needed in Terminal 3) 한 것으로 보아 수리를 요청하기 위해 전화한 것임을 알 수 있다. 따라서 정답은 (A)이다.

paraphrasing some urgent maintenance work 긴급 보수 작업 → a repair 수리

[어휘] cancelation 취소 missing 분실한 status (진행 과정상의) 상황

11.

시각 자료를 보시오. 어느 항공사가 영향을 받는가?
(A) Starway
(B) Olvera
(C) Toth Air
(D) Lemax

[해설] 대화에서 언급한 문제의 영향을 받게 되는 항공사를 시각 자료에서 찾는 문제다. 공항 터미널에서 통로로 가는 문이 열리지 않는다며 보수 작업을 요청하는 남자에게 여자가 몇 번 탑승구인지 묻자 B22 탑승구에 있다고(We're at Gate B22) 했다. 표에서 B22번 탑승구를 사용하는 항공사를 찾으면 Olvera이므로 정답은 (B)이다.

[어휘] be affected 영향을 받다

12.

남자는 무엇을 할 계획인가?
(A) 티켓을 확인하기
(B) 새로운 탑승구로 이동하기
(C) 공지문을 게시하기
(D) 승객들에게 탑승하라고 요청하기

[해설] 남자가 할 일을 묻는 문제로, 앞서 열리지 않는 문의 수리를 요청했던 남자가 대화 중반 자신이 문에 공지문을 붙여(I'll put a notice on the door) 사람들이 문을 억지로 열지 못하게 하겠다고 했다. 즉, 남자는 공지문을 게시할 계획이므로 정답은 (C)이다.

paraphrasing put a notice 공지문을 붙이다 → post a notice 공지문을 붙이다

[13-15] US-US

Questions 13-15 refer to the following conversation.

W: Hi, I'd like to reserve a seat on flight 932 to Toronto at 2 P.M. today.
M: Let me see if there are any seats available. ¹³Due to renovations on our airport, the number of flights going in and out has been temporarily reduced.
W: Yes, I heard about that. The thing is, ¹⁴I just found out about an urgent meeting that I have to attend tomorrow.
M: ¹⁵Unfortunately, the 2 P.M. flight is completely booked. There is one at 7:30 P.M. if that would work for you.
W: Okay, I'll take a seat on that one.

reserve 예약하다 due to ~ 때문에 temporarily 일시적으로, 임시로 reduce 줄이다, 축소하다 completely 완전히, 전적으로

13-15는 다음 대화에 관한 문제입니다.

여: 안녕하세요, 오늘 오후 2시 토론토 행 932 항공편 좌석을 예약하고 싶어요.
남: 좌석이 남아 있는지 볼게요. ¹³저희 공항 보수 공사 때문에 들어오고 나가는 항공편 수가 일시적으로 줄었습니다.
여: 네, 그 얘기는 들었어요. 실은 ¹⁴제가 내일 참석해야 하는 긴급 회의가 있다는 걸 방금 알았어요.
남: ¹⁵안타깝게도, 오후 2시 항공편은 모두 예약되었어요. 괜찮으시다면 저녁 7시 30분에 하나가 있어요.
여: 좋아요, 그 항공편의 좌석으로 주세요.

13.

남자는 무엇이 문제를 야기했다고 말하는가?
(A) 엔진 고장
(B) 다가오는 폭풍우
(C) 연료 가격 인상
(D) 보수 작업

[해설] 질문의 키워드 problem은 남자가 말한 항공편 수가 일시적으로 줄어든(the number of flights going in and out has been temporarily) 상황을 가리키는데, 이것은 공항 보수 공사 때문이라고(Due to renovations on our airport) 했다. 따라서 문제의 원인은 보수 작업이므로 정답은 (D)이다.

[어휘] failure 실패, 고장 incoming 도착하는, 들어오는 increased 증가한

14.

여자는 내일 무엇을 하기로 되어 있는가?
(A) 콘퍼런스에서 연설하기
(B) 회의에 참석하기
(C) 교육에 참석하기
(D) 일자리를 위해 면접을 보기

[해설] 질문의 핵심 키워드 tomorrow가 언급되는 부분에 집중한다. 여자는 내일 참석해야 하는 긴급 회의가 있다는 걸 방금 알았다고(I just found out about an urgent meeting that I have to attend tomorrow.) 했다. 즉, 내일 회의 참석이 예정되어 있으므로 정답은 (B)이다.

paraphrasing an urgent meeting that I have to attend 참석해야 하는 긴급 회의 → participate in a meeting 회의에 참석하기

15.

남자는 왜 "괜찮으시다면 저녁 7시 30분에 하나가 있어요"라고 말하는가?
(A) 다른 교통편을 추천하기 위해
(B) 여자에게 보안 절차를 알리기 위해
(C) 다른 옵션을 제시하기 위해
(D) 지연에 대해 사과하기 위해

[해설] 대화에서 주어진 표현이 나오기 이전의 상황은 여자가 오후 2시 항공편을 원하지만 공항 보수 공사로 인해 항공편이 줄어든 탓에 이 시간의 항공편은 모두 예약이 되었다는(the 2 P.M. flight is completely booked) 것이다. 따라서 남자가 다른 시간대의 항공편을 권하기 위해 "괜찮으시다면 저녁 7시 30분에 하나가 있어요"라고 말한 것이므로 정답은 (C)이다.

DAY 19 201

[어휘] inform A of B A에게 B를 알리다 security 보안, 안전 procedure 절차

[16-18] BR-BR

Questions 16-18 refer to the following conversation.

M: Hi, **¹⁶I just got off the bus from Baltimore and I think my wallet fell out of my pocket**. Can I go and check where I was sitting?
W: I'm sorry, but that bus has already gone to the service area. They'll be cleaning it momentarily. **¹⁷Can I see your ticket stub?**
M: Of course. I sat in seat 9A. Do you have a lost and found area that I should go to? All of my credit cards were in it.
W: **¹⁸You can wait in our station's office on the second floor if you like**. The cleaning crew normally brings all lost items there as soon as they're found.
M: Okay, thank you.

get off 떠나다, 출발하다 fall out of ~로부터 떨어지다 service (차량, 기계의) 정비[점검] momentarily 잠시 (동안), 곧 ticket stub 티켓 반쪽 lost and found 분실물 취급소 cleaning crew 청소부

16-18은 다음 대화에 관한 문제입니다.
남: 안녕하세요, ¹⁶제가 볼티모어에서 출발한 버스에서 방금 내렸는데 제 지갑이 주머니에서 떨어진 것 같아요. 제가 앉았던 곳에 가서 확인해봐도 될까요?
여: 죄송하지만 그 버스는 이미 정비 구역으로 갔어요. 곧 청소할 거예요. ¹⁷티켓 나머지 쪽을 보여 주시겠어요?
남: 물론입니다. 9A 좌석에 앉았어요. 제가 가볼 만한 분실물 취급 구역이 있나요? 제 신용카드가 전부 그 안에 있어요.
여: ¹⁸원하신다면 2층에 있는 저희 정류장 사무실에서 기다리실 수 있어요. 보통 청소부들이 분실물을 발견하는 대로 모두 거기로 가져가요.
남: 알겠습니다. 감사합니다.

16.
남자는 어떤 문제점을 언급하는가?
(A) 지갑을 잃어버렸다.
(B) 버스를 놓쳤다.
(C) 렌터카가 준비되지 않았다.
(D) 짐이 파손되었다.

[해설] 대화 초반, 남자는 버스에서 방금 내렸는데 지갑이 주머니에서 떨어진 것 같다고(I just got off the bus from Baltimore and I think my wallet fell out of my pocket.) 했다. 즉, 버스에서 지갑을 잃어버렸다는 말이므로 정답은 (A)이다.

[어휘] damaged 파손된

17.
여자는 무엇을 요청하는가?
(A) 예약 번호
(B) 출발역
(C) 수하물 영수증
(D) 티켓 반쪽

[해설] Can/Could I ~ 또는 Would/Could you ~ 같은 요청하는 표현을 잘 들어야 한다. 버스에서 지갑을 잃어버린 남자가 직접 버스에 들어가서 확인해보고 싶다고 하자 여자는 티켓의 나머지 반쪽을 보여 달라고(Can I see your ticket stub?) 했으므로 정답은 (D)이다. ticket stub은 버스를 타거나 공연장에 입장할 때 검표원이 표를 확인하고 고객에게 되돌려주는 티켓의 나머지 반쪽을 가리킨다.

18.
남자는 다음에 어디로 갈 것 같은가?
(A) 짐 찾는 곳으로
(B) 승객 휴게실로
(C) 정류장 사무실로
(D) 매표소로

[해설] 대화 후에 일어날 일을 묻는 문제의 단서는 주로 후반부에 나온다. 남자가 분실물 취급 구역이 있는지 묻자 여자가 2층의 정류장 사무실에서 기다려 보라고(You can wait in our station's office on the second floor if you like.) 했다. 따라서 남자는 대화가 끝난 후 정류장 사무실에 갈 것임을 유추할 수 있으므로 정답은 (C)이다.

[어휘] baggage claim area 짐 찾는 곳

[19-21] AU US

Questions 19-21 refer to the following conversation and train schedule.

Train Schedule				
	²⁰East Hampton	**²⁰Amityville**	Hartford	Brentwood
Red Line	5:05	5:15		5:45
Blue Line	5:10	5:20	5:35	

M: Attention passengers, please have your tickets out so I can check them.
W: Hi, this is my ticket. I'm trying to get to Hartford. **¹⁹Is this the right train?**
M: **¹⁹You must have taken the wrong train**. This one doesn't go directly there.
W: Oh, really? How can I get there?
M: **²⁰We just left East Hampton, so you'll have to transfer at the next stop.**
W: I see. Is there a long wait for that train? I'm a member of the Long Island Orchestra and **²¹I'm on my way to a performance and I'll be needing some time to rehearse.**
M: It usually comes every 5 minutes. You won't be late.

passenger 승객 directly 곧장, 똑바로 leave 떠나다, 출발하다 transfer 갈아타다, 환승하다; 환승 on one's way to ~으로 가는 길[도중]에 performance 공연, 연주 rehearse 리허설을 하다

202 기적의 토익 LC

19-21은 다음 대화와 열차 시간표에 관한 문제입니다.

열차 시간표				
	²⁰East Hampton	²⁰Amityville	Hartford	Brentwood
빨간색 노선	5:05	5:15		5:45
파란색 노선	5:10	5:20	5:35	

남: 승객 여러분들은 주목해 주십시오. 제가 확인할 수 있도록 티켓을 꺼내 주시기 바랍니다.
여: 안녕하세요, 여기 제 티켓이요. 저는 Hartford로 가려고 해요. ¹⁹이 열차가 맞나요?
남: ¹⁹열차를 잘못 타셨네요. 이 열차는 그곳으로 직행하지 않아요.
여: 아, 정말요? 그곳에 가려면 어떻게 해야 하나요?
남: ²⁰우리가 방금 East Hampton을 출발했으니까 다음 역에서 환승하셔야 해요.
여: 알겠습니다. 그 열차를 타려면 오래 기다려야 하나요? 저는 Long Island 오케스트라 단원인데 ²¹공연하러 가는 중이거든요. 리허설할 시간이 필요해요.
남: 보통 5분마다 와요. 늦지 않으실 거예요.

19.
여자에게는 어떤 문제가 있는가?
(A) 열차를 잘못 탔다.
(B) 콘서트가 매진되었다.
(C) 그녀의 티켓으로는 환승을 할 수 없다.
(D) 마지막 순간에 장소가 변경되었다.

[해설] 열차표를 확인하는 승무원인 남자와 열차 승객인 여자의 대화이다. 여자가 자신이 Hartford 행 열차를 탄 것이 맞는지 묻자 남자가 열차를 잘못 탔다고(You must have taken the wrong train.) 알려 주는 것으로 보아 정답은 (A)이다.

[어휘] at the last minute 마지막 순간에, 임박해서

20.
시각 자료를 보시오. 여자는 어디서 다른 열차로 환승할 것인가?
(A) East Hampton
(B) Amityville
(C) Hartford
(D) Brentwood

[해설] 여자는 자신의 목적지인 Hartford에 정차하지 않는 열차를 탄 상황으로, 남자는 현재 East Hampton을 출발했으니 다음 역에서 환승할 것을(We just left East Hampton, so you'll have to transfer at the next stop.) 제안했다. 시각 자료로 주어진 열차 시간표에서 East Hampton 다음 역을 찾으면 Amityville이므로 이 역에서 내려 Hartford에 정차하는 Blue Line을 타야 함을 알 수 있다. 따라서 정답은 (B)이다.

21.
여자는 왜 서두르는가?
(A) 사진 촬영에 참여해야 한다.
(B) 라이브 공연을 보러 가는 중이다.
(C) 회의에 늦었다.
(D) 연습할 시간이 필요하다.

[해설] 대화 후반, 여자는 Hartford 행 열차를 타려면 오래 기다려야 하는지 물으며, 연주를 하러 가는 중인데, 리허설할 시간이 필요하다고(I'm on my way to a performance and I'll be needing some time to rehearse) 덧붙였다. 즉, 여자는 공연 전 연습 시간이 필요해서 서두르고 있으므로 정답은 (D)이다.

paraphrasing I'll be needing some time to rehearse. 리허설할 시간이 필요할 것이다. → She needs time to practice. 연습할 시간이 필요하다.

[어휘] in a rush 서두르는 take part in ~에 참여[참가]하다 run late for ~에 늦다 practice 연습하다

PART 4 | 라디오 방송(radio broadcast)

출제 유형 01 지역 행사 안내 방송
| 풀이 방법 해석 |

여: Radio 9의 공공 서비스 안내입니다. Copperhead 주민 센터는 4월 9일 오후 2시부터 5시까지 특별 요리 워크숍을 열 예정입니다. 이 과정은 기본적인 요리 지식, 전문적인 조언, 그리고 당신이 집에서 해 볼 수 있는 몇몇의 빠르고 쉬운 요리법도 포함할 것입니다. 워크숍의 '직접 해보세요' 부분은 참석자들에게 특징 있는 요리를 해 볼 기회를 제공할 것입니다. 그 후에 여러분이 만든 요리가 무엇이든 댁으로 가지고 갈 수 있습니다. 자리는 한정되어 있고 예약은 온라인으로만 가능하므로 예약을 하기 위해 온라인에 접속해 주세요!

출제 유형 02 기업 소개 관련 방송
| 풀이 방법 해석 |

남: 지역 비즈니스 소식으로는, 새로운 멕시칸 레스토랑이 다음 주에 Sunset 가에 문을 엽니다. 주인인 Juan Trujillo는 식품 업계에서 20년 이상 일한 경험이 있습니다. 그는 푸드 트럭을 운영했었는데, 최근의 임대료의 하락 덕분에 그의 사업을 건물로 이전하기로 결정하였습니다. Juan's Upon A Time으로 불리는 그 레스토랑은 Trujillo 씨의 고향의 요리들을 전문으로 합니다. 인테리어는 멕시코의 전형적인 레스토랑에 있는 것처럼 느끼도록 설계되었습니다. 다음 달부터 Juan's Upon A Time은 배달 서비스도 시작할 것입니다.

연습 문제
01. (B) 02. (B) 03. (A) 04. (B) 05. (A) 06. (A)

01.
What information can the listeners get **from** the city's **Web site**?
(A) **Detours** (B) Event **schedules**

W: Thanks for listening to HBS Radio. We are only one week away from the annual Iron Valley Festival. It features a talent competition, a night market, and many outdoor activities for children. The detailed event schedules are posted on the city's Web site.

Traditionally, it begins with a street parade. So, there will be some **detours** downtown on the first day of the festival.

청자들은 시 웹사이트에서 어떤 정보를 얻을 수 있는가?
(A) 우회로 **(B) 행사 일정**

라디오 방송
여: HBS 라디오를 들어 주셔서 감사합니다. 연례 Iron Valley 축제가 일주일 앞으로 다가왔습니다. 재능 경연, 야시장, 그리고 어린이들을 위한 많은 야외 활동이 열릴 것입니다. 세부적인 행사 일정은 시의 웹사이트에 게재되어 있습니다. 전통적으로, 축제는 거리 행진으로 시작합니다. 그러므로, 축제의 첫날에는 시내에 우회로가 있을 것입니다.

02. [AU]

What event will be **taking place next week**?
(A) A **book signing** event   (B) A **job fair**

M: Welcome to the show. The Summer **Career Fair** will be **held** next week. Over 120 companies have **registered** to set up booths at the fair, and want to fill over 2,000 full-time and summer intern **positions**. Approximately 10,000 students and **graduates** are expected to **attend** it. This **anticipated** turnout is almost double the **previous** year's.

다음 주에 어떤 행사가 열릴 것인가?
(A) 책 사인회 행사   **(B) 구직 박람회**

라디오 방송
남: 방송에 오신 것을 환영합니다. 여름 직업 박람회가 다음 주에 열릴 것입니다. 120개가 넘는 회사들이 박람회에 부스를 설치하기 위해 신청했고, 2천 개 이상의 정규직과 여름 인턴직을 채용하고자 합니다. 거의 1만 명의 학생들과 졸업생들이 참석할 것으로 예상됩니다. 이 예상된 참석자 수는 지난해의 거의 두 배입니다.

03. [BR]

Who is **Patrick Hans**?
(A) A **worker** at the **hotel**   (B) A **radio** program **host**

W: Good evening WUNB Radio listeners, and welcome to the Redding Local news. Last Saturday, over 300 people **gathered** at Riverside Park to clean the Sacramento River Trail. The Seaside Redding Hotel sponsored this **annual** event and 56 employees **joined** this big cause. Patrick Hans, **manager** of the hotel's public relations, said that this shows how we can **pay back** the community for this beautiful nature.

Patrick Hans는 누구인가?
(A) 호텔의 직원   (B) 라디오 프로그램 진행자

라디오 방송
여: 안녕하세요, WUNB 청취자 여러분, Redding 지역 뉴스에 오신 것을 환영합니다. 지난 토요일에, 300명이 넘는 사람들이 Sacramento 강가의 길을 청소하기 위해 Riverside 공원에 모였습니다. Seaside Redding 호텔이 이 연례 행사를 후원했고 56명의 직원들이 이 대의를 위해 함께 했습니다. 호텔의 홍보 매니저인 Patrick Hans는 이것이 이 아름다운 자연에 대해 우리가 지역 사회에 되갚을 수 있는 방법을 보여 준다고 말했습니다.

니다.

04. [US]

What is **Cedarville Builders known** for?
(A) **Short construction** periods
(B) **Ecofriendly** building methods

M: Welcome to CBN radio's weekly news. Yesterday, Cedarville Builders officially announced that it **signed** a three-million-dollar **construction** contract with the city government for a new **high school**. Cedarville Builders was **founded** just three years ago, but it became one of the most **promising** construction companies with **environmentally friendly** construction methods.

Cedarville Builders는 무엇으로 유명한가?
(A) 짧은 건설 기간   **(B) 친환경적인 건설 방식**

라디오 방송
남: CBN 라디오의 주간 뉴스에 오신 것을 환영합니다. 어제 Cedarville Builders는 새 고등학교를 위해 300만 달러의 건설 계약을 시 정부와 체결했다고 공식적으로 발표했습니다. Cedarville Builders는 겨우 3년 전에 설립되었지만 친환경적인 건설 방식으로 가장 유망한 건설 업체 중 하나가 되었습니다.

05. [US]

What will the **listeners** likely **hear next**?
(A) **A game prediction**   (B) A **weather** update

W: And now for the Bedford City News. Today, the **final game** of the national college ice hockey league championship will be held at Oliver Ice Rink. It is the first time in the team's **history** that the Hornets **moved to** the final. We invite Mr. Palmer, **former** professional ice hockey player, to **analyze** both teams and **predict** the game. Mr. Palmer, which team do you think is **closer** to the championship trophy?

청자들은 다음에 무엇을 들을 것인가?
(A) 경기 예측   (B) 최신 날씨 정보

라디오 방송
여: 그리고 이제 Bedford 시 뉴스입니다. 오늘, Oliver 아이스링크에서 전국 대학 아이스하키 리그의 결승전이 열릴 것입니다. Hornets가 결승전에 올라간 것은 팀 역사상 처음입니다. 전 프로 아이스하키 선수인 Palmer 씨를 초대해서 두 팀을 분석하고 경기를 예측해 보겠습니다. Palmer 씨, 어느 팀이 결승 트로피에 더 가깝다고 생각하시나요?

06. [BR]

What event was held **yesterday**?
(A) A **hospital opening**   (B) A **music festival**

M: This is Paul Brown with the news updates. The grand **opening ceremony** of a children's **hospital** was held at Harrington Medical Center yesterday. After a **full year** of construction, the seven-story building has 30 wards with 200 beds for **patients** and state-of-the-art equipment for accurate diagnoses.

어제 어떤 행사가 어제 열렸는가?
(A) 병원 개장   (B) 음악 축제

라디오 방송
남: 저는 최신 소식을 전해 드리는 Paul Brown입니다. 어제 Harrington 의료 센터에서 아동 병원의 개장식이 열렸습니다. 한 해 동안의 건설 끝에, 그 7층짜리 건물은 환자들을 위한 200개의 침대와 정확한 진단을 위한 최신 기기를 갖춘 30개의 병동이 있습니다.

paraphrasing 정답 1. (c) 2. (b) 3. (a) 4. (c) 5. (a) 6. (b)

실전 문제
01. (D)	02. (A)	03. (D)	04. (B)	05. (D)	06. (C)
07. (A)	08. (B)	09. (D)	10. (B)	11. (D)	12. (A)
13. (B)	14. (D)	15. (C)	16. (D)	17. (D)	18. (A)
19. (C)	20. (C)	21. (B)	22. (A)	23. (B)	24. (D)

[01-03] AU
Questions 01-03 refer to the following broadcast.

M: Hello, you're listening to White Falls Local News. ⁰¹Today I'll be interviewing the actress Angelina Braxton. She is currently working with a special charity, for which ⁰²she goes around visiting sick young patients in hospitals around the country. The charity, Cures for Kids, has a social media Web site that will be covering the visits. ⁰³Through that Ms. Braxton will ask fans and supporters to donate to the cause of treating children suffering from various diseases.

currently 현재, 지금   charity 자선 단체   go around 돌아다니다   patient 환자   cure (병을) 치유하다: 치유, 치유법, 치유책   cover 다루다, 포함시키다   supporter 지지자, 후원자   donate 기부[기증]하다   cause 주의, 주장, ~ 운동   treat 치료하다   suffer from ~로 고통 받다   disease 질병, 질환

01-03은 다음 방송에 관한 문제입니다.
남: 안녕하세요, 여러분들은 White Falls 지역 뉴스를 듣고 계십니다. ⁰¹오늘 제가 배우 Angelina Braxton을 인터뷰할 예정입니다. 그녀는 현재 특별한 자선 단체와 함께 일하고 있는데요, ⁰²그녀는 전국을 돌며 병원의 아픈 어린 환자들을 방문합니다. Cures for Kids라는 자선 단체로, 이러한 방문을 다룰 예정인 소셜 미디어 웹사이트를 보유하고 있습니다. ⁰³이곳을 통해 Braxton 씨는 팬들과 지지자들에게 여러 질병으로 고통받고 있는 어린이들을 치료하는 운동에 기부해 달라고 호소할 것입니다.

01.
Angelina Braxton은 누구인가?
(A) 뉴스 기자
(B) 약사
(C) 의사
(D) 배우

[해설] 담화 초반, 방송 프로그램을 소개한 후 배우 Angelina Braxton

(the actress Angelina Braxton)을 인터뷰할 예정이라고 했으므로 정답은 (D)이다.

02.
Angelina Braxton은 어떤 종류의 프로젝트에 참여하고 있는가?
(A) 병원의 환자들 방문하기
(B) 콘서트에서 노래하기
(C) 새 영화 촬영하기
(D) 질병을 치료하기

[해설] Angelina Braxton이 현재 자선 단체와 함께 일한다고 한 후, 전국을 돌며 병원의 아픈 어린 환자들을 방문한다고(she goes around visiting sick young patients in hospitals around the country) 설명했다. 따라서 정답은 (A)이다.

paraphrasing she goes around visiting sick young patients in hospitals 병원의 아픈 어린 환자들을 방문하러 돌아다니다 → visiting hospital patients 병원의 환자들 방문하기

[어휘] shoot 촬영하다

03.
화자는 Angelina Braxton이 무엇을 할 것이라고 말하는가?
(A) 백신을 테스트하기
(B) 오디션을 개최하기
(C) 환자들을 인터뷰하기
(D) 기부를 요청하기

[해설] 담화 후반, Angelina Braxton이 할 예정인 활동이 언급된다. 팬들과 지지자들에게 여러 질병으로 고통받고 있는 어린이들을 치료하는 운동에 기부해 달라고 호소할 것이라고(will ask fans and supporters to donate the cause of treating children suffering from various diseases) 했으므로 정답은 (D)이다.

paraphrasing ask fans and supporters to donate 팬들과 지지자들에게 기부해 달라고 요청하다 → request donations 기부를 요청하기

[어휘] vaccine (예방) 백신   donation 기부, 기증

[04-06] US
Questions 04-06 refer to the following radio broadcast.

W: You're listening to Tech Talk Radio. Our studio guest today is ⁰⁴Dylan Harding, the owner of Harding's Employment Services. Mr. Harding has had tremendous success ⁰⁴pairing employers and workers together in a way that helps everyone. ⁰⁵He's here to tell us about the software he uses that tracks the data of his clients and recommends jobs that are available. ⁰⁶We have actually posted a link to download a demo version of the software. Please visit our Web site and click the link ⁰⁶to try out a trial version of it. It could prove to be very useful for your business.

owner 주인, 소유주   employment 고용   tremendous 엄청난   employer 고용주   track 추적하다   demo 견본, 전시용 제품   try out 시험적으로 사용해 보다   trial (최종 결정 전의) 시험, 실험   prove 입증[증명]하다   useful 유용한

DAY 19 205

04-06은 다음 라디오 방송에 관한 문제입니다.

여: 여러분은 Tech Talk 라디오를 듣고 계십니다. 오늘 저희 스튜디오의 손님은 **04Harding's 고용 서비스의 소유주인 Dylan Harding** 씨입니다. Harding 씨는 모두에게 도움이 되는 방법으로 **04고용주와 직원을 이어주는 것**으로 대단한 성공을 거두었습니다. **05그가 출연하여 고객들의 정보를 추적하고 자리가 난 일자리를 추천해주는, 그가 사용하는 소프트웨어에 대해 얘기해줄 것입니다. 06저희가 실제로 이 소프트웨어의 데모 버전을 다운로드 할 수 있도록 링크를 게시했습니다.** 저희 웹사이트에 방문하시어 링크를 클릭하시고 **06시험판을 사용해보세요**. 여러분의 사업체에 매우 유용하다는 것이 입증될 것입니다.

04.

Harding 씨는 어떤 종류의 사업체를 소유하고 있는가?
(A) 소프트웨어 디자인 회사
(B) 직업 소개소
(C) 엔지니어링 회사
(D) 소매 상점

[해설] 라디오 방송 프로그램의 일부로, 초대 손님인 Dylan Harding을 Harding's 고용 서비스의 소유주(owner)라고 소개하고, 그가 고용주와 직원을 이어주는(pairing employers and workers together) 일에 성공했다고 했다. 이로 보아 Mr. Harding은 구직자에게는 일자리를, 고용주에게는 직원을 소개해 주는 업체를 소유하고 있음을 알 수 있으므로 정답은 (B)이다.

[어휘] retail 소매

05.

Harding 씨는 어떤 종류의 소프트웨어에 대해 얘기할 것인가?
(A) 보안
(B) 재고 관리
(C) 일정 관리
(D) 데이터 추적

[해설] 질문의 핵심 키워드 software가 언급되는 담화 중반에 단서가 있다. 고객들의 정보를 추적하고 자리가 난 일자리를 추천해주는 소프트웨어(the software he uses that tracks the data of his clients and recommends jobs that are available)에 대해 얘기할 것이라고 했으므로 정답은 (D)이다.

[어휘] security 보안, 경비 inventory 재고, 재고 조사

06.

화자는 청자들에게 무엇을 하라고 요청하는가?
(A) 개인 정보를 제출하기
(B) 질문을 가지고 전화하기
(C) 데모를 다운로드 받기
(D) 일자리에 지원하기

[해설] 담화 후반, 화자는 소프트웨어의 데모 버전을 다운로드 할 수 있도록 링크를 게시했다며(We have actually posted a link to download a demo version of the software), 시험판을 사용해보라고(to try out a trial version of it) 했다. 즉, 데모 버전을 다운로드 하라는 것이므로 정답은 (C)이다.

[어휘] submit 제출하다 personal information 개인 정보 apply for ~에 지원하다

[07-09] BR

Questions 07-09 refer to the following broadcast.

W: Thank you for listening to WBS Radio. Don't forget that in just a few short weeks, **07the singer Camilla Suarez will be coming to put on a concert here in Crown Point. 08The show will begin at 5 P.M. on Sunday, July 2 at Regalia Stadium. Unfortunately, the stadium does not allow outside food or beverages.** There will be two opening performances before Camilla takes the stage. Who will be performing first has not yet been announced, but **09the tour manager has promised to post the lineup on Camilla's fan site by the end of the week, so be sure to check there.**

in just a few short weeks 단 몇 주 만에   put on 상연하다
stadium 경기장, 스타디움   allow 허용하다   outside 외부의
take the stage 무대에 오르다   promise to V ~하기로 약속하다

07-09는 다음 방송에 관한 문제입니다.

여: WBS 라디오를 들어주셔서 감사합니다. 단 몇 주만 지나면 **07가수 Camilla Suarez**가 이곳 Crown Point에 와서 콘서트를 할 것이라는 것을 잊지 마세요. **08공연은 Regalia 스타디움에서 7월 2일 일요일 오후 5시에 시작될 예정입니다. 안타깝게도, 이 스타디움은 외부 음식이나 음료 반입을 허용하지 않습니다.** Camilla가 무대에 오르기 전에 두 개의 오프닝 공연이 있을 예정입니다. 누가 첫 번째로 공연할지는 아직 발표되지 않았지만 **09투어 매니저가 주말까지 Camilla의 팬 사이트에 출연자 정보를 게시하겠다고 약속했으니** 그곳에서 꼭 확인하시기 바랍니다.

07.

담화의 주제는 무엇인가?
(A) 음악 콘서트
(B) 시상식
(C) 스포츠 경기
(D) 새로운 메뉴

[해설] 라디오 방송에서 가수 Camilla Suarez의 콘서트에 대해 소개하는(the singer Camilla Suarez will be coming to put on a concert) 담화로, 공연 일시와 장소를 비롯하여 관련 세부 정보를 제시하고 있다. 따라서 정답은 (A)이다.

08.

화자가 "안타깝게도, 이 스타디움은 외부 음식이나 음료 반입을 허용하지 않습니다"라고 말할 때 암시하는 것은 무엇인가?
(A) 참석자들이 미리 식사 예약을 해야 한다.
(B) 다과는 행사 장소에서만 구입해야 한다.
(C) 모든 종류의 식사 제한이 맞춰서 제공될 것이다.
(D) 사람들은 식사 직후에 운동하는 것을 피해야 한다.

[해설] 화자는 공연이 Regalia 스타디움에서 있을 거라고(The show will begin ~ at Regalia Stadium) 말한 후, 스타디움 밖에서 구입한 음식이나 음료를 가지고 공연장에 들어갈 수 없다고 했다. 즉, 먹을 것은 반드시 공연 장소인 스타디움 내에서만 구입해야 한다는 의미이므로 정답은 (B)이다.

[어휘] attendee 참가자   meal reservation 식사 예약   in advance 미리, 사전에   venue (행사의) 장소   dietary 음식물의, 식이 요법의   restriction 제한, 규제

09.

화자는 왜 청자들에게 웹사이트를 방문하라고 말하는가?
(A) 좌석을 예약하기 위해
(B) 주차권을 신청하기 위해
(C) 공연자의 프로필을 읽기 위해
(D) 공연 출연진을 보기 위해

[해설] 질문의 핵심 키워드인 Web site는 담화 후반의 Camilla's fan site를 가리킨다. 콘서트 투어 매니저가 주말까지 Camilla의 팬 사이트에 출연자 정보를 게시하겠다고 약속했다면서(the tour manager has promised to post the lineup on Camilla's fan site by the end of the week) 꼭 확인하라고 했다. 즉, 누가 공연에 나오는지 보려면 웹사이트를 방문하라는 것이므로 정답은 (D)이다.

[어휘] reserve 예약하다 apply for ~을 신청하다 performer 공연자 view 보다

[10-12] US

Questions 10-12 refer to the following broadcast.

> W: You're listening to *Personnel Perfection*, ¹⁰**the show developed exclusively for people working in the HR department.** If you're in charge of hiring new employees for your company, today's episode shouldn't be missed. Our special guest is ¹¹**Clara Cohen, who is an expert in social media platforms.** She'll tell you how to get the best pool of candidates, even on a small budget. ¹²**And don't forget that *Personnel Perfection* is holding its first-ever live conference** in Austin, Texas, on October 5. ¹²**Please join us there** for an opportunity to boost your professional development.

develop 개발하다 exclusively 독점적으로, 오로지 HR department 인사부 in charge of ~을 맡아서, 담당해서 hire 고용하다 expert 전문가 platform 플랫폼(컴퓨터 사용의 기반이 되는 하드웨어·소프트웨어의 환경) pool 이용 가능 인력 candidate 후보자 budget 예산 first-ever 생전 처음의, 사상 최초의 opportunity 기회 boost 신장시키다, 북돋우다 professional 전문적인, 직업의 development 발달, 성장

10-12는 다음 방송에 관한 문제입니다.
여: 여러분은 ¹⁰오로지 인사부에서 근무하는 분들을 위해 개발된 프로그램인 <Personnel Perfection>을 듣고 계십니다. 여러분이 만약 회사에서 신입 직원 채용을 담당하고 있다면 오늘 에피소드를 놓치시면 안 됩니다. 오늘의 특별 손님은 ¹¹소셜미디어 플랫폼의 전문가인 Clara Cohen 씨입니다. 그녀가 여러분께 심지어 적은 예산으로도 가장 우수한 후보 인력을 확보하는 방법을 알려 드릴 것입니다. ¹²그리고 <Personnel Perfection>이 10월 5일 텍사스, 오스틴에서 최초로 생방송 콘퍼런스를 개최한다는 것을 잊지 마세요. 그곳에서 우리와 함께하시어 여러분의 전문성을 신장할 기회를 가지세요.

10.

누구를 대상으로 하는 프로그램인가?
(A) 소규모 기업의 소유주들
(B) 인사부 직원들
(C) 영업 직원들
(D) 컴퓨터 기술자들

[해설] 오로지 인사부에서 근무하는 분들만을 위해 개발된 프로그램(the show developed exclusively for people working in the HR department)이라는 말로 프로그램을 소개하며 방송을 시작했다. 즉, 이 프로그램은 인사부 직원들을 대상으로 하므로 정답은 (B)이다.

paraphrasing people working in the HR department 인사부에서 근무하는 사람들 → Human resources workers 인사부 직원들

11.

Cohen 씨는 무엇을 전문으로 하는가?
(A) 언어 능력
(B) 교육 방법
(C) 개인 재무
(D) 소셜 미디어

[해설] Cohen 씨는 담화 중반, 오늘 에피소드의 특별 손님으로 언급된 Clara Cohen이다. Clara Cohen을 소셜미디어 플랫폼의 전문가(an expert in social media platforms)라고 소개한 것으로 보아 정답은 (D)이다.

paraphrasing specialize in ~을 전문으로 하다 → an expert in ~의 전문가

[어휘] specialize in ~을 전문으로 하다 method 방법 personal 개인의 finance 재정, 재무

12.

청자들은 무엇을 하라고 요청받는가?
(A) 행사에 참석하기
(B) 질문을 제출하기
(C) 대금을 보내기
(D) 상품을 검토하기

[해설] 요청/제안 사항은 주로 담화 후반부에 언급된다. 10월 5일 텍사스, 오스틴에서 최초로 생방송 콘퍼런스를 개최한다고(that *Personnel Perfection* is holding its first-ever live conference) 한 후, 그곳에서 함께해 달라고(Please join us there) 요청했다. 즉, 특정 행사에 참석할 것을 요청하고 있으므로 정답은 (A)이다.

[어휘] attend 참석하다 submit 제출하다 payment 지불, 지급 review 검토하다, 평가하다

[13-15] BR

Questions 13-15 refer to the following broadcast.

> M: You're listening to the local news broadcast on 99.3 FM. Yesterday, ¹³**the annual Greenville Summer Marathon** was held in Calhoun Park. About 1,500 athletes participated in ¹³**the 42-kilometer race**, up from about 1,300 compared to last year. As part of the event, ¹⁴**donations were collected from participants and spectators. These will be used to sponsor computer classes** for senior citizens at the local community center. ¹⁵**For updates about this and other events happening in the area, enroll in our station's text alert service by visiting www.greenvilleradio.com.** This is a free service for our listeners.

> broadcast 방송; 방송하다   local 지역의   annual 매년의, 연례의
> athlete 운동 선수   participate in ~에 참가하다   compared to
> ~와 비교하여   as part of ~의 일환으로   donation 기부, 기증
> collect 모금하다   participant 참가자   spectator (스포츠 행사
> 의) 관중   senior citizen 어르신   enroll in ~에 등록하다
> station 방송국

13-15은 다음 방송에 관한 문제입니다.
남: 여러분은 FM 99.3의 지역 뉴스 방송을 듣고 계십니다. 어제, **¹³연례 Greenville 여름 마라톤**이 Calhoun 공원에서 열렸습니다. 약 1,500명의 선수들이 **¹³42킬로미터 경주**에 참가했는데, 이는 약 1,300명이었던 작년에 비해 늘어난 숫자입니다. 행사의 일환으로, **¹⁴참가자와 관중으로부터 기부금을 모금했습니다**. 이것은 지역 문화 센터의 어르신들을 위한 **¹⁴컴퓨터 강좌를 후원하는 데 쓰일 예정입니다**. **¹⁵이를 비롯하여 이 지역에서 일어나는 다른 행사들에 관한 최신 정보를 원하시면 www.greenvilleradio.com을 방문하셔서 저희 방송국의 문자 알림 서비스에 등록하세요**. 이것은 우리 청취자들을 위한 무료 서비스입니다.

13.
방송은 어떤 종류의 행사에 관한 것인가?
(A) 개막식
(B) 장거리 경주
(C) 지역 사회 야유회
(D) 음악 공연

[해설] 방송에서 다루는 행사의 종류를 묻는 문제이다. 담화 초반의 연례 Greenville 여름 마라톤(the annual Greenville Summer Marathon)과 42킬로미터 경주(the 42-kilometer race) 같은 말로 보아 마라톤, 즉 장거리 경주에 대해 방송하고 있음을 알 수 있다. 따라서 정답은 (B)이다.

paraphrasing Marathon 마라톤 / the 42-kilometer race 42킬로미터 경주 → a long-distance race 장거리 경주

[어휘] long-distance 장거리의

14.
기부금은 무엇을 위해 쓰일 것인가?
(A) 연구 실시하기
(B) 스타디움 개조하기
(C) 정원에 나무 심기
(D) 강좌 개설하기

[해설] 기부금의 사용처를 묻는 문제이다. 담화 중반, 참가자와 관중으로부터 기부금을 모금하여(donations were collected from participants and spectators) 지역 문화 센터의 어르신들을 위한 컴퓨터 강좌를 후원하는 데 쓸 것이라고(These will be used to sponsor computer classes) 했다. 따라서 정답은 (D)이다.

paraphrasing sponsor computer classes 컴퓨터 강좌를 후원하기 → Holding some classes 강좌 개설하기

[어휘] conduct a study 연구하다   renovate 개조[보수]하다

15.
화자에 따르면, 청자들은 웹사이트에서 무엇을 할 수 있는가?
(A) 티켓 구매하기
(B) 의견 공유하기
(C) 최신 정보 신청하기

(D) 사진 보기

[해설] 담화 마지막에 웹사이트 주소가 언급되는데, 이 지역에서 일어나는 행사에 관한 최신 소식을 원하면 웹사이트에서 방문하여 문자 알림 서비스에 등록하라고(For updates about this and other events happening in the area, enroll in our station's text alert service by visiting www.greenvilleradio.com) 했다. 즉, 웹사이트에서 최신 정보 수신 신청을 할 수 있으므로 정답은 (C)이다.

paraphrasing enroll 등록하다 → sign up for 신청하다

[어휘] purchase 구매하다   share 공유하다   sign up for ~을 신청하다   view 보다

[16-18] US
Questions 16-18 refer to the following broadcast.

> W: Hello, and welcome back to Business Builders. If you're just joining us now, **¹⁶today's topic is ways to attract investors.** One listener called in during the break to tell me that **¹⁷he advertised his business on nearby highway billboards. Since then, the number of interested investors has more than doubled.** To discuss some more modern ideas, Marissa Bennett from Bennett Marketing is here. **¹⁸She's going to tell us what she thinks is the most effective way to promote your business these days.** Welcome to the show, Marissa.

> join 함께 하다, 합류하다   investor 투자자   break 쉬는 시간
> nearby 인근의   billboard (옥외의) 광고판   interested 관심이 있는   effective 효과적인   promote 홍보하다

16-18은 다음 방송에 관한 문제입니다.
여: 안녕하세요, Business Builders를 다시 찾아 주신 것을 환영합니다. 지금 막 저희와 함께 하신 거라면 **¹⁶오늘의 주제는 투자자들을 유치하는 방법입니다**. 쉬는 시간 동안 한 청취자 분께서 전화를 주셔서 **¹⁷인근 고속도로 광고판에 자신의 회사를 광고했다고 하셨는데요. 그때부터 관심을 보이는 투자자들의 수가 두 배 이상 늘었습니다**. 보다 새로운 아이디어에 대해 얘기 나누기 위해 Bennett 마케팅의 Marissa Bennett를 모셨습니다. **¹⁸그녀가 생각하는, 요즘 여러분의 사업체를 홍보하기 위한 가장 효과적인 방법에 대해 얘기해 줄 것입니다**. Marissa 씨, 우리 프로그램에 오신 것을 환영합니다.

16.
방송의 주제는 무엇인가?
(A) 장소 선정하기
(B) 투자자 유치하기
(C) 계약 협상하기
(D) 우수한 직원 모집하기

[해설] 담화 전반부에서 오늘의 주제는 투자자들을 유치하는 방법이라고(today's topic is ways to attract investors) 밝혔으므로 정답은 (B)이다.

[어휘] negotiate 협상하다   contract 계약(서)   recruit 모집하다, 뽑다

17.
화자가 "그때부터 관심을 보이는 투자자들의 수가 두 배 이상 늘었습니다"

라고 말할 때 암시하는 것은 무엇인가?
(A) 사업체가 합병에 동의해야 했다.
(B) 시청자를 겨냥하기 쉽다.
(C) 광고 비용이 너무 높지도 모른다.
(D) 방법이 효과가 있었다.

[해설] 한 청취자가 인근 고속도로 광고판에 자신의 회사를 광고했다는(he advertised his business on nearby highway billboards) 내용 뒤에 "그때부터 관심을 보이는 투자자들의 수가 두 배 이상 늘었습니다"라고 덧붙였다. 해당 표현은 광고판에 광고한 방법이 효과가 있었다고 말하기 위한 것이므로 정답은 (D)이다.

[어휘] merger 합병 audience 관중, 청중, 시청자 target 대상으로 삼다, 겨냥하다 cost 비용 method 방법 work well 효과가 있다

18.
화자는 다음에 무슨 일이 있을 것이라고 말하는가?
(A) 전문가가 자신의 생각을 공유할 것이다.
(B) 광고 후에 돌아올 것이다.
(C) 경연 대회가 발표될 것이다.
(D) 음악을 틀 것이다.

[해설] 앞으로 일어날 일을 묻는 문제의 단서는 주로 담화 후반에 제시된다. 화자는 Bennett Marketing의 Marissa Bennett가 출연해 그녀가 생각하는 사업체 홍보에 가장 효과적인 방법에 대해서 얘기할 것이라고 (She's going to tell us what she thinks is the most effective way to promote your business these days.) 했으므로 정답은 (A)이다.

[어휘] specialist 전문가 share 공유하다 thought 생각 commercial 광고 방송

[19-21] [BR]
Questions 19-21 refer to the following broadcast.

W: This is Eileen Ballard from KATR Radio. The Parks and Recreation Department is making repairs and improvements to [19]the town's forty-five miles of trails used for walking, jogging, and biking. In addition, [20]the local nonprofit organization Nature Now has just finished measuring the distances between all of the major landmarks in the system. They've added this information to a [21]convenient smartphone app that will help you to track how far you have gone. [21]You can download it for free from Nature Now's Web site. It'll be on my phone by the end of the day.

make a repair 수리하다 make improvements 개선시키다 trail 오솔길, 루트, 코스 used for ~에 사용하는 in addition 덧붙여, 게다가 local 지역의 nonprofit 비영리적인 measure 측정하다 distance 거리 landmark 주요 지형지물, 랜드마크 add 추가하다 convenient 편리한 track 추적하다

19-21은 다음 방송에 관한 문제입니다.
여: KATR 라디오의 Eileen Ballard입니다. 공원 및 위락시설 관리국이 [19]걷거나 조깅을 하거나 자전거를 탈 때 사용되는 우리 도시의 45마일 코스를 개보수할 예정입니다. 이에 더해서 [20]지역의 비영리 기구인 Nature Now가 시스템상의 모든 주요 랜드마크들 사이의 거리 측정을 막 끝냈습니다. 얼마나 멀리 이동했는지 추적하도록 도와줄 [21]편리한 스마트폰 앱에 이 정보를 추가했습니다. [21]Nature Now의 웹사이트에서 무료로 다운로드하실 수 있습니다. 오늘 안으로 제 전화기에도 다운받을 예정입니다.

19.
화자는 방송에서 무엇에 대해 얘기하는가?
(A) 자전거 경주
(B) 지하철 시스템
(C) 운동 코스
(D) 공원 폐쇄

[해설] 담화 초반, 공원 및 위락시설 관리국이 걷거나 조깅을 하거나 자전거를 탈 때 사용되는 코스(the town's forty-five miles of trails used for walking, jogging, and biking)를 개보수할 예정이라고 알렸다. 즉, 운동할 때 이용하는 코스의 개보수에 대해 다루고 있는 방송이므로 정답은 (C)이다.

paraphrasing trails used for walking, jogging, and biking 걷거나 조깅을 하거나 자전거를 탈 때 사용되는 코스 → exercise trails 운동 코스

[어휘] closure 폐쇄

20.
지역 자선 단체는 무엇을 했는가?
(A) 개선을 위한 기금을 모았다.
(B) 수상 후보로 지명되었다.
(C) 광범위한 측정을 했다.
(D) 새로운 웹사이트를 공개했다.

[해설] 질문의 핵심 키워드 local charity는 담화 중반의 the local nonprofit organization(지역의 비영리 기구) Nature Now를 가리키므로 이들이 한 일에 정답의 단서가 있다. 이들이 모든 주요 랜드마크들 사이의 거리 측정을 막 끝냈다고(has just finished measuring the distances between all of the major landmarks) 했으므로 이를 '광범위한 측정'으로 바꿔 표현한 (C)가 정답이다.

paraphrasing the local nonprofit organization 지역의 비영리 기구 → a local charity 지역 자선 단체 / measuring the distances between all of the major landmarks 모든 주요 랜드마크들 사이의 거리 측정 → taken extensive measurements 광범위한 측정을 했다

[어휘] charity 자선 단체 raise fund 기금을 모으다 nominate (후보자로) 지명[추천]하다 extensive 광범위한 take a measurement 치수를 재다 launch 출시하다

21.
화자는 왜 "오늘 안으로 제 전화기에도 다운받을 예정입니다"라고 말하는가?
(A) 설치 단계를 설명하기 위해
(B) 서비스를 지지하기 위해
(C) 지연에 대해 사과하기 위해
(D) 행사를 강조하기 위해

[해설] 지역의 비영리 기구가 측정한 주요 랜드마크들 사이의 거리 정보를 편리한(convenient) 이동 거리 추적 스마트폰 앱에 추가했으며, 이 앱을 그 비영리 기구 웹사이트에서 무료로 다운받을 수 있다고(You can download it for free from Nature Now's Web site) 한 후에 "오늘 안으로 제 전화기에도 다운받을 예정입니다"라고 덧붙였다. 즉, 화자 자신도 다운받고 싶을 만큼 이 앱에서 제공하는 서비스가 편리하고 유용하다는 것

DAY 19 209

을 강조하기 위해서 해당 표현을 사용한 것이므로 정답은 (B)이다.

[어휘] setup 설치 endorse (공개적으로) 지지하다 highlight 강조하다

[22-24] US

Questions 22-24 refer to the following radio broadcast.

> M: You're listening to K103 Radio. I'm your host, Louis Beck. Those visiting the Milford neighborhood today will notice a lot more activity than usual at 8th Street and Bailey Avenue, where the grand opening of Winifred's is being held. ²²**Winifred's is a dry-cleaning service that can clean any type of fabric.** There are several similar businesses in town, but ²³**Winifred's is the only one that is open twenty-four hours a day, seven days a week.** To celebrate the grand opening, ²⁴**the business is giving out coupons for twenty-five percent off any service to everyone who stops by the business today.**

host (TV·라디오의) 진행자 neighborhood 근처, 인근 notice (보거나 듣고) 알다 activity 움직임, 활기 grand opening 개점, 개장 fabric 직물, 천 similar 비슷한 business 사업체 in town 도심부에 있는 give out 나눠 주다 stop by (~에) 잠시 들르다

22-24는 다음 라디오 방송에 관한 문제입니다.
남: 여러분은 K103 라디오를 듣고 계십니다. 저는 진행자, Louis Beck입니다. 오늘 Milford 인근을 방문하시는 분들은 8번 가와 Bailey 가가 평소보다 훨씬 더 많이 북적이는 것을 보게 되실 텐데요, 이곳에서 Winifred's의 개점 행사가 열리고 있습니다. ²²**Winifred's는 어떤 종류의 직물이든 세탁이 가능한 드라이클리닝 서비스 업체입니다.** 시내에 비슷한 업체들이 여러 곳 있지만 ²³**Winifred's는 365일 24시간 내내 영업하는 유일한 곳입니다.** 개점을 축하하기 위해서 ²⁴**이 업체는 오늘 영업점에 들르는 모든 분들에게 어떤 서비스든 25퍼센트 할인 받을 수 있는 쿠폰을 나눠 드립니다.**

22.

무엇에 관한 방송인가?
(A) 드라이클리닝 업체
(B) 패션 잡지
(C) 옷 가게
(D) 직물 제조업체

[해설] 특정 거리가 북적이는 이유가 Winifred's의 개점 행사 때문이라고 한 후, Winifred's를 드라이클리닝 서비스를 제공하는 업체로(Winifred's is a dry-cleaning service) 소개했다. 이어서 이 업체의 특징과 개점 행사 세부 내용 등을 설명하고 있으므로 정답은 (A)이다.

> paraphrasing   a dry-cleaning service 드라이클리닝 서비스 업체 → a dry cleaner 드라이클리닝 업체

[어휘] dry cleaner 드라이클리닝 업체 fabric 직물

23.

화자에 따르면, 이 업체의 어떤 점이 특별한가?
(A) 이 지역에서 가격이 가장 저렴하다.

(B) 24시간 내내 영업한다.
(C) 무료 배송을 제공한다.
(D) 환경친화적이다.

[해설] 담화 중반, Winifred's가 365일 24시간 내내 영업하는 유일한 곳이라고(Winifred's is the only one that is open twenty-four hours a day, seven days a week.) 했으므로 정답은 (B)이다. around the clock은 '24시간 내내'라는 뜻이다.

> paraphrasing   open twenty-four hours a day, seven days a week 일주일 내내 하루 24시간 영업하는 → It is open around the clock. 24시간 내내 영업한다.

[어휘] around the clock 24시간 내내

24.

오늘 이 업체를 방문하는 사람들에게는 무엇이 주어질 것인가?
(A) 카탈로그
(B) 다과
(C) 무료 샘플
(D) 할인 쿠폰

[해설] 담화 마지막에서, 오늘 들르는 모든 사람들에게는 어떤 서비스든 25퍼센트 할인 받을 수 있는 쿠폰을 나눠준다고(the business is giving out coupons for twenty-five percent off any service to everyone who stops by the business today) 했으므로 정답은 (D)이다.

> paraphrasing   coupons for twenty-five percent off any service 어떤 서비스든 25퍼센트 할인 받을 수 있는 쿠폰 → a discount coupon 할인 쿠폰

[어휘] refreshments 다과

DAY 20

PART 3 박물관·공연장/교통수단

출제 유형 01 박물관·공연장

| 풀이 방법 해석 |

> 여: 안녕하세요, 제가 이 극장의 토요일 오후 연극 티켓이 이미 2장 있는데요, 합류하고 싶어 하는 다른 친구들이 몇 명 있어요. 4장 더 구매할 수 있을까요?
> 남: 죄송하지만, 그 공연의 티켓은 더 이상 남아 있지 않습니다. 하지만, 일요일 저녁 공연은 남은 좌석이 많아요.
> 여: 그러면, 6장의 티켓의 돈을 내는 대신 모두 함께 볼 수 있도록 이 티켓을 그 공연으로 바꿀 수 있을까요? 그리고 저희가 모두 서로의 옆에 앉을 수 있을까요?
> 남: 문제없습니다. 그나저나, 저녁 공연 후에는 출연진과 사진을 찍으실 수 있어요. 카메라 가져오는 것을 잊지 마세요!

출제 유형 02 교통수단

| 풀이 방법 해석 |

여: 안녕하세요, Jason. 여기서 당신을 만나서 반갑네요. 그건 제가 회사로 가는 셔틀버스를 타는 데 너무 늦지 않았다는 거니까요.
남: 안녕하세요, Olivia. 셔틀버스가 8시까지 도착하지 않는 건 이례적이네요. 10분 전에 여기 왔어야 해요. 제가 8시 40분에 시작하는 주간 회의에 늦을 것 같아 조금 걱정이 됩니다.
여: 제가 집에서 나오기 전에 교통 방송을 들었는데 버스의 경로에 자동차 사고가 있었대요. 그게 지연을 야기한 것 같아요.
남: 정말요? 그렇다면, Minsu에게 전화해서 오늘 우리를 태워 달라고 부탁해 볼게요. 그가 아직 집에 있길 바라요.

 연습 문제

01. (A)   02. (B)   03. (B)   04. (B)   05. (A)   06. (B)

01. US-AU

What caused the **detour**?
(A) **Construction** work   (B) A **car accident**

W: Good morning, Jason. How was your commute to the office today? There was an unexpected detour on Main Street. I was late this morning.
M: I listened to the local news and it said that resurfacing work started this morning. It won't be completed until next month. I commuted to the office by bicycle this morning. It will be good for my health.

무엇이 우회를 야기했는가?
(A) 공사 작업   (B) 자동차 사고

여: 안녕하세요, Jason. 오늘 회사로의 통근 어땠어요? Main 가에 예기치 못한 우회가 있었어요. 저는 오늘 아침에 늦었어요.
남: 지역 뉴스를 들었는데 오늘 아침에 도로 재포장 작업을 시작했대요. 다음 달까지 끝나지 않을 거예요. 저는 오늘 아침에 자전거를 타고 회사에 왔어요. 제 건강에 좋을 거예요.

02. BR-US

Where is the conversation most likely **taking place**?
(A) At a **post office**   (B) At a **theater**

W: Excuse me, I booked a ticket online for the 6:30 show. The confirmation e-mail said that I need to pick it up at the box office.
M: Okay. What's your last name? And would you please present a photo ID?

대화는 어디에서 이루어지고 있겠는가?
(A) 우체국에서   **(B)** 극장에서

여: 실례합니다, 제가 온라인으로 6시 30분 공연 티켓을 예매했어요. 확인 이메일에서 매표소에서 티켓을 수령하라고 하더라고요.
남: 알겠습니다. 성이 무엇인가요? 그리고 사진이 있는 신분증을 보여 주시겠어요?

03. BR-US

What does the **man offer to do**?
(A) **Give** a **discount coupon**
(B) **Sign** the **woman up** for a tour

M: Welcome to Bologna Museum. Here is your ticket and a guide map. Do you need anything else?
W: Yes, I want to learn more about Angela Russo's artwork. Do you have any audio guide services?
M: Unfortunately, we don't because it is a special exhibition. But we do offer a guided tour instead. You need to register for it first. Shall I do that for you?

남자는 무엇을 해주겠다고 하는가?
(A) 할인 쿠폰 주기   **(B)** 여자를 위해 투어 신청하기

남: Bologna 박물관에 오신 것을 환영합니다. 여기 티켓과 가이드 맵이 있습니다. 그 외에 필요한 게 있으신가요?
여: 네, Angela Russo의 예술 작품에 대해 더 알고 싶어요. 오디오 안내 서비스가 있나요?
남: 안타깝지만, 특별 전시라 그건 없습니다. 하지만 저희는 대신에 안내원이 있는 투어를 제공해요. 우선 그것을 신청하셔야 해요. 제가 그것을 해 드릴까요?

04. US-US

What does the **woman suggest doing**?
(A) **Renting** a car   (B) **Using** a **shuttle** bus

M: Jaime, do you think we need to rent a car during the conference?
W: That would be more convenient if we have something to be handled urgently. But we have a limited budget, so why don't we just use the hotel shuttle? During the conference, it runs every 30 minutes from our hotel to the conference center.

여자는 무엇을 할 것을 제안하는가?
(A) 자동차 렌트하기   **(B)** 셔틀버스 이용하기

남: Jaime, 우리가 학회 동안 차를 렌트할 필요가 있다고 생각해요.
여: 우리가 급하게 해결해야 할 게 있으면 더 편할 거예요. 하지만 우리는 한정된 예산이 있으니, 그냥 호텔 셔틀버스를 이용하는 게 어때요? 학회 동안, 우리 호텔에서 학회 센터까지 30분마다 운행해요.

05. BR-BR

What will the **man do next**?
(A) **Take** some **photos**   (B) **Buy** some **souvenirs**

M: The Centerville Ball Park is one of the oldest sports stadiums that I have ever visited.
W: Yes, I read on the board that it was constructed in 1922 and maintained with minimum renovations.
M: Wow, amazing. I'm going to go to the player's locker room and take some pictures before I stop by the gift shop.

남자는 다음에 무엇을 할 것인가?
(A) 사진 찍기   (B) 기념품 사기

남: Centerville 야구장은 제가 방문한 가장 오래된 스포츠 경기장 중 하나예요.
여: 네, 안내판에서 1922년에 지어졌고 최소한의 보수로 유지되어 왔다는 것을 읽었어요.
남: 와, 놀랍네요. 저는 기념품점에 들르기 전에 선수들의 탈의실에 가서 사진을 찍을 거예요.

06. [BR-AU]

What will the speakers take to the airport?
(A) Airport bus   (B) Subway

> W: We are supposed to get to the airport in an hour to pick up Mr. Kim. Do you think we need to get a taxi?
> M: I don't think so. The airport expressway is fine but there might be heavy traffic downtown. Therefore, we'd better take the subway to arrive on time.

화자들은 공항까지 무엇을 탈 것인가?
(A) 공항 버스   **(B) 지하철**

여: 우리는 Kim 씨를 태우기 위해 한 시간 내로 공항에 도착해야 해요. 우리 택시를 타야 할까요?
남: 안 그래도 될 것 같아요. 공항 고속도로는 괜찮지만 시내에 교통 체증이 있을 거예요. 그러므로, 우리는 제시간에 도착하기 위해 지하철을 타는 게 나을 것 같아요.

paraphrasing 정답 1. (c) 2. (b) 3. (a) 4. (b) 5. (c) 6. (a)

실전 문제

01. (C)   02. (B)   03. (C)   04. (C)   05. (A)   06. (A)
07. (A)   08. (C)   09. (D)   10. (B)   11. (A)   12. (D)
13. (B)   14. (B)   15. (C)   16. (D)   17. (C)   18. (B)
19. (B)   20. (D)   21. (C)

[01-03] [BR-US]

Questions 01-03 refer to the following conversation.

> W: Mr. Nichols, is this a good place for the ⁰¹**microphone for your solo**? I've put it right in the middle of the stage.
> M: Yes, that looks great. ⁰²**Do you happen to know about how many people will be in the audience** at tomorrow's show? I know ⁰¹**the rest of the members of my choir** are hoping for a good crowd.
> W: The tickets are nearly sold out. ⁰³**This is the first time that our theater has held an Internet-only promotional campaign.** It's been a success.
> M: I'm glad to hear that.

stage 무대   happen to V 우연히 ~하다   audience 청중, 관중   the rest of ~의 나머지   choir 합창단   good 상당한, 꽤 많은   crowd 사람들, 군중   nearly 거의   promotional campaign 홍보 캠페인

01-03은 다음 대화에 관한 문제입니다.
여: Nichols 씨, 여기가 ⁰¹**당신의 솔로를 위한 마이크** 자리로 괜찮을까요? 제가 무대 한가운데에 설치했는데요.
남: 네, 괜찮아 보여요. 내일 공연의 ⁰²**관객이 얼마나 될지 혹시 아시나요?** ⁰¹**우리 합창단의 나머지 단원들**이 관객이 많기를 바라고 있다는 걸 알거든요.
여: 티켓은 거의 매진되었어요. ⁰³**우리 극장에서 인터넷으로만 홍보 활동을 벌인 건 이번이 처음이에요.** 성공적이네요.
남: 그렇다니 기쁘네요.

01.

남자는 누구일 것 같은가?
(A) 극장 소유주
(B) 영화 감독
(C) 가수
(D) 기자

[해설] 남자의 직업을 묻는 문제로, 대화 초반 여자가 남자를 향해 당신의 솔로를 위한 마이크(microphone for your solo)라는 표현을 했고, 대화 중반 남자가 우리 합창단의 나머지 단원(the rest of the members of my choir)이라고 언급한 것으로 보아 남자가 합창단 소속이며 공연 중에 혼자 노래를 부르는 순서가 있음을 알 수 있다. 따라서 정답은 (C)이다.

02.

남자는 여자에게 무엇에 대해 물어보는가?
(A) 이용할 수 있는 장비
(B) 예상 참석자 수
(C) 조명 배치
(D) 리허설 시간

[해설] 대화 중반 남자가 여자에게 내일 공연의 관객이 얼마나 될지(how many people will be in the audience) 아냐고 묻는다. 즉, 관객 수를 궁금해하고 있으므로 (B)가 정답이다.

paraphrasing how many people will be in the audience 관객이 얼마나 될지 → The expected attendance 예상 참석자 수

[어휘] equipment 장비, 용품   expected 예상되는   attendance 출석, 참석; 참석자 수   lighting 조명 (시설)   arrangement 준비, 배치   rehearsal 리허설, 예행연습

03.

여자는 극장에서 처음으로 무엇을 했다고 말하는가?
(A) 단체 할인 요금을 제공했다.
(B) 웹사이트에서 공연을 방송했다.
(C) 오직 온라인으로만 광고했다.
(D) 매표소 운영 시간을 연장했다.

[해설] 대화에서 핵심 키워드 theater와 the first time이 언급된 부분에 집중해야 한다. 대화 후반 여자가 우리 극장에서 이번에 처음으로 인터넷으로만 홍보 활동을 벌였다고(This is the first time that our theater has held an Internet-only promotional campaign) 했으므로 (C)가 정답이다.

paraphrasing held an Internet-only promotional campaign 인터넷으로만 홍보 활동을 벌였다 → Advertised exclusively online 오직 온라인으로만 광고했다.

[어휘] rate 요금   broadcast 방송하다   exclusively 독점적으로; 오로지, 오직   extend 연장하다

[04-06] US-BR

Questions 04-06 refer to the following conversation.

W: Hello. **04I'm booked on a flight to Phoenix tomorrow around 8 P.M, but I need to take an earlier flight instead**, **06preferably in the early afternoon**.
M: I'm happy to help you with that, ma'am. **05You should have received a six-digit code as confirmation** that your booking was made. **05Do you have that?**
W: Yes, it's 315-870. And my name is Elizabeth Hedberg.
M: All right, let's see what's available. Hmm... **06all of the afternoon and late morning flights are fully booked**. There's one departing at 6 A.M.
W: I guess I'll have to go with that one. It's the only way I'll make it to my meeting.

book 예약하다; ~를 예약자 명단에 올리다 instead 대신에
preferably 오히려, 가급적(이면) digit 숫자 code 암호, 부호
confirmation 확인 make a booking 예약을 하다
fully booked 모두 예약이 된 depart 출발하다 make it 시간 맞춰 가다

04-06은 다음 대화에 관한 문제입니다.

여: 여보세요. 04제가 내일 저녁 8시경 피닉스 행 항공편을 예약했는데, 대신 더 이른 항공편을 타야 해서요. 06가급적이면 이른 오후로요.
남: 기꺼이 도와드리겠습니다, 손님. 예약이 되었음을 확인해주는 05여섯 자리 숫자를 받으셨을 거예요. 가지고 계신가요?
여: 네, 315-870이에요. 그리고 제 이름은 Elizabeth Hedberg입니다.
남: 좋습니다. 어떤 것을 이용할 수 있는지 보죠. 흠... 06오후와 늦은 오전 항공편은 모두 예약이 찼습니다. 오전 6시에 출발하는 것은 있어요.
여: 그것으로 해야 할 것 같네요. 그게 제가 회의에 맞춰 갈 수 있는 유일한 방법이에요.

04.

여자는 왜 이 업체에 전화하는가?
(A) 분실물을 신고하기 위해
(B) 환불을 요청하기 위해
(C) 항공편을 변경하기 위해
(D) 프로그램에 등록하기 위해

[해설] 전화 목적을 묻는 문제의 단서는 주로 대화 초반부에 나온다. 여자가 대화를 시작하면서 내일 저녁 8시경 피닉스 행 항공편을 예약했는데, 더 이른 항공편을 타야 한다고(I'm booked on a flight to Phoenix tomorrow around 8 P.M, but I need to take an earlier flight instead) 말하는 것으로 보아 항공편 예약을 변경하기 위해 전화한 것임을 알 수 있으므로 정답은 (C)이다.

paraphrasing take an earlier flight instead 대신에 더 이른 항공편을 타다 → change her flight 항공편을 바꾸다

[어휘] lost 잃어버린 refund 환불

05.

남자는 여자에게 무엇을 요청하는가?
(A) 확인 번호
(B) 여권 번호
(C) 선호하는 좌석
(D) 신용카드 번호

[해설] 항공편 변경을 원하는 여자에게 남자가 예약 확인용 여섯 자리 숫자(a six-digit code as confirmation)를 받았을 거라며 가지고 있는지(Do you have that?) 묻는다. 즉, 남자는 여자에게 확인 번호를 요청하고 있으므로 정답은 (A)이다.

[어휘] preference 선호, 선호하는 것

06.

남자는 왜 "오전 6시에 출발하는 것은 있어요"라고 말하는가?
(A) 해결책을 제시하기 위해서
(B) 일정 착오를 정정하기 위해서
(C) 지연에 대해 사과하기 위해서
(D) 언제 다시 전화할지 설명하기 위해서

[해설] 해당 표현은 더 이른 시간의 항공편으로의 변경을 원하는 여자에게 남자가 오후와 늦은 오전 항공편은 모두 예약이 찼다고(all of the afternoon and late morning flights are fully booked) 한 뒤 덧붙인 말이다. 즉, 여자가 원하는 시간대의 항공편은 모두 예약되었으므로 "오전 6시에 출발하는 것이 있어요"라는 말로 다른 해결 방법을 제시하는 것이므로 정답은 (A)이다.

[07-09] BR-US-AU

Questions 07-09 refer to the following conversation with three speakers.

W: Hi, Sheldon. Hi, Leon. One of our clients, Ms. Franklin, gave us two tickets to the **07Annual Classic Movie Festival** this Saturday. Are you interested in going?
M1: I'm a big fan of classic movies.
M2: Me, too. That would be a lot of fun.
W: Great! I wanted to reward you two for having the highest sales this past month. The first film is at 2 P.M.
M1: Leon, **08how about getting lunch together on that day** and then heading over to the film festival?
M2: **08That'll be perfect**. **09Ms. Choi, would you please call Ms. Franklin to thank her for us?**
W: Sure, Leon. I'll do that now.
M2: Thanks.

client 고객, 의뢰인 annual 매년의, 연례의 be interested in ~에 관심이 있다 reward 보상하다 head over to ~로 가다, ~로 향하다

07-09는 다음 세 명의 대화에 관한 문제입니다.

여: 안녕하세요, Sheldon. 안녕하세요, Leon. 우리 고객 중 한 분인 Franklin 씨가 이번 주 토요일에 있을 07연례 고전 영화제의 티켓 두 장을 주셨어요. 가는 데 관심 있어요?
남1: 전 고전 영화의 열렬한 팬이에요.
남2: 저도요. 정말 재미있을 거예요.
여: 잘됐네요! 지난 한 달간 판매 실적이 가장 높았던 두 분에게 보상을 하고 싶었어요. 첫 상영 시간은 오후 2시예요.
남1: Leon, 08그날 같이 점심 먹고 나서 영화제에 가는 게 어떨까요?

DAY 20 213

남2: ⁰⁸그게 딱 좋겠네요. ⁰⁹Choi, Franklin 씨에게 전화해서 저희가 고마워한다고 해 주시겠어요?
여: 물론이에요, Leon. 지금 그렇게 할게요.
남2: 고마워요.

07.
화자들은 어떤 종류의 행사에 대해 얘기하고 있는가?
(A) 영화제
(B) 영업 워크숍
(C) 음악 공연
(D) 미술관 개관

[해설] 대화의 주요 소재는 대화 초반에 드러난다. 대화 시작 부분 여자가 나머지 화자들에게 한 고객이 연례 고전 영화제(Annual Classic Movie Festival)의 티켓 두 장을 주었다며 관심이 있는지 묻는다. 이어지는 대화에서도 계속하여 이 영화제가 언급되므로 정답은 (A)이다.

[어휘] sales 영업 performance 공연, 연주회 gallery 미술관

08.
남자들이 하기로 결정하는 것은 무엇인가?
(A) 후기 읽기
(B) 일찍 사무실을 나서기
(C) 함께 식사하기
(D) 온라인으로 예약하기

[해설] 앞서 여자가 언급한 영화제에 대해 두 남자 모두 가고 싶다는 의사를 밝혔으며, 대화 후반 남자1이 남자2에게 그날 같이 점심을 먹고(how about getting lunch together) 영화제에 가자고 제안하자 이에 남자2도 적극 동의한다(That'll be perfect). 즉, 남자들은 함께 식사를 하기로 결정한 것이므로 정답은 (C)이다.

paraphrasing getting lunch together 함께 점심 먹기 → Have a meal together 함께 식사하기

09.
Leon은 여자에게 무엇을 하라고 요청하는가?
(A) 발표 연습하기
(B) 일정 업데이트하기
(C) 영수증 인쇄하기
(D) 고객에게 연락하기

[해설] 3인의 화자가 나누는 대화에서 특정 인물이 요청한 것을 묻는 문제이다. 우선 Leon의 이름을 부르며 그날 같이 점심을 먹고 영화제에 가자고 한 남자1의 말에 남자2가 답했으므로 남자2가 Leon임을 알 수 있으며, 이어 남자2가 여자에게 고객인 Franklin 씨에게 전화해서 고맙다고 전해 달라고(would you please call Ms. Franklin to thank her for us?) 했다. 따라서 정답은 (D)이다.

paraphrasing call 전화하기 → Contact 연락하기

[10-12] US-US
Questions 10-12 refer to the following conversation.

W: Mr. Wexler, we need to finalize the travel plans for ¹⁰our visit to Mumbai next week.
M: Our plane tickets are purchased, but we'll have to arrange transportation to the airport. ¹²We decided to book a taxi, right?
W: Yes, but... um... ¹¹under the new policy, we can only be paid back for up to fifty dollars of business expenses per day. ¹²Taking a taxi from the office would cost nearly twice that.
M: You know, the 408 bus runs every half hour.
W: All right. That sounds good to me.

purchase 구매하다 arrange 준비하다, 마련하다 policy 정책, 방침 pay back (돈을) 갚다, 돌려주다 up to (수, 정도) ~까지 business expenses 사무[영업] 비용 cost (비용이) ~이다 nearly 거의 run (버스, 기차 등이) 운행하다, 다니다

10-12는 다음 대화에 관한 문제입니다.
여: Wexler 씨, 우리가 ¹⁰다음 주 우리의 뭄바이 방문을 위한 여행 계획을 마무리 지어야 해요.
남: 우리 비행기 티켓은 구매했는데 공항으로 가는 교통편을 준비해야 해요. ¹²택시를 예약하기로 했었죠, 맞죠?
여: 네, 하지만... 음... ¹¹새로운 정책에 따르면 하루에 업무 비용을 50달러까지만 돌려받을 수 있어요. ¹²사무실에서 택시를 타면 거의 두 배의 비용이 들어요.
남: 있잖아요, 408번 버스가 30분 간격으로 운행해요.
여: 좋아요. 그거 괜찮네요.

10.
화자들은 다음 주에 무엇을 할 계획인가?
(A) 고객 감사 연회를 열기
(B) 함께 출장을 가기
(C) 새로 고용된 직원들을 교육하기
(D) 건물이 들어설 예상 부지를 둘러보기

[해설] 핵심 키워드 next week이 대화 초반 여자의 말에서 언급된다. 여자가 다음 주 우리의 뭄바이 방문(our client visit to Mumbai next week)을 위한 여행 계획을 마무리 지어야 한다고 했는데, 이어지는 대화에서 업무 비용(business expenses) 상환 등을 언급했다. 이로 보아 두 사람은 다음 주에 업무 관련 여행, 즉 출장을 갈 계획임을 알 수 있으므로 정답은 (B)이다.

[어휘] host 주최하다 banquet 연회 train 교육하다, 훈련시키다 hire 고용하다 potential 가능성이 있는, 잠재적인 site 현장, 부지

11.
여자의 말에 따르면, 이 회사는 최근에 무엇을 했는가?
(A) 상환 정책을 변경했다.
(B) 자동차 대여 계약을 취소했다.
(C) 몇몇 서비스 계약을 마무리 지었다.
(D) 직원들에게 보너스를 지급했다.

[해설] 업무 경비와 관련된 여자의 말에서 단서를 찾는다. 여자는 새로운 정책에 따르면 하루에 업무 비용을 50달러까지만 돌려받을 수 있다고(under the new policy, we can only be paid back for up to fifty dollars of business expenses per day.) 했다. 이것은 최근 회사의 정책이 변경되어서 상환받을 수 있는 업무 경비 금액의 한도가 줄었다는 의미이므로 (A)가 정답이다.

[어휘] reimbursement 변제, 상환, 배상 rental 임차, 대여 contract 계약 agreement 동의, 합의

12.
남자가 "408번 버스가 30분 간격으로 운행해요"라고 말한 이유는 무엇인가?

(A) 시대에 뒤진 세부 정보를 정정하기 위해서
(B) 여자에게 서두를 것을 권하기 위해서
(C) 여행 일정을 확인하기 위해서
(D) 계획 변경을 제안하기 위해서

[해설] 앞서 택시를 타는 것은 비용이 거의 두 배나 들 거라는(Taking a taxi from the office would cost nearly twice that) 여자의 말에 남자가 "408번 버스가 30분 간격으로 운행해요"라고 말했다. 즉, 비용 상환 문제에 대한 해결책으로 원래 택시를 타려던 계획을 변경해서 버스를 타자고 제안하기 위해 이렇게 말한 것이므로 정답은 (D)이다.

[어휘] correct 고치다, 수정하다 outdated 구식인, 시대에 뒤진 encourage 장려하다, 고무하다 itinerary 여행 일정

[13-15] AU-US

Questions 13-15 refer to the following conversation.

M: Hello?
W: Hi, Steve, it's Helen. ¹³**I have two tickets to the musical *Allowance* at Brookshire Theater on Friday**, but something came up and I can't go. ¹³**Would you like them?**
M: I live close to Brookshire Theater. ¹⁴**What time does the show start?**
W: It's a 7 P.M. show with a two hour running time.
M: Thanks for thinking of me, I really appreciate it. I can give you whatever you originally paid for them. ¹⁵**Shall we meet for lunch tomorrow?**
W: ¹⁵**Sure, that sounds good.** I'll bring the tickets.

running time (영화의) 상영 시간   pay for 대가를 치르다

13-15는 다음 대화에 관한 문제입니다.
남: 여보세요?
여: 안녕하세요, Steve. 저 Helen이에요. ¹³저한테 금요일 Brookshire 극장에서 하는 뮤지컬 <Allowance>의 티켓 두 장이 있는데 일이 생겨서 제가 못 가요. ¹³생각 있어요?
남: 저는 Brookshire 극장 근처에 살아요. ¹⁴공연이 몇 시에 시작하나요?
여: 저녁 7시 공연이고 2시간 동안 해요.
남: 저를 떠올려 주다니 감사해요. 정말 고마워요. 당신이 애초에 그 티켓을 구입하기 위해 얼마나 냈든 그만큼 보답할게요. ¹⁵내일 만나서 점심 먹을까요?
여: ¹⁵그래요, 그거 좋겠네요. 티켓을 가져올게요.

13.
여자는 남자에게 무엇을 제안하는가?
(A) 다가오는 공연에서의 역할
(B) 공연 티켓
(C) 식권
(D) 사무실까지 태워 주기

[해설] 대화 초반, 여자는 뮤지컬 티켓이 있으나(I have two tickets to the musical) 자신이 못 가게 되었다며 남자에게 이 공연을 보고 싶은 생각이 있는지(Would you like them?) 묻는다. 즉, 여자가 남자에게 공연 티켓을 주려고 하는 상황이므로 정답은 (B)이다.

paraphrasing musical 뮤지컬 → performance 공연

[어휘] role 역할 upcoming 다가오는, 곧 있을 meal voucher 식권 ride (차량, 자전거 등을) 타고 달리기[가기]

14.
남자가 "저는 Brookshire 극장 근처에 살아요"라고 말할 때 암시하는 것은 무엇인가?
(A) 운전 안내도가 필요하다.
(B) 제안에 관심이 있다.
(C) 극장 공연을 좋아하지 않는다.
(D) 티켓을 구매할 여유가 없다.

[해설] 여자가 Brookshire 극장에서 공연되는 뮤지컬 티켓이 있다며 남자에게 생각이 있는지 묻자, 남자가 "저는 Brookshire 극장 근처에 살아요"라고 말한 뒤 공연 시작 시간을 물어봄으로써(What time does the show start?) Brookshire 극장에서 공연을 보고 싶다는 의사를 밝혔다. 즉, 여자의 제안에 관심을 드러낸 것이므로 정답은 (B)이다.

[어휘] driving directions 운전 안내도 afford to V ~할 여유가 있다

15.
여자는 무엇을 하는 데 동의하는가?
(A) 사진을 찍기
(B) 좌석을 예약하기
(C) 남자와 식사를 하기
(D) 하루 동안 다른 사무실에서 일하기

[해설] 대화 후반, 남자가 함께 점심 식사를 할 것을 제안하자(Shall we meet for lunch tomorrow?) 여자가 수락했으므로(Sure, that sounds good.) 정답은 (C)이다.

paraphrasing Shall we meet for lunch tomorrow? 내일 만나서 점심 먹을까요? → Have a meal with the man 남자와 식사를 하기

[어휘] reserve 예약하다

[16-18] US-BR

Questions 16-18 refer to the following conversation.

M: Hi Mila, it's Ben. ¹⁶**I just wanted to remind you that tomorrow is the first day of our store's customer appreciation event.** Is the special aisle all set for our store members?
W: Oh, I'm glad you called. The special display counter did not arrive yet, but it won't take long to install and display the items. And, ¹⁷**don't you think we should postpone the monthly sales team meeting until after the event?**
M: That would probably be best. ¹⁸**I'll prepare a memo and send it out by this afternoon.**

appreciation 감사   aisle 복도, 통로   display 진열하다
postpone 미루다, 연기하다

16-18은 다음 대화에 관한 문제입니다.
남: 안녕하세요, Mila. Ben이에요. ¹⁶저는 그냥 내일이 우리 매장의 고객 감사 행사 첫날이라는 것을 상기시켜 드리고 싶었어요. 매장 회원들을 위한 특별 통로가 다 준비되었나요?
여: 오, 전화해 주셔서 기뻐요. 특별 전시 카운터가 아직 도착하지 않았지만, 설치하고 물건들을 진열하는 데 오래 걸리지는 않을 거예요. 그리고

¹⁷**월간 판매팀 회의는 행사 후로 미뤄야 하지 않을까요?**
남: 아마 그게 좋을 것 같아요. ¹⁸제가 회람을 준비해서 오늘 오후에 보낼게요.

16.
남자는 왜 여자에게 전화를 하였는가?
(A) 세일을 제안하기 위해
(B) 사업 동료를 소개하기 위해
(C) 약속 시간을 확인하기 위해
(D) 다가오는 행사에 대해 상기시키기 위해

[해설] 남자가 내일이 우리 매장의 고객 감사 행사 첫날이라는 것을 상기시켜 주고 싶었다고(I just wanted to remind you that tomorrow is the first day of our store's customer appreciation event) 전화를 건 이유를 말했으므로 (D)가 정답이다.

[어휘] propose 제안하다 introduce 소개하다 business associate 사업 동료, 동업자 confirm 확인하다 appointment 약속 upcoming 다가오는

17.
여자는 무엇을 하는 것을 제안하는가?
(A) 발표하는 것
(B) 포스터를 만드는 것
(C) 회의를 미루는 것
(D) 환불을 하는 것

[해설] 중후반부에 여자가 월간 판매팀 회의는 행사 후로 미뤄야 하지 않을지(don't you think we should postpone the monthly sales team meeting until after the event) 물었으므로 (C)가 정답이다.

[어휘] make an announcement 발표하다 create 만들다 issue a refund 환불하다

18.
남자는 무엇을 할 거라고 말하는가?
(A) 고객에게 연락
(B) 회람 발송
(C) 가격 조정
(D) 실수에 대해 사과

[해설] 대화 후반부에 여자가 회의를 미루는 것이 어떤지 묻자 남자가 좋을 것 같다며, 회람을 준비해서 오늘 오후에 보낸다고(I'll prepare a memo and send it out by this afternoon) 했으므로 (B)가 정답이다.

[어휘] adjust 조정하다 apologize 사과하다

[19-21] US-BR
Questions 19-21 refer to the following conversation and price list.

Stamford Museum of History	
History Musical (Ages 6 ~13)	$5.25
¹⁹Lecture: Local Historical Figures	$7.75
Movie: First Settlers	$8.50
Guided Artifact Tour	$9.90

W: Hello, and thank you for coming to the Stamford Museum of History.
M: Hi, I'd like one adult ticket, please.
W: Okay, would you like to attend any of our special events? This poster shows the prices for attending each event. The movie is very popular.
M: Actually, I'd rather listen to a talk. ¹⁹**I'll take a ticket for "Local Historical Figures".**
W: Alright, ²⁰**the next one starts at noon.** But you should probably get there by 11:45 because ²⁰**it might be hard to find seating at that time.**
M: Okay, great. ²¹**Do I need to present anything to get in?**
W: ²¹**Just your ticket.** Would you like to pay by cash or card?

price list 가격표 figure 인물 seating 좌석 present 제시하다 get in (안으로) 들어가다 by cash 현금으로 settler 정착민 artifact 공예품

19-21은 다음 대화와 가격표에 관한 문제입니다.

Stamford 역사 박물관	
역사 뮤지컬 (6세~13세)	5.25달러
¹⁹강연: 지역의 역사적 인물들	7.75달러
영화: 최초의 정착자들	8.50달러
가이드가 있는 공예품 견학	9.90달러

여: 안녕하세요, Stamford 역사 박물관에 와주셔서 감사합니다.
남: 안녕하세요, 성인 티켓 한 장 부탁드립니다.
여: 알겠습니다. 저희의 특별 행사에 참석하시겠어요? 이 포스터에 각 행사의 참석 비용이 나와 있습니다. 영화가 아주 인기가 많아요.
남: 실은, 저는 오히려 강연을 듣고 싶어요. ¹⁹**"지역의 역사적 인물들" 표를 한 장 주세요.**
여: 좋습니다. ²⁰**다음 강연은 정오에 시작해요.** 하지만 ²⁰그때에는 자리를 찾기 힘들지도 모르니까 아마도 11시 45분까지는 도착하셔야 합니다.
남: 알겠습니다. ²¹**입장할 때 제시해야 하는 것이 있나요?**
여: ²¹**티켓만 있으면 됩니다.** 현금으로 결제하시겠어요, 아니면 카드로 하시겠어요?

19.
시각 자료를 보시오. 남자는 특별 행사에 참석하기 위해 얼마를 지불할 것인가?
(A) 5.25달러
(B) 7.75달러
(C) 8.50달러
(D) 9.90달러

[해설] 대화 중반, 여자가 특별 행사 참석을 권하자 남자는 강연을 듣고 싶다며, "지역의 역사적 인물들" 표를 한 장 달라고(I'd rather listen to a talk. I'll take a ticket for "Local Historical Figures".) 했다. 가격표에서 이 행사의 가격을 확인하면 7.75달러이므로 정답은 (B)이다.

20.
여자는 정오의 행사에 대해 무엇이라고 말하는가?
(A) 방문자들 사이에서 인기가 많다.
(B) 좌석이 미리 배정된다.
(C) 박물관에서 할인을 해준다.
(D) 좌석을 찾기가 어려울 수도 있다.

[해설] 질문의 핵심인 키워드 noon이 여자의 대사에서 언급되는 부분에 집중한다. 여자는 다음 강연이 정오에 시작한다고(the next one starts at noon) 하면서 그 시간에는 자리를 찾기 힘들지도 모른다(it might be hard to find seating at that time)고 했다. 따라서 정답은 (D)이다.

[어휘] assign 배정하다, 배치하다   in advance 미리, 사전에

21.
여자는 남자가 무엇을 주어야 할 거라고 말하는가?
(A) 회원증
(B) 사진이 있는 신분증
(C) 티켓
(D) 영수증

[해설] 대화 후반부, 남자가 입장할 때 제시해야 하는 것이 있는지(Do I need to present anything to get in?) 묻자 여자는 티켓만 있으면 된다고(Just your ticket.) 했으므로 정답은 (C)이다.

paraphrasing have to provide 제공해야 하다 → need to present 제시해야 하다

PART 4 뉴스 보도

출제 유형 01 업계 소식 보도
| 풀이 방법 해석 |

남: 안녕하세요, 저는 Joshua Young입니다. 여러분은 최고의 TV 채널, BNF America에서 Business Update를 보고 계십니다. 전자 제품 회사인 OverSurge는 무선 단말기 업계에 충격을 주고 있습니다. 어떠한 선도 없이 떨어져 있어도 충전이 되는 배터리를 만들었습니다. 하나의 전력원이 동시에 50개의 배터리를 충전할 수 있습니다. 회사의 대변인인 Jessie Vaughn에 따르면, 배터리는 그 회사의 휴대폰에 쓰일 것이라고 합니다. 이 혁신적인 배터리가 장착된 첫 번째 휴대폰이 7월에 출시될 예정입니다.

출제 유형 02 연구 결과 보도
| 풀이 방법 해석 |

남: Economy Eagle에 오신 것을 환영합니다. 저는 TFW TV의 Jonathan Glavine입니다. 오늘 저희 방송은 소비자들의 소비 패턴에 대해 중점적으로 다루겠습니다. 성공적인 신생 기업이 있기는 하지만, 대부분 소비자들은 신생 기업의 제품이나 서비스의 신뢰도를 걱정합니다. 그들은 그래야 하죠. 회사가 매력적인 이름과 혁신적인 CEO가 있다고 해서 실패할 수 없는 건 아니니까요. 이제 성공하지 못했던 회사들의 몇 가지 보고서를 살펴보고, 왜 그런지를 설명드리겠습니다. 가끔은 가장 사소한 요인이 사업을 망하게 할 수 있습니다.

 연습 문제

01. (B) 02. (B) 03. (A) 04. (A) 05. (A) 06. (B)

01. [BR]
What is the **news** report **about**?
(A) A new **bookstore** opening
(B) A change in management

W: Welcome to Business World Today. This is Emilia Williams. Last Wednesday, the nationwide **bookstore chain** Owl's Nest announced that Maria Perez will start working as **chief** executive **officer** beginning September 20. Her extensive **experience** and valuable insight will **contribute** to bouncing up Owl's Nest's lagging sales.

뉴스 보도는 무엇에 관한 것인가?
(A) 새로운 서점 개업   **(B) 경영진의 변화**

뉴스 보도
여: Business World Today에 오신 것을 환영합니다. 저는 Emilia Williams입니다. 지난 수요일, 전국적인 서점 체인인 Owl's Nest가 9월 20일부터 Maria Perez가 최고 경영자로 일을 시작할 것이라고 알렸습니다. 그녀의 폭넓은 경험과 가치 있는 통찰력이 Owl's Nest의 뒤처지는 매출을 끌어 올리는 데 기여할 것입니다.

02. [AU]
What did Toys' Land experience in December?
(A) **Relocation** of its headquarters   **(B) A drop in sales**

M: Good morning. In today's business news, the city's largest toy **retailer**, Toys' Land, released its monthly sales **figures** and reported a significant sales **decline** of December compared to the same month of the **previous** year. Most industry experts are surprised by the almost 30% decrease **despite** the fact that December is the **peak season** for the toy industry.

Toys' Land는 12월에 무엇을 겪었는가?
(A) 본사의 이전   **(B) 매출 하락**

뉴스 보도
남: 안녕하세요. 오늘 비즈니스 뉴스에서는, 시의 가장 큰 장난감 소매업체인 Toys' Land가 월별 매출을 공개했고 지난해 같은 달과 비교했을 때 12월에 상당한 매출 하락을 보도했습니다. 대부분의 업계 전문가들은 12월이 장난감 업계의 성수기임에도 불구하고 거의 30퍼센트 감소한 것에 놀랐습니다.

03. [BR]
What is the **news** report **about**?
(A) A corporate merger   (B) A **marketing** campaign

M: And now for business news. There is a **widespread** rumor that DFO Digital and Lamington Electronics have been **negotiating** a merger deal. According to Mr. Smithson, an **industry** analyst, the **merger** would be expected to produce more than two billion dollars overall in annual revenue gains and cost savings. However, both companies officially denied it.

뉴스 보도는 무엇에 관한 것인가?
(A) 기업 합병   (B) 마케팅 캠페인

뉴스 보도
남: 그리고 이제 비즈니스 소식입니다. DFO Digital과 Lamington 전자가 합병을 위해 협상 중이라는 루머가 널리 퍼져 있습니다. 업계 분석가인 Smithson 씨에 따르면, 그 합병은 20억 달러 이상의 연간 소득과 비용 절감을 발생시킬 것이라고 예상했습니다. 하지만 두 회사 모두 합병을 공식적으로 부인했습니다.

04. [US]
What can the listeners do on Dr. Adams' Web site?
(A) Watch a video   (B) Download a survey result

W: Welcome to HBS's Health News. In a recent study conducted by Dr. Carol Adams, she indicates that an only 10-minute workout every day is effective enough to reduce body fat. 70% of the participants showed a fat reduction after one month of research. Dr. Adams suggests that all participants continued to do this after completion of the research. You can get more information about the 10-minute workout and watch a short video on her Web site.

청자들은 Adams 박사의 웹사이트에서 무엇을 할 수 있는가?
(A) 영상 시청하기   (B) 설문조사 결과 다운로드 받기

뉴스 보도
여: HBS의 건강 뉴스에 오신 것을 환영합니다. 최근 Carol Adams 박사가 실시한 연구에서, 그녀는 매일 10분간의 운동만으로도 체지방을 감소시키는 데 효과적이라고 시사했습니다. 참가자들의 70퍼센트가 한 달간의 연구 후에 지방 감소를 보였습니다. Adams 박사는 모든 참가자들이 연구의 완료 후에도 이것을 계속했다고 말했습니다. 여러분은 10분간의 운동에 대한 더 많은 정보와 짧은 영상을 그녀의 웹사이트에서 보실 수 있습니다.

05. [AU]
What are people encouraged to do?
(A) Use more efficient electronics
(B) Turn off unnecessary lights

M: Good afternoon. Tonight, I'll be talking about a new initiative by the city government. According to recent statistics on electricity usage, the amount of reserve power dropped by almost 7% on July 28. At that time, the energy department was taking measures in case of a blackout. Since summer is getting hotter, the government will draw up a budget to give a grant to those who replace their old air conditioner with more energy-efficient one.

사람들은 무엇을 하도록 권장받는가?
(A) 더 효율적인 전자제품 사용하기   (B) 불필요한 전등 끄기

뉴스 보도
남: 안녕하세요. 오늘 밤, 저는 시 정부의 새 계획에 대해 말할 것입니다. 최근 전기 사용에 대한 통계에 다르면, 보유 전력의 양이 7월 28일에 거의 7퍼센트로 떨어졌습니다. 그때, 에너지 부서는 정전에 대비하여 조치를 취하고 있는 중이었습니다. 여름이 더 더워지고 있으므로, 정부는 오래된 에어컨을 더 에너지 효율적인 것으로 교체하는 사람들에게 보조금을 주기 위해 예산을 편성할 것입니다.

06. [US]
What is the news report about?
(A) A construction project for a new apartment
(B) A recent increase in housing rent

M: In local news, a city official reported that the City of Battleston has experienced a large influx of newcomers over the past 18 months. This has caused monthly rent to soar up to 50%. A resident at Height Hill Apartment said that the landlord wants to raise the monthly rent to $600. His current monthly rental is $450. Most residents are worried about their housing next year.

뉴스 보도는 무엇에 관한 것인가?
(A) 새 아파트 건설 프로젝트   (B) 최근 주택 임대료의 상승

뉴스 보도
남: 지역 뉴스에서는, 한 시 공무원이 배틀스톤 시가 지난 18개월 동안 이주민들의 대량 유입을 겪고 있다고 발표했습니다. 이것은 월 임대료가 50퍼센트까지 상승하는 것을 야기했습니다. Height Hill 아파트의 한 주민은 건물주가 월 임대료를 600달러로 올리고자 한다고 말했습니다. 그의 현재 월 임대료는 450달러입니다. 대부분의 주민들은 그들의 내년 거주지에 대해 걱정합니다.

paraphrasing 정답 1. (a) 2. (c) 3. (b) 4. (c) 5. (b) 6. (a)

실전 문제

01. (B)	02. (D)	03. (A)	04. (C)	05. (D)	06. (A)
07. (D)	08. (C)	09. (A)	10. (C)	11. (B)	12. (C)
13. (A)	14. (C)	15. (B)	16. (A)	17. (D)	18. (B)
19. (B)	20. (C)	21. (A)			

[01-03] [BR]
Questions 01-03 refer to the following news report.

M: This is Edward Banks reporting for Channel 9 News. Today's top story is about **01 Chardon Corporation, the power tool manufacturing company**. It has plans to release a new line of power tools called Diligent Duty Tools which will all be equipped with **02 new batteries that last considerably longer than any other ones available on the market**. Many construction companies and DIY enthusiasts are anxiously awaiting the release of the product. Chardon Corporation says that **03 they will be available in hardware stores as of May 4th**. For Channel 9, I'm Edward Banks.

> power tool 전동 공구 manufacturing 제조업 release 공개하다, 출시하다: 공개, 출시 be equipped with ~을 갖추고 있다 last 지속하다 considerably 상당히 on the market 시장에 나와 있는 construction 건설, 공사 enthusiast 열광적인 팬 hardware store 철물점 as of ~부터

01-03은 다음 뉴스 보도에 관한 문제입니다.

남: Channel 9 News의 Edward Banks가 전해드립니다. 오늘의 첫 소식은 ⁰¹전동 공구 제조 회사인 Chardon 사에 관한 것입니다. 이 회사는 ⁰²시중에서 구입 가능한 다른 어떤 제품들보다도 상당히 더 오래 지속되는 새로운 배터리를 장착하게 될 Diligent Duty Tools라는 전동 공구 신제품 라인을 출시할 계획입니다. 많은 건설 회사들과 DIY 광들이 간절히 이 제품의 출시를 기다리고 있습니다. Chardon 사의 말에 따르면 ⁰³5월 4일부터 철물점에서 구입 가능할 것이라고 합니다. Channel 9의 Edward Banks였습니다.

01.

Chardon 사는 어떤 종류의 업체인가?
(A) 온라인 DIY 포럼 관리 회사
(B) 전동 공구 제조사
(C) 건설 회사
(D) 뉴스 방송사

[해설] Chardon Corporation이라는 회사에 대한 뉴스 보도이다. 보도 초반, 이 회사를 전동 공구 제조 회사(the power tool manufacturing company)로 소개했으므로 정답은 (B)이다.

paraphrasing manufacturing company 제조 회사 → manufacturer 제조사

[어휘] forum 포럼, (토론의) 장 administrator 관리자, 행정인 manufacturer 제조사 broadcaster 방송사, 방송인

02.

화자는 신제품 라인에 대해 어떤 점이 특별하다고 말하는가?
(A) 가격 면에서 쉽게 구매할 수 있을 것이다.
(B) 온라인으로 광고되고 있다.
(C) 비전문가가 사용하도록 고안되었다.
(D) 오래 지속되는 배터리가 특징이다.

[해설] 시판되는 어떤 제품들보다도 더 오래 지속되는 새로운 배터리(new batteries that last considerably longer than any other ones)를 장착하게 될 Diligent Duty Tools라는 전동 공구 신제품 라인을 출시할 계획이라는 말로 보아 신제품은 배터리가 오래 지속된다는 특징이 있다. 따라서 정답은 (D)이다.

paraphrasing batteries that last considerably longer than any other ones 다른 어떤 제품들보다도 상당히 더 오래 지속되는 배터리 → It features long-lasting batteries. 오래 지속되는 배터리가 특징이다.

[어휘] affordable (가격 등이) 알맞은, 감당할 수 있는 amateur 비전문가, 아마추어 feature 특별히 포함하다, 특징으로 삼다 long-lasting 오래 지속되는

03.

화자에 따르면, 5월 4일에 무슨 일이 있을 것인가?
(A) 제품 라인을 구매할 수 있을 것이다.
(B) 대규모 건설 작업이 시작될 것이다.
(C) 철물점의 주인이 바뀔 것이다.
(D) 공개 시연이 진행될 것이다.

[해설] 질문의 핵심 키워드 May 4th가 언급되는 담화 마지막을 보면, 5월 4일부터 철물점에서 제품 구입이 가능하다는(they will be available in hardware stores as of May 4th) 내용이 나온다. 따라서 정답은 (A)이다.

[어휘] massive 거대한 ownership 소유(권)

[04-06] US

Questions 04-06 refer to the following news report.

> W: Good morning, this is *Living Local*, Channel 5's new segment about arts, entertainment, and volunteer opportunities in the Wellington area. ⁰⁴**Today we turn our attention to the Wellington Community Center.** Event coordinator Craig Dalton will hold a series of painting classes for community members. ^{05, 06}**The paintings are to be donated to the City Hall Charity Auction in November**, and they are expected to be the hottest items.

> segment 단편, 조각, 부분 volunteer 자원봉사 opportunity 기회 event coordinator 행사 기획자 hold (행사를) 열다, 개최하다 a series of 일련의 donate 기부하다 charity 자선 단체 auction 경매

04-06은 다음 뉴스 보도에 관한 문제입니다.

여: 안녕하세요, 웰링턴 지역의 예술, 즐길거리, 자원봉사 기회에 대한 Channel 5의 새로운 코너인 <Living Local>입니다. ⁰⁴오늘은 웰링턴 지역 문화 센터로 관심을 돌려보겠습니다. 행사 기획자인 Craig Dalton 씨가 지역 주민들을 위해 일련의 그림 강좌를 엽니다. ^{05, 06}이 그림들은 11월에 시청 자선 경매에 기증될 예정이며, 가장 관심이 뜨거운 품목이 될 것으로 예상됩니다.

04.

화자는 어떤 종류의 시설에 대해 보도하는가?
(A) 극장
(B) 박물관
(C) 지역 문화 센터
(D) 관공서

[해설] 화자는 프로그램에 대한 간단한 소개를 한 후 오늘은 웰링턴 지역 문화 센터로 관심을 돌려보겠다는(Today we turn our attention to the Wellington Community Center.) 말로 오늘 다룰 내용을 밝혔다. 따라서 정답은 (C)이다.

05.

화자에 따르면, 강좌의 목적은 무엇인가?
(A) 예술 프로그램에 대한 관심을 끌어올리는 것
(B) 지역 예술가들을 홍보하는 것
(C) 도시를 아름답게 하는 것을 돕는 것
(D) 자선 경매를 후원하는 것

[해설] Craig Dalton 씨가 지역 주민들을 위해 여는 그림 강좌의 목적을 묻는 문제이다. 그림들이 11월에 시청 자선 경매에 기증될 예정이라고(The paintings are to be donated for the City Hall Charity Auction in November) 한 것으로 보아 자선 경매 후원이 목적임을 알 수 있다. 따

라서 정답은 (D)이다.

paraphrasing The paintings are to be donated for the City Hall Charity Auction 그림들이 시청 자선 경매에 기증될 예정이다 → to support a charity auction 자선 경매를 후원하는 것

[어휘] raise 올리다, 높이다 interest 관심, 흥미 promote 홍보하다 support 후원하다, 지지하다

06.

화자가 "그리고 가장 관심이 뜨거운 품목이 될 것으로 예상됩니다"라고 말할 때 암시하는 것은 무엇인가?
(A) 예술품이 경매에서 높은 가격으로 팔린다.
(B) 공공 장소는 에어컨이 필요하다.
(C) 그 행사는 과거에 성공적이었다.
(D) 많은 사람들이 도와주겠다고 자원했다.

[해설] 해당 표현에서 앞서 지역 주민을 위한 그림 강좌가 열리는데, 이 강좌에서 그린 그림들이 11월에 시청 자선 경매(the City Hall Charity Auction)에 기증될 것이라고 했다. 따라서 "가장 관심이 뜨거운 품목이 될 것으로 예상됩니다"라는 표현은 경매에서 그 그림들을 사고자 하는 사람들이 많아 높은 가격에 팔릴 것이라는 의미로 쓰였음을 알 수 있다. 정답은 (A)이다.

[어휘] artwork 예술품 public space 공공 장소 volunteer to V ~하겠다고 자원하다

[07-09] [BR]
Questions 07-09 refer to the following news report.

W: And now, the local news. **07The city council members of Levittown are preparing to vote on a bill that could charge fines for citizens who don't recycle properly.** Waste Removal & Reuse, the private firm that operates the city's recycling programs, has reported that sorting recyclables is an expensive process that could be easily avoided by simply having citizens separate materials when throwing them away. **08The company has offered to give out separate bins free of charge to each household,** but has asked for the council's assistance in enforcing the rule. We would like to hear your thoughts on the issue, **09so please post what you have to say on our social media page.**

city council 시 의회 vote on a bill 법안에 대해 투표하다 charge fine 벌금을 부과하다 properly 제대로, 적절히 waste 쓰레기, 폐기물 removal 없애기, 제거 reuse 재사용 private 사유의, 개인 소유의 operate 운용하다 sort 분류하다 citizen 시민 separate 분리하다, 나누다; 분리된 material 재료, 소재 throw away 버리다 give out 나눠주다 bin 쓰레기통 free of charge 무료로 household 가정 assistance in ~에 있어서의 도움 enforce 시행[실시]하다 issue 문제, 안건

07-09는 다음 뉴스 보도에 관한 문제입니다.
여: 다음은 지역 뉴스입니다. **07레빗타운 시 의회 의원들이 재활용을 제대로 하지 않는 시민들에게 벌금을 부과할 수 있는 법안에 대해 표결을 준비 중입니다.** 시의 재활용 프로그램을 운영하는 사기업인 Waste Removal & Reuse는 재활용품 분류는 비용이 많이 드는 과정인데, 이는 시민들이 쓰레기를 버릴 때 재질을 분류하기만 하면 쉽게 피할 수 있다고 알렸습니다. **08이 회사는 각 가정에 무료로 별도의 쓰레기통을 나눠주겠다고 제안하는** 한편 이 법규가 시행되도록 시 의회가 도와줄 것을 요청했습니다. 저희는 이 문제에 대한 여러분의 생각을 듣고 싶습니다. **09그러니 저희 소셜 미디어 페이지에 하실 말씀을 올려주시기 바랍니다.**

07.

뉴스 보도의 주제는 무엇인가?
(A) 대중교통 체계
(B) 다가오는 선거
(C) 쓰레기 처리 시설
(D) 재활용 법

[해설] 담화 초반에 단서가 있다. 시 의회 의원들이 제대로 재활용을 하지 않는 시민들에게 벌금을 부과할 수 있는 법안(a bill that could charge fines for citizens who don't recycle properly)에 대해 표결을 준비 중이라고 했고, 이어서 이러한 법안이 발의되게 된 원인을 제시하고 있으므로 정답은 (D)이다.

[어휘] election 선거 garbage 쓰레기 facility 시설

08.

화자에 따르면, 청자들에게 무엇이 배포될 예정인가?
(A) 새로운 기차표
(B) 연간 비용 보고서
(C) 재활용 쓰레기통
(D) 주차 허가증

[해설] 앞서 시의 재활용 프로그램을 운영하는 Waste Removal & Reuse이라는 업체를 언급한 후, 이 회사에서 각 가정에 무료로 별도의 쓰레기통을 나눠주겠다고 제안했다고(The company has offered to give out separate bins free of charge to each household) 했다. 이 통은 재활용품을 따로 버릴 수 있는 통을 의미한 것이므로 정답은 (C)이다.

paraphrasing separate bins 별도의 쓰레기통 → recycling bins 재활용 쓰레기통

[어휘] annual 연례의 expense 비용 permit 허용[허락]하다; 허가증

09.

화자는 청자들에게 무엇을 하라고 요청하는가?
(A) 의견을 게시하기
(B) 기부하기
(C) 지도 보기
(D) 투표하기

[해설] 요청/부탁 사항은 주로 담화 마지막에 제시된다. 앞서 언급한 법안 문제에 대한 청자들의 생각을 듣고 싶다며, 소셜 미디어 페이지에 할 말을 올려달라고(please post what you have to say on our social media page) 요청했으므로 정답은 (A)이다.

paraphrasing post what you have to say 할 말을 게시하다 → post their opinions 의견을 게시하기

[어휘] invite (정식으로) 요청하다 make a donation 기부하다 take a pledge 맹세하다 cast a vote 투표하다

[10-12] AU
Questions 10-12 refer to the following news report.

M: Here is some big news related to traffic. Edison Engineering has just announced a plan to run a high-speed express subway line from downtown Los Angeles directly to the airport. ¹⁰**The proposal would start drilling next month and be fully completed by the end of next year.** ¹¹**Edison Engineering's CEO Neil Marsh said that the line would greatly reduce the time spent travelling to and from the airport.** ¹²**So far, airline employees have expressed the most excitement**, as estimates suggest nearly an hour would be cut from their average daily commutes.

related to ~와 관련된 run 운행하다 express 급행의, 신속한; 나타내다, 표현하다 directly 곧장, 똑바로 proposal 제안, 제의 drill 구멍을 뚫다 fully 완전히, 충분히 complete 완료하다, 끝마치다 greatly 대단히, 크게 reduce 줄이다, 축소하다 so far 지금까지 express excitement 흥분을 표출하다 estimate 추정, 추산 nearly 거의 daily 매일의 commute 통근 (거리)

10-12는 다음 뉴스 보도에 관한 문제입니다.
남: 교통과 관련된 중요한 소식이 있습니다. Edison 엔지니어링은 로스앤젤레스 시내에서 공항으로 바로 가는 고속 급행 지하철 노선을 운행할 계획이라고 막 발표했습니다. ¹⁰이 계획은 다음 달 땅을 뚫기 시작하여 내년 말까지 완료됩니다. ¹¹Edison 엔지니어링의 CEO인 Neil Marsh 씨는 이 노선이 공항을 오가는 데 드는 시간을 크게 줄여줄 것이라고 말했습니다. ¹²지금까지는 항공사 직원들이 가장 큰 흥분을 드러냈는데요, 그들의 매일 평균 통근 시간이 거의 한 시간 가량 줄 것으로 추산되기 때문입니다.

10.
뉴스 보도에 따르면, 내년 말까지 무슨 일이 있을 것인가?
(A) 주요 공항이 확장될 것이다.
(B) 항공사가 새로운 VIP 서비스를 제공할 것이다.
(C) 새로운 지하철 노선이 완공될 것이다.
(D) 여행사가 더 많은 패키지 상품을 제공하기 시작할 것이다.

[해설] 새로운 지하철 노선 공사 계획을 알리는 뉴스 보도로, the end of next year, 즉 '내년 말'은 이 공사 계획이 완료되는(The proposal would ~ be fully completed by the end of next year.) 시점으로 언급되었다. 따라서 정답은 (C)이다.
[어휘] expand 확장하다

11.
Marsh 씨는 이 프로젝트의 이점이 무엇이 될 거라고 말하는가?
(A) 편안한 좌석
(B) 줄어든 이동 시간
(C) 자동화된 서비스
(D) 더 저렴한 요금

[해설] Mr. Marsh는 보도 중반에 언급되는데, 공사를 진행하는 Edison Engineering의 CEO로서 이 노선이 공항을 오가는 데 드는 시간을 크게 줄여줄 것이라고 말했다는(Neil Marsh said that the line would greatly reduce the time spent travelling to and from the airport.) 내용이 나온다. 따라서 정답은 (B)이다.

paraphrasing reduce the time spent travelling to and from the airport 공항을 오가는 데 드는 시간을 줄여줄 것이다 → reduced travel time 줄어든 이동 시간
[어휘] comfortable 편안한 automated 자동화된 fare (교통) 요금

12.
화자의 말에 따르면 누가 이 소식에 가장 흥분했는가?
(A) 건설 회사들
(B) 항공사 회원들
(C) 항공사 직원들
(D) 여행사 직원들

[해설] 보도 후반, 지금까지는 항공사 직원들이 가장 큰 흥분을 드러냈다고(So far, airline employees have expressed the most excitement) 했으므로 정답은 (C)이다.

paraphrasing have expressed the most excitement 가장 큰 흥분을 드러냈다 → most excited 가장 흥분한

[13-15] US
Questions 13-15 refer to the following broadcast.

M: This is Reece Webster reporting live from City Hall for Channel 5. In today's press conference, it was announced that ¹³**the proposal to build a new public library downtown has been approved. This project will be carried out next year** and could cost as much as one hundred million dollars, but there is already ¹⁴**one major issue. There is strong opposition from the majority of people living in Engleburg**, as they believe that the current main library branch is sufficient. ¹⁵**I'm here with Engleburg's mayor, Jessie Carter, who will be responding to my questions** about that as well as other aspects of the project.

press conference 기자회견 proposal 제안, 제의 downtown 시내에 approve 승인하다, 인가하다 carry out ~을 수행[이행]하다 issue 쟁점, 사안, 문제 opposition 반대, 항의 majority 다수 current 현재의, 지금의 branch 분관, 지점 sufficient 충분한 respond to ~에 대응하다 aspect 측면

13-15는 다음 방송에 관한 문제입니다.
남: 저는 시청에서 생방송으로 보도하고 있는 채널 5의 Reece Webster 입니다. 오늘 기자회견에서, ¹³시내에 새로운 공립도서관을 건설하는 제안이 승인되었다는 발표가 있었습니다. ¹³이 프로젝트는 내년에 시행될 예정이며, 1억 달러 상당의 비용이 들 것으로 보입니다만, 이미 ¹⁴한 가지 중대한 문제가 있습니다. ¹⁴Engleburg에 거주하는 주민들의 다수가 이에 격렬히 반대하고 있는데요, 이들은 현재의 중앙 도서관의 분관이면 충분하다고 생각하기 때문입니다. ¹⁵저는 Engleburg의 시장인 Jessie Carter 씨와 함께 있습니다. 그가 이에 대한 것은 물론 프로젝트의 다른 측면에 대한 ¹⁵제 질문에 답변해 주시겠습니다.

13.
Engleburg 시는 내년에 무엇을 할 것인가?
(A) 새 도서관을 건설하기

(B) 스포츠 토너먼트를 열기
(C) 관광 캠페인을 시작하기
(D) 국제 콘퍼런스를 열기

[해설] 시내에 새로운 공립도서관을 건설하는 제안이 승인됐고(the proposal to build a new public library downtown has been approved), 이 프로젝트는 내년에 시행될 예정이라고(This project will be carried out next year) 했다. 그런데 이 프로젝트에 대해 Engleburg 거주민들이 반대한다는 것으로 보아 도서관이 건설되는 곳이 바로 Engleburg임을 알 수 있다. 따라서 Engleburg 시에서 내년에 도서관을 새로 건설할 예정이므로 정답은 (A)이다.

paraphrasing build 건설하다 → construct 건설하기

[어휘] construct 건설하다 tournament 토너먼트, 승자 진출전 launch 시작[개시/착수]하다

14.

화자는 이 프로젝트의 어떤 문제를 언급하는가?
(A) 가격 인상이 예상된다.
(B) 자금이 충분하지 않다.
(C) 직원들이 충분히 많지 않다.
(D) 대부분의 주민들이 이에 반대한다.

[해설] 질문의 핵심 키워드 problem은 담화 중반에 언급된 issue에 해당한다. 화자는 한 가지 중대한 문제(one major issue)가 있다며, Engleburg에 거주하는 주민들의 다수가 이에 격렬히 반대하고 있다고 (There is strong opposition from the majority of people living in Engleburg) 설명했다. 따라서 (D)가 정답이다.

paraphrasing There is strong opposition from the majority of people living in Engleburg. Egleburg에 거주하는 주민들의 다수가 격렬히 반대한다. → Most residents oppose it. 대부분의 주민들이 이에 반대한다.

[어휘] funding 자금 resident 거주자, 주민 oppose 반대하다

15.

화자는 다음에 무엇을 할 것인가?
(A) 연락처를 주기
(B) 시 공무원을 인터뷰하기
(C) 개막식에 참석하기
(D) 현장을 답사하기

[해설] 담화 마지막, 화자는 자신의 질문에 답변해줄 Engleburg의 시장과 함께 있다고(I'm here with Engleburg's mayor, Jessie Carter, who will be responding to my questions) 했다. 즉, 담화 직후 보도 내용과 관련하여 시장을 인터뷰할 것이라는 말이므로 정답은 (B)이다.

[16-18] US

Questions 16-18 refer to the following news report.

W: You're listening to the local news update. If you love independent films, you won't want to miss this year's Spring Film Festival at the Warren Theater. ¹⁶**For the first time ever, some of the directors of the films will be in attendance.** The festival lasts for three days, and there are still ¹⁷**plenty of tickets available. You can get them by stopping by the box office.** Audience members are reminded that seating is on a first-come, first-served basis. ¹⁸**If you want a great view of the screen or if you have a particular seat in mind, there is no way to reserve it in advance.** The doors for the first film open at 6 P.M.

local 지역의, 지방의 independent film 독립영화
be in attendance (특별한 행사에) 참석하다 last 계속하다
plenty of 많은 stop by ~에 들르다 audience members 관람객 be reminded (of) (~을) 상기하다 on a first-come, first-served basis 선착순으로 particular 특정한, 특별한
there is no way to V ~할 수가 없다

16-18은 다음 뉴스 보도에 관한 문제입니다.
여: 여러분은 최신 지역 뉴스를 듣고 계십니다. 만약 여러분이 독립영화를 아주 좋아하신다면 Warren 극장에서 열리는 올해의 봄 영화 축제를 놓치고 싶지 않으실 겁니다. ¹⁶최초로, 일부 영화감독들이 참석할 예정입니다. 축제는 3일간 이어지며, 아직 ¹⁷티켓이 많이 남아 있습니다. 매표소에 들르셔서 구하시면 됩니다. 관람하실 분들은 좌석이 선착순으로 배정된다는 것을 알아두시기 바랍니다. ¹⁸스크린이 잘 보이는 자리를 원하신다거나 특별히 생각하고 있는 좌석이 있다 하더라도 미리 예약할 수 있는 방법은 없습니다. 첫 번째 영화의 입장은 저녁 6시에 시작합니다.

16.

올해 축제에서는 무엇이 달라졌는가?
(A) 특별 손님이 포함될 것이다.
(B) 새로운 기술이 시행될 것이다.
(C) 일주일간 지속될 것이다.
(D) 여러 개의 스크린을 사용할 것이다.

[해설] 지역에서 열리는 독립영화제에 대한 보도이다. 올봄에 개최될 이 영화제에는 처음으로 일부 영화감독들이 참석할 것이라고(some of the directors of the films will be in attendance) 했으므로 '영화감독들'을 '특별 손님들'로 표현한 (A)가 정답이다.

paraphrasing some of the directors of the films will be in attendance 일부 영화감독들이 참석할 것이다 → It will include special guests. 특별 손님이 포함될 것이다.

[어휘] include 포함시키다 implement 시행하다

17.

화자에 따르면, 청자들은 어떻게 티켓을 구할 수 있는가?
(A) 행사 기획자에게 이메일을 보냄으로써
(B) 극장 매표소에 전화함으로써
(C) 극장 웹사이트에 접속함으로써
(D) 직접 극장을 방문함으로써

[해설] 영화제 티켓을 구하는 방법은 담화 중반에 나온다. 티켓이 많이 남아 있으니 매표소에 들러서 구하면 된다는(You can get them by stopping by the box office.) 말은 직접 극장에 가야 한다는 의미이므로 정답은 (D)이다.

paraphrasing by stopping by the box office 매표소에 들름으로써 → by visiting the theater in person 직접 극장을 방문함으로써

[어휘] in person 직접

18.

화자는 왜 "첫 번째 영화의 입장은 저녁 6시에 시작합니다"라고 말하는가?

(A) 프로그램의 오류를 지적하기 위해서
(B) 청자들에게 빨리 도착할 것을 독려하기 위해서
(C) 다른 영화를 볼 것을 제안하기 위해서
(D) 티켓 구매 마감 시한을 강조하기 위해서

[해설] 좌석이 선착순으로 배정됨을 상기시키며 원하는 좌석이 있더라도 미리 예약할 수는 없다고(there is no way to reserve it in advance) 알린 다음에 해당 표현이 나왔다. 즉, "첫 번째 영화의 입장은 저녁 6시에 시작합니다"라고 특정 시간을 명시함으로써 관람객들이 이에 맞춰 서둘러 극장에 오도록 권유하고 있는 것으로 보이므로 정답은 (B)이다.

[어휘] point out 지적하다 emphasize 강조하다

[19-21] US

Questions 19-21 refer to the following news report and map.

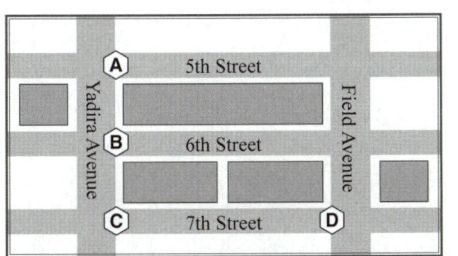

W: You're listening to the traffic report on Radio 820 AM. Most roadways are clear, as we're not into the rush hour yet. However, motorists traveling in the northern area of the city should be aware of a major traffic jam. [19]**A water pipe has burst**, forcing a temporary road closure. [20]**The affected intersection is at 7th Street and Yadira Avenue.** However, the surrounding streets are also heavily congested, so it's best to avoid the area if you can. We normally report on traffic at the top of each hour, but [21]**we'll be back in just fifteen minutes to give you an update on the traffic situation.**

roadway 도로, 차도 rush hour 혼잡 시간대, 러시아워 motorist 운전자 be aware of ~을 알다 major 주요한, 중대한 traffic jam 교통 체증 water pipe 송수관, 배수관 burst 터지다, 파열하다 force 어쩔 수 없이 ~하게 만들다 temporary 일시적인, 임시의 closure 폐쇄 affect 영향을 미치다 intersection 교차로, 교차 지점 surrounding 인근의, 주위의 heavily 심하게 congested 붐비는, 혼잡한

19-21은 다음 뉴스 보도와 지도에 관한 문제입니다.

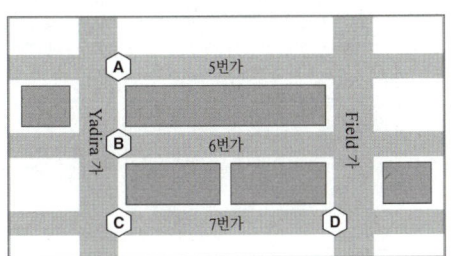

여: 여러분은 라디오 820 AM의 교통 방송을 듣고 계십니다. 아직 혼잡 시간대에 접어들지 않았기 때문에 대부분의 도로는 원활합니다. 그러나 도시 북부 지역에서 이동하는 운전자들은 심한 교통 체증을 느끼실 겁니다. [19]송수관 파열로 인해 어쩔 수 없이 도로가 일시적으로 폐쇄되었습니다. [20]이 영향을 받는 곳은 7번 가와 Yadira 가의 교차로입니다. 그러나 주변 도로 역시 정체가 심하므로 가능하다면 이 지역은 피하시는 게 최선입니다. 보통 때는 매시간 첫 번째 소식으로 교통 상황을 보도하지만, [21]**15분 뒤에 다시 돌아와서 교통 상황에 대한 최신 소식을 전해드리도록 하겠습니다.**

19.

무엇이 문제를 일으켰는가?
(A) 사라진 신호
(B) 고장 난 파이프
(C) 정전
(D) 교통 사고

[해설] 교통 정보를 전하는 보도로, 특정 지역의 교통 정체에 대해 언급한 후 송수관이 파열되어(A water pipe has burst) 도로가 폐쇄되었기 때문이라는 이유를 덧붙였다. 따라서 (B)가 정답이다.

paraphrasing A water pipe has burst 송수관이 파열되었다 → a broken pipe 고장 난 파이프

[어휘] signal 신호 power outage 정전

20.

시각 자료를 보시오. 화자는 어느 위치를 언급하는가?
(A) A 지점
(B) B 지점
(C) C 지점
(D) D 지점

[해설] 담화 중반, 화자는 앞서 언급한 송수관 파열로 인한 도로 폐쇄 때문에 7번 가와 Yadira 가에 있는 교차로가 영향을 받는다고(The affected intersection is at 7th Street and Yadira Avenue) 했다. 시각 자료로 주어진 지도에서 해당 지역을 찾으면 C 지점임을 알 수 있으므로 정답은 (C)이다.

[어휘] refer to ~를 언급하다, 가리키다

21.

청자들은 15분 뒤에 무엇을 들을 것인가?
(A) 다른 교통 보도
(B) 최신 스포츠 소식
(C) 일기 예보
(D) 국제 뉴스

[해설] 질문의 핵심 키워드 in fifteen minutes는 담화 마지막 부분에서 언급된다. 보통 때는 매시간 교통 정보를 전하지만 오늘은 15분 뒤에 다시 최신 교통 상황에 대해 전하겠다고(we'll be back in just fifteen minutes to give you an update on the traffic situation) 했으므로 청자들은 15분 뒤에 교통 정보를 또 듣게 된다. 따라서 정답은 (A)이다.

paraphrasing an update on the traffic situation 교통 상황에 대한 최신 소식 → another traffic report 다른 교통 보도